ENCYCLOPEDIA OF BUDDHISM

Editorial Board

ENCYCLOPEDIA OF BUDDHISM

Volume Two
M-Z
Appendix, Index

Robert E. Buswell, Jr., Editor in Chief

MACMILLAN
REFERENCE
USA™

THOMSON
GALE

New York • Detroit • San Diego • San Francisco • Cleveland • New Haven, Conn. • Waterville, Maine • London • Munich

THOMSON

GALE

Encyclopedia of Buddhism

Robert E. Buswell, Jr., Editor in Chief

For more information, contact
Macmillan Reference USA
300 Park Avenue South, 9th Floor
New York, NY 10010
Or you can visit our Internet site at
http://www.gale.com

Cover photograph of the Jo khang Temple in Lhasa, Tibet reproduced by permission. © Chris Lisle/Corbis.

The publisher wishes to thank the Vergleichende Sprachwissenschaft (Institute of Comparative Linguistics) of the University of Frankfurt, and particularly Dr. Jost Gippert, for their kind permission to use the TITUS Cyberbit font in preparing the manuscript for the *Encyclopedia of Buddhism.* This font was specially developed by the institute for use by scholars working on materials in Asian languages and enables the accurate transliteration with diacriticals of texts from those languages. Further information may be found at http://titus.fkidg1.uni-frankfurt.de.

LIBRARY OF CONGRESS CATALOGING-IN-PUBLICATION DATA

Encyclopedia of Buddhism / edited by Robert E. Buswell, Jr.
p. cm.
Includes bibliographical references and index.
ISBN 0-02-865718-7(set hardcover : alk. paper) — ISBN 0-02-865719-5 (Volume 1) — ISBN 0-02-865720-9 (Volume 2)
1. Buddhism—Encyclopedias. I. Buswell, Robert E.
BQ128.E62 2003
294.3'03—dc21
2003009965

This title is also available as an e-book.
ISBN 0-02-865910-4 (set)
Contact your Gale sales representative for ordering information.

Printed in the United States of America
10 9 8 7 6 5 4 3

M

MADHYAMAKA SCHOOL

The Madhyamaka school proclaims a middle way that rejects belief in the existence of an eternal self and inherently existent phenomena as well as the belief that such selves and phenomena do not exist at all. This school reinterprets the teaching of PRATĪTYASAMUTPĀDA (DEPENDENT ORIGINATION) to mean that because various causes and conditions produce phenomena, all are empty of any inherent existence. ŚŪNYATĀ (EMPTINESS) means that no phenomena and no persons are unoriginated and unrelated. Emptiness itself is empty. Since everything is empty, there is no real difference between good and bad, pure and impure, or SAṂSĀRA and NIRVĀṆA. These distinctions exist on the level of conventional truth and serve to introduce people to the ultimate truth that transcends dualistic language and conceptual thought. The liberating experience of meditation uncovers ultimate truth and destroys all attachment to erroneous conceptions of the self and the world.

The Madhyamaka school's influential teaching of emptiness endures in Buddhist traditions as diverse as the Tibetan DGE LUGS (GELUK) school and the East Asian CHAN SCHOOL and it continues to inspire debate among Western scholars whose interpretations of Madhyamaka's founder are equally diverse.

Early history: Nāgārjuna and his disciple Āryadeva

From the first century B.C.E. to the second century C.E., debate over the interpretation of the Buddha's teachings contributed to the writing of sūtras and scholastic ABHIDHARMA texts with new analyses of the Buddha's teachings. The authors of *abhidharma* works believed that the world contains a finite number of mental and physical phenomena (dharma) that have an inherent existence of their own (*svabhāva*) and that Buddhist saints (ARHATS) experience nirvāṇa through their insight into the nature of these phenomena. The movement that came to be known as the MAHĀYĀNA criticized the arhats' PATH as narrowly focused on their self-centered pursuit of nirvāṇa. BODHISATTVAS, who aspire to become buddhas, begin their path with the intention of working for the enlightenment of all beings. Mahāyāna supporters claim that the bodhisattva path is superior because it balances the individual pursuit of insight with great compassion for others. Although the origins of the Mahāyāna movement remain obscure, most scholars agree that it developed in monastic circles in India. No canon of Mahāyāna sūtras existed, nor, if statements in early Mahāyāna sūtras are to be taken at face value, would there have been interest in establishing one, since each sūtra proclaimed its own unique authoritative status.

Nāgārjuna and his major works. NĀGĀRJUNA, who composed treatises that incorporated the teachings of these diverse sūtras into a philosophical system, lived in a monastic community in southern India from about 150 to 250 C.E. The Madhyamaka (Middle Way) school of Buddhist philosophy takes its name from Nāgārjuna's belief that śūnyatā (emptiness) is the middle way between the extreme positions of nihilism and eternalism. Nihilism rejects belief in a transmigrating self that experiences the results of actions; eternalism believes in the eternal existence of such a self. Nāgārjuna, in *Ratnāvalī* (*Jewel Garland*) 1:44–5, explains that the eternalist view, which motivates people to do good in hope of a heavenly reward, is better than the nihilist view, but better still is the liberating insight into emptiness that repudiates both views. Nāgārjuna and his disciple, ĀRYADEVA (ca. 170–270 C.E.), were convinced that they were preserving the true middle way of the Buddha's teachings, while other Buddhists had strayed from it and adopted extreme positions.

Nāgārjuna's writings encompass several genres: letters, philosophical works, and hymns. His *Suhṛllekha* (*Letter to a Friend*), addressed to a South Indian Śātavāhana dynasty king, advises the king that since the world from the highest heavens down to worst hells is impermanent and painful, he should follow the eightfold path. Nāgārjuna encourages the king to develop insight into dependent origination and the FOUR NOBLE TRUTHS and to pursue meritorious actions with the intention of attaining buddhahood and creating his own buddha field, just as AMITĀBHA Buddha had. In the *Ratnāvalī,* Nāgārjuna discusses the bodhisattva's path and the goal of buddhahood in more detail. Through the cultivation of compassion and the six perfections, a bodhisattva advances on the ten stages that culminate in the inconceivable state of buddhahood. Although some people ridicule Mahāyāna beliefs, intelligent people use reason to accept the teaching of emptiness and achieve perfect enlightenment (4.67:99).

Nāgārjuna uses reason to prove that phenomena are empty of any inherent existence of their own in his most important philosophical work, the *Mūlamadhyamakakārikā* (*Root Verses on the Middle Way*). Emptiness (śūnyatā) means that nothing is created by itself or sustains itself without depending on various causes and conditions. Nāgārjuna's belief that all phenomena have arisen in dependence on causes and conditions is equivalent to saying that they are all empty of any inherent existence (24:18). He further explains this point of view in the *Śūnyatāsaptati* (*Seventy Verses on Emptiness*). While knowledge of emptiness is the proper means for relinquishing all extreme views, Nāgārjuna does not consider emptiness to be another view that somehow mediates between extreme positions. He refers to an early Mahāyāna scripture, the *Kāśyapaparivarta* (*The Section on Kāśyapa*), in which the Buddha asks whether a patient would be cured if the medicine a doctor uses to treat his symptoms remains in the body without being expelled (13:8). Kāśyapa replies that the patient's problems would become worse. Like the Buddha, Nāgārjuna regards emptiness as a therapeutic antidote to the ill effects of attachment to views and those who retain emptiness after it has achieved its purpose as incurable. He advocates insight into the emptiness of phenomena as a means for calming the mind and controlling its tendency to develop concepts (18:5). He describes (24:8–10) two types of truth—conventional and ultimate—and explains that without relying on conventional truth, which functions on the level of ordinary language and experience, the ultimate cannot be taught; and without understanding the ultimate, nirvāṇa is not achieved. Nirvāṇa and the cycle of death and rebirth (saṃsāra) cannot be differentiated (25:19–20) since emptiness characterizes both.

While the language and logic that Nāgārjuna uses in *Vigrahavyāvartanī* (*Warding off Arguments*) to criticize his opponents' views about the means of valid knowledge (*pramāṇa*) are as empty of substantive meaning as theirs, that does not impair their usefulness in exposing contradictions in their positions. Nāgārjuna has no thesis of his own to prove (vv. 29, 59), and he condemns the destructive psychological effects of attachment to views in his *Yuktiṣaṣṭikā* (*Sixty Verses on Reasoning*). He warns (vv. 47–52) that engaging in divisive debates produces the afflictions of desire and anger. Intelligent people who perceive phenomena to be like illusions and reflections, whose minds remain undisturbed, achieve nirvāṇa (vv. 55–58).

Nāgārjuna's collection of hymns praise the Buddha for his compassionate action and for his liberating knowledge of a world beyond conceptual discriminations. The *Acintyastava* (*Praise for the Inconceivable Buddha*) concludes (vv. 56–58) with the remarks that the Buddha's gift of the dharma, the nectar of his teaching, is that phenomena are empty. In the *Paramārthastava* (*Praise of the Ultimate*) he praises the Buddha, whom he describes as incomparable and beyond all words and all duality, although in the concluding verses Nāgārjuna asks how praise is possible when it and its object (like all phenomena) are empty.

Āryadeva and his major work. Nāgārjuna's main disciple, Āryadeva, in his major work, the *Catuḥśataka* (*Four Hundred Verses*), presents the path to the attainment of buddhahood, structured around the accumulation of the two requisites of merit and knowledge. The first eight chapters describe meritorious practices that gradually prepare the aspiring bodhisattva to receive knowledge about the empty and insubstantial nature of persons and phenomena, which the last eight chapters discuss in greater detail. Āryadeva utilizes the metaphor of illness and treatment in speaking about the actions of bodhisattvas and buddhas. They are skilled diagnosticians who provide the proper medication based upon a diagnosis of the illnesses that afflict SENTIENT BEINGS and remain patient when ignorant people, afflicted by illness, reject their medicine (5.11–13, 8.20). Throughout their career, but especially on the first stage of the path, bodhisattvas are encouraged to perfect the virtue of DĀNA (GIVING). The merit of donating material goods, however, is far surpassed by the gift of instruction in the dharma (5.7). The bodhisattvas' ability to discern the thoughts of others enables them to adapt the teaching to the capacities of each student. Only after the student is judged capable of understanding the most profound teachings, will these teachings be given (5.10). Āryadeva emphasizes that it is insight into the selfless and empty nature of all phenomena, rather than the performance of any meritorious action, that brings about the attainment of peace (8.11). The progressive method of instruction begins with the practices of generosity and moral conduct and culminates in peace (8.14). First, all demeritorious actions must be rejected, then the concept of a self, and finally all phenomena (8.15). There is no difference between the cycle of existence and nirvāṇa for a bodhisattva who has a powerful mind (8.22). The disciplined calming of the mind confers the power to realize nirvāṇa in the present life (8.23).

In the last eight chapters of the *Catuḥśataka,* Āryadeva refutes belief in permanent phenomena (atoms, the soul, time) and criticizes various theories about sense perception and causality. People who doubt and fear the Buddha's teachings on the selflessness of persons and phenomena cling to the less subtle views of Brahmin priests and naked ascetics (12.13–17, 19–22). The final chapter, a dialogue between teacher and student, considers the logical problems raised by the critics of emptiness. Āryadeva argues against the position that the negation of one thesis implies a commitment to the establishment of the opposite thesis (16.3–4, 7–8, 14). Statements about the existence of one thing and the nonexistence of another are unacceptable both on the conventional and ultimate level (16.16–18, 24). He concludes that no refutation can succeed against an opponent who refuses to hold any thesis (16.25).

Madhyamaka in Central Asia and East Asia. Little is known about Rāhulabhadra (ca. third century C.E.), a disciple of both Nāgārjuna and Āryadeva. One of his hymns, the *Prajñāpāramitāstotra* (*Praise of the Perfection of Wisdom*) is included in the Chinese text *Da zhidu lun* (*Treatise on the Great Perfection of Wisdom*). Because of the inclusion of this hymn, most scholars regard this text attributed to Nāgārjuna as a compendium of Madhyamaka philosophy compiled by Central Asian scholars, including its translator, KUMĀRAJĪVA (350–409/413). Kumārajīva also translated the three treatises (*san lun*), on which the Chinese branch of the Madhyamaka school was based: the *Zhong lun* (*Middle Treatise*), the *Shi'er men lun* (*Twelve Gate Treatise*), and the *Bai lun* (*Hundred Verses Treatise*), the first two attributed to Nāgārjuna and the third to Āryadeva. Kumārajīva's disciple SENGZHAO (374–414) composed original works that explain how the sage's calm and empty mind apprehends ultimate truth while still living in the world. The San Lun lineage ended in 623 with the death of Jizang (549–623), renowned for his commentaries on the three basic Madhyamaka treatises. A seventh-century Korean monk, Hyegwan, who studied with Jizang, brought these teachings to Japan, where they flourished briefly in the eighth century. Modern scholars appreciate the elegance of Kumārajīva's translations, although the academic schools founded in China and Japan to study them were not influential and did not survive after the eighth century.

Development of divisions within the Madhyamaka school

The distinction—Svātantrika versus Prāsaṅgika—often used to describe the views of later Madhyamaka writers developed late in Buddhist textual history, perhaps not until the eleventh century. These two classifications refer to the Svātantrika school's acceptance of independent (*svatantra*) inferences in philosophical debate and the Prāsaṅgika school's rejection of such inferences. The Prāsaṅgika school favors a *reductio ad absurdum* method that uses the opponent's own arguments to show the undesired consequences (*prasaṅga*) to which their opponents' theses invariably lead and that does not require proof of a contrary thesis. The Svātantrika school and Prāsaṅgika schools are associated with the works of BHĀVAVIVEKA and CANDRAKĪRTI, respectively.

Bhāvaviveka and his major works. Bhāvaviveka (ca. 500–570) wrote a lengthy commentary on Nāgārjuna's verses, the *Prajñāpradīpa* (*Lamp of Insight*), in which he criticized the *prasaṅga* method used in an earlier commentary, *Mūlamadhyamakavṛtti* of Buddhapālita (ca. 470–540 C.E.). Bhāvaviveka also wrote several original works, chief among them, the *Madhyamakahṛdayakārikā* (*Verses on the Heart of the Middle Way*) and his own commentary on this work, the *Tarkajvālā* (*Blaze of Reasoning*). In *Madhyamakahṛdayākarikā* 3:26 Bhāvaviveka uses syllogistic LOGIC to support the Madhyamaka position. He states that earth does not have any inherent existence from the perspective of ultimate reality (*paramārthataḥ*) because it is dependent on causes and conditions, like cognition. This syllogism has three parts—his thesis, the negative statement about inherent existence, and the reason—and an example. The thesis is a nonaffirming negation (*prasajyapratiṣedha*) and not an affirming negation (*paryudāsapratiṣedha*) because it is concerned only with denying that the earth has inherent existence and not with affirming that it has some other characteristic.

Bhāvaviveka's *Tarkajvālā* provides valuable information on the development of both Buddhist and Brahmanical thought. He defends the Madhyamaka school against its detractors through the use of inferences and syllogisms developed by the YOGĀCĀRA SCHOOL logician DIGNĀGA (ca. 480–540) and by the Brahmanical Nyāya logicians. In chapters four and five Bhāvaviveka refutes the positions of his Buddhist opponents; in chapters six through nine, he refutes, respectively, the positions of the Brahmanical philosophical schools Sāṃkhya, Nyāya-Vaiśeṣika, Vedānta, and Mīmāṃsā.

Candrakīrti and his major works. Candrakīrti (ca. 600–650) studied the works of Nāgārjuna and Āryadeva with students of Bhāvaviveka and Buddhapālita, and he supported Buddhapālita's position against Bhāvaviveka's criticism in his *Prasannapadā* (*Clear Words*) commentary on the *Mūlamadhyamakakārikā*. He also wrote commentaries on the *Śūnyatāsaptati*, the *Yuktiṣaṣṭikā*, and Āryadeva's *Catuḥśataka*. Candrakīrti's independent work, the *Madhyamakāvatāra* (*Introduction to the Middle Way*), presents a general introduction to the Madhyamaka school's ideas on the nature of the bodhisattva path and its goal of buddhahood. Candrakīrti is best known for his criticism of Bhāvaviveka's use of independent inferences in the *Madhyamakāvatāra* (6.12) and in the first chapter of the *Prasannapadā* (Pr 14–39) and for his criticism of the Yogācāra school's epistemological and logical views in the *Madhyamakāvatāra* (6. 34–78; Pr 58–75). He rejects as illogical the Yogācāra position that external objects are permutations of consciousness and that consciousness is reflexively aware of itself (*svasaṃvedana*). Candrakīrti knows the criteria set down by Dignāga for judging the soundness of an argument and applies them to demonstrate the flaws in his opponents' inferences and syllogisms. He is unwilling to support philosophical systems whose assertions are expressed positively or in the form of affirming negations. He rejects the distinctions Bhāvaviveka makes between theses established either conventionally or ultimately (6.12).

Candrakīrti distinguishes between conventional and ultimate truth in *Madhyamakāvatāra* (6:25–26). What ordinary people perceive as the object of their undamaged sense faculties is true from the conventional point of view; everything else is false. Eyes damaged by disease may produce false sense impressions. Water, mirrors, and the sun's rays may also produce false sense perceptions. These internal and external causes of false perception disturb the mental sense. Equally disturbing to the mental sense are non-Buddhist philosophers' views, which are not even conventionally true because ordinary people do not hold them. He describes conventional truth as the means, and ultimate truth as the goal (6:80). Candrakīrti concedes there are not really two truths but only one since the Buddha has said that nirvāṇa, which is nondeceptive, is the unique ultimate truth. Because conventional truth is deceptive it is not ultimately true.

Candrakīrti organizes his commentary on the *Catuḥśataka* around a debate between Āryadeva and various opponents. In the first half, he utilizes legal and political treatises, stories from the Hindu epics the *Rāmāyaṇa* and the *Mahābhārata,* and even secular love poetry in his demonstration of the superior merits of the Buddhist path. In the last half he critically examines the views of Buddhist and non-Buddhist opponents that lead people astray. These philosophers, he says in commenting on 12.4, talk about renunciation but they do not follow the right path and do not use the proper method. The proper method is the understanding of ultimate truth, namely, that all phenomena are empty of inherent existence. The cycle of death and rebirth ceases, he explains in his comments on 14:25, when consciousness no longer superimposes inherent existence on phenomena. What does not cease is the awakening of mind (*bodhicitta*) and the actions of a bodhisattva, which culminate in the ultimate knowledge of a buddha. The most influential work on the awakening of mind and the bodhisattva path is by ŚĀNTIDEVA.

Śāntideva and his major works. Śāntideva (ca. 685–763 C.E.) composed the *Śikṣāsamuccaya* (*Collection of Teachings*), a lengthy collection of excerpts from nearly one hundred Mahāyāna sūtras. His major work, the BODHICARYĀVATĀRA (*Introduction to the Conduct That Leads to Enlightenment*) traces the path of the bodhisattva from the initial resolution to become a buddha to the final dedication of merit after the completion of the six perfections. In the first chapter he distinguishes between the mind resolved upon awakening and the mind that proceeds toward awakening; the initial resolution creates merit but the merit of the bodhisattva actively proceeding toward awakening is unending (1:15–17). Chapter two and three describe the religious acts—offerings made to the Buddha, taking refuge in the Three Jewels, and the confession of faults—that the bodhisattva undertakes before setting out on the path. Chapter three describes the bodhisattva's request for buddhas in all directions to illuminate the world with their teachings (3:4–5) and the bodhisattva vows undertaken on behalf of all sentient beings (3:7–23). The fourth chapter indicates the strength of the bodhisattva's resolve to fulfill these vows. In chapter five Śāntideva begins his discussion of the six PĀRAMITĀ (PERFECTIONS). Chapter six's discussion of the perfection of patience concentrates on the avoidance of anger, the major impediment to the bodhisattva's resolution. Chapter seven focuses on the cultivation of vigor and chapter eight on meditation. In chapter eight Śāntideva explains how bodhisattvas meditate on the equality of self and others (8:89–119) and put themselves in the place of others by understanding that all suffering comes from selfish pleasures and all happiness from putting others' happiness first (8:120–131).

Śāntideva, in the lengthy ninth chapter on the perfection of wisdom, defends Madhyamaka beliefs against a multitude of objections from Buddhist and non-Buddhist opponents and refutes them. Śāntideva begins with a discussion of the two truths (9:2–8) and proceeds to refute the Yogācāra view of consciousness (11–34), *abhidharma* misconceptions about liberation and emptiness (40–56), and various wrong views about the self (57–87) and how feelings (88–101) and cognitions (102–5) arise. A detailed refutation of causality (114–37) is followed by his explanation of the emptiness of all phenomena and how insight into this teaching provides relief from the cycle of birth and death (138–167). The final chapter describes the dedication of merit derived from the bodhisattva's progress on the path to awakening.

The Yogācāra-Madhyamaka synthesis of Śāntarakṣita and Kamalaśīla. Śāntideva and Candrakīrti, both associated with the Prāsaṅgika wing of the Madhyamaka school, vigorously criticize Yogācāra beliefs. Two later Madhyamaka writers, Śāntarakṣita (ca. 725–790) and Kamalaśīla (ca. 740–795), found ways to incorporate some of these beliefs into their own systems. These scholars followed an example set two centuries earlier by the Yogācāra scholars Dharmapāla (ca. 530–561) and Sthiramati (ca. 510–570), who wrote commentaries on the Madhyamaka works of Nāgārjuna and Āryadeva. In the eighth-century monastic centers in eastern India, a synthesis of Yogācāra and Madhyamaka ideas came into prominence. The main figure associated with this movement is Śāntarakṣita. Like Bhāvaviveka, he uses logic to demonstrate the Madhyamaka position that phenomena lack inherent existence. Unlike Bhāvaviveka and his followers, Śāntarakṣita and his circle rejected the idea that external objects can be known even on the level of conventional truth. Madhyamaka and Yogācāra philosophers regard external objects as conceptual constructions. Śāntarakṣita (vv. 91–92 of *Madhyamakālamkāra, Eloquence of the Middle Way*) considers both object and subject as having the nature of consciousness, which is self-reflexive but still lacking in inherent existence. Śāntarakṣita concludes (v. 93) that Madhyamaka and Yogācāra taken together comprise the true Mahāyāna teachings. Śāntarakṣita's comprehensive *Tattvasaṃgraha* (Compendium of Truth) critically examines the beliefs of all schools of philosophy known to him: Nyāya, Mimāṃsā, Sāṃkhya, Advaita Vedānta, Jain, materialist, as well as the views of a variety Buddhist schools.

Kamalaśīla was Śāntarakṣita's disciple. In addition to his commentaries on Śāntarakṣita's *Madhyamakālaṃkāra* and *Tattvasaṃgraha,* he wrote independent works, the *Madhyamakāloka* (*Light of the Middle Way*) and the *Bhāvanākrama* (*Stages of Meditation*), a set of three works that concern the bodhisattva's practice of meditation. In the first *Bhāvanākrama* Kamalaśīla explains how the bodhisattva meditates first on compassion for all beings since compassion is the basic motivation for pursuing the path to buddhahood. The bodhisattva's practice encompasses both skillful means (the first five perfections) and wisdom, which is acquired through study, critical reflection, and meditative realization. The second and third *Bhāvanākrama* explains how the bodhisattva combines the practice of calming meditation (*śamatha*), which concentrates the mind, with insight meditation or VIPASSANĀ (SANSKRIT, VIPAŚYANĀ), which examines the meditative object and realizes the nonduality of subject and object. Śāntarakṣita and Kamalaśīla were major figures in the initial introduction of Buddhism into Tibet.

Madhyamaka in Tibet. Madhyamaka teachings were well established in central Tibet by the end of the eighth century. Śāntarakṣita first came to Tibet from Nepal around 763 and taught in Lhasa for four months until the hostility of the king's ministers forced him back to Nepal. He returned in 775 and supervised the construction of the first Tibetan monastery, BSAM YAS (SAMYE), and served as its abbot until his death. Bsam yas, according to Tibetan historical texts, hosted the BSAM YAS DEBATE between Śāntarakṣita's student Kamalaśīla and the Chinese monk Heshang Moheyan over the issue of the bodhisattva's pursuit of the gradual path toward awakening versus a sudden awakening. Moheyan prescribed meditation practices characteristic of the Chan school.

At Bsam yas teams of Tibetan translators and Indian and Chinese collaborators continued to translate Buddhist texts. By the end of the ninth century, they had completed translations of the works of Nāgārjuna and Āryadeva, as well as works of Buddhapalita, Bhāvaviveka, Candrakīrti, Śāntideva, Śāntarakṣita, and Kamalaśīla. These texts include several of the hymns attributed to Nāgārjuna, his letters and several of his philosophical treatises, the *Mūlamadhyamakakārikā*, the *Vigrahavyāvartanī*, the *Yuktiṣaṣṭika*, and the *Śūnyatāsaptati*, Buddhapālita's and Bhāvaviveka's commentaries on the *Mūlamadhyamakakārikā*, Candrakīrti's *Yuktiṣaṣṭikavṛtti* and *Śūnyatasaptativṛtti*, Śāntideva's *Bodhicaryāvatāra* and *Śikṣāsamuccaya*, Śāntarakṣita's *Madhyamakālaṃkāra*, and Kamalaśīla's *Madhyamakāloka* and *Bhāvanākrama*.

During the first dissemination of Buddhism in Tibet the views of Śāntarakṣita and Kamalaśīla's syncretistic Yogācāra-Madhyamaka school and the views of Bhāvaviveka flourished. Candrakīrti's interpretation of Madhyamaka presented a significant challenge to Bhāvaviveka's interpretation during the second dissemination of Buddhism in the tenth and eleventh centuries. The Indian scholar ATISHA (982–1054) arrived in western Tibet in 1042; at Mtho ling Monastery, he wrote his best-known work, the *Bodhipathapradīpa* (*Lamp for the Path to Awakening*) and a commentary that describes the Madhyamaka school's basic doctrines (vv. 47–51). He observes that people of slight abilities perform meritorious actions in hope of better rebirth, people of middling abilities seek nirvāṇa, and people of the highest ability seek buddhahood and an end to the suffering of all beings. Atisha identifies himself as part of a Madhyamaka lineage that includes Nāgārjuna, Āryadeva, Candrakīrti, Bhāvaviveka, and Śāntideva.

Although the study and teaching of Madhyamaka texts has a long history in Tibet, it is not until the late eleventh or early twelfth century that a clear distinction begins to develop between Svātantrika and Prāsaṅgika Madhyamaka. Pa tshab Nyi ma grags (b. 1055) translated three of Candrakīrti's major works: his early independent treatise on Madhyamaka, the *Madhyamakāvatāra*, and his commentaries on Nāgārjuna's and Āryadeva's major works. According to the Tibetan historians 'Go lo tsa ba and Gser mdog Pan chen, Spa tshab Nyi ma grags made the Prāsaṅgika viewpoint of Candrakīrti the dominant interpretation of the classical works of Nāgārjuna and Āryadeva from the twelfth century onward. Until Nyi ma grags translated *Prasannapadā* and clearly differentiated Candrakīrti's interpretation of Madhyamaka from Bhāvaviveka's, there had been no solid foundation for distinguishing between the two interpretations.

From the fourteenth through sixteen centuries scholars associated with all four of the major Tibetan schools—KLONG CHEN PA (LONGCHENPA) (1308–1363) of RNYING MA (NYINGMA) school; Red mda' ba (1349–1412), Rong ston (1367–1449), and Go ram pa (1429–1489) of the SA SKYA (SAKYA) school; Mi bskyod rdo je (1507–1554) and Padma dkar po (1527–1592) of the BKA' BRGYUD (KAGYU) school; TSONG KHA PA (1357–1419), Rgyal tshab, (1364–1432), and Mkhas grub (1385–1438) of the Dge lugs (Geluk) school—wrote works defining their positions on Madhyamaka philosophy. During this period, Dol po pa (1292–1361) of the Jo nang pa school developed his position on the teaching of emptiness, which incorporated insights from Yogācāra texts, particularly those concerned with the teaching of innate Buddha nature. He differentiated between the negative descriptive of emptiness, self-emptiness (*rang stong*), which regards all phenomena as lacking inherent existence, and a more positive description of emptiness, other-emptiness (*gzhan stong*), which refers to a truly existent ultimate reality that is beyond the limits of ordinary conceptualization. These medieval debates over positive and negative descriptions of emptiness recur in the works of contemporary scholars who study Madhyamaka thought.

The terse verses of Nāgārjuna's *Mūlamadhyamakakārikā*, which led to divergent interpretations among the classical schools of Madhyamaka thought, have also produced a spate of modern books and articles proposing various interpretations of his philosophy. Andrew Tuck's 1990 study, *Comparative Philosophy and the Philosophy of Scholarship: On the*

Western Interpretation of Nāgārjuna, associates the Western interpretation of Madhyamaka with whatever philosophical trends were current at the time. Nāgārjuna's nineteenth-century Western interpreters portrayed him as a nihilist. Twentieth-century interpretations, under the influence of modern analytical philosophy, focused on his use of logic and his skepticism about the use of language. Richard Hayes, in "Nāgārjuna's Appeal" (1994) concludes that twentieth-century scholarship on Madhyamaka largely corresponds to two distinct but traditional approaches: exegesis and HERMENEUTICS. The exegetical approach primarily focuses on the accumulation of philological, historical, and textual data, while the hermeneutic approach attempts to make that data relevant to the concerns of a modern audience.

Bibliography

Crosby, Kate, and Skilton, Andrew, trans. *The Bodhicaryāvatāra.* New York: Oxford University Press, 1996.

Garfield, Jay L. *The Fundamental Wisdom of the Middle Way: Nāgārjuna's Mūlamadhyamakakārikā.* New York: Oxford University Press, 1995.

Hayes, Richard. "Nāgārjuna's Appeal." *Journal of Indian Philosophy* 22 (1994): 363–372.

Hopkins, Jeffrey, trans. *Buddhist Advice for Living and Liberation: Nāgārjuna's Precious Garland.* Ithaca, NY: Snow Lion, 1998.

Huntington, C. W., Jr. *The Emptiness of Emptiness: An Introduction to Early Mādhyamika.* Honolulu: University of Hawaii Press, 1989.

Keenan, John P. *Dharmapāla's Yogācāra Critique of Bhāvaviveka's Mādhyamika Explanation of Emptiness.* Lewiston, NY: Mellen Press, 1997.

Lang, Karen. *Āryadeva's Catuḥśataka: On the Bodhisattva's Cultivation of Merit and Knowledge.* Copenhagen, Denmark: Akademisk Forlag, 1986.

Lindtner, Christian, *Nāgārjuniana: Studies in the Writings and Philosophy of Nāgārjuna.* Copenhagen, Denmark: Akademisk Forlag, 1982.

Ramanan, K. Venkata. *Nāgārjuna's Philosophy as Presented in the Mahāprajñāpāramitāśāstra.* Rutland, VT: Charles Tuttle, 1966.

Robinson, Richard. *Early Mādhyamika in India and China.* Madison: University of Wisconsin Press, 1967.

Ruegg, David Seyfort. *The Literature of the Madhyamaka School of Philosophy in India.* Wiesbaden, Germany: Harrassowitz, 1981.

Ruegg, David Seyfort. *Three Studies in the History of Indian and Tibetan Madhyamaka Philosophy.* Vienna: Arbeitskreis für Tibetische und Buddhistische Studien Universität Wien, 2000.

Sonam, Ruth. *Yogic Deeds of Bodhisattvas: Gyel-tsap on Āryadeva's Four Hundred.* Ithaca, NY: Snow Lion, 1994.

Sprung, Mervyn, trans. *Lucid Exposition of the Middle Way: The Essential Chapters from the Prasannapadā of Candrakīrti.* Boulder, CO: Prajña Press, 1979.

Tillemans, Tom J. F. *Materials for the Study of Āryadeva, Dharmapāla and Candrakīrti*, 2 vols. Vienna: Arbeitskreis für Tibetische und Buddhistische Studien Universitat Wien, 1990.

Tuck, Andrew. *Comparative Philosophy and the Philosophy of Scholarship: On the Western Interpretation of Nāgārjuna.* New York: Oxford University Press, 1990.

KAREN LANG

MA GCIG LAB SGRON (MACHIG LABDRÖN)

Ma gcig lab sgron (pronounced Machig Labdrön; ca. 1055–1149) was an eminent female Tibetan Buddhist teacher who codified and disseminated the ritual meditation system called severance (*gcod*, pronounced chö). Born in the southern Tibetan region of La phyi, Ma gcig lab sgron was recognized as a gifted individual even in her youth. According to her traditional biographies, she had a natural affinity for the *prajñāpāramitā* (perfection of wisdom) sūtras, spending much of her youth reading and studying their numerous texts and commentaries. For several years, she continued her education under Grwa pa mngon shes and Skyo ston Bsod nams bla ma in a monastic setting where she was eventually employed to use her skills in ritual recitation and exegesis. She then took up the lifestyle of a tantric yoginī, living as the consort of the Indian adept Thod pa Bhadra, eventually giving birth to several children, perhaps five in all. Vilified as a "nun who had repudiated her religious vows," Ma gcig lab sgron left her family and eventually met the famed Indian yogin who became her primary guru, Pha Dam pa sangs rgyas (d. 1105/1117), a contemporary of the famous Tibetan poet-saint MI LA RAS PA (1028/40–1111/23). Dam pa sangs rgyas transmitted to Ma gcig lab sgron the instructions of pacification (*zhi byed*) and the MAHĀMUDRĀ teachings. She combined these with her training in *prajñāpāramitā* and other indigenous practices, passing them on as the system of severance, principally to the Nepalese yogin Pham thing pa and her own son Thod smyon bsam grub.

The tradition of severance, like that of pacification, is commonly classified among eight important tantric traditions and transmission lineages that spread throughout Tibet—the so-called eight great chariot-like lineages of achievement (*sgrub brgyud shing rta chen po brgyad*), a system that prefigures the development of a fourfold sectarian division often noted in writings on Tibetan Buddhism. Ma gcig lab sgron herself described severance as a practice that severs (*gcod*) attachment to one's body, dualistic thinking, and conceptions of hope and fear. Although usually practiced by solitary yogins in isolated and frightening locations, severance liturgies are also performed by monastic assemblies, both accompanied by the ritual music of hand drum and human thigh-bone trumpet. The meditation, rooted in the theory of the *prajñāpāramitā* and *mahāmudrā,* also involves the visualized offering of the adept's body—flesh, blood, bones, and organs—as food for a vast assembly of beings, including local spirits and demons.

Ma gcig lab sgron is revered in Tibet as a ḌĀKINĪ goddess, an emanation of the Great Mother (Yum chen mo) and the bodhisattva Tārā. Her reincarnations have also been recognized in contemporary individuals, including the former abbess of the important Shug gseb Nunnery near Lhasa, Rje btsun Rig 'dzin chos nyid zang mo (1852–1953). Ma gcig lab sgron remains a primary Tibetan example of the ideal female practitioner and her tradition of severance continues to be widely employed among Tibetan Buddhist practitioners, both lay and monastic, of all sectarian affiliations.

See also: **Prajñāpāramitā Literature; Tibet; Women**

Bibliography

Edou, Jérôme. *Machig Labdrön and the Foundations of Chöd.* Ithaca, NY: Snow Lion, 1996.

Gyatso, Janet. "The Development of the Gcod Tradition." In *Soundings in Tibetan Civilization,* ed. Barbara Nimri Aziz and Matthew Kapstein. Delhi: Manohar, 1985.

Roerich, George N., trans. and ed. *The Blue Annals,* 2 vols. Calcutta: Royal Asiatic Society of Bengal, 1949. Reprint, New Delhi: Motilal Benarsidass, 1989.

ANDREW QUINTMAN

MAHĀBODHI TEMPLE

The history of Mahābodhi, the temple located at the site of the Buddha's enlightenment at BODH GAYĀ, is a contested one. According to the Chinese pilgrim XUANZANG (ca. 600–664 C.E.), the imposing structure visible during his lifetime was built over a smaller temple erected by King AŚOKA. A Bhārhut medallion shows a circular open structure enclosing the diamond throne and the bodhi tree above it. While the Aśokan pillar beside it suggests that it may represent the original Aśokan shrine, archaeological evidence for the latter is inconclusive. The large stone slab resembling the diamond throne of the Bhārhut relief recovered from the ruins might well be a conscious archaism.

The structural temple Xuanzang describes probably dates from the third to fifth centuries C.E. (late Kushan and Gupta dynasties). Myriads of tiered niches housing golden figures covered its soaring 170-foot high tower of whitewashed brick. Stringed pearl and celestial sages decorated its walls. A three-storied jeweled pavilion with projecting eaves abutted the east wall. Niches with ten-foot high silver figures of the bodhisattvas MAITREYA and Avalokiteśvara flanked the outside gate, while a Buddha image twice that size occupied the sanctuary's massive diamond throne. The Buddha's earth-touching gesture (MUDRĀ) represented the moment when the Buddha called the earth to witness his eligibility for enlightenment and MĀRA was defeated. The new structure necessitated the removal of the bodhi tree from the sanctuary to a location outside the temple, which Gupta inscriptions called a *mahāgandhakuṭī,* or the great fragrant chamber where the Buddha resides. Thus, in Bodh Gayā by the fifth century, the bodhi tree as the primary locus of the Buddha's living presence was replaced by his residence, throne, and image.

The present Mahābodhi temple is a late nineteenth-century restoration of dubious authenticity. It has a tall central tower with a high arch over the entrance and identical smaller towers on each of its four corners. Evidence from India, Burma, and Thailand indicates that corner towers were present before the eleventh century. This evidence consists of a small eleventh-century model of the Mahābodhi from eastern India and of its four Burmese and Thai re-creations beginning in the eleventh century. In referencing the directions and the four continents, the corner towers intensify the central tower's kinship with Mount Sumeru, thereby reinforcing the seat of enlightenment's increasing importance over the tree at Bodh Gayā. By contrast, in Sri Lanka the bodhi tree at Anurādhapura remains the prime relic of the enlightenment. No major enclosed structure has diminished or usurped its primacy as one of Sri Lanka's two major Buddha relic-shrines. Its preeminence probably derives from the belief that it is the sapling from the original bodhi tree that Aśoka's missionary son brought to the island together with Buddhism.

Bibliography

Beal, Samuel, trans. *Si-yu-ki: Buddhist Records of the Western World, Translated from the Chinese of Hiuen Tsiang* (A.D. *629)*. London: Trubner, 1884. Reprint, Delhi: Oriental Books Reprint Corp., 1969.

Bhattacharyya, Tarapada. *The Bodhgayā Temple.* Calcutta: Firma K. L. Mukhopadhyah, 1966.

Cunningham, Alexander. *Mahābodhi or the Great Buddhist Temple under the Bodhi Tree at Buddha-Gaya.* London, 1892.

Leoshko, Janice, ed. *Bodh Gayā: The Site of Enlightenment.* Bombay: Marg, 1988.

Mitra, Rajendralala. *Buddha-Gaya: The Great Buddhist Temple, the Hermitage of Sakya Muni.* Calcutta: Bengal Secretariat Press, 1878. Reprint, Delhi: Indological Book House, 1972.

Myer, Prudence. "The Great Temple at Bodhgaya." *Art Bulletin* 40 (1958): 277–278.

Leela Aditi Wood

MAHĀKĀŚYAPA

Mahākāśyapa (Pāli, Mahākassapa), a disciple of the Buddha, was of Brahmin descent. According to Buddhist legend, the Buddha was aware of a karmic connection between himself and Mahākāśyapa, and waited for him as his most distinguished disciple to accept him into the order. In the Mahāyāna sūtras, Mahākāśyapa readily understands the deeper meaning of the Buddha's teachings. Mahākāśyapa's supernormal powers and talents of meditation indicate his ability to penetrate to a soteriological layer of the dharma that is not accessible to the normal "hearers" (*śrāvaka*) of the Buddha or even to Buddhist saints, the arhats. The Chan school symbolized this capacity by showing Mahākāśyapa holding a lotus flower in his hand, which represents his grasp on the Buddha's teaching. Mahākāśyapa was made the first patriarch of the Chan school.

Legend holds that Mahākāśyapa became the head of the Buddhist community after the Buddha's *parinirvāṇa.* Shortly after the death of the Buddha, Mahākāśyapa convened the first Buddhist council near Rājagṛha, India, an event that is traditionally understood to have led to the codification of the Buddhist canon (Tripiṭaka). Mahākāśyapa also functions as the transmitter of the dharma from the Buddha to the future Buddha Maitreya. Buddhist tradition describes Mahākāśyapa as absorbed in the "attainment of cessation" (*nirodhasamāpatti*) deep inside Cockfeet Mountain (Kukkuṭapadagiri), where he keeps the garment of the Buddha, which he received from the hand of the master and will transfer to Maitreya as a symbol of the latter's legitimate succession.

See also: **Councils, Buddhist; Disciples of the Buddha**

Bibliography

Nyanaponika, Thera, and Hecker, Hellmuth. *Great Disciples of the Buddha: Their Lives, Their Works, Their Legacy.* Boston: Wisdom, 1997.

Ray, Reginald A. *Buddhist Saints in India: A Study in Buddhist Values and Orientations.* New York: Oxford University Press, 1994.

Max Deeg

MAHĀMAUDGALYĀYANA

Mahāmaudgalyāyana (Pāli, Mahāmoggallāna; Chinese, Mulian), a disciple of Śākyamuni Buddha, attained the enlightened status of an arhat, or saint. He is renowned for the magical powers he developed through meditation. Mahāmaudgalyāyana uses his powers to travel to other realms of the universe where he witnesses the happiness and suffering that living beings experience as a result of their karma (action). He also uses his magical powers to discipline monks, gods, nāgas, and other beings. Mahāmaudgalyāyana converted to Buddhism and entered the monastic order together with his childhood friend Śāriputra. They became the Buddha's two chief disciples in accordance with a prediction made to that effect many eons earlier by a previous buddha. Thus Mahāmaudgalyāyana and Śāriputra are sometimes depicted flanking the Buddha in Buddhist art. Mahāmaudgalyāyana predeceased the Buddha after being beaten by heretics. His violent death is attributed to bad karma; in a previous life he had killed his own parents.

Mahāmaudgalyāyana is most famous for liberating his mother from a bad rebirth as a hungry ghost. Beginning in the Tang period in China, this story became the basis for a popular annual Buddhist festival in East Asia called the Ghost Festival. During this festival, Buddhists make offerings to the monastic community, dedicating their merit to deceased ancestors in the hopes that these attain a better rebirth or greater comfort in their current rebirth. Mahāmaudgalyāyana is venerated in East Asia for his filial piety and shamanic powers. Like other arhats, Mahāmaudgalyāyana was also the focus of worship already in ancient and medieval India. In Burma (Myanmar) he is one of a set of eight arhats propitiated in protective rituals and he is also believed to grant his worshippers magical powers.

See also: **Disciples of the Buddha**

Bibliography

Malalasekera, G. P. "Mahā Moggallāna Thera." In *Dictionary of Pāli Proper Names* (1937–1938), 2 vols. New Delhi: Munshiram Manoharlal, 1995.

Strong, John S. *The Legend and Cult of Upagupta.* Princeton, NJ: Princeton University Press, 1992.

Teiser, Stephen F. *The Ghost Festival in Medieval China.* Princeton, NJ: Princeton University Press, 1988.

SUSANNE MROZIK

MAHĀMUDRĀ

The Sanskrit term *mahāmudrā,* which might be translated as "great seal," refers to a Buddhist doctrine describing the underlying nature of reality, the consummate practices of meditation, and the crowning realization of buddhahood. Although important for all of the later Tibetan sects, including the SA SKYA (SAKYA) and DGE LUGS (GELUK), *mahāmudrā* became principally associated with the many branches of the BKA' BRGYUD (KAGYU). The *mahāmudrā* tradition began with the Indian MAHĀSIDDHAS, or great adepts, including Tilopa (988–1069), NĀROPA (1016–1100), and Maitrīpa (ca. 1007–1085), and was disseminated in Tibet by such early Bka' brgyud masters as MAR PA (MARPA, 1002/1012–1097), MI LA RAS PA (MILAREPA, 1028/40–1111/23), and their followers.

According to the sixteenth-century Bka' brgyud exegete Bkra shis rnam rgyal (Tashi Namgyal, 1512–1587), the doctrine is called *great seal* because, "Just as a seal leaves its impression on other objects, so *mahāmudrā,* the ultimate reality, leaves its imprint upon all realities of SAṂSĀRA and NIRVĀṆA." It is a seal because it refers to "the inherent character or abiding reality of all things" (Namgyal, p. 92). The term in Tibetan, *phyag rgya chen po* (pronounced chagya chenpo) literally translates the Sanskrit and is traditionally explained in numerous ways. According to the *Phyag chen thig le* (Sanskrit, *Mahāmudrātilaka; The Seminal Point of Mahāmudrā*), *phyag* symbolizes the wisdom of emptiness and *rgya* the freedom from things of saṃsāra. *Chen po* stands for their union.

Mahāmudrā is commonly taught under the tripartite rubric of ground (in the sense of foundation), PATH, and fruition. This approach was summed up by the great nineteenth-century reformer Kong sprul Blo gros mtha' yas (Kongtrul Lodrö Thaye, 1813–1899) in the following way: "Ground *mahāmudrā* is the view, understanding things as they are. / Path *mahāmudrā* is the experience of meditation. / Fruition *mahāmudrā* is the realization of one's mind as buddha" (Nalanda Translation Committee, p. 83). Ground *mahāmudrā* expresses the primordially pure nature of the mind that normally goes unnoticed; it is likened to a jewel buried in the ground. Path *mahāmudrā* represents a wide variety of meditation practices. These can follow a systematic approach—as exemplified in numerous texts by the ninth Karma pa, Dbang phyug rdo rje (Wangchuk Dorje, 1604–1674)—incorporating preliminary practices (*sngon'gro*) with those of *mahāmudrā* serenity (*śamatha*) to still the mind, and *mahāmudrā* insight (*vipaśyanā*) to recognize the mind's nature. The practice of path *mahāmudrā* may also incorporate seemingly simple instructions such as resting free from exertion within naked awareness itself. Fruition *mahāmudrā* is the final result, the realization of phenomenal appearances and noumenal emptiness as nondual. This is not something newly produced, but rather the recognition of what is termed *ordinary mind* (*tha mal gyi shes pa*), the mind's innate clarity, purity, and luminosity. Such recognition is often described in vivid terms as being indestructible, youthful, fresh, shining, and experienced as great bliss.

Some Bka' brgyud scholars have divided *mahāmudrā* literature into two streams: sūtra *mahāmudrā* and TANTRA *mahāmudrā.* The former, based on Indian texts such as the *Uttaratantra-śāstra* (*Treatise on the Unexcelled Continuity*), describes a system centered primarily upon the cultivation of the six PĀRAMITĀ (PERFECTIONS) without the need for specific tantric initiation or practice. This approach—exemplified in the *Thar pa rin po che'i rgyan* (*Jewel Ornament of Liberation*), a text composed by Mi la ras pa's celebrated disciple Sgam po pa (Gampopa, 1079–1153)—was strongly criticized by Tibetan writers such as the renowned scholar SA SKYA PAṆDITA (SAKYA PAṆḌITA, 1182–1251). Tantra *mahāmudrā* is an approach in which the practices of *anuttarayoga,* or highest yoga tantra—such as those belonging to the system known as the Six Doctrines of Nāropa (*Nā ro chos drug*)—are used as a means for realization.

See also: **Tantra; Tibet**

Bibliography

Bstan 'dzin rgya mtsho (Dalai Lama XIV) and Berzin, Alexander. *The Gelug/Kagyu Tradition of Mahāmudrā.* Ithaca, NY: Snow Lion, 1997.

Dorje, Wangchug. *The Mahāmudrā Illuminating the Darkness of Ignorance,* tr. Alexander Berzin. Dharamsala, India: Library of Tibetan Works and Archives, 1978.

Nalanda Translation Committee. *The Rain of Wisdom.* Boston: Shambhala, 1980.

Namgyal, Takpo Tashi. *Mahāmudrā: The Quintessence of Mind and Meditation,* tr. Lobsang P. Lhalungpa. Boston: Shambhala, 1986.

Sgam po pa. *The Jewel Ornament of Liberation,* tr. Herbert V. Guenther. London: Rider, 1959. Reprint, Boston: Shambhala, 1971.

ANDREW QUINTMAN

MAHĀPARINIRVĀṆA-SŪTRA

The *Mahāparinirvāṇa-sūtra* (Pāli, *Mahāparinibbāna-sutta; Great Discourse on Extinction*) recounts the final months of the Buddha's life, his last acts and sermons to his disciples, his death, and the distribution of his relics. A canonical text, it was one of the early building blocks of the Buddha's biography, and versions exist in Pāli, Sanskrit, Tibetan, and Chinese. It should not be confused with the later MAHĀYĀNA sūtra of the same name.

See also: **Buddha, Life of the; Nirvāṇa Sūtra**

Bibliography

Walshe, Maurice, trans. "Mahāparinibbāna Sutta: The Great Passing." In *Thus Have I Heard: The Long Discourses of the Buddha.* London: Wisdom, 1987.

JOHN S. STRONG

MAHĀPRAJĀPATĪ GAUTAMĪ

According to the *Gotamī-apadāna* and the *Therīgāthā,* Mahāprajāpatī Gautamī (Pāli, Mahāpajāpatī Gotamī) was Siddhārtha Gautama's maternal aunt and foster mother. When Mahāprajāpatī was born, an astrologer predicted her leadership qualities and she was named Prajāpatī (Pāli, Pajāpatī), "leader of a large assembly." She and her sister Māyā were both married to Śuddhodana, the ruler of Kapilavastu. Māyā gave birth to a son who was named Siddhārtha and then died just seven days after his birth. After Māyā's death, Prajāpatī suckled the boy and raised him as her own child. Prajāpatī also gave birth to two children of her own, Nanda and Sundarīnandā.

Mahāprajāpatī is widely regarded as the first *bhikṣuṇī* and progenitor of the Buddhist order of NUNS (Bhikṣuṇī SAṄGHA). After Siddhārtha became "an awakened one" (a Buddha) and visited Kapilavastu, Mahāprajāpatī began to practice the dharma and achieved the stage of a stream enterer (*śrotāpanna*). According to tradition, she thrice requested the Buddha's permission to join the saṅgha, but was refused each time. Finally, she cut her hair, donned renunciant garb, and, accompanied by five hundred Śākyan noblewomen, walked to Vaiśālī where she once again sought admission to the order. This time, when ĀNANDA interceded on Mahāprajāpatī's behalf, the Buddha affirmed that women are indeed qualified to achieve the fruits of dharma (i.e., liberation), and granted her request.

The Buddha is said to have stipulated eight special rules (*gurudharma*) as the condition for Mahāprajāpatī's admission to the saṅgha. These rules, which later came to be applied to Buddhist nuns in general, make the Bhikṣuṇī Saṅgha dependent upon (and, to a certain extent, subordinate to) the Bhikṣu Saṅgha (order of monks) with regard to ordination, exhortation, admonishment, and reinstatement, thereby delimiting the nuns' independence.

In addition to being the first Buddhist nun and the leader of the Bhikṣuṇī Saṅgha from its origins, Mahāprajāpatī achieved higher spiritual attainments, including the six higher knowledges and supernormal powers. She often served as a trusted intermediary in communications between the *bhikṣuṇīs* and the Buddha. In the later part of her life, she reached the state of an ARHAT, as evidenced in her own verse, recorded in the *Therīgāthā:* "I have achieved the state where everything stops." Within the patriarchal social context of her time, Mahāprajāpatī became an exemplar of women's potential for leadership and spiritual attainment, and her achievements have inspired Buddhist WOMEN ever since.

Bibliography

Blackstone, Kathryn R. *Women in the Footsteps of the Buddha: Struggle for Liberation in the Therīgāthā.* Richmond, UK: Curzon Press, 1998.

Horner, Isaline Blew. *Women under Primitive Buddhism: Laywomen and Almswomen.* Delhi: Motilal Banarsidass, 1975.

Walters, Jonathan S. "The Buddha's Mother's Story." *History of Religions* 33 (1994): 350–379.

Walters, Jonathan S. "Gotamī's Story." In *Buddhism in Practice,* ed. Donald S. Lopez, Jr. Princeton, NJ: Princeton University Press, 1995.

KARMA LEKSHE TSOMO

MAHĀSĀṂGHIKA SCHOOL

The Mahāsāṃghika (or Mahāsāṅghika) school is believed to have emerged from the first major schism in the Buddhist order, at a council held in the fourth century B.C.E., more than a century after Gautama's death. The name, from *mahāsaṃgha,* "great(er) community," supposedly reflects the Mahāsāṃghikas' superior numbers, the Sthaviras being the minority party to the dispute. The split may have been caused by disagreements over the VINAYA, or the famous five theses of Mahādeva concerning the ARHAT, or the introduction of MAHĀYĀNA sūtras into the canon. Traditional accounts of these issues are obscure and conflicting. What is certain is that the Mahāsāṃghikas and their many subschools (Lokottaravādins, Prajñaptivādins, Pūrvaśailas, Aparaśailas, etc.) followed a conservative form of the vinaya, yet were responsible for many doctrinal innovations, chief of which is the theory known as *lokottaravāda.* This holds that the Buddha transcends all human limitations, and is thus above (*uttara*) the world (*loka*), his life as Gautama being a compassionate display.

Some Mahāsāṃghika ideas later flowed into Mahāyāna Buddhism, which is, however, now thought to have drawn its inspiration from many schools. Once well represented throughout the subcontinent, especially in the northwest (including present-day Afghanistan) and the south, the Mahāsāṃghikas eventually disappeared as a living ordination tradition. Now only parts of their canon survive, including the distinctively structured vinaya and what may be their *Ekottarikāgāma* (both in Chinese translation). Sections of the Mahāsāṃghika-Lokottaravādin Vinaya also survive in Sanskrit (notably the *Mahāvastu*), as do fragments of the literature of other subschools.

See also: **Mainstream Buddhist Schools**

Bibliography

Bareau, André. *Les sectes bouddhiques du petit véhicule.* Saigon, Vietnam: École Française d'Extrême-Orient, 1955.

Lamotte, Étienne. *History of Indian Buddhism: From the Origins to the Saka Era,* tr. Sara Webb-Boin. Louvain-la-Neuve, Belgium: Université catholique de Louvain, Institut Orientaliste, 1988.

Nattier, Janice J., and Prebish, Charles S. "Mahāsāṅghika Origins: The Beginnings of Buddhist Sectarianism." *History of Religions* 16 (1977): 237–272.

PAUL HARRISON

MAHĀSIDDHA

The Sanskrit term *mahāsiddha* ("great master of spiritual accomplishment" or "great adept") and the simpler, near synonymous form *siddha* (adept) refer to an individual who has achieved great success in tantric meditation. Buddhist traditions mainly associate siddhas with the transmission of tantric instructions throughout South, East, and, to some degree, Southeast Asia. They are especially important for the Buddhist schools of Nepal and Tibet, which commonly enumerate eighty-four *mahāsiddhas,* many of whom are regarded as founders of tantric lineages still in existence today.

Primarily active on the Indian subcontinent during the eighth to twelfth centuries, Buddhist siddhas are chiefly characterized by their possession of *siddhi* (success), yogic accomplishments of two types: the ordinary or mundane accomplishment of magical powers, and the supreme accomplishment of perfect enlightenment. Life stories of individual siddhas abound with examples of the first type of success: mastery over the physical elements and material world, superhuman cognition, even immortality. Siddhas are commonly associated with particular displays of accomplishment; for example, Virūpa's ability to stop the sun midcourse and Saraha's immunity to the heat of molten metal. According to tradition, however, such powers are mere by-products of tantric meditation, not the goal itself. Siddhas or *mahāsiddhas* qualified by the second type of accomplishment therefore stand as the VAJRAYĀNA enlightened ideal—a model for swiftly attaining realization and ultimate enlightenment through the practice of meditation and yoga.

While many siddhas were probably historical figures, records of their lives and teachings vary in depth and detail. The majority of these accounts are known from the rich corpus of biographical literature preserved in Tibetan, often based on oral and literary traditions from India. Prominent among them is the twelfth-century author Abhayadatta's *Caturaśītisiddhapravṛtti* (*Lives of the Eighty-Four Siddhas*)—extant in Tibetan translation—which presents brief vitae for numerous important masters (Robinson, 1979). The *Bka' babs bdun ldan* (*Seven Instruction Lineages*), written by the Tibetan historian Tāranātha (1575–1634), records elements of siddhas' lives as they pertain to the promulgation of important tantric lineages (Templeman). Several widely revered siddhas, such as the Bengali master NĀROPA (1016–1100), have been the subject of comprehensive biographies (Guenther).

Accounts of the *mahāsiddhas* generally portray individuated personalities while following tropes common to much of Buddhist sacred BIOGRAPHY—discontent and renunciation, practice of austerities, the overcoming of difficulties, and eventual realization. Siddhas were both male and female and represented all strata of Indian society: Some were born into royal families, others to uneducated laborers. Many began their lives as monks or scholars in one of the great Indian Buddhist universities. Most were compelled at a certain point to abandon their ordinary life, the monastery, or the throne, in favor of mountain solitude and a life of meditation and yogic practice. Some studied under a living master (occasionally another siddha), others received teachings through direct visions of the Buddha. After attaining siddhi, they often led the life of a wandering ascetic, or appeared in the guise of a yogin-madman, intentionally transgressing the normal parameters of religious practice. Siddhas often instructed their disciples through songs of realization (*dohā*), but hundreds of works—including tantric commentaries, liturgies, and meditation manuals—attributed to Indian adepts are also preserved in the Tibetan canon. As objects of meditation, devotional prayer, and religious art, the figures of the siddhas themselves form an important locus of religious practice throughout the Himalayan Buddhist world.

Well-known individuals among the traditional reckonings of eighty-four *mahāsiddhas* include Saraha and Maitrīpa, responsible for the spread of MAHĀMUDRĀ (great seal) instructions; Tilopa and Nāropa, earliest founders of the Tibetan BKA' BRGYUD (KAGYU) sect; and Virūpa, source for the Tibetan doctrine of path and fruition (*lam 'bras*) of the SA SKYA (SAKYA) sect.

See also: **Tantra**

Bibliography

Davidson, Ronald M. *Indian Esoteric Buddhism: A Social History of the Tantric Movement.* New York: Columbia University Press, 2002.

Guenther, Herbert V. *The Life and Teaching of Nāropa.* Boston and London: Shambhala, 1986.

Robinson, James B. *Buddha's Lions: Lives of the 84 Siddhas.* Berkeley, CA: Dharma Publications, 1979.

Robinson, James B. "The Lives of Indian Buddhist Saints: Biography, Hagiography and Myth." In *Tibetan Literature: Studies in Genre,* ed. José Ignacio Cabezón and Roger R. Jackson. Ithaca, NY: Snow Lion, 1996.

Templeman, David, trans. *The Seven Instruction Lineages.* Dharamsala, India: Library of Tibetan Works and Archives, 1983.

ANDREW QUINTMAN

MAHĀVASTU

The *Mahāvastu* (*Great Story*) recounts in both verse and prose the life of the Buddha from the perspective of the Lokottaravādins, a subgroup of the MAHĀSĀṂGHIKA SCHOOL. Written between the second century B.C.E. and the fourth century C.E. in Buddhist Hybrid Sanskrit, it embellishes many episodes of Śākyamuni's biography with *jātakas, avadānas,* and other legends, presenting him as a basically supernatural figure.

See also: **Avadāna; Buddha, Life of the; Jātaka**

Bibliography

Jones, J. J., trans. *The Mahāvastu,* 3 vols. London: Luzac, 1949–1956.

JOHN S. STRONG

MAHĀYĀNA

There are, it seems, very few things that can be said with certainty about Mahāyāna Buddhism. It is certain that the term *Mahāyāna* (which means "great or large vehicle") was in origin a polemical label used by only one side—and perhaps the least significant side—of a protracted, if uneven, Indian debate about what the real teachings of the Buddha were, that might have begun just before, or just after, the beginning of the common era in India. It is, however, not clear how soon this label was actually used outside of texts to designate a self-conscious, independent religious movement. The term does not occur in Indian inscriptions, for example, until the fifth or sixth century. It is also certain that Buddhist groups and individuals in China, Korea, Tibet, and Japan have in the past, as in the very recent present, identified themselves as Mahāyāna Buddhists, even if the polemical or value claim embedded in that term was only dimly felt, if at all.

But apart from the fact that it can be said with some certainty that the Buddhism embedded in China, Korea, Tibet, and Japan is Mahāyāna Buddhism, it is no longer clear what else can be said with certainty about Mahāyāna Buddhism itself, and especially about its earlier, and presumably formative, period in India. While it is true that scholars not so long ago made a series of confident claims about the Mahāyāna, it is equally clear that now almost every one of those claims is seriously contested, and probably no one now could, in good faith, confidently present a general characterization of it. In part, of course, this is because it has become increasingly clear that Mahāyāna Buddhism was never one thing, but rather, it seems, a loosely bound bundle of many, and—like Walt Whitman—was large and could contain, in both senses of the term, contradictions, or at least antipodal elements. But in part, too, the crumbling of old confidences is a direct result of the crumbling of old "historical" truisms about Buddhism in general, and about the Mahāyāna in particular. A few examples must suffice.

The old linear model and the date of the "origin" of the Mahāyāna

The historical development of Indian Buddhism used to be presented as simple, straightforward, and suspiciously linear. It started with the historical Buddha whose teaching was organized, transmitted, and more or less developed into what was referred to as *early Buddhism.* This Early Buddhism was identified as HĪNAYĀNA (the "small," or even "inferior vehicle"), THERAVĀDA (the teaching of the elders), or simply "monastic Buddhism" (what to call it remains a problem). A little before or a little after the beginning of the common era this early Buddhism was, according to the model, followed by the Mahāyāna, which was seen as a major break or radical transformation. Both the linear model and the rhetoric used to construct it left the distinct impression that the appearance of the Mahāyāna meant as well the disappearance of Early Buddhism or Hīnayāna, that, in effect, the former replaced the latter. If the development was in fact linear, it could, of course, not have been otherwise. Unfortunately, at least for the model, we now know that this was not true. The emergence of the Mahāyāna was a far more complicated affair than the linear model allowed, and "Early" Buddhism or Hīnayāna or what some now call—perhaps correctly—*mainstream Buddhism,* not only persisted, but prospered, long after the beginning of the common era.

The most important evidence—in fact the only evidence—for situating the emergence of the Mahāyāna around the beginning of the common era was not Indian evidence at all, but came from China. Already by the last quarter of the second century C.E. there was a small, seemingly idiosyncratic collection of substantial Mahāyāna sūtras translated into what Erik Zürcher calls "broken Chinese" by an Indoscythian, whose Indian name has been reconstructed as Lokakṣema. Although a recent scholar has suggested that these translations may not have been intended for a Chinese audience, but rather for a group of returning Kushan immigrants who were no longer able to read Indian languages, and although there is no Indian evidence that this assortment of texts ever formed a group there, still, the fact that they were available to some sort of Central Asian or Chinese readership by the end of the second century must indicate that they were composed sometime before that. The recent publication of, unfortunately, very small fragments of a Kushan manuscript of one of these texts—the *Aṣṭasāhasrikā Prajñāpāramitā* (*Perfection of Wisdom in Eight Thousand Lines*)—also points in the same direction. But the difficult question remains how long before they were translated into "broken Chinese" had these texts been composed, and here the only thing that can be said with some conviction is that, to judge by their contents, the texts known to Lokakṣema cannot represent the earliest phase or form of Mahāyāna thought or literature. They seem to presuppose in fact a more or less long development of both style and doctrine, a development that could have easily taken a century or more and, therefore, would throw the earliest phase of this literature back to about the beginning of the common era. The emergence of the Mahāyāna has—mostly as a matter of convention—therefore been placed there. But even apart from the obvious weaknesses inherent in arguments of this kind there is here the tacit equation of a body of literature with a religious movement, an assumption that evidence for the presence of one proves the existence of the other, and this may be a serious misstep.

The evidence for the Mahāyāna outside of texts

Until fairly recently scholars were content to discuss the emergence of the Mahāyāna almost exclusively in terms of literary developments, and as long as they did not look outside of texts the emergence of a Mahāyāna could indeed be placed—at least conventionally—around the beginning of the common era. But when they began to look outside of texts, in art historical or inscriptional or historical sources, for evidence of the Mahāyāna as a religious movement, or for evidence of actual Mahāyāna groups or cults in India, this became much more difficult. A good illustration of the issues involved here might be seen in the Indian evidence for what became first in China, and then in Japan, a major form of Mahāyāna Buddhism.

One of the Mahāyāna texts translated by Lokakṣema is called in Sanskrit the *Sukhāvatīvyūha-sūtra,* and a Chinese translation of it came to be a central text for East Asian PURE LAND BUDDHISM. According to the line of thought sketched above, since this text was translated already at the end of the second century it must have been composed in India sometime earlier and, by convention, around the beginning of the common era. Thus, if we limited ourselves to textual evidence, this form of Mahāyāna Buddhism must have emerged in India at that time. If, however, we look outside of texts there is simply no evidence for this. There is a large body of archaeological, art historical, and inscriptional evidence for Buddhist cult practice for this period, but absolutely nothing in it would suggest anything like East Asian Pure Land Buddhism, and no trace of the Buddha AMITĀBHA, the central figure and presumed object of devotion in this Buddhism. In the hundreds of Buddhist donative inscriptions that we have in India for the whole of the first five centuries of the common era, in fact, there is only a single certain, utterly isolated and atypical, reference to Amitābha, and it is as late as the second half of the second century. Among the hundreds of surviving images from the same period, images that testify to the overwhelming presence of the historical Buddha Śākyamuni as the focus of attention, there is again a single certain isolated image of Amitābha. There is a very small number of images or reliefs from Northwestern India (Gandhāra) that some scholars have taken as representations of Amitābha and his Pure Land, but there is no agreement here, and the images or reliefs in question may date from as late as the fifth century. In other words, once nontextual evidence is taken into account the picture changes dramatically. Rather than being datable to the beginning of the common era, this strand of Mahāyāna Buddhism, at least, appeared to have no visible impact on Indian Buddhist cult practice until the second century, and even then what impact it had was extremely isolated and marginal, and had no lasting or long-term consequences—there were no further references to Amitābha in Indian image inscriptions. Almost exactly the same pattern occurs on an even broader scale when nontextual evidence is considered.

The Mahāyāna and monastic Buddhism in the middle period

Although the history of Buddhism in India is in general not well documented, still, for the period from the beginning of the common era to the fifth to sixth centuries—precisely the period that according to the old scheme should be the "period of the Mahāyāna"—we probably have better sources than for almost any other period. Certainly, we have for this period an extensive body of inscriptions from virtually all parts of India. These records document the religious aspirations and activities of Buddhist communities throughout the period at sites all across the Indian landscape, and they contain scores of references to named Buddhist groups and "schools." But nowhere in this extensive body of material is there any reference, prior to the fifth century, to a named Mahāyāna. There are, on the other hand, scores of references to what used to be called Hīnayāna groups—the Sarvāstivādins, Mahāsāṃghikas, and so on. From this point of view, at least, this was not "the period of the Mahāyāna," but "the period of the Hīnayāna." Moreover, it is the religious aspirations and goals of the Hīnayāna that are expressed in these documents, not those of a Mahāyāna. There is, for example, a kind of general consensus that if there is a single defining characteristic of the Mahāyāna it is that for Mahāyāna the ultimate religious goal is no longer NIRVĀṆA, but rather the attainment of full awakening or buddhahood by all. This goal in one form or another and, however nuanced, attenuated, or temporally postponed, characterizes virtually every form of Mahāyāna Buddhism that we know. But, again, there is hardly a trace of this aspiration prior to the fifth century anywhere in the large body of Indian Buddhist inscriptions that have survived. Even more mediate goals associated with the Mahāyāna are nowhere represented. There is, for example, not a single instance anywhere in Indian inscriptions of a donor aspiring to REBIRTH in a Pure Land, and this is in startling contrast with what occurs in countries or communities—like LONGMEN in China—where Mahāyāna Buddhism was actually practiced and was important.

What is particularly disconcerting here is the disconnect between expectation and reality: We know from Chinese translations that large numbers of Mahāyāna sūtras were being composed in the period between the beginning of the common era and the fifth century. These texts were constructing, defining, and debating competing versions of a, or the, Mahāyāna, and articulating Mahāyāna religious ideas and aspirations. But outside of texts, at least in India, at exactly the same period, very different—in fact seemingly older—ideas and aspirations appear to be motivating actual behavior, and old and established Hīnayāna groups appear to be the only ones that are patronized and supported. In India at least, in an age when Mahāyāna Buddhas like Amitābha and AKṢOBHYA might have been expected to dominate, it is, in fact, the old Buddha Śākyamuni who everywhere remains the focus of attention—it is his image, for example, that is easily and everywhere found.

The Mahāyāna and the role of the laity

What to make of this disconnect remains, of course, a major conundrum for any attempt to characterize the Mahāyāna or to track its history and development—much of which might, in fact, have taken place outside India. But this is by no means the only disconnect that is encountered in trying to get a handle on the Mahāyāna. One of the most frequent assertions about the Mahāyāna—to cite another example—is that it was a lay-influenced, or even lay-inspired and dominated, movement that arose in response to the increasingly closed, cold, and scholastic character of monastic Buddhism. This, however, now appears to be wrong on all counts. While it is true that as it developed outside of India Mahāyāna Buddhism appears to have taken on at least the appearance of a more lay-oriented movement, a good deal of this appearance may be based on a misunderstanding or misrepresentation of the established monastic Buddhism it was supposed to be reacting to. It is, in fact, becoming increasingly clear that far from being closed or cut off from the lay world, monastic, Hīnayāna Buddhism—especially in its Indian, Sanskritic forms—was, very much like medieval Christian monasticism, deeply embedded in and concerned with the lay world, much of its program being in fact intended and designed to allow laymen and women and donors the opportunity and means to make religious merit. This in many ways remains the function of monastic Buddhism even today in modern Theravāda countries. Ironically, then, if the Mahāyāna was reacting to monastic Buddhism at all, it was probably reacting to what it—or some of its proponents—took to be too great an accommodation to lay needs and values on the part of monastic Buddhism, too pronounced a preoccupation with providing an arena for lay religious practices and all that that involved—acquiring and maintaining property, constructing institutions that would survive over time, and so on. The Mahāyāna criticism of monastic Hīnayāna Buddhisms may have been, in effect, that they had moved too far away from the radically individualistic and ascetic ideals that the proponents of the Mahāyāna favored. This view is finding increasing support in Mahāyāna sūtra literature itself.

The old characterization of the Mahāyāna as a lay-inspired movement was based on a selective reading of a very tiny sample of extant Mahāyāna sūtra literature, most of which was not particularly early. As scholars have moved away from this limited corpus, and have begun to explore a wider range of such sūtras, they have stumbled on, and have started to open up, a literature that is often stridently ascetic and heavily engaged in reinventing the forest ideal, an individualistic, antisocial, ascetic ideal that is encapsulated in the apparently resurrected image of "wandering alone like a rhinoceros." This, to be sure, is a very different Mahāyāna that is emerging. But its exploration is now still a work in progress. At this point we can only postulate that the Mahāyāna may have had a visible impact in India only when, in the fifth century, it had become what it had originally most strongly objected to: a fully landed, sedentary, lay-oriented monastic institution—the first mention of the Mahāyāna in an Indian inscription occurs, in fact, in the record of a large grant of land to a Mahāyāna monastery. In the meantime the Mahāyāna may well have been either a collection of marginalized ascetic groups living in the forest, or groups of cantankerous and malcontent conservatives embedded in mainstream, socially engaged monasteries, all of whom continued pouring out pamphlets espousing their views and values, pamphlets that we now know as Mahāyāna sūtras. We simply do not know.

The Mahāyāna and the misrepresentation of non-Mahāyāna literature

If, then, the notion of the Mahāyāna as a lay-inspired or oriented movement now seems untenable, the notion that it was a reaction to a narrow scholasticism on the part of monastic, Hīnayāna, Buddhism should have seemed silly from the start. Such a view was only even possible by completely ignoring an enormous collection of what are almost certainly the most culturally vibrant and influential forms of Buddhist literature. The representation of Hīnayāna Buddhism as narrowly scholastic rests almost entirely on a completely disproportionate, and undeserved, emphasis on the ABHIDHARMA. The *abhidharma* was almost certainly important to a narrow circle of monks. But *abhidharma* texts were by no means the only things that Hīnayāna monks wrote or read. They also wrote —especially it seems in what should have been "the Mahāyāna period"—an enormous number of stories, and they continued writing them apparently long after the early Mahāyāna sūtras were in production. Some of these stories are specifically called JĀTAKA and AVADĀNA and they have come down to us as separate collections—the Pāli *jātakas,* for example, which in bulk alone equals the *abhidhamma,* and the Sanskrit AVADĀNAŚATAKA—or embedded in vinayas or monastic codes, as is the case particularly in the enormous MŪLASARVĀSTIVĀDA-VINAYA where such monastic stories predominate. The amount of space given over to these stories in this vinaya alone makes the ABHIDHARMAKOŚABHĀṢYA look like a minor work.

Given the great amount of monastic energy that went into the composition, redaction, and transmission of this literature, and given its great impact on Indian Buddhist art, especially in what should have been "the Mahāyāna period," it is particularly surprising that the system or set of religious ideas that it articulates and develops has never really been taken seriously as representative of monastic Buddhism in India from the first to the fifth century. It contains—variously expressed and modulated—an uncomplicated, if not always consistent, doctrine of KARMA (ACTION) and merit that supports a wide range of religious activities easily available to both monks and laymen. It takes as a given the possibility of both monks and laymen interacting with and assisting the dead. It articulates in almost endless permutations what must have been a highly successful system of exchange and reciprocity between laymen and monks. It presents a very rich and textured conception of the Buddha in which he appears as almost everything from a powerful miracle worker to a compassionate nurse for the sick, but is also always the means to "salvation" or a better rebirth. The religious world of Buddhist story literature in addition offered to both monks and laymen easily available objects of worship—relics, stūpas, and images—and, again contrary to the old model, a fully developed conception and cult of the Buddha-as-Bodhisattva. The fact that all of this, and a great deal more that is religiously significant, is delivered in a simple, straightforward story form that was easily accessible makes it abundantly clear that a very large part of Hīnayāna monastic literature is anything but narrowly scholastic and off-putting. Indeed, in comparison with most Mahāyāna sūtra literature it appears to be positively welcoming, and it seems that the characterization "narrowly scholastic" fits far better with the Mahāyāna texts themselves. It is, for example, hard to imagine anyone but a confirmed scholastic reading the *Perfection of Wisdom in Eight Thousand Lines* for pleasure, and almost impossible to imagine anyone confusing it—or the vast majority of other Mahāyāna sūtras—with real literature. And yet, already long ago the French scholar Sylvain Lévi was able to characterize the enormous repository of monastic tales that is the *Mūlasarvāstivāda-vinaya* as not only a "masterpiece" of Buddhist literature, but of Sanskrit literature as a whole. Many of the issues here, however, involve something more than just literary form or style.

The scholasticism of the Mahāyāna

Both the assertion of the lay orientation of the Mahāyāna and of an increasingly inaccessible, scholastic monastic Buddhism, for example, are clearly linked to another of the early and persistent characterizations of both: Monastic Hīnayāna Buddhism was from very early on said to have been uninvolved in—indeed opposed to—ritual and devotion and focused exclusively on meditative practice and doctrine. The Mahāyāna, on the other hand, was somehow supposed to be the opposite, and to have been particularly marked by devotion. But while it is true that certain strands of the Mahāyāna in their later and largely extra-Indian developments came to be cast in increasingly devotional forms, it is by no means clear that this was so from the beginning, and hard to see how it could ever have been maintained that the Mahāyāna in its earlier

Indian forms was particularly devotional. Any such notion should have been easily dispelled by even a quick reading of the *Mūlamadhyamakakārikā* of NĀGĀRJUNA, the figure who has been taken—whatever his actual date—as the earliest individually named spokesman for the Mahāyāna in India. This is a work that is, in fact, decidedly scholastic, focused exclusively on a narrow band of doctrine, arcane, and very far from easily accessible: Even with long and laborious commentaries, both ancient and modern, much of it remains elusive. If it is, in fact, representative of the early forms of the Mahāyāna in India, then whatever that Mahāyāna was it could hardly have been a broad-based, easily accessible, lay-oriented, devotional movement. What seems to hold for Nāgārjuna's *Kārikās,* moreover, would seem to hold for much of Mahāyāna sūtra literature. Much of it also cannot be described as easily accessible, and most of it, perhaps, would only have been of interest to a certain type or types of monks.

The *Perfection of Wisdom in Eight Thousand Lines,* for example, as well as its ever-lengthening companion pieces in 10,000, 18,000, 25,000, and 100,000 lines, sometimes seem to be little more than unrelenting repetitions of long lists of technical doctrinal categories—that would, presumably, have been known by or of interest to only very learned monks—which are, again unrelentingly, said to be "empty." It is also not just the *Perfection of Wisdom* that can be so described. The *Kāśyapaparivarta* (*Chapter of Kāśyapa*), another Mahāyāna text that might be early, although it differs somewhat in format, is much the same in content: The whole first part of it consists of a long list of doctrinal items arranged in groups of fours. Some Mahāyāna sūtras—the SAṂDHINIRMOCANA-SŪTRA (*Sūtra of the Explanation of Mysteries*), for instance—can hardly be distinguished from technical treatise or śāstras. There are, of course, exceptions. The *Vimalakīrtinirdeśa* (*Teaching of Vimalakīrti*), for example, is commonly cited as one, but even then its atypicality is always noted and the contrast with other Mahāyāna sūtras emphasized. In contrast to the authors of other Mahāyāna sūtras its author, says Étienne Lamotte, "does not lose himself in a desert of abstract and impersonal doctrine" (p. v). There are also occasional lively vignettes elsewhere—for instance, the scene in the *Drumakinnararājaparipṛcchā* (*Questions of the Spirit King Druma*) where when the austere monk MAHĀKĀŚYAPA is so charmed by some heavenly music he cannot help himself and jumps up and dances, or the stories in the *Ratnakaraṇḍa-sūtra* (*Sūtra of the Basket of Jewels*) where Mañjuśrī makes MĀRA carry his begging bowl, or spends the rains-retreat in the King's harem—but these appear to be rare. What narrative or story elements occur in known Mahāyāna texts appear to be either polemics intended to make fun of other monks, as in the *Questions of Druma,* the *Basket of Jewels,* and in the *Teaching of Vimalakīrti*; or are simply unintegrated add-ons, like the story of Ever-Weeping in the *Perfection of Wisdom in Eight Thousand Lines*; or wholesale borrowings, as in the first part of the *Rāṣṭrapālaparipṛcchā* (*Questions of Rāṣṭrapāla*). Even with these possible exceptions, and bearing in mind that only a limited corpus of Mahāyāna sūtra literature has so far been studied, much of what has been studied seems positively dreary and is commonly said to be so in the scholarly backroom. Not only is there little narrative or story, there is also a very great deal of doctrinal, meditative and ascetic minutia—Lamotte's "desert." To learned monks—indeed very learned monks—this might have had great attraction, but how it would have struck anyone else remains imaginable, but unclear. What is clear, however, is that the scholasticism found from the beginning of Mahāyāna literature did not abate or go away, and already in India the Mahāyāna produced some very impressive, even mind-boggling, "philosophical" systems, like those lumped together under the heading Yogācāra. Works ascribed to the monk ASAṄGA play a key role in the Yogācāra, and a story preserved in BU STON's *History of Buddhism* about the reaction of Asaṅga's younger brother—himself a scholastic of the first order—might be instructive. He is supposed to have said:

> Alas, Asaṅga, residing in the forest,
>
> has practiced meditation for 12 years.
>
> Without having attained anything by this meditation,
>
> he has founded a system, so difficult and burdensome,
>
> that it can be carried only by an elephant.

The Mahāyāna and the move away from devotion and cult

None of this, of course, squares very well with the notion that the Mahāyāna was in India a popular devotional movement—if even learned monks found its scholasticism off-putting, any laity would almost certainly as well. But this is not the only thing that does not square. There is, for example, surprisingly little apparent interest in devotional or cult practice in the Mahāyāna sūtras that can, at least provisionally, be placed in the early centuries of the common era, and in what little there is there is a curiously anticultic stand.

One of the most visible characteristics of the Mahāyāna as it developed outside of India may well be an emphasis on a multiplicity of "present" Buddhas other than Śākyamuni, on the Buddhas Amitābha and Bhaiṣajyaguru in particular, less so on the Buddha AKṢOBHYA. But while there are early Mahāyāna sūtras devoted to the first and third of these that were composed, presumably, in India, these early texts contain really very little that would suggest any elaborate system of cult, WORSHIP, or RITUAL. It is, in fact, only in the sūtra devoted to Bhaiṣajyaguru, which cannot be early, that we get clear references to the use of cult images and set, specific ritual forms. There is, moreover, as already mentioned, only the barest certain trace of any devotion to Amitābha in the Indian art historical or inscriptional record, and none at all—or only very late—for Bhaiṣajyaguru or Akṣobhya. Unlike the great bodhisattvas, these buddhas seem never to have captured the Indian religious imagination in an immediate way. Rebirth in Amitābha's Pure Land was, to be sure, in India—as later in Nepal and Tibet—a generalized religious goal, but as such probably differed very little from other generic positive rebirths.

It is, however, not just in the early sūtras dealing with the new buddhas that it is difficult to find references to cult practice, to images—once erroneously thought to have been a Mahāyāna innovation—or even to the stūpa cult. They are surprisingly rare in all Mahāyāna sūtras until the latter begin their elusive transformation into TANTRA, and this process must start around the fourth century. The comparative rarity of references in this literature to the stūpa cult was particularly damaging to Akira Hirakawa's theory that tied the origin of the Mahāyāna to this cult, but his theory has been largely set aside on other grounds as well (i.e., a serious underestimation of the role of established monastic Buddhism [Hīnayāna] in the construction and development of the cult). It is in the literature of the latter, in fact, particularly in its vinaya and *avadāna* literatures, that the origin tales, the promotion, and the religious ideology of both the stūpa cult and the cult of images occur, not in Mahāyāna sūtras—if they refer to either it is at least clear that they take both as already established cult forms, and are in fact reacting to them, at first, at least, by attempting to deflect attention away from them and toward something very different. This attempt is most commonly articulated in passages that assert—to paraphrase—that it is good to fill the world with stūpas made of precious substances, and to worship them with all sorts of perfumes, incenses, and so on, but it is far and away, in fact infinitely, better and more meritorious to take up even a four-line verse of the doctrine, preserve it, recite it, teach it and—eventually, it now seems—write or copy it. Virtually the same assertion, using virtually the same language, is made in regard to religious giving—it is good to fill the whole world with jewels and give it as a gift to the Buddha, but it is far and away superior to take up, study and instantiate even a small part of the doctrine, or some practice, or a text. This, for example, is a constant refrain in the DIAMOND SŪTRA (*Vajracchedikā*).

Passages of this sort—and they are legion—are explicitly devaluing precisely what archaeological and inscriptional evidence indicates large numbers of Buddhist monks, nuns, and laypeople were doing everywhere in India in the early centuries of the common era: engaging in the stūpa cult and making religious gifts. They also appear to be inflating the value of what large numbers of Buddhist monks, nuns, and laypeople might well have not been doing, but what the authors or compilers of Mahāyāna sūtras wanted them to: seriously taking up or engaging with the doctrine. This looks very much like reformist rhetoric—conservative and the opposite of "popular"—and yet it, perhaps more than anything else, seems characteristic of a great deal and a wide range of Mahāyāna literature. Here too it is important to note that Gregory Schopen was almost certainly wrong—and his theory too must go the way of Hirakawa's—in seeing in these passages only an attempt by the "new" movement to substitute one similar cult (the cult of the book) for another similar cult (the cult of relics). That such a substitution occurred—and perhaps rather quickly—is likely, but it now appears that it is very unlikely that this was the original or fundamental intention. That intention—however precarious, unpopular, or successful—was almost certainly to shift the religious focus from cult and giving to doctrine, to send monks, nuns, and even laymen quite literally back to their books. That in this attempt the book itself was—again, it seems, rather early—fetishized may only be a testament to the strong pressures toward cult and ritual that seem to have been in force in Indian Buddhism from the beginning. The success of this attempt might well account for the fact—otherwise so puzzling—that it is very difficult to find clear and uncontested Mahāyāna elements in the Indian art historical and inscriptional record: If adherents of the Mahāyāna had in fact heeded the injunctions in their own texts, and turned away from cult and giving, they would have left few if any traces outside their large "pamphlet" or "tract" literature. But any success within Mahāyāna groups would also have to be set alongside the apparent failure to affect the mainstream Indian Buddhist tradition for a very long time: That tradition not only continued, but increased its construction and promotion of monastic cult sites and objects of devotion, and became increasingly entangled in religious gifts—land, cash endowments, and business enterprises. All our sources for the first five centuries make this clear. So too, it seems, did the Mahāyāna: When in the late fifth and early sixth centuries we finally get the first references to the Mahāyāna by name, it is, again, in association with large grants of land. There are still other possible indications that the Mahāyāna "reform" was not entirely successful even among its own ranks: A Mahāyāna text like, for example, the *Samādhirāja-sūtra* (*King of Concentrations Sūtra*) is still spending a great deal of space asserting the primacy of practice over worship, of realization over religious giving, and still fulminating against the accumulation of donations—preaching to the supposedly converted is probably never a good sign. It is also important to note that such assertions are not necessarily unique to the Mahāyāna. They occur sporadically (already?) in some Hīnayāna sources, both sūtra and vinaya, and are found even in works like Āryaśūra's JĀTAKAMĀLĀ. Such assertions may prove to be only an old Buddhist issue that the Mahāyāna revived.

The Mahāyāna and the new bodhisattvas

There is left, lastly, the one element that is associated with the Mahāyāna and that appears, perhaps more than anything else, to have had a major and lasting impact on Indian religious life and culture. It has already been noted that what evidence we have seems to suggest that the new Mahāyāna buddhas—Amitābha, and even less so Akṣobhya and Bhaiṣajyaguru—may never have really taken root in India, and the same would seem to hold for an almost endless list of Mahāyāna bodhisattvas or "aspirants to awakening." But two of these latter, starting from the fifth century, clearly caught on: the Bodhisattva Mañjuśrī and the Bodhisattva Avalokiteśvara, especially the latter. The first of these, the Bodhisattva Mañjuśrī, is certainly the earlier of the two. He, an exemplification of the new wisdom and emphasis on doctrine, occurs in some of the Mahāyāna sūtras that can be dated early, but never really as anything other than a model or ideal, and certainly not as an object of cult or devotion. It is only much, much later, when his character has changed, that cult images of Mañjuśrī occur, and even then—after the fifth century—they are not particularly numerous. It is quite otherwise with Avalokiteśvara. He comes later—perhaps considerably later—than Mañjuśrī, but already in the earliest textual references to him of any detail (probably in a late chapter of the LOTUS SŪTRA [SADDHARMAPUṆḌARĪKA-SŪTRA]), and the earliest undisputed art historical representations of him (probably some Gupta images from Sārnāth and some reliefs from the western cave monasteries), he appears as a "savior" figure, and he continues in this role, sometimes jostling with Tārā, a female competitor, until the "disappearance" of Buddhism from India.

The bodhisattva concept reflected in the late forms of Mañjuśrī and Avalokiteśvara is certainly important, but it remains unclear whether it is best seen as an organic development of specifically Mahāyāna ideas, or, rather, as a part of much larger developments that were occurring in Indian religion as a whole. What seems fairly sure, however, is that there was an earlier and much more prosaic—though none the less heroic—Mahāyāna conception of the bodhisattva as well. Simply put, this amounted to ordinary monks, nuns, and perhaps very committed laypersons taking a vow to replicate the career of Śākyamuni in all its immensity, committing themselves to, in effect, a long, if not endless, series of lifetimes spent in working for the benefit of others, of postponing their release and full enlightenment for the benefit of all. This ideal has had, of course, strong appeal in the modern West, but it also may account, at least in part, for the failure of the early Mahāyāna in India. At the least it asked too much—think what it would cost an individual just to become Saint Francis; at the worst such an ideal might well have appeared to religious women and men in India as counterintuitive, if not positively silly. What we know of such committed men and women would suggest that they were sternly conditioned to flee the very thing, the long cycle of rebirth, that they were being asked to embrace. In the end, however—and that is where we are—this may simply be yet another thing we do not really know about the Mahāyāna.

See also: **Madhyamaka School; Mainstream Buddhist Schools; Merit and Merit-Making; Prajñāpāramitā Literature; Relics and Relics Cults; Yogācāra School**

Bibliography

Bechert, Heinz. "Notes on the Formation of Buddhist Sects and the Origins of Mahāyāna." In *German Scholars on India,* Vol. 1. Varanasi, India: Chowkhamba Sanskrit Series Office, 1973.

Boucher, Daniel. "The Textual History of the Rāṣṭrapālaparipṛcchā: Notes on Its Third-Century Chinese Translation." In *Annual Report of the International Research Institute for Advanced Buddhology at Soka University for the Academic Year 2000.* Tokyo: International Research Institute for Advanced Buddhology, Soka University, 2001.

Conze, Edward. "Mahayana Buddhism." In *The Concise Encyclopaedia of Living Faiths,* ed. R. C. Zaehner. London: Hutchinson, 1959.

Deleanu, Florin. "A Preliminary Study on Meditation and the Beginnings of Mahāyāna Buddhism." In *Annual Report of the International Research Institute for Advanced Buddhology at Soka University for the Academic Year 1999.* Tokyo: International Research Institute for Advanced Buddhology, Soka University, 2000.

Dutt, Nalinaksha. *Aspects of Mahāyāna Buddhism and Its Relation to Hīnayāna.* London: Luzac, 1930.

Harrison, Paul. "Searching for the Origins of the Mahāyāna." *Eastern Buddhist* 28, no. 1 (1995): 48–69.

Hirakawa, Akira. "The Rise of Mahāyāna Buddhism and Its Relationship to the Worship of Stūpas." *Memoirs of the Research Department of the Toyo Bunko* 22 (1963): 57–106.

Lamotte, Étienne. "Sur la formation du Mahāyāna." In *Asiatica: Festschrift Friedrich Weller.* Leipzig, Germay: Harrassowitz, 1954.

Nattier, Jan. *A Few Good Men: The Bodhisattva Path According to the Inquiry of Ugra (Ugraparipṛcchā).* Honolulu: University of Hawaii Press, 2003.

Ray, Reginald A. *Buddhist Saints in India: A Study of Buddhist Values and Orientations.* New York and Oxford: Oxford University Press, 1994.

Sasaki, Shizuka. "A Study on the Origin of Mahāyāna Buddhism." *Eastern Buddhist* 30, no. 1 (1997): 79–113.

Schopen, Gregory. *Figments and Fragments of a Mahāyāna Buddhism in India: More Collected Papers.* Honolulu: University of Hawaii Press, 2003.

Shimoda, Masahiro. *A Study of the Mahāparinirvāṇasūtra: With a Focus on the Methodology of the Study of Mahāyānasūtras* (In Japanese, with English summary). Tokyo: Shunjūsha, 1997.

Silk, Jonathan A. "What, if Anything, Is Mahāyāna Buddhism? Problems of Definitions and Classifications." *Numen* 49 (2002): 76–109.

Stcherbatsky, Th. *The Conception of Buddhist Nirvāṇa* (1927). The Hague, Netherlands: Mouton, 1965.

Williams, Paul. *Mahāyāna Buddhism: The Doctrinal Foundations.* London and New York: Routledge, 1989.

Williams, Paul. *Buddhist Thought: A Complete Introduction to the Indian Tradition.* London and New York: Routledge, 2000.

Zürcher, Erik. *The Buddhist Conquest of China: The Spread and Adaption of Buddhism in Early Medieval China.* Leiden, Netherlands: Brill, 1959.

GREGORY SCHOPEN

MAHĀYĀNA PRECEPTS IN JAPAN

The term *Mahāyāna precepts* is usually used to differentiate lists of PRECEPTS or rules found in MAHĀYĀNA texts from those found in the VINAYA, the traditional source upon which monastic discipline was based. A large number of Mahāyāna texts contain such lists, some detailed and others very simple.

The history of Mahāyāna precepts in Japan was decisively influenced by the country's geography. Japan is an island country; during the Nara period, it was difficult to reach from the Asian mainland, and therefore difficult for ORDINATIONS to be performed in the orthodox manner, in rituals presided over by ten monks who had correctly received the precepts. GANJIN (688–763), for example, tried six times to lead a group of monks from China to Japan so that they could conduct a proper ordination. As a result, at least some monks resorted to self-ordinations, a Mahāyāna ritual in which monks would go before an image of the Buddha and perform confessions and meditate until they received a sign from the Buddha sanctioning their ordination, a sign that could occur either while they were awake or in a dream. In addition, government control of ordinations led other monks to use Mahāyāna precepts to ordain their followers. The most famous example of this is Gyōki (668–749), who used a set of Mahāyāna precepts, probably from the *Yogācārabhūmi,* to ordain groups of men and women who performed social works, such as building bridges and irrigation systems, activities specified in some sets of Mahāyāna rules.

The term *Mahāyāna precepts* was frequently used in a polemical manner to criticize the rules of the vinaya. However, most monks who adhered to the vinaya rules believed that they were following precepts that were largely or completely consistent with Mahāyāna teachings. Ganjin used an ordination platform that included an image of two buddhas sitting in a reliquary. This image is peculiar to the LOTUS SŪTRA (SADDHARMAPUṆḌARĪKA-SŪTRA) and indicated that Ganjin probably interpreted the vinaya in a manner consistent with Tendai teachings that enabled him to "open and reconcile" HĪNAYĀNA teachings of the MAINSTREAM BUDDHIST SCHOOLS with those of Mahāyāna so that no contradiction occurred. Moreover, Japanese monks were also ordained with the fifty-eight rules from a Mahāyāna text, FANWANG JING (BRAHMĀ'S NET SŪTRA). In this case, the Mahāyāna precepts were intended to supplement those found in the vinaya, thereby giving the practitioner a Mahāyāna perspective. As a result, virtually the entire history of Buddhist precepts in Japan could fall under the rubric of Mahāyāna precepts.

A decisive break with the rules of the vinaya occurred when SAICHŌ (767–822), founder of the Tendai School, argued that his monks should use the fifty-eight Mahāyāna precepts of the *Brahmā's Net Sūtra* for their ordinations. Saichō's main objective was to free his monks from administrative control of his adversaries in the Buddhist schools of Nara. His commitment to traditional standards of monastic discipline is revealed in a provision that Tendai monks "provisionally receive the Hīnayāna precepts" after twelve years on Mount Hiei. Because Saichō died before the court accepted his proposals, Tendai monks were left without clear instructions on how the terse precepts of the *Brahmā's Net Sūtra* were to be interpreted when they were the main basis of monastic discipline.

According to the *Brahmā's Net Sūtra,* when the major precepts of the sūtra were violated, confession, followed by a sign from the Buddha, served to restore the precepts. If a person did not receive a sign, the precepts could be received again. When esoteric Buddhist practices were used, a DHĀRAṆĪ (magical spell) might be sufficient to remove the karmic consequences of wrongdoing. Some later Tendai monks such as Annen (late ninth century) argued that the esoteric Buddhist precepts were predominant, but these were so abstract that they offered little concrete guidance to monks. Several centuries later, Tendai monks argued that the principles of the *Lotus Sūtra,* a vague set of recommendations, were sufficient to serve as precepts. Such interpretations meant that the Buddhist order of monks and nuns played little or no role in enforcing the precepts. In some cases, monastery rules might play a role in providing standards for behavior, but Tendai monastic discipline went into general decline.

A number of monks made efforts to revive monastic discipline. Monks such as Shunjō (1166–1227) traveled to China and brought back the practice of using ordinations based on the vinaya but interpreting the precepts in a Mahāyāna manner based on Tiantai teachings. Ninkū (1309–1388) tried to strengthen monastic discipline by emphasizing stricter adherence to the *Brahmā's Net* precepts. Instead of relying on the terse precepts found in that sūtra, he wrote detailed subcommentaries on the text, basing his interpretation of the precepts on a commentary by the de facto founder of the Chinese TIANTAI SCHOOL, ZHIYI (538–597). Kōen (1263–1317) was the center of another group based at Kurdani on Mount Hiei that tried to revive monastic discipline by reviving Saichō's twelve-year period of sequestration on Mount Hiei. At the end of the sequestration, a ritual called a "consecrated ordination" was conducted in which a monk and his teacher affirmed that they had realized buddhahood with this very body through their adherence to the precepts. Myōryū (1637–1690) and Reikū (1652–1739) used Saichō's statement allowing monks to "provisionally receive the Hīnayāna precepts" to argue that the vinaya could be used to supplement the *Brahmā's Net Sūtra.*

The issues and approaches that appeared in Tendai affected other schools in a variety of ways. Many Zen monks also strove to revive the precepts by using "Mahāyāna precepts." Eisai (1141–1215), often considered the founder of Rinzai Zen, deemed the precepts from the vinaya to be the basis of Zen and wrote several works on them. DŌGEN (1200–1253) used a unique set of sixteen Mahāyāna precepts for ordinations and wrote extensively on monastic discipline. The various Pure Land traditions interpreted the precepts in several ways, sometimes citing the DECLINE OF THE DHARMA (*mappō*) as a reason why they were no longer valid, as in the case of Shinshū. However, the various branches of the Jōdo school continued to use precepts in their ordinations even though monks frequently were not required to follow them. For NICHIREN, adherence to the *Lotus Sūtra* served as the precepts. In addition, the establishment of an "ordination platform of the original teaching" played a role in Nichiren's later thinking; the concept, however, was not clearly defined and has been interpreted in a variety of ways by later thinkers. Eison, founder of the Shingon Ritsu tradition, used a Mahāyāna self-ordination to establish a new lineage that followed the vinaya.

In the last few centuries, few Japanese monks have followed any set of precepts closely. However, discussions of the role of precepts have continued to be important, as is shown by the fierce arguments that ensued when the Meiji government made celibacy and meat-eating optional. Even though many monks did not observe these rules, the prestige lost by the new government ruling was important. In addition, the use of Mahāyāna precepts for lay believers should be noted. These are conferred on laity who wish to have ethical rules to guide their lives; these precepts are also used to ordain the dead so that they will have a good rebirth. In conclusion, although Japan is often described as a country where monks do not follow the precepts, they have discussed them continuously for well over a millennium.

See also: **Japan; Meiji Buddhist Reform**

Bibliography

Bodiford, William. *Sōtō Zen in Medieval Japan.* Honolulu: University of Hawaii Press, 1993.

Groner, Paul. "The *Fan-wang ching* and Monastic Discipline in Japanese Tendai: A Study of Annen's *Futsū jubosatsukai kōshaku.*" In *Buddhist Apocryphal Literature,* ed. Robert E. Buswell, Jr. Honolulu: University of Hawaii Press, 1990.

Groner, Paul. *Saichō: The Establishment of the Japanese Tendai School.* Honolulu: University of Hawaii Press, 2000.

Groner, Paul. "Vicissitudes in the Ordinations of Nuns during the Late Nara and Early Heian Periods." In *Engendering Faith: Women and Buddhism in Premodern Japan,* ed. Barbara Ruch. Ann Arbor: Center for Japanese Studies, University of Michigan, 2002.

Jaffe, Richard. *Neither Monk nor Layman: Clerical Marriage in Modern Japanese Buddhism.* Princeton, NJ: Princeton University Press, 2001.

PAUL GRONER

MAHĪŚĀSAKA

The Mahīśāsaka mainstream Indian Buddhist school, a subschool of the Sthavira branch, was prominent in southern India and was closely tied historically and doctrinally to the THERAVĀDA school. The term *Mahīśāsaka* is variously interpreted as referring to the name of the founder, a geographical locale, or to their role in governing or instructing the earth.

See also: **Mainstream Buddhist Schools**

COLLETT COX

MAINSTREAM BUDDHIST SCHOOLS

By several centuries after the death of the Buddha, the itinerant mendicants following his way had formed settled communities and had changed irrevocably their received methods of both teaching and praxis. These changes were inevitable, a consequence of the growth and geographic dispersion of the practicing communities. Confronted with new challenges and opportunities in an increasingly organized institutional setting, monks expanded and elaborated both doctrine and disciplinary codes, created new textual genres, developed new forms of religious praxis, and eventually divided into numerous sects or schools.

The character of mainstream Buddhist schools

Unfortunately, sources for this period, including documents, inscriptions, and archaeological evidence, are poor. Inscriptions and archaeological finds, while providing a priceless contemporaneous record, are limited in detail. Documentary sources, including chronicles, doxographies, translator records, narrative sections of canonical texts, lists of teachers or school lineages, and the diaries of Chinese Buddhist pilgrims who visited India from the fifth to seventh centuries C.E., provide greater detail, but postdate the emergence of schools by several centuries. As themselves products of the sectarian fragmentation that they describe, these documentary sources are colored by sectarian agendas. Nevertheless, they furnish valuable insight into the values and objectives of the developing Buddhist tradition.

A picture of the history of Buddhist schools depends upon reconstruction of the major events in the early history of Buddhism in India: the life of the Buddha; the communal recitations or councils; the so-called first schism; and the fragmentation of the monastic community after this initial schism. Also important are more general questions concerning the criteria by which various groups were distinguished from one another and the notion of what constituted a sect or school within the tradition. It is unclear whether the school names mentioned in traditional sources were intended to refer to independent groups distinguished on similar grounds. Nor is it clear whether the notion of what constituted a sect or school remained consistent in sources of different periods. For example, certain school names corresponded to separate communities of practitioners distinguished by distinct ordination lineages and collections of monastic disciplinary codes. Other names, especially those that appear in the doctrinal scholastic texts and later doxographical treatises, appear to have been used not to mark distinct communities of practitioners, but simply for heuristic purposes, to represent differences in doctrinal perspective or teaching lineage. As a result, different source texts emphasize different factors that contributed to sectarian fragmentation. These contributing factors include geographical separation, language differences, doctrinal disagreements, selective patronage, the influence of non-Buddhists, lineage loyalties to specific teachers, the absence of a recognized supreme authority or unifying institutional structure, varying degrees of laxness regarding or active disagreements over disciplinary codes, and specialization by various monastic groups in differing segments of Buddhist SCRIPTURE.

Further, the image of a harmonious early community from which distinct sects or schools emerged through gradual divergence in practice and in teaching must be questioned. Traditional sources attest to discord among the Buddha's disciples even during his lifetime, and relate that at the Buddha's death one monk, Subhadra, rejoiced since his followers would now be free to do as they liked. Similarly, accounts of the first communal recitation or council held soon after the Buddha's death record that one group of practitioners led by Purāṇa rejected the consensual understanding of the Buddha's teaching and preferred instead to transmit it as Purāṇa himself had heard it. Whether literally true or not, these stories affirm that the later traditions conceived of their own early history as involving both consensus and dissent.

The first schism

Virtually all later sources agree that the first schism within the early Buddhist community occurred with the separation of the MAHĀSĀṂGHIKA SCHOOL, or "those of the great community," from the remaining monks referred to as Sthaviras, or the "elders." Complex and inconsistent, these traditional sources postdate the first schism by several centuries and reflect the biases and viewpoints of separate transmission lineages. Hence, the actual circumstances for the first schism remain obscure and tied to other roughly contemporaneous events that later traditions connect with possibly three additional early councils. The first of these events, recorded in the monastic records of virtually all later schools, is the council of Vaiśālī, which most sources date to approximately one hundred years after the death of the Buddha. Monastic records suggest that this council was convened in response to a disagreement over certain rules of monastic discipline, but do not state that the council resulted in a schism. Later Pāli chronicles and the records of Chinese pilgrims and translators explicitly link the first schism with the outcome of either the first council immediately after the death of the Buddha or this second council of Vaiśālī. They relate that some participants would not accept the communal recitation of the teaching at the first council or the decisions concerning the rules of monastic discipline rendered at the second council. These dissenters, who constituted the adherents of the "great community" (*mahāsaṃgha*), recited a textual collection of their own and formed a separate Mahāsāṃghika school.

Other northern Indian Buddhist sources, all postdating the second century C.E., associate the first schism with yet another council, claimed to have been held at Pāṭaliputra during the mid-third century B.C.E. As a reason for this council, they cite discord over a doctrinal issue, specifically five points concerning characteristics of a "worthy one," or ARHAT. These five points suggest that arhats are subject to retrogression from their level of religious attainment or to limitations such as DOUBT, ignorance, various forms of assistance from or stimulation by others, or the employment of artificial devices such as vocal utterances in the practice of the PATH. Although these points have been interpreted in traditional and many modern sources as an attempt to downgrade the status of the arhat in general, it is possible that they reflect an attempt primarily to distinguish and to clarify specific stages in religious praxis. The later textual sources of the northern early Buddhist schools relate that the supporters of the five points were more numerous and hence were referred to as the Mahāsāṃghikas, "those of the great community"; the minority opponents were then referred to as the "elders," or Sthaviras.

Finally, Pāli sources record yet another council held in the third century B.C.E. at Pāṭaliputra under the auspices of King AŚOKA. According to these accounts, after years of discord within the monastic community, Aśoka convened a council under the direction of the Buddhist monk Moggaliputta Tissa in order to rectify monastic conduct and to root out heretical views. After questioning by Aśoka, sixty thousand monks were expelled from the community, and a select group of some one thousand monks were charged to set down the contents of the Buddha's true teaching. Moggaliputta Tissa is said to have recorded both the heretical views and their refutation in the Pāli scholastic text, the *Kathāvatthu* (*Points of Discussion*). Pāli sources also relate that at the conclusion of the council, Aśoka promulgated an edict inveighing against future divisions within the community and sent missionaries to spread the Buddha's teaching throughout his kingdom and beyond.

This particular account of a council at Pāṭaliputra, found only within Pāli sources, may reflect a conflict limited to the predecessors of the later THERAVĀDA school. However, the so-called schism edict promulgated during the reign of King Aśoka provides additional evidence of concern about discord within the Buddhist monastic community during the third century B.C.E. that was sufficient to warrant secular intervention. Despite differences in the scholarly interpretation of certain directives presented within the edict, it clearly condemns formal division within the monastic community (*saṅghabheda*) and declares that the community of monks and nuns should be united. Thus, this edict implies the presence of or at least the threat of divisions within a community that ideally should be united and stable.

Hence, the traditional sources do not paint a coherent picture of the reasons for the first schism, but instead offer two radically different possibilities, each reflected in later sectarian accounts. The Theravāda and Mahāsāṃghika sources cite differences in the monastic disciplinary code, and the Sarvāstivāda sources, differences in doctrinal interpretation. The former possibility finds support in the oldest Mahāsāṃghika account of the schism, the *Śāriputraparipṛcchā* (*Questions of Śāriputra)*. Here the Mahāsāṃghikas object to an attempt to tighten discipline through an expansion of the monastic disciplinary code and prefer instead to preserve the more restricted disciplinary rules as they stood.

Scholarly consensus also prefers the view that the earliest distinct Buddhist groups emerged not through disagreements over doctrine, but rather through differences in their lineages of ORDINATION (*upasampadā*) and in monastic disciplinary codes (VINAYA). While variety in doctrinal interpretation certainly existed even in the early period, the definition of formal division within the monastic community, which was eventually to be accepted by all groups, specifies monastic discipline as the key factor in the formation of independent groups. If this was indeed the case, then the names of schools reflecting differences in doctrinal interpretation, which are preserved in the later scholastic and COMMENTARIAL LITERATURE, cannot automatically be assumed to denote independent monastic communities, additionally defined by different ordination lineages and monastic disciplinary codes. These doctrinally distinguished school names may instead have functioned simply as heuristic labels, meaningful within the context of doctrinal interpretation, scholastic debate, and teaching lineages, but having limited significance in the life of the monastic community as a whole. Such an interpretation would be consistent with the reports of Chinese pilgrims that monks of different doctrinal persuasion resided together within the same monastery, where they were presumably unified by the same ordination lineage and monastic disciplinary code. Distinct monastic disciplinary codes (vinaya) of only six schools have been preserved: Mahāsāṃghika, MAHĪŚĀSAKA, DHARMAGUPTAKA, Theravāda, SARVĀSTIVĀDA AND MŪLASARVĀSTIVĀDA. Therefore, at the very least, these six school names denote independent groups with distinct lineages of authority and separate monastic communities. In general, relations even among schools distinguished on the basis of monastic disciplinary code were generally not hostile. All practitioners were to be accepted as disciples of the Buddha, and to be treated with courtesy, regardless of differing disciplinary or doctrinal allegiances.

Traditional mainstream schools

Traditional sources maintain that eighteen schools emerged following the first schism, but since more than thirty school names are recorded, the number eighteen may have been chosen for its symbolic significance. The variety of names points to different origins for the schools, including a geographical locale (e.g., Haimavata, "those of the snowy mountains"), a specific teacher (e.g., Vātsīputrīya, "those affiliated with Vātsīputra," or Dharmaguptaka, "those affiliated with Dharmagupta"), a simple descriptive qualification (e.g., Mahāsāṃghika, "those of the great community," or Bahuśrutīya, "those who have heard much"), or a distinctive doctrinal position (e.g., Sarvāstivāda, "those who claim that everything exists," or Vibhajyavāda, "those who make distinctions," or SAUTRĀNTIKA, "those who rely upon the sūtras"). The later doxographical accounts, each of which is colored by its own sectarian bias, do not agree on the chronology or on the order in which the schools emerged, but instead give temporal primacy to the particular group or school with which they were affiliated. They do, however, tend to agree on the basic filiation of the schools with either the Sthavira or the Mahāsāṃghika branch and generally concur that the additional schools were formed within a century or two of the first schism.

The Mahāsāṃghika branch. From the Mahāsāṃghika branch, according to tradition, initially arose three major groups, each of which was associated in later accounts with additional school names. One group, the Kaukkuṭika, may have derived its name from the Kukkuṭārāma Monastery in Pāṭaliputra. The name of a second group, the Ekavyavahārika (or Lokottaravāda) refers to "those who make a single utterance." Later sources interpret this name as reflecting the view that all phenomena can be described by one utterance, namely, the fact that all entities exist merely as mental constructs or provisional designations. However, the name could also be interpreted as referring to the distinctive doctrinal position of this school that the Buddha offers only one utterance, namely, a transcendent utterance. This interpretation would be consistent with an alternative or possibly later name for this group, Lokottaravāda, or "those who claim that (the Buddha and his utterance) are transcendent." Such a concern with the character of the utterance of the Buddha is also evident in the views associated with the schools that emerged from the first group of the Kaukkuṭika: namely, the Bahuśrutīya, who claimed that the Buddha offered both transcendent and ordinary teachings, and the Prajñaptivāda, or "those who offer provisional designations," which might also imply the claim that the Buddha utilized not simply transcendent utterance or absolutely true language, but also provisional designations or relative language.

Thus, the original Mahāsāṃghika branch appears to have been divided, at least in part, on the basis of a difference of opinion concerning the fundamental character of the Buddha's teaching, either as exclusively transcendent or as both transcendent and provisional. A third group emerging from the Mahāsāṃghika branch, the Caitya, centered in the region of Andhra in southern India, were presumably named in accordance with their practice of worship at shrines (caitya). They were also associated with a teacher, Mahādeva, who adopted and possibly reworked the five points concerning the characteristics of a "worthy one" that were cited by northern Indian Buddhist sources as the reason for the first schism between the Mahāsāṃghikas and the Sthaviras.

The Sthavira branch. Later accounts record as many as twenty or more schools that trace their origin to the Sthavira branch. Despite inconsistency in these accounts, the first to emerge was probably the Vātsīputrīya (or Saṃmatīya), also referred to as the PUDGALAVĀDA, or "those who claim that person(hood) (*pudgala*) exists." The Pudgalavādins were attacked vociferously by other Buddhists schools for violating the most basic of Buddhist teachings, namely, that no self is to be found (anātman). The opponents of the Pudgalavādins argued that animate beings exist only as a collection of components or SKANDHA (AGGREGATE), which are conditioned and impermanent. Any unifying entity such as personhood exists only as a mental construct or a provisional designation, which has no reality in itself. For the Pudgalavādins, this view was tantamount to nihilism. They saw a unifying entity of some type as a necessary basis for the notion of mutually distinct animate beings and for the continuity of their experience. Otherwise, the phenomena of moral action, REBIRTH, and religious attainment accepted by all Buddhists would be impossible. Consistent with this position, the Pudgalavādins also maintained the existence of an INTERMEDIATE STATE (*antarābhava*) after death, a transition state that links the aggregates of one lifetime with those of the next. Pudgalavāda positions that are presented and criticized in extant textual sources suggest that the Pudgalavādins did not simply defend the existence of personhood, but also used a distinctive method of argumentation that challenged the growing rigidity of stringent Buddhist scholastic analysis. Pudgalavāda arguments employ a sophisticated method of negative dialectics that continues certain tendencies in the earlier sūtra dialogues and stands in sharp contrast to their opponents' more straightforward, positivist methods.

Sarvāstivāda. Apart from the Pudgalavāda, the Sthavira branch was further divided into two groups: the Sarvāstivāda and the Vibhajyavāda. Evidence for an initial threefold split within the Sthavira branch among the Pudgalavādins, Vibhajyavādins, and Sarvāstivādins comes from two early scholastic treatises, the *Kathāvatthu* of the Theravādins and the *Vijñānakāya* (*Collection on Perceptual Consciousness*) of the Sarvāstivādins. Traditional sources date the *Kathāvatthu* to the period of King Aśoka (third century B.C.E.), but the presence in the *Kathāvatthu* of doctrinal positions associated with each of these three groups does not prove that adherents of these views formed separate schools at that time. The earliest inscriptional references to the name Sarvāstivāda, found in the northwestern regions of Kashmir and Gandhāra as well as in the north central region of Mathurā, date from the first century C.E. Both regions are connected by tradition with prominent early Sarvāstivāda teachers and later became strongholds of the Sarvāstivāda school.

Much of the Sarvāstivāda version of the Buddhist CANON is preserved in Chinese translations, including the complete monastic disciplinary code (vinaya), a portion of the dialogues (sūtra), and the complete collection of scholastic treatises (ABHIDHARMA), as well as many other postcanonical scholastic texts and commentaries. The presence of certain texts in multiple recensions confirms that the Sarvāstivāda school was not homogeneous, but was rather a vast group distinguished by regional, chronological, doctrinal, and other differences. This was most likely true of all early Buddhist schools. In the case of the Sarvāstivāda school, these internal distinctions are clearly demarcated in their scholastic texts by the attribution of distinct doctrinal positions to Sarvāstivāda groups of different regions.

Intragroup differences within the Sarvāstivāda school also may have led directly to the emergence of a Mūlasarvāstivāda school, whose separate monastic disciplinary code survives in Sanskrit, and to whom can probably be attributed other assorted sūtra dialogues and miscellaneous texts preserved in Chinese translation. The precise identity, however, of the Mūlasarvāstivādins remains elusive, and their relation to the Sarvāstivādins a point of scholarly disagreement. Some suggest that the Mūlasarvāstivādins represent merely a later phase in the development of the Sarvāstivāda sectarian stream. Others see the distinction as reflecting both geographical and chronological differences within the Sarvāstivāda school, which was widespread throughout northern India and Central Asia, and in particular in the northwestern region of Kashmir and Gandhāra and the north central region of Mathurā. In this latter view, when the Sarvāstivāda school of the northwest declined in prominence, the Sarvāstivādins of Mathurā became more significant and adopted the name Mūlasarvāstivāda (root Sarvāstivāda) to proclaim their status as the original Sarvāstivādins.

The Sarvāstivādins of northwest India were renowned for their scholarly study of Buddhist doctrine or *abhidharma.* From compiling voluminous treatises called *vibhāṣā,* commentaries on the most significant of their canonical *abhidharma* scriptures, those in the Kashmiri Sarvāstivāda branch eventually came to be called Sarvāstivāda-Vaibhāṣika. The last and best known of these *vibhāṣā* treatises is called the *Mahāvibhāṣā* (*Great Exegesis*). The later Sarvāstivāda summary digests and pedagogical manuals of *abhidharma* contain detailed discussions of all manner of doctrinal issues from ontology to religious praxis. The most controversial of these issues is the position from which the name Sarvāstivāda is derived: namely, *sarvam asti* or "everything exists," referring specifically to the existence of conditioned factors (dharma) in the three time periods of the past, present, and future. This assertion was motivated by the need to provide a basis for the commonly perceived efficacy of past and future causes and conditions. If past actions are accepted as conditions for the arising of present events, and past or future entities function as objects of recollection or presentiment, these past and future actions or entities must, the Sarvāstivādins claim, be admitted to exist. Attacked for violating the fundamental Buddhist doctrine of impermanence, the Sarvāstivādins responded with an elaborate ontology that attempted both to delimit the specific manner in which past and future factors exist and to preserve their conditioned and hence impermanent character.

Most prominent among the critics of this hallmark Sarvāstivāda position were the Sautrāntikas or Dārṣṭāntikas. The original meanings and referents of these names as well as their relationship to one another remain the subject of scholarly disagreement. Since no evidence survives of a separate Sautrāntika or Dārṣṭāntika monastic disciplinary code, they would appear to represent a particular doctrinal perspective, most likely the same doctrinal party within the Sarvāstivāda school. Proponents of this group may have used the term *Sautrāntika* (those who rely upon the sūtras) self-referentially, and their opponents among the Sarvāstivādins may have labeled them pejoratively as Dārṣṭāntika (those who employ examples). The Sautrāntika/Dārṣṭāntikas criticized orthodox Sarvāstivāda ontology as thinly veiled permanence and instead argued for a doctrine of extreme momentariness. They rejected unequivocally the existence of past and future factors, and equated the existence of present factors with an instantaneous exertion of activity. In contrast to the complex array of existent factors proposed by the Sarvāstivādins, the Sautrāntika/Dārṣṭāntikas claimed that experience is best described as an indistinguishable process. The name *Sautrāntika,* "those who rely upon the sūtras," also indicates a rejection of the authority that the Sarvāstivādins bestowed upon their separate canonical *abhidharma* collection.

Vibhajyavāda. The connotation of the term *Vibhajyavāda* has also been the subject of prolonged scholarly disagreement, largely because of the variety of senses in which the term was used over time. In the early sūtras, Vibhajyavāda occurs as a descriptive term for the Buddha, who, in reference to various specific issues, is said to "discriminate" carefully rather than to take an exclusivist position. In their accounts of the council at Pāṭaliputra, later Pāli sources use the term *Vibhajyavāda* to describe the correct teaching of the Buddha, and within Pāli materials the name continues to be used as one among several names for the Theravāda sect. A third-century C.E. inscription links the term *Vibhajyavāda* with the Sthaviras located in the regions of Kashmir, Gandhāra, Bactria, Vanavāsa (i.e., Karnataka), and the island of Sri Lanka. This connection between the Vibhajyavādins and the northwestern regions of Kashmir, Gandhāra, and Bactria clearly indicates that Vibhajyavāda was not simply another name for the Theravāda school. The Mahīśāsakas, Dharmaguptakas, and the Kāśyapīyas, attested in inscriptions from the Northwest, are all connected by later sources with the Vibhajyavādins. As a result, the name *Vibhajyavāda* might be best characterized as a loose umbrella term for those, excluding the Sarvāstivādins, who belonged to the original Sthavira branch.

A review of the many specific doctrinal views explicitly attributed to the Vibhajyavādins in the scholastic literature of the Sarvāstivādins supports this interpretation. These viewpoints do not form a coherent group, but rather are unified simply by virtue of being opposed to respective Sarvāstivāda positions. For example, the Vibhajyavādins are said to support that: thought is inherently pure; form (*rūpa*) occurs even in the formless realm (*ārūpyadhātu*); a subtle form of thought remains in states claimed to be without thought; PRATĪTYASAMUTPĀDA (DEPENDENT ORIGINATION) and the path (mārga) are unconditioned; there is no intermediate state (*antarābhava*) between rebirth states; clear comprehension (*abhisamaya*) of the FOUR NOBLE TRUTHS occurs in a single moment; worthy ones (arhat) cannot retrogress from their level of religious attainment; and finally, that the time periods (*adhvan*) are permanent in contrast to conditioned factors, which are impermanent. Various doctrinal positions attributed to the Mahīśāsakas, Dharmaguptakas, Kāśyapīyas, or the Dārṣṭāntikas are also assigned to the Vibhajyavādins, but each of these schools is characterized by views distinct from the others. For example, the Mahīśāsakas and the Dharmaguptakas disagreed on whether or not the Buddha should be considered as a part of the monastic community and on the relative merit of offerings to each. The Mahīśāsakas saw offerings to the community, which included the Buddha, as more meritorious, and the Dharmaguptakas advocated offerings to the STŪPA as representing the unsurpassed path of the Buddha, who is distinct from and far superior to the community.

Also associated with the Vibhajyavādins, the Theravāda school became dominant in Sri Lanka and Southeast Asia and survives there to the present day. The connection of the Theravāda school to the original Sthavira branch is clearly indicated by its Pāli name *thera,* which is equivalent to the Sanskrit, *sthavira,* and by close ties to the Mahīśāsaka school suggested by both textual and doctrinal similarities. Traditional sources claim that Buddhism was brought to Sri Lanka by the missionary Mahinda, either after the death of Buddha's direct disciple, ĀNANDA, or during the reign of Aśoka in the mid-third century B.C.E. By the fourth century C.E., the Theravāda school had divided into three subgroups, distinguished by their monastic centers: the Mahāvihāravāsins from the Mahāvihāra founded at the time of the introduction of Buddhism to Sri Lanka; the Abhayagirivāsins, dating from some two centuries later; and finally the Jetavanīyas, dating from the fourth century C.E.

The Theravāda textual collection, including both canonical and extensive extracanonical and commentarial texts, is the only early Buddhist collection extant, in toto, in an Indian language (Pāli). Theravāda doctrinal positions often accord with those attributed to the Vibhajyavādins, in opposition to those of the Sarvāstivādins. For example, like the Vibhajyavādins, the Theravādins claim that thought in its fundamental state is pure, that there is no intermediate state (*antarābhava*) between rebirth states, that clear comprehension (*abhisamaya*) of the four noble truths occurs in a single moment, and that worthy ones (arhat) cannot retrogress from their level of religious attainment. Perhaps the most distinctive view adopted by the Theravādins is that of a fundamental and inactive state of mind (*bhavaṅga*), to which the mind returns after each discrete moment of thought, and by which one rebirth state is connected with the next. Further, regarding the Sarvāstivāda claim that factors exist in the past and future, the Theravādins adopt the position that only present factors exist. However, on some positions the Theravādins agree with the Sarvāstivādins (e.g., that there are five possible rebirth states; that all forms of defilement are associated with thought), and on still others, they differ from both the Vibhajyavādins and the Sarvāstivādins (e.g., that NIRVĀṆA is the only unconditioned factor). Thus once again, a doctrinal picture of the various early Indian Buddhist schools reveals a complex mosaic of both shared and distinctive doctrinal positions.

Mahāyāna

The development of the MAHĀYĀNA must also be viewed in the context of the mainstream Buddhist schools. Differing scholarly opinions attempt to locate the origin of Mahāyāna variously within the confines of a particular mainstream Buddhist doctrinal school, in ascetic movements within mainstream Buddhist monasteries, or among lay religious practitioners. Although it is doubtful that any particular mainstream Buddhist school can lay claim to the Mahāyāna, it is clear that later Mahāyāna practitioners adopted the monastic disciplinary codes of mainstream Buddhist schools. Further, key doctrinal positions later associated with Mahāyāna can be traced to mainstream Buddhist doctrinal works: for example, the religious ideal of the BODHISATTVA; the six PĀRAMITĀ (PERFECTIONS) that are the cornerstone of Mahāyāna religious praxis; the theory of multiple forms of the Buddha; and a fundamental, subtle form of thought. But in more general terms, the methods of philosophical argumentation, areas of doctrinal investigation, and modes of communal religious life and praxis that were established in mainstream Buddhist schools determined the course of Buddhist inquiry and practice in India for some one thousand years.

See also: **Buddha, Life of the; Councils, Buddhist**

Bibliography

Bareau, André. *Les Sectes bouddhiques du Petit Véhicule.* Saigon, Vietnam: École Française d'Extrême-Orient, 1955.

Bechert, Heinz. "The Importance of Aśoka's So-Called Schism Edict." In *Indological and Buddhist Studies: Volume in Honour of J. W. de Jong on His Sixtieth Birthday,* ed. L. A. Hercus et al. Canberra: Faculty of Asian Studies, Australia National University, 1982.

Chau, Thich Thien. *The Literature of the Personalists of Early Buddhism,* tr. Sara Webb-Boin. Ho Chi Minh City: Vietnam Buddhist Research Institute, 1997.

Cousins, Lance S. "The 'Five Points' and the Origins of the Buddhist Schools." In *The Buddhist Forum: Volume II, Seminar Papers 1988–1990,* ed. Tadeusz Skorupski. London: Heritage, 1991.

Cousins, Lance S. "Person and Self." In *Buddhism into the Year 2000: International Conference Proceedings.* Bangkok and Los Angeles: Dhammakāya Foundation, 1994.

Cousins, Lance S. "On the Vibhajjavādins: The Mahiṃsāsaka, Dhammaguttaka, Kassapiya, and Tambapaṇṇiya Branches of the Ancient Theriyas." *Buddhist Studies Review* 18, no. 2 (2001): 131–182.

Cox, Collett. *Disputed Dharmas: Early Buddhist Theories on Existence.* Tokyo: International Institute for Buddhist Studies, 1995.

Lamotte, Étienne. *History of Indian Buddhism: From the Origins to the Saka Era,* tr. Sara Webb-Boin. Louvain, Belgium: Peeters Press, 1988.

Nattier, Janice J., and Prebish, Charles S. "Mahāsāṅghika Origins: The Beginning of Buddhist Sectarianism." *History of Religions* 16 (1977): 237–272.

Norman, K. R. "Aśoka's 'Schism' Edict." In *Collected Papers,* Vol. 3. Oxford: Pāli Text Society, 1992.

Sasaki, Shizuka. "Buddhist Sects in the Aśoka Period (1–8)" *Bukkyō Kenkyū* 18, 21, 22, 23, 24, 25, 27, 28 (1989–1999).

COLLETT COX

MAITREYA

Maitreya is the bodhisattva anticipated by all Buddhists traditions to become the next buddha of this world, Jambudvīpa. Currently dwelling in the Tuṣita heaven, Maitreya awaits rebirth at that time in the distant future when Śākyamuni Buddha's dispensation will have been completely forgotten.

Depicted as both BODHISATTVA and future buddha, Maitreya is frequently portrayed sitting Western-style with legs pendant, sometimes with ankles crossed. Another distinctive iconic attribute is a miniature STŪPA or funerary mound placed at the front of his head, recalling the legend that Śākyamuṇi Buddha's disciple MAHĀKĀŚYAPA remains suspended in meditation beneath a stūpa, awaiting Maitreya, to whom he will present Śākyamuṇi's robe and alms bowl, thus establishing the transmission of authority from one buddha to the next. East Asian Buddhists also recognize Maitreya in a particularly graceful form as the bodhisattva appearing in the lovely "pensive prince" pose and also as the "laughing buddha" ubiquitously encountered in the entryway of Chinese monasteries (and restaurants), the latter form based on the semihistorical sixth-century monk Putai, who was especially loved for his kindness to children.

A devotional cult focusing on Maitreya developed very early in India, later becoming especially prominent in Central Asia and China during the fifth and sixth centuries. Devotees sought to secure rebirth in Tuṣita, first to benefit from Maitreya's teaching there, and later to join him during his tenure as the next buddha. Although eventually eclipsed in East Asia by the more popular AMITĀBHA cult, anticipation of Maitreya's golden age continued to erupt periodically in millenarian movements that were intensely devotional and occasionally political as well.

See also: **Buddha(s); Millenarianism and Millenarian Movements**

Bibliography

Lancaster, Lewis. "Maitreya." In *The Encyclopedia of Religion,* ed. Mircea Eliade, vol. 9. New York: Macmillan, 1987.

Sponberg, Alan, and Hardacre, Helen, eds. *Maitreya, the Future Buddha.* Cambridge, UK, and New York: Cambridge University Press, 1988.

ALAN SPONBERG

MAṆḌALA

The Sanskrit noun *maṇḍala* is often translated as "circle" or "discoid object"; however, the term is also used to define visual and meditative images. Used in Hindu and Jain traditions as well as Buddhism, maṇḍalas are described as cosmoplans both in the external sense as diagrams of the cosmos and in the internal sense as guides to the psychophysical practices of an adherent. Fundamentally, however, they represent the manifestation of a specific deity (or group thereof) in the cosmos and as the cosmos. Maṇḍalas can include a few deities or thousands. Both figurative works, as well as those focusing on words, syllables, or attributes, are made. The principal deity, who is also its generative force, is usually placed at the center or core of the maṇḍala. Other deities, who function both independently and as manifestations of the essence and powers of the central image, are carefully placed to illustrate their relation to the primary icon. A maṇḍala can be understood, to some extent, as a web of forces radiating in and out of a self-contained and self-defined spiritual cosmos. Rites based on these icons presume a constant dialogue between the deity at the heart of the maṇḍala and the practitioner who moves, at least metaphorically, from the outside to its core. Once within, the practitioner identifies with the central deity, apprehends all manifestations as part of a single whole, and moves closer to the goal of perfect understanding or enlightenment.

Preserved principally in architectural structures and permanent material such as wood, stone, and paint, maṇḍalas are also made in ephemeral material such as sand or butter. The creation of a maṇḍala is integral to a RITUAL, during or after which it is sometimes destroyed. Both permanent and impermanent examples are used to decorate and sanctify monasteries and homes, in initiation rites for monks and rulers, and as the focus of visualization by clergy and other advanced practitioners and of worship by lay followers.

Groups of eight BODHISATTVAS assembled around a seated buddha (variously identified as Śākyamuni, AMITĀBHA, or Vairocana) are among the earliest and most widespread examples of maṇḍala imagery. Lists of eight great bodhisattvas occur in early MAHĀYĀNA texts, where they are described as protectors of the faithful and providers of mundane blessings, and are linked to a group of eight BUDDHAS. In later texts such groupings are identified as maṇḍalas. The first preserved visual examples of the Maṇḍala of Eight Great Bodhisattvas date from the sixth century, and the type was widespread from the eighth to the twelfth century. Examples include an interesting portable wooden shrine in the Nelson-Atkins Museum in Kansas City, Missouri; a group found along the interior walls of cave 11 at Ellora in India; a distinctive ninefold arrangement from cave 12 at the same site; versions from Chandi Mendut, Chandi Sari, and Chandi Pawon in Indonesia; a large mural in cave 25 in the Yulin grottoes in Gansu province in China; and images in Ldan ma brag in the Chamdo district and the Assembly Hall of Gra thang Monastery in Tibet. Later painted examples are found in both Korea and Japan.

Compositions of the Maṇḍala of Eight Great Bodhisattvas fall into three basic types: those in which the eight bodhisattvas are arranged in two sets of four to either side of the central Buddha; those in which the eight bodhisattvas encircle the central Buddha; and less common examples in which the nine figures in the maṇḍalas are arranged in groups of three placed one above the other. Of these, the circular arrangements, which provide prototypes for the inner sections of other maṇḍalas, are the most influential in later Buddhist art.

A Buddha surrounded by eight bodhisattvas forms the core of the Womb World Maṇḍala (Sanskrit, Garbhadhātu; Japanese, Taizōkai), whereas a ninefold arrangement is repeated in the structure of the Diamond World Maṇḍala (Sanskrit, Vajradhātu; Japanese, Kongōkai), examples of which are preserved since at least the eighth century. Found principally in Japan, these maṇḍalas are shown as a pair and are placed on the east and west walls of the inner precinct of a tem-

Maṇḍala of the Womb World. (Japanese hanging scroll, Kamakura period, thirteenth–fourteenth century.) The Brooklyn Museum of Art. Reproduced by permission.

ple. The Womb World (or Matrix) has 414 deities and symbolizes the possibility of buddhahood in the phenomenal world, while the Diamond World with 1,416 deities is a guide to the requisite spiritual practices.

Both the Womb World and the Diamond World maṇḍalas focus on Vairocana Buddha, and both are further subdivided into courts, each of which has its own primary and secondary deities and its own theme.

Maṇḍala of the Diamond World. (Japanese hanging scroll, Kamakura period, thirteenth–fourteenth century.) The Brooklyn Museum of Art. Reproduced by permission.

For example, in the Womb World Maṇḍala, Vairocana is seated in the center of an eightfold lotus containing four buddhas and four bodhisattvas. The maṇḍala unfolds from the center in twelve sections, each containing a central deity and attendant figures, symbolic of aspects of the cosmos or the process of spiritual development. The three courts to the east, reading from the center, include six deities surrounding a central triangle containing the burning fire of wisdom; the historical Buddha, Śākyamuni, thought to be a manifestation of Vairocana in the phenomenal world, with thirty-eight disciples; and at the outermost edge, Mañjuśrī, the Bodhisattva of Wisdom, with an entourage of twenty-three other figures.

Each maṇḍala is based on a different text: the Womb World on the *Mahāvairocana-sūtra* (*Great Vairocana Sūtra*) and the Diamond World on the *Vajraśekara* (*Diamond World*). The former was translated from Sanskrit into Chinese by the Indian Śubhakarasiṃha (637–735) in the eighth century, while the latter is based on a translation by Amoghavajra (705–774) during the same period. Together with Vajrabodhi (669–741), these monks are revered as the founders of the MIJIAO (ESOTERIC) SCHOOL of Buddhism in China. Examples of both maṇḍalas are said to have been brought to Japan from China in the early ninth century by the famed monk KŪKAI (774–835). As is more often than not the case with maṇḍalas, not all examples of these two conform precisely to these texts.

South or Southeast Asian evidence for either maṇḍala, and particularly for their use as a pair, is rare. It has been suggested that some figures in cave 6 at Aurangabad, a sixth- or seventh-century site in western India, can be understood to symbolize the Diamond and Womb World maṇḍalas. A variant of the Diamond World Maṇḍala is thought to underlie the structure and imagery of the famous ninth-century BOROBUDUR in Java. In addition, two examples of three-dimensional maṇḍalas, created using small (three- to five-inch) sculptures, have been found in Indonesia: a well-known late tenth- to early eleventh-century group from Nganjuk, and a slightly earlier assemblage from Surucolo.

Two divergent maṇḍala traditions are preserved after the eleventh century. One is associated with Indo-Tibetan Buddhism, the other with Japanese practices. The Indo-Tibetan examples reflect the spread of the Anuttarayoga or Unexcelled Yoga Tantra tradition from India to Tibet; however, with the exception of a few stone stelae, Indian prototypes are no longer extant.

A lotus flower, generally eight-petaled, fills the core of Indo-Tibetan maṇḍalas. The lotus is housed in a palacelike inner sanctuary with elaborate arched gateways at the four cardinal directions. The square palace is surrounded by an outer circle composed of rings of fire, *vajras* (ritual implements symbolic of the adamantine properties of the diamond), and lotus petals. The small figures that inhabit the graveyards or charnel grounds, often placed between the inner palace and the outer ring, are standard images in Tibetan maṇḍalas, and reflect early practices that led to the development of Anuttarayoga Tantra. The figures at the sides of the maṇḍala represent either teachers associated with its practices, or related deities.

Maṇḍalas are made as single works or in sets. A well-known series, based on the *Vajravali* (*Diamond Garland*) and commissioned by Ngor chen kun dga' bzang po (1382–1456), includes both single icons and paintings depicting four related maṇḍalas.

A seventeenth-century painting of the KĀLACAKRA Maṇḍala in the Museum of Fine Arts in Boston shows a large central maṇḍala surrounded by four smaller versions for related deities. The painting is based on the *Kālacakra Tantra* (*Wheel of Time Tantra*), a late text distinguished by its elaborate cosmology and the prophecy of an apocalyptic war ending in the triumph of Shambhala, a hidden Buddhist kingdom, and the enlightenment of the cosmos. The central palace has been divided into three structures, one symbolic of body, one mind, and one speech, the three primary components of the complicated Kālacakra system.

The twelve animals carrying circles filled with deities in the space between the middle and outer walls of the palace represent the days of the year according to the Kālacakra cycle. The tiny figures at the top of the painting are the kings of Shambhala, where the Kālacakra teachings were first taught and are preserved. The numerous small figures that provide the upper background for the five maṇḍalas represent lamas who have upheld the Kālacakra lineage. Those toward the bottom are various deities associated with the Kālacakra. Monks and lay patrons, involved in the creation of the work and possibly in its ritual use, are shown seated around an offering table at the lower left.

In addition to continuing early maṇḍala traditions, such as that of the eight bodhisattvas, Japanese Buddhism created several unique traditions, also known as maṇḍalas, that illustrate revered sites, such as the Kasuga shrine near Nara or Mount Kōya to the south of Osaka. Ascetics and others, some of whom were influenced by early forms of Esoteric Buddhism popular in Japan from the eighth through the twelfth centuries, frequently used such sites. Over time, the sharing of ideas and practices among these varied seekers and more settled monastic adherents led to the creation of a system known as HONJI SUIJAKU or "true-nature" manifestation. According to this system, native Shintō gods are manifestations of imported Buddhist deities, and the two become interchangeable. Paintings illustrating these complicated ideas include representations of famous scenic sites, with or without the Shintō shrines and Buddhist temples they house. Such paintings also include representations of both Shintō and Buddhist manifestations of the deities associated with these sites, as well as representations of the sacred animals or other emblems affiliated with the practices and beliefs of individual locations.

See also: **Stūpa**

Bibliography

Brauen, Martin. *The Maṇḍala: A Sacred Circle in Tibetan Buddhism,* tr. Martin Willson. Boston: Shambhala, 1998.

Leidy, Denise Patry, and Thurman, Robert A. F. *Maṇḍala: The Architecture of Enlightenment.* New York: Asia Society and Tibet House, 1997.

ten Grotenhuis, Elizabeth. *Japanese Maṇḍalas: Representations of Sacred Geography.* Honolulu: University of Hawaii Press, 1999.

DENISE PATRY LEIDY

MANTRA

Mantras, or incantations, magic formulas, or spells, were originally used in Vedic religion to invoke the gods during sacrificial rituals. They were used as spells and magic charms in mainstream Indian and East Asian Mahāyāna Buddhism, in which the word *mantra* was more less interchangeable with the word DHĀRAṆĪ. *Mantra* was translated into Chinese as *zhenyan* ("true word"). Mantra became so fundamental an aspect of tantric Buddhism, or VAJRAYĀNA, which rose in the seventh and eighth centuries, that it was initially called the "Mantrayāna."

Chanted in tantric ritual and practice, mantras are generally short combinations of syllables that have no direct or easily translatable meaning. The chanted sound of the formula, not the meaning, is the important factor. Mantras are powerful language understood to be the literal words or sounds of the Buddha. The word "mantra" is often combined or interchanged with the word *hṛdaya* ("heart"), so that it means something like "quintessence." A *hṛdaya-mantra* often begins with *oṃ* and ends with *svāhā, hūṃ,* or *phat.* This use of mantra is essentially the same as, and is often translated as "seed syllable," though that term is properly a translation of *bīja.* The best-known mantra among Tibetan and Mongolian Buddhists is OṂ MAṆI PADME HŪṂ, an invocation of the Bodhisattva Avalokiteśvara, who is depicted holding a jewel and a lotus—the exact meaning of which has long been a matter of popular and scholarly debate.

See also: **Dhāraṇī; Language, Buddhist Philosophy of; Tantra**

Bibliography

Strickmann, Michel. *Mantras et Mandarins: le bouddhisme tantrique en Chine.* Paris: Éditions Gallimard, 1996.

RICHARD D. MCBRIDE II

MAPPŌ. *See* **Decline of the Dharma**

MĀRA

Māra, whose name literally means "death" or "maker of death," is the embodiment of lust, greed, false views, delusion, and illusion. He is a virtually ubiquitous presence in Buddhist texts from the earliest accounts of the Buddha's enlightenment on. Māra stands as an active antagonist of the Buddha and his followers, as well as a powerful metaphor. Paradigmatically, Māra attempts to stop the Buddha in his quest for enlightenment.

In one of the earliest accounts of Māra's treachery, in the *Sutta Nipāta* (425–449), Māra approaches the about-to-be enlightened Buddha and attempts to convince him to abandon his efforts and to adopt the more conventional Brahmanical religious life, the life of sacrifice and good karma. The Buddha rejects this suggestion, and rebukes Māra and his minions. In later accounts of this episode found in the MAHĀVASTU (*Great Story*), LALITAVISTARA, *Nidāna-kathā* (*Story of Causation*), and the BUDDHACARITA (*Acts of the Buddha*), Māra sends his various armies, including his own daughters, to frighten and tempt the Buddha as he sits in meditation; all such efforts of course fail. Finally, Māra himself comes to the Buddha and calls into question his right to sit on the *bodhimaṇḍa,* the place of enlightenment, claiming that it is he, and not the Buddha, who is the rightful occupant of that position (due to his own past good karmic deeds). The Buddha then reaches out his hand and calls the earth goddess, Bhūdevī, to bear witness to his past good deeds; the earth quakes, the goddess appears, and Māra and his armies flee. This episode, known as the *Māravijaya*, or "defeat of Māra," became one of the most common modes of representing the Buddha in many parts of the Buddhist world, conveying as it does his defeat of the forces of temptation, lust, greed, avarice, torpor and sloth, and, ultimately, death itself. Māra also figures in the postenlightenment of the Buddha, when he deludes ĀNANDA at the moment when the Buddha's disciple is about to entreat the Buddha to remain on earth, preventing Ānanda from requesting that the Buddha stay until the end of the eon to teach. Māra then reminds the Buddha that he had promised to depart once the dharma and SAṄGHA were established, and so the Buddha agrees that this will be his final life.

Māra becomes a ubiquitous presence in Buddhist texts and iconography, standing as he does as the embodiment of *tṛṣṇā*, the grasping that fundamentally leads to further rebirth and, thus, further suffering. In Southeast Asia, it is the saint UPAGUPTA who defeats Māra, binding him with his own snares and converting him to Buddhism. In the Pure Land text, the *Bhaiṣajyaguruvaidūryaprabhārāja-sūtra* (*Sūtra of the Royal Lapis Healing Buddha*), the "healing Buddha" vows to free all beings caught by Māra's "heretical entrapments" and instill in them the correct views.

See also: **Buddha, Life of the; Divinities; Evil**

Bibliography

Boyd, James W. *Satan and Māra: Christian and Buddhist Symbols.* Leiden, Netherlands: Brill, 1975.

Ling, Trevor O. *Buddhism and the Mythology of Evil: A Study in Theravāda Buddhism.* London: Allen and Unwin, 1962.

JACOB N. KINNARD

MARATHON MONKS. *See* **Shugendō**

MAR PA (MARPA)

Mar pa (Mar pa Chos kyi blo gros, 1002/1012–1097) was a renowned translator and lay Buddhist master. He is revered as the Tibetan founder of the BKA' BRGYUD (KAGYU) sect of Tibetan Buddhism. According to many traditional Bka' brgyud texts, Mar pa is the reincarnation of the Indian MAHĀSIDDHA, or great adept, Ḍombī Heruka (ca. ninth–tenth century B.C.E.). Born in Tibet to wealthy landowning parents in the southern Tibetan region of Lho brag, Mar pa was a precocious child, characterized in his traditional biographies as having a volatile, though inwardly compassionate, personality. His parents addressed both qualities by sending the boy to study Sanskrit and Indian vernacular languages under the learned translator 'Brog mi Lotsāva Śākya ye shes (ca. 992/993–1043/1072) in western Tibet.

Because the resources for studying Buddhism in Tibet at the time were limited, Mar pa decided to seek instruction in India, a journey he would make three times over the course of his life. He first spent three years in Nepal, acclimating to the new environment and continuing his study of local languages. There he met two Nepalese teachers, Chitherpa and Paiṇḍapa, who offered many religious instructions but also encouraged Mar pa to seek out the master who would become his chief guru, the great siddha NĀROPA (1016–1100).

Nāropa first submitted Mar pa to a series of arduous trials, finally judging this perspicacious Tibetan to be a fit disciple. He studied under Nāropa at the forest retreat of Pullahari, receiving initiations and teachings of several important tantric lineages. Among these instructions is a collection known in Tibetan as the Six Doctrines of Nāropa (Nā ro chos drug). This elaborate system of tantric ritual and meditative disciplines includes the yogic practices of: (1) inner heat (*gtum mo*); (2) the illusory body (*sgyu lus*); (3) dreams (*rmi lam*); (4) radiant light (*'od gsal*); (5) the intermediate state (*bar do*); and (6) transference of consciousness (*'pho ba*).

Mar pa's second great master was the Indian siddha Maitrīpa (ca. 1007–1085), from whom he received instruction in the MAHĀMUDRĀ teachings and the tradition of *dohā*, or songs of spiritual realization. Although later disseminated in different forms among various Tibetan Buddhist sects, the Six Doctrines of Nāropa and *mahāmudrā* became central meditation systems for the Bka' brgyud. Mar pa received other tantric transmissions from Indian masters, such as Jñānagarbha and Kukkurīpā, as well.

Mar pa then returned to Tibet, where he married several wives (the most well known is Bdag med ma, who figures prominently in the life story of the renowned yogin MI LA RAS PA [Milarepa; 1028/40–1111/23]), established a home, and began his career as a Buddhist teacher and translator who was at the same time a landowner and farmer. Mar pa had planned to pass his dharma lineage on to his son Dar ma mdo sde (for whom Mi la ras pa's famous final tower was built), but the child died at a young age. Mar pa's accumulated instructions, which contributed to the formation of a new stream of Buddhist thought in Tibet known as new tantra (*rgyud gsar ma*), were later passed to several principal disciples including Mi la ras pa. At least twenty-four works translated from Sanskrit attributed to Mar pa are preserved in the Tibetan Buddhist canon.

See also: **Tantra**

Bibliography

Lhalungpa, Lobsang P., trans. *The Life of Milarepa.* New York: Dutton, 1977. Reprint, Boston: Shambhala, 1984.

Trungpa, Chögyam, and the Nalanda Translation Committee, trans. *The Life of Marpa the Translator.* Boston: Shambhala, 1986.

ANDREW QUINTMAN

MARTIAL ARTS

Modern historians of East Asia have noted the seemingly incongruous presence of martial monks in Buddhist monasteries at various moments in Asian history. This unusual conjunction has appeared ironic to many in the West, given the prominent place the renunciation of violence has had in Buddhist teachings and monastic PRECEPTS. On the other hand, to many Westerners who have taken up the practice of the Asian martial arts, this conjunction has been seen not as contradictory, but as essential to the modern rhetoric of spirituality and the martial arts. Zen Buddhism, in particular, has played an important role in this approach to the martial arts. Underlying these contradictory understandings has been a Western tendency to idealize and romanticize both Buddhism and the martial arts, removing them from their historical and institutional contexts. Abetting such tendencies has been an uncritical use of categories that have emerged over the past two centuries in the study of religion both in Asia and the West, including the category of religion itself. To understand the relationship of the martial arts to Buddhism, then, it is necessary to know something of the history and nature of Buddhist institutions in Asia, and, also of the ways in which Western perceptions of Eastern religion and spirituality have contributed to contemporary understandings and, in many cases, distortions of Asian Buddhism.

One of the definitive moments in becoming a Buddhist, either as a monastic or a layperson, is the act of taking a set of vows, which differ in character and total number depending on whether one remains a householder or receives ORDINATION as a monastic. Regardless, all Buddhists take a vow to abstain from harming living beings. One would be wrong, however, to regard these vows in general and nonviolence in particular as ends in themselves or as ethical absolutes. Rather, they seem to have been regarded as practical means to end suffering both for other living beings and for oneself. This fact has allowed for some flexibility in interpretation, as well as a degree of antinomianism. Faced with the dilemma of a vow of nonviolence and of allowing, for example, a mass murderer to continue wreaking havoc in the world—and at the same time adding to the sum of his own bad KARMA (ACTION) and implied future suffering—the compassionate act may be assassination, thus reducing the sum total of accumulated suffering. Such arguments have historically been offered by certain Buddhists to legitimate violence, in the assassination of a murderous Tibetan king in one instance. Though this example is somewhat extreme, in coming to terms with Buddhist ethics and practice, it suggests the importance of the historical and social contexts of Buddhist institutions.

Monasteries and warrior monks

Buddhist monasteries in Central Asia and the Far East, rather than existing as sites purely of otherworldly concerns, originated as institutions intimately embroiled in the affairs of society. Central Asian Buddhists introduced MONASTICISM to China sometime around the second or third centuries C.E. Monks accompanied Central Asian traders into China primarily to serve the ritual needs of their merchant patrons. At about the same time and for the next several hundred years, various Central Asian armies invaded north China, setting up their own generally short-lived dynasties. These kingdoms, like the merchants, employed the ritual services of Buddhist monks, now including many ethnic Chinese converts. Under such conditions, monastic institutions often found themselves caught in the ebb and flow of the political fortunes of their various sponsors. In addition, some monasteries, through their relationship with merchants and royalty, became wealthy in land and precious goods, making them frequent prey to marauding bands of warriors and bandits.

In the *Xu gaoseng zhuan* (645, *Continued Lives of Eminent Monks*), one of the earliest records of the lives of Buddhist monks in China, there are a number of ac-

Child monks perform kung fu (gongfu) exercises at Lingyanshan Monastery, Puli, Taiwan.

counts in which the monks' martial abilities are noted, sometimes in defending their own monasteries, sometimes in serving the interests of their royal patrons in other than ritual practices. Some early sources also suggest that monasteries sometimes admitted applicants more for their martial skills than for their devotion to meditation or a life of renunciation. It seems to have been common at this time for warriors who were demobilized at the end of a war or marked for vengeance among the defeated to seek cover and anonymity in the monastic system. Martially trained monks would have been of value in times of instability, and in such cases the maintenance of monastic vows would often have been a lesser priority. According to a fifth-century history of the Wei dynasty (*Wei shu*), several monasteries in the capital of Chang'an came under scrutiny in 438 for having developed large arsenals of weapons and posing a threat to public order.

As monasteries in China became more sinicized, they evolved bureaucratic modes of organization that closely paralleled those of Chinese civil administration. Hierarchical in structure, they were composed of various departments of monks with designated functions, such as lecturers, ritualists, and meditators. It is not surprising then that we find monks whose primary functions were to manage the fields and the wealth of their monastic establishments. Among their duties would be the protection of that wealth, and implicit in this was an incentive perhaps to cultivate martial skills. In fact, there is little evidence to suggest that more than a few monasteries developed such defense forces. However, one monastery that did respond to these incentives was the Shaolin Monastery, located at the foot of Mount Song, considered the central peak of China's five sacred mountains (*wu yue*), in Henan province. It is this monastery that has informed most later histories associating Chinese Buddhism with martial arts. According to the biography of the monastery's fifth-century founder, Fotuo, two of his first disciples were selected based not on their aptitude for traditional Buddhist cultivation practices, but for their acrobatic talents. While not explicitly martial, the ability of one of these disciples to balance precariously on a narrow well ledge while playing a sort of hacky-sack game with his feet bears close similarity to some of the martial exercises emphasizing balance exhibited in Shaolin martial forms.

By the seventh century the Shaolin Monastery had developed the cudgel as its weapon of choice. The heavy cudgel, while capable of great devastation, was neither metal nor sharp, and thereby was rhetorically legitimated as a nonweapon appropriate to Buddhist monks. According to popular histories, in 621 the monastery offered its cudgel-wielding monks, thirteen in all, to the service and ultimate victory of Li Shimin (d. 649), who became the first emperor of the Tang dynasty (618–907). Whether or not this tale is true, the monastery seems to have enjoyed imperial favor during the Tang dynasty, having been granted extensive land and wealth. Such increased holdings would have provided even greater incentive to maintain a martial presence in the monastery. Over the centuries, Shaolin monks developed other styles of combat, both armed and unarmed. By the fifteenth century, Shaolin had become synonymous in China with martial arts and has remained so to the present day.

The existence of monastic defense forces can also be found in Tibet and in medieval Japan, though in very different political and social circumstances and with different consequences. Some of the more important Japanese shrine-temple complexes and Buddhist sects, which were thoroughly integrated into the social and political ethos of the fourteenth and fifteenth centuries, built legions of monks trained in military skills and maintained militias not only to protect their existing wealth in land and power but also in some cases to expand it. The MONASTIC MILITIAS of Mount Hiei developed as a formidable force during this period, not only defending their own domains but also attacking the domains of neighboring monasteries and even attempting to intimidate the emperor in his Kyoto palace. Their existence, however, was abruptly ended in 1571 when Oda Nobunaga (1534–1582) surrounded Mount Hiei with his soldiers and slaughtered all the people associated with the monastery, including every man, woman, and child living on the mountain. He subsequently destroyed another Buddhist force, the legions of the Exclusive (Ikkō) Pure Land Buddhist sect, which had used its power to dominate entire provinces.

What emerges from this brief overview of early Buddhist history are two important observations about the relationship of Buddhist monasticism and the martial arts. First, the phenomenon of monastic warriors and militias, while a historical fact, was nonetheless relatively isolated in time and place. Second, there is no compelling evidence in the texts dating from the early periods to indicate that martial training was carried out in the context of traditional Buddhist ritual or cultivation practices such as meditation, sūtra explication, or chanting. Rather, martial training in Chinese, Japanese, and Tibetan monasteries appears to have been regarded not as a practice leading to awakening or liberation, but as an expedient deemed necessary in the circumstances in which many medieval Buddhist institutions found themselves.

Zen Buddhism and martial arts

Although there is little or no Buddhist doctrinal rationale for the activities of the monastic militias of the early period, the modern practice of Asian martial arts, particularly those that developed in Japan, are frequently characterized in terms that suggest modes of spiritual practice directly informed by the Buddhism of the CHAN SCHOOL (Japanese, Zen). Most contemporary martial arts have thus taken on a quasi-religious character. The student is encouraged to strive to attain a state of pure consciousness while in the midst of combat. In a psychological state of equanimity and oneness with the adversary, the student is assured that his or her actions will flow with effortless spontaneity. Initiations, practices, and successful progress are generally marked by formal rituals, including bowing, processions, and the award of certificates or insignia. These can be seen as stripped-down secularized versions of Asian religious rituals and practice. The distinction between the achievement of a state of awakening, understood as the ultimate goal of Buddhist practice, and the effortless defeat of an adversary in battle coalesce. The monk becomes warrior; the warrior becomes monk. Not surprisingly, many popular texts on martial arts trace their lineage to the Shaolin Monastery in China.

By the eight century, Shaolin Monastery had become identified with the fifth-century semilegendary figure of BODHIDHARMA, popularly regarded as the person who introduce Chan Buddhism to China. According to legend, Bodhidharma spent nine years meditating in a cave above Shaolin Monastery. However, the earliest text to mention Bodhidharma, the sixth-century *Loyang qielan ji* (*Record of Monasteries in Loyang*), describes him not as a wall-gazing meditation master, but as a wonder-working thaumaturge from the Western (barbarian) Lands. The thaumaturgic tradition in China contains accounts of such shamanlike characters performing prodigious feats of physical agility, such as leaping great distances. Though there is no suggestion that Bodhidharma performed martial feats, including him in this tradition makes clear that his skills placed him outside the exegetical or ritual spheres of the monastery and more firmly within a familiar Chinese tradition of religious eccentrics. Such an image was readily amenable to later martial traditions, particularly in Japan. The few works attributed to Bodhidharma give no indication of a concern with martial practices. Furthermore, as argued above, the Shaolin martial arts traditions bore only incidental relation to Chan Buddhist teachings.

While not detracting from the martial skill that many achieve in these arts, there remains the question of whether these achievements and the views of the modes and objectives of Zen practice that inform them accurately reflect Buddhist monastic practices in Japan or China now or in the past. In general, they do not. At best they represent successful adaptations of certain Buddhist meditative techniques to martial practices, and at worst they impart an aura of mystification that has less to do with Buddhism than with commercialization, nationalism, or self-promotion.

The rise of Japanese martial arts as they are known today only began to take shape in the closing decades of the nineteenth century following the collapse of the Tokugawa shogunate. The year 1868 marked the beginning of a thoroughgoing cultural revolution in Japan when the newly installed Meiji government sought to erase hundreds of years of local and state culture organized around a pervasive network of Buddhist temples and monks, and to replace this cultural substrate with the "rational" organs of the modern state. Temples were burned, images destroyed, and monks returned to lay status under the guise of destroying feudal superstition. State Shintō was declared the embodiment of the true spirit of the Japanese people and was, by definition, nonreligious, having been purified of the superstitious elements that had seeped into it due to the long presence of Buddhism in Japan. However, because "the spirit of the Japanese people" was somewhat ambiguous in meaning, an issue of great concern to the new national leadership was how to cultivate that spirit without religious institutions.

At this point the Zen Buddhists and particularly their secularized apologists were able to reenter the public discourse. Reinventing themselves as the embodiment of a distinctly Japanese form of rational modernity and the custodians of a spiritual practice free of religious superstition, they were able to inject such notions as no-mind (*mushin*), here generally understood as the sublimation of the self to the people (the state), into the physical training curriculums of Japan's schools. Moving into the twentieth century, these physical training curriculums took on an increasingly martial aspect and were highly amenable to the Japanese nationalism that was then emerging. Ironically, many of the notions put forward by these Zen advocates were in fact drawn more from Chinese Daoist and Confucian sources than they were from Buddhist traditions, specifically certain breathing practices and notions of self-sacrifice within an encompassing social hierarchy. Zen monks had been the primary conduits of such ideas into Japan as early as the twelfth century. Around the beginning of the twentieth century the suffix *dō*, from the Chinese *dao* (way), replaced many of the more mundane categorical Japanese terms for the martial arts. This revised vocabulary, including the terms *judō* (way of gentleness), *kendō* (way of the sword), and *budō* (martial way), was clearly intended to impart a spiritual significance not present in words denoting technique or art (*-jutsu*).

D. T. Suzuki (1870–1966), writing in English, emerged in the mid-twentieth century as the person most responsible for introducing these interpretations of Zen and its relation to the martial arts, among other themes, to the English-speaking world. Significantly, he was not a Zen priest but a scholar trained in the "science of religion" during an eleven-year stay in the United States under the tutelage of Paul Carus (1852–1919). During these years, Suzuki was exposed to the writings of William James on pure experience and Rudolph Otto on the nature of religion, and the influence of their ideas can be seen in his psychological interpretations of Zen Buddhism and the martial arts. Little wonder, then, that Suzuki's writings on Zen have struck many Westerners as exotic, and at the same time somehow familiar, drawing as they do on contemporary Western notions of religion and psychology. It should not be overlooked, however, that Suzuki's writings before World War II often revealed a distinctly nationalist slant. The Zen mind of pure experience was frequently represented as a unique capacity of the Japanese spirit, ultimately inaccessible to non-Japanese. Though the contradictory notion of a universal potential to experience the Zen mind can be found throughout his writings, this theme became pronounced only in his postwar writings. Suzuki did more to shape popular conceptions of Zen in the twentieth century than anyone else. However, much of his representation of Buddhism constitutes what must be considered an invented tradition, and it is this tradition that has permeated much of the Western understanding of the relationship between Buddhism and the martial arts.

The contemporary practice of the martial arts has clearly adapted some ideas and practices from the rich Buddhist heritage of Asia. But this does not make the objectives or the rationale of the martial arts Buddhist. In fact, much more of both the practice and rationale of contemporary martial arts are rooted in Chinese Daoism and Confucianism, as well as in modern notions of secular religion, sport, performance, and competition.

See also: **Confucianism and Buddhism; Daoism and Buddhism; Zen, Popular Conceptions of**

Bibliography

Bodiford, William M. "Religion and Spiritual Development: Japan." In *Martial Arts of the World: An Encyclopedia,* Vol. 2, ed. Thomas A. Green. Santa Barbara, CA: ABC-Clio, 2001.

Draeger, Donn F., and Smith, Robert W. *Asian Fighting Arts.* Tokyo: Kodansha International, 1969.

Grapard, Allan G. "Japan's Ignored Cultural Revolution: The Separation of Shintō and Buddhist Divinities in Meiji (*Shimbutsu Bunri*) and a Case Study (*Tōnomine*)." *History of Religions* 23, no. 3 (1984): 240–265.

Inoue, Shun. "Budō: Invented Tradition in the Martial Arts." In *The Culture of Japan as Seen through Its Leisure,* ed. Sepp Linhart and Sabine Frühstück. Albany: State University of New York Press, 1998.

Shahar, Meir. "Ming-Period Evidence of Shaolin Martial Procedure." *Harvard Journal of Asiatic Studies* (December 2001): 359–413.

Sharf, Robert H. "The Zen of Nationalism" (1993). In *Curators of the Buddha: The Study of Buddhism under Colonialism,* ed. Donald S. Lopez, Jr. Chicago: University of Chicago Press, 1995.

Suzuki, D. T. *Zen and Japanese Culture* (revised edition of *Zen Buddhism and Its Influence on Japanese Culture,* 1938). Princeton, NJ: Princeton University Press, 1959.

WILLIAM POWELL

MĀTṚCEṬA

Mātṛceṭa (second century C.E.) was a Sanskrit poet. A Śaivite convert to Buddhism, he is the author of: (1) *Varṇārhavarṇastotra (Hymn in Praise of the Praiseworthy)*, a poem in 386 stanzas (hence the subtitle *Catuḥśataka)* in praise of the Buddha, which survives in Sanskrit (incomplete) and Tibetan; (2) *Prasādapratibhodbhava* (*Inspired by Faith*), a poem in 153 stanzas (hence the subtitle *Śatapañcāśatka*) also in praise of the Buddha, which survives in Sanskrit, Tibetan, and Chinese; and (3) *Mahārājakaniṣkalekha* (*Letter to the Great King Kaniṣka*), a poem in 85 stanzas, surviving only in Tibetan translation, in which the aged Mātṛceṭa offers advice to the young Kaniṣka. A number of other works in the Tibetan Tanjur are attributed to Mātṛceṭa, but only a few further fragments remain of the original Sanskrit. Mātṛceṭa's poetry is notable for its terse, clear style, which heightens the intensity of his thought and feeling.

See also: **Sanskrit, Buddhist Literature in**

Bibliography

Bailey, D. R. Shackleton, ed. and trans. *The Śatapañcāśatka of Mātṛceṭa.* Cambridge, UK: Cambridge University Press, 1951.

Hahn, Michael, ed. and trans. *Invitation to Enlightenment: Letter to the Great King Kaniṣka and Letter to a Disciple by Candragomin.* Berkeley, CA: Dharma, 1999.

Hartmann, Jens-Uwe, ed. and trans. *Das Varṇārhavarṇastotra des Mātṛceṭa.* Göttingen, Germany: Vandenhoeck & Ruprecht, 1987.

PETER KHOROCHE

MEDICINE

Medicine has always been part of Buddhism. The central Buddhist teaching of the FOUR NOBLE TRUTHS is often described in terms of a medical paradigm by which suffering is the disease, desire its cause, cessation of desire its cure, and the Eightfold Path the method of its treatment. Although there is no evidence that medicine lay behind the formulation of the four noble truths, examples of the Buddha's role as healer, medical similes, and references to medical terminology occur throughout Buddhist literature.

Evidence suggests that the orthodox Hindu medical tradition of Āyurveda (the knowledge of longevity) owed its origins to a certain extent to the heterodox religions, which included Buddhism. Certain wandering ascetics collected useful medical information for the purpose of self-healing. Gradually, part of this medical knowledge was brought together and, eventually, became the beginning section of the chapter of medicines (*Bhesajjakhandha*) of the Buddhist monastic code (*Vinayapiṭaka; Basket of Discipline*) of the Pāli canon. Once established in the earliest canon, medicine became integral to Buddhist doctrine.

The monastic code of the Pāli canon provides two forms of medical information: *materia medica* and stories of treatments based on cases of diseases. The pharmacopeia, known as "the medicines requisite in sickness," consisted of the five basic medicinal substances permitted all monks—clarified butter, fresh butter, oil, honey, and molasses—as well as various fats, roots, extracts, leaves, fruits, gums, and salts. Although monks and nuns are normally forbidden to eat after noon, in cases of illness, certain foods were deemed medicines and could, therefore, be consumed at any time of the day.

The stories of medical treatments found in the monastic code are among the earliest examples of medical practice found anywhere in the world and illustrate the Buddha's rational and utilitarian approach to healing. Buddhists focused on concrete therapies rather than the theory of disease and medicine. The process was paradigmatic: A certain monk, suffering from a particular illness, came to the Buddha who, after careful consideration, sanctioned a treatment. This practical method of healing became the model for later medical manuals. These are among the first examples of the Buddha's role as healer. He provided cures for a variety of illnesses, ranging from demonic possession to sores on the feet, which were typically the kinds of maladies from which wandering ascetics might have suffered. Both the diseases and their cures bear a close affinity to their counterparts in the Sanskrit medical treatises.

The story of the semimythical physician Jīvaka Komārabhacca, found in another part of the Pāli VINAYA, discloses a similar paradigm of utilitarian medicine. Variations of this popular tale occur in Tibetan and Chinese Buddhist canonical literature. Jīvaka's extraordinary skill made him the physician to kings and to the Buddha.

Medicine grew along with Buddhism in India. Under the reign of King AŚOKA in the mid-third century B.C.E., Buddhism became a virtual state religion, and by royal proclamation basic medical care was provided to both humans and animals throughout the kingdom. By the seventh century C.E., medicine was part of the educational curriculum at major monastic centers in India. When Buddhism spread from India, medicine went with it and developed under indigenous influences.

In the early centuries C.E., Sri Lanka received the original monastic medical doctrines. New Buddhist medical treatises were composed, and certain monasteries maintained a type of clinic with medicinal baths. In the THERAVĀDA countries of Southeast Asia, traditional medicine remains closely connected to Buddhism.

In Central Asia, Buddhism was the vehicle for the transmission of Indian medicine to other parts of Asia. The original rational paradigm was the basis for new medical texts and manuals, which took the form of collections of formulas, each effective against several ailments. Originally composed in Sanskrit, they were translated into different Central Asian languages, and from those into Tibetan. Some manuals were even written on animal skins, which allowed doctors to carry them with ease and consult them when necessary. Certain Sanskrit medical treatises, translated into Tibetan, were incorporated into the Tibetan Buddhist canon. Indian medicine combined with Chinese, Persian, and indigenous Tibetan medical practices to yield Tibetan medicine. In China, where the cults of the healing buddhas and BODHISATTVAS found popularity, Buddhist medical doctrines were integrated with indigenous Chinese medicine. Similar trends were followed in Korea and Japan.

Early Buddhism's incorporation of medicine into its religious doctrine was unique and contributed to the religion's development. The practical care and medical attention that was given to all who required it helped provide the support and popularity necessary to sustain a religious movement through its various transformations in Asia.

Bibliography

Birnbaum, Raoul. *The Healing Buddha.* Boulder, CO: Shambhala, 1979.

Chattopadhyaya, Debiprasad. *Science and Society in Ancient India.* Calcutta: Research India Publications, 1977.

Filliozat, Jean. "La Médecine indienne et l'expansion bouddhique en Extrème Orient." *Journal Asiatique* 224 (1934): 301–307.

Liyanaratne, Jinadasa. *Buddhism and Traditional Medicine in Sri Lanka.* Kelaniya, Sri Lanka: University of Kelaniya, 1999.

Mitra, Jyotir. *A Critical Appraisal of Āyurvedic Material in Buddhist Literature.* Varanasi, India: Jyotirlok Prakashan, 1985.

Rechung Rinpoche Jampel Kunzang, trans. and ed. *Tibetan Medicine.* Berkeley: University of California Press, 1973.

Tatz, Mark, trans. *Buddhism and Healing: Demiéville's Article "Byō" from Hōbōgirin.* Lanham, MD: University Press of America, 1985.

Zysk, Kenneth G. "Buddhist Healing and Āyurveda: Some General Observations." In *Studies in Orientology: Essays in Memory of Prof. A. L. Basham,* ed. S. K. Maity, Upendra Thakur, and A. K. Narain. Agra, India: Y. K. Publishers, 1988.

Zysk, Kenneth G. "Indian Ascetic Traditions and the Origins of Āyurvedic Medicine." *Journal of the European Āyurvedic Society* 1 (1990): 119–124.

Zysk, Kenneth G. "New Approaches to the Study of Early Buddhist Medicine: Use of Technical Brāhmaṇic Sources in Sanskrit for the Interpretation of Pāli Medical Texts." *Pacific World,* New Series, no. 11 (1995): 143–154.

Zysk, Kenneth G. *Medicine in the Veda,* Vol. 1: *Indian Medical Tradition.* Delhi: Motilal Banarsidass, 1996.

Zysk, Kenneth G. "Mythology and the Brāhmaṇization of Indian Medicine: Transforming Heterodoxy into Orthodoxy." In *Categorisation and Interpretation: Indological and Comparative Studies from an International Indological Meeting at the Department of Comparative Philology, Göteborg University,* ed. Folke Josephson. Göteborg, Sweden: Meijerbergs Arkiv för Svensk Ordforskning 24, Göteborg University, 1999.

Zysk, Kenneth G. *Asceticism and Healing in Ancient India: Medicine in the Buddhist Monastery,* Vol. 2: *Indian Medical Tradition.* Delhi: Motilal Banarsidass, 2000.

KENNETH G. ZYSK

MEDITATION

In common usage, the word *meditation* approaches the meanings of the Indian Buddhist term DHYĀNA (TRANCE STATE): a shift in awareness typically carried out intentionally, in silence, and while holding the body in a static position (most characteristically sitting with legs crossed). Various practices of dhyāna are associated with notions of sainthood, wisdom, serenity, and extraordinary mental powers, such as the ABHIJÑĀ (HIGHER KNOWLEDGES). Additionally, the term suggests mental and bodily discipline, and is associated with systematic methods of self-cultivation, and with monastic or eremitical lifestyles.

Generally, Buddhist theories of meditation propose that the core of these practices consists in achieving a state of deep calm and concentration, called *samādhi,* which in turn can give rise to, or serve as the foundation for, a clear and accurate view (*vipaśyanā*) that discerns the real from the unreal. Furthermore, perfect calm and concentration can give rise as well to extraordinary visions and marvelous powers.

Wondrous powers arise when the mind is "concentrated, pure, translucent, spotless, free of trouble and confusion, supple." For instance, "from [one's] own body arises another body that has the constituents and shape of a material body but is made of mind. [And one] applies and directs this mind to the acquisition of wondrous powers. . . . Although [this person is] one, he becomes many, or having become many becomes one again; he becomes invisible, and then visible again" (*Dīghanikāya* 1, 77–78).

And, the perfect calm of a concentrated mind leads to extraordinary levels of knowing—especially an insight into reality that liberates the meditator from the bonds of DUḤKHA (SUFFERING). "He applies and directs this mind to that insight that comes from knowledge. He discerns clearly: 'my body is made of matter, . . . produced by a father and a mother, and continually renewed by boiled rice and juicy foods, . . . it is subject to decay, wear, dissolution, and disintegration. This consciousness of mine too depends on that body, is bound up in that body'" (*Dīghanikāya* 1, 76). With this, the meditator knows the reality of the FOUR NOBLE TRUTHS: This is suffering; this is the origin of suffering; this is the cessation of suffering; and this is the path leading to the cessation of suffering (*Dīghanikāya* 1, 83).

The literate elites generally regard as more estimable this second fruit of meditation: insight into the nature of reality and liberation from the bonds of suffering and REBIRTH. Nonetheless, meditation remains a practice for embodied beings, and is also valued for its putative transformative power on the world of embodiment.

The body

Insofar as the meditator assumes bodily postures that are considered to be those of the Buddha himself, in particular sitting cross-legged in the traditional lotus posture, the act of meditation is, in a manner of speaking, the actualization of the goal of meditation: to become like the Buddha. One is advised to "sit on a soft, comfortable seat," and to assume "the cross-legged posture," appropriately called "the posture of the Buddha Vairocana," or the half-lotus posture. Then, other aspects of body and mind need to conform to the ideal icon of a Buddha: (1) eyes neither open nor closed, and aimed at the tip of the nose; (2) body erect, without slouching or becoming too stiff; (3) mindfulness turned inward; (4) shoulders level; (5) head [erect] without bending [the neck] forward, backward, [or wavering] to either side, the nose in line with the navel; (6) teeth and lips [only] lightly closed, the tongue resting on the gums of the upper teeth; (7) breath inaudible, neither heavy nor too rapid, breathing in and out slowly and effortlessly (Kamalaśīla, *First Bhāvanākrama*). These instructions, written in the eighth century C.E. for a Tibetan audience, would not differ substantially from the instructions given to beginners in other Buddhist traditions.

Other postures may acquire a similar significance, whether they are explicitly linked to the technique of meditation or not. Thus, walking meditation reflects the gait and demeanor of the awakened, and monks are sometimes asked to sleep in the recumbent position of the Buddha in NIRVĀṆA, while they remain mindful of DEATH and liberation.

Some traditions expressed the connection between body and meditation more concretely by locating certain religious experiences or stages of meditation in different parts of the body. Such conceptions were central to the so-called Tantric tradition, especially in India, although the idea also has East Asian manifestations. In this meditation theory, several "spiritual nerve centers" (cakras) map out the interface between body and meditative experience. As many as eight and as few as five cakras are located along the spinal column, on what traditional anatomy regarded as two veins or pathways for spiritual energy. In the process of meditation this energy (conceived sometimes as a kind of fluid) was forced up or down these veins, concentrating alternatively in each one of the cakras: from the lowest in the area of the genitals or the sphincter, through the area of the solar plexus, the heart, the larynx, the eyes, and the crown of the head. Generally, the concentration of energy on the top cakra was regarded as the culmination of the meditation process, although each cakra had a distinct spiritual value.

A less technical location of meditation in the body occurs in the practice of mindfulness meditation, where the main exercise consists in cultivating a clear awareness of one's body, its breathing, its movements, its functions and feelings. In the Chan tradition, likewise, there is a common rhetoric of the body not only in an emphasis on proper posture, but also in the notion that nonconceptual thought is located in the belly (Japanese, *hara*), not in the head.

The body as object of meditation

The human body itself can become the object of meditation. Classical Indian texts describe various ways to think about or mentally analyze the body into its parts and processes. Some advise the meditator to sit next to a corpse and reflect on the meditator's own mortality, on the fragility and corruption of the body, and on the impossibility of discovering a permanent self in one's own material frame. This meditation is known as "cultivating the impure" (*aśubhabhāvanā*) because a greater part of the practice consists in understanding that the living body shares the foul nature of the rotting corpse. The practice continues in isolated pockets in THERAVĀDA countries, where monks now may have to visit a public hospital and sit in the morgue with the bodies of the unidentified and the indigent. The more common practice is to keep a skeleton or a skull in the monastery as a prop to aid in what may be termed "a reflection on one's self," vicariously using someone else's body to imagine one's own as the object of meditation.

In Tibet this tradition resonated with a number of local practices. In areas where the dead are disposed by exposure, a traditional meditation on the corpse was possible and occasionally practiced. But more characteristic of Tibetan Buddhism is the practice of *gcod* (*chöd*), a complex sequence of both performative and meditative actions meant to provoke various experiences of bodily dissolution. The meditator, instructed by an experienced master who knows the proper invocations and protective prayers, imagines himself being devoured by demons in a variety of settings called "feasts." In a "red feast," for instance, the body is visualized as being dismembered and cut up into bloody fragments, which are then offered to flesh-eating demons. A "white feast" transforms each part of the body into an idealized, pure part of a universe that will delight the gods. The new sanctified body becomes ambrosia and feeds benevolent deities.

Transforming the body into a spiritual body by ritual or meditation is a central notion in the TANTRAS. For instance, the ritual use of symbolic hand gestures, called MUDRĀ, sacred "seals," serve as a unifying principle for the transformation of the person through artistic representation, ritual performance, and meditation. Although many of these are even today common Indian hand gestures, they are regarded as the gestures of the Buddha himself, their association with the Buddha being confirmed by their appearance in Buddhist icons, and by the attribution of "secret" or mystical meanings the gestures.

Ritual acts, ritual frames

The theme of embodiment can also be used as a heuristic in understanding the connection of meditation to RITUAL. Most meditation practices occur within some sort of ritual or symbolic frame, and follow very

A monk meditates at a small stone altar on the grounds of the ruins at Sārnāth, India. © Chris Lisle/Corbis. Reproduced by permission.

specific instructions. In most cases meditation sessions are planned, prepared, and adorned, and thus tagged, in predictable fashion, as "proper meditation," or "meditation like that of the Buddha." Meditation sessions are usually seen as an integral part, if not the culmination, of a religious life that includes moral preparation and doctrinal definitions of what one should expect. Apart from the expectations of doctrine, ethical values, and cultural habits, Buddhist meditations are also usually announced and framed by ritual activities.

A long tradition of preliminaries associated with meditation rituals survives in various forms in East Asian and Tibetan practice. Custom, as well as ritual manuals, helped consecrate ritual practices as diverse as cleaning and adorning the place of meditation, setting up an altar or image, offering flowers and perfumed water, and framing the period of meditation with ancillary rituals, such as the sevenfold act of worship or the invocation of protective deities. In fact, meditation and ritual often form a web of activities that includes not only ostensible silent meditations and publicly performed ceremonies, but also activities such as chanting, recitation, and circumambulation that hold an ambiguous status between ritual and meditation, mechanical reading and deep reflection.

Special meditations are also sometimes regarded as preliminary or preparatory exercises. For instance, the Tibetan tradition often recommends the practice of the *sngon'gro* (*ngöndro,* preliminaries), which are divided into two types. The first is that of the four "outer preliminaries," which often serve as a standard or common meditation for the nonspecialist. This set of four consists of meditations of the "recollection" type, with reflection on the following four topics: the value of human rebirth, impermanence, the vicissitudes of KARMA (ACTION), and the suffering of living beings. The second type is formed by the five "inner preliminaries," which are construed as purificatory activities, each neutralizing or counteracting the effects of one of the major passions. Thus, pride is countered by taking refuge and performing ten thousand prostrations, jealousy by cultivating the aspiration to awaken for the sake of all living beings (the BODHICITTA), hatred by reciting the hundred-syllable mantra of Vajrasattva, craving by a MAṆḌALA offering, and delusion by visualizing one's teacher as identical with one's protective deity (a practice called *guru-yoga*).

Mental culture

The above reflections are not meant to minimize the significance of meditation as a technology of self-cultivation meant to affect mental states and traits, as well as the content of mind. India scholastics canonized an early schema (perhaps pre-Buddhistic) that saw meditation as combining two kinds of mental exercise. One exercise, dhyāna proper, involved techniques for the cultivation of calm (*śamatha*) and concentration (samādhi), and was the main ground for extraordinary powers, yet, by itself, it could not lead to liberation. The other, the exercise of the cognitive faculty (jñāna) in an act of accurate perception (*darśana*), involved the practice of calm, clear-minded observation (*vipaśyanā*) and the cultivation of discernment (prajñā).

Most Buddhist meditation theories consider both aspects of meditation necessary in the pursuit of liberation, but argue that correct insight is the uniquely Buddhist component in this joint practice. Nonetheless, techniques of calm and techniques of discernment often overlap. The ABHIDHARMA, for instance, tended to group together certain techniques and objects of meditation that were seen as primarily means toward the development of concentration, but could be used as props for discernment. Many of these lists are in fact mixed groupings of objects, styles, and states of meditation. One such inventory, explained by BUDDHAGHOSA in his *Visuddhimagga* (*Path of Purity*), lists forty "fields" of cultivation of meditation (each is a *kammaṭṭhāna,* working ground). The list includes heterogeneous categories, such as a hierarchy of meditative states (the four dhyānas), object-states (e.g., the boundless states or *brahmavihāra*), general objects (e.g., material or corporeal objects), and particular object-tools of meditation (that is, objects designed specially as aids to meditation).

Buddhaghosa's summary is thus a heterogeneous list describing various technical dimensions of meditation. For instance, among the "object-tools" of meditation are the all-inclusive or total objects, usually identified by their Pāli name *kasiṇa.* This device is a simple visual object that can become the single, neutral object of attention. For instance, a red *kasiṇa* is a circle of red sand or clay that is spread out on the ground before the meditator, who then focuses on it until he is able to displace all thoughts from the mind except the image of the red circle. The meditator continues the practice until he is able to keep in his mind the red circle even when he is away from the actual external *kasiṇa.* The outcome is regarded as a state of perfect calm and concentration that can serve as a foundation for special psychic powers or as a preliminary to insight meditation.

The mind: practices of recollection. Like meditation techniques and objects, meditative states cannot be easily classified as objects or states, processes or supports for sustained attention, nor can they be easily distinguished into states of serenity, processes of observation, or moments of insight. For example, the practice of MINDFULNESS (*smṛti*) can be used emblematically for concepts that encompass concentrated mental calm, as well as insightful observation, and that likewise straddle the distinction between object, process, and goal.

Broadly understood, mindful recollection includes a spectrum of mental states and exercises that the tradition conceives as "memory" or "bringing to mind" (the literal meaning of *smṛti*) and that overlap with practices of watchful recollection (*anusmṛti*). As a superordinate term *smṛti* refers broadly to three related practices: (1) vigilance with regard to one's own demeanor and behavior, (2) bringing to mind (recalling) and keeping in the mind (retaining) a prescribed object of meditation, and (3) constantly directing one's attention toward, and keeping in awareness, a prescribed object, especially the processes of one's body and mind.

The first usage, watching one's own behavior, arguably fits better in a discussion of the rules of monastic conduct and consists primarily of an effort to remain constantly aware of one's own demeanor, bodily posture, tone of voice, gaze, and so on, with a view to keeping mind and body (thoughts and senses) calm and restrained. This dimension of practice is totally ignored in Western accounts of Buddhist meditation but is amply described in classical literature under the rubrics of *saṃvara* (self-restraint) and *śikṣā* (training practices). Although often found as an integral part of monastic practice, its importance is suggested by both its pervasiveness on the ground and by influential classical treatments in works like ŚĀNTIDEVA's BODHICARYĀVATĀRA or the *Xiaozhiguan* attributed to ZHIYI, the systematizer of the Chinese TIANTAI SCHOOL.

Recollection practices of the second type (recalling and retaining prescribed objects of meditation) may be divided heuristically into the recollection of ideas, the recollection of sensory images, and the evocation of affective states. In the classical Indian practice of *anusmṛti* (recollection), the meditator is required to bring to mind one of six different ideal subjects: the Buddha, his teachings (dharma), the community of his noble disciples (saṅgha), good moral habits, generous giving, and heavenly beings (deva). The meditator first brings to mind the traditional description of the chosen topic, then reviews discursively the good qualities associated with the subject of meditation.

A practice that is not explicitly called *smṛti*, yet involves a systematic bringing to mind or an evocation of affect is "abiding in sublime abodes" (*brahmavihāra*, also called "boundless states"). Four such states are prescribed: benevolence, compassion, joy, and equanimity. In one of the most common forms (recommended and practiced in Theravāda circles) the meditator begins by developing thoughts of benevolence toward a person to whom the meditator is indifferent, then toward a friend, then an enemy, and finally all SENTIENT BEINGS, infusing the whole universe with feelings of benevolence. The meditator then proceeds to develop the other three feelings in the same manner.

A third type of *smṛti*, commonly known as "mindfulness practice" or "attention to mindfulness" (*smṛtyupasthāna*; Pāli, *satipaṭṭhāna*), may be called "mindfulness proper." It is the "recollection" or bringing to mind of bodily and mental states, and of the conditions to which these states are subject. Once "recollected" they are held in attention and observed with clear awareness.

Tradition prescribes four objects of mindfulness: body, sensations (bodily feelings), mind (thought and stream of consciousness), and dharmas (doctrinal truths and doctrinal ideas). However, tradition has it that all four are encompassed by the sole practice of "mindfulness of breathing" (*ānāpanasmṛti*), which can be undertaken in preparation for, or in conjunction with, the practice of the other four. One may argue that mindfulness proper is a type of insight practice (*vipaśyanā*), insofar as calm awareness is a requisite for keen observation. Observation is usually formulated as follows: "What is my body doing?" or "What is my mind doing at this moment?"

At the end of the nineteenth and the beginning of the twentieth century, several Buddhist monks from Myanmar (Burma) set out to reform the practice of Buddhist meditation. Leading figures like Ledi Sayadaw (1856–1923) and Sayagyi U Ba Khin (1889–1971) objected to what they perceived as an excessive emphasis on meditation as samādhi, that is, technically, as mental withdrawal and spiritual power. They proposed a putatively more direct meditation in which mindfulness was the primary technique and insight the ultimate goal. This, they felt, had been the teaching of the Buddha himself.

Presented in a variety of forms, this basic approach came to be known as "mindfulness" or "insight" (or by the original Pāli terms, *satipaṭṭhāna* and *vipassanā*). The prototypical practice was mindfulness of breathing, but other forms of mindful awareness and recollection were emphasized. Insight meditation lent itself to lay practice, and soon came to satisfy the aspirations of the new secular, middle-class audience that appeared in modern Southeast Asia, and of young Western disciples who came to Asia in search of the dharma.

The mind: calm and insight. Contemporary advocates of mindfulness/insight methods regard such practices as distinctive or self-contained practices, as suggested in canonical texts like the *Satipaṭṭhāna-sutta* (*Majjhimanikāya* 1, 55–63). However, the most common scholastic position in classical times was to suppose that one needed techniques for making body and mind supple and malleable, serene and focused, as a basis for mental culture.

In this context, the word *samādhi* denotes a family of techniques shared by other religious systems of India, but normative Buddhist literature generally regards these techniques as preparatory or foundational, and not as aims in themselves. Although, in practice, many even today pursue states of samādhi for their own sake, the higher, normative goal is insight, which is believed to lead to liberation from suffering and from the cycle of rebirth.

Insight is not a simple "looking" or "seeing," but rather a review of reality or truth. Insight is therefore not easily separated from doctrine and doctrinal reflection. The classical Indian tradition sometimes accepts the possibility that there can be insight without the cultivation of serenity. An integration of both is not a given, and it is neither simple nor necessary, yet most traditions acknowledge the need for both, even when one is emphasized more than the other. Generally, the theoretical integration is based on two assumptions: that a preparatory calming of the mind will allow for clear insight, and that the objects used as the foundation for calm can also be used as objects of investigation by means of insight. The goal of insight is discernment or clear understanding (prajñā), and this discernment would never arise without the cultivation (*bhāvanā*) of insight accompanied by the cultivation of perfect calm and concentration.

Meditation in Mahāyāna

Most Buddhist currents and religious groups in India—whether they were identified as *nikāya* (so-called MAINSTREAM BUDDHIST SCHOOLS) or MAHĀYĀNA communities—tended to model meditation on elements found in a common pool of practices. These corresponded in their rough outlines to the techniques summarized in the formula of the forty *kammaṭṭhāna,* and they are also found in practice manuals (so-called *yogācāra* or *yogāvacāra* manuals). Sometimes these recommendations were incorporated into larger treatises on doctrine and practice, like the encyclopedic *Yogācārabhūmi* attributed to ASAṄGA.

Thus, Mahāyāna meditation in India followed some variants of the common background of practices found in non-Mahāyāna traditions. Mahāyāna texts recommend, for example, the practice of the boundless states, the meditation on the corpse (*aśubhabhāvanā*), and mindfulness practices. Many of these practices were transported to Mahāyāna regions outside India in versions that seldom differed significantly from the accounts found in the Indian texts we possess.

Nevertheless, a number of innovations occurred in Mahāyāna, in India and beyond. Emphasis on ŚŪNYATĀ (EMPTINESS) led some Mahāyāna authors to criticize the notion that the corpse was impure or foul (*aśubha*), arguing that it was better to conceive of it as empty of both substance and characteristics. In the same vein, the classical meditation on mental states (*citta*), which had earlier focused on a clear distinction between mental states that are good or healthy (*kuśala*) and those that are noxious or unhealthy (*akuśala*), shifted according to Mahāyāna dialectic, and the meditator asked himself whether his own thoughts, good or bad, could be located anywhere: "Where did they come from, where will they go, where are they located, inside of me, outside, or somewhere in between?"

Śāntideva describes in his *Bodhicaryāvatāra* a psychologically complex meditation on no-self and compassion that became a classic in Tibet and has been admired in the West for almost a century. The meditation has two parts: identification of self with others, and reversing roles between self and others. In the first part, the meditator explores the boundaries of the self and the preconceptions that make us set such boundaries. For instance, one is to reflect on the fact that suffering is the same in all beings, so that our natural impulse to avoid suffering makes more sense as a desire to protect all living things from suffering than in any selfish desire to protect ourselves at the expense of others.

In the second part of the meditation, Śāntideva imagines another person, one who is less fortunate than he is. Then he assumes the role of this other person and imagines this person looking back at Śāntideva first with envy, then reproaching him for his pride and for his insensitivity in regarding the less fortunate as inferiors, instead of as the only reason for his existence, for only those in pain justify one's existence since service to others is the only meaning of the Buddhist's life.

A group of texts written approximately a century later, Kamalaśīla's three *Bhāvanākramas,* also describe uniquely Mahāyāna practices. These three essays borrow extensively from the Yogācāra tradition. The second essay establishes clearly a uniquely Mahāyāna use of the boundless states (*āpramāṇya*) as a way to generate the great compassion that will motivate the meditator to seek the awakening of a buddha. The same texts also summarize meditations on emptiness that progress from an *abhidharmic* analysis of matter, through a *yogācāra* analysis of mind and its contents, and culminate in a state of samādhi that is devoid of any conceptual contents (*ānimittasamādhi*). The latter state is the gateway to the liberating knowledge that is nondual (*advayajñāna*).

Tantric practices

The Buddhist textual and ritual traditions that are usually called *Tantric* expanded on some of the practices outlined above and adopted practices that may have been autochthonous to the localities where Tantra grew roots. The typical Tantric meditation session is a pastiche or a stratified event, in which elements from different periods and currents of the tradition intermingle. Such a session, called a *sādhana* (realization, empowerment) is typically a mixture of evocation and visualization overlaying a classical Mahāyāna liturgy.

Three characteristics of Tantric meditation stand out in a sādhana; two of them are evident to an outside observer, one is apparent only to the practitioner. First, meditation exercises can take the form of complex liturgies. These are ritual events that may or may not include meditation proper, since often the representation or performance of the liturgical process is considered as effective as, equivalent to, or inducive of events internal to the practitioner. Yet, silent, private meditation may incorporate these ritual elements as inner, or mental, rituals. The dividing line between a meditation embedded in a ritual and a liturgy meant to display publicly the structure and power of the meditation is often blurred.

Second, one cannot escape the obvious emphasis on the senses that pervades Tantric practice. Sight is both stimulated and used by a number of multicolored props, offerings, and ritual implements, and by the maṇḍala (a graphic representation that in part maps out the ritual and any internal processes of meditation). The sense of smell is stimulated by the frequent use of incense and flowers. The ear is involved through recitation and through the focusing of the ritual and the meditation on specific ritual formulas and "mystical" formulas (mantras) and syllables (*bījas*).

The third characteristic is less palpable. Tantric liturgical-meditative events are often presumed to depend on or to induce an inner sensory process in the practitioner. This process is sometimes called "visualization," since instructions often ask the meditator to "see" something in his or her heart or mind. This object is to be retained in the mind for a prescribed time, to the exclusion of everything else, and serves some of the functions of the *kasiṇa.*

Although some Western observers have questioned the meaning of these instructions, it seems clear that the practitioner is being asked to view something in the mind. Whether this is at all possible is not as critical as understanding that many people think it is possible. Once the picture is in the mind one can look at it, view it, and contemplate it; or one can become one with the object.

The inner process is also called *sādhana,* and it may be construed as a "realization" because it implies that the vision is, or should be made to become, something that is real or that can be appropriated or incorporated into one's person. The meditator, for instance, is asked to perceive mentally, in his own heart, the first vowel, *A,* which gradually turns into the orb of the moon. In the middle of this moon he should see a lovely blue lotus. On the filaments of this lotus he will see the spotless orb of a second moon, upon which appears the yellow seed-syllable (*bīja*) *Tāṁ.* Thereupon, the meditator sees rays of light issuing from this yellow seed-syllable, and this mass of rays destroys the darkness of the world's delusions, illuminates all the endless worlds that exist in the ten directions, and gathers the numberless, measureless families of buddhas and bodhisattvas from the whole universe, bringing them before the meditator.

Such visualizations often lead to meditations of the insight type that we have seen before: The mental picture of a buddha, for instance, is examined by asking questions regarding the substantiality of the image, and of the buddha it represents.

The evocation of deities in contexts that shade off from simple invocation to visualization, and from apotropaic and propitiatory prayer to meditations of identity, was especially popular among Tibetan Buddhists. It is sometimes called *deity yoga* in the West, in accordance with a free English translation of the Tibetan term *lha'i mgnong rtogs* ("realization" or "actualization" of the deity). In a deity-yoga sādhana, the meditator invokes and visualizes the physical appearance (including shape, sound, and smell) of his or her own meditation deity (the chosen or assigned object of meditation), which is also the person's main protective deity, the "chosen" tutelary deity (*yi dam*; Sanskrit, *iṣṭadevatā*). As a step into higher meditations the practice is indistinguishable from a basic sādhana, but as a devotional practice it is perhaps the most popular of all meditations in circles that follow Tibetan traditions of meditation. A meditation of this type is the *nyungne* (*bsnyung gnas*), which is especially popular among the laity and is devoted to the bodhisattva of compassion, Avalokiteśvara. This ritual meditation is usually carried out during the days celebrating the birth, enlightenment, and death of the Buddha. The *nyungne* is a two-day fasting retreat for laypersons, led by a monk. Although the primary objective appears to be strengthening the vows and precepts of the bodhisattva and the invocation of Avalokiteśvara's compassionate assistance, the model for the liturgy is still that of a deity-yoga sādhana inviting the bodhisattva to make himself present before and inside the meditator.

Another form of Tantric practice, a syllable or a full phrase (of the mantra genre), recited aloud or mumbled, becomes the focus for the development of concentration and insight. These Sanskrit syllables often represent sacred presences, and by extension embody and therefore invoke and appropriate them (that is, fuse or exchange the identities of meditator and deity).

In Japanese Tantric practice, as modeled, for instance, in the Shingon tradition, the syllable *hrī* is taken to represent the name, person, and presence of AMITĀBHA. When the syllable is drawn or recited, the believer presumes that the Buddha Amitābha has been invoked or, better yet, that he is present. The set of all syllables, and therefore of all buddhas, bodhisattvas, and deities, is contained in the primary vowel sound *A.* This syllable is regarded as the origin and essence of all syllables, and hence of all language and every-

A twelfth-century statue of the Buddha seated in meditation position, at Polonnaruva, Sri Lanka. (Sri Lankan, 1153–1186.) The Art Archive/British Museum/The Art Archive. Reproduced by permission.

thing constructed and generated by language. Its invocation therefore brings forth not an individual buddha, but the totality or essence of what is real (*dharmadhātu*).

Tantric meditation blends the themes and instruments of ritual, sound, and language, combining them with the ideas of serenity and insight, all in a process rooted in a conviction that deities can be made manifest before or assimilated into the meditator. This is then not only meditation of speech, but also meditation of visual imagery; yet it is also a technique for inviting holy, ideal beings to come, as guests, before the meditator, and then gradually share their identity with that of the meditator. Additionally, this identity is usually reduced to the emptiness of all things, which is, paradoxically, what is ultimately real, stable, and foundational.

Other uses of the word

Belief in the transformative power of word and syllable is not limited to Tantra. A different sort of invocation is found in the practice of calling on or calling out the name of the Buddha Amitābha. Indian notions of the sacred name found fertile ground in East Asia, where they tended to cluster around the cult of this buddha in particular, whose invocation has become synonymous with Buddhist devotionalism.

In China, where the East Asian tradition has its roots, one may chant either the name of the Buddha Amitābha or the equivalent of the Sanskrit expression "homage to the Buddha Amitābha" (*namo 'mitābhāya buddhāya*; Chinese, *namo Amito-fo*), which has been turned into a sacred name or "the Name." The recitation is conceived as devotion or devotional surrender, but can also be conceived as meditation embedded in traditions of mental culture and moral-ascetic cultivation. In the latter function, the recitation may be part of a visualization exercise in which the meditator imagines or images the paradise of Amitābha, the Pure Land.

Traditional understandings of meditation on the name include conceiving of it as concentrated wish or devotion, as meditation on the true name or essence of the Buddha, or as an aid to visualizing Amitābha's Western Paradise. Additionally, the recitation of the sacred name has been used as part of Chan meditation practice.

The Chan use of language in meditation is less explicit that it is in Tantric tradition, as the Chan tradition claims to have access to an experience that is nonconceptual and free from the boundaries of language. Yet important strands of the tradition claim that this nonconceptual mode of being is achieved through a peculiar use of words. Although ostensibly the ultimate meaning of *Chan* is "an independent transmission that is outside doctrinal teaching, and does not rely on words," Chan has had much to do with words, and has developed a specialized language of the unspoken and the ineffable.

The Chan traditions (*chanzong,* or *Zen* in contemporary Western parlance) began to develop an approach that was described as a method of no-method, but which was in fact a radical method, using a rhetoric of iconoclasm and paradox. The tradition conceives enlightenment as already present in the mind, or, rather, as the mind itself being already enlightened and therefore requiring no cultivation, no meditation. Some strands of the tradition argue accordingly that method and meditation are superfluous; truth must be grasped directly, without mediation; delusion and suffering are nothing but a mistake, and if one abandons the mistake, the true mind manifests itself. Such extreme statements perhaps were put into practice among a limited circle of disciples and for a short time during the Tang dynasty (618–907 C.E.), but, in theory, this rhetoric remained in the tradition as an ideal description of Chan.

Be that as it may, the most characteristic Chan use of language developed in the Song dynasty (960–1279 C.E.) and is known in the West as the KŌAN—borrowing the Japanese pronunciation (kōan) of the Chinese *gong'an.* The term refers today to a key word or phrase used as the pivot or focus for meditation and believed to be derived directly from the words of ancient masters. The key phrase is usually found in an anecdotal or legendary exchange between disciple and master. These dialogues are known as "question and answer" (Japanese, *mondō*; Chinese, *wenda*) and are for the most part presented as vignettes of incidents or anecdotes of dialogues from the lives of great Chan masters. The incident or exchange was regarded as a "public case" (the meaning of *gong'an*), hence a "court precedent" embodying the wisdom of the greatest judges of what is true enlightenment, that is, the great meditation masters of the past. The master's "verdict" or judgment was the key phrase (*huatou*) in the anecdote.

In the Japanese Rinzai tradition, the meditator memorizes the anecdote with its key phrase (both called *kōan* in common parlance) and uses the phrase as the focus of concentrated attention. In China, Korea, and Vietnam, it is common to reserve the cases for study, reflection, commentary, or debate, and make the focus of meditation a more general or all-encompassing question, such as: "What is it?" "Who is it?" "Who is reciting the sūtras?" In this phrasing, the *it* and the *who* are the focus of concentrated attention.

Whatever the assigned question might be, the meditator is expected to cultivate undistracted awareness of the kōan during sitting meditation and then "take it with him wherever he goes." This is reminiscent of the *kasiṇa* exercise, in the sense that the person is expected to become one with, and think of nothing but, the object of meditation.

But the exercise also develops insight because the phrase becomes an object of inquiry as part of the question formulated in the kōan (e.g., "What is *this*?") The answer has to be nondiscursive: a gesture or a sound, or perhaps even the right unquestioned and unreflective word. A common reply is an interjection. Among the interjections, some have become classical answers on the same plane with other sayings of the great masters. One such word is *ho!* (Japanese, *katsu!*), a Chinese monosyllabic expression indicating a sharp scolding or sarcastic surprise. The Chan master Can of Boyun Wuliangsi states,

> Throughout the twenty-four hours of the day, walk with your key phrase (*huatou*), stand with your key phrase, sit with your key phrase, lie down with your key phrase. Your mind should feel just like a thorn bush, so you cannot swallow such notions as "person," "self," "delusion," etc. Whether you are walking, standing, sitting, or lying down, turn your entire body into a ball of DOUBT . . . . Then, upon hearing some sound or seeing some shape or color, most certainly you will shout, "Ho!" This single sound takes you to the end. (*Taishō* 2024, vol. 48, 1100a2–7)

The system remained permeable to various influences from the literature and philosophy of the countries in which kōan were used. For instance, beginning with the Ming dynasty (1368–1644), Pure Land recitation was often used as a kōanlike topic. Master Zhiji advised,

> Recite the name of the Buddha Amitābha once, or three, or five, or seven times. Then turn back silently and ask yourself, "Where does this recitation of the name of the Buddha arise?" Or ask yourself, "Who is this reciting the name of the Buddha?" If you have doubts, simply have doubts . . . . Investigate it carefully, inquire into it thoroughly. (*Taishō* 2024, vol. 48, 1102b18–23)

The practice of Zen meditation, although idealized sometimes as a path of lonely self-discovery, requires constant coaching, prodding, and questioning by a qualified Zen master. In the Japanese Rinzai Zen tradition, interactions between the disciple and the meditation instructor take place in private interviews known as *sanzen* (Zen practiced by visiting) or *dokusan* (private visit). The interview can be frightening to the novice because the master traditionally sits on a cushion with his teaching rod lying at his feet, in a dark room, with a single candle illuminating the room from behind the master's back. The disciple must bow before the master and immediately give or demonstrate his understanding of the meditation exercise. Any exchange taking place in *dokusan* is considered secret because it is believed to embody transmission from mind to mind.

Although tradition sometimes suggests that all kōans ultimately have the same meaning, it is not uncommon to organize kōans in graded or step-wise presentations, or to prescribe them for different purposes (including the healing of specific diseases). Collections composed mostly during the Song dynasty also generated much debate as to the meaning of kōans and the proper explanation or "answer" to the riddle implicit in the fact that a kōan cannot have a "discursive" meaning.

In Japan, approximately after the seventeenth century, kōans were systematized into a curriculum of Zen training that included, for instance, traditional correct answers to the kōans. The plan also incorporated some kōans of Japanese origin, such as the famous, "What is the sound of one hand," attributed to HAKUIN EKAKU (1686–1768). The disciple is expected to come up with the correct answer to a given kōan, which will then be accepted or rejected by the master. Once the answer is accepted, the master assigns a different kōan. The rigidity of the system and a number of abuses were often criticized, the most thorough and devastating criticism coming at the beginning of the twentieth century.

The contexts of meditation

What we conceive as "Buddhist meditation" may involve a spectrum of beliefs and practices embedded in both the private and the public lives of Buddhists. Moreover, as outlined above, meditation practice and doctrine, inner meditation processes, and external ritual overlap significantly and reinforce each other.

Unlike ritual, meditation is, in practice, open-ended and subject to missing its ultimate goal, even when technically correct. To express it differently, meditation is supposed to have a transformative effect, but in actual practice, the effect may come about gradually, imperfectly, or not at all. Both the experience of the struggle, the failures and frustrations, and the pragmatic quest for the right technique, time, and intensity of practice are topics worth exploring.

The full range of meditation includes many experiences. We have noted already some of the more abstract: notions of truth, polemical and philosophical insights, and the experience of preparation, retreat, or ritual frames. But, as a personal journey, meditation meets many obstacles: a person's frustration with meditation; sleepiness or overexcitability during meditation; physical pain, fatigue, or discomfort; and the disappointment of making no progress. For people who practice meditation these obstacles are equally important experiences. Sometimes they are either commented upon in meditation instruction, or used for meditation itself.

Needless to say, meditation, like other aspects of the religious life, also has its social contexts and its interpersonal correlates. In its social contexts, meditation can have many meanings and functions. Similarly, the goals of meditation can vary considerably even in the lifetime of one individual. Such goals may be associated with traditions of hygiene, health, and healing, or with those of wonder-working. Meditation is also often closely associated with the visionary quest, the quest for visions of hidden or distant worlds, HEAVENS and HELLS. It is also associated with ASCETIC PRACTICES, withdrawal, or escape. In all of these functions the tendency is to see meditation as essentially the concentration of spiritual power.

Buddhists can, and often do, appeal to the experience of meditation as a justification or a foundation for their beliefs, values, and practices, regardless of their willingness or capacity to actually practice meditation. But it is also true that many Buddhists see meditation as a value in itself, as an ideal that may be difficult to achieve, too difficult for most of us, but nevertheless as a spiritual discipline that represents the highest accomplishment that a human being is capable of achieving. A Buddhist expressing this second view of meditation can also consider meditation as essentially a practice, something to be done or accomplished, and therefore, as something that is not merely a belief or an ideal.

See also: **Bodhi (Awakening); Chan School; Nenbutsu (Chinese, Nianfo; Korean, Yŏmbul); Psychology; Vipassanā (Sanskrit, Vipaśyanā); Yogācāra School**

Bibliography

Beyer, Stephan. *The Cult of Tārā: Magic and Ritual in Tibet.* Berkeley, Los Angeles, and London: University of California Press, 1973.

Beyer, Stephan V., ed. and trans. *The Buddhist Experience: Sources and Interpretations.* Encino, CA: Wadsworth, 1974.

Beyer, Stephan V. "The Doctrine of Meditation in the Hīnayāna" and "The Doctrine of Meditation in the Mahāyāna." In *Buddhism: A Modern Perspective,* ed. Charles S. Prebish. University Park: Pennsylvania State University Press, 1975.

Blacker, Carmen. "Methods of Yoga in Japanese Buddhism." In *Comparative Religion: The Charles Strong Trust Lectures,* ed. John Bowan. Leiden, Netherlands: Brill, 1972.

Blofeld, John. *The Tantric Mysticism of Tibet: A Practical Guide.* New York: Dutton, 1970.

Blofeld, John Eaton Calthorpe. *Mantras: Sacred Words of Power.* London: Allen and Unwin, 1977.

Bronkhorst, Johannes. *The Two Traditions of Meditation in Ancient India.* Stuttgart, Germany: Verlag, 1986; 2nd revised edition, Delhi: Motilal Banarsidass, 1993 (mistakenly identified as "first edition" on the copyright page).

Cleary, Thomas. *Stopping and Seeing: A Comprehensive Course in Buddhist Meditation by Chih-I.* Boston: Shambhala, 1997.

Conze, Edward, ed. and trans. *Buddhist Meditation.* London: Allen and Unwin, 1956.

Gómez, Luis O. "Prayer: Buddhist Perspectives" and "Spirituality: Buddhist Perspectives." In *Encyclopedia of Monasticism,* Vol. 2, ed. William M. Johnston. Chicago: Fitzroy Dearborn, 2000.

Griffiths, Paul J. "Indian Buddhist Meditation." In *Buddhist Spirituality: Indian, Southeast Asian, Tibetan, Early Chinese,* 2 vols., ed. Yoshinori Takeuchi. New York: Crossroad, 1993.

Jamgon Kongtrul Lodro Tayé (Kong-sprul Blo-gros-mtha'-yas). *Jamgon Kongtrul's Retreat Manual,* tr. Ngawang Zangpo. Ithaca, NY: Snow Lion, 1994.

King, Winston L. *Theravāda Meditation: The Buddhist Transformation of Yoga.* University Park: Pennsylvania State University Press, 1980.

Kornfield, Jack. *Living Dharma: Teachings of Twelve Buddhist Masters.* Boston: Shambhala, 1996. Previously published as *Living Buddhist Masters,* Santa Cruz, CA: Unity Press, 1977.

Minoru Kiyota, ed., assisted by Elvin W. Jones. *Mahāyāna Buddhist Meditation: Theory and Practice.* Honolulu: University of Hawaii Press, 1978.

Nyanaponika Thera. *The Heart of Buddhist Meditation.* London: Rider, 1962.

Sharf, Robert H. "Buddhist Modernism and the Rhetoric of Meditative Experience." *Numen* 42 (1995): 228–283.

Sharf, Robert H. "Experience." In *Critical Terms for Religious Studies,* ed. Mark C. Taylor. Chicago: University of Chicago Press, 1998.

Sharf, Robert H., and Sharf, Elizabeth Horton. *Living Images: Japanese Buddhist Icons in Context.* Stanford, CA: Stanford University Press, 2001.

Singh Khalsa, Dharma, and Stauth, Cameron. *Meditation as Medicine: Activate the Power of Your Natural Healing Force.* New York: Pocket Books, 2001.

Tambiah, Stanley J. "The Cosmological and Performative Significance of a Thai Cult of Healing through Meditation." *Culture, Medicine, and Psychiatry* 1, no. 1 (1977): 97–132.

Thrangu, Khenchen. *The Practice of Tranquility and Insight: A Guide to Tibetan Buddhist Meditation.* Ithaca, NY: Snow Lion, 1993.

Vajirañāna, Paravahera (Mahāthera). *Buddhist Meditation in Theory and Practice: A General Exposition According to the Pāli Canon of the Theravāda School* (1962). Kuala Lumpur, Malaysia: Buddhist Missionary Society, 1975.

Yamasaki, Taiko. *Shingon: Japanese Esoteric Buddhism,* translated and adapted by Richard and Cynthia Peterson, ed. Yasuyoshi Morimoto and David Kidd. Boston: Shambhala, 1988.

LUIS O. GÓMEZ

MEIJI BUDDHIST REFORM

The collapse of the Tokugawa regime and the wave of changes accompanying the restoration of imperial rule and the formation of a new government at the start of the Meiji period (1868–1912) stimulated directly and indirectly numerous significant changes in Japanese Buddhism. The harsh critiques of Buddhism by Confucians, Nativists, and Shintōists during the waning years of the Tokugawa period (1600–1868) and at the start of Meiji culminated in the state-mandated separation of Buddhist and local elements of worship (which came to be identified as Shintō), triggering a brief but exceedingly violent suppression of Buddhism that lasted until 1871. Numerous Buddhist clerics were forcibly laicized, monastery lands were confiscated, and many temples and works of Buddhist art were destroyed. Even after the overt violence subsided, Buddhists were left reeling by an end to state support, government-mandated institutional centralization and restructuring, and the end to state enforcement of traditional protocols of Buddhist discipline, particularly the prohibitions against such clerical infractions as eating meat, marriage, and abandoning clerical dress or tonsure. An additional threat to Buddhism was posed by the growing influence in Japan of foreign Christian missionaries and Japanese Christian converts, who, along with domestic critics of Buddhism, characterized Buddhism as decadent, corrupt, impotent, and outdated.

Buddhists responded to the challenges of the Meiji period at the denominational, clerical, and lay levels. At the institutional level, leaders of the main Buddhist denominations availed themselves of the growing centralization of denominational governance in an effort to end the clerical abuses that they believed had helped bring Buddhism to its troubled state. Such leaders as Fukuda Gyōkai (1809–1888), Shaku Unshō (1827–1909), and Nishiari Bokusan (1821–1910) called on the Buddhist clergy to voluntarily preserve traditional Buddhist praxis, especially adherence to the PRECEPTS, and to ground themselves thoroughly in traditional Buddhist learning. These reform efforts gave rise to the adoption of strict new denominational rules and the creation of centers for clerical education that evolved into such sectarian universities as today's Ryūkoku, Ōtani, and Komazawa universities. The main branches of the Jōdo Shinshū, in particular, sponsored travel and study in Europe and the United States by such important contributors to the construction of modern Japanese Buddhism and Buddhist studies as Akamatsu Renjō (1841–1919), Kitabatake Dōryū (1820–1907), Shimaji Mokurai (1838–1911), Nanjō Bun'yū (1849–1927), and Takakusu Junjirō (1866–1945).

Groups of clerics, working independently of the denominations, began movements that aimed to reform clerical practice, meld Buddhist and Western styles of PHILOSOPHY and scholarship, and restructure denominational governance. Notable among the cleric-led movements that sought to extend Buddhist morality into day-to-day social life were Kiyozawa Manshi's (1863–1903) Jōdo Shin-based "spiritualist" movement (*Seishin shugi*); the pro-temperance Hanseikai (Self-reflection Society), which was led by such Nishi Honganji notables as Takakusu Junjirō, MURAKAMI SENSHŌ, INOUE ENRYŌ, and Furukawa Rōsen (1871–1899); and Shaku Unshō's Tokkyōkai (Morality Society). Other clerical reformers, for example, Kuruma Takudō (1877–1964), Tanabe Zenchi, and Nakazato Nisshō, worked for the acceptance of clerical marriage and the creation of an educated Buddhist clergy that was totally engaged with family, social, and national affairs.

Lay Buddhist movements, stimulated by the growth of a literate middle class, were also a major feature of the religious landscape during the Meiji era. Such former clerics as Inoue Enryō, Ōuchi Seiran (1845–1918), Daidō Chōan (1843–1908), and Tanaka Chigaku (1861–1939) founded new lay Buddhist organizations that ran the political gamut from liberal to very conservative. These groups variously sought to create a new Buddhism that would play an integral role in the daily lives of their members, give Buddhism intellectual parity with Western religion, philosophy, and science, and, at the same time, provide solid ideological support for the new Japanese nation-state. Ōuchi's Sonnō Hōbutsu Daidōdan (Great Association for Revering the Emperor and Worshipping the Buddha) and Tanaka Chigaku's Nichiren-based, lay religious groups that evolved into Kokuchūkai (National Pillar Society) were vehemently anti-Christian and strongly nationalistic. These movements served as influential models for many of the Buddhist-based new religious movements that arose in the first half of the twentieth century.

See also: **Clerical Marriage in Japan; Japan**

Bibliography

Collcutt, Martin. "Buddhism: The Threat of Eradication." In *Japan in Transition,* ed. Marius Jansen and Gilbert Rozman. Princeton, NJ: Princeton University Press, 1986.

Grapard, Allan G. "Japan's Ignored Cultural Revolution: The Separation of Shintō and Buddhist Divinities in Meiji (Shinbutsu Bunri) and a Case Study: Tonomine." *History of Religions* 23 (February 1984): 240–265.

Ketelaar, James Edward. *Of Heretics and Martyrs in Meiji Japan.* Princeton, NJ: Princeton University Press, 1990.

Snodgrass, Judith. *Presenting Japanese Buddhism to the West: Orientalism, Occidentalism, and the Columbian Exposition.* Chapel Hill: University of North Carolina Press, 2003.

RICHARD M. JAFFE

MERIT AND MERIT-MAKING

Merit (*puṇya*; Chinese, *gongde*; Japanese, *kudoku*) is karmic virtue acquired through moral and ritual actions; it is widely regarded as the foundation of Buddhist ethics and salvation. Although Jōdo Shinshū, the Shin (true) PURE LAND SCHOOL of Japanese Buddhism, rejects the efficacy of meritorious acts, the vast majority of Buddhist communities affirm the soteriological effects of good actions. As indicated by the term *merit-making,* virtue is the deliberate result of human consideration and conduct.

Buddhist literature widely attests to the making and consequences of merit. The JĀTAKA tales tell stories of how people benefit from their virtues and suffer from their vices. "Be quick in goodness," counsels the *Word of the Doctrine* (DHAMMAPADA), "from wrong hold back your thought." In *Milinda's Questions* (MILINDAPAÑHA), the Buddhist monk Nāgasena tells King Milinda that those who are pure in heart, refined and straight in action, and free from the obstacles of craving will see NIRVĀṆA. In these Pāli texts, merit accrues from moral actions.

In MAHĀYĀNA literature, the importance of morality is affirmed, but the notion of merit is extended to the idea of benefits obtained largely through ritual actions. Since ritual involves magical power exceeding that of moral effort, the benefits are greater. The LOTUS SŪTRA (SADDHARMAPUṆḌARĪKA-SŪTRA; Japanese, *Myōhō rengekyō*), for example, describes the magnificent benefits that will fall on those who do no more than read, recite, copy, and uphold the sūtra. Their benefits will be without limit or measure, far exceeding the merits acquired through moral practices such as almsgiving, patience, and gentleness. An investment in ritual actions yields greater benefits than merits realized through moral effort.

The relationship between ritual benefits and moral merits varies according to different traditions and teachers, but in most cases both are affirmed and are indicated by the single Japanese term *kudoku,* which literally means "the virtue of effort." In order to specify the particular value of Buddhist effort, as opposed to all other human actions, the idea of the "field of merit" (*puṇyakṣetra*; Chinese, *futian*; Japanese, *fukuden*) identifies Buddhism as the field within which merit and benefits can be realized and even multiplied. The Chinese and Japanese terms extend even further beyond the idea of ritual benefits to suggest divine blessings. The field of blessings is identified variously with the Buddha, the SAṄGHA (monastic community), and the dharma—that is, the entirety of Buddhism itself—and is defined even more specifically as particular deities, texts, or objects such as relics, all of which have the power to grant blessings. Despite the emphasis on ritual benefits and divine blessings, the merit of moral action is seldom forgotten. In the category of the "three fields of blessings," for example, the first field involves reverence to the BUDDHAS, the second calls for repaying obligations to parents and teachers, and the third requires acts of compassion to help the poor and the sick. The value of any act, therefore, depends not just on the person carrying out the act but on the recipient as well. More merit and benefit will accrue by giving to buddhas rather than humans, humans rather than animals, monks rather than laypersons, and the poor rather than the rich.

Benefits and blessings, the related virtues of merit, are enjoyed as rewards for one's efforts, but they can also be dedicated or transferred to others. Like economic transactions, merit can be transferred from one account to another. In *Milinda's Questions,* Nāgasena argues that only the merits of good deeds can be transferred to others; the results of evil deeds cannot. Many rituals close with a section on the transfer of merit (*pariṇāmanā*; Japanese, *ekō*) to all sentient beings and to ancestors. Far from being fixed, karmic merit is transactional: Bad KARMA (ACTION) acquired in the past can be extinguished or offset by merit accrued in the present, and the karmic accounts of the dead can be augmented by a transfer of merit from the living. Rendering karmic aid to the dead is particularly important for those who might be reborn in the HELLS, where they will face the Ten Kings of Hell, who will surely indict them for lack of merit. Even for those whose lives were clearly meritorious, transferring merit assured their general well-being, and is a key element in the postmortem care of ANCESTORS. The best reason for transferring merit to the deceased is to help them gain rebirth in the pure land, the heavenly paradise in Buddhist COSMOLOGY.

Since these transfers take place through formal rituals, monks and nuns, acting as agents brokering the transfer, receive donations for their services. This economic support has been an essential part of the institutional life of Buddhism; in addition to being the foundation of Buddhist morality and salvation, the belief in merit and the transfer of merit is a cornerstone for sustaining the clergy and their monasteries.

Sparrows are freed by a merit-maker during the Thai new year festival in Bangkok, Thailand, 1999. AP/Wide World Photos. Reproduced by permission.

Merit can also be transferred between people without the ritual services of a cleric. Passing merit directly between people technically does not constitute a transfer of merit, which requires the ritual intervention of a monk or nun and is limited to the merit of good deeds. These direct karmic interchanges are better described as exchanges of merit taking place through personal relationships. In these situations, it is commonly believed that harm done to another will result in harsh retribution. Wrongdoing represents a loss of merit from the perpetrator to the victim, who thereby has the right to retaliate, often in the form of curses. Misfortunes are commonly interpreted to be retributions and even revenge inflicted by those who have been wronged. In Japan, aborted fetuses, for example, are said to be able to inflict harm on the parents who terminated their lives. Resolution of this problem takes the form of a ritual (MIZUKO KUYŌ) through which a transfer of merit (*ekō*) from the parents to the fetus provides proper recompense. An exchange of bad karma through personal relationships can be corrected through a transfer of merit.

As a moral commodity, merit is quantifiable. Chanting the name of the Buddha produces merit, and greater numbers of repetitions result in greater merit. In both China and Japan, people kept merit books in which they recorded the number of times they performed a ritual. Accumulated merit could be applied to oneself or transferred to a group, to ancestors, or to particular persons, such as the emperor. Quantification also permitted simplification, and practices such as reciting the Buddha's name became popular among lay believers who did not have the resources for more complex rituals. The conflation of merit, benefits, and blessings meant that the rewards of virtue could be enjoyed in this life as well as the next, and testimonies abound about how people gained worldly boons from their moral and ritual practices.

With the exception of Jōdo Shinshū, all schools of Buddhism affirm the acquisition of worldly benefits through merit-making. In Japan, the ritual essentials are extremely simple, consisting of short petitionary prayers and the purchase of good luck amulets and charms. In the teaching of karma, nothing can happen by luck or chance, everything is the result of human deliberation and action. The belief in the power of amulets to produce benefits and blessings is often criticized by intellectuals and scholars as a form of magic that contradicts the doctrine of karma. Defenders of the practice, however, point out that it is precisely the law of karma that is at work when believers create merit by purchasing and venerating amulets. Benefits—and they include health, wealth, business success, good grades, family harmony, traffic safety, safe childbirth, and a host of other good things in life—result from the virtue of acquiring amulets and believing in the divine power it represents. Since amulets are believed to be consecrated with the power of specific deities, the worldly benefits are received as divine blessings.

While there is clearly an element of magical thinking associated with amulets, few people believe that the mere possession of charms will produce the desired effects without any exertion of effort on their part. Japanese students, for example, purchase amulets for good grades, but do not believe that they are thereby relieved of having to study for an exam. Right action is still necessary in order to create merit, which can be complemented by divine blessings, but is not abrogated.

Set within the larger context of the teaching of karma, merit and merit-making comprise a cogent system in which moral action produces merit, ritual performance generates benefits, and the buddhas and bodhisattvas grant blessings to those who earn them through their efforts and can share the fruits of their virtues with the living and the dead in hopes of gaining a good rebirth and, ultimately, entry into nirvāṇa.

See also: **Amulets and Talismans; Death; Ghosts and Spirits; Rebirth**

Bibliography

Brokaw, Cynthia J. *The Ledgers of Merit and Demerit: Social Change and Moral Order in Late Imperial China.* Princeton, NJ: Princeton University Press, 1991.

Kalupahana, David. *Buddhist Philosophy: A Historical Analysis.* Honolulu: University of Hawaii Press, 1975.

Reader, Ian, and Tanabe, George J., Jr. *Practically Religious: Worldly Benefits and the Common Religion of Japan.* Honolulu: University of Hawaii Press, 1998.

Teiser, Stephen F. *The Scripture on the Ten Kings and the Making of Purgatory in Medieval Chinese Buddhism.* Honolulu: University of Hawaii Press, 1994.

GEORGE J. TANABE, JR.

MIJIAO (ESOTERIC) SCHOOL

The Esoteric school (Chinese, Mijiao) of Buddhism was introduced to China as part of the general spread of MAHĀYĀNA Buddhism that took place in the third and fourth centuries of the common era. The earliest forms of Esoteric Buddhist practice consisted of incantations and DHĀRAṆĪ, as found in a number of canonical and essentially exoteric sūtras belonging to the Mahāyāna tradition. The gradual development toward esotericism in Indian Mahāyāna Buddhism is reflected in Chinese translations, which preserve the largest number of early Esoteric Buddhist scriptures. In the course of its development in China, Esoteric Buddhism evolved from a ritualistic appendix on the exoteric scriptures to full-scale Esoteric Buddhist scriptures that propagated a wide range of practices and beliefs with ritualized magic at the center. In the course of this development the Esoteric Buddhist tradition adapted a number of Daoist beliefs and practices, while at the same time greatly contributing to the development of that rival religious tradition.

During the Tang dynasty (618–907) Esoteric Buddhism reached its zenith in terms of influence and popularity, and its lore and ritual practices were adopted by most Buddhist traditions in China. Esoteric Buddhism under the Tang was chiefly represented by the Zhenyan (True Word) school, which propagated a systematic and highly elaborate form of Esoteric Buddhism. Its leading patriarchs were Śubhākarasiṃha (637–735), Vajrabodhi (669–741), and Amoghavajra (705–774), all of whom were of foreign ancestry. All three teachers served as preceptors for a succession of Chinese rulers. The teachings and rituals of the Zhenyan school were based on a large number of sūtras and scriptures, most of which propounded the use of MUDRĀS, MAṆḌALAS, and visualizations, as well as incantations of magical formulas in the forms of MANTRAS and dhāraṇīs. The main teachings and practices focused on the *Mahāvairocana* (*Great Sun*) and the *Vajraśekhara* (*Vajra Pinnacle*), sūtras that exemplify the *kriyā* (action [i.e., rite]) and *caryā* (ritual performance) stages according to the later classification of Esoteric Buddhism. In other words, the school focused on the initial or preliminary stages of practice in accordance with mature Tantric Buddhist doctrine. The antinomian practices commonly associated with the later Tantric tradition, including meat-eating, the drinking of alcohol, and ritual sex (i.e., the conscious breaking of the conventional Buddhist PRECEPTS), were not practiced by the teachers of the Zhenyan school. However, in the ritual cycles relating to the Vajrasattva cult as propagated by Amoghavajra, there is evidence of tendencies toward antinomianism.

The centers of Zhenyan Buddhism were situated in the twin capitals of Chang'an and Luoyang, and included a series of famous monasteries such as Anguosi, Da Xingshansi, and Qinglongsi. During the late eighth and early ninth centuries, Mount Wutai in Shanxi province, with its hundreds of monasteries and hermitages, was a flourishing center of Zhenyan Buddhism. It was during this period that the Japanese monks SAICHŌ (767–822), the founder of the Japanese Tendai (Chinese, Tiantai) school, and KŪKAI (774–835), who established Zhenyan in the form of SHINGON BUDDHISM in Japan, studied under Esoteric Buddhist masters in China.

The Huichang persecution of Buddhism of 844 to 845 destroyed most of the important Buddhist monasteries in Chang'an and Luoyang, and, while it seriously crippled the Zhenyan school, it did not cause lasting damage to the development of Esoteric Buddhism in China. Although the Zhenyan tradition declined, Esoteric Buddhist practices in nonsectarian and more unstructured forms continued to flourish in the provinces. In particular, Sichuan in the southwestern part of China saw the rise of a strong Esoteric Buddhist tradition that continued well into the Southern Song dynasty (960–1279). Yunnan, which at that time was ruled by the Dali kingdom (937–1253), also saw the rise of a distinct form of Esoteric Buddhism that incorporated influences from China, Tibet, and Burma.

During the early Song, a new wave of translations of Buddhist scriptures introduced the first full-fledged tantras to Chinese soil, including the *Mañjuśrīmūlakalpa* (*Fundamental Ordinance of Mañjuśrī*), the *Hevajra-tantra* (*Tantra of Hevajra*), and the *Guhyasamāja-tantra* (*Tantra of Guhyasamāja*). However, it appears that the antinomian practices expounded in these scriptures did not win many adherents among the Chinese Buddhists. In contrast, the Tanguts, a people of Tibeto-Burmese stock, who had founded the Xixia dynasty (1038–1223) in present-day Ningxia and Gansu provinces, followed a mixture of Sino-Tibetan Buddhism that included Esoteric Buddhism in its Tantric form. Here the higher yoga and *annuttarayoga* tantras were taught. Tibetan lamas served as imperial preceptors to the Tangut rulers.

During the Yuan (1260–1368) and early Ming (1368–1644) dynasties, Esoteric Buddhism in the form of Tibetan Lamaism was introduced in China, where it remained influential for several centuries. Under the Qing dynasty (1644–1911), Lamaism became the official religion of the Manchu rulers, who favored a succession of important lamas from Tibet and Mongolia. During this period, a number of important Tibetan and Mongolian tantric texts were translated into Chinese.

See also: **China; Daoism and Buddhism; Esoteric Art, East Asia; Exoteric-Esoteric (Kenmitsu) Buddhism in Japan; Persecutions; Tantra; Tiantai School**

Bibliography

Chou I-liang. "Tantrism in China." *Harvard Journal of Asian Studies* 8 (1945): 41–332.

Lü Jianfu. *Zhongguo Mijiao shi* (*The History of Esoteric Buddhism in China*). Beijing: Zhongguo Shehui Kexue Chubanshe, 1995.

Orzech, Charles D. "Seeing Chen-yen Buddhism: Traditional Scholarship and the Vajrayāna in China." *History of Religions* 29, no. 2 (1989): 87–114.

Osabe Kazuo. *Tō Sō Mikkyō shi ronkō* (*Essays on the History of Esoteric Buddhism during the Tang and Song*). Kobe, Japan: Eiden bunshōdō, 1963.

Osabe Kazuo. *Tōdai Mikkyō shi no zakkō* (*History of Esoteric Buddhism during the Tang Dynasty*). Kobe, Japan: Eiden bunshōdō, 1971.

Shi Jinbo. *Xixia fojiao shilu* (*An Abbreviated History of Buddhism under the Xixia*). Yinchuan, China: Ningxia renmin chubanshe, 1988.

Sørensen, Henrik H., ed. *The Esoteric Buddhist Tradition: Selected Papers from the 1989 SBS Conference*. Copenhagen and Aarhus, Denmark: Seminar for Buddhist Studies, 1994.

Strickmann, Michel. *Mantras et mandarins: Le bouddhisme tantrique en Chine*. Paris: Éditions Gallimard, 1996.

Xiao Dengfu. *Daojiao yu mizong* (*Daoism and Esoteric Buddhism*). Taipei, Taiwan: Xinwenfeng, 1993.

Yoritomi Motohiro. *Chūgoku mikkyō no kenkyū* (*Studies in Chinese Esoteric Buddhism*). Tokyo: Daitō shuppan sha, 1980.

HENRIK H. SØRENSEN

MI LA RAS PA (MILAREPA)

Mi la ras pa (pronounced Milarepa, 1028/40–1111/23) was a highly revered Tibetan yogin. He is considered an early founder of the BKA' BRGYUD (KAGYU) sect of Tibetan Buddhism. Mi la ras pa is esteemed throughout the Tibetan cultural world as an exemplar of religious dedication, perseverance through hardship, and meditative mastery. His life story has been the subject of a vast hagiographic tradition in Tibet. The most famous biographical account (Lhalungpa 1977) and collection of spiritual songs (Chang 1962), both composed in the late fifteenth century, remain extremely popular within the Tibetan Buddhist world. The themes associated with his biographical tradition—purification of past misdeeds, FAITH and devotion to the guru, ardor in MEDITATION and yogic practice, and the possibility of attaining buddhahood in a single lifetime—have influenced the development of Buddhist teaching and practice in Tibet, and the way they have been understood in the West.

Mi la was his clan name; *ras pa* is derived from the word for a single cotton robe (*ras*) worn by Tibetan anchorites—an attire Mi la ras pa retained for most of his life. The name is therefore an appellation, perhaps translated as "The Cotton-Clad Mi la."

Although his dates are debated, biographies agree that Mi la ras pa was born to a prosperous family in the Gung thang region of southwestern Tibet. At an early age, after the death of his father, he and his family were dispossessed of their wealth and home by Mi la ras pa's paternal aunt and uncle, and thereby reduced to a life of poverty and privation. At the behest of his mother, Mi la ras pa studied black magic in order to exact revenge upon his relatives, and he eventually murdered a great number of people. Later, feeling contrition and realizing the magnitude of his misdeeds, he sought to redeem himself from their karmic effects through the practice of Buddhism. He studied briefly under several masters before meeting his principal guru, the great translator of Indian texts MAR PA (MARPA) (1002/1012–1097). Mar pa, however, did not immediately teach Mi la ras pa, but rather subjected him to continual abuse, forcing him to undergo various ordeals, such as the famous trial of constructing immense stone towers. Pushed to the brink of utter despair, Mi la ras pa even contemplated suicide. Mar pa finally assuaged his disciple, revealing that the trials were actually a means of purifying previous negative karma. He explained that Mi la ras pa was, from the beginning, his disciple as prophesied by the Indian master NĀROPA (1016–1100). Mi la ras pa received numerous tantric initiations and instructions—especially those of MAHĀMUDRĀ and the practice of yogic inner heat (*gtum mo*)—together with the command that he should persevere against all hardship, meditating in solitary caves and mountain retreats.

Mi la ras pa spent the rest of his life practicing meditation in seclusion and teaching small groups of disciples, mainly through poetry and songs of realization. He had little interest in philosophical discourse and no tolerance for intellectual pretension. His songs are composed in vernacular idioms, abandoning the highly ornamental formal structures of classical poetry in favor of a simple, direct, and often playful style. According to tradition, he was active across southern Tibet from Mount KAILĀŚA (KAILASH) to Bhutan. Dozens of locations associated with the yogin have become important pilgrimage sites and retreat centers. Foremost among Mi la ras pa's disciples were Sgam po pa Bsod nams rin chen (Gampopa Sonam Rinchen, 1079–1153) and Ras chung pa Rdo rje grags (Rechungpa Dorje Drak, 1084–1161).

See also: **Tibet**

Bibliography

Chang, Garma C. C., trans. *The Hundred Thousand Songs of Milarepa*, 2 vols. New Hyde Park, NY: University Books, 1962. Reprint, Boston: Shambhala, 1999.

Lama Kunga Rinpoche and Cutillo, Brian, trans. *Drinking the Mountain Stream*. Novato, CA: Lotsawa, 1978. Reprint, Boston: Wisdom, 1995.

Lama Kunga Rinpoche and Cutillo, Brian, trans. *Miraculous Journey*. Novato, CA: Lotsawa, 1991.

Lhalungpa, Lobsang P., trans. *The Life of Milarepa*. New York: Dutton, 1977. Reprint, Boston: Shambhala, 1984.

ANDREW QUINTMAN

MILINDAPAÑHA

The *Milindapañha*, or *Milinda's Questions*, is a Pāli text that, though normally regarded as extracanonical, is nonetheless accepted in Myanmar (Burma) as part of the *Khuddakanikāya* of the Pāli canon. Possibly based on a Sanskrit or Prakrit original, it dates prior to the fourth century C.E., when it—or the Sanskrit original—was translated into Chinese. Some even surmise that the original text was written in Greek.

In general, the text records a series of conversations between the Buddhist monk Nāgasena and the Bactrian Indo-Greek king Milinda (also called Menander), who ruled northwestern India from Sāgalā (modern Siālkot) during the second century B.C.E. Its main thrust lies in eighty-one dilemmas, couched in Socratic dialogue, in which Milinda seeks to reconcile what appear to him to be contradictory statements by the Buddha in the Pāli canon. Most notable of these is Milinda's inability to reconcile the supposed doctrine of anattā (Sanskrit, anātman; no-self) and the Buddha's belief in REBIRTH, which Nāgasena skillfully resolves with his account of the chariot, in which he demonstrates that the terms *self* and *chariot* are simply concepts superimposed upon what is in fact merely a collection of parts.

Although clearly regarded as authoritative by the scholar BUDDHAGHOSA, who quotes from it in his *Visuddhimagga* (*The Path of Purification*) and other commentaries (Horner, vol. I, p. xx), the text seemingly evinces Sarvāstivādin influence in maintaining that both nibbāna (NIRVĀṆA) and space are without cause, whereas for the Theravāda only nibbāna is non-compounded.

See also: **Pāli, Buddhist Literature in**

Bibliography

Horner, I. B., trans. *Milinda's Questions*, 2 vols. London: Luzac, 1963–1964.

PETER MASEFIELD

MILLENARIANISM AND MILLENARIAN MOVEMENTS

Like most religious traditions, Buddhism has an understanding of time, both cyclic and linear, and a developed tradition of thought concerning the eventual end of the world. Within Buddhism, this tradition centers around the person of MAITREYA bodhisattva, who was identified early on as the future successor to Śākyamuni Buddha. Particularly in the MAHĀYĀNA tradition, Maitreya came to be viewed as a messianic figure. In East Asia, the arrival of Maitreya was linked both to the apocalyptic end of the current epoch and the initiation of a future epoch in which the world would be transformed into a paradise. Historically, the worship of Maitreya has served as the seed both for general utopian longing and armed movements meant to usher in the millennium.

Judeo-Christian and Buddhist millenarianism

Millenarianism is a branch of utopianism, one specifically concerned with the arrival (or return) of a divinely portended messianic figure and the subsequent establishment of an earthly kingdom of peace and plenty. The term itself derives from the Christian belief in a thousand-year reign of Christ preceding the final judgment, leading to anticipation that the apocalypse would occur in the year 1000 C.E. For most Western readers, the concept of millenarianism is closely connected to the Judeo-Christian tradition, both the Jewish belief in the arrival of a messiah and the related Christian belief in Armageddon and the return of Christ Triumphant as described in the Book of Revelation. There is an inherent danger in relying too heavily on these conceptions of the millennium to understand similar ideas in Buddhism. The scriptural portents given by prophets of the Old and New Testaments provide a very specific picture of the arrival of the messiah and the nature of the judgment, reward, and punishment, none of which fits precisely with those of Buddhism or has much significance for millenarian movements in Buddhist history.

At the same time, however, certain elements of Judeo-Christian millenarianism are conceptually similar to those seen in other traditions (including what might be termed *political millenarianism,* such as the anticipated return of a mythical ruler), suggesting that millenarian thought and movements involve certain universal themes. The first such element is a system of reckoning cosmic time. In most traditions, time is composed of three parts: epochs of the mythical past, the current age, and the distant future. These three epochs are separated by events of cosmic significance in which the old order is destroyed or altered completely, and thus the recorded history of humankind falls primarily inside the second age. In the Judeo-Christian tradition, the pivotal event that marked the commencement of the age of humans was the expulsion of Adam and Eve from the Garden of Eden. Human history progresses in a linear fashion from that point, reaching its culmination in the arrival or return of the messiah, at which point humankind as a whole will be subjected to its final judgment.

The second element is the conception of the post-millennial paradise, which is depicted in very physical, earthly terms. Jewish messianism has historically produced a wide spectrum of ideas and movements, but is most fundamentally predicated on the physical return of the Jews to Palestine. The Christian Book of Revelation, as well, emphasizes the physicality of the millennium, with resurrection of the body and the founding of the Kingdom of God on earth. This type of millenarianism, which is predicated on the arrival of a sacred figure from heaven, is referred to as the *descending* motif. It is distinguished from belief in a postmortem paradise, often described as a place where purified souls await the final apocalypse. The ascent of souls to this heavenly kingdom marks this as the *ascending* motif.

Maitreya in South and Central Asia

Millenarian thought and devotion to Maitreya have appeared in almost every manifestation of the Buddhist tradition and may reflect pre-Buddhist themes. The arrival of a messianic and triumphant figure is based on the Indian ideal of the cakravartin, a virtuous universal monarch who is divinely destined to unify the earthly realm. Both the Buddha himself and Buddhist political figures such as King AŚOKA and the Japanese prince SHŌTOKU were identified with this monarch. Early contact between Buddhism and Zoroastrianism (from Iran and Bactria) may have influenced this belief with the addition of beliefs concerning Mithra, a deity associated with apocalyptic change, and the image of Saošyant, a divine savior who would appear on earth at the end of twelve cosmic cycles, purge the world of sin, and establish an immortal material paradise. Scholars are undecided as to the exact relation of these traditions to the development of Buddhist millenarianism and Maitreya worship.

Maitreya is not discussed in any of the canonical South Asian texts and is mentioned only tangentially in the canonical literature of the THERAVĀDA, but he catapults to prominence in the MAHĀVASTU (*Great Story*), a central text of the MAHĀSĀṂGHIKA SCHOOL. This text, which outlines the theory of bodhisattvas as supernatural beings, places Maitreya at the head of a list of future buddhas. The Mahāyāna sūtras continue in this line, portraying Maitreya as a worthy monk, who spent lifetimes developing in wisdom and preaching the dharma before being reborn as a bodhisattva in the Tuṣita heaven, where he awaits his incarnation as the buddha of the next epoch.

This latter event, however, is spoken of in relatively vague terms, and it is destined to occur only in the very distant future (five billion years, by some accounts), according to cycles of growth and decay. An early Buddhist idea says that the universe oscillates between growth and decay in cycles called *kalpas.* All things, from the dharma to human life span (which can be as long as eighty thousand years or as short as ten) depend on this cycle, which is currently in an advanced state of decay, a phenomenon known as the DECLINE OF THE DHARMA. Once the nadir of this cycle has passed, the universe will again begin a period of growth, and as it approaches its peak, a cakravartin king will appear to usher in Maitreya's advent and the Maitreyan Golden Age.

This formulation is significant because it placed the return of Maitreya in the distant future and says that the human world must first pass the nadir of the cosmic cycle before this can happen. Because things would get worse before they got better, people placed their hopes on the ascending motif of individual salvation, such as rebirth in the Pure Land or Tuṣita heaven, rather than the millennium.

Buddhist millenarianism in China

It was in China that the worship of Maitreya and tradition of longing for a distant golden age evolved into millenarian movements. This transformation happened for three reasons. First, when Buddhism took root in China during the first few centuries C.E., it encountered a well-established tradition of Daoist millenarianism. This tradition encompassed many of the elements that would come to be associated with Buddhist millenarianism in East Asia, such as the tripartite division of sacred time. The Daoist millenarian tradition was focused on the immanent return of a transcendent manifestation of Laozi called Lord Lao on High (*taishang laojun*), who would establish a millennial kingdom called the Great Peace (*taiping*). From the second through fourth centuries C.E., this belief served as the seed for a number of sizable rebellions, including one that was able to establish a viable, although short-lived, state in the mountainous southwest.

The second innovation was the restructuring of the theory of cosmic rise and decline so as to place the enthronement of Maitreya Buddha at the nadir of the cycle, rather than at its peak. These ideas were developed in Chinese apocryphal sūtras from the sixth century, which discussed the arrival of Maitreya as a vast cleansing that would see a cosmic battle between bodhisattvas and demons, following which a pure and perfect world would be created. This reinterpretation not only made the arrival of the millennial event more immanent, it also located it at the lowest point of human suffering. This new eschatology was especially appealing during times of demographic crisis, such as war or famine, which were now felt to portend the end of the age. Although such crises also fueled the ascending motif of Buddhist utopianism, the belief that the individual soul would find postmortem salvation in the Pure Land, Maitreya soon came to be distanced from this vision and closely associated with the descending motif of the apocalypse. This belief also provided inspiration for those who would take action to hasten along the millennium by causing the destruction that marked the end of the cycle.

The third innovation was the participation of Chinese political actors in worship of Maitreya and reinterpretation of the cakravartin, not as a precursor to the arrival of Maitreya, but as Maitreya himself. In part, this was facilitated by the pre-Buddhist belief in the divine significance of Chinese rulers as beneficiaries of the "mandate of heaven." As early as the fourth century, rulers of the Chinese Northern Wei dynasty (386–534) were identified as Buddhist deities, first as TATHĀGATAS and later as Maitreya. The most famous instance occurred in the late seventh century, when the empress Wu Zhao (625–705) revealed her identity as Maitreya Buddha in order to bolster her highly contested claim to the throne.

This politicization of Maitreya worship was soon turned against its masters, and came to take on the distinctly antistate stance that it has held ever since. The earliest known instances both occurred in the year 613, when two separate individuals each proclaimed themselves to be Maitreya Buddha and raised the flag of rebellion. In the eighth and eleventh centuries, large-scale uprisings were mounted under the slogan of ending the decaying epoch of Śākyamuni and ushering in the arrival of the new buddha. Finally, in the early fourteenth century, a collection of religious societies devoted to the Maitreyan vision rose in rebellion against the Mongol Yuan dynasty (1279–1368), and the leader of one of these groups, Zhu Yuanzhang (1328–1398), founded the Ming (meaning "bright," an allusion to the Buddhist ideal of divine KINGSHIP, the *vidyārājas*; Chinese, *ming wang*) dynasty in 1368.

White Lotus sectarianism

The Ming dynasty brought organized Buddhism under close state control, while lay devotion became increasingly integrated into a syncretic mixture of Buddhism, Daoism, and Confucianism known as the Three Teachings. Particularly during the Ming and Qing dynasties (mid-fourteenth through early twentieth centuries), this mixture took shape in a tradition of popular teachings known collectively as White Lotus sectarianism.

Although the White Lotus encompassed a number of independent teachings, the tradition as a whole developed through a medium of scriptures known as "precious scrolls" (*baojuan*), which were composed by the hundreds over the course of these six centuries. The earliest known text, dating from 1430, expounds a basic version of the White Lotus eschatology, including a tripartite division of sacred time, punctuated by periods of apocalyptic calamity between epochs, and the role of Maitreya as the buddha of the millennial third epoch. However, although Maitreya is occasionally mentioned in these scriptures in connection with the change of epoch, he is not the primary figure. Rather, the characteristically sectarian contribution to this scheme is a supreme deity called the Eternal Venerable Mother (*wusheng laomu*), from whom all life emanates, and who has sent a series of teachers to earth in order to save humankind from its own wickedness. This must be accomplished before the end of the second epoch, at which point, those of her human children who have cultivated goodness and purified themselves will be called to join the Dragon Flower Assembly and invited to dwell in a millennial paradise ruled over by Maitreya and the Eternal Venerable Mother.

As was the case with later Maitreyan millenarianism, the eschatological vision of the White Lotus sect sees the decay and destruction of the human order as precursors of the epochal change. Moreover, this process can be hastened by human action in the form of armed rebellion. Thus, the White Lotus tradition was strictly banned, most energetically by the Ming emperor who himself had ridden just such an uprising to power. The most notable period of White Lotus activity was during the nineteenth century, when a number of such teachings, such as the Eight Trigrams (*bagua*) and Primal Chaos (*hunyuan*) teachings, rose in rebellion, often spurred on by the claim of a leader to be the reincarnation of Maitreya. Such claims persisted well into the middle of the twentieth century, when groups such as the Way of Pervading Unity (*yiguandao*) prophesied that a Communist victory over the Nationalist forces would prompt the early arrival of the millennium. Even among those groups active during this period with no organizational or doctrinal ties to the White Lotus tradition, such as the mid-nineteenth-century Taipings or the Boxers five decades later, the themes of millennial world renewal are easily linked to the larger tradition of Maitreya worship.

Agrarian utopianism in Japan

In Japan, as well, native utopian ideals promised a coming age of peace and plenty. As had been the case in China, Buddhist millennialism in Japan grafted onto an extant tradition, restructuring elements so as to incorporate Buddhist terminology and figures such as Maitreya. However, in the Japanese tradition, this millennium was not premised on epochal change or the violent destruction of the world order, and as a consequence, did not serve as the inspiration for revolt as often as it did in China.

One characteristic of Japanese belief was the location of the promised land on earth, either on a mountaintop or across the sea. The pre-Buddhist cult of mountain worship was taken up and transformed by various sects of Japanese Buddhism, who established sacred mountains as the home of Maitreya and the location of the millennial paradise. The deathbed utterance of KŪKAI (774–835), the deified founder of the esoteric Shingon school, that he would descend to earth with Maitreya, has prompted the belief that he remains alive and in deep meditation on Mount Kōya. This and other sacred mountains, such as Fuji and Kimpu, became regarded as gates to the Pure Land, and were the home of ascetics known as *yamabushi,* who dwelled between heaven and earth. Similarly, another tradition prophesied the arrival of Maitreya by ship, prompting a tradition of popular folk worship in anticipation of the triumphal arrival of Maitreya in a ship laden with rice.

See also: **Apocrypha; Cosmology; Monastic Militias; Nationalism and Buddhism; Politics and Buddhism; Pure Land Buddhism; Sanjie Jiao (Three Stages School); Syncretic Sects: Three Teachings**

Bibliography

Baumgarten, Albert I., ed. *Apocalyptic Time.* Boston and Leiden, Netherlands: Brill, 2000.

Haar, B. J. ter. *The White Lotus Teachings in Chinese Religious History.* Honolulu: University of Hawaii Press, 1992.

Hori, Ichirō. *Folk Religion in Japan: Continuity and Change* (1968), ed. Joseph M. Kitagawa and Alan L. Miller. Chicago: University of Chicago Press, 1994.

Naquin, Susan. *Millenarian Rebellion in China: The Eight Trigrams Uprising of 1813.* New Haven, CT: Yale University Press, 1976.

Overmyer, Daniel. *Folk Buddhist Religion: Dissenting Sects in Late Traditional China.* Cambridge, MA: Harvard University Press, 1976.

Overmyer, Daniel. *Precious Volumes: An Introduction to Chinese Sectarian Scriptures from the Sixteenth and Seventeenth Centuries.* Cambridge, MA: Harvard University Press, 1999.

Ownby, David. "Chinese Millennial Traditions: The Formative Age." *American Historical Review* 104, no. 5 (1999): 1,513–1,530.

Seidel, Anna. "The Image of the Perfect Ruler in Early Taoist Messianism: Lao-tzu and Li Hung," *History of Religions* 9, nos. 2–3 (1969/1970): 216–247.

Sponberg, Alan, and Hardacre, Helen, eds. *Maitreya: The Future Buddha.* Cambridge, UK, and New York: Cambridge University Press, 1988.

THOMAS DUBOIS

MIND.
See **Consciousness, Theories of**

MINDFULNESS

Mindfulness (Sanskrit, *smṛti*; Pāli, *sati*) is a spiritual practice that is common to both early Buddhism and early Jainism. It plays a particularly important role in the former. Two conspicuously different forms of mindfulness are found near each other in the standard description of the PATH to liberation that occurs numerous times in the early canonical sermons: one in preparatory exercises and the other in meditation proper. During the former the (hypothetical) practitioner "acts consciously while going and while coming, while looking forward and while looking backward, while bending his limbs and while stretching them, while carrying his clothes and alms-bowl, while going, while standing, while sleeping, while waking, while speaking and while remaining silent." However, at some point the practitioner sits down, folds his legs, holds his body erect, and applies mindfulness. Applying mindfulness (Sanskrit, *smṛtyupasthāna*; Pāli, *satipaṭṭhāna*) is the precondition for the four stages of dhyāna (trance state) that follow. Indeed, mindfulness accompanies the practitioner in all of them, the fourth being characterized by "purity of equanimity and mindfulness." Clearly mindfulness in its highest degree of purity is required for the next step: reaching liberating insight.

As happens frequently in the Buddhist canon, a number of sermons present mindfulness itself or, more precisely, the applications of mindfulness as the way to liberation. Some of these sermons have *smṛtyupasthāna* or *satipaṭṭhāna* in their title, and distinguish four applications of mindfulness: (1) on the body; (2) on feelings; (3) on the mind; (4) on the dharmas. The Pāli *Satipaṭṭhāna-sutta* of the *Majjhima Nikāya* makes the highest promises to those who practice mindfulness: "If anyone should develop these four applications of mindfulness in such a way for seven days, one of two fruits could be expected for him: either final knowledge here and now, or if there is a trace of clinging left, non-return."

Mindfulness also figures in the noble eightfold path, at the seventh place, just before meditative concentration (samādhi). This position agrees with the account found in the standard description of the path to liberation, where mindfulness is a precondition for and an accompaniment of the four stages of dhyāna.

No doubt as a result of subsequent attempts to organize the received teachings of the Buddha, mindfulness came to be incorporated in various lists. It is, for example, the first of the seven "members of enlightenment" (*bodhyaṅga*). However, the list of seven members of enlightenment is itself an item in a longer list that altogether contains thirty-seven so-called aids to enlightenment (*bodhipakṣyadharma*). The artificial nature of this enumeration can be seen from the fact that this long list also, and separately, contains the four applications of mindfulness, plus mindfulness as included in the five faculties (*indriya*), in the five forces (*bala*), and in the noble eightfold path. That is to say, mindfulness by itself accounts for eight of the thirty-seven aids to enlightenment.

See also: **Dhyāna (Trance State); Meditation**

Bibliography

Bronkhorst, Johannes. "Dharma and Abhidharma." *Bulletin of the School of Oriental and African Studies* 48 (1985): 305–320.

Gyatso, Janet, ed. *In the Mirror of Memory: Reflections on Mindfulness and Remembrance in Indian and Tibetan Buddhism.* Albany: State University of New York Press, 1992.

JOHANNES BRONKHORST

MIRACLES

The English word *miracle* (from the Latin *miraculum,* meaning "object of wonder") has traditionally been used in a Christian context to refer to an extraordinary event that cannot have been brought about by human power alone or by the ordinary workings of nature and hence must be ascribed to the intervention of God. For most Christian theologians, only God can perform miracles; the function of saints, in heaven close to God, is to act as intermediaries on behalf of a supplicant to request a miracle from God. Hence, according to a strict Christian interpretation of the word, there are no miracles in the Buddhist tradition. A looser definition of the term, however, harking back to its original meaning as "object of wonder," allows miracles to be understood as extraordinary events that, because they cannot be explained by ordinary human powers or the everyday functioning of nature, evoke a sense of wonder. This looser definition proves useful to describe a wide variety of phenomena, including omens and other extraordinary changes in the natural world, acts of the Buddha and his disciples, and supernormal powers acquired through MEDITATION—all common throughout Buddhist literature.

Miracles in the life of the Buddha

Paradigmatic miracles occur in accounts of the life of the Buddha, well-known wherever Buddhism is practiced. Although there is much diversity in detail, accounts of the Buddha's birth generally describe it as a marvelous event, different in almost every way from an ordinary birth. The Buddha was conceived in a dream in which his mother saw a white elephant enter her womb, an event accompanied by earthquakes and other auspicious omens. Unlike other women in ancient India who gave birth sitting down, the Buddha's mother gave birth standing up, the infant emerging not from the womb, but from his mother's right side, causing her no pain. At birth the infant was bathed by streams of water that fell from the sky, after which he immediately took seven steps and declared in a loud voice, "I am the chief in the world."

Later, as the child matures, marvelous events accompany him throughout his life as he receives the assistance of gods who through various devices help him to pursue his fated life as a seeker of truth. At the moment when Śākyamuni is enlightened and becomes a buddha, the earth shakes, the heavens resound with the sound of drums, and flowers fall from the sky. As a buddha, Śākyamuni was believed to possess the standard set of supernormal powers or ABHIJÑĀ (HIGHER KNOWLEDGES) accruing to those of high spiritual attainments, including the power to know details of his previous lives, the ability to see the past lives of others, the power to read minds, and other magical powers, such as the ability to fly. In the course of his teachings, the Buddha demonstrates these powers repeatedly, frequently, for instance, recounting events that took place in the previous lives of members of his audience in order to explain the workings of KARMA. Similarly, the Buddha performed two famous miracles at the city of Śrāvastī in order to win converts. After admonishing his own disciples for displaying their magical powers in public, the Buddha declared that, in their place, he would perform a miracle at the foot of a mango tree to demonstrate his superiority to proponents of false teachings. On hearing this, his opponents uprooted all of the mango trees in the vicinity so that he would be unable to fulfill his vow. In response, the Buddha took the seed of a ripe mango, and no sooner planted it in the ground than it sprouted and in an instant grew into an enormous tree. This done, he fulfilled his promise to perform a miracle by the mango tree when he rose into the sky and emitted water and fire from his body in spectacular fashion.

Finally, the Buddha's NIRVĀṆA is accompanied by a number of marvelous events. When the Buddha predicts his own death, vowing to enter nirvāṇa in three months time, the earth quakes once again. Three months later, as the Buddha lay down to die, flowers fell from the sky. At the moment he entered nirvāṇa, there was a great earthquake and loud peals of thunder. Some of those present then attempted to light the funeral pyre, but were unable to do so. Later, when the disciple MAHĀKĀŚYAPA, who had been away, arrived on the scene, the pyre miraculously caught fire of itself, leaving behind relics that were themselves later attributed with miraculous powers.

Many attempts, of varying degrees of sophistication, have been made to root out all that is miraculous, and hence historically suspect, in accounts of the Buddha's life in order to derive a more sober, believable narrative, or to interpret miracles in the Buddha's life as rhetorical tools for explaining Buddhist doctrines. For the vast majority of Buddhists, however, marvelous events were and are an integral part of any biography of the Buddha. In general, Buddhists have interpreted these literally, as signs of the Buddha's unique attainments. Indeed, some of the phenomena described above, such as the Buddha's power to see the previous lives of others, are recounted in such a matter-of-fact manner that they are miraculous only in a weak sense. In other words, however fantastic such powers may appear to a modern skeptic, from the perspective of the tradition, they are more commonsensical than marvelous.

Disciples of the Buddha

Many of the Buddha's disciples were credited with supernormal powers and associated with miraculous events. Mahākāśyapa, as a product of his determined cultivation of the most trying austerities, could fly. ŚĀRIPUTRA attained the "dharma eye," allowing him to perceive the past lives of others. MAHĀMAUDGALYĀYANA, called "foremost of those who have supernormal powers," could vanish from one place and appear in another in an instant.

Later figures in Indian Buddhism possessed marvelous powers as well. UPAGUPTA, for instance, to prove a point, once caused a drought of twelve years. The powerful King AŚOKA (third century B.C.E.), who was at first hostile to Buddhism but eventually became its greatest patron, was, according to legend, converted upon seeing the supernormal powers of a monk his executioners could not kill.

Miracles in the spread of Buddhism

Miracles continued to play a prominent role in the history of Buddhism as it spread beyond India. Legends of the founding of Buddhism in other lands are typically tied to miraculous events. In Sri Lanka, it is said that the Buddha himself visited the island at a time when it was dominated by demons. Traveling directly to a grand meeting place of these demons, the Buddha hovered above them in the sky, calling up rain, winds, and darkness, and thereby terrifying the demons to such an extent that they conceded dominion of the island to him. In China, the introduction of Buddhism was linked to Emperor Ming of the Han dynasty (r. 58–75) who, according to the legend, had a marvelous dream in which he saw a golden deity flying through the air. The following day, when he asked his ministers to explain the dream, one informed him that he had heard of a deity called the Buddha whose body was of golden color and who could fly. The emperor then dispatched envoys to obtain more information about the Buddha, thereby initiating the introduction of Buddhism to China. In Japan, the introduction of the first Buddhist image was followed by widespread pestilence, prompting the emperor to have the image destroyed. This act was followed by the miraculous appearance of a large log of camphor wood that emitted the sound of Buddhist chants. Impressed, the emperor gave orders that the wood be fashioned into two Buddhist images, thus assuring the successful introduction of Buddhist devotion to Japan.

Miracles and monks

Throughout the Buddhist world, accounts of holy Buddhist monks are laced with miraculous events and descriptions of their marvelous powers. Many of these are patterned on accounts of the Buddha, noting a monk's auspicious birth and the omens that followed his death. It is said, for instance, that when the prominent Chinese monk Hongren (602–675) was born a bright light filled the room, and that when he died the sky turned dark and mountains trembled, as they did every year on the anniversary of his death. Other monks are credited with the standard supernormal powers of being able to read minds, levitate, and recognize the past lives of others. For example, according to one biography, the Korean monk WŎNHYO (617–686) once appeared at one hundred places at the same time. Holy monks are often thought to have special powers over nature, taming wild animals and changing the weather. The twelfth-century Vietnamese monk Tịnh Giới, for instance, received the title Rain Master after provoking rain during a serious drought, something other eminent monks of the time were unable to accomplish. The Japanese monk KŪKAI (774–835) was also said to be able to provoke rain through his mastery of Buddhist ritual. To this day, stories circulate of miraculous events associated with prominent or mysterious monks, nuns, and lay Buddhist figures, living and dead.

In addition to miracles provoked by individuals, countless miracles are associated with Buddhist objects. Buddhist scriptures are said at times to protect their owners from fire, Buddhist images come to life in dreams to offer warnings and advice, and prayers to relics result in miraculous cures. Such stories permeate Buddhist culture, only a small portion of the total ever being written down or otherwise reaching beyond the local level.

Explanations for miracles

Scholastic Buddhist literature does not group all of the phenomena discussed here into one category; there is no well-attested Buddhist term equivalent to *miracle.* Buddhist writers have expounded at length on the classic set of supernormal powers accruing to holy men, but have shown less interest in proposing a general theory of miracles. In some cases, the miraculous was explained according to local theories. In East Asia, for instance, recourse was often made to the Chinese concept of resonance (*ganying*) by which animals, the weather, and so on respond to a person of high attainments or an event of extraordinary significance just as one string on a musical instrument responds naturally to another. More frequently, wondrous events are simply recorded without a sustained attempt at explanation. In fact, many Buddhist texts and teachers make a point of downplaying the significance of supernatural events. They insist that supernormal powers are a by-product of cultivation and not its goal. The Buddha himself upbraided his disciples for displaying their powers in public. Nonetheless, the allure of the marvelous made it an exceptional rhetorical tool. That is, Buddhist texts are at pains to demonstrate the extraordinary powers of, for instance, the Buddha, before going on to dismiss these powers as child's play and peripheral to the far greater goals of enlightenment and release from suffering.

There has never been a strong tradition of skepticism toward miracles within Buddhist circles, though those hostile to Buddhism were always ready to discount Buddhist claims to the marvelous. For the most part, Buddhists have always accepted the supernormal powers of the Buddha and the potential of Buddhist figures and objects to provoke miracles. In modern times, however, it has become commonplace for Buddhist writers to strip away miraculous events from ancient Buddhist writings in an attempt to reveal a historical core to a given legend. While not in itself unreasonable, this approach is often accompanied by the assumption that miraculous stories emerge in response to the demands of an unsophisticated laity, steeped in popular superstition. In fact, for most of Buddhist history, miracle stories have been popular at all social levels and accepted as literally true by even the most erudite of monks.

The future of Buddhist miracles is uncertain. Even Buddhist leaders skeptical of accounts of miracles have not made concerted efforts to disprove Buddhist miracles or discourage the propagation of stories of marvelous, supernatural events associated with Buddhism, suggesting that miracles will continue to occupy a place of importance in Buddhist culture for the foreseeable future.

See also: **Buddhahood and Buddha Bodies; Buddha, Life of the; Disciples of the Buddha; Relics and Relics Cults**

Bibliography

Gómez, Luis O. "The Bodhisattva as Wonder-Worker." In *Prajñāpāramitā and Related Systems: Studies in Honor of Edward Conze,* ed. Lewis Lancaster. Berkeley, CA: Berkeley Buddhist Studies Series, 1977.

Kieschnick, John. *The Eminent Monk: Buddhist Ideals in Medieval Chinese Hagiography.* Honolulu: University of Hawaii Press, 1997.

Nakamura, Kyoko Motomochi. *Miraculous Stories from the Japanese Buddhist Tradition: The Nihon ryōiki of the Monk Kyōkai.* Cambridge, MA: Harvard University Press, 1973.

Ray, Reginald A. *Buddhist Saints in India: A Study in Buddhist Values and Orientations.* Oxford: Oxford University Press, 1994.

Thomas, Edward J. *The Life of Buddha as Legend and History* (1927). London: Routledge and Kegan Paul, 1975.

Woodward, Kenneth L. *The Book of Miracles: The Meaning of the Miracle Stories in Christianity, Judaism, Buddhism, Hinduism, and Islam.* New York: Simon and Schuster, 1999.

JOHN KIESCHNICK

MIZUKO KUYŌ

Mizuko kuyō is a Japanese rite performed at Buddhist temples for the repose of aborted fetuses. *Mizuko,* literally "water child," is the modern term used for fetus, and *kuyō* refers to rituals for making offerings. *Mizuko kuyō* was popular particularly in the 1970s and 1980s, and is still performed at many Buddhist temples.

Japanese Buddhists are divided in their attitudes toward *mizuko kuyō*. The Shin (true) Pure Land school (Jōdo Shinshū) is opposed officially to this rite on the grounds that it is based on the superstitious fear that spirits of the dead can curse the living. Others criticize the rite as a moneymaking scheme made popular through advertisements designed to make women feel guilty about abortions and the anguish of the aborted fetuses, who will surely curse those who killed them. Defenders of the rite argue that *mizuko kuyō* provides the same ritual service that funeral and memorial rites do in commemorating and caring for the deceased.

Associated with *mizuko kuyō* is the practice of dedicating a sculpted image of Kṣitigarbha (Japanese, Jizō), the BODHISATTVA who protects children, by tying a baby bib around its neck. Parents inscribe the bib with the name of the child, and often include words of apology and regret. While some of these words can be interpreted as expressions of guilt arising from the clear sense of moral wrongdoing, they more often express sadness and regret for having done something circumstantially unavoidable but not morally reprehensible.

See also: **Abortion**

Bibliography

Hardacre, Helen. *Marketing the Menacing Fetus in Japan.* Berkeley: University of California Press, 1997.

LaFleur, William R. *Liquid Life: Abortion and Buddhism in Japan.* Princeton, NJ: Princeton University Press, 1992.

GEORGE J. TANABE, JR.

MODERNITY AND BUDDHISM

No religion has a greater claim to embodying modernity than Buddhism. This assertion can be supported by examining what is meant by *modernity,* and by relating this modernity to the doctrinal characteristics of Buddhism. The term *modernity* derives from Latin *modernus,* which itself derives from the adverb *modo,* a term that since the fifth century C.E. was equivalent to *nunc* (now). During the European Middle Ages one's status as *modernus* required distinguishing oneself from the *antiqui.* Modernity, then, is to be understood as requiring an act of self-conscious distantiation from a past in which ignorance or naiveté prevailed. More specifically, modernity has required moving from an organic to a mechanic conception of the cosmos and society, from hierarchy to equality, from the corporate to the individual, and from an understanding of reality in which everything resonates with everything else to an understanding built around precision and the increasing differentiation of domains. Ultimately, *modernity* has had to do with the perpetual questioning of one's presuppositions. In terms of religion, modernity has generally involved the rejection of a symbolic view of reality and of anthropomorphic conceptions of the divinity, and, even more radically, the rejection of any notion of transcendence. When discussing modernity in the context of Western history, this process has been understood above all as involving a movement away from religion. Both in Christian and Buddhist terms, however, such a view is problematic to the extent that the process of differentiation has involved less a movement away from religion than the coming into being of two separate domains, the religious and the secular.

Concepts of modernity and causality

The concept of modernity has been used in a Buddhist context, mainly when studying reform movements of the nineteenth and twentieth centuries. The concept of modernity has not been used, however, when studying the emergence of the movement or the characteristics of the dharma. The main reason for this has to do with the assumption that although the time of modernity's birth may be uncertain, its place of birth, the West, is certain. Against this view it is worth considering whether instead of thinking in terms of one modernity, one should think in terms of multiple modernities. Thinking in terms of multiple modernities forces us to consider the differences between a modernity that combines heightened reflexivity and technological development, as in the West since at least the seventeenth century, and a modernity understood mainly in cultural terms. This means that even as we seek to identify the constitutive elements of modernity, we must keep in mind that those characteristics are not found all at once. For example, in the world in which Buddhism appeared there was no technological equivalent to the Buddha's concern with causality. On the other hand, as we shall see below, one can establish a correlation between the Buddhist analysis of reality in terms of dharmas and the use of coins in northern India in the sixth century B.C.E.

Causality is present at the beginning of Buddhism, when, according to the *Mahātanhāsaṇkhāya-sutta* of the *Majjhimanikāya,* the Buddha teaches: "When this exists, that comes to be; with the arising of this, that arises." Causality is similarly present as the principle that underlies the relation among the FOUR NOBLE TRUTHS: DUḤKHA (SUFFERING), the cause of suffering, the cessation of suffering, and the PATH that leads to that cessation. The counterpart of a causal chain whose components can be identified is a conception of the world based on the principle of correlation, a conception in which various aspects of reality resonate with each other, allowing those who can manipulate such correlations to claim special rights and powers for themselves. The Buddha rejected such an organic understanding of society, which was exemplified by the brahmins' claims to have been born from the mouth of the primordial being, Puruṣa. According to the *Assalāyana-sutta* of the *Majjhimanikāya,* the Buddha ridiculed those claims, pointing out that brahmin women give birth just like everybody else. This issue is related to the contrast between the Buddhist and the traditional Indian understanding of language. While the former regards the connection between words and reality as arbitrary, so that words are understood as labels, the latter, being a "sonic" view of reality, regards the connection between words and reality as involving an intrinsic connection between the very sound of words and the things named by them.

It is this assumption of a nonarbitrary connection between words and things that underlies the belief in the efficacy of RITUAL and of practices generally labeled as magic. It is worth noticing in this regard the Buddha's refusal to be considered a magician in the sense of being a *māyāvin,* a possessor of māyā (understood in this context as "fraud" or "deceit")—this, despite the fact that he was believed to possess supernatural or magic powers (*ṛddhi*) and was known as *daśabala* (endowed with ten powers). The Buddhist rejection of the ritual powers claimed by brahmins and by priests in general is still present today, for, at least in theory, Buddhist monks are not supposed to have sacramental powers analogous to those that depend on a person's birth or those that Catholic priests claim to have obtained through ordination. The distance established between monks and sacramental powers is further demonstrated by the fact that the return of monks to lay status is common, especially in Southeast Asia. It is true that throughout the Buddhist world, including Sri Lanka and southeast Asia, monks engage in ritual practices, such as the *paritta* ceremony, the selling of AMULETS AND TALISMANS, and the preparation of astrological charts, love philters, and the like. But it is also true that when seeking to return to a scripturally-based religion, Buddhist reform movements have been able to find canonical support for the rejection of what reformers considered superstitious practices.

Subjectivity and intentionality

The condemnation or at least mistrust of ritual practices, especially of the wasteful expenditures associated with them, has been central to attempts at modernization. Equally important have been efforts to move religious practices away from the material world and toward a spiritual realm, a realm that has frequently been equated with the domain of morality. All these processes are ultimately linked to an emphasis on subjectivity, will, and intentionality. We encounter all of them in Buddhism, long before they became the preoccupation of medieval Christians. We find an early example when the Buddha advises Sigālaka to engage

Young monks take a computer class at Ban-Thaton Temple in northern Thailand in 1995. © Gilles Mingasson/Getty Images. Reproduced by permission.

in ethical behavior and avoid dissipation instead of engaging in elaborate ritual practices. We also encounter it more than two millennia later when, intent on modernizing their country, southeast Asian kings such as Mongkut (r. 1851–1868) and Chulalongkorn (1868–1910) sought to curtail ritual expenditures, labeling them as wasteful and superstitious. That a Thai king such as Mongkut sought to reform the SAṄGHA in the process of centralizing power and modernizing his country is typical of attempts at modernization. Equally typical—whether in Thailand, in Myanmar (Burma), or in Reformation Europe—is the fact that reformers have usually shown an extreme unease toward ritual and consider themselves as having returned to the original, textually-based teachings of their religion. Indeed in Thailand, the monks around Mongkut (himself an ex-monk) called themselves the Thammayut (Dhammayuttika, "those adhering to doctrine"). Connected to these twin processes of centralization of power and curtailing of ritual activities is the delimitation of a religious realm, analogous to that found in the West since the eighteenth century. Once again, we find examples of this delimitation in Southeast Asia, partly as the result of the desire to emulate the degree of development demonstrated by colonial powers, and ultimately to counteract the colonial powers' activities.

The emphasis on intentionality is found in the acknowledgment, present since the earliest day of Buddhism, that in order for an action to be considered blameworthy, one has to be aware of what one is doing. This distinguishes Buddhism radically from the archaic approach found in the Hindu world, according to which one incurs guilt regardless of one's intentions. What is peculiar to Buddhism is the coexistence of an emphasis on intentionality and a radical rejection of a reified self. Indeed, what distinguishes Buddhism from all other religious systems is a processual understanding of reality combined with the rejection of reification, an understanding and a rejection that find their culmination in the concept of anātman (no-self).

But rejection of the notion of self does not entail lack of concern for subjectivity. The reverse is in fact the case, as Buddhist intellectual elites have devoted considerable effort to exploring in theory and in practice various levels of awareness. Contrary to common assumptions, however, meditative practices do not always have as their goal a calm mind (*śamatha*). In the context of a discussion of the connection between Buddhism and modernity it is significant to note that the mental states that are the goal of VIPASSANĀ (SANSKRIT, VIPAŚYANĀ) meditation—awareness, discrimination, analysis—are congruent with the analytical attitude that allows one to master the world. In more general terms, the exploration of one's subjectivity can be said to constitute a central component of one's attempt to distance oneself from the tyranny of the past. But this exploration of levels of consciousness did not lead Buddhists to a mastery of the physical world similar to the one that occurred in the West since the scientific revolution, bringing us back to the point made at the beginning of this entry about the need to distinguish a modernity that takes place mainly in cultural terms from one that encompasses economic and technological attainments. It should be added that one of the components of the Buddhist revival that has taken place in Sri Lanka has involved a revival of *vipassanā* meditation among the urban middle classes.

Institutional modernity

There are intimations of Buddhist modernity not just at the philosophical or psychological level, but also at the institutional level. We have already seen how throughout Buddhist history attempts were made to put distance between monks and supernatural powers. A further step in that direction was taken when it was determined that position in the saṅgha would depend exclusively on seniority, and that decisions would be made by majority vote or consensus. Another significant characteristic of the saṅgha is the fact that, in principle, administrative positions could not be inherited because monks were expected to be celibate. It goes without saying that to a greater or lesser extent all these regulations were breached in practice. We know, for example, that monks had property and that they were able to keep prebends within the family by passing administrative positions from uncle to nephew. Similarly, one needs to keep in mind that the seniority system is overruled by GENDER considerations, insofar as even the most junior monk is considered senior to even the most senior nun. Despite this, gender-based taboos prevalent in South Asia generally do not apply to Buddhists; for example, whereas menstruating women are not allowed to enter Hindu temples, their Buddhist counterparts can enter their own temples. More generally, it is important to note that even when disregarded in practice, that certain regulations had to be honored at least in theory establishes an abstract legal framework. Even more significant is the fact that such a framework was not transcendentally legitimized.

The economics of modernity

It would be worthwhile to examine the conditions that may have contributed to the emergence of this radically modern understanding of the world. In broad swathe, the process of urbanization, political centralization, and monetarization of the economy that took places in northern India in the sixth century B.C.E. can be understood as constituting a radical change that required a readjustment of the ideological system that includes religion. In this sense, Buddhism can be understood as a critique of the new order, but also as a commentary. Money, for example, can be related both to asceticism and to the concept of dharma. Money is in some ways analogous to asceticism because it symbolizes the solidification of labor, and, insofar as it is not spent, money constitutes a deferral of the satisfaction of one's desires. Money is also related to the concept of dharma in that just as all of reality can be analyzed in terms of dharmas, all economic interactions—labor, commodities, one's position in the world in relation to labor—can be analyzed using money as the means of universal convertibility. In a hierarchical society in which one's chances in life were determined by one's position in the hierarchy, money, as the ultimate solvent, can have liberating effects. In this regard, insofar as it dissolves qualitative relationships into quantitative ones, money dissolves hierarchies, and in that sense it functions as does language in relation to sensory objects: as a label, as a mere designation. That in a society such as India the cash nexus can be liberating can be seen even today in the case of the B. R. AMBEDKAR Buddhists of Maharashtra: As Timothy Fitzgerald shows, besides being highly literate and resisting actively the power of brahmins and Marathas, Ambedkar Buddhists are willing to work only for cash.

Given the importance of money in Buddhism, it is not surprising that it was urban groups, above all merchants, who identified most readily with this approach to life. This was also the case for the land-based *gahapati,* who were also early supporters of the saṅgha. The *gahapati* are especially relevant, not only because they constituted networks of traders who can be regarded as having helped the expansion of Buddhism; as interstitial groups, the *gahapati* are also significant for comparative purposes, given analogous developments in the eastern Mediterranean at the time of the birth of another successful world religion, Christianity. Considering the importance of trade and traders in the early history of Buddhism, it is at first surprising to find that the rules of discipline kept monks from handling the ultimate leveler, money. But such rules can be understood as rendering visible the autonomy of the economic realm, as well as the relatively new reality of money as the embodiment of labor.

Suspicion toward transcendence, an emphasis on contractual arrangements, and a tendency toward analysis and abstraction—all these characteristics can easily be shown to have been disregarded in practice long before the advent of the Mahāyāna. Thus, for every Mongkut one can point to *dharmārajas,* such as the rulers of Angkor. Similarly, the modernization of Thailand can be contrasted to the rigidity of southeast Asian polities whose Buddhist-based systems of legitimation interfered with attempts to resist colonial aggression. Likewise, we can see the rationalization of everyday life challenged, either by the materiality of popular ritual or by the utopian emphasis on subjectivity and inner freedom cultivated by the middle classes. In conclusion, we may apply to Buddhism what we have written about modernity in general—namely, that the fundamental ambiguity at its core is revealed by the tension between the two strands at work in the cultivation of subjectivity: on the one hand the self-centered rationality of individualism, and on the other the ideal of internal freedom and ceaseless self-exploration exemplified by mystics.

See also: **Colonialism and Buddhism; Economics**

Bibliography

Benavides, Gustavo. "Modernity." In *Critical Terms for Religious Studies,* ed. Mark C. Taylor. Chicago: University of Chicago Press, 1998.

Bond, George D. *The Buddhist Revival in Sri Lanka: Religious Tradition, Reinterpretation and Response.* Columbia: University of South Carolina Press, 1988.

Fitzgerald, Timothy. "Politics and Ambedkar Buddhism in Maharashtra." In *Buddhism and Politics in Twentieth-Century Asia,* ed. Ian Harris. London and New York: Pinter, 1999.

Gombrich, Richard. *Theravāda Buddhism: A Social History of Buddhism from Ancient Benares to Modern Colombo.* London and New York: Routledge and Kegan Paul, 1988.

Gombrich, Richard, and Obeyesekere, Gananath. *Buddhism Transformed: Religious Change in Sri Lanka.* Princeton, NJ: Princeton University Press, 1988.

Harris, Ian, ed. *Buddhism and Politics in Twentieth-Century Asia.* London and New York: Pinter, 1999.

Harvey, Peter. *An Introduction to Buddhist Ethics: Foundations, Values, Issues.* New York and Cambridge, UK: Cambridge University Press, 2000.

Tambiah, S. J. *World Conqueror and World Renouncer. A Study of Buddhism and Polity in Thailand against a Historical Background.* New York and Cambridge, UK: Cambridge University Press, 1976.

GUSTAVO BENAVIDES

MOHE ZHIGUAN

The *Mohe zhiguan* is a work by ZHIYI (538–597). It was transcribed from his lectures by his disciple Guanding (561–632), and it is considered one of the "Three Great Works of Tiantai" and a comprehensive manual of Tiantai practice. The title means "The Great Calming and Contemplation," *zhi* and *guan* being the Chinese translations of the traditional Buddhist terms *śamatha* and *vipaśyanā* (Pāli, *vipassanā*). In Chinese, the first term means literally "stopping," the latter "contemplating"; for both Zhiyi distinguishes "relative" and "absolute" types. Relative stopping and contemplating are each interpreted, in typical Tiantai manner, as having three aspects:

1. Stopping as putting an end to something.
2. Stopping as dwelling in something.
3. Stopping as an arbitrary name for a reality that is ultimately neither stopping nor nonstopping.

1. Contemplation as comprehending something.
2. Contemplation as seeing through something.
3. Contemplation as an arbitrary name for a reality that is ultimately neither contemplation nor noncontemplation.

The first sense of stopping corresponds to the second sense of contemplation (ending something as seeing through it); the second sense of stopping corresponds to the first sense of contemplation (dwelling in something as comprehending it); and the third senses of both correspond to each other (each is a provisional name for an absolute reality that can be described alternately as quiescent, illuminating, both, or neither). On the basis of this interpervasion of stopping and contemplating, Zhiyi establishes the "absolute (or perfect-sudden) stopping and contemplating." Zhiyi first gives an overview of the ritual procedures for practice in the "four samādhis": the "constantly sitting," "constantly walking," "half sitting and half walking," and "neither sitting nor walking" samādhis. The first three are specific ritual practices, during which Tiantai doctrinal contemplations were to be simultaneously applied. The fourth samādhi, known also as the "samādhi of following one's own attention," while also associated with particular texts and practices, was more broadly applicable. This involved the contemplation of each moment of subjective mental activity (good, evil, or neutral) as it arose, and the application of the Tiantai three truths doctrine to see its nature as empty, provisionally posited, and the mean—that is, as the absolute ultimate reality that pervades and includes, and is identical to, all other dharmas.

After this overview, Zhiyi describes "ten vehicles of contemplation." The first of these ten vehicles is the contemplation of (1) the realm of the inconceivable. It is here that Zhiyi gives his famous teaching of "the three thousand quiddities inherently entailed in each moment of experience" (*yinian sanqian*). All possible determinacies are here to be seen not as "contained" in or "produced by" a single moment of experience, but as "identical to" each moment of experience, just as a thing is identical to its own characteristics and properties, or to its own process of becoming and perishing. As a supplement to this practice, Zhiyi then describes nine other contemplations of the same object in terms of (2) *bodhicitta,* (3) skillful pacification of the mind, (4) universal refutation of all dharmas, (5) recognition of obstructions and throughways, (6) adjustment of aspects of the way, (7) curative aids, (8) understanding stages of progress, (9) forbearance, and (10) freedom from attachment to spiritual attainments. The text applies these ten methods first to one's own conditioned existence as such, and then to other more specific objects of contemplation, such as KARMA (ACTION), illnesses, defilements, and so on.

See also: **Tiantai School; Vipassanā (Sanskrit, Vipaśyanā)**

Bibliography

Donner, Neal. "Chih-i's Meditation on Evil." In *Buddhist and Taoist Practice in Medieval Chinese Society,* ed. David W. Chappell. Honolulu: University Press of Hawaii, 1987.

Donner, Neal. "Sudden and Gradual Intimately Conjoined: Chih-i's T'ien-t'ai View." In *Sudden and Gradual: Approaches to Enlightenment in Chinese Buddhism,* ed. Peter N. Gregory. Honolulu: University of Hawaii Press, 1987.

Donner, Neal, and Stevenson, Daniel B. *The Great Calming and Contemplation: A Study and Annotated Translation of the First Chapter of Chih-i's Mo-ho chih-kuan.* Honolulu: University of Hawaii Press, 1993.

Hurvitz, Leon. *Chih-i (538–597): An Introduction to the Life and Ideas of a Chinese Buddhist Monk.* Brussels: Institut Belges Des Hautes Etudes Chinoises, 1980.

Ng Yu-kwan. *T'ien-t'ai Buddhism and Early Mādhyamika.* Honolulu: University of Hawaii, 1993.

Stevenson, Daniel. "The Four Kinds of Samādhi in Early T'ien-t'ai Buddhism." In *Traditions of Meditation in Chinese Buddhism,* ed. Peter N. Gregory. Honolulu: University of Hawaii Press, 1986.

BROOK ZIPORYN

MONASTIC ARCHITECTURE

The monastery has been and remains the core of Buddhist communal life in all parts of Asia. Designated religious space first appeared in India in the late centuries B.C.E., and the importance, size, and complexity of Buddhist monastery buildings increased as the religion traveled eastward across Central Asia to China, Korea, and Japan. Always constructed with local materials, monastery architecture adapted itself to every region of Asia, from desert sands to snow-covered mountains, and the individual structures changed according to the worship requirements of every branch and school of Buddhist Asia. Yet its fundamental purpose as a setting for Buddhist worship and education has remained constant through more than two millennia.

Monastic architecture in South Asia

The origins of the Buddhist monastery lie in residential architecture at the time of the historical Buddha, Gautama Siddhārtha. According to legend, a merchant once offered the Buddha and his congregation sixty dwellings for meditation and retreat. Thereafter it became fashionable for wealthy lay devotees to offer large complexes of buildings to accommodate the needs of monastic life. Although each structure was probably made of perishable materials, such as bamboo, thatch, and wood, the buildings included dwellings, private cells, porches, storehouses, privies, promenades, wells, bathing chambers, and halls of unspecified purposes. The same multiplicity of building functions, usually in a secluded location but close enough to the greater population to allow for alms collection, would remain standard for monastery architecture in East Asia. The conversion of residential space into Buddhist space, including the donation of residences for transformation into monasteries, would also become common in East Asia.

Three structures named in Sanskrit texts or inscriptions of the last centuries B.C.E. are associated with early Indian Buddhist monastic architecture: the vihāra, the caitya, and the STŪPA. All were constructed of enduring materials and were derived from vernacular architecture in which rooms of a covered arcade enclose an open courtyard. In a Buddhist context, *vihāra* refers to the residential cells of monks and the courtyard they define. Because a resident monastic population is fundamental to religious life, the Sanskrit term *vihāra* can, in certain instances, be translated as "monastery." The first meaning of *caitya* is mound or pedestal, but the concept of a locus for elevation quickly gave way to a more general meaning of "sacred place." In the vocabulary of Buddhist architecture, *caitya* is most often an adjective for hall (*caityagṛha*), and the most common form of caitya is a rock-carved worship cave with a stūpa inside. Some of the best examples of this kind of caitya hall are at Lmas Ṛṣi in the Barabar Hills and Bhājā and the nearly adjacent site, Karlī, both about one hundred kilometers southeast of Mumtaz (Bombay). Dated to around the third century B.C.E., the first century B.C.E., and the first century C.E., respectively, the exterior entry to each is marked by a pointed, horseshoe-shaped arch known as a caitya arch. The same archway appears in relief sculpture from contemporary stūpas at Bhārhut and SĀÑCĪ.

Although each is best known for its monumental stūpa and in some cases *toraṇa* (gateways) with relief sculptures recounting the life and legends of the Buddha, the monasteries Sāñcī in Madhya Pradesh, Amarāvatī and Nāgārjunikoṇḍa in Andhra Pradesh, and Taxila in present-day Pakistan included all three types of monuments in the late centuries B.C.E. and early centuries C.E. Moreover, all remained sacred sites of Buddhism to which architecture would be added through their history. Temple 17 at Sāñcī, for instance, built four centuries after the monastery's famous stūpa, is an excellent example of a Gupta temple.

Rock-carved monastic architecture

Full-scale monastic complexes were also carved into natural rock in India. Most famous are the caitya and vihāra of AJAṆṬĀ in Aurangabad, Maharashtra. Consisting of twenty-eight caves excavated over ten centuries, Ajaṇṭā includes some of the best examples of architecture of the Gupta period (ca. fourth to seventh centuries), the stylistic pinnacle in Buddhist art production in India. Two distinctive cave types and all three architectural forms are preserved there. The majority of caves are vihāra-style, consisting of monastic cells enclosing a central, open, squarish space or an interior with pillars arranged in grid pattern. Caitya-style caves at Ajaṇṭā (numbers 9, 10, 19, and 26) are elliptical in shape with pillar-defined arcades and a stūpa at the interior end of the ellipse. Like the majority of caves at Ajaṇṭā, all the caitya-caves are MAHĀYĀNA. That is, the Buddha image is represented, often seated on in a stūpa, in the caitya chapels. In plan, it is hard to differentiate between a Mahāyāna and pre-Mahāyāna caitya- or vihāra-style cave. Inside they are immediately distinguishable, the early ones having an unornamented stūpa for circumambulation at the deepest point in the cave and the later ones with the Buddha image represented not only on the stūpa but in other sculpture and murals.

Rock-cut monasteries and temple complexes were constructed in India through the course of Buddhist history. The details of architectural style were often of the period, so that a Gupta monastery might house a building whose structure, minus the iconographic decoration, would be hard to distinguish from a contemporary Hindu temple. In general, it can be said that Hindu architecture surged and Buddhist monastery construction began to wane after the Gupta period. By that time, however, monks and travelers from the east had come to India to study, and Indian Buddhists had traveled eastward. The midway points where meetings between Chinese and Indian monks occurred resulted in some of the most extraordinary Buddhist monasteries known. Monasteries in these points of encounter in former Chinese and Russian Turkestan, the present-day Xinjiang Uygur Autonomous Region of China, and the republics of Kyrgyzstan, Tajikistan, Kazakhstan, Uzbekistan, and Turkmenistan, survive as ruins in oases of the death-defying mountain ranges, deserts, and barren wasteland that characterize CENTRAL ASIA.

Almost every oasis had a Buddhist presence, although chronologies of the sites and their architecture are sketchy. It is similarly difficult to trace the movement of Buddhist sects from one to another. Datable materials suggest Buddhist monasteries propagated in Central Asia by the third century C.E. and survived until other religions, such as Islam, or invasions of peoples, such as the Mongols, destroyed them. Like most construction in Central Asia, monastery buildings were almost without exception mud brick. Some of the earliest Buddhist monasteries in Central Asia are in Miran on the southern SILK ROAD in eastern Xinjiang province. An inscription and paintings date Buddhism in Miran to the second century C.E. Both freestanding temples and stūpas survive.

Buddhism was present in China by the first century C.E., and a growing number of sites such as the rock-carved elephant at Lianyun'gang in Jiangsu province attest to this fact. By the fourth century, Buddhist CAVE SANCTUARIES inspired by Indian models were carved in several regions of Xinjiang, in China proper, and at oases in China's westernmost territory. Most famous among the cave monasteries are, from west to east, Kizil, Kumtura, and Bezeklik in Xinjiang; the Mogao and other cave-temple groups in the DUNHUANG region and Maijishan in Gansu province of Western China; and YUN'GANG, Tianlongshan, Xiangtangshan, LONGMEN, and Gongxian in the north central Chinese provinces of Shanxi, Hebei, and Henan. Additional cave sanctuaries have been studied in China in the last two decades of the twentieth century, in particular in Gansu, the Ningxia Hui Autonomous Region, and southeastern China, giving way to redating and refinement of chronologies. Still, it is not possible to suggest a clear path of transmission of Buddhism and its monasteries. Rather, monastery remains suggest that, from the third or fourth centuries through the ninth or tenth centuries, monks traveled and dwelt in Buddhist sites from Afghanistan, Persia, Turkmenistan, and Uzbekistan in the West to Central China in the East, alongside practitioners of other faiths; their monasteries consisted of rock-cut caitya halls, freestanding temples, and stūpas. The earliest monastery remains in China date to the fifth century. As far as can be determined, the dominant structures in early Chinese monasteries were a stūpa and Buddhist worship hall, with the stūpa often towering as a major monument in a town or city.

Monastic architecture in China

By this time, the stūpa had become four-sided in plan, closer in appearance to multistory Chinese towers of the late B.C.E. and early C.E. centuries than to circular stūpas of India or Central Asia. The Northern Wei (386–534) capital at Luoyang in Henan province contained 1,367 Buddhist structures or building complexes. Its two most important monasteries were Jimingsi, which had a seven-story pagoda, and Yongningsi, whose wooden pagoda rose 161 meters in nine stories. Each side of each story had three doors and six windows and was supported by ten pillars. The doors were vermilion lacquer, held in place with golden nails. Golden bells hung from each corner of each level. The great Buddha hall directly to its north was fashioned after the main hall of audience of the Luoyang palace. It contained a three-meter golden Buddha. Also following imperial architecture, Yongningsi was enclosed by a 212-by-301 meter mud-earth wall, 3.3 meters thick, with a gate on each side; its main gate, seven bays across the front, was sixty-six meters high and rose three stories. Yongning Monastery is said to have contained a thousand bays of rooms, among which were monks' quarters, towers, pavilions, and the main Buddha hall and pagoda behind one another at the center.

The oldest wooden architecture in China survives at four monasteries in Shanxi province of the late eighth and ninth centuries of the Tang dynasty (618–907). Still resembling palace architecture, Buddhist halls also became models for sarcophagi in the Tang period. The most important monasteries were commissioned by the emperor or empress, usually for national capitals or sacred Buddhist peaks.

It was still common in the Tang dynasty for imperial residential architecture to be transformed into a Buddhist monastery. The residence of the Prince of Wei, son of the second Tang emperor, was transformed in 658 into a monastery of more than four thousand bays of rooms with thirteen major Buddhist halls arranged around ten courtyards. One hall measured 51.5 by 33 meters at the base. It was not the main hall, which was considerably larger. By the Tang dynasty, it is possible to associate building plans with Buddhist ceremonies. Halls used for ordination of Zhenyan (Shingon in Japan) monks were divided into front and back areas, the private back space for the initiation rite in which the Womb and Diamond World MAṆḌALAS were removed from the wall and placed on a low central table or the floor. Other halls had a central inner space for the altar and images and an enclosing

The Mogao Caves at Dunhuang, China, also known as the Cave of the Thousand Buddhas. © Wolfgang Kaehler/Corbis. Reproduced by permission.

ambulatory defined by pillars. Both hall types and full-scale monasteries are depicted in Buddhist murals and paintings on silk of the period.

From the Song (960–1279), Liao (907–1125), and Jin (1125–1234) dynasties, monasteries with numerous buildings survive all over China. As was the case earlier, a pagoda or multistory pavilion and main Buddha hall on the same building line dominated some monasteries. Tenth- or eleventh-century monasteries with pagodas or pavilions as their focus include Dule Monastery in Hebei province, whose pavilion and front gate date 984; Fogong Monastery in Shanxi, whose 67-meter pagoda, the tallest wooden pagoda in China today, dates 1056; and Fengguo Monastery in Liaoning, whose main hall was built in 1013.

One of the most extensive lines of main structures survives at Longxing Monastery in Zhengding, Hebei province, where a hall to the Sixth Patriarch HUINENG, a hall to Śākyamuni Buddha, an ordination platform, and a pavilion to Avalokiteśvara known as Dabei or Foxiang Pavilion stood on the main axial line behind the front gate; pairs of side halls, pavilions, and towers framed each major courtyard in front of one of the axially-positioned structures. The pairing of pagodas and pavilions on either side in front of a main hall became standard in tenth- to thirteenth-century Chinese Buddhist monasteries. Shanhua Monastery in Datong in Shanxi province consisted of a front gate, a hall of the three deities, and a main hall along its main building line, along with two pairs of halls and a pair of pavilions joined to the covered arcade that enclosed it. One of the pavilions at both Shanhua and Longxing monasteries contained the sūtra collection of each monastery. A sūtra hall, often a pavilion or other multistory structure, was another standard feature in Chinese monasteries of this middle period.

By the Southern Song dynasty (1127–1279), centered in Hangzhou, monasteries of the CHAN SCHOOL dominated Buddhist architecture. The major monasteries of this meditative school were dominated by seven halls arranged along a north-south line: a front gate, a Buddha hall, a Vairocana hall, a dharma hall, abbot's quarters, and a room for seated meditation. Buildings for mundane affairs, such as storage halls and dormitories, filled the space on either side of the main building line. Monks' quarters sometimes contained a single huge bed on which monks meditated and slept.

By the thirteenth century, monastery architecture in China was marked by great variety. The lack of consistency can in part be explained by numerous Buddhist schools and by an increasing syncretism in Buddhist and Daoist worship that gave rise to new sects. Often a twelfth- or thirteenth-century Buddhist monastery was architecturally indistinguishable from a Daoist one until one entered the halls and saw the statues and paintings. In addition, Daoist precincts could be constructed at Buddhist monasteries and Buddhist precincts at Daoist temple complexes.

Lamaist monasteries in China

By the fourteenth century, Lamaist Buddhist architecture also was present on the Chinese landscape. The most representative structure of a Lamaist Buddhist monastery is the bulb-shaped pagoda known as a *dagoda,* often painted white. The Lamaist pagodas of Miaoying Monastery, built in 1279, and in Beihai Park, built in 1651, still rise above much of the rest of Beijing's architecture. Lamaism and its architecture dominated the regions of China adjacent to Tibet, the center of this branch of Buddhism, in particular the areas of Sichuan and Gansu and regions adjacent to them in Ningxia Hui, Qinghai, and Inner Mongolia. Patronized by the Manchu rulers of the last Chinese dynasty, Qing (1644–1911), some of the most creative architecture of China's last three imperial centuries stands at Lamaseries. The most purely Tibetan monasteries, in Qinghai and Sichuan, include multistory stone buildings with small windows and flat roofs, the style famous on the mountainous terrain of Tibet. The Sino-Tibetan style of Inner Mongolia, Ningxia, and Gansu, represented by Wudangzhao in Baotou or Xilituzhao in Hohhot, both in Inner Mongolia, is characterized by the axial arrangements seen in Chinese monasteries but with great sūtra halls in the block style of Tibet, as well as numerous funerary pagodas. Often several buildings are interconnected into one block-like structure, but roofs may be of Chinese glazed ceramic tile.

Ta'er Monastery in Qinghai is of this type. Most impressive are the Sino-Tibetan Lamaseries of Chengde (formerly Jehol) in Hebei province. Site of a summer palace of the Qing emperors, Chengde had twelve temple complexes, known as the Eight Outer Temples after the eight offices through which they were administered in the eighteenth century. Often the monasteries contain Chinese-style architecture in the front and Tibetan-style buildings behind. One monastery even had architecture that replicated the POTALA palace in Tibet. Dominated by great sūtra halls, traditional buildings dedicated to, for example, the four divine kings, are also present at the Eight Outer Temples. This kind of regionalism in architecture was widespread in Qing China, giving way not only to scores of residential styles among the "minority" peoples of the empire, but also to Sino-Burmese Buddhist monasteries in Xishuangbanna in southwestern Yunnan province near the border with Myanmar. Traditional Buddhist monasteries never disappeared from China. Yonghegong, a princely palace in the heart of Beijing that was turned into a lamasery during the eighteenth century, with its main halls painted red and golden rooftops on an axial line, represents a Chinese-style lamasery. In other parts of China, Chan monasteries continued to be built and restored, especially at historically sacred locations, such as the four great peaks: These include Wutai in Shanxi province, dedicated to Mañjuśrī; Putuo, the unique island setting off the coast of Ningbo, dedicated to Avalokiteśvara; Emei in Sichuan, dedicated to Samantabhadra; and Jiuhua in Anhui, dedicated to Kṣitigarbha. The later monasteries of traditional sects retained axial arrangements but were larger than their pre-fourteenth century predecessors, with two new hall types, the diamond hall and the hall of divine kings. Both halls were incorporated into Lamaist construction in China. Also new in the fourteenth century were brick halls, nicknamed "beamless" halls, which stood in sharp contrast to the ubiquitous wooden buildings of Chinese construction.

Monastic architecture in Korea

Since initial contacts in Northeast Asia, things Chinese were transmitted to the Korean peninsula. Buddhism entered Korea from China officially in 372. Although not every Chinese Buddhist school became popular in Korea, most were known to Korean monks who traveled to China or through Chinese Buddhist missionaries. Korean Buddhist monasteries thus contained the standard structures of Chinese monasteries. A standard plan in Korean Buddhist monasteries has an entry gate with a pair of divine kings on each side, followed by a dharma hall and main hall.

Buddha halls, pagodas, and cave sanctuaries all are found in Korea. Korea's best-known Buddhist monasteries, Pulguksa and SŎKKURAM, both in the outskirts of Kyŏngju, capital of the unified Silla kingdom

(668–935), borrow from monastery traditions of China and represent two distinctly Korean types of Buddhist architecture at the same time. Pulguksa consists of a front gate and two halls directly behind it, and smaller halls dedicated to buddhas or bodhisattvas in their own precincts. The entry and most of the enclosing corridors of the monastery, however, are elevated on stone foundations. Pulguksa's twin pagodas are also made of stone, the predominant and uniquely Korean material of early pagodas. Sŏkkuram is Korea's most famous Buddhist cave sanctuary. The greatest concentration of Buddhist rock-carved niches and worship spaces in Korea is on Namsan (South Mountain), also in the vicinity of Kyŏngju. The largest monastery in Korea is T'ongdosa, located between Kyŏngju and Pusan. One of the most noteworthy monasteries is Haeinsa, where an extensive set of woodblocks of the Korean CANON survives.

Monastic architecture in Japan

Early Buddhist monasteries in Japan are believed to have followed the patterns of continental East Asia, transmitted directly from China or from China by way of Korea. Much can be learned about East Asian monasteries from Japan's monasteries because more pre-ninth-century wooden architecture survives in Japan than anywhere else in East Asia. As was the case in contemporary China and Korea, the main structures of Japanese monasteries of the Nara period (710–784) were the Buddha hall and pagoda. Their arrangements, however, signaled distinctive types believed to follow regional variations in Korea and probably also in China. At Shitennōji in Osaka, for example, whose plan dates before the Nara period, to 593, the pagoda and hall are on an axial line, matching the arrangement that was implemented in China at Yongning Monastery in the late fifth or early sixth century. At Hōryūji and Kawaharadera, the pagoda and main Buddha hall, known in Japan as *kondō,* were built side by side.

At Asukadera, south of Nara in Asuka and dated to the sixth century, three *kondō* enclosed a dominant central pagoda on all but the south side. Yet another Nara-period plan included twin pagodas on either side in front of the main hall. Eighth-century monasteries of Japan also inform us of the range of buildings in an active temple complex of the early period in East Asia.

The Great Buddha Hall at Tōdaiji, in Nara, Japan, built in 1692. It replaced an original of 752 that was twice destroyed by fire. © Robert D. Fiala, Concordia University, Seward, Nebraska. Reproduced by permission.

The Phoenix Hall, at the Byōdōin, Kyoto, Japan. Built in 1053, it was intended as a three-dimensional representation of the Sukhāvatī Pure Land—the Western Paradise—of Amitābha. © Sakamoto Photo Research Laboratory/Corbis. Reproduced by permission.

Hōryūji, for instance, had a gatehouse, *kondō,* pagoda, and covered arcade connected to the gatehouse at its core, as well as a south gate, lecture hall, monks' dormitories, sūtra library, bell tower, refectory, and administrative offices, and a separate precinct with an octagonal hall dedicated to Prince SHŌTOKU (574–621).

The Great Eastern Monastery in Nara (Tōdaiji) had south and middle gates, its main Buddha hall, another gate, a lecture hall, and monks' quarters on the main building line, and twin pagodas, halls for ceremonies of the second and third moons of the year, an ordination hall, and a treasure repository located elsewhere. None of these buildings was unique at Hōryūji or Tōdaiji. Monasteries could also include shrines to monks or monk-founders, halls to individual buddhas or bodhisattvas, gardens, bathhouses, and anything else that offered full-service life and education to the monastic and sometimes lay community. Coincident with the move of the main capital to Heian (Kyoto) at the end of the eighth century, esoteric Buddhist schools rose in Japan. In contrast to monasteries of the Nara capital, early Heian-period monasteries had smaller buildings located in remote, often mountainous settings. Not only were the clergy kept distant from court affairs, the new mountain monasteries were primarily for esoteric Buddhist schools, especially Tendai and Shingon, which had been transmitted to Japan from China at the turn of the ninth century.

Although monastery structures in the middle part of the Heian period remained small in comparison to their Nara counterparts, decoration became lavish. The change corresponded to the surge in PURE LAND BUDDHISM, whose monasteries often included a re-creation of the Buddha's paradise, or Pure Land, in the form of a hall with lotus pond in front of it. The PHOENIX HALL (AT THE BYŌDŌIN) in Uji, once the residence of one of Japan's wealthiest families, and the Golden Hall of Chūsonji in Hiraizumi are typical Fujiwara-period (951–1086) monastery buildings.

By the end of the Heian period, however, monasteries that were much less ornate became popular. Single-bay square halls dedicated to AMITĀBHA, Buddha of the Western Paradise, were common. Austere monastery construction was characteristic of the next period of Japanese history, the Kamakura (1185–1333). Austerities were suited to Zen, the dominant form of Buddhism among the military rulers of Japan. Five great Zen monasteries and countless small ones covered the mountainous village of Kamakura; these were modeled after the great Chan mountain monasteries of Southern Song China. The front gate of a Zen monastery was two stories with a triple entry and access to the second floor, where statues of the sixteen arhats often were found. The main hall was known as the *butsuden,* or Buddha hall. Public ceremonies were held in the *butsuden,* whereas lectures and other assemblages of monks took place in the dharma hall, a structure also found in Chinese monasteries of the eleventh century. Both in Kamakura and in Kyoto, Zen monasteries consisted of public reception space used chiefly by the main abbot, abbot's quarters, halls for study and meditation, a hall for sūtra recitation, a hall dedicated to the monastery founder, and usually gardens. The abbot's quarters traced its origins to a humble single-bay square hut (*hōjō*), the kind of dwelling used by the earliest Indian Buddhists, but the structure became increasingly important and lavish by the end of the Kamakura period.

Yet another hall type in Zen monasteries was the *shariden,* the relic hall. Examples of all these structures remain in Kamakura and most survive at one of the best examples of Zen architecture outside Kamakura—Tōfukuji in Kyoto. Whereas some Kamakura-period monastery architecture originated in two areas of China's southeastern coast, and came to be known as Indian style or Tang style, in contrast to native Japanese style, monastery architecture of the fourteenth and fifteenth centuries displayed a uniquely Japanese architectural aesthetic. As represented by the monasteries of the Silver and Golden pavilions, Ginkakuji and Kinkakuji in Kyoto, the return of the Japanese capital to Kyoto was coincident with a return to luxurious living among the military lords of Japan's Muromachi period (1338–1573).

Buddhist monasteries continue to be built and restored in China, Korea, and Japan at the beginning of the twenty-first century, and are preserved as historic relics in India and Central Asia.

See also: **Central Asia, Buddhist Art in; China, Buddhist Art in; Himalayas, Buddhist Art in; Hōryūji and Tōdaiji; Japan, Buddhist Art in; Korea, Buddhist Art in; Monasticism; Southeast Asia, Buddhist Art in**

Bibliography

Mitra, Debala. *Buddhist Monuments.* Calcutta: Sahitya Samdad, 1971.

Prip-Møller, Johannes. *Chinese Buddhist Monasteries: Their Plan and Its Function as a Setting for Buddhist Monastic Life.* Copenhagen, Denmark: G. E. C. Gad; London: Oxford University Press, 1937.

Sarkar, H. *Studies in Early Buddhist Architecture of India.* New Delhi: Munshiram Manoharlal, 1966.

Seckel, Dietrich, *The Art of Buddhism,* tr. Ann Keep. New York: Greystone Press, 1968.

Soper, Alexander. *The Evolution of Buddhist Architecture in Japan.* Princeton, NJ: Princeton University Press, 1942.

Suzuki Kakichi. *Early Buddhist Architecture in Japan,* tr. Mary N. Parent and Nancy S. Steinhardt. Tokyo, New York, and San Francisco: Kodansha International, 1980.

Zhongguo jianzhu yishu quanji (universal history of the art of Chinese architecture), Vol. 12: *Fojiao jianzhu* (Buddhist architecture). Part 2: *The North.* Beijing: China Building Industry Press, 2002. Part 2: *The South,* Beijing: China Building Industry Press, 1999.

NANCY SHATZMAN STEINHARDT

MONASTICISM

The term *monasticism* is derived from the Greek word *monos,* which means "single" or "alone." Despite the etymology, the majority of Buddhist monastics are not hermits or solitary wanderers. Monastics, even those who may choose to take up a solitary life from time to time, belong to the Buddhist SAṄGHA or community. The range of Buddhist monastic communities is quite extensive, including everything from extremely large and wealthy urban monasteries, to mid-size and small village monasteries, to forest, cave, and mountain monasteries.

Buddhist monasticism has its origins in India and dates back to the lifetime of Śākyamuni Buddha. The earliest members of the monastic order appear to have led lives that alternated between wandering from place to place in groups and residing in parks and groves donated by kings and wealthy merchants. Some Buddhist scholars, such as Sukumar Dutt, have argued that the wandering lifestyle was gradually transformed into a more permanently settled monastic existence as a result of the Buddha's requirement that MONKS and NUNS cease wandering during the monsoon season. Other Buddhist scholars, such as Mohan Wijayaratna, have argued that the first monastic complexes were the result of the desire of wealthy laypeople to donate land and permanent structures to the saṅgha. Although scholars debate the origins of monasteries, they do agree that with the advent of permanent structures, there arose a class of monastics who remained in the monasteries permanently to act as caretakers and administrators.

Texts and archeological evidence reveal that shortly after the death of the Buddha, there were eighteen large Buddhist monasteries near the city of Rājagṛha alone. The records of Chinese Buddhist pilgrims point to the existence, during the fifth to seventh century C.E., of great Buddhist monasteries and monastic universities in India that housed thousands of monastics from a variety of Buddhist traditions. The monasteries quickly became wealthy institutions endowed with land, buildings, and numerous possessions.

The Buddhist monastic order was originally made up of ordained male and female monastics. During the medieval period, however, the lineage of fully ordained nuns died out in the THERAVĀDA order. Although the formal order was gone, some women did continue to live as novices in nunneries. While novice nuns in certain countries (such as the *dasa sil mātāvas* in Sri Lanka) often lack the recognition and support that is so essential to their survival, novice nuns in other countries (such as the *śrāmaṇerikā* in Tibet) have enjoyed a wider network of support and a greater recognition of their status. Since the 1980s there have been moves to reintroduce the lineage of fully ordained nuns in certain Theravāda countries such as Sri Lanka and Thailand, though this effort has often met fierce opposition from the male order.

By the medieval period all Buddhist monastic orders had died out in India. By that time, Buddhist monasticism had already become a pan-Asian phenomenon. Within the last century Buddhist monastic institutions have not only been reestablished in India, but have also been founded throughout North and South America, Africa, Europe, and Australia.

Monasticism and the saṅgha

In Buddhism, the monastic order is referred to as the saṅgha, which, in its strictest sense, refers specifically to MONKS and NUNS. The saṅgha began when the Buddha accepted his first five disciples shortly after his enlightenment. As the monastic order grew and the religion spread in an ever-widening radius, numerous disciplinary rules were put forth to govern the lives of the monks and nuns. Even though the rules, which are found in the VINAYA section of the Buddhist CANON, are very complex, the underlying intention is straightforward: to help guide the lives of monks and nuns on a spiritual PATH and to create a unified group of monastics. The Buddhist monastic order functions to preserve and teach the Buddhist doctrine and, by dictating how to live in accordance with the way taught by Śākyamuni Buddha, the order's rules provide an historical link to the past.

The Buddha originally functioned as the head of the monastic order. At the time of his death he refused to appoint a successor; instead, the Buddhist teachings and disciplinary code were said to take the place of a central authority. Lacking a leader who could maintain doctrinal and disciplinary congruity, the saṅgha split into several monastic traditions in the centuries following the death of the Buddha. The early splits in the saṅgha were often based on disputes regarding discipline and led to the formation of separate vinaya texts. Within the first millennium following the death of the Buddha and continuing to the present, the disputes often related to doctrinal and disciplinary issues, thus resulting in the growth of Buddhist sects and schools centered around particular doctrines, texts, monastic leaders, and practices.

The lack of a central authority in Buddhism may be seen as problematic and as the cause of internal disputes and divisions. In a more positive light, the openness to interpret Buddhist practice and doctrine has led to a staggering range of Buddhist monastic institutions and types of monastic vocations, thus contributing to the adaptation of the tradition through time and space. As the order expanded geographically over time, adjustments were needed to make the tradition and the monastic institution acceptable to the people living in the various countries where the religion was introduced. For example, while monks of the Theravāda order (such as those living in Sri Lanka, Myanmar, Thailand, Laos, and Cambodia) are prohibited from farming and must receive their food directly from the laity, the monks from the CHAN SCHOOL of East Asia are encouraged to grow their own food, an idea that is closely related to the Confucian ideal of not being a parasite to society.

Categories of monastics

Buddhist monasteries house many different categories of Buddhist monastics, from postulants seeking admission into the saṅgha to the abbot of a monastery. Prior to becoming a monk or nun, a person seeking admission into the saṅgha usually spends a probationary period, ranging from several days to several years, in

Thicksay Monastery, Leh, Ladakh, India, 1997. © Don Farber 2003. All rights reserved. Reproduced by permission.

the monastery where he or she is seeking ORDINATION. During this period, the postulant learns about the practice of monastic life, is involved in various menial and demanding tasks around the monastery, and is in charge of taking care of the needs of the other monastics. This period allows the postulant as well as the monks and nuns of the monastery to ascertain whether monastic life is an appropriate choice.

Traditionally, entrance into the Buddhist saṅgha follows a two-step process in which the postulant first becomes a novice (*śrāmaṇera, śrāmaṇerikā*) before becoming a fully ordained monk (bhikṣu) or nun (*bhikṣunī*). To become a novice, one must be old enough to scare away crows (usually interpreted to be seven to eight years of age). Novices must follow ten basic injunctions or PRECEPTS:

1. Not killing
2. Not stealing
3. Not engaging in sexual activity
4. Not lying
5. Not taking intoxicants
6. Not eating after midday
7. Not watching shows or listening to musical performances
8. Not wearing garlands or perfume
9. Not sleeping on high beds
10. Not handling gold or silver (understood to be money)

Monks and nuns who remain in the order may choose, once they reach twenty years of age, to take a second, more formal "higher" ordination (*upasampadā*). As "fully ordained" monastics, monks and nuns are required to follow a greater number of precepts that not only elaborate the ten novice precepts, but also deal with subjects of decorum, dress, and demeanor. Even though the number of precepts differ between the various regions and schools as determined by the vinaya code that is followed, monastics rarely follow all of the precepts, and in some traditions in Japan and Tibet, for example, a married clergy was deemed acceptable and even preferable.

The categories of monks and the stages of ordination outlined above are often traced back to Indian Buddhist practices. In actuality, many variations exist regarding ordination and the categories of monastics. One such variation pertains to whether or not becoming a fully ordained monastic is a permanent or temporary commitment. Another important variation concerns the *upasampadā* ordination: While in most Theravāda countries there are social pressures for novices to take the *upasampadā* ordination once they reach the appropriate age, the majority of monks in China choose to remain novices, possibly due originally to a lack of monasteries able to administer the monastic precepts. Moreover, most East Asian monastics, after becoming fully ordained, take another set of precepts called BODHISATTVA vows derived from the FANWANG JING (BRAHMĀ'S NET SŪTRA), which, in accordance with the MAHĀYĀNA tradition, are based on a commitment to lead all beings to enlightenment.

Daily monastic routines

Monastic daily routines are often centered around four types of activities: studying, practicing MEDITATION, performing RITUALS, and fulfilling assigned monastery duties. Outside of these activities, Buddhist monastics have also involved themselves, from time to time, in politics and in social service activities like the construction of shelters for the homeless, schools, animal shelters, and hospitals.

Generally, daily monastic routines include activities such as cleaning the monastery; performing a variety of monastery duties; honoring the Buddha, his teachings (dharma), the monastic community (saṅgha), and one's own teacher; studying; chanting; and meditating. In addition to being restricted by the monastic code, the daily monastic routines are further limited by the actual Buddhist tradition, monastery, rank of the monastic, and time of the year. For instance, while certain meditation-oriented monasteries might dedicate the majority of the day to the practice of meditation, the daily routine of other monasteries might focus more heavily on studying Buddhist texts and performing rituals. In addition to these differences, monastic routines vary between Buddhist traditions and countries. Whereas Theravāda monks from Thailand, Myanmar (Burma), or Laos might go out in the early morning to collect alms and must refrain from eating after midday, Mahāyāna monks from China, Taiwan, Korea, and Japan rarely seek alms and may partake in an evening meal (sometimes called a "medicine meal"). Daily monastic routines may also change depending upon the time of year. For example, whereas monks living in certain Sŏn (Chinese, Chan) monasteries in Korea might meditate for over fourteen hours a day during the retreat seasons (summer and winter), they may devote little time to meditation during the nonretreat season. During this time, monks often visit other monasteries, travel on PILGRIMAGES, and engage in various other projects around the monastery, such as gardening, farming, and construction work.

Buddhist monastic routines are also punctuated by monthly rituals and ceremonies that may vary in form and content between the different Buddhist traditions. One such monthly ritual commonly practiced in the Theravāda tradition is the *poṣadha* (Pāli, *uposatha*) ritual, which is held semimonthly on new moon and full moon days. In this ritual, the disciplinary code is recited and the members of the monastic community are asked whether or not they have broken any of the precepts. This confessional ritual creates a sense of unity within the monastic community and encourages self-scrutiny and monastic purity, which are necessary for spiritual progress.

The *poṣadha* ritual is slowly gaining in renewed popularity in certain Mahāyāna countries such as Taiwan and Korea. In monasteries where the ritual is not practiced, other monthly and semimonthly rituals may take its place. It is common in the Korean Sŏn tradition, for instance, that every fortnight during the new and full moons days the abbot gives a lecture and may even administer the bodhisattva precepts to the monks. Usually this lecture covers various aspects of the Buddha's or other famous Buddhist monks' teachings, as well as brief instructions on meditation.

Yearly rituals and celebrations also play an important role in monastic routines. One of the most popular and important annual Buddhist ceremonies is the celebration of the Buddha's birth, enlightenment, and death. This ceremony usually occurs during the full moon of the fourth lunar month (usually late April or early May) of each year. In anticipation of this very important celebration, monks in the week leading up to the full moon begin thoroughly cleaning the monastery and decorating it with handmade paper lanterns. During this ritual, the laity flock to their local monastery, where they wander in and around the monastic buildings, meet with the monks and nuns, partake in certain rituals, and attend lectures on various aspects of the Buddha's life and teachings.

Relationship between the monastic institution and the laity

The survival of the Buddhist monastic order depends on two factors: men and women who desire to take up the monastic life and the LAITY who support them. From the earliest period, it was the laity who funded the construction of the first Buddhist monasteries in India and beyond.

Despite the fact that a monastic "goes forth" (*pravrājita*) from society when he or she enters the saṅgha, monks and nuns remain deeply connected to the laity in a symbiotic manner. The laity ideally supplies the four requisites (food, clothing, shelter, and medicine) to the monks and nuns in exchange for guidance and spiritual support in the form of sermons and the performance of rituals. The interaction between monastics and the laity varies considerably depending on the type of monastery: Whereas residents of forest, cave, and mountain monasteries tend to have more limited contact with the laity, monastics living in village and city monasteries often have close ties with the laity. Indeed, along with serving as centers where the laity could receive instructions on Buddhist doctrine and practices, these urban and village monasteries functioned and may still function as educational centers that teach religious and secular subjects.

Underlying the symbiotic relationship between the monastic order and the laity is the very important concept of merit. As the monastic order is made up of people who represent, perpetuate, and follow the teachings of the Buddha, the monastic institution itself is said to be the highest field of merit and therefore most worthy of offerings. According to this system, donating to the monastic order is one of the most wholesome acts a person can perform and anything donated to the saṅgha increases the donor's store of merit. Not only does this merit ensure good fortune and more propitious rebirths in the future, it can also be transferred to others who need it, such as a deceased relative.

See also: **Chanting and Liturgy; Councils, Buddhist; Economics; Festivals and Calendrical Rituals; Merit and Merit-Making; Repentance and Confession**

Bibliography

Bunnag, Jane. *Buddhist Monk, Buddhist Layman: A Study of Urban Monastic Organization in Central Thailand.* Cambridge, UK: Cambridge University Press, 1973.

Buswell, Robert E., Jr. *The Zen Monastic Experience: Buddhist Practice in Contemporary Korea.* Princeton, NJ: Princeton University Press, 1992.

Dutt, Sukumar. *Early Buddhist Monachism: 600 B.C.–100 B.C.* London: Kegan Paul, 1924.

Gombrich, Richard. *Precept and Practice: Traditional Buddhism in the Rural Highlands of Ceylon.* Oxford, UK: Clarendon, 1971.

Gunawardana, R. A. L. H. *Robe and Plough: Monasticism and Economic Interest in Early Medieval Sri Lanka.* Tucson: University of Arizona Press, 1979.

Henry, Patrick G., and Swearer, Donald K. *For the Sake of the World: The Spirit of Buddhist and Christian Monasticism.* Minneapolis: Fortress Press, 1989.

Lamotte, Étienne. *History of Indian Buddhism: From the Origins to the Śaka Era,* tr. Sara Webb-Boin. Paris: L'Institute Orientaliste de Louvain, 1988.

Olivelle, P. *The Origin and the Early Development of Buddhist Monachism.* Colombo, Sri Lanka: Gunasena, 1974.

Samuel, Geoffrey. *Civilized Shamans: Buddhism in Tibetan Societies.* Washington, DC: Smithsonian Institution, 1993.

Schopen, Gregory. *Bones, Stones, and Buddhist Monks: Collected Papers on the Archeology, Epigraphy, and Texts of Monastic Buddhism in India.* Honolulu: University of Hawaii Press, 1997.

Silber, Ilana F. *Virtuosity, Charisma, and Social Order: A Comparative Sociological Study of Monasticism in Theravāda Buddhism and Medieval Catholicism.* Cambridge, UK: Cambridge University Press, 1995.

Spiro, Melford E. *Buddhism and Society: A Great Tradition and Its Burmese Vicissitudes,* 2nd edition. Berkeley: University of California Press, 1982.

Welch, Holmes. *The Practice of Chinese Buddhism: 1900–1950.* Cambridge, MA: Harvard University Press, 1967.

Wijayaratna, Mohan. *Buddhist Monastic Life: According to the Texts of the Theravāda Tradition,* tr. Claude Grangier and Steven Collins. Cambridge, UK: Cambridge University Press, 1990.

JEFFREY SAMUELS

MONASTIC MILITIAS

Monastic militias (Chinese, *sengping*; Korean, *sŭngbyŏng*; Japanese, *sōhei*) is a generic term for armed members of the SAṄGHA or the private armed forces employed by Buddhist monasteries. The term *monastic militia* is not a Buddhist one, but was coined by Confucian historians and its use cannot be attested earlier than circa 1451 in Korea, 1682 in China, or 1715 in Japan. Although the term is relatively late, it can be used to retrospectively designate earlier phenomena. Buddhist scriptures prohibit the use of force and the taking of life. Nonetheless, East Asian history records many instances during times of political conflict, regional unrest, dynastic change, or foreign invasion when Buddhist institutions relied on armed forces to defend their interests. During the years from 1553 to 1555, for example, Chinese monastic forces fought alongside government troops to repel coastal raiders. Likewise, in 1592 Korean Buddhist monks formed armed bands to help fight invading Japanese armies.

Neither Chinese nor Korean examples, however, have been as historically prominent or as well studied as those of early and medieval Japan. Throughout most of that period the institutions of secular government in Japan derived legitimation from the divine protection of buddhas (enshrined in temples) and local gods (placated at shrines), while the temples and shrines engaged in the secular activities of controlling large tracts of land and the people who worked thereon. Beginning in the tenth century, major shrines (such as Ise) developed the tactic of protesting unfavorable government actions by sending armed bands of men to the capital, where they would parade the divine body of the gods in front of the residences of terrified government officials. Major Buddhist centers (Mount Hiei, Onjōji, Kōfukuji, Tōdaiji, etc.) soon adopted this tactic. By the end of the eleventh century, they were directing their armed forces not just to protest government authorities but also to attack one another.

Mount Hiei, the main center of the Japanese Tendai school, became infamous for its men of arms. During the twelfth century they repeatedly attacked and burned Onjōji, a rival Tendai center. English-language accounts of these conflicts frequently render the term *sōhei* as "warrior monks," although membership in those armed bands was not limited to the clergy, but consisted primarily of laborers (*shuto, jinin,* etc.) in various degrees of servitude to the temples and shrines. The warlord Oda Nobunaga (1534–1582) campaigned to eliminate the military power of Japanese Buddhist institutions beginning with Mount Hiei, which he torched in 1571. His successor Toyotomi Hideyoshi (1537–1598) successfully concluded this campaign in 1585 when he defeated the Shingon school's stronghold of Negoroji and eradicated monastic militias from Japan.

See also: **Hyujŏng; Martial Arts; War; Yujŏng**

Bibliography

Adolphson, Mikael S. *The Gates of Power: Monks, Courtiers, and Warriors in Premodern Japan.* Honolulu: University of Hawaii Press, 2000.

Hirata Toshiharu. "Akusō ni tsuite." In *Shūkyō shakaishi kenkyū,* ed. Risshō Daigaku Shigakkai. Tokyo: Yūzankaku. 1977.

Kuroda Toshio. *Jisha seiryoku: mō hitotsu no chūsei shakai.* Tokyo: Iwanami Shoten, 1980.

McMullin, Neil. *Buddhism and the State in Sixteenth Century Japan.* Princeton, NJ: Princeton University Press, 1984.

Nishigaki Harutsugu. "Ritsuryō taisei no kaitai to Ise jingū." *Chichō* 56 (1955): 37–51.

WILLIAM M. BODIFORD

MONGOLIA

In the late twelfth and early thirteenth centuries, a confederation of Mongol tribes rose up in Outer and Inner Mongolia under the leadership of Genghis Khan (Chinggis Khan, named Temujin, 1162?–1227). Though the Mongols had certainly had contact with Buddhist neighbors (Jurchen, Tanguts, and Chinese), Genghis continued to support indigenous shamanist practices. However, following his death in 1227 and the subsequent conquest of China and much of Central and Western Asia by his sons and grandsons, Buddhism—specifically Tibetan Buddhism—began to have a significant impact on Mongolian concepts of rulership and empire.

Buddhism during the Mongol Yuan dynasty (1260–1368)

Genghis's son Ogodei (r. 1229–1241) established a Mongol empire that stretched from Korea (occupied in 1238) to present-day Poland and Hungary (1241). Ogodei's second son, Gödan Khan, invaded Tibet several times and in 1244 brought three prominent Tibetan SA SKYA (SAKYA) lamas as guests (or hostages) to his court in Liangzhou (modern Gansu province). They were SA SKYA PAṆḌITA (SAKYA PAṆḌITA, 1182–1251), head of the Sa skya pa, and his two nephews, 'Phags pa (1235–1280) and Phyag na rdo rje (1239–1267). Under duress, Sa skya Paṇḍita wrote a letter to Tibet's great nobles and lamas praising Gödan Khan, but he also initiated him into Tibetan Buddhist practice, thereby trading political control of Tibet for spiritual authority over the Mongol khan. Mongol rule over Tibet was formally achieved in 1252 by Ogodei's nephew, Möngke (r. 1251–1259), whose guru was the BKA' BRGYUD (KAGYU) master, miracle worker, and eventual second KARMA PA, Karma Pakshi (1204–1283).

Möngke's successor and brother, Kublai Khan (Qubilai Khan, r. 1260–1294) followed Gödan Khan's example when he proclaimed himself emperor of the Chinese Yuan dynasty in 1260. Urged by his wife Chabi, Kublai allowed 'Phags pa to initiate him into the *Hevajra Tantra* on the promise that he would gain the intelligence and compassion of the great protector Mahākāla. Tibetan VAJRAYĀNA Buddhism offered worldly benefits to the emperor as well. By naming 'Phags pa *guoshi* (national preceptor) and, ten years later, *dishi* (imperial preceptor), the two reigned side-by-side as "sun and moon" in an ostensibly balanced *yon mchod* (patron-lama) relationship. 'Phags pa acted as the Mongols' agent in Tibet and as head of their Zongshiyuan (court of the general administration of Buddhism), the office in charge of religious institutions throughout the empire. Kublai's protection and patronage of the Tibetan Sa skya pa signaled his auspicious status as a world-ruling Buddhist cakravartin (wheel-turning king), though he also encouraged an atmosphere of religious tolerance, even sponsoring debates at court between Buddhists and Daoists. In 1345 Kublai was posthumously celebrated at the Juyongguan, a grand stone stūpa-gate constructed northeast of the Mongol capital at Dadu (modern Beijing), where a multilingual inscription asserted his identity as "benevolent king" and "Mañjuśrī-emperor." Kublai's representation as an emanation of Mañjuśrī, the bodhisattva of wisdom, who, it was believed, dwelled in China's Wutaishan (Five Terrace Mountains in modern Shanxi province), was a strategic move designed to solidify waning Mongol control over north China.

Mongolian Buddhism after the fall of the Yuan dynasty (late fourteenth to sixteenth centuries)

The Mongol Yuan dynasty was not long able to rule China effectively after Kublai's death, however. By the middle of the fourteenth century, they had lost control of southern China and, in 1368, the Yuan was toppled by a former Chinese Buddhist monk, Zhu Yuanzhang, who founded the Ming dynasty. With the collapse of their East Asian empire, the Mongols retreated beyond the Great Wall. Evidence of their continued devotion to Buddhism is sparse in the centuries following the end of the Yuan. Buddhist practice was mainly limited to the Genghisid aristocracy, who retained limited political control in the Chahar region of eastern Inner Mongolia as the Northern Yuan. In the late sixteenth century, however, as the Ming dynasty began to decay, a number of khans moved to rebuild the Mongol empire. Among them was a Western Mongol of the Tumed tribe, Altan (the Golden) Khan (r. 1543–1582). Altan drove the Northern Yuan east to Liaodong, captured Ogodei's old Outer Mongolian capital, Kharakhorum, and forged an alliance with the Ming. Altan was not a blood descendant of Genghis Khan, however, which proved to be an obstacle in his attempts to forge a new Mongolian confederation. Following an initiation into Tibetan Buddhism presaged in a dream, in 1577 he arranged to meet the DGE LUGS (GELUK) lama Bsod nams rgya mtsho (1543–1588) at Kokonor, in modern Qinghai province (Amdo). Bsod nams rgya mtsho was in the direct lineage of TSONG KHA PA (1357–1419), the founder of the Dge lugs order. At Kokonor the two exchanged titles: Bsod nams rgya mtsho recognized Altan as Kublai Khan's incarnation, and Altan gave Bsod nams rgya mtsho a new title, Dalai (meaning "ocean" in Mongolian) Lama. Bsod nams rgya mtsho became the third in the DALAI LAMA lineage, with two of his predecessors posthumously named as the first and second. This exalted title and Mongol support gave the Dge lugs pa an advantage in their ongoing struggles with the Bka' brgyud pa, who were advisers to the Tibetan kings, and the Sa skya pa. The Mongols had once again become an essential component in the power structure of Tibetan Buddhism.

To honor Bsod nams rgya mtsho, Altan Khan built a monastery, Byang chen theg chen chos 'khor gling, at his capital Koke qota (modern Hohhot in Inner Mongolia). There, following Altan's decree prohibiting shamanist practices, the third Dalai Lama used the fire MAṆḌALA of Mahākāla to burn *ongod,* shamanist ancestral images. By Altan Khan's order, the deities of Tibetan Buddhism quickly replaced many of the spirits of shamanism, while in the following decades the shamanist spirits of important Mongolian mountains were incorporated whole into an expanding Buddhist pantheon.

The Dge lugs pa's willingness to ally themselves with Mongol khans brought other candidates forward. Among them was Genghis's descendant, Abadai Khan of the Outer Mongolian Khalkha tribe, who met with Bsod nams rgya mtsho at Koke qota in 1576 or 1577, where he was entitled as khan. Abadai Khan returned to Khalkha to found the Tusheet khanate and to build Erdeni Zuu, a monastery at Ogodei's old capital of Kharakhoram modeled on Altan Khan's monastery in Koke qota. After failing to recruit Dge lugs pa lamas to come to Khalkha for his monastery's consecration, Abadai enlisted local Sa skya pa lamas. As a result, Erdeni Zuu continued to be allied with the Sa skya pa, even long after the Khalkha khans solidly came to support the Dge lugs pa.

In 1588 the third Dalai Lama died en route to Mongolia. Altan Khan, sensing a brilliant opportunity, pushed to have his own great-grandson recognized as the fourth Dalai Lama, who was named Yon tan rgya mtsho (1589–1617). Despite this prestigious coup, through the first decades of the seventeenth century Inner Mongolia remained contested ground. The Northern Yuan emperor, Ligdan Khan (r. 1605–1634), a devout Buddhist, patronized the Sa skya pa and supported a complete Mongolian translation of the *Bka' 'gyur* (a project later emulated in a woodblock printed version by the Manchu Kangxi emperor, r. 1660–1723). In 1617 Ligdan was given a golden image of Mahākāla that was said to have been made by 'Phags pa and used in Kublai's campaigns against south China. Ligdan enshrined it at the center of his capital in Chahar. As he retreated west in the face of Manchu incursions in 1634, the Mahākāla and all the powers that accompanied it fell into Manchu hands. In 1636 they took the image and installed it in the center of their ancestral capital, Mukden, later moving it to Beijing.

Mongolian Buddhism and the Manchus

Meanwhile, in Tibet, the fifth Dalai Lama enlisted the support of Gushri Khan of the Qoshot, who had established himself in the Kokonor region. In 1642 Qoshot troops defeated the rivals of the fifth Dalai Lama and the Dge lugs, most notably the king of Gtsang. This year traditionally marks the beginning of the Dalai Lamas' rule over Tibet. However, it was only with the death of Gushri Khan in 1656 that the fifth Dalai Lama became the unrivaled ruler of Tibet.

Some years earlier, in 1639, Abadai's son, the Tusheet Khan Gombodorji (1594–1655), had had his own young son, known as Öndür Gegen or Zanabazar (1634–1723), initiated as a Buddhist monk at Erdeni Zuu before a convocation of Khalkha lords. The boy traveled to Tibet with a large retinue in 1651, where the fifth Dalai Lama recognized him as an incarnation of the famous historian Tāranātha (1575–1634), a member of a rival order, the Jonang pa, who had spent years missionizing in Mongolia. The Dalai Lama gave Öndür Gegen the title Rje btsun dam pa (Mongolian, Bogdo Gegen) and charged him with establishing the Dge lugs pa in Khalkha. Öndür Gegen is credited with building numerous monasteries, the primary of which was a traveling collection of yurts, Urga (from Mongolian *örgöö,* "palace") or Da Khuree (Great Circle), where he reigned as Rje btsun dam pa Khutukhtu (Mongolian for incarnate lama) of Urga. He also designed rituals; established religious festivals, among them the annual Maitreya Festival; borrowed from the Panchen Lama's monastery, Bkra shis lhun po; and produced brilliant paintings and sculptures. In 1691, pressed by the onslaughts of Galdan, khan of the Western Mongolian Dzungar tribe, Öndür Gegen led the Khalkha lords to Dolonnor, Inner Mongolia, to seek the protection of the Qing Kangxi emperor. The emperor and his lama subsequently spent considerable time together in Beijing and at Wutaishan. When first the emperor and then Öndür Gegen died in 1723, the latter's remains were enshrined at imperial expense at a new, palatial Chinese-style monastery, Amarbayasgalant khiid (hermitage), south of Lake Baikal.

The Qing emperors, following the Mongols' precedent, were recognized by the fifth Dalai Lama as emanations of Mañjuśrī. They maintained close diplomatic relations with the great lamas of Tibet and Mongolia. During the eighteenth and nineteenth centuries, hundreds of Mongolian lamas flooded into the Qing capital at Beijing, where they were mainly housed at the Huangsi (Yellow Monastery) and the Yonghegong (Palace of Harmony). The lineage that forged the closest ties to the Qing emperors was that of the Lcang skya Khutukhtus, who were granted primacy over the Dge lugs pa Buddhists of Inner Mongolia. Particularly effective was the third incarnation, Rol pa'i rdo rje (1719–1786). Born in Amdo of a Monguor (Tibetanized Mongol) family, Rol pa'i rdo rje was brought to the Songzhu Monastery in Beijing as a child during the reign of the Yongzheng emperor (r. 1723–1735) and raised with Yongzheng's eventual heir, Hongli, who reigned as the Qianlong emperor (r. 1736–1795). Qianlong's reign marks the height of Mongolian and Tibetan Buddhist prestige and power at the Qing court. Rol pa'i rdo rje initiated the emperor into the *Cakrasaṃvara Tantra* in 1745, taught him Tibetan and Sanskrit, and accompanied him on regular pilgrimages to Wutaishan. Rol pa'i rdo rje was also an invaluable adviser in the emperor's efforts to control the process of incarnation among the powerful lineages of Tibet and Mongolia, and in his many projects in Buddhist art,

The monastery of Erdeni Zuu in Kharakhorum, Mongolia, founded in 1585. It is now a museum. © Nik Wheeler/Corbis. Reproduced by permission.

architecture, translation, and publishing in Beijing, Chengde (Jehol), Dolonnor, and beyond.

The Mongolian lineages of the Rje btsun dam pa Khutukhtus of Urga and the lCang skya Khutukhtus of Beijing and Inner Mongolia, as well as many other Mongolian lineages, were perpetuated through incarnation into the twentieth century. The Qing closely controlled this process to the end of the dynasty and found all the Rje btsun dam pa Khutukhtus after Öndür Gegen's immediate successor in Tibet. Few of Öndür Gegen's incarnations (with the exception of the fourth) exhibited his spiritual or political brilliance; in fact, few lived to reach adulthood. The eighth in the line (1870/1–1924) was brought to Urga from Tibet in 1876 and eventually found himself enthroned as Bogdo Khan, a Mongolian title previously reserved for the Qing emperors, upon the fall of the Qing empire in 1912. He played a dual role as leader of the Mongolian Dge lugs pa and head of the new (Outer) Mongolian state until his death from syphilis in 1924. His incarnation, the ninth Bogdo Gegen, was found shortly after, but by then Mongolia was in the midst of political chaos and the new incarnation was forced into exile.

Mongolian Buddhism in the twentieth century

Through the 1930s and 1940s Buddhist themes were deployed as propaganda by various contending forces. Among them were the Japanese, who during their occupation of Manchuria claimed Japan was Shambhala; the Russians, who made the same claim about the Soviet Union, even as others hinted that V. I. Lenin was an incarnation of Glang dar ma, the apostate ninth-century Tibetan king; and the Chinese, who spread rumors that the PANCHEN LAMA, then in exile in China, would invade Mongolia leading the armies of Shambhala. Other would-be rulers, among them Jamtsarano, a Buriat Mongol and a practicing Buddhist, urged a revitalization of Buddhism that would recapture the principles of Śākyamuni. His renewal movement failed to convince the new communist-led government of the People's Republic of Mongolia, however, and, in 1937, following the precedent set by Joseph Stalin's repression of the Russian Orthodox Church, Buddhism was banned. The Mongolian government executed thousands of lamas, burned monasteries to the ground, and destroyed religious books and images. Beginning with the collapse in 1991 of the Soviet Union, to which the People's Republic of Mongolia was tied as an unofficial satellite, Buddhism began to resurface in both Outer Mongolian and in Russian Buriatia. Gandantegchinling, the main monastery in Ulan Bator (located at the last site of Urga); Amarbayasgalant khiid, where Öndür Gegen's remains were once enshrined (and whence they were apparently stolen); Erdeni Zuu; and other monasteries in Outer Mongolia began to rebuild their monastic populations, both through the return of former monks, by then elderly, and the entrance into monastic life of new initiates. By contrast, in Inner Mongolia, an autonomous region of the People's Republic of China, Buddhism has been submitted to the same Chinese state control as exists in Tibet.

Bibliography

Bawden, Charles R. *The Modern History of Mongolia.* London: Weidenfeld and Nicolson, 1968. 2nd revised edition, London and New York: Kegan Paul, 1989.

Berger, Patricia, and Bartholomew, Terese. *Mongolia: The Legacy of Chinggis Khan.* San Francisco: Asian Art Museum of San Francisco, 1995.

Dharmatala, Damcho Gyatsho. *Rosary of White Lotuses, Being the Clear Account of How the Precious Teaching of Buddha Appeared and Spread in the Great Hor Country,* tr. Piotr Klafkowski. Wiesbaden, Germany: Harrassowitz, 1987.

Farquhar, David. "Emperor as Bodhisattva in the Governance of the Ch'ing Empire." *Harvard Journal of Asiatic Studies* 38, no. 1 (1978): 5–35.

Grupper, Samuel. "The Manchu Imperial Cult of the Early Ch'ing Dynasty: Texts and Studies on the Tantric Sanctuary of Mahakala at Mukden." Ph.D. diss. Indiana University, Bloomington, 1979.

Heissig, Walther. "A Mongolian Source to the Lamaist Suppression of Shamanism in the Seventeenth Century." *Anthropos* 48, nos. 1–2 (1953): 1–29; nos. 3–4 (1953): 493–536.

Heissig, Walther. *The Religions of Mongolia,* tr. Geoffrey Samuel. Berkeley: University of California Press, 1980.

Jagchid, Sechin. "Buddhism in Mongolia after the Collapse of the Yuan Dynasty." In *Traditions religieuses et para-religieuses des peuples altaiques.* Paris: Presses Universitaires de France, 1972.

Moses, Larry W. *The Political Role of Mongol Buddhism.* Bloomington: Asian Studies Research Institute, Indiana University, 1977.

Pozdneyev, Aleksei M. *Mongolia and the Mongols,* tr. John Roger Shaw and Dale Plank. Bloomington: Indiana University, 1971.

PATRICIA BERGER

MONGOLIA, BUDDHIST ART IN. *See* **Himalayas, Buddhist Art in**

MONKS

The English word *monk* derives from the Latin *monachus,* originally referring to a religious hermit, but eventually coming to mean instead a male member of a religious order living in a community of other renunciants devoted to the performance of religious duties. Similarly, while terms for monk in the Buddhist tradition (Sanskrit, *bhikṣu* or *śramaṇa*; Pali, *bhikkhu* or *samaṇa*) are rooted in words connoting mendicancy and austerity, the Buddhist monk is more generally understood as a member of a community of religious renunciants (the SAṄGHA) who has undergone a formal ORDINATION ceremony conducted by a quorum of fully ordained monks. In addition to the fully ordained monk (bhikṣu), novice monks (*śrāmaṇera*) may also be considered members of the monastic community.

Hence, one way to understand what it means to be a Buddhist monk is to examine the collective to which monks belong, a line of inquiry readers can pursue under entries for saṅgha and MONASTICISM. It is equally useful, however, to focus on smaller groups or types of monks within this larger community, and to examine the most common motivations for becoming a monk—subjects not necessarily covered in compendia of monastic regulations or discussions of the history of the monastic community as a whole.

Ascetics

One such type is the ascetic monk, who devotes himself to physical austerities. Almost all monks are ascetics in a loose sense of the term, since becoming a monk involves renunciation of certain sensual pleasures, usually including avoidance of sex, adornment, and alcohol. But some monks are drawn to the challenge of greater acts of self-denial. These may involve fasting, sleep deprivation, self-mutilation, and various other sorts of physical trials. Reasons for a man to pursue such a life are various, including an attempt to purify the body, to experiment with states and insights achieved through mortification of the body, a desire for the prestige that society renders ascetic virtuosi, and even, in some cases, dementia and masochism. One or more of these factors coalesce in the ascetic, one type of Buddhist exemplar.

The Buddha himself is an ambivalent model for the ascetic monk. In one of the most memorable episodes in accounts of the Buddha's life, he rejects extreme austerities after nearly starving himself to death, and, much to the dismay of his disciples, begins to take food after realizing that enlightenment cannot be achieved on an empty stomach. In the context of ancient India, with its strong traditions of severe asceticism, the Buddha cannot be said to have promoted an extreme variety of self-mortification. Nevertheless, the stories of the Buddha's ascetic feats before this realization, including acts he committed in previous lives, have inspired many to follow his earlier example. Another important early exemplar of the ascetic path was the Buddha's disciple MAHĀKĀŚYAPA, known as "the foremost of those who observe the austere discipline." Mahākāśyapa engaged in long bouts of uninterrupted meditation, isolated in a cave, and wearing only robes made of coarse rags, cast off by others. So immune was he to sensual concerns that, according to one account, he once accepted and ate an offering from a leprous woman into which a piece of her rotted finger had accidentally fallen.

For monks outside of India, more proximate models for ASCETIC PRACTICES are readily found in accounts of local monks in Tibet, Thailand, China, Vietnam, and elsewhere. Supernormal powers are one of the byproducts of ascetic practice. Mahākāśyapa, for instance, was said to be able to fly. Stories of strange and wondrous abilities are often attached to such figures and are among the reasons monks have chosen to pursue ascetic training. In modern times, Buddhists throughout the world have, following a general trend, become increasingly uncomfortable with extreme forms of asceticism, but the ascetic impulse at some level continues to provide a key motivation for men to become monks and for the laity to follow them.

Scholars

If the ascetic lifestyle appeals to those attracted to physical and at times even anti-intellectual practice, the model of the scholar monk provides inspiration for men drawn to the study and explanation of Buddhist doctrine, ritual, and history. For much of the history of Buddhism, monasteries were centers of learning, equipped with excellent libraries and staffed with erudite monks. Indeed, in premodern Sri Lanka and Burma (Myanmar), monasteries served as schools for neighboring children, providing basic EDUCATION in reading and writing as well as Buddhist knowledge. Even in China, with its strong tradition of secular learning, candidates preparing for the imperial civil service examinations would often study in monasteries for the discipline and tranquility, not to mention books, to be found there. As in the case of asceticism, a model for the scholar-monk could readily be found among the Buddha's most prominent disciples in the person of ŚĀRIPUTRA, known among the Buddha's disciples as "foremost in wisdom." Praised for his prodigious memory, astute questioning, and ability to refute false doctrines in pointed debate, Śāriputra was also the paradigmatic saint of the most abstruse, formal branch of Buddhist knowledge, ABHIDHARMA. All cultures where Buddhism is practiced have produced monks known for their erudition, primarily in Buddhist learning, but also in fields not directly related to Buddhism, such as painting, poetry, calligraphy, engineering, and medicine. The Japanese monk KŪKAI (774–835), for instance, in addition to his considerable contributions to the development of Buddhist thought in Japan, is also known as one of Japan's greatest calligraphers, poets, and lexicographers, credited with compiling the oldest extant dictionary in Japan and even, some claim, with inventing the *kana* syllabary—the foundation of modern written Japanese. In modern times it is not uncommon for scholastically inclined monks to pursue academic degrees at home and abroad, and to teach in secular institutions.

Administrators

While not, at first glance, as glamorous as the otherworldly ascetic or the brilliant scholar, the institutional leader, responsible for monastic administration and the performance of ceremony is essential to the survival of the saṅgha. On a mundane level, monastic administrators are charged with soliciting funds and overseeing the performance of ritual for lay patrons. They also set standards for the monastery, in some cases earning a monastery a reputation for rigor, intellectual activity, or splendor of ceremony. Institutional leaders may be either conservative monks, determined to maintain traditional standards, or reformers, intent on introducing change to the Buddhist order or to society in general. In the twentieth-

Monks at a ceremony at Biechuan Monastery, Guangdong, China, 1987.

century, Buddhists have turned to such reform monks to meet the challenge of finding new sources of revenue with the emergence of radically different national economies, and of opposing or incorporating new intellectual and social trends, including socialism, feminism, and the findings of modern science. Leading Buddhist monks now establish universities and hospitals, instigate missionary programs abroad, and at times exercise considerable political influence. In Taiwan and Sri Lanka, monks have stood for political office. Less directly, but more importantly, leading monks shape the political opinions of their followers and control substantial economic resources. While some express discomfort with the prestige and power that accrue to institutional leaders, seemingly at odds with the traditional monastic imperative to renounce such values, others see them as admirable and necessary for protecting and disseminating Buddhist beliefs and practices.

Eccentrics and degenerates

Standing outside these conventional types, on the margins of the monastic community, are monks known for their eccentricity. The "holy fool," a monk who appears to be mad or stupid but is in fact enlightened, is a stock figure in much of Buddhist art and literature. Such figures are often credited with supernatural powers to foresee the future, heal the sick, and influence the weather. The fifth-century Chinese thaumaturge, Baozhi, for instance, was known to wander the streets making incomprehensible statements. Only later were his statements understood to have predicted important events. In modern times, some monks are known for their bizarre, unpredictable behavior and willingness to break monastic regulations on the grounds that a full appreciation of doctrines of nonduality and emptiness renders conventional restrictions moot. Attitudes toward such figures are necessarily ambivalent, as it is often difficult to distinguish between an enlightened holy man, beyond the ken of ordinary morals, and a charlatan.

Individual monks may be more drawn to one of the types of monks described above over another, but few monks would openly challenge the legitimacy of any of them: Ascetics, scholars, institutional leaders, and even enlightened eccentric monks are all, for the most part, positive images. Equally prominent in all cultures where Buddhism is practiced, however, is the negative image of the corrupt, degenerate monk. In Buddhist writings, perhaps the most famous bad monk was DEVADATTA, cousin and disciple to the Buddha, who out of envy and ambition tried repeatedly to thwart the Buddha's goals, at one point even attempting to poison him, an act for which he was, in the end, consigned to hell. Equally vile was Mahādeva, said to have had sex with his mother before killing both his parents, after which he sought ordination in a desperate attempt to redeem himself. As a monk, his most significant act was to propose five controversial theses that led to dissension within the saṅgha. Legends such as these probably grew out of attempts to vilify proponents of rival schools or factions. Descriptions of malicious, insincere monks are common in Buddhist writings, where they are condemned and employed as a pedagogical device to inspire more noble monks to avoid their example. Because of this rhetorical aspect in such stories, one must be cautious before accepting accounts of immoral monks as accurate descriptions of real behavior, even when such accounts come from Buddhist sources.

Outside of Buddhist sources, the corrupt monk is also a stock figure in non-Buddhist literature, where monks are often portrayed as only pretending to accept Buddhist principles of renunciation and detachment in order to better achieve the most base and worldly aims. The characteristics of such monks depend in part on the mores of their country of origin. In China, for instance, where vegetarianism is an important part of the monk's identity, monks are often portrayed as secretly satisfying their cravings for meat and wine. And sexually depraved, insatiable monks appear in the literature of all cultures where Buddhism is practiced. Again, it is often difficult to assess the accuracy of such characterizations. While from ancient times to the present there have no doubt always been monks of questionable ethics ready to violate their vows for selfish intent, many such accounts are products of lay fantasy rather than accurate descriptions of actual monks.

Grouping the entire monastic community into a few ideal types masks its diversity. In addition to joining the saṅgha for ascetic training, to investigate Buddhist doctrine, to promote Buddhist institutions, or for less lofty motives, some join because of social obligation, whether out of the custom of becoming a monk for a short period as in Thailand and Burma, or to fulfill a vow made by one's parents. Men become monks after failing in the secular world or after becoming disillusioned with secular success. They may seek tonsure out of a yearning for tranquility, contempt for the materialism and pettiness of ordinary society, or out of a sense of boredom. In short, the list of reasons for becoming a Buddhist monk is long and varied. It is in part because of this diversity of character and motive that the monastic vocation has held such an enduring appeal for so many and that monks have played such an influential role in all of the societies in which Buddhism is or was once prevalent.

See also: **Disciples of the Buddha; Nuns; Wilderness Monks**

Bibliography

Bechert, Heinz, and Gombrich, Richard, ed. *The World of Buddhism: Buddhist Monks and Nuns in Society and Culture.* London: Thames and Hudson, 1984.

Buswell, Robert E., Jr. *The Zen Monastic Experience: Buddhist Practice in Contemporary Korea.* Princeton, NJ: Princeton University Press, 1992.

Kieschnick, John. *The Eminent Monk: Buddhist Ideals in Medieval Chinese Hagiography.* Honolulu: University of Hawaii Press, 1997.

Lopez, Donald S., Jr., ed. *Buddhism in Practice.* Princeton, NJ: Princeton University Press, 1995.

Ray, Reginald A. *Buddhist Saints in India: A Study in Buddhist Values and Orientations.* Oxford: Oxford University Press, 1994.

Welch, Holmes. *The Practice of Chinese Buddhism, 1900–1950.* Cambridge, MA: Harvard University Press, 1967.

JOHN KIESCHNICK

MOZHAO CHAN (SILENT ILLUMINATION CHAN)

Used as a derogatory term by its critics, "silent illumination" Chan (Chinese, mozhao Chan; Japanese, mukoshō Zen) designates an approach to practice and enlightenment that strongly emphasizes the inherently enlightened buddha-nature (TATHĀGATAGARBHA) in all SENTIENT BEINGS. Silent illumination Chan advocates an objectless, still MEDITATION, in which all dualisms disappear and enlightenment naturally manifests itself.

The term *silent illumination* was first used in Chinese Chan (Korean, Sŏn; Japanese, Zen) circles in the first half of the twelfth century, probably introduced by the great Chan master of the Caodong tradition, Hongzhi Zhengjue (1091–1157). However, the term was made infamous by Hongzhi's contemporary Dahui ZONGGAO (1089–1163) of the Linji Chan tradition, who vehemently attacked what he called the "heretical silent illumination Chan" of his day as a quietistic form of meditation, lacking in wisdom and enlightenment. Dahui Zonggao countered with his own *kanhua* Chan meditation (literally "Chan of observing the key phrase" or "KŌAN introspection Chan"), and he succeeded in imbuing the term *silent illumination* with strongly negative connotations that came to characterize it in all of East Asian Buddhism.

Hongzhi is the only Chan master on record who used *silent illumination* in a positive sense, although it is possible that the term was expunged from the records of other Caodong masters after Dahui's attacks. In his writings and recorded sayings, Hongzhi often lyrically extols the realm of enlightenment that manifests in quiet meditation, as in the opening lines of his famous poem "Mozhao Ming" ("Inscription on Silent Illumination"), where he writes: "In complete silence, words are forgotten; total clarity appears before you." However, in this poem and elsewhere, Hongzhi stresses that although there is no need to strive for an enlightenment experience, the meditator must not fall into a murky and unthinking state of mind; transcendent wisdom will naturally manifest itself only in an alert mind. To Hongzhi, silent illumination was by no means a passive or thought-suppressing exercise.

Other Caodong masters around the time of Hongzhi can be shown to have embraced similar teachings, beginning with the reviver of the Song-dynasty (960–1279) Caodong tradition, Furong Daokai (1043–1118). There is, however, no evidence that a special silent illumination approach characterized the Caodong Chan tradition from the time of its reputed founder, Dongshan Liangjie (807–869), although this has often been assumed.

In the thirteenth century the Japanese monk DŌGEN (1200–1253) received a transmission in the Chinese Caodong tradition and founded the Japanese Sōtō sect of Zen. Dōgen did not use the term *silent illumination*, but his *shikantaza* (just sitting) meditation practice can clearly be seen as influenced by the silent illumination of the twelfth-century Caodong tradition, although there is no agreement among scholars as to the extent of this influence. The Japanese Rinzai (Chinese, Linji) sect of Zen, which became heir to Dahui Zonggao's *kanhua* Chan, has occasionally accused the Sōtō sect of practicing silent illumination, but the Sōtō sect has never used the term for its own teachings. In Korean Sŏn, *kanhua* (Korean, *kanwha*) Chan dominated early on, and silent illumination Chan never had an impact. Although *kanhua* Chan became the standard for meditation in China shortly after Dahui Zonggao and was even adopted in the late Song Caodong tradition, silent illumination style meditation is still recognized as legitimate in Chinese Chan.

See also: **Chan School**

Bibliography

Leighton, Taigen Daniel, ed. and trans. (with Yi Wu). *Cultivating the Empty Field: The Silent Illumination of Zen Master Hongzhi.* San Francisco: North Point Press, 1991.

Schlütter, Morten. "Silent Illumination, Kung-an Introspection, and the Competition for Lay Patronage in Sung-Dynasty Ch'an." In *Buddhism in the Sung,* ed. Peter N. Gregory and Daniel Getz. Honolulu: Hawaii University Press, 1999.

MORTEN SCHLÜTTER

MUDRĀ AND VISUAL IMAGERY

With the exception of the earliest phases of Indian Buddhist art, when the presence and achievements of the Buddha were represented by symbols, such as a STŪPA (burial mound), footprints, or an empty throne, the study of Buddhist art is generally that of figural representations. BUDDHAS, BODHISATTVAS, and other deities are invariably depicted as idealized anthropomorphic images, and their physical perfection—defined differently in various places and times—reflects their spiritual advancement. Indian images of the Buddha emphasize intellectual concepts, represented by, for example, the wide breast and narrow waist of a lion, or the long legs of a gazelle. In addition, physical marks, such as the *uṣṇīṣa* (a cranial protuberance), the *ūrṇā* (a tuft of hair or "third eye" between the eyebrows), webbed fingers, and wheels on the soles of the feet, further distinguish a buddha from other beings. Symbols such as the lotus, emblematic of purity, or the wheel, indicative of preaching, are ubiquitous in Buddhist art.

The first anthropomorphic images of the Buddha stressed his role as a teacher, showing him wearing the monk's long skirt covered by a full shawl. By the eighth century, crowned and bejeweled buddhas were also represented. Such icons, which parallel monastic practices in which a crown was placed on the head of a monk during initiation, are one way of representing the numerous transcendent buddhas of the later pantheon. Like the earlier icons, bejeweled buddhas are physically perfect. Gestures, postures, and implements are used to distinguish them from one another.

Mudrās in Buddhist imagery

The enthroned Buddha seated in a meditative or lotus posture (*padmāsana*) on a tenth- or eleventh-century Indian sculpture holds his proper right hand in a gesture of meditation and his proper left in the gesture of touching the earth (*bhūmisparśamudrā* [Figure 1, d]). The earth-touching gesture illustrates a specific moment in Śākyamuni's sacred biography when he was challenged by MĀRA, the personification of EVIL. To defend his right to seek enlightenment, the Buddha-to-be Śākyamuni reached down to touch the ground, calling upon the earth as witness to validate the propriety of his quest. The earth responded thunderously, and Māra was vanquished. Known generically as *mudrās,* such gestures, which have long roots in Indian culture, may derive from early dance traditions or from other forms of physical communication. Śākyamuni is known to have used one in an early JĀTAKA tale (a story detailing one of the lives he lived before he become a buddha) in order to communicate with a potential wife. Sixteen such gestures are listed in an early Buddhist text, while three hundred are found in a later work.

The four smaller standing buddhas on this same sculpture illustrate additional moments in Śākyamuni's life: Moving clockwise from the lower left are Śākyamuni's descent from the Heaven of the Thirty-Three Gods (Trāyastriṃśa), which he visited to preach to his mother; the first sermon; the story of a monkey's offering of honey to the Buddha; and the taming of the mad elephant Nālāgiri, sent by his evil cousin DEVADATTA to kill him. These events, from a standardized group of scenes called the Eight Great Events in a buddha's life, can be interpreted both as historical records and as paradigms for the process of enlightenment. For example, the taming of the mad elephant is sometimes understood as a symbol of the mastery of certain aspects of the self that must be disciplined.

The specific historical moments illustrated by the four smaller buddhas are identified by the postures of the figures, the objects they hold in their hands, and their hand gestures or mudrās. For example, the gesture of fearlessness (*abhayamudrā* [Figure 1, a]) often identifies the moment when Śākyamuni tamed the mad elephant. In this mudrā, the right hand is held upward with the palm facing outward, illustrating the act of teaching and signifying the Buddha's ability to grant fearlessness to his followers.

Most of the mudrās found in Buddhist texts are not used in the visual arts, but instead are performed in personal devotions and as an aspect of RITUAL. In general, deities with their hands held up and open are actively engaged in the cosmos, while those with closed hands, or hands held close to the body, are in a transcendent state. The gesture of appeasement or argumentation (*vitarkamudrā* [Figure 1, b]) in which the thumb and index, middle, or ring finger of the upraised right hand are shown touching, indicates teaching, and is one of the most common in visual imagery. Teaching is also defined by upraised hands with the thumb and index fingers of both hands touching each other, a gesture known as "turning the wheel of the law" (*dharmacakramudrā* [Figure 1, f]). Hands placed on the lap, one above the other, with palms upward (*dhyānamudrā* [Figure 1, e]) indicate concentration or meditation. Donors and other devotees have clasped palms, a universal symbol of prayer, known as the gesture of worship (*añjalimudrā* [Figure 1, c]).

Bodhisattvas

Hand gestures and postures are also used to identify the innumerable bodhisattvas found in the Buddhist pantheon. In early Buddhism, the term *bodhisattva* is used to define an individual who, like Śākyamuni, is on the path to enlightenment. The aristocratic clothing and jewelry worn by these figures indicate their active engagement in the world, while the same accoutrements worn by the great bodhisattvas in later traditions suggest their transcendence. These later figures, a primary theme in the visual arts, are revered for their decision to remain accessible to and guide the devout.

MAITREYA is a bodhisattva in the present age, and will become a buddha in the next. As a bodhisattva, he is identified by the stūpa that is found in his headdress, which indicates that he carries on the legacy of the current buddha Śākyamuni. The white lotus he holds and the small figure of the Buddha AMITĀBHA in his headdress identify Avalokiteśvara, the personification of compassion. Mañjuśrī, the personification of wisdom, rides a lion and holds a blue lotus that bears a copy of a "perfection of wisdom" (*prajñāpāramitā*) text. Mañjuśrī is sometimes paired with Samantabhadra (whose name means "universal kindness") on an elephant. In addition, Kṣitigarbha, or the Bodhisattva of the Earth

FIGURE 1

Six common ddhist Mudras

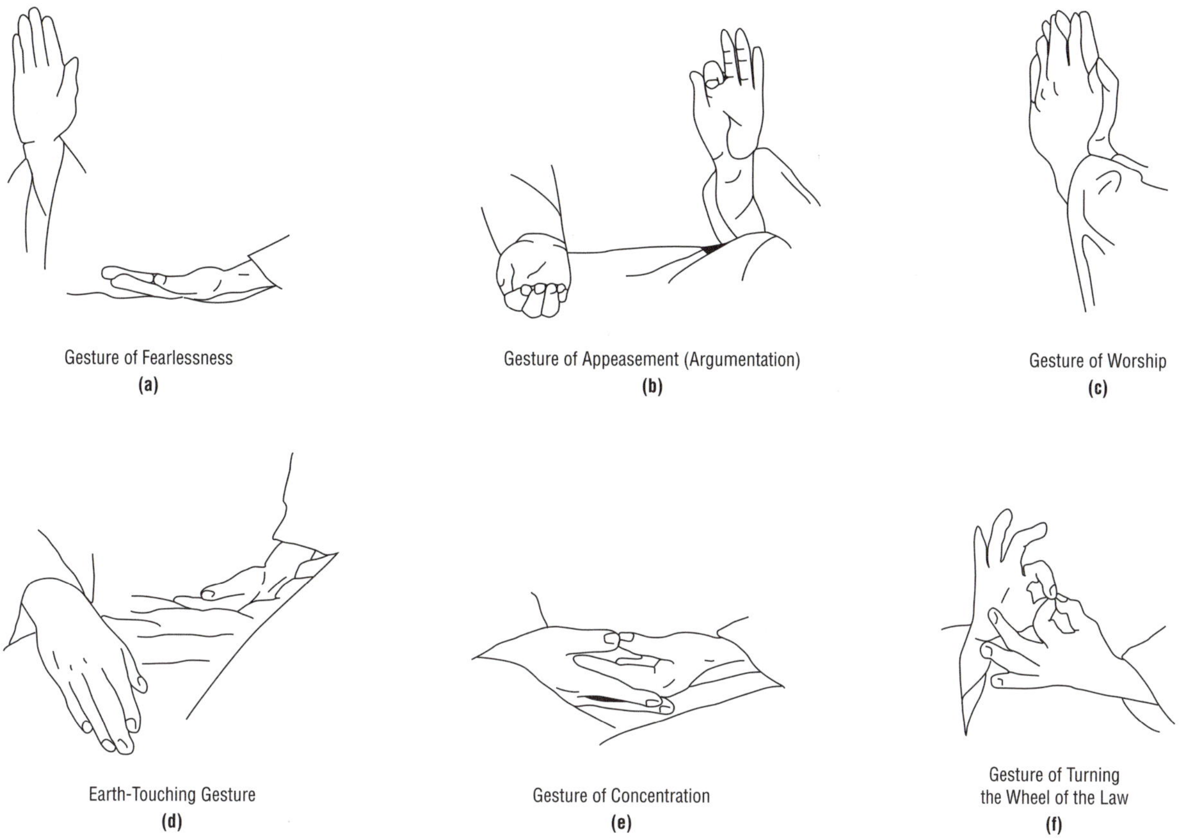

SOURCE: Adapted from Eliade, et al. (1987), vol. 10, p. 135.

Womb, who is generally portrayed as a monk, plays an important role in Central and East Asia, where he is revered as a guide to paradise, a protector from the torments of hell, and, at times, the special guardian of travelers, and women and children.

By the sixth century, the major bodhisattvas had acquired multiple manifestations. For example, Avalokiteśvara, who eventually became the most widely revered deity in Asia, has both an eleven-headed form (*Ekadaśamukha*) and one with one thousand hands and one thousand eyes (*Sahasrabhujasahasranetra*). In Chinese culture, Avalokiteśvara occasionally takes female forms, which led to his misrepresentation as a Buddhist "madonna" in early Western studies of the religion. Mañjuśrī and Samantabhadra also have manifestations distinguished by multiple arms and heads. The former, whose name means "pleasing to behold," is invariably depicted as a young prince, and often wears a necklace made of tiger claws, commonly used in India to protect children.

Some images show Mañjuśrī with one head and four hands, seated in a lotus posture. As befits his role as a bodhisattva, he is active, leaning slightly to the right. Mañjuśrī brandishes a truncated sword in his primary right hand, and a lotus supporting a text in his left. His secondary right hand once held an arrow that was paired with a bow in the left. The first two implements illustrate his capacity to defeat egoism, the second his ability to confound ignorance. Often called Tīkṣṇa-Mañjuśrī, this manifestation of the Bodhisattva of Wisdom is prevalent in the Himalayas and China, but not elsewhere in Asia.

Female deities found in later Buddhist traditions are sometimes understood as buddhas and sometimes as bodhisattvas. Of these, Tārā, who takes many forms, some green, some white, is the most prominent. She is frequently linked with Avalokiteśvara and is revered in Tibet. Others include Prajñāpāramitā, the personification of wisdom, and Uṣṇīṣavijaya, the embodiment of the cranial protuberance on the Buddha's head.

Guardians and other figures

A wide array of protectors is found in Buddhist iconography. The guardians of the four cardinal directions, derived to some extent from early Indian nature spirits known as *yakṣas*, are the earliest and most longstanding. After the sixth century, they are usually shown wearing heavy armor and carrying weapons and other attributes in the arts of Central and East Asia. Door or entranceway guardians (*dvārapālas*), on the other hand, are shown in active, almost threatening, postures, and wear only the dhoti, a skirtlike Indian garment. The five wisdom kings (*vidyārāja*), who manifest the powers of the transcendent Buddha Vairocana, are commonly found in East Asian traditions beginning in the eighth century. They are characterized by Indian clothing, weapons, and terrifying expressions.

Related figures, often based on Hindu Śaivism, such as Hevajra, Cakrasaṃvara, and Yamantaka-Vajrabhairava, are common in Tibetan traditions, where they serve as both protectors and the focus of individual practices. Yamantaka-Vajrabhairava is a terrifying manifestation of Mañjuśrī, whose benign head appears at the top of his stack of nine faces. His primary face, which is that of a buffalo, is a reference to Yama, the Hindu god of death, who rides this animal. Yamantaka-Vajrabhairava's adoption of this face illustrates his ability to transcend the state of death. He has thirty-four arms, many of which hold ritual implements, and sixteen legs. The garland of severed heads, and the human beings and animals that he tramples, illustrate negative states that must be conquered in the quest for enlightenment. His embrace of Vajravetali signifies the union of compassion and wisdom, the two penultimate Buddhist virtues. Known as father-mother, or *yab-yum*, such icons are common in Tibet.

Tibetan Buddhism preserves the use of a system of five buddha families to help structure the enormous pantheon that had evolved by the eleventh and twelfth centuries. The Tibetan system derives from one used in eastern India (Bihar, West Bengal, and Bangladesh) during this period, and is loosely based on an earlier grouping of three families. Each family is headed by one of the five major transcendent buddhas: AKṢOBHYA, Amoghasiddhi, Vairocana, Amitābha, and Ratnasambhava. Each of the five buddhas and the various members of his family have an associated color, vehicle, attribute, gesture, and direction.

Sculpted and painted portraits of famous monks, both historical and semilegendary, are found in Tibet, China, Korea, and Japan. Other commonly portrayed figures include ARHATS, enlightened disciples of the Buddha who became popular in China in the ninth and tenth centuries, and spread from there to Korea, Japan, and Tibet. In addition to representations in sculpture and painting, arhats are often shown as a theme in the decorative arts. Found in groups of sixteen, eighteen, or five hundred, they are depicted either as gruesome figures or as handsome young men. The MAHĀSIDDHAS, a group of semihistorical adepts often credited with the creation of the later esoteric traditions practiced in Tibet, are commonly found in paintings from that part of Asia.

See also: **Bodhisattva Images; Buddha Images; Buddha, Life of the, in Art; China, Buddhist Art in; Himalayas, Buddhist Art in; Huayan Art; India, Buddhist Art in; Indonesia, Buddhist Art in; Japan, Buddhist Art in; Korea, Buddhist Art in; Robes and Clothing; Southeast Asia, Buddhist Art in**

Bibliography

Eliade, Mircea, ed. *The Encyclopedia of Religion*, 16 vols. New York: Macmillan, 1987.

Mallmann, Marie-Thérèse de. *Introduction a l'iconographie du tantrisme bouddhique*. Paris: Librarie Adrien-Maisonneuve, 1975.

Saunders, E. Dale. *Mudrā: A Study of Symbolic Gestures in Japanese Buddhist Sculpture*. Princeton, NJ: Princeton University Press, 1985.

Snellgrove, David L., ed. *The Image of the Buddha*. London: Serindia; Paris: UNESCO, 1978.

DENISE PATRY LEIDY

MŪLASARVĀSTIVĀDA.

See **Sarvāstivāda and Mūlasarvāstivāda**

MŪLASARVĀSTIVĀDA-VINAYA

The *Mūlasarvāstivāda-vinaya* is one of the six extant Buddhist monastic codes, or VINAYAS. There is some controversy about how to understand its title, and thereby its place among the various vinayas. It could be read as "The Root (or Original) Monastic Code of the Group that Teaches that All Exists," or it could be read as "The Monastic Code of the Root (or Original) Group that Teaches that All Exists." However it be taken, it is almost certain that the presence of *mūla* in the title reflects a polemical claim on the part of its compilers or their group.

Although again there is some controversy, the best available evidence would seem to indicate that, in the form that we have it, it was probably compiled in the first or second century C.E. in northwest India. Several scholarly studies have suggested that, in comparison with the other vinayas, the *Mūlasarvāstivāda-vinaya* often seems to contain some very early material or accounts that are markedly undeveloped when compared with those found elsewhere. "Very early," however, is relative since this vinaya, like all the surviving vinayas, appears to have been redacted late, centuries after the time of the Buddha, and to presuppose a fully developed and very sophisticated form of monasticism.

One of the most striking characteristics of the *Mūlasarvāstivāda-vinaya* is its enormous size. It has been called "monstrous" and has been said to be about four times longer than any other vinaya. Its Tibetan version, in traditional format, fills thirteen large volumes and consists of more than four thousand leaves or eight thousand "pages." In addition to this Tibetan version, which appears to be complete, the *Mūlasarvāstivāda-vinaya* survives in a partial (but still massive) Chinese translation, and significant parts of it have also come down to us in Sanskrit. Very little of this monster has been translated into English; a little more has been translated into German.

This vinaya, like all vinayas, contains a huge number of major rules and minor regulations meant to govern everything from ORDINATION to how to use the latrine. But this vinaya also contains rules detailing how monks should lend money on interest or borrow money from laymen, how they should warehouse and sell rice, take images in procession into town, make up parts of canonical texts, and a host of other things not commonly presented as integral parts of Buddhist monasticism.

Rules per se, however, take up a relatively limited space in this huge collection. It also contains a significant number of texts that elsewhere are found in the sūtra collection. More importantly, perhaps, it is stuffed with stories and narrative tales. On this account one scholar has even called it "one of the masterpieces of Sanskrit literature," and it has certainly been a source that later authors and artists drew on heavily for their subjects, and that scholars will be mining for a very long time.

See also: **Sarvāstivāda and Mūlasarvāstivāda**

Bibliography

Schiefner, F. Anton von. *Tibetan Tales Derived from Indian Sources,* tr. W. R. S. Ralston. Boston: Osgood, 1882.

Schopen, Gregory. *Buddhist Monks and Business Matters: More Collected Papers.* Honolulu: University of Hawaii Press, 2003.

GREGORY SCHOPEN

MURAKAMI SENSHŌ

Murakami Senshō (1851–1929) was a Jōdo Shinshū, Ōtani branch cleric and scholar of Buddhism. He was born in Tanba (Hyōgo prefecture) in Japan, the eldest son of an Ōtani-branch Jōdo Shin cleric. Murakami received a classical Confucian and Buddhist education at academies in Himeji and at the Higashi Honganji in Kyoto. He took the surname Murakami when he married into the family of Murakami Jōkai, a Shin cleric in Mikawa. Murakami went on to hold teaching positions successively at the Sōtōshū Daigakurin, the Ōtani Kyōkō, and finally, Tokyo Imperial University, where he became a lecturer in Indian philosophy.

In an effort to further scholarship of Buddhism that was historically sound, pan-sectarian in scope, and sympathetic to the tradition, Murakami, together with Washio Junkyō (1868–1941) and Sakaino Kōyō (1871–1933), founded the important journal *Bukkyō shirin* (*Buddhist History*), one of the earliest academic journals devoted to the humanistic study of Buddhism in Japan. Murakami also published the pathbreaking, pan-sectarian study of Japanese Buddhist history, *Dainihon Bukkyōshi* (*History of Japanese Buddhism*). Most controversially, in his book describing the doctrines fundamental to all streams of Buddhism, *Bukkyō tōitsu ron* (*The Unity of Buddhism*), and more fully in *Daijō bussetsu ron hihan* (*Critique of the Argument that Mahāyāna Is the Teaching of Śākyamuni Buddha*), Murakami advanced the radical thesis that MAHĀYĀNA Buddhism was not the direct teaching of Śākyamuni Buddha. Rather, he contended that Mahāyāna was a development of Śākyamuni's teaching and that all other BUDDHAS and BODHISATTVAS for example, AMITĀBHA (Amida) and Mahāvairocana (Dainichi), were, unlike the historical Śākyamuni, abstract expressions of the historical Buddha's ideal qualities. Hostile reactions to his book from the Buddhist establishment, particularly his own Shin denomination, forced Murakami to renounce his status as a Shin cleric in 1901. He reconciled with the Shin establishment, however, reclaiming his clerical status in 1911.

See also: **Buddhist Studies**

Bibliography

Vita, Silvio. "Interpretations of Mahāyāna Buddhism in Meiji Japan: From Religious Polemics to Scholarly Debate." *Transactions of the International Conference of Orientalists in Japan* 31 (1986): 44–57.

RICHARD M. JAFFE

MYANMAR

The modern state of Myanmar, also known as Burma, is geographically the largest and westernmost country of mainland Southeast Asia. Its population of approximately forty-seven million as of the year 2000 is comprised of more than one hundred nationalities, the largest of which include the majority Bamar or ethnic Burmans, the Rakhine (Arakanese), the Shan, the Kayin (Karen), and the Mon. As a convention in English, members of all of these nationalities receive the designation *Burmese* as citizens of the country. The vast majority of the Burmese people, regardless of their ethnic affiliation, subscribe to THERAVĀDA Buddhism as their traditional faith. So pervasive is the influence of this religion on the people of Myanmar that it is often said that to be Burmese is to be Buddhist. Indeed, historically it was Theravāda Buddhism more than any other force that drew the many peoples of Myanmar together into a single civilization, so much so that even non-Buddhist citizens of the country acknowledge the centrality of Theravāda ethical, social, and political conceptions to the fabric of Burmese life.

Historical background

Burmese chroniclers trace the origin of Theravāda Buddhism in their country to the Buddha himself, who they assert personally converted the inhabitants of Lower and Upper Myanmar. These regions are the respective homelands of the Mon and the ancient Pyu people, precursors of the modern Bamar and the nationalities most closely associated with the evolution of Burmese Buddhism. Burmese sources further equate the Mon homeland with Suvaṇṇabhūmi and the Pyu-Bamar homeland with Aparanta, identifications that allow them to claim for their country two missions from King AŚOKA (ca. 300–232 B.C.E.). Reflecting a long-standing cultural rivalry with Sri Lanka, the same sources emphasize that the two missions restored an already established Theravāda tradition in Myanmar, whereas the simultaneous single Aśokan mission to Sri Lanka merely established Theravāda Buddhism on the island for the first time. As a final claim to primacy, the Mon identify the great Pāli commentator BUDDHAGHOSA as a native son.

Although Theravāda Buddhism has a long history in Myanmar, there is little evidence of its presence in the country before the fourth century C.E. In addition, that which has been uncovered does not support the traditional portrayal of early Burmese Buddhism as uniformly Theravāda. Rather it shows an eclectic mix of traditions that included multiple forms of Buddhism, Brahmanism, and indigenous animist cults. Excavations at the ancient Pyu capital of Śrīkṣetra, for example, unearthed images of VIṢṆU, MAHĀYĀNA bodhisattvas, and Pāli and Sanskrit Buddhist inscriptions. Seventh-century Chinese travelogues note that the city supported Sthaviravāda (Theravāda), Mahāsāṃghika, Mūlasarvāstivāda, and Saṃmatīya monks and that the Pyu observed the custom of ordaining all youths as novices in the Buddhist religion.

During this early period Myanmar absorbed cultural influences chiefly from South India, though important contacts were also maintained with Sri Lanka. Beginning in the ninth century, by which time the Bamar had begun to replace the Pyu in Upper Myanmar, Bengal emerged as a major source of Indian influence in the region. Large numbers of Buddhist votive tablets bearing Mahāyāna imagery and Sanskrit inscriptions written in north Indian script were imported and produced locally at this time. Bengali influence waned by the twelfth century as a consequence of the Muslim conquest of north India, a development that encouraged the expansion of Burmese ties with Sri Lanka. The Sri Lanka connection facilitated the introduction of new reformist strands of Sinhalese Theravāda Buddhism that in time emerged as the majority Buddhist tradition of mainland Southeast Asia. This process proceeded incrementally and did not complete itself in Myanmar until the eighteenth century.

In 1057 C.E., the Bamar king of Pagan, Anawrahta (Pāli, Anuruddha), conquered the Mon kingdom of Thaton in Lower Myanmar, inaugurating the first Burmese empire (1057–1287). Tradition states that he carried off to his capital Pāli texts, relics, and orthodox monks, and that he adopted Theravāda Buddhism as the sole religion of his domain. To prepare for this, Anawrahta suppressed an already established sect of heretical Buddhist monks known as the Ari, who, though notorious for their wickedness, had enjoyed the traditional support of his forefathers. Whatever the historical accuracy of the legend, epigraphic and archaeological evidence indicates that Anawrahta was more eclectic than portrayed. He assisted the Sinhalese king Vijayabāhu I to reinstate a valid Theravāda ordination line in Sri Lanka; at the same time he circulated in his own kingdom votive tablets adorned with Mahāyāna imagery. Anawrahta also supported a royal cult of *nat* or spirit propitiation dedicated to the very deities said to have been worshipped by the Ari monks.

In 1165 the Sinhalese king Parakkamabāhu I reformed the Theravāda SAṄGHA of Sri Lanka by abolishing the Abhayagiri and Jetavana monasteries and compelling all worthy monks to be reordained in the Mahāvihāra fraternity. Within two decades, this reformed Sinhalese tradition was established at Pagan and elsewhere in the Burmese empire. The Burmese monarch extended patronage to the imported Sinhalese order but did not compel the native saṅgha to unite with it. As a consequence, the Burmese monastic community split into two groups, an indigenous unreformed faction called the Myanma saṅgha, and the reformed Sinhalese faction called the Sīhala saṅgha. The Sīhala saṅgha was revered for its discipline and scholarship, though it fractured repeatedly, giving rise to a pattern of saṅgha disunity that has been characteristic of Burmese monasticism ever since.

In the thirteenth century a powerful community of forest-dwelling monks emerged from the Myanma saṅgha, whose discipline was lax when viewed by Sinhalese standards. Modern scholarship has identified these as the Ari monks of the chronicles. Ruins of their headquarters at Minnanthu near Pagan include temples decorated with Mahāyāna and tantric imagery, suggesting that the forest dwellers were votaries of these traditions. The Tibetan historian Tārānātha (1575–1634) states that Buddhist TANTRA was introduced to Pagan from Bengal by this time and inscriptions indicate that as late as the fifteenth century the Myanma saṅgha received, along with Pāli scriptures and commentaries, Mahāyāna and tantric works as donations to its libraries.

Ascendancy of Sinhalese orthodoxy

Toward the end of the thirteenth century the Pagan empire began to disintegrate. The Mon broke away and established the kingdom of Rāmañña in Lower Myanmar, while the Bamar divided Upper Myanmar into several smaller states, chief of which was the kingdom of Ava. The monastic community remained divided throughout the region. In the fourteenth and fifteenth centuries, new waves of reformed Theravāda Buddhism emanating from Sri Lanka were introduced into Southeast Asia via Lower Myanmar. In 1476 Dhammazedi, the Mon king of Rāmañña, adopted these reforms, compelling all monks in his realm to be reordained in the new more stringent Sinhalese order and to be educated according to a standardized curriculum.

Dhammazedi's reformed saṅgha was favored by two succeeding Burmese empires, the Taungoo (1531–1752) and the Konbaung (1752–1885), though rival monastic fraternities were allowed to flourish unmolested. It was during this period of relative stability that the village monastery became the basic institutional unit of the Burmese saṅgha and assumed its traditional role as village center and school for village youth. It was principally through this institution, which facilitated literacy and the propagation of a standardized Buddhist ethos, that the cultural integration characteristic of Burmese civilization was achieved. In 1791 the Burmese monarchy ordered Dhammazedi's reforms imposed uniformly throughout the empire, thus unifying the Burmese saṅgha for the first time. Although monastic unity was short lived and did not survive the demise of the Konbaung dynasty, all contemporary monastic fraternities in Myanmar trace their lineages back to Dhammazedi's reforms and share a common interpretation of the monastic code. Buddhism was disestablished as the state religion under the British colonial government (1885–1947) to the detriment of saṅgha discipline. State oversight of religious affairs was restored at Burmese independence in 1947, and has remained in place under both the original democratic government and the subsequent military junta that has ruled the country since 1962.

In addition to overseeing monastic affairs, Burmese kings devoted themselves to the acquisition of Buddha relics (Pāli, *dhātu*; Burmese, *dat-daw*) and to the preservation of Buddhist texts. These three together (relics, texts, and monks) are the physical embodiments

The golden spire of the Shwedagon pagoda in Yangon (Rangoon), Myanmar (Burma). © David Cumming; Eye Ubiquitous/Corbis. Reproduced by permission.

of the Buddha, the *dhamma* (Sanskrit, dharma; teachings), and the saṅgha—the three JEWELS (Pāli, *tiratana*) at the center of Buddhist devotional practice. Within the precincts of every capital were grand pagodas (Burmese, *zedi*) housing relics that functioned as palladia of the state, and during periods of imperial unity, the shrines of subjugated territories were often restored and embellished as signs of the emperor's piety and magnanimity. Myanmar's most magnificent shrine, the gilded SHWEDAGON pagoda in Yangon (Rangoon), reached its present monumental dimensions through a process of repeated expansion at the hands of rival monarchs. Since Pagan times Burmese kings took upon themselves the task of promoting monastic learning and preserving accurate copies of the Theravāda CANON—the Pāli *tipiṭaka*. The most recent recensions of the *tipiṭaka* in Myanmar were produced during two Buddhist councils; the first convened by King Mindon in 1871 and the second convened by Prime Minister U Nu in 1954. Since at least the fifteenth century, officially edited *tipiṭakas* have formed the core curriculum of state administered monastic examinations.

The Burmese synthesis of traditions

Buddhism in Myanmar combines several key elements from its variegated past to produce a unique form of Theravāda orthodoxy. Occupying the center is the Pāli textual tradition with its beliefs, practices, and institutions as interpreted by the Burmese Theravāda saṅgha, and supported by the state and the general populace. There are, in addition, important rites and beliefs that derive from non-Pāli sources but are regarded as wholly orthodox. Prominent among these is the *shinpyu* ceremony, the obligatory temporary ordination of boys as Buddhist novices, and the simultaneous ear-piercing ceremony for girls, rites of passage that can be traced back to the Buddhist initiation ceremonies of the ancient Pyu. The popular cult of Shin Upagot (Sanskrit, UPAGUPTA), an immortal ARHAT and remover of obstacles, and the cave-shrine of Alaung-daw Kathapa near the city of Monywa, which allegedly contains the sacred corpse of MAHĀKĀŚYAPA (Pāli, Mahākassapa), both have their origins in Sanskrit Buddhist traditions. The famous water festival of Thin-gyan, which marks the Burmese New Year in April, was adapted from the Hindu New Year festival of Holi, with Buddhist elements taken from Pāli scripture interpolated into the festival's legend.

For purely worldly concerns, Burmese seek the assistance of a host of *nats* or spirits. Considered morally ambiguous at best, *nats* may be nature deities or the ghosts of legendary persons who died violent deaths and whose energies can be tapped in exchange for veneration. At the national level the belief system is organized into the cult of the Thirty-Seven Lords, which originally was a royally administered cult of spirit propitiation that tied pre-Buddhist regional deities and their human devotees into a hierarchical web of ritual obligation paralleling the political order. *Nat* worship often entails the offering of alcohol and blood sacrifice (chickens), for which reason it is regarded even by its votaries as falling outside of Buddhism. Nevertheless the *nat* pantheon is conceived of in entirely Buddhist terms and it is situated within the lower strata of the Buddhist cosmos as articulated by the normative tradition.

Burmese Buddhism as a salvific system can be divided into three general types or PATHS. The first and most traditional of these is the path of merit-making whereby one strives to accumulate merit (Pāli, *puñña*; Burmese, *kuthol*) through the observance of PRECEPTS

(Pāli, *sīla*), the performance of meritorious deeds, and acts of DĀNA (GIVING) directed especially toward religious persons and objects, such as monks and pagodas. The goal of merit accumulation is repeated for happy rebirth as a human or god, with NIRVĀṆA (Pāli, nibbāna) or final liberation at most a very distant goal in the mind of the practitioner. The majority of Burmese Buddhists, both lay and ordained, have happy rebirth as their preferred goal, an orientation that has been typical of Buddhists in Myanmar since at least the Pagan period.

The second system is the path of VIPASSANĀ (SANSKRIT, VIPAŚYANĀ) or insight meditation. *Vipassanā* meditation, when successfully practiced, leads to the attainment of BODHI (AWAKENING), or enlightenment, and nirvāṇa, either in this life or in a not-too-distant future life. Practitioners of *vipassanā* in Myanmar typically meditate privately and join meditation centers (Burmese, *wipathana yeiktha*) during retreats. The observance of precepts and a general moral lifestyle is considered a necessary foundation for insight practice. *Vipassanā* meditation was revived in Myanmar in the early eighteenth century and by the late twentieth century was widely popular among all classes throughout the country.

The third salvation system is called *weikza-lam* or the path of the Buddhist wizard. This is an esoteric system of powerful occult sciences requiring initiation by a master. The goal of this path is to become a *weikza* or *weikza-do* (from the Pāli *vijjādhara*), which is a kind of semi-immortal magician or wonder-worker. The *weikza* vows to remain in the world for the benefit of the faithful until the advent of the future Buddha MAITREYA (Pāli, Metteyya), at which time the *weikza* will attain nirvāṇa or take a vow to become a perfect buddha himself. As a service, he acts as teacher to human disciples, instructing them in the recitation of spells, the casting of runes, alchemy, and *samatha* (Sanskrit, *śamatha*) or tranquility meditation. *Weikza* practitioners typically eschew *vipassanā* meditation on the basis that it could potentially cut short their career by causing them to attain nirvāṇa too quickly. In its methodology and goals, the *weikza-lam* shows striking similarities to the tantric Buddhist MAHĀSIDDHA tradition of medieval Bengal. Because it proposes an alternative soteriology to that contained in Pāli sources, the *weikza-lam* is sometimes viewed with suspicion by the religious authorities.

See also: **Esoteric Art, South and Southeast Asia; Folk Religion, Southeast Asia; Southeast Asia, Buddhist Art in**

Bibliography

Aung Thwin, Michael. *Pagan: The Origins of Modern Burma.* Honolulu: University of Hawaii Press, 1985.

Bischoff, Roger. *Buddhism in Myanmar: A Short History.* Kandy, Sri Lanka: Buddhist Publication Society, 1995.

Duroiselle, Charles. "The Ari of Burma and Tantric Buddhism." *Annual Report of the Arhaeological Survey of India* (1915–1916): 79–93.

Htin Aung, Maung. *Folk Elements in Burmese Buddhism.* Oxford: Oxford University Press, 1962.

Mendelson, E. Michael. *Saṅgha and State in Burma: A Study of Monastic Sectarianism and Leadership,* ed. John P. Ferguson. Ithaca, NY: Cornell University Press, 1975.

Ray, Nihar Ranjan. *Sanskrit Buddhism in Burma.* Amsterdam: H. J. Paris, 1937.

Spiro, Melford E. *Buddhism and Society: A Great Tradition and Its Burmese Vicissitudes.* Berkeley: University of California Press, 1982.

Than Tun. "Mahākassapa and His Tradition." *Journal of the Burma Research Society* 42, no. 2 (1959): 99–118.

PATRICK A. PRANKE

MYANMAR, BUDDHIST ART IN

Burma, renamed Myanmar in 1989, is the largest mainland country in Southeast Asia. Burma has a continuous tradition of Buddhist art from the early centuries of the common era to the present. The principal forms of this art involve the construction of monuments, either stūpas or temples, which embody the main artistic media: architecture, painting, and sculpture, in addition to the decorative arts. Despite the large number of monuments and other vestiges of this tradition, Burmese art history has remained a neglected area of study.

Early history, 600–800 C.E.

Between the fifth and eight centuries C.E. the Irrawaddy valley was settled by a people known as the Pyu, sometimes described as the Proto-Burmese, who migrated from southwest China. Living in walled city-states, their civilization was documented by imperial Chinese chroniclers who marveled at the Pyu's sophistication in matters of music, dance, jewelery making, textile production, and religious life. Archaeological finds at Śrī Kṣetra, the largest Pyu city near the modern town of Prome (Pyay), and Beik-than-myo, which literally translates as "Viṣnu City," indicate a mixed religious life derived from the Indian subcontinent. This had elements of Sanskritic and Pāli Buddhism. In addition, various Hindu images have been found indicating that Pyu religious life incorporated a number of cults and movements. The workmanship of these images, particularly the gold work on the reliquary casket found at the Khin Ba mound, is exquisite and bears testimony to the accounts of the Chinese chroniclers. The principal Buddhist monuments found at Śrī Kṣetra, large stūpas like the Be-be-gyi, are said to derive from colossal Sri Lankan prototypes; cave temples, such as the Lei-myet-hna, were made of brick and are precursory to the monuments found at Pagan. They share similar structural systems, incorporating the pointed arch and voussoir brick patterns.

Along the southern Burma coastline the Mon civilization enjoyed good maritime contacts with India and acted as a conduit for the ingress of Buddhism into the Irrawaddy valley. Iconographic finds at Thaton and the other Mon sites indicate a mixed religious life derived from the subcontinent. Portable votive plaques made of terra-cotta illustrate principal scenes from the life of the Buddha; relief stone sculptures are in the Mon-Dvārāvatī style, which is also found in southern Thailand. Bronzes and other portable images brought from the subcontinent also have been found. There are no surviving temples or original stūpas from this period. The Mon possessed their own script, and their knowledge of Pāli texts was significant to the development of art at Pagan.

Pagan, 1000–1300 C.E.

The Pyu city of Śrī Kṣetra fell to a Chinese raid in 832 C.E., after which a new state emerged to dominate the middle part of the Irrawaddy valley at Pagan. Early Pagan STŪPAS, such as the Nga-kywe-na-daung, or temples, such as the Alo-pyi, are of Pyu origin. By the eleventh century C.E., Pagan under King Anawartha came to dominate much of the valley and annexed the Mon kingdom of Thaton. As a consequence, both Mon and Pāli texts appeared for the first time at Pagan. These provided the basis for cycles of religious paintings and sculpture. Inside temples, THERAVĀDA texts, tales of the life of the Buddha, and JĀTAKA stories were depicted. Along the terraces of stūpas, terra-cotta plaques, usually glazed, illustrated *jātaka* stories. As with the Pyu cities, religious life at Pagan appears to have been mixed, even eclectic, with Theravāda, MAHĀYĀNA, and Brahmanic elements coexisiting. It is significant that Pagan's rise coincided with the decline of Buddhism in India and elsewhere. The wealth and patronage of Pagan kings attracted both scholars and artists to court, whether from the MAHĀYĀNA world of Pāla Bengal or the Theravāda heartland of Sri Lanka. By the beginning of the twelfth century the Pagan kings had firmly embraced Theravāda, and epigraphy describes the "purification" of the country's religious life. Theravāda notions of KINGSHIP styled the Pagan kings as *dhammarāja* and *khammarāja*—protectors of Buddhism granting them legitimacy in their imperial mission to unite all Burma. Pagan kings in turn promoted the faith through the lavish and profuse construction of monuments.

According to the United Nations Educational, Scientific, and Cultural Organization (UNESCO) survey completed in 2000 there are 2,217 standing monuments at Pagan; in addition there are numerous mounds indicating collapsed monuments. An earlier survey by an eighteenth-century king had listed over 4,000 monuments. The palace-city was walled and moated and covered a relatively small corner of the twenty-five-square-mile site. The principal architectural forms are the stūpa and the temple, with a number of hybrid forms integrating both these types. Monastery complexes, library structures, and ordination halls are to be found, either as part of, or independent of, larger temple complexes. Nearly all of these monuments were constructed with brick. Monuments were endowed, whether by the king and royal family or by courtier families, with considerable grants of glebe land and "pagoda slaves" for the maintenance of these foundations into posterity. The greater dedications were collegiate centers of study and scholarship. Most of the wooden monasteries, which, along with the palaces and domestic buildings, were made from perishable materials, have been lost. It may be that the decline of Pagan in the late thirteenth century was the result of the strain of having much of the national economy dedicated to the service of these monuments and their incumbents. Considerable information on the extent and costs of such dedications is contained in contemporary epigraphy.

Burmese Buddhism, from Pagan times to the present, has been described as *kammatic*, the main preoccupation, from the king to humblest subject, being the earning of merit to ensure a favorable REBIRTH in the next existence. Coupled to this, the royal dedication of colossal monuments was seen as an act of communal merit-earning that would benefit the entire nation. (This thinking has remained current with successive postindependence military regimes, who, like the kings of Pagan, dedicate a large part of the national product to Buddhist building activities.) Linked to this was the belief that enlightenment is too difficult for most people to attain and therefore the objective in merit-making is to be reborn when the future Buddha Metteya (MAITREYA) appears on earth, for an encounter with Metteya brings instant and easy enlightenment. This messianic belief, whose origins can be found in Pyu sculptures, gave rise to a pentagonal plan for monuments that reached its zenith in the construction of the virtuoso Dhamma-yazika stūpa at Pagan.

During the three centuries of artistic activity at Pagan there were three principal phases in which art and architecture evolved. During the early period, Pyu temple types, such as the Abe-yadana or Naga-yon, housed paintings and sculpture clearly derived from Pāla Bengal that illustrate textual sources originating from Sri Lanka but captioned in the Old Mon language. Coupled with imperial expansion was a proselytizing movement of conversion to the Theravāda way, and this art was essentially educational. By 1150, with the construction of the That-byin-nyu and Dhamma-yan-gyi temples under Sithu I, a transitional period becomes evident in the Pagan temple, whereby a clear Burmese idiom emerges in architecture, painting, and sculpture. At the same time, the Old Burmese language is written for the first time as captions beneath wall paintings. Bronze work, perhaps derived from the Arakan, achieves a succinct beauty rarely paralleled in Buddhist art. Temples grow taller, lighter, and more spacious compared with the darker, more mystical early types. By 1200, late period temples, such as Sula-mani or Hti-lo-min-lo, with the main shrine on the upper level, display a virtuoso technical sophistication and quality of craftsmanship. Likewise, painting and sculpture pass from an early period style that is, in spiritual terms, highly charged to a late period style that is supremely confident, yet in execution delicate and in effect delightful.

Iconography from this period betrays the mixed origins of Pagan Buddhism and by the mid-eleventh century the dominance of the Theravāda tradition. Bodhisattva, *dvārapāla, garuḍa,* nāga, and other "sacred beasts" of the Hindu-Buddhist pantheon abound mainly as decorative elements in great cycles of narrative paintings depicting the life of the Buddha, the *jātaka,* and other Theravāda tales. During the early period, Buddhist "purifications" of ancient animist cults were absorbed into the new state religion, as were Hindu deities, as supporters of the faith. These spirit or *nat* cults survive to this day, and such "folk art" combined with ritual, costume, and dance is a rich potential area of anthropological study.

Post-Pagan, 1300–1752

Following the Mongol incursion of 1278, Pagan fell into economic decline and into the power vacuum stepped Shan-Tai tribes who were responsible for much of the desecration of the temples at Pagan. Later converted to Buddhism, the art and architecture of the Shan states is a rich potential source of study with distinct styles of architecture, sculpture, and decoration more akin to Thailand than Burma. Likewise for the Arakan, a kingdom on the Bay of Bengal that remained independent until the late eighteenth century with its capital at Mrauk-U and its own highly original styles betraying the proximity of India. By the sixteenth century the Burmese under the First Ava dynasty had reasserted itself at Toungoo. They established capitals at Pegu, which they captured from the Mons, who had regained lost territories following the decline of Pagan, and then at Ava in 1637. During this period the country was reunified and Thailand invaded several times. Little of architectural interest survives from this period, with the exception of various royal stūpas that have since been remodeled. Sculpture from this period can be heavy and crude in execution. The first mural paintings since the end of Pagan may be seen at the Thi-loka-guru (1672) caves at Sagaing and at the Hpo-win-daung caves in the Chindwin valley. These paintings, like the sculpture of this period, are naïve yet vividly entertaining. Early carved wood monasteries at Mingkin show an excellence of decorative work, and Ava period temples, though technically less ambitious than Pagan temples, reveal fine stucco work in the Pagan tradition.

The Konbaung dynasty, 1752–1885

It was not until the rise of the Konbaung dynasty in 1752 that a true revival of the arts in Burma is evident. The Konbaung kings were conscious of their own Pagan heritage; indeed, they set about the first restorations of monuments there and dedicated a number of new monuments at Pagan. Compared with the more restrained classical idiom of Pagan, the art of the Konbaung has a distinctly rococo tendency. Decoration can be highly florid; stucco carvings adorning temple pediments tend to be flamboyant. The principal Konbaung monuments are found in the area around present-day Mandalay, in the vicinities of the sites of the three former Konbaung capitals at Ava, Amarapura, and Mandalay itself, established in 1855. Under the Konbaung,

Kyaiktiyo Pagoda hangs on a cliff top in Mon state, Myanmar (Burma). Pilgrims must hike seven miles up a jungle mountain path to reach it. The twenty-four-foot-tall stūpa atop the rock is said to contain a hair from the Buddha's head. AP/Wide World Photos. Reproduced by permission.

woodcarving flourished, as seen in a number of splendid carved wood monasteries, including Shwe Kyaung in Mandalay and Bagaya Kyaung in Ava. The unfinished Mingun Pagoda, built by the megalomaniacal King Bodawhpaya in 1790, is said to be the largest brick structure in the world, and its bell is the largest working bell in the world. Across the Irrawaddy from Mandalay, the pilgrimage center of Sagaing contains a number of Ava, Konbaung, and colonial-period dedications revealing the high levels of craftsmanship achieved in the decorative arts during these periods. Illustrated manuscripts (secular and religious), glass mosaic work, textiles, lacquer ware, and silversmithing are but a few of the crafts that flourished.

The sixth conquest of AYUTTHAYA in Thailand in 1767 resulted in the relocation of a number of Thai artists in Burma whose work includes the redecoration of the Upali Thein at Pagan. Chinese influences appeared in the works of Bagyidaw. The hand of Italian engineers employed by King Mindon can be seen in a number of Italianate pavilions at the new Mandalay palace and in a number of religious dedications, notably the Atu-ma-shi Monastery, destroyed by fire in an 1890 war and since reconstructed. Following the British annexation of Upper Burma in 1886, the Buddhist arts underwent something of a renaissance as a result of increased prosperity coupled with the liberation of a devout mercantile class from sumptuary controls. Splendid monastery complexes, such as the Ma-so-shin and Myin-wun-taik monasteries, were constructed in the 1890s with traditional ground plans and pseudo-Palladian facades. The classical arcades of the Yakhine Maha-myat-muni Hpaya-gyi, the principal pagoda of modern Mandalay, dedicated in 1784 but largely rebuilt in the colonial period, again reveal this European influence. In the mural paintings found within the Hpaya-gyi, early portrayals of Europeans, railway trains, and steamboats are depicted in classical Konbaung style.

See also: **Cave Sanctuaries; Merit and Merit-Making; Monastic Architecture; Myanmar; Shwedagon**

Bibliography

Aung Thaw. *Historical Sites in Burma.* Rangoon: Ministry of Union Culture, 1972.

Harvey, G. E. *A History of Burma from Earliest Time to 10 March 1824.* London: Frank Cass and Co., 1925.

Luce, G. H. *Old Burma—Early Pagan,* 3 vols. Locust Valley, NY: J. J. Augustin, 1969–1970.

Pichard, Pierre. *Inventory of Monuments at Pagan,* 8 vols. Paris: UNESCO; Gartmore, Scotland: Kiscadale Publications, 1992–2002.

Spiro, Melford E. *Buddhism and Society: A Great Tradition and Its Burmese Vicissitudes.* New York: Harper and Row, 1972.

Strachan, Paul. *Pagan: Art and Architecture of Old Burma.* Whiting Bay, Scotland: Kiscadale Publications, 1989.

Than Tun. *Essays on the History of Buddhism in Burma,* ed. Paul Strachan. Whiting Bay, Scotland: Kiscadale Publications, 1988.

PAUL STRACHAN

MYŌE. *See* **Kōben**

MYSTICISM. *See* **Bodhi (Awakening); Meditation**

N

NĀGĀRJUNA

The Indian philosopher Nāgārjuna (ca. second century C.E.) is probably the single most important Buddhist philosopher. Nothing reliable is known about his life; modern scholars do not accept the traditional account whereby Nāgārjuna lived for some six hundred years and became a Tantric wonderworker (siddha), although it is believed that Nāgārjuna was the teacher of ĀRYADEVA (ca. 170–270 C.E.). There is moreover a debate over which works can be attributed to this Nāgārjuna, with some agreement on:

Madhyamakakārikā (*Verses on Madhyamaka*), Nāgārjuna's main work, still extant in Sanskrit;

Vigrahavyāvartanī (*Countering Hostile Objections*), verses extant in Sanskrit together with an autocommentary, a reply by Nāgārjuna to his critics.

Save for a few fragments, the following works survive only in Tibetan and, in some cases, Chinese translation:

Yuktiṣaṣṭikā (*Sixty Verses on Reasoning*);

Śūnyatāsaptati (*Seventy Verses on Emptiness*);

Vaidalyaprakaraṇa (*The Treatise That Grinds into Little Pieces*), an attack on the categories of the Hindu epistemologists;

Ratnāvalī (*The Jewel Garland*), a long epistle apparently to a king (a shorter royal epistle attributed to Nāgārjuna is the *Suhṛllekha [Letter to a Friend]*);

Catuḥstava (four hymns).

Nāgārjuna saw his philosophy as itself part of the spiritual project of enlightenment, of "seeing things the way they really are" (*yathābhūtadarśana*). His arguments should be placed in the context of Buddhist philosophy (preceding ABHIDHARMA thought), which he both presupposed and the ontology of which he trenchantly criticized. It was Nāgārjuna who first explained philosophically the concept of ŚŪNYATĀ (EMPTINESS). According to Nāgārjuna, emptiness is a property (a *-ness*) possessed by each thing without exception. It is the property of lacking intrinsic existence (*niḥsvabhāvatā*) as a result of being one way or another, the result of causal processes. Existing is nothing more than an intersecting point of causal factors. Nāgārjuna sought to demonstrate this by asserting that if something—say, a table—*were* more than just an intersecting point of causal factors, it would prove resistant to analytical deconstruction. Absolutely nothing can resist the process of analytical deconstruction, investigating its coherence through reasoning. Thus Nāgārjuna's works embody arguments in the style of a skeptic, debunking concepts like existence and nonexistence, causation, perception, time, motion, and even religious concepts like the Buddha, or enlightenment itself. Nāgārjuna also offers methodological reflections on what he is doing, why he is not a nihilist or even really a skeptic, and how his practice fits into the overall Buddhist project. For Nāgārjuna this project is a deep "letting-go," which nevertheless also facilitates compassionate reengagement.

Nāgārjuna was enormously influential in India. The MADHYAMAKA SCHOOL of philosophy, which he probably founded, was the earliest of the two great Indian schools of MAHĀYĀNA thought. In Tibet, Madhyamaka is said to represent the highest philosophical standpoint, the final truth. In East Asian Buddhism, the influence of emptiness can be seen in Chinese and Japanese art, in poetry, in the martial arts, and even, ostensibly, in Japanese business practice.

In the West, attempts have been made to compare Nāgārjuna's thought with Immanuel Kant, G. W. F. Hegel, or Francis Herbert Bradley, and more recently with Jacques Derrida (deconstruction, particularly of egocentricity) and Ludwig Wittgenstein (liberation of others from philosophical predicaments that result from fundamentally confused preconceptions; return to the everyday world of praxis). Emptiness has also been portrayed as a philosophy of relativity, or ecological cosubsistence.

Bibliography

Bhattacharya, Kamaleswar, ed. and trans. *The Dialectical Method of Nāgārjuna (Vigrahavyāvartanī),* critically ed. E. H. Johnston and Arnold Kunst. Delhi: Motilal Banarsidass, 1978.

Hayes, Richard. "Nāgārjuna's Appeal." *Journal of Indian Philosophy* 22 (1994): 299–378.

Inada, Kenneth K. *Nāgārjuna: A Translation of His Mūlamadhyamakakārikā, with an Introductory Essay.* Tokyo: Hokuseido Press, 1970.

Lindtner, Christian. *Nāgārjuniana: Studies in the Writings and Philosophy of Nāgārjuna.* Copenhagen, Denmark: Akademisk Forlag, 1982.

Potter, Karl H., ed. *Buddhist Philosophy from 100 to 350 A.D.,* Vol. 8: *Encyclopedia of Indian Philosophies.* Delhi: Motilal Banarsidass, 1999.

Ruegg, David S. *The Literature of the Madhyamaka School of Philosophy in India.* Wiesbaden, Germany: Harrassowitz, 1981.

Tola, Fernando, and Dragonetti, Carmen. *On Voidness: A Study on Buddhist Nihilism.* Delhi: Banarsidass, 1995.

Williams, Paul. *Mahāyāna Buddhism: The Doctrinal Foundations.* London and New York: Routledge, 1989.

Williams, Paul, with Tribe, Anthony. *Buddhist Thought: A Complete Introduction to the Indian Tradition.* London and New York: Routledge, 2000.

PAUL WILLIAMS

NARA BUDDHISM

The term *Nara Buddhism* refers to Buddhist scholarship and monasteries in Nara, the first permanent capital of Japan, during the Nara period (645–794 C.E.). From the time of the official introduction of Buddhism to Japan in the mid-sixth century, the Japanese acquired a wide variety of Buddhist scriptures and other texts from Korea and China, where doctrinal schools had developed. By the Nara period, Buddhism in Japan was classified into six philosophical schools. These schools did not comprise exclusive sectarian organizations, but were custodians of doctrinal traditions studied freely by monks and nuns.

The six doctrinal traditions were: (1) the *Jōjitsu,* which denied the permanent reality of the self and the world; (2) the *Kusha,* which denied the permanent reality of the self but not the world; (3) the *Sanron,* which asserted that the self and the world are empty; (4) the *Hossō,* which asserted the nature of reality as a function of the mind; (5) the *Kegon,* which linked all existences into a web of connections; and (6) the *Ritsu,* which taught the precepts governing the lifestyle of monks and nuns. Large monasteries such as Tōdaiji, Kōfukuji, and Tōshōdaiji served as home bases for these schools.

Nara Buddhism was incorporated into the government, which enforced a legal code for monks and nuns. The code prohibited clergy from practicing and propagating Buddhism in the countryside and restricted them to their home monasteries. The government also limited the annual number of monks receiving ordination, which could only be carried out at an officially sanctioned ordination platform. The court conferred ranks on leading monks, thus creating a sense of gratitude and obligation as well as a chain of command used to regulate the clerical community. The official system gave rise to illegal monks, who were often self-ordained and worked freely among the people.

The court also created a national system, the PROVINCIAL TEMPLE SYSTEM (KOKUBUNJI, RISHŌTŌ). The central monastery was Tōdaiji, which established a branch monastery in each of the provinces. This national system emphasized the power of the court as the central political authority, and also placed Buddhism in the service of the nation. The provincial monasteries were dedicated to the ritual protection of the country.

Large families and clans also built private monasteries. Kōfukuji, for example, was the clan monastery for the powerful Fujiwara family. At the family level, Buddhist rites were conducted for the well-being of the clan, and for commemorating their ancestors. Nara Buddhism thus consisted of the national system, family monasteries, and illegal monks working among the people.

Late in the Nara period, the monk DŌKYŌ (d.u.–772) gained political power through an intimate relationship with a reigning empress, and attempted to usurp the throne. The scandal highlighted the significant power and influence that the Nara Buddhist establishment had gained, and the court, for many reasons including its concern about Buddhist interference, decided to move the capital out of Nara. The new permanent capital was located in Heian-kyō (now known as Kyoto), and while Nara continued to be an important site for Buddhist learning and practice, new forms of Buddhism, namely Tendai (Chinese, TIANTAI SCHOOL) and Shingon, arose in the succeeding Heian period (794–1185).

See also: **Japan; Japanese Royal Family and Buddhism; Nationalism and Buddhism; Shingon Buddhism, Japan**

Bibliography

de Bary, William Theodore; Keene, Donald; Tanabe, George; and Varley, Paul. *Sources of Japanese Tradition,* 2nd edition, Vol. 1. New York: Columbia University Press, 2001.

Kitagawa, Joseph M. *Religion in Japanese History.* New York: Columbia University Press, 1966.

GEORGE J. TANABE, JR.

NĀROPA

Nāropa (1016–1100) was an Indian tantric adept and scholar who is counted among the eighty-four MAHĀSIDDHAS, or great adepts. He is widely revered in Tibet for his tantric instructions. According to one of his traditional biographies, Nāropa was born to royal parents in a brahman family of Bengal. At the age of eleven he traveled to Kashmir in northwest India and after a brief period of Buddhist study, he was forced to marry at the age of seventeen. The marriage lasted only eight years, after which the couple divorced by mutual consent; Nāropa's former wife (or sister according to some sources) has been identified as Niguma, who became an influential tantric teacher in her own right. Nāropa received monastic ordination and in 1049 entered the Buddhist university of Nālandā, in present-day Bihar. He excelled as a scholar and subsequently served a term as abbot and senior instructor at Nālandā, where he was given the name Abhayakīrti.

In 1057, however, he reached a turning point in his career. One day, in the midst of his philosophical studies, he was surprised by a vision of an old, haggard woman—in reality a ḌĀKINĪ goddess. She challenged the level of his spiritual insight and, through her provocative intervention, the prodigious scholar realized that although he understood the literal words of his religious texts, he did not yet fathom their underlying meaning. The woman compelled Nāropa to abandon his post at the university and seek his destined spiritual master, the great tantric adept Tilopa (988–1069), a figure about whom scant historical information exists. During his extended search across northern India, Nāropa repeatedly encountered Tilopa in various guises, although he was unable to recognize the guru in his true form. Finally, as Nāropa was driven to the brink of despair and even suicide, Tilopa revealed himself and accepted the seeker as a worthy disciple.

In the ensuing years, Tilopa famously subjected Nāropa to a series of twelve greater and twelve lesser trials, inflicting upon him the most terrible forms of abuse and physical punishment. Nāropa persevered, however, eventually coming to understand these ordeals as a means for purifying his past negative actions. Among the seminal instructions Tilopa taught were the Four Transmissions (*bka' babs bzhi*). Although the list varies according to different sources, the four are often enumerated as the transmissions of illusory body (*sgyu lus*), dreams (*mi lam*), radiant light (*'od gsal*), and inner heat (*gtum mo*). Nāropa later codified these instructions and transmitted them to his own principal disciples, including the Tibetan translator MAR PA (MARPA; 1002/1012–1097), who then carried them to Tibet. This system, known in Tibetan as the Six Doctrines (or Yogas) of Nāropa (Nā ro chos drug), was promulgated by numerous Buddhist sects, but became especially associated with the BKA' BRGYUD (KAGYU). The Bka' brgyud sect subsequently came to view Nāropa as an important founder of their lineage. Several works of spiritual songs and tantric commentarial literature attributed to Nāropa are preserved in the Tibetan Buddhist canon.

See also: **Tibet**

Bibliography

Guenther, Herbert V. *The Life and Teaching of Nāropa.* Boston and London: Shambhala, 1986.

Mullin, Glen H. *Tsongkhapa's Six Yogas of Nāropa.* Ithaca, NY: Snow Lion, 1996.

Mullin, Glen H. *Readings on the Six Yogas of Nāropa.* Ithaca, NY: Snow Lion, 1997.

ANDREW QUINTMAN

NATIONALISM AND BUDDHISM

Buddhists traditionally maintained close ties with established political authority, which typically meant KINGSHIP. When the global system of nation-states began to develop in earnest during the nineteenth century, Buddhists too began to engage in nationalist imaginings. The linear, progressive, and essentialist concept of nation is a modern construct. Researchers have attributed the following characteristics to nationalism: global industrialization, the development of print capitalism and of modern science and technology, and the pursuit of status and respect.

There is an affinity between modernity and nationalism and between Buddhism and nationalism. For example, "Zen nationalism" was born through the process of interaction between Japanese Buddhism and Western modernity. As a way of defending Buddhism during the MEIJI BUDDHIST REFORM, the Japanese created what they termed New Buddhism, a "modern, cosmopolitan, humanistic, and socially responsible" form of the tradition (Sharf, "Buddhist Modernism," p. 247). Robert Sharf notes that the contemporary version of Zen Buddhism is an offspring of this New Buddhism. Japanese Zen Buddhists employed Western discourse to create the new tradition and eventually presented it as being superior to Western modernity. This universalizing discourse of Zen implied the cultural superiority of Japanese Buddhism.

Similarly, the universalism of religion and the particularism of nationalism go hand in hand, despite their apparent differences. Religion remains a strong force, if not an active accomplice, in the formation of nationalism. Kenneth Wells points out that Korean Protestants, for example, had no difficulty in retaining their identities as both Koreans and Protestants. Korean Protestants fused their religion and nationalism by trying to incorporate their Christian beliefs into the process of nation building. The same may also be said for Buddhist nationalism.

Buddhist responses

During the latter half of the nineteenth and the first half of the twentieth centuries, most Buddhists in Sri Lanka, China, Korea, and Japan faced similar political and social changes due to the colonial expansion of the West. To these Asian Buddhists, who had theretofore enjoyed stability, Western invasions initiated crises that threatened the survival of the religion. The rapid influx of Western civilization brought about chaotic disturbances to the traditional social and political equilibrium; Asian Buddhists could no longer enjoy their privileged status in the traditional order. Some Asian intellectuals began to believe that their traditional religions, including Buddhism, were superstitious and backward, and thus obstacles to the modernization process. Under these circumstances, Buddhist institutions throughout Asia soon became the target of attack and they found themselves surrounded by rapidly secularizing societies.

The survival of Buddhism depended largely on the capability and willingness of Buddhists to adapt their religion not only to Western modernity but also to the new political structure of nation-states that emerged as a result of interaction with the West. In particular, the rapid dissemination of Christianity awakened Buddhists to the imminent nature of the challenges they were facing. Whether Buddhism could demonstrate its viability in this new context became a pivotal point for the continuance of the religion.

Buddhists participated in nationalist movements, often embracing nationalism in the name of modernization. Buddhism was reappropriated in terms of issues central to Protestantism and the Enlightenment, namely, anticlericism, this-worldly engagement, rational and pragmatic inclination, and individualism. In this process of reappropriation, religious identity was formed and intensified. The emergence of religious identity instilled national pride in many Buddhists. Buddhism was regarded as their indigenous heritage vis-à-vis the imported Western religion of Christianity.

In Sri Lanka, the challenge of Christian missionaries sharpened the Buddhist sense of self-identity. It took much time and prolonged attack from Christian missionaries before the Sinhala Buddhists entered into polemical debates with them. Before the 1860s Buddhists did not react in any organized way to the hostile attacks of Christianity. With the developing self-awareness prompted by the need to respond to Christian inroads, however, Buddhists began to refute the coexistence of variant religious practices that characterized their traditional religion. Buddhists tried to purge such popular elements as spirit cults, magic, and astrology from their practices. They took a fundamentalist approach, attempting to return to what they considered to be canonical Buddhism.

Furthermore, the history of organized Buddhism in Sri Lanka was identified with the history of the nation, and Buddhism was promoted as a way to defend the

Monks carrying Vietnamese flags march past the mausoleum of Ho Chi Minh during an Independence Day parade in Hanoi, Vietnam, 2000. AP/Wide World Photos. Reproduced by permission.

nation from the colonial West. ANAGĀRIKA DHARMAPĀLA (1864–1933), a lay celibate, urged the Sinhalese to restore their true identity as Buddhists by discarding foreign influences. Buddhist intellectuals adopted nationalism in order to confer cultural identity and ethnic consciousness on the Sinhalese.

In China, under the name of modernization, the state campaigned to eradicate "superstitious" practices and to convert religious properties for public purposes. The late Qing dynasty (1644–1911) targeted Buddhist properties as financial resources to rebuild the country and to defend against the threat imposed by Western imperial powers. The Chinese Buddhist establishment, which already had suffered severe devastation during the Taiping rebellion in the mid-nineteenth century, faced the persistent recurrence of violence. The state withdrew its official protection of Buddhism in 1900 and issued a general order to convert temple property to schools.

Under these circumstances, Chinese Buddhists also presented Buddhism as their traditional religion and attempted to use their religion to counterbalance the challenges of Christianity and Western cultural encroachment. Liang Qichao (1873–1929) contended that the Chinese made Buddhism their own by creating their own indigenous schools of Buddhist philosophy and practice. In his presentation of the tradition, Chinese Buddhism encompassed both philosophical and religious attributes, while Christianity rested on the delusive beliefs of a shallow philosophy.

In Japan, the Meiji state (1868–1912) supported the active importation of Western civilization. Under the guise of modernization, the state inflicted severe blows to the Buddhist establishment. Starting in the mid-seventeenth century, anti-Buddhist measures had begun in individual domains. The Meiji government carried out these anti-Buddhist policies nationwide, equating Buddhism with the previous Tokugawa regime and forging a distinctive Shintō national ideology by separating Shintō from Buddhism. The Office of Proselytization was set up by Shintō propagandists in 1869 to promote Shintō as the national creed. The separation of Buddhism and Shintō led to a massive anti-Buddhist movement that resulted in the destruction of great numbers of Buddhist institutions. The government further developed its policy of disestablishing Buddhism in 1871 and 1872.

Japanese Buddhists offered their services to the government in order to soften the ongoing persecution. They tried to prove Buddhism's value by supporting national policies. Japanese Buddhists claimed that Buddhism was the indigenous religious practice of Japan and that the Japanese version of the religion was the consummation of all previous developments within Asian Buddhism. They also promoted Buddhism as a way to defend their nation against the incursions of Christianity. Along with growing nationalist sentiments, they identified themselves as protectors of Japanese tradition against the encroachments of Western culture, including Christianity.

Korean Buddhists developed their sense of national identity around the turn of the twentieth century, beginning with the opening of the nation to the Western world in 1876 and the subsequent colonization by Japan in 1910. Awakened by the influx of Western modernity, and threatened by the rapid growth of Christianity and Japanese Buddhism on the peninsula, Korean Buddhists developed a sense of their own independent identity. They attempted to present Buddhism as a source of national identity by identifying it as the backbone of Korean history and culture. They began to consolidate their own identity as distinct from that of Japanese Buddhists, in particular, and to write their own history.

Overall, Buddhist nationalism arose in response to the influx of Western civilization. Buddhists presented the religion as being useful to the nation and reclaimed its status as a traditional religion, in opposition to the imported Christian traditions of the West.

The problematic nature of Buddhist nationalism

For an understanding of Buddhist nationalism, however, a more nuanced approach is needed. When the ethnicity of the rulers was the same as that of the governed, Buddhist nationalism posed no difficulties. Japanese Buddhists, for instance, became faithful followers of state policies, identifying themselves with the nation-state. By the mid-Meiji period, Buddhism managed to present itself as the essence of Japanese culture. Buddhist leaders actively joined the state's military policies. They endorsed and rationalized imperial policies during the Sino-Japanese War (1894) and the Russo-Japanese War (1904). They sent war missionaries to the battlefields to comfort soldiers. They also organized the Buddhist Society for the Defense of the Nation during World War I and became involved in the state's war effort during the Pacific War.

In contrast, Buddhists under colonial governments displayed confusing behaviors in their development of nationalism. The Buddhist clergy in Sri Lanka, for example, pursued formal recognition from, and the patronage of, the colonial government. They asked persistently for state intervention in the maintenance and supervision of Buddhist temporalities. Kitsiri Malalgoda suggests that these ties with foreign rulers account for the fact that the Sinhala Buddhist revival movements did not develop into a concerted movement for national independence. The Chinese SAṄGHA also showed ambivalence when their religious interests and national interests diverged. Chinese monasteries voluntarily subjected themselves to Japanese Buddhist schools to protect their property. They rushed to register their monasteries with major Japanese Buddhist denominations to solicit protection from the Japanese consulate. The Chinese saṅgha was accused of collaborating with the Japanese after the Japanese commenced a campaign of military conquest in 1937.

During the colonial period, the Korean Buddhist saṅgha also maintained close ties with the Japanese regime, seeking favors from it. The majority of Korean Buddhist leaders tacitly or overtly acquiesced to the Japanese policy of "Japan and Korea Are One Entity," which aimed to eradicate Korean identity. Some Korean monks gave lectures in support of the Japanese war effort during the 1940s and even made consolatory visits to the Japanese imperial army, submitting to the demands of the Japanese regime.

The political ambivalence and impotence of Buddhists resulted in liaisons with those in power, no matter who they were. Japanese Buddhists followed imperialist policies out of their collective interest in protecting their establishments and in consonance with their traditional subservience to political authority. The saṅgha's traditional dependence on the ruling court produced further confusion among Sinhala, Chinese, and Korean Buddhists. This ambivalence toward the state attests to the complexity of Buddhist nationalism.

This complexity derives partly from the fact that the concept of nation is unstable and a source of contention. There are many different versions of *nation* and *nationalism,* such as the nation-state and the "ethnic nation." Japanese Buddhists identified the state with nation, faithfully supporting its policies. In comparison, Sri Lanka developed its own version of nation, while recognizing the confinement of the colonial state. Likewise, Korean Buddhists also separated nation from state. At the same time, the Japanese colonial state did not entirely deny the development of ethnic nationalism, as long as the nation-state was not threatened. After 1930 the Japanese regime even participated in the creation of national identity for Koreans. For the efficient operation of the nation-state, the Japanese colonial government felt that it needed to create homogeneous national subjects, even as it treated Koreans as second-class citizens.

Asian Buddhists forged their religious identity and redefined the role of Buddhism in response to Western modernity and the concept of the nation-state. Buddhists adopted social tactics and nationalist stances in order to prove the utility of the religion, so that the status of Buddhism in society would be improved. The accommodations they reached with colonial powers, however, account for the Buddhists' insensitivity to, and occasional collaborations with, imperial war, social injustice, and military occupation.

See also: **Christianity and Buddhism; Colonialism and Buddhism; Shintō (Honji Suijaku) and Buddhism**

Bibliography

Anderson, Benedict. *Imagined Communities: Reflections of the Origin and Spread of Nationalism.* London: Verso, 1983. Revised edition, 1991.

Bond, George. *The Buddhist Revival in Sri Lanka: Religious Tradition, Reinterpretation, and Response.* Columbia: University of South Carolina Press, 1988.

Buswell, Robert E., Jr. "Imagining 'Korean Buddhism': The Invention of a National Religious Tradition." In *Nationalism and the Construction of Korean Identity,* ed. Hyung Il Pai and Timothy R. Tangherlini. Berkeley, CA: Institute of East Asian Studies, 1998.

Gellner, Ernest. *Nations and Nationalism.* Oxford: Blackwell, 1983.

Gombrich, Richard, and Obeyesekere, Gananath. *Buddhism Transformed: Religious Change in Sri Lanka.* Princeton, NJ: Princeton University Press. 1988.

Greenfeld, Liah. "Transcending the Nation's Worth." *Daedalus* 122, no. 3 (1993): 47–62.

Heisig, James, and Maraldo, John, eds. *Rude Awakenings: Zen, the Kyoto School, and the Question of Nationalism.* Honolulu: University of Hawaii Press, 1995.

Ketelaar, James. *Of Heretics and Martyrs in Meiji Japan: Buddhism and Its Persecution.* Princeton, NJ: Princeton University Press, 1990.

Lopez, Donald S., Jr., ed. *Curators of the Buddha: the Study of Buddhism under Colonialism.* Chicago: University of Chicago Press, 1995.

Malalgoda, Kitsiri. *Buddhism in Sinhalese Society 1750–1900: A Study of Religious Revival and Change.* Berkeley: University of California Press, 1976.

Sharf, Robert. "Buddhist Modernism and the Rhetoric of Meditative Experience." *Numen* 42 (1995): 228–283.

Sharf, Robert. "Whose Zen? Zen Nationalism Revisited." In *Rude Awakenings: Zen, the Kyoto School, and the Question of Nationalism,* ed. James W. Heisig and John C. Maraldo. Honolulu: University of Hawaii Press, 1995.

Welch, Holmes. *The Buddhist Revival in China.* Cambridge, MA: Harvard University Press, 1968.

Wells, Kenneth. *New God, New Nation: Protestants and Self-Reconstruction Nationalism in Korea, 1896–1937.* Honolulu: University of Hawaii Press, 1990.

Wright, Arthur F. "Buddhism in Modern and Contemporary China." In *Religion and Change in Contemporary Asia,* ed. Robert F. Spencer. Minneapolis: University of Minnesota Press, 1971.

PORI PARK

NENBUTSU (CHINESE, NIANFO; KOREAN, YŎMBUL)

Nenbutsu, also transcribed as *nembutsu* (Chinese, *nianfo*; Korean, *yŏmbul*), is the religious practice in PURE LAND BUDDHISM of chanting or invoking the name of the Buddha Amida (Sanskrit, AMITĀBHA or Amitāyus; Chinese, Amituo). There are many buddhas whose names can be chanted, but in practice, *nenbutsu* typically refers to chanting Amida's name. In Japan, the practice consists of reciting the six-character formula *Namu Amida Butsu* (Chinese, *Namo Amituo fo*), "Homage to Amida Buddha." This invocation can be spoken once or repeatedly. Commonly it is intoned as a melodic chant, but can also be uttered in ordinary intonation. It is sometimes used as an ancillary practice in meditative trance or visualization, but more frequently it is performed as an independent and self-contained practice. Buddhist liturgy, especially of the Pure Land tradition, typically contains sections or interludes of *nenbutsu* chanting.

Religious chanting, which was common in Buddhism from an ancient period, no doubt influenced the development of the *nenbutsu.* But another influence was the practice of reflecting or meditating on the Buddha. In fact, *nenbutsu* literally means thinking on the Buddha or keeping him in mind (*Buddhānusmṛti*). To that extent, it does not explicitly denote verbal activity. But since chanting sacred syllables or names often accompanied meditation, the practice of intoning the Buddha's name coalesced with the idea of keeping him in mind. Over the centuries there emerged two primary views of *nenbutsu* chanting: One treated it as an aid to visualizing the Buddha, which was considered a practice leading to enlightenment; the other treated it as an act resulting in birth in Amida's Pure Land paradise. The two, however, often overlapped. In Japan, the verbal practice eventually overshadowed visualization, so that *nenbutsu* came to mean invoking Amida's name without necessarily meditating on him, though mental awareness of the Buddha was always considered one aspect of saying his name.

See also: **Buddhānusmṛti (Recollection of the Buddha); Chanting and Liturgy; Pure Land Schools**

Bibliography

Andrews, Allan A. "Pure Land Buddhist Hermeneutics: Hōnen's Interpretation of Nembutsu." *Journal of the International Association of Buddhist Studies* 10, no. 2 (1987): 7–25.

Fujiwara, Ryosetsu. *The Way to Nirvana: The Concept of the Nembutsu in Shan-tao's Pure Land Buddhism.* Tokyo: Kyoiku Shincho Sha, 1974.

Hori, Ichiro. "Nembutsu as Folk Religion." In *Folk Religion in Japan: Continuity and Change,* ed. Joseph M. Kitagawa and Alan L. Miller. Chicago: University of Chicago Press, 1968.

Pas, Julian. *Visions of Sukhāvatī: Shan-tao's Commentary on the Kuan Wu-Liang-Shou-Fo Ching.* Albany: State University of New York Press, 1995.

JAMES C. DOBBINS

NEO-CONFUCIANISM. *See* **Confucianism and Buddhism**

NEPAL

Like most of the Himalayan region, the valley called Nepal was a frontier zone until the modern state's creation in 1769. The area absorbed and interpreted Indic cultural influences from the south and, later, from the Tibetan region to the north. This entry will discuss the history of the early Indic traditions in the Kathmandu valley, the Tibetan Buddhist lineages originating from the Tibetan plateau, the Newar-supported MAHĀYĀNA traditions, and the recently imported THERAVĀDA tradition.

Early Buddhism in the Licchavi era

The earliest historical records of the central Himalayan region—more than two hundred Sanskrit inscriptions made by kings of a ruling dynasty who referred to themselves by the name Licchavi—are found in the Nepal valley beginning in 464 C.E. These inscriptions indicate that Hindu temple institutions existed alongside Buddhist monastic traditions in a harmonious relationship confirmed by the Chinese pilgrim XUANZANG around 640 C.E. This relationship has endured up to the present day. The Licchavi inscriptions reveal connections between the Nepal valley and the traditions of monasticism and patronage that originated across the Gangetic plain from the time of the Buddha. There are references in the inscriptions to MONKS and NUNS from over a dozen discrete saṅghas residing in land-owning vihāras (monasteries) and enjoying the support of prominent local merchants and caravan leaders. The most frequently mentioned saṅgha is that of the MAHĀSĀṂGHIKA SCHOOL.

These early monasteries were centers of a predominantly Mahāyāna culture, with the inscriptions providing only a few hints of Vajrayāna practice. Monastic precincts reveal verses of praise addressed to Śākyamuni and other buddhas, as well as shrines to the celestial bodhisattvas Manjuśrī, Vajrapāṇi, Samantabhadra, and—most frequently—Avalokiteśvara. Donations of STŪPAS, in several instances by nuns, are also mentioned. Nepal's earliest monasteries charged monks with maintaining law and civic order in settlements built on lands donated to them, a custom that is unattested in Indian sources. Examples of similar duties are also found in the records of the residents (*mandalis*) of contemporaneous Hindu temples.

Tibetan monasticism across the Himalayan highlands

Tibetan texts recount how great Indian sages came up through the Nepal valley to establish Buddhist traditions on the Tibetan plateau. Later legends describe their subduing demons and establishing communities of devotees. Although the history of these first Himalayan monasteries remains obscure, some may have been established by the great siddha PADMASAMBHAVA (ca. late eighth century) or his disciples. Texts composed to recount the lives of ATISHA (982–1054) and

Nepalese lay Buddhists circumambulate the Bodhanath Stūpa in Kathmandu, Nepal, 1997.

MAR PA (MARPA; 1002/1012–1097) describe their sojourns visiting still-recognized valley locations.

Once Buddhism was firmly established in central Tibet as a result of its second introduction (ca. 1050 C.E.), the northernmost settlements of modern highland Nepal became sites where monasteries were established by every major school of Tibetan Buddhism. These areas include Humla in the far west, as well as (from west to east) Dolpo, Lo-Mustang, Nyeshang, Nupri, Manang, Langtang, Helambu, Solu-Khumbu, and Walung. Local boys interested in training to become senior monks would travel to central Tibet and return to maintain local institutions that typically sheltered, at most, a dozen or so monks whose main occupation was ritual service. This same pattern occurred for the BON faith in a few of these regions.

There was a second level of connection with the monastic networks of central Tibet established among the Tibeto-Burman–speaking peoples living in the mid-hills, including the Magars, Gurungs, Tamangs, and Sherpas. Many of these peoples followed the RNYING MA (NYINGMA) school and relied on householder lamas to perform Buddhist rituals for their villages. To train for this service, young men typically lived for several years as apprentices with elder householder lamas or in the regional highland monasteries. Most returned to marry and maintain shrines established as their family's own property. Thus, most "Buddhist monasteries" among Tibeto-Burman peoples were (and are) family shrine-residences, and sons usually succeed their fathers as local Buddhist ritualists.

By the early Malla era (1350 C.E.) Tibetan monks came to the Nepal valley to acquire tantric initiations, ritual practices, and texts from resident masters (Newars and others), traditions they conveyed up to the highlands. Some Tibetan monks also established branch monasteries affiliated with the main Tibetan schools; the first were located near the monumental stūpas at Svayambhū and Bauddha. Notable Tibetan teachers probably influenced the practices of Newar Buddhists.

Although the Hindu state of Nepal, which was established in 1769, did not favor Buddhism and tried to make Buddhists conform to brahmanical laws, the traditions and loyalty of most Buddhist ethnic groups has endured, as have Nepal's family-based monasteries. Since 1990 the strength of Buddhist identity that is held together by these institutions among the Tibeto-Burman groups has become the basis of ethnic nationalism directed against the high caste dominated Hindu state.

The Kathmandu valley is now one of the most important centers of Tibetan Buddhism in the world for several reasons. First, one of the world's largest concentrations of Tibetan refugees has settled in the Kathmandu valley, where they have focused on building institutions for their communities. Some of the profits generated by the carpet-weaving industry have been used to expand the initial structures and build new monasteries. Second, since about 1970, many of the most affluent Tibeto-Burman Buddhists from Nepal have chosen to establish homes in the valley, both for business and political purposes. Prominent donors from this community have bought lands and built monasteries that have drawn monks or nuns from their home regions. Finally, as Tibetan Buddhism has become increasingly attractive to Westerners, prominent Tibetan lamas funded by their donations have established "dharma centers" that in most ways resemble traditional monasteries. Here one can find textual study and meditation being pursued by both ethnic Tibetans and Westerners clad in monastic robes.

Newar Buddhism (1000 C.E. to the present)

By the early Malla era, the valley had become an important regional center active in domesticating an indigenous Indic Mahāyāna Buddhism. Nepalese monks developed a highly ritualized Buddhist culture among the Newars, whose life-cycle rites, Mahāyāna festivals, and temple ritualism reached high levels of articulation. It was VAJRAYĀNA Buddhism and tantric initiation that assumed the highest position in local understanding, though only a few practiced esoteric traditions. MONASTIC ARCHITECTURE reflects this development: In the large courtyards that define the monastic space, the shrines facing the entrance have, on the ground floor, an image of Śākyamuni, but on the first floor above is the *āgama*, a shrine with a Vajrayāna deity, with access limited to those with tantric initiation.

By the later Malla era (1425–1769 C.E.), when Hindu shrines and law were in the ascendancy, Newar Buddhism underwent many changes and assumed roughly the form extant today. This era was marked by the building of many new vihāras, but there was also a literal domestication of the saṅgha, wherein former monks became householders. These Newar householder monks called themselves *Bare* (from the Sanskrit term *vande* or *vandanā*, an ancient Indic term of respect for monks), adopted the names *śākyabhikṣu*, and *vajrācārya*, and began to function as endogamous castes. This meant that one had to be born into the saṅgha and, with a few exceptions, everyone else was prohibited from being admitted. Thus, ordination into celibate monastic life was possible only in the local Tibetan saṅghas. The Newar saṅghas were probably transforming their tradition to conform to caste laws and thereby preserve the social and legal standing of the Buddhist community, as well as their extensive monastic land holdings. Since that time, those wanting to become adult members of the Newar saṅgha must first undergo (in local parlance) śrāvaka-styled celibate ordination (usually taking three days), then Mahāyāna-styled initiation into what is referred to as the bodhisattva saṅgha.

Many contemporary Newar monasteries, especially in Patan, still bear the name of their founding patrons, some dating back to the early Malla period. Local Buddhist monks, like Hindu *paṇḍitas* (scholars), were especially active in manuscript copying; by the modern era, Buddhist monastic libraries had became a vast repository of Sanskrit texts.

Unlike the monastic institutions of Tibet that fostered in-depth philosophical inquiry and vast commentarial writings, Newar monks produced few original contributions to Buddhist scholarship. The Newar saṅgha's focus was the performance of rituals drawing upon deities and powers of the Mahāyāna-Vajrayāna Buddhist tradition. Like married Tibetan monks of the Rnying ma order, *vajrācārya* priests serve the community's ritual needs, with some specializing in textual study, medicine, astrology, and meditation. Lifelong ritual relations link householders to family *vajrācārya* priests, which some have called "Buddhist brahmins." Their ritual services are vast, including Buddhist versions of Hindu life-cycle rites (saṃskāra), fire rites (*homa*), daily temple rituals (*nitya pūjā*), MANTRA chanting protection rites, merit-producing donation rites, stūpa rituals, chariot festivals (ratha jātra), and tantric initiation (*abhiṣeka*). Some of these cultural performances were noted centuries ago in India. In Kathmandu's Itum Bāhā one can still observe monks rapping on wooden gongs to mark time, a monastic custom begun over two thousands years ago in ancient India. The "Mahāyāna cult of the book" endures as well. In this and many other respects, Newars continue the evolutionary patterns of ritual practice and lay ideals of later Indic Buddhism. Claims that "Indian Buddhism died out" defy geography and ignore the ongoing survival of Newar Buddhism.

Once the Newar kings were ousted by the Shah dynasty from Gorkha that unified the modern state in 1769, discrimination against Buddhists and changes in land tenure laws undermined the tenancy system that had supported the domesticated Newar monastic institution. At its peak, Newar Buddhists had established over three hundred monasteries. Today, roughly 10 percent have all but disappeared and more than 50 percent are in perilous structural condition. The majority of the monasteries, however, still function and most of the remainder can still be located using modern records.

The cities of Kathmandu and Patan both have a system of main monasteries (*mu bāhā*), eighteen and fifteen, respectively; each monastery is linked to one or more satellite monasteries. Every householder monk is ordained in one of these monasteries, though they may reside in one of the several hundred branch monasteries affiliated with the main monasteries. A system of rotation requires that each ordained male perform the monastic daily ritual duties periodically. Bhaktapur and other smaller towns in the Kathmandu valley also have *bāhās,* but each is an independent entity. Newar monasteries are now ruled by the senior male members of their individual saṅghas, which makes reform or innovation within the local saṅgha difficult. From the Shah-era conquest in 1769 until the present, Newar Mahāyāna Buddhism has been gradually weakening as a cultural force due to the loss of landed income and leadership. Yet despite the decline of the monasteries as buildings and institutions, much is still preserved in the elaborate monastic architecture, the thousands of archived texts, and the wealth of cultural observances.

The typical Newar *bāhā* is situated around a courtyard. The main entrance, often ornamented by a tympanum, usually has small shrines dedicated to the monastery guardians Ganesh and Mahākāla, which flank the passageway leading into the main courtyard. Opposite the entrance is the main shrine building. On the ground floor is the *kwāpa dyah,* usually Śākyamuni Buddha, flanked by images of his two great disciples, MAHĀMAUDGALĀYANA and ŚĀRIPUTRA. Stairs within the main shrine building lead to the *āgama,* a tantric shrine that is opened only to adults who have received the appropriate Vajrayāna initiation. The windows and the door, including another tympanum, are often adorned by elaborate wood carvings.

One of the most important changes that Shah rule brought to the middle hill regions of the country was the expansion of trade, and this was commonly in the hands of Newars who migrated to trade towns. The thousands who left the valley brought their prominently Buddhist culture with them. Thus, in towns such as (from east to west) Daran, Dhankuta, Chainpur, Bhojpur, Dolakha, Trisuli, Bandipur, Pokhara, Palpa, and Baglung, Newar Buddhists built *bāhās* as branch institutions of those in their home cities.

Theravāda Buddhism

Since the mid-twentieth century, Newars who have become disenchanted with their form of Mahāyāna monasticism have supported the establishment of Theravāda Buddhist reform institutions in the Kathmandu valley. Inspired by teachers from Sri Lanka, Burma, Thailand, and India, Newars "entered the robes" and some founded institutions in the large cities that are dedicated to the revival of Buddhism based upon textual study, popular preaching, and lay meditation.

Beginning with the Ānandakuṭī Monastery at Svayambhū for monks and the Dharmakīrti dormitory for nuns in central Kathmandu, Newars have been ordained and have renounced the householder life to live in these institutions. Technically, the ancient order of nuns has died out in Theravāda countries; the term *anagārika* is used locally, although the women conform to most vinaya rules, including celibacy.

Theravāda institutions have been instrumental to promoting the modernist "Protestant Buddhism" originating in colonial Sri Lanka. These institutions have subtly critiqued Newar and Tibetan Mahāyāna beliefs and practices, while seeking to revive the faith by promoting textual study and vernacular translations, scheduling popular preaching, and spreading the practice of lay meditation. Other independent meditation centers started by Goenka, a lay teacher from India, have since the early 1980s gained considerable popularity. Theravāda monasteries and meditation centers are now found in most major towns of the Kathmandu valley of Nepal.

See also: **Himalayas, Buddhist Art in; Newari, Buddhist Literature in**

Bibliography

Dowman, Keith. "A Buddhist Guide to the Power Places of the Kathmandu Valley." *Kailash* 9, nos. 3–4 (1982): 183–291.

Gellner, David N. *Monk, Householder and Tantric Priest: Newar Buddhism and Its Hierarchy of Ritual.* Cambridge, UK: Cambridge University Press, 1992.

Hutt, Michael. *Nepal: A Guide to the Art and Architecture of the Kathmandu Valley.* Boston: Shambhala, 1994.

Lewis, Todd T. "Newars and Tibetans in the Kathmandu Valley: Ethnic Boundaries and Religious History." *Journal of Asian and African Studies* 38 (1989): 31–57.

Lewis, Todd T. *Popular Buddhist Texts from Nepal: Narratives and Rituals of Newar Buddhism.* Albany: State University of New York Press, 2000.

Lienhard, Siegfried. "Nepal: The Survival of Indian Buddhism in a Himalayan Kingdom." In *The World of Buddhism,* ed. Heinz Bechert and Richard F. Gombrich. New York: Facts on File, 1984.

Locke, John K. "The Vajrayāna Buddhism in the Kathmandu Valley." In *The Buddhist Heritage of Nepal.* Kathmandu, Nepal: Dharmodaya Sabba, 1986.

Ramble, Charles. "How Buddhist Are Buddhist Communities? The Construction of Tradition in Two Lamaist Communities." *Journal of the Anthropological Society of Oxford* 21, no. 2 (1990): 185–197.

Riccardi, Theodore, Jr. "Buddhism in Ancient and Early Medieval Nepal." In *Studies in the History of Buddhism,* ed. A. K. Narain. New Delhi: B. R. Publishing, 1980.

Slusser, Mary S. *Nepal Mandala.* Princeton, NJ: Princeton University Press, 1982.

Snellgrove, David. "Buddhism in Nepal." In *Indo-Tibetan Buddhism,* Vol. 2. Boston: Shambhala, 1987.

Toffin, Gerard. *Societe et religion chez les Newar du Nepal.* Paris: CNRS, 1984.

TODD T. LEWIS

NEPAL, BUDDHIST ART IN. *See* **Himalayas, Buddhist Art in**

NEWARI, BUDDHIST LITERATURE IN

Beginning with Sanskrit inscriptions dating from the fifth century C.E., the large mid-montane Himalayan valley called Nepal has been a vibrant cultural center where both Hindu and Buddhist traditions have flourished. What is called "Nepal" today was formed after 1769 when the modern Shah state expanded across the region, conquering the valley city-states and making Kathmandu its capital. The first cities and religious monuments of this valley were built by the Newars, the earliest attested ethnic group of the region. Newars speak a nontonal Tibeto-Burman language called *Newari* in the Euro-American world, but referred to by Newars as *Nepāl Bhāṣā,* using Sanskritic terminology, or *Newā: Bhāy* in the spoken vernacular. This language has been thoroughly influenced by Sanskrit vocabulary, especially in the technical terms imported from the Indic traditions that shaped Newar culture. Newari texts have similarly been written using north Indian-derived scripts, the earliest on palm leaves (*tāra patra*), and from the seventeenth century onward on paper made from the daphne plant. In the latter form, the texts were written on stacked rectangular pages, or in the format of a folded book (*thyā sāphu*). Many such books were illustrated with finely rendered miniature paintings, some with fifty to one hundred images.

Since this valley was from its origins a Himalayan trade and pilgrimage center, and later a refuge for Buddhist monks fleeing the destruction of north Indian monasteries in the wake of the Muslim conquests that ended in 1192 C.E., many monasteries in Kathmandu, Bhaktapur, and Patan became centers of manuscript veneration, archiving, and copying. From this era onward, Tibetan scholars visited Nepal to obtain Sanskrit manuscripts and, in some cases, to confer with Nepalese *paṇḍitas.* There have been many Newar Buddhist scholars—especially among the "householder monk" groups calling themselves *śākyabhikṣus* and *vajrācāryas*—who could read and utilize Sanskrit, making it an important local language for the indigenous Buddhist elite. Some notable *paṇḍitas* up through the modern era also composed works in Sanskrit.

The vast holdings of Sanskrit manuscripts in the Kathmandu Valley have remained central to the modern academic study of Buddhism, beginning with the texts sent to Calcutta and Europe by the official British resident in Nepal from 1825 to 1843, Brian Hodgson. Many ancient Sanskrit texts survived only in Nepal. Though one might include these works as a literature used by the Newar Buddhist religious elite and other literati, the remainder of this entry focuses on the religious texts composed in the Newari vernacular.

The Newar saṅgha's widespread familiarity with Sanskrit, and especially the use of Sanskrit mantras and religious terminology, explains the existence of the many hundreds of manuscripts rendered in a bilingual

(Sanskrit and Newari) format. While the elite ritualists, adepts, and scholars used Sanskrit texts to guide their ritual practices, tantric meditations, and philosophical studies, they also redacted relevant Indic works into their own language and composed treatises in their own lingua franca. The Newar literati devised over ten calligraphic scripts, especially for manuscripts used for ritual "book pūjā" purposes: *Newā Lipi* since the ninth century, and *Rañjana* since the fourteenth century.

Vernacular Buddhist literature in Nepāl Bhāsā mirrors the distinctive cultural traditions of Newar Buddhism, which was centered on a saṅgha of "householder monks" and their focus on intricate ritual and popular narratives more than scholasticism, with VAJRAYĀNA practices important for the elite. Accordingly, no vinaya or early canonical works are extant in the bilingual collections and only fragments of any Buddhist scholastic treatises (*śastra*) have been identified. More common are MAHĀYĀNA "classics" such as the *Prajñāpāramitā-sūtra* (*Perfection of Wisdom Sūtra*), BODHICARYĀVATĀRA *(Introduction to the Conduct That Leads to Enlightenment)*, and the LOTUS SŪTRA (SADDHARMAPUṆḌARĪKA-SŪTRA).

Especially numerous are texts devoted to the celestial BODHISATTVA Avalokiteśvara, such as the *Kārandavyūha* (*Description of the Basket*). The most locally influential text in this genre is the *Guṇakaraṇḍavyūha* (*Description of the Garlanded Basket*), a Sanskrit work originally composed in Nepal that has been widely translated into Newari.

Several other important works were composed by local scholars in Sanskrit and translated into numerous Newari editions. First is the *Bhadrakalpa Avadāna* (*Glorious Stories of This Auspicious Era*), a text that recounts the Buddha's return to his hometown Kapilavastu. More important in the indigenous worldview is the *Svayambhū Purāṇa* (*The Sacred Account of Svayembhū, the Self-Existent*). It has a curious title for a Buddhist text, indicating the strong influence of Hindu traditions in Nepal. But this text recounts the Buddhist origins of the valley as a hierophany of the Ādi-Buddha as a flaming lotus in a lake, one subsequently visited by buddhas of former ages of the world. In the current era, this lake is finally drained by the Bodhisattva Mañjuśrī to form the Kathmandu Valley and opened to settlement by his disciples, making the *Svayambhū Purāṇa* a work simultaneously of Mahāyāna Buddhology and ethnic origins. This text was later expanded to include the history of tantric teachers entering the domain and to discuss the history of related sacred sites. Most important among these is the sacred hilltop now called Svayambhū Mahācaitya.

The most common manuscript genres in Newar Buddhist literature are popular narratives (JĀTAKAS and AVADĀNAS) and ritual texts. "Folklorists" in the Newar saṅgha collected, redacted, and "trans-created" (to use Kamal Prakash Malla's term) the classical tales from the JĀTAKAMĀLĀ (*Garland of Jātakas*), AVADĀNAŚATAKA (*A Hundred Glorious Deeds*), and MAHĀVASTU (*Great Story*). Some stand alone due to their popularity. These include the *Simhalasarthabāhu Avadāna,* the *Maṇicūḍa Avadāna,* the *Vīrakūśa Avadāna,* the *Kavirakumār Avadāna,* and the *Viśvantara Jātaka*; such texts have been used up to the present day by *paṇḍit*-storytellers who attract audiences for evening performances during the Newar Buddhist monsoon holy month, Gunlā. Interestingly, several of these Newar *avadāna* anthologies, such as the *Vicitrakarṇika Avadāna,* have no known classical source.

Given the embedding of story recitations into many ritual texts, it is difficult to separate the genres. Newar *panditas* have typically labeled their ritual guides as *vidhi* (directive) or *kriyā* (performance), and these span a vast repertoire from life-cycle rites and building construction rites to festival practices, temple observances, and tantric initiations. Special Mahāyāna rites called *vratas* have their own textual guides, including those dedicated to the beneficent Tārā, the fierce protector Mahākāla, the Buddhist earth mother Vasundhārā, and many others. By far the most common text in this category is that outlining the *Aṣṭamī Vrata* and dedicated to Avalokiteśvara. Of special prominence in this Newar literature are guidebooks for making 100,000 clay stūpas, the *Lakṣacaitya Vidhi,* and for the old-age ritual (*bhīmaratha kriyā*) for elders reaching seventy-seven years and seven months, which includes making a STŪPA and reciting the *Uṣṇīṣavijayā dhāraṇī.* Also important are after-death guidebooks for utilizing the *Durgatipariśodhana Tantra's* salvific mantra and a sand MAṆḌALA made by a *vajrācārya* ritualist.

Even more numerous, and variable, are the *mantra-dhāraṇī* collections. The most widespread single text is the *Pañcarakṣā* (*Five Protectors*), which provides recitations and visualizations of five protectors, each with stories testifying to their pragmatic efficacies. Other works, many reflecting the compiler's own fields of ritual expertise, are simply lists of recitations for specific purposes. These span all spheres of human experience: worshiping, memorizing, singing, healing, attracting love, rainmaking, injuring. Related to this are collections of devotional songs that can be sung by priests or by worshipers playing drums and other instruments.

Modern published literature

The printing press expanded the possibilities of Newar Buddhist piety, as devotees continue to make books for merit, memorialize the dead, pen new translations, and create hundreds of new magazines that disseminate works of scholarly interpretation and Buddhist revivalism. In these forums, partisans of traditional Newar Buddhism, as well as advocates of the THERAVĀDA movement, have sought to promote their traditions. Leading *vajrācārya* priests have continued their tradition of composing ritual guide pamphlets and anthologies for their colleagues, with such publications numbering over a thousand since 1950. Since about 1960, Theravādin scholars have published Newari translations of nearly the entire Pāli canon. Traditional *paṇḍitas* and private scholars have likewise published their own new complete Newari translations of the Mahāyāna classics, including the *Aṣṭasāhasrikā Prajnāpāramitā* by Jog Muni Vajrācārya (Kathmandu, 1968), the LALITAVISTARA by Nisthananda Vajrācārya (1978), the BODHICARYĀVATĀRA by Dibyabajra Bajrācārya (1986), and the *Saddharmapuṇḍarīka-vaipulyasūtra* by Saddharmarāja Vajrācārya (1989). Special mention should be made of *Sugata Saurabha* (*The Sweet Fragrance of the Buddha*), a book-length life of the Buddha that was written in Newari by Nepal's greatest twentieth-century poet, Chittadhar Hridaya. Newar poets have also composed songs for *bhajan* singing that have been widely published and used.

Finally, since 1950, a vast library of Newari scholarly publications has come into being. These works concern local epigraphy, texts, temples, and cultural traditions. Most notable among indigenous scholars is Hem Rāj Shākya, whose monographs on the Svayambhū stūpa (1977), the *Samyak* festival (1980), and other monuments testify to the Newars' vigorous love of their own culture and the continuing high regard in Newar society for literary works on Buddhism. The views of a medieval copyist are still discernible at the beginning of the twenty-first century: "I have written this manuscript painstakingly. Try your best to protect and preserve this MSS from oil stains, fire, and thieves. Look after it as you would your own offspring because while writing this mss my backbone, my head, and my eyesight have all bent downward" (Vaidya and Kamsakar, p. iv).

See also: Nepal

Bibliography

Lewis, Todd T. "Mahāyāna *Vratas* in Newar Buddhism." *Journal of the International Association of Buddhist Studies* 12, no. 1 (1989): 109–138.

Lewis, Todd T. "The *Nepāl Jana Jīvan Kriyā Paddhati*: A Modern Newar Guide for Vajrayâna Life-Cycle Rites." *Indo-Iranian Journal* 37 (1994): 1–46.

Lienhard, Siegfried, ed. *The Songs of Nepal: An Anthology of Nevar Folksongs and Hymns.* Honolulu: University of Hawaii Press, 1984.

Locke, John. "The Uposadha Vrata of Amoghapāsha Lokeshvara." *L'Ethnographie* 83, nos. 100–101 (1989): 109–138.

Malla, Kamal Prakash. *Classical Newari Literature.* Kathmandu: Nepal Study Centre, 1981.

Tatelman, Joel. "'The Trials of Yashodharā': The Legend of the Buddha's Wife in the Bhadrakalpāvadāna." *Buddhist Literature* 1 (1999): 176–261.

Vaidya, Janak Lal, and Kamsakar, Prem Bahadur. *A Descriptive Catalogue of Selected Manuscripts Preserved at the Aśā Saphū Kuthi.* Kathmandu: Cvasāpāsā, 1990.

TODD T. LEWIS

NICHIREN

Nichiren (1222–1282) is regarded as the founder of the Hokke (Lotus) or NICHIREN SCHOOL, one of several new Buddhist movements that emerged in Japan's Kamakura period (1185–1333). Of humble origins, Nichiren was ordained at age sixteen at Kiyosumi Temple in Awa province (now Chiba prefecture) and trained especially in the Tendai school's teachings of the LOTUS SŪTRA (SADDHARMAPUṆḌARĪKA-SŪTRA) and in esoteric Buddhism. Later he studied in Kamakura, site of the new shogunate or military government, and at the great Tendai center on Mount Hiei, as well as at other major Buddhist temples in western Japan. Eventually he based himself in Kamakura and won followers among the eastern warriors. Nichiren's early writings are critical of PURE LAND BUDDHISM, especially the newly popular Pure Land doctrine of HŌNEN (1133–1212), which he saw as undermining traditional Tendai emphasis on the *Lotus* and esoteric teachings. Over time, however, Nichiren developed a doctrine of exclusive devotion to the *Lotus Sūtra*, which he regarded as the Buddha's highest teaching and the sole vehicle for realizing buddhahood now in the final dharma age (*mappō*). He advocated chanting the DAIMOKU or title of the *Lotus Sūtra* in the formula "Namu Myōhō-renge-kyō," and he devised a calligraphic MAṆḌALA, depicting the assembly of the *Lotus Sūtra,* as an object of worship (*honzon*) for his followers. While defining himself in opposition to the established Buddhism of his day, Nichiren also creatively assimilated into his *Lotus* exclusivism many older elements of both exoteric and esoteric Buddhist thought and practice.

Based on MAHĀYĀNA and especially Tendai teachings of the profound interrelationship between persons and their outer world, Nichiren saw contemporary disasters, including famine, epidemics, and Mongol invasion attempts, as karmic retribution for collective rejection of the Lotus in favor of "inferior" teachings; conversely, he asserted, the spread of faith in the *Lotus Sūtra* would transform this world into a buddha land. This conviction underlay his commitment to *shakubuku,* an assertive approach to spreading the dharma by directly critiquing opposing views. Nichiren's repeated criticisms of the Buddhist establishment and of its patrons in government incurred the wrath of the authorities; he himself was twice exiled and attempts were made on his life, while his followers were arrested, banished, and in a few cases executed. Undeterred, Nichiren urged defiance of worldly authority when it contravenes Buddhist truth, and he valorized encounters with harsh trials. Undergoing such persecution, he taught, serves to eradicate past evil deeds, proves the validity of one's practice, and guarantees the realization of buddhahood. Nichiren's ideal of establishing the buddha land in the present world has inspired modern followers, who have assimilated it to a range of political agendas as well as social and humanitarian projects. Today more than forty religious organizations claim association with him, including traditional schools and new religious movements.

See also: **Exoteric-Esoteric (Kenmitsu) Buddhism in Japan; Kamakura Buddhism, Japan; Tiantai School**

Bibliography

Habito, Ruben L. F., and Stone, Jacqueline I., eds. *Revisiting Nichiren.* Special issue of *Japanese Journal of Religious Studies* 26, nos. 3–4 (1999).

Lamont, H. G. "Nichiren." In *Kodansha Encyclopedia of Japan,* Vol. 5. Tokyo: Kodansha, 1983.

Stone, Jacqueline I. "Nichiren and the New Paradigm." In *Original Enlightenment and the Transformation of Medieval Japanese Buddhism.* Honolulu: University of Hawaii Press, 1999.

Watanabe Hōyō. "Nichiren." In *The Encyclopedia of Religion,* Vol. 10, ed. Mircea Eliade. New York: Macmillan, 1987.

Yampolsky, Philip B., ed. *Selected Writings of Nichiren,* tr. Burton Watson and others. New York: Columbia University Press, 1990.

Yampolsky, Philip B., ed. *Letters of Nichiren,* tr. Burton Watson and others. New York: Columbia University Press, 1996.

JACQUELINE I. STONE

NICHIREN SCHOOL

The term *Nichiren school* (Nichirenshū) broadly denotes the entire Buddhist tradition deriving from the medieval Japanese teacher NICHIREN (1222–1282). It comprises more than forty independent religious institutions, including traditional temple denominations, lay associations, and new religious movements. Originally a monk of the Tendai tradition, Nichiren did not regard himself as the founder of a new sect, nor did he designate his following by any particular sectarian name. Because he taught exclusive faith in the LOTUS SŪTRA (SADDHARMAPUṆḌARĪKA-SŪTRA), after his death, his following became known as the Lotus sect (Hokkeshū). The name Nichirenshū came into broad usage from around the late sixteenth century.

Present organization and observances

The largest of the Nichiren Buddhist temple denominations takes Nichirenshū as its legal name and has its head temple at Kuonji at Mount Minobu in Yamanashi Prefecture, where Nichiren spent his last years. Other Nichiren Buddhist denominations include, for example, Hokkeshū (Shinmon, Honmon, and Jinmon branches), Honmon Butsuryūshū, Honmon Hokkeshū, Kenpon Hokkeshū, Nichiren Honshū, Nichiren Kōmonshū, Nichiren Shōshū, and Nichirenshū Fuju Fuse-ha. Many of these temple organizations trace their history back to the original monastic lineages established by Nichiren's immediate disciples, which underwent repeated schisms during the fourteenth through sixteenth centuries due to geographic separation, institutional rivalry, and differences of doctrinal interpretation. The nineteenth century saw the flourishing of Nichiren Buddhist lay associations (*kōchū* or *kō*), sometimes independent of priestly guidance, which were the predecessors of today's Nichiren- or *Lotus Sūtra*-based lay organizations. Of these latter groups, the most prominent are Reiyūkai, Risshō Kōseikai, and SŌKA GAKKAI, which number among

A Nichiren priest paying respect to Mount Fuji from atop neighboring Mount Minobu, Japan, 1991.

Japan's largest "new religions." To an extent not seen in other Buddhist sects, the religious energy of modern Nichiren Buddhism has shifted to lay movements.

Despite considerable differences of interpretation and ritual observance, all these various groups revere Nichiren and the *Lotus Sūtra* and recite the title or DAIMOKU of the *Lotus* in the formula "Namu Myōhō-renge-kyō," as Nichiren taught. (The actual pronunciation of the *daimoku* may vary slightly according to the particular group.) This practice, deemed especially suited to the present era, known as the "Final Dharma age" (*mappō*), is said to manifest individuals' innate potential for buddhahood and lead to positive transformation of the world. Reciting portions of the *Lotus Sūtra* and chanting the *daimoku* are performed at all formal ceremonies and constitute the basic practice of both clergy and laity. In addition to annual rites conducted by temples of all Buddhist sects, such as New Year's observances and memorial services for the dead at the equinoxes and during the summer Obon festival, Nichiren Buddhist temples and lay societies perform ritual observances on dates sacred to their tradition, usually transposed from the lunar to the Western calendar. These include Nichiren's birthday (celebrated February 16); the date of his first sermon, said to mark the founding of the Nichiren school (April 28); commemorations of various persecutions that Nichiren faced in propagating his teachings; and the day of his death or NIRVAṆĀ (October 13).

The founder Nichiren

Nichiren is often counted as one of the founders of the "new Buddhism" of the Kamakura period (1185–1333). He was born in Kominato in Awa Province (Chiba prefecture) in humble circumstances. At age twelve he entered a nearby temple, Seichōji or Kiyosumidera, for study and was ordained four years later, in 1237. Driven by a desire to understand the truth of the

Buddha's teachings, he spent the next sixteen years studying at major monasteries, including the great Tendai Buddhist center at Mount Hiei near Kyoto, the imperial capital. Later he based himself in Kamakura, seat of the newly established shogunate or military government, where he proselytized among warriors of middle and lower rank. Nichiren's early teachings draw heavily on Tiantai/Tendai thought grounded in the *Lotus Sūtra* and its commentaries, as well as on esoteric Buddhism. His early teachings also championed traditional Buddhist institutions over and against the growing influence of the new Pure Land sect founded by HŌNEN (1133–1212). Over time, however, Nichiren increasingly stressed that only the *Lotus Sūtra* leads to liberation during this Final Dharma age, and he began to dissociate himself from the Tendai Buddhist establishment, which he saw as having adulterated devotion to the *Lotus* with the practice of provisional teachings no longer suited to the times. Based on Tendai doctrines of the nonduality of persons and their environment, Nichiren interpreted the disasters of his day—including famine, epidemics, and Mongol invasion attempts—as karmic retribution for people having abandoned the *Lotus Sūtra* in favor of lesser teachings; conversely, he held, the spread of faith in the *Lotus* would transform this world into the Buddha land. This theme informs his famous admonitory treatise, *Risshō ankoku ron* (*On Establishing the Right [Dharma] and Bringing Peace to the Land*), delivered to the shogunate in 1260, as well as his later writings.

Convinced of the pressing need to communicate his message, Nichiren adopted *shakubuku*, a confrontational method of teaching the dharma by directly rebuking attachment to provisional teachings, whether through writing, preaching, or religious debate. Nichiren's mounting criticism of other forms of Buddhism, and of government officials for supporting them, soon incurred the anger of the authorities. He was exiled twice, to the Izu peninsula (1261–1263) and to Sado island (1271–1274), and was once nearly beheaded during the so-called Ryūkō or Tatsunokuchi persecution of the twelfth day, ninth month, 1271. Several of his followers were imprisoned or had their lands confiscated. Nichiren considered these trials a proof of the righteousness of his convictions and asserted the need to uphold the *Lotus Sūtra* in the face of opposition, even at the cost of one's life. His mature teachings were developed during his exile to Sado and his subsequent reclusion on Mount Minobu (1274–1282), where he devoted his last years to writing and to training successors. More than a hundred of his writings, including personal letters and doctrinal essays, survive in his own hand.

Nichiren's teachings

Nichiren adopted the TIANTAI SCHOOL doctrine of reality as "three thousand realms in a single-thought moment" (*ichinen sanzen*) to explain the theoretical basis upon which ordinary people can realize buddhahood, and their surroundings become the buddha land. In terms of practice for the Final Dharma age, however, Nichiren understood "the single thought-moment being three thousand realms," not as a formless principle to be discerned within one's own mind, as in Tiantai meditation, but as manifested in concrete form as the "three great secret dharmas" (*sandai hihō*). Derived from the "origin teaching" (*honmon*) or latter half of the *Lotus Sūtra*, regarded as the preaching of the original or primordially enlightened Buddha, these three constitute the core of Nichiren's teaching. They are:

(1) The *daimoku*. For Nichiren, the five characters *Myō-hō-ren-ge-kyō* (in Japanese pronunciation) that comprise the *Lotus Sūtra*'s title are not merely a name but embody the essence of all Buddhist teachings and are the seed of buddhahood for all beings. All the practices and resulting virtues of the primordial Buddha are encompassed in these five characters and are "naturally transferred" to the practitioner in the moment of FAITH and practice. That is, the practitioner and the original Buddha are identified in the act of chanting the *daimoku*.

(2) The *honzon*, or object of worship. Nichiren's *honzon* has the two inseparable aspects of the "Buddha," the primordial Śākyamuni of the origin teaching, enlightened since the beginningless past, and the "dharma," the truth of "Myōhō-renge-kyō," to which this Buddha is awakened. Nichiren gave this object of worship iconic form as a calligraphic MAṆḌALA of his own devising. "Namu Myōhō-renge-kyō" is inscribed down its center, while to the left and right are written the characters for the names of the two buddhas, Śākyamuni and Prabhūtaratna, along with the names of other representatives of those present at the assembly of the *Lotus Sūtra*. This maṇḍala depicts the realm of the primordial Buddha, which, Nichiren taught, ordinary persons can enter through faith. More than 120 of these maṇḍalas, inscribed for individual followers and their families, survive in Nichiren's handwriting. Various configurations of sculpted images representing the original Buddha and his *Lotus* assembly were also used by later Nichiren followers.

(3) The *kaidan*, or ordination platform. This designates the place of practice. Nichiren's own writings do not explain it in detail, and considerable controversy has surrounded its interpretation. Nichiren himself may well have envisioned the *kaidan* as an actual physical structure, supplanting the other, court-sponsored ordination platforms of his day, to be erected by imperial authority at some future time when people had widely embraced faith in the *Lotus Sūtra.* At the same time, the *kaidan* has often been interpreted metaphorically, to mean that wherever one embraces faith in the *Lotus Sūtra* is the buddha land.

Although he taught devotion to the *Lotus* as a self-contained, exclusive practice, Nichiren understood that practice as encompassing all possible benefits: realization of buddhahood, assurance for one's next life, eradication of sin, cultivation of merit, and protection and blessings in this world.

Contributions to Japanese culture

A key element of Nichiren's legacy is his doctrine of *risshō ankoku* (establishing the right [dharma] and bringing peace to the land), which holds that faith in the *Lotus Sūtra* can manifest the buddha land in this present world. This ideal supports the value of positive engagement with society and may have contributed to the growth of mercantile culture in Japan's medieval cities. In the mid-fifteenth century, half the population of Kyoto—the majority of them manufacturers, tradespeople, and moneylenders—is said to have belonged to the Nichiren school. Since the late nineteenth century, Nichiren's goal of transforming this world into a buddha land has been assimilated to a range of political and social goals. During Japan's modern imperial period (1868–1945), some Nichirenist lay societies, such as the Kokuchūkai (Pillar of the Nation Society), established in 1914 by Tanaka Chigaku (1861–1939), interpreted Nichiren's *risshō ankoku* ideal in terms of Japanese nationalism and deployed it to legitimize the armed expansion of empire. In the post–World War II period, especially among the new religious movements, it has been interpreted as a spiritual basis for the antinuclear movement, efforts for global peace, and a range of humanitarian endeavors. Nipponzan Myōhōji, a small Nichiren Buddhist monastic order, embraces absolute pacificism and engages in peace marches and civil protest, while Nichiren- or *Lotus*-based lay organizations, notably Sōka Gakkai and Risshō Kōseikai, support the United Nations as NGO (nongovernmental organization) members and engage in relief work and civic projects. This side of Nichiren Buddhism lends itself to contemporary emphasis on Buddhist social engagement.

Another, less well-recognized contribution of the Nichiren school lies in its history of committed individuals, beginning with Nichiren himself, who risked official displeasure for the dharma's sake. Once well established, most Nichiren Buddhist institutions, both past and present—like religious institutions more generally—have tended to take a conciliatory stance toward existing authority and support the status quo. Nonetheless, Nichiren's teaching that one must uphold the *Lotus Sūtra* even in the face of persecution from the country's ruler created a moral space exterior to worldly authority, from which that authority could be criticized and, if necessary, opposed. This attitude of defiance has periodically resurfaced, often on the part of those who saw themselves as reformers within the Nichiren school, seeking to revive the founder's spirit. Medieval hagiographies celebrate the stories of those monks of the tradition who, in imitation of Nichiren, admonished high officials to take faith in the *Lotus Sūtra* for the country's welfare and were imprisoned or tortured as a result. A later example is the Nichiren *fuju fuse* (neither receiving nor giving) movement of the late sixteenth and seventeenth centuries, whose monks—until driven underground—resisted official controls imposed on religious institutions, refusing to accept alms from rulers who were not *Lotus* devotees or to participate in public religious ceremonies for their benefit. Similarly, during the 1940s, leaders of both Honmon Hokkeshū and Sōka Gakkai were imprisoned for their defiance of wartime government religious policy, which mandated displays of reverence for state Shintō. Nichiren's intransigent spirit and his example of unwavering loyalty to a transcendent truth have also inspired individuals, linked only tenuously to the Nichiren tradition or even outside it altogether, who have faced official sanctions for their beliefs. These include the Christian leader Uchimura Kanzō (1861–1930) and the socialist activist Senoo Girō (1890–1961).

See also: **Engaged Buddhism; Kamakura Buddhism, Japan; Original Enlightenment (Hongaku)**

Bibliography

Dolce, Lucia Dora. "Esoteric Patterns in Nichiren's Interpretation of the *Lotus Sutra.*" Ph.D. diss. University of Leiden, 2002.

Habito, Ruben L. F. "Lotus Buddhism and Its Liberational Thrust: A Rereading of the *Lotus Sutra* by Way of Nichiren." *Ching feng* 35, no. 2 (1992): 85–112.

Habito, Ruben L. F., and Stone, Jacqueline I., eds. *Revisiting Nichiren.* Special issue of *Japanese Journal of Religious Studies* 26, nos. 3–4 (1999).

Lamont, H. G. "Nichiren Sect." In *Kodansha Encyclopedia of Japan,* Vol. 5. Tokyo: Kodansha, 1983.

Murano, Senchū. "Nichirenshū." In *The Encyclopedia of Religion,* Vol. 10, ed. Mircea Eliade. New York: Macmillan, 1987.

Petzold, Bruno. *Buddhist Prophet Nichiren: A Lotus in the Sun,* ed. Shotaro Iida and Wendy Simmons. Tokyo: Hokke Jānaru, 1978.

Rodd, Laurel Rasplica. *Nichiren: Selected Writings.* Honolulu: University of Hawaii Press, 1980.

Stone, Jacqueline I. "Rebuking the Enemies of the *Lotus*: Nichirenist Exclusivism in Historical Perspective." *Japanese Journal of Religious Studies* 21, nos. 2–3 (1994): 231–259.

Stone, Jacqueline I. *Original Enlightenment and the Transformation of Medieval Japanese Buddhism.* Honolulu: University of Hawaii Press, 1999.

Tanabe, George J., and Hori, Kyōtsū, eds. *Writings of Nichiren Shōnin: Doctrine 2.* Tokyo: Nichirenshu Overseas Promotion Association, 2002.

Watanabe Hōyō. "Nichiren." In *The Encyclopedia of Religion,* Vol. 10, ed. Mircea Eliade. New York: Macmillan, 1987.

Yampolsky, Philip B., ed. *Selected Writings of Nichiren,* tr. Burton Watson and others. New York: Columbia University Press, 1990.

Yampolsky, Philip B., ed. *Letters of Nichiren,* tr. Burton Watson and others. New York: Columbia University Press, 1996.

JACQUELINE I. STONE

NIKĀYA. *See* **Āgama/Nikāya**

NINE MOUNTAINS SCHOOL OF SŎN

The Nine Mountains school of Sŏn (Korean, Kusan Sŏnmun) is a comprehensive term referring to the nine monastic centers of the Korean Sŏn school (Chinese, CHAN SCHOOL), which were established from the eighth through the ninth centuries. Each of the nine schools takes its name from the mountain on which its central monastery is located: Kajisan, founded by Toŭi (d. 825); Silsangsan, founded by Hongch'ŏk (fl. 826); Tongnisan, founded by Hyech'ŏl (785–861); Sagulsan, founded by Pŏmil (810–889); Pongnimsan, founded by Hyŏnuk (787–869); Sajasan, founded by Toyun (797–868); Hŭiyangsan, founded by Chisŏn Tohŏn (824–882); Sŏngjusan, founded by Muyŏm (799–888); and Sumisan, founded by Iŏm (869–936).

According to tradition, Chan Buddhism was first introduced into Korea by the Silla monk Pŏmnang (fl. 632–646), who putatively studied in China under the Fourth Patriarch Daoxin (580–651), then returned to Silla and transmitted the teachings to Sinhaeng (d. 779), who also went to China, where he studied under Chigong (Chinese, Zhigong; 703–779), a Korean disciple of Puji (651–739), the second patriarch of the Northern Chan school. Sinhaeng thus imbibed both the "gradual teachings" of the Northern school and the "sudden teachings" of the so-called Southern school, passing them on to his disciples Chunbŏm (d.u.), Hyeŭn (d.u.), and finally Chisŏn Tohŏn (824–882), who founded the Hŭiyangsan school in 879.

Though sectarian rivalries certainly existed, the underlying kinship of the nine schools was recognized, and they were referred to collectively as the Chogye (Tsao-hsi) school, an allusion to Caoxi mountain, the residence of the sixth patriarch HUINENG (638–713). In point of fact, the Nine Mountains school was more doctrinally diverse than the name would indicate. This is because of the traditional emphasis placed on lineage in Korean Buddhism: For a new school to be included among the mountain schools, the founder had to have studied in China first; if he belonged to a mountain school before leaving for China, he was still considered a member of that school on his return, regardless of the new doctrine he brought back. A number of Nine Mountains adherents brought back new doctrines that were taught and practiced in Korea but were not given separate identities as schools.

One feature of Korean Sŏn is the dominance of the "sudden teachings" of the so-called Southern Chan school. Seven of the nine schools were founded by monks who studied under first generation successors of Mazu DAOYI (709–788), the founder of the Hongzhou school of Chan. Thus it was only natural that the "sudden teachings" became the dominant doctrinal feature of traditional Korean Sŏn. This orientation continues in contemporary Korean Buddhism.

See also: **Chogye School; Korea**

Bibliography

Buswell, Robert E., Jr. *The Formation of Ch'an Ideology in China and Korea: The Vajrasamādhi-Sūtra, A Buddhist Apocryphon.* Princeton, NJ: Princeton University Press, 1989.

Buswell, Robert E., Jr. *Tracing Back the Radiance: Chinul's Korean Way of Zen.* Honolulu: University of Hawaii Press, 1991.

Cho, Sungtaek. "Buddhist Philosophy, Korean." In *Encyclopedia of Philosophy,* Vol. 2. London and New York: Routledge, 1988.

SUNGTAEK CHO

NIRODHA. *See* Four Noble Truths

NIRVĀṆA

The most common term used by Buddhists to describe a state of freedom from suffering and rebirth, *nirvāṇa,* is one of the most widely known Buddhist words outside Asia. It is found in dictionaries as an English word, *nirvana,* and has acquired a patina that makes many assume its meaning is obvious. Yet, it is a word about which Buddhists themselves have never reached agreement.

The term *nirvāṇa*

The quest for the real or original "idea of nirvāṇa" often masks our preconceptions about what is reasonable or desirable in religious doctrine and practice, or, for that matter, what we expect from Buddhism (Welbon). It may be that when we ask: "What is nirvāṇa?" we seek to answer the wrong question. Instead we need to ask: How have Buddhists used the term? With what polemical or apologetic purposes? What human aspirations might these uses reveal?

The word's etymology already reveals the concept's ambiguity and polysemy. The Sanskrit term *nirvāṇa* is an action noun signifying the act and effect of blowing (at something) to put it out, to blow out, or to extinguish, but the noun also signifies the process and outcome of burning out, becoming extinguished, cooling down, and hence, allaying, calming down, and also taming, making docile. Technically, in the religious traditions of India, the term denotes the process of accomplishing and experiencing freedom from the unquenchable thirst of DESIRE and the pains of repeated births, lives, and deaths.

The word contains a problematic metaphor, an image of denial that only suggests what nirvāṇa is not (fire, heat, ardent craving, and repeated pain), but offers only limited clues as to what might be the term's referents or discursive contexts. Furthermore, the semantic overlap between "extinguishing" and "cooling down" does not solve the question of what are the exact means and the end result of putting out this fire. These uncertainties encapsulate much of the doctrinal debates over nirvāṇa.

The religious uses of the term *nirvāṇa* perhaps precede the beginnings of Buddhism, and may have been imported into Buddhism with much of its semantic range from other śramaṇic movements. It has had wide currency in Indian religions as a more or less central concept among the Jains, the Ājīvikas, the Buddhists, and certain Hindu strands. In different religious traditions its meanings range from composure in calm detachment (or in samādhi) to liberation from suffering, and from "escape from this world to a world of bliss" to the utter "rest" of dying out (e.g., as in Jain ritual suicide). *Nirvāṇa* can also be associated in the same breath with an impersonal absolute and a personal deity (as it is in the *Bhagavadgītā*).

Early definitions

For the most part, definitions found in Buddhist scriptural literature emphasize the cooling down of craving, aversion, and unawareness (*Suttanipāta* 4, 251–252). In a typical scriptural passage a nun puts out an oil lamp and characterizes the act as a *nibbāna* (the Pāli equivalent of Sanskrit *nirvāna*): "As I pull down the wick-pin and put out the flame of the lamp, ah, indeed, it is like my mind made free!" (*Therīgāthā* 116). The canonical explanatory metaphor speaks of a flame that is blown out, or of a fire that burns out when it runs out of fuel or is denied its fuel. However, in this context extinction means relief, calm, rest, and not the annihilation of being. In an Indian setting, fire is mostly hot and uncomfortable, or it is associated with a raging destructive forest conflagration during the dry months before the monsoon; it is not a symbol of life, but a symbol of painful desire.

A passage depicting an encounter between the Buddha and the wandering ascetic Vacchagotta explains that a buddha (here called a tathāgata) is liberated when "all cogitation, all worry and rumination, all me-making and mine-making as well as the penchant to conceit are extinguished, no longer desired, stopped, abandoned, no longer grasped" (*Majjhimanikāya* 1, 486). When someone is liberated in this way one cannot say that *he will* reappear or that *he will not* reappear after DEATH. It is like a fire that dies out; it does not go anywhere (*Majjhimanikāya* 1, 486–487). In the same way the Buddha is free "from those bodily forms and sensory images which a person seeking to characterize him would use to recognize [him as a] Tathāgata. They are cut off at the root, . . . so that they will not rise again in the future. The Tathāgata is free from any representations of bodily forms and sensory images, he is profound, immeasurable, unfathomable like the ocean" (*Majjhimanikāya* 1, 487–488). Needless to say, the same is declared about the other four constituents of the human person: sensations, thoughts, habits, and consciousness—that is, all five SKANDHA (AGGREGATES) have been uprooted by the TATHĀGATA.

As is often the case, here the question is what a buddha is after death. The connection of nirvāṇa to death is central to understanding the term, and one of the most common contexts for its usage. The Buddha's death is one of the defining moments of his life and person—one of the earliest events in the biography to be recorded, and the signal moment in the liberation from REBIRTH (and redeath). Especially with reference to the Buddha or persons regarded as having led an unusually holy life, *nirvāṇa* is synonymous with death, needless to say, a death that is peaceful and liberating. When a saint dies he "puts out the fire" (*parinirvāti* or *parinirvāyati*).

In other contexts, terms expressing profound, stable calm or mental concentration may be synonymous with *nirvāṇa.* In both cases the word suggests an ideal and desirable state of detachment and the paradoxically powerful presence of that which is absent: the dead saint or a serene demeanor. Thus, nirvāṇa is suggested by both a tranquil demeanor and the presence or miraculous appearance of relics, or by a reliquary mound (STŪPA). Such monuments, like images of the reclining Buddha that serve as models for the way a monk must lie—ready for death and liberation—remind us of how real the absence that is nirvāṇa can be and how close it is to relaxed sleep.

Within this broader context, one must locate a range of meanings in the metaphor of "blowing out," which suggests a number of different kinds of extinction, cooling down, or freedom from the turmoil and raging fires of human existence. It is freedom from rebirth by virtue of the *extinction* of everything that defines the person as subject to birth, death, and suffering (that is, the skandhas). Yet, this extinction can be understood as cessation or relinquishment, or both. Additionally, the encounter with Vacchagotta suggests that it is a freedom from a way of thinking, a type of self-definition and self-consciousness (and freedom from the attitudes generated by this way of thinking). Hence, "extinction" could also be freedom from the turbulence of the mind, from the fire generated by churning ideas of self and possession. This conception of nirvāṇa as extinguishing a form of knowing one's self (the fuel) overlaps with the notion of freedom from desire and aversion (the heat of the fire). Finally, nirvāṇa, like the extinguished fire, cannot be imagined: Such is the ineffable state of a liberated buddha, and the mysterious condition of being absent in death yet present as the tathāgata. The tradition will waver between all these meanings, sometimes integrating them, at other times preferring one over the other.

Some of the most important components of the metaphor appear in what is arguably one of the earliest strata of textual Buddhism, the *Aṭṭhakavagga* of the *Suttanipāta.* Here, the preferred Pāli term is *nibbuti,* a synonym for *nibbāna* that is usually rendered in Sanskrit as *nirvṛti* (extinction, perfect rest, and contentment). This word may be a distortion of *nivṛti* (to put a lid on, to arrest), but is most likely a transformation of *nivṛtti* (stop turning around, bring to rest), a form attested in the scholastic literature. A poem in the *Aṭṭhakavagga* (*Suttanipāta* 915 ff.) links *nibbuti* to the state of peace (*santipadam*) attained by the person who cools down (*nibbāti*—perhaps "blows out his own fire"). The poem also describes the goal as a state of detached solitude (*viveka*) in which one gains a special insight (*Suttanipāta* 915), and one no longer dwells in or holds on to (*anupādiyāno*) anything in the world.

Specifically addressed at monks, the poem advises that they mindfully dedicate themselves to the practice of putting away or taming (vinaya) the thirst within, uprooting the conceptions and mental fabrications (*papañcasaṁkhā*) that depend on one's ideas about oneself (*Suttanipāta* 916). The text describes the practice that leads to peace as remaining mindful and discerning the dharma. Significantly *dharma* in this poem is not some conception of truth or reality; it is rather a practice: observing with detachment common ideas about one's self (being better or inferior to others, being equal to others) and being mindful of the life of the world-renouncer.

The connection with MINDFULNESS (*smṛti/sati*) reminds us not only of the close connection of nirvāṇa to ideas of mental cultivation, but also signals the fact that *nirvāṇa* is also a term for the calm demeanor of the awakened or of those on the way to awakening. The young Gautama is said to be *nirvṛta* (*nibbuto*) in contexts describing his appearance or demeanor, and not his attainment of liberation. In such contexts, the word means not only that he is "calm," but also that he appears to be "serenely content." This usage suggests the common Buddhist metaphor of the wild elephant or the elephant in rut that, once tamed, becomes calm and acquires the grace that derives from training.

Tradition offers more than a definition by negation (i.e., what *nirvāṇa* is not). Extinction is not only a state of absence of sorrow and absence of desire; it is bliss. But it is also an active process: a coming to rest, a stopping (*nirodha*), and a cooling down. Definitions by negation can be understood as apophatic moves, attempts to speak of the unknowable, the ineffable. One cannot speak of the Tathāgata after he has left behind the conditions of rebirth, one can only say that he is not born and that he does not die, and so on. Finally, some descriptions come closer to telling us what nirvāṇa is: It is the unchanging (*Udāna* 80–81); it is the unconditioned, the true, the auspicious, the secure, the refuge, the pure state of health (*Suttanipāta* 4, 369–373). This range of perceptions corresponds to the ambiguity of the original metaphor, and, needless to say, becomes fertile ground for much speculation. One is always at liberty to try to imagine in what sense any given human being or human activity is closer to or further away from nirvāṇa.

Theories of nirvāṇa

In a constant struggle to understand the unfathomable state of the liberated Buddha, the tradition develops a number of theories. According to a classical view, "thirst" (*tṛṣṇā,* the insatiable craving for existence and sensual satisfaction), is completely eliminated with BODHI (AWAKENING), and thus the root cause for future rebirth is destroyed. When this happens, the person experiences "nirvāṇa with residual attachment factors" (*sopadhiśeṣanirvāṇa*); that is, freedom from desire has been attained and freedom from rebirth is assured, but the person must still remain in the world of suffering until the moment of death, when he will be free from any possibility of further rebirth. In other words, awakening causes the extinction of thirst and thus removes the causes for future rebirth, but does not remove the preexistent causes that continue to propel the individual in his or her present existence until the moment of death. Some caveats apply to the idea that final nirvāṇa is assured after awakening because one may bring a potent cause, a karmic condition that has not matured yet and will cause further rebirth until this cause bears its fruit. Hence, a person may achieve awakening and still be reborn once more in this world or in one of the HEAVENS.

However, when death occurs for a person who has achieved this first level of nirvāṇa, the nirvāṇa with residual factors, it is almost a foregone conclusion that there will be no more rebirth—at the moment of death this person will attain "nirvāṇa with no residue of attachment factors" (*nirupadhiśeṣanirvāṇa*). In Western literature, this final state is sometimes called *parinirvāṇa,* but this special usage of the term may be relatively recent (Thomas).

Full awakening implies, by necessity, the first level of nirvāṇa, yet nirvāṇa and awakening (bodhi) are not exact synonyms. Although the tradition itself at times blurs the distinction, one may separate the two as follows. Nirvāṇa is the affective, soteriological, and eschatological dimension of buddhahood: It is release from passion, desire, agitation, anger, birth and death, and any future rebirth. Bodhi, on the other hand, is the cognitive dimension of the experience: It is insight, perfect understanding, freedom from the veils of desire, aversion, and confusion, and, in some interpretations, omniscience. Despite their importance, throughout most of the history of Buddhism the concepts of awakening and nirvāṇa have been neither the sole nor the orienting goals of Buddhist doctrine and practice. At times they appear as defining principles, in tandem or competing with each other, but often they occur as placeholders and signs of orthodoxy or as a background to complex webs of doctrines and practices.

Turning provisionally to related scholastic formulations, one of the central concerns appears to have been the connection between the absolute or uncaused goal of nirvāṇa and the practices that constitute the PATH (necessarily a chain of causes and effects). Expressed abstractly, if nirvāṇa is not caused, then how can it be attained? If it is the absence of birth and death, is it the absence of life? If it is not a form of existence, then, how can it be bliss? The MILINDAPAÑHA attempts to address some of the problems, arguing that there is no cause for the arising of nirvāṇa (it is *ahetuja* like empty space), but its attainment is the fruit of following the path (*Milinda* 267–271). Similarly, the *Abhidharmakośa* (II.55) goes to great lengths to argue that nirvāṇa has no cause and no effect: It is the saint's attainment of nirvāṇa that is caused by the practice of the path.

The *Abhidharmakośa* (IV.8 and II.55) argues that liberation in nirvāṇa is the supreme good (*śubhaḥ paramataḥ*) and yet is not an entity (*abhāvamātra*—"not a thing in any way"). It is a conscious or intentional cessation, and yet it is somehow the goal of all the virtues and goodness of a buddha. Moreover, the *Abhidharmakośa* (II.55) seems to distinguish the cessation (*nirodha*) of dharmas that is the result of an intentional process (nirvāṇa proper) from other forms of cessation or nonexistence (such as that of a burned out fire).

The tendency to conceive of nirvāṇa as a nonstate or a state that is not within the sphere of that which exists is also suggested by the classical Indian notion that a yogin in meditation can achieve a cessation of life (a subtle state of death, as it were) called *nirodhasamāpatti* (Griffiths). Although such mental states are not the same as the final liberation of nirvāṇa, they are considered "analogous" to nirvāṇa (*Abhidharmakośa* II.44). This tallies well with common Indian ideas about the nature of samādhi as an alternative reality or a state that is outside the normal parameters of being and life. A parallel association can be seen in the contemporary custom of calling the tombs of Hindu saints their "samādhi."

Despite the apparent synonymy of *nirvāṇa* with the calm of meditation, the Buddhist tradition generally seeks a liberation that is for all time (or timeless) and not only a temporary state of serenity in samādhi. Thus, an early distinction separates liberation of mind (*cetovimukti*—perhaps liberation [only] in the mind) from liberation through insight (*prajñāvimukti*). Technically, the first is experienced by an ARHAT during the phase of traversing the path, and the second is attained at the moment of attaining the fruits of arhatship. This implies a distinction between an inner peace achieved during transitory states of mental recollection, and nirvāṇa proper, which is only possible after complete liberation through insight.

Further developments and polemical issues

However, the neatness of scholastic speculation may hide the disarray of competing views of nirvāṇa. Although an exact chronology is not possible, a later summary of conflicting concepts of nirvāṇa is found in a list of "mistaken ideas" in the LAṄKĀVATĀRA-SŪTRA, which criticizes those who conceive of nirvāṇa as:

> A state in which thought and mental states are no longer active because the skandhas, *dhātus* and *āyatanas* have ceased . . . or when one is no longer aware of past, present, or future, just as when a lamp is extinguished, . . . or when a fire runs out of fuel; others say liberation is going to another place or state when one stops discriminating sense objects, as when a wind stops blowing; others . . . say it is the destruction of the view that there is a knower and a known . . . ; others imagine nirvāṇa to be the destruction of the self, the living thing, the person . . . ; others, the extinction of merit and demerit, the destruction of the afflictions by means of knowledge . . . ; others, seeing the true nature of things as they are in their self-nature, such as the many colors on the peacock, variously formed precious stones. (pp. 182–187, § LXXIV)

A variety of interpretations of nirvāṇa can be attested historically as well, especially in MAHĀYĀNA. But, arguably, major differences appeared at an early stage in the development of *nikāya* Buddhism (the so-called HĪNAYĀNA schools). Buddhists advocating teachings like those of the Lokottaravāda, for instance, assumed that a buddha's nirvāṇa not only continues to exist beyond or after temporary states of samādhi but that it exists *before* time and existence, in an atemporal state, attained as it were since beginningless time.

Echoes of this view appear, for instance, in the so-called TATHĀGATAGARBHA doctrine, whose proponents argued that the Buddha's perfect nirvāṇa was already present in every sentient being. Buddhas exist in a permanent state of bliss, a nirvāṇa free from the self only in the sense that it lacks the negative qualities of selfhood. This state is the opposite of the impermanent, the impure, and the painful, and embodies the innate purity of a buddha-seed or buddha-nature present in most (if not all) SENTIENT BEINGS (an important polemic being fought over the presence or absence of this capacity in a particular group of people, the ICCHANTIKA).

Nirvāṇa also becomes the focus of polemical attempts to define Mahāyāna by contrast to a purported Hīnayāna. Mahāyāna apologetes distinguished the nirvāṇa of BODHISATTVAS from that of śrāvakas. The views of the latter are present in a polemical caricature to serve as the straw man for the promotion of Mahāyāna ideals: Śrāvakas are portrayed as aspiring to an imperfect and selfish state of peace. While they seek release from suffering only for themselves, the bodhisattva seeks awakening for the sake of all sentient beings.

This turn is arguably the beginning of a major shift in the position of nirvāṇa within the Buddhist conceptual edifice. One sees this shift in Śāntideva's resolution: "Nirvāṇa means to renounce all things, and my mind is set on attaining nirvāṇa; if I must renounce everything, it would be better to give it all to other sentient beings" (*Bodhicaryāvatāra* III.11).

At times this polemical stance is expressed by suggesting that bodhisattvas value awakening and compassionate engagement far more than their own liberation in nirvāṇa. But, another formulation, perhaps stemming from a different polemic, states that in some sense SAṂSĀRA and nirvāṇa are the same. This is usually traced back to aphorisitic statements of NĀGĀRJUNA (ca. second century C.E.), but it may be treated as another one of those background concepts that appear in many other formulations of Mahāyāna doctrine. The identity encapsulates both an ontology and a SOTERIOLOGY. As an ontology, it may be taken to imply that liberation from suffering takes place in the world (hence freedom from attachment to nirvāṇa), but in a world transformed by an awakened vision (hence detachment from saṃsāra). The stage of such vision and freedom is liberation (hence, a "higher" nirvāṇa).

Yogācāra scholastics proposed that the bodhisattva's nirvāṇa is a "nirvāṇa that has no foothold" (*apratiṣṭhitanirvāṇa*) in either nirvāṇa (perfect peace, rest) or saṃsāra (the turmoil of transmigration). This doctrine may be historically a spin-off of early ideas of the bodhisattvas' activity in saṃsāra or ontological reflections on the bodhisattva vow, but doctrinally it can be conceived as a development of the principle of the identity of saṃsāra and nirvāṇa, and also it seems to be linked to the idea of nirvāṇa as an act of generosity proposed by ŚĀNTIDEVA (ca. 685–763).

The idea of nirvāṇa with no foothold is also extended to buddhas, whose compassion could not conceivably allow them to "depart into nirvāṇa" while other sentient beings continue to suffer. As expressed succinctly by CANDRAKĪRTI (ca. 600–650) in one of the concluding verses to his *Madhyamakāvatāra* (XI.51): "With a mind to liberate those in pain, you have made the world the object of your compassion. Blessed, Compassionate One, out of love, you turn away from your own nirvāṇa forsaking its peace." The passage could be interpreted as an exhortation to forsake certain notions of nirvāṇa: doctrinal and practical conceptions of peace and relief from suffering that entail world-denial.

Another common, perhaps background, Mahāyāna conception, which may in fact have ancient roots in *nikāya* Buddhism, is the doctrine of "innate or natural" nirvāṇa (*prakṛtinirvāṇa*), according to which all things are already, and have been since beginningless time, in perfect peace. The world as it is and has always been is not polluted or polluting, does not cause our attachments and fettered relationships, does not cause suffering. This is taken to be synonymous with saying "all things are empty." This doctrine may be implicit in early canonical teachings about the natural luminescence (*prakṛtiprabhāsvaratā*) of the tranquil mind.

However, many of the above ideas also overlap with so-called mind-only theories of liberation (sometimes subsumed under the rubric *Yogācāra*), with their historical interconnections remaining obscure. The mind-only approach to liberation and reality is epitomized in a statement of the *Laṅkāvatāra-sūtra*:

> The all-knowing [buddhas] describe nirvāṇa as a turning back or stopping (*vyāvṛtti*) of the functions of consciousness, occurring when one understands that there is nothing but what appears as thought itself, when one no longer clings to external objects, existent or nonexistent, . . . when one sees the condition of things as they are . . . with the mind dwelling in neither subject nor object. (pp. 184–185, § LXXIV)

The conundrum implicit in the metaphors of extinction has not been avoided, for the same text describes the Buddha's liberation with another metaphor of the same family:

> [All functions of consciousness] are active (*pra-vṛt-*) or cease (*ni-vṛt-*) impelled by the wind of sense objects, which are appearances in thought itself, like waves on the ocean. Therefore, when the mind consciousness (*manovijñāna*) has been turned back or stopped, all seven forms of consciousness are stopped. . . . When a flooded stream subsides and dries out, no waves arise; in the same manner when the multifarious manifestations of consciousness cease [consciousness] is no longer active. (p. 127 and stanza 181, § LIII)

Mahāyāna doctrine in India contributed to the intellectual underpinnings of tantric theories of the process and goals of liberation. One can express the connection syllogistically, if not historically, by stating that, if all things are inherently or naturally already in nirvāṇa, then the body and the passions perhaps are in some way expressions of liberation, embodiments of peace. Doctrinally, tantric views of nirvāṇa fit within the range of Mahāyāna doctrines described above. Sometimes it is proposed that the bodhisattva, like a skillful magician, knows that the world is a magical apparition and hence is not tainted by the world, and, furthermore, can interact with the world in some way like a magician or wonder-worker. At other times, it is emptiness and compassion that define the bodhisattva's and the yogin's liberation, with compassion and a skillful use of liberating strategies (UPĀYA) eclipsing the renunciation and liberation as world denial. At other times, the body as such is the location for nirvāṇa, so that a homology between the body, speech, and mind of the practitioner and that of the buddha becomes the basis for ritual and meditation, and emptiness replaces concepts of the serene ineffable.

Whether the acceptance of the world and the passions is seen as a skillful use of liberating strategies (*upāya*) or as a redefinition of nirvāṇa (as the peace of accepting the passions without clinging to them), a redefinition of traditional Buddhist ascetic views of the body took place, and some of the older ideas of nirvāṇa had to shift position within the puzzle of Buddhist doctrine. Such shifts in emphasis and perspective find expression today among a few pockets of Buddhists in Nepal, in Tibetan communities (in Tibet and in exile), and among East Asian Buddhists.

Summary interpretation

One may argue, by way of conclusion, that nirvāṇa is one of those shifting foundations that believers see as solid rock, but history reveals as shifting sands. And yet, one must wonder how else it could have been with a concept that attempts to make intelligible so many questions about human presence and awareness, passion and serenity, and passion and death. Abstractly, one may say that the idea of nirvāṇa has had three distinguishable, though overlapping, functions in the development of Buddhist belief and practice. First, nirvāṇa appears to be the defining fulcrum for understanding the path as a way to peace through calm abiding. Second, nirvāṇa is the placeholder for various attempts at understanding a liberation that is peace and calm as something more than a temporary psychological state: liberation, timeless felicity, but, above all a deathless state that is nevertheless often associated with saintly death or the last moment in the holy path. Last, but equally important, nirvāṇa served as a stable reference point, as placeholder, for the tradition as it struggled to define its own identity against competing Buddhist and non-Buddhist communities of belief. Thus, even if one's main hope is rebirth in a paradise, that paradise must exist to facilitate nirvāṇa. More generally, *nirvāṇa* is one of those words that also embody the struggle to understand the possibility of perfection, of inner peace, and of freedom from the turmoil of our own desires and conflicted views of ourselves. It is not surprising that for all the many attempts to understand nirvāṇa as a psychological state or a state of body or mind, most traditions continue to give a special value to death in nirvāṇa or nirvāṇa in death, for the enigmas of full freedom and unending bliss seem to push imagination to a realm beyond the normal range of the experience of living humans.

Bibliography

Collins, Steven. *Nirvāṇa and Other Buddhist Felicities: Utopias of the Pāli Imaginaire.* New York and Cambridge, UK: Cambridge University Press, 1998.

Griffiths, Paul. *On Being Mindless: Buddhist Meditation and the Mind-Body Problem.* La Salle, IL: Open Court, 1986.

Kasulis, Thomas. "Nirvāṇa." In *The Encyclopedia of Religion,* Vol. 10, ed. Mircea Eliade. New York: Macmillan, 1987.

La Vallée Poussin, Louis de. *The Way to Nirvāṇa: Six Lectures on Ancient Buddhism as a Discipline of Salvation.* Cambridge, UK: Cambridge University Press, 1917.

La Vallée Poussin, Louis de. "Nirvāṇa." In the *Encyclopaedia of Religion and Ethics,* Vol. 9, ed. James Hastings. New York: Scribner's, 1927.

Thomas, Edward Joseph. *Nirvāṇa and Parinirvāṇa.* Leiden, Netherlands: Brill, 1947.

Welbon, Guy Richard. *The Buddhist Nirvāṇa and Its Western Interpreters.* Chicago: University of Chicago Press, 1968.

LUIS O. GÓMEZ

NIRVĀṆA SŪTRA

The core text of the Mahāyāna Mahāparinirvāṇa-sūtra was completed in Kashmir around 300 C.E., but over the next century additional material enlarged it to three or four times its original length. Today only fragments remain of the original Sanskrit text, but we have a complete Chinese translation of the extended sūtra by Dharmakṣema. Finished in 421, it became one of the most influential religious texts in East Asia. Tibetan translations appeared later (P. 788, D. 120), but this scripture had relatively little impact in Tibet.

Echoing and at one point even citing the LOTUS SŪTRA (SADDHARMAPUṆḌARĪKA-SŪTRA), the *Nirvāṇa Sūtra* affirms that the Buddha's death or *parinirvāṇa* did not mean his destruction, but occurred to illustrate that the true body of a buddha (*buddhakāya*) is uncreated (*asaṃskṛta*) and eternal, and to provide relics for veneration. Arguing against the Yogācāra categorization of SENTIENT BEINGS by their differing spiritual potentials, the *Nirvāṇa Sūtra* asserts that all sentient beings equally possess the same potential for buddhahood. Rendered in Chinese as *buddha-nature,* this far-reaching doctrine implies that the core nature of each individual is that of a buddha, but mental afflictions (*kléṣa*) prevent most from realizing it.

Although earlier Buddhist literature described sentient beings as plagued by ANITYA (IMPERMANENCE), DUḤKHA (SUFFERING), nonself, and impurity, in this sūtra, buddha, NIRVĀṆA, and by extension the buddha-nature within everyone are all characterized by permanence, joy, self, and purity. Despite our experience, there is thus another "great self" within us, and the sūtra even uses the term *true ātman.*

East Asian Buddhism was also profoundly affected by the *Nirvāṇa Sūtra*'s advocacy of vegetarianism and its overt inclusion of the ICCHANTIKA in its doctrine of universal salvation. *Icchantika* are individuals devoid of faith or morality, some of whom even slander the dharma. Like most other sūtras, the first part of the *Nirvāṇa Sūtra* excludes them, but beginning with chapter nine, the *Nirvāṇa Sūtra* repeatedly asserts that *icchantika* also have the buddha-nature.

Bibliography

de Jong, J. W. "Review of the Mahāyāna Mahāparinirvāṇa-sūtra Translated by Kosho Yamamoto." *Eastern Buddhist,* Vol. 9 (new series), no. 2 (1976): 134–136.

Matsuda Kazunobu. "New Sanskrit Fragments of the Mahāyāna Mahāparinirvāṇa-sūtra in the Stein/Hoernle Collection: A Preliminary Report." *Eastern Buddhist,* Vol. 20 (new series), no. 2 (1987): 105–114.

Ming-Wood, Liu. "The Doctrine of Buddha-Nature in the Mahāyāna Mahāparinirvāṇasūtra." *Journal of the International Association of Buddhist Studies* (Wisconsin), Vol. 5 (1982): 63–94.

Yamamoto Kosho, trans. *The Mahāyāna Mahāparinirvāṇa-sūtra: A Complete Translation from the Chinese Classical Language in 3 volumes.* Oyama, Japan: Karinbunko, 1973.

MARK L. BLUM

NO-SELF. *See* **Anātman/Ātman (No-Self/Self)**

NUNS

Buddhist nuns, like nuns and MONKS of other religious orders, renounce sexual activity, marriage, and household life. As renunciants, they voluntarily make a commitment to abide by a given number of PRECEPTS, or rules of conduct. To regulate their involvement with the affairs of the world, they agree to accept a subsistence standard of food, shelter, clothing, and medicine. The lay community provides these requisites; in return, the nuns provide teachings, advice, and a model of discipline and contentment.

To leave the household life (*pravrajya*) and become a member of the Buddhist order (SAṄGHA), a woman must first obtain the permission of her parents, husband, or guardian. There are four stages in the process of becoming a fully ordained nun (Sanskrit, *bhikṣuṇī*; Pāli, *bhikkhunī*). The first three stages of the process are administered by, and at the discretion of, the Bhikṣuṇī Saṅgha. Candidates first receive the ten precepts of a *śrāmaṇerikā* (novice), then the precepts of a *śikṣamāṇā* (probationary nun), and finally the precepts of a *bhikṣuṇī* (fully ordained nun). The purpose of the two-year probationary period as a *śikṣamāṇā*, a stage that is not required for monks, is twofold. First, it ensures that candidates for *bhikṣuṇī* ordination are not pregnant and, second, it allows time to provide the candidates with thorough training. The final stage in the process of becoming a fully ordained nun involves receiving the *bhikṣuṇī* precepts for a second time from the Bhikṣu Saṅgha. It is unclear whether this second *bhikṣuṇī* ordination indicates that bhikṣus have the final authority for *bhikṣuṇī* ordinations or whether they simply confirm the ordination the candidates have already received from the *bhikṣuṇīs.*

Precepts and practice

Bhikṣuṇīs and those in training abide by the precepts of the *Bhikṣuṇīprātimokṣa-sūtra.* The first five categories of the precepts are common to both bhikṣus and *bhikṣuṇīs.* Arranged according to the seriousness of the transgression, they are: (1) *pārājika* (defeats that entail expulsion from the saṅgha); (2) *saṅghāvaśeṣa* (remainders that entail suspension); (3) *niḥsargikā-pātayantikā* (abandoning downfalls that entail forfeiture); (4) *pātayantika* (propelling downfalls or lapses); and (5) *śaikṣā* (faults or misdeeds). An additional category, the *pratideśanīya* (offenses requiring confession), prohibits *bhikṣuṇīs* from begging for specific foods, unless they are ill. There are also seven *adhikaraṇa-śamatha* (methods of resolving disputes) for both bhikṣus and *bhikṣuṇīs.*

In all schools of VINAYA (monastic discipline), there are considerably more precepts for *bhikṣuṇīs* than for bhikṣus. Because the Bhikṣu Saṅgha was already quite well organized by the time the Bhikṣuṇī Saṅgha was established some years later, the *bhikṣuṇīs* were expected to follow most of the bhikṣu precepts. In addition, approximately one hundred precepts were formulated on the basis of wrongdoings that occurred among the nuns. The four *pārājikas,* which are common to both bhikṣus and *bhikṣuṇīs,* are to refrain from: (1) sexual intercourse, (2) taking what is not given, (3) taking a human life, and (4) telling lies, especially about one's spiritual attainments. There are four additional *pārājikas* that *bhikṣuṇīs* are required to refrain from: (5) bodily contact with a lustful man; (6) arranging to meet a man with amorous intentions; (7) concealing a *pārājika* of another *bhikṣuṇī;* and (8) obeying a bhikṣu who has been expelled from the saṅgha. (For a bhikṣu, to touch a woman, sit in a secluded place with a woman, or follow an expelled bhikṣu is an offense in the next suspension category.) In the second category of precepts, *saṅghāvaśeṣa,* there are seventeen for *bhikṣuṇīs* in the DHARMAGUPTAKA and THERAVĀDA schools and twenty in the Mūlasarvāstivāda. The *saṅghāvaśeṣas* in the Dharmagupta school prohibit *bhikṣuṇīs* from such actions as matchmaking, baselessly accusing someone of a *pārājika,* making an accusation against a layperson, knowingly ordaining a thief, absolving a suspended *bhikṣuṇī* without permission, traveling alone, refusing to accept admonishments, creating a schism in the saṅgha, and so on.

Bhikṣuṇīs, like bhikṣus, are required to hold three primary ritual observances: (1) *poṣadha,* the bimonthly recitation of the PRĀTIMOKṢA; (2) *pravāraṇā,* the invitation at the end of the rains-retreat (*vārṣa*); and (3) *kaṭhina,* the distribution of robes that concludes the rains-retreat. Traditionally, *bhikṣuṇīs* primarily devoted themselves to teaching, meditating, and other means of mental cultivation toward the goal of liberation. In modern times, they have also become active in translating, publishing, and a wide variety of other social welfare activities.

The lineage of full ordination for women

According to Buddhist accounts, the order of Buddhist nuns began five or six years after the order of monks when MAHĀPRAJĀPATĪ GAUTAMĪ, Buddha Śākyamuni's maternal aunt and foster mother, requested admission to the saṅgha. After the Buddha refused her request three times, she and a contingent of five hundred noblewomen shaved their heads, donned mendicants' robes, and walked barefooted to Vaiśālī to demonstrate their determination. When the Buddha's attendant ĀNANDA pressed their case and asked whether women were equally capable of achieving the fruits of the dharma, the Buddha confirmed that they were. He consequently granted Mahāprajāpatī's request to join the order, purportedly on the condition that she agree to accept eight special rules (*gurudharma*): (1) a *bhikṣuṇī* ordained even one hundred years must rise and pay respect to a bhikṣu even if he was ordained that very day; (2) *bhikṣuṇīs* must not hold their rains-retreat in a place where there is no bhikṣu; (3) *bhikṣuṇīs* must request instruction from the bhikṣus twice each month; (4) at the conclusion of the rains-retreat, *bhikṣuṇīs* must declare the faults they have seen, heard, and suspected before the order of bhikṣus; (5) suspended *bhikṣuṇīs* must be reinstated before a quorum of twenty bhikṣus and twenty *bhikṣuṇīs;* (6) the ordination of *bhikṣuṇīs* must be conducted by both orders (first by ten *bhikṣuṇīs* and then by ten bhikṣus); (7) *bhikṣuṇīs* must not revile bhikṣus; and (8) *bhikṣuṇīs* must not admonish bhikṣus, although bhikṣus may admonish *bhikṣuṇīs.* Although it is unlikely that these eight rules were actually imposed by the Buddha, they are cited as the source of the unequal status of nuns and monks in Buddhist societies.

Accounts indicate that, following Mahāprajāpatī's ordination, thousands of women became nuns. Among these early nuns, many were renowned for their extraordinary attainments: Khemā for wisdom, Dhammadinnā for teaching, Paṭācārā for monastic discipline, Kisā Gautamī for asceticism, Nandā for meditation, Bhaddā for past-life recall, and Uppalavaṇṇā for supernormal powers. During the Buddha's time, many nuns were said to have achieved the fruits of practice, including the state of an ARHAT, or liberation. Examples of their songs of realization are included in the *Therīgāthā* (*Verses of the Bhikṣuṇī Elders*).

There is evidence that the Bhikṣuṇī Saṅgha continued to exist in India until about the tenth century, though in dwindling numbers and with less support than the order of monks. According to the Sinhalese chronicle *Dīpavaṃsa,* the Bhikṣuṇī Saṅgha in Sri Lanka was established in the fourth century B.C.E. when Saṅghamittā, daughter of King AŚOKA, traveled from India especially to transmit the *bhikṣuṇī* precepts to Queen Anulā and hundreds of Sinhalese women. Around the eleventh century, the Bhikṣuṇī Saṅgha died out in Sri Lanka due to droughts and the Chola invasions from India. Before that time, however, in the fifth century C.E., the *bhikṣuṇī* lineage was transmitted from Sri Lanka to China. Sri Lankan *bhikṣuṇīs* headed by a *bhikṣuṇī* named Devasarā traveled in two delegations to Nanjing, where they administered the ordination to Jingjian and several hundred other Chinese nuns. From China, the *bhikṣuṇī* lineage was gradually

Nuns of Jamyang Choling Institute, Dharamsala, India. Courtesy of Karma Lekshe Tsomo. Reproduced by permission.

transmitted to Korea, Vietnam, and Taiwan, where it still thrives.

Buddhist nuns in contemporary society

In 2003 there were an estimated 125,000 Buddhist nuns, including at least 35,000 *bhikṣuṇīs.* Nuns in China, Korea, Taiwan, and Vietnam follow the Dharmagupta lineage school of vinaya, which is the only *bhikṣuṇī* lineage in existence today. In these traditions, a woman who wishes to become a nun first requests the rite of leaving home (*pravrajya*), shaves her head, dons the robes, and receives the ten precepts of a *śrāmaṇerikā* (novice nun). After a period of training, a *śrāmaṇerikā* who is at least twenty years old may then request *bhikṣuṇī* ordination. The two-year probationary period as a *śikṣamāṇā* is currently observed only in stricter monasteries. According to the vinaya, nuns are required to receive their novice ordination and monastic training under the guidance of qualified *bhikṣuṇī* masters; in Taiwan, however, it is not uncommon for women to receive ordination and train under bhikṣu masters. Ideally, *bhikṣuṇī* ordination is conducted by a full quorum of ten *bhikṣuṇīs* and ten bhikṣus, in rites supervised in the morning by the *bhikṣuṇīs* and in the afternoon of the same day by the bhikṣus. Occasionally, *bhikṣuṇī* ordinations are conducted by high-ranking bhikṣus without the formal participation of *bhikṣuṇī* ordination masters and such ordinations are accepted as legitimate, if not technically correct.

As far as is known, the Bhikṣuṇī Saṅgha was never officially established in Cambodia, Japan, Laos, Mongolia, Thailand, or Tibet. Although there is evidence to document that *bhikṣuṇīs* existed in earlier times in Myanmar, Nepal, and Sri Lanka, these orders unfortunately died out long ago. In countries where *bhikṣuṇī* ordination is not currently available, nuns do not have the same status, nor do they receive the same patronage or access to religious education as monks. In recent years, inspired by an international Buddhist women's movement, conditions for nuns in all countries have begun to improve markedly.

In the Theravāda countries of Cambodia, Laos, Myanmar, Sri Lanka, and Thailand, and in Theravāda communities in Bangladesh, Indonesia, and Nepal, nuns receive eight, nine, or ten precepts. These nuns are celibate, shave their heads, take no solid food after noon, and generally maintain the lifestyle of a *bhikṣuṇī*, but are not regarded as members of the saṅgha. Nuns in Cambodia, Laos, and Thailand wear white robes; in

Cambodia they are known as *donchee,* in Laos as *maikao,* and in Thailand as *maechee.* Nuns in Myanmar wear pink robes with an orange underskirt and brown shawl over the left shoulder, and are known as *tila shin* (possessors of morality). Nuns in Sri Lanka wear orange or brown robes, and are known as *dasasīlāmātā* (ten-precept mothers). In these traditions, emphasis is placed on monastic discipline, meditation practice, and dissemination of the Buddha's teachings.

Recently, the standards of Buddhist education among Theravāda nuns have improved considerably and the contributions that nuns have made and continue to make to society are being more widely recognized. Interest in achieving equal opportunities for full ordination for women has increased, both among nuns and laypeople. In Sri Lanka, an estimated four hundred nuns have become *bhikṣuṇīs* since 1988, first by attending ordinations held in Los Angeles, Sārnāth, and BODH GAYĀ, and more recently in ordinations held in Sri Lanka itself. Many nuns in Theravāda countries hesitate to press for *bhikṣuṇī* ordination for two primary reasons. First, *bhikṣuṇīs* are prohibited from handling money and are expected to maintain themselves by a daily alms round. Thus, their survival literally depends on receiving sufficient support from the lay community. Judging by the history of nuns in India and Sri Lanka, where the Bhikṣuṇī Saṅgha may have died out due, in part, to famine, sufficient support for nuns is never certain. Second, according to the stipulations of the eight *gurudharmas, bhikṣuṇīs* are subordinate to the bhikṣus in a number of ways. Some nuns have very legitimate fears that the independence nuns presently enjoy may be compromised if the *bhikṣuṇīs* are beholden to, or come under the domination of, the Bhikṣu Saṅgha.

In Japan, nuns receive the BODHISATTVA precepts of the FANWANG JING (BRAHMĀ'S NET SŪTRA), which are similar to the ten precepts of a *śrāmaṇerikā,* and they follow a celibate monastic lifestyle. In 590 C.E., three nuns named Zenshin-in, Zenzo-ni, and Kenzen-ni traveled from Japan to the Paekche kingdom of Korea, where they received the *śrāmaṇerikā, śikṣamāṇā,* and *bhikṣuṇī* ordinations successively. These nuns returned to Japan, but were unable to conduct a *bhikṣuṇī* ordination there because they did not constitute the required minimum of five *bhikṣuṇī* precept masters. When the Tiantai monk GANJIN (Jianzhen) came to Japan in 754 C.E., three *bhikṣuṇīs* accompanied him, but they were also too few in number to conduct a *bhikṣuṇī* ordination. Thus, the Bhikṣuṇī Saṅgha was never established in Japan. Nevertheless, numerous nunneries and several thousand nuns exist throughout Japan today, primarily in the Jōdo, Tendai, Shingon, Nichiren, Sōtō, and Rinzai Zen schools. Together with several million devoted laywomen, they play essential roles in preserving and disseminating Japanese Buddhist culture.

In Tibet and, more recently, in Mongolia, nuns take thirty-six precepts, which are a detailed enumeration of the ten precepts of a *śrāmaṇerikā.* Although there is mention of *bhikṣuṇīs* in Tibetan historical records, there is no evidence that a Bhikṣuṇī Saṅgha was ever established in Tibet. In the Tibetan tradition, which is followed by nuns throughout the Tibetan cultural region, nuns wear robes identical to those of the monks. These nuns are recognized as members of the saṅgha but, as novices, they do not generally receive the same education, esteem, or material support as do monks. Nuns and devoted laywomen nevertheless receive the bodhisattva precepts, receive teachings on both the sūtras and tantras, and engage in a variety of practices, including prostrations, meditation, MAṆḌALA offerings, and MANTRA recitation.

Conditions for study and practice seem to be most conducive for nuns in those traditions that have living *bhikṣuṇī* lineages. In Korea, the training for a prospective *bhikṣuṇī* lasts up to six years, and places a high value on sūtra studies, vinaya studies, and meditation. The monastic year is divided into four seasons. Summer and winter are spent in intensive meditation and retreat; spring and autumn are spent cultivating, harvesting, and preparing the food needed during the meditation seasons, as well as performing other tasks required to maintain the monastery. Educational standards among Korean nuns have improved dramatically in recent decades and nuns are increasingly taking leading roles in Buddhist education, youth activities, and other social welfare programs.

Nuns are also prominent in the resurgence of Buddhism that is currently taking place in Taiwan. Full ordination and a wide range of educational opportunities are available to Taiwanese nuns, including Buddhist studies programs in several hundred colleges, institutes, and universities. Nuns in Taiwan are active in social service activities, health care, and the arts. In addition to founding and directing numerous temples and institutions for Buddhist education and training, nuns have founded and maintain libraries, museums, orphanages, medical centers, care homes, and women's shelters. Although nuns substantially outnumber monks in Taiwan, monks generally hold the

Master Cheng Yen (Zhengyan), Buddhist nun and founder of the Tz'u-chi (Compassionate Relief) Society, the largest charity in Taiwan, 1993. © Don Farber 2003. All rights reserved. Reproduced by permission.

leadership positions in Buddhist organizations. Nevertheless, nuns in Taiwan are widely respected for the exemplary work they do to propagate Buddhism and benefit society.

The unequal status of nuns in Buddhism has become a topic of concern in recent years, especially as Buddhist teachings gain popularity in Western countries and encounter modern ideals of GENDER equality. Although only a few hundred Western women have become Buddhist nuns so far, the subordinate status of women in Buddhist societies has stimulated efforts to improve conditions for women within the various Buddhist traditions by providing more equitable opportunities for religious education, ordination, and meditation training. With improved facilities, nuns will undoubtedly assume more positions of spiritual and institutional leadership in the years to come. As nuns gain greater representation within the various Buddhist traditions, a reevaluation and restructuring of hierarchically ordered institutions is inevitable.

See also: **Ascetic Practices; Monasticism; Women**

Bibliography

Arai, Paula. *Women Living Zen: Japanese Sōtō Buddhist N* New York: Oxford University Press, 1999.

Barnes, Nancy Schuster. "Buddhist Women and the Nuns' der in Asia." In *Engaged Buddhism: Buddhist Liber Movements in Asia,* ed. Christopher S. Queen and Sall King. Albany: State University of New York Press, 199

Bartholomeusz, Tessa. "The Female Mendicant in Buddhis Lanka." In *Buddhism, Sexuality, and Gender,* ed. José I cio Cabezón. Albany: State University of New York P 1992.

Bartholomeusz, Tessa. *Women under the Bō Tree: Buddhist N in Sri Lanka.* Cambridge, UK: Cambridge University P 1994.

Blackstone, Kathryn R. *Women in the Footsteps of the Bud Struggle for Liberation in the Therīgāthā.* Richmond, Curzon Press, 1998.

Dresser, Marianne, ed. *Buddhist Women on the Edge: Con porary Perspectives from the Western Frontier.* Berkeley, North Atlantic Books, 1996.

Falk, Nancy. "The Case of the Vanishing Nuns: The Frui Ambivalence in Ancient Indian Buddhism." In *Unsp Worlds: Women's Religious Lives in Non-Western Culture* Nancy Falk and Rita Gross. San Francisco: Harper, 197

Findly, Ellison Banks, ed. *Women's Buddhism, Buddhi Women: Tradition, Revision, Renewal.* Boston: Wisdom, I

Grimshaw, Anna. *Servants of the Buddha: Winter in a Himal Convent.* Cleveland, OH: Pilgrim Press, 1994.

Gross, Rita M. *Buddhism after Patriarchy: A Feminist His Analysis, and Reconstruction of Buddhism.* Albany: State versity of New York Press, 1993.

Havnevik, Hanna. *Tibetan Buddhist Nuns.* Oslo: Norwe University Press, 1990.

Hirakawa, Akira. *Monastic Discipline for the Buddhist Nuns English Translation of the Chinese Text of the Mahāsāṃgh Bhikṣuṇī-Vinaya.* Patna, India: K. P. Jayaswal Research stitute, 1982.

Kabilsingh, Chatsumarn. *Thai Women in Buddhism.* Berk CA: Parallax Press, 1991.

Murcott, Susan. *The First Buddhist Women: Translations Commentaries on the Therigatha.* Berkeley, CA: Par Press, 1991.

Norman, K. R., trans. *The Elders' Verses II: Therīgāthā.* Lon Luzac, 1966.

Rhys-Davids, Caroline Augusta Foley, and Norman, K. R. *ems of Early Buddhist Nuns* (*Therīgāthā*). Oxford: Pali Society, 1989.

Tsai, Kathryn Ann. *Lives of the Nuns: Biographies of Chinese dhist Nuns from the Fourth to Sixth Centuries.* Honolulu: versity of Hawaii Press, 1994.

Tsomo, Karma Lekshe. *Sisters in Solitude: Two Traditions of Buddhist Monastic Ethics for Women, a Comparative Analysis of the Dharmagupta and Mūlasarvāstivāda Bhikṣuṇī Prātimokṣa Sūtras.* Albany: State University of New York Press, 1996.

Tsomo, Karma Lekshe, ed. *Buddhist Women across Cultures: Realizations.* Albany: State University of New York Press, 1999.

Tsomo, Karma Lekshe, ed. *Innovative Women in Buddhism: Swimming against the Stream.* Richmond, UK: Curzon, 2000.

Watkins, Joanne C. *Spirited Women: Gender, Religion, and Cultural Identity in the Nepal Himalaya.* New York: Columbia University Press, 1996.

Willis, Janice Dean. *Feminine Ground: Essays on Women and Tibet.* Ithaca, NY: Snow Lion, 1989.

KARMA LEKSHE TSOMO

NYINGMA. *See* **Rnying ma**

O

OBON. *See* Ghost Festival

OṂ MAṆI PADME HŪṂ

Oṃ maṇi padme hūṃ is the MANTRA of the bodhisattva Avalokiteśvara. In recitation, rotation, and writing, the six-syllable mantra, as it is popularly known, is deeply embedded in daily life throughout the Tibetan cultural sphere. It is an invocation to the bodhisattva in the guise of Maṇipadma (the final e is a vocative case ending to the feminine noun). It might therefore be rendered "Oṃ O [thou who] hast a jewel and lotus Hūṃ." This interpretation, though familiar to Tibetan exegetes since at least the ninth century, has largely eluded Westerners, who have commonly misconstrued its meaning as some variation of "Hail to the jewel in the lotus."

While multiple Avalokiteśvara DHĀRAṆĪ and mantra were in circulation by the third century C.E., the six-syllable mantra seems to have first appeared in the *Kāraṇḍavyūha-sūtra.* This text, composed as early as the fifth century C.E., offers extensive description of the mantra's power, chief among them rebirth in the pure realms contained within the hair pores of Avalokiteśvara. According to legend, a copy of the *Kāraṇḍavyūha-sūtra*—or alternatively simply the six syllables contained in a jeweled casket (kāraṇḍa means casket)—fell out of the sky onto the roof of the semi-historical sixth-century Tibetan king Lha tho tho ri. The sūtra was translated some time before 812, as it is included in the Ldan dkar ma catalogue of imperial-period translations published in that year. Although comparable mantras associated with Avalokiteśvara are found in several DUNHUANG texts, usage of the six-syllable mantra appears to have gained wide popularity only in the eleventh century.

Tibetans traditionally interpret the mantra and its six syllables in terms of numerical correspondences, such as to the six realms of existence. Oral recitations of the mantra, commonly counted on prayer beads, are said to prevent REBIRTH in the six realms and purify even the gravest of sins. Recitation is often supplemented by simultaneous spinning of the well-known prayer wheel (*maṇi 'khor lo, chos 'khor lo,* or *lag 'khor*). This is a device that allows the practitioner to activate the mantra's efficacy through spinning the wheel. According to tradition a single revolution produces an amount of merit equal to reading all of the Buddha's discourses; ten revolutions purify an amount of sin equal to Mount Meru, and so forth. The mantra is also written, engraved, and painted on rocks, its physical presence understood to offer protection to those nearby.

Western travelers to Tibet have been fascinated by the prevalence of the mantra since the thirteenth century, when the Franciscan missionary William of Rubruck observed the continual chanting of *on mani baccam,* as he recorded it. The mantra, and its ubiquitous mistranslation, Jewel in the Lotus, has over the centuries worked its way into the Western fascination with all things Eastern, engendering any number of mystical (including sexual) interpretations, and seeping into various Western countercultural movements, spiritual and otherwise.

A trail of "maṇi" stones bearing sacred inscriptions along a Buddhist pilgrimage route in Kashmir in the Himalayas. © Hulton Archive by Getty Images. Reproduced by permission.

See also: Heart Sūtra

Bibliography

Imaeda, Yoshro. "Note préliminaire sure la formule *Oṃ maṇipadme hūṃ* dans les manuscripts tibétains de Touen-houang." In *Contributions aux études sur Touen-houang,* ed. Michel Soymié. Geneva, Switzerland: Librairie Droz, 1979.

Kyabje Yonzin Trijang Dorje Chang Losang Yeshe Tenzin Gyatso Pal Zangpo. "The Significance of the Six Syllable Mantra *OM MA NI PAD ME HUM.*" *Tibet Journal* 7, no. 4 (1982): 3–10.

Lopez, Donald S., Jr. *Prisoners of Shangri-La: Tibetan Buddhism and the West.* Chicago: University of Chicago Press, 1998.

Martin, Dan. "On the Origin and Significance of the Prayer Wheel, According to Two Nineteenth-Century Tibetan Literary Sources." *Journal of the Tibet Society* 7 (1987): 13–29.

Studholme, Alexander. *The Origins of Oṃ Maṇipadme Hūṃ: A Study of Kāraṇḍavyūha Sūtra.* Albany: State University of New York Press, 2002.

Verhagen, P. C. "The Mantra '*Oṃ maṇi-padme hūṃ*' in an Early Tibetan Grammatical Treatise." *Journal of the International Association of Buddhist Studies* 13, no. 2 (1990): 133–138.

ALEXANDER GARDNER

ORDINATION

Ordination, the ceremony by which men and women accept the more than two hundred rules of the Buddhist VINAYA and are thus defined as clerics, has been immensely important throughout the entire Buddhist tradition, even as its definitions, functions, and salience have differed over time and space. Ordination ceremonies are roughly the same for men and women, except that those for women often include additional requirements that subordinate NUNS to MONKS. The ordination of women was completely halted in the eleventh to the thirteenth centuries in Southeast Asian Buddhism, and recent efforts to introduce the nun's ordination from China and Taiwan have not yet been widely accepted. In ancient India and medieval Tibet and East Asia, the emergence of MEDITATION and esoteric (tantric) INITIATION lineages has reduced the salience of ordinations. Japanese Buddhism is well known—even infamous throughout the Buddhist world—as the only national tradition to have rejected celibacy and avoidance of intoxicants, a development that has had some impact on modern Korean and Taiwanese Buddhism as well.

In addition to conventional types of ordination, the ceremony was sometimes applied (or, more often, the five PRECEPTS administered) to gods and spirits as Buddhism competed with and amalgamated native religious traditions during its expansion throughout Asia. In Japan from late medieval times on funerals for laypeople often included posthumous ordination, and in modern Southeast Asia the ordination of trees has been used to protect forests from logging. Given the diversity of attitudes and approaches, it is not surprising that modern Western Buddhists have generally interpreted the ordination ritual and the associated vows abstractly, and only a few Western Buddhist have undertaken lifetime maintenance of the full monastic precepts.

Description of the ordination ceremony

Entrance into the SAṄGHA occurs in two stages, the first being the novice's ordination involving ten precepts, by which the novice becomes a *śramaṇera* or *śramaṇerikā.* In Southeast Asia this step may be taken as early as age seven; in East Asia one may not formally become a novice until age nineteen, even though one may have lived within the monastic community from a very young age. Short-term novitiates of a few weeks or months are common in Southeast Asia. Short-term higher ordinations are also common; the term is usually a summer rains-retreat period or longer. There is no particular onus on those who do not go on to full ordination. (The ritual described in this section is based on the unpublished translation by Gregory Schopen of the ordination ritual found in the MŪLASARVĀSTIVĀDA-VINAYA.)

The full or higher ordination (*upasampadā*), by which one becomes a bhikṣu or *bhikṣunī,* can occur only at or after age twenty (dated from conception). In the primitive saṅgha there was presumably a generally accepted core of about 150 rules in the monastic code (PRĀTIMOKṢA), but the diversification of ordination lineages has led to divergences in many of the minor rules. Hence THERAVĀDA monks in Southeast Asia observe 227 rules (Theravāda nuns once observed 311), Tibetan monks observe the 258 rules (the nuns 354) of the *Mūlasarvāstivāda-vinaya,* and Chinese and Korean monks observe the 250 rules (the nuns 348) of the *Dharmaguptaka-vinaya.* East Asian monks also accept the bodhisattva vows derived from the FANWANG JING (BRAHMĀ'S NET SŪTRA), a formal part of ordination, and in most Japanese schools these vows have entirely supplanted the prātimokṣa rules.

The ordination ceremony must involve all the monks in a given local saṅgha, and no one can enter or leave during the proceedings; usually a separate temporary boundary (*sīma*) is established for the duration of the ceremony. There should be an assembly of ten or more fully ordained monks (or, in border regions, five monks) and a vinaya master to serve as preceptor. The ceremony begins with the ordinand paying reverence to the monks, then entreating the preceptor to confer ordination on him. The ordinand then takes possession of his robes, or the cloth for their making, declaring to the preceptor that they are of appropriate material and cut. If the robes have not yet been made, the ordinand declares his intention to wash, cut, dye, and sew them properly from the material provided. The same process occurs for the bowl.

The ordinand then moves out of hearing range but stays within sight so that the officiant can ask the ordinand's private instructor about his appropriateness for ordination. The private instructor then goes over to the ordinand and, after reminding him not to be embarrassed by the questions, ascertains whether the ordinand is free from any of the impediments to ordination. These include questions about the individual's age, gender, genital completeness, and authorization by his parents (if living), and his identity as other than slave, criminal, eunuch, hermaphrodite, or despoiler of nuns. The questions also confirm that the ordinand has not been a member of another religious group or suffered expulsion from another saṅgha; has not murdered his father, mother, or an ARHAT; has not caused a split in the saṅgha or wounded the Buddha; is not a magically created phantom or animal; is not in debt (beyond the ability to pay at point of ordination); is not suffering from any illness (giving a long list); and is someone who is now fully entered into the religious life, including the practice of chastity.

Buddhist novices from a hill tribe in northern Thailand pray as they walk past their families during an ordination ceremony in Bangkok, 2001. © AFP/Corbis. Reproduced by permission.

Upon returning to the assembly the private instructor informs them of the ordinand's absence of any obstacles. The candidate is then brought forward and, after reverence to the Buddha and the elders of the community, the private instructor entreats the assembly three times to confer ordination on him. As a member of the saṅgha in full standing, the officiant then restates this entreaty as a formal resolution to the community. Following this, the same questions placed privately are now posed to the candidate before the entire group, and upon his successful responses the officiant formally moves that the assembly ordain him. The time of this event is measured (using pegs of specified size) on a sundial, so as to determine the new monk's exact seniority.

The ordinand is then made to affirm that he can maintain his asceticism for the rest of his life, including the four supports (*niśraya*) of clothing, food, housing, and medicine. He also confirms that he can maintain celibacy in both mind and body, and avoid stealing, killing, and lying. In the text of the Mūlasarvāstivāda ordination, the injunctions against such errors are lengthy and emphatic, with particular attention on the transgression of claiming false knowledge or attainment of spiritual truths, cosmic realities, meditative states or yogic powers, or achievement of arhatship. The ordinand affirms that he will not revile, offend, chastise, or deride others, even when others do so to him.

After all this, the officiant finally declares that the ordinand has now been properly entered into the religious life by a preceptor, two teachers, the agreement of the saṅgha, and a formal action (the ceremony) involving three inviolable motions. The ceremony does not immediately end with this declaration, but continues with injunctions to the new monk to maintain his training, to treat his preceptor as his father just as the preceptor will treat the monk as son, to respect those senior to him, to strive for the direct realization of Buddhist truths, to learn the monastic rules not covered yet in the bimonthly saṅgha meeting, and to maintain attentiveness with all aspects of the dharma.

Historical variations in Buddhist ordination

Ordination was used in the early years of Buddhism to define the membership of the saṅgha and induce members to adhere to a uniform religious lifestyle, both differentiating the Buddhist order from other religious groups and inspiring its members with a shared sense of identity as formally accepted descendents of the Buddha. As the Buddhist movement diversified, there developed multiple ordination lineages, called *nikāyas* (literally, segment or division), each with slightly different interpretations of the vinaya regulations. Since these *nikāyas* also predominated in different geographical areas and developed sometimes very different sets of ABHIDHARMA philosophical texts, they functioned as separate MAINSTREAM BUDDHIST SCHOOLS.

There is no evidence for any variant approach to ordination in the early MAHĀYĀNA vocation, but with the emergence of master–student initiation lineages in the Kashmiri meditation tradition (fourth century C.E. and thereafter) and the Indian tradition of TANTRA (ca. sixth century C.E. and thereafter), the relative significance of ordination declined somewhat. The Tibetan saṅgha maintains the use of ordination as an important threshold of entry into the practice of Buddhism, but greater emphasis is placed on tantric initiation lineages and the identification of *tulkus* (reincarnated sages). In an analagous fashion, local monastery relationships and both CHAN SCHOOL and esoteric (tantric) initiation lineages changed the religious salience of ordination in East Asia. More drastic changes occurred in modern Japan, where the Buddhist clergy have redefined ordination as a more lofty but less demanding dedication to Mahāyāna ideals not requiring maintenance of the rules of celibacy.

In the early years of Buddhism in each of the cultural realms of East Asia (China, Korea, Japan, and Vietnam), there was great emphasis on proper training in Buddhist vinaya (monastic regulations) and the correct ordination of monks and nuns. DAO'AN (312–385) devised a set of monastic rules himself, but was happy that it could be displaced by portions of the *Sarvāstivāda-vinaya* introduced toward the end of his life. The entire *Four Part Vinaya* (*Sifen lü*) of the Dharmaguptaka school, which was to become the most widely used version in China, was translated in 414 by Buddhayaśas and Zhu Fonian; complete vinayas of four other mainstream Buddhist schools were translated during the next decade or so. The insights of the pilgrim and translator XUANZANG (ca. 600–664) on contemporary Indian practices upon his return to China in 649, as well as his suggestion that all Chinese monks needed to be ordained anew, caused substantial uneasiness among his peers. This was one of the motivations behind an ordination platform movement initiated by the great historian and vinaya specialist DAOXUAN (596–667), who in the very last year of his life had visions of the Buddha's ordination platform at Jetavana. Although entirely contrary to Indian historical realities, the *sīma* boundary of the Indian ordination was reinterpreted as a Chinese-style raised platform. Daoxuan's example inspired other Chinese monks to build platforms and confer ordinations on the surface of what was effectively a caitya or monumental embodiment of the Buddha. A famous account of just such an ordination, or at least the sermons associated with it, is found in the PLATFORM SŪTRA OF THE SIXTH PATRIARCH (LIUZU TAN JING). After a major rebellion in China in 755, both government and rebels sponsored the ordination of Buddhist monks for fund-raising purposes; each ordinand paid a hefty fee but then received a lifetime exemption from taxation. In the Song dynasty (960–1279) blank ordination certificates were sometimes traded for financial speculation, but the government eventually eradicated all such abuses. It is generally held that government control of ordination negatively influenced the quality and independence of the Chinese saṅgha.

Several developments contributed to a change in the status and function of ordination in Chinese Buddhism. Based on the voluminous vinaya writings of Daoxuan, the Chinese tradition consolidated on the use of the Dharmaguptaka school's *Four Part Vinaya.* It was only during the Song dynasty, though, that the Chinese vinaya tradition really became formalized as an independent "school," and even here this word denotes a social reality very different from the *nikāyas* of Indian Buddhism. That is, a handful of major "public monasteries" in China were designated as vinaya centers, meaning that they were the ones where most but not all sophisticated study of the vinaya tradition occurred, and where all Chinese monks and nuns were ordained. The official ordination process became a large-scale affair involving not only the ceremony of vow-taking and induction itself, but a lengthy period of preliminary training in liturgy (recitation of scriptures, use of bells, drums, and other ritual implements, etc.) and deportment (wearing of robes, monastic etiquette, etc.). All Chinese monks and nuns were, and still are, united by their experience of this rite of passage, but the scale and formality of the event came to mean a reduced significance in contrast with other monastic relationships. That is, monks and nuns are far more likely to identify with the "disciple lineages" based on the local monasteries and teachers where they initially trained in Buddhism, to which they often returned after the weeks-long ordination ritual. In addition, elite segments of the monastic population also identify more profoundly with Chan and MIJIAO (ESOTERIC) SCHOOL initiation lineages. The use of *moxa* or incense to burn marks on the heads of Chinese ordinands seems to have begun around the sixteenth century.

There are various accounts, if only from later sources, describing the efforts taken by fourth- to fifth-century Korean Buddhists to establish proper vinaya practices there. Missionaries from Koguryŏ (northern Korea) and Paekche (southwestern Korea) were the earliest ordained monks in Japan. The earliest ordained Japanese Buddhists were women sent to Paekche in the late sixth century, the choice of women perhaps deriving from their function as priestesses or shamanesses (*miko*) in ancient Japanese society. The quest for orthodox vinaya regulations and qualified ordination masters preoccupied early Japanese Buddhists as much as it had their Chinese and Korean counterparts in earlier centuries, although here the source of canonical praxis was China rather than India. A great advance occurred with the arrival of the vinaya specialist Jianzhen (Japanese, GANJIN; 688–763) in Japan in 753. He had been frustrated many times in his efforts to reach Japan, becoming blind in the process. Although the Japanese government installed him in a magnificent monastery (Tōshōdaiji, still one of the most beautiful sites in Nara) and had him lead a spectacular ordination ceremony at a platform on the grounds of Tōdaiji, the "Great Eastern Monastery" that housed the Daibutsu or Great Buddha, Ganjin was frustrated by the Japanese refusal to consider ordination as much more than an elaborate ritual.

This tendency to disregard the 250 regulations of the *Four Part Vinaya* was carried even further by SAICHŌ (767–822), who argued that the government should allow his newly founded Tendai school to ordain monks without reference to the vinaya, which Saichō rejected as being "hīnayāna." Saichō's goal was to maintain control over the training of his own students, who frequently did not return from their ordinations in Nara; his wishes were granted just after his death, and the subsequent growth of Mount Hiei and the Tendai school as a whole meant that fewer and fewer Japanese clergy took vows based on the vinaya. In the early thirteenth century the Pure Land priest SHINRAN (1173–1262), who like many important Kamakura-period figures had trained for a period at Mount Hiei, declared himself to be "neither priest nor layperson" and publicly married. Although there was a short-lived movement to revitalize Buddhism through strict maintenance of the precepts at about the same time, marriage eventually became the norm for priests in Shinran's True Pure Land school (Jōdo shinshū). Although many Japanese priests in other schools maintained widely recognized but technically illicit marriage relationships throughout the late medieval period, it was only with the government's disestablishment of Buddhism in 1872 that a broad spectrum of the Japanese clergy renounced celibacy.

See also: **Mahāyāna Precepts in Japan; Monasticism**

Bibliography

Bunnag, Jane. *Buddhist Monk, Buddhist Layman: A Study of Urban Monastic Organization in Central Thailand.* Cambridge, UK: Cambridge University Press, 1973.

Coleman, Mary T. *Monastic: An Ordained Tibetan Buddhist Speaks on Behalf of Full Ordination for Women.* Los Angeles and Charlottesville, VA: Dharma Institute, 1995.

Dickson, J. F. "The Admission and Ordination Ceremonies." In *Buddhism in Translations,* by Henry Clarke Warren. New York: Atheneum, 1963 (1896). Reprinted from *Journal of the Royal Asiatic Society* (1874): 1–16.

Groner, Paul. *Saichō: The Establishment of the Japanese Tendai School.* Berkeley: Center for South and Southeast Asian Studies, University of California at Berkeley, 1984.

Gutschow, Kim. "What Makes a Nun? Apprenticeship and Ritual Passage in Zanskar, North India." *Journal of the International Association of Buddhist Studies* 24, no. 2 (2001): 187–215.

Heirman, Ann. *Rules for Nuns According to the Dharmaguptakavinaya: The Discipline in Four Parts.* New Delhi: Motilal Banarsidass, 2002.

Holt, John. *Discipline: The Canonical Buddhism of the Vinayapitaka.* New Delhi: Motilal Banarsidass, 1981.

Horner, Isaline Blew. *Women under Primitive Buddhism: Laywomen and Almswomen.* London: Routledge, 1930.

Kieffer-Puelz, Petra. "Die buddhistische Gemeinde." In *Der Buddhismus I. Der indische Buddhismus und seine Verzweigungen,* ed. Heinz Bechert et al. Stuttgart: Kohlhammer, 2000.

Lévy, Paul. *Buddhism: A "Mystery Religion"?* London: School of Oriental and African Studies, University of London, 1957.

Mendelson, E. Michael. "Initiation and the Paradox of Power: A Sociological Approach." In *Initiation: Contributions to the Theme of the Study-Conference of the International Association for the History of Religions Held at Strasburg, September 17th to 22nd 1964,* ed. C. J. Bleeker. Leiden, Netherlands: Brill, 1965.

Olivelle, Patrick. *The Origin and Early Development of Buddhist Monachism.* Colombo, Sri Lanka: Gunasena, 1974.

Sangharakshita. *Forty-Three Years Ago: Reflections on My Bhikkhu Ordination, on the Occasion of the Twenty-Fifth Anniversary of the Western Buddhist Order.* Glasgow, Scotland: Windhorse Publications, 1996.

Seneviratne, H. L. "L'ordination bouddhique à Ceylan." *Social Compass* 20 (1973): 251–56.

Tambiah, Stanley J. *Buddhism and the Spirit Cults in North-East Thailand.* Cambridge, UK: Cambridge University Press, 1970.

Thanissaro Bhikku, trans. *The Buddhist Monastic Code: The Patimokkha Training Rules,* 2 vols. Valley Center, CA: Metta Forest Monastery, 1994.

Tiyanavich, Kamala. *Forest Recollections: Wandering Monks in Twentieth-Century Thailand.* Honolulu: University of Hawaii Press, 1997.

Tsomo, Karma Lekshe, ed. *Sisters in Solitude: Two Traditions of Buddhist Monastic Ethics for Women—A Comparative Analysis of the Chinese Dharmagupta and the Tibetan Mūlasarvāstivada Bhikṣuṇī.* Albany: State University of New York Press, 1996.

Wachirayanawarorot. *Ordination Procedure.* Bangkok, Thailand: Mahamakut Rajavidyalaya [Mahamakut Educational Council], 1973.

Welch, Holmes. *The Practice of Chinese Buddhism.* Cambridge, MA: Harvard University Press, 1967.

Wijayaratna, Mohan. *Buddhist Monastic Life According to the Texts of the Theravāda Tradition.* Cambridge, UK: Cambridge University Press, 1990.

Wijayaratna, Mohan. *Les moniales bouddhistes: naissance et développement du monachisme féminin.* Paris: Cerf, 1991.

Yen Kiat, Bhikku. *Mahayana Vinaya.* Bangkok, Thailand: Wat Bhoman Khunnarama, 1960.

JOHN R. MCRAE

ORIGINAL ENLIGHTENMENT (HONGAKU)

The doctrine of original enlightenment (Japanese, *hongaku*) dominated Tendai Buddhism from roughly the eleventh through the early seventeenth centuries and profoundly influenced medieval Japanese religion and culture. This doctrine holds that enlightenment or the ideal state is neither a goal to be achieved nor a potential to be realized but the real status of all things. Not only human beings but ants and crickets, even grasses and trees, manifest innate buddhahood just as they are. Seen in its true aspect, every aspect of daily life—eating, sleeping, even one's deluded thoughts—is the Buddha's conduct.

Especially since the latter part of the twentieth century, considerable controversy has arisen over the cultural significance and ethical implications of this doctrine. Some scholars see in original enlightenment thought a timeless Japanese spirituality that affirms nature and accommodates phenomenal realities. Others see it as a dangerous antinomianism that undermines both religious discipline and moral standards. Beginning around the 1980s an intellectual movement known as CRITICAL BUDDHISM (HIHAN BUKKYŌ) has denounced original enlightenment thought as an authoritarian ideology that, by sacralizing all things just as they are, in effect bolsters the status quo and legitimates social injustice. Such sweeping polemical claims, however, have tended to inflate the term *original enlightenment* beyond its usefulness as an analytic category and to ignore its specific historical context within medieval Tendai.

Terms and texts

No scholarly consensus exists as to the best way to translate the word *hongaku.* In addition to "original enlightenment," the expressions "original awakening," "innate awakening," "primordial enlightenment," and others are also used (for the pros and cons of various translations, see Jacqueline I. Stone, *Original Enlightenment and the Transformation of Medieval Japanese Buddhism,* p. 369, n. 1). The term *original enlightenment* has its locus classicus in the AWAKENING OF FAITH (DASHENG QIXIN LUN), attributed to the Indian master AŚVAGHOṢA (ca. 100 C.E.), but was probably composed in China around the sixth century. There, *original enlightenment* (Chinese, *benjue*; Japanese, *hongaku*) refers to the potential for enlightenment even in deluded persons, and forms a triad with the terms *nonenlightenment* (*bujue, fukaku*), the deluded state of those ignorant of that potential, and *acquired enlightenment* (*shijue, shikaku*), the actualizing of that potential through Buddhist practice. In medieval Japanese Tendai literature, however, *original enlightenment* no longer denotes merely a potential but indicates the true status of all things just as they are.

Original enlightenment thought as a distinct Tendai intellectual tradition appears to have had its inception around the mid-eleventh century, when *hongaku* teachings began to be passed down from master to disciple in the form of oral transmissions (*kuden*). Eventually, these transmissions were written down in a few sentences on single sheets of paper called *kirikami,* which were in turn compiled to form larger texts, attributed retrospectively to great Tendai masters of the past, such as SAICHŌ (767–822), ENNIN (794–864), or GENSHIN (942–1017). Thus the precise dating of any specific collection, or of the ideas contained in it, is extremely difficult. In the thirteenth through fourteenth centuries, the doctrines of these oral transmission collections began to be systematized; Tendai scholars also began to produce commentaries on traditional Tiantai texts and on the LOTUS SŪTRA (SADDHARMAPUṆḌARĪKA-SŪTRA) itself, reinterpreting them from a *hongaku* perspective. It is only from about the fourteenth to fifteenth centuries that the dating and authorship of some of this literature can be established with relative certainty.

Major ideas

Original enlightenment doctrine has been described as a pinnacle in the development of MAHĀYĀNA concepts of nonduality. In particular, it is indebted to the great totalistic visions of the HUAYAN SCHOOL and the TIANTAI SCHOOL, in which all things, being empty of fixed substance, interpenetrate and encompass one another. Another important influence on the development of original enlightenment doctrine was tantric Buddhism, particularly its claim that all phenomena—forms, colors, sounds, and so on—are the activities of a primordial or cosmic Buddha who pervades the universe. The noted scholar Tamura Yoshirō (1921–1989) observed that, in original enlightenment thought, the absolute realm of abstract truth or principle (*ri*) and the conventional realm of concrete actualities (*ji*) are conflated. In other words, there is no reality beneath, behind, or prior to the phenomenal world; the moment-to-moment arising and perishing of all things, just as they are, are valorized absolutely as the expressions of original enlightenment. This idea is commonly expressed by such phrases as "all dharmas are the buddhadharma," "the defilements are none other than enlightenment," and "SAṂSĀRA is none other than NIRVĀṆA."

From this perspective, the buddhas represented in the sūtras, radiating light and endowed with excellent marks, are merely provisional signs to inspire the unenlightened. The "real" buddha is all ordinary beings. Indeed, "he" is not a person at all, whether historical or mythic, but the true aspect of all things. This buddha is said to be "unproduced," without beginning or end; to "constantly abide," being always present; and to "transcend august attributes," having no independent form apart from all phenomena just as they are. This view of the buddha is associated with the "origin teaching" (*honmon*) of the *Lotus Sūtra,* which describes Śākyamuni Buddha as having first achieved awakening at some point in the unimaginably distant past. Reinterpreted from the standpoint of *hongaku* thought, this initial attainment by Śākyamuni in the remote past becomes a metaphor for the beginningless original enlightenment innate in all.

Practice and enlightenment

This reinterpretation has significant implications for Buddhist practice. According to conventional views, enlightenment is attained as the culmination of a linear process in which the practitioner gradually accumulates merit, extirpates defilements, and eventually reaches awakening. Original enlightenment literature describes this view as the perspective of "acquired enlightenment," which "proceeds from cause (practice) to effect (enlightenment)"; it is judged to be, at best, an expedient to encourage the ignorant, and at worst, a deluded view. Original enlightenment doctrine reverses this directionality to "proceed from effect to cause." In other words, practice is seen, not as the cause of an enlightenment still to be attained, but as the expression of an enlightenment already inherent. One could also express this as a shift from a linear to a maṇḍalic view of time, in which practice and enlightenment are simultaneous.

Original enlightenment doctrine has often been criticized as leading to a denial of religious discipline: Why practice, if one is already enlightened? While the danger of this sort of antinomian interpretation certainly exists, original enlightenment thought is more accurately understood as representing a transformation in how practice is understood. It opposes instrumentalist views of practice as merely a means to achieve something else, and instead redefines practice in nonlinear terms as the paradigmatic expression of the nonduality of the practitioner and the buddha.

Moreover, despite its thoroughgoing commitment to a nondual perspective, original enlightenment doctrine distinguishes between the experiential state of knowing (or even simply having faith) that "all dharmas are the buddhadharma" and that of not knowing it. It is only on the basis of insight into nondual original enlightenment that such statements as "saṃsāra is precisely nirvāṇa" can be made. Based on such insight or faith, however, not only formal Buddhist practice but all other activities of daily life can be seen as constituting the buddha's behavior.

Hongaku doctrine and medieval Japanese culture

Original enlightenment teachings developed within, and also contributed to, a broader medieval tradition of "secret transmission," deriving largely from private master-to-disciple initiation into the ritual procedures transmitted within lineages of esoteric Buddhism. In time, knowledge, not only of ritual and doctrine, but of poetry, the visual and performing arts, and also many crafts came to be handed down through master–disciple lineages. The "orally transmitted teachings" of original enlightenment thought were similarly elaborated and passed down within specific Tendai teaching lineages. Chief among these were the Eshin and Danna lineages; each had several sublineages. Despite conventions of secrecy, evidence points to considerable exchange among lineages and to individual monks receiving transmissions from more than one teacher.

The premises of original enlightenment doctrine were also assimilated to other vocabularies and influenced the broader culture. One such area of influence was Shintō theory. From around the mid-Heian period (794–1185), local deities (*kami*) had been understood as "traces" or manifestations projected by the universal buddhas and bodhisattvas as a "skillful means" to benefit the people of Japan. This view clearly subsumed *kami* worship within a Buddhist framework. Original enlightenment thought, with its emphasis on concrete actualities as equivalent to absolute principle, set the stage for a revalorization of the *kami* as equal, or even superior, to buddhas, and thus played a key role at the theoretical level in the beginnings of formal Shintō doctrine.

Original enlightenment thought also influenced the development of medieval aesthetics, especially poetic theory. Though the composition and appreciation of verse were vital social skills in elite circles, many clerics saw poetry as a distraction for the committed Buddhist because it involved one in the world of the senses and the sin of "false speech." Original enlightenment ideas provided one of several "nondual" strategies by which poets, many of whom were monks and nuns, reclaimed the composition of verse, not only as a legitimate activity for Buddhists, but, when approached with the proper attitude, as a form of Buddhist practice in its own right. From this perspective, poetry, or art more generally, was seen, not as a second-level representation of a higher, "religious" truth, but as an expression of innate enlightenment.

See also: **Exoteric-Esoteric (Kenmitsu) Buddhism in Japan; Kamakura Buddhism, Japan; Poetry and Buddhism; Shingon Buddhism, Japan; Shintō (Honji Suijaku) and Buddhism; Shugendō; Tantra**

Bibliography

Groner, Paul. "A Medieval Japanese Reading of the *Mo-ho chih-kuan*: Placing the *Kankō ruijū* in Historical Context." *Japanese Journal of Religious Studies* 22, nos. 1–2 (Spring 1995): 49–81.

Habito, Ruben L. F. *Originary Enlightenment: Tendai Hongaku Doctrine and Japanese Buddhism.* Tokyo: International Institute for Buddhist Studies, 1996.

Hubbard, Jamie, and Swanson, Paul L., eds. *Pruning the Bodhi Tree: The Storm over Critical Buddhism.* Honolulu: University of Hawaii Press, 1997.

LaFleur, William R. "Symbol and *Yūgen*: Shunzei's Use of Tendai Buddhism." In *Flowing Traces: Buddhism in the Literary and Visual Arts of Japan,* ed. James H. Sanford, William R. LaFleur, and Masatoshi Nagatomi. Princeton, NJ: Princeton University Press, 1992.

Shirato, Waka. "Inherent Enlightenment (*hongaku shisō*) and Saichō's Acceptance of the Bodhisattva Precepts." *Japanese Journal of Religious Studies* 14, nos. 2–3 (1987): 113–127.

Stone, Jacqueline I. "The Contemplation of Suchness." In *Religions of Japan in Practice,* ed. George J. Tanabe, Jr. Princeton, NJ: Princeton University Press, 1999.

Stone, Jacqueline I. *Original Enlightenment and the Transformation of Medieval Japanese Buddhism.* Honolulu: University of Hawaii Press, 1999.

Sueki, Fumihiko. "Two Seemingly Contradictory Aspects of the Teaching of Innate Enlightenment (*Hongaku*) in Medieval Japan." *Japanese Journal of Religious Studies* 22, nos. 1–2 (Spring 1995): 3–16.

Tamura, Yoshirō. "Japanese Culture and the Tendai Concept of Original Enlightenment." *Japanese Journal of Religious Studies* 14, nos. 2–3 (June–Sept. 1987): 203–210.

JACQUELINE I. STONE

OXHERDING PICTURES

This is a series of Chan (Japanese, Zen) school illustrations of a boy chasing and taming a wild ox that symbolizes the process of seeking and attaining enlightenment by means of self-discipline and self-transformation. Through the ten paintings that are titled and accompanied by verse commentaries, a narrative of the awakening process unfolds. The boy represents a seeker, and the ox represents the chaotic, unharnessed tendencies of the mind or ego that has the potential to be transformed into a vehicle for realizing true spiritual awareness.

What is known as the *Ten Oxherding Pictures* is not a single collection of illustrations, but multiple versions of the series of pictures and poems. The best known are two early versions developed in the eleventh or twelfth century during the Song dynasty of China: one by Puming, which is probably the oldest, and the other by Kuoan. These are included in the main supplement to the Chinese Buddhist canon, the *Xu zang jing* (*Supplemental Buddhist Canon*), but they have been reproduced and modified on numerous occasions. Revision of the paintings and comments was especially popular in Tokugawa-era Japan, and new versions have been produced in the modern period as well. A well-known version by Kuo'an is transcribed by Nyogen Senzaki and Paul Reps and illustrated by Tomikichiro Tokuriki in a way that is similar to the originals, but with some interesting differences.

The early version by Puming is titled as follows:

1. *Undisciplined.*
2. *Discipline Begun.*
3. *In Harness.*
4. *Faced Round.*
5. *Tamed.*
6. *Unimpeded.*
7. *Laissez Faire.*
8. *All Forgotten.*
9. *The Solitary Moon.*
10. *Both Vanished.*

The other early series by Kuo'an is titled as follows:

1. *Searching for the Ox.*
2. *Seeing the Traces.*
3. *Seeing the Ox.*
4. *Catching the Ox.*
5. *Herding the Ox.*
6. *Coming Home on the Ox's Back.*
7. *The Ox Forgotten.*
8. *The Ox and the Man Both Gone Out of Sight.*
9. *Returning to the Origin.*
10. *Entering the World.*

In both sets, subtle details in the landscape and the coloring of the boy, ox, trees, moon, and other background elements change to reflect the changing state of mind of the seeker, who gradually attains enlightenment.

The main difference in the versions hinges on the sequence of events and the religious implications in the final outcome. In the Puming version, the boy tames the ox and the two coexist in a paradisiacal state, and then move into a mystical realm. By the penultimate picture, the ox is gone, and in the last, the boy also disappears, leaving an empty circle. In the Kuoan version, the empty circle appears in the seventh picture, but by the end the boy, without the ox, reenters the ordinary world to apply his enlightenment in the marketplace.

See also: **Chan School**

Bibliography

Miyuki, Mokusen. "Self-Realization in the Ten Oxherding Pictures." In *Self and Liberation: The Jung/Buddhism Dialogue,* ed. Daniel J. Meckel and Robert L. Moore. New York: Paulist Press, 1992.

Reps, Paul. *Zen Flesh, Zen Bones,* collected by Paul Reps and tr. by Paul Reps and Nyogen Senzaki. Boston: Charles E. Tuttle Publishing, 1957.

Suzuki, D. T. *The Manual of Zen Buddhism.* London: Rider and Company, 1950.

STEVEN HEINE

P

PADMASAMBHAVA

Active in the late eighth century, Padmasambhava (Lotus Born) is widely revered throughout the Himalayan regions under the title Guru Rinpoche. He is of particular importance to the followers of the RNYING MA (NYINGMA) school of Tibetan Buddhism, who consider him the "Second Buddha" and a founder of their school. Today Padmasambhava is the focus of many rituals. The tenth day of each lunar month is devoted to him. At monasteries of the Rnying ma school, these days are observed with ritual feasting, and sometimes religious dances (*'chams*) are performed to pay homage to the Indian master's eight manifestations (*gu ru mtshan brgyad*). Many Buddhist monasteries are decorated with paintings of these same eight forms.

The influences of this renowned master on Tibetan Buddhism have been both historical and inspirational. Initially in the eighth century he seems to have played a crucial role in the establishment of Buddhism in Tibet. Since then he has appeared to Tibetans in revelations and visionary encounters. As a result of the latter inspirational role, visionary biographies of Padmasambhava abound, and his historical activities have become heavily mythologized.

Historically, relatively little is known of this master. He seems to have come from Oḍḍiyāna, a kingdom probably located in the northwest of India. The late eighth century was an unusually creative period in the development of tantric Buddhism. In particular, these years saw the arrival of the Mahāyoga class of TANTRAS. Remarkable for their transgressive practices and imagery, the Mahāyoga tantras taught the violent means for subjugating demons and harmful spirits. Padmasambhava seems to have specialized in these new Mahāyoga practices. Traveling through the Himalayan regions of India and Nepal, his reputation was enhanced by his activities around Kathmandu valley, were he is said to have stayed in retreat for some years at Muratika, Yang le shod, and the Asura cave. Around this time, the Tibetan king, Khri song lde btsan (r. 755–797), was working to construct Tibet's first Buddhist monastery, BSAM YAS (SAMYE). On the recommendation of the Indian scholar Śāntarakṣita, the king invited Padmasambhava to assist with subjugating the indigenous Tibetan spirits opposed to the foreign religion. Padmasambhava accepted the invitation, and his activities around Bsam yas were considered crucial to the establishment of Buddhism as the state religion of Tibet.

This basic narrative is embellished with many legendary details in the later visionary biographies received as *gter ma* (treasure) texts after the eleventh century. One early biography that was particularly influential was the *Zang gling ma* (*Copper Colored Mountain*) discovered by Nyang ral nyi ma'i 'od zer (1124–1192). Named after the paradise for which Padmasambhava is believed to have departed Tibet, this biography describes the master's miraculous birth from a lotus blossom at the center of Lake Danakośa in Oḍḍiyāna. Initially raised by the king Indrabodhi, the youth is said to have renounced his royal trappings to live as a Buddhist ascetic. Various legendary adventures are then recounted, including Padmasambhava's meeting with his first consort, the Indian Mandārāva, at the Lotus Lake (Mtsho Padma) in Himachal Pradesh. While residing near Kathmandu, he is said to have gathered the scattered practice traditions for the deity Vajrakīlaya into a single, all-powerful system. In

Padmasambhava, who played a crucial role in the establishment of Buddhism in Tibet in the eighth century. (Tibetan *thang ka* [scroll painting], nineteenth century.) The Art Archive/Private Collection Paris/Dagli Orti. Reproduced by permission.

Tibet, he used his tantric powers to convert the local spirits into protectors of the Buddhist faith. As reward for his work, the Tibetan king offered Padmasambhava a second consort, named Ye shes tsho rgyal. This powerful woman would eventually become a cult figure in her own right. Together with her, Padmasambhava is said to have concealed his most secret teachings as hidden *gter ma,* to be revealed by later generations of Tibetans at the appropriate times. The future revealers of these *gter ma* were understood to be reincarnations of Padmasambhava's students, so that the process of revelation was, in part at least, one of remembering long-forgotten teachings once received from the great master.

Later biographies added still more detail, and the places visited by Padmasambhava continued to multiply. Over the centuries the legend grew as Padmasambhava's myth was replayed in various border regions. As new regions were converted to Buddhism, narratives would often surface describing Padmasambhava's alleged visits to sites crucial to those regions. According to such narratives, Padmasambhava visited these sites to subjugate the local non-Buddhist spirits, thus preparing the ground for the future conversion of the regions to Buddhism. Many such sites have remained sacred and are still PILGRIMAGE destinations for Buddhists throughout Tibet, Nepal, India, and Bhutan. Thus, Padmasambhava's primary importance has become twofold: as the inspirational source for the *gter ma* revelations and as a legendary tamer of local spirits.

See also: **Apocrypha; Tibet**

Bibliography

Douglas, Kenneth, and Bays, Gwendolyn. *The Life and Liberation of Padmasambhava: The bKa' thang shel brag ma as Recorded by Yeshe Tsogyal,* 2 vols. Berkeley, CA: Dharma, 1978.

Guenther, Herbert V. *The Teachings of Padmasambhava.* New York: Brill, 1996.

Gyatso, Janet. "The Logic of Legitimation in the Tibetan Treasure Tradition." *History of Religions* 33, no. 2 (1993): 97–134.

Rinpoche, Dudjom. *The Nyingma School of Tibetan Buddhism: Its Fundamentals and History,* 2 vols., tr. Gyurme Dorje and Matthew Kapstein. Boston: Wisdom, 1991.

JACOB P. DALTON

PĀLI, BUDDHIST LITERATURE IN

The term *Pāli,* used today in both Buddhist and Western cultures as a designation of a language, is a relatively modern coinage, not traceable before the seventeenth century. An earlier name given to this language in Buddhist literature is Māgadhī, the language of the province Magadha in Eastern India that roughly corresponds to the modern Indian state Bihār. The only Buddhist school using this language is the THERAVĀDA in Sri Lanka and Southeast Asia. Theravādins erroneously consider Pāli to be the language spoken by the Buddha himself.

During the nineteenth century, Western scholarship discovered that Pāli is not an eastern Middle Indic language and has little relationship to Māgadhī, which is known from other sources. By comparing the languages used in the inscriptions of AŚOKA (third century B.C.E.), it is possible to demonstrate that Pāli, while preserving some very old Eastern elements, is clearly based on a western Middle Indic language, one of the languages that developed out of Vedic Sanskrit, which was used in India roughly until the time of the Buddha (ca. fourth century B.C.E.). Although Pāli is clearly younger than the time of the Buddha, it is the oldest surviving variety of Middle Indic.

The dialect used by the Buddha himself when instructing his disciples is unknown and irretrievably lost. It might have been some early variety of Māgadhī. The oldest Buddhist language, which can be traced by reconstruction, is Buddhist Middle Indic, a lingua franca that developed much later than the lifetime of the Buddha. Buddhist Middle Indic is the basis of Pāli and the Buddhist Hybrid Sanskrit used by the MAHĀSĀṂGHIKA Lokottaravādins.

Even though Pāli, as an artificial language, was never actually a vernacular of any part of India, it was by no means a "dead" language. Changes in the phonetic shape of Pāli, most likely introduced by Buddhist grammarians at various times, can be observed, although dating them is problematic. None of these changes were far-reaching, although they seem to have continued well into the sixteenth century, if not later.

The oldest literature preserved in Pāli is the CANON of the Theravāda Buddhists, the only Buddhist canon extant in its entirety in an Indian language. Consequently, it is linguistically the oldest form of Buddhist scriptures known. This, of course, does not mean that other scriptures in different younger languages or translations necessarily preserve only later developments of Buddhist thought and tradition. Though generally conservative, Pāli literature probably developed over several centuries before it was committed to writing. According to the Theravādins, this redaction happened during the first century B.C.E. in Sri Lanka, when various disasters decimated the number of Buddhist monks and threatened the oral tradition. Like the Vedic texts, early Buddhist literature was composed during a period of pure orality in India, before script was introduced during the reign of Aśoka. This early oral tradition has left obvious traces in the written literature, particularly in the numerous formulas typical of oral composition, which were used to facilitate memorization.

The writing down of the Theravāda canon is related in Theravāda church history as preserved in two chronicles (VAṂSA) composed in Pāli: the *Dīpavaṃsa* (*Chronicle of the Island*, ca. 350 C.E.) and the later *Mahāvaṃsa* (*Great Chronicle*, late fifth century C.E.). Both give a legendary history of political and religious events in Sri Lanka; the latter, which was extended several times, ends with the British conquest in 1815.

Tipiṭaka (Threefold Basket)

According to the Theravāda tradition, the texts committed to writing comprised the complete *Tipiṭaka* (Sanskrit, *Tripiṭaka*), the *Threefold Basket*—the designation for the canon in all Buddhist schools. Although a similar name is also used by the Jains for their holy scriptures, the choice of the term *basket* for a collection of texts cannot be explained. The Threefold Basket is, however, not the oldest division of the canonical texts. An earlier division into *nine limbs* (*nava aṅga*) was abandoned at a very early date, most likely when the collection of texts grew into a large corpus and had to be regrouped following different principles.

Vinayapiṭaka (Basket of Discipline). Each of the Tipiṭaka's three parts are made up of collections of texts concerning three different aspects of Buddhist community life and teaching. The first part of the Tipiṭaka is the *Vinayapiṭaka* (*Basket of Discipline*), which is further divided into three parts. At the beginning is the *Suttavibhaṅga* (*Explanation of the Sutta*), an old commentary in which the *sutta* itself is embedded. *Sutta* here does not mean, as in later usage, a discourse of the Buddha, but a set of 227 rules (*Pāṭimokkha*; Sanskrit, PRĀTIMOKṢA) regulating the life of each individual monk. Some of these rules are among the oldest Buddhist texts preserved, with parallels in the Vinaya or monastic codes of other schools. The meaning of the title *Pāṭimokkha* is unclear. This text must be recited twice each month by monks in every monastery. In spite of its age, an early development of this text can be traced. Brief rules, such as "in drinking alcohol, there is an offense," eventually developed into much longer and legally complicated formulations. The original brevity reflects the original meaning of *sutta* (Sanskrit, sūtra), "[set of] brief rule(s)." The first four rules describe offenses entailing an expulsion from the order (*pārājika*, concerning a chasing away [of a monk from the community]). The offenses described in the following rules are increasingly less grave. The seventh and last groups of offenses contain rules for general civilized behavior, and an appendix enumerates methods to settle disputes. All the rules are embedded in frame stories, which describe the occasion that necessitates the creation of such a rule. The commentary explains single words of the rules and develops their legal applications.

The second part of the *Vinayapiṭaka*, the *Khandhaka* (sections), contains rules governing the life of the community as a whole. The *Khandhaka*, which is divided into twelve parts, begins with the enlightenment of the Buddha and the founding of the Buddhist order (SAṄGHA) and ends with the reports on the first two councils at Rājagṛha and Vaiśālī, respectively. The tenth part of the *Khandhaka* is devoted to the foundation of the order of NUNS, to which the Buddha agreed only after much hesitation.

The third and much later part of the *Vinayapiṭaka* is a handbook, the *Parivāra* (ca. first century C.E.). This handbook comprises a collection of texts containing brief summaries of the Vinaya, among them an interesting collection of difficult legal questions called *Sedamocanakagāthā* (*Sweat Producing Verses*).

Suttapiṭaka (Basket of the Discourses). The second part of the Tipiṭaka, the *Suttapiṭaka* (*Basket of the Discourses*) is divided into four older parts, which are mentioned in the *Vinayapiṭaka*'s report of the first council, and a fifth later addition. The name *Suttapiṭaka*, however, does not occur in the report on the council describing the formation of the canon. Single texts were called *veyyākaraṇa* (explanation) or *dhammapariyāya* (discourse on the teaching) before the name *sutta*(*nta*) was introduced at an uncertain date.

The first part of the *Suttapiṭaka* is made up of twenty-four texts called the *Dīghanikāya* (*Group of Long Discourses*). The *Dīghanikāya* contains, among other things, discussions with the six heretics, and one of the most famous Buddhist texts, the *Mahāparinibbāna-sutta*

(Sanskrit, MAHĀPARINIRVĀṆA-SŪTRA; *Great Discourse on the Nirvāṇa*), the longest text in the canon and the first lengthy literary composition in ancient India.

The second part of the *Suttapiṭaka*, the *Majjhimanikāya* (*Group of Middle Length Discourses*), comprises 152 texts in which different aspects of Buddhist teaching are explained in the form of dialogues. The last two groups (*nikāya*), the *Saṃyuttanikāya* (*Connected Discourses*) and the *Aṅguttaranikāya* (*Discourses Increasing by One*), are structurally unique; the mostly short texts (according to the tradition about 7,500 in the *Saṃyuttanikāya* and almost 10,000 in the *Aṅguttaranikāya*) are the first attempts to present the teaching in a more systematic form. Topics in the *Aṅguttaranikāya* are arranged by number: The first book contains items existing only once, the last one items existing eleven times. (The last two *suttantas* of the *Dīghanikāya* follow a similar method for arranging texts.) The first part of the *Saṃyuttanikāya*, the *Sagāthavagga* (*Section Containing Verses*), stands apart, containing some old views that are occasionally close to Vedic concepts.

The *Khuddakanikāya* (*Group of Small Texts*), is an unsystematic collection of partly very old, partly very young texts. The *Khuddakanikāya*'s famous DHAMMAPADA (*Words of the Doctrine*), a collection of 423 verses, is one of the most popular texts with Buddhist monks and laypersons. The *Khuddakanikāya* also includes one of the oldest parts of the canon, the *Suttanipāta* (*Group of Discourses*), a collection of small independent texts, mostly in verse. It seems likely that some titles quoted in an inscription of Aśoka are in fact referring to texts of this collection. If correct, this is the oldest Indian epigraphical evidence for extant Buddhist texts.

Another collection mentioned in early inscriptions are the JĀTAKA stories. Some of the 547 stories, which describe the former lives of the Buddha as BODHISATTVA (Pāli, *Bodhisatta*), are illustrated and provided with titles in the bas-reliefs of Bharhut in India. Only the jātaka verses are part of the Tipiṭaka. The collection of prose stories, called *Jāṭṭakatthavaṇṇanā* (*Explanation of the Birth Stories*), is regarded as a commentary and was composed in its present form about a millennium later than the verses, which, for the most part, are not specifically Buddhist. The best known is the 547th, the *Vessantara jātaka* (Sanskrit, VIŚVANTARA), which describes the last birth of the Bodhisattva, before he ascends to the Tuṣita heaven, from where he is reborn on earth to reach enlightenment.

Among the other collections in the *Khuddakanikāya* are the *Verses of the Elders* (*Thera-* and *Therīgāthā*), which are supposed to have been spoken by disciples of the Buddha. Those ascribed to "elder nuns" (*Therīgāthā*) are the oldest literature known from ancient India supposed to have been composed by women. As such they are unique in Middle Indic as well as in Sanskrit literature. Some texts of the *Khuddakanikāya* are early commentaries, with one text, the *Paṭisambhidāmagga* (*Path of Discrimination*), which would fit better into the third part of the canon, the *Abhidhammapiṭaka*.

Abhidhammapiṭaka (Basket Concerning the Teaching). The title *Abhidhamma* is interpreted later by Buddhists as "Higher Teaching." The seven texts of this final part of the canon comprise the *Kathāvatthu* (*Text Dealing with Disputes*), where conflicting opinions on different points of the Buddhist teaching are discussed. According to tradition, this text was composed during the reign of Aśoka by Moggalliputta Tissa. Therefore, this is the only text in the canon with an author and a date. The other texts of the *Abhidhammapiṭaka* mostly contain enumerations of different *dhammas* elaborated by unfolding a summary (*mātikā*), which appears at the beginning of the respective text. as the frame of an *Abhidhamma* text. Parts of the *Vinayapiṭaka*, and particularly the *Sāṃyuttanikāya*, can be similarly condensed and are handed down as "skeleton texts" to be unfolded in recitation. The last *Abhidhamma* text, the *Paṭṭhāna* (*Conditional Relations*), can be expanded in such a way that it becomes infinite, as the commentary says.

Commentaries and subcommentaries

The Tipiṭaka was the object of explanatory commentaries at an early date. According to tradition, both Tipiṭaka and commentary, the *Aṭṭhakathā* (*Explanation of the Meaning*), were brought to Sri Lanka by Mahinda during the time of Aśoka (third century C.E.). The commentary actually preserved is a revision of an earlier, now lost, explanation of the Tipiṭaka composed in old Sinhalese Prākrit.

During the fifth century C.E., BUDDHAGHOSA composed his still valid handbook of Theravāda orthodoxy for the Mahāvihāra in Anurādhapura. This *Visuddhimagga* (*Path to Purification*) is the centerpiece of Buddhaghosa's commentaries on the first four *nikāyas*. As stated in the respective introductions, each of the four commentaries comprises a full explanation of the Buddha's teaching in combination with the *Visuddhimagga*. Contrary to the claims of the Theravāda tradition, Buddhaghosa wrote, or supervised the writing, only of these texts, huge in themselves. The commentaries on the *Vinaya-piṭaka*, on the *Abhidhammapiṭaka*, and on part of the *Khuddakanikāya* are anonymous.

A commentary of uncertain date (probably between 450 and 600 C.E.) on seven of the collections of the *Khuddakanikāya* was composed by Dhammapāla (although Lance Cousins has recently suggested Jotipāla as the author of this commentary). It is important to note that Dhammapāla's sequence of *Khuddakanikāya* texts deviates from the one common in the Mahāvihāra, and that he used a different recension of two texts, suggesting that he was following traditions of South Indian Pāli literature, which probably flourished through the first millennium C.E., but is now almost completely lost.

Subcommentaries constitute another layer of Pāli literature. After older subcommentaries on the *Abhidhammapiṭaka* (ascribed to Ānanda) and on Buddhaghosa's commentaries (ascribed to Dhammapāla), the next subcommentaries were written during the reign of Parakkamabāhu I (r. 1153–1186), who reformed and unified the Buddhist order in Sri Lanka. Consequently, much weight was put on explaining the *Vinayapiṭaka*. This task was entrusted by the king to Sāriputta and his disciples.

Pāli literature in Southeast Asia

With Theravāda also firmly established in Southeast-Asia (Burma [Myanmar], Thailand, and Cambodia), new branches of Pāli literature developed. During a short period in the late fifteenth and early sixteenth centuries, Pāli literature flourished in Chiang Mai (Northern Thailand). A chronicle of Buddhist teaching concentrating on developments in Southeast Asia, the *Jinakālamālinī* (*Garland of the Epochs of the Conquerer*) by Ratanapañña, and subcommentaries to the *Vinayapiṭaka* and *Abhidhammapiṭaka* by Ñāṇakitti indicate a remarkable, but short-lived, literary activity. At the same time, cosmological texts such as the *Cakkavāḷadīpanī* (*Elucidation of the World Systems*), composed in 1520 by Sirimaṅgala, brought new elements into Pāli literature.

Another literary genre that flourished in this period (and that remains particularly popular in Thailand) is the jātaka. Numerous apocryphal jātakas were written in vernacular languages, as well as in Pāli. The best known Pāli collection is the *Paññāsajātaka* (*Fifty Jātakas*), which formally imitates the canonical collection. This was also the time when the oldest extant Pāli manuscripts were copied in ancient Lān Nā (Northern Thailand). Palm leaf manuscripts are also known from Sri Lanka and Burma, mostly copied during the eighteenth and nineteenth centuries. A singular exception is a fragment of a Pāli manuscript preserved in Kathmandu containing four folios from the *Vinayapiṭaka* written during the eighth or ninth century in Northern India.

In Burma, a long and fruitful philological activity began with Aggavāmsa's *Saddanīti* composed in 1154. This grammatical treatise deeply influenced the whole later Pāli tradition. Strong emphasis was also put on explaining the *Abhidhammapiṭaka* and on writing handbooks on *Abhidhamma* matters.

Conclusion

It is striking that the older Pāli literature is almost exclusively confined to the canon and its commentaries. Handbooks on the *Vinayapiṭaka* or *Abhidhammapiṭaka*, such as those written by Buddhadatta, a contemporary of Buddhaghosa, or on HERMENEUTICS, such as the *Peṭakopadesa* (*Instruction Concerning the Tipiṭaka*) and the *Nettipakaraṇa* (*Guide to Interpretation*), both predating Buddhaghosa, are rare exceptions, as are the chronicles. It is only after the twelfth century that Pāli literature began to develop outside (and beside) the canon. However, these later literary activities, particularly the later literature from Southeast Asia, are comparatively little studied. When Pāli studies began in Europe with the publication of a Pāli grammar by Eugène Burnouf (1801–1852) and Christian Lassen (1800–1876) in 1826, emphasis was on research on older literature. The canon was first printed after T. W. Rhys Davids (1834–1922) founded the Pāli Text Society in 1881; the society continues to publish translations and canonical and commentarial texts in Pāli.

See also: Entries on specific countries; **Commentarial Literature; Languages; Sinhala, Buddhist Literature in**

Bibliography

Gombrich, Richard. "What Is Pāli? Introduction To." In *A Pāli Grammar*, by Wilhelm Geiger, tr. Bata-Krishna Ghosh, rev. and ed. K. R. Norman. Oxford: Pali Text Society, 1994.

Lienhard, Siegfried. *A History of Classical Poetry: Sanskrit, Pāli, Prakrit.* A History of Indian Literature, vol. 3, facs. 1. Wiesbaden, Germany: Harrassowitz, 1984.

Norman, K. R. *Pāli Literature: Including the Canonical Literature in Prakrit and Sanskrit of All the Hinayana Schools of Buddhism.* A History of Indian Literature, vol. 7, facs. 2. Wiesbaden, Germany: Harrassowitz, 1982.

Oberlies, Thomas. *Pāli: A Grammar of the Language of the Theravāda Tipiṭaka.* Berlin: de Gruyter, 2001.

von Hinüber, Oskar. *A Handbook of Pāli Literature.* Berlin: Gruyter, 1996.

von Hinüber, Oskar. *Entstehung und Aufbau der Jātaka-Sammlung.* Mainz: Akademie der Wissenschaften und der Literatur, 1998.

von Hinüber, Oskar. "Structure and Origin of the Pātimokkha-sutta of the Theravadins." *Acta Orientalia Academiae Scientiarum Hungaricae* 51 (1998): 257–265.

von Hinüber, Oskar. "Lān Nā as a Centre of Pāli Literature during the Late Fifteenth Century." *Journal of the Pali Text Society* 26 (2000): 119–138.

OSKAR VON HINÜBER

PANCHEN LAMA

The Panchen Lamas are the second most powerful religious and secular figures in Tibet, after the Dalai Lamas. The word *pan* is a short form of the Sanskrit word *paṇḍita* (scholar), and *chen* is a Tibetan word that means "great." Although the institution of Panchen Lama, like the DALAI LAMA, is part of the DGE LUGS (GELUK) tradition in its origins, its power and authority extend beyond the confines of that particular sect.

The line of Panchen Lamas begins with the abbots of Bkra shis lhun po (pronounced Tashilunpo) Monastery in Gzhi ka rtse (Shigatse), the largest city in Gtsang (Tsang) in west central Tibet. Bkra shis lhun po was founded by Dge 'dun grub (Gendun Drup, 1391–1474), a student of the great scholar-saint TSONG KHA PA (1357–1419). Dge 'dun grub, who was posthumously named the first Dalai Lama, was instrumental in extending the influence of the fledgling Dga' ldan pa (Gandenpa, later called Dge lugs pa) sect beyond the east central region centered around Lhasa.

The first named Panchen Lama was Blo bzang chos kyi rgyal mtshan (Lobsang Chökyi Gyaltsen, 1567–1662), the teacher of the fourth and fifth Dalai Lamas and the force behind the coalition that in 1642 defeated the Karma pas and their Gtsang patrons. Following that defeat, the center of power moved decisively from Gtsang to the new government called the Tuṣita Palace (Dga' ldan pho brang) seated in the POTALA palace in Lhasa. As an expression of gratitude for his help, the fifth Dalai Lama (1617–1682) named his teacher the abbot of Bkra shis lhun po Monastery and bestowed on him the title Panchen Lama.

As with the Dalai Lamas, a number of important figures were subsequently and retroactively named earlier reincarnations of Blo bzang chos kyi rgyal mtshan. The most important of them was Mkhas grub dpal bzang po (Kaydrub Pelzangpo, 1385–1438), one of the two closest disciples of Tsong kha pa. Following him was Bsod nams phyogs kyi glang po (Sonam Chokyi Langpo, d. 1504?) and Blo bzang don grub (Lobsang Dondrub, 1505–1566). According to this manner of calculation, Blo bzang chos kyi rgyal mtshan became the fourth Panchen Lama, and the present disputed child incarnation of the Panchen Lama, Dge 'dun chos kyi nyi ma (Gendun Chökyi Nyima, b. 1990), is the eleventh.

In some early English accounts the Panchen Lamas are called Tashi Lamas, a confusion between the name of the person and Bkra bzhis lhun po Monastery; in Chinese publications, they are called Panchen Erdini, a Mongolian word that means "precious jewel." This latter title was first bestowed on the fifth Panchen Lama, Blo bzang ye shes (Lobsang Yeshay, 1663–1737) in 1731 by the Manchu-Chinese emperor Kangxi.

After the death of the seventh Dalai Lama in 1758, the sixth Panchen Lama, Blo bzang dpal ldan ye shes (Lobsang Palden Yeshay, 1738–1780) was regarded by the Manchus as the foremost Tibetan spiritual leader because of his great learning and rectitude. He was repeatedly invited to Beijing. He finally assented and died there from smallpox in 1780.

Although the relationship between the Dalai Lamas and Panchen Lamas in the seventeenth and eighteenth centuries was cordial, the traditional antagonism between western Gtsang and the east central regions of Tibet, centered in Gzhi ka rtse and Lhasa, respectively, soon reappeared. The Manchus, and later the Chinese Communist Party led by Mao Zedong, exploited this tension to counter the power of the Dalai Lamas.

The relationship between the thirteenth Dalai Lama, Thub bstan rgya mtsho (Tubten Gyatso, 1876–1933), and the ninth Panchen Lama, Thub bstan chos kyi nyi ma (Tubten Chökyi Nyima, 1883–1937), was severely strained according to Melvyn Goldstein in *A History of Modern Tibet* (1989) when the Dalai Lama attempted to tax the Panchen Lama's estates to help pay for a new modern army. The Panchen Lama's retainers saw this as a veiled attack on the institution of the Panchen Lama, and this in turn led the Dalai Lama's government to accuse the Panchen Lama of treason. The ninth Panchen Lama then fled to China where he remained until his death.

The tenth Panchen Lama, Chos kyi rgyal mtshan 'phrin las rnam rgyal (Chökyi Gyaltsen Tinlay

In 1995 the Dalai Lama, in his Indian exile, announced that a boy named Dge 'dun chos kyi nyi ma was the new Panchen Lama. China, asserting its authority, repudiated the choice and later declared another boy to be the true Panchen Lama. Here the Chinese nominee, six-year-old Rgyal mtshan nor bu (Gyaltsen Norbu), is escorted into the Xihuang Monastery in Beijing in 1996. AP/Wide World Photos. Reproduced by permission.

Namgyel, 1938–1989), like the fourteenth Dalai Lama, Bstan 'dzin rgya mtsho (Tenzin Gyatso, b. 1935), was born in 'A mdo, the far northeastern region of Tibet. The tenth Panchen Lama was educated traditionally and was given a position in the Chinese government. In 1959, when the Dalai Lama fled to India, the Chinese government urged the Panchen Rinpoche to assume the Dalai Lama's position, but he declined to do so. He further antagonized the increasingly repressive Communist China government in 1962 with a seventy-thousand-character petition detailing the appalling conditions in Tibet and asking for an end to persecution and a genuine acceptance of religious freedom. This petition, later published as *A Poisoned Arrow: The Secret Report of the 10th Panchen Lama,* eventually led to his imprisonment for ten years. After his release from prison in February 1981, the Panchen Lama was reinstated; until his death in Gzhi ka rtse in 1989, he worked with the central and regional authorities for the betterment of Tibet. Tibetans consider the tenth Panchen Lama a great patriot, and pictures of him, which are allowed by the Chinese government, are widely found.

At the beginning of the twenty-first century, two claimants vie for the title of eleventh Panchen Lama. In May 1995 in Dharmasala, India, the fourteenth Dalai Lama announced that a six-year-old boy from Tibet, Dge 'dun chos kyi nyi ma, was the reincarnation of the Panchen Lama. He had named the boy chosen by Bya bral (Chadrel) Rin po che, a religious official from Bkra bzhis lhun po and the head of the committee originally constituted by the Chinese government to search for the Panchen Lama's reincarnation. To demonstrate its sole authority over important Tibetan institutions, China repudiated the choice and later that year declared another boy, Rgyal mtshan nor bu (Gyaltsen Norbu), a six-year-old from Hla ri ri in Nag chu in northeastern Tibet, to be the true Panchen Lama. Since 1996 Dge 'dun chos kyi nyi ma and his family have been detained despite the efforts of the international community to secure their release.

See also: **Lama; Tibet**

Bibliography

Goldstein, Melvyn. *A History of Modern Tibet, 1913–1951: Demise of the Lamaist State.* Berkeley: University of California Press, 1989.

Panchen Lama X. *A Poisoned Arrow: The Secret Report of the 10th Panchen Lama.* London: Tibet Information Network, 1998. Available online at www.tibetinfo.co.uk/pl-opening .htm.

Richardson, Hugh, and Snellgrove, David. *A Cultural History of Tibet.* London: Weidenfeld and Nicholson, 1968.

Smith, E. Gene. "Introduction." In *The Autobiography of the First Panchen Lama Blo-bzang-chos-kyi-rgyal-mtshan,* ed. Ngawang Gelek Demo. Delhi: Ngawang Gelek Demo, 1969.

GARETH SPARHAM

PARAMĀRTHA

Paramārtha (Zhendi; 499–569) was one of the most influential translators of Buddhist philosophical texts in China. Born Kulanātha in Ujjain in north central India to a brahmin family, Paramārtha traveled in 545 to

Funan (modern Cambodia), where there was active support for Buddhism. He was brought to Nanhai (modern Canton) in 546. From there he was summoned to the Liang capital at Jiankang (modern Nanjing) by Emperor Wu, a great patron of Buddhism. Shortly after his arrival, the capital was sacked and Emperor Wu was overthrown. Paramārtha fled the chaos, traveling southeast to Fuchun in modern Zhejiang province, where his translation career appears to have begun in earnest. He translated the *Shiqi di lun* (*Treatise on the Seventeen Stages [of the Bodhisattva Career]*) in 550 with the assistance of over twenty monks. Two years later he returned to Jiankang, now under the newly inaugurated reign of Emperor Yuan, and translated the SUVARṆAPRABHĀSOTTAMA-SŪTRA (*Golden Light Sūtra*), again with the help of over twenty monastic assistants. A number of additional sūtras and treatises are attributed to Paramārtha and his associates, including the *Mile xia sheng jing* (*Sūtra on Maitreya's Descent [from Heaven]*), the RENWANG JING (HUMANE KINGS SŪTRA), and the AWAKENING OF FAITH (DASHENG QIXIN LUN). The latter two texts are widely believed by modern scholars to be APOCRYPHA, that is, texts produced in China but claiming legitimacy as authentic discourses of the Buddha.

Paramārtha's most notable contribution is in being the first person to widely disseminate YOGĀCĀRA SCHOOL thought in China. To this end he translated several important treatises by the Indian founders of this school, ASAṄGA (ca. 320–390) and VASUBANDHU (fourth century C.E.). These include *Viṃśatikā* (*Twenty Verses*), *Triṃśika* (*Thirty Verses*), *Madhyāntavibhāga* (*On Distinguishing the Extremes from the Middle*), and *Mahāyānasaṃgraha* (*Compendium of Mahāyāna*). Scholars have long noted, however, that Paramārtha was no mere translator; by all appearances he added much of his own commentarial exegesis. In particular, Paramārtha attempted to synthesize Yogācāra and TATHĀGATAGARBHA thought into a single philosophical system. One of Paramārtha's most notable contributions in this regard is the positing of a ninth level of consciousness (the *amalavijñāna,* immaculate consciousness), which transcends the evolutionary consciousness and storehouse consciousness posited by the Yogācāra school. For Paramārtha, this immaculate consciousness is the true source of all reality, the means to overcome the defilements that afflict the lower levels of consciousness, and thus it is identified with the tathāgatagarbha, the sine qua non for enlightenment.

Despite a prodigious teaching and translation career, Paramārtha deeply lamented the chaotic conditions of sixth-century China, culminating in a thwarted suicide attempt in 568. The death of his closest disciple later that same year further debilitated Paramārtha; he died in February 569. Nonetheless, Paramārtha's work laid the philosophical foundation not only for the Faxiang (Yogācāra) school in China, but for the intellectual developments of the Huayan, Tiantai, and Chan traditions of the Sui and Tang dynasties as well.

See also: **Chan School; Consciousness, Theories of; Faxiang School; Huayan School; Tiantai School**

Bibliography

Demiéville, Paul. "Sur l'authenticité du Ta Tch'eng K'i Sin Louen." *Bulletin de la Maison Franco-Japonaise* 2, no. 2 (1929): 1–78. Reprinted in *Choix d'études bouddhiques, 1929–1970.* Leiden, Netherlands: Brill, 1973.

Paul, Diana Y. *Philosophy of Mind in Sixth-Century China: Paramārtha's "Evolution of Consciousness."* Stanford, CA: Stanford University Press, 1984.

DANIEL BOUCHER

PĀRAMITĀ (PERFECTION)

Pāramitā (Pāli, *pāramī*; Tibetan, *pha rol tu phyin pa*; Chinese, *boluomi*) refers to the spiritual practice accomplished by a BODHISATTVA. The term has been interpreted variously as meaning, for example, "perfection," "to reach the other shore," or "to cross over." In Japanese Buddhism the term has been used to indicate the spring and autumn equinox. The literal meaning of the Tibetan *pha rol tu phyin pa* is "to reach the other shore," a meaning with which the Chinese translation *dao bian* agrees. Traditionally, the term *pāramitā* comprises four groups: the group of six pāramitās; the group of ten pāramitās; the group of four pāramitās; and the perfections of esoteric Buddhism. However, the constituents of each grouping differ according to the sūtra or śāstra in which they are discussed.

The understanding of pāramitā in the sense of "to reach the other shore" suggests that one goes from the ordinary world of SAṂSĀRA (this shore) to the realm of NIRVĀṆA (the other shore). Depending on the text, this formula may mean, for example, that a buddha is one who has reached the other shore already, while an ordinary being is one who has not yet reached the other shore (*Maitreyaparipṛccha-sūtra*). "Reaching the other shore" may mean that, in accordance with one's practice, one attains the final goal with nothing remaining, or that one reaches reality-as-it-is (just as all streams finally return to the ocean), or that one attains the incomparable fruition (of awakening).

The group of six pāramitās includes DĀNA (GIVING), *śīla* (ethical behavior), *kṣānti* (patience), *vīrya* (endeavor or effort), DHYĀNA (contemplation or meditation), and PRAJÑĀ (WISDOM). *Dāna* means to give an ordinary gift, to give the gift of the dharma, or to give the gift of mental peace and tranquility to another. *Śīla* means to honor and practice proper ethical behavior. *Kṣānti* means to endure hardship. *Vīrya* means to strengthen one's mind and body and to practice continuously the other five perfections. Dhyāna means to focus one's mind and make it firm and stable. Prajñā means to awaken to the defining characteristics of existence. Of these, the first five can be understood to describe the practices manifested in a bodhisattva's activities of KARUṆĀ (COMPASSION) and the last a bodhisattva's wisdom. Because prajñā is so foundational to the other five perfections, it is referred to as the "mother of all buddhas."

When four more perfections—UPĀYA (appropriate action), *praṇidhāna* (vow), *bala* (strength), and jñāna (understanding)—are added to the former six, the grouping of ten pāramitās is established. *Upāya* means that a bodhisattva assists SENTIENT BEINGS by means of utilizing his expertise (*upāyakauśalya*). *Praṇidhāna* means that having become awakened, a bodhisattva makes the highest vow to save all sentient beings from the round of saṃsāra. *Bala* refers to the power to guide sentient beings to proper spiritual practices. *Jñāna* refers to the attainment of peace that comes with awakening and the instruction of sentient beings to attain the all-inclusive wisdom. Along with perfecting one's self, these ten perfections serve the purpose of benefiting all sentient beings. These comprise the bodhisattva's spiritual practices completed on each of the ten stages of the *Daśabhūmika-sūtra*.

The group of four pāramitās refers to an explanation of the perfections found in the *Śūraṅgama (samādhi)-sūtra* and includes *permanent perfection*—a perfection that is completely everlasting; *bliss perfection*—a perfection that is completely peaceful; *material perfection*—a perfection that has the nature of being completely substantive; and *pure perfection*—a perfection that has the nature of being wholesome. These four can be understood to comprise the four virtues of one who has attained nirvāṇa (the extinction of the cause of suffering).

The perfections of esoteric Buddhism are focused on Vairocana Buddha who is located at the center of the Vajradhātumaṇḍala. These postulate *vajra-pāramitā* (diamond scepter perfection) in the East, *ratna-pāramitā* (jewel perfection) in the South, *dharma-pāramitā* (doctrine perfection) in the West, and *kāma-pāramitā* (desire perfection) in the North.

Aside from these, THERAVĀDA Buddhism, in texts such as *Cariyapiṭaka, Buddhavaṃsa,* and *Dhammapadaṭṭhakathā,* postulates the following ten perfections: *dāna* (charity), *sīla* (ethical behavior), *nekkhamma* (liberation), *paññā* (wisdom), *viriya* (endeavor or effort), *khānti* (patience), *sacca* (truth), *adhiṭṭhāna* (resolve), *mettā* (loving kindness), and *upekkhā* (equanimity).

See also: **Mahāyāna; Maṇḍala; Prajñāpāramitā Literature**

Bibliography

Conze, Edward, trans. *The Large Sūtra on Perfect Wisdom.* Berkeley and Los Angeles: University of California Press, 1975.

Dayal, Har. *The Bodhisattva Doctrine in Buddhist Sankrit Literature.* London: Kegan Paul, Trench, Trubner, 1932.

Dutt, Nalinaksha, ed. *Bodhisattvabhūmiḥ.* Patna, India: K. P. Jayaswal Research Institute, 1978.

Kawamura, Leslie, ed. *The Bodhisattva Doctrine in Buddhism.* Waterloo, ON: Wilfrid Laurier University Press, 1981.

Ogihara, Unrai, ed. *Bodhisattva-bhūmi: A Statement of Whole Course of the Bodhisattva.* Tokyo: Sankibo Buddhist Book Store, 1971.

LESLIE S. KAWAMURA

PARISH (DANKA, TERAUKE) SYSTEM IN JAPAN

Parish temples (alternately *dannadera, dankadera,* or *bodaiji*) constitute over 90 percent of Buddhist temples in contemporary Japan. These terms have their etymology in the Sanskrit word DĀNA (GIVING) and were used during the medieval period to refer to major temple patrons. The broader concept of a "parish" in Japan, however, emerged during the Tokugawa period (1603–1868) as the predominant Buddhist temple affiliation method for ordinary lay members. The practice of organizing Buddhist adherents into parishes stems from the Tokugawa government's anti-Christian (*Kirishitan*) campaigns and ordinances of 1613 and 1614. Christianity, which had achieved a foothold in certain regions during the sixteenth century through the efforts of Portuguese and Spanish missionaries, was increasingly seen by the new Tokugawa regime as a subversive force and a threat to their hegemony. The threat of Christianity, as seen from the perspective of government officials, lay less with its biblical teachings and doctrines, than with the issue of Christian loyalty to God and the pope rather than to the Tokugawa government's secular authority. This led to a ban on Christianity in 1614.

To ensure that no Japanese person remained a Christian, the government ordered "Investigations of Christians" (*Kirishitan aratame*) to be conducted in each domain. Former Christians were certified by the local Buddhist temple and village officials as no longer Christians but as parish members of a Buddhist temple. The first surveys of Christians, begun in 1614, were followed by more extensive surveys ordered by the government in 1659 in which not only the parish temple, but the village *goningumi* (a unit of five households sharing mutual responsibility) were required to attest that no one in their group was a Christian. By 1670 the practice of temple investigation and registration (*tera-uke seido*) had become almost universal when a standardized temple registration certificate was adopted by Buddhist temples across all regions of Japan. This document certified that parishioners were neither Christians nor Nichirenfuju fuse members (a sect of Nichiren Buddhism banned by the government in 1669). Although the Buddhist temple held primary responsibility for monitoring and reporting on its parishioners to the village head, each village head had to gather these certificates in order to compile reports called *shūmon aratamechō* (Registry of Religious Affiliation), also known as *shūmon ninbetsuchō* or *shūshi aratamechō.*

These registries helped authorities monitor and control the populace by using Buddhist temples and local authorities to maintain detailed records, weeding out any persons who might be a potential threat to the government. From the perspective of the average parishioner, the practice of temple registration legally obligated them ritually and economically to their parish temple under the threat of being branded a "heretic," which continued to have meaning even as the possibility of Christian subversion of the government disappeared.

Temple membership was not an individual affair; rather, the unit of religious affiliation was the emergent unit of social organization, the "household" (*ie*). Thus, from the mid-Tokugawa period onward, the term *danka* (used interchangeably with *danna*), which includes the Chinese character for *household,* became the dominant term for parish households. For each household, the main benefit of membership was the funerary and ongoing memorial services that temples provided for all household members. Temple grounds also served as the location for the family gravestones. Thus, once a family registered as a member of a particular temple, that affiliation continued for successive generations during which sect changes were virtually impossible.

Parish temples emphasized parishioners' obligation toward the temple in terms of financial support and attendance of funerals and ancestral rites. Whether it be to pay for rituals or temple construction, it is clear that parishioners were not simply asked to support their parish temple, they were obligated to do so. The consequences of not doing so resulted in parishioners being branded heretics.

In ritual terms, the parish temple also became virtually synonymous with "funerary Buddhism," where DEATH rituals, as opposed to meditation, sūtra study, or prayers for worldly benefits, became the main ritual practice. Beyond the funeral proper, Buddhist parish priests performed death rites throughout the year. Memorial services were routinely performed for thirty-three years following a death. Services were also performed for various classes of deceased people, such as hungry ghosts (Sanskrit, preta), ANCESTORS, and women and children who had died during childbirth. Large festivals for the dead, such as the summer Obon festival for ancestors or the Segaki festival for hungry ghosts, marked important moments in each temple's annual ritual calendar. This preoccupation with ritualizing death was intimately tied to the emergence of the Buddhist parish temples during the Tokugawa period. Hereditary parishioners, who associated the parish temple with the proper maintenance of funerary rites and family customs, provided the ritual and economic backbone of Buddhist temples. The parish system in Japan, originally established as a method to monitor Christians, eventually became the basic organizational structure for Japanese Buddhism into the modern period.

See also: **Nationalism and Buddhism; Temple System in Japan**

Bibliography

Marcure, Kenneth. "The *Danka* System." *Monumenta Nipponica* 40, no. 1: 39–67.

Tamamuro Fumio. "Local Society and the Temple-Parishioner Relationship within the Bakufu's Governance Structure." *Japanese Journal of Religious Studies* 28, nos. 3–4 (2001): 260–292.

Williams, Duncan. "Representation of Zen: A Social and Institutional History of Sōtō Zen Buddhism in Edo Japan." Ph.D. diss. Harvard University, 2000.

DUNCAN WILLIAMS

PARITTA AND RAKṢĀ TEXTS

Paritta (protection) or *rakṣā* (Pāli, *rakka*; protection) are protective texts that keep a person who chants them safe from evil spells, menacing other-worldly creatures, and the dangers of knives, guns, disease, betrayal, fire, and poison. *Parittas* like the *Ratana, Maṅgala, Mora, Dibbamanta, Khandha, Dhajagga,* and *Āṭānāṭiya suttas* are some of the most common texts used in Southeast Asian Buddhism. *Rakṣās* like the *Pañcarakṣā* and sections of the *Candragarbha-sūtra* also fall under this protective invocational genre and are well known by practitioners in India, Tibet, and East Asia. They are important in daily monastic and lay Buddhist life, and collections of these texts, such as the *Pirit Pota* in Sri Lanka or the *Jet Tamnān* in Laos, are found in most homes and monasteries. Any Buddhist who regularly attends monastic ceremonies, or requests monks to bless his or her property or endeavors is familiar with these Pāli and Sanskrit texts, which often serve as subjects for sermons. *Paritta* and *rakṣā* literature has long been associated with ritual action and protective implements, such as sacred string, holy water, candles, AMULETS AND TALISMANS, incense, knives, engraved metal *manta* (Sanskrit, MANTRA) texts—rolled and worn around the neck (Thai, *takrut*)—and the like. *Paritta* and *rakṣā* literature is also the subject of decorative and ritual art in Tibet and East Asia.

Primary textual sources abound for those interested in Buddhist protective texts. There are several places in the earliest Pāli *suttas,* chronicles, and commentaries from the third century B.C.E. to the sixth century C.E. that mention how *parittas* were employed during protective ceremonies. For example, the commentary on *Ratana-sutta* mentions that ĀNANDA sprinkled water from the Buddha's alms bowl as he went through Vesāli reciting the *sutta.* Older canonical texts from the third century B.C.E. to the third century C.E. that also describe *parittas* being used in ceremonies are mentioned in the *Mahāvaṃsa* (VII 14) when the Buddha is said to have permitted the use of a protective chant to cure a snakebite in the *Vinayapiṭaka* (II 109–110). As Peter Skilling points out, the *Āṭānāṭiya-sutta* of the *Dīghanikāya* is a protective *paritta.* The MILINDAPAÑHA (150, 27) states that the Buddha himself sanctioned the use of these protective texts. The *Dhammapadaṭṭhakathā* (III 6) includes a story in which the Buddha recommends the use of a protective *manta* for monks who are afraid of tree spirits.

Although the differences between the uses of *paritta* texts of South and Southeast Asia and their counterparts—the *rakṣā* texts of India, Tibet, and East Asia—have not been adequately explored, certain MAHĀYĀNA sūtras contain sections that could be called protective texts. Some texts that fall under this rubric are sections of the *Sikṣāsamuccaya* and *Aṣṭasāhasrikāprajñāpāramitā,* as well as tantric (Tibetan, *rgyud*) texts in the Tibetan Kanjur, such as the *Mahāsitavanasūtra* and *Bhadrakara-sūtra.* In East Asia, chapter 21 of the LOTUS SŪTRA (SADDHARMAPUṆḌARĪKA-SŪTRA), on the supernatural powers of the tathāgata, is also considered a protective text.

The five goddesses of Tibetan and East Asian Buddhism also are the focus of protective texts known loosely as the *Pañcarakṣā.* These texts are hymns that praise and request the protective power of the five goddesses (Mahāprātisārā, Mahāsāsrapramardiṇī, Mahāmantrānudhāriṇī, Mahāmantrānusāriṇī, and Mahāmāyūrī). The last, Mahāmāyūrī, became the focus of her own cult, and popular protective texts, such as the fourth-century *Mahāmāyūrī-Vidyārājñī,* were used to invoke her in ritual. These five deities are especially popular among Newar Buddhists in the Kathmandu Valley of Nepal, but they are also depicted on murals in the AJAṆṬĀ cave complex in India and are the subject of elaborate MAṆḌALAS in Tibet and China. In the various *mikkyo* (esoteric) schools of Japan, Mahāmāyūrī, in particular, is a *myōō* (radiant wisdom ruler) and she is depicted riding on the back of a peacock (who has the ability to kill snakes) and holding two fruits that ward off evil spirits and protect against illness.

In Southeast Asia *parittas* are part of everyday Buddhist monastic and secular life. In modern Thailand *parittas* are chanted at a number of ceremonies and especially at house, water buffalo, and even motorcycle blessings. In northeastern Thailand these ceremonies often involve a quorum of four monks who chant while holding a white cord that connects their hands to everyone in the room. This cord is also wrapped around a Buddha image and often surrounds the whole room or even the whole house. One end of the cord is submerged in a bowl of water and, after the chanting, a handful of leaves is placed in the water and then used to flick water over those objects to be blessed and the people who attend the ceremony. Protective *yan* (Sanskrit, *yantra*) are drawn with moistened white powder and sealed with small gold leaves and the exhalation of the monk who has chanted. The power of *parittas* lies in their sound and in their role in a protective ceremony, and less (or not at all) in their semantic meaning. In fact, their meaning often has nothing to do with their role and result in a ritual.

The numbers of mantras (Pāli, *manta*) in the various *paritta* collections varied widely before the printing of modern prayer books like the *Royal Chanting Book of Thailand,* the various *Gu Meu Phra Song* of modern Laos, and the *Catubhānavāra* in Burma (Myanmar). Still, the *Ratana, Maṅgala,* and *Dibbamanta parittas* have remained at the core of these collections for centuries. The parameters of the *Rakṣā* genre in Tibet and East Asia are more difficult to define and this genre overlaps in content and function with that of DHĀRAṆĪ. Both groups of texts play a significant role in the ritual life of Buddhists across the various schools in Asia.

Bibliography

Becchetti, Catherine. *Le Mystère dans les Lettres: Étude sur les yantra bouddhiques du Cambodge et de la Thaïlande.* Bangkok, Thailand: Edition des Cahiers de France, 1991.

Bizot, François, and Lagirarde, François. *La Pureté par les mots.* Paris: École Française d'Extreme-Orient, 1996.

De Silva, Lily. "Paritta: A Historical and Religious Study of the Buddhist Ceremony for Peace and Prosperity in Sri Lanka." *Spolia Zeylanica (Bulletin of the National Museums of Sri Lanka),* 36:1 (1981).

Khanna, Madhu. *Yantra.* London: Thames and Hudson, 1979.

Nginn, P. S. *Les fêtes profanes et religieuses.* Vientiane, Laos: Éditions du Comte Litteraire, 1967.

Saddhatissa, H., trans. *The Suttanipāta.* London: Curzon, 1985.

Saso, Michael. *Homa Rites and Maṇḍala Meditation in Tendai Buddhism.* New Delhi: South Asia Books, 1991.

Skilling, Peter. "The Rakṣā Literature of the Śrāvakayāna." *Journal of the Pāli Text Society* 15 (1992): 110–180.

Skilling, Peter. *The Mahāsūtras.* Cambridge, MA: Wisdom, 1994.

Snodgrass, Adrian. *The Matrix and Diamond World Maṇḍalas in Shingon Buddhism.* New Delhi: Aditya Prakashan, 1988.

Spiro, Melford. *Burmese Supernaturalism.* Englewood Cliffs, NJ: Prentice Hall, 1967.

Strickmann, Michel. *Mantras et mandarins: le bouddhism tantrique en Chine.* Paris: Gallimard, 1996.

Terwiel, B. J. *Monks and Magic: An Analysis of Religious Ceremonies in Central Thailand.* London: Curzon, 1975.

JUSTIN MCDANIEL

PATH

From the inception of their tradition, Buddhists have conceived of their soteriological regimens as analogous to a "path" (mārga). Buddhists from different traditions invariably believed in the power of the mārga to provide a tested and viable passage to NIRVĀṆA, and to replicate in those who followed its course verifiable transformative experiences. The idea that religious life primarily involves one's own personal effort in walking an explicit path of training distinguishes the MAINSTREAM BUDDHIST SCHOOLS from those religions that place pride of place on adherence to stipulated doctrines or the saving grace of a transcendent "other."

The teachings of the Buddha were often referred to as "traces of [the Buddha's] footsteps or tracks" (*pratipadā*), because they were seen as being deliberately left behind by him after he had personally traversed the highway to liberation.

The path is more than a descriptive account of absolute paradigms of religious ideals *in illo tempore*; it also defines prescriptive parameters for religious behavior and spiritual attainment in mundane time, which allows Buddhists of different traditions to articulate their religious experiences in mutually intelligible language. The notion of path helps to organize a highly illusive and subjective realm of personal experience according to normative standards, and provides a heuristic model upon which Buddhist teachers could ground their pedagogy and claim a sense of continuity within the transmitted tradition.

The notion of path contains the simultaneous implication of constancy and elasticity. The Buddha is said to have professed that he was but one of the many enlightened beings since time immemorial who had walked on this same "ancient path," making his role more that of a restorer than an innovator. Ever accessible and enduringly relevant to human quandaries, Buddhists describe this path as being discoverable even by those in future eons who were bereft of the benefit of direct Buddhist instruction, seeing the periodic resurrections of the timeless Dharma by future BUDDHAS as a virtual certainty and a reassuring prospect. In this regard, the metaphor of path represents something that is unalterably reliable, a constant that will forever exist, whether or not it is discovered. Since the conundrums besetting all SENTIENT BEINGS are presumed to be the same throughout the ages, attributable to primordial nescience (avidyā) and craving (*tṛṣṇā*), the solution thereof is presumed to be immutable and eternally applicable as well.

On the other hand, the path is also construed by some as elastic and open to potential elaborations and even modifications. It is more than the Buddha's account of an unchanging, settled course of action to be passively retraced by future generations. The Buddhist path was also seen as in some way originally and ingeniously devised by the Buddha, who had judiciously and expediently plotted its guideposts with considerations specific to both time and individual. This utilitarian view of the path allows for the possibility of different paths with different approaches, so long as they lead to the appropriate goal or the general wellbeing and betterment of sentient beings. Many Buddhists therefore conceive the path as open to renewal and reinvention by the spiritually qualified in order to address changing religious needs, an approach consistent with the Buddhist strategy of employing diverse UPĀYA (skillful means) in the edification of even the least spiritually inclined. The path as a historical reality, too, was never statically suspended outside the contexts of history, but constantly evolves in dynamic interaction with social and cultural changes. This intrinsic resilience is particularly evidenced by the new categories of soteriological schemata that Buddhism formulated as the religion was transplanted to different geographical regions or responded to the emergence of new traditions.

This tendency to formulate mārga systems as an afterthought to newly arisen doctrines and ideals is contrary to the common expectation that the path should exclusively provide practical guides to the realization of enlightenment. In actuality, the development of new programs of praxis has often been instigated by polemical agendas or by an impulse to provide a sense of coherence, self-containment, and legitimacy to an ideology that a faction was promoting. Rather than spiritual maps, then, path schemata could at times serve more as hermeneutical devices to relegate or promote, to exclude or incorporate, different teachings and traditions, like KŪKAI's ten abodes of the mind (*jūjūshin*), which subsumes the whole of Buddhism in a schema that privileges his own school of SHINGON BUDDHISM (Buswell and Gimello, p. 20), or as ceremonies of ritualized and formalized behavior that invoke and reaffirm ancient mystical paradigms, like the initiation procedures into the Sōtō Zen transmission of the mind (Bodiford, pp. 423–424).

The emergence of the MAHĀYĀNA movement led to a plethora of new, elaborate mārga systems. Among these, the status traditionally assigned to the Buddha underwent significant upgrading as the gaping distinction of the BODHISATTVA path and its goal of buddhahood from mainstream Buddhist SOTERIOLOGY and its ideal of arhatship became the hallmark of Mahāyāna's dramatic self-idealization. Correspondingly, the path that led to such an infinitely more elevated religious goal was also framed quite differently in both quality and projected duration. The arduous and protracted crucibles that a bodhisattva is supposed to endure are exemplified and organized in the uniquely Mahāyāna scheme of the ten stages or grounds (*bhūmi*) of the bodhisattva path: the stages of joy, immaculacy, splendor, brilliance, invincibility, immediacy, transcendence, immovability, eminence, and dharmacloud. In this schema, each stage is primarily defined by marvelous powers, transcendental wisdom, and altruistic qualities in increasingly mythic proportion and is to be completed in exponentially greater numbers of eons. The Mahāyāna tradition's understanding of its soteriological objectives similarly was expanded immeasurably to embody the loftiest inspirational models, rather than strictly prescribing something that is readily accessible in the here and now. Buddhahood, the radically reenvisioned product of this expansively reconstituted path, stood in the most hyperbolic contrast to the now polemicized HĪNAYĀNA ideal personality of the ARHAT, in terms of a buddha's near-omnipotent capacity to save all beings and his myriad other wondrous qualities.

Doctrinal implications of the path

Just as a path is delineated according to fixed coordinates, the Buddhists maintained that their religious path is based on the bedrock of certain cosmically operative laws that are eternal, inviolate, and efficacious. According to Buddhism, these laws—such as KARMA

(ACTION) and its fruition, anātman (no-self) and ŚŪNYATĀ (EMPTINESS), and PRATĪTYASAMUTPĀDA (DEPENDENT ORIGINATION) or the conditioned coarising of suffering and of psychophysical existence—are discernible and logical, and open to rational and meditative scrutiny, because they are the organizing principles of reality itself rather than the haphazard and fantastic figments of personal mystical experiences. Since the Buddhist spiritual path was said to pattern itself after these universal principles, the path is also held out to be fundamentally rational and logical in that it is propounded on the grounds of a proper diagnosis of human problems, the accurate pinpointing of the source of those problems, the prognosis of a problem-free condition, and the solution tending to the eradication of the problem—the contents of the paradigmatic Buddhist soteriological formula, the FOUR NOBLE TRUTHS.

In distinction to non-Buddhist soteriological solutions—which are seen as either futile or at least inefficient because of their failure to properly identify and base their solutions on operative and governing natural laws—the four noble truths represent instead an attempt to plot religious development in accordance with certifiable causal relations so that the path is specifically and efficaciously tailored to target the real cause of suffering. The noble eightfold path by the same token is understood to be "right," not so much because it stands in opposition to what is morally wrong but because it is proclaimed on the principle of the middle way—a religious attitude grounded on the experientially sensible, which is free from the extremes of such categorical assertions as eternalism and nihilism, dogmatism and skepticism, self-indulgence and self-denial, and so on (Kalupahana, pp. 121 and 152). Denouncing blind FAITH in hearsay, metaphysical reasoning, and divine revelation, the Buddha was widely seen by his followers not as a purveyor of arbitrary ritual injunctions but as one whose direct experiential insight conforms well to both reason and the observable principles of all phenomena (Jayatilleke, pp. 169–204). Just as the word *Dharma* in its Indian religious and philosophical context represents both the underlying principles governing all phenomena and the religious teachings deriving thereon, the term *mārga* to a large extent is synonymous and connotes the same dual implication. The four noble truths therefore anchor personal religious action on external natural laws, making the realization of "the way things are" equivalent to the attainment of ultimate liberation and purification.

Although reason and analysis were rarely presumed in the Buddhist tradition to be sufficient in themselves to engender liberating insight—in fact some schools of Buddhism at times saw them as impediments to be transcended before genuine, nonconceptual wisdom could set in—a consistent attempt was made to integrate the conative aspect of the path with its cognitive aspects. In other words, the four noble truths were enumerated in such a way so as to make them congruous with the Buddha's analysis of existential realities as encapsulated in the scheme of, say, *pratītyasamutpāda*, so that Buddhist praxis is presented as an ineluctable course of action deriving from the proper understanding of the way things are.

These are not just "truths" in the sense that they are distinguished from what is rationally incoherent or incompatible with epistemological facts. Buddhists have always viewed this "proper understanding" to be more than just a neutral intellectual assent to what is factual: It actually carries a compelling ethical dimension that informs and structures religious behavior so that the latter is carried out in accordance with the ethical efficacy of the external natural laws. Thus, to see reality is to understand the imperative to walk the path, in the same manner that these reified Buddhist sets of truths, like the twelvefold chain of dependent origination and the four noble truths, were not intended to be metaphysical expositions, but instead psycho-ethical analyses that helped to galvanize spiritual action. This was the reason that the Buddha proclaimed that penetration into any one of the noble truths amounts to penetration into all four: Since the fourth noble truth is the prescribed praxis (conative) after the diagnosis and prognosis of the problem were identified in the first three truths (cognitive), the conative and cognitive aspects of the path are in this way seen to be complementary and mutually validating. In this framework of understanding, to divorce one's religious action from empirical insight is to continue to allow the assertion of, and the search for, the wrongly posited absolutistic substance (*svabhāva*) to further create delusions that are in turn the propelling force of wrong actions and SAṂSĀRA.

On the other hand, Buddhist soteriological programs often conversely posit PRAJÑĀ (WISDOM) as the consummating finality of the mārga rather than the path's initial guiding vision. This seeming ambivalence on whether cognitive exercise of insight or purificatory practice constitutes the body of the path gives rise to variant explanations of BODHI (AWAKENING) as, alternatively, the result of a gnoseological realization of reality, the overcoming and abandonment of mental defilements, or the spontaneous maturation of wholesome karmic seeds. Take, for example, the penchant of mainstream Buddhist schools to define spiritually accomplished people in four distinct gradations: the so-called four noble persons of *stream-enterer, once-returner, nonreturner,* and *arhat.* At least within this scheme, the completion of the path is characterized as entailing both an epiphanic instant of insight *and* the extended application of explicit procedures of mental purification. The progression from the first to the fourth grades of perfection is usually defined in terms of the eradication of ten specific psychological "fetters" (*saṃyojanaprahāṇa*). The abandonment of the first three fetters—the view of an (abiding) personality, belief in the efficacy of rites and rituals (and other religious exertions that are causally irrelevant to the removal of suffering), and skeptical DOUBT—is associated with the establishment of right view and is said to be achieved at the very moment when supramundane knowledge is ignited (once the false view of personality is eliminated, the other two fetters vanish instantly). But the remaining seven fetters, such as lust and ill will, are generally said to be so deep-seated and lingering that they could only be subdued, attenuated, and eventually eradicated through the enactment of a full soteriological regimen.

Different models of the path

The path's functionality can be understood structurally in several models. The first assumes the path constitutes the simultaneous cultivation of various mutually balanced activities, each indispensably addressing and governing a particular aspect of the spiritual life. One such soteriological program is the noble eightfold path (*ārya-aṣṭāṅgikamārga*) of right view, right intention, right speech, right conduct, right livelihood, right effort, right mindfulness, and right concentration. Its layout of the constituent practices on the path does not necessarily imply the sequential order in which these stages are to be cultivated, but is rather an indication that the Buddhist path enjoins a holistic lifestyle that comprehensively tends to all facets of an individual's daily activity, whether mental, physical, verbal, or spiritual.

The second model conceptualizes the path as a spiraling, self-augmenting process, with each step in the soteriological program being implicitly embodied and reinforced by subsequent steps. Each round of this spiraling path goes through the same constituent sets of practices, but with all of them becoming correspondingly strengthened in foundational and supportive power to the other sets. The rationale behind the working principle of the "three trainings" (*trīṇi śikṣāni*) is illustrative of this model of upwardly spiraling spiritual progression. The first of these trainings, *morality* (*śīla,* consisting of basic ethical codes like nonviolence, rules on the use of daily requisites, such as moderation in eating, and the restraint of the senses and of other grossly distracting and disquieting activities), is understood to condition one's mental and physical states so that they become amenable to the second training: *mental absorption* (samādhi) or *tranquility* (*śamatha*), whose highly refined cultivation of concentration and equanimity requires a pliant and elated psychophysical state that is not dulled by immoderation or burdened with anguish. Minimizing mental hindrances correspondingly magnifies the mental clarity that is the direct result of tranquility practice; this makes possible the exercise of the third training: *prajñā* (wisdom) or *insightful discernment* (VIPASSANĀ; SANSKRIT, VIPAŚYANĀ) of the impermanent, unsatisfactory, selfless nature of existential reality. The transcendent wisdom kindled thereby in its turn deepens the practitioner's conviction to establish himself or herself on a firm moral foundation, rendering in him or her a profoundly subtle and harmonious mindset that is reinforcing and naturally compatible with the first training. This positive loop feeds on itself, building momentum as each of the constituent trainings conduces to more advanced ones and, at the same time, injects new vigor into, and qualitatively reorients, the antecedent ones.

Since the noble eightfold path has often been organized and interpreted in the framework of the three trainings (e.g., right intention as belonging to the first training in morality, right concentration to training in tranquility, and so on), it shows that traditional Buddhist HERMENEUTICS sought to correlate at least some of these alternative mārga schemata. In fact, all these modular understandings of the Buddhist path have large areas of overlap and each soteriological scheme could be readily classified into more than one model.

Third, contrary to what the metaphor of a "path" would intuitively suggest, the Buddhist mārga has been depicted in a "sudden," or subitist, model by some traditions, entailing a momentous spiritual vision that instantaneously transports the practitioner beyond the conditioned (*saṃskṛta*) realm of gradual, deliberate exertions. Robert E. Buswell, Jr., and Robert Gimello describe several scenarios in which such an "anti-*mārga*" model prevailed:

> Thus do Buddhist texts abound in such seeming self-contradictions as the claim that the fruit (*phala*) of prac-

> tice is actually a prevenient cause (*hetu*) of its own causal practices, the assertion that practice and realization are really indistinguishable from each other, the claim that sudden realization precedes and enables gradual practice, and even the conviction that all prideful confidence in the sufficiency of one's "own power" (*jiriki*) as exercised in "difficult practices" (*nangyō*) must be relinquished humbly in the "easy practice" (*igyō*) whereby one accepts the "other power" (*tariki*) of the transcendent. (Buswell and Gimello, p. 24)

The final proposed model conceptualizes the path as a linear sequence of increasingly refined stages of psycho-ethical amelioration from rudimentary to more advanced practices, with former steps succeeded by those that follow and abandoned after they have served their purpose. This pragmatic view of the nature of religious practice lends itself to the traditional Buddhist reluctance to assign absolutistic and overriding value to any set of practices as an end in itself. Like the individual footsteps that form a track, the different practices suitable at different points in spiritual development are not to be mistaken as definitive endpoints, but only as onward-leading phases in a continuous process of development that one passes through rather than abides in.

In this depiction of the path as a linear progression, the ultimate value of spiritual practices has little to do with insuperable religious ideals in and of themselves. Their worth lies instead in their value in producing and sustaining more advanced forms of cultivation. If one unduly clings to these transitional trainings after they have served their purpose, they would only become self-inhibiting affectations and conceptual burdens rather than the expedient, liberating devices they were meant to be—hence, the ubiquitous parable in Buddhist texts of the person letting go of the raft as soon as the river is crossed and the famous maxim "even what is good has to be abandoned, let alone what is evil" (*dhammā pi . . . pahātabbā pageva adhammā*).

Such a model of successive advancement is found in the so-called five paths paradigm: the path of equipment, the path of preparation, the path of seeing, the path of cultivation, and the path of completion (alternately called the path beyond instruction), with each "path" serving as a preparatory and prerequisite step to its immediately subsequent path. At the most elementary path of equipment, one is expected to engage in meritorious actions that will plant the wholesome karmic seeds that are conducive and necessary to spiritual maturation. But after one has arrived at the second path of preparation, where one is supposed to apply oneself to more refined, formal trainings, such as mental cultivation, the actions appropriate to the first path would now be a distraction, rather than a help. Once one has entered the stage of cultivation, which entails the actualization and implementation of the proper dharma one "sees" on the preceding path, one need not revert back to the former stage to repeat the awakening experience, because the insight engendered thereby is generally held out to be final and not liable to regression.

It is practically inconceivable to try to understand the Buddhist doctrinal outlook and programs of practice without appreciating and making reference to their conception of the path. Its modal varieties and richness in meanings were naturally the result of many centuries of development, reflecting the perennial Buddhist fascination with the theme and its diverse interpretations, but the basic assumptions and spiritual ethos it carries, as outlined previously, have also given Buddhism whatever degree of consistency it has enjoyed.

See also: **Psychology**

Bibliography

Bodiford, William. "Dharma Transmission in Sōtō Zen: Manzan Dōhaku's Reform Movement." *Monumenta Nipponica* 46, no. 4 (1991): 423–451.

Bronkhorst, Johannes. *The Two Traditions of Meditation in Ancient India.* New Delhi: Motilal Banarsidass, 1993.

Buswell, Robert E., Jr., and Gimello, Robert M., eds. *Paths to Liberation: The Mārga and Its Transformations in Buddhist Thought.* Honolulu: University of Hawaii Press, 1992.

Gethin, Rupert. *The Buddhist Path to Awakening: A Study of the Bodhi-Pakkhiyā Dhammā.* Leiden, Netherlands: Brill, 1992.

Gethin, Rupert. *The Foundations of Buddhism.* Oxford and New York: Oxford University Press, 1998.

Gregory, Peter N., ed. *Traditions of Meditation in Chinese Buddhism.* Honolulu: University of Hawaii Press, 1986.

Gregory, Peter N., ed. *Sudden and Gradual: Approaches to Enlightenment in Chinese Thought.* Honolulu: University of Hawaii Press, 1987.

Jayatilleke, J. N. *Early Buddhist Theory of Knowledge.* Delhi: Motilal Banarsidass, 1963.

Kalupahana, David J. *A History of Buddhist Philosophy: Continuities and Discontinuities.* Honolulu: University of Hawaii Press, 1992.

King, W. L. *Theravāda Meditation: The Buddhist Transformation of Yoga.* University Park: Pennsylvania State University Press, 1980.

Mahāthera Henepola Gunaratana. *The Jhānas: In Theravāda Buddhist Meditation.* Kandy, Sri Lanka: Buddhist Publication Society, 1988.

Ñāṇārāma. *The Seven Stages of Purification and The Insight Knowledges: A Guide to the Progressive Stages of Buddhist Meditation.* Kandy, Sri Lanka: Buddhist Publication Society, 1983.

Ruegg, David S. *Buddha-nature, Mind, and the Problem of Gradualism in a Comparative Perspective: On the Transmission and Reception of Buddhism in India and Tibet.* London: School of Oriental and African Studies, 1989.

Takeuchi, Yohinori, et al., eds. *Buddhist Spirituality: Indian, Southeast Asian, Tibetan, Early Chinese.* New York: Crossroad, 1997.

Thanissaro Bhikkhu. *The Wings to Awakening.* Barr, MA: Dhamma Dana, 1996.

Vetter, Tilmann. *The Ideas and Meditative Practices of Early Buddhism.* Leiden, Netherlands: Brill, 1988.

WILLIAM CHU

PATIENCE. *See* **Pāramitā (Perfection)**

PERSECUTIONS

Buddhism has been the object of persecution throughout its history. While this often involved direct religious persecution (e.g., persecution at the hands of dominant iconoclastic religions because of the devotional focus on the BUDDHA IMAGE), if one investigates the context of any particular episode, one may detect nonreligious factors that led to, allowed for, or exacerbated persecution. Such factors include the role of Buddhism in authorizing secular power and acting as the potential and actual supporter of political rivals; the power of Buddhist institutions as wealthy landowners, including the suspected and actual use of fortresslike monasteries as banks or armories; the involvement of monastic groups in warfare, including militarized monks and MONASTIC MILITIAS; Buddhism's role as a mediator of political views at the grassroots level; Buddhism's international dimension and potential representation of foreign rather than national interests, along with its emphasis on PILGRIMAGE within and beyond national boundaries; the fact that important sacred sites, objects of devotion, or esteemed religious leaders could develop into rival foci of power or could reflect local rather than national interests; and Buddhism's traditional role in EDUCATION, making it the source of potentially conflicting views and independent thinking. The fact that it is possible to draw selectively on aspects of Buddhism to affirm virtually all types of governance and political ideology has also contributed to its continued entanglement in power struggles in the huge transformations that have swept the modern world.

In some cases, persecutions were aimed against the representatives of the religion itself—the institutions, texts, sacred sites, or people. At other times, persecutions were waged against groups with which Buddhism overlapped or was coterminous.

Bāmiyān

The relative roles of religious persecution and the broader factors listed above can be hard to identify. Let us take by way of example the well-publicized attack on the remaining traces of Buddhism in Afghanistan, the demolition in BĀMIYĀN by the Taliban in March 2001 of the two colossal Gandhāran Buddha statues from the third and fourth centuries C.E. Taliban foreign minister Wakil Ahmad Mutawakel described this act as an internal religious affair, stating that "false idols" should be destroyed according to Islamic teachings. While some Islamic scholars point out that Islam does not prescribe the destruction of idols, and some demonstrate that the images of Hinduism and Buddhism are not idols in the sense intended in the Qur'an, iconoclasm within Islam can be based both on the injunctions on Muslims not to worship idols and on repeated historic precedents, starting with Muhammad's destruction of the images around the Ka'ba. A 1996 Taliban ruling against idolatry prohibited portraits in public places. Nevertheless, since the Bāmiyān statues had been standing for centuries in a predominantly Muslim country, since some Islamic powers have advocated tolerance toward sacred objects of other religions, and since the Taliban had as recently as 1999 identified the statues as part of the pre-Islamic heritage of Afghanistan rather than as current objects of idolatry, one must look for further causes underlying this event.

In addition to the reactionary Islam represented by the Taliban, there are two other significant factors. One is the Taliban's long-standing suppression of the Hazara community in the region of Bāmiyān. The other is the international isolation of the Taliban—only Pakistan recognized the Taliban's right to govern. In addition, in February 2001 the United Nations imposed new sanctions on Afghanistan for harboring terrorists. The importance of the Bāmiyān statues for world her-

A visitor in 1997 approaches one of the two giant Buddha statues carved from the face of a cliff at Bāmiyān, Afghanistan. © Muzammil Pasha-Files/Reuters/Getty Images. Reproduced by permission.

Taliban soldiers and visiting journalists before a niche that had contained one of the giant Buddha statues at Bāmiyān after their destruction in March 2001. © Sayed Salahuddin/Reuters/Getty Images. Reproduced by permission.

itage meant that they were destroyed as "false idols" in a political sense; the destruction served as a message of the Taliban's defiance to the world.

Premodern persecutions

Puṣyamitra. Our ability to interpret the reasons behind a persecution depends very much on the nature of our sources. The earliest recorded episode of the persecution of Buddhism came at the hands of the Indian king Puṣyamitra in the second century B.C.E. The event is related in Buddhist literary works that reached their current form centuries later. Puṣyamitra was a brahmin who murdered and usurped the position of the last king of the Mauryan empire. The most famous Mauryan king had been AŚOKA, who lived a century earlier. The legend of Aśoka's patronage of Buddhism has been perpetuated in Buddhist traditions and continues to provide a role model for Buddhist rulers to this day. Among other great acts of piety, Aśoka had the relics of the Buddha redistributed throughout his vast empire and re-enshrined under eighty-four thousand new STŪPAS, the commemorative funerary structures that form the fulcrum of the sacred landscape of Buddhism. Puṣyamitra desired to become even more legendary than Aśoka. Realizing that he could not compete in virtue, he decided to match virtue with vice, and set about destroying monasteries and stūpas, burning books, and massacring monks and nuns.

The destruction of the glories and institutions associated with the royal lineage that Puṣyamitra had replaced can be understood in terms of his wish to undermine rival sources of authority. Puṣyamitra himself celebrated the horse sacrifice, the supreme ritual demonstration of dominion in brahmanical Hinduism, the dominant rival of Buddhism for much of its history in South and Southeast Asia. Nevertheless, the narrative also reflects another model—that of traditional Indian drama in which adverse events result from the vices of the king. According to this narrative, Puṣyamitra is driven by jealousy, and although the immediate victims of his persecutions are Buddhists, his acts backfire. Puṣyamitra sets a bounty on the head of all Buddhist monks, and an ever growing number of heads are presented to him. But the inexhaustible supply of heads is the product of a miracle rather than real beheadings, and the resulting bounty payouts bankrupts the royal treasury. When Puṣyamitra later tries to destroy the bodhi tree, its protective spirit has Puṣyamitra and his armies crushed to death beneath a mountain.

This theme of the cruel but ultimately self-destructive whims of kings is widely attested elsewhere in Buddhist literature. It is a recurrent theme in the JĀTAKA tales, which teach morals through stories of the Buddha's former births. The VINAYA also describes the dangers for monks of associating with kings, an association that has proved both a source of Buddhism's success and a trigger for its suppression.

Zoroastrian persecution. The earliest persecution for which there is contemporaneous historical evidence took place under the Sassanian dynasty, which came to power in Iran in the third century C.E. The context was the centralization of power. We know most about Sassanian efforts to reform and unify the indigenous Persian religion of Zoroastrianism by establishing a single Avestan canon, destroying all royal sacred fires other than its own, establishing a new calendar, and replacing cult images with sacred fires. The iconoclasm extended to images of other religions. Although Zoroastrianism and Buddhism had coexisted peacefully in Iran since the Kushan period (first to early third century C.E.), the dominant Zoroastrianism felt increasingly threatened by other proselytizing religions, including Christianity, Buddhism, and Judaism. The Sassanian high priest Kirder proudly records in an inscription that Buddhists, along with Jews, Brahmins, various types of Christians, and Manichaeans were being removed from the land. The eleventh-century Muslim historian Al-Biruni, who made use of Zoroastrian sources, claims that Buddhism was widespread in Iran until this persecution. The long-term result of Sassanian iconoclasm and the subsequent rise to dominance of Islam, heavily influenced by Zoroastrianism, is that the only traces of Buddhism in the region are cave temples and place names, such as Naubihar, which means "new Buddhist monastery."

The White Huns. Further pre-Islamic persecution of Buddhism took place under the White Huns, also known as the Huna or Hephthatlites. This tribe, thought to have originated in southwestern Mongolia, invaded areas of Central Asia and India during the fifth and sixth centuries. The invasion of Afghanistan in 515 C.E. by Mihirakula (502–542) devastated Buddhist strongholds in the Gandhāran region along the SILK ROAD. The resulting diminished state of Buddhism can be traced in the accounts of successive Chinese pilgrims. At the beginning of the fifth century C.E., the Chinese monk FAXIAN documents the flourishing state of Buddhism in the region. In 520, after the Mihirakula attacks, Song Yan records monasteries in ruins and heavy population losses, which had become total desertion and ruination by the time XUANZANG traveled that route in the seventh century. Nevertheless, finds of coins from later periods in stūpas of the region indicate that patronage of Buddhism did continue beyond this date.

The demise of Buddhism in India. The most famous persecution of Buddhism was that which led to its demise in India, namely, the series of Islamic expansions into the subcontinent from the eighth to the fourteenth centuries. The conquest of the remaining Pāla and Sena dynasties of Bengal and Bihar in the twelfth to the thirteenth centuries brought an end to the last powerful Buddhist kingdoms of India and sent many Buddhists fleeing to safer regions in the Himalayas and mainland Southeast Asia. Although the increasing popularity of other Indian religions, such as devotional Hinduism, and the merging of non-institutional Buddhist practice into the broader Indian religious milieu are important factors in the disappearance of Buddhism in India, several Muslim chronicles of the time portray the impact of repeated massacres, the looting of monasteries, the destruction of Buddhist images, and the burning of books, people, and libraries.

These events had a major impact on the shape of Buddhism in other regions. In particular, they eliminated the South Asian mainland as a source of Buddhism for East, Central, and Southeast Asia. Tibetan and Newar Buddhism preserved most fully the features of Indian Buddhism of the medieval period. Meanwhile, the Sri Lankan victory over the Hindu kingdoms of South India, led Sri Lanka to become the dominant source of Buddhist authority in mainland Southeast Asia, while in insular Southeast Asia, Islam became the dominant religion. Buddhism was not completely eliminated from the South Asian mainland at this time. It has continued to maintain a presence in peripheral regions in the Himalayas, mostly dominated by the culture and Buddhism of Tibet. To a limited extent, Buddhism also retained a presence until the seventeenth and eighteenth centuries in other pockets, including port areas on the southeast coast, where people traded with THERAVĀDA countries.

Premodern East and Central Asia

In regions often regarded as the strongholds of Buddhism beyond India, namely Tibet, China, Korea, and Japan, periods of flourishing patronage of Buddhism have nevertheless often given way to (sometimes severe) persecution.

The first diffusion of Buddhism to Tibet ended with the ninth-century civil war between factions loyal to the indigenous BON religion on the one side and Buddhism on the other, an episode remembered in Buddhist histories as the beginning of two centuries of persecution.

In China, arguments against Buddhism almost always related to its status as a foreign religion that therefore undermined Confucian values, the emperor, and the state. The golden era of longevity of pre-Buddhist emperors is adduced as testimony to Buddhism's intrinsic threat to stability. The first recorded Chinese persecution took place under Emperor Wu or Taizi (r. 423–452) of the Northern Wei dynasty (386–534). During the suppression of a rebellion in 446, a cache of arms was discovered at a Buddhist monastery, and Buddhism was seen as loyal to the rebels. Further discoveries indicative of lax monastic practices, including wealth banked at the monastery by locals, were cited as additional reasons for subsequent persecution in which monks and nuns were executed, as was any person who harbored them. Buddhist images were smashed, and monasteries, pagodas, and books were burnt. Although a gradual relaxation took place, Buddhism was proscribed again during the Northern Zhou dynasty (557–588).

State domination of Buddhism continued under the Tang dynasty (618–907) and ORDINATION was forbidden in 845 during the so-called Huichang persecution. Over 260,000 monks and nuns were forcibly returned to lay life and hundreds of monasteries were destroyed. After this time, restrictions controlled the number of ordinations allowed and set age limits, prohibiting adult males under the age of forty from being ordained. Periodic crackdowns on monasteries and ordinations occurred during the twelfth century under the Song dynasty (960–1279). The leaders of the Ming dynasty (1368–1644), which imposed hard labor for unauthorized ordinations in the fifteenth century, also persecuted Tibetan Buddhists in Chinese territories. Successive Chinese governments from the fourteenth to the eighteenth century suppressed, often brutally, intermittent rebellions led by the White Lotus Society, a secret millenarian religious group that appealed to the poor and predicted the advent of the future buddha Maitreya.

Mongol invasions of Korea in the thirteenth century devastated the country, destroying Buddhist monasteries, art, and the famous Koryŏ Buddhist canon. Because the wealth accumulated by the monasteries during centuries of state support gave them too strong an influence in national affairs, the Chŏson dynasty (1392–1910) officially promoted Confucianism. The dynasty's anti-Buddhist sentiment developed into full-scale persecution in the fifteenth century. Buddhism suffered again, as did other aspects of Korea's culture and economy, after the Japanese invasions in the sixteenth century. Further persecution occurred during the Japanese occupation beginning in 1910, during which Japanese forms of Buddhism were advanced to supplant Korean forms, especially in urban centers.

In Japan, the militarization of monasteries and their participation in feudal power structures led to competition between schools. By the eleventh century, rivalries among Tendai and Nara monasteries frequently resulted in armed conflicts. Buddhist figures that were regarded as threats to national stability, including HŌNEN (1133–1212) and NICHIREN (1222–1282), were suppressed or sent into exile. In further reaction to its militarization and political involvement, Buddhism was suppressed in the sixteenth to seventeenth centuries, particularly under the warlord Oda Nobunaga (1534–1582), who destroyed thousands of temples and massacred their inhabitants.

The founding of the Tokugawa military government in 1603 brought stability to the Buddhist establishment in Japan. All families had to register with a Buddhist temple; affiliation became fixed and the temples administered taxes. This development came at the expense of Christian missionaries who were associated with European political ambitions and were thus persecuted as a first step in Japan's two hundred years of isolationism. When the Meiji regime assumed power in 1868, its first act was to disestablish Buddhism and to separate the worship of local gods from Buddhist temples. These policies, which created Shintō as an independent religion, resulted in the destruction of thousands of Buddhist temples.

School rivalry in Sri Lanka

Persecution resulting from rivalries between different Buddhist traditions also occurred in Sri Lanka before the twelfth-century unification of the Mahāvihāra by Parākramabāhu I. After unification, monks of rival schools took fresh ordination in the Mahāvihāra, losing all previous rank. The Pāli canon came to be treated as orthodox, while the Abhayagirivihāra and Jetavana became associated with the more inclusive MAHĀYĀNA texts.

The *Nikāyasaṅgraha* also records the third-century persecution of the Abhaygirivihāra by Goṭhābhaya, who burned their books and branded (marked as criminals) the expelled monks. The *Mahāvaṃsa* records how Goṭhābhaya's successor, Mahāsena, temporarily reversed royal patronage in favor of the Abhayagirivihāra. The *Nikāyasaṅgraha* further records the decimation of the mysterious blue-robe sect, a form of tantric Buddhism, in Southern India under King Śrī Harṣa: "Pretending to be convinced, he sent for the blue-robed brethren and their books, and having got them with the books into a house, he made a fire-offering of house and all" (Fernando, p. 19).

These chronicles, which are recorded in the Mahāvihāra tradition, naturally attribute persecution of their own tradition to evil monks, and the persecution of rivals as a triumph over corruption. Nevertheless, the process described appears to be similar in each case. After consecration of a king, particularly after victory in a major military campaign, the king sought to "purify" the saṅgha in emulation of Aśoka.

European colonial period

From the sixteenth to the twentieth century, the European colonial powers managed to undermine Buddhism through a subtle structure of institutional persecution. Mechanisms for the implicit promotion of Christianity included the establishment of secular and Christian education systems designed for colonial administration, the rewarding of conversion with promotion and employment, nonsupport for state-saṅgha interaction, and failure to set protocols for lay support of Buddhism. Active persecution also occurred, particularly in the early days of European colonization. These patterns were especially evident in Sri Lanka, beginning with the suppression of Buddhism by Portuguese Catholics in the sixteenth century, and continuing through the active and then implicit promotion of Protestantism, first by the Dutch and later by the British.

Attitudes favoring Christians continued to influence events even after the colonial period. Suppression of Buddhism by the American-backed government in the former French colony of South Vietnam led to the well-known Buddhist SELF-IMMOLATION protests in 1963. The Catholic government was in power in part because of Vatican pressure on the United States to prevent the democratic elections that would have given mandate to the moderate Marxist Ho Chi Minh. President Diem aimed to destroy rival religious groups by passing legislation that gave preferential status to Catholics and prevented the practice and teaching of other religions. The persecution of the majority Buddhist population, including the torture and murder of tens of thousands of Vietnamese and the incarceration in concentration camps of hundreds of thousands, came to a head when Diem prohibited the carrying of religious banners on the Buddha's birthday. This restriction contrasted with the flying of the Vatican flag in celebration of the Catholic archbishop, who was Diem's brother, only a few days earlier. Diem's troops fired directly into Buddhist crowds, and mass hunger strikes and other protests followed. The self-immolation of the monk Thich Quang Duc in 1963 in full view of the international press brought the plight of Vietnamese Buddhists to the world's newspapers and television screens, eventually forcing the U.S. government to publicly distance itself from Diem's religious policies.

Communism

The most significant ideology affecting religions in twentieth-century Asia has been communism. Although Buddhism sometimes fared marginally better than other religions, the overall damage has been great because many of the areas affected by communism were traditional Buddhist strongholds.

Some non-communist governments, such as those in Thailand and Indonesia, actively encouraged particular forms of Buddhism by way of defense against communism. In Thailand this entailed undermining some forms of Buddhist practice, including WILDERNESS MONKS whose traditional domain was the poor and remote northeast, which bordered countries with Marxist governments. This is an example of the persecution of a group within Buddhism because it was believed to be coterminous with a different target, namely communist insurgents. Other governments, such as that of China, which occupied Tibet and eastern Southeast Asia, have actively persecuted Buddhism. Maoist terrorists in Nepal have also targeted religion.

Communist China did not initially seek to wipe out religion, but to wean people from it gradually as economic and social reforms made the prop of religion unnecessary. In fact, the 1949 constitution advocated freedom of religious belief, and Buddhist institutions were harnessed for welfare work and to educate society about new government policies. The younger generation of monks was particularly enthusiastic, given that the highest ethical value of Buddhism—compassion—could find expression in the ideals of egalitarianism and social uplift, which communism espoused.

Nevertheless, this cooperation with communism undermined the distinctive features of most forms of Buddhism. Monks and nuns had to abandon their traditional "unproductive" roles and undertake activities that were traditionally prohibited for Buddhist monastics, such as farm and factory work. Through the land reform act of 1950, feudal land ownership was replaced by communalization, and monasteries and nunneries lost their sources of revenue. Monasteries were turned into factories, communal food halls, military bases, and government education centers. Furthermore, the government made little distinction between "religion" and "superstition" when attempting to suppress the latter. Government-controlled Buddhist organizations discouraged festivals, offerings to deities, and the burning of paper money for the deceased—all key features of traditional Buddhism. The policy that loyalty to the state was a higher value than religious belief meant that religious activities could be discouraged as a hindrance to productivity.

Moreover, measures taken to ensure that all religious statements were in line with party politics eliminated freedom of expression. The Communist government monitored the recruitment of monks, and their freedom of movement, necessary for pilgrimage, was severely restricted. In a short time, Buddhism was effectively dismantled and transformed into an instrument of the state. By the commencement of the Cultural Revolution in 1966, any pretext of religious tolerance was abandoned, and all personal or material expressions of religion were outlawed and destroyed.

The enactment of these policies in Tibet moved at a slower pace. Communist China's 17-Point Plan, negotiated with Tenzin Gyatso, the fourteenth DALAI LAMA, in 1950, protected religion and monasteries from communalism, and China pursued a policy of gradual transformation from the top, with the involvement of highly esteemed Buddhist leaders. This approach changed when Mao Zedong encouraged rapid collectivization during the mid-1950s. Opposition to these reforms led to a bloody uprising involving monks from prestigious monasteries in Lhasa. The Chinese army responded with force, the Dalai Lama fled to India, and China abandoned its more lenient policy on Tibet. Religious property was confiscated, religious buildings were destroyed, and monks and nuns were imprisoned, disrobed, or put to alternative work. Still, it was not until the Cultural Revolution that the practice of Buddhism by individuals, so central to Tibetan culture, was banned outright in Tibet, as elsewhere in China. After the late 1970s, Chinese policy toward Tibetan Buddhism gradually softened in the hope of persuading Tibetans to accept Chinese rule. The failure of negotiations with the Tibetan government in exile, however, has triggered a hardening of control since the mid-1990s.

The Chinese pattern of initially using Buddhism for its own ends, then suppressing it, has been mirrored in other communist countries. The saṅgha of Laos had already become politicized, with French encouragement, as part of its defense against the Japanese from the 1920s until the1940s. When Laos was returned to French colonial occupation in 1946, active members of the Lao Issara, the national independence movement, sought refuge in Thailand. The saṅgha, meanwhile, could promote anticolonial sentiment as an aspect of Buddhist teaching, while also collecting funds for Lao Issara under the cover of the traditional donations given to temples on holy days. After independence, the royalist government of Laos formed a coalition with the Marxist party, the Pathet Lao, in 1957. The Pathet Lao then negotiated the Ministry of Religious Affairs as one of its portfolios, allowing the Pathet Lao to further politicize the saṅgha in its favor.

Monastic teachings reach all levels of society, and the infiltration of the saṅgha by Pathet Lao cadres was relatively straightforward because of the tradition of unrestricted ordinations. Those seeking ordination often came from the same groups most susceptible to Marxist ideology: young men from relatively poor rural backgrounds, who traditionally sought ordination as a means of education and social advancement, but who were excluded from the secular education and economic development experienced by the urban elite. When the royalist government responded by instituting tighter controls on monks, the Pathet Lao could play the defender of religious freedom. By this time, it was too late for the royalist party to regain the authority it once had amongst the saṅgha. When the Pathet Lao formed its own government in 1975, it used the saṅgha to legitimize its increasing monopoly on power. Monks fled to Thailand to avoid being sent to reeducation camps that effectively turned Buddhist preaching into education in government ideology, and the rigorously controlled saṅgha lost credibility among the laity, which had traditionally supported it and from whom its members were recruited.

The persecutions of the Khmer Rouge in Cambodia were far more extreme than those of the Pathet Lao. As part of the Khmer Rouge goal to transform Cambodia into a truly socialist republic within the space of a few years, Pol Pot oversaw the wholesale destruction of Cambodian society and culture between 1975 and 1978. People were reeducated to not give alms to monks, monks were forcibly laicized, Buddhist rituals were forbidden, and monasteries and libraries were destroyed. Any monk suspected of resistance was executed. Few Cambodian monks survived these years of hard labor, mass starvation, and extermination, which saw the death of an estimated one quarter of the Cambodian population. Although some monks found refuge abroad, more than 90 percent of Cambodia's Buddhist literary heritage was extirpated.

Religion continued to be heavily controlled under the Vietnamese-backed government after 1979, and it is only since the reinstatement of the monarchy in 1991 that Buddhism entered a phase of revival in Cambodia.

The modern world's improved communications, the attendant potential for state intervention, and the mass availability of educational systems that embody an intellectual disdain toward religion, have meant that, to some extent, Buddhism had already begun to lose esteem even before communists came to power. Even where Buddhism is not under attack, modernity has undermined the dominant traditional Buddhism of ritual and worship in favor of philosophy and those aspects of Buddhism that can be mapped onto modern scientific thought and global ethics. To some extent Buddhism has been defended because of the role it has played as a motivating force and as a form of cultural identity. During the twentieth century, these aspects of Buddhism were harnessed both by independence movements that brought to an end the European colonial era and by nationalist governments that drew their mandate from an ethnically Buddhist majority.

See also: **Christianity and Buddhism; Colonialism and Buddhism; Communism and Buddhism; Decline of the Dharma; Islam and Buddhism; Meiji Buddhist Reform; Millenarianism and Millenarian Movements; Modernity and Buddhism; Politics and Buddhism; Shintō (Honji Suijaku) and Buddhism; Syncretic Sects: Three Teachings**

Bibliography

Ball, W. "How Far Did Buddhism Spread West?" *Al Rafidan* 10 (1989): 1–11.

Boyce, Mary. *Zoroastrians: Their Religious Beliefs and Practices.* London and New York: Routledge and Kegan Paul, 1979. Revised reprint, 1987.

Bush, Richard C. *Religion in Communist China.* Nashville, TN: Abingdon Press, 1970.

Buswell, Robert E., Jr. "Buddhism under Confucian Domination: The Synthetic Vision of Sŏsan Hyujŏng." In *Culture and the State in Late Chosŏn Korea,* ed. Jahyun Kim Haboush and Martina Deuchler. Cambridge, MA: Harvard University Asia Center, 1999.

de Groot, J. J. M. *Sectarianism and Religious Persecution in China.* Amsterdam: Johannes Müller, 1903.

Fernando, C. M. *The Nikāya Saṅgrahawa.* Colombo, Sri Lanka: H. C. Cottle, 1908.

Geiger, Wilhelm, and Bode, Mable Haynes, trans. *The Mahāvaṃsa or The Great Chronicle of Ceylon.* London: Pali Text Society, 1912.

Geiger, Wilhelm, trans. (German). *Cūlavaṃsa: Being the More Recent Part of the Mahāvaṃsa,* tr. C. Mabel Rickmers (English). London: Pali Text Society, 1929.

Goldstein, Melvyn C., and Kapstein, Matthew T., eds. *Buddhism in Contemporary Tibet: Religious Revival and Cultural Identity.* Berkeley: University of California Press, 1998.

Grapard, Allan G. "Japan's Ignored Cultural Revolution: The Separation of Shinto and Buddhist Divinities in Meiji (*Shinbutsu bunri*) and a Case Study (*Tōnomine*)." *History of Religions* 23, no. 3 (1984): 240–265.

Harris, Ian, ed. *Buddhism and Politics in Twentieth-Century Asia.* London: Pinter, 1999.

Ketelaar, James E. *Of Heretics and Martyrs in Meiji Japan: Buddhism and Its Persecution.* Princeton, NJ: Princeton University Press, 1990.

Lamotte, Étienne. *History of Indian Buddhism: From the Origins to the Saka Era,* tr. Sara Webb-Boin. Louvain-la-Neuve, Belgium: Institut Orientalist, 1988.

Stuart-Fox, Martin. *Buddhist Kingdom, Marxist State: The Making of Modern Laos.* Bangkok, Thailand: White Lotus, 1996.

Warder, A. K. *Indian Buddhism.* Delhi: Motilal Banarsidass, 1970.

Warikoo, K., ed. *Bamiyan: Challenge to World Heritage.* New Delhi: Bhavana Books, 2002.

KATE CROSBY

PERSON. *See* **Anātman/Ātman (No-Self/Self); Pudgalavāda**

PHILOSOPHY

Within the Buddhist tradition there exist enormously sophisticated systems of thought. Whether these systems should be regarded as "philosophy" or "theology" or something else is a difficult question and a topic of much debate. *Philosophy* is a Western word and concept, derived from the Greek origins of Western thinking, and no traditional Buddhist language had a word analogous to *philosophy* prior to the modern era. The Buddhist term most closely related is DHARMA, which means something like *truths* or *teachings,* especially teachings about how to live.

It is often said that the Buddhist teachings are more philosophical than religious because of their open spirit of inquiry and their lack of a central concept of God. In this sense, *philosophy* means "overarching ideas about the nature of the world and the meaning of human life that guide daily living." By this definition, much Buddhist dharma is indeed philosophy. But it is important to recognize that this is not what professional philosophers in the modern West mean by that term. For most contemporary philosophers, philosophy is concerned with logical analysis and the structure of human thinking. Although a few Buddhists have taken up these issues, especially in India, they have done so under the guidance of what they take to be larger and more important questions that are ultimately ethical and spiritual (e.g., What is excellence of human character? What is enlightenment and how can it be achieved?). Logic and analysis have no standing on their own as Buddhist concerns. One reason for this is that early Buddhist sūtras depict the Buddha rejecting abstract philosophical speculation in preference for practical techniques of self-transformation. Another reason is that very early in the Buddhist tradition philosophers attained a high level of psychological sophistication. Through the rigors of meditative practice, they came to realize that what one considers to be true—no matter how good one is at logical analysis—is shaped and conditioned by the state of one's character. What this means is that desires, intentions, and thoughts of a certain kind will inevitably lead a person to reason out the truth of the matter in ways that are in part preshaped by those same desires, intentions, and thoughts.

Therefore, in much Buddhist thought, truth is not simply a matter of logic or reason, since both logic and reason are themselves dependent on other factors. For Buddhists, realizing the truth is the result of a great deal of internal work beyond analytical reasoning, and it is for this reason that philosophy in the Buddhist tradition is best classified as a subcategory under "means to awakening" or, more appropriately, under "MEDITATION." Most analytical thinking in the Buddhist tradition takes place in the context of meditation, which can be divided into two overarching categories: *śamatha* (calming) and VIPASSANĀ (SANSKRIT, VIPAŚYANĀ; contemplation). Contemplation, or insight meditation, is a conceptual practice focusing on the analysis of the world and one's internal conceptions of it. Most Buddhist philosophical writings are intended to be used in this kind of meditative practice, and most of them were written within a monastic setting. Buddhist philosophy, therefore, has a practical intention: It is meant to open and transform the mind of the meditator and lead, ultimately, to BODHI (AWAKENING). The idea of philosophical thinking outside of that spiritual and ethical setting is utterly foreign to Buddhist culture.

Issues

Among the many issues prominent in Buddhist "philosophy," the following are most instructive for getting a sense of how this tradition of thought is shaped: No-self, change and causality, morality and ethics, and philosophy and truth.

No-self. The idea for which Buddhists are perhaps best known is the claim that there is no self (anātman); that what we take to be the true inner core of a human being is actually an illusory process of constant change. This idea runs against the grain of ordinary thinking, not just in Western cultures but in Asia as well. The Buddhist critique of the concept of the self is based on the conclusion that in fact people never experience an unchanging inner core, and that their ideas about that core are derived from a quite natural tendency to understand themselves through their desires and attachments. Although the idea of the self that was rejected in early Buddhism was quite specific—the concept of ātman in the Hindu *Upaniṣads,* the unchanging core that undergirds all experience—the development of this critique in the history of Buddhist philosophy extends far beyond the specifics of that initial rejection. The basic anātman position is that there exists no controller, no possessor, no constant self behind experience, which means that it is not that "I" have a body and thoughts and feelings but that "I am" these elements at any given moment in the process of life. Rejecting the unchanging self does not mean that no one is here; the idea of no-self is the Buddhist effort to explain who or what is here, and how that person can best live.

In order to clarify the rejection of self, early sūtras posit the five SKANDHA (AGGREGATES), the five components that make up a person: physical body, feelings, conceptions, volition, and self-consciousness. Sūtras explain how these five components of the self are always changing, always dependent on one another, and therefore not constant, not stable, and not the unchanging foundation that one assumes. Although languages posit an "I" behind these fluctuating states, no such background possessor is ever present to experience. Buddhist sūtras challenge meditators to examine their own experience, and to locate the truth of the posited self. The Buddhist critique of the concept of the self is unique among the world's religions, and it provided a powerful starting point for the history of Buddhist philosophy.

Change and causality. Perhaps the most basic philosophical principle in Buddhist philosophy is the claim that all things are characterized by ANITYA (IMPERMANENCE); that is, all things are subject to change, including birth and death. The initial context for this realization was the FOUR NOBLE TRUTHS, where suffering is caused by desires for and attachments to things that are always changing and passing away. Failure to recognize the ubiquity of impermanence and failure to adjust one's life accordingly lead inevitably to poor judgment and subsequent suffering.

That moral context for reflection on change was just the beginning. Later Buddhist philosophers took the basic principle of impermanence as the starting point for a wide variety of reflections on the nature of the always changing world. Closely associated with the idea of impermanence was the concept of PRATĪTYASAMUTPĀDA (DEPENDENT ORIGINATION), the Buddhist explanation for how it is that things change. Change is not random; it is caused and conditioned by other surrounding factors. The principle of dependent origination states that all things arise, change, and pass away dependent upon the influence of other things. Nothing, therefore, is self-sufficient; everything depends. Buddhist thinkers took this principle to be an example of the "middle way" between two logically unacceptable views—eternalism, the view that things exist permanently and on their own, and annihilationism, the view that things have no existence at all. *Pratītyasamutpāda* falls between those extreme views by affirming that things exist within a larger process of dependence. Although these ideas certainly could be applied to the natural world, and on occasion were, their most important application concerned the workings of the mind. How is it possible, Buddhist philosophers asked, to live an enlightened life, in touch with the way things really are and free of delusion, greed, and hatred? That possibility, like any other, they concluded, arises dependent on the requisite conditions. Living your life in accordance with those conditions gives rise to the state of NIRVĀṆA. The principles of impermanence and dependent origination are the most basic ideas in Buddhist philosophy.

Morality and ethics. Like all Buddhist philosophy, Buddhist ETHICS is articulated in the context of meditation, and set in the framework of the quest to eliminate the devastating effects of suffering by achieving the state of human excellence called nirvāṇa. Suffering and enlightenment are the central ethical issues. Ethics is a practical matter of shaping one's life in accordance with the wisdom of the Buddha's realization. Far from making Buddhist ethics simple, this setting in the domain of practice gave rise to a voluminous philosophical literature on how it is that human life ought to be lived. One difference between Buddhist ethics and modern Western moral philosophy is the Buddhist focus on everyday life, on choices that people habitually make all of the time. The idea behind this focus is that one's character is formed in every act one undertakes, especially in the acts that one performs over and over. This is where the Buddhist concept of KARMA (ACTION) functions most forcefully. Modern Western ethics has focused almost exclusively on exceptional situations, on perplexing moral dilemmas that arise occasionally in a person's lifetime when major choices need to be made. As a consequence of this focus, very little attention has been given to how one achieves a state from which major decisions will be made with integrity. From a Buddhist ethical perspective, how one makes major choices in life depends almost entirely on how one has cultivated oneself throughout one's life. Buddhist enlightenment, therefore, depends on daily acts of morality and meditation on the virtues that sustain them. This focus can be seen clearly in the lists of virtues that function in the context of meditation, including, for example, the "four immeasurables" (loving kindness, compassion, sympathetic joy, and equanimity) or the "six PĀRAMITĀ (PERFECTIONS)" (generosity, morality, tolerance, effort, concentration, and wisdom).

Philosophy and truth. The pursuit of truth in Buddhist philosophy is not so much an effort to formulate general doctrines about the world as it is to change people's lives, to enlighten. Philosophy is therefore not a theoretical activity abstracted from life, but rather a practical matter of articulating a way of living, placed in the service of human liberation. As a form of meditation, theoretical thinking is linked to other forms of spiritual practice. The link is important in Buddhism because truth is not simply the product of logical analysis. The quality of someone's analysis of the world depends for Buddhists on the purification of their minds and characters. It is not possible, they reason, for someone entangled in personal desires and self-centeredness to encounter the truth, no matter how intelligent they are. Truth in Buddhist meditative contexts is more a matter of how clearly someone can see the ways in which their own minds falsify reality based on attachments and self-absorption. Understanding this psychological prerequisite to truth, calming and insight meditation begin to open the mind to the possibility of truthful understanding.

Traditions and styles

Buddhist philosophy has unfolded over a two-thousand-year history, and continues today, perhaps as strongly as ever. Over these many centuries, numerous traditions and styles of philosophy have thrived. The following are a few of the best known and most representative.

Abhidharma. ABHIDHARMA, meaning higher or extended dharma, is an early Buddhist philosophical literature that has scriptural status. These texts differ from sūtras in the same way that systematic philosophical analysis differs from practical religious teachings. Abhidharma is "extended" beyond the first communication of dharma by pursuing a comprehensive vision and analytical rigor. Abhidharma works, such as BUDDHAGHOSA's famous Pāli text *Visuddhimagga* (*Path to Purification*), attempt to lay out the underlying structures of the Buddhist dharma by providing lists, definitions, and descriptions of what might be encountered in meditative experience. Abhidharma breaks ordinary experience down into its component parts—dharmas—the final building blocks of human experience. The Abhidharma is the earliest and most widely known form of Buddhist philosophy.

Madhyamaka. NĀGĀRJUNA, the second century C.E. founder of the MADHYAMAKA SCHOOL, is the most famous of all Buddhist philosophers. His philosophical tradition, which developed for many centuries in MAHĀYĀNA Buddhist cultures such as China and Tibet, began as an extension and correction of Abhidharma thinking. Nāgārjuna's philosophy of ŚŪNYATĀ (EMPTINESS) is derived from a systematic thinking through of the earlier concept of dependent origination. From this point of view, the Abhidharma effort to list the ultimate building blocks of human experience was misguided. If all things lack independence, arising dependent on other equally dependent things, then nothing can be found to possess the secure and permanent status that earlier Buddhists had sought. In this sense, Madhyamaka extends the Buddhist analysis of existence one step further—all existing things are "empty" of permanent and self-constituting natures. Although things do indeed exist, this philosophy seeks to articulate the way in which they exist, and, like other forms of Buddhist philosophy, to use this analysis for the purpose of awakening.

Yogācāra. Often considered the culmination of Buddhist philosophy in India, the YOGĀCĀRA SCHOOL represented a renewed effort to accomplish a systematic account of experience in the style of Abhidharma, but now employing the Madhyamaka critique. Granting that all components of experience are "empty," philosophers such as ASAṄGA (ca. 320–390 C.E.) and VASUBANDHU (fourth century C.E.) sought to explain how it is that impermanent and dependent factors come together to shape the world as it is. Their basic thesis was that the primary factor upon which experience depends is the mind; since all experience is the mind's experience, understanding the complexities of the mind was the most important philosophical task. Well-known for their thesis that reality is "mind only," Yogācārins based their analysis on meditative experience. They broke the mind down into eight types of consciousness and the three fundamental "natures" of mind, constructing what is perhaps the most sophisticated statement of Buddhist psychology.

Huayan. One of several innovative philosophical schools that began in China and subsequently influenced Buddhism throughout East Asia, the HUAYAN SCHOOL came to prominence during the early Tang dynasty (618–907) as a philosophical articulation of the meaning of certain Mahāyāna sūtras, most notably the HUAYAN JING (*Avataṃsaka-sūtra, Flower Garland Sūtra*). This sūtra is unusual in communicating the experiences of enlightened BODHISATTVAS, rather than the Buddha, but the focus of the text is on what the world looks like from the perspective of awakening. Reality is "emptiness," articulated in Huayan as the enormously complex interplay of all elements in existence, each dependent on all others. Each aspect of the world receives its particular shape through the influence of all other aspects, while its seemingly insignificant influence radiates out into every dimension of the universe. Huayan philosophy is staggering in its complexity and sophistication, and it is currently exerting a profound theoretical influence on the field of ecological studies.

Kyoto school. Working under the influence of modern Western philosophy, a group of twentieth-century Buddhist philosophers in Japan has attained international recognition. Nishida Kitarō, Tanabe Hajime, and Nishitani Keiji, all former professors at Kyoto University, are the most famous thinkers in this school. Although their philosophical writings are too complex and diverse to summarize, all of them sought to articulate a philosophical vision of reality in the modern Western sense, while simultaneously subordinating this vision to the quest for spiritual awakening, as has been the custom throughout the history of Buddhism. Philosophical thinking has its goal in self-awakening, and its truth is the effectiveness with which it accomplishes that primary task. The translation of these works of philosophy into Western languages has provided non-Buddhists throughout the world with substantial examples of the sophistication of the long and impressive tradition of Buddhist philosophy. It may very well be that the influence of Buddhist philosophy on world affairs is only now in its opening stages.

See also: **Anātman/Ātman (No-Self/Self); Consciousness, Theories of; Dharma and Dharmas; Logic; Psychology**

Bibliography

Collins, Steven. *Selfless Persons: Imagery and Thought in Theravāda Buddhism.* Cambridge, UK: Cambridge University Press, 1982.

Eckel, Malcolm David. *To See the Buddha: A Philosopher's Quest for the Meaning of Emptiness.* Princeton, NJ: Princeton University Press, 1992.

Garfield, Jay. *The Fundamental Wisdom of the Middle Way: Nāgārjuna's Mūlamadhyamakākarikā.* Oxford: Oxford University Press, 1995.

Gethin, Rupert. *The Foundations of Buddhism.* Oxford: Oxford University Press, 1998.

Griffiths, Paul. *On Being Mindless: The Classical Doctrine of Buddhahood.* Albany: State University of New York Press, 1994.

Kalupahana, David. *Buddhist Philosophy: A Historical Analysis.* Honolulu: University of Hawaii Press, 1976.

Keown, Damien. *The Nature of Buddhist Ethics.* Basingstoke, UK: Palgrave, 2001.

Nagao, Gadjin. *Madhyamaka and Yogācāra: A Study of Mahāyāna Philosophies.* Albany: State University of New York Press, 1991.

Williams, Paul. *Buddhist Thought: A Complete Introduction to the Indian Tradition.* London: Routledge, 2000.

Wright, Dale. *Philosophical Meditations on Zen Buddhism.* Cambridge, UK: Cambridge University Press, 1998.

DALE S. WRIGHT

PHOENIX HALL (AT THE BYŌDŌIN)

The extant Phoenix Hall (Hōōdō) of Byōdōin is located on the west bank of the Uji River southeast of Kyoto. Regent Fujiwara Yorimichi (990–1074) transformed an inherited villa into the (now lost) Main Hall of Byōdōin in 1051, his sixtieth year. The unprecedented Phoenix Hall, consecrated in 1053, was built as a three-dimensional representation of the depiction of Amida's Sukhāvatī Pure Land, as found in the *Guan Wuliangshou jing* (*Visualization Sūtra*). With its birdlike wings and tail, the Phoenix Hall faces east and was designed to be viewed from a small palace on the opposite shore. The hall and its central Amida (AMITĀBHA) icon served as the focus of meditation and as a backdrop to ceremonies. Narrative paintings depicting the nine stages of REBIRTH adorned the doors and walls surrounding the icon, each showing a seasonal landscape as the setting for a "descent of Amida" (*raigō*) to recognizably Japanese devotees. Above the walls, fifty-two small wood-carved bodhisattvas and musicians complete the effect of Amida's descent.

Mimi Yiengpruksawan has made a convincing case that the Phoenix Hall was the private domain of

Yorimichi and his descendants, rather than the quasi-public focus of the temple. Esoteric Tendai ceremonies were carried out in front of the Main Hall icon, Dainichi Nyorai, while the Phoenix Hall appears to have been Yorimichi's private devotional chapel where he himself could meditate upon Sukhāvatī. After his death, his daughter Kanshi lived at Byōdōin and carried out ceremonies on behalf of her father and other relatives, both at the temple's sūtra repository and at the Phoenix Hall.

See also: **Japan, Buddhist Art in**

Bibliography

Akiyama Terukazu. "The Door Paintings in the Phoenix Hall of Byōdōin as Yamatoe." *Artibus Asiae* 53, nos. 1– 2 (1993): 144–167.

Yiengpruksawan, Mimi Hall. "The Phoenix Hall at Uji and the Symmetries of Replication." *Art Bulletin* 77, no. 4 (1995): 648–672.

KAREN L. BROCK

PILGRIMAGE

The practice of journeying to locations of special significance is a common feature of many religious traditions and it has played a formative role in the history of Buddhism. Given this rich pilgrimage tradition, there are several ways to approach the subject of pilgrimage in Buddhism. These range from analytical perspectives that highlight the distinctive histories and social dynamics of individual pilgrimage sites in the diversity of cultures shaped by Buddhism, to perspectives reflecting a broader comparative framework. These latter approaches emphasize features common to a number of Buddhist pilgrimages, and to religious pilgrimage in general. This entry examines Buddhist pilgrimage from several angles and is organized in three sections: historical overview, pilgrimage practices, and contemporary perspectives.

Historical overview

We cannot say with assurance when pilgrimage first became a part of Buddhist tradition. However, the fact that the canonical collections of several early Buddhist schools include a sūtra in which Gautama Buddha himself exhorts his followers to visit sites associated with his life indicates the centrality that pilgrimage came to have in the early centuries of the Buddhist movement. This passage occurs in the MAHĀPARINIRVĀṆA-SŪTRA, which narrates the Buddha's last days before his final passing away. In the Pāli version, four places identified with pivotal events in his life (birth, enlightenment, first teaching, and final passing away) are described as worthy of being seen and productive of strong religious feeling, and the passage concludes by promising that anyone who dies while undertaking such a journey with serene joy will be reborn in a blissful heavenly realm.

The earliest archeological evidence of Buddhist pilgrimage comes from inscriptions commissioned by the Indian emperor AŚOKA in the third century B.C.E. There are also later textual traditions that give Aśoka a formative role in the creation of a Buddhist sacred geography through the enshrinement of Gautama Buddha's relics in eighty-four thousand relic monuments throughout his empire. According to the Rummindeī pillar edict in Nepal, Aśoka visited the site of the Buddha's birth and erected a commemorative pillar there. Another inscription may refer to Aśoka's pilgrimage to the site of the Buddha's enlightenment at BODH GAYĀ, and a third, located at Nigālī Sāgar in Nepal, tells of Aśoka's visit to and enlargement of the relic monument of the former Buddha Koṇāgamana, suggesting that a devotional cult centered on the lives of previous BUDDHAS had also emerged at this time.

The history of Buddhist pilgrimage becomes clearer during the Śuṅga period (second to first centuries B.C.E.) with the relic monuments at Bhārhut and SĀÑCĪ, where we also find extensive donative inscriptions. These remains suggest the existence of well-developed regional pilgrimage centers supported by a wide range of donors, including lay and monastic men and women. Significantly, neither Bhārhut nor Sāñcī is identified with the presence of Gautama Buddha during his lifetime. Instead, the sites have been rendered religiously powerful through the enshrinement of relics, and through vivid artistic representations of scenes from the Buddha's biography, including his past lives.

The sites attested in the Aśokan inscriptions and in the Śuṅga-era monuments point to the two primary means through which particular locations became the focus of special religious devotion: claims that the Buddha himself visited them during his lifetime and later enshrinements of physical objects that represent him, either through alleged historical continuity (bodily remains or objects he used) or visual evocation (sculptures and paintings). These were not mutually exclusive options, as many sites were associated with events in the Buddha's life and with later relic and

Husband-and-wife pilgrims praying on their way to a Nichiren temple in Japan, around 1925. © Hulton Archive by Getty Images. Reproduced by permission.

image enshrinements; some were associated with the presence of previous buddhas, as well. As many scholars have noted, there was a close relationship between the development of a comprehensive Buddha BIOGRAPHY, which was not a part of the earliest tradition, and the emergence of pilgrimage sites.

Buddhism was first transmitted into China around the beginning of the common era. Beginning around 400 C.E., we find the earliest surviving accounts of Chinese Buddhist pilgrims to India. These testify to the emergence of major pilgrimage routes, extending through CENTRAL ASIA and northwest India into the Ganges basin, which attracted pilgrims from distant lands. Among the most prominent of these monk-pilgrims were FAXIAN (ca. 337–418) and XUANZANG (ca. 600–664), each of whom traveled to India through Central Asia and spent many years collecting texts and visiting important religious centers throughout the Indian subcontinent and beyond. Faxian's account testifies to the great proliferation of places that had come to be associated with events in Gautama Buddha's life, particularly those of a miraculous character, and to the number of relic monuments attributed to Aśoka's great relic distribution.

Faxian also spent two years in Sri Lanka, and he mentions the tradition that Gautama Buddha visited the island in order to pacify the nāgas residing there, a tradition narrated in detail in the monastic histories of the island (e.g., *Dīpavaṃsa, Mahāvaṃsa*). On one of his sojourns, the Buddha is said to have visited and consecrated a number of different locations around the island and these form the nucleus of what was eventually defined as an authoritative list of sixteen Sri Lankan pilgrimage sites. Narrative traditions of a similar character later developed in Southeast Asia, linking the movement and enshrinement of relics and images with locations in the region already sacralized by legendary visits of Gautama Buddha.

As Buddhist traditions spread throughout Asia and became institutionalized through royal patronage and popular support, the network of Buddhist pilgrimage expanded in two senses. On the one hand, monks and nuns throughout the Buddhist world traveled back to the Buddhist heartland for access to texts, to places of religious power associated with buddhas and other powerful religious figures, and to centers of Buddhist learning (thus a centripetal force). An analogous, centrifugal movement drew Buddhist relics and images (and in some cases, Gautama Buddha himself, as recounted in later texts) outward to create new centers of pilgrimage in what had been the territorial margins of Buddhist tradition. In many cases these new devotional centers were established in places long regarded as religiously powerful because of the presence of local or regional deities, places often marked by striking natural features such as mountains, lakes, and caves. Typically, these "pre-Buddhist" beings were not simply replaced, but instead subdued and converted into guardians of Buddhist sacralia. Such centers of pilgrimage undoubtedly brought together devotees with diverse religious identities and forms of practice, thus facilitating the integration of Buddhist ideas and practices into broader religious milieux.

The fluidity of interaction that pilgrimage so effectively orchestrates has contributed greatly to the expansion and adaptation of Buddhist traditions outside the land of its origins. Buddhist pilgrimages are generally voluntary undertakings motivated by a range of individual concerns, including the acquisition of merit, the need for purification and expiation, and hopes for healing, increased prosperity, fertility, and so on. They also commonly bring together people from diverse social and religious groups. As a result, they have frequently encouraged the interplay of different symbolic systems and behaviors, thus facilitating the adaptation of Buddhist traditions to new historical circumstances. In the case of Chinese pilgrimage sites, for example, it is difficult to determine what defines a "Buddhist" pilgrimage, since popular beliefs and practices were drawn from Daoism and Confucianism, as well as Buddhism, and these seemingly exclusive religious designations are meaningful only when referring to professional elites. Thus these sites have commonly enabled a multivocality of meanings and a diversity of practices to flourish side by side with varying degrees of integration.

Pilgrimage practices

Certainly the most salient feature of pilgrimage is movement. A minimal definition of pilgrimage is a journey to a place of special religious significance, and movement here means the movement of individual bodies away from the places where they typically reside and toward a center of intensified religious power. A pilgrimage is usually an exceptional undertaking, often involving significant disruption of the pilgrim's ordinary life and frequently entailing some element of physical discomfort or ordeal. Among the more striking examples are the protracted journeys of the early Chinese pilgrims to India; Faxian was away for fifteen years, Xuanzang for sixteen. The degree of difficulty and danger faced by the pilgrim obviously varies widely; in addition, specific Buddhist pilgrimage sites have been more or less accessible at different historical periods. The availability of cars, buses, and planes has clearly transformed the pilgrimage experience for many modern participants.

As was the case for the early Chinese pilgrims, the goal of the journey was often not a single site of religious significance, but rather the completion of a pilgrimage route punctuated with a succession of sites, each with its distinctive associations. Japanese Buddhist pilgrimages, such as those to Shikoku and Saikoku, typically involve the clockwise completion of an extensive pilgrimage circuit; these reflect the common Buddhist practice of circumambulation (Sanskrit, *pradakṣiṇa*) in which one ritually honors a person or object of religious authority by circling them clockwise, thus keeping the right side of the body facing them. Circumambulation of sacred mountains is a prominent feature of Tibetan Buddhist pilgrimage, with some pilgrims going so far as to complete an entire circuit, sometimes hundred of miles long, with a succession of full-body prostrations.

Other forms of ritualized devotion include various forms of offering, such as flowers, incense, light in the form of candles or lamps, gold leaf, and so on, as well as the recitation of appropriate chants or MANTRAS. Offering rituals are often not limited to the Buddhist figures represented at Buddhist shrines; as noted above, other supernatural beings and forces are commonly believed to reside in pilgrimage sites and these are also venerated, sometimes in fulfillment of a special vow to honor the deity in return for a specified benefit. Finally, a broad range of Buddhist figures are deemed worthy of veneration by pilgrims, including buddhas, BODHISATTVAS, and ARHATS. In some Chinese Chan Buddhist communities, the miraculously mummified bodies of deceased teachers became the object of pilgrimage.

One of the fundamental organizing principles of pilgrimage is the contrast between the heightened power and purity of the pilgrimage site and the space around it, and this is reflected in special modes of bodily

Tibetan Buddhist pilgrims circle Kailāśa (Mount Kailash) in southwestern Tibet. © Galen Rowell/Corbis. Reproduced by permission.

deportment. Many pilgrims wear special clothing that clearly distinguishes them from non-pilgrims. The hierarchical classification of the body according to standards of purity, with right favored over left and higher over lower (head/feet), structures much devotional behavior, such as circumambulation and offering rituals. Social hierarchy is present, as well, in the authority exercised by experienced pilgrims over novices, and by local officiants and guides who mold the behavior of the visiting devotees. Hierarchies of purity and sacrality are also commonly reflected in the spatial and architectural organization of pilgrimage centers; this may explain why mountains and other elevated locations are so frequently the "natural" settings for pilgrimage. Pilgrimage traditions in some cases also define time, as well, by their connections with calendars of religious observance. Many Tibetan pilgrimages operate on a twelve-year cycle, while visits to a number of Sri Lankan pilgrimage sites are organized around a calendar of full-moon-day observances.

Contemporary perspectives

Considerable scholarship has been devoted to pilgrimage, much of it focused on Christianity. Victor Turner's theory of pilgrimage as a "liminoid phenomenon" has been the most influential general theory of pilgrimage. Turner asserts that pilgrimage places its participants in an ambiguous social status that frees them from some of the dominant social structures of their regular lives and enables particular kinds of personal transformation to occur. In part this transformation takes the form of a heightened group identification among people who would normally be socially distinguished. The "betwixt and between" character of pilgrims' social status also renders them more emotionally vulnerable to the powerful symbolic systems that dominate pilgrimage sites, a vulnerability often heightened by physical ordeal. This model, which knits together social and psychological factors, and which attempts to take into account both the cognitive and affective dimensions of pilgrim's experiences, is sufficiently flexible to illuminate many specific pilgrimages from various religious traditions. As many scholars have noted, however, this approach also emphasizes the commonality of pilgrims' experience, and may mask the divisive social and political forces that often constellate around pilgrimage centers.

In Sri Lanka, for example, Buddhist pilgrimage tradition played an important role in the nineteenth- and twentieth-century Buddhist revival in response to British colonial rule; it has also heightened conflict between Sinhalas and Tamils. In Tibet, the pilgrimage tradition centered on Mount KAILĀŚA (KAILASH), which identifies it as Mount Meru and Śiva's abode, has long drawn pilgrims from Hindu, Buddhist, and Jain traditions who venerate it with circumambulation. In the wake of the Chinese occupation of Tibet, however, pilgrimage was prohibited for nearly two decades beginning in 1962; since the early 1990s restrictions have been relaxed somewhat, and increasing numbers of Western practitioners of Buddhism are making this arduous pilgrimage to the "center of the world" as new Buddhist communities are established in Europe and North America.

See also: **Merit and Merit-Making; Relics and Relics Cults; Space, Sacred**

Bibliography

Coleman, Simon, and Elsner, John. *Pilgrimage: Past and Present in the World Religions.* Cambridge, MA: Harvard University Press, 1995.

McKay, Alex, ed. *Pilgrimage in Tibet.* Richmond, UK: Curzon Press, 1998.

Morinis, Alan, ed. *Sacred Journeys: The Anthropology of Pilgrimage.* Westport, CT: Greenwood Press, 1992.

Naquin, Susan, and Yü, Chün-fang, eds. *Pilgrims and Sacred Sites in China.* Berkeley: University of California Press, 1992.

Nissan, Elizabeth. "Polity and Pilgrimage Centres in Sri Lanka." *Man* (New Series) 23, no. 2 (1988): 253–274.

Reader, Ian, and Swanson, Paul L., eds. "Pilgrimage in Japan." *Japanese Journal of Religious Studies* 24, nos. 3–4 (1997): 225–452.

Turner, Victor, and Turner, Edith. *Image and Pilgrimage in Christian Culture: Anthropological Perspectives.* New York: Columbia University Press, 1978.

KEVIN TRAINOR

PLATFORM SŪTRA OF THE SIXTH PATRIARCH (LIUZU TAN JING)

The *Liuzu tan jing* (*Platform Sūtra of the Sixth Patriarch*) is the capstone text of the early CHAN SCHOOL of Chinese Buddhism. The sūtra resolves hotly contested issues of earlier decades in a charmingly instructive narrative. At its heart is a verse competition between Shenxiu (ca. 606–706) and HUINENG (ca. 638–713), in which the latter becomes sixth patriarch in spite of being an illiterate and socially declassé layman from the far south of China. The entire story is fictional—Shenxiu had long since left the "fifth patriarch" Hongren's (601–674) monastic training center when the events supposedly took place—but the text's imaginative dramatization of Chan spiritual training has been almost universally accepted. Composed originally around 780 (the approximate date of the DUNHUANG version), the *Platform Sūtra* is an important source for understanding both the Chinese monastic institution and the state of evolution of Chan mythology at that time. Although the text did not remain universally popular throughout the medieval and premodern period—the Japanese Zen master DŌGEN (1200–1253) was particularly critical of it—it is widely read and cited throughout East Asian Buddhism today.

In the opening anecdote, Hongren instructs his students to compose verses demonstrating their understanding of Buddhism, with the author of the best verse becoming his successor. After some consternation, Shenxiu submits:

> The body is the bodhi tree.
> The mind is like a bright mirror's stand.
> At all times we must strive to polish it
> and must not let dust collect.

The response by Huineng, a menial laborer at the monastery for the preceding eight months, reads:

> Bodhi originally has no tree.
> The mirror also has no stand.
> The buddha-nature is always clear and pure.
> Where is there room for dust?

The Dunhuang manuscript actually contains two slightly different versions of Huineng's response. Further editorial adjustment is shown in later versions from the tenth and thirteenth centuries, which reduce this contribution to a single verse with a famous third line, "Fundamentally there is not a single thing."

The *Platform Sūtra* has generally been misread as a clear-cut validation of a subitist "Southern school" associated with Huineng. However, the text actually outlines a three-level movement from an initial assertion about Buddhist practice, through a deconstruction of that assertion using the rhetoric of ŚŪNYATĀ (EMPTINESS), to a profoundly nuanced restatement of the initial assertion. Shenxiu taught the constant or perfect practice of the PATH of the BODHISATTVA, by which he meant that one should always remain in meditation and always work to help other SENTIENT BEINGS. If he had actually used the metaphor of the mirror as given here, polishing the mirror would be a standard procedure of ethical training, not a gradualistic device for progressing toward enlightenment.

Huineng's verse contains no reference to suddenness, but is rather a deconstructive move implying a more profound understanding of Shenxiu's initial "perfect teaching." The balance of the *Platform Sūtra* explains this more profound understanding using such expressions as the "formless precepts" and metaphoric reinterpretations of "sitting in meditation."

Bibliography

McRae, John R. *The Northern School and the Formation of Early Ch'an Buddhism.* Honolulu: University of Hawaii Press, 1986.

McRae, John R., trans. *The Platform Sūtra of the Sixth Patriarch.* Berkeley, CA: Numata Center for Buddhist Translation and Research, 2000.

Yampolsky, Philip B. *The Platform Sūtra of the Sixth Patriarch: The Text of the Tun-huang Manuscript with Translation, Introduction, and Notes.* New York and London: Columbia University Press, 1967.

JOHN R. MCRAE

POETRY AND BUDDHISM

The effect of Sanskrit Buddhist poetics and prosody on Chinese language and culture is one of the most profound characteristics of the introduction of Buddhism to East Asia. Indian Buddhist poetry formally begins with the poet and philosopher AŚVAGHOṢA (ca. first or second century C.E.), who composed the earliest surviving examples of the *kāvya* literary style of Sanskrit poetry, the BUDDHACARITA (*Acts of the Buddha*) and *Saundarananda.* Prior to Aśvaghoṣa, Buddhists employed Pāli and other local languages in metrical arrangement. The Sanskrit used in Aśvaghoṣa's poetry, however, is highly literary and displays linguistic artistry more in accordance with later Jaina or Hindu poets of the Gupta period (320–540). Sanskrit *kāvya* poetry and poetics spread to Burma (Myanmar), Thailand, Cambodia, and the Malay Archipelago before affecting the reception of Buddhism in China, Japan, and Tibet.

Buddhists introduced notions of resonance, repetition, a system of four tones (as opposed to five or seven), meter, and poetic defects (Sanskrit, *doṣa*)—all of which generated discussion on the mechanics of poetics among East Asian aristocrats. Indian and Central Asian Buddhist literature incorporated religious verse or *gāthās* (Chinese, *jie* or *jietuo*), one of the twelve divisions of the tripiṭaka according to genre. In addition to *gāthās, geya* (Chinese, *qiye*)—the verse summaries of tenets presented in sūtra literature—captivated monastic and lay Buddhists in China because of the *śloka* meter, with four quarter verses of eight syllables each.

Because of the difficulty in dating most Indian texts, it is nearly impossible to ascertain which specific Indian texts or figures were influential in China. But, scholars do know that the genre of composing poems of eulogy or praise (Chinese, *zan* or *jiesong*) for religious or secular reasons, with five to seven Chinese characters to a line, was instigated on the basis of Sanskrit *gāthās.*

During the period of disunion of the Wei, Jin, and Northern and Southern dynasties (220–589), Buddhist ideas and literature spread throughout East Asia as composing poetry became the principal literary art. While most East Asian poets did not study the Sanskrit language, many familiarized themselves with the principles of accurately rendering the sounds of Sanskrit into Chinese—using Indian Siddham (Chinese, *xitan*) script in order to chant sūtras or DHĀRAṆĪ. In the monastic estates, where lay and monastic elites assembled, the massive project of translating Buddhist texts into Chinese prompted men like the Buddhist poet Xie Lingyun (385–433) to work on a standardized system for the transcription of Sanskrit sounds. Xie's system was later used by literati to compose standard rhyme dictionaries for composing poetry.

Chinese literati came to write about poetics and the mechanics of composition in a genre of writing called *shihua.* Although it was not until the Song (960–1279) dynasty that the genre became pervasive, early authors in China based their theories on Sanskrit analogues transmitted through Buddhism. KŪKAI (774–835), the famous transmitter of EXOTERIC-ESOTERIC (KENMITSU) BUDDHISM IN JAPAN, composed the most comprehensive treatise on both Sanskrit and Chinese poetics in his *Bunkyō hifuron* (*A Treatise [Comprising] a Mirror for Literature and a Repository of Rare [Verses and Expressions]*). Kūkai's mastery in languages has made his *Bunkyō hifuron* the principal reference work on Buddhist poetry and inspired generations of East Asian poets.

The Tang (618–907) and Song dynasties are traditionally recognized for their poets and poetry. During these dynasties, Buddhist monks and lay officials like Hanshan, Guanxiu, Juefan Huihong (1071–1128), Wang Wei (701–761), and Su Shi (1036–1101) all associated with the emergent CHAN SCHOOL (Korean, Sŏn; Japanese, Zen) to make poetry a conspicuous and permanent aspect of Buddhist practice.

See also: **Canon; Chinese, Buddhist Influences on Vernacular Literature in; Japanese, Buddhist Influences on Vernacular Literature in; Languages; Sanskrit, Buddhist Literature in**

Bibliography

Demiéville, Paul. "Le Tch'an et la poésie chinoisie." In *Choix d'études bouddhiques.* Leiden, Netherlands: Brill, 1973.

Lienhard, Siegfried. *A History of Classical Poetry: Sanskrit, Pali, Prakrit.* Wiesbaden, Germany: Harrassowitz, 1984.

Mair, Victor H., and Mei, Tsu-lin. "The Sanskrit Origins of Recent Style Prosody." *Harvard Journal of Asiatic Studies* 51, no. 2 (1991): 375–470.

GEORGE A. KEYWORTH

POLITICS AND BUDDHISM

Siddhārtha Gautama was himself a prince, who nonetheless rejected political power, abandoning his royal inheritance along with his family and material comforts. In the biographies of the Buddha there is thus a strong sense of dichotomous contrast: The "world" (of family, wealth, and politics) must be renounced in the pursuit of enlightenment. MONKS and NUNS were instructed to refuse or minimize involvement with the political leadership. Nonetheless, ORDINATION was a political statement with political consequences, since the ordinand claimed to be opting out of the power structures of the (lay) world. Indeed one measure of the holiness of a Buddhist saint has been a distance from the centers of political power. Even monks who were intimately involved in political lobbying and who lived lives of urban comfort nonetheless retained some of the symbolism of the poor mountain or forest renunciant.

There are scriptural cases of the Buddha's dealings with rulers, generally in the contexts of teaching them the dharma and receiving donations. Bimbisāra, king of Magadha during the Buddha's lifetime, is remembered as a pious disciple and generous donor who gave land for the SAṄGHA and sponsored the creation of the first Buddha image.

More influential was the example of King AŚOKA (third century B.C.E.), ruler of the Mauryan dynasty, who converted to Buddhism and promoted its spread throughout much of India. His conversion came after a famously bloody war campaign, and the violence of his earlier military career is often thought to lie behind his religious fervor. His policy of conquest by force (*digvijaya*) was replaced by an idea of conquest by righteousness (*dharmavijaya*). Much of the image of Aśoka as personally pious dates from later sources, which blend into hagiographic idealization. Aśoka's official pronouncements are known from the extant edicts carved in rocks and distributed throughout his empire, often on display in Buddhist monasteries. He also sponsored religious sects other than Buddhism, and the dharma teachings that the edicts emphasize are fairly nonspecific exhortations to law-abiding social conduct. Aśoka did recommend sūtras to read, and he

A monk participating in a Mother's Day protest against nuclear weapons testing prays at the entrance to the Nevada test site in 2000. AP/Wide World Photos. Reproduced by permission.

seems to have intervened in a schism, forcing schismatic monks to wear white robes and be removed from the orthodox saṅgha. According to traditional Sinhalese accounts, he took a role in the Council of Pāṭaliputra (250 B.C.E.), which formalized a schism between the Sthaviras (elders) and the MAHĀSĀṂGHIKAS (Great Assembly). Aśoka became a model of the righteous Buddhist king, and temples to King Aśoka were founded throughout East Asia.

Some kings have chosen to be ordained as monks. Some of the Japanese emperors lived as monk-recluses (in their palaces). As another example, King Mongkut of Siam (1804–1868) was hurriedly ordained a monk a week before his father's death, and was thereby sheltered from succession struggles. Instead, Mongkut's half-brother reigned for twenty-seven years, and upon his death, Mongkut disrobed and ascended the throne for a further seventeen-year reign. During his time as a monk, Mongkut founded a reform sect of Thai Buddhism, which has continued to enjoy royal favor.

The ideal ruler

The ideal ruler was described as cakravartin (wheel-turning king or universal ruler) and *dharmarāja*, or as a bodhisattva. Cakravartins have the thirty-two marks of a great man, rule in accordance with dharma, and preside over an age of peace. Buddhist rulers have claimed the right to purify the religion and to judge the teachings. In China, the emperor presided over debates between representatives of Buddhism, Daoism, and Confucianism, pronouncing the winner at the end of the day. Various state laws provided some legal backing, such as tax exemptions, to monastic institutions. Conceding that the ruler has a legitimate role to play in reducing the bad karma of crime, the saṅgha has performed rituals to protect the ruler and the state.

Many rulers in Asia, even pro-Buddhist rulers, have sought to control aspects of the saṅgha. Taking on the role of the cakravartin, rulers have at times "purged" the saṅgha of its "impurities" by enforcing stricter controls on entry (quotas on ordinations, or added stipulations), by extending secular law into the jurisdiction of the VINAYA (monastic code), and by expelling certain monks and nuns. In some cases, then, attacks on clerical institutions have been phrased in pro-Buddhist terms. In other cases, there was no such rationalization and the goal was simply the extermination of the saṅgha. Such violent anticlerical PERSECUTIONS have occurred sporadically throughout history, but perhaps the best known include the persecution during the Huichang period in China (ca. 842–845), the Communist-inspired iconoclasm of the Chinese Cultural Revolution (1966–1976), and the violence in Tibet since the 1950s. In Japan, the slaughter of monks during the civil warfare of the sixteenth and seventeenth centuries, and the anti-Buddhist movements of the early Meiji (1868–1870s), come to mind.

The ideal ruler is a lavish patron, funding monastery construction and large publication projects. Many rulers in Asia have indeed donated land and other wealth for the establishment of monasteries, with a variety of motives. Undoubtedly the popular perception of the ruler as pious, the complicity of the monastic institutions in state propaganda, and the conspicuous displays of wealth all helped to legitimate the reign. The doctrine of merit (Sanskrit, *puṇya*; Chinese, *gongde*) made economic wealth religiously significant, as donations became the very substance of the saṅgha. The construction of large Buddha images, such as the colossal Buddha at Tōdaiji in Nara, dedicated in 752 C.E., was also a powerful means of asserting political jurisdiction. The Tōdaiji image was built from donations gathered throughout the imperial domain, and in both its material contributions and its iconographic symbolism, consolidated the sense of a unified imperial nation.

The imperial states of Asia were often intimately involved in the process of importing the dharma. Even when the state ideology was non-Buddhist or anti-Buddhist in orientation, rulers made donations out of political expediency, and many officials of the state were committed to Buddhism in a "private" capacity. Imperial women in particular were often sponsors of Buddhism.

Monks were sometimes desirable subjects for rulers. The great translator of Sanskrit texts, KUMĀRAJĪVA (350–ca. 409/413), was one of the spoils of war in conflicts between Chinese and Central Asian states. Well-traveled monks lent prestige and foreign intelligence to a regime; they also embodied a certain magical auspiciousness. According to the account by XUANZANG (ca. 600–664) of his travels to India, rulers of the kingdoms he passed through often wanted him to stay. King Harsha (r. 606–647) paid his respects to Xuanzang, convened a debating tournament and declared him the winner, and released him only after much delay. When Xuanzang returned to China, he was welcomed by Emperor Gaozong (r. 649–683), who attempted to press the monk into political service. Failing that, he urged Xuanzang to record his travels.

Buddhism as a political problem

Buddhism has at times been perceived as a political danger. Various versions of millennial Buddhism have been seen as challenges to the state, and in some cases truly were. The idea of the DECLINE OF THE DHARMA (also known by the Japanese term *mappō*) described the declining, or degenerating, capacity of human beings to achieve enlightenment as they grew increasingly remote from Śākyamuni Buddha. Various time frames were projected, with most orthodox estimates placing the decisive "end of the dharma" in the distant future. However, some popular millennial movements have posited the arrival or imminence of the end. In some cases Buddhists concluded that FAITH in AMITĀBHA Buddha was the only viable option in such a degenerate age, but in other cases it was believed that the messianic figure MAITREYA was present or soon would be present.

Mappō assumed political importance both as a critique of government, since corrupt government was one indication of the decline, and also as an element of movements actively opposing the state. Though orthodox traditions posit the arrival of the next buddha, Maitreya, in the remote future, the notion of a messiah who incarnates in a corrupt world to wash away the existing order has been taken more immediately at a popular level. In the fourteenth century, the White Lotus society developed expectations of the imminent arrival of Maitreya that required a cleansing of the evil political regime. The White Lotus Rebellion, which occurred in China from 1796 to 1805, was just such an attempt. Many states have been suspicious of religious secret societies, including those with Buddhist roots. In some cases Buddhist institutions openly maintained large standing armies; in Japan, powerful monasteries accumulated land holdings so large that they effectively became feudal domains, complete with taxation and militias. When Japan was unified by force in the sixteenth century, it was inevitable that warlords such as Oda Nobunaga (1534–1582) came to face Buddhist institutions in battle, especially the Jōdo shinshū. During the Tokugawa period (1600–1868), local monasteries and temples came to function as organs of the state, so that anti-Buddhism overlapped with nativism and new versions of Shintō. The strong association of Buddhism and the Tokugawa regime led to a persecution and widespread destruction of Buddhism in the years after the Meiji restoration of 1868.

The relations of monk and ruler

Although the saṅgha has had much to gain from good relations with political rulers, in an ideal sense monks are supposed to be uninterested in material wealth. The legendary story of BODHIDHARMA meeting Emperor Wu of the Liang (r. 502–550) has the great patriarch of the CHAN SCHOOL bluntly dismissing the salvific potency of all the emperor's wealth: All the donations to build temples and copy scriptures produced no merit at all. Furthermore, the ideal monk was supposed to be unaffected by the threat of violence represented by the ruler. Lore has developed in which the heroic monk casually brushes aside any hint of fear. The monk SENGZHAO (374–414), for example, faced with the threat of execution, recited a verse to the ruler:

> The four elements originally have no master;
> The five skandhas are basically empty.
> When my head meets the white blade,
> It will merely be like beheading the spring wind.

Placed in a situation of conflict with the civil authorities, threatened with the possibility of physical punishment and death, Sengzhao used his words to convey a simple message: The body is empty, so killing me would be useless and cannot even frighten me; you ultimately cannot kill me, because there is no "me" to kill. The basic trope then, is the use of the idea of ŚŪNYATĀ, (EMPTINESS) during a display of virtuous bravado in the face of an overbearing ruler.

This ability to speak truth to power was in part derived from Buddhist anthropology and the cultivation of nonattachment, but also from the position of the monk as "outside" or "beyond" the world. Indeed, at times the foreignness of Buddhism was embraced and displayed: Monks—even native-born monks—described themselves as *fangwai zhi bin* (guests from outside the boundaries) who come from outside the imperial domain. The analogy of exteriority is evident also in the term *chujia* (left the household), although this was also quite literally true—clerics were indeed absent from the home. As Stephen Teiser remarks: "The power of monks—their ability to enrich substantially the welfare of the family—depends upon their social placement outside of the family" (p. 205). The same could be said of their placement outside of the political realm.

There were moments when the ritual practices of clerics were in direct physical contact with other, incompatible, systems of behavior. For example, in China, Confucian imperial guest ritual conflicted with the vinaya—as when a monk refused to bow to the ruler. Yet at these moments of obvious physical presence, we find the otherness of the monk admitted, indeed emphasized. The claim of belonging to some authority "outside the boundaries" was at the same time the claim to a site within the realm, from which to speak of the ruler as if from outside his realm.

The strength of this assertion relied on the tradition of legal privileges accorded to foreign visitors (for example, visiting princes). Hereditary kinship with the ruler of a foreign state brought a number of privileges, such as partial noncompliance with imperial ritual, and partial extraterritoriality. Buddhist discourses often analogized monks to high-ranking representatives of a "ruler," the Buddha. Monks are the Buddha's "sons," his "crown princes," and so should, by analogy, have diplomatic immunity or extraterritoriality. Buddha is an emperor (of the dharma), and monks (his heirs) are princes, and thus the authoritative ambassadors of his words. In China, even as heaven

Tibetan monks demonstrating in front of the U.S. Capitol for the cause of religious freedom in Tibet in 1998. AP/Wide World Photos. Reproduced by permission.

mandates just rulership (*tianming*), the just ruler receives Buddha's charge or mandate for improving society and maintaining moral conduct: The model ruler is a "wheel-turner" who is responsible for law and order. There was a division of labor between the Buddha and the cakravartin, with the Buddha delivering beings from the world to a salvation "outside the world" (*fangwai*), and the cakravartin working "in the world" to reduce bad karma.

Law and party politics

Imperial domain requires territory and more or less demarcated spatial boundaries (physical or imagined), within which there is jurisdiction; applicable laws were those determined by the emperor and his ministers, scholars, and magistrates, and the military and police power needed to enforce those laws. At times the monastic institutions and the state contested areas of jurisdiction. For example, if a monk commits murder, the saṅgha is entitled to disrobe him, but not to send him to prison; the state may wait until the monk is disrobed before arresting him, or may claim a right to reach directly into the monastery. Similarly, state law codes have recognized the status of the cleric in a variety of ways, sometimes affording the ordained a dispensation not to perform military service, or acknowledging the Buddhist educational qualification as equivalent to secular educational degrees. In Thailand, degrees from Buddhist universities have gained qualified recognition from the government; for example, these degrees are fully accredited for those who disrobe and serve as military chaplains. Thai law prescribes penalties on those who impersonate a monk.

There have also been explicitly Buddhist political parties. SŌKA GAKKAI, a Nichiren Shoshū-derived movement founded in 1930 in Japan, has been politically active, especially after World War II. In 1964 Sōka Gakkai leader Ikeda Daisaku established the political party Kōmeitō, formally unaffiliated but closely aligned with Sōka Gakkai. Officially dissolved in 1994 but reformed in 1998 as the New Kōmeitō, it has remained small but influential. In Sri Lanka as well, Buddhist nationalism has become a powerful political force. In India, the lawyer and politician B. R. AMBEDKAR (1891–1956) campaigned for the rights of untouchables, and shortly before his death led a mass conversion to Buddhism. There has also been a global mobilization of Tibetan Buddhist adherents against the Chinese occupation of Tibet. These and many other cases show that despite elements of other-worldly rhetoric, Buddhism is easily enlisted in political causes.

See also: **Communism and Buddhism; Councils, Buddhist; Japanese Royal Family and Buddhism; Kingship; Law and Buddhism; Meiji Buddhist Reform; Millenarianism and Millenarian Movements; Monastic Militias; Nationalism and Buddhism; Shintō (Honji Suijaku) and Buddhism**

Bibliography

Orzech, Charles D. *Politics and Transcendent Wisdom: The Scripture for Humane Kings in the Creation of Chinese Buddhism.* University Park: Pennsylvania State University Press, 1998.

Smith, Bardwell L., ed. *Religion and the Legitimation of Power in South Asia.* Leiden, Netherlands: Brill, 1978.

Smith, Bardwell L., ed. *Religion and Legitimation of Power in Sri Lanka.* Chambersburg, PA: ANIMA, 1978.

Smith, Bardwell L., ed. *Religion and Legitimation of Power in Thailand, Laos, and Burma.* Chambersburg, PA: ANIMA, 1978.

Tambiah, Stanley J. *World Conqueror and World Renouncer: A Study of Buddhism and Polity in Thailand against a Historical Background.* Cambridge, UK: Cambridge University Press, 1976.

Teiser, Stephen. *The Ghost Festival in Medieval China.* Princeton, NJ: Princeton University Press, 1988.

Zürcher, E. *The Buddhist Conquest of China: The Spread and Adaptation of Buddhism in Early Medieval China.* Leiden, Netherlands: Brill, 1959.

ERIC REINDERS

PORTRAITURE

Representations of MONKS, NUNS, and members of the LAITY flourished in East Asian and Tibetan Buddhist traditions. In pre-Buddhist Han China, portraits of exemplary figures past and present derived from historical, biographical, and eulogistic texts. Ancient Chinese concepts of *portrait* are encompassed by the words *xiang* (Japanese, *zō*), *zhen* (Japanese, *shin*), and *ying* (Japanese, *ei*). Where a caption named a figure, both words and image called to mind the larger story of that individual; a likeness was not essential. Yet most modern definitions of portraiture mandate that the subject be an individual, and that the representation be based on observed reality. Within Buddhist contexts, the word *xiang* also denotes BUDDHA IMAGES (*foxiang*; Japanese, *butsuzō*), as well as representations of local deities (*shen*; Japanese, *kami*). Combinations like *zhenxiang* (Japanese, *shinzō*), and *yingxiang* (Japanese, *eizō*) stress the importance of resemblance and truth, not merely to appearances but also to the spirit. Like devotional icons, portraits consecrated in formal ceremonies embodied the living aura of their subjects. As such, they too, served as the focus of offerings and ceremonies.

Lineages and patriarchs

In China early Buddhist portraiture featured genealogies or lineages that trace a particular history of dharma transmission. At the Kanjingsi cave chapel at LONGMEN (ca. 720–730), a procession of twenty-nine patriarchs of the "western lands" (i.e., India) carved in larger than life relief surround the central image of Śākyamuni. This artificial group, found in a text of the Northern CHAN SCHOOL, begins with Śākyamuni's senior disciple MAHĀKĀŚYAPA and ends with BODHIDHARMA, putative founder of Chan in China. Although individually lifelike and varied, these depictions recall the Han tradition of exemplar portraits. LINEAGE portraits, in both painting and sculpture, spread to both Japan and Tibet. In mid-eighth century Japan at Tōdaiji, the patriarchs of each of the six competing schools of Buddhism were painted on wooden cabinets holding sūtras promoted by each school. Zhang Shengwen's *Long Roll of Buddhist Images* (1173–1176, National Palace Museum, Taipei), painted for the kingdom of Dali in southwestern China, incorporated a succession of Chan portraits showing each master seated in a landscape setting. In Tibet, the founders of the four Tibetan orders appeared as the large central figure in *thang kas* (*thanka*; painted hanging scrolls), surrounded by smaller depictions of their teachers and Buddhist deities. No matter how convincing or lifelike, such images were imaginary and deified representations of semilegendary and long-dead masters created to legitimize particular lineages.

The impulse to remember and venerate the sanctity of one's own teacher led to the creation of individual portraits from life and the writing of hagiographies. Numerous Chinese tales and images exemplify efforts to preserve the corpses of venerated saints, both through natural mummification and a complex practice of preservation by desiccation and cloth soaked in lacquer. Corpses encased in such a coating, placed within sūtra-mausoleums or separate temple halls, became objects of veneration for both temple and pilgrims. The mummy of the sixth Chan patriarch HUINENG (ca. 638–713) is the most famous extant example, while the life-sized hollow dry lacquer image of GANJIN (Chinese, Jianzhen; 688–763) may be an example of a sculpted image substituted for a "failed mummy." At Tōshōdaiji in Nara, Japan, Ganjin's portrait served as a relic of the strong connection between a revered teacher and his surviving students, as well as a portrait of the temple's founder. In the thirteenth century, VINAYA school revivalists venerated Ganjin as their patriarch and erected a portrait hall for the image. Many portraits of individual monks commemorate their leadership talents and patronage activities, as for instance Hongbian (late ninth century), whose clay portrait was installed in a small chapel at DUNHUANG. Not a mummy, the image contained a bag of ashes, while a record of his activities was inscribed in a neighboring chapel.

A conflation of these strains of portraiture appears with KŪKAI (774–835), who studied Zhenyan (SHINGON BUDDHISM, JAPAN) teachings in Chang'an from 804 to 806. Kūkai brought back to Japan seven life-size individually painted portraits of his immediate predecessors that incorporated written biographies. After Kūkai's death, his followers added his own portrait to make a set of eight Shingon patriarchs. These paintings were copied and disseminated to Shingon temples throughout Japan, where they became an essential component in main halls and on pagoda walls.

Portraiture blossomed in thirteenth-century Japan as a result of an increased awareness of Buddhist history and fresh contact with Chinese teachers. Students of Pure Land, Vinaya, and Chan teachings brought back portraits of their teachers from China. These depicted formally dressed abbots seated in elaborate cloth-decorated chairs, holding attributes of their status and character. Often drawn from life, these paintings frequently bore inscriptions by the sitter. These individual portraits were venerated in Japanese monasteries, and when the subject died, they became the focus of memorial ceremonies. As the lineages of these teachers spread throughout Japan, copies proliferated. At some temples, separate portrait/memorial halls enshrined painted or sculpted images of founders. Perhaps the strongest manifestations of the lineage/memorial portrait tradition are the countless portraits of Chan abbots. Abbot portraits occupied central altar space in the various subtemples of Zen monasteries in Japan, where sculpted founder portraits replaced buddha images as the central object of devotion.

Donors and lay believers

Buddhist portraiture was not confined to representations of lineages, patriarchs, and abbots. In ancient India, famous lay patrons, both men and women, abound in illustrated narratives, occasionally with identifying inscriptions. Relief carved images of lay patrons also appear on the gates to stūpa mounds. While neither of these types of representation qualify as portraiture, they can be seen as precursors to donor images of royalty and prominent families found in the cave-chapels of Dunhuang and Longmen in China. At the POTALA in Lhasa, a large ninth-century sculpted statue of King Srong btsan sgam po (Songtsen Gampo, ca. 627–649) suggests that the making of sculpted donor portraits may have been more common than extant evidence suggests. Many of the workshop-produced paintings found at Dunhuang depict generic lay donors, with space left to record names, dates, and vows. The genres of ancestor and commemorative portraits flourished in China long after Buddhism waned among the elite classes.

In Japan, however, portraits of the lay elite survive in considerable numbers. Numerous sculpted portraits of Prince SHŌTOKU (574–622) at different ages commemorate his role in establishing Buddhism. The hollow bodies of the sculptures often contain copies of the sūtras he promulgated, as well as donations from patrons. Several pious emperors received the tonsure upon abdicating the throne; thus their portraits show them with shaven heads in monk's clothing. Their descendants enshrined these portraits in private chapels or in temples they founded.

Throughout Japan's medieval period, numerous portraits of the aristocratic and military elite were created at their deaths to be hung in mortuary temples (*bodaiji*). Documentary sources tell of painters summoned to sketch their likenesses, either before or after death. These sketches served as the basis for life-size portraits, usually painted but occasionally carved. Family memorial portraits also included representations of prominent women, retired empresses and military wives, and even boys who had died young. The portraits frequently incorporated written biographies or eulogies, or the Buddhist name conferred on the deceased. Although memorial portraits depict their subjects in finery appropriate to their station, such portraits were not secular in function or place of display. The families of the deceased provided material support, often including the personal possessions of the deceased, to these mortuary temples for memorial ceremonies as well as care of family burial sites.

See also: **Arhat Images; Bodhisattva Images; Buddha, Life of the, in Art; Chan Art; China, Buddhist Art in; Japan, Buddhist Art in**

Bibliography

Guth, Christine M. E. "Portraiture." In *Japan's Golden Age: Momoyama,* ed. Money L. Hickman. Dallas, TX: Dallas Museum of Art, 1996.

Levine, Gregory P. "Switching Sites and Identities: The Founder's Statue at the Buddhist Temple Kōrin'in." *Art Bulletin* 83, no. 1 (2001): 72–104.

Mori, Hisashi. *Japanese Portrait Sculpture,* translated and adapted by W. Chie Ishibashi. Tokyo and New York: Kodansha International, 1977.

Phillips, Quitman E. *The Practices of Painting in Japan, 1475–1500.* Stanford, CA: Stanford University Press, 2000.

Sharf, Robert H. "The Idolization of Enlightenment: On the Mummification of Ch'an Masters in Medieval China." *History of Religions* 32, no. 1 (1992): 1–31.

Sharf, Robert H. "On the Ritual Use of Ch'an Portraiture in Medieval China." *Cahiers d'Extreme-Asie* 7 (1993–1994): 149–219.

Sharf, Robert H., and Sharf, Elizabeth Horton, eds. *Living Images: Japanese Buddhist Icons in Context.* Stanford, CA: Stanford University Press, 2001.

Spiro, Audrey. *Contemplating the Ancients: Aesthetic and Social Issues in Early Chinese Portraiture.* Berkeley: University of California Press, 1990.

KAREN L. BROCK

POTALA

The Potala palace, one of Tibet's largest and best known landmarks, is an enormous fortresslike structure located in the Tibetan capital Lhasa. The Potala served as the winter residence of the DALAI LAMAS and as the locus of the Tibetan government from the seventeenth century to the fourteenth Dalai Lama's flight from Tibet in 1959. In thirteen floors said to contain more than one thousand rooms, the Potala encompasses an elaborate conglomeration of residential chambers, reception and assembly halls, temples, reliquary chapels, monastic quarters, and offices. Located atop a small hill called Mar po ri on the northwestern edge of Lhasa, the palace's full name is the Summit Palace of Potala (Rtse po ta la'i pho brang). The name refers to Mount Potalaka in India, which is revered as the abode of the compassionate BODHISATTVA Avalokiteśvara, who is believed to manifest in the figure of the Dalai Lamas.

The earliest foundations of the palace date to the Tibetan king Srong btsan sgam po (r. ca. 614–650), who moved his capital to Lhasa from the south, erecting an eleven-storied structure on Mar po ri in 637 that served as the center for his court. Some ten centuries later, in 1645, the fifth Dalai Lama (1617–1682) began renovations to this structure, planning a new ecclesiastic residence and offices for the Dga' ldan pho brang—the central Tibetan government—all to be moved from the nearby 'Bras spungs (pronounced Drepung) Monastery. These additions included the so-called White Palace, composed mainly of administrative and residential quarters, and the upper Red Palace containing rooms used for religious purposes, which now include the reliquary tombs of the fifth and seventh through thirteenth Dalai Lamas. Construction continued for many decades and was not finished until the close of the seventeenth century. According to Tibetan histories, the fifth Dalai Lama's adroit regent Sangs rgyas rgya mtsho (1653–1705) kept news of the hierarch's death secret for more than twelve years in order to bring this monumental project to completion. Jesuit missionaries Albert Dorville and Johannes Grueber published sketches of the partially erected Potala palace, which they witnessed while passing through Lhasa in 1661.

For nearly three hundred years, the Potala served as an epicenter of Tibetan religious and political power. The outer facade was shelled by occupying Chinese troops in 1959, the time of the fourteenth Dalai Lama's

The Potala palace is the traditional residence of the dalai lamas in Lhasa, Tibet. © Corbis. Reproduced by permission.

flight into exile in India. Since then, much of the Shol village, a frequent destination of the flamboyant sixth Dalai Lama (1683–1707), located at the palace's foot, has been systematically dismantled. Although the Potala's structural damage was subsequently repaired, the vacant palace remains a potent symbol for the absence of Tibet's principal religious and political leader.

The Potala's massive structure also continues to play a central part in contemporary Tibetan religious practice. It forms the northern boundary of the large circumambulation route around Lhasa called the *gling skor* (pronounced ling khor) or sanctuary circuit. Pilgrims visit the palace daily, winding through its many inner chambers, reciting prayers and presenting offerings at its many hundreds of shrines. In 1994 the Potala was named a UNESCO World Heritage Site.

See also: **Tibet**

Bibliography

Bishop, Peter. "Reading the Potala." In *Sacred Spaces and Powerful Places in Tibetan Culture: A Collection of Essays*, ed. Toni Huber. Dharamsala, India: Library of Tibetan Works and Archives, 1999.

Larsen, Knud, and Sinding-Larsen, Amund. *The Lhasa Atlas: Traditional Tibetan Architecture and Townscape.* Boston: Shambhala, 2001.

ANDREW QUINTMAN

PRAJÑĀ (WISDOM)

With KARUṆĀ (COMPASSION), prajñā (wisdom) is one of two virtues universally affirmed by Buddhists. Broadly, prajñā is correct discernment of any object; specifically, it is intellectual and experiential insight into soteriologically significant truths, whether metaphysical (e.g., categories of DHARMAS, the functioning of KARMA, the realms of SAṂSĀRA) or ontological (e.g., no-self, emptiness, the natural purity of mind). Virtually all Buddhist traditions affirm that wisdom is a prerequisite to enlightenment, and that a buddha possesses the maximum possible wisdom, or gnosis (jñāna).

Like many Indian religious teachers of his era, the Buddha apparently regarded the "sentient condition" (repeated, uncontrolled REBIRTH in unsatisfactory realms) as rooted primarily in misapprehension of reality. For early Buddhists, ignorance (avidyā) was, with desire and aversion, one of the three poisons that perpetuate SAMSĀRA, the cycle of rebirth; it was also the first of the twelve factors of PRATĪTYASAMUTPĀDA (DEPENDENT ORIGINATION) that account for continued rebirth. This ignorance misconstrues both the details and the ultimate nature of the world and of persons. In particular, the belief that one is or has a permanent, independent self leads to desire and aversion, thence to unskillful actions and unpleasant results, including rebirth. In fact, both philosophical and meditative investigation reveals that, because there is nothing anywhere in the conditioned world that is permanent, there can be no such self. The recognition of this fact of no-self (anātman) is the antidote to ignorance, that is, wisdom. When one realizes experientially, with insight MEDITATION founded on one-pointed concentration, that there is no self, one no longer creates desire or aversion for the sake of that self, and one begins to uproot defilements, becoming an ārya, whose enlightenment is assured.

In THERAVĀDA and other mainstream Buddhist texts, both canonical and commentarial, wisdom is, with morality (*śīla*) and concentration (samādhi), one of three indispensable Buddhist trainings. Wisdom itself is commonly divided into that gained through study of written and oral teachings, reflection upon the meaning of those teachings, and meditative internalization of those meanings. This list and its sequencing show that in most Buddhist contexts both philosophical and experiential wisdom were valued, but that experiential wisdom, gained through insight meditation, was considered superior. Most great Theravāda and Śrāvakayāna texts—from the Sūtra and ABHIDHARMA Piṭakas to scholastic masterworks such as BUDDHAGHOSA'S *Visuddhimagga* (*Path to Purification*) and VASUBANDHU'S ABHIDHARMAKOŚABHĀṢYA (*Treasury of Abhidharma*) (both ca. fifth century C.E.)—provided a more or less systematic categorization of the dharmas or phenomena into which Buddhists analyze reality, while also stressing the limitations of intellectualism and the necessity for meditative scrutiny of oneself and the world, especially so as to negate the idea of a subsisting self.

Despite caveats about scholasticism, Theravāda and Śrāvakayāna philosophers sometimes reified dharmas and their categorizations, and many MAHĀYĀNA texts evidently were written to counter this tendency. The earliest and most influential was the PRAJÑĀPĀRAMITĀ LITERATURE, which focused on wisdom as the sixth and culminating PĀRAMITĀ (PERFECTION) that a BODHISATTVA must master en route to full buddhahood. This literature described wisdom as the nonconceptual realization that not just the self, but the very dharmas that constitute the person and the world are intrinsically empty. The bodhisattva must also perfect such methods (UPĀYA) as generosity, morality, patience, effort, and contemplation, but does so while bearing in mind their emptiness. Other Mahāyāna sūtras promoted wisdom in other ways, seeing it as the realization of nonduality, sameness, lack of intrinsic nature, mind-only, the interpenetration of all dharmas, or the stainless primordial mind. However they described the object of wisdom, these sūtras shared an emphasis on the ultimate inconceivability of reality and the primacy of experiential over intellectual approaches to wisdom.

Far from ending philosophical debate, however, the Mahāyāna sūtras spawned countless commentaries and treatises, which systematically analyzed both the subjective and objective aspects of wisdom, from YOGĀCĀRA SCHOOL enumerations of types of consciousness, to Pramāṇa school analyses of epistemic authority, MADHYAMAKA SCHOOL debates about the place of reason in arguments for emptiness, and TATHĀGATAGARBHA-tradition evocations of a pure buddha-wisdom lying dormant in every sentient being. Scholar-monks examined the relation of wisdom to *bodhicitta*, compassion, and skillful means; the way to arrive at a "middle view" that avoided the extremes of eternalism and nihilism; the balance to be struck in meditation between concentration and analysis; and what is known by a buddha's perfect gnosis. By the late first millennium C.E., north India was dotted with great monastic universities emphasizing a scholarly approach to wisdom.

Not surprisingly, countercurrents developed. East Asian Chan traditions focused on direct transmission and nonconceptual realization of perfect wisdom. Indian and Tibetan tantric movements developed dramatic ritual and meditative practices to bring about a wisdom consciousness that simultaneously realizes emptiness, sees forms, and experiences bliss. Chan and tantric traditions themselves sometimes embraced scholasticism, and were in turn reformed by contemplatives, such as HUINENG (638–713) in the CHAN SCHOOL and Saraha (late first millennium C.E.) in TANTRA, who sought to return wisdom to its home in nonconceptual meditative experience. Meditative schools, however, sometimes adopted irrationalism or antinomianism, and so were opposed by others, including ZONGMI (780–841) in China and TSONG KHA PA (1357–1419) in Tibet, who insisted that philosophical training was a prerequisite to attaining experiential wisdom through meditation.

Wisdom was not restricted to philosophers and contemplatives; it became accessible to ordinary Buddhists through art and ritual. Content aside, texts were often believed to impart wisdom and protective power simply by virtue of being containers of the dharma, and they were worshipped accordingly. Certain doctrinal formulas were inscribed on steles and statuary; for example, "Of those dharmas arising from causes, the tathāgata has described the cause, and also their cessation—thus spoke the Great Ascetic." Wisdom was condensed into DHĀRAṆĪS and MANTRAS, which evoked power and knowledge in the practitioner, and served as purifiers in confession rituals. Wisdom also was deified, sometimes as male, as in the bodhisattva Mañjuśrī, whose widespread cult is centered at Wutaishan in China, but more often as female, as in Prajñāpāramitā, who is "mother of the Buddhas," or Vajrayoginī, who symbolizes the tantric gnosis experiencing emptiness and bliss simultaneously.

Wisdom remains central to contemporary Buddhism, especially as Buddhist traditions enter the modern world. Insight meditation (*vipassanā*) is practiced more widely than ever before, Buddhist views are compared with one another and with Western ideologies, and old debates continue about how to describe the object of wisdom, balance intellectual and experiential approaches to wisdom, and apply wisdom to living life in the world with real intelligence and freedom.

See also: **Bodhicitta (Thought of Awakening)**

Bibliography

Buddhaghosa, Bhadantacariya. *The Path of Purification: Visuddhimagga*, tr. Bhikku Ñyāṇamoli. Boulder, CO: Shambhala, 1976.

Collins, Steven. *Selfless Persons: Imagery and Thought in Theravāda Buddhism.* Cambridge, UK: Cambridge University Press, 1982.

Lancaster, Lewis, ed. *Prajñāpāramitā and Related Systems.* Berkeley: University of California Press, 1997.

Napper, Elizabeth. *Dependent Arising and Emptiness: A Tibetan Buddhist Interpretation of Mādhyamika Philosophy Emphasizing the Compatibility of Emptiness and Conventional Phenomena.* London and Boston: Wisdom, 1989.

Pettit, John W. *Mipham's Beacon of Certainty: Illuminating the View of Dzogchen, the Great Perfection.* Boston: Wisdom, 1999.

Ruegg, David Seyfort. *The Literature of the Madhyamaka School of Philosophy in India.* Wiesbaden, Germany: Harrassowitz, 1981.

Williams, Paul. *Mahāyāna Buddhism: The Doctrinal Foundations.* London and New York: Routledge, 1989.

Yampolsky, Phillip B., trans. *The Platform Sūtra of the Sixth Patriarch.* New York: Columbia University Press, 1967.

ROGER R. JACKSON

PRAJÑĀPĀRAMITĀ LITERATURE

One of the earliest records of the MAHĀYĀNA school's discourse in Indian Buddhism is to be found in the family of texts known as the Prajñāpāramitā, often translated as "Perfection of Wisdom." These texts appear in several forms. Some were similar in content but were characterized by expansion. Titles were later added to these expansions, based on the length of each. The oldest of this group was designated as 8,000 lines and the largest as 100,000. There were those numbering 18,000 and 25,000 lines. Another group of texts was formed in the opposite fashion, by contraction. The great length of the earlier texts created problems of how to preserve and use documents that covered hundreds of palm leaves or strips of birch bark. One solution was to look for ways to present the core of the teaching in shortened formats. Out of this grew the texts that are most often recited in monasteries and Buddhist ceremonies in East Asia, the so-called DIAMOND SŪTRA and HEART SŪTRA. One further development was added by the tantric movement. In this form, MANTRAS and DHĀRAṆĪ dominated, and the smallest of the contractions appeared in which the doctrine of the Prajñāpāramitā was contained in the single letter *A*.

There is very little known about the community of monastics who produced these texts that were to become a primary source for Mahāyāna development. The lack of inscriptions, archeological finds, and mixed reports from early Chinese pilgrims suggest that the documents were not the result of a large institutional structure. From internal evidence within the texts that gave high praise to the practice of making written copies, it may be that this discourse was transmitted mainly through the emerging technology of writing. The early years of Buddhism, after the time of the Buddha, was based on an oral tradition and a large organization of monasteries. The use of written manuscripts may have allowed a small group to disseminate these particular ideas without reliance on more traditional oral methods.

Within the texts, the teaching is mainly done through the use of dialogue between well-known figures, including the Buddha and his major followers. The subject matter revolves around long established debates over the nature of perception and cognition. The list of terms seldom varies from the *Mātṛkā* (seed) categories set up in the ABHIDHARMA groups. The innovation found in the Prajñāpāramitā is the emphasis given to the momentary and unique nature of each moment of cognition and the insights regarding this process achieved by a special group of adepts known as BODHISATTVAS.

See also: **Sanskrit, Buddhist Literature in**

Bibliography

Conze, Edward. *The Prajñāpāramitā Literature.* The Hague, Netherlands: Mouton, 1960.

Conze, Edward, trans. *The Perfection of Wisdom in Eight Thousand Lines and Its Verse Summary.* Bolinas, CA: Four Seasons Foundation, 1973.

Lancaster, Lewis, ed., and Gómez, Luis, assoc. ed. *Prajñāpāramitā and Related Systems: Studies in Honor of Edward Conze.* Berkeley: University of California Regents, 1977.

Lopez, Donald S. *Elaborations on Emptiness: Uses of the Heart Sūtra.* Princeton, NJ: Princeton University Press, 1996.

LEWIS LANCASTER

PRĀTIMOKṢA

The prātimokṣa (Pāli, *pātimokkha*), presumably the oldest section of the VINAYA, contains the disciplinary code that regulates the life of the SAṄGHA, the Buddhist monastic community. The etymology of the term *prātimokṣa* is uncertain, but it denotes the highest standard of conduct for Buddhist monastics. In the early days of the Buddhist community, the prātimokṣa was apparently a simple profession of faith in the Buddha's primary teachings that was recited periodically by the expanding saṅgha. Later, the term came to refer to the corpus of disciplinary rules that developed gradually over time as the saṅgha grew and regulations were formulated in response to specific incidents of misconduct.

The prātimokṣa is recited twice a month, on the full moon and new moon days, at an observance known as saṅgha *poṣadha* (Pāli, *uposatha*). This observance is a rite of confession in which the actual confession of faults precedes the recitation of precepts and declaration of purity. The *Bhikṣuprātimokṣa* is recited by fully ordained MONKS and the *Bhikṣuṇīprātimokṣa* is recited by fully ordained NUNS in separate observances; novices and laypeople are not permitted to attend. The semimonthly obligatory recitation of the prātimokṣa is a means of reviewing the ethical guidelines and rules of etiquette that the monks and nuns voluntarily agree to observe, and a time for them to reaffirm their purity with regard to the prohibitions. This liturgical observance, conducted within a *sīmā* (ritually established boundary), is a way to ensure harmony within the saṅgha and between the saṅgha and the laity. Rituals of REPENTANCE AND CONFESSION and specific procedures for expiating offenses are prescribed. The importance of the PRECEPTS is evident in the Buddha's declaration that the prātimokṣa would guide the saṅgha after he passed away.

The prātimokṣa precepts found in the vinaya (monastic discipline) regulate the lives of Buddhist monastics who have received the *upasaṃpadā* (full ORDINATION), as well as novices and probationers who are in training. The precepts give detailed instructions that regulate ethical decision making, food, clothing, shelter, furnishings, and other material requisites, as well as the rules that govern etiquette and personal interactions. The extant texts of all schools of vinaya list five categories of precepts that are common to both bhikṣus and *bhikṣuṇīs*: (1) *pārājika* (defeats that entail expulsion from the saṅgha, such as killing a human being or engaging in sexual intercourse); (2) *saṅghāvaśeṣa* (remainders that entail suspension, such as acting as a go-between or baselessly accusing someone of a *pārājika*); (3) *niḥsargika-pātayantika* (abandoning downfalls that entail forfeiture, such as keeping excess robes or engaging in business activities); (4) *pātayantika* (propelling downfalls or lapses, such as intentionally telling a lie or eating at an improper time); and (5) *śaikṣā* (faults or misdeeds, such as wearing the robes improperly or eating in a careless fashion). There is one additional category for bhikṣus, the two *aniyatadharma* (individually confessed downfalls), and one for *bhikṣuṇīs*, the eight *pratideśanīya* (offenses requiring confession). The seven *adhikaraṇa-śamatha* (methods of resolving disputes) are included in the prātimokṣas of both bhikṣus and *bhikṣuṇīs*. These seven methods include assembling the parties to the dispute, remembering events, admitting one's responsibility, resolving matters by a majority decision, and so forth.

Diverse schools of vinaya (*nikāyas*) developed in India within a few hundred years after the Buddha's *parinirvāṇa,* but the prātimokṣa rules and procedures of all these schools are thought to derive from the rules of discipline that were originally recited at the first of the Buddhist councils. Although the substance of the precepts is fundamentally the same, the specific numbers of precepts vary slightly from one school to another, for a variety of reasons. For example, (1) local communities had different interpretations of monastic discipline and there was no central authority to adjudicate them; (2) the precepts were transmitted orally and in different languages for several hundred years before they were written down; and (3) as the Buddhist community spread to different geographical and cultural areas, some precepts were adjusted in accordance with local customs. These schools are in almost complete agreement concerning the precepts, exhibiting only minor differences.

Of the roughly eighteen schools of vinaya that developed in India, three lineages of prātimokṣa are still in existence today. The THERAVĀDA Vinaya is preserved in Pāli and practiced by bhikṣus in Bangladesh, Burma, Cambodia, Laos, Thailand, and Sri Lanka; although the *Bhikṣuṇīprātimokṣa* exists in Pāli, there is no living lineage of *bhikṣuṇīs* in the Theravāda tradition. The *Dharmaguptaka-vinaya* is preserved in Chinese and practiced by bhikṣus and *bhikṣuṇīs* in China, Japan, Korea, Taiwan, and Vietnam. The MŪLASARVĀSTIVĀDA-VINAYA is preserved in Tibetan and practiced by bhikṣus in Bhutan, the Indian Himalayas, Mongolia, Nepal, and Tibet; although the *Bhikṣuṇīprātimokṣa* exists in Tibetan, there is no living lineage of *bhikṣuṇīs* in the Tibetan tradition. In the Theravāda tradition, there are 227 precepts for bhikṣus and 311 for *bhikṣuṇīs*; in the Dharmagupta, there are 250 for bhikṣus and 348 for *bhikṣuṇīs*; and in the Mūlasarvāstivāda, there are 258 for bhikṣus and 354 for *bhikṣuṇīs.*

The *Bhikṣuṇīprātimokṣa-sūtra* exists in all three of these vinaya schools, but a living lineage of *bhikṣuṇīs* exists only in the Dharmagupta school. Tens of thousands of *bhikṣuṇīs* in China, Korea, Taiwan, and Vietnam today regulate their lives by the *Bhikṣuṇīprātimokṣa* of the Dharmagupta school. In all three extant vinaya schools, the number of precepts for *bhikṣuṇīs* is considerably greater than for bhikṣus. The Bhikṣu Saṅgha was quite well organized and influential by the time the Bhikṣuṇī Saṅgha was established five or six years later, so the *bhikṣuṇīs* were naturally expected to follow the majority of the bhikṣus precepts, in addition to new precepts occasioned by specific misbehavior among the nuns. In the first category of precepts, the *pārājikas,* there are four that are common to both bhikṣus and *bhikṣuṇīs.* They are to refrain from: (1) sexual intercourse, (2) taking what is not given, (3) taking a human life, and (4) telling lies, especially about one's spiritual attainments. The four additional *pārājikas* for *bhikṣuṇīs* are to refrain from: (5) bodily contact with a lustful man; (6) arranging to meet a man with amorous intentions; (7) concealing a *pārājika* of another *bhikṣuṇī*; and (8) obeying a bhikṣu who has been expelled from the saṅgha. Of the second category of precepts, *saṅghāvaśeṣas,* bhikṣus in all schools have thirteen, whereas *bhikṣuṇīs* in the Dharmagupta and Theravāda have seventeen, and *bhikṣuṇīs* in the Mūlasarvāstivāda have twenty. Some *saṅghāvaśeṣas* are similar for bhikṣus and *bhikṣuṇīs* (e.g., acting as a go-between, baselessly accusing someone of a *pārājika,* refusing to accept admonishments, creating a schism in the saṅgha), while others are dissimilar.

Broadly interpreted, there are eight types of prātimokṣa precepts: bhikṣu (fully ordained monk), *bhikṣuṇī* (fully ordained nun), *śikṣamāṇā* (probationary nun), *śrāmaṇera* (male novice), *śrāmaṇerikā* (female novice), *upāsaka* (layman), *upāsikā* (laywoman), and *upavāsatha* (one-day lay observance). There is no counterpart to the *śikṣamāṇā* (probationary nun) ordination for monks. The first seven categories of prātimokṣa precepts generally entail a lifetime commitment, except in countries such as Thailand where temporary ordination is offered. The eighth type of prātimokṣa precepts, *upavāsatha,* is the observance of eight precepts for twenty-four hours by laypeople. The aim of all types of prātimokṣa precepts is to cultivate restraint of the senses as a means to achieve liberation.

See also: **Councils, Buddhist; Festivals and Calendrical Rituals**

Bibliography

Davids, T. W. Rhys, and Oldenberg, Hermann, trans. *Vinaya Texts,* parts 1–3. Delhi: Motilal Banarsidass, 1974.

Dhirasekera, Jotiya. *Buddhist Monastic Discipline: A Study of Its Origin and Development in Relation to the Sutta and Vinaya Piṭakas.* Sri Lanka: Ministry of Higher Education, 1982.

Horner, Isaline Blew. *The Book of Discipline,* 6 vols. London: Routledge and Kegan Paul, 1982.

Prebish, Charles S. *Buddhist Monastic Discipline: The Sanskrit Prātimokṣa Sūtras of the Mahāsaṃghikas and Mūlasarvāstivādins.* University Park: Pennsylvania State University Press, 1975.

Tsomo, Karma Lekshe. *Sisters in Solitude: Two Traditions of Buddhist Monastic Ethics for Women, a Comparative Analysis of the Dharmagupta and Mūlasarvāstivāda Bhikṣuṇī Prātimokṣa Sūtras.* Albany: State University of New York Press, 1996.

Vajirañāṇavarorasa, Somdetch Phra Māha Samaṇa Chao Krom Phrayā. *The Entrance to the Vinaya: Vinayamukha,* 3 vols. Bangkok, Thailand: Mahāmakuṭ Rājavidyālaya Press, 1969–1983.

Wijayaratna, Mohan. *Buddhist Monastic Life According to the Texts of the Theravāda Tradition,* tr. Claude Grangier and Steven Collins. Cambridge, UK: Cambridge University Press, 1990.

KARMA LEKSHE TSOMO

PRATĪTYASAMUTPĀDA (DEPENDENT ORIGINATION)

The theory of dependent origination (*pratītyasamutpāda;* Pāli: *paticcasamuppāda*), which literally means "arising on the ground of a preceding cause," could well be considered the common denominator of all Buddhist traditions throughout the world, whether THERAVĀDA, MAHĀYĀNA, or VAJRAYĀNA. The canonical texts of the Theravāda tradition portray ŚĀRIPUTRA (the Buddha's disciple) as saying that "whoever understands dependent origination understands the teaching of the Buddha, and whoever understands the teaching of the Buddha understands dependent origination" (M. i, 190–191). In the Vajrayāna tradition, a similar view is expressed by the fourteenth DALAI LAMA (1935–) who stated in his 1990 book, *Freedom in Exile,* that the fundamental precept of Buddhism is this law of dependent origination. No matter what the tradition, one can clearly see the importance attributed to the theory: It renders it a fundamental tenet of Buddhism, indispensable for realizing and understanding the implications of Buddhist philosophy.

The theory of dependent origination is usually divided into twelve links (*nidāna*), each of which conditions the following link. The order presented in Table 1 is traditionally refered to as the normal order (*anuloma*), which illustrates the process of the development of SAṂSĀRA. The *pratītyasamutpāda* is also often presented soteriologically in reverse order (*pratiloma*), which simply indicates that if one link is eradicated, the next is also eradicated.

The chain of dependent origination is often approached as a causal theory. One usually speaks of causality when one says "there being this, that appears." Yet it is necessary to stress that a substantial "cause" from which the "effect" was generated cannot be deduced from dependent origination. The *Saṃyuttanikāya (Connected Discourses;* S.ii.87–88) explains that fertile soil, water, and light are necessary conditions for the growth of a sapling, but none of these factors alone will yield the expected result. Similarly, each of the links of the chain of dependent origination is necessary for the production of the next element, yet none can definitely be perceived as sufficient on its own.

TABLE 1

The twelve links of the chain of dependent origination

1. Ignorance 2. Karmic activities	PAST
3. Consciousness 4. Mind and matter 5. Six sense-doors 6. Contact 7. Sensation 8. Craving 9. Attachment 10. Becoming	PRESENT
11. Birth; rebirth 12. Old age, death	FUTURE

Since this complex chain of causation is always said to give rise to suffering, the deactivation of any of the twelve links of this chain is bound to break the causal process and to eliminate suffering. According to the Pāli canon, both the chain of dependent origination and the five SKANDHA (AGGREGATE) are responsible for suffering. The Buddha stated repeatedly that the root of all suffering lies in the five aggregates, which represent the psychophysical constituents of the individual. This is further evidenced by the *Mahāvagga* of the *Aṅguttaranikāya* (*Discourses Increasing by One*), where an intimate relation between the five aggregates and the theory of dependent origination is established. In this specific discourse, a description of the FOUR NOBLE TRUTHS is offered in terms of dependent origination. Therein, the first noble truth follows the standard canonical rendering and ends with the following phrase: "in short, the five aggregates are suffering" (A. i, 177). Yet the description of the two following truths does not comply with the paradigmatic rendition.

Instead, they are depicted in terms of the theory of dependent origination. The noble truth concerned with the arising of suffering is simply explained by the *pratītyasamutpāda* in normal order (*anuloma*), while the noble truth of cessation of suffering is defined by dependent origination in reverse order (*pratiloma*). It is clear then that dependent origination, traditionally seen as an explanation for the arising and the eradication of suffering, is intimately related to the theory of the five aggregates.

The Theravāda tradition holds that certain links of the chain of causation are limited either to the past, present, or future. In other words, and as illustrated in Table 1, different links constitute different temporal divisions. Although this chronological division is not expressed explicitly in the Pāli canonical literature itself, it is supported by the *Abhidhammatthasaṅgaha (Compendium of Philosophy)* of Anuruddha, a South Indian Buddhist philosopher (ca. eleventh–twelfth century C.E.). What is unclear, however, is the delineation and theoretical distinction among these three divisions. Since the past is nothing but the aging of the present, and the present the actualization of the future, each temporal division has to be seen as the paraphrasing of, or a different perspective on, the two other divisions. Since these divisions are merely arbitrary, the links of dependent origination that were classified under a certain time period could have been easily classified under another. What comes under "past" could have been under "future" or "present," and vice versa. Therefore, it becomes evident that elements belonging to a specific time period represent a process similar to the one reflected by the elements belonging to another. Ignorance and karmic activities operate on the same principles as birth and old age and death, and as the eight middle links. The physical and psychological elements at work in the individual remain the same whether in the past, present, or future. Stated differently, the theory of dependent origination could run thus: Within one life span (links 11–12; birth and old age and death), one keeps generating karmic activities (link 2) because of ignorance (link 1), and this generation of karmic activities due to ignorance is more easily understandable by examining the process described by the eight middle links.

Equally striking is that the division of the chain of causation into three time periods implies the presence of the five aggregates in each of these periods, since an "individual" (composed of the five aggregates) must experience this process within each of the periods; this is the perspective put forth by VASUBANDHU (fourth century C.E.) in his ABHIDHARMAKOŚABHĀṢYA (AbhK. iii, 20). This suggests that the theory of dependent origination is not merely a soteriological tool, indicating how the individual ought to proceed in order to attain liberation from the causal process of saṃsāra, but also a psychological chart mapping the working of the mind.

See also: **Duḥkha (Suffering)**

Bibliography

Dalai Lama XIV. *Freedom in Exile: The Autobiography of the Dalai Lama.* New York: HarperCollins, 1990.

Lamotte, Étienne. "Conditioned Co-Production and Supreme Enlightenment." In *Buddhist Studies in Honour of Walpola Rahula,* ed. Somaratna Balasooriya et al. London: Gordon Fraser, 1980.

Macy, Joanna. "Dependent Co-Arising: The Distinctiveness of Buddhist Ethics." *Journal of Religious Ethics* 7, no. 1 (1979): 38–52.

Silburn, Lilian. *Instant et cause: Le discontinu dans la pensée philosophique de l'Inde.* Paris: Librairie Philosophique J. Vrin, 1955.

Tanaka, Kenneth K. "Simultaneous Relation (sahabhū-hetu): A Study in Buddhist Theory of Causation." *Journal of the International Association of Buddhist Studies* 8, no. 1 (1985): 91–111.

MATHIEU BOISVERT

PRATYEKABUDDHA

In the early tradition of the Pāli canon the *paccekabuddha* (Sanskrit, pratyekabuddha) refers to a male individual who has attained enlightenment or insight (*bodhi*; hence, *buddha*) by himself. In contrast to a *sammāsambuddha* (Sanskrit, *samyaksaṃbuddha*), which is a completely enlightened person, a pratyekabuddha keeps enlightenment for himself (*pratyeka*) and does not embark on a career of preaching it to others. In early Buddhist COSMOLOGY, buddha era and nonbuddha era follow each other. During a buddha era, an enlightened being like the historical Buddha (Siddhārtha Gautama) is born, attains enlightenment, and eventually preaches the FOUR NOBLE TRUTHS that he has discovered. He then starts a dispensation on the basis of his compassion for other suffering beings. A pratyekabuddha also attains enlightenment by his own effort, but does not have the energy to preach or establish a Buddhist dispensation because, as the canonical texts explain, he lacks the compassion of a fully enlightened buddha. Even so, he is considered a teacher, albeit a silent one, teaching by the example of his life and actions.

The figure of the pratyekabuddha may have been the result of integration in early Buddhist history of pre-Buddhist ascetics, who had been revered by the people as saints and sages. By incorporating them into Buddhist history, early Buddhist communities were able to establish a kind of continuity with the pre-Buddhist period. At the same time, they were able to acknowledge the possibility of enlightened persons in other eras and cultures.

Pratyekabuddhas therefore have a special, but limited, place in Buddhist ideology. A fully enlightened person, a buddha, finds the eternal truths of the Buddhist message by himself and starts a period of Buddhism. A pratyekabuddha, on the other hand, will not preach and will have no followers. Like a pratyekabuddha, an ARHAT is a person who attains the highest state of enlightenment. However, according to Buddhist tradition, the arhat did not reach this stage by his or her own efforts, but rather came to understood the four noble truths and traveled the PATH as taught by the Buddhist tradition. In the MAHĀYĀNA tradition, the paths of arhat, pratyekabuddha, and buddha are initially all considered as leading to NIRVĀṆA, but the path of a buddha is believed to be the only worthy goal, the One Vehicle of Supreme Buddhahood, which will eventually be attained by all.

See also: **Ascetic Practices; Buddhahood and Buddha Bodies**

Bibliography

Kloppenborg, Ria. *The Paccekabuddha: A Buddhist Ascetic.* Leiden, Netherlands: Brill, 1974.

Wiltshire, Martin G. *Ascetic Figures before and in Early Buddhism: The Emergence of Gautama as the Buddha.* Berlin and New York: de Gruyter, 1990.

RIA KLOPPENBORG

PRATYUTPANNASAMĀDHI-SŪTRA

Pratyutpannasamādhi-sūtra, an early MAHĀYĀNA meditation text, was first translated into Chinese by Lokakṣema in 179 C.E. The full Sanskrit title is *Pratyutpanna-buddha-saṃmukha-avasthita-samādhi-sūtra,* which translates as "the scripture of the meditation in which one comes face-to-face with the buddhas of the present," that is, buddhas now inhabiting other worlds. The principal objectives of this encounter are to hear the dharma from the buddha of one's choice and to be reborn with him in his world after death. The text's use of AMITĀBHA in Sukhāvatī as a paradigm case suggests links with PURE LAND BUDDHISM, but practitioners may seek to encounter and be taught by any buddha of the present. The sūtra thus provides a means and a rationale for continuing scriptural revelation. After purifying themselves, practitioners meditate on the buddha's virtues and visualize his physical person (using the standard list of thirty-two marks and eighty features), while seated facing the appropriate direction (e.g., west for Amitābha). Doing this continuously for up to seven days and nights, they eventually see the desired vision, either in the waking state or in dreams. Interestingly, the sūtra itself undercuts an excessively literal understanding of the process or undue emotional attachment to its results by deconstructing them in terms of the doctrine of ŚŪNYATĀ (EMPTINESS), thus representing a merging of various currents of Mahāyāna Buddhist thought and practice.

Evidence for the practice in India is slim, although many sources extol the salvific value of such visions of the buddhas. In East Asia, however, the *pratyutpannasamādhi* and its derivatives are well attested elements in the meditative and ritual repertoire of Buddhism.

Bibliography

Harrison, Paul. "Buddhānusmṛti in the Pratyutpanna-buddha-saṃmukhāvasthita-samādhi-sūtra." *Journal of Indian Philosophy* 6 (1978): 35–57.

Harrison, Paul. *The Samādhi of Direct Encounter with the Buddhas of the Present: An Annotated English Translation of the Tibetan Version of the Pratyutpanna-Buddha-Saṃmukhāvasthita-Samādhi-Sūtra with Several Appendices Relating to the History of the Text.* Tokyo: International Institute for Buddhist Studies, 1990.

PAUL HARRISON

PRAYER

Buddhists, like many other religious people, usually pray *to* someone or something, and they pray *for* the realization of certain goals. Sometimes Buddhists pray using their body alone (a simple bow in front of an altar); sometimes they use words (the recitation of a verse of homage or devotion, a verbal petition or a supplication). Buddhist prayer can also be done in the mind. Buddhists pray in private, individually in public, or together with others as a joint activity.

Buddhists pray to a variety of beings, both human and nonhuman. The object of prayer can be the historical Buddha, or one of a seemingly infinite number of transhistorical BUDDHAS or BODHISATTVAS. When THERAVĀDA Buddhists, for example, prostrate before a Buddha statue, this might be considered an act of praying with the body. If, in addition, they chant the most famous Pāli worship formula, "Homage to the worthy one, the lord, the completely awakened one," that might be considered to involve a verbal prayer as well. If this is further accompanied by thoughts of the Buddha's greatness, or by feelings of gratitude or devotion, this might be considered to involve the mind in prayer. In the Chinese and Japanese Pure Land tradition, the practice of *nenbutsu* (*nianfo*), the recollection of the Buddha AMITĀBHA and his pure land, is quintessentially a mental action, but it is usually accompanied by the repeated recitation of a prayer-formula, "Homage to the Buddha Amitābha."

Prayers can also be directed to human beings, both living and not. For example, Tibetan Buddhists practice what is popularly called *guru devotion.* Mentally, this involves the cultivation of an attitude in which the teacher comes to be seen as a buddha. Verbally, guru devotion can be done through the simple repetition of the guru's name. In more elaborate rituals, for example, in the "worship of the guru" (*bla ma mchod pa*), the living or deceased guru, whose presence is ritually invoked, becomes the object of the adept's devotions: Offerings are made, the guru is requested not to forsake the world and to continue to teach the doctrine, and he or she will also be asked to impart blessings on the adept.

Buddhists also direct their prayers at special things. For example, the widespread practice of "going for refuge to the three jewels" can be seen not only as a prayer to the buddha and the SAṄGHA, but also to the dharma (a holy, but inanimate, object). Sometimes a specific scripture will become an object of prayer and devotion, as in the Sino-Japanese cults of the LOTUS SŪTRA (SADDHARMAPUṆḌARĪKA-SŪTRA). The worship of STŪPAS or relics might also be said to be forms of prayer directed at something, rather than at someone.

Besides praying to what we might call "transcendental" objects, however, Buddhists also pray to the various DIVINITIES (devas) that are believed to inhabit the world. These can be quite extraordinary beings, like the great gods of the Hindu pantheon, or the protectors of the dharma. They can also be lesser, though nonetheless powerful, spirits associated with a particular region or place. Tantric Buddhists developed elaborate prayer rituals to propitiate both dharma protectors and indigenous spirits. In many of these rituals practitioners visualize themselves in the form of an enlightened deity, who then demands, rather than requests, the cooperation of the protector. This is important, lest it be thought that all forms of Buddhist prayer requires the adept to assume a position of humility and submission before the object to whom the prayer is directed.

Finally, Buddhists pray for a variety of things that range from worldly goals (e.g., a good harvest, children, protection from harm, health, money, erudition, love) to the most sublime (enlightenment). They pray for a better REBIRTH (e.g., as a human or god) or, as is widespread in Mahāyāna Buddhism, they pray to be reborn in a pure land. When one engages in prayer for one's own sake, this is often conceptualized in terms of the dual activities of purification and the accumulation of merit. For example, Tibetan Buddhists spin prayer wheels, metal cylinders that rotate on their axes and that contain MANTRAS (Tibetans themselves call these objects *maṇi wheels*). The spinning of prayer wheels is often done during other activities, almost as a reflex, and would appear not to involve any conscious goal. However, Tibetans generally believe that the movement of sacred objects (in this case, printed mantras) generates merit for the mover, and so the goal of merit-making is at the very least implied in the spinning of prayer wheels.

Buddhists also believe in the efficacy of prayers for the sake of others, both living and dead. The Mahāyāna in particular stresses the importance of praying for others, as in the practice of "dedicating one's merits" for the benefit of all sentient beings, which can also be seen as an act of prayer.

See also: **Merit and Merit-Making; Nenbutsu (Chinese, Nianfo; Korean, Yŏmbul); Refuges; Relics and Relics Cults**

Bibliography

Griffiths, Paul J. "A Hymn of Praise to the Buddha's Good Qualities." In *Buddhism in Practice,* ed. Donald S. Lopez, Jr. Princeton, NJ: Princeton University Press, 1995.

Makransky, John. "Offering (*mChod pa*) in Tibetan Ritual Literature." In *Tibetan Literature: Studies in Genre,* ed. José I. Cabezón and Roger R. Jackson. Ithaca, NY: Snow Lion, 1996.

Sharf, Robert. "The Scripture on the Production of Buddha Images." In *Religions of China in Practice*, ed. Donald S. Lopez, Jr. Princeton, NJ: Princeton University Press, 1995.

Williams, Paul. *Mahāyāna Buddhism: The Doctrinal Foundations.* London: Routledge, 1989.

José Ignacio Cabezón

PRECEPTS

Precepts within Buddhism are rules and guidelines intended to properly shape the mind and its manifestations in physical and verbal behavior so as to facilitate progress on the PATH to liberation. The term *precepts*, although a valid rendering of one sense of the Sanskrit word *śīla* (Pali, *sīla*), fails to convey the full range and force of that word, which properly refers to the morality or virtue that constitutes one of the prerequisite foundations for ultimate spiritual attainment. The cultivation of *śīla* in this broad sense represents one of three required forms of training (*trīṇi śikṣāṇi*), along with concentration and wisdom, that correspond to the noble eightfold path. Although the precepts appear as external prescriptions and are often couched in negative terms, their goal and the proper thrust of Buddhist morality is the natural and positive embodiment of right action, speech, and livelihood. The various categories of precepts that will be discussed below are therefore not to be seen as ends in themselves, but rather as necessary steps in training for awakening. As steps, these categories distinguish between the lay and monastic life stations, between males and females, as well as between different levels of progress and commitment in religious life.

The five, eight, and ten precepts

The most basic moral prescriptions in Buddhism are often identified with the categories of five, eight, and ten precepts, which are generically known as rules of training (Sanskrit, *śikṣāpada*; Pāli, *sikkhāpada*). The five precepts address the moral obligations of all Buddhist laypersons and are sometimes taken along with the three REFUGES in a formal ceremony. They are thus viewed, much like monastic precepts, as a set of vows that call for abstention: (1) from the taking of life, (2) from stealing, (3) from sexual misconduct, (4) from lying, and (5) from intoxicants. Laypersons seeking to express greater dedication to the Buddhist path and further growth in moral training can take on observance of the eight precepts. Besides adopting a stricter interpretation of the first five precepts in which observance of the third precept requires complete abstinence from sexual activity, adherence to the eight precepts further entails: (6) refraining from eating after midday, (7) avoiding singing, dancing, and music, as well as use of perfume, and (8) refraining from the use of luxurious beds. Observance of these eight rules conventionally takes place only for limited periods, often on six days each month, arranged around the full and new moon days that coincide with the bimonthly confessional ceremonies (Sanskrit, *poṣadha*; Pāli, *uposatha*) in the monastic community.

In contrast to the categories of five and eight precepts that pertain to the moral training of laypersons, the category of ten precepts sets forth a basic moral vision for Buddhist monastics. Those entering the monastic order take these ten precepts in a "going-forth" ceremony (*pravrajyā, pabbajā*) through which they become novices (*śrāmaṇera, sāmaṇera*). The ten precepts resemble an expanded form of the eight precepts, which involves adherence to the five precepts, including a strict ban on all sexual activity, and further entails vowing to refrain: (6) from eating after midday, (7) from singing, dancing, and music, (8) from wearing jewelry and using perfumes, (9) from sleeping on luxurious beds, and (10) from handling gold and silver.

The monastic disciplinary code

Whereas the ten precepts set forth a basic moral compass for MONKS and NUNS, the monastic disciplinary code (PRĀTIMOKṢA, *pātimokkha*), consisting of a greatly enlarged number of more than two hundred precepts, historically has been a determining factor in shaping the Buddhist monastic order (SAṄGHA) as an institution. These precepts, which constitute the central content of the VINAYA-*piṭaka* in the Buddhist CANON (Tripiṭaka, Tipiṭaka), function on different levels.

On the one hand, the monastic code has an obvious moral dimension. Many of these precepts are simply a further elaboration of the moral principles laid out in the ten precepts, and therefore reinforce the continued moral training of monastics after their ORDINATION. At the same time, the aim of these precepts has been to preserve the Buddhist saṅgha's image as a model of rectitude in the eyes of the lay community. Thus, the Buddha is recorded as having established some of the precepts as a result of incidents in which the conduct of monks threatened to cause scandal in those for whom the monastic community was to provide moral guidance and upon whom the monastic community relied for its physical support.

From another perspective, these precepts have an institutional dimension. In practical terms, many of the precepts in the prātimokṣa have the concrete goal of ensuring order and smooth functioning in the everyday affairs of the community. More fundamentally, however, the very existence of the whole Buddhist community is premised upon the stability of the saṅgha, which in turn is dependent upon the valid conferral of the precepts in ordination. The vinaya specifies that the prātimokṣa are to be formally taken (*upasaṃpadā*) in the presence of a requisite number of properly ordained monks. Furthermore, the candidates were required to fulfill conditions that were ascertained through a set of questions during the ceremony. Finally, there were specifications with regard to the site of ordination, which DAOXUAN (596–667), founder of the Chinese Vinaya school (Lüzong), developed into a detailed set of specifications for the erection of an ordination platform. Absence of these key conditions was thought to invalidate this crucial ceremony that marks the passage to status as a fully ordained monk or nun. Great attention, therefore, has been paid through history to ensure the validity of this process. A striking example of such concern took place in Japan in the eighth century when questions about proper ordination cast the validity of the whole Buddhist order, which had existed in Japan for over a century, into doubt. Consequently, the Chinese ordination master GANJIN (Jianzhen, 688–763) was invited to Japan. After five failed attempts, he finally arrived in Japan in 754, erected an ordination platform according to specifications in Nara before the great Tōdaiji, and performed a properly prescribed ordination, thus ensuring the legitimacy of the saṅgha in Japan.

The centrality of the prātimokṣa for the moral discipline of monks and nuns and the cohesion of the saṅgha is symbolically expressed through fortnightly confessional ceremonies (*poṣadha, uposatha*) at which monastics in a locality are required to gather together (with monks and nuns meeting separately) for a recitation of the precepts of the prātimokṣa. The recital of each precept is accompanied by a required confession before the community of any instance of transgression. The shared recognition and adherence to a particular articulation of the prātimokṣa evident in these ceremonies has been the token of unity for communities of the saṅgha through history, while disagreement with regard to the precepts has led historically to the creation of new communities with their own separate prātimokṣa. Unlike Christianity, in which doctrinal disagreements often inspired the rise of new groups, sectarian division within early Buddhism is thought to have been largely premised on differing approaches to the discipline.

One of the historical results of these divisions was the production of divergent prātimokṣa contained within different versions of the *vinaya-piṭaka*. There currently exist in various languages versions of the vinaya from six different schools: SARVĀSTIVĀDA AND MŪLASARVĀSTIVĀDA, DHARMAGUPTAKA, MAHĀSĀṂGHIKA, MAHĪŚĀSAKA, and THERAVĀDA. Of these, three have contemporary relevance: The Theravāda tradition observes the precepts in its Pāli version of the vinaya; the East Asian tradition of Buddhism has largely adhered to the precepts of the Dharmaguptaka Vinaya (*Sifen lü*) for over a thousand years; and discipline in the Tibetan Buddhist tradition is based on the vinaya of the Mūlasarvāstivāda. Each of these differs with regard to the number of precepts constituting the prātimokṣa. For full ordination, the Theravāda Vinaya contains 227 rules for monks (or 311 for nuns), the Dharmaguptaka 250 (or 348), and the Mūlasarvāstivāda 258 (or 354). Today only East Asian Buddhism continues to preserve a tradition of fully ordained nuns.

The precepts of the prātimokṣa are grouped in categories that are arranged in descending order of seriousness according to the gravity of an offense. The most serious category (*pārājika*) contains offenses that require immediate expulsion from the saṅgha with no possibility of reinstatement in one's lifetime. For monks, this category involves four major offenses: sexual intercourse, stealing, murder, and false claims with regard to one's spiritual attainment. The prātimokṣa for nuns legislates four more offenses in this category, including intimate touching of men, holding hands with men, hiding the serious offenses of other nuns, and following a censured monk. The second category (*saṅghāvasesa*) concerns offenses that call for discipline falling short of expulsion but requiring temporary forfeiture of one's full status as a monk or nun and removal from the community for a period of time. This category contains thirteen offenses for monks that include sexual impropriety, erecting dwellings, slander, and causing dissension in the saṅgha. For nuns, this category in the Dharmaguptaka Vinaya holds seventeen precepts, including prohibition from serving as a marriage broker. The remaining categories of the prātimokṣa address less serious offenses calling for punishments that range from confiscation of inappropriate items and confession before the whole community to confession before one person. Although the different versions of the vinaya listed above vary in the number of categories and precepts, they nevertheless manifest a remarkable similarity.

Mahāyāna precepts

The MAHĀYĀNA tradition from its inception paid great heed to training in morality and the observance of precepts. This emphasis was incorporated into the bodhisattva path as an essential element of the PĀRAMITĀ (PERFECTION) that the bodhisattva was expected to cultivate. The second of these perfections calls for dedication to morality and strict adherence to the precepts. This dedication has often been expressed simply through observance of traditional precepts. Mahāyāna monks and nuns, for example, have ordinarily taken and adhered to the full precepts of the prātimokṣa. In time, however, Mahāyāna came to develop precepts that were unique to the bodhisattva vocation. The most famous articulation of such precepts is that found in the FANWANG JING (BRAHMĀ'S NET SŪTRA), an apocryphal text thought to have been produced in China. This scripture sets forth fifty-eight precepts, dividing them into ten major and forty-eight minor rules that besides emphasizing the basic moral orientation of the five precepts also stress the bodhisattva's obligation to care for all beings. They further call for extreme ASCETIC PRACTICES, such as the burning of limbs, thus marking a significant departure from the discipline of the prātimokṣa.

These bodhisattva precepts were administered to lay persons and monastics alike. Monks and nuns customarily would take these precepts in a separate ceremony following the administration of the prātimokṣa in ordination. Historically, the Mahāyāna tradition rarely called attention to the disparity between these "Mahāyāna precepts" and the "precepts" of the vinaya. The founder of the Japanese Tendai school, SAICHŌ (767–822), however, made just such a distinction. In attempting to firmly establish the Tendai teaching that he had brought back from China, Saichō asked permission of the court to build an ordination platform on Mount Hiei. Tendai monks ordained on this platform were not to receive the customary precepts but only the bodhisattva precepts, thereby ensuring that their ordination was a purely "Mahāyāna" one. When the Japanese court granted Saichō's request shortly after his death, the Japanese Tendai school and the traditions that grew out of it adopted an approach to precepts that differed from that taken by the rest of the Buddhist world.

See also: **Councils, Buddhist; Ethics; Festivals and Calendrical Rituals; Mahāyāna Precepts in Japan; Repentance and Confession**

Bibliography

Gethin, Rupert. *The Foundations of Buddhism.* Oxford: Oxford University Press, 1998.

Groner, Paul. *Saichō: The Establishment of the Japanese Tendai School.* Berkeley: Center for South and Southeast Asian Studies, University of California at Berkeley, 1984.

Harvey, Peter. *An Introduction to Buddhist Ethics: Foundations, Values and Issues.* Cambridge, UK: Cambridge University Press, 2000.

Holt, John Clifford. *Discipline: The Canonical Buddhism of the Vinayapiṭaka,* 2nd edition. Delhi: Motilal Banarsidass, 1995.

Matsunaga, Daigan, and Matsunaga, Alicia. *Foundation of Japanese Buddhism,* Vol. 1. Los Angeles: Buddhist Books International, 1974.

Prebish, Charles. *Buddhist Monastic Discipline.* University Park: Pennsylvania State University Press, 1975.

Welch, Holmes. *The Practice of Chinese Buddhism 1900–1950.* Cambridge, MA: Harvard University Press, 1967.

DANIEL A. GETZ

PRINTING TECHNOLOGIES

Since at least the eighth century C.E., printing technologies have been used to promulgate Buddhist teachings, preserve Buddhist literature, and protect Buddhist people and their sacred sites and possessions. Most of the techniques that will be discussed below were not developed originally by Buddhists, but were an outgrowth of the rich cultural, intellectual, and religious traditions of China and their spread eastward to Korea and Japan and, subsequently, to the West.

Dhāraṇī and the origin of Buddhist print culture

The earliest technique employed for printing Buddhist texts was xylography, which used reverse-image characters carved on woodblocks to print pages of text. The exact process that led to the development of woodblock printing is unknown, although the earliest advances in print culture and technology took place in medieval China after the invention of paper in about 105 C.E. Printing from blocks of wood is commonly considered to be the first true printing technology, although printing with stamps and seals (*yin*), from

A monk holds a hand-carved wooden printing block of the Buddhist canon in the xylograph repository at Haeinsa in Taegu, South Korea. © Leonard de Selva/Corbis. Reproduced by permission.

which the common term for printing is derived, had long been performed. The process leading to the development of xylography is presumed to be an extension of the practice of cutting wooden Daoist charms in order to make impressions on clay (early fourth century C.E.) and, later, covering them with the red ink of cinnabar or vermilion to make imprints on white paper (early sixth century C.E.).

The earliest examples of Buddhist printing involve a type of charm or spell called a DHĀRAṆĪ. To date, the oldest printed material that has been discovered is the Korean *Mugu chŏnggwang taedarani kyŏng* (Chinese, *Wugou jingguang datuoluoni jing*; *Great Dhāraṇī Scripture of Flawless, Pure Light*), a scroll, nearly twenty feet long and three and a half inches wide, produced from about twelve woodblock pages printed on bamboo paper. Executed with great skill, it was rolled together and placed in the relics container of a stone pagoda at Pulguk Monastery in Kyŏngju, Korea, in 751, and was discovered in 1966. Scholars believe that it was printed sometime between 704 and 751 in either Kyŏngju or Luoyang, China. The next oldest examples of printed material are the remnants of the Japanese *Hyakuman-tō darani* (*Dhāraṇī of the Hyakuman Pagodas*), which were printed around 770 to commemorate the end of a long civil war. These dhāraṇī are copies of the first four of the six dhāraṇī included in the *Great Dhāraṇī Scripture of Flawless, Pure Light.* They were made from copper blocks printed on small scrolls of yellowish hemp paper. Although technically inferior to the Korean dhāraṇī, the *Hyakuman-tō darani* was a great achievement; 3,076 of the printed dhāraṇī are preserved at HŌRYŪJI in Nara, Japan.

Xylography

Most Buddhist texts in traditional East Asia were printed using xylography or woodblock printing. After the dhāraṇī scriptures, the DIAMOND SŪTRA (*Vajracchedikāprajñāpāramitā-sūtra*) of 868, which was discovered at DUNHUANG in 1907, is the oldest known printed book. It was printed for merit and for everyday use on seven woodblock pages and pasted on a foot-wide scroll sixteen feet long. Other dhāraṇī texts and versions of the *Diamond Sūtra* that were placed as relics in Buddhist sculptures and pagodas during the tenth and eleventh centuries have been discovered in China, Korea, and Japan. Pasting printed pages onto scrolls gave way to the folded book in the ninth or tenth century. Stitched books, bound with such materials as bamboo and horsehair, were introduced in the tenth or eleventh century and are still used for some Buddhist writings.

The impetus for carving the entire Buddhist CANON on woodblocks may be traced to an imperially sanctioned xylographic edition of Confucian classics made between 932 and 953 under the auspices of the Later Shu state in Sichuan. During the early Song period, an official edition of the Chinese Buddhist canon was carved on woodblocks between 972 and 983 in Chengdu—5,048 volumes in 130,000 blocks. A dynastically sponsored printing revolution followed in Asia for the next several hundred years. The Khitans, Jurchens, Tanguts, and Koreans all carved and printed Buddhist canons either in Chinese characters or in native scripts.

Lithography

Long before the development of xylography, exact copies of important literature and beautiful calligraphy were produced by making rubbings from stone inscriptions. The Confucian classics were carved in stone in 175 C.E. The first stone carvings of Buddhist scriptures were made during the Northern Qi period (550–577) around the capital at Ye. A grand project of preserving the Buddhist scriptures was begun during the end of the Sui period (581–618) at Yunju Monastery on Fangshan in northern China southwest of present-day Beijing. In dread of the impending DECLINE OF THE DHARMA (*mofa*) and the corruption and loss of the Buddhist religion, the monk Jingwan (d. 639) vowed to carve the entire canon of Buddhist scriptures onto stone as a means of preserving them for all time. The stone tablets were stored in mountain caves and underground caches near the monastery at Shijing shan (Stone Scripture Mountain). The project continued through the Tang (618–907), Liao (907–1125), and Jin (1125–1234) dynasties due to both imperial and local support. More than four thousand stone tablets from nine caves and ten thousand buried tablets of the Fangshan lithic canon have been identified.

Movable type

Although movable type was invented in China, Korean artisans perfected the techniques associated with this method of printing. In China, movable earthenware type was made in the mid-eleventh century; later, type made of tin was cast, but it is not known whether these were used by Buddhists. Movable wooden type was invented by the beginning of the fourteenth century (at the latest), but examples of printing by this process are difficult to differentiate from xylography. Pieces of a wooden Uigur-script font were found at Dunhuang and dated to about 1300.

The type mold was invented in either China or Korea, probably during the early thirteenth century prior to the Mongolian invasions. The earliest reference to printing with movable metal type is found in the colophon to a woodblock print of the Korean *Nammyŏng Ch'ŏn hwasang song chŭngdo-ga sasil* (*Buddhist Master Nammyŏng Ch'ŏn's Laudatory Commentary on the "Song Verifying Enlightenment"*). The colophon says that the text was originally printed with cast metal type in Korea in 1234. The oldest extant example of metal type printing is the *Pulcho chikchi simch'e yojŏl* (*Essentials in which the Buddhas and the Patriarchs Point to the Essence of the Mind*), which was printed in 1377 at Hŭngdŏk Monastery in Ch'ŏngju in central Korea. The type was made using the lost-wax type-casting method, which seems to have been the earliest process for making movable metal type. One drawback to this method is that each piece of type has a slightly different shape, so the printed result lacks aesthetic balance.

During the late fourteenth and early fifteenth centuries, a more advanced method of casting metal type using wooden models, called *mother type* (*moja*), was developed by the Chosŏn government of Korea. The precision of the wooden mother types was such that the shapes of all the pieces were alike. The technology of movable metal type was transmitted from Korea back to China and later to Japan. The first book printed with movable type in Japan was made in 1595. After the creation and promulgation of the Korean alphabet in 1446, some of the earliest books published with movable metal type in the Korean vernacular were episodes of the Buddha's life and hymns honoring Śākyamuni written and printed in 1447 and 1448. During the ensuing centuries in Korea, metal type editions of Buddhist scriptures and illustrated vernacular expositions of Buddhist scriptures were produced, the most common being the LOTUS SŪTRA (SADDHARMAPUṆḌARĪKA-SŪTRA), the *Diamond Sūtra,* and the *Fumu enzhong jing* (*Sūtra on the Profound Kindness of Parents*; Korean, *Pumo ŭnjung kyŏng*). These same scriptures, as well as the *Shiwang jing* (*Sūtra of the Ten Kings*), were also printed widely in contemporary China and Japan, usually from woodblocks, with a few printed from movable type.

Computer-age print culture

Computer technology's coming of age at the end of the twentieth century has created new possibilities for preserving Buddhist literature, and making it accessible electronically over the Internet. Many web sites provide access to Buddhist scriptures in a variety of canonical languages and vernacular translations that are machine readable and easily searchable. The development of unicode fonts and digital imaging in the late 1990s made it possible to digitize the Chinese Buddhist canon. The Chinese Buddhist Electronic Text Association (www.cbeta.org) has developed a searchable electronic text of the *Taishō shinshū daizōkyō* (*Revised Version of the Canon, Compiled during the Taishō Era,* 1924–1935). The Research Institute of the Tripiṭaka Koreana (www.sutra.re.kr) has created an electronic font that duplicates exactly the calligraphy of the *Koryŏ taejanggyŏng* (*Korean Buddhist Canon* or *Tripiṭaka Koreana*), enabling researchers to view the texts of the canon as though they were original woodblock prints.

See also: **Canon; Merit and Merit-Making; Relics and Relics Cults; Scripture**

Bibliography

Carter, Thomas Francis, and Goodrich, L. Carrington. *The Invention of Printing in China and Its Spread Westward,* 2nd edition. New York: Ronald Press, 1955.

Hickman, Brian. "A Note on the *Hyakumantō Dhāraṇī.*" *Monumenta Nipponica* 30, no. 1 (1975): 87–93.

Lancaster, Lewis R. "The Rock Cut Canon in China: Findings at Fang-shan." In *Buddhist Heritage: Papers Delivered at the School of Oriental and African Studies in November 1985,* ed. Tadeusz Skorupski. London: Institute of Buddhist Studies, 1989.

Ra Kyung-jun. "Early Print Culture in Korea," tr. Richard D. McBride II. *Korean Culture* 20, no. 2 (1999): 12–21.

Twitchett, Denis. *Printing and Publishing in Medieval China.* New York: Frederic C. Beil, 1983.

RICHARD D. MCBRIDE II

PROVINCIAL TEMPLE SYSTEM (KOKUBUNJI, RISHŌTŌ)

Twice in Japanese history the state has established a provincial temple system for the purpose of political unification and state legitimation. In emulation of the national temple network instituted in seventh-century China, Emperor Shōmu (701–756 C.E.) set out in 741 to enhance the state's power through the authority of Buddhism. One official temple (*kokubunji*) was designated in each of the sixty-seven provinces; Tōdaiji in Nara was the network's central temple. These were each to be staffed by twenty clerics who would pray for the state's protection. Provincial nunneries (*kokubunniji*) were also established, each housing ten nuns to pray for the atonement of wrongdoing. This system declined when the capital was moved from Nara to Kyoto in 794. None of the provincial *kokubunji* emerged as temples of national importance.

The brothers Ashikaga Takauji (1305–1358) and Tadayoshi (1306–1352), the founders of the second shogunate, implemented another system of provincial temples. At the urging of Zen cleric and shogunal adviser Musō Soseki (1275–1351), temples called *ankokuji* were designated between about 1338 and 1350 in every province to mourn victims of ongoing warfare. Pagodas containing religious relics contributed by the imperial court were also constructed in each province. Called *rishōtō,* they were usually five stories in height and were erected at Shingon or Tendai (Chinese, Tiantai) temples. *Ankokuji* were mainly family temples of prominent local warriors within the Five Mountain (Gozan) Zen network. The conceptual precedent for this temple-pagoda system was the *kokubunji,* but there were also antecedents in Chinese and Indian Buddhist practice. The countrywide establishment of temples and pagodas also bespoke territorial control, reflecting Ashikaga political ambitions. With the shogunate's decline at the end of the fifteenth century, the temple-pagoda system weakened; today twenty-eight pagodas remain, but no temples.

See also: **Hōryūji and Tōdaiji; Japan**

Bibliography

Collcutt, Martin. *Gozan: The Rinzai Zen Monastic Institution in Medieval Japan.* Cambridge, MA: Harvard University Press, 1981.

Tamura, Yoshio. *Japanese Buddhism: A Cultural History.* Tokyo: Kosei, 2000.

SUZANNE GAY

PSYCHOLOGY

It has become so common, if not trite, to speak of "Buddhism as a psychology" that the idea no longer seems peculiar or surprising in either Asia or the West. The parallel is not totally spurious or devoid of heuristic value: Important aspects of Buddhist doctrine and practice may be construed as efforts at understanding human psychology. Yet, it would be imprudent to accept uncritically the accuracy of this parallelism. The present entry summarizes some of the reasons why we have come to assume that there are overlaps in perspective and goals that seem to argue for an interpretation of Buddhism as a "psychology," and some of the reasons why this seeming parallelism can be misleading.

Why Buddhism and psychology?

Early in the twentieth century Buddhism became associated in the Western imagination with the objectives of Western psychology. This presumed connection has also been accepted by many Asian exponents of Buddhist doctrine. In suggesting a parallel we often imagine "psychology" as an idealized source of unassailable truths about better living and human happiness, and perhaps with the mythic, almost mystical, power that many Westerners attribute to the disciplines and discourses of Buddhism. The vagueness of many of these comparisons may also be attributed in part to the fact that there is no autonomous Buddhist discipline of psychology—that is, a discrete genre of discourse (let alone a scientific discourse) corresponding to the many meanings that the term *psychology* has in contemporary academic and popular conversation. Conversely, contemporary scientific discourse does not as yet have a language to speak reliably about the wide range of concepts and practices that we intuitively call "Buddhist psychology."

The temptation to link observations and normative conceptions about Buddhism with our ideas about psychology does not reflect a single view of Buddhism. "Buddhism as psychology" is usually grounded on ideas that include a number of separate, at times overlapping, and at times competing, conceptions about religion and spirituality. First, it is common to imagine Buddhism as a therapy, as a way to heal a sick soul—a mind in error or a person in pain. Second, some consider Buddhist theories of mind parallel to Western psychological inquiry—perhaps conflating somehow a broad spectrum of Buddhist doctrines with the equally diverse set of Western philosophical and empirical psychologies. Third, since the inception of the Western discipline of psychology, religion has been seen as one among other objects to be understood with the methods of scientific psychology (e.g., in both Wilhelm Wundt and Sigmund Freud). Yet, simultaneously, religion (and perhaps Buddhism in particular) has been regarded as somehow coextensive with many of the doctrines and goals of popular psychologies. Hence, as a fourth historical connection, one must note that several of the above factors have helped to anchor in our collective mind the otherwise imprecise modern ideal of an ahistorical "spirituality" that transcends the "traditional dogmas" of institutional religions.

Buddhism as psychology: Traditional views

Traditional Buddhist sources often compare the Buddha to a physician; his dharma is the prescription that cures all ills. The preferred interpretation of this metaphor imagines this cure as a healing of the mind—repairing a mind otherwise immersed in an error that leads to repeated, almost interminable, suffering across many lives. But the cure also entails a transformation of other aspects of the person: bodily demeanor, behavior toward others and care of self, emotion and desire. In other words, Buddhists may be suggesting that important parts (if not the most important or core aspects) of their religious practice can be seen as a project of comprehensive behavioral modification, with "behavior" including body, speech, and mind. However, this transformation of body and mind is also taken to entail the development of extraordinary powers that are not within the usual Western conception of the mental. Such special faculties include the capacity to transform and replicate the body, the power to know past lives, and so forth.

Even if it is conceived as purely the healing of an afflicted human mind, the Buddha's cure is believed to have the power to remove all suffering, because the total removal of the error, and of the mental turmoil arising from the error, leads to the end of REBIRTH and the elimination of all DUḤKHA (SUFFERING) of mind and body. In this sense, Buddhism is primarily a psychology if we assume that the cure is fundamentally a mental cure, or if we imagine the desired state of health as being "psychological" in the sense that it encompasses the totality of the human being as a sentient being capable of intentional behavior. Or, one may also adopt the popular notion that all physical ills are ultimately psychosomatic, so that "psychological" mental culture is simultaneously a technique of the whole person. Additionally, the concept of "psychology" may be applied to Buddhism by extending the notion of mental disease beyond the apparent limits that death imposes on an individual body, and beyond the limitations of the mind of a single individual in a single existence.

Thus, generally speaking, the Buddhist tradition may be interpreted as a religious tradition with a prominent emphasis on the mind and liberation of the mind, but still a tradition for which the release from all suffering—if not the total release from an inherently painful embodiment—is the ultimate goal. Significant exceptions are found in traditions that have either sidelined the schemata of rebirth or have demythologized it. This is the case, for instance, with the MADHYAMAKA SCHOOL and traditions that adopt similar rhetorical or dialectic understandings of the dichotomy between rebirth (SAṂSĀRA) and liberation (NIRVĀṆA). In such traditions it is not at all clear that belief in "rebirth" is to be taken to imply the acceptance of a psychosomatic process existing outside of, or independently from, the imaginative faculties of the individual. The Madhyamaka school, for instance, offers tantalizing, yet paradoxical and baffling claims that rebirth and all the suffering that it brings is only the construction of mind or language, and that suffering disappears when it is shown to be a mistaken notion.

Be that as it may, the most common normative principle in elite Buddhism is the belief that liberation is the consequence of a cognitive and affective shift, brought about not so much by an intellectual effort, but by contemplative exercises, and ascetic and moral training, that entail radical transformations of the person. In other words, changes in behavior and belief are understood to derive their liberating power from changes that can be described as "psychological" only in the broadest possible sense of the idea of "psychology": shifts in the way in which a person perceives what is real, worthy, desirable, or satisfying, or changes in passion and affect, in behavior and demeanor, and in the bodily, sensory, and intellectual faculties. Such changes are "psychological" also in the sense that they are behavioral, they require modifications in the mode and orientation of a person's mental, verbal, and bodily action.

A certain "primacy of mind" is a common, and at times dominant, orientation in elite Buddhist doctrines of self-cultivation, soteriology, and ontology. One may also state with a certain degree of confidence that this elite characterization of the tradition has a mythic value even outside the small circles of monastic specialists who engage in the practice of MEDITATION or in formulating the theory of meditation and sainthood. This makes Buddhism a tradition in which ideals and techniques of psychological or psychosomatic self-cultivation play a central role as markers of religious identity and continuity of tradition.

A philosophy of mind

But the question then arises as to whether or not there will be any heuristic or practical value in understanding this psychological orientation—or, for that matter, explicit Buddhist theories about the structure and the vicissitudes of the "mental"—as significantly parallel to Western psychological inquiry, or as viable alternatives that can be compared by means of common criteria of truth or effectiveness. The systematic exploration of such parallels can take us simultaneously in various directions and across difficult issues of epistemology and the philosophies of mind and science. This is fertile ground for future research, but we shall explore in this entry only cursorily what there is in the Buddhist tradition, if anything, that may be called a "psychology."

Buddhism shares with other Indian systems of religion and philosophy an interest in how the human self is constituted, including the nature and origin of the mental and the bodily broadly understood (*nāmarūpa*), as well as the nature of awareness (*vijñapti*) and consciousness (*vijñāna*). Early Buddhist speculation separated itself from other early śramaṇic systems by formulating unique theories about the embodied self (*jīva* and *kāya*) and the state of a liberated being (TATHĀGATA), as well as by formulating critiques of those who denied the consequences of intentional actions (*kriyā*), or of those who overemphasized the pervasiveness of moral causation.

Related to these broad issues were, on the one hand, early theories of liberation and the PATH, and, on the other, structural conceptions of the mind-body complex, which sought to explain the origins, processes, and ultimate liberation of this complex by identifying the components and arrangement of mental states and processes. Some, presumably early, texts show attempts to reduce the sentient person to elementary substances, such as water, fire, earth, air, and space. But, among the most influential of the protoscientific theories are the structural theories of SKANDHA (AGGREGATE), *dhātu* (sensory domains), and *āyatana* (sense faculties). The three theories show obvious signs of having originated independently from each other, but one can still treat them, as the tradition does, as three components of a single theory, which is summarized below.

We may assume naively that each human person (*pudgala*) is a single living (*jīva*) and a sentient entity (*sattva*) that is the objective referent of the word "self" (ātman). Buddhist introspection and inference, however, claim that the real referent for this idea is a constellation of phenomenal, transient entities that can be summarized under five headings or "sets" (skandha). Strictly speaking, these sets are "aggregates" of related phenomena held together *in* the idea of a single self *by* our own persistent grasping (*upādāna*). The five—matter, sensation, conceptions/perceptions, habitual tendencies, and awareness—include body (matter, sensations, habitual tendencies) and mind (sensation, conception, habitual tendencies, and awareness). The mental components can also be analyzed in terms of a sensorium that includes a mental sense sphere and organ (manas), resulting in a hierarchical system of six senses (*āyatana*), with mind as gatekeeper. The system is further analyzed into twelve sensory elements, each sense faculty being paired with an organ and an object (the object being internal for the mind sense). These twelve are called *dhātu* (perhaps "domain" or "basis").

The system of the twelve sense *dhātus* maintains the close connection between body and mind already noted (organ and input, in fact, appear to be placed on a similar ontological plane). The connections are further developed by proposing three faculties and processes of awareness (*vijñāna*) for each domain (*dhātu*). This additional layer of analysis emphasizes the privileged status of the mind, insofar as mental awareness (consciousness proper) occupies a higher position in the hierarchy, serving as the center for both sensory and mental processes.

Early speculations about the constitution of the self used these analytic categories to explain how a human person (*sattva*) could be constituted, in the absence of a simple, autonomous, and unitary self (ātman). In psychological terms, this may seem to undermine our experience of being an autonomous agent capable of its own perceptions, ideas, sensation, and feelings, with the capacity to choose the path to liberation. But the tradition insists that intentionality, moral responsibility, and personal continuity can be explained by using the above building blocks.

Attempts to explain the natural illusion of the elemental reality of self and will led to the creation of theories of mind. Such theories developed as speculation entered the more systematic stage of the ABHIDHARMA and as the Buddhist philosophical schools engaged other Indian philosophical systems in a centuries-long polemical dialogue. In the *abhidharma* literature the psychological categories of the sūtra literature were organized according to canonical sets and analytic categories. Systems of terminological matrices (*mātṛkā*) helped organize sets of terms in concepts like the *Dhammasaṅganī* and the *Dhātukāya* (*Taishō* 1540). In the latter work, for instance, canonical terms for mental states are reorganized under categories such as universally present states and states only present when the mind is confused and afflicted (*kliṣṭa*). The universally present states or processes (sensation, conception, volition, etc.) are also organized into six groups of six each (so-called hexads) that correspond to the inner and outer spheres (*āyatana*) of sentience: factors of consciousness, of sense contact, of sensation, of perception, of conception, and of drive (or DESIRE, *tṛṣṇā*).

In the *abhidharma*, the apparent unity of the self is explained by a variety of theories, but the most common types (which are not necessarily mutually exclusive) are theories of causal continuity and theories of the location of awareness. The first is epitomized by the concept of *santāna*—the cause and effect series of bodily and mental events that constitutes a human life and personality. The second is illustrated by the concept of *ādāna* or *ālaya* (site, container, holder), according to which past experiences leave traces on a foundation or base of the personality (the *āśraya*), so that their proximity and interaction can create the illusion of a single person.

Ethics and liberation as theories of mind

Both types of theories share in varying degrees a general Buddhist tendency to see intentionality or will (*cetanā*) as the governing force behind the causal series, and various levels of the mind as the locus for the encoding and "storage" of karma and its consequences. These models generate, and attempt to explain, a variety of problems that can be covered only briefly in this entry. One may mention, as representative examples, the doctrine of *vāsanā* (traces), the theory of unmanifest processes (*avijñapti*), and the problem of mentation and mental construction (*prajñapti*).

The doctrine of *vāsanā* was fundamental to Buddhist "moral psychology" in India, and represented an attempt to explain both moral habits (propensities) and the process of karmic traces and consequences. The interaction between mental states and consequent suffering was seen as a process whereby intention and its behavioral manifestations left faint traces (*bīja*, planted seeds) that constituted a system of habitual and mostly unconscious drives. The process was summarized in the metaphor of a cloth impregnated by a perfume or a dye (the technical sense of the term *vāsanā*). In the same way that the perfume instills some of its properties on the cloth, and that the cloth retains the faint aroma, intentional action leaves traces in the human causal chain. The predisposition as trace is known as *anuśaya,* and as manifest character and mental state it is known as *kleśa* (a term that means both "stain" or "dye" and "torment"). The character state and the action generate and maintain habitual tendencies and cause future karmic effects. The *kleśas* may be regarded as a psychological condition, whereas KARMA (ACTION) is an ostensive or behavioral cause, although it too generates latent or potential consequences. The two constitute the pervasive ruling conditions (*adhipati-pratyaya*) for all suffering, and of the sentient being's beginningless wandering in the realm of rebirth.

The category of *kleśa* subsumes under a single rubric habits of emotion, intentionality, and cognition, such as three fundamental unhealthy mindsets: concupiscence, animosity, and delusion (the *Dhātukāya's* inventory includes five: the cravings of sense desire, craving for nonsensuous pleasures, craving for disembodied bliss, animosity, and DOUBT). The idea is found outside Buddhism (e.g., in the *Yogasūtras*) and constitutes a common assumption of religious moral psychology in India: Unhealthy frames of mind are at the root of suffering; healthy mindsets are at the root of liberation. The idea presupposes a virtue epistemology in which attitudinal character flaws are intertwined with errors of cognition, and error is abandoned and replaced with certainty only if the whole person cultivates and masters the highest moral, attitudinal, attentional, and cognitive virtue.

However, Buddhist philosophers often separate, at least theoretically, the processes that transcend the *kleśas* (meditative processes, or *bhāvanā*) from those that transcend error (cognitive-meditation process of correct seeing and discernment, or *darśana*). In the MAHĀYĀNA tradition, the distinction is summarized in the idea that rending the veil of the *kleśas* (*kleśa-āvaraṇa*) is only part of the process of liberation. A separate cognitive shift is needed, overcoming the obscuration caused by a veil that covers the objects of cognition (the veil called *jñeya-āvaraṇa*), a veil maintained by the habitual tendency to cognize by way of dualities: being/nonbeing, self/object, and so forth.

The preceding theoretical constructs sometimes parallel and sometimes overlap with the idea that acts of mentation and acts of manifest behavior generate bodily changes that, although unseen, are powerful determinants of future experience and behavior. This unmanifest transformation is known as *avijñapti* ("lacking the capacity to make itself noticeable," hence, that which is "unnoticed, unreported, latent, not manifest") and is a type of material or bodily change. Generally mental states are, by definition, nonmanifest, and Buddhist thinkers do not appear to have explored the possibility of unconscious conflicts or processes.

The theory of the *avijñapti* and the *vāsanās* do not appear to have cross-fertilized in any significantly productive manner. Although both theoretical constructs explain in part how contradictory, unexpected, or unwilled behavior can occur, they were not used to explain inner conflict or struggles between the forbidden and the tolerated. Nonetheless, one may argue that Buddhist philosophers, especially in India, struggled with the idea that some of the most potent determinants of human experience and behavior are not readily accessible to consciousness, much less to willful control. Thus, suffering in general was understood to be more than simply the awareness of painful states, cognitions, and vicissitudes: The most powerful and pervasive form of suffering is understood only by the saints, for it is the innately or inherently painful nature of the very construction (*saṁskāra-duḥkhata*) of the person's psychosomatic makeup. It is the profound ache behind the conscious and unconscious, the ever-frustrated attempt to hold on to the false idea of a self. Suffering is, therefore, like desire and delusion, a pervasive free-floating drive, a thirstlike unquenchable drive that pushes us not only toward sense-enjoyment, but toward wanting to be and wanting not to be.

These principles help explain in part the process by which a sentient being effects psychosomatic movements in the direction of either psychic health or psychic "dis-ease." However, to explain the possibility of liberation, the scholastics had to propose explanations for the possibility of error. With regard to this problem, the fundamental question for the Buddhist philosopher was how one could see a self where there was none, or see an object of desire and pleasure in phenomena that were inherently undesirable and painful. Furthermore, if our perception of the world is in essence a construct of mentation (*abhisaṃskṛta*), one needed to explain the process of verbal and mental reification that led to delusion and suffering.

The theory made a common assumption that convention constructs, or at the very least, distorts reality—either through a process of discursive elaboration (*prapañca*) or conceptual imagination (*vikalpa*). A key term behind such theories was that of "conventional designation" or "provisional conceptual distinctions" (*prajñapti*). The idea led in some schools to the denial of a correspondence theory of truth and to a phenomenalistic theory of perception and conception.

The idea of conventional reality as construct seems to have followed three distinct, but at times overlapping, lines of inquiry: one epistemological-linguistic, one phenomenalistic, and the other mentalistic (sometimes called idealistic). The linguistic view is relevant to psychology in the sense that it presupposes that mind itself is constructed (*vikalpita*), or, at the very least, conditioned by discursive thought (so that, for instance, we will perceive what words tell us to perceive or what the inner interplay between desire and mental chatter drive us to think). This is generally the tendency in the Madhyamaka traditions. The phenomenalistic view, represented by schools that have been identified with the SAUTRĀNTIKA traditions, is a theory of representation: Perception is an inner, mental process in which one becomes aware of the mental representation of external things (an almost natural derivative of the hierarchy of the six senses). From extreme phenomenalistic positions one can easily slide into an idealistic understanding of how the apparently real can feel real yet be an illusion: If the mind needs only an inner representation of the world to feel like it knows an external world, then all of conventional reality may very well exist in the mental sphere, perhaps only as mere mentation (*vijñapti*).

Perhaps the most significant derivatives of this third line of speculation were the positions adopted among followers of the YOGĀCĀRA SCHOOL. The idea of the real as mere mentation (*vijñaptimātratā*), originally proposed by ASAṄGA (ca. 320–390 C.E.) and VASUBANDHU (fourth to fifth century C.E.) was developed by Dharmapāla (sixth century C.E.), who attempted to explain how there could be both an ultimately real inner world (consciousness) and a world that is objective (external to the mind) and ordered (subject to causes and conditions). Dharmapāla developed further the school's idea of a consciousness that is the repository (ĀLAYAVIJÑĀNA) of karmic traces, manifesting itself in eight forms of consciousness: the consciousness corresponding to each of the five sense organs, mental consciousness (*manovijñāna*), a foundational but still deluded consciousness (*kliṣṭamanovijñāna*), and the ground consciousness (*ālayavijñāna*).

This eightfold division of consciousness has been arguably the most influential Buddhist topography of the mind. Its applications extend, naturally, into the questions of what makes the mind become pure, and whether or not there is an inherently pure level of consciousness (*amalavijñāna*) or a mind that is inherently awakened. The schema was central to theories of the path, even among those East Asian Buddhists for whom the theory of karma and the doctrine of rebirth had lost its earlier importance—as was the case, for example, in the use of the theory to explain Zen SATORI (AWAKENING) in HAKUIN EKAKU (1686–1768).

Also important in scholastic theories of the development of mind was the difficult concept of the "basis" (*āśraya*) for the action and transformations of karma. According to this conception, all aspects of the psychosomatic person are in constant transformation; if the person follows the path of the buddhas to its completion, this basis is transformed or inverted (*āśrayaparāvṛtti*), so that it is perfectly pure and the normal faculties become the special powers and knowledges of a buddha.

Systematic reflections on the nature of mind overlap with ontological speculation, but the above three theories of error and true knowledge also provide at least part of the foundation for the ethical, contemplative, and soteriological dimensions of Buddhist theory and practice. For instance, the transformation of the psychosomatic basis (*āśrayaparāvṛtti*) is believed to result, predictably, in a radical transformation of cognition (jñāna): body and mind become the living wisdom (active cognition) of a buddha. This wisdom has five aspects. It is perfectly and constantly aware of the true nature of things (*dharmadhātu-jñāna*); it is a serene, mirrorlike reflection of all things (*ādārśa-jñāna*); it cognizes the semblance and equivalence of all things (*samatā-jñāna*); yet, it discerns clearly (*pratyavekṣā-jñāna*) and engages freely in the work of a buddha (*kṛtyupasthāna-jñāna*). Furthermore, this wisdom is all-knowing, all-compassionate, and free from any notion of a self. With such implications to be derived from at least one Buddhist theory of mind, the Western observer needs to be constantly aware of the nuances that separate the intent and underlying question in Buddhist speculation from those that tend to drive Western psychological research.

Comparing psychological theories

What may appear as a similar interest in the disphase between conscious and unconscious storage and retrieval is not understood in Buddhism as a question of psychoneurology or intrapsychic conflict, but as a distinction between memory and karmic causation. The contemporary reader may understand karma as a kind of memory—an inscription of a trace upon the self, which, once recovered informs consciousness of a previous psychic event—but one needs to note the ethical and soteriological meanings that the Buddhist discovers in such processes. One may imagine (by projecting on the Buddhist tradition a psychodynamic schema) that the process by which awareness is fostered and transformed to achieve awakening is some sort of transformation of the repressed; but even granting this stretching of Buddhist doctrine, the most common Buddhist conceptions of what is "healthy" (*kuśala*) about this process would not come close to contemporary views of mental health as autonomy, acceptance, and enjoyment of human sexual desire, and the like.

Furthermore, for most traditional Buddhist elites, the traces left on consciousness by human action remain and develop as part of an inexorable law of moral responsibility and retribution that is only transcended by a path out of our imperfections, not by a simple acceptance of human shortcomings or a celebration of the body and the emotions. Moreover, the final discovery of the forgotten and the unraveling of its meaning is reached through extrasensory perception, and only by those who attain the yogic power of the remembrance of past lives (*jāti-smara*). Most traditional Buddhist philosophers, unlike Western empirical psychologists, took it as a given that the extrasensory perception of a yogi (*yogipratyakṣa*) is a valid source of empirical evidence—in fact, one that needs no corroboration and is not open to falsification when the cognizer is one of those deemed awakened.

Nonetheless, one could argue that it is precisely in the soteriological and moral dimensions of Buddhist psychology that one may find avenues of thought that complement or challenge some contemporary views of mental health. Of particular theoretical and historical importance are those Buddhist theories dealing with the techniques of meditation—arguably the most typically Buddhist "therapeutic" techniques and the place where Buddhism as religion and ethical system can be said to become a way of overcoming "dis-ease," and therefore, as perhaps a psychological cure or a therapy. Theories of meditation often attest to the keen psychological awareness of those who reflected on Buddhist doctrine and practice. In their application, these theories at times suggest the techniques of Western psychosocial healing practices, despite an apparent difference in their presuppositions and goals.

Meditation, consciousness, and healing

Buddhist theories of meditation are concerned with the transformation of rigid habits and turbulent states of mind that may roughly correspond to contemporary notions of maladaptive or dysfunctional behaviors; but the underlying theory and questions hiding behind diverging ideas of dysfunction may be disparate enough to make comparison difficult. The meditator seeks to make the mind pliable, aspiring to achieve a "tranquil flow of mind" (*upekṣā*) that is effortless and free from the extremes of mental turpitude and excitation (*laya* and *auddhatya*). A mind that is in such a state is no longer dominated by the mind's usual tendencies toward inertia (*dauṣṭhulya*) and unrest (*kleśa*). Nonetheless, although the goal is a state free of confusion and anguish, freedom from distress and dysphoria is not here a condition for increased autonomy and adaptation in negotiating inner drives and outer social reality, as it is generally understood in Western psychologies, but a condition often described as desireless, free of conceptual constructs, and empty (the three "doors to liberation," *vimokṣamukha*).

Defects of thought (*doṣa*) are superseded by cultivating antidotes or opposite states (*pratipakṣa*) that lead to a removal of both the veils (of *kleśa* and of the object of knowledge), and hence lead to liberation. But such antidotes are also substitute behaviors, that is, they are virtues, and they transform the confused person into the person of serene insight. But the state of liberation, at least as understood by the major scholastic systems, is not comparable to Western ideas of individual autonomy, adaptive acceptance of the body and its drives, and resolution of intrapsychic and interpersonal conflict. It is liberation from rebirth, hence, from birth, aging, and death, as well as from desire and suffering. Furthermore, in systems following traditional Mahāyāna scholastic definitions, liberation is accompanied by the omniscience and the miraculous powers of a buddha, or at the very least the superior wisdom and wonder-working powers of the BODHISATTVA.

In the classical Buddhist view of "mental health," most normal desires are seen as a sort of madness, and as a "delusion" originating in a beginningless round of past lives; full health is accomplished only when one becomes a full buddha, or when it is approached gradually as one matures in the bodhisattva's spiritual career. It is difficult to imagine how such a view of "mental health" (perhaps, better: "absence of dis-ease") is commensurable with contemporary Western notions, which do not value the renunciation or the denial of desire.

However, some Buddhist doctrinal positions deviate in varying degrees from the above characterization. Important currents within the Chan and Tantric traditions qualify their understanding of renunciation (or are openly critical of the denial of desire) and tend to focus on the problems of self-deception and the tyranny of conceptual constructs and dualities, including the duality between desire and desirelessness, holy and mundane. Nonetheless, even these traditions tend to preserve monastic institutions and practices that draw a boundary between the transcendence of duality of the religious specialist and the need to negotiate dualities and ambivalences in lay life. In this context, acceptance of desire appears to be a stepping stone in the direction of a different form of desirelessness, and not necessarily an acceptance of our instinctual drives in the sense that the West has come to conceive of it after the psychoanalytic revolution.

An ambiguous acceptance of desire may be postulated in the case of the Chan tradition, where despite its iconoclastic rhetoric of immediacy and nonduality, a strict ethos of self-control and unrelenting effort points at least toward a transcendence of individual will (pace radical or mad monks like the fifteenth-century Japanese Zen monk IKKYŪ). In TANTRA, where desire is to be transformed rather than abandoned, the transformation is framed in ritual and symbolic contexts that can hardly be assimilated into contemporary notions of the tolerance of strong affect and intrapsychic conflict (such framing occurs even in the radical antinomian rhetoric of the *Caryāgīti*). In both traditions it may be more accurate to speak of a paradoxical inversion of the normal order of ascetic denial, but not of an acceptance of desire as conceived in the more common contemporary assumptions about psychological well-being.

Nonetheless, much needs to be explored if we are to be able to understand the significance of the insights offered by Buddhist concepts of self-deception and delusion. Such insights include the recognition of a connection between suffering and misuses of language and conceptual labeling, as well as the obsessive quality of unawareness or error. These are elements suggested, for instance, by the speculations of the Madhyamaka school, where desire and unawareness seem to coalesce in the concept of obstinate dwelling in error (*abhiniveśa*). This idea of an inertia that favors a persistent dwelling in distorted perception seems to echo Western concepts like those of neurotic paradox and the repetition compulsion.

The above digressions suggest that much remains to be understood, not only about the history of Buddhist understanding of desire and its obstinate clinging to imagined objects, but also about the implications of variations within Buddhism. It is not at all clear, for instance, that we are yet in a position to understand the psychological implications (or for that matter, the health valence) of the full spectrum of Buddhist attitudes toward cognition and emotion, and the role of ethical and contemplative discipline in the relief of distress.

Perhaps as an attempt to circumvent some of the above difficulties, some researchers have looked at only one narrow cross section of Buddhist practice by studying selected meditative states. In the last quarter of the twentieth century, researchers investigated the effects of meditation practice on psychophysiological states. Using contemporary physiological and psychological measures, Japanese researchers established a connection between Zen meditation and neural and physiological states associated with rested, wakeful attention (Kasamatsu and Hirai 1966; Hirai 1978 and 1989). Subsequent studies have confirmed and expanded on their results (summarized in Murphy and Donovan).

The most interesting and robust result of these studies was the accumulation of evidence that showed that meditation is not a type of hypnosis, catalepsy, or a "catatonic state," as had been proposed earlier in the twentieth century. By measuring the brain waves of meditators, these experimenters determined that the brain of a subject in deep meditation (especially, but not exclusively, an experienced meditator) emits patterns of alpha and theta waves that are distinct from those emitted by subjects that were anxious, under hypnosis, or in deep sleep. This result of electroencephalographic (EEG) measurements suggests that the meditator is in fact in a state of "calm awareness," as claimed by Buddhist tradition. Subsequent MRI and SPECT studies suggest similar conclusions (Newberg et al.).

These investigations suggest that meditation techniques affect the body as well as the mind, lowering, for instance, blood pressure and galvanic skin pressure. The studies also confirm something noted by the tradition: The obvious importance of the body does not diminish the importance of the mind; a particular way of controlling the body is a precondition of, and perhaps entails, a particular state of mind.

For the tradition, even for those branches that give the body an explicit central role, the mind is paramount; and yet, paradoxically, the goal of Buddhist meditation is often presented as an experience of no-mind. Something about the presumed psychological makeup of the meditator is lost, erased, or shown to be an error or an illusion. Hence the theme of "extinction" or "cessation" that is so common to many theories of meditation. One attains a serene and clear awareness of a state that may be legitimately described as "mindless." Yet, different Buddhist traditions understand the "mindless" in different ways—from a literal absence of thought (P. J. Griffiths) to various notions of freedom from speech in speech (as in the Chan and Tantric traditions). And even in the latter traditions there is much room for variation, from the early Chan notion that the arising of a single thought generates a world of conceptual constructs and confusion to the acceptance of a higher form of discrimination that gains new value after one awakens to nonduality—as in the Yogācāra's five buddha-jñānas or in the MAHĀMUDRĀ stage of noncultivation (*sgom med*).

However, these studies have not looked at a number of potential sources for disconfirming evidence or falsification. For instance, it is not clear that they have considered the significance of failure to progress in meditation (who succeeds and when) or cases of psychological distress or physical illness due to meditation (phenomena that are amply documented in Buddhist literature), or the significance of differences among expert meditators regarding the meaning and content of the experiences that correspond to the brain measurements and readings. In fact, it is not at all clear that even expert meditators agree on the significance of various states of mental concentration or samādhi (Sharf 1995 and 1998). One may argue that the psychological significance or goals of meditation point to using body and mind to re-create a new self; one assumes a specific bodily and mental posture, persisting in it until the mind is serene and focused, or one focuses the mind on what appears at first to be the self, in order to dissolve misconceptions about the self, including the misconception of imagining that who we are is identical to this self whom we hold so dear. But this summary of traditional understandings raises a number of questions regarding the significance of neuropsychological and physiological studies of meditation. First, where in these studies do we find any evidence about self and conceptions of the self? Second, the tradition itself is not in complete agreement as to what it is that remains or comes to light once the delusions of self are removed.

Furthermore, the neurological focus still needs to explain what to the Buddhist is paramount: Transformations of mind and self have significant ethical and soteriological implications. Such implications include a vast and complex path theory explaining how one becomes a buddha, and, for instance, acquires the three modes of wisdom described above. These expectations cannot be dismissed or demythologized by assuming an objective cerebral or psychological referent.

Buddhism and scientific psychology

As a corollary to the above, one returns to the question of what in Buddhism may be considered parallel to Western ideas about how one heals intrapersonal and interpersonal distress—and to the related question of whether or not there is a Buddhist tradition similar to Western clinical psychology and psychiatry. Despite the existence of medical traditions in Buddhist countries (T. Clifford), little was done until recent times to create a dialogue between medicine and Buddhist practice, let alone a systematic study of mental diseases and the Buddhist goal of relieving all "dis-ease." There are multiple cultural and institutional reasons for this apparent lack, including the fact that the very notion of mental disease is a relatively recent Western creation. Nonetheless, some Buddhist practices and systems of belief may be considered parallel to Western techniques for healing through the modification of thought and behavior, and conversely, Western specialists have adapted Buddhist ideas with greater or lesser open acknowledgment of their depth.

Historically, one should mention the Swiss psychiatrist Carl G. Jung (1875–1961) as the pioneer. Despite certain ambivalence about "the Orient" (Gómez 1995), Jung borrowed generously, especially in his analysis of "mandala symbolism," which combined traditional Buddhist and Hindu understandings about the significance of the MAṆḌALA with keen clinical observations.

In recent times we have seen the development of biofeedback and behavioral techniques that involve ideas of self-monitoring (Rokke and Rehm) and mindful reassessment of experience (Smyth), and of relaxation as a natural response to specific stimuli (Benson and Klipper), techniques that echo, explicitly or implicitly, Buddhist serenity and MINDFULNESS techniques (de Silva 1984, 1985, and 1986). These efforts go well beyond some of the soft formulations found in the literature of self-help, spirituality, New Age, and pop psychology. In fact, the implicit and the avowed recognition of the influence of Buddhist ideas and attitudes extends beyond associations with contemporary popular expectations. We now count several systematic, and successful attempts to integrate aspects of Buddhist theories of cognition and meditation into empirically testable clinical theory. The most explicit use of Buddhist models is seen in Zindel Segal's mindfulness-based cognitive therapy for depression (Segal et al.). This technique incorporates both the behavioral and the cognitive aspects of mindfulness meditation into the treatment of depression, including the practice of mindfulness of breath (*ānāpānasati*) as a way to refocus or shift attention away from distorting patterns of cognition and emotion toward adaptive schemas.

Less explicitly linked to Buddhist practice, but now amply tested as an effective therapy is Marsha Linehan's *dialectic cognitive-behavioral therapy* or DBT (Linehan 1993a and 1993b). This system is a subtle integration of empirically based cognitive-behavioral strategies and a number of elements of Buddhist theory of knowledge and meditation. Linehan, for instance, conceives the processes of dysfunction and therapy in part through the lens of her own experience with Zen practice, but also through her own nontraditional understanding of the practice. The process is a dialectic because it assumes and relies on the "fundamental interrelatedness or wholeness of reality" and the placement of individual experience within a whole of relationships. This means, on the one hand, that the client needs "to accept herself as she is in the moment and the need for her to change" (1993b, pp. 1–2), but also that change requires the cultivation of "core mindfulness skills" through which the client learns to observe and accept without judgment even those behaviors or interpersonal deficits that need to be changed.

Jeffrey Schwartz, who was also inspired in part by his Buddhist practice, has adapted similar mindfulness techniques into the treatment of obsessive-compulsive disorder. In this particular technique, one may posit that Schwartz's behavioral strategy is a variant of Buddhist uses of attention and selective inattention, including the confrontation of disgust and negative emotions while in a serene state. Here Buddhist techniques may be understood as equivalent to Western systematic desensitization, and exposure with response prevention. Yet, although both traditions follow similar paths in reorienting the suffering individual toward a revaluation of the causes of distress and disgust, Schwartz highlights the Buddhist practice of detached, nonjudgmental awareness, rather than the purposeful increase in anxious tension built into exposure techniques.

Unlike attempts to link Buddhism to psychology by demanding a softening of the strictures of scientific research, these applications respond to a critical reflection on Buddhist conceptions followed by systematic clinical trials and empirical testing. But they also represent a willingness to follow the theory and technique in whichever direction is required to achieve effectiveness, including the use of techniques and belief systems that would have been totally foreign to traditional Buddhists.

However, one should note that the danger of missing a valid parallel is as great as the danger of accepting spurious correspondences. An important component of Linehan's technique called "distress tolerance skills" (1993a) parallels psychodynamic concepts of affect tolerance and affect dysregulation (Riesenberg-Malcolm). One would be tempted to regard these principles as unrelated (at least genetically) to any Buddhist technique of self-cultivation, except that a wide range of Buddhist practices pursue similar goals. One may mention, in passing, the contemplation of objects of disgust (corpse meditation or *aśubhabhāvanā*), as well as the use in the TIANTAI SCHOOL of repentance rituals that both move away from distress and remorse by contemplating emptiness and approach emptiness by contemplating the passions and their effects.

Commensurability and dialogue

The use of Buddhist techniques or beliefs as points of departure for contemporary psychologies or as a partner in scientific dialogue raises issues of commensurability: Are Buddhist psychological conceptions in some way commensurate with Western ideas of psychology and can there be a fruitful dialogue between the two? An obvious risk is to read psychological (scientific) literature the same way one reads religious literature: as statements of eternal truth. But equally tempting is the tendency to read psychological studies as confirmations or equivalents to Buddhist doctrinal speculation and religious practice.

Psychological "conclusions" are essentially provisional heuristic tools, with two functions: prediction and explanation, which are in turn validated (the probability of their disconfirmation reduced) when they themselves set the direction for further research and observation. There are, of course, good reasons to doubt their total independence from culture and the sociology of knowledge, but one risks misunderstanding their scope if one chooses to ignore the research protocols that underlie scientific statements about human psychosomatic processes.

Similarly, religious discourse and practice has its own protocols, and these must be thoroughly understood before one draws comparisons. Even today, practicing Buddhists tend to reject an interpretation of their beliefs and practices that may feel "reductionistic." As already noted, a psychoneurological explanation may ring true, but for it ultimately to have heuristic value or applicability beyond its conceptual conclusions it must account for the belief systems (the truths and myths of tradition) and the actual practices (ritual and contemplative patterns and events) cherished by the believers themselves.

Nonetheless, one may begin to consider, speculatively at this point in our understanding of the issue, ways in which Buddhist traditions may be seen to contain insights or techniques that may help illuminate contemporary problems of psychology. As suggested above, such illumination could be in a number of areas of philosophical and psychological inquiry: theories of consciousness and the unconscious, such as the theories of perception, emotion, and mental health. Some of these issues have been discussed in an ongoing series of symposia involving Western scholars, scientists, and the fourteenth DALAI LAMA.

The discussions point toward interesting possibilities for the future, and the participation of the Dalai Lama also reminds us of the frame of reference within which Buddhist psychological theories have developed —and arguably will continue to develop. Buddhist theories of mind speak of health and "dis-ease," but they also have ethical concerns that do not always overlap with the concerns of Western psychologists. The Buddhist may, for instance, be concerned with total liberation from the bonds of desire that have enslaved us for millions of rebirths, whereas the Western psychologist may be seeking an adaptive compromise in this single life. The Buddhist meditator may value unquestioned acceptance of a teacher's wisdom, whereas the Western psychologist may be interested in the matter of power differentials and authority in the relationship between therapist and client.

Most likely the majority of scientific psychologists, whatever their theoretical leanings, would not want to describe Buddhist doctrine and practices as equivalent to any one of the Western psychologies. Conversely it is difficult to imagine how a person committed to Buddhism in belief, practice, or both would want to reduce his or her preferred set of beliefs and practices to anything similar to what is considered scientific or empirical. And yet, if history is an effective teacher, we may expect to find an increasing cross-fertilization between both styles of studying and healing the human being as a unity of body and mind.

See also: **Anātman/Ātman (No-Self/Self); Chan School; Consciousness, Theories of; Sentient Beings**

Bibliography

Austin, James H. *Zen and the Brain: Toward an Understanding of Meditation and Consciousness.* Cambridge, MA: MIT Press, 1988.

Benson, Herbert, and Klipper, Miriam Z. *The Relaxation Response.* New York: Avon, 1976.

Birx, Ellen. *Healing Zen.* New York: Viking, 2002.

Block, Ned; Flanagan, Owen; and Guzeldere, Guven. *The Nature of Consciousness: Philosophical Debates.* Cambridge, MA: MIT Press, 1998.

Bstan Dzin Rgya Mtsho (Tenzin Gyatso, Dalai Lama XIV). *MindScience: An East-West Dialogue,* ed. Daniel Goleman and Robert A. F. Thurman. Boston: Wisdom, 1991.

Bstan Dzin Rgya Mtsho (Tenzin Gyatso, Dalai Lama XIV). *Gentle Bridges: Conversations with the Dalai Lama on the Sciences of Mind,* ed. Jeremy W. Hayward and Francisco J. Varela. Boston: Shambhala, 1992.

Bstan Dzin Rgya Mtsho (Tenzin Gyatso, Dalai Lama XIV), with Daniel Goleman et al. *Worlds in Harmony: Dialogues on Compassionate Action.* Berkeley, CA: Parallax, 1992.

Bstan Dzin Rgya Mtsho (Tenzin Gyatso, Dalai Lama XIV). *Healing Anger: The Power of Patience from a Buddhist Perspective,* tr. Geshe Thupten Jinpa and Sonam Thupten Jinpa. Ithaca, NY: Snow Lion, 1997.

Bstan Dzin Rgya Mtsho (Tenzin Gyatso, Dalai Lama XIV). *Transforming the Mind: Teachings on Generating Compassion,* tr. Geshe Thupten Jinpa. London: Thorsons, 2000.

Bstan Dzin Rgya Mtsho (Tenzin Gyatso, Dalai Lama XIV). *Healing Emotions: Conversations with the Dalai Lama on Mindfulness, Emotions, and Health,* ed. Daniel Goleman. Boston: Shambhala, 2003.

Chalmers, David J. *The Conscious Mind: In Search of a Fundamental Theory.* Oxford and New York: Oxford University Press, 1996.

Chang, Ruth, ed. *Incommensurability, Incomparability, and Practical Reason.* Cambridge, MA: Harvard University Press, 1998.

Chen, X. "How Do Scientists Have Disagreements about Experiments? Incommensurability in the Use of Goal-Derived Categories." *Perspectives on Science* 2 (1994): 275–301.

Chen, X. "Thomas Kuhn's Latest Notion of Incommensurability." *Journal for General Philosophy of Science* 28 (1997): 257–273.

Chen, X.; Andersen, H.; and Barker, P. "Kuhn's Theory of Scientific Revolutions and Cognitive Psychology." *Philosophical Psychology* 11 (1998): 5–28.

Churchill, J. "The Bellman's Map: Does Antifoundationalism Entail Incommensurability and Relativism?" *Southern Journal of Philosophy* 28 (1990): 469–484.

Claxton, Guy, ed. *Beyond Therapy: The Impact of Eastern Religions on Psychological Theory and Practice.* London: Wisdom, 1986.

Claxton, Guy. "Neurotheology: Buddhism, Cognitive Science and Mystical Experience." In *The Psychology of Awakening: Buddhism, Science, and Our Day-to-Day Lives,* ed. Gay Watson, Stephen Batchelor, and Guy Claxton. York Beach, ME: Weiser, 2000.

Clifford, Michael D. "Psychotherapy and Religion." In *The Encyclopedia of Religion,* Vol. 12, ed. Mircea Eliade. New York: Macmillan, 1987.

Clifford, Terry. *Tibetan Buddhist Medicine and Psychiatry: The Diamond Healing.* Delhi: Motilal Banarsidass, 1994.

Cornwell, John, ed. *Consciousness and Human Identity.* New York: Oxford University Press, 1998.

Csikzentmihalyi, Mihalyi. "The Concept of Flow." In *Play and Learning,* ed. Brian Sutton-Smith. New York: Gardner Press, 1979.

Damasio, Antonio. *The Feeling of What Happens: Body and Emotion in the Making of Consciousness.* New York: Harcourt, 1999.

D'Aquili, Eugene G., and Newberg, Andrew B. *The Mystical Mind: Probing the Biology of Religious Experience.* Minneapolis: Fortress Press, 1999.

Davidson, Richard J., ed. *Anxiety, Depression, and Emotion.* New York: Oxford, 2000.

Davis, Martha; Robbins Eshelman, Elizabeth; and McKay, Matthew. *The Relaxation and Stress Reduction Workbook,* 5th edition. Oakland, CA: New Harbinger, 2000.

de Silva, Padmal. "Buddhism and Behaviour Modification." *Behaviour Research and Therapy* 22, no. 6 (1984): 661–678.

de Silva, Padmal. "Early Buddhist and Modern Behavioral Strategies for the Control of Unwanted Intrusive Cognitions." *Psychological Record* 35, no. 4 (1985): 437–443.

de Silva, Padmal. "Buddhism and Behaviour Change: Implications for Therapy." In *Beyond Therapy: The Impact of Eastern Religions on Psychological Theory and Practice,* ed. Guy Claxton. London: Wisdom, 1986.

de Silva, Padmal. "Buddhist Psychology: A Review of Theory and Practice." *Current Psychology: Research and Reviews* 9, no. 3 (1990): 236–254.

de Silva, Padmal. "Buddhism and Counselling." *British Journal of Guidance and Counselling* 21, no. 1 (1993): 30–34.

de Silva, Padmal. "Buddhist Psychology: A Therapeutic Perspective." In *Indigenous Psychologies: Research and Experience in Cultural Context,* ed. Uichol Kim. Thousand Oaks, CA: Sage, 1993.

DeCharms, Christopher. *Two Views of Mind: Abhidharma and Brain Science.* Ithaca, NY: Snow Lion, 1998.

Deikman, A. J. "Experimental Meditation." *Journal of Nervous and Mental Disease* 136 (1963): 329–343.

Deikman, A. J. "De-automatization and the Mystic Experience." *Psychiatry* 29 (1966): 324–338.

Deikman, A. J. "Implications of Experimentally Produced Contemplative Meditation." *Journal of Nervous and Mental Disease* 142, no. 2 (1966): 101–116.

Deikman, A. J. Review of *Freedom from the Self: Sufism, Meditation, and Psychotherapy,* by M. Shafii. *Journal of Nervous and Mental Disease* 174, no. 8 (1986): 503–504.

Dennett, Daniel C. *Kinds of Minds: Toward an Understanding of Consciousness.* New York: Basic Books, 1996.

Dreyfus, Georges. "Is Compassion an Emotion? A Cross-Cultural Exploration of Mental Typologies." In *Visions of Compassion: Western Scientists and Tibetan Buddhists Examine Human Nature,* ed. Richard J. Davidson and Anne Harrington. London: Oxford University Press, 2002.

Edelman, Gerald M., and Tononi, Giulio. *A Universe of Consciousness: How Matter Becomes Imagination.* New York: Basic Books, 2000.

Eisenberg, Nancy. *Altruistic Emotion, Cognition, and Behavior.* Hillsdale, NJ: Erlbaum, 1986.

Ellis, Ralph D. *Questioning Consciousness: The Interplay of Imagery, Cognition, and Emotion in the Human Brain.* Philadelphia: John Benjamins, 1995.

Epstein, Mark. *Thoughts without a Thinker: Psychotherapy from a Buddhist Perspective.* New York: Basic Books, 1995.

Farthing, G. William. *The Psychology of Consciousness.* Englewood Cliffs, NJ: Prentice-Hall, 1992.

Faure, Bernard. *Chan Insights and Oversights: An Epistemological Critique of the Chan Tradition.* Princeton, NJ: Princeton University Press, 1995.

Fingarette, Herbert. *Self-Deception.* Berkeley and Los Angeles: University of California Press, 2000.

Firestone, Robert W.; Firestone, Lisa A.; and Catlett, Joyce. *Creating a Life of Meaning and Compassion: The Wisdom of Psychotherapy.* Washington, DC: American Psychological Association, 2003.

Fisher, Seymour, and Fisher, Rhonda L. *The Psychology of Adaptation to Absurdity: Tactics of Make-Believe.* Tuxedo Park, NY: Erlbaum, 1993.

Flack, William F., Jr., and Laird, James D., eds. *Emotions in Psychopathology Theory and Research.* New York: Oxford University Press, 1998.

Forman, Robert K. C. *The Problem of Pure Consciousness: Mysticism and Philosophy.* New York: Oxford University Press, 1990.

Forman, Robert K. C., ed. *The Innate Capacity: Mysticism, Psychology, and Philosophy.* New York: Oxford University Press, 1998.

Goleman, Daniel. *Destructive Emotions: How Can We Overcome Them? A Scientific Dialogue with the Dalai Lama.* New York: Bantam Books, 2003.

Gómez, Luis O. "'Oriental' Wisdom and the Cure of Souls: Jung and the Indian 'East.'" In *Curators of the Buddha,* ed. Donald S. Lopez. Chicago: University of Chicago Press, 1995.

Gómez, Luis O. "Healing Suffering by Healing Consciousness: The End of Suffering in Buddhist Discourse." In *Pain and Its Transformations,* ed. S. Coakley and A. Kleinman. Cambridge, MA: Harvard University Press, 2003.

Greenberg, Leslie S. *Emotion-Focused Therapy: Coaching Clients to Work through Their Feelings.* Washington, DC: American Psychological Association, 2002.

Griffiths, Paul E. "Emotions." In *The Blackwell Guide to Philosophy of Mind,* ed. Stephen P. Stich and Ted A. Warfield. Malden, MA: Blackwell, 2003.

Griffiths, Paul J. *On Being Mindless: Buddhist Meditation and the Mind-Body Problem.* La Salle, IL: Open Court, 1986.

Guenther, Herbert V. *Philosophy and Psychology in the Abhidharma.* Lucknow, India: Buddha Vihara, 1957.

Guggenbühl-Craig, Adolf. *Power in the Helping Professions* (1971), tr. Myron B. Gubitz. Woodstock, CT: Spring Publications, 1999.

Gyatso, Janet, ed. *In the Mirror of Memory: Reflections on Mindfulness and Remembrance in Indian and Tibetan Buddhism.* Albany: State University of New York Press, 1992.

Gyatso, Janet. "Healing Burns with Fire: The Tacilitations of Experience in Tibetan Buddhism." *Journal of the American Academy of Religion* 67, no. 1 (1999): 113–147.

Harvey, Peter. *The Selfless Mind: Personality, Consciousness, and Nirvana in Early Buddhism.* Richmond, UK: Curzon, 1995.

Hill, Peter C. "Toward an Attitude Process Model of Religious Experience." *Journal for the Scientific Study of Religion* 33, no. 4 (1994): 303–314.

Hirai, Tomio. *Zen and the Mind: Scientific Approach to Zen Practice.* Tokyo: Japan Publications, 1978.

Hirai, Tomio. *Zen Meditation and Psychotherapy,* revised edition of *Zen and the Mind* (1978). Tokyo: Japan Publications, 1989.

Hood, Ralph W., Jr., ed. *Handbook of Religious Experience.* Birmingham, AL: Religious Education Press, 1995.

Houshmand, Zara; Livingstone, Robert B.; and Wallace, B. Alan, eds. *Consciousness at the Crossroads: Conversations with the Dalai Lama on Brain Science and Buddhism.* Ithaca, NY: Snow Lion, 1999.

Humphrey, Nicholas. *A History of the Mind.* New York: Simon and Schuster, 1992.

Hunt, Harry. *On the Nature of Consciousness: Cognitive, Phenomenological, and Transpersonal Perspectives.* New Haven, CT: Yale University Press, 1995.

Jaini, Padma. Nabh. S. "The *Sautrāntika* Theory of *Bīja.*" *Bulletin of the School of Oriental and African Studies* 22, no. 2 (1959): 236–249.

Jayasuriya, W. F. *The Psychology and Philosophy of Buddhism.* Colombo, Sri Lanka: Y.M.B.A. Press, 1963.

Jayatilleke, K. N. *Early Buddhist Theory of Knowledge.* London: Allen and Unwin; New York: Humanities Press, 1963.

Johansson, Rune E. A. *The Psychology of Nirvana.* London: Allen and Unwin, 1969; New York: Anchor Books, 1970.

Jones, Stanton L. "A Constructive Relationship for Religion with the Science and Profession of Psychology: Perhaps the Boldest Model Yet." In *Religion and the Clinical Practice of Psychology,* ed. Edward P. Shafranske. Washington, DC: American Psychological Association, 1996.

Joseph, R.; Newberg, Andrew B.; Alper, Matthew; et al. *NeuroTheology: Brain, Science, Spirituality, Religious Experience,* 2nd edition. Berkeley and Los Angeles: University of California Press, 2003.

Jung, Carl Gustav. *Concerning Mandala Symbolism,* tr. R. F. C. Hull. Princeton, NJ: Princeton University Press, 1959.

Kasamatsu, A., and Hirai, T. "An EEG Study on the Zen Meditation (Zazen)." *Folia Psychiatrica et Neurologia Japonica* 20, no. 4 (1966): 315–336.

Kasamatsu, A., and Hirai, T. "An EEG Study on the Zen Meditation (Zazen)." *Psychologia* 12, nos. 3–4 (1969): 205–225.

Kaszniak, Alfred W., ed. *Emotions, Qualia, and Consciousness.* London: World Scientific, 2001.

Klein, Anne C. *Knowledge and Liberation: Tibetan Buddhist Epistemology in Support of Transformative Religious Experience.* Ithaca, NY: Snow Lion, 1986.

Kobayashi, K. "The Effect of Zen Meditation on the Valence of Intrusive Thoughts." *Dissertation Abstracts International* 43, no. 1-B (July 1982): 280.

Langer, Ellen J. *Mindfulness.* Reading, MA: Addison-Wesley, 1989.

Laplanche, Jean. *Life and Death in Psychoanalysis,* tr. Jeffrey Mehlman. Baltimore: Johns Hopkins University Press, 1976.

Lati Rinbochay and Napper, Elizabeth. *Mind in Tibetan Buddhism: Oral Commentary on Ge-shay Jam-bel-sam-pel's Presentation of Awareness and Knowledge* (1980), translated and edited by Elizabeth Napper. Ithaca, NY: Snow Lion, 1986.

Linehan, Marsha M. *Cognitive-Behavioral Treatment of Borderline Personality Disorder.* New York: Guilford Press, 1993a.

Linehan, Marsha M. *Skills Training Manual for Treating Borderline Personality Disorder.* New York: Guilford Press, 1993b.

Lusk, Julie T., ed. *Thirty Scripts for Relaxation Imagery and Inner Healing.* Duluth, MN: Whole Person, 1992.

Lycan, William G. *Consciousness and Experience.* Cambridge, MA: MIT Press, 1996.

Macrae, J. "Therapeutic Touch as Meditation." In *Spiritual Aspects of the Healing Arts,* compiled by Dora Kunz. Wheaton, IL: Theosophical Publishing House, 1985.

Mahāsi Sayadaw. *The Progress of Insight through the Stages of Purification: A Modern Pali Treatise on Buddhist Satipatthana Meditation,* tr. Nyanaponika Thera. Kandy, Sri Lanka: Forest Hermitage, 1965.

Matilal, Bimal Krishna. *Perception: An Essay on Classical Indian Theories of Knowledge.* Oxford and New York: Oxford University Press, 1986.

Miller, William R., ed. *Integrating Spirituality into Treatment: Resources for Practitioners.* Washington, DC: American Psychological Association, 1999.

Molino, Anthony. *The Couch and the Tree: Dialogues in Psychoanalysis and Buddhism.* New York: North Point Press, 1998.

Murphy, Michael, and Donovan, Steven. *The Physical and Psychological Effects of Meditation: A Review of Contemporary Research with a Comprehensive Bibliography, 1931–1996,* 2nd edition. Sausalito, CA: Institute of Noetic Sciences, 1997.

Newberg, Andrew; D'Aquili, Eugene G.; and Rause, Vince. *Why God Won't Go Away: Brain Science and the Biology of Belief.* New York: Ballantine, 2001.

Obeyesekere, Gananath. *Imagining Karma: Ethical Transformation in Amerindian, Buddhist, and Greek Rebirth.* Berkeley and Los Angeles: University of California Press, 2002.

Ortony, Andrew; Clore, Gerald L.; and Collins, Allan. *The Cognitive Structure of Emotions.* Cambridge, UK: Cambridge University Press, 1988.

Otis, L. S.; Shapiro, Deane H., Jr.; and Walsh, Roger N. "Adverse Effects of Transcendental Meditation." In *Meditation: Classic and Contemporary Perspectives,* ed. Deane H. Shapiro and Roger N. Walsh. New York: Aldine, 1984.

Parfit, Derek. *Reasons and Persons.* Oxford: Clarendon, 1984.

Renik, Owen, ed. *Knowledge and Authority in the Psychoanalytic Relationship.* Northvale, NJ: Jason Aronson, 1998.

Riesenberg-Malcolm, Ruth. *On Bearing Unbearable States of Mind.* London and New York: Routledge, 1999.

Rokke, Paul D., and Rehm, Lynn P. "Self-Management Therapies." In *Handbook of Cognitive-Behavioral Therapies,* ed. Keith S. Dobson. New York and London: Guilford Press, 2001.

Rubin, Jeffrey B. "Psychoanalytic Treatment with a Buddhist Meditator." In *Object Relations Theory and Religion: Clinical Applications,* ed. Mark Finn and John Gartner. Westport, CT, and London: Praeger, 1992.

Rubin, Jeffrey B. *Psychotherapy and Buddhism: Toward an Integration.* New York: Plenum Press, 2000.

Sanderson, C., and Linehan, M. M. "Acceptance and Forgiveness." In *Integrating Spirituality into Treatment: Resources for Practitioners,* ed. William R. Miller. Washington, DC: American Psychological Association, 1999.

Schmithausen, Lambert. "On the Problem of the Relation of Spiritual Practice and Philosophical Theory in Buddhism." In *German Scholars on India,* Vol. 2, ed. Cultural Department, Embassy of the Federal Republic of Germany. Bombay: Embassy of the Federal Republic of Germany, 1976.

Schmithausen, Lambert. *Ālayavijñāna: On the Origin and Early Development of a Central Concept of Yogācāra Philosophy.* Tokyo: International Institute for Buddhist Studies, 1987.

Schumaker, John F., ed. *Religion and Mental Health.* New York: Oxford University Press, 1992.

Schwartz, Jeffrey M. *Brain Lock: Free Yourself from Obsessive-Compulsive Behavior.* New York: HarperCollins, 1996.

Scott, Alwyn. *Stairway to the Mind: The Controversial New Science of Consciousness.* New York: Copernicus, 1995.

Searle, John R. *The Mystery of Consciousness.* New York: New York Review of Books Press, 1997.

Segal, Zindel V.; Williams, J.; Mark, G.; and Teasdale, John D. *Mindfulness-Based Cognitive Therapy for Depression: A New Approach to Preventing Relapse.* New York and London: Guilford Press, 2000.

Serres, Michel. *Les cinq sens: Philosophie des corps mêlés.* Paris: Grasset et Fasquelle, 1985.

Shafranske, Edward P., ed. *Religion and the Clinical Practice of Psychology.* Washington, DC: American Psychological Association, 1996.

Shapiro, Deane H., Jr. "Adverse Effects of Meditation: A Preliminary Investigation of Long-Term Meditators." *International Journal of Psychosomatics* 29 (1992): 62–66.

Shapiro, Deane H., Jr., and Walsh, Roger N., eds. *Meditation: Classic and Contemporary Perspectives.* New York: Aldine, 1984.

Sharf, Robert H. "Buddhist Modernism and the Rhetoric of Meditative Experience." *Numen* 42 (1995): 228–283.

Sharf, Robert H. "Experience." In *Critical Terms for Religious Studies,* ed. Mark C. Taylor. Chicago: University of Chicago Press, 1998.

Singh Khalsa, Dharma, and Stauth, Cameron. *Meditation as Medicine: Activate the Power of Your Natural Healing Force.* New York: Pocket Books, 2001.

Sinha, Jadunath. *Indian Psychology,* 2nd edition, 2 vols. Calcutta: Sinha, 1958, 1961.

Smith, J. C. "Meditation as Psychotherapy: A Review of the Literature." *Psychological Bulletin* 82 (1975): 557–564.

Smyth, Larry D. *Clients Manual for the Cognitive-Behavioral Treatment of Anxiety Disorders,* 2nd edition. Havre de Grace, MD: RTR, 1999.

Stocker, Michael, and Hegeman, Elizabeth. *Valuing Emotions.* New York and Cambridge, UK: Cambridge University Press, 1996.

Tart, Charles T., ed. *Altered States of Consciousness,* 3rd edition. San Francisco: HarperCollins, 1990.

Varela, Francisco J., ed. *Sleeping, Dreaming, and Dying: An Exploration of Consciousness with the Dalai Lama.* Boston: Wisdom, 1997.

Varela, Francisco J. "Steps to a Science of Inter-Being: Unfolding the Dharma Implicit in Modern Cognitive Science." In *The Psychology of Awakening: Buddhism, Science, and Our Day-to-Day Lives,* ed. Gay Watson. York Beach, ME: Weiser, 2000.

Waddell, Norman, trans. *Wild Ivy: The Spiritual Autobiography of Zen Master Hakuin.* Boston: Shambhala, 1999.

Wall, Patrick. *Pain: The Science of Suffering.* New York: Columbia University Press, 2000.

Wallace, Benjamin, and Fisher, Leslie E. *Consciousness and Behavior,* 4th edition. Boston: Allyn and Bacon, 1999.

Wallace, Robert Keith. "Physiological Effects of Transcendental Meditation." *Science* 167 (1970): 1,751–1,754.

Walsh, Robert N. "Meditation." In *Handbook of Innovative Therapy,* 2nd revised edition, ed. Raymond J. Corsini. New York: Wiley, 2001.

Walsh, Roger, and Vaughn, Frances. *Paths beyond Ego: The Transpersonal Vision.* Los Angeles: Jeremy P. Tarcher, 1993.

Watson, Gay. *The Resonance of Emptiness: A Buddhist Inspiration for a Contemporary Psychotherapy.* Richmond, UK: Curzon, 1998.

Watson, Gay, ed. *The Psychology of Awakening: Buddhism, Science, and Our Day-to-Day Lives.* York Beach, ME: Weiser, 2000.

Weiskrantz, Lawrence. *Consciousness Lost and Found: A Neuropsychological Exploration.* New York: Oxford University Press, 1997.

Wilber, Ken; Engler, Jack; and Brown, Daniel P., eds. *Transformations of Consciousness: Conventional and Contemplative Perspectives on Development.* Boston: Shambala, 1986.

Wolman, Benjamin B., and Ullman, Montague. *Handbook of States of Consciousness.* New York: Van Nostrand Reinhold, 1986.

Wood, Thomas E. *Mind Only: A Philosophical and Doctrinal Analysis of Vijñānavāda.* Honolulu: University of Hawaii Press, 1991.

Wright, Crispin; Smith, Barry C.; and Macdonald, Cynthia, eds. *Knowing Our Own Minds.* Oxford: Oxford University Press, 1998.

Yasuo, Yuasa. *The Body: Toward an Eastern Mind-Body Theory.* Albany: State University of New York Press, 1987.

Zangpo, S., and Feuerstein, G. "The Risks of Visualization: Growing Roots Can Be Dangerous." *Quest* (Summer 1995): 26–30, 84.

LUIS O. GÓMEZ

PUDGALAVĀDA

The Pudgalavāda was a group of schools sharing the doctrine that the person (*pudgala*) or self (ātman) is real. The earliest Pudgalavāda school was the Vātsīputrīya; from the Vātsīputrīya came the Dharmottarīya, Bhadrayānīya, Sāṃmitīya, and Ṣaṇṇagarika. Of these schools, the Vātsīputrīya and Sāṃmitīya were the most important.

Very little of their literature has survived. This circumstance, together with their apparent denial of the Buddhist doctrine of nonself, has created the impression that they were an eccentric minority on the fringe of Buddhism. But in fact they were in the mainstream; XUANZANG (ca. 600–664) tells us that roughly a quarter of the monastic population in India in the seventh century C.E. was Pudgalavāda.

They agreed with other Buddhists that the self is neither the same as the five SKANDHA (AGGREGATES) nor separate from them, but affirmed the self as "true and ultimate." They thought of the self as conceptual yet real, real because for the purposes of kindness and compassion the self was not reducible to the skandhas, and apparently because the self was a reflection of the timeless reality of NIRVĀṆA in the flux of the skandhas. As a fire can exist locally only through its fuel, so the self can exist as a particular person only through the skandhas. As the fire vanishes when the fuel is exhausted, but cannot be said to be either existent or nonexistent, having "gone home" to its timeless source, so the self that has attained nirvāṇa, vanishing at death, cannot be said either to exist or not to exist.

See also: **Anātman/Ātman (No-Self/Self); Mainstream Buddhist Schools**

Bibliography

Priestley, Leonard C. D. C. *Pudgalavāda Buddhism: The Reality of the Indeterminate Self.* Toronto, ON: Centre for South Asian Studies, University of Toronto, 1999.

Thien Chau, Thich. *The Literature of the Personalists of Early Buddhism,* tr. Sara Boin-Webb. Delhi: Motilal Barnasidass, 1999.

LEONARD C. D. C. PRIESTLEY

PURE LAND ART

Visions of PURE LANDS are premised upon the Mahāyāna COSMOLOGY of multiple worlds in "ten directions," each presided over by one buddha and each constituting a blissful alternative to the Sahā world of impurity in which we live. The Western Land of Bliss (Sukhāvatī) associated with AMITĀBHA Buddha epitomizes the notion of the pure land. The term *pure land* is thus used in a narrow sense to refer to Amitābha's Land and in a broader sense to refer to domains associated with BUDDHAS of other directions. Visual representation of pure lands, a major theme in the Buddhist art of East Asia, takes three major forms: (1) sculptural representations of Amitābha Buddha with his retinue; (2) BIANXIANG (TRANSFORMATION TABLEAUX) showing paradise scenes or pictures of the descent of Amitābha to usher the deceased to the Land of Bliss; and (3) landscape and architectural simulation of the Western Paradise.

Western Pure Land evoked through the Amitābha image

The Amitābha image, with its evocation of the Western Pure Land, dates back to at least the fourth century in China, culminating in its veneration by HUIYUAN (334–416) and his followers on Mount Lu. There was a remarkable lack of doctrinal coherence underlying the early practice, which took its cues largely from sūtras tangential to Amitābha's Pure Land. Chief among them is the PRATYUTPANNASAMĀDHI-SŪTRA, which emphasizes the role of BUDDHA IMAGES, including images of Amitābha, as an expedient agency for achieving the state of contemplation, rather than as cultic icons in their own right. In early cases involving Amitābha images, stone chambers were chosen as the topographic setting for such meditative activities, as a means of "traveling," in the words of a devotee named Liu Yimin around 400 C.E., "to the most distant region (of the Western Paradise) . . . to settle for the great repose (of Nirvāṇa) as the final term."

Such pure land aspirations gained momentum during the fifth and sixth centuries in China. However, the majority of buddha icons made during this period depicted Śākyamuni, MAITREYA, and the Śākyamuni/Prabhūtaratna pair. A new trend emerged in northern China in the 460s: Of the variety of buddha images made by lay commoners, about 17 percent were Amitābha icons, which received little patronage from monks and nuns. It was not until a century later that the SAṄGHA's interest in Amitābha icons overrode their interest in icons of Śākyamuni and Maitreya. The change suggests that the pure land cult associated with Amitābha was a movement that began from the bottom up. It largely tallied with the early indifference shown by the learned Buddhist community during this period toward Amitābha Pure Land sūtras, as indicated by the initial absence of scholarly commentary regarding them. Early donors of Amitābha images were unclear about the location of Amitābha's Pure Land in the Buddhist cosmological scheme. Amitābha images were often integrated into the imagined afterlife encounter with Maitreya, the future Buddha. In southern China, Amitābha images were cast in gilded bronze, with the largest statues reported to be sixteen feet tall. In the north, stone was the favored medium.

Transformation tableaux of the Western Pure Land

It is not clear when pure land pictures first appeared in China. A mural in cave 169 at Binglingsi, executed in 420, contains the earliest painted icon of Amitāyus, but shows no topographic features of the Western Paradise. The earliest surviving example of a pure land picture in China is a set of topographic tableaux carved on the back of the nimbus of icons from the Wanfosi at Chengdu. The oldest of these survives in an ink rubbing, dated 425, with the pure land scene largely missing. A sixth-century relief carving, similar in design, on the back of double bodhisattvas from the same site, preserves a complete composition. It is based on the "Life Span" and "The Universal Gateway" chapters of the LOTUS SŪTRA (SADDHARMAPUṆḌARĪKA-SŪTRA). In the middle is the assembly gathered at the bird-shaped Vulture Peak, where Śākyamuni announces that, at the end of a kalpa, fire and terror engulf the human world, while his pure land remains intact, where halls, pavilions, gardens, and groves are "adorned with gems," and "jeweled trees abound in flowers and fruit, and living beings enjoy themselves at ease." The composition is thus divided into two contrasting parts: below, scenes of calamities; above, the pure land. Human figures appear in the lotus pond, a scene of rebirth associated with a pure land. The carving is often hailed as a precursor to later representations of the Western Pure Land. The composition also anticipates pictures of the "White Path to Paradise," which are typically divided into two realms: Below is the impure mundane world of the east, teeming with suffering beings from the six REALMS OF EXISTENCE; above is the Western Pure Land. In between is a symmetrically divided river. To the left and south is the pool of fire of anger and violence; to the right and north is the river of greed and desire. Flanked by these two engulfing rivers is a thin white path that leads to the Western Paradise. Śākyamuni, on one side of the river, urges the devotee to cross, while Amitābha and his retinue beckon on the other shore. Shandao's commentary on the *Guan Wuliangshou jing* (*Contemplation of the Buddha of Limitless Life Sūtra*) presents a matching textual account. However, pictures of this kind are found only in surviving Japanese hanging scrolls of the Kamakura period (1185–1333).

Another notable early painting of a pure land, executed around the early seventh century, appears in cave 420 at DUNHUANG. Based in part on the *Lotus Sūtra,* the mural shows Vulture Peak on the right and Śākyamuni passing into nirvāṇa in the middle. Issuing from the foot of Vulture Peak is a winding river dotted with lotuses, with a boat and numerous ducks crossing to the other shore. Flanking the river are an array of nine buddhas and various buddha-lands. The scene draws on the "Life Span" chapter of the NIRVĀṆA SŪTRA, translated by Dharmakṣema in 423 C.E., which describes an "Eastern world named Joy and Beautiful Sound," a pure land. Both the Wangfosi carving and the Dunhuang mural demonstrate the tenuous relationship between early pictures of pure lands and the Amitābha sūtras. The pictures arose out of a topographic imagination that was driven by soteriological interest and cued by scriptures.

As the cult of the Amitābha Pure Land gained currency during the second half of the sixth century, its pictorial representation took more definitive shape. Two compositional prototypes emerged during the Northern Qi period (550–577). The first is the "Amitābha with Fifty Bodhisattvas," a picture allegedly acquired by the five bodhisattvas of the Kukkutārāma Monastery from the Western Paradise, and dubiously claimed to have been transmitted by the Indian monk Kāśyapa-mātaṅga (d. 73 C.E.) to China. Cao Zhongda of the Northern Qi is said to have specialized in pictures of this type, which continued to appear into the seventh century. A painting on the east wall of cave 332 at Dunhuang shows a gigantic tree dominated by the Amitābha triad. Fifty reborn souls appear as bodhisattvas perched on various tree branches; two other figures are each wrapped in a lotus bud.

The second compositional prototype represents the more popular model. It is exemplified by a large spread of relief sculpture from cave 2 of South Xiangtangshan, now at the Freer Gallery in Washington, D.C. The composition contains all the key elements of subsequent Western Paradise tableaux. Three haloed deities—Amitābha in the middle, with Avalokiteśvara and Mahāsthāmaprāpta on each side—constitute the Western triad. In front of them are three ponds. In the middle pond, four human figures emerge respectively from a lotus—the extent to which they break out of the lotus bud indicates the ranking order of their classes in the merit-based three-tiered hierarchy of rebirth, as described in the Larger SUKHĀVATĪVYŪHA-SŪTRA. Each of the two side ponds shows a figure—either a bodhisattva or a Buddha disciple—bathing in the "jeweled ponds" to cleanse the impurities of the world of transmigration before entering the Land of Bliss. The pond motif has since become a distinctive feature of Amitābha's Pure Land. This design grew into a major compositional form in the seventh century, as exemplified by the Amitābha tableau in cave 220 at Dunhuang, dated 642 C.E., and in the Golden Hall of Hōryūji in Japan.

Western Pure Land pictures developed new forms in the seventh and eighth centuries. The threefold gradation of rebirths in the pure land based on the Larger *Sukhāvatīvyūha-sūtra* evolved into a ninefold scheme —three grades, each subdivided into three degrees— as pure land tableaux incorporated the *Guan Wuliangshou jing.* An early example is a seventh-century wall painting in cave 431 at Dunhuang, which contains vignettes of the descent of Amitābha or his delegates to fetch the dying person to the Western Paradise. In its early phase, the composition took the form of a horizontal band measuring 1 by 15.4 meters, a form apparently adapted from the hand scroll format, and it emphasizes narrative actions rather than pure land scenes. In the early eighth century, a triptych form took

A bas-relief in limestone representing Amitābha's Western Paradise. (Chinese, Northern Qi dynasty, sixth century.) Freer Gallery of Art Library. Reproduced by permission.

shape. The two side panels depict the story of Ajātaśatru, a prince who puts his father, King Bimbisāra, and his mother, Queen Vaidehī, under house arrest. In response to the queen's appeal, the Buddha appears and teaches her sixteen ways of visualization. This royal family drama and the scenes of visualization often occupy two side columns that flank the central paradise scene in triptychs. The side vignettes set the *Guan Wuliangshou jing* tableau apart from the Amitābha tableau. Their identification on the basis of sūtra(s) is in fact tenuous since the *Guan Wuliangshou jing* does not include the description of the Western Pure Land that appears in the Amitābha sūtras.

Other pure lands

Pure land tableaux are not limited to the Western Paradise. In MAHĀYĀNA cosmology, there are "pure lands of ten directions." Tableaux depicting other pure lands include those of the Medicine Buddha (Bhaiṣajyaguru) of the East; Maitreya, often associated with north; and those described in sūtras not pertaining to particular pure lands. There is even a tableau of pure lands of the ten directions as identified by its cartouche in cave 158 at Dunhuang. The tableau of the Pure Land of the Bhaiṣajyaguru of the East features scenes of lamp-lighting, "Nine Violent Deaths," and "Fulfillment of Twelve Great Vows"

FIGURE 1

Pure land tableaux

North: Tableau of Maitreya's Pure Land

West: Tableau of Amitābha's Pure Land

East: Tableau of Bhaiṣajyaguru's Pure Land

South: Tableau of Śākyamuni's Buddha Land

SOURCE: Author.

made by the Bodhisattva Bhaiṣajyaguru before he becomes a buddha. The tableaux of Maitreya Pure Land (a somewhat misleading term since Maitreya's domain is considered by some scriptures as an impure land) are of two types: Maitreya's ascent to Tuṣita Heaven, and Maitreya's descent into Jambudvīpa to preach under the dragon-flower trees. Gaining popularity in the Tang dynasty, the tableau of Maitreya's descent includes miracle scenes, such as "Seven Harvests after One Sowing," "Clothing Growing Out of Trees," "Five-Hundred-Year-Old Women Getting Married," and so on. Regardless of the kind of pure land being depicted, most of the tableaux largely follow the compositional model of Amitābha's Pure Land, with the exception of certain distinctive features associated with a particular buddha realm.

Pictorial programs of pure land tableaux

During the seventh and eighth centuries, tableaux of pure lands were integrated into larger pictorial programs. The documented set of pure land tableaux in the five-story pagoda at the Kōfukuji in Japan is a typical example current in the eighth century (Figure 1). A temporal scheme, mapped out by way of spatial opposition, underlies the iconographic program. The Bhaiṣajyaguru tableau suggests the present, the Amitābha tableau the future (afterlife); the Śākyamuni land signals the present, the Maitreya land the future (afterlife). Thus, the entire program maps out a symbolic cosmos for the spirit of the deceased to cross the boundary between this and the other world. The topographic continuum may also underlie the spatial opposition between different pure land tableaux. Placing the *Lotus Sūtra* tableau opposite the Western Pure Land scene may imply a progressive transition from the wilderness of the earthly terrain to the order of the afterlife domain. It is therefore misleading to identify these pure land tableaux on the basis of the sūtras they appear to "illustrate."

Pictures of the Buddha's welcoming descent

A significant detail of the *Guan Wuliangshou jing* tableau forms the basis of a new development. The last three of the sixteen visualizations, as exemplified by seventh-century vignettes in cave 431 at Dunhuang, show the descent of the Buddha or his delegates to dying devotees to escort their spirits to the Western Paradise. These vignettes anticipated the pictures of the Buddha's welcoming descent (*raigō*), which became popular in Japan beginning in the twelfth century. The early descent paintings, exemplified by a set of three hanging scrolls in Jūhakka-in at Mount Kōya, show the frontally seated Amitābha, surrounded by his entourage on a swirl of clouds, descending toward the implied viewer. A compositional variation of this image gained popularity, especially in the Kamakura period. In this variation, Amitābha and his heavenly attendants on streaming clouds sweep down diagonally from the upper left to the lower right toward the dwelling of the dying devotee. Their swift movement is dramatized by sharp-angled trailing clouds blazing through space, often set against precipitous peaks, as shown in a scroll at Chion-in. Amitābha's seated posture also changes to an upright stance to reinforce the

The Phoenix Hall at the Byōdōin, Kyoto, Japan. Built in 1053, it was intended as a three-dimensional representation of the Sukhāvatī Pure Land—the Western Paradise—of Amitābha. © Archivo Iconografico, S.A./Corbis. Reproduced by permission.

sense of his instantaneous arrival. Amitābha in such a composition may also be replaced by other buddhas, such as Maitreya.

Related to the descent pictures in the Kamakura period is a new type of design known as "Amitābha Crossing the Mountains." The composition shows the radiant bust-length Amitābha trinity towering over mountain peaks in the horizon. Premised upon the association of Amitābha Pure Land with the west, the radiant icon evokes the setting sun. Standard textbook accounts correlate the development of the descent pictures to the doctrinal lineage of Pure Land school teaching laid out by Shandao and explicated and propagated in Japan by GENSHIN (942–1017), HŌNEN (1133–1212), and SHINRAN (1173–1262). It is more fitting to see teachings by Genshin and his followers not as the determining source for image-making, but as collaborative testimony to the collective aspiration that finds different channels of expression.

Spatial installation of pure lands

Both sculptures and paintings are often integrated into spatial simulation of pure lands. An early-seventh-century Chinese monk named Zhenhui is said to have built a "pure land" dominated by a square high altar overlooking a ground of lapis lazuli with crisscrossing paths bounded by golden ropes. An elaborate surviving example of a pure land simulation is the PHOENIX HALL (AT THE BYŌDŌIN) near Kyoto, built in the mid-eleventh century. Its interior houses an Amitābha statue in the center, surrounded on four sides with wooden panels depicting painted scenes of the nine degrees of rebirth. In front of the hall is a pond, a key feature of the topography of the Western Paradise. Moreover, the architectural design of the Phoenix Hall itself evokes a winged bird, another feature associated with the Amitābha land.

As the general trend of Buddhist art gradually turned more toward esoteric charms and invocations, Amitābha Buddha was increasingly assimilated into MAṆḌALA designs; written characters invoking prayer formulae replaced iconic images and visionary tableaux. With the loss of its topographic character, pure land art also lost its distinction.

See also: **Central Asia, Buddhist Art in; China, Buddhist Art in; Hōryūji and Tōdaiji; Japan, Buddhist Art in; Korea, Buddhist Art in; Pure Land Buddhism; Pure Land Schools**

Bibliography

Fukuyama, Toshio. *Heian Temples: Byodo-in and Chuson-ji*, tr. Ronald K. Jones. New York: Weatherhill, 1976.

Mochizuki, Shinkō. *Chūgoku Jōdo kyōrishi* (History of the Chinese Pure Land doctrinal teaching). Kyoto: Hōzōkan, 1942.

Nakamura Kōji. "Saihō jōdohen no kenkyū" (Studies in transformation tableaux of the Western Pure Land), parts 1–29. *Nihon bijutsu kōgei* no. 491 (August 1979): 84–90, through no. 519 (December 1981): 31–35.

Nakamura Kōji. "Wagakuni no jōdo hensō to Tonkō" (The transformation tableaux of pure land in Japan and Dunhuang). In *Chūgoku sekkutsu Tonkō Bakkōkutsu* (Chinese grottos: Mogao cave shrines at Dunhuang), Vol. 3. Tokyo: Heibonsha, 1982.

Okazaki, Jōji. *Pure Land Buddhist Painting*, tr. Elizabeth ten Grotenhuis. Tokyo, New York, and San Francisco: Kodansha International and Shibundo, 1977.

Tsukamoto, Zenryū. "Jōdohenshi gaisetsu" (A historical survey of the transformation tableaux of pure lands). *Bukkyō geijutsu* (*Ars Buddhica*) 26 (1955): 27–41.

Tsukamoto, Zenryū. *Jōdoshu shi, bijutsuhen* (History of the Pure Land sect: art history volume), Vol. 7 of *Tsukamoto Zenryū chosaku shū*. Tokyo: Daitō, 1975.

Wang, Eugene. "Transformation in 'Heterotopia': The Longhuta and Its Relief Sculptures." *Orientations* 29, no. 6 (1998): 32–40.

Wang, Eugene. "Watching the Steps: Peripatetic Vision in Medieval China." In *Visuality before and beyond the Renaissance: Seeing as the Others See*, ed. Robert Nelson. New York: Cambridge University Press, 2000.

Wang, Eugene. *Shape of the Visual: Imaginary Topography in Medieval Chinese Buddhist Art*. Seattle: University of Washington Press, 2004.

Wu Hung. "Reborn in Paradise: A Case Study of Dunhuang Sūtra Painting and Its Religious, Ritual and Artistic Context." *Orientations* 23, no. 5 (1992): 52–60.

Wu Hung, and Ning Qiang. "Paradise Images in Early Chinese Art." In *The Flowering of a Foreign Faith: New Studies in Chinese Buddhist Art*, ed. Janet Baker. New Delhi: Marg, 1998.

EUGENE Y. WANG

PURE LAND BUDDHISM

Pure Land Buddhism signifies a wide array of practices and traditions within MAHĀYĀNA Buddhism directed to the Buddha AMITĀBHA (Amitāyus) and his realm, Sukhāvatī (Land of Bliss), which came to be referred to in Chinese as the *Pure Land* (*jingtu*; Japanese, *jōdo*). Mahāyāna recognized the existence of innumerable BUDDHAS and even BODHISATTVAS who presided over their own buddha-fields (*buddhakṣetra*), realms that they had purified or were in the process of purifying. Early on, some of these buddhas and their pure lands were singled out as the objects of particular scriptural and liturgical distinction. For example, the *Askṣobhyavyūha-sūtra* suggests that AKṢOBHYA and his buddha-field Abhirati in the eastern quadrant of the universe achieved a significant cultic status in Mahāyāna's early period. It was, however, Amitābha and his buddha-field in the west that ultimately came to attract the overwhelming preponderance of attention, particularly in East Asia, and to a modified extent in the VAJRAYĀNA Buddhism of the Tibetan cultural area. It is to this tradition, focused on Amitābha and his paradise Sukhāvatī, that the term *Pure Land Buddhism* conventionally applies.

Pure Land and Mahāyāna Buddhism

The Buddha Amitābha and his Land of Bliss were already amply attested to in early Mahāyāna scriptures. The story of Amitābha as found in the Longer SUKHĀVATĪVYŪHA-SŪTRA rehearsed elements that were fundamental to the Mahāyāna vision: the bodhisattva vocation with its initial set of vows and subsequent accumulation of merit through austerities, the attainment of supreme enlightenment, and the creation of a land through stored merit for the salvation of all SENTIENT BEINGS. Consequently, the practices affiliated with the Pure Land tradition were reflective of Mahāyāna values and were inextricably embedded within a complex of cultivational and liturgical regimens that prevailed throughout the Mahāyāna tradition.

Mahāyāna contains a soteriological paradox that historically led to wide disparities with regard to Pure Land practice, as well as to contrasting views on the nature and function of that practice. On the one hand, Amitābha's Pure Land itself was the result of cultivation of the bodhisattva PATH, thus serving as an example that encouraged emulation in all of those seeking the Pure Land. They too were expected to assiduously follow that path, rigorously engaging in the requisite spiritual disciplines and austerities, all the while attending to the welfare of all sentient beings. On the other hand, the Pure Land as a place of refuge and liberation was a creation of Amitābha's beneficent vows to save all sentient beings and as such became a goal for those seeking liberation not through their own effort but through faith in Amitābha's salvific power. Strengthening this latter view was the belief that grew up in some Mahāyāna circles that the dharma had entered into an age of decline in which the diminished capacities of adherents were no longer adequate to meet the rigorous demands of the traditional bodhisattva path. Thus, only through easier practices and through Amitābha's assistance could people hope to attain liberation. While the sectarian Pure Land movement that developed in Japan embraced the latter perspective, an overall examination of Pure Land tradition reveals that both of these seemingly contradictory perspectives have prevailed alongside each other for most of the tradition's history, and therefore both must be taken into account for a balanced approach to Pure Land developments. The requirement for an even-handed historical view in Pure Land also necessitates avoiding the facile distinction between monastic and lay practice that associates members of the monastic community with the rigors of the bodhisattva path and lay adherents with an easier course. Indeed, the very argument for easier practice came from members of the monastic community, while, conversely, we find laics in history emulating liturgical and meditative practices that had monastic origins.

Mindful recollection of the Buddha

Pure Land practice was initially predicated on the aspiration common throughout Mahāyāna to achieve proximity to a buddha either through a meditative vision or through REBIRTH in his Pure Land. This aspiration derived from a latent sense of regret frequently voiced in Buddhist scriptures with regard to Śākyamuni's departure and subsequent absence from this world, as well as from the abiding hope that liberation could be more easily achieved in the presence and under the tutelage of a buddha. This goal of seeking access to a buddha was thought to be best achieved through a practice known as "mindful recollection of the Buddha" (BUDDHĀNUSMṚTI), a discipline that had roots in early Buddhism and became a common feature in Mahāyāna scriptures. This meditative discipline most simply refers to the practice of calling to mind and concentrating on the qualities of a buddha, but in reality it embraces a wide range of contemplative objects and techniques. In the Pure Land tradition, the practice sometimes entailed concrete visualization of the Buddha Amitābha, his attendant bodhisattvas Avalokiteśvara and Mahāsthāmaprāpta, or the Land of Bliss. Then again, in contrast to these tangible visualizations, the practice at other times required a meditation on the formless and empty nature of the Buddha's ultimate reality, the *dharmakāya.* Meditative concentration was achieved by such diverse practices as fixing the mind on one or many aspects of the Buddha Amitābha's appearance, concentrating on the name of the Buddha, or vocally intoning that name through chant or speech. Furthermore, the practitioner could engage in the process through a variety of postures including sitting, standing, walking, or lying down.

The practice of *buddhānusmṛti* was accorded a central cultivational role in sūtras that dealt with Amitābha and his Pure Land. An early Mahāyāna scripture, the PRATYUTPANNASAMĀDHI-SŪTRA, called for an uninterrupted meditation on the Buddha Amitāyus for seven days and nights, promising that the Buddha would appear before the adherent at the end of that period. The previously mentioned Longer *Sukhāvatīvyūha-sūtra,* in presenting the conditions for rebirth, set forth the exclusive recollection of the Buddha of Measureless Life (Amitāyus), if even for ten moments of thought, as a requirement for all levels of spiritual capacity. Another scripture of non-Indian provenance, the *Guan Wuliangshou jing* (*Contemplation of the Buddha of Limitless Life Sūtra*), had as its main content the explication of thirteen different visualizations on various attributes of the Buddha and his Pure Land.

Meditative practice in East Asia and Tibet

The Chinese translation of the Sanskrit word *buddhānusmṛti* was *nianfo* (Japanese, *nenbutsu*), a term burdened with ambiguity as to the form of practice it denotes. In many contexts, *nianfo* commonly signifies a mental recollection of a Buddha's attributes. This discipline was also called *nianfo sanmei* (the *samādhi* of *buddhānusmṛti*), an expression that reinforced a contemplative emphasis by alluding to the meditative trance in which the Buddha would appear. In yet other contexts, the term *nianfo* came to refer to invoking the Buddha's name vocally. Despite this seeming contrast, it must be kept in mind that the recitation of the name, whether voiced or silent, chanted or spoken, was originally but one method of several in the mindful recollection of the Buddha. Steering away from this contemplative emphasis, the sectarian traditions of Japanese Pure Land Buddhism, Jōdo shū and Jōdo Shinshū, appealed to a distinction made by the Chinese monk Shandao (613–681), assigning recitation of the name a separate and superior status among the various practices. This recitation conventionally expressed as *Namo Amituo Fo* (Japanese, *Namu Amida Butsu*), a formula that was drawn from the *Guan Wuliangshou jing*, therefore came to eclipse all other practices within the sectarian Pure Land traditions. Western scholarship until recently has focused largely upon these traditions and therefore has tended to overlook the ongoing importance of the meditative tradition in East Asia, as well as in Tibet. Since the centrality of the vocal invocation as a distinct practice within the sectarian traditions is treated in other entries, the discussion below will avoid the bifurcation of the two practices and assume that the invocatory practice constituted one method of several within the practice of mindful recollection.

In China the practice of recollecting the Buddha was present from the outset of Pure Land belief. The scholar-monk HUIYUAN (334–416), whom the Chinese Buddhist tradition came to regard as the initiator of the Pure Land movement and therefore its first patriarch, founded a society of monks and elite gentry in 402 C.E. that adopted the buddha recollection of the *Pratyutpannasamādhi-sūtra* as its core practice. More than a century later, ZHIYI (538–597), the founder of the TIANTAI SCHOOL, incorporated the same sūtra's practice into his four-fold system of meditative practice. Zhiyi's system, which had as its goal the contemplative apprehension of ultimate reality, integrated the meditations into liturgical regimens performed in daily ritual cycles. These performances often included preparation of the ritual site, personal purification, offerings of flowers and incense, invitation and invocation of the deities, physical obeisance, confession of sins, and application of merit. In the Constantly Walking Samādhi, the second of the four practices, Zhiyi structured the *Pratyutpannasamādhi-sūtra*'s practice of mindful recollection around a strenuous ordeal that required the practitioner to continuously circumambulate an image of Amitābha in a dedicated hall throughout a period of ninety days, leaving the premises only to attend to bodily functions.

Zhiyi's liturgical and contemplative regimens continued to exert influence on the development of Pure Land in the Tiantai school in China, as well as its Japanese counterpart, the Tendai school. Zhiyi's ninety-day retreat was promoted by such prominent Tang-dynasty (618–907) figures as Chengyuan (712–742) and Fazhao (d. 822), who also created a musically based ritual for the community on Mount Wutai. During the Song dynasty (960–1279), the Tiantai monk Zunshi (964–1032), emulating the liturgical patterns established by Zhiyi, developed a number of rites and practices dedicated to Amitābha and to the achievement of rebirth in his Pure Land. Zunshi's rituals, which included a longer and a shorter penitential ceremony, came to hold a place of honor in subsequent ritual practice that has survived into the modern era.

During the aforementioned historical developments within the Tiantai school, the practice of recollection on Amitābha shifted in focus from the *Pratyutpannasamādhi-sūtra* to emphasis on the *Guan Wuliangshou jing*. Members of the Tiantai school in the Song dynasty consequently constructed retreats called Sixteen Visualization Halls that were based on the *Guan Wuliangshou jing* and consisted of a central hall at the middle of which stood an image of Amitābha. Around this cultic focal point were arranged a series of cells for retreatants dedicated to extended periods of ritual and contemplative practice.

The Tiantai school was not alone in promoting the practice of recollecting the Buddha as a Pure Land discipline. Members of the Huayan and Chan traditions also contributed to the understanding of the practice. Common to all these traditions, however, was a hierarchical ranking of the various practices signified by the term *nianfo*. Characteristic of this type of ranking was the fourfold distinction set forth by the great Chan–Huayan scholar ZONGMI (780–841), who assigned the recitation of the name to the lowest position, with contemplation of a sculpted or painted image, visualization either of a single attribute or of the whole body of the Buddha, and contemplation of the truly real (that is, apprehension of the *dharmakāya*) following in ascending order. Implicit in this categorization and others like it in other traditions is the notion that what is ultimately apprehended in contemplation is the identity of Buddha and his field with one's own mind. This identity constituted part of a comprehensive idealistic philosophical system embraced by some members of the Tiantai, Huayan, and Chan traditions. These philosophers saw all reality as ultimately reducible to mind, and in some cases applied this idealistic approach to Pure Land. One of the most famous of such articulations of mind-only Pure Land was that produced by the Chan scholar YANSHOU (904–975). Members of the Chan school sometimes adopted this view as the basis of a polemic that argued for the superiority of the goals and practices of Chan over the aspiration to rebirth and its attendant practices found within Pure Land.

In Tibetan Buddhism, although the devotion to Amitābha did not acquire the same degree of prominence as in East Asia since his cult coexisted alongside practices dedicated to other buddhas and their pure lands, the contemplation of Amitābha and his realm, nevertheless, historically has come to occupy a significant position in tantric practice. During the twelfth to the fourteenth centuries, Sukhāvatī figured prominently in visions of RNYING MA (NYINGMA) masters among whom Dam pa Bde gshegs (1122–1192) developed a tantric *sādhana* for visualizing Amitābha, along with a prayer for rebirth in his land. The BKA' BRGYUD (KAGYU) tradition accorded special significance to a tantric technique called "transference" (*'pho ba*), in which consciousness at the moment of DEATH could be projected to a desired realm of rebirth. Later in history this goal was explicitly linked to the attainment of Sukhāvatī. Yet another type of Pure Land contemplation is found in a "sleep exercise" (*nyal bsgom*), made popular by the SA SKYA (SAKYA) order. In this practice, the adept before sleep visualizes himself as a deity in Sukhāvatī before a seated Amitābha. The visualization, which culminates in a dissolving of Amitābha into the adept, is practiced with the belief that it will lead to eventual rebirth in Sukhāvatī.

Other practices

The various meditative disciplines described above have occupied a significant but by no means exclusive position in the tradition of Pure Land practice. Sometimes, general Buddhist merit-gaining activities, such as the strict observance of PRECEPTS, the chanting or copying of scriptures, the commissioning of carved images, and other forms of donative activity, have been imbued with Pure Land significance. Also throughout Mahāyāna traditions are found prayers and, in Vajrayāna, the recitation of DHĀRAṆĪ that seek rebirth for oneself and members of one's family. More proper to the original Mahāyāna vision, Pure Land practice has often been integrated into the larger context of the bodhisattva vocation with its concomitant host of activities aimed at the acquisition and transference of merit as well as at the aiding of all sentient beings. In Pure Land accounts, we find devotees taking the bodhisattva precepts and engaging in bodhisattva acts, such as the building of bridges and the digging of wells, the releasing of living creatures destined for slaughter, the conversion of people from taking of life, the eating of meat, the providing of hostels for travelers, and the burial of the dead. On a more extreme note, some Pure Land adherents undertook the physical austerities (*dhūta*) enjoined in the bodhisattva precepts and Mahāyāna scriptures, such as the LOTUS SŪTRA (SADDHARMAPUṆḌARĪKA-SŪTRA). Practitioners burnt fingers, limbs, and sometimes even their entire person both as acts of devotion to the *Lotus Sūtra* and as deeds done in the hope of rebirth in Pure Land. Beyond these acts of SELF-IMMOLATION, religious suicide within Pure Land found expression in Kamakura Japan when devotees drowned themselves in expectation of rebirth.

The goal of rebirth in the Pure Land made the period directly preceding and that immediately following death a critical time fraught with both danger and opportunity in the determination of one's future destiny. This resulted in the creation of deathbed and funerary practices that aided the dying and the newly deceased in the attainment of Pure Land. The content of one's last thoughts were thought to be the crucial factor in determining one's next rebirth, and thus deathbed rites were designed to assist the dying in forging a karmic link with the Pure Land by fixing their mind on Amitābha. Depending on the dying person's disposition, deathbed rituals might involve repentance, the chanting of sūtras, or, most importantly, mindful recollection of Amitābha (*nianfo, nenbutsu*), deriving largely from the promise of the *Guan Wuliangshou jing* that ten uninterrupted thoughts on the Buddha would lead to rebirth even for those who had accumulated a lifetime of evil karma. Increasingly, this latter practice was interpreted in terms of vocally reciting the Buddha's name. The dying person was encouraged to intone the Buddha's name, and, if that was no longer possible, it was done for him or her by assistants. He or she would be often placed in front of an image of Amitābha and given a cord to hold that was attached to Amitābha's right hand. This symbolic link portended both the aspirant's hope for rebirth and the grace and power of the Buddha flowing through the connection. Funeral rites in East Asia and in the Tibetan cultural area have often attended to the theme of rebirth in Sukhāvatī through liturgical expression and prayers.

Underpinning deathbed and funeral practices was a promise articulated in Amitābha's nineteenth vow that at the moment of death Amitābha and his attendant bodhisattvas would appear before the devotee. In Japan, this belief inspired the creation of artistic and ritual representations of this crucial event signifying the attainment of rebirth. *Raigōzu*, paintings depicting Amitābha and his retinue descending on a white cloud to meet the dying devotee, became popular during the Heian period. The same period also witnessed the widespread enactment of *mukaekō*, a ceremony in which the Buddha's coming was recreated in song and dance accompanied by verbal chanting of the *nenbutsu*.

The focus upon the events surrounding a devotee's death similarly gave rise to prognosticatory practices aimed at discerning evidence confirming the successful attainment of rebirth. Among the numerous signs accompanying the death of a devotee, deathbed and postmortem accounts report apparitions, DREAMS, the presence of fragrances or auras at the moment of death, the preservation of the devotee's body, or the discovery of relics (*śarīra*) in the ashes of the adherent's cremated body. The narration of these auspicious signs became a central element in collections of Pure Land biographies that proliferated in China and Japan with the development of Pure Land belief.

These compendia offer windows through time on Pure Land adherents from a wide range of religious and social positions. The biographical collections include hagiographies of monks and laity, men and women, elite and poor. Besides their edificatory role, the collections were historically instrumental in creating a sense of Pure Land as a unified tradition, a perception that was reinforced by the Chinese Pure Land biographical collections of the Song period, which constructed a patriarchal lineage for the tradition.

Pure Land societies

Although the meditative practices enumerated above could be understood as suited for solitary cultivation, it is equally important to emphasize the communal settings in which Pure Land came to flourish. Chinese Buddhists traditionally traced the origins of Pure Land in China back to the aforementioned Huiyuan, who in 402 C.E. on Mount Lu organized a society of 123 members drawn from the monastic community and the gentry elite. The members of this society took a solemn vow before an image of Amitābha that whoever achieved the Pure Land first would aid those remaining behind in attaining rebirth. This association, which was later named the White Lotus Society (*Bailian she*), became a paradigm in the formation of societies (*jieshe*) that proliferated particularly during the Song dynasty. Many of these later societies differed from Huiyuan's confraternity in a number of significant ways. Their membership was drawn not from the elite alone but from a wider societal spectrum, including women and people of the lower classes. The size of these societies was sometimes in the thousands, far exceeding the modest size of Huiyuan's society. Furthermore, these associations often engaged in practices that did not always explicitly or exclusively address Amitābha and the Pure Land or that differed from the meditative emphasis in Huiyuan's group. Lastly, some of these societies were founded and led by lay people rather than monks. This is notably the case of the White Lotus movement founded by Mao Ziyuan (d.u.) in the twelfth century.

This period in which Pure Land associations multiplied in China also witnessed a proliferation of similar associations in Korea and Japan. The Korean monk CHINUL (1158–1210), who is best known for the Koryŏ period (918–1392) revival of the Sŏn (Chan) tradition, is credited with initiating a movement of religious societies (*kyŏlsa*; Chinese, *jieshe*) that drew inspiration from the Chinese movement of the same era. In Heian Japan, the scholar Yoshishige Yasutane (d. 1002), who is famous for compiling the first Japanese collection of Pure Land biographies, and the Tendai monk Genshin (942–1017), renowned for his seminal work on Pure Land, the *Ōjōyōshū* (*Essentials of Rebirth*), were active in establishing and participating in societies such as the *Kangakue* (Society for the Advancement of Learning) and the *Nijūgozammaie* (Twenty-five [Member] Samādhi Assembly) that had a Pure Land orientation. Besides regular gatherings in which the name of Amitābha was recited, the *Nijugozammaie* also provided support for sick and dying members, adopting many of the deathbed practices discussed above. In contrast to these associations with elite membership, groups with members from all social strata were enlisted by the itinerant holy men (*hijiri*) who spread Pure Land practice among the masses. Perhaps the most famous of these was Kūya (903–972), who proclaimed the vocal recitation of the Buddha's name from street corners.

See also: **Buddhānusmṛti (Recollection of the Buddha); Decline of the Dharma; Nenbutsu (Chinese, Nianfo; Korean, Yŏmbul); Pure Lands; Pure Land Schools**

Bibliography

Dobbins, James C. "Genshin's Deathbed Nembutsu Ritual in Pure Land Buddhism." In *Religions of Japan in Practice*, ed. George J. Tanabe, Jr. Princeton, NJ: Princeton University Press, 1999.

Foard, James; Solomon, Michael; and Payne, Richard M., eds. *The Pure Land Tradition: History and Development.* Berkeley: Center for South and Southeast Asian Studies, University of California at Berkeley, 1996.

Getz, Daniel A. "T'ien-t'ai Pure Land Societies and the Creation of the Pure Land Patriarchate." In *Buddhism in the Sung*, ed. Peter N. Gregory and Daniel A. Getz. Honolulu: University of Hawaii Press, 1999.

Gómez, Luis O., trans. *The Land of Bliss: The Paradise of the Buddha of Measureless Light: Sanskrit and Chinese Versions of the Sukhāvatīvyūha Sutras.* Honolulu: University of Hawaii Press, 1996.

Stevenson, Daniel. "The Four Kinds of Samādhi in Early T'ien-t'ai Buddhism." In *Traditions of Meditation in Chinese Buddhism,* ed. Peter N. Gregory. Honolulu: University of Hawaii Press, 1986.

Stevenson, Daniel. "Deathbed Testimonials of the Pure Land Faithful." In *Buddhism in Practice,* ed. Donald Lopez. Princeton, NJ: Princeton University Press, 1995.

Stevenson, Daniel. "Pure Land Buddhist Worship and Meditation in China." In *Buddhism in Practice,* ed. Donald Lopez. Princeton, NJ: Princeton University Press, 1995.

Williams, Paul. *Mahāyāna Buddhism: The Doctrinal Foundations.* London: Routledge, 1989.

Zürcher, Erik. *The Buddhist Conquest of China,* 2 vols. Leiden, Netherlands: Brill, 1959.

DANIEL A. GETZ

PURE LANDS

The English term *Pure Land* is used as a handy equivalent for the East Asian notion of a purified buddha-field, a large extent of space made pure and beautiful by the presence of a BUDDHA or BODHISATTVA. In its specific usage the phrase "the Pure Land" is one such purified world, the buddha-field of the Buddha AMITĀBHA. The English term has no Indian antecedent and is a direct translation of Chinese *jingtu* (pure field, pure land), or its Japanese equivalent *jōdo.*

Buddha-fields, pure and impure

Buddhist cosmology depicts a universe formed of multiple worlds (*lokadhātu*) of varying sizes and characteristics. Some of these worlds have never had a buddha, but others are the special fields of practice (*kṣetra*) of individual bodhisattvas, who, upon attaining awakening, will make this territory the field within which they exert their saving power and share their immeasurable merit in their role as perfect buddhas.

Called *buddha-fields* (*buddhakṣetra*), these worlds are made beautiful and perfect by the meritorious power of the buddhas that inhabit them and by the power of that buddha's solemn bodhisattva vows. However, buddha-fields may have varying spiritual climates or degrees of perfection, and they are accordingly classified as *pure* or *mixed.* Worlds where the saving action of a buddha has not yet had its effect, or those that lack a buddha and are therefore technically not yet buddha-fields, are sometimes known as *impure* worlds. The world we inhabit, known as the Sahā World, is considered one such imperfect world, despite the effects of Śākyamuni's awakening and ministry. Other worlds have been completely "purified" by various buddhas and bodhisattvas, and are held as models of what a fully purified world, a pure land, would be.

As long as a bodhisattva is still seeking full awakening, his "field" is not a "pure land"; thus, *pure* or *purified* denote the result of a long process by which the bodhisattva transforms a common world into a paradise or an ideal and marvel-filled world. This realm is "pure" in the sense that evil, disease, and suffering have been eliminated by the bodhisattva's vows and actions; but it is also said that the field is "adorned" because it is made rich and beautiful with extraordinary marvels and treasures (jewel trees, charming ponds, spiritually uplifting music, etc.). Such a perfect world is a paradise-like place in which believers hope to be reborn after they die at the end of their present life of suffering.

Those pure lands are places of maximum bliss (Chinese, *jile*; Japanese, *gokuraku*), paradisiacal lands, but they must be distinguished from other Indian notions of heavenly and earthly paradises. The imagery used to describe pure lands is indeed similar to the language used to describe the heavenly blissful realms of the gods (*devaloka*), the royal cities of universal monarchs, and the carefree life in the mythical land of Uttarakuru. However, unlike a pure land, these other paradisiacal realms are not completely free from the pains of REBIRTH, nor are they places favorable to the attainment of the final rest of NIRVĀṆA.

Buddhist paradises

The conception of a pure land is also different from Western notions of paradise: A pure land is not technically a place of pristine innocence before "the Fall," nor is it the place or time for the souls or resurrected bodies of the blessed to dwell with a creator after death or after the restoration of the original paradise at the end of time. Pure lands are worlds parallel to ours, existing at the same time as our world, but perfected for the express purpose of allowing living beings the opportunity to pursue liberation in a favorable environment. They are places where one can escape from (in fact one will dwell outside of) the six REALMS OF EXISTENCE described in Buddhist COSMOLOGY. Perhaps one point of similarity to some Western conceptions of heavenly glory is the idea that pure lands are communities of saints, and that their inhabitants may influence the course of life in our world—primarily through the saving power of the buddha presiding over the pure land, but also because, as bodhisattvas, the inhabitants of a pure land may descend upon our lowly world or travel outside the pure land to worship buddhas and save SENTIENT BEINGS in many faraway universes.

Although the purification of a world system is the work of only one bodhisattva, and there can be only one buddha presiding over a pure land, the number of pure lands in the universe is as great as many times the grains of sand in the Ganges River. Scriptural texts, however, usually mention only ten pure lands by name, one for each of the main and intermediate points of the compass, and at the zenith and the nadir. But a more common number of pure lands is four, one for each of the main directions of the compass.

Only a few of these lands seem to have a clear mythology associated with a system of worship and belief. Among the purified fields associated with specific myths and texts or connected to special practices one must mention above all the western Pure Land of Buddha Amitābha, called Sukhāvatī (Blissful). But also of historical significance are the eastern Pure Land of AKṢOBHYA, Abhirati (Enchantment), and the eastern land of Bhaiṣajyaguru, Vaiḍūryanirbhāsa (Shining like Beryl). Still, the most famous is unquestionably Amitābha's Sukhāvatī; it is the most common referent of the phrase "the Pure Land" (Chinese, *jingtu*; Japanese, *jōdo*, or for that matter, *jile* and *gokuraku*). Thus, the hope of being reborn in Amitābha's Pure Land is often synonymous with "Pure Land belief."

The Buddha Amitābha (Japanese, Amida) obtained this pure land as the result of the solemn vows (in East Asia traditionally counted as forty-eight) he made when, as the bodhisattva Dharmākara, he promised to seek enlightenment in order to create a paradise where those who heard his name and believed in him could be reborn. The hope of rebirth in Sukhāvatī and faith in Amitābha's saving grace, like beliefs and practices associated with other pure lands, is firmly grounded in generalized MAHĀYĀNA beliefs such as the bodhisattva vows, the saving powers of buddhas and bodhisattvas, the theme of bodhisattvas traveling to visit distant buddha-fields where they worship myriad buddhas, and the power of the transfer of merit.

Sukhāvatī is depicted as a paradise, that is, a garden-like enclosure, the inhabitants of which know nothing but beauty and bliss. In marvelous gardens and groves, birds and plants preach the dharma, and the presence of the Buddha Amitābha is accessible to living beings in varying degrees and guarantees the effortless attainment of nirvāṇa. Living beings from impure lands who hear the name of the Buddha Amitābha and have faith in his vows will be reborn in his pure land immediately after they die in their own world.

In some cases the mythology allows for pure lands that are not technically purified worlds—thus, MAITREYA, the buddha of the future, transforms the place he inhabits into a pure land by virtue of his presence. Yet his place of dwelling forms part of our world, for it is the heaven of the deities known as Tuṣita, located among the heavenly planes that rise above Mount Meru; once reborn in this world Maitreya will inhabit a royal city, Ketumatī, that also shares some features with conceptions of the pure lands. East Asian Buddhists have identified other locations in our world as technically pure lands; this is the case, for instance, of the Vulture Peak near Rājagṛha, where it is said that Śākyamuni preached the Mahāyāna sūtras, or of Avalokiteśvara's mythic island dwelling called Potalaka. Additionally, the literature mentions many more abstract notions of purified worlds, such as Vairocana's Lotus Pure Land.

Imagining pure worlds

Of course, even pure lands presumed to be outside our world are given a concrete, if mythical, location (Sukhāvatī is trillions of worlds away), and they have very concrete topographic and material characteristics (Sukhāvatī is completely flat, Abhirati has mountains). Yet, this does not preclude metaphoric or atopic understandings of the reality of the pure land. Many Buddhists have rejected or qualified the notion of a distant pure land, or at the very least have emphasized the importance of "purifying" or transforming our own world. Some equate the purification of one's own mind with the purification of society at large, so that this, our world of suffering and conflict, can or should become the pure land. These views were particularly important in the development of traditions fusing meditation with FAITH in the pure land, but the idea of the pure land as a state in this life rather than, or in addition to, being a distant place recurs throughout the history of Mahāyāna Buddhism. Buddhists have argued at times that our world can be a pure land, either by virtue of the power of a pure mind (a key concept in the *Vimalakīrtinirdeśa*), or because the practice of the dharma can transform a human society into a holy land (a common theme in the mythology of Buddhism

Amitābha in the Western Paradise, from a painting at Dunhuang. (Chinese, ca. 618–907.) © Pierre Colombel/Corbis. Reproduced by permission.

generally). The first of these ideas is not only an anagogic understanding of the concept, but also a psychological or epistemological understanding of the ideals of purity, beauty, and perfection. The second conception has social implications and may overlap with millenarian hopes that have appeared throughout the history of Buddhism.

The idea of a "pure land of the mind" pervades the CHAN SCHOOL tradition even among those who do not adopt pure land practices. In his *Zazen wasan* (*Hymn in Praise of Zazen*) the Japanese Zen Master HAKUIN EKAKU (1686–1768) states that "the pure land is near at hand" for one who practices dhyāna, and that for one who experiences no-mind, "this very world is the Pure Lotus Land." In a more systematic way the idea appears in Tiantai theological writings, and even among the Chinese founders of pure land theology and practice. Thus, Shandao (613–681) explains that even while still in this world one is reborn in the pure land the moment one recites the *nianfo* (Japanese, *nenbutsu*). Such conceptions may resurface under favorable social conditions, as may have been the case among the reformers of Buddhism during the Chinese Republican period, or some of the Meiji and Taishō Japanese Pure Land thinkers, and perhaps in the *myōkōnin* movement of the same period of rapid modernization and rising nationalistic fervor.

The East Asian concept of the pure land does not have an exact equivalent in the Buddhist literatures of Tibet and Southeast Asia. However, one may speak of a pan-Asian Buddhist belief in a purified and beautified paradise that offers ease of life, freedom from suffering, and the opportunity for a long life dedicated to spiritual pursuits in the presence of a buddha. In Tibet this belief is generally firmly set in the scholastic edifice of Mahāyāna and tantric ritual practice, and does not take the independent life that it took in East Asia. The pure land figures prominently in appeals to Amitāyus (Amitābha's alter ego) for long life, and for a sojourn in the pure land as a respite from the sorrows of this world.

Graphic representations of different pure lands played an important role in East Asian iconography and religious architecture, such as on the murals at DUNHUANG. Similar motifs appear as MAṆḌALAS (Japanese, *mandara*) or schematic representations of the pure land, be it Amitābha's land, as in the *Taima Mandara* (based on the *Guan Wuliangshou jing, Contemplation of the Buddha of Limitless Life Sūtra*), or one of the representations of mythic geographies, as in the Kumano Mandara. The practice of using images of Amitābha for making believers at the moment of their death mindful of their hope of being reborn in his pure land also resulted in a variety of representations. The most famous among these are depictions of Amitābha's descent with his retinue of bodhisattvas "coming to meet" (*raigō*) and welcome believers who are on their deathbeds.

The idea of a pure land plays a symbolic and iconic role that goes well beyond the technical theological sense of the concept. The concept has a more general manifestation: a paradisiacal or utopic place in which bliss and enlightenment are possible through the beneficent agency of a supremely enlightened and virtuous being, namely a buddha. In this broader sense, earthly locations and religious monuments may be seen as equivalents or embodiments of pure lands. For instance, the temple of Byōdōin in Uji, Japan, represents a pavilion in Amitābha's Pure Land. The POTALA in Lhasa represents the pure abode of Spyanras gzigs (Chenresik; Avalokiteśvara); the Potala is itself reproduced in the summer palace of the Manchu emperors in Jehol. A combination of several of these themes is seen in the temple complex of Jōruriji, near Nara, Japan, a Shingon temple named after Bhaiṣajyaguru's Pure Land. In this complex, two buildings arranged around a pond represent the pure lands of Amida (Amitābha—to the west) and Yakushi (Bhaiṣajyaguru—to the east); believers position themselves on the eastern bank of the pond, which represents our impure world, and look across to the Amida temple (iconically representing the pure land as depicted in the *Guan Wuliangshou jing*. Additionally, specific topographic configurations may be understood as pure lands. This is the case in Japan where, for instance, the Jōdosan peak in Tateyama and the three mountains of the Kumano shrine are regarded as literal and ritual pure lands.

The great variety of conceptions and representations of the concept need not be interpreted as an overflowing of the narrow boundaries of the more technical conception of a purified buddha-field. In earthly or iconic representations the idea of a pure land retains its mythic and metaphoric sense of a place made pure and beautiful by the saving presence of extraordinary holiness, especially the marvelous effects of the sacred presence—in person, icon, or memory—of a buddha or a bodhisattva. One may nevertheless summarize the above themes within five categories of pure land: (1) extraterrestrial pure lands of the future, objects of faith and goals of hope for rebirth—today the most common conception of the pure land; (2) cosmographic pure lands, that is, adorned extraterrestrial fields of the many buddhas and bodhisattvas of the universe; (3) topographic pure lands, which form part of concrete locations within mythic geographies; (4) millenarian, utopic, or ideal pure lands requiring a radical transformation of the present world in which we live; and (5) metaphoric or psychological pure lands, which are summarized by the phrase "a pure mind is the pure land."

See also: **Dhyāna (Trance State); Heavens; Hells; Pure Land Art; Pure Land Buddhism; Pure Land Schools**

Bibliography

Fujita, Kōtatsu. "Pure and Impure Lands." In *The Encyclopedia of Religion*, ed. Mircea Eliade, Vol. 12. New York: Macmillan, 1987.

Gómez, Luis O., trans. and ed. *The Land of Bliss: The Paradise of the Buddha of Measureless Light: Sanskrit and Chinese Versions of the Sukhāvatīvyūha Sūtras* (1996), 3rd printing, corrected edition. Honolulu: University of Hawaii Press, 2000.

Kloetzli, Randy. *Buddhist Cosmology, from Single World System to Pure Land: Science and Theology in the Images of Motion and Light.* Delhi: Motilal Banarsidass, 1983.

Lamotte, Étienne, trans. and ed. *L'enseignement de Vimalakīrti.* Louvain, Belgium: Institut Orientaliste, 1962. English translation: *The Teaching of Vimalakīrti*, tr. Sara Webb-Boin. London: Pāli Text Society, 1976.

MacCulloch, J. A. "Blest, Abode of the (Japanese)." *Encyclopaedia of Religion and Ethics*, 2 (1927): 700b–702a.

Rowell, Teresina. "The Background and Early Use of the *Buddha-kṣetra* Concept." *Eastern Buddhist* 6 (1933): 199–246, 379–431; and 7 (1936): 131–145.

Sadakata, Akira. *Buddhist Cosmology: Philosophy and Origins*, tr. Gaynor Sekimori. Tokyo: Kosei, 1997.

LUIS O. GÓMEZ

PURE LAND SCHOOLS

The MAHĀYĀNA sūtras developed considerable lore based on the idea of different buddhas and bodhisattvas dwelling in buddha-fields (*buddhakṣetra*). It is common for practitioners to meditate on, make offerings to, chant sūtras about, and recite the name or MANTRA of a particular BUDDHA or BODHISATTVA. These

Mahāyāna expressions developed out of the *darśana* complex, which is well documented in the earliest materials, and were seen as part of the overall institutional fabric of Indian Mahāyāna. (Buddha *darśana* refers to "seeing" the buddha and entering his nirvanic power, which leads to spriritual progress.) The core Mahāyāna idea is to cultivate a *darśanic* relationship with the buddha and thus gain awakening, or one could aim at future birth in the buddha-field. The genre of Mahāyāna literature that developed these ideas was instrumental in the formation of the tantras. AMITĀBHA Buddha and his accompanying bodhisattvas, Avalokiteśvara and Mahāsthāmaprāpta, are the focus of the Pure Land tradition in East Asia.

Pure Land teachings in China

In China, the institutionalization of the Pure Land teachings and the first line of transmission began with the founding of the White Lotus Society by HUIYUAN (334–416) on Mount Lu. This society's practice was based on the PRATYUTPANNASAMĀDHI-SŪTRA. The lead devotee was Liu Yimin, one of the eighteen sages of Mount Lu, who wrote the society's manifesto and a collection of chants. The area became a center of Pure Land teachings.

The *Larger* SUKHĀVATĪVYŪHA-SŪTRA, a major text in the tradition, had been translated twice by the mid-third century. In 402 the *Amitābha Sūtra* (also called the *Amida Sūtra* or *Smaller Sukhāvatīvyūha-sūtra*) and later the *Daśabhūmikavibhāṣā* (*Treatise on the Ten Stages*), attributed to NĀGĀRJUNA (ca. second century), were translated by KUMĀRAJĪVA (350–409/413). The *Guan Wuliangshou jing* (*Contemplation of the Buddha of Limitless Life Sūtra*) is claimed by tradition to have been translated between 424 and 453, though it is probably a Chinese or Central Asian composition. Once these three major sūtras and one main commentary became available, the Pure Land teachings moved away from being solely based on the *Pratyutpannasamādhi-sūtra*.

Tanluan (476–542) became interested in Pure Land teaching through the influence of Bodhiruci (sixth century), who translated the *Jingtu lun* (*Discourse on the Pure Land*) attributed to VASUBANDHU (fourth century) in 531. Tanluan wrote an extensive commentary to this work, as well as *Zan Amitofo ji* (*Verses in Praise of Amida Buddha*) and *Lüe lun anlejingtu yi* (*An Abridged Discourse on the Pure Land of Peace and Bliss*). Tanluan accepted the *Daśabhūmikavibhāṣā*'s distinction of the difficult PATH (the path of sages) and the easy path (the Pure Land path). He believed that Amitābha's Pure Land was the ultimate reality; that reciting Amitābha's name (Chinese, *nianfo*; Sanskrit, *buddhānusmṛti*) eliminates negative karma; and that the practice of *nianfo* requires a mind of true "confidence." He also described how an accumulation of positive karma aids rebirth and is distributed when returning to aid sentient beings, and he accepted the divisions of the dharmakāya into a dharma-nature aspect and an expedience aspect. Tanluan coined the term *other power*, meaning not relying on one's false notion of a self and its abilities but on the nirvanic power of Amitābha, a refinement of the Mahāyāna concept of *adhiṣṭhāna* (base, power, approach, establish). According to Japanese sources, this constitutes a second transmission lineage.

One of the greatest successors in Tanluan's line is Daochuo (562–645), who, inspired by Tanluan's writings, wrote *Anle ji* (*A Collection of [Passages Concerning Birth in the Land of] Peace and Bliss*), and promoted the idea of the DECLINE OF THE DHARMA and the idea that the *nianfo* samādhi was the highest samādhi. Shandao (613–681) was the most influential master in this lineage. At first he studied on Mount Lu and achieved some success practicing according to the *Pratyutpannasamādhi-sūtra*. He later became Daochuo's disciple and was able to attain the *nianfo* samādhi. Shandao reaffirmed Tanluan's and Daochuo's positions while developing further the overall doctrine. Although he discussed many Pure Land practices, he placed great emphasis on *nianfo*; he taught that *nianfo* was sufficient for rebirth in the Pure Land and that Amitābha was a *saṃbhogakāya* buddha. Shandao delineated three types of confidence: sincere confidence, deep confidence, and confidence that seeks rebirth. Shandao also taught visualization methods and repentance, and developed the famous parable of the two rivers (fire-anger and water-greed) and the white path (the Pure Land path leading from SAṂSĀRA to NIRVĀṆA) over the rivers. On the near side Śākyamuni stands, indicating that we should cross. On the far side, Amitābha stands, indicating that we should come.

A third line of Pure Land began with Cimin (680–748), who had traveled in India and began spreading Pure Land teachings after his return. Cimin composed *Jingtu cibei ji* (*The Pure Land Compassion Collection*; partially extant), *Xifang zan* (*Western Quarter Chant*), and *Pratyutpannasamādhi Chant*. His teachings emphasized meditation, study, recitation, and precepts.

The line that developed from the *Pratyutpannasamādhi-sūtra* also become part of the TIANTAI SCHOOL as ZHIYI

(538–597) incorporated it into his system of practice. Zhiyi was a devotee of Amitābha (and other buddhas). In addition, he worked on the problem of classifying the different types of Pure Lands and developed the *constant walking samādhi,* which is focused on Amitābha, a core practice for Tiantai.

From the Tang dynasty on, Tiantai forms of Pure Land practice were influenced by developments both within the school and from outside. Tiantai followers helped make Pure Land part of daily life during the Song dynasty (960–1279) and thereafter by forming White Lotus societies and engaging in other activities to spread the tradition.

The Pure Land teachings were also influential in the CHAN SCHOOL. The Tiantai form influenced the fourth Chan patriarch Daoxin (580–651). Xuanshi, a disciple of the fifth patriarch, Hongren (688–761), founded the Southern Mountain Chan of the Nian Fo Gate school. Baizhang (749–814) incorporated Pure Land practices into his Chan rules, which are the behavioral code for Chan monasteries. YANSHOU (904–975) was influenced by Cimin's line. Of particular note is Yinyan Longqi (1592–1673), who became the founder of the Ōbaku Zen school in Japan. The idea of Pure Land practice even becomes the KŌAN, "Who recites the *nian fo.*"

There were many significant figures in Chinese Buddhist history who, although masters of different teachings such as Huayan and Sanlun, were influential in the overall development of Pure Land thought and practice. In fact, Pure Land teachings became so ubiquitous in Chinese Buddhism that to speak of them as a *school* is a misnomer.

Pure Land teachings in Japan

Gyōgi (668–749), while cultivating donations for the building of Tōdaiji in Nara, spread the Pure Land teachings to the populace by publicly reciting the *nenbutsu* (Chinese, *nianfo*) and teaching people about the Pure Land in their homes. Chikō (709–780), a resident of Nara's Gangōji, wrote a now lost commentary to Vasubandhu's *Discourse* and had a MAṆḌALA painted after his vision of the Pure Land. These are the major Pure Land activities during the early period.

SAICHŌ (767–822), the founder of Tendai (Chinese, Tiantai) in Japan, introduced the teachings on Amitābha associated with this line of transmission. ENNIN (794–864), Saicho's main disciple in addition to those mentioned above, learned the "*nianfo* in five movements" while in China. Upon his return to Japan, he blended the "constant walking samadhi" with the "five movements" and created the nonstop (*fudan*) *nenbutsu.* He also seems to have known some esoteric aspects of Amitābha lore. With these beginnings Tendai became the fountainhead of Pure Land teachings in Japan for many centuries with masters like Ryōgen (912–985), Ryōnin (1072–1134), and many more. Of special distinction is the great master and prolific writer GENSHIN (942–1017), who composed some twenty works on Pure Land teachings, including the celebrated *Ōjōyōshū* (*Essentials for Birth*).

The Heian period witnessed Amitābha sages who helped spread the teachings to the general population. Several of these are historically significant. Kōya (903–972), a Tendai monk, performed many good works and taught the *nenbutsu* in the Nagoya, Kyoto, and northern Japan. Senkan (918–983), Kōya's disciple, wrote *Gokurakukoku Mida wasan* (*Sukhāvatī Realm Amida Chant*) and many other works. Kōya strictly observed the PRECEPTS and established eight rules and ten vows for his disciples. In addition, masters associated with many other schools of Japanese Buddhism also practiced and promoted Pure Land teachings.

The Kamakura period saw an emphasis on finding the one primary practice that was sufficient for awakening, an effort that brought theretofore exclusive practices to the fore and led to a simplification of considerable lore throughout Japanese Buddhism. The first major figure to address this effort as it related to Pure Land teachings was HŌNEN (1133–1212), a learned Tendai priest. He wrote a commentary to Genshin's work, which became the standard of interpretation. In 1198 Hōnen wrote *Senchaku hongan nenbutsu shū* (*Passages on the Selection of the Nenbutsu in the Original Vow*), which explained the essentials of the *nenbutsu* way, including exclusive recitation, theory of the Pure Land lineage, emphasis on the three sūtras, and welcoming by Amitābha at the time of death. Hōnen's writings generally accepted the interpretation of the Shandao line. He also transmitted the bodhisattva precepts, and his teachings formed the basis of the Jōdo school.

Among Hōnen's important disciples, SHINRAN (1173–1262) is of particular note. Like Hōnen, Shinran was first trained as a Tendai scholar-practitioner. He lived as an openly married priest and propagated Pure Land teachings near eastern Tokyo. He wrote a number of works including *Kyōgyōshinshō* (*Teaching, Practice, Faith, and Attainment*). A new sect (Jōdo Shinshū) was based on his interpretations of the Pure Land teachings. Shinran considered Amitābha to be the *Adi* Buddha, and he emphasizes "other power," exclusive *nenbutsu,* crosswise transcendence (instant and gradual attainment of awakening with Pure Land birth), the disadvantages of the path of sages, and the advantages of the Pure Land path. He also emphasized one vehicle (the *nenbutsu*), the dharma ending age, and that "confidence" or "faith" is endowed by the Tathāgata, is Buddha-nature, and is the key to liberation.

The last great Pure Land master of the Kamakura period was IPPEN CHISHIN (1239–1289), who studied under a second-generation disciple of Hōnen. Ippen had an awakening while in retreat at Kumanojin-ji and afterward spread the "dancing nenbutsu" teaching, which expresses the joy of the liberating power of Amitābha. The Ji school is based on his teachings.

Although Chinese and Japanese practices and interpretations have developed along different lines, taken as a whole they help form a rich fabric for the tapestry of the greater Pure Land tradition.

See also: **Buddhānusmṛti (Recollection of the Buddha); Hōryūji and Tōdaiji; Kamakura Buddhism, Japan; Nenbutsu (Chinese, Nianfo; Korean, Yŏmbul); Pure Land Buddhism**

Bibliography

Foard, James; Solomon, Michael; and Payne, Richard K.; eds. *The Pure Land Tradition: History and Development.* Berkeley: Regents of the University of California, 1996.

Haar, B. J. ter. *The White Lotus Teachings in Chinese Religious History.* Honolulu: University of Hawaii Press, 1992.

Inagaki, Hisao. *The Three Pure Land Sūtras.* Kyoto: Nagata Bunshodo, 1994.

Ono, Gemmyo. "On the Pure Land Doctrine of Tz'u-Min." *Eastern Buddhist* 5, nos. 2–3 (1930): 200–210.

A. W. BARBER

R

RĀHULA

Rāhula was the son of Siddhārtha Gautama, the Buddha-to-be. On hearing the news of Rāhula's birth, according to paracanonical literature, Siddhārtha Gautama immediately decided to renounce the world and go forth into homelessness, considering the birth of a son an obstruction in his search for truth. The name *Rāhula* literally means "little Rāhu"; Rāhu is the demon formerly believed to obstruct the sun and the moon and thus cause eclipses. When the Buddha visited his hometown for the first time after his realization of buddhahood, his former wife sent Rāhula to his father to ask him for his inheritance. Not receiving any response, Rāhula followed the Buddha, repeating his request, until eventually the Buddha had his son ordained by his chief disciple ŚĀRIPUTRA.

As a monk, Rāhula proved extremely conscientious, well-behaved, and eager to put into practice what he was taught. The Pāli canon contains a number of important discourses addressed to Rāhula, and it was while listening to the Buddha's *Cūla-Rāhulavādasutta* (*Shorter Discourse of Advice to Rāhula*) on not-self (anātman) and disenchantment (*nirvidā*) that Rāhula realized arhatship. The account of his winning ultimate freedom that is given in the Chinese version of the *Ekottarāgama* (*Discourses Increasing by One*) differs: Having received from the Buddha the decisive advice, Rāhula practiced MINDFULNESS of breathing, experienced DHYĀNA (TRANCE STATE), and obtained the three kinds of ABHIJÑĀ (HIGHER KNOWLEDGES), culminating in penetrating insight. Thus his mind was freed from all malign influences.

Tradition has it that Rāhula died before his father. In his lifetime, he was esteemed foremost among the Buddha's disciples in his eagerness to train.

See also: **Disciples of the Buddha**

Bibliography

Huyên-Vi, Thich; Bhikkhu Pāsādika; and Boin-Webb, Sara. "Ekottarāgama (XV): Translated from the Chinese Version (Taishō, Vol. 2, 581b29 ff.)." *Buddhist Studies Review* 10, 2 (1993): 213–222.

Malalasekera, G. P. "Rāhula Thera." In *Dictionary of Pāli Proper Names,* Vol. 2. London: Indian Text Series, 1937–1938.

BHIKKHU PĀSĀDIKA

REALMS OF EXISTENCE

The Sanskrit term *gati* (literally "manner of going") refers to the different "destinies" or realms of existence that await beings at death and into which they will be reborn as a result of the particular KARMA (ACTION) that has dominated their lives. The older Buddhist texts (followed by the exegetical texts and manuals of such schools as the THERAVĀDA and Sarvāstivāda) preserve a list of five basic realms: HELLS, hungry ghosts, animals, human beings, and gods. But it was always recognized that these five—and especially the last—represented broad categories. Thus we find different hells listed and different types of hungry ghosts distinguished, as well as a whole hierarchy of gods (deva).

Some Buddhist schools and some MAHĀYĀNA sūtras speak of six basic realms of existence, adding the asuras (jealous gods) to the list. Other schools, although in effect also recognizing rebirth as an asura as a significant and distinctive form of existence, refused to allow an actual list of six *gatis* on the grounds that such a list was not given in the earliest sūtras.

There is an old tradition (continued now especially in Tibetan Buddhism) of representing the six realms graphically as forming six segments of a wheel of existence: at the top, the heavenly realms of the gods, and moving clockwise, the jealous gods (separated by the wishing tree), animals, hells, hungry ghosts, and humans. The outer rim of the wheel is formed of the twelve links of PRATĪTYASAMUTPĀDA (DEPENDENT ORIGINATION). At the hub, driving the whole process, are a cock (greed), a snake (hatred), and a pig (ignorance).

See also: **Cosmology; Divinities; Ghosts and Spirits; Heavens**

Bibliography

Reynolds, Frank E., and Reynolds, Mani B., trans. *Three Worlds According to King Ruang: A Thai Buddhist Cosmology.* Berkeley: University of California Press, 1982.

Sadakata, Akira. *Buddhist Cosmology: Philosophy and Origin.* Tokyo: Kosei, 1997.

RUPERT GETHIN

REBIRTH

Rebirth (Sanskrit, *punarāvṛtti, punarutpatti, punarjanman,* or *punarjīvātu*), also called transmigration and reincarnation, is the belief common to all Buddhist traditions that birth and death occur in successive cycles driven by ignorance (avidyā), DESIRE (*tṛṣṇā*), and hatred (*dveṣa*). The cycle of rebirth, termed SAṂSĀRA, is beginningless and ongoing, and it is determined by the moral quality of a person's thoughts and KARMA (ACTION). The effects of good moral actions lead to wholesome rebirths, and the effects of bad moral actions lead to unwholesome rebirths.

Origins of the doctrine

Scholars have long debated the origins of the theory of rebirth among the religions of India. Some trace the belief to the ritual models inscribed in the ancient literature of the Vedas and Brāhmaṇas, which rested firmly on belief in the efficacy of ritual sacrifice as a means to secure a place in heaven. To guarantee positive future results these sacrificial acts were required to be perpetually reenacted. The conceptual parallels in this ancient model of a continuous cycle of ritual action have led some scholars to suggest that the mechanics of Vedic ritual should be seen as the precursor to later Indian theories of karma, saṃsāra, and rebirth. Other more controversial suggestions have been that rebirth doctrine originated among the ancient non-Aryan tribal groups of India. Still others theorize that the doctrine was formulated by followers of the *saṃnyāsin* (renouncer) traditions affiliated with the broad-based *śramaṇa* (mendicant) movement that began to emerge in India around the sixth century B.C.E., a movement that included the early Buddhists and Jains.

Rebirth and the problem of no-self

The Buddhist doctrine of rebirth differs fundamentally from the idea generally upheld in Hinduism and Jainism, both of which accept the existence of an eternal and substantial self or soul (ātman in Hinduism, *jīva* in Jainism) that transmigrates from life to life. Buddhism, by contrast, rejects the notion of an absolute self. Fundamental to its understanding of rebirth is the doctrine of no-self (anātman)—the idea that in saṃsāra, which is forever in flux, impermanent, and constantly changing, there can be no permanent, unchanging, independent self or soul.

But if there is no absolute self, how does Buddhism resolve the problem of transmigration and of the continuity of karma between one life and the next? The early Buddhist schools in India offered a variety of responses to this conundrum. One school, the Vātsīputrīya (also known as the PUDGALAVĀDA), went so far as to propose the concept of an inexpressible personal entity (*pudgala*) that traveled from life to life, a concept that seemed to contradict the fundamental tenet of anātman. Other schools, such as the Sarvāstivāda, posited the existence of an ethereal entity (called a *gandharva*) composed of subtle forms of the five SKANDHA (AGGREGATES) that passed through an INTERMEDIATE STATE (*antarābhava*) between death and the next birth. In the early period of Buddhism in India, concepts like *pudgala* and *antarābhava* were subjects of much controversy.

Not all of the schools accepted such ideas. The THERAVĀDA, for example, denied the existence of an intermediate state and argued instead for the existence of an inactive mode of deep consciousness (*bhavaṅga*) that forms a causal link (Sanskrit, *pratisandhi*; Pāli, *paṭisandhi*) between one life and the next. In this view, the first moment of consciousness in a new birth is simply the direct conditioned effect of the final moment of consciousness of the immediately previous existence.

Rebirth and cosmic causality

In basic Buddhist doctrinal terms, an answer to the difficult question of rebirth in light of the cardinal teaching of "no-self" is to be located in how Buddhism understands causality, the way one thing leads to another. One Buddhist formula describes it as follows: "When this exists, that exists; from this arising, that arises. When this does not exist, that does not exist; from this ceasing, that ceases." Technically speaking, this principle of causality is explicated by the formal doctrine of PRATĪTYASAMUTPĀDA (DEPENDENT ORIGINATION), which holds that all phenomena, including the "self" and the surrounding world, arise out of a network of relationships dependent upon other causes and conditions. The self, therefore, is not to be understood as an essential, independent entity moving from one life to the next, but rather as a manifestation of a complex of causes and conditions, both mental and physical, themselves interdependent and continually in flux.

The doctrine of dependent origination is graphically depicted as a circular chain consisting of twelve conditioned and conditioning links (*nidāna*): (1) ignorance, the inability to perceive the truth of ANITYA (IMPERMANENCE) and dependent origination, conditions (2) karmic formations, from which comes (3) consciousness, which leads to (4) mind-and-body (name and form) and then (5) the six senses (sources); the gateway of the six senses leads to (6) sensory contact that creates (7) sense impressions or feelings; these lead to (8) attachment; attachment leads to (9) grasping, which in turn gives rise to (10) becoming; becoming culminates in (11) birth, from which follow (12) aging and death, and the cycle begins again. In sequence, these twelve links generate life cycles within the perpetual process of saṃsāra driven by karma. In this way, the twelvefold chain of dependent origination describes the process of rebirth. Birth and death, then, are to be understood as nothing more or less than oscillating links in the ongoing chain of cause and effect. Rebirth is a configuration of a new cluster of causes and conditions propelled by previous karmic impulses. The process is compared to lighting one candle with the flame of another; the former flame is not the same as the latter and yet there is still a transfer of the flame. Like lighting a new candle, rebirth is simply the movement of a continuum of ever-changing mental and physical complexes from one physical support to another. It is this particular notion of causality that lies at the heart of the Buddhist understanding of rebirth.

The engine of rebirth is karma, the good and bad actions of body, speech, and mind that have been performed not only in the immediately preceding life but also many lifetimes ago. The cumulative moral quality of a person's karma determines the quality of each successive life. There is widespread consensus among Buddhists everywhere, however, that the state of a person's mind at the moment of death can actually be the most significant factor in setting the course for the future rebirth. It is usually the case that the mind at death tends to be occupied by whatever habitual thoughts and actions were most familiar in life or by whatever actions are performed just prior to death. For this reason, Buddhism recommends the cultivation of proper mindfulness and the performance of virtuous activities at the time of dying, which are all designed to insure a favorable rebirth. To be sure, the concern of the vast majority of ordinary Buddhists is less about the achievement of liberation from the cycle of saṃsāra and more about the attainment of a better position within that cycle. A good rebirth, according to Buddhism, is birth in one of the three higher realms of saṃsāra, that of gods (deva), demigods (asura), and human beings (*manuṣya*), with human birth deemed the most precious. Rebirth in the other three realms, of animals (*tiryak*), ghosts (preta), and hell beings (*naraka*), is regarded as terribly unfortunate. In all Buddhist cultures, certain merit-enhancing actions are performed at death to assure favorable circumstances in the next life. In the most general terms, these actions include the dedication of merit, almsgiving, and the recitation of Buddhist scriptures.

Methods for ensuring a wholesome rebirth

In China and Japan, much emphasis is placed on rebirth in a buddha's pure land, such as AMITĀBHA's pure land of Sukhāvatī, the Land of Bliss. Although there are multiple explanations for how best to ensure rebirth in one of these pure lands, in general it requires faith and a sincere aspiration to be reborn there. The repeated chanting of the name of the particular buddha of that realm or the recitation of his scripture at the moment of dying is also recommended. In addition, Chinese Buddhists at the time of death sometimes offer ritual paper money, popularly called "spirit money," to the postmortem bureaucrats and executive officers who are believed to abide in the afterlife. It is thought that this monetary offering will lessen the deceased's karmic debts and secure passport to a more favorable rebirth. The burning of such "hell notes" as an offering for the benefit of the dead is also practiced among Buddhists in Burma (Myanmar) and Vietnam.

In Japanese Buddhism, posthumous ORDINATION, the monastic ordination of the dying on their deathbed, is commonly practiced as a means to guarantee salvation and a better rebirth. In this way it can be said that all Buddhists in Japan die as MONKS or NUNS. Tibetan Buddhism also recognizes the value of virtuous actions and proper MINDFULNESS at the moment of death. In Tibet, special rituals are performed to actually guide the deceased's consciousness through the perilous pathways of the intermediate state (Tibetan, *bar do*) and into the next life. These funerary rituals are inscribed in specific Tibetan Buddhist liturgical manuals, some of which have achieved notoriety in Western-language translations, such as the TIBETAN BOOK OF THE DEAD.

In all of these Buddhist deathbed practices an underlying principle is at work. Virtuous actions performed at the moment of death by the dying and by surviving relatives can positively affect a person's future destiny. In other words, a good death leads to a good rebirth.

See also: **Anātman/Ātman (No-Self/Self); Cosmology; Death; Hinduism and Buddhism; Intermediate States; Jainism and Buddhism**

Bibliography

Jamgon Kongtrul Lodrö Tayé. *Myriad Worlds: Buddhist Cosmology in Abhidharma, Kālacakra, and Dzog-chen,* tr. and ed. by the International Translation Committee founded by the V.V. Kalu Rinpoche. Ithaca, NY: Snow Lion, 1995.

O'Flaherty, Wendy Doniger, ed. *Karma and Rebirth in Classical Indian Traditions.* Berkeley: University of California Press, 1980.

Sadakata, Akira. *Buddhist Cosmology: Philosophy and Origins,* tr. Gaynor Sekimori. Tokyo: Kōsei, 1997.

Teiser, Stephen F. *The Scripture of the Ten Kings and the Making of Purgatory in Medieval Chinese Buddhism.* Honolulu: University of Hawaii Press, 1994.

Tenzin Gyatso (Dalai Lama XIV). *The Meaning of Life: Buddhist Perspectives on Cause and Effect,* tr. and ed. Jeffrey Hopkins. Boston: Wisdom, 2000.

BRYAN J. CUEVAS

REFUGES

At the beginning of virtually every Buddhist ritual performed in South and Southeast Asia, whether public or private, the following Pāli invocation is chanted:

Buddhaṃ saranaṃ gacchāṃi.

Dhammaṃ saranaṃ gacchāmi.

Sanghaṃ saranaṃ gācchami.

The translation is:

I go to the Buddha as a refuge.

I go to the *dhamma* as a refuge.

I go to the saṅgha as a refuge.

Taking refuge in the triratna (triple gem) is usually first chanted by a monk and then repeated by the laity. It is a collective confessional statement in which the three "jewels" of the *śāsana* (tradition or teaching) are publicly affirmed, a declaration that the Buddha discovered the truth and made it known to the SAṄGHA, who have preserved and embodied it.

Taking refuge in the triratna is often a prelude to the acceptance of basic PRECEPTS. Observing the *pañcaśīla* (fivefold morality) is regarded as normative for all pious Buddhists. Indeed, it is an ancient moral formula shared with other Indian religious śramaṇa (renunciant) and Brāhmaṇa (priestly) traditions and comprises the cardinal principles encoded within the monastic *Vinayapiṭaka* (*Book of Discipline*). This code includes prohibitions against taking life, against taking what is not given, against lying about spiritual achievement, against engaging in sexual misconduct, and against imbibing intoxicants—five basic precepts for Buddhists. *Aṭṭhaśīla,* the taking of eight precepts by laity on full-moon days, includes observing the five precepts plus three more: not taking solid food after noon, wearing only white clothes without ornamentation, and sitting and lying only on mats.

See also: **Ordination; Vinaya**

Bibliography

Carter, John Ross. *On Understanding Buddhists: Essays on the Theravāda Tradition in Sri Lanka.* Albany: State University of New York Press, 1993.

Gombrich, Richard. *Precept and Practice: Traditional Buddhism in the Rural Highlands of Ceylon.* Oxford: Clarendon Press, 1971.

JOHN CLIFFORD HOLT

RELICS AND RELICS CULTS

Relic veneration has been virtually ubiquitous in the history of Buddhist traditions. The reputed remains of the historical Buddha, as well as those of other BUDDHAS, BODHISATTVAS, and even DISCIPLES OF THE BUDDHA, have been the objects of WORSHIP in a variety of locations and eras. Such remains have usually taken the form of granulated ashes or bones, and have often been seen as possessing a sheen similar to, if not identical with, JEWELS. In some contemporary Buddhist traditions, believers search for relics among the cremated remains of deceased masters; if found, such remains will sometimes be divided for distribution among affiliated monasteries.

Meaning and early historical context

The term that is usually used to refer to relics in Sanskrit Buddhist literature is *śarīra,* which refers to the body. Less frequently, *dhātu,* a word with multiple and complex senses, is used. Relics have been a focus of veneration for Buddhists since, it would seem, the passing of the historical Buddha Śākyamuni himself. The MAHĀPARINIRVĀNA-SŪTRA (Pāli, *Mahāparinibbāna-sutta; Great Discourse on the Extinction*) depicts the relics of the Buddha as remaining at his cremation pyre. Monarchs of northern India vied to obtain the relics for enshrinement, leading to a dispute that was prevented only by a Brahman named Droṇa, who divided the remains into eight portions for distribution. Archaeological investigations at reliquary sites, such as Vaiśālī and Piprāhwā in northern India, have further confirmed that the practice of relic veneration existed prior to the time of King AŚOKA (third century B.C.E.).

According to the Pāli *Kaliṅgabodhi-jātaka,* funerary mounds housed three types of relics of the Buddha: bodily relics (*sarīrika-cetiyam*), use or contact relics (*uddesika-cetiyam*), and commemoration relics (*pāribhogika-cetiyam*). In general, Buddhist traditions have interpreted the bodily relics to be granulated ashes, as well as remains of teeth, hair, and flesh. Use or contact relics were objects believed to be associated with the Buddha, such as his begging bowl and staff. The relics of commemoration, a category that presumably developed later than the others, consisted of images of the Buddha.

Relics were signs that simultaneously represented DEATH and the conquest of death. As emphasized by Peter Brown in the context of the veneration of saints' relics in Western Mediterranean Christendom of the third to sixth centuries, the reputed remains of saints provided believers with hope; the presence of the relic, as an instantiation of the "special dead," provided a kind of proof of existence beyond death and alleviated anxieties concerning what seemed to be radical finitude. For Buddhists, relics, especially those of the historical Buddha, served as a sign of death and the subjugation of death.

On the one hand, the Buddha was subject to the universal law of ANITYA (IMPERMANENCE), like all other beings. Moreover, relics, like the living community of MONKS, constituted a "field of merit," so that making offerings to relics and reliquaries enabled believers to accumulate great merit (*puṇya*). Indeed, a conceptual relationship existed in Buddhist literature between relic veneration and the actions of the Buddha during previous lives as a BODHISATTVA. In particular, JĀTAKA tales describe acts of giving on the part of the bodhisattva, such as the offering of his body or other valuable objects on behalf of other beings, which served as a model of ideal giving. Thus, sites associated with the offering of the bodhisattva's body became locations for construction of relic STŪPAS, and Buddhist literature depicted the construction of reliquaries in response to such actions. In fact, homilies that invoked tales of the Buddha's sacrifice were probably made at stūpas in order to encourage believers to give lavish offerings to reliquaries.

On the other hand, relics represented the Buddha's conquest of death through his attainment of *parinirvāṇa;* they were an index of his former presence. Indeed, as Gregory Schopen has noted, the relics and the reliquary constituted a "legal person" because the Buddha was viewed as a living entity on the site and the rightful owner of objects offered at the stūpa. One Buddhist text forbade the appropriation of even a robe given to a reliquary, warning against its exchange for money, because no object of the stūpa could have a price. Other writings went so far as to identify the theft of reliquary property with the five acts of immediate retribution within the Buddhist community (Schopen 1987, pp. 206–208).

In addition, the transfer of relics to increasingly disparate locations made it possible for Buddhists to venerate holy figures without going on long-distance pilgrimages. Buddhists throughout Asia were clearly concerned about their access to sites associated with the historical Buddha, and remains reputedly of him or those close to him were highly valued. Through the local veneration of relics, Buddhists could gain merit

A monk carries a miniature stūpa containing a tooth believed to have been the Buddha's. It was put on display in Taiwan in 1998. Here it is escorted from the airport by an official party led by the Taiwanese prime minister. AP/Wide World Photos. Reproduced by permission.

equivalent to that accrued through PILGRIMAGE to sacred sites like BODH GAYĀ and Lumbinī Garden. Thus, the presence of reputed relics bridged the temporal gap between contemporary believers and the historical Śākyamuni, whose life grew increasingly distant with the passage of time.

In fact, for Buddhists, the mobility of relics offered a new mode of relationship with Śākyamuni, the early disciples, and later Buddhist saints. Insofar as relics could be easily transported across long distances, these objects (like the images and amulets studied by Stanley Tambiah in contemporary Thai Buddhism) were "repositories of power." They constituted the burning energy (*tejas*) manifested in the body of the Buddha and other holy beings, as well as in images of them. Indeed, the transfer of relics to, and their discovery in, Southeast Asia and East Asia became so common that one might argue, as Brown has noted in the context of Christendom, that "Translations—the movement of relics to people—and not pilgrimages—the movement of people to relics—hold the center of the stage in late-antique and early-medieval piety" (pp. 89–96). Throughout the history of early Buddhism, as well as later MAHĀYĀNA and TANTRA Buddhism, relics of one form or another were venerated in a vast variety of locales, and constituted a form of veneration that complemented efforts at pilgrimage.

The increasing dissemination of *śarīra*

The categories of Buddhist relics include not only bodily remains of the historical Buddha and other saints, but a variety of other objects. For example, image consecration in Buddhism included the common practice of inserting relics inside of the images.

In works associated with the rise of Mahāyāna Buddhism, the words of the Buddha as embodied in sūtras were represented as *śarīra* or *dhātu*. As the Mahāyāna came to prioritize worship of "the book" as manifesting the presence of the Buddha, sūtras as relics came to be considered superior to physical remains. Moreover, insofar as the practice of venerating bodily relics had developed earlier and was historically dominant, the discussions of relics in sūtras of the early and middle Mahāyāna were ambivalent, both antagonistic toward the practice and modeling it. Scriptures such as the early *Aṣṭasāhasrikāprajñāpāramitā-sūtra* (*Perfection of Wisdom in 8,000 Lines*) thus stressed the fundamental importance of relic veneration, while at the same time emphasizing that because sūtras are the dharma of the Buddha, their veneration is, ultimately, superior to that of physical remains.

In this context, such "dharma" relics came to be inserted in stūpas throughout Asia by the early centuries of the common era. In most cases, only portions of the scripture were included. The verse most often enshrined described PRATĪTYASAMUTPĀDA (DEPENDENT ORIGINATION): "Those dharmas which arise from a cause: the Tathāgata has declared their cause, and that which is the cessation of them; thus the great renunciant has taught." Thus, the words of the Buddha, when inserted in reliquaries, revivified his presence, and works such as the *Pratītyasamutpāda-sūtra* described the great merit of inserting such verses even into miniature stūpas.

By roughly the middle of the first millennium, the emergent Mahāyāna DHĀRAṆĪ sūtras (incantatory formulae scriptures) proclaimed that dhāraṇī should be deposited in stūpas and interpreted as relics. Indeed, as noted by Yael Bentor, the contents of scriptures such as the *Guhyadhātu* equate their very presence with that of the Buddha and his relics (p. 252). The practice of inserting dhāraṇī in stūpas occurred in parts of China, Tibet, Korea, and Japan, in addition to the Indian subcontinent.

The Shingon school of the Japanese tantric tradition, which inherited the practice of venerating relics from Chinese Buddhism, stressed the importance of the bodily relics that the founder KŪKAI (774–835) brought back from China. Over time, the Shingon school developed innovative interpretations of relics. The so-called *Last Testament* (*Go-yuigō*) of Kūkai, from roughly the tenth century, describes how Buddha relics and a variety of precious substances and herbs can be combined to produce a wish-fulfilling "jewel" (Japanese, *nyoi hōju*; Sanskrit, *cintāmaṇi*). Likewise, some scriptures describe how, in the event that "authentic" relics cannot be obtained for ritual use, relics can be constructed from a variety of precious stones, pebbles, or medicines.

Buddhist kingship and the ritual use of relics

As noted above, Buddhist tradition told of the efforts of monarchs to obtain relics of the Buddha on the occasion of his cremation. Moreover, King AŚOKA's construction of reliquaries, and the wealth of literature describing him constructing eighty-four thousand stūpas throughout the Indian subcontinent, consolidated the narrative foundations for a long history of royal patronage of relics, as well as for a wide variety of ritual uses.

The *Aśokāvadāna* (*Legend of Aśoka*) had the greatest influence on the development of Buddhist traditions concerning the ideal of the wheel-turning king (cakravartin) and his relationship with relics. In particular, the motif of the ruler's construction and protection of reliquaries arose out of Aśoka's effort to give exhaustively to the Buddhist community, and the centerpiece of his actions is his construction of stūpas. As a wheel-turning king, Aśoka is the chief supporter of the "wheel of dharma," the teachings of Buddhism; to fulfill that duty, he cares for the body of the Buddha in the form of relics. In symbolic terms, as suggested by Paul Mus, when a king constructs stūpas to house relics, he and his kingdom become a kind of living reliquary. To the extent that stūpas constitute *mesocosms* (cosmic centers for the ritual invocation of the absent Buddha), the Buddhist king may also be conceived of as a symbol of the Buddha.

The construction of stūpas and their veneration by rulers and aristocrats continued with the spread of Buddhism. Rulers in China, especially those of the Wei of the mid-fifth to sixth centuries, gave elaborately to the Buddhist community, a relationship epitomized by the sponsorship of the construction of stūpas and images. Emperor Wen (r. 581–604) of the Sui dynasty took imitation of Aśoka's patronage to great lengths, going so far as to sponsor the construction of multiple stūpas enshrining Buddha relics for distribution to monasteries throughout the land.

Imperial patronage of relic veneration in China, Sri Lanka, and other areas of Asia constituted both a demonstration of the rulers' largess and a response to the fervor of local Buddhists. For example, the writings of Chinese pilgrims such as FAXIAN (ca. 337–418) indicate that the Chinese were aware of the practice among Asian rulers of conducting relic processions to

The Buddha's finger relic, in a miniature gold pagoda. In 2002 it was taken from Famensi in Xi'an, China for display in Taiwan. AP/Wide World Photos. Reproduced by permission.

bolster their authority, and the large crowds that attended such processions gave evidence of faith among the populace. Indeed, a famous tract by Han yu (768–824) argued forcefully against welcoming the relic of the Buddha's finger from FAMENSI into the Chinese imperial palace in 819. Han yu demonstrated in his criticisms of believers' behavior the extent of their devotion, whereby some burned their heads and fingers, and discarded clothing and large numbers of coins. On the occasion of another procession of Buddha relics in 873, worshippers variously offered their arms, fingers, and hair in acts that symbolically matched the bodily sacrifices that Śākyamuni as a bodhisattva had made in the *jātaka* tales.

In Japan, the royal government, in a gesture similar to that of Emperor Wen, sponsored the presentation of Buddha relics throughout the land. In this case, however, the offerings were made to celebrate royal accession to shrines of the native deities (*kami*), with relic veneration being incorporated directly into cults associated with royal authority. Moreover, clerics of the Shingon school held an annual royal rite in the palace Shingon'in chapel in veneration of the relics brought back by Kūkai, suggesting that monastic Buddhists, together with the royal family and aristocracy, saw the veneration of relics as key to the annual renewal of the ruler's body and of the realm. At the same time, possession of the relics legitimized the Shingon lineage internally and vis-à-vis the royal family. By at least the thirteenth century, the relics of Shingon were seen as indispensable to royal authority; by the fourteenth century, clerics of both the Shingon and Tendai tantric traditions identified the wish-fulfilling jewel with the regalia of the sovereign.

See also: **Merit and Merit-Making; Printing Technologies; Reliquary; Self-Immolation**

Bibliography

Bentor, Yael. "On the Indian Origins of the Tibetan Practice of Depositing Relics and *Dhāraṇīs* in Stūpas and Images." *Journal of the American Oriental Society* 115, no. 2 (1995): 248–261.

Boucher, Daniel. "The *Pratītyasamutpādagāthā* and Its Role in the Medieval Cult of the Relics." *Journal of the International Association of Buddhist Studies* 14, no. 1 (1991): 1–27.

Brown, Peter. *The Cult of the Saints: Its Rise and Function in Latin Christianity.* Chicago: University of Chicago Press, 1981.

Faure, Bernard. *The Rhetoric of Immediacy: A Cultural Critique of Chan/Zen Buddhism.* Princeton, NJ: Princeton University Press, 1991.

Mus, Paul. *Barabadur: esquisse d'une histoire du bouddhisme fondée sur la critique archéologique des textes,* 2 vols. Hanoi, Vietnam: Imprimerie d'Extreme-Orient, 1935. Reprint, New York: Arno Press, 1988.

Ruppert, Brian D. *Jewel in the Ashes: Buddha Relics and Power in Early Medieval Japan.* Cambridge, MA: Harvard University Asia Center and Harvard University Press, 2000.

Schopen, Gregory. "Burial '*Ad Sanctos*' and the Physical Presence of the Buddha in Early Indian Buddhism: A Study in the Archaeology of Religions." *Religion* 17 (1987): 193–225.

Schopen, Gregory. *Bones, Stones, and Buddhist Monks: Collected Papers on the Archaeology, Epigraphy, and Texts of Monastic Buddhism in India.* Honolulu: University of Hawaii Press, 1997.

Strong, John S. *The Legend of King Aśoka: A Study and Translation of the Aśokāvadāna.* Princeton, NJ: Princeton University Press, 1983.

Tambiah, Stanley Jeyaraja. *The Buddhist Saints of the Forest and the Cult of Amulets: A Study of Charisma, Hagiography, Sectarianism, and Millennial Buddhism.* New York: Cambridge University Press, 1993.

Trainor, Kevin. *Relics, Ritual, and Representation in Buddhism: Rematerializing the Sri Lankan Theravāda Tradition.* New York: Cambridge University Press, 1997.

BRIAN O. RUPPERT

RELIQUARY

As the focus of worship in early Buddhist monasteries, every STŪPA or pagoda had a foundation deposit, usually sealed within a stone casket or small chamber beneath the central mast, and hence inaccessible once the stūpa was raised above it.

Reliquary deposits were placed either in a vault centrally located in the foundations of a pagoda or higher up in a chamber within the structure. Such deposits were made at the time of construction, but those in the foundation vault would be recovered and reconsecrated whenever it became necessary to rebuild the structure above them (e.g., when a pagoda built of wood burnt down and was rebuilt). Exceptionally, as at FAMENSI, the vault would be accessible on other occasions.

Many deposits have been revealed through excavation and conservation projects in the second half of the twentieth century. The earliest examples, like the earliest pagoda (Songyuesi ta at Dengfeng in Henan province, dated 520) are from the Northern Wei dynasty (386–534). At this date, the reliquary container is a cubical stone chest, no more than thirty centimeters in height, with a chamfered stone lid. The relics or *sheli* (the Chinese rendering of the Sanskrit *śarīra*) are tiny crystalline grains, usually enclosed in a very small glass bottle. This in turn is enclosed within other containers, and accompanied by wrappings of silk and offerings of various kinds, including precious objects and coins. Among the latter it is common to find coins minted a decade or so earlier in Byzantium or the Sassanian empire, which had come to China through trade along the SILK ROAD.

In the seventh century, the shape of the reliquary was changed into the form of a Chinese coffin, with arched lid, higher at one end than the other, a Sinicized form that was to persist until the end of the twentieth century, when clear plastic containers of this form were used to reconsecrate the four relics found in the Famensi pagoda deposit.

The most recently discovered reliquary deposit was recovered during excavation of the Leifengta, on the shores of the West Lake in Hangzhou, the brick core of which collapsed in 1924. Excavated in 2001, the foundation chamber contained an iron chest (the domed and flat-sided one-piece cover extending to the flat square base with raised inner flange) with its contents intact. The relics inside were contained in a miniature one-story stūpa of silver, dedicated by the ruler of the eastern state of Wu-Yue in the tenth century, set on a gilt-bronze circular tray with floral decoration. A seated bronze image of Śākyamuni supported on a dragon, bronze mirrors, coins, and exquisite jade carvings were also found inside the iron chest. The rulers of Wu-Yue are said to have dedicated eighty-four thousand such miniature stūpas. One reliquary deposit, the Wanfosi at Jinhua in Zhejiang province, contained no fewer than twenty-one of them.

Relic deposits, often dated and containing, besides the relic grains themselves, Buddhist images and scriptures; wooden, lacquered and inlaid containers; and countless objects made of precious materials, provide some of the most fascinating evidence of Buddhist devotion. In the eyes of Buddhist devotees, relics were of equal if not greater importance than scriptures and images. The great traveler and translator XUANZANG (ca.

600–664) brought 150 relic grains, as well as seven images and 657 chapters of Buddhist scriptures, from his sixteen-year journey to India.

See also: **Relics and Relics Cults; Ritual Objects**

Bibliography

Wang, Eugene Y. "Of the True Body: The Famensi Relics and Corporeal Transformation in Tang Imperial China." In *Body and Face in Chinese Visual Culture,* ed. Wu Hung et al. Cambridge, MA: Harvard Asia Center and Harvard University Press, 2003.

Whitfield, Roderick. "Buddhist Monuments in China: Some Recent Finds of Śarīra Deposits." In *The Buddhist Heritage: Papers Delivered at the Symposium of the Same Name Convened at the School of Oriental and African Studies, University of London, November 1985,* ed. Tadeusz Skorupski. Tring, UK: Institute of Buddhist Studies, 1989.

RODERICK WHITFIELD

RENNYO

Rennyo (1415–1499) was the eighth head of the Honganji temple of the Jōdo Shinshū tradition of PURE LAND BUDDHISM in Japan. The Shinshū, which originated in the teachings of SHINRAN (1173–1263), emerged during Rennyo's period as the largest and most powerful Buddhist movement in Japan. Rennyo is largely credited with the Shinshū's expansion and success in the fifteenth century and with building Honganji from a minor temple in Kyoto into a formidable institution.

Early in his career Rennyo's initiatives incensed rivals at the Tendai monastic complex on Mount Hiei outside Kyoto, which dominated religious affairs in the region. Its agents attacked and destroyed Honganji in 1465, and sent Rennyo fleeing into the provinces, where he spent the next decade and a half proselytizing. Gradually, he built up a massive following, especially among peasants, and he popularized Shinshū teachings though his *ofumi* (pastoral letters), which were circulated and read aloud in congregational meetings. The message he proclaimed was that faith in Amida (AMITĀBHA) Buddha assures birth in the Pure Land where Buddhist enlightenment is certain. Rennyo also taught that the *nenbutsu,* the Pure Land practice of reciting Amida's name, was a palpable expression of coalescence with the Buddha and indebtedness to him. People in this religious state, he claimed, live a life of peace and assurance, and are inspired to follow rules of upright conduct. This message lay behind the popularization of the Shinshū throughout Japan. In the early 1480s Rennyo fulfilled his dream of rebuilding Honganji as a magnificent temple complex on the outskirts of Kyoto. It became the site of a huge annual memorial service on the anniversary of Shinran's death, in which Shinshū pilgrims came from around the country to participate.

See also: **Nenbutsu (Chinese, Nianfo; Korean, Yŏmbul); Pure Land Schools**

Bibliography

Dobbins, James C. *Jōdo Shinshū: Shin Buddhism in Medieval Japan,* (1989). Reprint, Honolulu: University of Hawaii Press, 2002.

The Rennyo Shonin Reader. Kyoto: Jōdo Shinshū Hongwanji-ha, 1998.

Rogers, Minor L., and Rogers, Ann T. *Rennyo: The Second Founder of Shin Buddhism.* Berkeley, CA: Asian Humanities Press, 1991.

Weinstein, Stanley. "Rennyo and the Shinshū Revival." In *Japan in the Muromachi Age,* ed. John Whitney Hall and Toyoda Takeshi. Berkeley: University of California Press, 1977.

JAMES C. DOBBINS

RENWANG JING (HUMANE KINGS SŪTRA)

The *Renwang jing* (*Humane Kings Sūtra*) is one of the more influential of the East Asian "apocryphal" scriptures—texts that purported to be translations of Indian works, but were actually composed in China and Korea. Although its full title indicates that it is a transcendent wisdom (*prajñāpāramitā*) text, it is better characterized as a blend of transcendent wisdom, YOGĀCĀRA SCHOOL, and TATHĀGATAGARBHA teachings. The *Renwang jing* is unusual in that its target audience is the rulership, rather than lay practitioners or the community of monks and nuns. Thus, whereas the interlocutors in most scriptures are ARHATS or BODHISATTVAS, the discussants in this text are the kings of the sixteen ancient regions of India. The foregrounded teachings, rather than meditation and wisdom, are humaneness and forbearance, these being the most applicable religious values for the governance of a Buddhist state.

A second "translation" was supposedly carried out a few centuries after the appearance of the original version by the monk Amoghavajra (Pukong, 705–774), one of the most important figures in the Chinese MIJIAO (ESOTERIC) SCHOOL. But this new version was actually just a rewrite, since there was no original Sanskrit version. This second version of the text (T 246), while based mostly on the original version (T 245), contains new sections that include teachings on MAṆḌALA, MANTRA, and DHĀRAṆĪ. In the same way that other apocryphal works, such as the FANWANG JING (BRAHMĀ'S NET SŪTRA), came to hold a special authoritative position in the subsequent development of Buddhism in Korea and Japan, as well as China, the *Renwang jing* became the standard model text in these East Asian countries for Buddhist-based state protection and statecraft.

See also: **Apocrypha; Kingship; Politics and Buddhism; Prajñāpāramitā Literature**

Bibliography

Orzech, Charles. *Politics and Transcendent Wisdom: The Scripture for Humane Kings in the Creation of Chinese Buddhism.* University Park: Pennsylvania State University Press, 1998.

A. CHARLES MULLER

REPENTANCE AND CONFESSION

Repentance and confession have been a part of the practice of Buddhism from its beginning, and several distinctive forms have evolved for different contexts. Indian Buddhism developed at least three forms: (1) communal repentance and confession within the monastic SAṄGHA; (2) metaphysical repentance of one's karmic past to a supramundane buddha; and (3) meditational repentance of incorrect attachments and understanding. Chinese Buddhists developed public and elaborate forms of repentance and confession; these have cosmic dimensions to relieve the suffering of both the living and the dead.

Indian Buddhism

When disciples of the Buddha first left their family lives for full-time practice, they adopted a set of guidelines that were recited in a twice-monthly ceremony called *poṣadha* (Pāli, *uposatha*). During this gathering, monks recited the rules of discipline (PRĀTIMOKṢA) as a check and support for their individual practice. Participation in the group recitation required purity, so prior confession and restitution were required by monks and nuns if they had violated any rules. Although expulsion resulted from violation of the more serious *pārājika* rules (no killing, stealing, sexual intercourse, or lying about one's spiritual achievements), lesser rule violations could be remedied by confession and other supportive behavior.

When *saṅghādisesa* (Sanskrit, *saṅghāvaśeṣa*) rules were broken, for example, recovery required confession to a community of at least twenty monastics, plus a probationary two-week seclusion for reflection and reform. *Saṅghādisesa* rules set prohibitions against disruptive behaviors, such as failing to accept admonitions, speaking in envy, gossiping about another, or repudiating the Buddha, dharma, and saṅgha. Violation of the *nissaggiya pācittiyas* (Sanskrit, *naiḥsargika-prāyaścittika*) rules also required confession, but only to a minimum of five monastics, plus forfeiture of an article that had been wrongly obtained, such as a robe, bowl, or rug. Confession was required to only one or more monastics for breaking rules against telling laity about the misbehavior of monks, bad manners, carelessness, not keeping an accepted invitation, or abusing others by scolding, tickling, or degrading them. Similarly, violations of a fifth category of rules dealing with food required only confession. Lesser rules dealing with ETIQUETTE did not require confession at all.

Confession did not excuse the violator from the penalties of rule breaking; rather, confession was a matter of truth-telling and of inviting appropriate penalties for rectifying the situation. A monk or nun could confess only to other monastics, and confession was not a public event open to the laity. By contrast, the rite of *pavāraṇa*, which occurred after the annual rainy-season retreat, publicly examined the wrongs that monks and nuns had committed during the three-month retreat. The confession and public repentance involved in *pavāraṇa* differed from the private whispered confession of the *prātimokṣa*. Thus, repentance and confession within the Buddhist monastic community served not only to support individual practice, but also to maintain the unity of the monastic community and its good reputation with the laity.

A second form of repentance and confession arose as a way to cope with bad KARMA (ACTION) and had a very different goal from maintaining monastic purity. These confessions referred to unexpiated guilt resulting from unknown or unremembered past wrongs, and were a plea for forgiveness to alleviate suffering and harm in the present life. The goal was not merely to escape the social penalties of rule breaking, but to avoid the larger karmic consequence of wrongful actions, thoughts, and attitudes. Such a confession of karmic wrongs is given a mythological framework in the "Chapter on Confession" in the Mahāyāna SUVARṆAPRABHĀSOTTAMA-SŪTRA (*Sūtra of Golden Light*). According to this chapter, during the vision of a shining drum, verses came forth that proclaimed the power of the drum to suppress many woes, and a confession of all previous wrongs was uttered to supramundane, compassionate buddhas. Even the name *Survarṇaprabhāsa* (Golden Light) was believed to destroy all evil deeds done over thousands of eons. But the most striking feature of this form of Buddhist confession was the theistic function of the buddhas, who were asked to give protection and to forgive all evil deeds. This text presents an endless time span, the recognition of possible unexpiated guilt, a request for forgiveness, supramundane compassionate buddhas as sources for forgiveness, and the use of the name of the *Suvarṇaprabhāsa* to destroy all evil actions and their consequences.

The worldview expressed by this ritual extends beyond the present social world of the monastery to invoke karmic history and draw on supramundane powers, such as the force of compassionate buddhas and the magical power of dhāraṇī, to rectify a harmful situation. In this worldview, wrongs from previous rebirths not only affect one's present REBIRTH, but also relate directly to the Buddha, who can intercede and offer relief and support. Repentance is not primarily communal, but rather devotional and directed to a cosmic, transhistorical figure, and thus it can be called "metaphysical repentance." It was this kind of repentance that later evolved into large public rituals in China.

A third form of repentance and confession is based on the *Sūtra of Meditation on Bodhisattva Samantabhadra*. In this text, the wrongs to be eliminated are from both the remembered and the unknowable past, but the method of repentance and confession goes beyond pleading for mercy and help. Instead, the text offers instruction for visualization of the Bodhisattva Samantabhadra, and leads to instruction about all the karma and wrongs of former lives that can then be confessed. In addition, the devotee systematically reviews the functioning of each of the sense organs, followed by a recitation of ritual repentance (said three times) for all inner attachment and external wrongdoing. Samantabhadra's "law of repentance" says that attachment to phenomena perceived by the senses causes one to fall into the cycle of birth and death.

Whereas meditative inspection of the sense-fields is the main basis for regretting and rectifying past wrongs, the final dimension of personal transformation is the development of a new understanding based on contemplating the "real mark of all things," namely, their emptiness of enduring distinguishing attributes (*lakṣaṇa*). This contemplation of the emptiness and signlessness of dharmas is the locus classicus for the idea of "formless repentance" found in Chinese CHAN SCHOOL texts like the PLATFORM SŪTRA OF THE SIXTH PATRIARCH (LIUZU TAN JING). Since this contemplation removes bad karma and frees one from past wrongs and present attachments based on exposure to enlightened awareness, just as "the sun of wisdom disperses dew and frost," then this could be called *insight repentance.*

Insight repentance differs from the confessional model of early Buddhism to correct wrong actions in the present through penance, exclusion, probation, restitution, or confession. Instead, for Chan Buddhists, wrongs are to be "cast aside by your own true Buddha nature" through an inner change, and inner transformation by enlightenment corrects all "past, future, and present" wrong actions and thoughts. As a result, many Zen practitioners in the West daily recite: "All the evil karma ever created by me since of old, on account of my beginningless greed, hatred, and ignorance, I now confess openly and fully."

Chinese Buddhism

All three forms of Indian repentance were adopted in China. The great Chinese vinaya master DAOXUAN (596–667) grouped the causes of repentance into three categories: violations of monastic codes, violations of phenomena (immoral behavior), and violations of principle (wrong attitudes, perceptions, and understanding). The Tiantai monk ZHIYI (538–597) was influential in developing the metaphysical and insight repentance methods. In his *Fahua sanmei chanyi* (*Lotus Samādhi Techniques*), Zhiyi presents the Lotus Samādhi ritual as a dialectic between the *Meditation on Samantabhadra Sūtra* and the "Chapter on Peaceful Practices" in the LOTUS SŪTRA (SADDHARMAPUṆḌARĪKA-SŪTRA). The first text instructs practitioners to repent sins from the six senses, whereas the second text states that bodhisattvas do not make distinctions, nor do they practice any dharmas. Zhiyi argues that these two texts complement one another, and he shows how they switch positions, with the second advocating remembering, reciting, and explaining the scriptures, while the first advocates "formless repentance," as in the statement "Since one's own mind is void of itself, there is no subject of demerit or merit." This "formless repentance" not only became popular in Chan Buddhism, but also led to a reduction of repentance in Japanese Buddhism to the single act of recognizing the emptiness of all things—doer, deeds, and karma.

Zhiyi emphasized, however, that both "practices of form" and "formless practice" are preliminary, but at the time of realization, both methods are discarded. Instead, based on the statement in the NIRVĀṆA SŪTRA that "In the mind that is 'one moment of thought' one is able to name and evaluate each of the incalculable birth-and-deaths," Zhiyi asserts that at every moment one is to understand three truths: emptiness, the value of provisional worldly truth that includes precepts and repentance, and an inclusive middle path. As a result, one empathizes with the pain of all beings and causes them to cross over to unboundedness.

This inclusion of others into one's repentance caused a dramatic increase in repentance rituals in China. Shioiri Ryōdō (1964) observed the remarkable fact that the Chinese pilgrims who traveled most extensively in India—FAXIAN (ca. 337–418), XUANZANG (ca. 600–664), and YIJING (635–713)—reported only two public Buddhist repentance rituals in India and Southeast Asia. By comparison, Chinese Buddhist repentance rituals are prominent as regular public ceremonies, so that more than one-fourth of the ritual texts collected among contemporary Chinese Buddhist practitioners by Kamata Shigeo (1986) are repentance texts. These ceremonies pervade the Chinese Buddhist liturgical year and constitute a major bond between the monastic elite and the laity, and between the world of Buddhism and Chinese society.

The Chinese transformed Buddhist repentance practices because they believed that the sufferings of the dead can be visited upon the living, and the actions of the living can transform the sufferings of the dead. Chinese Buddhists also assumed that a conspicuous public display of regret and anguish over previous wrongs would influence cosmic powers to show mercy. As a result, public repentance during the GHOST FESTIVAL to relieve the suffering of deceased family members became a major ritual in Chinese society from medieval times to the present (Teiser, 1988).

See also: **Festivals and Calendrical Rituals; Precepts**

Bibliography

De Visser, M. W. *Ancient Buddhism in Japan: Sūtras and Ceremonies in Use in the Seventh and Eighth Centuries A.D. and Their History in Later Times,* Vol. 1. Leiden, Netherlands: Brill, 1935.

Eberhard, Wolfram. *Guilt and Sin in Traditional China.* Berkeley: University of California Press, 1967.

Eckel, M. David. "A Buddhist Approach to Repentance." In *Repentance: A Comparative Perspective,* ed. Amitai Etzioni and David W. Carney. New York: Rowman and Littlefield, 1997.

Kamata Shigeo. *Chūgoku no Bukkyō girei* (Chinese Buddhist Ceremonies). Tokyo: Daizo shuppan, 1986.

Kuo Li-ying. *Confession et contrition dans le bouddhisme chinois de Ve au Xe siècle.* Paris: L'École Française d'Extrême-Orient, 1994.

Prebish, Charles S. *Buddhist Monastic Discipline: The Sanskrit Prātimokṣa Sūtras of the Mahāsāṃghikas and Mūlasarvāstivādins.* University Park: Pennsylvania State University Press, 1975.

Rhys Davids, T. W., and Oldenberg, Hermann. *Vinaya Texts, Part I: The Pātimokkha, The Mahāvagga I–IV. Sacred Books of the East,* Vol. 13. Delhi: Motilal Banarsidass, 1996 (reprint of the Oxford University Press edition, 1885).

Shioiri Ryōdō. "Chūgoku Bukkyō ni okeru raisan to butsumei kyōten" (Repentance Rituals and Scriptures of the Buddha's Name in Chinese Buddhism). In *Bukkyō shisōshi ronshū: Yūki Kyōju shoju kinen.* Tokyo: Daizo Shuppan, 1964.

Teiser, Stephen. *The Ghost Festival in Medieval China.* Princeton, NJ: Princeton University Press, 1988.

Teiser, Stephen. *The Scripture on the Ten Kings and the Making of Purgatory in Medieval Chinese Buddhism.* Honolulu: University of Hawaii Press, 1994.

Tsomo, Karma Lekshe. *Sisters in Solitude: Two Traditions of Buddhist Monastic Ethics for Women.* Albany: State University of New York Press, 1996.

DAVID W. CHAPPELL

RITUAL

In the Pāli *nikāyas* there are four stages to final liberation: (1) stream-enterer (*sotāpanna*), who has glimpsed NIRVĀṆA and will attain full liberation in no more than seven rebirths; (2) once-returner (*sakadāgāmin*), who will be reborn only once more; (3) nonreturner (*anāgāmin*), who will have at most one more lifetime in a celestial pure abode; and (4) ARHAT, who is fully liberated in this life. Each of these stages is associated with the elimination of progressively more subtle fetters (*saṃyojana*). The three lower fetters are removed upon entering into the stream: (1) wrong view in the reality of the self (*sakkāyadiṭṭhi*); (2) doubt concerning the Buddha and his teaching; and (3) attachment to rules and observances (Pāli, *sīlabbataparāmāsa*; Sanskrit, *śīlavrataparāmarśa*), whether ritual or ascetic, in the belief that these themselves are liberative.

During the nineteenth century, modernizing apologists emphasized the rational and ethical qualities of Buddhism and, in keeping with assumptions common to Western religious culture, focused on issues of belief and doctrine. This version of Buddhism interpreted the elimination of the fetter of attachment to rules and observances as a comprehensive rejection of ritual practices. Based on this selective reading of Pāli sources, Buddhism was portrayed as a tradition in which ritual played no role. Claiming that Śākyamuni Buddha rejected all ritual practice, this interpretation of Buddhism gave privileged position to MEDITATION, so much so that today Buddhism is often simply identified with meditation. The distinction of meditation and ritual as mutually exclusive categories, however, is an artificial one that has its roots in Western religious culture rather than in Buddhism.

Rather than rejecting ritual, however, Śākyamuni appears to have rejected animal sacrifice, which forms the core of Vedic ritual and the religious authority of the brahman priests who perform such sacrifices. Historically, many Buddhist activities, such as the prātimokṣa recitation, were ritualized early in the history of the tradition. By the third through sixth centuries C.E. ritual practices were well established among Indian Buddhist practitioners.

While use of the term *ritual* seems to indicate a specific category, such that there ought to be a clear way in which one can identify what is and what is not a ritual, scholars still do not agree on a general definition of *ritual.* It is instead more useful to think in terms of *ritualization,* that is, a process by which certain activities are regularized both in performance and periodicity. Rather than a bounded category, or a simply stipulative definition, ritualization suggests a range of degrees to which activities have been regularized. Over the course of Buddhist history, important activities, including individual religious practices (sādhana), have been ritualized.

Basic model for Buddhist rituals

Elements of what became known as the unexcelled worship (*anuttarapūjā*) are found as early as the late second century C.E. The other name for this is the seven-limbed pūjā (*saptāṅgā* pūjā), since rituals of this kind often employed seven elements. This latter name is somewhat misleading in that the number of possible elements was more than seven, and the number of elements in particular rituals might be more or less than seven. The standard elements from which rituals could be constructed include: praise (*vandanā*), WORSHIP (*pūjanā*), confession of faults (*deśana*), rejoicing in the merits of others (*modanā*), requesting the buddhas to teach (*adhyeṣaṇā*), requesting the buddhas to remain in this world (*yācanā*), transfer of merit (*pariṇāmana*), arising of *bodhicitta* (*bodhicittotpāda*), taking refuge (*śaraṇagamana*), making vows (*praṇidāna*), and sacrifice of oneself (*ātmatyāga*).

Another kind of ritual organization is found in many tantric Buddhist rituals. These rituals are constructed symmetrically around the symbolically central action of ritualized identification between the practitioner and the deity evoked; this is called *deity yoga.* The five steps of these rituals are:

- **purification**—preparation of the practitioner
- **construction**—preparation of the ritual site
- **encounter**—inviting, greeting, and feasting the deity
- **identification**—meditative union, or ritual identification
- **dissociation**—recapitulates the first three steps:
- **departure of the deity**: corollary of encounter
- **dissolution of the ritual site**: corollary of construction
- **departure of the practitioner**: corollary of purification

A number of different categories of ritual practice are known. Early eighth-century translations into Chinese by Bodhiruci list three categories: *śāntika,* for protection; *pauṣṭika,* for increase of benefits; and *abhicāraka,* for domination. By the end of the ninth century, an additional two categories are evidenced: *vaśīkaraṇa,* for attraction; and *aṅkuśa,* for acquisition. These categories inform both the Indo-Tibetan and East Asian traditions. In Tibetan ritual traditions, a set of four appears to have become the standard grouping, while in East Asia the standard grouping comprises all five. These categories establish a complex set of associations for ritual performance: for ex-

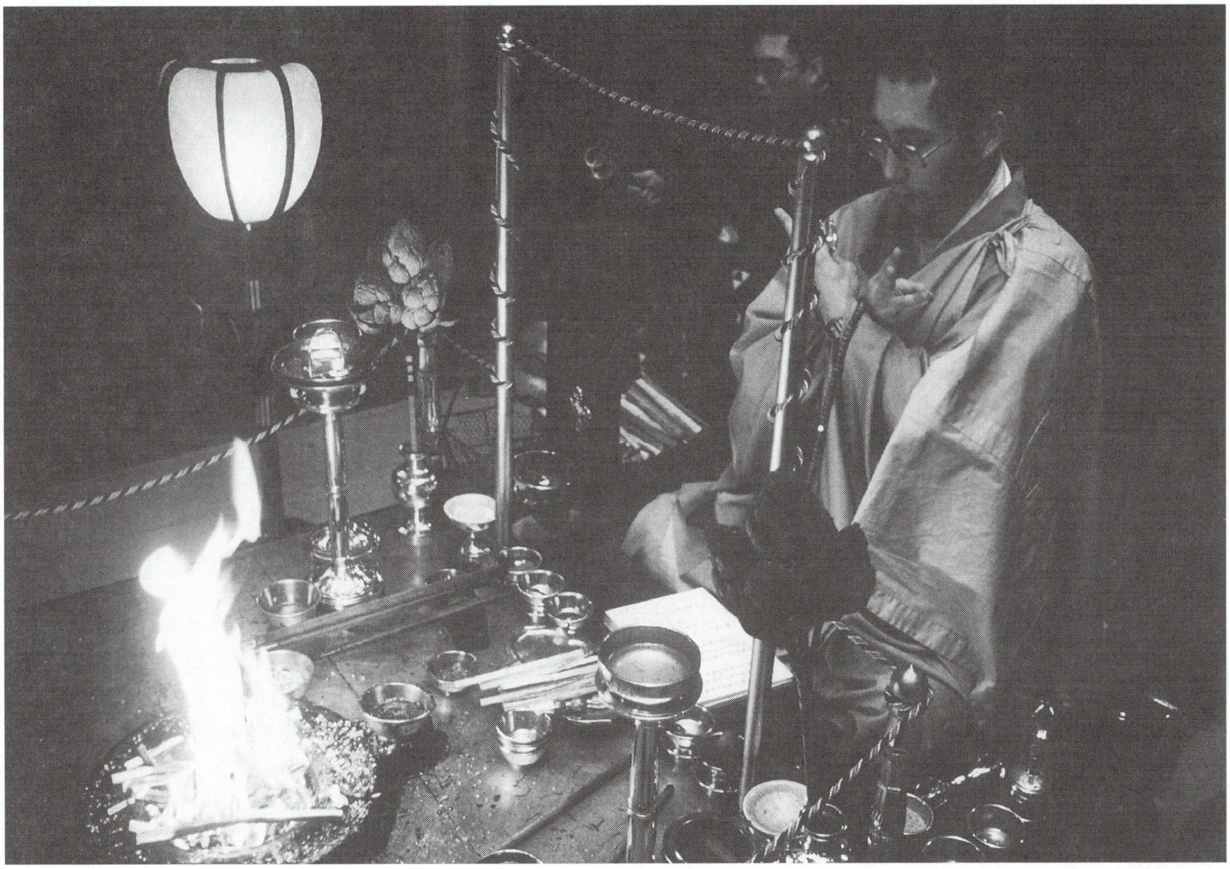

A Shingon priest performs a *homa* ritual ceremony at Takamuruin, Kōyasan, Japan. © Don Farber 2003. All rights reserved. Reproduced by permission.

ample, the time of day for performing the ritual, the color of the practitioner's clothing, and the kind of altar to be employed.

An exemplary ritual: *homa*

Originating in the Vedic tradition, *homa,* or fire ritual, is found in both Hindu and Buddhist tantra. Within the Buddhist world *homa* is found wherever the tantric tradition has taken root, including Mongolia, China, Tibet, Japan, and Bali. The ritual comprises a series of offerings made into a fire built on the altar. The mouth of the altar hearth is homologized to the mouth of the deity and to the practitioner's mouth, while the fire is the deity's digestive fire and the fire of wisdom (prajñā) that purifies defilements (*kleśa*).

The *homa* ritual demonstrates the way in which rituals are organized according to a basic metaphor. *Homa* is a feast for the deities who are evoked in the course of the ritual. This ritual metaphor is found in many tantric Buddhist rituals, and evidences the connection between them and their Vedic sources, which also serve as ritual feasts.

In addition to the ritual metaphor and *homa*'s organization, specific elements within the ritual highlight the continuity of practice across more than three millennia and multiple religious cultures. These include an opening offering to Agni, the Vedic god of fire and sacrifice; implements used (e.g., two ladles for making offerings); and the varieties of materials offered, most emblematically, clarified butter (ghee). The processes of cultural adaptation are reflected in the use of various substitutes, such as sesame oil (Japanese, *goma abura*) for ghee. The widespread practice of the *homa* ritual indicates the central place that ritual holds in much of the Buddhist tradition. Rather than being purely rational and ethical, Buddhism has therefore always maintained a crucial role for ritual in its religious culture and practice.

See also: **Initiation; Ordination; Ritual Objects; Tantra**

Bibliography

Aune, Michael B., and DeMarinis, Valerie, eds. *Religious and Social Ritual: Interdisciplinary Explorations.* Albany: State University of New York Press, 1996.

Bell, Catherine. *Ritual Theory, Ritual Practice.* New York and Oxford: Oxford University Press, 1992.

Bell, Catherine. *Ritual: Perspectives and Dimensions.* New York and Oxford: Oxford University Press, 1997.

Bentor, Yael. *Consecrations of Images and Stūpas in Indo-Tibetan Tantric Buddhism.* Leiden, Netherlands: Brill, 1996.

Bentor, Yael. "Literature on Consecration (*Rab gnas*)." In *Tibetan Literature: Studies in Genre,* ed. José Ignacio Cabezón and Roger R. Jackson. Ithaca, NY: Snow Lion, 1996.

Beyer, Stephan. *The Cult of Tara: Magic and Ritual in Tibet.* Berkeley and Los Angeles: University of California Press, 1978.

Cabezón, José Ignacio. "Firm Feet and Long Lives: The *Zhabs brtan* Literature of Tibetan Buddhism." In *Tibetan Literature: Studies in Genre,* ed. José Ignacio Cabezón and Roger R. Jackson. Ithaca, NY: Snow Lion, 1996.

Cozort, Daniel. "*Sādhana* (*sGrub thabs*): Means of Achievement for Deity Yoga." In *Tibetan Literature: Studies in Genre,* ed. José Ignacio Cabezón and Roger R. Jackson. Ithaca, NY: Snow Lion, 1996.

Egge, James R. *Religious Giving and the Invention of Karma in Theravāda Buddhism.* Richmond, UK: Routledge Curzon, 2002.

Gombrich, Richard F. *How Buddhism Began: The Conditioned Genesis of the Early Teachings.* London and Atlantic Highlands, NJ: Athlone, 1996.

Kohn, Richard J. *Lord of the Dance: The Mani Rimdu Festival in Tibet and Nepal.* Albany: State University of New York Press, 2001.

Makransky, John. "Offering (*mChod pa*) in Tibetan Ritual Literature." In *Tibetan Literature: Studies in Genre,* ed. José Ignacio Cabezón and Roger R. Jackson. Ithaca, NY: Snow Lion, 1996.

Payne, Richard K. *The Tantric Ritual of Japan: Feeding the Gods, The Shingon Fire Ritual.* Delhi: International Academy of Indian Culture, 1991.

Payne, Richard K. "The Tantric Transformation of Pūjā: Interpretation and Structure in the Study of Ritual." In *India and Beyond: Aspects of Literature, Meaning, Ritual, and Thought,* ed. Dick van der Meij. London and New York: Kegan Paul, 1997.

Payne, Richard K. "Tongues of Flame: Homologies in the Tantric Homa." In *The Roots of Tantra,* ed. Katherine Anne Harper and Robert L. Brown. Albany: State University of New York Press, 2002.

Wallis, Glenn. *Mediating the Power of Buddhas: Ritual in the Mañjuśrīmūlakalpa.* Albany: State University of New York Press, 2002.

Weber, Claudia. *Buddhistische Beichten in Indien und bei den Uiguren: Unter besonderer Berücksichtigung der uigurischen Laienbeichte und ihrer Beziehung zum Manichäismus.* Wiesbaden, Germany: Harrassowitz, 1999.

RICHARD K. PAYNE

RITUAL OBJECTS

The VINAYA relates that the historical Buddha permitted his ordained mendicants only four possessions—three robes and a begging bowl. These simple, functional objects served as the first Buddhist ritual implements since they were the primary material means to clearly distinguish the members of the monastic community from the laity. Initiates could not be ordained until they had properly received them. Over the succeeding centuries, as Buddhism was transmitted throughout Asia, the number of permissible possessions increased to six—three robes, a begging bowl, a stool, and a water strainer—and then to eighteen, including a censer and staff. Moreover, as the rituals of the religion became increasingly elaborate, greater numbers of implements were required. Although different regions frequently interpreted the forms of these objects in culturally specific ways, implements often had their origins in secular Indian modes of veneration and ornamentation.

Implements of ornamentation

Indian Buddhists correlated sacred adornment with the manifestation of the supernatural. In decorating the interior of halls that housed the object of WORSHIP, they hoped to realize the appearance of the paradises in which the deities were believed to dwell, as described in the sūtras. Thus, elaborate decoration and exquisite craftsmanship came to characterize the implements that adorned the halls.

As images of the Buddha and other members of the Buddhist pantheon became the focus of worship, implements were employed to demarcate the sacred space in which they were enshrined. For example, canopies, which derived from the parasols used by the ancient Indian elite, were suspended over the deity. Garlands of flowers that likewise had been used by the South Asian nobility for personal adornment were draped over images. In northern climates the festoons were reinterpreted in openwork plaques of fabric, leather, or metal, and ornamented with semiprecious stones. Today in Japan these symbolic floral offerings, which are known as *keman,* continue to be hung from the beams of the interiors of image halls. In addition banners known as *ban,* which had been adapted in luxurious textiles or gilt bronze from ancient battle standards signifying victory over one's enemies, fly from dragon-headed poles both in the interior and exterior of the halls.

A monk holds prayer beads at the Rumtek Monastery near Gangtok, Sikkim, seat of the Bka' brgyud (Kagyu) school of Tibetan Buddhism. © Ric Ergenbright/Corbis. Reproduced by permission.

Vessels for offerings

In India the primary offerings made to the Buddha and stūpas were incense, flowers, and candles. The Japanese *Darani jikkyō* (*Sūtra of Collected Dhāraṇī*) explains that incense and perfumed water were used to purify, flowers to pay homage, and light to illuminate the darkness of ignorance. Offerings of food symbolized the giving of alms. In East Asia a set of three metal vessels for these offerings—a candlestick, incense burner, and flower vase—were placed on the main altar in front of an image. In some Buddhist sects the set of three was replaced by a more elaborate set of five, including two candlesticks, two flower vases, and an incense burner.

Ritual implements in the Japanese liturgical context

The great diversity in the practice of Buddhism in Asia has resulted in a great variety of rituals and of ritual implements. Study of contemporary Buddhist ritual practice in Japan, which closely follows that on the continent in earlier centuries, reveals that most sectarian differences ultimately are outweighed by fundamental similarities. The ceremonies begin with a call to worship, marked by the striking of a large bronze bell. During the procession of monks into the hall, the chief officiant holds a long-handled censer—an emblem of his authority. In the CHAN SCHOOL (Zen) the chief officiant may alternatively wield an animal-hair *wisk* or a scepter with a foliate end. After making obeisance to the deity, he seats himself on a raised, square ritual platform (*raiban*). To his left and right are two small tables, generally crafted from lacquer, which hold ritual implements and texts.

During the introductory section of the service, stylized chanting is accompanied by the shaking of a monk's staff (*shakujō*) and the strewing of flower petals from openwork baskets (*kekō*) in order to purify the ritual space. During the main part of the ceremony the deity is summoned, praised, and hosted, after which prayers are made. Expressions of appreciation are then communicated to the deity and the celebrant then promises that the benefits accrued from the ritual will be shared with others. During the service the celebrant frequently strikes a metal chime (*kei*), which is suspended from a lacquer stand to the right of the *raiban*, to punctuate the different sections of the liturgy. This percussion instrument generally takes the form of an inverted chevron with a raised lotus boss.

Esoteric ritual implements

Implements are essential to the performance of esoteric Buddhist rituals. Derived in form from ancient Indian weapons, esoteric ritual implements are believed to imbue the officiant with extraordinary powers and thus assist the individual in the quest to join Buddhist deities in the quest for enlightenment.

As in MAHĀYĀNA ritual, the practitioner sits on a ritual dais, but esoteric ritual employs a ritual platform, on which are placed a great variety of implements and which in turn is placed in front of the painting or sculpture that is the focus of the rite. In India this platform would have been formed from earth over a seven-day period and then later destroyed. In China and Japan it took a more permanent form in wood. The implements used in esoteric rituals can generally be divided into four categories: those for protecting the practitioner, those for purifying the deity and officiant, those for holding offerings, and those for providing musical accompaniment. The most

Monks rotate prayer wheels at the Ivolginski Datsan Temple in Buryatiya, eastern Siberia. © Oleg Nishikin/Getty Images. Reproduced by permission.

important are those that protect and empower the practitioner and the ritual space. These are placed on the ritual altar and include the various forms of *vajra,* the *vajra* spikes placed at the four corners to support a five-colored rope, the cakra placed in the center, and crossed *vajra* at the four corners.

Most frequently composed of clawlike opposed outer prongs and a sharply notched profile, *vajra* resemble stylized thunderbolts. The most common form is one with three prongs on each end, said to symbolize the three mysteries of body, speech, and mind. Other *vajra* include the five-prong form, symbolizing the five wisdoms of the five buddhas, and the single-prong form, symbolizing the universal truth. The implements are usually fashioned from gilt bronze, but esoteric texts specify that they may also be made from gold, silver, copper, iron stone, rock crystal, acacia, sandalwood, and purple sandalwood.

The cakra was believed to be one of the seven treasures of a cakravartin or universal monarch. Said to miraculously precede him into battle, conquering foes in the four directions, the cakra resembles a wheel. Different texts mention cakra with a varying number of spokes. Those with four spokes symbolize the FOUR NOBLE TRUTHS and those with six symbolize the realms of existence. In Japan, where it is called a *rimpō,* the wheel most often takes an eight-spoked form that was thought to symbolize the eightfold PATH. The crossed *vajra* (known in Japanese as *katsuma*) resembles two intersecting three-pronged *vajra.* Based upon an Indian weapon that was hurled, this metal implement is believed to provide protection in the four directions.

The second category of implements used in esoteric rituals are those that hold various materials used in the ritual to purify the deity and the officiant. Most often they consist of a set of covered containers for water and powdered incense, which are placed near the ritual dais. A third category includes vessels for holding the offerings to be made to the deity. These consist of a censer for burnt incense offerings and the six vessels, which hold offerings of sacred water, floral garlands, powdered incense, and light. Generally made from gilt bronze, they are placed in sets along the four sides of the ritual dais. Vases for offerings of flowers

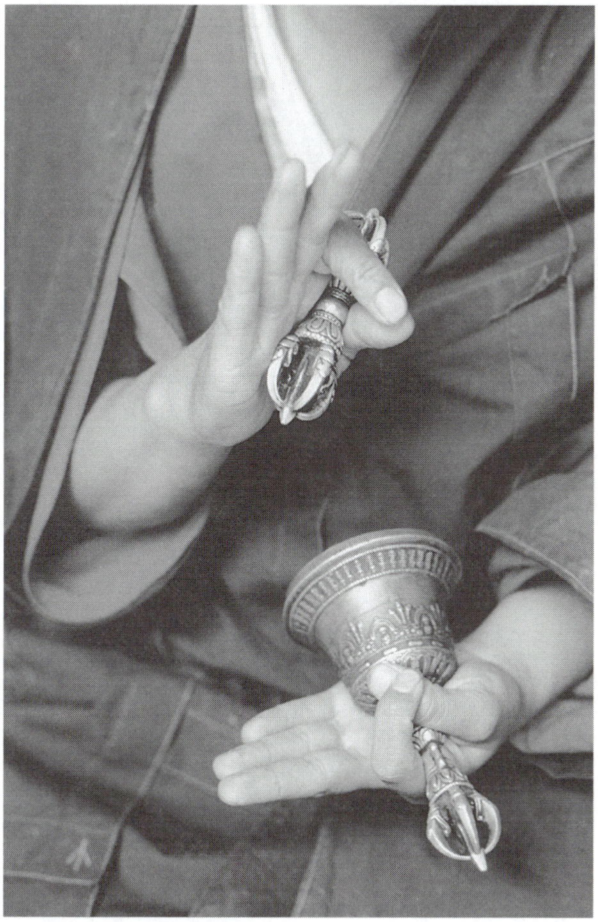

A monk holding a *vajra* rings a small bell as an aid to ritual chanting at a monastery in Bhutan. © Hulton/Archive by Getty Images. Reproduced by permission.

and vessels for offerings of food are positioned in the four corners.

The final group includes various musical implements such as bells and cymbals used to gain the attention of the deity, entertain it with sound, and then to provide it with melodious accompaniment upon its departure. Bells are also used to awaken the enlightened mind of the practitioner. Although single examples are frequently used in rituals, handheld bells also occur in sets of five, consisting of a single-pronged *vajra*-handled bell, a three-pronged *vajra*-handled bell, a five-pronged *vajra*-handled bell, a jewel-handled bell, and a pagoda-handled bell. The five bells are placed on the ritual altar, along with *vajra* of similar forms. The five *vajra* represent the *samaya* form of the five wisdom buddhas and their secret wisdom, while the five bells represent their outwardly directed teachings.

A metal ritual tray, frequently raised, is placed on the ritual altar in front of the practitioner. On it is placed a set of implements to be utilized during the ceremony. Usually a single-pronged *vajra,* a three-pronged *vajra,* and a five-pronged *vajra* surround a *vajra*-handled bell, but the arrangement of the implements and the placement of the tray itself vary according to sect and to school.

Bibliography

Morse, Anne Nishimura, and Morse, Samuel Crowell. *Object as Insight: Japanese Buddhist Art and Ritual.* Katonah, NY: Katonah Museum of Art, 1995.

Reynolds, Valrae. *From the Sacred Realm: Treasures of Tibetan Art from the Newark Museum.* New York and Munich, Germany: Prestel, 1999.

Yamasaki Taikō. *Shingon: Japanese Esoteric Buddhism,* translated and adapted by Richard Peterson and Cynthia Peterson. Boston and London: Shambhala, 1988.

ANNE NISHIMURA MORSE

RINZAI ZEN. *See* **Chan School**

RNYING MA (NYINGMA)

The Rnying ma (ancient) school is one of the four main schools of Tibetan Buddhism, the other three being the BKA' BRGYUD (KAGYU), the SA SKYA (SAKYA), and the DGE LUGS (GELUK). According to the Tibetan historical tradition, Buddhism arrived into Tibet in two waves. The "early spread" (*snga dar*) arrived over the seventh to the ninth centuries, during the height of the Tibetan empire, and the "later spread" (*phyi dar*) came after the late tenth century. Adherents of the Rnying ma school trace their roots back to Buddhism's early spread, while followers of the three newer (*gsar ma*) schools adhere to those traditions that arrived during the later spread. In this way, the Rnying ma school is defined in juxtaposition to the other schools of Tibetan Buddhism; *Rnying ma* as a term only began to be used in the eleventh century, after the later spread had begun.

From an early date, criticisms were leveled against the tantric traditions of the Rnying ma pa (adherents of the Rnying ma school). The period that separated the two waves of Buddhism (roughly 842–978 C.E.) witnessed the collapse of the Tibetan empire and a subsequent breakdown of any centralized authority. Buddhist monasteries throughout Tibet lost their official patronage and were closed down. Traditional

Tibetan histories unanimously portray these years as a "dark period," a time of degeneration for Buddhism when, freed from the watchful eye of authoritative Buddhist institutions, the scattered local communities went astray. The response among the new schools was to reimport Buddhism from India, while the Rnying ma pa claimed that their Buddhism was a pure strand that had survived intact since the glory days of the Tibetan empire and Buddhism's earlier spread. In the competitive atmosphere of Buddhism's later spread, a TANTRA's legitimacy depended on its being a translation from an Indian original. Many Rnying ma tantras came under suspicion for being Tibetan APOCRYPHA. A fair number of new works were certainly composed in Tibet, particularly during the creative disorder of the dark period.

Perhaps the most successful of the post-tenth-century Rnying ma pa responses to these accusations was their development of the "treasure" (*gter ma*) revelation system. Received in visionary encounters or discovered hidden in the physical landscape, these revelations were timely teachings attributed to the legendary (usually Indian) masters of the early imperial period. In this way, new Rnying ma works could surface under the protection of a canonical Indian origin. The Rnying ma school shares the system of treasure revelation with the non-Buddhist BON religion of Tibet, but generally speaking, none of the other schools made use of this strategy.

Also unique to the Rnying ma school and Bon is their highest category of Rnying ma teachings, called *Atiyoga* or *Rdzogs chen* (*Great Perfection*). This was the highest of the Rnying ma school's nine vehicles (*theg pa dgu*), a hierarchical schema for organizing Buddhist teachings according to the sophistication of the view each advocated. After the eleventh century, the Rnying ma pa focused increasingly on the Atiyoga class of teachings, and the writings from this period are some of the most creative in Rnying ma literature. The development of Rdzogs chen culminated in the systematizing works by KLONG CHEN PA (LONGCHENPA) (1308–1363). This fourteenth-century master was also instrumental in sealing a new relationship between Rdzogs chen and PADMASAMBHAVA, the eighth-century tantric master who was instrumental in bringing Buddhism to Tibet. Since the eleventh century, the Rnying ma pa had looked to Padmasambhava as their principal founding father, but this master does not appear to have enjoyed a particularly close association with Rdzogs chen until the fourteenth century. Before that, the most influential Rdzogs chen works were usually attributed to two other masters of Tibet's early imperial period, Vairocana or Vimalamitra. By the end of the fourteenth century, however, Padmasambhava reigned supreme in the minds of the Rnying ma pa, over almost all aspects of their school.

In the seventeenth century the Rnying ma school became embroiled in the political turmoil that led to the fifth DALAI LAMA's takeover of Tibet. The family of the fifth Dalai Lama (1617–1682) had maintained close contacts with the Rnying ma pa, particularly with the followers of the Northern Treasures (*byang gter*). As the Dalai Lama rose to power in the mid-seventeenth century, he brought his Rnying ma pa associates with him. Under his patronage, the period witnessed a sudden surge in large, new Rnying ma monasteries being founded throughout central and eastern Tibet.

This proliferation of monasteries engendered a shift in the character of the Rnying ma school toward large-scale monastic institutions and elaborate public festivals. The changes were spearheaded by a close associate of the Dalai Lama, Gter bdag gling pa (1646–1714), the founder of Smin grol gling Monastery. This master, together with his brother, Lochen Dharmaśrī (1654–1717), conducted extensive historical research into the Rnying ma school's past; on the basis of his findings he formulated a new ritual tradition that could be shared by all of the new monasteries.

With the death of the fifth Dalai Lama and his regent, the Rnying ma pa lost their protection, and in 1717 the Mongolian Dzungars, themselves dogmatic supporters of the Dalai Lama's own Dge lugs school, invaded central Tibet. During their short time there, the Dzungars looted the new Rnying ma monasteries of Rdo rje brag and Smin grol gling, executing the head lamas. But the work accomplished at Smin grol gling survived this blow, and the Rnying ma pas' resolve to consolidate their school only strengthened over the next two centuries. An important element in this trend came with the late-eighteenth-century revelation of the *Klong chen snying thig* treasure cycle by 'Jigs med gling pa (1730–1798). 'Jigs med gling pa came from Khams in eastern Tibet, and his teachings were quickly adopted by all of the large new monasteries throughout this region.

The *Klong chen snying thig* (*Seminal Heart of the Great Expanse*) also inspired many of the great nineteenth-century lamas of eastern Tibet who were involved in the new nonsectarian (*ris med*) movement. This movement was based in Sde dge, the cultural capital of the

TOP: A Buddhist monastery in the mountains above Tetang, Nepal. © *Macduff Everton/Corbis. Reproduced by permission.*

RIGHT: The Sku 'bum (Kumbum) ("place of one hundred thousand images") stūpa at the Dpal 'khor chos sde (Palkhor Chode) Monastery in Rgyal rtse (Gyantse), Tibet. © *Craig Lovell/Corbis. Reproduced by permission.*

TOP: The wooden cover or "title page" of the *Prajñāpāramitā-sūtra* (*Perfection of Wisdom Sūtra*). The manuscript is in Tibetan, translated from Sanskrit; the text on the cover is in Mongolian. Tibetan, eighteenth century, gold on blue paper with carved and gilt wooden covers. *Victoria & Albert Museum. Reproduced by permission.*

BOTTOM: Illuminated title page from the Tibetan translation of the *Vinayavibhaṅga* (*Explanation of the Monastic Discipline*). The figure on the left is Kāśyapa, senior disciple of the Buddha; on the right is Tsong kha pa (1357–1419), founder of the Dge lugs (Geluk) school of Tibetan Buddhism. Tibetan, gold ink on paper. *The British Library. Reproduced by permission.*

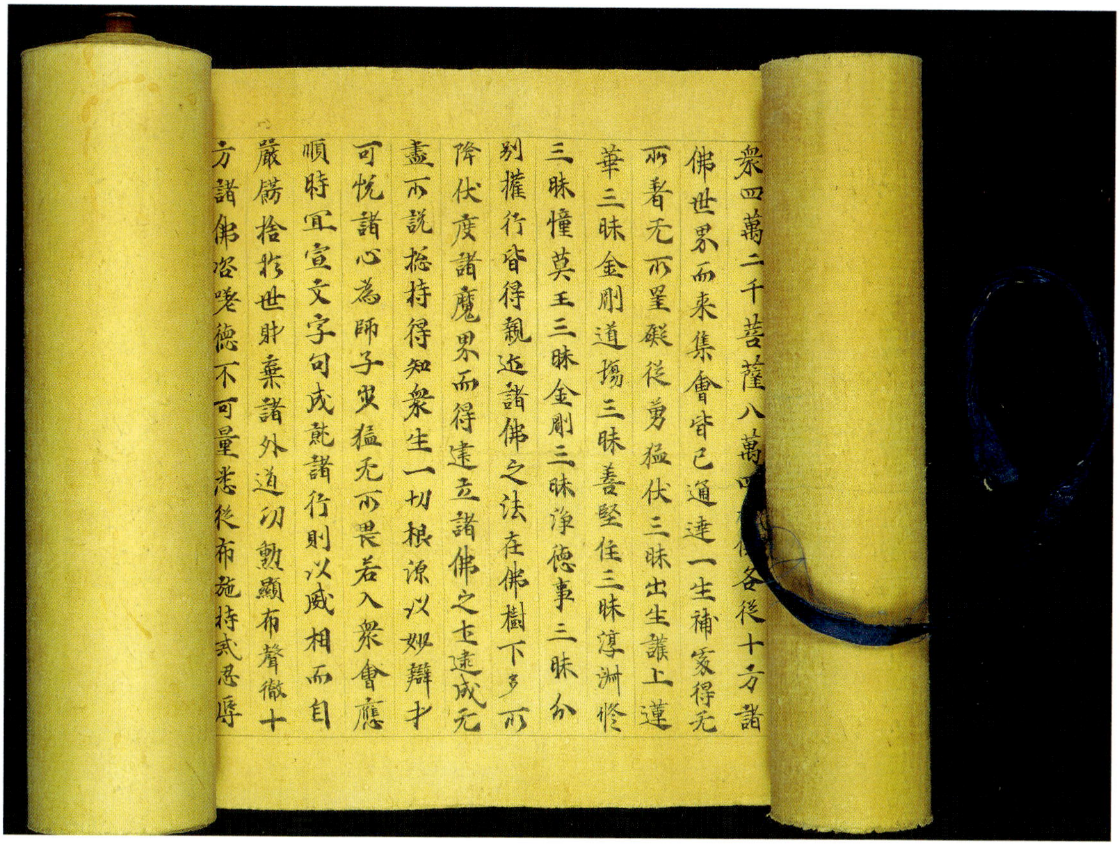

TOP: The *Ratnakūḍaparipṛcchā* (*Ratnakūḍa's Questions*), in Chinese translation. This work is the forty-seventh scripture in the collection known as the *Mahāratnakūṭa-sūtra* or *Great Heap of Gems Sūtra*, a collection of early Mahāyāna sūtras. Chinese, Western Jin dynasty (265–316 C.E.), ink on paper scroll, with wooden roller. *The British Library. Reproduced by permission.*

BOTTOM: Illuminated manuscript of the *Aṣṭasāhasrikāprajñāpāramitā-sūtra* (*Perfection of Wisdom in 8,000 Lines*), in Sanskrit, from the Vikramaśīla Monastery in Bihar. The figures depicted are the bodhisattvas Avalokiteśvara (top), seated on a lion's back, and Maitreya. Indian, ca. 1145 C.E., ink and gouache on palm leaves with wooden covers. *The British Library. Reproduced by permission.*

Vaiśravana, Dharma-protector of the north, with Śrīdevī (the goddess Splendor) and attendants. Chinese, Tang dynasty (618–907), painting on silk from Dunhuang. *Copyright The British Museum. Reproduced by permission.*

The horrific celestial buddha Śaṃvara with his female partner. Above Śaṃvara are depicted the buddhas Dīpaṃkara, Śākyamuni, and Maitreya; below is Amitābha Buddha flanked by green and white Tārās, protective female deities. Tibetan, eighteenth century, painting on cloth with silk border. *Copyright The British Museum. Reproduced by permission.*

TOP: The Procession of the Buddha's Tooth Relic. This image is one of six in a scroll depicting an annual event in Kandy. Here the temple elephant carries the reliquary casket, surrounded by the faithful. Sri Lankan, ca. 1796–1815, watercolor on paper. *The British Library. Reproduced by permission.*

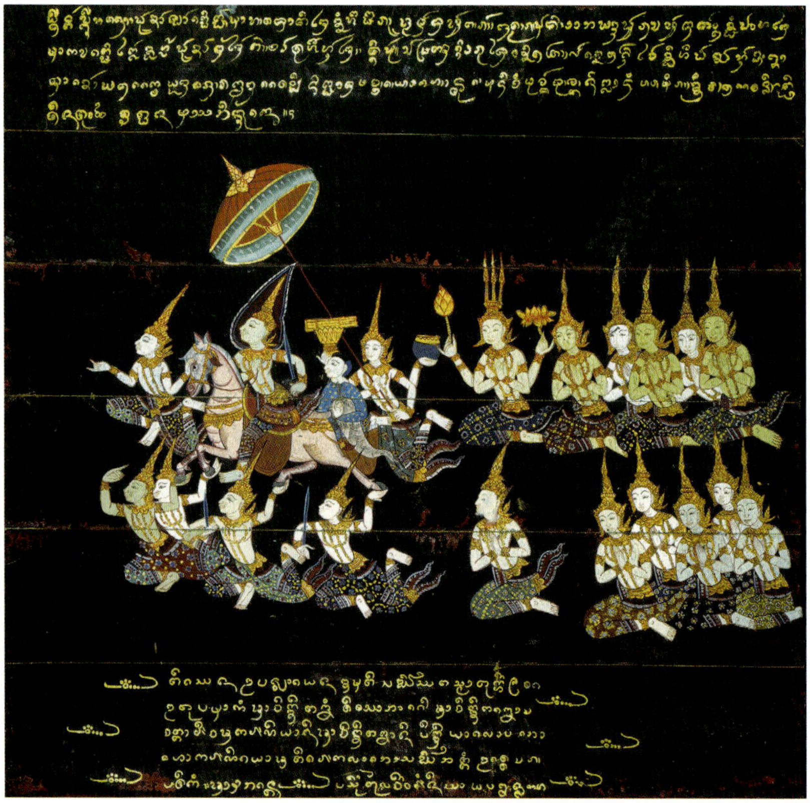

RIGHT: Illustrated manuscript of the *upasampadā* (ordination ceremony), in Pāli. The image depicts Siddhārtha being carried away from household life on his horse by the gods. Thai, late nineteenth century, painting and gold script on stiffened cloth. *The British Library. Reproduced by permission.*

TOP: Nichiren (1222–1282), founder of the Nichiren school, was an opponent of the established Japanese Buddhist schools of his day. Here he is shown calming the sea on his way into exile on Sado Island following a failed insurrection in 1271. Japanese, ca. 1830. Woodblock color print by Utagawa Kuniyoshi (1797–1861). *Copyright The British Museum. Reproduced by permission.*

LEFT: The *Pañcarakṣā* (*Five Protective Hymns*). This decorated manuscript was donated to the Tarumūla Monastery in Kathmandu by a wealthy merchant named Jayarāma and his family, who are depicted making offerings to the Buddha in the bottom panel. Nepalese, 1676, gold and gouache on blue paper, gouache on wood. *The British Library. Reproduced by permission.*

The seventh–eighth-century stūpa at the Mahābodhi Temple at Bodh Gayā. © *David Cumming; Eye Ubiquitous/Corbis. Reproduced by permission.*

region. In reaction to the growing sectarianism throughout Tibet, those involved sought out common ground between the schools and developed massive new literary collections that could be shared by all the schools of Tibetan Buddhism. The Rnying ma philosophy of Rdzogs chen played a particularly important role in this movement. The shape of today's Rnying ma school derives directly from the efforts of these nonsectarian masters of the nineteenth century.

See also: Tibet

Bibliography

Germano, David. "Architecture and Absence in the Secret Tantric History of the Great Perfection (*rdzogs chen*)." *Journal of the International Association of Buddhist Studies* 17, no. 2 (1994): 203–335.

Rinpoche, Dudjom. *The Nyingma School of Tibetan Buddhism: Its Fundamentals and History,* tr. Gyurme Dorje and Matthew Kapstein. Boston: Wisdom, 1991.

Smith, E. Gene. *Among Tibetan Texts: History and Literature of the Himalayan Plateau.* Boston: Wisdom, 2001.

Thondup, Tulku. *Masters of Miracles and Meditation: The Longchen Nyingthig Lineage of Tibetan Buddhism.* Boston: Shambala, 1996.

JACOB P. DALTON

ROBES AND CLOTHING

Buddhist robes (*kāṣāya;* Chinese, *jiasha;* Japanese, *kesa*) originally reflected the ideals of a life of poverty and simplicity. The VINAYA or monastic codes permitted a monk only three rectangular pieces of cloth of different sizes for use as religious robes. The small-, medium-, and large-sized robes were worn alone or in combination with each other. These rectangular mantles had no tailoring and simply wrapped around the body. They resembled the clothing of ordinary people and therefore used distinctive colors, materials, and fabrication to distinguish the wearer as one who had left the ordinary world to embark upon the path to enlightenment. As Buddhism spread throughout Asia, the robes delineated in greater detail such things as rank and sectarian affiliations through further variations in color, materials, and fabrication. The robes also came to be regarded as merit-making objects themselves, requiring special treatment, much like any other ritual object.

Regulations for early Buddhist robes

To differentiate Buddhist robes from the ordinary white robes of common people, the robes were dyed. Texts do not concur on the exact colors to be used, but most prohibit the use of undiluted primary colors. However, there is consensus that the preferred color is *kāṣāya,* which literally means impure, and came to refer to a reddish-yellow or brownish-yellow saffron or ocher color. THERAVĀDA monks still regularly wear this color; MAHĀYĀNA monks wear it less often. The actual shades vary, but the use of impure or mixed coloring is essential and emphasizes the teaching of nonattachment and nonpreference even for the color of one's robes. The use of impure or muddied color was such an important characteristic that the word, *kāṣāya,* became the common name for the robes themselves.

According to the PRECEPTS, the actual material for Buddhist robes was not as important as the humble origins of the material. The best material was that which had no value to others, such as unwanted and soiled rags. The precepts urged monks to be wearers of robes taken from the dust heap. While acceptable materials included silk, cotton, wool, hemp, and even fur, the most important characteristic was that they be tattered and defiled in some way, such as having been charred by fire, gnawed by rats, used as a shroud for the dead, or stained with menstrual blood, mucus, urine, or feces. Texts also caution against the use of embroidery and ornate weaving, a proscription later ignored. Plain, common materials are best, but the primary requirement is that they should not engender covetousness or attachment.

The third distinguishing feature of Buddhist robes is that they should be sewn from many pieces. Against charges that robes of whole cloth might reflect sensual enjoyment, the Buddha announced that robes made of uncut cloth should not be worn. Although in later passages of the Vinaya the Buddha allowed two of the three robes to be made of whole cloth, the standard *kāṣāya* was a patchwork marked by horizontal and vertical divisions. The Vinaya reference to patterns of rice fields bordered by embankments inspired the patchwork design of the *kāṣāya.*

Robes were patched together in vertical columns, always odd in number, and edged by a binding. The smallest of the three regulation robes had five columns, each comprised of one long and one short panel; the medium-sized robe had seven columns, each comprised of one short and two long panels; and the largest and most formal robe either had nine columns, each made up of two long and one short panel, or twenty-five columns, each comprised of four long and one short panel. Figure 1 shows the pattern for a seven-columned medium-sized *kāṣāya*. Variations based on odd numbers of columns between nine and twenty-five also exist, and there are legends of unusual robes with more columns. Small square patches reinforce the material at the four outer corners and at spots where cords are attached. Buddhist robes did not have any kind of fastening until the disciple ĀNANDA's robes were blown by a breeze, and in order to maintain modesty the Buddha permitted the use of cords and buckles of wood, bone, or shell. Braided cords and buckles were common in East Asia, but not in Southeast and South Asia.

The precepts also reinforce the idea of the robe as ritual object regulated in size, shape, and methods of stitching. Moreover, various texts recommend that each stitch be accompanied by a bow or a MANTRA (incantation), and advise that robes be cleaned with purified water and stored on high shelves surrounded by flowers and incense. Before Japanese Sōtō Zen monks don their robes, for example, they make three prostrations, place the folded robe on top of their heads and chant a verse in praise of the robe as a garment of liberation. Clearly the color, materials, and fabrication transform common robes into mantles of piety that represent humility and require respect.

Buddhist robes as insignias of status, occasion, and sectarian affiliation

Despite the Buddha's exhortations, changes occurred. One of the most noticeable was the East Asian practice of bordering the patched panels with a dark material, forming a robe of striking contrasts. Most significantly, the colder climates and customs of dress in East Asia led to the use of tailored garments worn beneath the *kāṣāya*. Established by the sixth century in China, these underrobes consisted of an upper garment that had neckband sleeves falling to the wrist, and a piece of pleated cloth used for a skirt, which Indian Buddhists had also used. In East Asia these two pieces eventually were sewn into a single kimono-like garment. In Japan a culotte type of skirt was also worn. The use of these underrobes changed the function of the *kāṣāya* in East Asia. *Kāṣāya* were no longer needed for warmth and modesty, but rather were used to convey rank, status, occasion, and sectarian affiliation.

The colors of a *kāṣāya* distinguished rank, status, and the level of formality of the occasion. To move from white to saffron robes signaled the advance from layman to monk in Thailand, just as the first level of novices in Japan today wear black and are permitted ocher robes only after receiving the formal transmission. East Asian Buddhists created complex systems of ecclesiastical ranks and offices modeled after those used at the imperial court, and they assigned certain colors to specific ranks. Martin Collcutt in *Five Mountains* (1981) describes the ranks and titles within medieval Japanese Zen monasteries. He notes that ordinary monks wore black underrobes and *kāṣāya*, but abbots wore robes of color. These colors depended not just on the individual's rank but also on the status of the particular monastery. For example, only abbots of the senior monastery of the highest status were permitted to wear deep-purple robes.

The propriety of colorful robes was debated at various times. However, religious leaders as divergent as PARAMĀRTHA (499–569), an Indian monk and translator of the sixth century, and DŌGEN (1200–1253), the founder of Sōtō Zen Buddhism in thirteenth-century Japan, affirmed that while muddy ocher may be best, robes of blue, yellow, red, black, purple, or a combination of these colors were permissible. Occasion also governed the selection of the robe's color. For example, in 1561 the New Pure Land sect decreed that henceforth their monks would wear white underrobes for happy events such as weddings, black underrobes for solemn occasions such as funerals, and colored underrobes for other ceremonial functions.

Another indication of a monk's rank was the quality of the *kāṣāya* material. Many *kāṣāya* for high-ranking monks in East Asia were made of exquisite brocades decorated with gold leaf, gold threads, and embroidery. These refinements were justified as marks of respect appropriate for robes that were devotional objects rather than ordinary garments. The precepts themselves also permit the use of donated materials, which could be refined, and this led to greater diversity of materials. The Vinaya relates the story of Jīvaka, who received an especially beautiful cloth from a king. When he asked the Buddha if it were permissible to wear such a cloth, the Buddha approved, saying that the monks were free to wear rag robes or to accept householders' garments, although it would be best to cut them. The status and fervor of the donor as well as the rank of the recipient were reflected in the quality of the donations, and thus donors contributed the most valuable materials they could afford. During the seventeenth through nineteenth centuries in Japan, for example, believers donated fragments of bright and richly decorated theatrical garments for monks to

FIGURE 1

Seven-columned kāṣāya

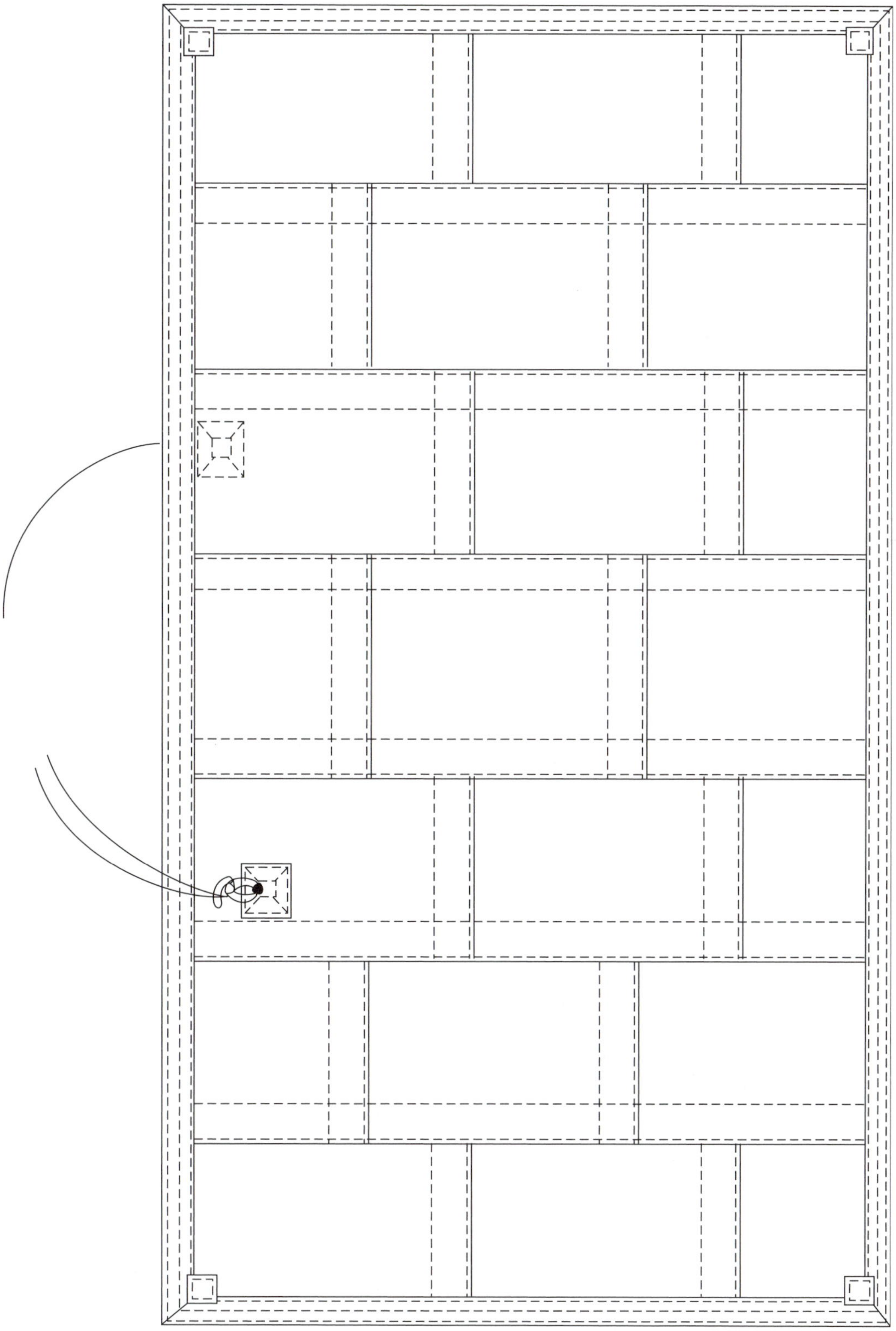

SOURCE: Adapted from Kyūma (1994), p. 48.

patch together for robes. In modern times, Japanese congregations sometimes solicit funds to provide their monks with beautiful and expensive *kāṣāya,* which can cost up to $100,000. Even these fabrics, however, are still cut or overstitched to resemble the patchwork required by the Buddha's directive.

Other indications of rank and formality of occasion include the number of columns in the *kāṣāya,* five columns for ordinary monks and occasions, and seven and nine columns for high-ranking monks and more formal events. Even the fastening cords were color coded to rank. Certain accessories also emphasized rank. The head scarf or hood that was worn initially by important Tiantai monks, for example, originated from the story that ZHIYI (538–597), the Chinese founder of TIANTAI SCHOOL Buddhism, received a gift of a sleeve from the emperor to wear on his head for protection against the severe cold as he administered the PRECEPTS. Recalling this legend, the Japanese emperor also gave a sleeve for use as a hood to SAICHŌ (767–822), who introduced Tiantai (Japanese, Tendai) Buddhism to Japan. Later, other sects adopted the sleevelike headdress.

Sectarian regulations were complex and underwent many revisions in the twentieth century. Japanese underrobes, for example, often have crests that symbolize particular sects, and sometimes *kāṣāya* incorporate scenes from the life of the sect's founder. Also in Japan, the abbreviated, folded *kāṣāya* forming long narrow bands vary in style according to sect. They are worn across the chest in the NICHIREN SCHOOL or sect, and as circlets around the neck in the New Pure Land sect, while Zen sects retain the use of a biblike abbreviated *kāṣāya.* Laypeople also wear the abbreviated *kāṣāya* around their necks as badges of affiliation and piety. While Buddhist robes convey shared ideals and meanings, it is clear that the color, materials, and fabrication can also distinguish the wearers from one another.

Buddhist robes as devotional objects

Kāṣāya are also objects of spiritual charisma that function as devotional objects and amulets. The robes of great religious teachers are passed down to disciples as evidence of transmission of the teachings, and they function as proof of spiritual LINEAGE. DŌGEN, in the chapter on "The Merits of the Buddhist Robe" in his *Shōbōgenzō* (*Treasury of the True Dharma Eye*), argues that *kāṣāya* are more important than Buddhist relics. The association of robes with relics is suggested too by the occasional deposit of robes within Buddhist sculptures along with sūtras and other valuable objects. Dōgen further argues that the Buddha himself told his monks to think of their robe as a STŪPA, that is, as a reliquary. And, in fact, relics and other precious objects were sometimes sewn into the backs of the robes. *Kāṣāya* were also visualized as altars, with the patches in the four corners representing the four Heavenly Kings that protect the four corners of the altar. The central patch was considered the seat of the Buddha, and the two patches on either side as the attendants to the Buddha.

The *kāṣāya* derives its spiritual worth from its ability to induce enlightenment and create merit. Tales of its power abound from India to Japan. Two famous examples include the story of Utpalavarnā, a prostitute in a previous life, who had once dressed herself in a *kāṣāya* as a joke. Despite her many sins, this action, even though it was in jest, produced sufficient merit to eventually lead her to enlightenment. Similarly, a JĀTAKA tale tells of the Buddha's previous life as a lion that was tricked into allowing a hunter to approach because the hunter had disguised himself and hid his weapons within a *kāṣāya.* Realizing the ruse, the lion nevertheless sacrificed himself rather than hurt a person dressed in Buddhist robes. In short, the *kāṣāya* produced merit and provided protection, and laypeople sometimes made miniature *kāṣāya* to carry with them as amulets at all times.

The Buddhist robe is layered with meanings. It can symbolize simplicity or splendor and can convey identities of place and position. As Dōgen suggested, its essential importance lies in the fact that wearing this humble robe plants the seed of enlightenment and destroys the poisonous arrows of delusion.

See also: **Etiquette; Merit and Merit-Making; Relics and Relics Cults**

Bibliography

Collcutt, Martin. *Five Mountains: The Rinzai Zen Monastic Institution in Medieval Japan.* Cambridge, MA: Harvard University Council on East Asian Studies and Harvard University Press, 1981.

Dōgen Zenji. *Shōbōgenzō,* tr. Nishiyama Kosen. Tokyo: Nakayama Shobo, 1988.

Faure, Bernard. "Quand l'habit fait le moine: The Symbolism of the Kāṣāya in Sōtō Zen." *Cahiers d'Extreme-Asie* 9 (1995): 335–369.

Griswold, A. B. "Prolegomena to the Study of the Buddha's Dress in Chinese Sculpture." *Artibus Asiae* 26, no. 2 (1963): 85–131.

Kennedy, Alan. *Manteau de Nuages: Kesa Japonais.* Paris: Reunion des Musée Nationaux, 1992.

Kyūma, Echū. *Kesa no hanashi.* Kyoto: Hōzōkan, 1994.

Till, Barry, and Swart, Paula. *Kesa: The Elegance of Japanese Monks' Robes.* Victoria, BC: Art Gallery of Greater Victoria, 1996.

WILLA JANE TANABE

RYŌKAN

Ryōkan (Taigu, 1758–1831) was the eldest son of a prosperous family in a port town of northwest Japan. He was ordained at the age of seventeen as a Sōtō Zen monk. After ten years of monastic training and five years of wandering Ryōkan returned to his home district, where he lived alone in a mountain hermitage. He maintained no ties to the Buddhist institutions, preferring a life of simplicity and poverty, writing poetry and practicing solitary meditation. He supported himself by the traditional practice of begging for alms, often stopping to play with children or to drink with the farmers. Gradually his fame spread and he became widely known as a poet and calligrapher. Scholars and writers traveled from far away to see him. The last three years of his life he became close friends with Teishin, a beautiful young nun who was an accomplished poet.

Ryōkan's poetry describes the fleeting details of his rural life with both joy and sadness, adding occasional references to Buddhism and classical allusions. He wrote in both Japanese and literary Chinese, often bending or ignoring rules of composition in favor of common speech. Beneath this surface of transparent simplicity is Ryōkan's great erudition in the most ancient classics of both Japanese and Chinese poetry. His unparalleled popularity in contemporary Japan comes both from his poetry and from the ideal of his life. Ryōkan is seen as one who achieved religious awakening in the midst of ordinary events, living a life that embodied the ideal of the unity of the mundane and transcendent.

See also: **Japanese, Buddhist Influences on Vernacular Literature in; Poetry and Buddhism**

Bibliography

Abé, Ryūichi, and Haskel, Peter. *Great Fool, Zen Master Ryōkan: Poems, Letters, and Other Writings.* Honolulu: University of Hawaii Press, 1996.

Yuasa, Noboyuki. *The Zen Poems of Ryōkan.* Princeton, NJ: Princeton University Press, 1981.

DAVID E. RIGGS

S

SAHA WORLD. *See* **Cosmology**

SAICHŌ

Saichō (767–822), posthumously known as Dengyō Daishi, was the founder of the Japanese Tendai (Chinese, Tiantai) school. He was a prolific scholar, and is best known for his efforts to reform monastic regulations and to create a new system of ordination for monks.

Soon after he was ordained in the capital city of Nara, Saichō began studying and meditating at Mount Hiei, just northeast of Kyoto, in 785. When the capital moved to Kyoto in 794, Saichō was no longer distant from the political center. Enryakuji, which he built atop of Mount Hiei, became the training ground for Japan's most illustrious Buddhist monks for the next four centuries. Although Enryakuji was a Tendai monastery, Saichō's original interests, as well as later developments, incorporated a diverse body of Buddhist practices, including Japanese Zen and Pure Land, and a strong emphasis on tantric Buddhism. Saichō's initial vision for a monastic center was motivated by his desire to purify and strengthen the spirit of Buddhist practice in Japan. He eventually proposed that Tendai monks be exempted from the government requirement to be ordained in Nara and, moreover, that Mount Hiei should house a center where monks could be ordained under Mahāyāna precepts that traditionally made no distinction between monastic and lay practitioners. His criticism of the doctrine and practice of the Nara Buddhist schools, particularly Hossō, resulted in strong opposition to his proposals. Nonetheless, the new ordination center was built shortly after his death. As a result, the Tendai school became a sectarian institution independent from Nara, and its monks became free from the vinaya.

See also: **Mahāyāna Precepts in Japan; Nara Buddhism; Tiantai School**

Bibliography

Abé, Ryūichi. "Saichō and Kukai: A Conflict of Interpretations." *Japanese Journal of Religious Studies* 22, nos. 1–2 (1995): 103–137.

Groner, Paul. *Saichō and the Establishment of the Japanese Tendai School.* Honolulu: University of Hawaii Press, 2000.

Weinstein, Stanley. "The Beginnings of Esoteric Buddhism in Japan: The Neglected Tendai Tradition." *Journal of Asian Studies* 34, no. 1 (1974): 177–191.

DAVID L. GARDINER

SAKYA. *See* **Sa skya (Sakya)**

ŚĀKYAMUNI. *See* **Buddha(s); Buddha Images**

SAMĀDHI. *See* **Meditation**

SAṂDHINIRMOCANA-SŪTRA

Probably originally composed sometime around the fourth century B.C.E. in India, the *Saṃdhinirmocana-sūtra* (*Discourse Explaining the Thought or Sūtra on*

Unfurling the Real Meaning) is today extant only in Chinese and Tibetan versions (Chinese, *Jie shenmi jing*; Tibetan, *Dgongs pa nges par 'grel pa'i mdo*). As its title indicates, the text claims to provide definitive explanations for contradictory statements in earlier sūtras. It is divided into ten chapters, each of which has a main interlocutor who asks the Buddha to explain the intentions behind earlier statements attributed to him. All of the interlocutors are identified as BODHISATTVAS on the tenth stage (*bhūmi*), and the discourse is set in a heavenly realm. These tropes are apparently intended to establish the text as the definitive statement on contentious doctrinal issues.

The first four chapters focus on a discussion of the ultimate truth (*paramārtha*). The fifth contains a seminal description of the *storehouse consciousness* (ĀLAYA-VIJÑĀNA), and the sixth explains the notion of the *three characteristics* (*trilakṣaṇa*) of phenomena (imputational, other-dependent, and thoroughly real). The seventh chapter is mainly concerned with outlining principles of Buddhist HERMENEUTICS, and the eighth focuses on MEDITATION theory and practice. The ninth chapter describes the bodhisattva PATH, and the final chapter is concerned with the characteristics of buddhahood, the culmination of the practices the text describes.

The *Saṃdhinirmocana-sūtra* became the main scriptural source for the YOGĀCARA SCHOOL, one of the two main philosophical traditions of Indian MAHĀYĀNA Buddhism (the other being Madhyamaka). It figures prominently in the thought of ASAṄGA (ca. 320–390), VASUBANDHU (fourth century C.E.), and their commentators, and inspired a voluminous literature in Tibet that is based on TSONG KHA PA's *Legs bshad snying po* (*Essence of Good Explanations*).

Bibliography

Powers, John. *Hermeneutics and Tradition in the Saṃdhinirmocana-sūtra.* Leiden, Netherlands: Brill, 1993.

Powers, John, trans. *Wisdom of Buddha: The Saṃdhinirmocana-sūtra.* Berkeley, CA: Dharma, 1995.

JOHN POWERS

SAMGUK YUSA (MEMORABILIA OF THE THREE KINGDOMS)

The *Samguk yusa* (*Memorabilia of the Three Kingdoms*) is a collection of myths, anecdotes, and short stories from ancient Korea, mostly from the kingdom of Silla. The text was compiled around 1285, after the Mongol subjugation of Korea, by the Buddhist monk Iryŏn (Kim Kyŏnmyŏng, 1206–1289) and contains at least one later insertion by his disciple Mugŭk (d.u.). Little is known about the text prior to 1512. The title word *yusa* (Chinese, *yishi*) suggests that the text was meant to serve as an unofficial supplement to an official work, perhaps the *Samguk sagi* (*Historical Records of the Three Kingdoms*), compiled by Kim Pusik between 1136 and 1145. *Samguk yusa* is roughly modeled after the *Lidai fabao ji* (*Record of the Dharma-Jewel over Successive Generations,* ca. 780) and the *Taiping guangji* (*Expanded Tales of the Taiping Era,* compiled 977–978) in form and content.

The *Samguk yusa* is comprised of five chapters. The first chapter begins with a dynastic chronology and follows with the foundation myths of the native Korean kingdoms and other traditional narratives dating from before Silla's conquest of the other kingdoms. The second chapter contains tales from the peninsular wars for unification, as well as postunification dynastic and other tales. The third chapter is comprised of two sections subtitled "The Flourishing of the Dharma" and "Stūpas and Images," which present the Buddhist perspective of the transmission of the religion to the peninsula and tales about the miraculous founding and history of particular sacred or cultic sites. The fourth chapter, "Exegetes," contains hagiographies of eminent Silla scholastic monks. The fifth chapter is divided into four subsections titled (1) "Divine Spells," hagiographies of Buddhist monks who specialize in working miracles through chanting DHĀRAṆĪ and sūtras; (2) "Thaumaturges," stories of individuals, particularly Buddhist monks, who possess magic powers; (3) "Escape and Seclusion," stories of people who escaped this mortal realm; and (4) "Filial Piety and Virtue," traditional narratives of filial sons and virtuous daughters.

See also: **Korea; Korean, Buddhist Influences on Vernacular Literature in**

Bibliography

Ha, Tae-Hung, and Mintz, Grafton K., trans. *Samguk Yusa: Legends and History of the Three Kingdoms of Ancient Korea.* Seoul: Yonsei University Press, 1972.

RICHARD D. MCBRIDE II

SAṂSĀRA

Saṃsāra (wandering) is a term referring to the beginningless cycle of birth, DEATH, and REBIRTH and a process characterized by mental and physical DUḤKHA (SUFFERING). This ongoing series of lives is determined by the moral quality of an individual's thoughts and KARMA (ACTION) in this life and in previous lives. It is generally postulated that within saṃsāra the effects of good moral actions lead to wholesome rebirths, while the effects of bad moral actions lead inevitably to unwholesome rebirths. Liberation (NIRVĀṆA), release from the cycle altogether, is achieved only by those individuals who gain correct insight and realization of the truth of the Buddha's teachings.

Saṃsāra is divided cosmologically into five (sometimes six) distinct realms of existence, within which living beings are reborn in dependence upon their karma. These places of rebirth include the realms of DIVINITIES (deva), human beings (*manuṣya*), animals (*tiryak*), spirits of the dead or hungry ghosts (preta), and the hells (*naraka*). When the list of five realms is expanded to six, the place of demigods (asura) is added below the god realm. Life in any one of these realms is never eternal and never free from the prospect of suffering. Whether wandering temporarily in the higher realms of gods and humans or in the lower realms of animals, ghosts, and the denizens of hell, all living beings experience the sufferings of birth, death, and rebirth. Saṃsāra and the realms of rebirth are depicted in paintings of the wheel of life (*bhavacakra*), which are especially common in Tibet.

Liberation from the cycle of saṃsāra is not always the immediate goal of Buddhism. In some Buddhist traditions, particularly in East Asia, greater emphasis is placed on rebirth in a buddha's pure land (Chinese, *jingtu*; Japanese, *jōdo*). The pure lands are purified buddha-fields (Sanskrit, *buddhakṣetra*) or paradises, which are free from mental and physical suffering and watched over by a particular buddha. Dissenting opinions exist about the exact location of the PURE LANDS. Some place them within the realms of saṃsāra, and others place them outside the cycle altogether. Rebirth in one of the pure lands is determined less by karma and more by sincere FAITH and aspiration to be reborn there. The compassionate assistance of the buddha who resides in the pure land is also a decisive factor in securing rebirth in such an auspicious realm. Among the most popular pure lands are AMITĀBHA's Land of Bliss (Sukhāvatī) and AKṢOBHYA's Land of Delight (Abhirati).

See also: **Cosmology**

Bibliography

Jamgön Kongtrul Lodrö Tayé. *Myriad Worlds: Buddhist Cosmology in Abhidharma, Kālacakra, and Dzog-chen.* Ithaca, NY: Snow Lion, 1995.

Sadakata, Akira. *Buddhist Cosmology: Philosophy and Origins,* tr. Gaynor Sekimori. Tokyo: Kōsei, 1997.

BRYAN J. CUEVAS

SAMYE DEBATE. *See* **Bsam yas Debate**

SĀÑCĪ

Sāñcī's extensive monastic complexes occupy a hilltop near the prosperous Indian town of Vidiṣa, where major road and river routes intersect. Its many freestanding pillars, STŪPAS, temples, assembly halls, and monastic residences (vihāras) date from the reign of King AŚOKA (third century B.C.E.) to around 1200 C.E., making it one of the oldest and most constantly occupied extant Buddhist sites. A small flat-roofed Gupta temple (ca. fourth century C.E.) is probably the earliest extant stone temple in South Asia. Many structures were erected on the foundations of earlier ones. Begun during Aśoka's rule, an apsidal temple complex (no. 40) was enlarged in Śuṅga times (ca. second to first centuries B.C.E.) and again later. Four quadrangular dry-masonry vihāras belong to the seventh century C.E. Two of these were double-storied, while another incorporated a stone-faced temple with a northern-style tower in its eastern wall. As at AJAṆṬĀ, Sāñcī's early stūpas are unadorned and austere, while a Buddha image graces its Gupta stūpa. Here too, Buddha images do not replace stūpas; rather the two coexist.

Dominating the hilltop, the Great Stūpa's core of Mauryan bricks and the edict pillar beside it suggest Aśoka may have built it as part of his legendary redistribution of the Buddha's bodily relics (*śarīra*). During the Śuṅga period, the stūpa was doubled in size to its present diameter of thirty-six meters. A railed berm accessed by a double staircase was also added to the dome, and an identical but more massive stone railing with openings at the cardinal directions enclosed the sacred precinct. These unadorned railings defined circumambulatory passages where Buddhist devotees could perform the basic rite of worshiping their lord's relics.

In the Śātavāhana period (ca. 150 C.E.), towering gateways consisting of two pillars bearing three architraves were erected at each railing opening. Every surface was carved with tumultuous and naturalistic reliefs that constantly threaten to break free from their architecturally defined, linear frames and the rock matrix. In comparison with Bhārhut (first century B.C.E.), Sāñcī has proportionately more narrative scenes of Aśoka and of animals worshiping the Buddha's living presence in relics such as the bodhi tree and the stūpas, as well as more scenes from the Buddha's life and far fewer JĀTAKAS. Sāñcī's narratives typically include scenes of worshiping crowds moving freely in space. Style and meaning cohere in expressing the unselfconscious and unrestrained joyousness that often characterizes devotional worship (bhakti). Loaded up with auspicious actions, motifs, and figures, Sāñcī's gates simultaneously honor the sacred precinct and protect its liminal openings against negative powers seeking to enter. What better way to do so than by representing and invoking the power of worship?

The Great Stūpa's six hundred short inscriptions in Prakrit attest to a pattern of collective, multiple donation typifying early Buddhist patronage. Accounting for a third of all donations, monks and nuns form the largest donor group. Next come merchants crisscrossing the subcontinent. Donors include a guild of ivory-carvers and the Śātavāhana king's chief artisan.

See also: **Cave Sanctuaries; India, Buddhist Art in; Monastic Architecture; Relics and Relics Cult**

Bibliography

Cunningham, Alexander. *The Bhilsa Topes; or, Buddhist Monuments of Central India* (1854). Reprint, Varanasi, India: Indological Book House, 1966.

Dehejia, Vidya, ed. *Unseen Presence: The Buddha and Sanchi*: Bombay: Marg, 1966.

Maisey, Fredrick Charles. *Sanchi and Its Remains: A Full Description of the Ancient Buildings, Sculptures, and Inscriptions* (1892). Reprint, Delhi: Indological Book House, 1972.

Marshall, John Hubert. *The Monuments of Sāñchī*. London: Probsthain, 1940.

Marshall, John Hubert. *A Guide to Sanchi,* 3rd edition. Delhi: Manager of Publications, 1955.

LEELA ADITI WOOD

SAṄGHA

The saṅgha (community) is the third of the three Buddhist REFUGES, or JEWELS (*triratna*), of BUDDHA, DHARMA, and saṅgha. The word *saṅgha* literally means "that which is well struck together"; it derives from a Sanskrit root, *han* (to strike), with the prefix *sam* conveying a sense of togetherness and completeness. The idea is that the true Buddhist community is well hammered together, impervious to schism, and in perfect harmony. From the very earliest period the undisputed focus of Buddhist WORSHIP has been the saṅgha, together with the Buddha and dharma, and the statement *buddhaṃ śaraṇaṃ gacchāmi, dharmaṃ śaraṇaṃ gacchāmi, saṅghaṃ śaraṇaṃ gacchāmi* (I go for refuge to the Buddha, I go for refuge to the dharma, I go for refuge to the saṅgha) has been the primary, shared affirmation of Buddhists.

Idealized community

The traditional explanation of saṅgha describes it not as a community of ordinary monks and nuns belonging to a Buddhist order, but as a special community of eight noble beings called *āryas* (Pāli, *ariyas*) who carry in their hearts the liberating dharma. They are described in the *Ratana-sutta* of the *Cullavagga* of the *Sutta Nipāta* (II.1.6–7), one of the very earliest Buddhist teachings: "The eight persons praised by the virtuous are four pairs. They are the disciples of the Buddha and are worthy of offerings. Gifts given to them yield rich results . . . free from afflictions they have obtained . . . the state beyond death. This is the precious saṅgha jewel."

The first pair of noble beings are those who have reached, or are on their way to, the state of the ARHAT (one worthy of praise and offerings). The arhats, like the Buddha, have found liberation from unending SAṂSĀRA (the cycle of birth and death). The three other pairs of noble beings are those who, if not arhats, have reached, or are on their way to, the state of *anāgāmin*; that is, they are nonreturners to this ordinary world, which is dominated by sense gratification. If they are not yet at that stage of development, they have reached, or are on their way to, the state of *sakṛdāgāmin* (once-returners), and they will return once more to this ordinary world. The fourth pair of noble beings are *srota-āpannas*, stream-enterers, who have obtained, or are on their way to obtaining, a state where they may return to this ordinary world up to seven more times before they reach the goal of liberation at the end of the PATH. They are called *stream-enterers* because the stream of the dharma, the understanding of the FOUR NOBLE TRUTHS that systematize the content of the Buddha's liberating teaching, has become one with the stream of their minds. In this traditional understanding of the saṅgha, the Buddha, as an arhat, is a member of the saṅgha, and embodies the dharma as well.

The salvific function of the saṅgha has been much discussed. Traditional explanations liken it to a nurse who helps a patient take the medicine (the dharma) that is prescribed by the Buddha, who is likened to a perfect doctor. Early Indian Buddhism (*Majjhimanikāya* 75, 105), perhaps drawing on ancient Indian medical theory (e.g., *Caraka-saṃhitā* 9.19), claims that the Buddha or TATHĀGATA (one who knows things as they are) can only teach disciples the path to the end of suffering, he cannot "wash away the sufferings of others by hand" (*Udanavārga*). The suffering person effects his or her own cure by putting into practice the eightfold path to freedom taught by the Buddha. Salvific power resides in the dharma, not in the Buddha or in the saṅgha, and according to early Buddhist texts, not in monks or nuns, either as individuals or as a group.

History of the early community

The earliest parts of the Buddhist canon extant in Pāli suggest that the original historical community consisted of those engaging in ascetic endeavors as śramaṇas (Pāli, *samaṇa*) and *pravrājika* (Pāli, *pabbajita*; those gone forth into homelessness). Buddhist ascetics were distinguishable from other similar groups of mendicants primarily by their dislike of intellectual disputation, their avoidance of extreme asceticism, their shared admiration for Gautama Śākyamuni, and a commitment to mental cultivation or MEDITATION (*Sutta Nipāta* 2). Whereas the very earliest members of the community had no fixed monasteries, and sheltered under trees or in caves, the difficulty of traveling during the rainy season soon led members to take shelter in permanent buildings. It is likely that householders and wealthy patrons who originally gave alms without discrimination to all religious mendicants, be they Jainas, Ājīvikas, or orthodox followers of the Veda, over time began to favor the followers of Gautama Buddha and to understand themselves as responsible for their sustenance and well-being. This led to the basic division of the community into bhikṣu (Pāli, bhikkhu; MONKS) and *bhikṣuṇī* (Pāli, *bhikkhunī*; NUNS), words that literally mean "beggars," and *upāsaka* and *upāsikā* (male and female LAITY). According to tradition, ĀNANDA, the personal attendant of Gautama, asked that women be admitted into the community, and the first Buddhist nun was MAHĀPRAJĀPATĪ GAUTAMĪ, the Buddha's aunt.

Entrance into the community was originally earned simply by answering the Buddha's call to come forward. When charismatics like ŚĀRIPUTRA and MAHĀMAUDGALYĀYANA, with considerable followings of their own, became Gautama's disciples, the community grew considerably larger. Even before Gautama's demise it is probable that senior members of the community were allowed to induct new members by having them recite the refuge formula (I go for refuge to the Buddha, etc.) three times. Gradually a more complex *upasampadā* (ritual ordination) came into being. By that time, ORDINATION meant ordination as a monk or nun, and for practical purposes the Buddhist community became equivalent to the community of monks and nuns, though the community of the four assemblies (monks, nuns, and male and female laity) was also recognized.

The history of the community of Buddhist monks and nuns over its first five hundred years is primarily a history of *saṃgīti* (councils) and *nikāya* (ordination lineages or schools). Immediately after the death of the Buddha, members of the fledgling community met in what was later called the First Council to record the Buddha's teachings. Probably the earliest codification of community rules, the PRĀTIMOKṢA, was formulated at about that time. Prātimokṣa may originally have meant "anti-dissipatory," and its recitation was the main factor connecting the various *nikāyas*, which were already growing separate because of geography, loyalty to particular charismatic monks, and minor disagreements over discipline.

The Second Council took place about a hundred years after the death of the Buddha. By that time the basic constitution of the community of monks and nuns, and most of the rules and rituals relating to monastic discipline and procedure, had already been codified. The texts in which this codification is found are together called the VINAYA (discipline). These texts comprise the first of the three sections of the *tripiṭaka* (the Buddhist CANON). The *Vinaya Piṭaka* consists of three main sections: (1) the *Vinaya-vibhaṅga*, a list of personal rules for the different levels of ordination along with stories about how they came into being; (2) the *Skandhaka* (Pāli, *Khandhaka*), an explanation of the rules governing community procedures, such as admission to the order and the conducting of the rains-retreat; and (3) the *Parivāra*, a compendium of additional materials.

The vinaya texts list seven different sets of rules for junior and senior members of the community. Besides the rules for the bhikṣus and *bhikṣuṇīs* (fully ordained monks and nuns), there are also sets of rules for male and female novices. The further special set of rules for probationary nuns probably reflects a stage in the gradual elimination of the female component of the community. The *bhikṣuṇī* component of the community eventually died out in India, though it has continued in China and Korea to the present day.

The morality expected of all members of the monastic community is given in the prātimokṣa. At its core are four basic rules of defeat (*pārājika*): to refrain from taking life, from taking what is not offered freely, from sexual activity, and from lying about spiritual attainments. Transgression of any of these rules entails expulsion from the order. The different *nikāyas* list slightly different totals for the number of rules, ranging from about 350 for the full *bhikṣuṇī* down to about thirteen for novices. Among these rules are some that enjoin on members of the community the yellow-, maroon-, or blue-colored robes, the begging bowl, the *kuṭi* (monastic cell), and dietary habits such as not eating in the afternoon and not keeping food overnight.

The first major split in the saṅgha occurred between the MĀHĀSĀṂGHIKAS (the Great Assembly, or Majorityists) and the Sthaviras (elders). Since most of what we know about the early history of the Buddhist order comes from the *Mahāvaṃsa* (*Great Chronicle*), a history written in Pāli from the particular viewpoint of monks of the ancient Mahāvihāra monastery in Sri Lanka (the *nikāya* from which the present-day THERAVĀDA school understands itself to originate), there has been a tendency to overemphasize the differences between different Buddhist *nikāyas*, and to see them as sects fundamentally opposed to each other, rather than as different saṅghas, each connected through the same basic prātimokṣa.

The community of Buddhist monks and nuns has never been a monolithic entity. It is possible that its basic decentralized structure, characterized by the absence of a strong central ruler in favor of consensual assemblies, reflects the customs of the Śākyas, part of the Vṛji (Pāli, Vajji) confederation in the area of north-central India where Śākyamuni ("the sage of the Śākyas") was born. Although diversity was an integral part of the Buddhist community from an early period, the early *nikāyas* were careful to formulate themselves in ways that avoided formal schism. Even after the Māhāsāṃghika/Sthavira schism, there was no fundamental split in the saṅgha, and it is an error to imagine that the split into HĪNAYĀNA and MAHĀYĀNA Buddhism was based on irreconcilable differences between these early *nikāyas*.

There were at least eighteen early Buddhist *nikāyas*, some of which give their names to later schools of Buddhist practice and philosophy. Many, if not all, recited the prātimokṣa in their own vernacular language, and it is likely that each also had a vinaya, and perhaps an entire *tripiṭaka*. The complete *tripiṭaka* of the Mahāvihāra *nikāya*, or Theravāda school, written in Pāli, became available to European-language scholars in the nineteenth century.

Although the original versions of the *Vinaya Piṭaka* of many of the other schools have been lost, except for occasional texts and fragments, some are extant in Chinese and Tibetan translation. Among them, the *Dharmaguptaka-vinaya* in particular was followed in China and countries strongly influenced by Chinese Buddhism, and the MŪLASARVĀSTIVĀDA-VINAYA was followed in Tibet and the regions influenced by it.

Each saṅgha was (and still is to a great extent) defined by a shared recitation of the prātimokṣa at a bimonthly *poṣadha* (Pāli, *uposatha*; confession or restoration-of-morality ceremony) carried out while scrupulously following *karmavacana* (Pāli, *kammavācā*; prescribed formula) and ritual action dictated by tradition. Also defining of a community are two other ritual activities: setting up the *sīmā* (established boundaries) for the *varṣavāsa* (rains-retreat; Pali, *vassavāsa*) and the ritual crossing of those boundaries at the end of the retreat. This custom probably dates back to the original followers of Gautama and to the places where buildings were located for groups of monks and nuns to spend the rainy season. A minimum of ten, or in some cases five, fully ordained members of a saṅgha constitute the required quorum. The presence or absence of these defining acts of a saṅgha is the basic criterion for deciding whether or not the *śāsana* (Pāli, *sāsana*; Buddhist teaching) is or is not present in a particular region. Members of different communities keep basically the same rules, but they do not attend each others' ceremonies and they do not form a single saṅgha, except in the sense that they symbolize, through their clothes and adherence to the rules in the prātimokṣa, the community of noble beings described above.

Tibetan monks sitting together during a ceremony at a monastery in Himachal Pradesh, India. © Lindsay Hebberd/Corbis. Reproduced by permission.

Mahāyāna and Tantric saṅghas

We can see clearly in Edward Conze's translation of the *Large Sūtra on Perfect Wisdom* (p. 66 ff.) that the idealized Mahāyāna community is based on the eight noble beings. In addition to the eight noble beings of earlier Buddhism, however, the Mahāyāna community also includes BODHISATTVAS and buddhas. These are theoretically infinite in number, but best known amongst them are the eight bodhisattvas, including Mañjuśrī, Avalokiteśvara, Kṣitigarbha, and so on, and the buddhas AKṢOBHYA, AMITĀBHA, and Vairocana. These noble bodhisattvas and buddhas are sometimes called "celestial" because they are located not in this ordinary world, but on a *bhūmi* (high spiritual level) or in a fabulous *buddhakṣetra* (buddha-field or pure land).

Mahāyāna tradition holds that bodhisattvas and buddhas are not motivated by NIRVĀṆA, the partial freedom from REBIRTH attained by the eight noble beings. They instead produce BODHICITTA (thought of enlightenment), attain *samyaksaṃbodhi* (right and perfect enlightenment), become buddhas, and work for countless ages for the benefit of the world. Noble bodhisattvas are on their way to attaining, and buddhas have actually attained, an everlasting enlightenment that shows itself in manifold ways appropriate for the benefit of the world. The Mahāyāna scriptures therefore claim that the Buddhist community is present in the world to a much greater degree and in many different forms compared to the community of the eight noble beings that is described in the scriptures of the MAINSTREAM BUDDHIST SCHOOLS.

In Buddhist TANTRA, the idealized community is understood to be pervaded by the nature of the guru and further augmented by VIDYĀDHARA (knowledge holders or sorcerers). *Vidyādhara* are said to be highly motivated bodhisattvas who utilize esoteric meditation, including sexual pleasure, to quickly attain high spiritual goals. Also given importance in the idealized tantric community are wrathful female figures (ḌĀKINĪ), personal meditation deities (*iṣṭadevatā*), and dharma protectors (*dharmapāla*).

The differences between actual historical Mahāyāna and pre-Mahāyāna communities have not been conclusively determined. The records of early Chinese travelers in India suggest that both functioned equally as communities of monks, sometimes even including members of the same *nikāya.* As for the historical tantric communities, they are also largely an object of speculation. Ronald Davidson has suggested tribal origins for some of them. It is likely that some tantric saṅghas formed around charismatic tantric masters (*vajrācārya*) and held ritual meetings (*gaṇacakra*) and other rites as a group. David Gellner has shown that such groups still exist amongst the Newar Buddhists of Nepal.

Modern Buddhist communities

There has been a tendency in European writing since the end of the colonial period to associate Buddhist saṅghas with the emergence and legitimization of the nation-state. Thus it is customary to talk about the Thai saṅgha, Burmese saṅgha, Tibetan Buddhists, Chinese Buddhists, and so on. While this approach clearly has some descriptive value, it is misleading if it suggests a basic change from earlier *nikāya* structure. For example, in modern Sri Lanka the three *nikāyas* are divided on the basis of caste and do not cross each other's boundaries; in Tibet *nikāyas* are divided on the basis of regions, monastic colleges, or sects that may have strong antipathy to each other. Nevertheless, it is clear that for the majority of Buddhists in those countries such differences do not preclude the various communities from being perceived as equally authentic Buddhist saṅghas; taken together in an undifferentiated manner, each saṅgha is esteemed as highly as the idealized community of the eight noble beings itself.

Among new converts to Buddhism in Western countries there are widely differing views about what a Buddhist saṅgha entails. It is probably best understood as any group that meets together and that is joined by a shared Buddhist faith, or any group linked by its members' devotion to a particular Buddhist teacher. The British founder of the Friends of the Western Buddhist Order is particularly insistent that his group's Aristotelian friendship between members of the same sex is what makes his an authentic Buddhist community. Groups strongly influenced by Western Christian notions define the saṅgha as a group with a shared level of commitment to social action.

See also: **Councils, Buddhist**

Bibliography

Conze, Edward, ed. and trans. *The Large Sūtra on Perfect Wisdom, with the Divisions of the Abhisamayālaṅkāra.* Berkeley and Los Angeles: University of California Press, 1975.

Davidson, Ronald. *Indian Esoteric Buddhism: A Social History of the Tantric Movement.* New York: Columbia University Press, 2003.

Gellner, David N. *Monk, Householder, and Tantric Priest: Newar Buddhism and Its Hierarchy of Ritual.* Cambridge, UK: Cambridge University Press, 1992.

Horner, I. B., trans. *The Book of the Discipline (Vinaya Piṭaka),* 6 vols. London: Pāli Text Society, 1938–1966.

Prebish, Charles. *Buddhist Monastic Discipline: The Sanskrit Prātimokṣa Sūtras of the Mahāsāṃghikas and Mūlasarvāstivādins.* University Park: Pennsylvania State University Press, 1975.

GARETH SPARHAM

SANJIE JIAO (THREE STAGES SCHOOL)

The Sanjie jiao (Three "Levels" or "Stages") movement begun by the Chinese monk Xinxing (540–594 C.E.) is perhaps best known because its teachings and practices were suppressed as heretical numerous times over the two-hundred-plus years of its history. Banned from the official scriptural canon as apocryphal (*weijing*), Sanjie writings were lost until discoveries of numerous manuscripts at DUNHUANG and elsewhere in the early twentieth century. In spite of opposition, the movement remained popular for several centuries, attracting the aristocracy as well as throngs of commoners.

The movement takes its name from its central teaching, which divides SENTIENT BEINGS into three levels of spiritual capacity: the "wise, the in-between, and the stupid," as the *Wei-Shu* (eighth century) put it. Xinxing taught that the people of his era were entirely of the third level, blinded by prejudice and hatred and therefore incapable of a correct understanding of the Buddha's teachings. Whereas sentient beings of superior capacity could benefit from the varied teachings of the different schools (*biefa*), the degenerate beings of the third level needed to rely on the universal teachings (*pufa*) of ultimate truth that transcend distinctions of truth and falsity, purity and impurity. Xinxing was also influenced by the doctrine of the DECLINE OF THE DHARMA, according to which people's capacity for practice decreases as the time from the historical Buddha increases.

Equally important for Xinxing was the doctrine of universal buddha-nature or TATHĀGATAGARBHA. This teaching asserts that all sentient beings are fundamentally of the same nature as the fully awakened buddha and will one day realize that nature. From these doctrines came the Sanjie practice of "recognizing the evil" in oneself while cultivating "universal respect" for the inherent buddhahood of all other sentient beings.

The Sanjie community was headquartered at Huadu and four other monasteries in the capital city of Chang'an, though it had communities throughout China. In their monastic life, members followed a typical regimen that included a wide variety of contemplative practices, penitentiary rituals, veneration of the buddhas, devotional liturgies, chants, the seeking of alms, and the like. Perhaps reflecting their emphasis on recognizing the evil in oneself, Sanjie communities were extremely rigorous in these practices and punished even small infractions. The best-known Sanjie institution was the charitable Inexhaustible Storehouse (*Wujinzang*), which lent goods free of interest to the poor and needy.

In spite of its popularity, Sanjie was suppressed five times between 600 and 725. It is hard to know the exact reasons behind the suppressions, for there was nothing particularly radical or socially dangerous about Sanjie teachings, practices, or institutions—indeed, they were typical of many other groups of the time. There was also no common theme linking the suppressions: Some edicts banned Sanjie texts from the canon, others aimed at its institutional base at Huadu Monastery, and others attacked unspecified practices. The reign (684–705) of Empress Wu saw both imperial support for the Inexhaustible Storehouse and suppression of Sanjie scriptures, though none of the attacks ever actually eliminated the movement. The treatment Sanjie received does show the political nature of religious institutions and the important yet ephemeral nature of orthodoxy.

See also: **Apocrypha; China; Persecutions**

Bibliography

Buswell, Robert E., Jr., ed. *Chinese Buddhist Apocrypha.* Honolulu: University of Hawaii Press, 1990.

Hubbard, Jamie. *Absolute Delusion, Perfect Buddhahood: The Rise and Fall of a Chinese Heresy.* Honolulu: University of Hawaii Press, 2001.

JAMIE HUBBARD

SANSKRIT, BUDDHIST LITERATURE IN

Buddhist literature in Sanskrit is a large and diverse category. It consists of both canonical and noncanonical materials, the latter ranging from anonymous narrative collections and ritual manuals through technical treatises, poetry, and plays written by known individuals. Two distinct languages are used in this category: Sanskrit and so-called Buddhist Hybrid Sanskrit. Sanskrit is the ancient prestige language of Indian culture, first known through collections of hymns called Vedas dating from the second millennium B.C.E., and later systematized in a generative grammar by Pāṇini (fourth century B.C.E.). In brahmanical Hindu religion, Sanskrit is seen as the natural language, that which would be spoken by any person if not trained in a vernacular as a child, and as such represents reality more closely than external phenomena perceived through the senses. The ability to compose in Sanskrit—requiring precise control of its complex inflectional system, and in verse the capacity to reproduce artfully a variety of metrical patterns—was seen as the epitome of educated civilization. Buddhist Hybrid Sanskrit (hereafter BHS) is the language of a text called the MAHĀVASTU and of most MAHĀYĀNA sūtras, that is, discourses attributed to the Buddha. It has been denoted by this name since the publication of a dictionary and grammar of the language by Franklin Edgerton, but has also been called "Buddhist Sanskrit," "mixed Sanskrit," and "the *gāthā* dialect" (reflecting the fact that it is most commonly found in the verses, *gāthā*, of Mahāyāna discourses). The origin and nature of BHS is disputed, Edgerton preferring to view it as the result of an incomplete process of translation into Sanskrit of materials originally composed in a vernacular, *prakrit.* This was not a formal attempt at translation but a gradual process of influence reflecting the prestige of Sanskrit proper in the broader community (Edgerton, sect. 1.34). BHS texts vary in character, particularly in the degree to which they employ vernacular grammatical forms. Later BHS texts are identified as such largely through their vocabulary, their grammar being that of standard, if simple, Sanskrit. In the eyes of traditionally trained paṇḍits and even some Western scholars, BHS has appeared to be a highly incorrect, even barbaric, language requiring correction. The work of defining BHS continues, as texts are edited anew with greater sensitivity.

Canonical literature

Whereas for the MAINSTREAM BUDDHIST SCHOOLS, the CANON was defined in terms of an exclusive *tripiṭaka,* both the Mahāyāna and VAJRAYĀNA traditions utilized a more flexible, inclusive concept of canon that allowed, alongside the *tripiṭaka,* the incorporation of a large number of texts claiming to be BUDDHAVACANA,

(WORD OF THE BUDDHA). This is indicated by their opening with the phrase *evaṃ mayā śrutaṃ* ("Thus have I heard"), indicating that each text is understood to have been recited by the Buddha's disciple ĀNANDA at the First Council. Modern scholarship situates these texts as new if anonymous compositions, the chronology of which tracks the evolution of Mahāyāna and Vajrayāna, respectively. The inclusiveness of later Indian Buddhism regarding canonicity also means that it is difficult to know the precise total extent of the literature. The Pāli canon by tradition has been fixed since the first century B.C.E. and the exact content is well known, as revealed in the fifth-century C.E. commentaries attributed to BUDDHAGHOSA and others. There is no comparable clarity for the Mahāyāna or Vajrayāna, and even now there exists no comprehensive catalogue of works for either tradition. The nearest we have are the ancient CATALOGUES OF SCRIPTURES of the Chinese and Tibetan translated canons, none of which are exhaustive. This situation makes it difficult to write with conclusive authority on many aspects of this literature as a whole.

This situation is further complicated in that the major portion of canonical Buddhist literature in Sanskrit has been lost since the time of Muslim depredations in northern India (eleventh through twelfth centuries C.E.) and is now known only through ancient translations made into Tibetan, Chinese, and other languages. The exceptions to this have come from two sources: archaeological or antiquarian recovery of ancient manuscripts or their active preservation through copying in Nepal. Notable among the former are numerous manuscripts recovered from the oases of Central Asia, the small library of about fifty texts found in Gilgit in the 1930s, Rāhula Sāṅkṛtyāyana's photographs made in the 1930s in Tibet of very early Sanskrit manuscripts originally transported there in the medieval period to assist translation work, and the recovery in the 1990s of very early manuscripts from Afghanistan, such as those in the collection of Martin Schøyen in Oslo (Braarvig). Typical of the latter category from Nepal are numerous manuscripts of nine canonical texts called the *navadharma* (the nine teachings), along with a wide range of tantric ritual texts. The bulk of Buddhist Sanskrit literature known today has been preserved in Nepal (Mitra).

Āgama collections. The *āgama* collections are the functional equivalents of the *nikāyas* of the Pāli canon—thus there were long (*dīrgha*), middling (*madhyama*), thematic (*saṃyukta*), incremental (*ekottara*), and miscellaneous (*kṣudraka*) collections in Sanskrit. The *āgama* collections contain Sanskrit versions of many of the texts found in the Pāli collections, and are understood to have been the śrāvaka canon as utilized on the Indian subcontinent by śrāvaka lineages other than that of the THERAVĀDA school. Overall the *āgamas* contained a larger number of texts than the *nikāyas* and arranged them in a different sequence. Unlike other Buddhist literature in Sanskrit that has no śrāvaka parallels, this category offers enormous potential for comparative study to differentiate the ideas and concerns of the śrāvaka schools. Regrettably, the *āgamas* do not survive in their entirety and are largely known through translations of them made into Chinese (Lamotte, pp. 153 f.). Until recently the only exceptions to this were individual sūtras—for example, the MAHĀPARINIRVĀṆA-SŪTRA (Waldschmidt) and fragments recovered from long abandoned Buddhist sites in Central Asia—but this has changed with the discovery in Afghanistan in the late 1990s of an almost complete manuscript of the *Dīrghāgama,* probably belonging to the Mūlasarvāstivāda school (Hartmann).

Vinaya and *abhidharma*. Although there were seven canonical ABHIDHARMA texts in Sanskrit belonging to the Sarvāstivāda school, these are now lost in their original language. The Sanskrit VINAYA collections have fared better, and two works in particular warrant mention. The first of these is the MŪLASARVĀSTIVĀDA-VINAYA, which has mostly survived in a single manuscript discovered at Gilgit. This massive text is a compilation of narratives and case law offering numerous insights into the preoccupations and realia of monastic life in medieval India (Panglung). With this we can compare the *Mahāvastu,* a wonderful collection of narratives and lore built around a biography of the Buddha that describes itself as belonging to the vinaya of the Lokottaravāda branch of the MAHĀSĀṂGHIKA SCHOOL (Jones). This too contains interesting and important parallels to material found in the Pāli canon.

Mahāyāna. Mahāyāna sūtras form a diverse body of literature produced between the first century B.C.E. and the fifth century C.E. The earliest examples are thought to be the perfection of wisdom texts, *Aṣṭasāhasrikā-prajñāpāramitā* and *Ratnaguṇasaṃcaya-gāthā,* in prose and verse, respectively. These expound a critique of the *abhidharma* and the teaching of the real existence of dharmas and promote the BODHISATTVA as the ideal Buddhist. While many Mahāyāna sūtras are now only known in Tibetan and Chinese translations, we are well endowed with manuscripts of the *navadharma*, which includes the following sūtras: *Saddharmapuṇḍarīka* (*Lotus Sūtra*), *Aṣṭasāhasrikā-prajñāpāramitā*, LAṄKĀVATĀRA-SŪTRA, *Daśabhūmiśvara*, *Gaṇḍavyūha*, *Samādhirāja*, and SUVARṆAPRABHĀSOTTAMA-SŪTRA; plus the LALITAVISTARA, a *śrāvakayāna* biography of the Buddha that is built around guides to the main pilgrimage sites of the Buddha's life (Foucher), and the *Guhyasamāja-tantra*, a Vajrayāna work. These texts and others express a range of doctrinal views and a number of them were among those considered authoritative and thus expounded by Mahāyāna doctrinal traditions, such as the MADHYAMAKA SCHOOL and the YOGĀCĀRA SCHOOL.

Vajrayāna. From the middle of the first millennium C.E. until the demise of institutional Buddhism in India in the twelfth century, there began to appear Buddhist tantric works, written in Sanskrit, employing instrumental magic and ritual to achieve specific goals. Retrospectively these have been assigned to four classes: *kriyā* or "action" TANTRAS; *caryā* or "conduct" tantras, dominated by the *Mahāvairocanābhisaṃbodhi Tantra* (*Tantra on the Perfect Awakening of Mahā-Vairocana*); *yoga* or "meditation" tantras, dominated by the *Sarvatathāgatatattvasaṃgraha* (*Compendium on the Essence of all the Tathāgatas*); and the *anuttarayoga* or "supreme meditation" tantras, among which is included the *Guhyasamāja Tantra* (*Tantra on the Secret Assembly*). The last tantra composed in India before the final demise of institutional Buddhism there was the eleventh-century *Kālacakra Tantra*, a major work seeking not just soteriological goals but also offering a defense against contemporary Muslim domination. Texts in the higher classes of tantra tend toward asserting feminine representations of the ideal, employing antinomian practices (e.g., consumption of forbidden substances, sexual transgression of monastic rules and caste boundaries), and, although written in relatively normal Sanskrit, employ a secret or allusive vocabulary called *sandhyabhāṣā*, in which actual referents are disguised by euphemisms and elaborate symbolism. A minor example of this appears in the opening phrase of the *Guhyasamāja Tantra*, which forgoes the familiar formula and asserts instead that the Buddha delivered the tantra while residing in the "vagina of the Vajra Lady," which is understood to mean "while residing in the wisdom of enlightenment."

Commentaries. This entire body of canonical material inspired COMMENTARIAL LITERATURE usually composed by known historical individuals, although this too has fared badly and relatively little survives in its original language. There is no definitive catalogue of Sanskrit commentaries, but it has been estimated in relation to the Tibetan canon that, of 120 commentaries translated into Tibetan, only ninety remain current; allowing for duplications, these offer comment on only thirty-four, or 10 percent, of the sūtras extant in the same canon (Schoening). Commentaries vary widely in length, from single folios to several volumes, and some sūtras have attracted much more attention than others—the HEART SŪTRA, a short Perfection of Wisdom text, having seven commentaries. There are also subcommentaries on primary commentaries, the *Abhisamayālaṃkāra* apparently inspiring something in excess of twenty.

Noncanonical literature

Canonical materials alone do not exhaust Buddhist literature in Sanskrit. In fact, the larger part of the field is made up of noncanonical materials, which are even more diverse than their canonical counterparts. In the following survey, the subcategories employed are by no means exclusive, merging in some cases with each other and with canonical materials.

Narrative. Narrative is a, if not the, dominant genre of Buddhist literature, and happily many examples have survived into the present day. The canonical literature already reviewed is replete with narrative materials that were redacted to form new compilations of pure narrative, such as the AVADĀNAŚATAKA (*One Hundred Stories of Edifying Deeds*) and the DIVYĀVADĀNA (*Divine Stories of Edifying Deeds*), the latter probably redacted from the *Mūlasarvāstivāda-vinaya*. The *Avadānaśataka* subsequently inspired further cycles of verse renderings of sets of its stories, which were composed probably in the second half of the first millennium C.E. These texts, clearly the result of a concerted attempt to revise the entire *Avadānaśataka* by what was probably a tradition of specialists in this kind of narrative literature, were termed *mālā* (garlands), and typically employ a frame story involving a dialogue between the emperor AŚOKA and a monk named UPAGUPTA (Strong).

Ritual texts. The Nepalese community has preserved a host of ritual texts of a variety of kinds. Many of these are transmitted from Indian originals and include compendia of meditation texts giving guidance on the visualization and worship of buddhas, bodhisattvas, and various tantric figures, such as the *Sādhanamālā* and *Niṣpannayogāvalī*. There are also more miscellaneous collections covering a range of activities, such as building monasteries (e.g., the *Kriyāsaṃgraha*).

Treatises. Often attracting attention before the more extensive narrative and ritual materials, there are important treatises, śāstras, compiled by known historical individuals in order to expound specific doctrinal positions, sometimes doctrines voiced in sūtra sources. Among these we should note the encyclopedic ABHIDHARMAKOŚABHĀṢYA (*Treasury of Higher Teaching*) of VASUBANDHU, which sets out a survey of Sarvāstivāda doctrine, which it then critiques from a SAUTRĀNTIKA viewpoint in an autocommentary. Some treatises offer exegeses of the work of earlier scholiasts; thus CANDRAKĪRTI's *Prasannapadā* is effectively a commentary on NĀGĀRJUNA's *Mūlamadhyamakakārikā* (*Foundational Verses on the Middle Way*), both being core textual authorities in the exegesis of Madhyamaka doctrine. By contrast, Vasubandhu's *Viṃśatikā* and *Triṃśikā* (*Twenty Verses* and *Thirty Verses*) expound doctrine de novo. ŚĀNTIDEVA's BODHICARYĀVATĀRA (*Introduction to the Conduct of a Bodhisattva*) systematically outlines in evocative poetry the nature of a bodhisattva's practice and exemplifies the crossover into material that we might otherwise classify as purely poetic (Crosby and Skilton).

Poetry and drama. Sometimes undeservedly attracting less attention are splendid works of self-consciously high literary merit. These include AŚVAGHOṢA's second-century C.E. BUDDHACARITA, a verse biography of the Buddha, and *Saundarananda*, the earliest examples of Sanskrit *kāvya* (high poetry) that have survived. Regrettably we have lost Aśvaghoṣa's dramas, which included an account of the conversions of ŚĀRIPUTRA and MAHĀMAUDGALYĀYANA, and they are known now only through manuscript fragments from Central Asia. Similar to these are the prose and verse *kāvya* JĀTAKAMĀLĀ of ĀRYAŚŪRA (fourth century C.E.), a retelling of thirty-four *jātaka* stories in elegant court style. His *Pāramitāsamāsa* (*Compendium of the Perfections*) is an important parallel to Śāntideva's *Bodhicaryāvatāra* (Meadows). Another important work is the *Nāgananda* of Harṣa, a seventh-century king, a complete drama that retells the story of the bodhisattva as Jīmutavāhana. This last is notable in that its author was not a Buddhist, a distinction shared with the *Avadānakalpalatā*, a cycle of 108 Buddhist stories retold in verse by the eleventh-century Kashmiri poet Kṣemendra. All these examples are characterized by the reworking of existing narratives from canonical sources, but this crossover can also be seen in the elegant *kāvya* meters sometimes employed in the composition of some canonical literature. Numerous original compositions in verse survive mainly in translation. Often concerned with praise, they are called *stotra* (hymns), chief among which must be the works of Mātṛceta (second century C.E.), two of which were memorized by all monks in India, according to the Chinese pilgrim YIJING (635–713).

Nepalese Buddhist literature in Sanskrit. While the composition of Buddhist literature died out in India after the Muslim conquests of the twelfth century C.E., it continued in Nepal, where cultural continuity was retained and in fact heavily augmented by refugees from the Buddhist homelands in northeastern India. Of later composition in Nepal are various *pārājika* texts, describing ritual means whereby one might avoid the negative consequences of various kinds of killing, and demonstrating a Hindu-Buddhist syncretism. Of greater literary merit are seven large verse compositions that retell materials familiar from Indic sources, such as the *Avadānaśataka* and *Mahāvastu,* but which also borrow heavily from śāstra-type material, such as the *Bodhicaryāvatāra.* These include the *Svayambhūpurāṇa, Bhadrakalpāvadana, Vicitrakarṇikāvadāna,* and the *Guṇakāraṇḍavyūha.* These all reuse the frame story of Upagupta and Aśoka, familiar from the Indian *avadānamālās,* but supplement it with a further framing device involving two monks, Jināśrī and Jayaśrī. These texts also incorporate values of Nepalese Buddhism, while the *Svayambhūpurāṇa* goes so far as to localize the Buddhist sacred landscape and mythology in Nepal.

See also: **Āgama/Nikāya; Languages; Pāli, Buddhist Literature in**

Bibliography

Braarvig, Jens; Harrison, Paul; Hartmann, Jens-Uwe; Kazunobu Matsuda; and Sander, Lore; eds. *Buddhist Manuscripts of the Schøyen Collection,* 2 vols. Oslo: Hermes, 2000 and 2002.

Crosby, Henrietta Kate, and Skilton, Andrew, trans. *The Bodhicaryāvatāra.* Oxford: Oxford University Press, 1995.

Edgerton, Franklin. *Buddhist Hybrid Sanskrit Grammar and Dictionary.* New Haven, CT: Yale University Press, 1954.

Foucher, Alfred. *La vie du Bouddha, d'après les textes et les monuments de l'Inde* (1949). Paris: Maisonneuve, 1987.

Hartmann, Jens-Uwe. "Further Remarks on the New Manuscript of the Dīrghāgama." *Journal of the International College for Advanced Buddhist Studies* 5 (2002): 98–117.

Hodge, Stephen, trans. *The Mahā-Vairocana-Abhisambodhi Tantra: With Buddhaguhya's Commentary.* London: Routledge Curzon, 2003.

Jones, J. J., trans. *The Mahāvastu,* 3 vols. London: Luzac, 1949–1956.

Lamotte, Étienne. *History of Indian Buddhism from the Origins to the Śaka Era* (1958), tr. Sara Webb-Boin. Louvain, Belgium: Peeters Press, 1988.

Meadows, Carol. *Ārya-Śūra's Compendium of the Perfections: Text, Translation, and Analysis of the Pāramitāsamāsa.* Bonn, Germany: Indica et Tibetica Verlag, 1986.

Mitra, Rajendralal. *The Sanskrit Buddhist Literature of Nepal* (1882). Delhi: Motilal Banarsidass, 1981.

Panglung, Jampa L. *Die Erzälstoffe des Mūlasarvāstivāda-Vinaya Analysiert auf grund der Tibetischen Übersetzung.* Tokyo: Reiyukai Library, 1981.

Schoening, Jeffrey D. "*Sūtra* Commentaries in Tibetan Translation." In *Tibetan Literature: Studies in Genre,* ed. José I. Cabezón and Roger R. Jackson. Ithaca, NY: Snow Lion, 1996.

Skorupski, Tadeusz. *Kriyasamgraha: Compendium of Buddhist Rituals.* Tring, UK: Institute of Buddhist Studies, 2002.

Strong, John. "The Buddhist Avadānists and the Elder Upagupta." *Mélanges chinois et bouddhiques* 22 (1985): 862–881.

Waldschmidt, Ernst. *Das Mahāparinirvāṇasūtra,* 3 vols. Berlin: Akademie Verlag, 1950–1951.

Wayman, Alex. *Yoga of the Guhyasamājatantra: The Arcane Lore of Forty Verses, a Buddhist Tantra Commentary.* Delhi: Motilal Banarsidass, 1977. Reprint, 1991.

Winternitz, Maurice. *A History of Indian Literature* (1933), Vol. 2: *Buddhist and Jain Literature,* tr. V. Srinivasa Sarma. Delhi: Motilal Banarsidass, 1983. Reprint, 1999.

ANDREW SKILTON

ŚĀNTIDEVA

The MADHYAMAKA SCHOOL philosopher and poet Śāntideva is generally thought to have lived some time between 685 and 763 C.E., although this is by no means conclusive. The claim that he was a prince from North India who fled royal consecration repeats a traditional Buddhist theme and has no independent support. Śāntideva adhered to the MAHĀYĀNA tradition. His spiritual poem the BODHICARYĀVATĀRA (*Introduction to the Conduct That Leads to Enlightenment*) indicates that he was particularly devoted to the bodhisattva Mañjuśrī. His other great work is the *Śikṣāsamuccaya* (*Compendium of Doctrines*), which consists in the main of valuable quotations from many Mahāyāna Buddhist scriptures (sūtras) arranged to illustrate aspects of the Mahāyāna PATH. The *Śikṣāsamuccaya* is an important Sanskrit source for sections of sūtras that no longer survive in their Sanskrit originals.

In the traditional (mainly Tibetan) hagiographies, Śāntideva appears to be quite ordinary although actually a figure of advanced spiritual attainment. One story goes that he seemed to the monks of Nālandā Monastery simply to laze around doing nothing. They asked him to give a recitation before the monastery, then tried to erect the teacher's seat so high that Śāntideva could not reach it. With one hand he magically lowered the seat, sat on it, and asked what they wanted him to recite. At the request for something new (for a change) Śāntideva began to create spontaneously his *Bodhicaryāvatāra,* undoubtedly the single greatest Indian poem about cultivating the Mahāyāna spiritual life. When he had nearly reached the end he ascended into the air and disappeared, although his voice could still be heard.

See also: **Sanskrit, Buddhist Literature in**

Bibliography

Bendall, Cecil, and Rouse, W. H. D., trans. *Śikṣā Samuccaya: A Compendium of Buddhist Doctrine.* Delhi: Motilal Banarsidass. Reprint of 1922 edition.

Crosby, Kate, and Skilton, Andrew, trans. *Śāntideva: The Bodhicaryāvatāra.* Oxford: Oxford University Press, 1995.

Ruegg, David S. *The Literature of the Madhyamaka School of Philosophy in India.* Wiesbaden, Germany: Harrassowitz, 1981.

Tsonawa, Losang Norbu, trans. *Indian Buddhist Pandits from "The Jewel Garland of Buddhist History."* Dharamsala, India: Library of Tibetan Works and Archives, 1985.

Wallace, Vesna A., and Wallace, B. Allan, trans. *A Guide to the Bodhisattva Way of Life (Bodhicaryāvatāra).* New York: Snow Lion, 1997.

Williams, Paul. *Mahāyāna Buddhism: The Doctrinal Foundations.* London and New York: Routledge, 1989.

Williams, Paul, with Tribe, Anthony. *Buddhist Thought: A Complete Introduction to the Indian Tradition.* London and New York: Routledge, 2000.

PAUL WILLIAMS

ŚĀRIPUTRA

Śāriputra (Pāli, Sāriputta), a disciple of Śākyamuni Buddha, attained the enlightened status of an ARHAT, or saint. Śāriputra is renowned for his wisdom and his expertise in ABHIDHARMA.

Because of his reputation for wisdom, Śāriputra frequently appears in Mahāyāna sūtras as a prime representative of the HĪNAYĀNA. The Buddha predicts Śāriputra's future buddhahood in the LOTUS SŪTRA (SADDHARMAPUṆḌARĪKA-SŪTRA), a famous Mahāyāna scripture. Originally Śāriputra and his childhood friend MAHĀMAUDGALYĀYANA were students of Sañjayin, a non-Buddhist teacher. Śāriputra and Mahāmaudgalyāyana promised each other that whoever attained knowledge of liberation first would inform the other. One day Śāriputra met a Buddhist monk named Aśvajit (or Upasena in some texts). Attracted by Aśvajit's serene countenance and flawless comportment, Śāriputra converted to Buddhism. Śāriputra attained the dharma-eye when Aśvajit recited a four-line verse summary of Buddhist teachings on ANITYA (IMPERMANENCE). Mahāmaudgalyāyana converted to Buddhism upon seeing a physically transformed Śāriputra, exclaiming: "Venerable One, your senses are serene, your face is at peace, and the complexion of your skin utterly pure. Did you reach the deathless state?" (*Catuṣpariṣatsūtra,* quoted in Strong, 2002, p. 50).

At Śāriputra's and Mahāmaudgalyāyana's ordination, the Buddha proclaimed that they would be his two chief disciples in accordance with a prediction made to that effect many eons ago by a previous buddha. Thus the two are sometimes depicted flanking the Buddha in Buddhist art. Śāriputra predeceased the Buddha. Like other arhats, Śāriputra was already the focus of worship in ancient and medieval India. In Burma (Myanmar) he is one of a set of eight arhats propitiated in protective rituals and he is also believed to grant his worshippers wisdom.

See also: **Disciples of the Buddha**

Bibliography

Malalasekera, G. P. "Sāriputta Thera." In *Dictionary of Pāli Proper Names* (1937–1938), 2 vols. New Delhi: Munshiram Manoharlal, 1995.

Strong, John S. *The Legend and Cult of Upagupta.* Princeton, NJ: Princeton University Press, 1992.

Strong, John S. *The Experience of Buddhism: Sources and Interpretations,* 2nd edition. Belmont, CA: Wadsworth, 2002.

SUSANNE MROZIK

SARVĀSTIVĀDA AND MŪLASARVĀSTIVĀDA

The term *Sarvāstivāda* means "those who claim that everything exists"; *Mūlasarvāstivāda* means "root Sarvāstivāda." The Sarvāstivāda school, one of the largest and most important mainstream schools of Indian Buddhism, a subschool of the Sthavira branch, is first attested in inscriptions dating from the first century C.E. and was to become prominent throughout northern India and Central Asia, in particular in the northwestern regions of Kashmir and Gandhāra and the north central region of Mathurā. Traditional sources connect each of these regions with a prominent early Sarvāstivāda teacher: Kashmir with Madhyāntika, and Mathurā with Upagupta. Later, both regions became strongholds of the Sarvāstivāda school, but scholarly disagreement persists as to which region was the original home of the sect.

A substantial portion of the Sarvāstivāda version of the Buddhist canon is preserved in Chinese translation, including the complete monastic disciplinary code (VINAYA), a portion of the dialogues (sūtra), the complete collection of canonical scholastic treatises (ABHIDHARMA), as well as other postcanonical scholastic texts and commentaries that contain detailed examinations of virtually all aspects of early Indian Buddhist doctrine. The most important of these doctrinal discussions is the hallmark position, "everything exists" (*sarvam asti*), from which the name, *Sarvāstivāda,* derives. Here the Sarvāstivādins suggest that "everything," that is all conditioned factors (dharma), "exist" and can exert causal efficacy in the three time periods of the past, present, and future. This position was attacked by rival Buddhist groups as a violation of the fundamental Buddhist position of ANITYA (IMPERMANENCE). In response, the Sarvāstivādins developed an elaborate ontology that specified the manner in which past and future factors exist while attempting to preserve their impermanent character.

Multiple recensions of extant Sarvāstivāda texts, as well as references in their scholastic literature to the variant doctrinal positions of different groups of Sarvāstivādins, indicate that internal divisions existed within the larger Sarvāstivāda school. These divisions reflected regional, chronological, doctrinal, and possibly other differences. Regional variation might also explain the origin of one notable Sarvāstivāda group, the Mūlasarvāstivāda. The Mūlasarvāstivādins possessed their own separate monastic code, extant in Sanskrit, and can also possibly be affiliated with certain sūtra dialogues and other miscellaneous texts extant in Chinese translation. While the exact relationship between the Sarvāstivādins and the Mūlasarvāstivādins remains unclear, it is possible that the Mūlasarvāstivādins represented either a later phase in the development of the Sarvāstivāda sectarian stream or perhaps specifically those Sarvāstivādins who were centered in the region of Mathurā. After the decline in prominence of the Sarvāstivādins within the northwestern region of Kashmir and Gandhāra, the Sarvāstivādins of Mathurā may have adopted the name Mūlasarvāstivāda, or "root Sarvāstivāda," to assert their status as the preeminent or original Sarvāstivādins.

See also: **Mainstream Buddhist Schools; Mūlasarvāstivāda-vinaya**

Bibliography

Cox, Collett. *Disputed Dharmas: Early Buddhist Theories on Existence.* Tokyo: International Institute for Buddhist Studies, 1995.

Frauwallner, Erich. *Studies in Abhidharma Literature and the Origins of Buddhist Philosophical Systems,* tr. Sophie Francis Kidd. Albany: State University of New York Press, 1995.

Lamotte, Étienne. *History of Indian Buddhism: From the Origins to the Saka Era,* tr. Sara Webb-Boin. Louvain, Belgium: Peeters Press, 1988.

COLLETT COX

SA SKYA (SAKYA)

The monastery of Sa skya (Sakya) was founded in southern Tibet in 1073 by the master Dkon mchog rgyal po (Könchog Gyalpo, 1034–1102), a member of the ancient 'Khon (Khön) family from which the leaders of the Sa skya tradition have always come. Beginning with Dkon mchog rgyal po's son, Sa chen Kun dga' snying po (Sachen Kunga Nyingpo, 1092–1158), the next five great patriarchs of the 'Khon lineage are known as the Five Early Patriarchs of Sa skya (*sa skya gong ma lnga*).

Sa chen Kun dga' snying po mastered a huge variety of Buddhist teachings, both in the sūtra-based MAHĀYĀNA (Great Vehicle) tradition and the TANTRA-based VAJRAYĀNA (Adamantine Vehicle). The Sa skya school that developed after his time is distinguished by the teaching and practice of the various transmissions collected by Sa chen. For example, at the age of twelve Sa chen experienced a vision of the bodhisattva Mañjuśrī, from whom he received a teaching known as "Parting from the Four Attachments" (*Zhen pa bzhi bral*). These instructions became the basis of the practice of "mind training" (*blo sbyong*) in the Sa skya school, and have continued to be used for meditation on the key points of the Mahāyāna tradition.

The most significant tantric systems of the Sa skya tradition are connected to the *Hevajra Tantra* and the *Cakrasaṃvara Tantra.* From among these, the esoteric instructions of the great Indian adept Virūpa's "Path with the Result" (*Lam 'bras*) are a complete system of theory and meditation based on the tantric scriptures associated with the *Hevajra Tantra.* Sa chen received these teachings from the yogin Zhang ston Chos 'bar (Zhangdön Chöbar, 1053–1135), and the "Path with the Result" has continued to be the most important Vajrayāna transmission practiced in the Sa skya school. Sa chen wrote the first texts to explain the "Path with the Result," which had previously been an oral tradition in both India and Tibet.

Sa chen was succeeded by two of his sons: Bsod nams rtse mo (Sönam Tsemo, 1142–1182) and then Grags pa rgyal mtshan (Trakpa Gyaltsen, 1147–1216). Bsod nams rtse mo wrote a number of important works, especially in the field of tantric study and practice. Grags pa rgyal mtshan wrote many extremely influential treatises concerning the esoteric instructions of the Sa skya tradition, and his works formed the basis for the development of the Sa skya approach to tantric study and meditation. During the lifetime of Sa chen and his sons, the Sa skya school remained concentrated at Sa skya Monastery, but during the following generations a major expansion occurred.

Sa skya Paṇḍita Kun dga' rgyal mtshan (Sakya Paṇḍita Kunga Gyaltsen, 1182–1251) succeeded his uncle, Grags pa rgyal mtshan, as the head of the Sa skya tradition. Several of Sa skya Paṇḍita's literary compositions became very important for the Sa skya school, including his *Sdom gsum rab dbye* (*Clear Differentiation of the Three Codes*). In about 1244 Sa skya Paṇḍita was summoned to the court of the Mongol prince Göden Khan at Liangzhou in China. During the final years of his life, Sa skya Paṇḍita taught Buddhism at the Mongol court, where he also completed an important treatise on Mahāyāna Buddhism entitled *Thub pa'i dgongs gsal* (*Elucidating the Intention of the Sage*).

Sa skya Paṇḍita was succeeded by his nephew, 'Phags pa Blo gros rgyal mtshan (Pakpa Lodro Gyaltsen, 1235–1280), the fifth Early Patriarch of Sa skya. In 1253 'Phags pa met Qubilai Khan (1215–1294), who later became the first emperor of the Yuan dynasty in China. Qubilai Khan requested from 'Phags pa the complete Hevajra initiation in 1258, marking the beginning of Vajrayāna Buddhism in Mongolia. Three years later Qubilai Khan granted 'Phags pa the title of national preceptor (*guoshi*), thereby appointing him the leading Buddhist master in the empire. This precedent for a patron-priest relationship between Chinese emperors and Tibetan Buddhist masters would have great repercussions in subsequent centuries.

Several important subdivisions later developed within the Sa skya tradition. Two of these are most significant: the Ngor pa (Ngorpa) subsect established by Ngor chen Kun dga' bzang po (Ngorchen Kunga Zangpo, 1382–1456) and the Tshar pa (Tsarpa) subsect following the teachings of Tshar chen Blo gsal rgya mtsho (Tsarchen Losel Gyatso, 1502–1566). It is customary to refer to the Sa skya, Ngor pa, and Tshar pa traditions when discussing the entire range of the Sa skya school.

In 1429 Ngor chen established the monastery of E waṃ Chos ldan (Ewam Chöden) at Ngor, where he instituted strict monastic rules. Ngor chen specialized in the tantric systems practiced in the Sa skya school and wrote many treatises based on the definitive works of the early 'Khon masters of Sa skya. His compositions formed the basis for the distinctive interpretations of the Ngor pa school, the first lasting subdivision of the Sa skya tradition. The Ngor pa tradition became extremely influential in the eastern regions of Tibet, where it enjoyed the royal patronage of the ruling house of Sde dge (Derge).

The Tshar pa tradition takes its name from the great yogin Tshar chen Blo gsal rgya mtsho. This tradition is distinguished by its emphasis on a special esoteric transmission of the ancient tantric teachings of Sa skya, which came to be known as the "explication for disciples" (*slob bshad*), in contrast to the "explication for the assembly" (*tshogs bshad*). This esoteric transmission had previously been taught only to small groups of students and was seldom written down until the time of Tshar chen and his main disciples, who wrote a number of crucial texts. Some of the specific points of the Tshar pa explication were at first quite controversial, but they were eventually accepted by all Sa skya and Ngor pa teachers and taught more widely than before.

At the beginning of the twenty-first century the Sa skya school is perhaps strongest in the Tibetan communities of India and Nepal, where most of the great teachers of the tradition resettled in the 1960s following the Chinese occupation of Tibet. In the modern establishments of India and Nepal, teaching, study, and meditation continue to be freely practiced according to the ancient traditions of Sa skya. The leader of the Sa skya school, His Holiness Sa skya Khri 'dzin (Sakya Trizin), Ngag dbang kun dga' theg chen dpal 'bar (Ngawang Kunga Tegchen Palbar, b. 1945), is the forty-first patriarch of Sa skya. From his residence in India, he frequently travels in Southeast Asia, Europe, and North America, constantly spreading the traditional Sa skya teachings.

See also: **Sa skya Paṇḍita (Sakya Paṇḍita); Tibet**

Bibliography

Davidson, Ronald. "Preliminary Studies on Hevajra's Abhisamaya and the Lam-'bras Tshogs-bshad." *Tibetan Buddhism: Reason and Revelation,* ed. Steven Goodman and Ronald Davidson. Albany: State University of New York Press, 1992.

Deshung Rinpoche. *The Three Levels of Spiritual Perception,* tr. Jared Rhoton. Boston: Wisdom, 1995.

Jackson, David. *The Entrance Gate for the Wise (Section III).* Vienna: Arbeitskreis für Tibetische und Buddhistische Studien Universität Wien, 1987.

Jackson, David. *Enlightenment by a Single Means.* Vienna: Der Österreichischen Akademie der Wissenschaften, 1994.

Ngorchen Konchog Lhundrub. *The Beautiful Ornament of the Three Visions,* tr. Lobsang Dagpa, Ngawang Samten Chophel (Jay Goldberg), and Jared Rhoton. Ithaca, NY: Snow Lion, 1991.

Sakya Paṇḍita Kunga Gyaltshen. *A Clear Differentiation of the Three Codes: Essential Distinctions among the Individual Liberation, Great Vehicle, and Tantric Systems,* tr. Jared Douglas Rhoton. Albany: State University of New York Press, 2002.

Stearns, Cyrus. "Sachen Kunga Nyingpo's Quest for The Path and Result." *Religions of Tibet in Practice,* ed. Donald S. Lopez, Jr. Princeton, NJ: Princeton University Press, 1997.

Stearns, Cyrus. *Luminous Lives: The Story of the Early Masters of the Lam 'bras Tradition in Tibet.* Boston: Wisdom, 2001.

CYRUS STEARNS

SA SKYA PAṆḌITA (SAKYA PAṆḌITA)

Sa skya Paṇḍita Kun dga' rgyal mtshan (Sakya Paṇḍita, 1182–1251) was revered as the greatest early scholar of the SA SKYA (SAKYA) sect of Tibetan Buddhism. He is accorded the distinction of being the fourth of the five great Sa skya teachers, and is noted for his conservative polemics against what he saw as unwarranted Tibetan innovations.

Precocious as a youth, Sa skya Paṇḍita was identified early to follow in the footsteps of his 'Khon clan predecessors. His great-grandfather, 'Khon Dkon-mchog rgyal po (Khön Könchok gyelpo, 1034–1102) had founded Sa skya Monastery in 1073 C.E., and the edifice had increased in fame and fortune under succeeding teachers. Sa skya Paṇḍita's uncle, Grags pa rgyal mtshan (Drakpa Gyeltsen, 1147–1216), directed much of his early education and was concerned mostly with the tantric system. In distinction, his nephew's interest clearly moved toward the scholastic texts that had gained much currency and authority in Tibet throughout the twelfth century. Accordingly, Sa skya Paṇḍita was sent to Central Tibet in 1200 C.E. to study with Tibetan teachers who emphasized the texts of YOGĀCĀRA SCHOOL idealism, the philosophical works of the MADHYAMAKA SCHOOL, and the works on LOGIC and epistemology of DHARMAKĪRTI (ca. 650 C.E.) and his followers. The greatest influence, though, on Sa skya Paṇḍita was destined to come through his meeting with the Kashmiri master Śākyaśrībhadra (1140s–1225) and his retinue of Indian and Kashmiri teachers fleeing the Muslim persecution of Buddhism taking place in India at the time.

Together with the other scholars, Śākyaśrībhadra instructed Sa skya Paṇḍita in the Sanskrit curriculum employed in the great Indian monasteries of the period. The topics emphasized the scholastic syllabus (ABHIDHARMA, VINAYA, PRAJÑĀPĀRAMITĀ LITERATURE, Madhyamaka, logic and epistemology, etc.), as well as a well-rounded education in the literature and, especially, poetics current in India. Scholastic pedagogy emphasized the memorization of texts and the debate of their contents, so that the learned were expected to become expert in the defense of specific propositions.

In the more than one hundred compositions of his received œuvre, Sa skya Paṇḍita demonstrated his commitment to Indian scholastic Buddhism. David Jackson in his 1987 book *The Entrance Gate for the Wise* (vol. 1, pp. 39–48) identifies five works of special influence:

1. *Mkhas pa rnams 'jug pa'i sgo* (*Entrance Gate for the Wise*) is a pedagogical text that instructs the student in the primary skills—composition, exposition, and debate—of late Indian monasteries.
2. *Legs par bshad pa rin pa che'i gter* (*Treasury of Aphoristic Jewels*) is a delightful collection of homilies and remains Sa skya Paṇḍita's best known work; it is still memorized by Tibetans and establishes a common discourse for much of Tibetan culture.
3. *Tshad ma rigs gter* (*Treasury of Epistemology*), with its autocommentary, is Sa skya Paṇḍita's major statement on epistemology; it is dedicated to the refutation of the innovations of Tibetan scholars, especially Phywa pa Chos kyi seng ge (Chapa Chökyi Sengé, 1109–1169).
4. *Thub pa'i dgongs gsal* (*Clarifying the Sage's Intention*) is dedicated to the bodhisattva path as understood in late Mahāyāna scholasticism.
5. *Sdom gsum rab dbye* (*Clear Differentiation of the Three Codes*) is a synthetic work on the vows of the monk, the bodhisattva, and the tantric practitioner.

Through these and other works, Sa skya Paṇḍita challenged what he perceived as non-Indian innovations, especially those he identified as coming from Chinese influence or indigenous Tibetan sources.

Sa skya Paṇḍita's reputation for learning and sanctity eventually drew Mongol interest, and he was ordered by Göden Khan to the Mongol camp in 1244 C.E. He spent his last days in Mongol hands, instructing his nephew, 'Phags pa (Pakpa, 1235–1280), who was destined to become the first monk ruler of Tibet and the fifth of the five great Sa skya teachers.

See also: **Tibet**

Bibliography

Bosson, James E. *A Treasury of Aphoristic Jewels: The Subhasitaratnanidhi of Sa Skya Pandita in Tibetan and Mongolian.* Bloomington: Indiana University Publications, 1969.

Jackson, David P. *The Entrance Gate for the Wise (Section III): Sa-skya Pandita on Indian and Tibetan Traditions of Pramāṇa and Philosophical Debate,* 2 vols. Vienna: Arbeitskreis für Tibetische und Buddhistische Studien, 1987.

Jackson, David P. *Enlightenment by a Single Means: Tibetan Controversies on the "Self-Sufficient White Remedy."* Vienna: Der Österreichischen Akademie der Wissenschaften, 1994.

Kuijp, Leonard W. J. van der. *Contributions to the Development of Tibetan Buddhist Epistemology from the Eleventh to the Thirteenth Century.* Wiesbaden, Germany: Franz Steiner Verlag, 1983.

Sakya Paṇḍita Kunga Gyaltshen. *A Clear Differentiation of the Three Codes: Essential Distinctions among the Individual Liberation, Great Vehicle, and Tantric Systems,* tr. Jared Douglas Rhoton. Albany: State University of New York Press, 2001.

Stearns, Cyrus. *Luminous Lives: The Story of the Early Masters of the Lam 'Bras Tradition in Tibet.* Boston: Wisdom Publications, 2001.

RONALD M. DAVIDSON

ŚĀSTRA. *See* **Commentarial Literature**

SATIPAṬṬHĀNA-SUTTA

The *Satipaṭṭhāna-sutta* (*Discourse on the Foundations of Mindfulness*) is one of the most important expositions of Buddhist meditation in the Pāli canon and in the THERAVĀDA school. The discourse enumerates twenty-one meditation practices for the cultivation of MINDFULNESS (Pāli, *sati*; Sanskrit, *smṛti*) under a fourfold rubric called the four foundations of mindfulness. The four foundations are extolled as the one path leading to the realization of NIRVĀṆA. The first foundation, "contemplation of the body" (*kāyānupassanā*), includes fourteen practices: mindfulness of breathing, mindfulness of postures, full awareness of bodily actions, contemplation of bodily impurities, contemplation of elements, and nine cemetery meditations. The second foundation, "contemplation of feeling" (*vedanānupassanā*), consists of one practice: mindfulness of sensations (pleasant, unpleasant, neutral). The third foundation, "contemplation of mind" (*cittānupassanā*) is also a single practice: mindfulness of states of mind, such as lust, hatred, and liberation. The fourth foundation, "contemplation of mind-objects" (*dhammānupassanā*), includes five meditations on specific categories of dharmas: the five hindrances, the five SKANDHA (AGGREGATES), the six sense bases, the seven enlightenment factors, and the FOUR NOBLE TRUTHS. In every exercise, the practitioner is directed to observe the object of meditation simply as it is with bare attention and without attachment.

The text claims that correct practice of the four foundations of mindfulness will lead to enlightenment in as little as seven days. An expanded version of this text named the *Mahāsatipaṭṭhāna-sutta* is also found in the Pāli canon. Since the beginning of the twentieth century, the *Satipaṭṭhāna-sutta* has become especially influential as the scriptural foundation for the modern revival and popularization of insight meditation practice (*vipassanā*) in the Theravāda countries of South and Southeast Asia.

See also: **Vipassanā (Sanskrit, Vipaśyanā)**

Bibliography

Bhikkhu Ñāṇamoli and Bhikkhu Bodhi, trans. "The Foundations of Mindfulness." In *The Middle Length Discourses of the Buddha: A Translation of the Majjhima Nikāya.* Boston: Wisdom, 1995.

Nyanaponika Thera. *The Heart of Buddhist Meditation (Satipaṭṭhāna): A Handbook of Mental Training Based on the Buddha's Way of Mindfulness.* London: Rider, 1962.

PATRICK A. PRANKE

SATORI (AWAKENING)

Satori (Chinese, *wu*) is a term used principally in the CHAN SCHOOL to designate momentary episodes of transforming disclosure or insight that prompt further progress on the PATH. A practitioner may experience multiple satori, which may be of greater or lesser intensity. One's first satori, sometimes defined as "seeing one's [buddha] nature" (Chinese, *jianxing*; Japanese, *kenshō*), is typically regarded as especially important. Popular conceptions of Zen tend to portray satori as a sudden breakthrough in which intuition solves an otherwise intractable problem or dilemma. In Japanese Buddhist contexts, satori and its verb form *satoru* (to discern, to comprehend) frequently translate the Chinese terms *jue* (to become aware), *wu* (to comprehend), and *zheng* (to authenticate). Although *satori* is commonly translated as "awakening" or "enlightenment," it is to be distinguished from the related term BODHI (AWAKENING).

See also: **Zen, Popular Conceptions of**

ROBERT M. GIMELLO

SAUTRĀNTIKA

The term *Sautrāntika* means "those who rely upon the sūtras." The Sautrāntika mainstream Indian Buddhist school represented a dissenting doctrinal party within the Sarvāstivāda school, which was referred to by their Sarvāstivādin opponents as Dārṣṭāntika. The Sautrāntika school rejected the authority of a separate ABHIDHARMA collection and adopted a doctrinal position of extreme momentariness, whereby only present activity exists.

See also: **Mainstream Buddhist Schools**

COLLETT COX

SCRIPTURE

The word *scripture* (from the Latin *scribere,* "to write or to compose") is typically used to refer to written texts, usually the written, foundational texts of a religious tradition. But few religions had written texts in their earliest historical period. Instead, those fundamental texts were committed to writing only after they had been transmitted orally, often for several hundreds of years. Buddhism fits this pattern of development. According to the tradition, immediately after the death of the Buddha, MAHĀKĀŚYAPA, one of the Buddha's senior disciples, convened a council of five hundred ARHATS. At that time, those monks who had heard the Buddha speak were said to have recited all of the Buddha's discourses from memory, and specific monks were then charged with the responsibility of transmitting specific discourses verbatim to their students. According to traditional historical accounts, this is the way in which Buddhist scripture was preserved in the earliest period. Whether this narrative represents historical fact or whether it is an attempt on the part of the tradition to legitimize the authenticity of its scriptures by tracing them back to the original source in an unbroken lineage is, of course, uncertain. However, it would appear that in India monks did orally transmit texts attributed to the Buddha from master to disciple in distinct lineages over several hundreds of years. This continued to be the case even after these oral texts were finally committed to writing and compiled into, for example, the Pāli Buddhist CANON sometime in the first century B.C.E. The fourth century C.E. scholar monk VASUBANDHU speaks of such oral lineages of transmission (and of their corruption) in his important text, the *Vyākhyāyukti* (*Science of Exegesis*).

What are the Buddhist scriptures? The simple answer is that scriptures are texts that have the status of being considered BUDDHAVACANA (WORD OF THE BUDDHA). Sūtras are paradigmatic examples of scriptures. A sūtra (literally "thread," "measuring line," or "standard," from the Sanskrit root *sūtr,* "to string together," "to compose") in its most general sense is a discourse of a buddha. However, the category of scripture is actually much broader than that of sūtra. Thus, while all sūtras are scripture, not all scriptures are sūtras (see below). Scriptures are often distinguished from śāstras, which are works, usually of a more synthetic and commentarial nature, that are based on, in the sense of being second-order expositions of, scriptural material. Not all scriptures are considered to be the word of the historical Buddha Śākyamuni, since there are some scriptures that are said to be spoken by other buddhas. Moreover, not everything that is spoken by a buddha is considered to be scripture. For example, the Tibetan tradition generally considers the works attributed to MAITREYA, the future Buddha, to be śāstras, and not sūtras. What is more, it is often the case that a work that is not a scripture may have a more exalted status, playing a more pivotal role in a particular Buddhist tradition than do actual scriptures. Take once again the works of Maitreya, or those of NĀGĀRJUNA (ca. second century C.E.), which, despite their status as śāstras, are immensely important for much of the later Indian, Chinese, and Tibetan traditions. All of this is to say that there is a certain arbitrariness concerning what is and what is not a Buddhist scripture, and that in the end a "scripture" may be no more and no less than what a specific Buddhist community considers to fall within the purview of that category.

Scriptures and canons

By comparison to the Torah, Bible, and Qur'an, the set of texts that comprise the Buddhist scriptural canon is mammoth. The Pāli canon, for example, consists of over forty large volumes, and the scriptural portions of the Chinese and Tibetan canons are over twice that size. Given the heterogeneous nature of Buddhism, moreover, different Buddhist schools have different collections of texts that they consider to be the Buddha's word. For example, the Theravāda tradition of Southeast Asia generally considers only those works contained in the Pāli canon (*tipiṭaka*) to be the Buddha's word. The *tipiṭaka,* or "three baskets," consists of the *sutta* (Sanskrit, sūtra), the VINAYA, and the abhidhamma (Sanskrit, ABHIDHARMA). The *sutta* basket, although the most thematically heterogeneous collection in so far as it deals with a wide range of subjects, is nonetheless relatively coherent in terms of style. A *sutta* or sūtra is a discourse or sermon usually on a specific topic delivered by the Buddha at a particular time, in a particular location, and to a specific audience. All of these—time, place, and audience—are identified in the preamble of a sūtra. Sūtras also tend to begin characteristically with the opening line, "Thus have I heard," signaling once again the oral/aural nature of the original transmission of scripture. The vinaya basket is more thematically coherent in so far as it is a collection of texts dealing with the monastic discipline of monks and nuns. It contains texts that discuss the life of the Buddha and the history of the order, texts that list monastic vows, narrative accounts of how the various vows were set forth by the Buddha, ritual formulas (for example, for ORDINATION), and so forth. The *abhidharma* basket, by contrast, is more philosophical, often elaborating lists of technical terms (for example, the psychophysical constituents of the self and the world), their definitions and their grouping. Since it is a more derivative, manipulated, one might almost say artificial genre, there arose the question even in ancient times of whether or not *abhidharma* texts should be considered the actual word of the Buddha, with different schools taking different positions on the issue.

Although there were questions even from very early times about which texts should and should not be considered the buddha's word (and hence scripture), the issue truly came to the fore with the rise of the MAHĀYĀNA, or Great Vehicle. The Mahāyāna emerged (or, according to the tradition, reemerged) in the first centuries of the common era in India. It maintained that the Buddha had actually taught a much wider set of doctrines and practices than those preserved in the earlier scriptures, but that these texts had been hidden until the world was ripe for their revelation. Mahāyānists thus made a case for an expanded scriptural corpus that included a wider range of texts. Although it is not clear whether this new corpus of texts ever achieved a canonical completeness or finality as a separate and distinct collection that had the same level of authority as the earlier canon, there is evidence that some Mahāyānists did have a notion of the so-called *Vaipulya* (*Extensive Works*) as a kind of Mahāyāna canon, possibly subsumed within the sūtra basket.

Following this same pattern, several centuries later the TANTRA (also known as the Mantrayāna or Vajrayāna) emerged as a movement within Indian Buddhism (more specifically, as a submovement within the Mahāyāna), claiming scriptural status for its own set of texts, this time called not sūtras but tantras. Like the former, the tantras were considered to be the word of the historical Buddha, or else the word of one or another of a variety of deities that, like the buddha, were fully enlightened beings. And here too one sometimes finds use of the "hidden text" trope to explain why these scriptures had not existed in the world heretofore. But tantrics also at times resorted to other strategies to explain why their scriptural texts had never existed in this world, strategies that were not unknown to the earlier Mahāyāna. For example, in some instances, rather than having been hidden, the texts were claimed to have been revealed anew to accomplished yogis or siddhas in visions or in otherworldly journeys to heavenly realms. In this way one finds in some tantras a theme that is common to other religious traditions, namely, the notion of a heavenly library, access to which is granted only to spiritually advanced individuals.

As mentioned above, the corpus of texts that came to have the status of "scripture" varied from one Buddhist tradition to another. Hence, the Pāli, the Tibetan, and the Chinese canons, to take three examples, are quite different, even if there is some overlap between the three. For example, the Chinese canon has a section called *āgama,* which contains many of the sūtras also found in the Pāli canon (even if the Chinese texts are translations of different—Sanskrit, and not Pāli—versions of these texts). Likewise, the Tibetan canon contains a great deal of vinaya material that is thematically similar to material found in the vinaya sections of both the Chinese and the Pāli canons, even if the texts are not exactly the same. But of course both the Chinese and the Tibetan canons include Mahāyāna sūtras that are absent from the Pāli canon, and the Tibetan canon, in addition, includes many tantras that are not found in any other collection of Buddhist scriptural material. Theravāda Buddhists, who follow the Pāli canon, consider much of what is found in the Chinese and Tibetan scriptural collections to be apocryphal, that is, inauthentic because it is not the Buddha's word. And likewise, Chinese Mahāyāna Buddhists will consider much of the scriptural material found in the tantric portions of the Tibetan Buddhist canon to be apocryphal. And even among Tibetans there were controversies over whether certain texts were authentic, such as certain tantras of the RNYING MA (NYINGMA) school, and the so-called treasure texts (*gter ma*) that were said to have been hidden and later found in a variety of sites in Tibet. This is important to point out, lest it be thought that there is consensus among different Buddhists concerning what constitutes scripture. Despite the fact that there are some contemporary collections of translated texts that bear this name, there is in reality no such thing as a single "Buddhist Bible."

The uses of scripture

That being said, there is a great deal of similarity in the ways that different Buddhist traditions use scripture.

First, scriptures are memorized. Sometimes they are memorized for no other reason than that memorizing the Buddha's word is considered a virtuous activity that brings much merit. In Thailand, for example, those (albeit few) monks who have managed to memorize the entire Pāli canon have an exalted status in the society, even being recognized with an official title by the government. Sometimes scriptures are committed to memory so as to be used liturgically, as is the case with the HEART SŪTRA in the East Asian Tibetan traditions. In each of these cases it is possible that the person who is memorizing the text will not understand the meaning of the scripture, and this tells us that scriptures cannot be reduced to their content or meaning, since they are put to many uses that have nothing to do with their meaning. For example, scriptures are often displayed on altars, where they serve as a representation of the second of the three jewels, the jewel of the dharma, and where, in that capacity, they serve as an object of worship and devotion. In large monasteries in Tibet, for example, it is common for ambulatories to exist below shelved scriptures, permitting the devout to receive the merit and blessing of the dharma by walking underneath (in a squatting position that indicates subservience to and respect for) the physical texts located above them. In addition, in some Buddhist traditions scriptures are often taken in procession into the fields before sowing or harvesting as a way of blessing the earth and assuring a good crop. Sometimes portions of scripture will be tattooed onto the body, sometimes they are worn in the form of AMULETS AND TALISMANS, and sometimes they are burnt and ingested, all of this as a way of protecting the bearer or consumer of the text from evil or harm. All of these might be called "magical" or "popular" uses of scripture, wherein the physicality of the text (its sound and its material quality) are the principal focus of the various practices. It would be mistaken to consider these practices to belong exclusively to the LAITY, since MONKS and NUNS also engage in them.

In addition to these popular practices, however, there are also what might be called the more elite uses of scripture. Here it is the content or meaning of the text that is the focus, and this is the object of concern of religious virtuosi, usually, though increasingly not exclusively, male monastics. In India the process of appropriating scriptural material in this fashion was systematized in the doctrine of the "three ways of gaining knowledge": through hearing, thinking, and MEDITATION. First, the scripture is heard. Since the earliest form of scripture was oral, the only access that monks had to scripture was through hearing it spoken or recited. This spoken text was then usually memorized, and thus internalized linguistically. Once this had been accomplished, the monk was expected to begin the process of critically scrutinizing the meaning of the words. This would involve questioning the text, allowing doubts to emerge, and resolving those doubts through reasoning. Finally, once a stable form of certainty had been reached by pondering the meaning of the text, it was expected that that meaning would become the focus of one's meditation, so that the doctrinal content of the scripture would be internalized in such a way that it had a permanent transformative impact on the person of the practitioner. This process that begins with language and proceeds through critical reflective practices culminating in transformative experience is paradigmatic of the Buddhist scholastic approach to the study of scripture. It became the quintessential mode of elite appropriation of scriptural texts in much of later Indian, Tibetan, and East Asian Buddhism, and it is in large part what gave rise to the vast commentarial tradition, that is, to scriptural exegesis.

Although most Buddhist scholastics tended to follow the pattern of scriptural study just mentioned, it must be pointed out that there were also differences. For example, Indian and especially Tibetan Buddhist institutions tended to develop broad curricula that encouraged the study of many different scriptural texts (or their at times quasi-canonical commentaries). By contrast, in East Asia one finds that, rather than seeking diversified scriptural curricula, specific schools tended to focus on a particular scriptural text or on a small group of texts. Hence we find a focus on the LOTUS SŪTRA (SADDHARMAPUṆḌARĪKA-SŪTRA) on the part of the TIANTAI SCHOOL of East Asia. In a similar fashion, the Chinese HUAYAN SCHOOL developed an elaborate system of metaphysics and hermeneutics around the HUAYAN JING (*Avataṃsaka-sūtra, Flower Garland Sūtra*). PURE LAND SCHOOLS likewise had their own canon-within-the-canon in the form of the SUKHĀVATĪVYŪHA-SŪTRA.

It would be mistaken to think that all Buddhist schools are univocally in favor of scriptural study, however. For example, those forms of Japanese Buddhism that derive from NICHIREN (1222–1282) tended to downplay the study of the content of the *Lotus Sūtra*, believing, rather, that the appropriate practice in the present "degenerate age" should be the recitation of the DAIMOKU title of the sūtra (*Myōhō-renge-kyō* in Japanese). An even more ambivalent attitude toward scriptural study is found among certain (though by no means all) branches of the CHAN SCHOOL, wherein the study of scripture (especially for the beginning practitioner) is seen as having the potential to mire the mind in language and in the dichotomies of thought. In these traditions, then, scriptural study is eschewed in favor of meditation, or else permitted only after the adept has a strong foundation in meditative practice. Interestingly, this inverts scholastic Buddhism's classical order of praxis by advocating a movement from experience to words.

See also: **Āgama/Nikāya; Apocrypha; Canon; Catalogues of Scriptures; Commentarial Literature; Merit and Merit-Making; Printing Technologies; Relics and Relics Cults**

Bibliography

Bond, George D. "Two Theravāda Traditions of the Meaning of 'The Word of the Buddha.'" *Mahabodhi* 83 (1975): 402–413.

Buswell, Robert E., Jr., ed. *Chinese Buddhist Apocrypha.* Honolulu: University of Hawaii Press, 1990.

Cabezón, José Ignacio. *Buddhism and Language: A Study of Indo-Tibetan Scholasticism.* Albany: State University of New York Press, 1994.

Coward, Harold. "Scripture in Buddhism." In *Sacred Word and Sacred Text: Scripture in World Religions.* New York: Maryknoll, 1988.

Eimer, Helmut, and Germano, David, eds. *The Many Canons of Tibetan Buddhism.* Leiden, Netherlands: Brill, 2002.

Lancaster, Lewis. "Buddhist Literature: Its Canons, Scribes, and Editors." In *The Critical Study of Sacred Texts,* ed. Wendy Doniger O'Flaherty. Berkeley, CA: Berkeley Religious Studies Series, 1979.

Lopez, Donald S., Jr. *Buddhist Hermeneutics.* Honolulu: University of Hawaii Press, 1992.

Ray, Reginald. "Buddhism: Sacred Text Written and Realized." In *The Holy Book in Comparative Perspective,* ed. Frederick M. Denny and Rodney L. Taylor. Columbia: University of South Carolina Press, 1985.

Smith, Wilfred Cantwell. "The Buddhist Influence." In *What Is Scripture? A Comparative Approach.* Minneapolis: Fortress, 1993.

JOSÉ IGNACIO CABEZÓN

SELF. *See* Anātman/Ātman (No-Self/Self)

SELF-IMMOLATION

Self-immolation refers to ASCETIC PRACTICES that include the voluntary termination of life or the offering of parts of the body. The most commonly encountered types of self-immolation in Buddhism are autocremation (the deliberate incineration of one's own body) and the burning off of fingers. Buddhist literature refers to such practices by a variety of terms that may best be rendered as "abandoning the body." In the popular imagination, the best-known examples of self-immolation are the Vietnamese monks who burned themselves to death between 1963 and 1975 to protest the anti-Buddhist policies pursued by the government of South Vietnam. The autocremation of Thích Quang Du'c on June 11, 1963, was captured by the American reporter Malcolm Browne in a series of photographs that have been frequently reproduced. Autocremation by Vietnamese Buddhists continues to be reported in the 1990s and early years of the twenty-first century.

Self-immolation is best attested in Chinese Buddhist sources, which record hundreds of cases dating from the late fourth to the mid-twentieth century. Very few of these acts can be understood as political protest. The offering of fingers is still recognized and carried out as an ascetic practice by monks in China and Korea.

Chinese Buddhist sources contain many accounts of monks, nuns, and laypeople who encouraged insects to feed on their blood, cut their own flesh (particularly the thigh), burned incense on their skin, or burned their fingers, toes, or arms. These practices did not always result in death, but they were still classified as heroic examples of "abandoning the body." There are also accounts of people who starved themselves to death, disemboweled themselves, drowned in rivers or oceans, leapt from cliffs or trees, or fed themselves to wild animals. Although drowning seems to have been more common in Japan, autocremation was the most commonly attested form of self-immolation in China. The preparations for autocremation usually involved the construction of a funeral pyre, inside which the monk or nun would sit. The body was often wrapped in oil-soaked cloth to expedite the burning process, and frequently the autocremator would also consume oil and incense for several days or even months beforehand. Autocremation was usually a public event witnessed by a large audience. In the early medieval period (fifth to seventh centuries C.E.) Chinese emperors and senior officials often attended and later eulogized these dramatic acts.

Autocremation was primarily a Sinitic Buddhist creation that first appeared in late fourth-century China. As practiced in China, autocremation was not a continuation of an Indian custom. Rather, it developed after a particular interpretation of certain Indian texts was combined with indigenous traditions, such as burning the body to bring rain, a practice that long predated the arrival of Buddhism in China. The most influential textual models were some of the bloodier JĀTAKA tales and the twenty-third chapter of the LOTUS SŪTRA (Chinese, *Miaofa lianhua jing*; Sanskrit, *Saddharmapuṇḍarīkasūtra*), in which the Bodhisattva Bhaiṣajyagururāja (Medicine-King) burns his body in offering to the buddhas and to the sūtra itself. The literary precedents for the practice of self-immolation found in Indian Buddhist sources are often extremely graphic, even if they were intended only rhetorically. These have been well studied by Hubert Durt and Reiko Ohnuma. The validity of self-immolation was reinforced by the production of Chinese apocryphal sūtras that vindicated the practice, by the composition of biographies of self-immolators, and, in time, their inclusion in the Buddhist canon as exemplars of heroic practice.

Self-immolation was often controversial and attracted opposition from Confucians and sometimes from the state. The Confucian revivalist Han Yu (768–824), in his famous *Lun Fogu biao* (*Memorial on the Buddha Relic*), warned Emperor Xianzong (r. 805–820) in 819 that he should not honor the Buddha's relic because this would trigger a mass outbreak of religious fervor, causing people to burn the tops of their heads and set fire to their fingers. An edict promulgated in 955 by Emperor Shizong (r. 954–959) of the Later Zhou explicitly prohibited self-immolation for both saṅgha and laity. Within Buddhism, the strongest objection came from the eminent monk YIJING (635–713), who wrote a lengthy diatribe against autocremation in his *Nanhai jigui neifa zhuan* (*An Account of the Dharma Sent Back from the Southern Seas*). Much later the Ming dynasty cleric ZHUHONG (1532–1612) included a heartfelt and extremely critical essay on the practice of burning the body in his *Zheng'e ji* (*Rectification of Errors*, 1614). The most coherently and passionately argued defense of self-immolation is that of Yongming YANSHOU (904–975) in his *Wanshan Tonggui ji* (*The Common End of the Myriad Good Practices*). For Yanshou self-immolation is primarily a manifestation of DĀNA (GIVING), and as the ultimate expression of this PĀRAMITĀ (PERFECTION) it is grounded in ultimate truth rather than at the level of conventional phenomena.

Bibliography

Benn, James A. "Where Text Meets Flesh: Burning the Body as an 'Apocryphal Practice' in Chinese Buddhism." *History of Religions* 37, no. 4 (1998): 295–322.

Durt, Hubert. "Two Interpretations of Human-Flesh Offering: Misdeed or Supreme Sacrifice." *Journal of the International College for Advanced Buddhist Studies* (*Kokosai Bukkyōgaku daigakuin daigaku kenkyū kiyo*) 1 (1998): 236–210 (sic).

Gernet, Jacques. "Les suicides par le feu chez les bouddhistes chinois de Ve au Xe siècle." *Mélanges publiés par l'Institute des Hautes Études Chinoises* 2 (1960): 527–558.

Jan, Yün-hua. "Buddhist Self-Immolation in Medieval China." *History of Religions* 4 (1965): 243–265.

Ohnuma, Reiko. "The Gift of the Body and the Gift of the Dharma." *History of Religions* 37, no. 4 (1998): 323–359.

Orzech, Charles D. "Provoked Suicide and the Victim's Behavior." In *Curing Violence*, ed. Mark I. Wallace and Theophus H. Smith. Sonoma, CA: Polebridge Press, 1994.

JAMES A. BENN

SENGZHAO

Practically the entire life of the important early Chinese MADHYAMAKA SCHOOL philosopher Shi Sengzhao (374–414 C.E.) was connected to KUMĀRAJĪVA (350–409/413) and Kumārajīva's translation workshop in Chang'an. Coming from a poor family, Sengzhao earned his living as a copyist. This provided him with an excellent education in the Chinese classics, as well as Daoist and Buddhist scriptures. Recognized as a distinguished literatus by age twenty, he was fascinated with Kumārajīva even before Kumārajīva arrived at Chang'an. In fact, according to his biography, Sengzhao traveled to Guzang to meet his world renowned mentor, by whose side he spent the next twenty years serving as disciple and interpreter.

Many of Kumārajīva's translations bear the literary style of Sengzhao, who is said to have had the primary responsibility for editing Kumārajīva's translations, adapting them to the taste of the literary elite in Chang'an. Sengzhao is also responsible for putting together a catalogue of Kumārajīva's translations, including some ninety titles, which circulated in Chang'an as late as the sixth century and which were later absorbed into the comprehensive catalogues *Chu sanzang jiji* (*Collection of Records about the Production of the Tripiṭaka*) and *Kaihuang Sanbao lu* (*Catalogue of the Three Treasures of the Kaihuang [Era]*).

Sengzhao made multiple contributions to the world of early medieval Chinese Buddhism. One is his ten-fascicle commentary to the *Weimojie suo shuo jing* (*Sūtra of Vimalakīrti's Discourses*; Sanskrit, *Vimalakīrtinirdeśa-sūtra*), which elevates lay Buddhism above the monastic path of the clergy. Sengzhao is known to have been converted to Buddhism by this sūtra. His commentary, written to Kumārajīva's translation of this text, reportedly inspired hundreds of Chang'an literati to practice Buddhism. Another contribution is a collection of philosophical treatises in which the Madhyamaka philosophy of NĀGĀRJUNA (ca. second century C.E.) was expounded through the use of devices and language provided by traditional Chinese thinkers, particularly those of the Xuanxue (Dark Learning) school. Several such treatises were collected by later editors of the Tripiṭaka under the name of ZHAO LUN (*The Treatises of [Seng] zhao*). Other works attributed to Sengzhao, such as *Zongben yilun* (*Treatise on the Foundational [Principles of the Doctrine]*) and the apocryphal *Baozanglun* (*Treasure Store Treatise*), circulated as independent treatises. The greatest philosophical importance of Sengzhao's writings is the introduction to China of the Madhyamaka ideas of Nāgārjuna as they were shaped by Kumārajīva's understanding of these issues. Sengzhao's own Daoist mystical inclinations contributed to the great emphasis placed on the idea of the TATHĀGATAGARBHA (buddha-nature) in Kumārajīva's translated texts, thus paving the way for the next phase in the development of Chinese Buddhist thought.

See also: **Catalogues of Scriptures**

Bibliography

Ch'en, Kenneth. *Buddhism in China: A Historical Survey.* Princeton, NJ: Princeton University Press, 1964.

Liebenthal, Walter, trans. and ed. *Chao lun, The Treatises of Seng-chao: A Translation with Introduction, Notes, and Appendices,* Vols. 1 and 2, second revised edition. Hong Kong: Hong Kong University Press, 1968

Sharf, Robert H. *Coming to Terms with Chinese Buddhism: A Reading of the Treasure Store Treatise.* A Kuroda Institute book. Honolulu: University of Hawaii Press, 2002.

T'ang Yung-t'ung. *Han Wei Liang-Chin Nan-pei ch'ao fo-chiao-shih.* Shanghai: Shangwu yinshuguan, 1938.

TANYA STORCH

SENTIENT BEINGS

Sentient beings is a term used to designate the totality of living, conscious beings that constitute the object and audience of the Buddhist teaching. Translating various Sanskrit terms (*jantu, bahu jana, jagat, sattva*), *sentient beings* conventionally refers to the mass of living things subject to illusion, suffering, and rebirth (SAṂSĀRA). Less frequently, *sentient beings* as a class broadly encompasses all beings possessing consciousness, including BUDDHAS and BODHISATTVAS.

The Pāli *nikāyas* and the Sarvāstivāda Abhidharma differentiate the mass of deluded beings subject to saṃsāra into a hierarchy of five paths or destinations of REBIRTH based upon KARMA (ACTION): DIVINITIES (deva), humans (*manuṣya*), animals (*tiryak*), spirits of the dead (preta), and denizens of hell (*naraka*). An alternative list of six categories, which was attributed to the Vātsīputrīyas and gained popularity in East Asian and Tibetan Buddhism, places a class of demonic beings (asura) between humans and gods.

All of these beings reside in the three realms of existence (*tridhātu*) that comprise the entirety of the Buddhist universe. The realm of desire (*kāmadhātu*) is residence for beings from all the categories, while the realm of form (*rūpadhātu*) and the realm of formlessness (*ārūypadhātu*) are reserved for gods of higher achievement. Among these paths of rebirth, the denizens of hell, spirits of the dead, and animals are regarded as unhappy destinies, while rebirth as humans and gods (as well as asura in the list of six) are considered desirable, most importantly because it is only through the human and deva destinies that enlightenment can be obtained.

Although the Buddhist message from its inception held as its goal the liberation of sentient beings from the cycle of rebirth, the concern for sentient beings took on even greater urgency with the emergence of the MAHĀYĀNA tradition, since all called to this tradition's bodhisattva vocation were entrusted with the welfare and ultimate liberation of all sentient beings. The compassion, transfer of merit, and cultivation of UPĀYA (skill in means) that are central in the cultivation of the bodhisattva path are all concerned with the salvation of sentient beings. The Mahāyāna tradition furthermore came to maintain that all sentient beings possessed the buddha-nature, which meant that all inherently had the potential to become enlightened. In later developments in East Asian Buddhism the possession of this nature was extended to insentient existents as well.

See also: **Cosmology; Ghosts and Spirits; Karuṇā (Compassion); Merit and Merit-Making; Tathāgatagarbha**

Bibliography

Gethin, Rupert. *The Foundations of Buddhism.* Oxford: Oxford University Press, 1998.

Matsunaga, Daigan, and Matsunaga, Alicia. *The Buddhist Concept of Hell.* New York: Philosophical Library, 1972.

Sadakata, Akira, et al. *Buddhist Cosmology: Philosophy and Origins,* tr. Gaynor Sekimori. Boston: Charles E. Tuttle, 1997.

DANIEL A. GETZ

SEXUALITY

From the earliest beginnings of the religion, Buddhist thinkers have recognized the human drive for sensual gratification as an extremely powerful force. This recognition, however, is difficult to characterize. While sexuality has usually been viewed suspiciously, as a primary obstacle on the PATH to salvation, some Buddhists have claimed that, used properly, desire and pleasure can offer a shortcut to enlightenment for the advanced practitioner. Also, since laypeople have always been an essential part of the Buddhist community, fertility cults embracing a fecund sexuality have played an important part in the repertoire of ritual and iconography.

This entry outlines the tension in Buddhism between antipathy toward sex and the celebration of it. As a religious tradition that has spread widely to diverse geographical regions over the course of some two and a half millennia, Buddhism cannot be said to have one fixed view of sex and sexuality. While it is impossible to delineate a single Buddhist attitude regarding sexuality, one can observe in specific doctrinal and historical moments tendencies typical of the tradition as a whole.

The celibate ideal: Buddha, arhat, monk, and nun

Hagiographies of the Buddha, in their treatment of his early years as the prince Siddhārtha Gautama, place great emphasis on the sensual nature of his royal amusements. Having received a prophecy that the prince would either become a universal monarch or a great renunciant, Siddhartha's father, King Śuddhodāna, uses every means at his disposal to keep his son's mind firmly focused on the pleasures of this world. Essentially, the young man is held prisoner in a garden of earthly delights. With sumptuous palaces and a large harem, Siddhārtha has every opportunity to indulge in the pleasures of the flesh. The women of celestial beauty who dote on the young prince, foremost among them his lovely wife, Yaśodhara, are quite prominently featured. Lavish gyneceum scenes are depicted in the written, illustrated, and carved biographical representations of the Buddha's life. Every libidinal urge he may have is gratified immediately. And yet, he feels malaise in this paradisiacal setting.

Life in the palace compound is cloying and confining, so Siddhartha asks his charioteer to take him on a tour outside the gates. There he sees various signs of impermanence, which further disturb him, and he decides to leave his life of royal ease and with it the world of sexuality. As the prince escapes the palace by night, he sees his women, usually so poised and bewitching, sleeping in various states of dishevelment. Like so many corpses they lie, their poses wholly unflattering, threads of drool hang from the corners of their lolling mouths. The sight fills him with disgust as he beats a hasty retreat. After years of hard work in mental, spiritual, and physical cultivation, Siddhārtha finds himself on the verge of enlightenment. MĀRA, wishing to entice Siddhārtha from the fulfillment of his aim, sends his daughters to tempt the great man. Although they are beautiful as they dance provocatively and flirt with him, Siddhārtha is unmoved. Even after the women undergo a series of transformations in an attempt to accord with a full range of male tastes in women, Siddhārtha remains steadfast in his pursuit of the goal of enlightenment.

Vulnerability to sexual temptation remains a barometer of spiritual fallibility in the Buddhist tradition far beyond this foundational story. Some accounts suggest that the first schism in the Buddhist monastic community was occasioned in large part by a debate concerning the nature of the enlightened person, the ARHAT. In the course of the debate, a monk named Mahādeva proposed that arhats are limited in their powers of omniscience, clairvoyance, and continence. Among the five assertions this monk made is that although the arhat has put an end to rebirth, escaping the round of SAṂSĀRA, he is still subject to nocturnal emissions or so-called wet dreams. To make such a claim was to suggest that the perfected person was still subject to lustful thoughts, if only in his dreams. For some members of the community, this was heresy. Similarly, the story of the One-Horned Saint, a tale well known in Buddhist Asia from India to Japan, describes a religious virtuoso who has obtained many magical powers (*abhijñā*) as a result of his training and austerities. While flying through the air one day, he is distracted by the sight of the white thighs of a woman who has hiked up her dress to wash clothes by a river. The sage tumbles from the sky, bereft of his supernatural abilities. In one moment of sexual arousal, all the fruits of years of discipline are lost. He marries the washerwoman and settles down to a life more ordinary. In this story, the control of sexual urges is presented as a kind of litmus test for spiritual attainment.

For the monastic community, the threat of sexual temptation was recognized as a serious obstacle to progress on the Buddhist path. For this reason, the disciplinary codes for MONKS and NUNS, the VINAYA, are quite explicit and exhaustive in the varieties of sexual activity they proscribe. The monk's rule clearly states that genital, oral, manual, or anal sex is absolutely prohibited, be it with humans, divine beings, or animals. These acts will result in expulsion from the Buddhist order (SAṄGHA), as will making a lustful remark to a woman about her pudenda or her anus. Intentionally emitting semen (nocturnal emissions excepted) or causing someone else to do so will result in temporary suspension from the order. The nun's rule is similarly detailed.

Yet, while celibacy and complete sexual abstinence was an ideal for the clergy, for the LAITY, sexuality was an essential and celebrated aspect of life. In the different geographical and cultural areas where it flourished, Buddhism often assimilated itself to autochthonous fertility cults, enlisting local deities into the Buddhist pantheon. Thus, although proscribed for monks and nuns, lay sexuality was not merely tolerated as a necessary evil, but could, in fact, be lauded as a positive good. In some parts of Southeast Asia, where temporary ordination of young men is common, time spent as a monk is understood to increase one's fertility and virility.

Sexuality and the lay Buddhist

The earliest surviving Buddhist STŪPA, the great stūpa at SĀÑCĪ in central India, was built around the third century B.C.E. In its richly carved decorative railings and gates, which date from a few centuries later, the modern viewer is afforded a glimpse into the sumptuous world of ancient Buddhist sexuality. These stone fences and doors are adorned with frankly seductive statues of female tree sprites (*yakṣī*) and male–female pairs in attitudes of erotic play or union (*maithuna*). The gracefully arched pose of the *yakṣī* as she grasps the branches of a mango tree is echoed in ancient Indian representations of the Buddha's mother, Māyā, as she painlessly delivers the bodhisattva from her side. The person of Lady Māyā is a telling indicator of Buddhist ambivalence toward sexuality. The bodhisattva, the Buddha-to-be, must choose for his mother a woman who is the epitome of sexual attractiveness and fecundity, and yet she must die ten days after bearing him so that there can be no chance of her being defiled by any subsequent sexual intercourse.

In every Buddhist culture, lay donors and supporters of Buddhism far outnumbered monastics. The institution of the family has been a focus of Buddhist theory and practice in every context—from India, to Thailand, to Korea. Lay worshippers who visited the Sāñcī stūpa and similar sites like Bhārhut, while they no doubt also sought proximity to the relics of the Buddha enshrined within the monument, would have been keenly interested in these visual representations of gods and goddesses who had ensured sexual fulfillment and safe childbirth long before the advent of Śākyamuni.

New stories were created to demonstrate the Buddhist nature of such deities. These deities, whom people were accustomed to worshipping, were given new Buddhist identities and thus existing loyalties and devotions were brought into the Buddhist fold. One popular pairing was Pāñcika (Kubera), King of the Tree Sprites, and Hāritī, a ravenous demoness converted by Śākyamuni. Statues of this couple, often surrounded by small children, gave the laity a positive vision of their own sexually engaged lives with the attendant blessings of progeny that belies the stereotype of Buddhism as a pessimistic and world-denying faith.

Wherever Buddhism spread, a similar kind of conquest through assimilation occurred. For instance, in Japan, popular tales recounting the origins of Buddhist deities often incorporated local gods and goddesses and more often than not involved a story of star-crossed lovers. Medieval Buddhist interpretations of Japan's cosmogonic myth placed particular emphasis on the lesson of the creative power of sexual union. Laypeople saw no contradiction between adherence to the Buddhist teachings and an active sex life; native fertility cults survived in Buddhist guise.

And yet, it was not only the laity who sought sexual fulfillment. In many MAHĀYĀNA countries, members of the saṅgha, specifically monks, saw fit to embrace women as wives or lovers either in secret or publicly. The bodhisattva Avalokiteśvara is said to have visited the thirteenth-century Japanese monk SHINRAN (1173–1263) to assure him that she would remove from him the obstacle of sexual desire by transforming into a woman and becoming his wife. In today's

Japan, most Buddhist monks (often called *priests* in English to distinguish them from celibates) are married. In the VAJRAYĀNA or tantric contexts of Nepal and Tibet, there has long existed a special class of married clergy. While to some, both within and outside the Buddhist community, this may seem like a violation of the rule of the saṅgha, by many it is understood as much more than a mere concession to human nature. For Shinran, the attempt to live a life unsullied by sex marked a kind of striving that smacked of hubris. For others, particularly within the Vajrayāna, sexuality is a powerful force for transformation, an aspect of the path of purification, an aid to enlightenment.

Sexuality as obstacle, sexuality as opportunity

While sexuality was often understood as a negative force associated with desire, some attempted to harness its power as a tool. As a fundamental drive numbered among the *kleśa* (afflictions, passions), sexuality was regarded with much disdain and suspicion, but there were those who felt that sensual desire was a door to liberation. Others used the senses to distance themselves from sexual instincts. One MEDITATION practice that spread, in one form or another, across Buddhist Asia, sought to cut off sexual desire at its root. Here, in typically androcentric fashion, sexual desire figured as the desire of a man for a woman.

In these graveyard meditations, the monk would observe the fresh corpse of a young woman, a potential object of lust, as it proceeded through the stages of decomposition. As the body would begin to bloat, the skin to discolor, as maggots and wild animals hastened the process of the dissolution of the corpse, the monk was invited to reflect upon the true nature of the body. What had been so bewitching became an object of repulsion. A strain of misogyny that locates the origins of male desire in the female body is common to monastic legal codes and didactic literature. Thus, men's lust for sexual gratification is blamed on the women who are the objects of their attraction. Behind this is the insistence in orthodox or mainstream Buddhism that sexual desire must be suppressed in order to attain the goal of awakening. A common description of the body is that it is a bag of skin filled with blood and pus, urine and excrement.

Some Buddhists, primarily those of the Mahāyāna schools, have taken a different tack, at least rhetorically. While actual sexual activity was always the exception within the monastic community, the nondualist doctrines of the Mahāyāna called the traditional preoccupation with purity into question. In the tantric conception of the Vajrayāna and the transcendentalist philosophy of immanence advocated by some in the CHAN SCHOOL, the afflictions (*kleśa*) themselves are equivalent to BODHI (AWAKENING), the realm of suffering (saṃsāra) in which one lives is no different than the goal of enlightenment (nirvāṇa). The phenomenal world is, just as it is, ŚŪNYATĀ (EMPTINESS). In such a philosophical context, it is impossible to define sex as "dirty," or as somehow able to impede enlightenment, which is understood to be an indwelling and immanent quality of mind. Awakening has nothing to do with stifling urges like sexuality; what is essential is to transform one's outlook on the world. Correct understanding is, therefore, more important than what one does with one's body. To the person who has deeply understood emptiness, no act creates attachment, no act is defiling. In fact, when used properly, sex can teach the practitioner about nondualism and the eradication of the sense of an independent self.

In some traditions sex has been understood as a liberative technique, numbered among the UPĀYA (skillful means) of the bodhisattva. In tantric Tibetan Buddhism in particular, there is an elaborate system of sexual yoga. Whether the sexual encounter between the male practitioner and the ḌĀKIṆĪ is properly meant to be understood as taking place in the physical world or in the mind of the devotee or in some other realm is a matter subject to much debate, but the literature outlining these practices is rich in sensual imagery and detailed in its description of the male and female body. Considerable attention is focused on sexual techniques and postures. Also remarkable is the iconography associated with this practice of union. While most often associated with the Tibetan cultural region, ideas of the religious benefits of conscious and controlled sexual union also appear in other contexts, for instance, the TACHIKAWARYŪ school of Japanese tantra, which was persecuted as heretical.

Buddhist views of homosexuality

The question of Buddhist views toward homosexuality is a complex one. One might want to argue that homosexuality is for the Buddhist problematic in precisely the same way that heterosexuality is; desire is, ipso facto, nonconducive to liberation and contributes to a false notion of the independence and permanence of the self. In the monastic codes there are sanctions against almost any imaginable kind of sexual activity, and homosexual acts are by no means exempt. However, male homosexuality is given special attention.

This is evident in the extensive vinaya discussion of the somewhat ambiguous figure of the *paṇḍaka*. While this term has often been translated as "eunuch," there is good reason to understand it to mean a man who is sexually inclined toward other men.

In Japan there is substantial evidence that some Buddhists understood homosexuality, or more specifically relationships between adult male monks and their boy pages, to be a natural part of the monastic life. There are numerous popular tales from the medieval period describing these affairs. Usually the stories end in tragedy and the monk regrets his excessive attachment to the boy, but nowhere is the propriety of the homosexual relationship per se called into question.

See also: **Family, Buddhism and the; Gender; Women**

Bibliography

Bloss, Lowell W. "The Buddha and the Nāga: A Study in Buddhist Folk Religiosity." *History of Religions* 13, no. 1 (1973): 36–53.

Cabezón, José Ignacio, ed. *Buddhism, Sexuality, and Gender.* Albany: State University of New York Press, 1992.

Faure, Bernard. *The Red Thread: Buddhist Approaches to Sexuality.* Princeton, NJ: Princeton University Press, 1998.

Jaffe, Richard. *Neither Monk nor Layman: Clerical Marriage in Modern Japanese Buddhism.* Princeton, NJ: Princeton University Press, 2002.

Perera, L. P. N. *Sexuality in Ancient India: A Study Based on the Pāli Vinayapiṭaka.* Kelaniya, Sri Lanka: Postgraduate Institute of Pāli and Buddhist Studies, 1993.

Shaw, Miranda. *Passionate Enlightenment: Women in Tantric Buddhism.* Princeton, NJ: Princeton University Press, 1994.

Wilson, Liz. *Charming Cadavers: Horrific Figurations of the Feminine in Indian Buddhist Hagiographic Literature.* Chicago: University of Chicago Press, 1996.

HANK GLASSMAN

SHINGON BUDDHISM, JAPAN

Shingon refers to a major Japanese Buddhist school devoted to esoteric Buddhism. Shingon's doctrine is built around two essential theories developed by KŪKAI (774–835), based on his interpretation of the *Mahāvairocana-sūtra* (Japanese, *Dainichikyō*) and the *Tattvasaṃgraha* or *Vajraśekhara-sūtra* (or *Tantra*; Japanese, *Kongōchōkyō*): the dharmakāya's preaching of the dharma (*hosshin seppō*), and the practice of the three mysteries (*sanmitsu gyō*). According to Kūkai, the cosmic Buddha Mahāvairocana, whose body consists of the six great elements (earth, water, fire, wind, space, and consciousness), is none other than the dharmakāya (law body). The constant, harmonious interaction between the six elements creates all things in the universe; everything in the world, made up of the six elements uniquely combined, is the manifestation of the dharmakāya. Thus, the dharmakāya permeates the universe, and all sorts of movements in the world are understood as the dharmakāya's manifestation of the dharma.

This secret revelation of the dharma can be captured by the study of the ritual system of the three mysteries: the mysteries of the body (MUDRĀ), speech (MANTRA), and mind (MAṆḌALA). The study of mudrās teaches practitioners to recapture in their bodies the cosmic movement of the six great elements by forming sacred gestures with their hands, arms, and legs. Mantras enable practitioners to manipulate the syllables that symbolically represent the six elements and their combinations, and to create the intertwining of the elements in the phonic actions of the mantras chanted. Meditation on the maṇḍala creates in the minds of practitioners sacred images whose colors and shapes illustrate the six elements in their constant, concerted, engendering acts. The mastery of the discipline of the three mysteries therefore teaches Shingon practitioners not only to decipher dharmakāya Mahāvairocana's secret language, but also to engage in the dhamakāya's eternal creation of the universe.

This mode of understanding the relationship between the universe and individuals, the macrocosm and microcosm, led to the development of Shingon as a spiritual and religious "technology." When applied to the area of physiology, the practice of the three mysteries enables practitioners to ritually simulate the body, speech, and mind of the cosmic Buddha, which, because of the intrinsic identity between the creating force and created objects, effaces the distinction between the practitioner and the dharmakāya (*sokushin jōbutsu*; literally, "to achieve buddhahood in this very body"). The same technology can be employed as medicine in that it can serve as a method to restore the optimal balance between the six elements in the body of a patient. When applied outwardly to the environment, the practice of the three mysteries provides the means to change the course of natural events. Or, in the field of human affairs, it serves as a political technology to be used in diplomacy and warfare. All these elements have influenced the course of the development of the Shingon school in Japanese history.

The incipient Shingon school in the early Heian period of the ninth century grew rapidly due largely to the adoption by the royal court of esoteric Buddhist rituals for performing diverse ceremonies, especially the rites for the emperor's coronation, legitimation, and empowerment. The Shingon school also built an alliance with the schools of NARA BUDDHISM, which found Shingon's orientation toward ritual studies complementary to their doctrinal, text-based study of Buddhism. Tōnain'in subtemple at Tōdaiji was established in 875 as a center for the combined study of the Shingon and Sanron schools by the monk Shōbō (832–909). In the mid-Heian period (tenth and eleventh centuries), new centers of Shingon ritual studies, such as Daikakuji, Kajūji, Ninnaji, and Daigoji, in the vicinity of the Heiankyō (Kyoto), were founded by the emperors and members of the imperial family. Shingon monks at these monasteries vied with one another in developing sophisticated and complex theories and practice of esoteric rituals to better serve the imperial court and the aristocracy. Ningai (951–1045) is celebrated for his rainmaking ritual, which is said to have been used during the great droughts of 1015 and 1018, and on nine other occasions. These developments during the Heian period were important in forming the Shingon school's strong orientation in ritual studies. By the end of the period, thirty-six ritual lineages within Shingon had been established, with each lineage holding its own distinct claim for its dharma transmission.

The study of Shingon doctrine developed only from the latter part of the Heian period. Kakuban (1094–1143) was the first to develop a systematic interpretation of Kūkai's doctrinal works. During the Kamakura period (1185–1333), Kakukai (1142–1223), Dōhan (1178–1252), Raibō (1279–1330), and other scholar-monks of Mount Kōya and Tōji, two institutions founded by Kūkai, took the lead in developing a gamut of doctrinal treatises and exegeses on the essential scriptures of the Shingon school. Raiyu (1226–1304) inherited Kakuban's scholarship and founded Mount Negoro Monastery as another major center for Shingon doctrinal studies. Negoro later developed into the headquarters of the Shingi Shingon school, which was largely responsible for the spread of Shingon into the provinces of eastern Japan in the medieval and early modern periods.

During this period the spread of numerous legends depicting Kūkai as a charismatic, miracle-making savior further raised the prestige of Mount Kōya and Tōji. The alliance of the Shingon school with the Nara Buddhist schools continued to grow. It was often the scholar-monks of the Nara monasteries whose combined mastery of Shingon gave rise to the most innovative use of the knowledge of esotericism; they include Hōssō master Jōkei (1155–1213), Kegon master Myōe KŌBEN (1173–1232), and Shingon-ritsu nun Shinnyo (1211– ?). Master Eizon of Saidaiji (1201–1290) and his disciple Ninjō (1217–1303) are particularly renowned for saving beggars, lepers, and outcasts. This was also the time in which *kami*, the local Japanese gods, became integral within the esoteric Buddhist pantheon, playing the role of the guardians of Buddhism. Eizon's esoteric Buddhist ritual service in 1281 at Iwashimizu, where the god HACHIMAN is enshrined, was praised by the court, the warrior government, and the masses for its claimed power to protect the nation from the Mongol invasion.

Political turmoil during the Muromachi and Sengoku periods (1333–1600) significantly weakened the institutional and economic foundation of the Shingon monastaries. However, the influence of Shingon on late medieval culture and art, especially in Japanese poetry and poetics, remained essential. A significant number of celebrated *waka* and *renga* poets of the period, including Shinkei (1406–1475) and Sōgi (1421–1502), were esoteric Buddhists. In the early modern period, the religious policy of the Tokugawa shogunate prohibited Buddhists from studying more than one discipline. Thus, one significant characteristic of Shingon since inception—its combined study with exoteric schools—ceased, and the Shingon school was reduced to a sectarian institution. The forceful separation of the worship of local gods from Buddhism and the creation of Shintō as the official religion of the nation by the Meiji government deprived Shingon of another important quality. In 1868 the Shingon ritual was eliminated from the emperor's coronation ceremony, and the esoteric ritual lost its relevance to the official business of the state. At the beginning of the twenty-first century, Shingon continues to exist as an affiliation of eighteen independent subschools—the largest among them are the Mount Kōya school, the Chizan school, and the Busan school. However, with its sophisticated symbolism of visual signs and representations that are grounded in unique semiotic and linguistic theories, Shingon continues to exert its influence on modern and contemporary Japanese art, literature, and philosophy.

See also: **Exoteric-Esoteric (Kenmitsu) Buddhism in Japan; Japan; Japanese Royal Family and Buddhism; Kamakura Buddhism, Japan**

Bibliography

Abé, Ryūichi. *The Weaving of Mantra.* New York: Columbia University Press, 1999.

Dobbins, James C. "Envisioning Kamakura Buddhism." In *Re-Visioning Kamakura Buddhism,* ed. Richard K. Payne. Honolulu: University of Hawaii Press, 1998.

Hakeda, Yoshito. *Kūkai: Major Works.* New York: Columbia University Press, 1976.

Orzech, Charles. *Politics and Transcendent Wisdom.* University Park: Pennsylvania State University Press, 1998.

Rambach, Pierre. *The Secret Message of Tantric Buddhism.* New York: Rizzoli, 1979.

Sharf, Robert. *Coming to Terms with Chinese Buddhism: A Reading of the Treasure Store Treatise.* Honolulu: University of Hawaii Press, 2002.

ten Grotenhuis, Elizabeth. *Japanese Mandalas: Representations of Sacred Geography.* Honolulu: University of Hawaii Press, 1999.

Yamasaki Taiko. *Shingon: Japanese Esoteric Buddhism,* translated and adapted by Richard and Cynthia Peterson; ed. Yasuyoshi Morimoto and David Kidd. Boston: Shambhala, 1988.

RYŪICHI ABÉ

SHINRAN

Shinran (Zenshin, Shakkū; 1173–1263) was a Pure Land Buddhist teacher of medieval Japan and founder of the Jōdo Shinshū (Shin Buddhism) tradition. His teachings focused on FAITH (*shinjin*) in conjunction with the practice of the *nenbutsu,* invoking Amida (AMITĀBHA) Buddha's name, as the basis for birth in the Pure Land, where he believed Buddhist enlightenment is immediate. Shinran considered the Buddha's power, rather than human effort, to be the motive force behind all true religious practice and behind enlightenment itself. The Shinshū, in accord with Shinran's own example, broke with the Buddhist tradition of clerical celibacy, and allowed priests to marry and have families. Three centuries later, Shinran's modest following grew into a huge and powerful Buddhist school headed by Honganji in Kyoto, which originated at his gravesite.

Shinran spent the first twenty years of his career as a Tendai monk on Mount Hiei, but in 1201, after a hundred-day religious retreat at the Rokkakudō chapel in Kyoto, he abandoned monastic life and became the disciple of HŌNEN (1133-1212). In 1207 Shinran was banished to Echigo province (present-day Niigata prefecture) in a general suppression of Hōnen's Pure Land movement that occurred after provocative behavior by certain followers. Shinran never saw his teacher again, and for over twenty-five years he lived away from Kyoto. The last two decades of this period were spent in the Kanto region (around modern-day Tokyo), where Shinran became a peripatetic Pure Land teacher. His marriage occurred shortly before, or soon after, his banishment. Shinran continued to dress in Buddhist clerical robes and shaved his head as priests do, even while living with his wife, Eshinni (1182–ca. 1268), and their children.

The gist of Shinran's teaching is that Amida Buddha has vowed to bring all living beings to enlightenment, and the power of his vow surpasses any religious practice humans can perform. Thus, the consummate religious state is single-hearted reliance on Amida, or faith. This faith is none other than the Buddha operating in a person, rather than a person's own created mental condition. The *nenbutsu,* likewise, is an act initiated by Amida, as well as an extension of him in the world. When people hear Amida's name it awakens them to his grand vow, and when they intone the *nenbutsu* their practice coalesces with Amida's compassionate activity. The upshot of this teaching is that Amida's saving power extends to everyone without differentiation: clerical or lay, male or female, good or evil. In fact, evildoers are a prime object of Amida's vow (*akunin shōki*).

Shinran returned to Kyoto in the early 1230s. By that time he had completed a preliminary draft of his magnum opus, *Kyōgyōshinshō* (*Teaching, Practice, Faith, and Attainment*). He spent the rest of his days in Kyoto, but remained in touch with his Kanto followers through letters and occasional visits on their part. In old age he dedicated himself to study and writing, completing his *Kyōgyōshinshō* and composing a variety of other Buddhist works, including *wasan* hymns. His wife and most of their children moved to Echigo in the 1250s to live on property she inherited. But Shinran remained in Kyoto with their youngest daughter Kakushinni (1224–1283), who looked after him in his last years. He died in Kyoto in 1263, chanting Amida's name and surrounded by followers. Many revered him as an earthly manifestation of Amida Buddha or of Kannon (Avalokiteśvara) Bodhisattva.

See also: **Japan; Kamakura Buddhism, Japan; Nenbutsu (Chinese, Nianfo; Korean, Yŏmbul); Pure Land Buddhism; Pure Land Schools**

Bibliography

Bloom, Alfred. *Shinran's Gospel of Pure Grace.* Tucson: University of Arizona Press, 1965.

Dobbins, James C. *Jōdo Shinshū: Shin Buddhism in Medieval Japan* (1989). Reprint, Honolulu: University of Hawaii Press, 2002.

Hirota, Dennis, et al., trans. *The Collected Works of Shinran,* 2 vols. Kyoto: Jōdo Shinshū Hongwanji-ha, 1997.

Keel, Hee Sung. *Understanding Shinran: A Dialogical Approach.* Fremont, CA: Asian Humanities Press, 1995.

Ueda, Yoshifumi, and Hirota, Dennis. *Shinran: An Introduction to His Thought.* Kyoto: Hongwanji International Center, 1989.

JAMES C. DOBBINS

SHINTŌ (HONJI SUIJAKU) AND BUDDHISM

Any investigation into the relationships of Shintō and Buddhism in Japan cannot ignore the effects of the anti-Buddhist persecutions and forced separation of Buddhist monasteries and *kami* shrines that occurred during the Meiji era (1868–1912). Such an inquiry can be further strengthened by understanding the premodern contexts. This entry will attempt to do precisely that by discussing how Buddhist concepts and ritual techniques served (or were adapted) to articulate the significance of various kinds of gods and spirits in premodern Japan.

Received interpretations and their problems

According to received definitions, Shintō is the autochthonous religious tradition of Japan. Its origins can be traced to animistic beliefs dating from the remotest antiquity. Its main features are an animistic belief in the sanctity of nature, shamanic practices, ancestor cults, respect for authority and communal value, and a strong capacity to integrate and homogenize foreign elements. Standard accounts also present the history of Japanese Buddhism as a gradual process of "Japanization," that is, of Buddhism's integration within the supposedly dominant Shintō system of beliefs and ritual practices. These kinds of accounts are heavily influenced by a nativist ideology of Japanese religion and do not reflect actual historical processes. In order to disentangle the complex relationships between Buddhism and local cults in the Japanese archipelago from ideological stereotypes, it is necessary to begin with an analysis of the term *Shintō* itself. As Kuroda Toshio has made clear, *Shintō* did not mean the same things throughout history. In particular, it did not designate an established system of religious institutions and their beliefs and rituals until after the eighteenth century.

Shintō, most likely pronounced "jindō" until at least the fifteenth century, was essentially a Buddhist concept indicating the realm of local deities as related to, but distinct from, Indian deities of the Buddhist pantheon, which were usually referred to as *ten* or *tendō.* It was only since the second half of the Edo period (1600–1868) that more or less autonomous Shintō institutions began to develop, mainly centered on the Yoshida house in Kyoto (see below) and several schools of Confucian studies. However, Shintō as an independent religious tradition begins only in 1868 with the so-called separation of *kami* and buddhas (*shinbutsu bunri*). This forceful separation, carried out upon orders emanating from the government, was one of the first acts in the Japanese process of modernization, and amounted to the artificial creation of two separate religious traditions, namely, Shintō and Japanese Buddhism. Subsequently, Shintō's development was directly related to the policy and imperial ideology of the new Japanese state in what is known as *State Shintō* (*kokka Shintō*)—a formation that was disbanded after the end of World War II.

In practice, *shinbutsu bunri* was not a mere "separation." It defined what was "Buddhist" and what was "Shintō," meaning that which was supposedly autochthonous in the religious world of the time. "Buddhist" elements (such as images with Buddhist flavor worshiped as the body of a *kami,* architectural elements, Buddhist scriptures offered to the *kami,* and so forth) were set apart and, in many cases, destroyed. "Shintō" elements, on the other hand, were systematized and "normalized." Many local shrines were destroyed; the *kami* enshrined in several others were replaced by *kami* listed in the *Kojiki* (*Record of Ancient Matters*), an early eighth-century text that had become the bible of the nativists. Sacerdotal houses that had been in charge of services to the *kami* in certain locales for several generations were replaced by state-appointed officers who were followers of the nativist scholar Hirata Atsutane's (1776–1843) brand of religious nationalism. Local rituals were replaced by authorized ceremonies that were related to a newly created cult for the emperor. People were forced to attend to new holidays that were related to state-sanctioned events. In this way, a new religion, supposedly autochthonous and with roots in a remote Japanese past before the arrival of Buddhism, was created and propagated among the people. After a few years of prohibition, Buddhism reorganized itself as a religion that was concerned with funerals and the moral education of the citizens of the new Japanese state.

Buddhist appropriation of Japanese local deities

The Buddhist appropriation of local *kami* is not a typically Japanese phenomenon: Local guardian gods and fertility gods are worshiped at Buddhist monasteries throughout Asia. Monastery gods are perhaps the original forms of adoption of local divinities in a Buddhist context. The interactions between Buddhism and local deities in Japan went through several phases, according to patterns that seem to be common to most Buddhist cultures. Japanese *kami* were first subjugated or converted to Buddhism, then transformed into dharma protectors, and finally organized in a hierarchical structure, a phase that involved a redefinition of the place of the *kami* in the Buddhist cosmology as manifestations of buddhas and bodhisattvas.

At first, local *kami* were envisioned by Buddhists as dangerous entities that needed to be saved from their deluded condition and guided toward enlightenment; this implied acts of subjugation or conversion. Two legends exemplify this stage well. One day in 763 the *kami* of Tado village is said to have manifested itself through an oracle and requested to be converted so as to be liberated from its *kami* condition. A Buddhist monastery (*jingūji*) was built in the area where the *kami* resided, and special services were held for the *kami*'s salvation. Another tale reports how a giant tree, believed to be the abode of a *kami,* fell to the ground and rolled into a river, where it was carried by the current. Every time the tree was stranded, epidemics struck the area. Finally, a Buddhist monk cut the fallen tree into pieces and carved three images of the BODHISATTVA Kannon (Avalokiteśvara) out of them (one of these images is said to be the Kannon at Ishiyamadera near Kyoto). Immediately, the epidemics ceased and the images generated good fortune and miracles. In both tales local *kami* are described as dangerous, violent entities, and sources of calamity to the local people. In contrast, Buddhism is presented as a pacifying and ordering force. At a subsequent stage, converted *kami* turned into protectors of the Buddhadharma and guarantors of the peace and prosperity in their respective locales. *Kami* were also gradually organized into a hierarchical structure, with the deities of twenty-two imperially sponsored shrines at the top, regional shrines at the middle, and village shrines at the bottom. There were in addition various orders of local deities that granted particular kinds of protection.

These stages (subjugation or conversion of local divinities, their inclusion within the Buddhist system as protectors, and their redefinition as manifestations of sacred, translocal Buddhist entities) are usually presented as moments in a linear process of evolution, but it is important to emphasize that in practice they amounted to different modes of interaction rather than separate historical stages. As such they often overlapped. A local *kami* could be seen as a manifestation of a buddha or a bodhisattva, but at the same time it functioned as the protector of a specific locale, and Buddhist rituals were performed in front of it to secure its salvation.

The field of Japanese local deities and its complexity

Kami are usually understood as local, autochthonous Japanese deities. They are often described in animistic terms as supernatural forces abiding in natural entities such as trees, rocks, mountains, and waterfalls. However, the situation in premodern Japan was more complicated. Not all *kami* were animistic entities. In fact, scholars can identify a historical variety of *kami,* including royal deities, divinities of local clans (more or less related to royal deities), village spirits (which often had no name and no clearly defined shape), and imported deities (from India, Korea, and China). Royal deities, in particular those listed in the *Kojiki* and the early eighth-century *Nihon shoki* (*Chronicles of Japan*), were worshipped by the emperor as part of his sacerdotal duties. Interestingly, Buddhism was largely unconcerned with those deities, except for the most important ones among them—the *kami* of the Ise shrines. Japanese Buddhists devoted great efforts instead to domesticate and incorporate within their system local tutelary spirits. Clan divinities were largely treated as tutelary deities, and as such they were included in the Buddhist system in the ways discussed above.

In premodern Japan there were a large number of local tutelary deities (*chinju*), ranging from household gods (such as the deities of the hearth), to village gods (such as paddy deities, *ta no kami*), to provincial and national protectors such as HACHIMAN, Kumano, Kasuga, and Sannō. The sanctuaries of these gods were normally affiliated with major Buddhist institutions (such as the large monasteries in Nara and Kyoto), were sponsored by the royal court and local gentry, and were often centered in sacred mountains where

SHUGENDŌ mountain ascetics resided. In addition there were monastery gods (*garanjin,* such as Idaten, the son of Śiva, but also arhats) and dharma protectors (*gohōjin*), even though this distinction was, in most cases, purely theoretical. These orders of deities were not clearly distinguished and, in practice, they often overlapped. The case of Nichira is particularly interesting. Originally a Korean general who became the tutelary deity of Mount Atago, which was considered a Japanese manifestation of bodhisattva Jizō (Kṣitigarbha), Nichira came to be treated as an ARHAT. The name *Nichira* was interpreted as an abbreviation for the Japanese words *nichi* from *Nippon* (Japan) and *ra* from *rakan* (arhat). Arhats were the protectors of some Zen monasteries in Japan.

As the case of Nichira indicates, not all *kami* were autochthonous, or originally Japanese. Buddhist priests brought to Japan deities from India, Korea, and China. Some of them were quickly "naturalized" and became very popular. Even today, many popular *kami* include foreign deities such as Benten (Sanskrit, Sarasvatī), Daikokuten (Sanskrit, Mahākāka), Shinra (Korean, Silla), Myōjin (probably of Korean origin), and other minor deities of Chinese origin related to yinyang and polar star cults. In addition, new deities were created under the influence of Buddhism. The two most popular *kami* in modern times, Hachiman and Inari, were produced by Buddhist combinatory doctrines and rituals. Hachiman, in particular, is said to have been the tutelary deity of a clan in southern Japan, but was recognized by the state in the eighth century as a great bodhisattva (*daibosatsu*) who promised to protect the country and ensure the diffusion of Buddhism there. He was also one of the protecting deities of the Tōdaiji, the largest monastery in Nara. Since then, he has always been one of the main protecting deities of Japan.

Finally, premodern *kami* were usually not singular subjectivities, but plural entities that combined historical human beings, deities from various places in Asia, and Buddhist supernatural beings. Hachiman, for example, is both a *kami* and a bodhisattva, a king and a holy being: He is the deified aspect of Emperor Ōjin (who is said to have reigned in the late fourth to early fifth centuries) and at the same time a Japanese manifestation of Amida (Sanskrit, AMITĀBHA), or, according to some sources, of Śākyamuni. Analogously, the *kami* Inari began as an agricultural spirit bringing prosperity, later became the tutelary deity of the Fushimi area near Kyoto, and finally was envisioned as the Japanese manifestation of the Indian cannibal ogresses known as ḌĀKINĪ. Inari is variously represented as an old man, a white fox, or a beautiful woman.

With the development of increasingly complex hierarchies of protection and classification of divinities, we also see the formation of new interpretations about their functions and their modes of interaction with human beings. In general, buddhas and bodhisattvas were in charge of supramundane benefits (such as better rebirths and ultimate salvation), whereas the *kami* dealt specifically with worldly benefits and material prosperity. Furthermore, buddhas were normally benevolent, whereas the *kami* were in charge of punishing those who did not respect the deities. However, in medieval Japan a more nuanced vision developed, according to which buddhas and *kami* together administer punishments against their enemies. On the other hand, in some cases, such as in certain Shintō esoteric rituals, the *kami* provided a form of soteriology. In addition, refusal to worship the *kami* was considered a subversive act by the establishment and a revolutionary act by reform movements. In this way, the structure of the Buddhist pantheon was directly connected with visions of social order and morality.

Japanese *kami* as manifestations of Buddhist sacred beings

Buddhism interacted with Japanese deities in a way that finds no equivalent in most other Buddhist cultures (though there are very few comparative studies of Buddhist interactions with local deities). Around the eleventh to twelfth centuries, *kami* began to be envisioned as Japanese manifestations (Japanese, *gongen*; Sanskrit, *avatāra*) of bodhisattvas or other deities of the Indian pantheon brought to Japan by Buddhism. The capacity of manifesting themselves in many forms is a feature of the gods of classical Indian mythology that was later attributed also to buddhas and bodhisattvas; in Japan, this feature was used to explain the status of the *kami*. This logic of manifestation was commonly defined as *honji suijaku* and *wakō dōjin*. The term *honji suijaku* (literally, "the original ground and its traces") was originally used by the Chinese Tiantai patriarch ZHIYI (538–597) in his exegesis of the LOTUS SŪTRA (SADDHARMAPUṆḌARĪKA-SŪTRA). According to Zhiyi, the first fourteen chapters of the scripture contain the provisional "trace-teaching" of the historical Buddha, whereas the final fourteen chapters are the ultimate "original teaching" of the eternal Buddha. In medieval Japan, *honji suijaku* was employed to mean that Indian and Buddhist entities constitute the "original ground" (*honji*) of their Japanese manifestations as local *kami*, defined as "traces" (*suijaku*).

The expression *wakō dōjin* (literally, "to soften one's radiance and become the same as dust") can originally be found in the Chinese classic *Daode jing* (*The Way and Its Power*), where it refers to the way in which the Dao, the supreme principle, manifests itself in the world. The idea here is that the supreme principles (in this case, buddhas and bodhisattvas) cannot show their true forms in this world, but require a "coarsening" that makes them understandable to human beings. The "coarse" forms of buddhas and bodhisattvas were, of course, those of the Japanese *kami*. The underlying implication of both these expressions, as explained by several medieval texts, was that the Japanese people are too difficult to convert and too ignorant to understand buddhas and bodhisattvas in their "normal" forms. Therefore, they require rough manifestations to guide them to salvation. For example, according to *honji suijaku* logic, the sun goddess Amaterasu was envisioned as a manifestation of Mahāvairocana, the universal Buddha of esoteric Buddhism; Hachiman was a manifestation of Amitābha; and so forth.

The idea that Japanese deities were local manifestations of translocal deities proved enormously productive. By the fifteenth century, some Buddhist authors were arguing that the *kami* were in fact the primary, original forms of divine beings, while buddhas and bodhisattvas were Indian local manifestations of these original Japanese models. This reversal of dominant Buddhist ideas was at the basis of a new Shintō movement, of a strong nativist character, that stressed the superiority of all things Japanese against imported cultural elements. The center of this nativist reversal of the *honji suijaku* paradigm was the Yoshida shrine in Kyoto. Its priest, Yoshida Kanetomo (1435–1511), had collected a number of doctrines and rituals about the *kami*, mostly related to the then dominant esoteric Buddhism (*mikkyō*), and tried to establish his own tradition by getting rid of the most visible Buddhist features. Gradually, the Yoshida tradition became the point of reference for nativist thinkers, anti-Buddhists, and *kami* priests disgruntled with the Buddhist establishment still dominating their shrines. These were the people and the groups that contributed to the constitution of a Shintō discourse as distinct from Buddhism during the Edo period in a process whose final stage was the early Meiji separation of Shintō from Buddhism.

However, in medieval Japan not all *kami* were considered manifestations of Indian sacred entities. In the second half of the Kamakura period (1192–1333), the *kami* were divided into three categories that were based on ORIGINAL ENLIGHTENMENT (HONGAKU) thought: (1) *kami* of original enlightenment, such as Amaterasu of Ise; (2) *kami* of nonenlightenment (*fukaku*), such as the violent *kami* of Izumo shrine; and (3) *kami* of acquired enlightenment (*shikaku*), such as Hachiman. Even though this classification was probably devised to enhance the status of the Ise shrines and their deities, it is interesting to note that the *kami* are here thought to embody modalities of Buddhist soteriology and that some of them represent an obscure realm of ignorance and violence untouched by Buddhism.

This latter point was further developed during the Kamakura period when authors began to define a distinction between "provisional deities" (*gonsha*) and "true deities" (*jissha*). Whereas provisional deities were considered to be benevolent, true deities were described as violent and dangerous entities that threatened the peace and security of local people. This distinction indicates that in medieval Japan divinities still existed that had not been integrated within the Buddhist system and that were described as chaotic forces (much as local deities before the arrival of Buddhism). The attitude of the Buddhists toward true deities was complex. Some warned local people not to worship them, since they were outside of Buddhism and therefore were irrelevant to the process of salvation; others suggested that these deities should be propitiated, while still others argued that human beings could not easily tell the difference between one category of deities and the other, and it was thus best to worship them all.

Esoteric Buddhism and *kami* cults

Honji suijaku and original enlightenment (*hongaku*) were essential parts of premodern Japanese esoteric Buddhism (*mikkyō*), especially in its configuration known as EXOTERIC-ESOTERIC (KENMITSU) BUDDHISM. In fact, esoteric Buddhism played a fundamental role in the transformation of the *kami* and their inclusion within the Buddhist cosmology and salvation process. In particular, esoteric Buddhist MAṆḌALA provided an important model for the systematization of the realm of sacred beings in Japan. The external sector of the Womb Maṇḍala (*taizōkai mandara*) contains a number of non-Buddhist divinities ranging from Brahmā, Śiva, and INDRA, to more animistic entities such as the gods of fire, water, and wind, and violent spirits and demons (YAKṢA). These divinities constituted the template for the organization of the premodern Japanese pantheon: As part of maṇḍala they were provisional manifestations of the Buddha, and therefore entitled to a place in the Buddhist cosmos. In other words, Buddhism provided in Japan a new and broader cosmological framework in which to insert all (or most) forms of local sacred entities. During the Middle Ages, furthermore, maṇḍalas were also used as conceptual models to represent the sacred space of *kami* shrines. In these images, the *kami* are usually represented both as "traces" (*suijaku*) with their earthly forms (animals, human beings) and as "original grounds" (*honji*), that is, buddhas and bodhisattvas.

Esoteric Buddhism also influenced doctrines and rituals concerning the *kami*. Several schools of esoteric Shintō teachings developed at major cult sites, such as the Ise outer shrine, Hie shrine (affiliated with the Tendai monastery Enryakuji), and the Shingon monastery Ōmiwadera (or Daigorinji). They all discussed issues of the *honji suijaku* paradigm, each from its own sectarian perspective and with its own Buddhist vocabulary. At the same time, these centers also developed a vast body of esoteric rituals dealing with the *kami*. Especially significant among them were initiation rituals on *kami* matters (*jingi kanjō* or *shintō kanjō*), directly modeled on esoteric initiation rituals (*denbō kanjō*), but also rituals for specific professions (e.g., carpenters, merchants, farmers) involving deities of the *honji suijaku* universe. In this respect, the previously discussed Yoshida tradition has a particular position in that it absorbed several elements from esoteric Buddhism (such as the *goma* fire ceremony and the notion of originals and traces), but developed them in an anti-Buddhist direction.

See also: **Cosmology; Folk Religion, Japan; Ghosts and Spirits; Japanese Royal Family and Buddhism; Local Divinities and Buddhism; Meiji Buddhist Reform; Shingon Buddhism, Japan; Shugendō; Space, Sacred**

Bibliography

Breen, John, and Teeuwen, Mark, eds. *Shintō in History: Ways of the Kami.* Richmond, UK: Curzon Press, 2000.

Gellner, David N. "For Syncretism: The Position of Buddhism in Nepal and Japan Compared." *Social Anthropology* 5, no. 3 (1997): 277–291.

Grapard, Allan G. "Institution, Ritual, and Ideology: The Twenty-two Shrine-Temple Multiplexes of Heian Japan." *History of Religions* 27, no. 3 (1988): 246–269.

Grapard, Allan G. *The Protocol of the Gods: A Study of the Kasuga Cult in Japanese History.* Berkeley, Los Angeles, and London: University of California Press, 1992.

Hardacre, Helen. *Shintō and the State, 1868–1988.* Princeton, NJ: Princeton University Press, 1989.

Iyanaga Nobumi. *Daikokuten hensō* (Bukkyō shinwagaku 1). Kyoto: Hōzōkan, 2002.

Kageyama Haruki. *The Arts of Shintō,* translated and adapted by Christine Guth. New York and Tokyo: Weatherhill, 1973.

Ketelaar, James E. *Of Heretics and Martyrs in Meiji Japan: Buddhism and Its Persecution.* Princeton, NJ: Princeton University Press, 1990.

Kuroda Toshio. "Shintō in the History of Japanese Religion." *Journal of Japanese Studies* 7, no. 1, 1981: 1–21.

Matsunaga, Alicia. *The Buddhist Philosophy of Assimilation: The Historical Development of the Honji-Suijaku Theory.* Rutland, VT, and Tokyo: Sophia University Press, 1969.

Murayama Shūichi. *Honji suijaku.* Tokyo: Yoshikawa Kōbunkan, 1974.

Naumann, Nelly. *Die einheimische Religion Japans,* 2 vols. Leiden, Netherlands: Brill, 1988–1994.

Rambelli, Fabio. "Buddha's Wrath: Esoteric Buddhism and the Discourse of Divine Punishment." *Japanese Religions* 27, no. 1 (2002): 41–68.

Satō Hiroo. *Amaterasu no henbō: Chūsei shinbutsu kōshōshi no shiza.* Kyoto: Hōzōkan, 2000.

Scheid, Bernhard. *Der Eine und Einzige Weg der Götter: Yoshida Kanetomo und die Erfindung des Shintō.* Vienna: Verlag der Österreichischen Akademie der Wissenschaften, 2001.

Teeuwen, Mark. *Watarai Shintō: An Intellectual History of the Outer Shrine in Ise.* Leiden, Netherlands: Research School CNWS, 1996.

Teeuwen, Mark, and Rambelli, Fabio, eds. *Buddhas and Kami in Japan: Honji Suijaku as a Combinatory Paradigm.* London and New York: Routledge Curzon, 2003.

Teeuwen, Mark, and Scheid, Bernhard, eds. *Tracing Shintō in the History of Kami Worship.* Special issue of *Japanese Journal of Religious Studies* 29, nos. 3/4 (2002).

FABIO RAMBELLI

SHŌBŌGENZŌ

Shōbōgenzō (*Treasury of the Eye of the True Dharma*) is a collection of essays, in several premodern redactions, by the early Japanese Zen monk DŌGEN (1200–1253). The title, which denotes the CHAN SCHOOL (Japanese, Zen) tradition, derives from an expression indicating the awakening traditionally said to have been transmitted by the Buddha Śākyamuni to his disciple MAHĀKĀŚYAPA.

CARL BIELEFELDT

SHŌTOKU, PRINCE (TAISHI)

Prince Shōtoku (*taishi,* 574–622) was a semilegendary prince who from the earliest stages of Japanese history has been revered as a cultural hero, as a Buddhist patron, as a civilizing ruler, and as a Japanese incarnation either of the Chinese TIANTAI SCHOOL monk Huisi (Japanese, Eshi; 515–577) or of the BODHISATTVA Avalokiteśvara. The earliest written accounts (dating from the eighth century) credit Shōtoku with mastering Buddhism and Confucianism under the tutorage of the Korean teachers Hyeja (Japanese, Eji) and Kakka (Japanese, Kakuka); serving as regent for his aunt, Suiko (r. 593–628); establishing a system of twelve court ranks to replace ranks based on familial status; composing a *Seventeen Article Constitution* that expresses basic governmental ideals along with pious Buddhist and Confucian sentiments; constructing statues of the Four Heavenly Kings (*shi tennō,* gods of the four directions who protect Buddhist kingdoms); as well as lecturing on or authoring commentaries on three MAHĀYĀNA Buddhist scriptures: the LOTUS SŪTRA (SADDHARMAPUṆḌARĪKA-SŪTRA; Japanese, *Hokekyō*), the *Vimalakīrtinirdeśa* (*Yuimagyō*), and *Queen Śrīmālā Sūtra* (*Shōmangyō*). Significantly, the central figure of the *Vimalakīrti Sūtra* is a wise layman (like Shōtoku), and the central figure of the *Queen Śrīmālā Sūtra* is a female ruler (like Suiko). In addition, many Buddhist temples important in early Japanese history traditionally have claimed Shōtoku as their founding patron. These temples include Shitennōji, Gangōji (also known as Hōkōji or Asukadera), Hōryūji, Chūgūji, and countless others. These claims helped to legitimate the strong relationship between the royal court and institutional Buddhism throughout most of premodern Japanese history. Moreover, reverence for Shōtoku played a significant role in the lives of many subsequent Japanese Buddhist leaders, such as SAICHŌ (767–822) and SHINRAN (1173–1263).

In modern times Shōtoku has been promoted as a paradigm of ideal Japanese virtues, especially those of harmony (*wa*), nationalism, and a strong imperial rule. The prominence afforded him by many modern textbook accounts of ancient Japan can sometimes foster a one-dimensional view of the complex process by which the early Japanese state emerged.

See also: **Hōryūji and Tōdaiji; Japanese Royal Family and Buddhism; Kingship; Nationalism and Buddhism**

Bibliography

Deal, William E. "Hagiography and History: The Image of Prince Shōtoku." In *Religions of Japan in Practice,* ed. George J. Tanabe, Jr. Princeton, NJ: Princeton University Press, 1999.

Ito, Kimio. "The Invention of Wa and the Transformation of the Image of Prince Shōtoku in Modern Japan." In *Mirror of Modernity: Invented Traditions of Modern Japan,* ed. Stephen Vlastos. Berkeley: University of California Press, 1998.

Kanaji, Isamu. "Three Stages in Shōtoku Taishi's Acceptance of Buddhism." *Acta Asiatica* (Tokyo), no. 47 (1985): 31–47.

Kusunoki, Masazumi. "The Seventeen Article Constitution of Prince Shōtoku: Its Contemporary Significance," tr. Larry L. Hanson. *Ex Oriente* (Tokyo), no. 6 (1993): 1–34.

Nishimura, Sey. "The Prince and the Pauper: The Dynamics of a Shōtoku Legend." *Monumenta Nipponica* (Tokyo) 40, no. 3 (1985): 299–310.

Ōyama, Seiichi. *Shōtoku taishi to Nihonjin* (Prince Shōtoku and Japanese identity). Nagoya, Japan: Fūbaisha, 2001.

WILLIAM M. BODIFORD

SHUGENDŌ

Shugendō is a syncretistic Japanese Buddhist tradition of mountain ASCETIC PRACTICES that incorporates elements from shamanism, indigenous Japanese folk beliefs concerning mountains and spirits of the dead, and Daoist magic. The word *Shugendō* literally translates as "the way of cultivating supernatural power." Its practitioners are known as *yamabushi* (those who "lie down" in the mountains) or *shugenja* (ascetics, or "those who cultivate power"). Although their role has evolved and changed over the years, these figures were expected to accumulate religious power by undergoing severe ascetic practices in the mountains, such as fasting, meditating, reciting spells or Buddhist texts, sitting under waterfalls, gathering firewood, abstaining from water, hanging over cliffs to "weigh" one's sins, retiring in solitary confinement to caves, and performing rituals such as fire ceremonies. *Shugenja* then drew on this power to provide services, such as guiding pilgrims, performing religious rites, and demonstrating superhuman feats like walking on fire, as well as divination, exorcism, and prayers.

Historical development and characteristics

In pre-Buddhist Japan, religious activities included shamanistic trances, communication with spirits, and festivals and rites celebrating the descent of the agricultural deities from the mountains in the spring and their return to the mountains after the autumn harvest. Mountains were also believed to be the residence of the dead. As Buddhism was being assimilated into Japanese society in the sixth century (if not earlier), ascetics entered mountainous areas to undergo religious austerities. These persons were not always Buddhist monks, but included an assortment of solitary hermits, diviners, exorcists, "unordained" Buddhist specialists (*ubasoku*), and wandering religious figures (*hijiri*). The most famous of these was En-no-Gyōja (En the Ascetic, also known as En-no-Ozunu; ca. seventh century), a prototypical ascetic with shamanic powers and the semilegendary founder of Shugendō, stories of whose activities are in evidence at almost every mountainous area with an ascetic tradition.

By the early Heian period (ninth century) many Buddhist ascetics, especially those associated with the tantric schools, entered Mount Hiei and Mount Kōya (the headquarters of the Tendai and Shingon Buddhist schools), as well as other mountains such as Mount Kimbu in the Yoshino region. Various mountainous areas throughout Japan developed their own traditions, among them Hakusan and Mount Fuji in central Japan, the Haguro peaks in the north, Mount Ishizuchi in Shikoku, and Mount Hiko in Kyushu. Each had its own religious history, its own set of deities, its own web of associations with other sacred sites, and its own community of Shugendō practitioners. *Shugenja* from these areas performed religious services and guided pilgrims to popular sacred sites like Mitake and Kumano. These *shugenja* gradually became organized by the middle of the Heian period (tenth century), usually in connection with the pilgrimages of retired emperors and aristocrats. In time its institutional structure formed two major pillars: the Honzan-ha headquartered at Shōgo-in and affiliated with Tendai Buddhism, and the Tōzan-ha headquartered at Kōfukuji and Daigoji and affiliated with Shingon Buddhism. In this way the older shamanistic and mountain ascetic practices were incorporated within the teachings and practices of tantric Buddhism, and Shugendō came to represent a large portion of the dominant syncretistic worldview of medieval Japan. In the early modern period (lasting from the seventeenth century to the nineteenth century) the role of most *shugenja* shifted from that of ascetic wanderer to that of someone settled in a local society as *oshi* (teacher) or *kitōshi* (a diviner who offers "prayers").

Today Shugendō represents only a shadow of its former self, though Shugendō-related activities, such as the *kaihōgyō* Tendai practice of "circumambulating the peaks" on Mount Hiei and Shugendō-influenced rituals and activities in some of the new religious movements of Japan, are still practiced. A syncretistic mix of traditions, Shugendō was outlawed in the late nineteenth century as part of the attempt by the Japanese government to "purify" Shintō of its "foreign" elements. Shugendō specialists were forced to identify themselves either as Buddhist monks or Shintō priests. With the postwar declaration of religious freedom in the second half of the 1940s, Shugendō organizations recovered their independence and many activities, such as the Yoshino-Kumano pilgrimage along the Ōmine range and the seasonal retreats at Haguro, have been revived by their former institutional centers.

Buddhist aspects of Shugendō

Buddhist aspects of Shugendō are reflected in its doctrinal and ethical teachings, rituals, COSMOLOGY, and ascetic practices. These are based mainly on tantric Buddhism as it evolved in the Tendai and Shingon traditions in Japan. Examples include the reinterpretation of traditional Buddhist categories, such as the ten realms of existence (from hell to Buddha) and the six PĀRAMITĀ (PERFECTIONS), in terms of the physical and spiritual progress made by ascetics as they advance through the mountain trails and trials. Fire ceremonies (*goma*) and other Buddhist rituals also underwent transformation. Cosmological and symbolic significance was assigned to Shugendō geographical sites based on the configuration of the womb realm (*taizōkai*) and diamond realm (*kongōkai*) MAṆḌALAS. In this way the mountains came to be identified with the body of the cosmic Buddha Mahāvairocana (Japanese, Dainichi), and entering the mountains took on the added meaning of becoming integrated with the Buddha and attaining enlightenment. The belief that buddhahood can be attained within this life is a central tenet of Shugendō faith and a major goal of its practice. Traditional Buddhist and Buddhist-like figures (buddhas, BODHISATTVAS, and guardian deities) were incorporated into Shugendō worship, along with completely new figures. Especially important is Fudō (*myōō*; the unmovable), a fiery and angry looking representation of the role of the cosmic Buddha in destroying the passionate afflictions of this world. Fundamental Buddhist practices such as MEDITATION (seated, walking, or otherwise on the move) and the recitation of sūtras belong to the basic activities of Shugendō. Thus, while it is misleading to speak of Shugendō only in terms of Buddhism, its adherents consider themselves Buddhists and it is not inaccurate to consider it part of the Buddhist tradition.

See also: **Japan; Shintō (Honji Suijaku) and Buddhism; Space, Sacred**

Bibliography

Earhart, H. Byron. *A Religious Study of the Mount Haguro Sect of Shugendō.* Tokyo: Sophia University, 1970.

Miyake Hitoshi. *Shugendō: Essays on the Structure of Japanese Folk Religion,* ed. H. Byron Earhart. Ann Arbor: University of Michigan Center for Japanese Studies, 2001.

Renondeau, Gaston. *Le Shugendō: Histoire, doctrine, et rites des anachorètes dits Yamabushi.* Paris: Imprimerie Nationale, 1965.

Rotermund, Hartmut O. *Die Yamabushi: Aspekte ihres Glaubens, Lebens und ihrer sozialen Funktion im japanischen Mittelalter.* Hamburg, Germany: de Gruyter, 1968.

Swanson, Paul L. "Shugendō and the Yoshino-Kumano Pilgrimage." *Monumenta Nipponica* 36, no. 1 (1981): 55–84.

Swanson, Paul L., and Tyler, Royall, eds. "Shugendō and Mountain Religion in Japan." Special issue of *Japanese Journal of Religious Studies* 16, nos. 2–3 (1989).

PAUL L. SWANSON

SHWEDAGON

According to Burmese accounts the Shwedagon pagoda was constructed in 585 B.C.E. It has since been, and is still being, much embellished. Successive Mon and Burmese kings and queens added their weights in gold to the spire as it rose higher and higher through the centuries. The finial or *hti* is encrusted with enormous rubies and diamonds. The Shwedagon finally reached its present height of 326 feet in the fifteenth century under the patronage of the Pegu queen Shin Sawbu. According to tradition, the Buddha gave eight of his hairs to two Mon merchants who returned to their land and dedicated the pagoda. The Shwedagon is now the most famous shrine in Burma and truly a wonder of the world. Best visited at night, one enters another world of gilded spires and tinkling bells, flickering candles, and reverberating gongs.

The pagoda rises from the 190-foot high Dagon Hill and has four main entrances—one to each cardinal point—with long covered stairs, commanded at their feet by giant *chinthé* lions, and lined with pagoda shops selling flowers and religious paraphernalia. The south and east stairs have been remodeled recently. The main terrace was leveled by the Pegu kings in the fifteenth century; it covers fourteen acres and is paved with marble slabs. The main STŪPA has a circumference of 1,421 feet; the base is octagonal, each side lined with eight subsidiary stūpas for a total of sixty-four. At each corner is a *manothiha* or sphinx. Octagonal terraces rise for eighty feet; only one terrace above the main platform is accessible, and only to monks and male Buddhists. Above these are the circular bands that rise to the *hti* finial.

Opposite the covered *zaung-dan* (stair halls) are the four principal shrines dedicated to each of the four BUDDHAS who have manifested themselves during the present eon. Filling the platform are several hundred shrines and temples, mostly dating from the colonial period and Rangoon's development as a mercantile capital. There are shrines erected by various merchant guilds, including the Chinese Buddhist Community. A fire in 1931 destroyed many of these pavilions and they were subsequently rebuilt. There are many fine examples of traditional wood carving. Surrounding the main stūpa are planetary shrines for the days of the week with their corresponding animals. There are countless other shrines, statues, and symbolic objects on site. Divine beasts are everywhere, as are *nats* (spirits). The Mahā Ghaṇṭā, a great bell cast by King Singu in 1779, is especially notable. It weighs twenty-three tons, has a diameter of over six feet, and stands seven feet high. In 1825 the British attempted to send the bell to London as booty, but while loading it onto a ship it fell into the Rangoon River and was abandoned there. Later an association of pious Burmese salvaged it from the riverbed and were allowed to replace it in the Shwedagon. There is another larger bell, the Mahatisadda Ghaṇṭā, that weighs forty tons; it was donated by King Tharawaddy in 1848 and is the second-largest bell in Burma.

See also: **Monastic Architecture; Myanmar; Myanmar, Buddhist Art in; Southeast Asia, Buddhist Art in**

Bibliography

Moore, Elizabeth; Meyer, Hansjorg; and U Win Pe. *Shwedagon: Golden Pagoda of Myanmar.* London: Thames and Hudson, 1999.

Win Pe. *The Shwedagon.* Rangoon: Printing and Publishing Corporation, 1972.

PAUL STRACHAN

ŚIKṢĀNANDA

Śikṣānanda (652–710), a native of Khotan, was one of the major translators of MAHĀYĀNA sūtras into Chinese. Conversant with both Mahāyāna and mainstream Buddhist scriptures, as well as with non-Buddhist texts, Śikṣānanda came to China with a complete set of the HUAYAN JING (*Avataṃsaka-sūtra; Flower Garland Sūtra*) in Sanskrit after learning that Empress Wu (r. 690–705) had sent envoys to Khotan to search for the Sanskrit edition of the scripture and its translators. Under Empress Wu's auspices, Śikṣānanda joined the translation team that undertook the translation and retranslation of nineteen Mahāyāna scriptures, including the *Huayan jing* and the LAṄKAVĀTĀRA-SŪTRA (*Discourse of the Descent into Laṅka*). The newly translated *Huayan jing,* completed in 699 in a total of eighty fascicles, was said to be a literal translation, closer in both style and language to Buddhabhadra's sixty-fascicle translation from the early fifth century than to the more recent translation of XUANZANG (ca. 600–664).

In 704 Empress Wu allowed Śikṣānanda to return to Khotan, but he was summoned back to Chang'an in 708. Zhongzong (r. 705–710), then the reigning emperor, and all the monks in the capital greeted Śikṣānanda at Kaiyuan Gate with banners and parasols. Apparently in poor health at this time, Śikṣānanda was unable to take on any additional translation assignments and died in 710 at the age of fifty-nine. His body was cremated and his remains were escorted back to Khotan. His followers built a seven-story pagoda at the cremation site and named it "Pagoda of the Trepiṭaka Huayan" to commemorate him.

See also: **Kumārajīva; Paramārtha**

Bibliography

Ch'en, Kenneth. *Buddhism in China: A Historical Survey.* Princeton, NJ: Princeton University Press, 1964.

Song Gaoseng zhuan (*Biographies of Eminent Monks Compiled in the Song Dynasty*). Beijing: Zhonghua shuju, 1987.

CHI-CHIANG HUANG

SILENT ILLUMINATION CHAN.

See **Mozhao Chan (Silent Illumination Chan)**

SILK ROAD

Buddhism spread from India to Central Asia and China via an overland network of major and minor routes popularly called the Silk Road. This network connected Buddhist centers in Northwest India, western Central Asia, the Tarim basin, and China during the first millennium C.E. In the broadest sense, the silk routes extended from China to the Mediterranean, incorporating routes through Syria, Mesopotamia, and Iran. Primary routes in western Central Asia ran through Margiana and the Oxus River (Amu Darya) valley, reached Bactria in northern Afghanistan or branched northward to Sogdiana, and continued to the Tarim basin in eastern Central Asia. Capillary routes through the Karakoram mountains in northern Pakistan directly linked the silk routes of eastern Central Asia with the major arteries for trade and travel in Northwest India. Northern and southern routes around the Tarim basin rejoined at DUNHUANG, the westernmost outpost of the Chinese empire, and proceeded through the Gansu corridor to central China.

The transmission of Buddhism from India to Central Asia and China corresponded with the development of the silk routes as channels for intercultural exchanges. Chinese contacts with the "Western Regions" (*Xi-yu*) of Central and South Asia expanded during the Han dynasty (206 B.C.E.–220 C.E.). By 111 B.C.E., the Han controlled the Gansu corridor to Dunhuang, and garrisons and irrigated agricultural oases around the Tarim basin were established in the first century B.C.E. Although Chinese control of these areas fluctuated, prosperous trade in luxury items (including silk) and dynamic cultural exchanges continued.

Chinese historical chronicles of the Han period refer to the gradual migration of Yuezhi nomads from the area around Dunhuang through the Tarim basin to Bactria in the second century B.C.E. The Kushans, a branch of the Yuezhi, advanced from Bactria across the Hindu Kush into Northwest India in the first century C.E. By the second century C.E. during the reign of Kanishka, the Kushan empire controlled the routes that connected northern India with the silk routes. Kushan control accelerated economic and cultural contacts and stimulated the movement of Buddhism beyond South Asia to Central Asia and China.

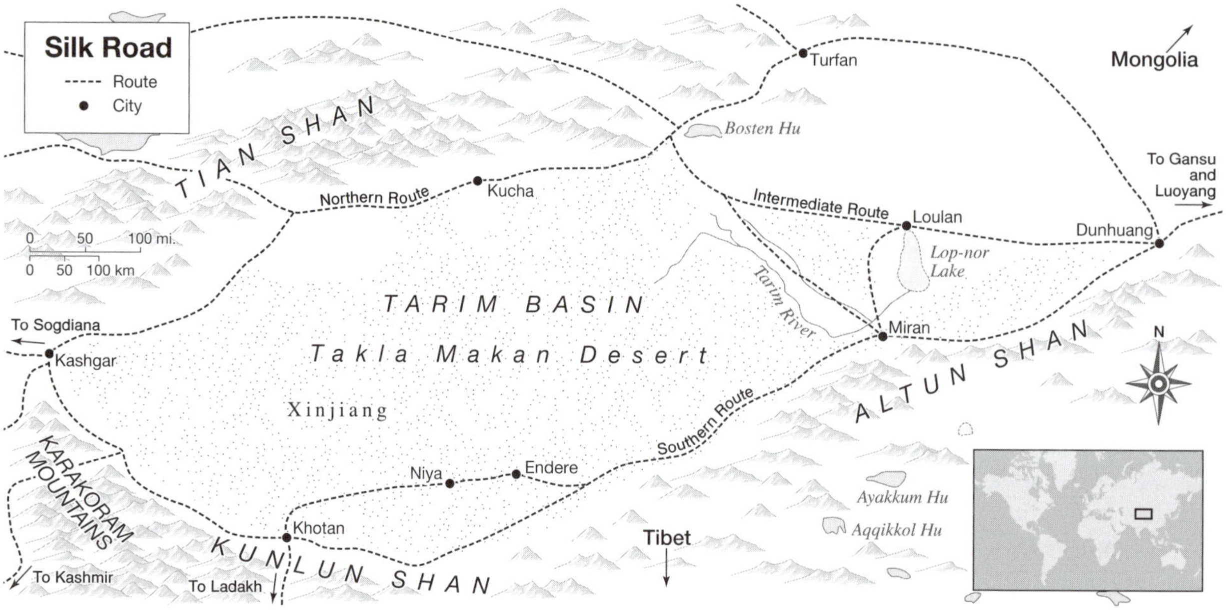

The Silk Road: trade routes through eastern Central Asia. XNR Productions, Inc. Reproduced by permission of the Gale Group.

Translators of early Chinese Buddhist texts came to China from western Central Asia and Northwest India via the silk routes. AN SHIGAO, Lokakṣema, and other Parthian, Sogdian, and Indian translators arrived in Luoyang beginning in the middle of the second century C.E. Buddhist monasteries emerged near irrigated oases at Khotan, Kucha, Turfan, and Dunhuang on the northern and southern branches of the silk routes during the third to fifth centuries C.E. Certain scholarly monks, including DHARMARAKṢA (ca. 233–310 C.E.) from Dunhuang and KUMĀRAJĪVA (350–409/413 C.E.) from Kucha, came directly from Buddhist centers in the Tarim basin. Many anonymous monks who traveled between India and China along the silk routes were responsible for the transmission of Buddhism outside the monastic community. Chinese pilgrims to India returned with manuscripts, relics, and stories about sacred places in the Buddhist heartland. FAXIAN (ca. 337–418 C.E.) and XUANZANG (ca. 600–664 C.E.) were the most famous Chinese pilgrims; their accounts contain valuable details about social political, and religious conditions in Central Asia and India.

STŪPAS (reliquaries), cave paintings, and manuscripts discovered by Aurel Stein and other explorers in the early twentieth century illustrate the role of the Silk Road as a path for the expansion of Buddhism. Stūpas at Buddhist sites on the southern route in the Tarim basin adopted architectural features from Northwest India. A Gāndhārī manuscript of the *Dharmapada* (Pāli, DHAMMAPADA) from Khotan and approximately one thousand Kharoṣṭhī documents from Niya, Endere, and Loulan show that the Gāndhārī language continued to be used along the southern silk route until the fourth century C.E. Numerous Buddhist paintings in caves along the northern silk route display close stylistic affinities with the art of Gandhāra, western Central Asia, and Iran, while others incorporate Chinese and Turkish elements. The distribution of Buddhist Sanskrit manuscripts from the second to sixth centuries C.E. indicates that Buddhist centers along the northern silk route were generally affiliated with MAINSTREAM BUDDHIST SCHOOLS (particularly the Sarvāstivāda), but the MAHĀYĀNA tradition was prevalent in southern silk route centers such as Khotan. After the sixth century, Buddhist literature was written in Central Asian vernacular languages, including Khotanese Saka, Tocharian, Sogdian, Uighur, Tibetan, and Mongolian. Buddhist artistic and literary traditions continued to flourish in Central Asia along with Zoroastrian, Manichaean, and Nestorian Christian traditions in the middle to late first millennium C.E.

Despite this historical legacy, with the exception of the surviving Buddhist traditions in Tibet and Mongolia, Buddhism disappeared from the Silk Road regions of Central Asia as these areas gradually Islamicized in the second millennium C.E.

See also: **Cave Sanctuaries; Central Asia; Central Asia, Buddhist Art in; China; Gāndhārī, Buddhist Literature in; India, Northwest; Languages; Pilgrimage**

Bibliography

Härtel, Herbert, and Yaldiz, Marianne. *Along the Ancient Silk Routes: Central Asian Art from the West Berlin State Museums.* New York: Metropolitan Museum of Art, 1982.

Klimburg-Salter, Deborah. *The Silk Route and the Diamond Path: Esoteric Buddhist Art on the Trans-Himalayan Trade Routes.* Los Angeles: UCLA Arts Council, 1982.

Liu, Xinru. *Ancient India and Ancient China: Trade and Religious Exchanges, A.D. 1–600.* Delhi: Oxford University Press, 1988. Reprint, 1997.

Liu, Xinru. *The Silk Road: Overland Trade and Cultural Interactions in Eurasia.* Washington, DC: American Historical Association, 1998.

McRae, John, and Nattier, Jan, eds. *Buddhism across Boundaries—Chinese Buddhism and the Western Regions.* Honolulu: University of Hawaii Press, 2004.

Nattier, Jan. "Church Language and Vernacular Language in Central Asian Buddhism." *Numen* 37 (1990): 195–219.

Rhie, Marylin Martin. *Early Buddhist Art of China and Central Asia,* Vol. 1: *Later Han, Three Kingdoms, and Western Chin in China and Bactria to Shan-shan in Central Asia.* Leiden, Netherlands: Brill, 1999.

Sander, Lore. "Buddhist Literature in Central Asia." In *Encyclopaedia of Buddhism,* ed. G. P. Malalasekera, Vol. 4, fascicle 1. Colombo, Sri Lanka: Government of Ceylon, 1981.

Zürcher, Erik. *The Buddhist Conquest of China: The Spread and Adaptation of Buddhism in Early Medieval China,* 2 vols. Leiden, Netherlands: Brill, 1959.

JASON NEELIS

SINHALA, BUDDHIST LITERATURE IN

Sinhala is the language of 72 percent of the population of Sri Lanka. Sinhala is considered part of the Indo-European family of languages, but recent scholarship has revealed a strong Dravidian influence as well. No written documents exist of the period before the coming of Buddhism in the third century B.C.E.; with Buddhism, a written literature developed. The earliest extant records are cave and rock inscriptions in a Brāhmī script dating from around 200 B.C.E., which list the names of Buddhist donors who supported cave dwelling monks. This connection between the language and the religion, established very early, gave rise over time to a vigorous Buddhist literature.

As far back as the first century B.C.E., Buddhist monks at Aluvihāre in central Sri Lanka committed Buddhist texts to writing. Monasteries quickly developed into centers of literary and intellectual activity, and a substantial collection of religious works, commentaries, exegetical writings, and historical records appeared in Pāli, Sanskrit, and the local vernacular. Most of the early works have not survived, but scholars know of their existence from references in later texts and from rock inscriptions. The only extant works from before the eighth century C.E. are the historical chronicles the *Dīpavaṃsa* (fourth century C.E.), the *Mahāvaṃsa* (sixth century C.E.), and its continuation the *Cūlavaṃsa* (twelfth century C.E.), which were all written in Pāli, though based on records from the Sinhala. These chronicles, written by monks, constitute a chronology of Sinhala kings (from the time of the founder Vijaya to the time of the authors), their major victories and defeats, and their peacetime activities, especially their meritorious deeds in support of Buddhism. The chronicles present a blend of historical information, religious exhortation, and political nationalism, all done with remarkable literary skill, thus constituting a record of what the authors perceived as the establishing of a Buddhist nation on the island of Sri Lanka.

The evidence of the chronicles, and references in later works and inscriptions, all suggest the existence of a flourishing literary tradition, even during this early period. Jayabahu Dharmakirti, writing in the thirteenth century in his *Nikāyasaṃgrahaya* (*Collection of Writings on the Books of the Doctrine*), lists the names of twenty-eight monks and nine lay writers well known for composing religious works, commentaries, glossaries, translations, and other works between the fifth and thirteenth centuries. Unfortunately, all that remains from the first to eighth centuries C.E. are graffiti poems on the mirror wall of the rock fortress at Sigiriya. These short casual scribbles of visitors to Sigiriya between the seventh and ninth centuries C.E. (many of whom included their names and identities) do not represent the major literary tradition of the time. However, their skill and verve indicate the widespread nature and vitality of a tradition where soldiers, artisans, monks, and women (in addition to more traditional scholars) could all write poems.

Sinhala literature from the tenth to the thirteenth centuries was strongly influenced by the classical court literature of India. The major Sinhala poetical works of the period are the *Muvadevāvata* (*The Story of the Bodhisattva's Birth as King Mukhadeva,* [twelfth century]), the *Sasadāvata* (*The Story of the Bodhisattva's Birth as a Hare,* [twelfth century]), and the *Kavsiḷumiṇa*

(*The Crown Jewel of Poetry*), attributed to King Parakramabahu II (thirteenth century). These works are classical in style, and present stories of the past births of the Buddha.

The oldest extant prose work in Sinhala is on rhetoric, the *Siyabaslakara* (*The Ornaments of One's Language*), ascribed to King Sena I (r. 832–851). The *Dhampiyātuvā gätapadaya* (*Commentary on the Blessed Doctrine*), a commentary on words and phrases in the Pāli DHAMMAPADA, was composed in the tenth century. The *Sikhāvalaňda* (*The Mark of Sign of the Precepts*) and *Sikhāvalaňda vinisa* (*An Examination of the Signs of the Precepts*), a summary of precepts on priestly discipline, also belong to this period.

Sinhala prose works from the twelfth and thirteenth centuries can be described as "intermediate texts." Though still classical in form they were closer in idiom to the spoken vernacular. The *Saddhamaratnāvaliya* (*The Jewel Garland of the True Doctrine*) by the monk Dharmasēna, the *Amāvatura* (*The Nectar Flow* or *The Flowing Nectar* [*of the Doctrine*]) and *Dharmapradīpikāva* (*The Light of the Doctrine*) by the monk Gurulugōmi, the *Butsaraṇa* (*The Protection* [or *Refuge*] *of the Buddha*) by Vidyācakravarti, the Sinhala *Thūpavaṃsa* (*The Chronicle of the Stūpas*), the *Daladāsirita* (*An Account of the Tooth Relic* [*of the Buddha*]), the *Pūjāvaliya* (*The Garland of Worship*), the *Pansiya Panas Jātaka Pota* (*The Book of Five Hundred and Fifty Birth Stories* [*of the Buddha*]), the monk Vīdāgama Maitrēya's *Buduguṇālaṃkāraya* (*An Elaboration of the Buddha's Virtues*), and the *Lōväda saṃgrahaya* (*A Collection of Writings for the Betterment of the World*) all belong to this tradition. They are Buddhist works intended for the edification of ordinary people and so had the flavor and style of popular sermons. Works on rhetoric, such as the *Sidat Saṃgarāva* (*A Collection of Writings on Grammar*), the *Siyabas lakuṇa* (*The Marks or Signs of One's Language*), and the *Dandyālaṃkāra sanna* (*Commentary on Dandin's Theory of Ālaṃkāra*) and works on prosody, such as the *Elusandäs lakuṇa* (*The Mark of Signs of the Original Sinhala* [*elu*]), were also composed during this period.

If the thirteenth century saw a flowering of Sinhala prose literature, the fourteenth and fifteenth centuries saw a flowering of poetry as the process of secularization that had begun with prose continued into poetry. These Sinhala poems were written by monks using Buddhist themes, but they were modeled on classical Sanskrit court literature and thus became more secular in content. The most famous of a spate of *sandēsa* (message poems) from this period were the *Sälalihini sandēśaya* (*The Message Poem Carried by the Salalihini Bird*) and the *Parevi sandēśaya* (*The Message Poem Carried by the Pigeon*) by the monk Toṭagamuvē Sri Rāhula, who also wrote the *Kāvyaśēkhera* (*The Crown of Poetry*). Two other well-known writers of the age were the monk Vidāgama Maitrēya, who wrote the *Buduguṇālaṃkāraya,* and the monk Vëttëve, who wrote the *Guttila Kāvya* (*The Poem of Guttila*). Increasing secularization resulted in a shift away from the earlier heavy Sanskritization of the language.

Unfortunately, Sinhala literary and linguistic creativity was short lived. The arrival of Western European powers and subsequent colonial conquest by the Portuguese, Dutch, and British in succession from the sixteenth to the twentieth centuries resulted in a period of decadence in Sinhala literature. The only poet of significance during the sixteenth century was Alagiyavanna Mohoṭṭāla, who wrote the *Kusa Jātaka* (*The Story of the Birth of the Bodhisattva as King Kusa*), the *Dahamsoňda kāvya* (*The Poem on the Good Doctrine*), the *Subhāsita* (*Auspicious Thoughts*), and some panegyrics.

In the mid-eighteenth century there was a brief literary and religious revival in the central kingdom of Kandy, which had not yet been conquered by Western powers. It was spearheaded by the monk Welivitiye Saranakara, and produced a considerable body of work in Pāli, Sanskrit, and Sinhala. This literary renaissance was short lived, however; the British conquered the entire island in 1815, colonial rule was established, and Sinhala language and literature became stagnant once again.

When the first stirring of political nationalism occurred in the late nineteenth and early twentieth centuries it took the form of a literary and religious revival, and the long-standing Sri Lankan connection between religion, literature, and the national identity resurfaced. The phenomenal increase in literary activity was at first entirely religious, but eventually newer genres influenced by Western contact came to prominence, and a modern secular literature was born.

See also: **Pāli, Buddhist Literature in; Sri Lanka**

Bibliography

Geiger, Wilhelm. *A Grammar of the Sinhalese Language.* Colombo, Sri Lanka: Royal Asiatic Society, 1938.

Godakumbure, C. E. *Sinhalese Literature.* Colombo, Sri Lanka: Colombo Apothecaries, 1955.

Obeyesekere, Ranjini. *Sinhala Writing and the New Critics.* Colombo, Sri Lanka: Gunasena, 1974.

Obeyesekere, Ranjini. "A Survey of the Sinhala Literary Tradition." In *Modern Sri Lanka: A Society in Transition,* ed. Tissa Fernando and Robert N. Kearney. Syracuse, NY: Maxwell School of Citizenship and Public Affairs, Syracuse University, 1979.

Obeyesekere, Ranjini, trans. *The Jewels of the Doctrine: Stories of the Saddharmaratnāvaliya.* Albany: State University of New York Press, 1991.

Obeyesekere, Ranjini, trans. *Portraits of Buddhist Women: Stories from the Saddharmaratnāvaliya.* Albany: State University of New York Press, 2001.

Reynolds, C. H. B., ed. *An Anthology of Sinhalese Literature up to 1815.* London: Allen and Unwin, 1970.

RANJINI OBEYESEKERE

SKANDHA (AGGREGATE)

According to Buddhist texts, the entire universe, including the individual, is made up of different phenomena (dharma). Although all these phenomena of existence are reduced to transitory entities by the theory of anātman (no-self), Buddhism classifies these phenomena into different categories, including the conventionally accepted concept of "person." The three concepts of bases (*āyatana*), elements (*dhātu*), and aggregates (skandha; Pāli, *khandha*) constitute different schemes for classifying the various phenomena. Although the aggregates are nothing but a "convenient fiction," the Buddha nevertheless made frequent use of the skandha when asked to explain the elements at work in the individual.

According to this scheme, what is conventionally called a "person" can be understood in terms of five aggregates, the sum of which must not be mistaken for a permanent entity since beings are nothing but an amalgam of ever-changing phenomena. The five aggregates are variously translated as matter or form (*rūpa*); sensation, emotion, or feeling (*vedanā*); recognition or perception (*saṃjñā*); karmic activity, formation, force, or impulse (saṃskāra); and consciousness (*vijñāna*). *Rūpa* is made of four primary elements (*mahābhūta*): air, fire, water, and earth. It is also described as an amalgam of twenty-three secondary elements, which include the five sense organs, as well as their respective objects. *Vedanā,* on the other hand, refers to the actual experience of the senses, always qualified as being either pleasant, unpleasant, or neutral. The term *saṃjñā* is assigned to the mental faculty that imposes categories upon the sensory stimuli, which interprets what is sensed. The fourth aggregate, saṃskāra, is probably the hardest to grasp because of the various meanings associated with the term. It is a force, karmic energy, that generates all the other aggregates; the theory of PRATĪTYASAMUTPĀDA (DEPENDENT ORIGINATION), for example, stipulates that on account of saṃskāra, *vijñāna* and the other links of the chain emerge. Saṃskāra can therefore be seen as the driving force, the fuel, or the energy that keeps the five aggregates bound together within the cycle of life and death (SAṂSĀRA). Saṃskāra is not only a causal factor; its signification includes everything that has been caused. Each of the five aggregates is therefore a saṃskāra in the sense that it is conditioned. The last aggregate is *vijñāna* (consciousness), the faculty responsible for apprehending what manifests itself through each of the six senses.

As with each of the links of the theory of dependent origination, the five aggregates are mutually dependent on one another. They need to be perceived from a cyclical perspective, where the last (*vijñāna*) is a key factor in the emergence of the first (*rūpa*). This causal process points to the everlasting cycle of saṃsāra as opposed to NIRVĀṆA, which, in the THERAVĀDA tradition, is defined as a state totally devoid of the aggregates, beyond mind and matter.

See also: **Anātman/Ātman (No-Self/Self); Consciousness, Theories of; Dharma and Dharmas**

Bibliography

Bodhi, Bhikkhu. "Khandha and Upādānakkhandha." *Pāli Buddhist Review* 1, no. 1 (1976): 91–102.

Boisvert, Mathieu. *The Five Aggregates; Understanding Theravāda Psychology and Soteriology.* Waterloo, ON: Wilfrid Laurier University Press, 1995.

Collins, Steven. *Selfless Persons: Imagery and Thought in Theravāda Buddhism.* Cambridge, UK: Cambridge University Press, 1982.

Gethin, R. M. "The Five Khandhas: Their Theatment [sic] in the Nikāyas and Early Abhidhamma." *Journal of Indian Philosophy* 52 (1986): 35–53.

Hamilton, Sue. *Identity and Experience: The Constitution of the Human Being According to Early Buddhism.* London: Luzac Oriental, 1996.

MATHIEU BOISVERT

SLAVERY

The definition of the word *slavery* and the identification of terms such as Sanskrit *dāsa* and corresponding vocabulary in other languages is contentious. If one understands the concept in terms of obligations, or power relations, however, slaves may be seen as those who owed obligations to many, but were owed few or none by others, thus avoiding the complications introduced by seeing slaves, as in classical law, as things (*res*). Of course, since the socioeconomic systems of different places and periods vary radically, it is impossible to generalize; in particular, the ties that many people in the premodern world had to the land meant that donations of property to Buddhist monasteries included the labor of those attached to that land. Whether or not such individuals are called *serfs*, their limited autonomy with respect to the state and to society is clear. In this sense, discussions of slavery can hardly be separated from those of land ownership or practices such as corvée labor, and in each case the whole complex must be investigated in light of the large-scale economic systems within which Buddhist institutions existed.

While it is important to distinguish actual practices within Buddhist institutions from attitudes toward these practices as found in Buddhist literature, what can be said clearly is that there is almost no indication in any premodern Buddhist source, scriptural or documentary, of opposition to, or reluctance to participate in, institutions of slavery. It is true that the Buddhist monastic codes (VINAYA) of all sects are unanimous in stipulating that it is not permissible to ordain a slave, but the reasons for doing so clearly lie not in any opposition to slavery but rather in the well-recognized reluctance of the Buddhist communities to interfere in previously established relations of social obligation, since it is also forbidden to ordain debtors, those in royal or military service, and so on. Again, when Buddhist texts speak of restrictions on the monastic ownership of slaves, they do so virtually without exception in the context of restrictions on individual rather than corporate ownership of wealth in general, and not with the intention of singling out slave ownership as somehow different from any other type of ownership. Indeed, in Buddhist literature of all varieties, stock descriptions of wealth, even that gifted to the Buddha, regularly include both male and female slaves along with silver, gold, fields, livestock, and so on. Some texts, emphasizing the moral obligation to receive whatever is given in reverence, declare that it is an offense not to accept such offerings, the lists of which regularly include slaves.

Although there is a lack of sufficient sources to offer detailed proof, references in the accounts of Chinese pilgrims, as well as several inscriptional sources, make it clear that at least some Buddhist monasteries in India owned slaves. The sources are much better for other areas of the Buddhist world, and here too they are virtually unanimous. There is copious inscriptional and documentary evidence for the institutional monastic ownership of slaves from Sri Lanka, Cambodia, Burma, Thailand, Korea, China, and Japan; Central Asian documents frequently refer to slaves privately owned by individual monks. For example, in Koryŏ-period Korea (918–1392), the Buddhist monastic institution was one of the major slaveholders on the Korean peninsula during the late fourteenth century; the founders of the succeeding Chosŏn dynasty (1392–1910) transferred eighty-thousand monastery slaves to public ownership, leaving "only" one slave for every twenty monks. Slaves were also, however, owned by individual monks, and these remained unaffected by this legislation. Although it is worth stating that the general socioeconomic situation in theocratic Tibet was such that direct parallels are difficult to draw, there can be little doubt that comparable institutions existed there, whether or not the individuals in question were always called *bran* (slave).

Although the details of every circumstance are different, we are compelled to conclude that here, as in so many other cases, individual Buddhists and Buddhist institutions were, much more frequently than not, fully integrated into the societies in which they existed, not challenging the structures or customs of those societies, but on the contrary, often working to strengthen them.

See also: **Economics; Monasticism; Persecutions**

Bibliography

Agrawala, Ratna Chandra. "Position of Slaves and Serfs as Depicted in the Kharosthi Documents from Chinese Turkestan." *Indian Historical Quarterly* 29/2 (1953): 97–110.

Law, B. C. "Slavery as Known to Early Buddhists." *Journal of the Ganganatha Jha Research Institute* 6/1 (1948): 1–9.

Salem, Ellen. "The Utilization of Slave Labor in the Koryŏ Period: 918–1392." In *Papers of the First International Conference on Korean Studies 1979.* Songnam: The Academy of Korean Studies, 1980.

Singh, Madan Mohan. "Slavery as Known from the Buddhist Pali Sources." *Indian Historical Quarterly* 39/1–2 (1963): 1–12.

JONATHAN A. SILK

SŌKA GAKKAI

Sōka Gakkai (Society for Value Creation), Japan's largest lay Buddhist organization, was founded by the educator Makiguchi Tsunesaburō (1871–1944) in 1930 and reestablished after World War II by its second president, Toda Jōsei (1900–1958). In 2002 it claimed 8.21 million member households; its worldwide umbrella organization, Sōka Gakkai International (SGI), headed by the Sōka Gakkai's spiritual leader and former third president Daisaku Ikeda (1928–), claimed more than twelve million members in 185 countries and territories. Beginning as a lay association of Nichiren Shōshū, a small sect within the NICHIREN SCHOOL, Sōka Gakkai became independent in 1991 after longstanding tensions with the Nichiren Shōshū priesthood. In ethos and organizational style, it bears more similarity to Japan's so-called New Religions than to traditional temple denominations.

Sōka Gakkai stresses faith, practice, and study of the teachings of NICHIREN (1222–1282) as the key to personal happiness and world peace. Members enshrine a copy of Nichiren's MAṆḌALA in their homes and twice daily recite portions of the LOTUS SŪTRA (SADDHARMAPUṆḌARĪKA-SŪTRA) and also chant the *Lotus Sūtra*'s title, or DAIMOKU, *Namu Myōhō-renge-kyō*. (In Sōka Gakkai, as in some other Nichiren groups, "Namu" is usually pronounced "Nam" in actual recitation.) This practice is said to manifest innate buddhahood, bringing about a positive character transformation known as "human revolution," and to contribute directly to realizing an ideal society. To help implement its social vision, Sōka Gakkai established a political party, the Kōmeitō (Clean Government Party), in 1964, sparking controversy over religion–state relations. Sōka Gakkai officially separated from Kōmeitō in 1970 but remains the party's chief supporter. The organization encourages proselytizing, chiefly through personal contacts and neighborhood discussion meetings. Sōka Gakkai also undertakes a range of cultural, educational, and humanitarian activities and is an NGO (nongovernmental organization) member of the United Nations.

Bibliography

Machacek, David, and Wilson, Bryan, eds. *Global Citizens: The Sōka Gakkai Buddhist Movement in the World.* New York: Oxford University Press, 2000.

Métraux, Daniel A. *The Sōka Gakkai Revolution.* Lanham, MD: University Press of America, 1994.

Métraux, Daniel A. "The Soka Gakkai: Buddhism and the Creation of a Harmonious and Peaceful Society." In *Engaged Buddhism: Buddhist Liberation Movements in Asia,* ed. Christopher S. Queen and Sallie B. King. Albany: State University of New York Press, 1996.

Murata, Kiyoaki. *Japan's New Buddhism: An Objective Account of the Soka Gakkai.* New York and Tokyo: Weatherhill, 1969.

JACQUELINE I. STONE

SŎKKURAM

Sŏkkuram (Stone Grotto Hermitage) is a Buddhist shrine located in Korea on the slope of Mount T'oham in Kyŏngju City in South Kyŏngsang province. According to the SAMGUK YUSA (MEMORABILIA OF THE THREE KINGDOMS, 1279), Prime Minister Kim Taesŏng (d. 774) constructed Sŏkkuram in 751 C.E. during the reign of King Kyŏngdŏk (r. 742–776) to honor his mother from a previous incarnation.

The manmade, keyhole-shaped, cavelike structure is constructed with granite blocks covered with earth. The inner sanctuary is circular with a hemispherical domed ceiling containing a lotus capstone and twenty-eight clump-stones representing the sun and the stars of the cosmos. The MAHĀYĀNA Buddhist iconographic program is mixed with esoteric elements. The main buddha, perhaps an image of Śākyamuni, seated in the *padmāsana* position with the earth-touching MUDRĀ, is a monumental sculpture in the round. Carved in relief on the sanctuary wall are fifteen standing deities: an eleven-headed Avalokiteśvara, Samantabhadra, Manjuśrī, INDRA, Brahmā, and ten ARHAT disciples of Śākyamuni. The upper niches of the wall contain ten seated figures: Vimalakīrti, Kṣitigarbha, Avalokiteśvara, and other esoteric BODHISATTVAS, one of whom holds a three-prong *vajra.* Fourteen guardian deities are depicted in the front area: four heavenly kings, two Dvārapāla guardians, and the eight-set guardians, including Asura, Garuḍa, and Nāga.

The Buddha's full fleshy face is softly modeled with a benign spiritual expression. The *tribaṅga* (three-bending)-posed bodhisattvas are elegantly tall figures wearing three-plaque crowns with double-U pattern scarves. The international Tang style is apparent in the thin clothes and fluid folds. The complex but precise iconometry of the cave and the figures creates a sense of harmony in the monument.

See also: **Cave Sanctuaries; Huayan Art; Korea, Buddhist Art in; Monastic Architecture; Stūpa**

Bibliography

Harrell, Mark. "Sokkuram—Buddhist Monument and Political Statement in Korea." *World Archaeology* 27, no. 2 (October 1995): 318–335.

Hwang Su-young. *Sokkuram Cave Temple.* Photos by Ahn Jang-heon. Seoul: Yekyong Publications, 1989.

Kang Woo-bang. "Bulguksa Temple and Seokbulsa Temple." *Korea Journal* 41, no. 2 (Summer 2001): 320–344.

Park Hyounggook. "A Discussion on the Sculptured Images in Niches at the Sŏkkuram Cave Temple of Kyŏngju—with a Focus on the Restoration of Vimalakīrti, Mañjuśri and Eight Bodhisattvas." *Ars Buddhica* no. 239 (July 1998): 50–72.

JUNGHEE LEE

SŎN SCHOOL. *See* Chan School

SOTERIOLOGY

Soteriology (from Greek *sōtēr,* "healer") is the study of salvation. Soteriology is an important area of theology, especially in Christianity. Although it is a problematic term for Buddhists, most of whom (with the notable exception of Pure Land Buddhists) do not see salvation as occurring primarily through the agency of an external power, soteriology is being adopted in contemporary Buddhist scholarship to denote the study of the Buddhist PATH.

DAN COZORT

SŌTŌ ZEN. *See* Chan School

SOUTHEAST ASIA, BUDDHIST ART IN

The earliest Buddhist art in Southeast Asia dates to about the sixth century C.E. These sculptures, primarily BUDDHA IMAGES, show close stylistic and iconographical relationships with Indian images. Contact between Southeast Asia and India occurred earlier, by the beginning of the common era as attested by Chinese literary sources and small scattered finds, such as Indian coins and glyptics. The motivation for contact was trade, primarily between India and China, with Southeast Asia being initially less a destination than a stopover between them. Southeast Asia was exposed to both Indian religions—Buddhism and Hinduism—during this process, not in terms of proselytization or colonization but from haphazard meetings of locals with Indian merchants and crew. While this perhaps helps to explain the late appearance of Buddhist art in Southeast Asia, it does not explain how thoroughly Buddhism and its art, from the sixth century on, were adopted and indigenized within the region.

The modern nation-states of Southeast Asia are a poor model for organizing geographically the early Buddhist art. The people who made the earliest Buddhist art were the Pyu, Mon, Khmer, and Cham peoples on the mainland. These categories are not clear-cut, and are linguistically based on vernacular inscriptions. The Indonesian islands and the Malay Peninsula present a number of linguistic groups as well.

The mainland: Pyu, Mon, Khmer, and Cham

The Pyu lived in central and northern areas of Burma, with Śrī Ksetra (modern Prome) offering the most Buddhist artifacts. These include three enormous tube-shaped brick stūpas (the Bawbawgui STŪPA is 150 feet tall) and several small brick temples that housed Buddha images. In addition, many metal and stone images of the Buddha and thousands of clay votive tablets were found. The discovery of twenty gold leaves (each 6-1/2 by 1-1/4 inches) bound as a manuscript, with sections from the *abhidamma* and *vinayapiṭaka* inscribed in Pāli, suggests relationships with THERAVĀDA traditions. Indeed, some scholars feel this is the earliest extant Pāli manuscript, dating on the basis of its epigraphy to around the fifth century C.E.

The Mon lived in southern Burma and in Thailand. They, like the Pyu, were predominantly Buddhists, and they also inscribed in stone Pāli verses that relate closely to texts. The presence of images of bodhisattvas and some JĀTAKA reliefs indicate that the Mon were aware of Sanskrit Buddhist traditions as well. The Mon in Thailand (whose "kingdom" is often referred to as Dvāravatī) had a brilliant sculptural tradition and have left extensive numbers of Buddhist images in stone, bronze, and clay. In addition, they produced several unique image types, including stone wheels of the law (*dharmacakra*) that were raised on pillars, as well as depictions of the Buddha riding on the back of a winged figure, which are as yet unexplained. Dozens of Mon sites, such as Nakhon Pathom and Ku Bua, have been identified, but no complete architectural remains survive. From archaeological evidence we know it was brick architecture, and it included at Nakhon Pathom the Chula Phatom Chedi (stūpas are referred to in Southeast Asia as *chedi*), which was decorated with stucco and terra-cotta *jātaka* reliefs dating to around the eighth century.

The Khmer lived in Cambodia, as well as in the northeastern parts of Thailand and in the Delta area of Vietnam. They, unlike the Pyu and Mon, were predominantly Hindus until the twelfth century, although Buddhism was present as well. The Khmer founded the famous Angkor dynasty in 802 C.E., which ruled not only Cambodia but much of the mainland for almost five hundred years. The pre-Angkorian period, however, produced some of the most remarkable Hindu and Buddhist sculpture ever made. The Buddhist images were primarily of the Buddha and two bodhisattvas, Avalokiteśvara and MAITREYA. The stone sculptures, dating to the seventh and eighth centuries, tend to be cut out into three dimensions, so that the arms, held by stone supports, extend into space. The three-dimensional quality of Khmer sculpture continued for centuries, in part reflecting the use of these images at the center of small shrines, where they were meant to be seen from all sides. The inscriptions and the art indicate that Buddhism was of much lesser importance than Hinduism during the ninth to twelfth centuries. The Khmer king Jayavarman VII (r. 1181–ca. 1220) made a radical shift from royal support of Hinduism to Buddhism in the twelfth century.

Under Jayavarman VII, the Khmer ruled more of mainland Southeast Asia than ever before, from coastal Vietnam up to the Thai-Burmese border. Jayavarman built monuments with inexhaustible energy. He constructed the BAYON, a temple that was rebuilt perhaps three times during his reign, in his royal city of Angkor Thom. Each of the kings of Angkor constructed a temple mountain in the form of a stepped pyramid, upon which they set an image of a Hindu god, usually Śiva, thus establishing the king's personal relationship with the deity. The Bayon is Jayavarman's temple mountain, and the deity he placed at its center was neither Śiva nor VIṢṆU, but the Buddha seated in meditation on the coils of a seven-headed snake (nāga). The king also built two enormous temples dedicated to his parents, one for his mother in the guise of the goddess Prajñāpāramitā and one to his father as Lokeśvara (a form of Avalokiteśvara). Indeed, these three deities (the Buddha on the snake, Prajñāpāramitā, and Avalokiteśvara) were represented repeatedly in art as a triad, and were central to Buddhism under Jayavarman.

The Bayon has a circle of shrines that surrounds the central 140-foot tower in which the Buddha on the snake was housed. Placed in these shrines were images of local and regional deities brought to the capital from locations throughout the empire. These deities were placed in subordination to Jayavarman's Buddha. The temple has fifty-four towers that are crowned by enormous faces. These faces, numbering some two hundred, are arranged so that they look axially. The city itself, Angkor Thom, is surrounded by a wall about two miles square with five gates, each gate topped by four directional faces. Although scholars have tried to interpret these faces, no theory has been completely convincing. One possibility is that the faces are those of the bodhisattva Lokeśvara, who as Lord of the World sees everywhere with a look of KARUṆĀ (COMPASSION). That Jayavarman felt such compassion for all living things is stated in his inscriptions and seen in his building of 102 hospitals throughout the kingdom. In addition, the Bayon has extensive sculptural reliefs in surrounding galleries. These reliefs, however, do not depict stories from Buddhist texts but are mostly scenes of battles that Jayavarman undertook against the Cham, as well as interesting genre scenes, such as cockfights and markets. The reliefs also show that both Śiva and Viṣṇu were under worship.

Of the hundreds of other monuments Jayavarman built, the Neak Pean (coiled serpents) is notable. It consists of a square pond, 230 feet on each side, faced with stone steps and a circular stone island with a shrine in the center. Two carved snakes entwine the base of the island. There are four smaller directional ponds surrounding the central pond; these are connected with channels so that water could flow out of the central pond into the four side ponds. The water flowed through the stone heads of a human (east), lion (south), horse (west), and elephant (north). This symbolism apparently indicates that the pond was considered a duplicate of the Himalayan lake Anavatapta from which the four celestial rivers of India flow. The central shrine has three false doors carved with images of Avalokiteśvara, to whom the shrine was dedicated. A three-dimensional stone horse to which human figures cling is placed in the water; this is an image of Avalokiteśvara in his form as the horse Balaha, who

The twelfth-century Khmer Bayon Temple at Angkor Thom, Cambodia, has fifty-two (originally fifty-four) "face towers." Each contains four images, which likely represent the all-around compassion of Avalokiteśvara looking in all directions. © Robert D. Fiala, Concordia University, Seward, Nebraska. Reproduced by permission.

attempted to rescue shipwrecked sailors. We know from a thirteenth-century Chinese visitor that the waters of Neak Pean were believed to wash away sin.

The Cham sites are in mid- and southern Vietnam (the kingdom called Champa). The earliest Indian-related inscription, in Sanskrit, in Southeast Asia comes from Vo Canh in south Vietnam, dating to around the third century C.E. The earliest extant Indian-related images are much later, from the seventh century, and are entirely Hindu. A Buddhist monastery, however, was built at Dong Duong in central Vietnam in the ninth and tenth centuries. The Buddhism was MAHĀYĀNA with tantric elements, apparently something of a local school. The stone sculptures include figures performing unique gestures and wearing unique clothing and ornaments. Both Tārā and Avalokiteśvara were of importance, and in 1978 a metal image of Tārā, almost fifty inches tall, was found, indicating that large metal images were also being made at the time. The style of the Dong Duong sculptures is highly unusual within the Southeast Asian artistic tradition, with such characteristics as a single long eyebrow and the use of wormlike designs for hair and halos.

Indonesia and the Malay Peninsula

The art history of Buddhism becomes even more complex when turning to Indonesia and the Malay Peninsula. As on the mainland, both Hinduism and Buddhism were introduced simultaneously from India as a result of trade. Two of the earliest Indian-related Southeast Asian kingdoms were founded in the fifth century C.E. on the islands, one in Borneo and one in Java. The inscriptions by the "kings" from both mention brahmanical rites and indicate the appeal Hinduism had for the local Southeast Asian chiefs as a means to increase their power through using a shared Indian religious vocabulary.

These two kingdoms apparently disappeared, with Indian religions reappearing in central Java in the eighth century. During about a two-hundred-year period (ca. 730–950), hundreds of monuments in brick and stone were built and thousands of images were made in stone and metal. It was during this Central Javanese period that the Buddhist monument BOROBUDUR was erected (ca. 800–830). Few Buddhist monuments have been studied as extensively as Borobudur. It is an enormous structure, measuring 370 feet square and 113 feet tall. Built over a small hill, it consists of millions of cut volcanic stone blocks that rise like a pyramid in four square and three round terraces. There are 1,300 relief panels that illustrate a series of Indian texts, including *jātakas* and life stories of Śākyamuni Buddha from the LALITAVISTARA. Placed in niches and in stūpas are 504 life-size Buddha images, each cut in the round. In addition, about 1,472 small stūpas, 72 large perforated stūpas, and an enormous single closed stūpa at the top decorate the structure.

A Mahāyāna monument, with perhaps tantric aspects, Borobudur has defied any single interpretation of its meaning and use. As with the Dong Duong Buddhism and art mentioned above, or the Dvāravatī buddhas on flying figures, Southeast Asian Buddhists at Borobudur developed a type of Buddhism that was local and unique. Unlike East Asian Buddhists, Southeast Asian Buddhists did not in the ancient period translate Indian texts into local vernaculars, nor, as far as we know, did they produce their own Buddhist texts. They used the Indian texts in the original Sanskrit or Pāli. The result is that we have Indian texts but Southeast Asian art, art that is Indian-related but consistently local in style and iconography. In short, we often have no way to know the extent to which local understanding is hidden under the Indian guise.

There are other important Buddhist monuments in Central Java. Candi Sewu, which probably dates to the end of the eighth century, was dedicated to the bodhisattva Mañjuśrī. It had a central cella with four attached directional subshrines, and was surrounded by 250 smaller shrines. This maṇḍalic organization is seen as well at Borobudur, with the organization of the Buddha images into a seven-Buddha system differentiated by their hand gestures (MUDRĀ) and directional placement. During the Central Javanese period both Hinduism and Buddhism coexisted, with the complex of Loro Jonggrang dedicated to Śiva, Viṣṇu, and Brahmā being constructed at about the same time as Borobudur.

During the Central Javanese period enormous numbers of both Buddhist and Hindu images were caste in bronze, gold, and silver. The closeness in style and iconography that many of these metal images shared with images from the Pāla period (eighth to twelfth centuries) sites in India has long been observed. The Pāla kings were among the last major patrons of Buddhism in India, and it was under them that the great Eastern Indian monastery complexes such as Nālandā flourished. There is also inscriptional and historical evidence for frequent interchange between these monasteries and those in Indonesia.

Sometime around the middle of the tenth century Central Java appears to have been abandoned, and artistic work ceased. The cause may have been the eruption of the volcano of Mount Merapi. The Central Javanese court moved to eastern Java, with a very different type of art and architecture developing there under several different kingdoms. By the sixteenth century, Islam had become dominant throughout the Indonesian islands, except in Bali.

Buddhism continued throughout the Eastern Javanese period (tenth to fifteenth centuries), but it was not as important as Śaivism. Tantric beliefs and rituals became paramount in both Buddhism and Śaivism, and the two religions blended in many ways. The Buddhist KĀLACAKRA rituals were performed, and the kings were identified as Śiva/Buddha after death. The images in the temples in the forms of Buddhist deities, such as Prajñāpāramitā, were intended to represent the kings and queens after death when they became absorbed into the deity. Indeed, this use of images of deities as "portrait" statues of both the god and the royal person is what took place under Jayavarman VII at Angkor at about the same time, and it can be found in Champa as well. The Khmer, Cham, and Javanese royalty used images of deities in a similar way, a practice probably from the earliest adoption of Indian-related art.

There is a corpus of Buddhist art found on the island of Sumatra, but mainly at sites in what is today the southern area of the Thai peninsula; this art is loosely labeled as "Śrīvijaya" in style, with dates from the seventh to thirteenth centuries. Śrīvijaya enters history in the seventh century with several inscriptions in Sumatra. At the same time the Chinese monk-pilgrim YIJING (635–713) tells us that he spent several years in Śrīvijaya, initially in 671 to learn Sanskrit on his way to India, and then for two extended periods from 685 to 695 (with a brief return to China in 689) to translate texts and write his memoirs. Śrīvijaya continued to exist for almost five hundred years, and inscriptions on the peninsula mention it. The problem has been to find it. The place Yijing lived appears to be Palembang in Sumatra, but it has been only since the late 1970s that any archaeological evidence has been found there. Much of Śrīvijaya would have been

An aerial view of the monument at Borobudur in Java, Indonesia. © Charles and Josette Lenars/Corbis. Reproduced by permission.

built in bamboo and thatch, with people living on boats that left no trace.

Most of the Buddhist art associated with Śrīvijaya has been found in peninsular Thailand from such cities as Chaiya and Nakhon Si Thammarat. The art shares such general characteristics as being Mahāyāna in theme, with Avalokiteśvara being very popular. But rather than seeing this material, which is generally varied in style, as belonging to Śrīvijaya, it is more helpful to locate and discuss it by region because the existence of a hegemonic empire based in Śrīvijaya is questioned today.

The Burmese, Thais, Laotians, and Vietnamese

Besides the Khmer of modern Cambodia, there are other linguistic groups that dominate mainland Southeast Asia today: the Burmese, Thais, Laotians, and Vietnamese. Each of these groups, and the modern nations they have created, was predominantly Buddhist. The Burmese appear in history around the eleventh century. The Pyu kingdoms ended in the ninth, but the Mon continued for a time to share power with the Burmese. The Burmese looked to Sri Lanka for Theravāda Buddhist monks and texts, and they built one of the greatest Buddhist sites in the world at Pagan on the Irrawaddy River. Fueled by a veritable frenzy of merit-making through giving to the SAṄGHA, some two thousand brick monuments (temples and stūpas) were built over a two-hundred-year period. Although most of these monuments are abandoned today, some, such as the ANANDA TEMPLE, continue in serve worshipers.

The Ananda was built by King Kyanzittha at the beginning of the twelfth century. As with the Bayon and Borobudur, the Ananda is impressive in its size and complexity. It takes the form of a Greek cross, with four directional entrances, each of which leads to a standing wood buddha image. The buddhas stand against a solid central masonry block that is 175 feet square. The buddhas, each thirty-one feet tall, are identified as four earthly buddhas: Kakusandha (Sanskrit, Krakuccanda; north), Koṇāgamana (Sanskrit, Kaṇakamuni; east), Kassapa (Sanskrit, Kāśyapa; south), and Gotama (Sanskrit, Gautama; west). There are two inner galleries flanked by niches in which stone sculptures are placed, and on the outside of the building are extensive series of glazed stone tiles, including 912 tiles depicting *jātakas* that are arranged in tiers on the roof, which rises to a height of 172 feet.

Myanmar (Burma), like Thailand, is a Buddhist nation today, and Buddhism is officially sponsored by the government. The famous SHWEDAGON pagoda (stūpa) in Rangoon is constantly thronged with worshipers, as are Buddhist monuments everywhere, and images of the Buddha, mostly in bronze, are being produced in great quantities. Contemporary Thailand shares many Buddhist traditions with Burma, including its Theravāda Buddhism. It is not clear when the Mon in central Thailand (Dvāravatī) ceased making images, perhaps as early as the ninth century, but the Mon had a kingdom in northern Thailand at Haripunchai until the thirteenth century. This is approximately the time that the Thais first appear in history, when they revolt against their Khmer overlords and establish the first Thai kingdom of SUKHOTHAI. Like the Burmese, they looked to the Mon of lower Burma and the Sri Lankans for their Buddhism.

Sukhothai in north central Thailand has many Buddhist monuments, but they are not on the scale of Pagan or Angkor, and most are in ruins today. But this area developed a new style of Buddha image known for its lithe, melting lines, which remains the favored style of the Thais, who continue to produce thousands of Buddha images in the style. Sukhothai's political power waned quickly, as AYUTTHAYA, another Thai kingdom founded in 1350, soon dominated much of Thailand, and was to control much of Cambodia as well. The Khmer abandoned Angkor as the capital in 1431 because of Thai attacks. By then Theravāda Buddhism, already present during the reign of Jayavarman VII, had spread throughout Cambodia and Laos. The famous Angkor Wat, built in the twelfth century as the temple mountain of Suryavarman II and dedicated to the Hindu god Viṣṇu, was converted in the fourteenth century to a Buddhist monastery.

Finally, the Vietnamese have an extended Buddhist tradition. It is not, however, with India and Sri Lanka that we find relationships, but with China. China held northern Vietnam (Dai Viet) as a province for over a thousand years. The Vietnamese gained independence in the eleventh century. The Cham, in central and southern Vietnam, were in constant warfare with the Vietnamese, who relentlessly pushed them south until they completely collapsed in the nineteenth century. Vietnamese Buddhist art is best discussed in conjunction with that of China.

The Ananda Temple at Pagan, Myanmar (Burma), is white with gilded spires. It rises to a height of 172 feet. © Robert D. Fiala, Concordia University, Seward, Nebraska. Reproduced by permission.

See also: **Buddha, Life of the, in Art; Esoteric Art, South and Southeast Asia; Indonesia and the Malay Peninsula; Indonesia, Buddhist Art in; Monastic Architecture; Myanmar, Buddhist Art in**

Bibliography

Boisseler, Jean. *The Heritage of Thai Sculpture.* Bangkok, Thailand: Asia Books, 1975.

Boisseler, Jean. *Trends in Khmer Art* (1956), tr. Natasha Eilenberg and Melvin Elliott. Ithaca, NY: Cornell University, Southeast Asia Program, 1989.

Brown, Robert L. *The Dvaravati Wheels of the Law and the Indianization of South East Asia.* Leiden, Netherlands: Brill, 1986.

Chihara, Daigoro. *Hindu-Buddhist Architecture in Southeast Asia.* Leiden, Netherlands: Brill, 1996.

Diskul, M. C. Subhadradis, ed. *The Art of Śrīvijaya.* New York and Kuala Lumpur, Malaysia: Oxford University Press, 1980.

Fontein, Jan, et al. *The Sculpture of Indonesia.* Washington, DC: National Gallery of Art, 1990.

Frédéric, Louis. *The Temples and Sculpture of Southeast Asia,* tr. Arnold Rosin. London: Thames and Hudson. 1965.

Geslan-Girard, Maud, et al. *Art of Southeast Asia,* tr. J. A. Underwood. New York: Harry N. Abrams, 1998.

Gosling, Betty. *Sukhothai: Its History, Culture, and Art.* Singapore and New York: Oxford University Press, 1991.

Guillon, Emmanuel. *Cham Art: Treasures from the Dà Nang Museum, Vietnam,* tr. Tom White. London: Thames and Hudson, 2001.

Jacq-Hergoualc'h, Michel. *The Malay Peninsula: Crossroads of the Maritime Silk Road,* tr. Victoria Hobson. Leiden, Netherlands: Brill, 2002.

Jacques, Claude. *Angkor.* Cologne, Germany: Konemann, 1999.

Jacques, Claude, and Freeman, Michael (photographs). *Angkor: Cities and Temples,* tr. Tom White. Bangkok, Thailand: River Books; London: Thames and Hudson, 1997.

Jessup, Helen Ibbitson, and Zephir, Thierry, eds. *Millennium of Glory: Sculpture of Angkor and Ancient Cambodia.* Washington, DC: National Gallery of Art, 1997.

Lopetcharat, Somkiart. *Lao Buddha: The Image and Its History.* Bangkok, Thailand: Siam International Book Company, 2000.

Luce, Gordon H. *Old Burma—Early Pagan,* 3 vols. Locust Valley, NY: J. J. Augustin, 1970.

Mazzeo, Donatella, and Antonini, Chiara Silvi. *Ancient Cambodia.* New York: Grosset and Dunlap, 1978.

Moore, Elizabeth; U-win Pe; and Mayer, Hansjörg (photographs). *Shwedagon: Golden Pagoda of Myanmar.* London: Thames and Hudson, 1999.

Nou, Jean-Louis, and Frédéric, Louis. *Borobudur.* New York: Abbeville Press, 1994.

Rawson, Philip. *The Art of Southeast Asia.* London: Thames and Hudson, 1995.

Siribhadra, Smitthi, and Moore, Elizabeth. *Palaces of the Gods: Khmer Art and Architecture in Thailand.* Bangkok, Thailand: River Books, 1997.

Soekmono, R. *The Javanese Candi: Function and Meaning.* Leiden, Netherlands: Brill, 1995.

Strachan, Paul. *Pagan: Art and Architecture of Old Burma.* Whiting Bay, UK: Kiscadale, 1989.

Thaw, Aung. *Historical Sites in Burma.* Rangoon, Myanmar: Ministry of Union Culture, 1972.

Wales, H. G. Quaritch. *Dvāravatī: The Earliest Kingdom of Siam.* London: Quaritch, 1969.

Woodward, Hiram. *The Sacred Sculpture of Thailand.* Baltimore, MD: Walters Art Gallery, 1997.

Woodward, Hiram. *The Art and Architecture of Thailand from Prehistoric Times through the Thirteenth Century.* Leiden, Netherlands: Brill, 2003.

ROBERT L. BROWN

SPACE, SACRED

One way to investigate the historical and geographical spread of Buddhism in Asia is to focus on the creation, uses, and transformations of sites that religion characterized as sacred. Every Asian country where Buddhism became a major cultural force was remarkably affected by the production of its sacred spaces. While referring to continental examples, this entry will focus on JAPAN, where such creations and transformations occurred in a massive and profound manner.

Indian Buddhism

The original sacred space acknowledged by all schools of Buddhism is the actual site where the historical Buddha is said to have to have achieved BODHI (AWAKENING), BODH GAYĀ in northeastern India, as is attested by the fact that sculpted depictions of the site in question were made before the Buddha himself was ever represented. The symbolism attached to this site formed a kind of anchor that most subsequent notions and practices referred to, consciously or not. A secondary, early form of sacred space involved PILGRIMAGES undertaken by monastic or lay figures who wished to "follow the footsteps" of the historical Buddha; many of these footsteps are described in a vast number of sūtras, most of which begin with a statement identifying sites where the Buddha would have given his teachings. These sites are still visited by Buddhists from around the world, which seems to indicate that sacred space is not to be separated from practices and ideas linked to salvation (SOTERIOLOGY). One can see throughout Asia, for example, stones in which imprints of the soles of the Buddha's feet have been engraved with a variety of symbols. Borrowed from pre-Buddhist Indian mythology, this feature of footprints left by divine entities stands for the notion that each Buddhist school is a "way" or "PATH" that is said to be a replica of the process whereby the Buddha reached NIRVĀṆA, or, as became fairly common later, that the footprints in question are "traces" that the post-nirvāṇa Buddha would have left on the ground wherever local traditions claimed he would have manifested himself, preached, or performed supernatural deeds.

One of the earliest aspects of the production of Buddhist sacred space in India was, perhaps, the construction of STŪPAS, stone monuments that were used as reliquaries and soon became objects of veneration. As time passed and the legend of the Buddha's life took shape, some of these stūpas were adorned with bas-relief representations of important moments presumed to have taken place during the Buddha's life and, later, with events that would have occurred in his former lives. Originally venerated as repositories of relics (physical supports for memories held to be true), stūpas became memorials constructed and adorned in such a way that they would evoke specific recollections of the Buddha's path, elicit intended readings of major experiences in the Buddha's life, and support practices, such as circumambulation (walking clockwise around any Buddhist site of cult). As MONKS and NUNS engaged in austerities and built retreats, cave complexes were dug at the base of cliffs; some were plain cells, others were sanctuaries adorned with paintings or statues. Among the many cave complexes scattered throughout Asia, Ellora and AJAṆṬĀ in India and DUNHUANG in China are, perhaps, the most famous. Monasteries also came to be erected on or near such sites. Their scope, sometimes immense, attests to the patronage Buddhism enjoyed on the part of rulers or wealthy merchants, as can be seen in the stupendous monastery complexes of Pagan and Rangoon in Myanmar (Burma), Angkor Wat and Angkor Thom in Kampuchea (Cambodia), BOROBUDUR in Java, Lhasa in Tibet, the various capital cities of China, and many others.

Pilgrims prostrating themselves at the site of the Buddha's enlightenment in Bodh Gayā, India. © Alison Wright/Corbis. Reproduced by permission.

Monasteries

The construction of monasteries (*tera, ji,* or *ji-in*) in Japan began shortly after Buddhism was recognized by the court in the mid-sixth century C.E. The layout of these structures shows Chinese and Korean influences, while some aspects of the organization of their space reveals their relation to the COSMOLOGY and cosmography described in the ABHIDHARMA literature of early Buddhism. Typically, the four corner pillars of a monastery represent the abodes of the Four Heavenly Kings (Japanese, *shitennō*), who are said to protect the east, south, west, and north corners of Mount Sumeru, the mountain located at the center of the Buddhist cosmos. Toward the back of such a monastery is a platform called *shumidan* (platform of Mount Sumeru), on which statues of buddhas and bodhisattvas are placed. Some monastery architecture, then, was based on cosmographic principles, but these cultic sites became sacred only after *eye-opening* rites (Japanese, *kaigen shiki, kaigen kuyō*), in which a ritualist paints in an iris or otherwise sanctifies the sense of vision—both in the sense that BUDDHAS and BODHISATTVAS bless devotees by establishing visual contact and in the sense that anyone is blessed by looking at a buddha or bodhisattva. Furthermore, the transformation of a statue into a living icon required a ritualized exchange of breath between an officiating monk and a statue, and recent discoveries of relics and fashioned replicas of internal organs in statues prove that what was thought to be representations were, by ritual fiat, living entities and sacred spaces par excellence.

Most of Japan's earliest Buddhist monasteries were erected in plains or cities. Starting in the eighth century, however, monasteries were built on the sides of or near the summits of mountains, and concepts of sacred space thereby gained more intricate meanings, as did spatial, ritualized practices. An obvious but perhaps simplistic indication to this effect is the fact that fourteen Japanese mountains bear the name Misen, which refers to Mount Sumeru. Seventeen bear the name Ben[zai]ten, the Buddhist form of the Vedic deity Sarasvatī. Twenty-two bear the name Fudō, the king of sapience Acala, an important deity in esoteric Buddhism. Twenty-seven bear the name Kyōzuka (sūtra-burial mounds), although many more mountains bearing different names were also sites of sūtra-burial. Twenty-nine bear the name Buddha, either as a title or as the name of the historical Buddha, Śākyamuni. Another twenty-nine bear the name Jizō (Kṣitigarbha bodhisattva). Thirty-one bear the name Dainichi nyorai (Mahāvairocana tathāgata). Thirty-two bear the name Kokuzō (Ākāśagarbha bodhisattva). Forty-three bear the name Yakushi (the buddha of medicine, Bhaiṣajyaguru). Fifty-four bear the name Kannon (the bodhisattva of compassion, Avalokiteśvara). And 101 mountains are simply named *gongen* (avatar), a term used to refer to a local native deity that is considered to be a manifestation of a buddha or bodhisattva. Several hundred other such examples of the occupation of striking features of Japan's topography by the Buddhist pantheon attest to the creation of Buddhist sacred landscapes. This naming of mountains on the basis of buddhas, bodhisattvas, various Buddhist or Indian deities, and local Japanese deities should not be given too much weight, however, for it merely suggests certain aspects of topophilia and does not account for the fact that thousands of mountains were the object of more complex sacralization by means of Buddhist rituals, narratives, and other techniques described below.

Ritualized geography

As MAHĀYĀNA Buddhism evolved around the beginning of the common era, one finds important statements concerning the actual site where the Buddha achieved awakening. In *Dazhidu lun* (*Treatise on the Great Perfection of Wisdom*) attributed to NĀGĀRJUNA, for example, this site is referred to as *bodhimaṇḍa* (site of awakening; Japanese, *dōjō*), and it is described as consisting of an immense diamond protruding at the base of the tree where the Buddha would have sat in meditation. In later writings the term *bodhimaṇḍa* came to denote not only the physical site where the Buddha reached awakening, but the psychological situation or "mental space" he would have attained or produced through meditation. As a consequence, this term became an important aspect of the properties of sacred space in the context of ritualized practices, in which spiritual or subjective states were always linked to material or objective sites. Indeed, countless manuals detailing how rituals must be conducted contain an important section called "visualization of the site of practice/space of awakening" (*dōjōkan*), which details how a ritual platform (*dan*) must be constructed and consecrated, as well as specific steps in the ritualized meditations that are supposed to lead to a visualization of the residence of a given buddha or bodhisattva that is thereby made to occupy the space of the ritual platform, as well as the mind of the ritualists.

In a number of cases in Japan, such ritualized practices and exercises in visualization were projected onto mountains, which were then regarded as the *dōjō* of a certain buddha or bodhisattva, that is, its site of residence, manifestation, and practice. The oldest Japanese document detailing this process of identification of a mountain with the abode (Pure Land) of a bodhisattva was written by KŪKAI (Kōbō Daishi, 774–835) in 814. Kūkai describes therein the first ascent of Mount Futara (today called Nantaizan and located in Nikkō) by the monk Shōdō, who, reaching the summit of its volcanic dome, envisioned it as the abode of Kannon (Avalokiteśvara, the bodhisattva of compassion). Shōdō then sculpted a representation of Kannon, which can be seen today in Chūzenji, located at the foot of that mountain. Kūkai's rationale for identifying Mount Futara with Kannon's residence was the toponym, which allowed an association between the Japanese name of the mountain, Futara, and the Japanized version of Kannon's Pure Land, Fudaraku (Sanskrit, Potalaka). The entire area surrounding this mountain subsequently became a major site of SHUGENDŌ (Japan's mountain religion), and ever more intricate practices continued, over the centuries, to elaborate the sacred character of the region. Such identifications of pure lands of buddhas and bodhisattvas with Japanese mountains reached full development with the nationwide spread of Shugendō, and ultimately led to the notion that Japan, in its entirety, was the actual residence of buddhas and bodhisattvas as well as other deities and their retinues. Kūkai also wrote texts concerning the rituals used in the establishment of sacred grounds where monasteries were built; the term for these grounds, *kekkai* (bounded realm), refers to a ritually purified area that can range from a ten-foot square hut, as in the tea ceremony, for example, to large geographical areas over which the government or individuals relinquished all control, as in the case of sacred mountains.

Several doctrinal propositions undergirded this geohistorical process. First, a central tenet of Shingon esoteric Buddhism (*tōmitsu*) held that this world is the manifestation of its central buddha, Mahāvairocana (Japanese, Dainichi). Second, and very closely related to the former proposition although structurally different, the Shingi-Shingon branch of esoteric Buddhism created by Kakuban (1094–1143) held that this world is the Pure Land of buddhas and bodhisattvas (*mitsugon jōdo*, Pure Land adorned with mysteries). Third, a doctrine issued from Tendai esoteric circles (*taimitsu*) proposed that this world's flora could achieve buddhahood (*sōmoku jōbutsu*), and this proposition enjoyed a spectacular success in the medieval period and evolved to the point that, in some cases, the flora was regarded as the Buddha itself (*sōmoku zebutsu*). Fourth, various PURE LAND SCHOOLS proposed that certain geographical locations were gates to the transcendental Pure Land of the buddha Amida (Sanskrit, AMITĀBHA) or of various bodhisattvas, with an emphasis on Kannon. As a consequence, quite a few monastery gardens and buildings were built as physical replicas of various scriptural descriptions of the Pure Lands.

Last but not least, the medieval assumption that many local deities, the indigenous *kami* of Shintō who were objects of cult in precise locations, were manifestations of buddhas and bodhisattvas became a major social practice. Known as HONJI SUIJAKU (Buddhist deities leaving their traces in the form of Shintō deities), this assumption and the related set of practices were responsible for a systematic association between Buddhist and non-Buddhist deities and their respective cultic sites, and for the addition of Buddhist notions of sacred space to native sentiments and practices. Nowhere was this system of associations, as well as the former four doctrinal points, more evident than in the development of pilgrimage and the formulation of Shugendō.

Shugendō

An amalgamation of Buddhist, Daoist, and Japanese native notions and practices, Shugendō slowly arose and became a loose institutional system in the eleventh century, by which time official records indicate the presence of its practitioners (called *shugenja* or *yamabushi*) in many parts of Japan, including the imperial court, where they served as thaumaturges and healers. Shugendō's dominant features include tenets and practices that are central to both Shingon and Tendai forms of esotericism, as well as longstanding, pre-Buddhist notions of sacred space. Mountains that had been regarded as the abode of gods (many of them, incidentally, female entities), or as gods themselves, became objects of worship on the part of these mountain ascetics, but they also came to be treated as off-limits to all but male ascetics. Women were only allowed up to the point of certain boundaries marked by engraved stones or wooden boards that read *nyonin kekkai* (limit for women). Some peaks became the object of ritualized ascents, while mountain ranges became the object of highly ritualized peregrinations, the goal of which was to realize buddhahood in this body by becoming one with the land, each and every feature of which was conceived of as a repository or natural form of the Buddha's teachings. Eventually, several hundred mountains became sacred to Shugendō practitioners.

The main organizational characteristic of the Shugendō practitioners' ascents and peregrinations was to associate a given trek through mountain ranges with the ritual acts and meditations monks of esoteric Buddhism engaged in when using MAṆḌALAS. Two main maṇḍalas were used in both Tendai and Shingon esoteric branches: the Adamantine maṇḍala (*kongō-kai mandara*), which was drawn as geometric elements containing iconographic representations as well as symbols in order to represent the essential character of the absolute knowledge of the buddha Mahāvairocana (Dainichi nyorai), and the Matrix maṇḍala (*taizō-kai mandara*), which represented the various objects of that knowledge. There were many other maṇḍalas, dedicated to single deities and known as *besson mandara*, many of which were also used in Shugendō. Elaborate rituals led to the achievement of mystic identification with the deities shown in these maṇḍalas: Following a specific course through a given maṇḍala, ritualists engaged in the practice of the triple mystery of the body, speech, and mind. Buddhahood was supposed to be reached when distinctions between the knower and the known (subject and object) were annihilated. In Shugendō, this ritual process was projected over fairly large geographical areas: One mountain range would be considered the natural form of one maṇḍala, and a nearby range was considered the natural form of the other maṇḍala. Each peak rising in these ranges, as well as some of the boulders, springs, waterfalls, and other topographic features, were regarded as the residence of one of the many deities represented in the maṇḍalas, and the practitioners would spend several weeks peregrinating through such "natural maṇḍalas" while dedicating rituals to these deities. Practitioners usually followed one maṇḍala course through a given range in spring, the other maṇḍala course through a nearby range in autumn, and a summer retreat in the central mountain. Sacred space, then, encompassed vast areas that were to be crossed ritually, and stood as guarantor of physical and spiritual salvation. Such "mandalized" areas were established along several ranges, from the northernmost part of Honshū Island to the southernmost part of Kyushu Island, and they ranged from relatively small areas to the entirety of Japan. Related mandalization processes also occurred in Tibet; further research should indicate whether other countries engaged in similar processes of sacralization.

Another major technique used in Shugendō to produce sacred space was to consider individual mountains or entire mountain ranges as the natural embodiments of Buddhist scriptures. The Katsuragi range in the Kansai area, for example, was crossed by practitioners who stopped at twenty-eight caves adorned with statues or where scriptures had been interred; each cave was supposed to symbolically represent one of the twenty-eight chapters of the LOTUS SŪTRA (SADDHARMAPUṆḌARĪKA-SŪTRA). On Kyushu Island, the Kunisaki peninsula was regarded as the lotus pedestal on which the Buddha preached the *Lotus Sūtra*; eventually, twenty-eight monasteries, each corresponding to a chapter of the scripture, were built on the slopes of the peninsula, and there too peregrinations leading to these monasteries were held to enable one to grasp the multiple meanings of the sūtra (this peregrination is still performed once every twelve years). Also in northern Kyushu, Mount Hiko was regarded as the site where MAITREYA (Japanese, Miroku), the next Buddha, would achieve buddhahood. Scriptures describe the palace where Maitreya awaits this moment as being composed of forty-nine chambers, and on and around Mount Hiko forty-nine caves were made to correspond to these chambers. As time passed, two mountains ranges extending north and northwest from Mount Hiko were treated as natural maṇḍalas. Furthermore, Mount Hiko itself was regarded as the natural embodiment of a Tendai doctrine known as the Four Lands (*shido kekkai*), which were progressive spiritual stages reached in a ritualized meditation on the *Lotus Sūtra.* In this case, the mountain was divided into four superimposed zones, each separated by a sacred gate (*torii*), and life was strictly regulated therein. In the lowest zone, ascetics and laypeople could commingle and reside; in the second zone, only ascetics could reside; in the third zone, which consisted of a variety of caves and sites for austerities, neither residences nor women were allowed.

The fourth zone, which encompassed the triple summit of the mountain, could be visited only by ascetics who had completed fifteen maṇḍala courses through the mountain ranges, but even they could not stay for long, for no bodily fluid, of any kind, was to defile the sacred space in question. The study of Shugendō has barely begun in Western countries, but it is obvious that this unique system was instrumental in the formation of concepts and practices related to the notion that sacred space is, in fact, the entirety of the natural world. These features illustrate a historical process whereby reverence for discrete "sites of cult" was enhanced by Shugendō rituals and concepts, and evolved into a "cult of sites" that is representative of premodern Japanese culture.

Pilgrimage routes

Eventually, many of these sites became pilgrimage stops for both priests and laity. Pilgrimages are structurally different from the mandalized peregrinations Shugendō practitioners performed, however, and a single case will serve to illustrate this important difference. In central Japan's Kii peninsula, Shugendō practitioners went through two mandalized courses, one leading from Yoshino, located in the north, to Kumano, located in the southernmost part of the peninsula, and one leading from Kumano to Yoshino. Only male ascetics could engage in these mandalized peregrinations. But there was also a pilgrimage to Kumano, which emperors, aristocrats, warriors, and commoners alike engaged in. Its course, however, was radically different: It entailed following the western coast of the peninsula in a southerly direction, and then entering the mountainous ranges of the southern part of the peninsula to eventually reach Kumano. This pilgrimage course was marked by ninety-nine sites dedicated to protectors of various deities. In other words, Kumano was considered a sacred space by all, but it could be reached only by different roads, one "professional" (the mandalized peregrination), and the other, "common" (the pilgrimage). Furthermore, since Kumano came to be regarded as the Pure Land on earth of Kannon, the bodhisattva of compassion, it was placed at the head of yet another pilgrimage, dedicated to Kannon's thirty-three manifestations, each worshiped in different monasteries connected by pilgrimage roads in central Japan. This pilgrimage was so popular that it was duplicated in many areas of Japan: Today there are at least fifty-four different pilgrimage courses dedicated to these thirty-three forms of Kannon.

Starting in the medieval period, religious narratives detailing the origins, supernatural events, and the topography of Japan's famed sacred sites were elaborated and written down. This fairly large body of literature indicates that sacred space cannot be separated from sacred time, that the history of these cultic sites is an intrinsic feature of their sacredness, and that lo-

Monks in the Sacred Caves at Pak Ou, Laos. © Christophe Loviny/Corbis. Reproduced by permission.

cal topography, natural features (in particular, sources of water), Buddhist monasteries, shrines to local gods, and narratives formed a single coherent whole. In other words, sacred spaces were fundamentally associated with postulated recollections of the past and ritualized practices, all tied up in attitudes and acts of devotion or piety that have been collectively referred to as *geopiety* by the human geographer J. K. Wright and *topophilia* by Yi-Fu Tuan.

In contemporary Japan, about one hundred different pilgrimage courses linking more than five hundred monasteries in all parts of the country attest to the complexity of sacred space and exemplify the equally complex nature of the Japanese people's spiritual and emotional attachments to their land. Shikoku Island, for instance, boasts of several mountains that were objects of Shugendō practices, and it is also the site of Japan's most famous pilgrimage. Kūkai, the founder of the Shingon school of esoteric Buddhism, was born there in the late-eighth century and he practiced austerities in some of these mountains. During the medieval period, Kūkai became the object of a nationwide cult, and a pilgrimage dedicated to him was established around Shikoku Island; it consists of a course linking eighty-eight monasteries, and is still quite popular. Each monastery is sacred, obviously, but so is the entire course, and many pilgrims consider Shikoku Island itself to be sacred.

Historical, social, and economic aspects

Sacred spaces, however, have a history. To take one example, Japan's highest mountain, Mount Fuji, was originally regarded as the abode of one local god; when Buddhism took charge of the cult around the twelfth century, the mountain came to be viewed as the abode of three buddhas and bodhisattvas and of that god as well, and it became a center of Shugendō. By the seventeenth century, however, Shugendō's influence waned (for political reasons), and Mount Fuji became the object of mass pilgrimages on the part of laypeople, as a consequence of which the understandings of the mountain's sacred character radically changed. Another example of major historical changes is the Ise Shrine, located on the eastern coast of the Kii peninsula. It is composed of an Inner Shrine dedicated to the ancestral god of the imperial house, and of an

Outer Shrine dedicated to a god of food. During the medieval period, these sanctuaries became the object of complex associations with esoteric Buddhism, which viewed them as yet another manifestation of the Adamantine and Matrix maṇḍalas. Ise subsequently became the object of mass pilgrimages, and for several centuries pilgrims were escorted by professional religious guides (*onshi*, or *oshi*), who gave instructions concerning the varied features of these sites of cult's sacred features, ranging from trees, rivers, and waterfalls, to caves, monasteries, and shrines. In the early modern period, however, Buddhism became the object of critiques that led, ultimately, to the separation of theretofore unified Shintō-Buddhist cults throughout Japan. The thirty-seven Buddhist monasteries of Ise were destroyed at the end of the nineteenth century, and today Ise is regarded as a Shintō cultic site, with no trace of Buddhism whatsoever.

It is important, therefore, to stress that the term *sacred space* is sometimes misleading because its oft-found emphasis on spirituality tends to generate an avoidance of the universally present material features of its historical production, as well as an avoidance of the many conflicts it caused or witnessed in the course of history. That is, the sacredness of certain sites or regions was instituted or maintained through various forms of an occupation of land (one of which was control over the people who lived there), and this socio-historical fact suggests that studies of the term *sacred space* need to include historical, social, and economic aspects. Japan's (and other countries') shrines and monasteries were established on pieces of land that used to belong to an individual or the government. Measured on the basis of a technique called, in Japanese, *shiichi* (four corners), the area where they were to be erected was ritually cleansed and propitiated, and the individual or ruling entity that entrusted that area to religious authorities thereby gave up all and any control over it, especially taxes. In order to meet the monasteries' needs for regular maintenance and repair, as well as in order to enhance their visibility and prestige, individuals or rulers commended land estates to them, and cultic sites became powerful economic entities. During the medieval period this estate system eroded and fell apart, and religious authorities had to look for different funding sources and traveled across the land in search of financial assistance while chanting the sacred character of their sites of cult and encouraging people to engage in pilgrimage.

Pilgrimage, then, arose in a specific social and economic climate, and the narratives mentioned earlier played a great part in this development. Still today, pilgrimages have an important economic dimension that is all too often ignored in the analysis of sacred space, and the long but sometimes violent history of the sacred sites visited by pilgrims should be critically assessed in light (or shadow) of the stable myths that are often attached to the notion of sacred space.

See also: **Cave Sanctuaries; Consecration; Kailāśa (Kailash); Monasticism; Relics and Relics Cults**

Bibliography

Grapard, Allan G. "Flying Mountains and Walkers of Emptiness." *History of Religions* 21, no. 3 (1982): 191–221.

Grapard, Allan G. "Japan's Ignored Cultural Revolution: The Separation of Shintō and Buddhist Divinities in Meiji (*shimbutsu bunri*) and a Case Study: Tōnomine." *History of Religions* 23, no. 3 (1984): 240–265.

Grapard, Allan G. "Lotus in the Mountain, Mountain in the Lotus: Rokugo Kaizan Nimmon Daibosatsu Hongi." *Monumenta Nipponica* (Tokyo) 41, no. 1 (1986): 21–50.

Grapard, Allan G. "The Textualized Mountain–Enmountained Text: The Lotus Sūtra in Kunisaki." In *The Lotus Sūtra in Japanese Culture,* ed. George J. Tanabe, Jr., and Willa Jane Tanabe. Honolulu: University of Hawaii Press, 1989.

Grapard, Allan G. *The Protocol of the Gods: A Study of the Kasuga Cult in Japanese History.* Berkeley: University of California Press, 1992.

Grapard, Allan G. "Geosophia, Geognosis, and Geopiety: Orders of Significance in Japanese Representations of Space." In *NowHere: Space, Time and Modernity,* ed. Roger Friedland and Deirdre Boden. Berkeley: University of California Press, 1994.

Grapard, Allan G. "Geotyping Sacred Space: The Case of Mount Hiko in Japan." In *Sacred Space: Shrine, City, Land,* ed. Benjamin Z. Kedar and R. J. Zwi Werblowsky. New York: New York University Press, 1998.

Higuchi, Tadahiko. *The Visual and Spatial Structure of Landscapes,* tr. Charles Terry. Cambridge, MA: MIT Press, 1988.

Huber, Toni. *The Cult of Pure Crystal Mountain: Popular Pilgrimage and Visionary Landscapes in Southeast Tibet.* New York: Oxford University Press, 1999.

Miksic, John. *Borobudur: Golden Tale of the Buddhas.* Singapore: Periplus, 1990.

Statler, Oliver. *Japanese Pilgrimage.* New York: Morrow, 1983.

Tuan, Yi-Fu. *Topophilia: A Study of Environmental Perception, Attitudes and Values.* Englewood Cliffs, NJ: Prentice Hall, 1974.

ALLAN G. GRAPARD

SRI LANKA

Sri Lanka is home to the world's oldest continuing Buddhist civilization. Brāhmī inscriptions etched in stone on drip ledges above natural caves in the country's North-Central province indicate that hermitages have been dedicated by Buddhist LAITY for the meditation needs of monks since the third century B.C.E. Moreover, the fourth- and fifth-century C.E. monastic chronicles, the *Dīpavaṃsa* (*Chronicle of the Island*) and the *Mahāvaṃsa* (*Great Chronicle*), contain a series of myths in which the Lankan king Devanāṃpiya Tissa (third century B.C.E.), a contemporary of the Indian emperor AŚOKA, is said to have been converted to the Buddha's teachings by Aśoka's own missionary son, Mahinda. Thus, from inscriptions and monastic literary traditions, it is known that by the third century B.C.E. lineages of forest monks supported by Buddhist laity were established on the island in the region that became Lanka's political center for thirteen subsequent centuries. Since Aśoka is also thought to have provided support for Devanāṃpiya Tissa's abhiṣeka (coronation), it would seem that Buddhism became formally associated with Lanka's KINGSHIP by this time as well. For more than two millennia, until the British dethroned the last Lankan king in 1815, a symbiotic relationship entailing mutual support and legitimation between the Lankan kings and the Buddhist SAṄGHA (community) was sustained, either as an ideal or in actual practice.

Over the course of this long history, other forms of Buddhism joined the predominant THERAVĀDA bhikkhu (monk) and *bhikkhunī* (nun) saṅghas, which the *Mahāvaṃsa* asserts were established by Aśoka's children, Mahinda and his sister Saṅghamittā, respectively, and whose lineages were preserved by the Theravāda Mahāvihāra *nikāya*. These included the cults of MAHĀYĀNA BODHISATTVAS such as Avalokiteśvara, and the teachings of several Mahāyāna schools and of tantric Buddhist masters associated with Mahāvihāra's rival in Anurādhapura, the Abhayagiri *nikāya*, which were established and thrived, particularly during the seventh through the tenth centuries C.E.

The Anurādhapura period

FAXIAN (ca. 337–ca. 418 C.E.), the itinerant Chinese Buddhist pilgrim, has provided a valuable description of fifth-century Anurādhapura, reporting that approximately eight thousand Buddhist monks then resided in the capital city. Faxian also reports that a public ritual procession of the *Daḷadā* (tooth-relic of the Buddha) was celebrated annually, that the cult of Śri Mahābōdhi (a graft of the original bodhi tree at BODH GAYĀ in India) was regularly venerated and lavishly supported by the laity and the king, and that Lankan kings had built massive STŪPAS to commemorate the Buddha and his relics. Well before Faxian's time and long thereafter, the city of Anurādhapura had become a politically powerful and cosmopolitan center whose successful economy had been made possible through the development of sophisticated hydraulic engineering and through the establishment of trade with partners as far flung as China in the east and Rome in the west. Furthermore, the city had become the administrative pivot of the three great monastic *nikāyas* (chapters) of the Lankan Buddhist saṅgha: the Theravāda Mahāvihāra; and the more doctrinally eclectic Abhayagiri and Jetavana chapters, each of which systematically established a vast array of affiliated village monasteries and forest hermitages throughout the domesticated rice-growing countryside. During the first millennium C.E., the three *nikāyas* in Anurādhapura and their affiliated monasteries dominated every facet of social, economic, educational, and cultural life. Some have argued that just as Lankan polity was expected to be the chief patron supporting the saṅgha, so the saṅgha functioned as a "Department of State" for the kingship. Perhaps somewhat exaggerated, that assertion does point to the extent to which Buddhist institutions became the basic social infrastructure in Lanka for many centuries.

Given the congenial relationship between polity and religion, the Anurādhapura period witnessed the fluorescence of an economically advanced and artistically sophisticated culture. Although the only surviving examples of painting are the frescos of heavenly maidens (perhaps *apsaras*) found at Sīgiriya, thousands of free-standing stone sculptures of the Buddha, scores of stone-carved bas-reliefs, and hundreds of bronzes are still extant, including the famous colossal images at Avukana and the meditative Buddhas that remain within the ruins of the Abhayagiri monastic complex at Anurādhapura. Early anthropomorphic images of the Buddha in Lanka bear a stylistic, and sometimes material, affinity with Buddha images created at Amarāvatī in south India, while images from the later Anurādhapura period, such as the eighth-century Avukana image, reflect the development of a distinctive Lankan style that emphasized the significance of the Buddha as a *mahāpuruṣa* (cosmic person).

The *Mahāvaṃsa* asserts that the Buddhist CANON (*Tripiṭaka*; Pāli, *Tipiṭaka*) was first committed to writing during the reign of King Vaṭṭagāmiṇī Abhaya in the first century B.C.E. at Aluvihāra just north of Matale, inaugurating, perhaps, the tradition of inscribing Buddhist texts on to *ola* leaves, a tradition of committing the dharma to handwriting that continued into the nineteenth century. In rare instances, texts were also inscribed on gold or copper plates, such as the gold leaves bearing an eighth-century fragment of a Sanskrit *Prajñāpāramitā-sūtra* (*Perfection of Wisdom Sūtra*), found within the massive STŪPA at Jetavana in Anurādhapura in the early 1980s.

In addition to the Pāli *Tipiṭaka* and the Pāli monastic chronicles *Dīpavaṃṣa* and *Mahāvaṃsa*, the fifth and sixth centuries were the backdrop for the commentaries produced by BUDDHAGHOSA. His *Visuddhimagga* (*Path of Purification*), an elaborate and precise exegesis of *sīla* (*śīla*; English, morality), samādhi (meditation), and *paññā* or PRAJÑĀ (WISDOM)—the three elemental principles of practice that Buddhaghosa regarded as the bases of the Buddha's "noble eightfold PATH"—eventually became an enduring centerpiece of normative orthodoxy for Theravāda in Sri Lanka and later in Southeast Asia. The *Visuddhimagga* stressed the interrelated and dependent nature of *sīla*, samādhi, and *paññā*, and the fundamental reality of *paticcasamupāda* or PRATĪTYASAMUTPĀDA (DEPENDENT ORIGINATION).

The Polonnaruva era

Beginning with the Polonnaruva era (eleventh through thirteenth century C.E.), and especially during the reign of Parākramabāhu I (1153–1186 C.E.), when the saṅgha was reunified after its demise by south Indian Cōḷa invaders who had demolished Anurādhapura in the late tenth century, Theravāda became the exclusive form of doctrinal orthodoxy patronized by the kingship in Sri Lanka. It was specifically this reconstituted Theravāda that was exported to Burma (Myanmar) in the eleventh century and subsequently into northern Thailand, spreading from those regions to become the dominant religion of mainland Southeast Asia. What was not reconstituted at Polonnaruva, however, was the *bhikkhunīsaṅgha*, a sorority that had thrived during the Anurādhapura centuries and had spread its lineage as far as China. Yet Polonnaruva became a marvelous city for a span of about 150 years before it was sacked by another south Indian invasion. Although its beautiful stūpas could not rival the size of the Abhayagiri, Jetavana, and Ruvanvälisāya topes in Anurādhapura, and although its sculptures lacked the plastic fluidity of times past, the architecture, literature, and educational institutions of Polonnaruva were unparalleled anywhere in South or Southeast Asia at that time. The massive *Alahena* monastic university, a bastion of Theravāda orthodoxy, at one time housed as many as ten thousand monks.

It was also at Polonnaruva and in the courts of kings who soon followed, such as Parākramabāhu II at thirteenth-century Daṁbadeṇiya, that new literary innovations were cultivated, in part due to the stimulus and presence of Hinduism and Sanskrit literature, and in part due to the maturation of the Sinhala language itself. At Polonnaruva, the Hindu temples built by the Cōḷa invaders had not been destroyed by the reconquering Sinhalas in the eleventh century because the queens of the Sinhala kings, who were brought from south India, were nominally Hindu, as were their relations and retinues. Thus, the royal court headed by a Sinhala Buddhist king was heavily influenced by a classical Sanskritic or Hindu presence seen not only in the substance and style reflected in contemporary sections of the *Cūḷavaṃsa* (*Minor Chronicles*, the sequel to the *Mahāvaṃsa*), but also in the cultic life and sculptural creations of Polonnaruva, which included the veneration and depiction of Hindu deities such as VIṢṆU and Śiva. In this context, Guruḷugōmi, a Buddhist *upāsaka* (layman), composed the first Sinhala works of prose, including the *Amāvatura* (*The Flood of Nectar*), a reworking of the life of the Buddha aimed at demonstrating his powers to convert others to the truth of dharma. Since the *Amāvatura* seems to have been written in a conscious effort to avoid using Sanskrit words, some have suggested that his writings reflect an antipathy for an ever-growing Hindu influence on Sinhala Buddhist culture in general. The late Polonnaruva era also marks the creation of many other important Sinhalese Theravāda Buddhist classics, including the *Butsaraṇa* (*Refuge of the Buddha*), the *Pūjāvaliya* (*The Garland of Offerings*), and the *Saddharma Ratnāvaliya* (*The Garland of Jewels of the Good Doctrine*), all didactic and devotional works.

Hinduization of Buddhist culture in Sri Lanka

While the destruction of institutional Buddhism at Anurādhapura and the reconstruction of the saṅgha at Polonnaruva may have led in general to the eclipse of Mahāyāna and tantric cults in Lanka, invasions from south India beginning in the tenth century and the increasing numbers of military mercenaries who followed during the politically volatile thirteenth and fourteenth centuries only increased the presence and influence of Hindu cults in the Sinhala Buddhist religious culture of the era. During the fourteenth century, when a retreating Buddhist kingship established its capital in the Kandyan highlands at Gampola, Hindu deities such as Viṣṇu, Skanda, the goddess Pattinī, and Ganesha, as well as a host of other local deities associated with specific regions and natural phenomena, were incorporated into an evolving pantheon of Sinhala deities. They were recast as gods whose warrants for acting in the world on behalf of Buddhist devotees were subject to the sanctioning of the Buddha's dharma. The highest of these deities, worshipped within the same halls where the Buddha was worshipped or in adjacent shrines (*devālāyas*) , came to be styled as BODHISATTVAS, or "buddhas in-the-making," and a vast literature of ballads, poems, and sagas in Sinhala, some inspired by the Sanskrit purāṇas (mythic stories), was created to edify devotees over the ensuing several centuries.

By the fifteenth century, the island had been again reunified politically by Parākramabāhu VI, whose capital at Kōṭṭe on the southwest coast became the hub of an eclectic renaissance of religious culture epitomized by the *gamavāsi* (village-oriented monk) Śrī Rāhula, whose linguistic dexterity (he was known as "master of six languages") and concomitant affinities for popular religious and magical practices, refracted the syncretic character of religion at the time. Śrī Rāhula is perhaps best remembered for writing two classical Sinhala *sandēśaya* poems styled after the Sanskrit poet Kālidāsa's *Meghadhūta* (*Cloud Messenger*) that, while glorifying the Buddha as the "god beyond the gods," appealed directly to the gods for divine assistance in sustaining the well-being of the Buddhist KINGSHIP and its administration. Vīdāgama Maitreya, a WILDERNESS MONK (*araññavāsi*) and one of Parākramabāhu's childhood mentors, wrote the *Buduguṇalāṃkāraya* (*In Praise of the Buddha's Qualities*) as a scathing critique of the increasing Hinduization of Buddhist culture. These two great monks, both of whom were deeply involved in competing trajectories of court and monastic cultures, represent an ancient and continuing tension regarding the nature of the monastic vocation: as a matter of caring for the "welfare of the many" (the village monk) or engaging in the "rhinoceros-like solitary life" of a forest meditator.

Colonial and postcolonial eras

By the sixteenth century, the Portuguese had begun to interfere with the court at Kōṭṭe and eventually converted King Dharmapāla to Christianity, exacerbating an increasingly fractious political context that led in the 1590s to the establishment of a new line of Sinhala Buddhist kings in highland Kandy, a new capital city replete with a supportive cast: a *bhikkhusaṅgha* whose lineage was imported from Burma, a new *Daḷadā Maligāvā* (Palace of the Tooth-Relic), and *devālāyas* for the gods who had emerged as the four protective guardian deities of the island. The Kandyans colluded with the Dutch in the mid-seventeenth century to oust the Portuguese. Despite one war in the 1760s during the reign of Kīrti Śrī Rājasiṃha, the Kandyans and the Dutch managed to coexist for a century and a half producing, in effect, distinctive highland and lowland Sinhala cultures. The former styled itself as more purely Sinhala Buddhist, despite the fact that by this time the Kandyan kings were ethnically Tamil, owing to the continuing practice of securing queens from Madurai. But it is remarkable how "Buddhacized" this last line of Lankan kings became. Kīrti Śrī and his brother Rājādi who succeeded him, were responsible for the last great renaissance of Theravāda: first, by reconstituting what had become a decadent saṅgha by introducing a fresh lineage from Thailand that became known as the dominant Siyam Nikāya; second, by appointing a monastic head (*saṅgharāja*) in the person of the learned monk Saraṇamkara, who reemphasized the importance of monastic literary education and moral virtue; third, by providing the means to hold a calendar of Buddhist public rites, including the still annually held *äsaḷa perahära* procession of the *Daḷadā* and the insignia of the guardian deities in Kandy; and fourth, by refurbishing virtually every Buddhist monastery in the kingdom, a commitment that resulted in the artistic birth of the Kandyan school of Buddhist monastery painting.

After the British established their colonial hegemony in the early nineteenth century, Buddhist culture atrophied for several decades. Its revival toward the end of the century was catalyzed in part by the establishment of two new low-country monastic *nikāyas*, the Amarapura and the Rāmañña. Both, in contrast to the Siyam Nikāya, established new lineages from Burma, claimed to be more doctrinally orthodox, emphasized the practice of meditation, and recruited novices without regard to caste. A series of public religious debates between Buddhist monks and Anglican clergy in the low country also fueled the revitalization. Moreover, the revival gained momentum with the arrival of Henry Steel Olcott (1832–1907), an American theosophist who organized and established many

A young novice monk bathes another after their heads were shaved as part of an ordination ceremony at a monastery in Colombo, Sri Lanka. © Anuruddha Lokuhapuarachchi/Reuters/Getty Images. Reproduced by permission.

Buddhist schools modeled on the successful missionary schools administered by the Anglicans. Olcott wrote a widely disseminated "Buddhist Catechism," designed and distributed a Buddhist flag, and helped to organize a liturgical year celebrating full moon days as Buddhist holidays. One of Olcott's early and enthusiastic followers, the ANAGĀRIKA DHARMAPĀLA (1864–1933), transformed the religious revival into a religio-nationalist cause by founding in 1891 the Mahābodhi Society, which sought to regain Buddhist control of Buddhist holy sites in India. In addition, Dharmapāla published his influential *Return to Righteousness* (a detailed excursus on lay Buddhist conduct and spiritual realization aimed at purifying Buddhism of its colonial and popular "contaminations"), and he inspired the laity to emulate their colonial masters' work ethic. Some have argued that Olcott and Dharmapāla successively set into motion a new lay Buddhist religious ethic comparable to the lay-oriented religious culture of Protestant Christianity, a "Protestant Buddhism," so called because of its emphasis on unmediated individual lay religious practice and the importance attached to integrating the significance of spiritual teachings into everyday life.

Aside from "Protestant Buddhism," at least three other features marked the character of Buddhism in twentieth-century Sri Lanka. The first is the reemphasis given to meditation for both monks and laypersons, especially methods of insight (VIPASSANĀ [SANSKRIT, VIPAŚYANĀ]) practice made popular by Burmese masters. The second is the establishment of Buddhist-inspired welfare institutions, such as Sarvodaya, founded in the 1950s by A. T. Ariyaratne (1931–) to reawaken village culture and to stimulate rural economies and social services. The third is the increasing politicization of Buddhism in the postcolonial era, most notably the patterns that can be traced to the pivotal national elections of 1956 when

S. W. R. D. Bandaranaike (1899–1959) and his newly formed Sri Lanka Freedom Party won a landslide election on promises of "Sinhala only" as the national language and Buddhism as the state religion. This posture on language and religion (the basic constituents of ethnic identity in South Asia), as well as other subsequent "Sinhala Buddhist" based education and economic policies, were enacted to redress perceived inequalities resulting from earlier British colonial policies that had favored Tamil interests and disenfranchised the Sinhalese. In turn, these changes became reasons for Tamil alienation, feeding an enduring ethnic conflict dividing Sinhalas and Tamils during the final decades of the twentieth century. In this context, some influential Buddhist monks have colluded with Sinhala politicians to resurrect the ancient rhetoric of the *Mahāvaṃsa* and proclaim Lanka as the exclusive and predestined domain of the Buddhadharma. Others have marched for peace and coexistence.

See also: **Mainstream Buddhist Schools; Sinhala, Buddhist Literature in; Sri Lanka, Buddhist Art in**

Bibliography

Bartholomeusz, Tessa. *Women under the Bo Tree: Buddhist Nuns in Sri Lanka.* Cambridge, UK: Cambridge University Press, 1994.

Bond, George. *The Buddhist Revival in Sri Lanka: Religious Tradition, Reinterpretation, and Response.* Columbia: University of South Carolina Press, 1988.

Carrithers, Michael. *The Forest Monks of Sri Lanka: An Anthropological and Historical Study.* Oxford: Oxford University Press, 1983.

Geiger, Wilhelm, ed. and trans. *The Cūḷavaṃsa,* 2 vols. Colombo, Sri Lanka: Government Printer, 1953.

Geiger, Wilhelm, ed. and trans. *The Mahāvaṃsa.* London: Pāli Text Society, 1964.

Gombrich, Richard. *Precept and Practice: Traditional Buddhism in the Rural Highlands of Ceylon.* Oxford: Clarendon Press, 1971.

Gombrich, Richard, and Obeyesekere, Gananath. *Buddhism Transformed: Religious Change in Sri Lanka.* Princeton, NJ: Princeton University Press, 1988.

Gunawardana, R. A. L. H. *Robe and Plough: Monasticism and Economic Interest in Early Medieval Sri Lanka.* Tucson: University of Arizona Press, 1979.

Holt, John Clifford. *Buddha in the Crown: Avalokitesvara in the Buddhist Traditions of Sri Lanka.* New York: Oxford University Press, 1992.

Holt, John Clifford. *The Religious World of Kīrti Śrī: Buddhism, Art, and Politics in Late Medieval Sri Lanka.* New York: Oxford University Press, 1996.

Kemper, Steven. *The Presence of the Past: Chronicles, Politics, and Culture in Sinhala Life.* Ithaca, NY: Cornell University Press, 1992.

King, Winston Lee. *Theravāda Meditation: The Buddhist Transformation of Yoga.* University Park: Pennsylvania State University Press, 1980.

Malalasekera, G. P. *The Pāli Literature of Ceylon.* Colombo, Sri Lanka: M. D. Gunasena, 1958.

Malalgoda, Kitsiri. *Buddhism in Sinhalese Society, 1750–1900: A Study of Religious Revival and Study.* Berkeley: University of California Press, 1976.

Obeyesekere, Gananath. *The Cult of the Goddess Pattini.* Chicago: University of Chicago Press, 1984.

Seneviratne, H. L. *The Work of Kings: The New Buddhism in Sri Lanka.* Chicago: University of Chicago Press, 1999.

Von Schroeder, Ulrich. *Buddhist Sculptures of Sri Lanka.* Hong Kong: Visual Dharma Publications, 1990.

JOHN CLIFFORD HOLT

SRI LANKA, BUDDHIST ART IN

During the twenty-five hundred years of Sri Lanka's history, its royal capital has been located in a number of places. In chronological order they were Anurādhapura (ca. 500 B.C.E.–1000 C.E., North-Central province); Polonnaruva (1000–1235 C.E., North-Central province); Daṁbadeṇiya (1232–1272 C.E., North-Western province); Yāpahuwa (1272–1284 C.E., North-Western province); Kuruṇēgala (1293–1341 C.E., North-Western province); Gampola (1341–1411 C.E., Central province); Koṭṭē (1411–1597 C.E., Western province); and Kandy (1480–1815 C.E., Central province). Sri Lanka's Buddhist art is often analyzed in terms of these different periods. Of these eras, the Anurādhapura and Polonnaruva periods offer the most important surviving examples of early Buddhist art. The instability of the kingship and the wars that prevailed during the other periods resulted in less art surviving from those eras.

Of these less copious periods, the Yāpahuwa rock fortress is a remarkable monument from the Yāpahuwa period. From the Kandy period, the king's palace and the Tooth-Relic Temple at Kandy, one of the most important Buddhist PILGRIMAGE sites in the country, have survived. Gadalādeniya and Lankātilaka, two temples from the Kuruṇēgala period that still stand near the city of Gampola, are famous for their architectural features and intricate carvings.

Some of the important architectural structures and features from the Anurādhapura and Polonnaruva periods include the STŪPA or *dāgäba* (symbolic burial mounds of the Buddha with relics enshrined), *bodhighara* (bodhi tree shrines), *āsanaghara* (shrines enclosing huge rectangular stone slabs that symbolize the throne of the Buddha), *vatadāge* (circular relic shrines), and *chētiyaghara* (circular shrines built around stūpas, sheltering the monument).

The sacred bodhi tree shrine from Anurādhapura, one of Sri Lanka's most venerated Buddhist sites, has a long history dating back to the third century B.C.E. According to the Sri Lankan chronicles, the Buddhist nun Saṅghamitta, who was the daughter of Emperor AŚOKA (mid-third century B.C.E.), brought a sapling of the original bodhi tree from BODH GAYĀ and planted it in this location at Anurādhapura. There are both literary and inscriptional references to bodhi tree shrines in Sri Lanka from the early Anurādhapura period onward. A well-preserved structure of a bodhi tree shrine dating from the Anurādhapura period still stands at Nillakgama in the Kuruṇēgala district. The structure includes two square stone walls with an entrance on one side, demarcating the shrine, which was inside.

Famous examples of circular relic shrines include those at Thūpārāma (Anurādhapura), Medirigiriya (Polonnaruva), and Tiriyāyi (Trincomalee), all dating to the seventh to tenth centuries. In Pulukunāvi (Batticaloa district) there are remains of an early *āsanaghara*, an architectural feature referred to in ancient literature and inscriptions. The remains of the largest chapter house for Buddhist monks stand in the ancient city of Anurādhapura. Such chapter houses, of which numerous ruins have been found throughout Sri Lanka, were called Uposathaghara in the ancient literature and Pohotaghara in inscriptions.

Before the introduction of BUDDHA IMAGES, worship of the Buddha using aniconic symbols was common in Sri Lanka from about the third century B.C.E. to the second century C.E., as it was in contemporary India. A large number of stone footprints of the Buddha have been found in Buddhist monasteries from the early common era. A considerable number of *bodhigharas* and *āsanagharas* from the Anurādhapura period are also evidence of a tradition dating back to an aniconic phase of Buddhism.

Early Sri Lankan artists appear to have been influenced by three main Indian artistic traditions: Amarāvati (or Āndhra), Gupta, and Pallava. Of these, the Amarāvati school of art from the Āndhra region of India was the earliest and the most influential. Almost all surviving art in Sri Lanka beginning in about the first century C.E. shows the strong impact of the Amarāvati style. During the fifth to sixth centuries and sixth to seventh centuries, styles deriving from Gupta and Pallava, respectively, begin to appear in Sri Lanka.

The unique early art of Sri Lanka includes numerous seated and standing buddha images, including some monumental buddha statues. There are also gigantic stūpas, some with highly ornate frontispieces called *vāhalkada,* which consist of four rectangular architectural projections at the base of the stūpa facing the four cardinal directions. Further early Sri Lankan art includes *sandakadapahana* (moonstones), *dvārapāla* (guardstones), and the renowned Sigiriya paintings of beautiful damsels from the fifth century C.E.

The earliest Buddhist edifices in Sri Lanka are natural rock shelters prepared and dedicated by lay devotees from the third century B.C.E. to the first century C.E. as residences for Buddhist monks during the earliest phase of Buddhist monastic activity in the region. Most of these CAVE SANCTUARIES include short formulaic dedicatory inscriptions declaring the donation. These rock shelters are devoid of any carvings, sculptures, or paintings; if there once were paintings, rain and weathering washed them away long ago.

The eminent Sri Lankan archaeologist and epigraphist Senarat Paranavitana (1896–1972) published more than one thousand of these early Brāhmī cave inscriptions from almost three hundred early monastic sites scattered throughout Sri Lanka. Using the number of caves with inscriptions as an index, the largest of these early Buddhist rock monasteries are Mihintale, with 75 inscriptions (Anurādhapura district, North-Central province); Situlpavvuwa, with 59 inscriptions (Hambantota district, Southern province); Rajagala, with 46 inscriptions, (Ampāra district, Eastern province); Periya Puliyankulama, with 34 inscriptions (Vavuniya district, Northern province); and Ritigala, with 33 inscriptions (Anurādhapura district, North-Central province).

Stūpas or *dāgäba* begin to appear from about the second century B.C.E. onward, simultaneous with the earliest phase of Buddhist cave construction. Early Sri Lankan stūpas are of gigantic proportions. The three largest are from Anurādhapura, the earliest capital of

Sri Lanka: Ruvanvälisăya, from the second century B.C.E., has a diameter of 294 feet at the base and was originally 300 feet tall; Abhayagiriya, from the first century B.C.E., has a diameter of 325 feet and a height of 325 feet; and Jetavana, from the third century C.E., has a diameter of 367 feet and was originally 400 feet tall. Until Anurādhapura was abandoned in the tenth century, these three stūpas were enlarged a number of times by successive kings.

The earliest Buddhist art in Sri Lanka appears in the relief carvings of the stūpa *vāhalkada* (frontispiece). The earliest of these relief carvings date to the first and second century C.E. and are found on the *vāhalkada* of the Kantaka Cētiya (stūpa) at Mihintale, eight miles east of Anurādhapura. Mihintale is the site where Buddhism was believed to have been first introduced to Sri Lanka by Buddhist missionaries from India, who were led by the arhat Mahinda during the mid-third century B.C.E.

Unfortunately, little art from the earliest period has survived because the stūpas were enlarged in various phases through the centuries. With the exception of the Kantaka Cētiya, surviving relief carvings of all other stūpas are late in date and can probably be assigned to the second to fourth centuries C.E. For example, the carvings at Dīghavāpi stūpa (Ampara district, Eastern province) date to the second century C.E.; those at Dakkhina stūpa (Anurādhapura) and Yaṭāla stūpa (Humbantota district, Southern province) date to the second to third centuries C.E.; those at Ruvanvälisăya (Anurādhapura) to the third century C.E.; those at Abhayagiri stūpa (Anurādhapura) to the third or fourth centuries C.E.; and those at Jetavana stūpa (Anurādhapura) to the late third century.

The main images appearing in Sri Lankan frontispieces include DIVINITIES, such as Sūrya and INDRA; YAKṢAS with attendants, such as Kubera and Vaiśravana; *yakṣinīs* or other females with attendants; Gaja Lakṣmi, the goddess of prosperity; nāgas in complete serpent form, often with five or seven cobra hoods; *nāgarājas* in human form, often with five or seven cobra hoods; *nāginīs*, female serpent figures in human form with cobra hoods; and stone pillars depicting the *kalpavṛkṣa* or the tree of life. Figures of yakṣas, nāgas, elephants, lions, bulls, and birds were shown emanating from this tree of life. Attached to these frontispieces were stone pillars topped by elephants, lions, bulls, and horses (Von Schroeder, pp. 80–95). All these early works are related to the late Amarāvatī tradition of the Āndhra region in India.

The earliest available buddha images in Sri Lanka appear to be no older than the 250 C.E. to 350 C.E. period. A few seated buddha images from this period have been found at Anurādhapura at the sites of Abhayagiri Stūpa and Thūpārāma Stūpa (Von Schroeder, p. 113). Seated buddha statues become increasingly common in many parts of Sri Lanka beginning in the fifth to sixth centuries. The majority of them show the direct impact of the Amarāvatī school. The seated buddha statues at Abhayagiri Vihāra, Pankuliya Vihāra, and Asokārama Vihāra (all at Anurādhapura), datable to between the sixth and ninth centuries, are a few well-known examples. The majority of the seated buddha statues found in Sri Lanka are in the samādhi (meditative) posture.

According to the available evidence, most of the standing buddha images from Sri Lanka also date from the fifth to sixth centuries C.E. and later. There are monumental standing buddha images carved in rock and stone at Avukana (42 feet, ninth century, Anurādhapura district); Sassēruva (38 feet, eighth to ninth centuries, Kuruṇēgala district); Buduruvāgala (44 feet, ninth to tenth centuries, Monarāgala district); Dōva Rajamahāvihāra (38 feet, ninth to tenth centuries, Badulla district); Maligāvila (30 feet, eighth century, Monaragala district), and Lankātilaka and Tivanka (26 feet, twelfth century) at Polonnaruva. The twelfth-century Gal Vihāra, or "rock temple," at Polonnaruva is a unique monument carved out of solid rock and famous for its monumental recumbent and standing rock-cut statues in the round.

There are a number of monumental MAHĀYĀNA rock-cut and standing stone statues in the round. They include the eighth-century Dam̆bēgoda stone image in the round at Māligāvila; at 45 feet in height, this image, believed to be Avalokiteśvara, is the largest bodhisattva statue in the world. The 13-foot Kushtarājagala rock-cut relief at Väligama (Southern province), which dates to the ninth or tenth century, is also believed to be an image of Avalokiteśvara. There are also two groups of rock-cut reliefs at Buduruvāgala. One group includes a 12-foot Sudhanakumāra on the left, a 24-foot Avalokiteśvara in the middle, and a 20-foot Tārā at the right; the other group includes a 22-foot Vajrapāni at the left, a 25-foot MAITREYA in the middle, and a 20-foot Avalokiteśvara at the right. These images all date to the ninth or tenth centuries (Von Schroeder, pp. 292–295).

Other early Buddhist art of Sri Lanka from the Anurādhapura period was influenced by the Gupta and

A recumbent Buddha statue at the twelfth-century Gal Vihāra (Rock Temple) at Polonnaruva, Sri Lanka. The temple and statuary are carved out of the living rock. The Art Archive/Musée Guimet Paris/Dagli Orti. Reproduced by permission.

Pallava traditions of India. The famous Mithuna or "loving couple" figure, which dates to the fifth to sixth centuries, from the so-called Isurumuniya Monastery of Anurādhapura is a well-known example of Gupta influence. The "man and the horse head" figure (sixth or seventh century) from the same monastery is considered to have been influenced by the Pallava tradition. Beautifully carved *dvārapālas* (guardstones) from the sixth to tenth centuries flank the entrances to Buddhist monasteries from Anurādhapura and many other parts of Sri Lanka; these are unique examples of both Gupta and Pallava artistic influences. The *sandakadapahana* (moonstone), an elaborately carved half-circle stepping stone placed at the entrance to a Buddhist monastery, is unique to Sri Lanka. At the center of these stone ornaments is a lotus flower from which emanate concentric half circles of vegetable, animal, bird, and flame motifs. Although the most refined moonstones are from the late Anurādhapura period, the carving of moonstones continued into the Polonnaruva period and later.

Although secular in nature, Sigiriya's elegant symmetrical gardens (fifth century) and water gardens are the earliest such examples in South Asia. Almost contemporary to the famous AJAṆṬĀ paintings from India, the renowned fifth-century rock paintings at Sigiriya, which was built by King Kāśyapa as a palace city, are masterpieces of early Sri Lankan art. On the western face of the Sigiriya rock, about four hundred feet above the ground, there are twenty-two extant paintings of beautiful women voluptuously depicted, most with their breasts exposed. Two images in particular appear prominently in these paintings: an elite lady standing alone holding a flower or an elite lady accompanied by a handmaiden. The meaning of these images is controversial. Ananda Coomaraswamy

(1877–1947) was of the view that they are celestial nymphs or Apsarās. Senarat Paranavitana, however, proposed that they symbolize the clouds (*megha*) and lightning (*vijju*) surrounding Mount KAILĀŚA (KAILASH). His theory was that the builder of Sigiriya fortress, King Kāśyapa, lived there as Kuvera, the god of wealth in Hindu and Buddhist literature, who is supposed to dwell at Ālakamanda on Mount Kailāśa. But some evidence points in another direction. The ladies holding flowers and accompanied by handmaidens appear to be popular motifs in art throughout west, central, and south Asia prior to Sigiriya times. It is possible that the Sigiriya paintings are an adaptation in a Sri Lankan context of this internationally popular subject. Given Sri Lanka's flourishing role as a trade center connecting the eastern and western trade routes during the fourth through sixth centuries, such a sharing of international art motifs was quite possible.

See also: **India, Buddhist Art in; Sri Lanka**

Bibliography

Coomaraswamy, Ananda Kentish. *History of Indian and Indonesian Art.* Leipzig, Germany: Hiersemann; London: Goldston; New York: Weyhe, 1927. Reprint, New York: Dover, 1985.

Coomaraswamy, Ananda Kentish. *Mediaeval Sinhalese Art,* 2nd edition. New York: Pantheon, 1956.

Paranavitana, Senarat. *Sigiri Grafitti, Being Sinhalese Verses of the Eighth, Ninth, and Tenth Centuries,* 2 vols. London and New York: Oxford University Press, 1956.

Paranavitana, Senarat. "Civilization of the Early Period: Religion and Art." In *University of Ceylon History of Ceylon.* Colombo, Sri Lanka: Colombo University Press, 1959.

Paranavitana, Senarat. "The Significance of the Paintings of Sigiri." *Artibus Asiae* 24, nos. 3/4 (1961): 382–387.

Paranavitana, Senarat. *Inscriptions of Ceylon,* Vol. 1: *Containing Cave Inscriptions from 3rd Century B.C. to 1st Century A.D. and Other Inscriptions in the Early Brāhmī Script.* Colombo, Sri Lanka: Dept of Archaeology, 1970.

Priyanka, Benille. "New Research in the Early Art History of Sri Lanka: The Sigiriya Paintings Reinterpreted." Paper presented in honor of the opening of the Sri Lankan consulate in Los Angeles, organized by the Southern Asian Art Council of the Los Angeles County Museum of Art, February 17, 2000.

Von Schroeder, Ulrich. *Buddhist Sculptures of Sri Lanka.* Hong Kong: Visual Dharma, 1990.

BENILLE PRIYANKA

STŪPA

The Monier-Williams *Sanskrit-English Dictionary* defines the word *stūpa* as "a knot or tuft of hair, the upper part of the head, crest, top, summit"; also "a heap or pile of earth, or bricks etc." Opinions about the etymology of the word *stūpa* differ, and the root √*stūp,* "to heap up, pile, erect," seems to have been a late invention in order to explain the term. Although now inextricably linked to Buddhism, originally the stūpa was not exclusively a Buddhist structure, but also a Jaina monument.

Generally the terms *stūpa* and *caitya,* said to derive from *cita,* "a funeral pile," are used interchangeably. Both terms indicate a mound of earth surrounded by a wooden railing, marking the place of the funeral pyre of a significant person. While the meaning of *caitya* may also mean observances "relating to a funeral pile or mound," the term *stūpa* designates the actual structure. Originally, stūpas contained relics, mainly ash, of a saintly person, and later other objects, such as crystal beads.

Buddhist texts narrate how the Buddha's relics were divided into eight portions; these were distributed to different kingdoms within India and stūpas were built over them. These relics were redistributed during the third century B.C.E. by AŚOKA not only as an act of homage to the Buddhist faith, but also to ensure the Buddha's protection over his extensive empire. Thus, thousands of stūpas were built as a remembrance of the Buddha and of the crucial episodes of his life; for example, the stūpa at Sārnāth commemorated the Buddha's first sermon. In time, stūpas were erected as an homage to any past or future buddha, or to any Buddhist saint.

Basically a stūpa consisted of a circular platform (*meḍhī*) on which was erected a solid masonry hemisphere, or *aṇḍa* (egg), made of unburnt bricks. In its center was a small space for a receptacle containing relics. On the summit of the plain *aṇḍa,* and aligned with the reliquary, was raised a shaft surmounted by one or more *chattravali* (parasols), a mark of royalty that later assumed a complex metaphysical meaning. The surface of the dome was finished with a thick layer of plaster. Because it was customary to circumambulate the stūpa as a part of worship, a *pradakṣiṇapatha* (processional path) was provided both on the *meḍhī* and at ground level by enclosing the monument within a *vedika* (wooden railing), leaving enough space for walking. The *vedika,* which, at least in theory, should be a perfect circle, was interrupted by L-shaped entrances at the four cardinal points, creating a cosmological diagram in the form of an auspicious *svastika* cross. An example of this early type of stūpa is that at Svayambhu Nath near Kathmandu; this stūpa has been worshiped for more than two thousand years.

This basic architectural scheme bears, in its simplicity, an infinite potential for variations dictated by local traditions, materials, and religious trends. Its crucial importance in the development of sacred buildings throughout Buddhist Asia, extending roughly from today's eastern Afghanistan throughout Central, East, and Southeast Asia, cannot be overestimated.

Early Pāli texts do not pay much attention to the actual building of a stūpa because its construction, maintenance, and worship were the concern of the LAITY. Later, however, the building process became the focus of intense metaphysical speculation. Each part of the stūpa, beginning from the terraces at its base, to the number of parasols on the *chattravali*, became imbued with a profound meaning, variously interpreted by different schools.

Central India: Stūpas at Sāñcī and Bhārhut

The greatest artistic expressions of early Buddhist tradition are the monuments at SĀÑCĪ and Bhārhut, in Madhya Pradesh, seats of two of the most important Buddhist communities from the third century B.C.E. Among the oldest surviving stūpas is Stūpa II at Sāñcī, which dates from the Śuṅga period (second to first centuries B.C.E.). This simple monument housed the relics of several Buddhist teachers; the relics were enclosed in caskets and buried within the stūpa's solid mass. Of great interest are the interior and exterior surfaces of the stone *vedika*, obviously a replica of a wooden prototype, embellished with sets of vigorously carved medallions. Especially elaborate are the reliefs on the pillars flanking the L-shaped entrances at the four cardinal points.

Dating from this early period is the now ruined *mahāstūpa* (great stūpa) discovered by Alexander Cunnigham in 1873 at Bhārhut. The conspicuous size of the monument, whose diameter measures more than twenty meters, the care lavished on the decoration of the sandstone *vedika*, some three meters in height, and the monumental *toraṇas* (entryways) bear witness to the affluence of this commercial town, located on one of the major trade routes of ancient India. Although inscriptions on the *vedika* and the eastern *toraṇa* proclaim that they were erected during the Śuṅga period (possibly between 100 and 80 B.C.E.), the stūpa is probably earlier in date, because it was customary to add *vedikas* and *toraṇas* to earlier buildings. The *toraṇa* consists of two upright pillars supporting three architraves spanning the entry to the stūpa complex. The crossbars of the *vedika* are adorned with medallions displaying floral motifs, human figures, and JĀTAKA scenes. On the *vedika*'s terminal uprights are carved single figures, including standing warriors, equestrian figures, and *yakṣīs* clutching a tree. Animals, plants, creepers, geometrical motifs, and scenes from Buddha's life are among the subjects carved on the *toraṇa.* Most of the remains of this railing are now displayed at the Indian Museum in Calcutta and in the Allahabad Museum.

The celebrated Sāñcī Stūpa I was built between the third century B.C.E. and the first century C.E., with additions of the fifth century C.E. This imposing monument, measuring 36.6 meters in diameter, rises on top of the hill at Sāñcī. The solid hemisphere is truncated at the top by a *harmikā* (pedestal supporting the shaft of the umbrella) crowned by a three-tiered stone umbrella and set within a square railing. A circular terrace accessed by two staircases runs along the base of the *aṇḍa.* At ground level is a stone-paved circumambulation path encircled by a *vedika* that is interrupted at the four cardinal points by imposing *toraṇas.*

The present stūpa, dating from roughly the second century B.C.E., encases an older one that was built probably a century earlier. Its plain surface contrasts with the wealth of images carved on the *vedika.* Medallions display floral, animal, and bird motifs, as well as human figures and mythical beings. The balustrade is divided into four sections defined by the L-shaped *toraṇas,* which were erected in the first century C.E. These are similar in design and construction technique to those at Bhārhut, and they are covered with sculptures, whose liveliness and variety of subject matter are unsurpassed. The most famous scenes illustrate episodes from the *jātakas* and from the life of the Buddha.

As in the case of the previous monuments, Gautama is never represented in human form, but by emblems, such as an empty throne beneath the bodhi tree, footprints, the triratna (three REFUGES), and finally the stūpa. Salient events of his life and career have pride of place, such as his birth, the temptation of MĀRA, the first sermon at Sārnāth, the conversion of the Kāśyapa brothers, and the miracles at Śrāvastī and Kapilavastu. Episodes that followed his death (e.g., the fight over the Buddha's relics) have also been illustrated. The predecessors of Gautama, the buddhas of antiquity, have been incorporated in the iconographic program of the four *toraṇas* and are represented either by stūpas or bodhi trees. Apart from scenes related to Gautama's life, there are others depicting everyday life, music, dance, sports, and the like. These three early stūpas, of seminal importance in the formation of early Indian sculpture, exemplify two opposing facets of early Buddhist art: On the one hand, there is the strict adherence to aniconic representation of the Buddha; on the other hand, there is the unstoppable, exuberant flow of narrative. The last addition to Sāñcī Stūpa I occurred in the fifth century C.E. when four Buddha images in teaching MUDRĀ were placed against its walls, facing the entrances. Each figure is flanked by attendants.

Western Deccan

An interesting development occurred during the second and first centuries B.C.E., when a number of Buddhist cave complexes were excavated in the Western Ghats (e.g., Bhājā and Bedsā). These consisted of one or more caitya halls, pillared apsidal halls that contained a stūpa, and rock-cut cells, some of which served as accommodation for the monks and nuns. This architectural innovation brought the recluses into closer contact with the stūpa, which had to be included in their daily ritual, and eventually became the focus of worship.

An early example of this type of architecture is the monastic complex at Bhājā (Maharashtra), which consists of a large caitya hall with a monolithic stūpa and a substantial number of smaller cells. On epigraphical and stylistic grounds, it is probable that the main phase of the works took place between 100 and 70 B.C.E. This is possibly the earliest caitya hall of this region. It is divided into three naves by slightly inward-sloping octagonal columns, thus providing a circumambulatory passage around the stūpa. The light penetrates from the door above, which opens a horseshoe window, one of the many elements that derive from wooden architecture (the horseshoe window is part of the door). This basic model was followed in Buddhist rock-cut architecture of Western India until the seventh century C.E.

Gandhāra region

Buddhism was introduced in the Bactro-Gandhāra regions at the time of Aśoka. By around 130 B.C.E. the Śakas took control of this area in present-day Pakistan and Afghanistan, and at the turn of the common era, the Parthians moved in from Iran. One of the legacies of the Śaka-Parthian domination was the terrace-stūpa. The circular base disappeared, to be replaced by a square terrace whose basement was adorned with classical elements inherited from the Hellenistic world: columns, pilasters, entablatures, and niches. In the first century C.E. the Kushan dynasty established its power over the territory of the Śaka-Parthians, and in the wake of their political influence Buddhism spread, not only throughout their territory, but also to adjacent countries, including Central Asia and China. By this time the MAHĀYĀNA doctrine had introduced a new conception of the Buddha, in which he was seen as the epitome of wisdom, truth, and compassion, and as such, his person was worthy of worship. This led to a crucial artistic development: the almost contemporaneous creation of the Buddha image in the two main cultural centers of the Kushan empire, the Gandhāra region, and Mathurā (Uttar Pradesh), the southern capital of the empire.

Among the numerous stūpas and monastic establishments built in this period is the second-century terrace-stūpa at Guldara in Afghanistan, a massive construction resting on an imposing square base adorned with pilasters, and a substantial superstructure now ruined. Also from this period is the large monastic establishment at Takht-i-Bahi in Pakistan, whose stūpa is completely destroyed but for its base. Its elongated appearance, however, can be reconstructed by examining smaller stūpas found in the region.

By this time the primordial hemispherical stūpa had developed into a towerlike monument by way of multiplying the layers of the base, elongating the *aṇḍa* into a domelike cylinder, and stretching the *chattravali* to a considerable length, either by multiplying the chattras or compressing them into a compact conical spire.

Another innovation was the tower-stūpa, which plays a determinant role in the evolution of the stūpa into the East Asian pagoda. The massive cross-shaped foundations of the famous Kanishka tower-stūpa at Shahji-ki-Dheri, near Peshawar, are still preserved. According to the reports of Chinese pilgrims, this building was characterized by superimposed wooden "stories" with cornices, windows, and niches, as well as a copper mast carrying thirteen copper umbrellas. It was probably from this model that the Chinese pagoda evolved.

The Deccan: Amarāvatī and Nāgārjunakoṇḍa

In most of peninsular India and Sri Lanka, the stūpa kept its hemispherical shape and continued to be erected on a circular platform. Among the numerous

Reliefs depicting events from the life of the Buddha adorn the gate leading to this first-century B.C.E. stūpa at the great monastic complex of Sāñcī at Vidiṣa near Bhopal, India. © Adam Woolfitt/Corbis. Reproduced by permission.

Buddhist sites in the eastern Deccan, two are noteworthy: Amarāvatī and Nāgārjunakoṇḍa (Andhra Pradesh). The stūpa at Amarāvatī achieved its final form in the second and third centuries C.E. during the Śātavāhana and Ikṣvāku periods. Almost nothing is preserved of this monument, which was the largest in the eastern Deccan, apart from an earthen mound and a surrounding pathway defined by upright slabs. A number of celebrated finely sculpted limestone slabs that have survived depict this lavishly decorated monument with imposing projecting gateways in the four directions. Among the distinctive features of this structure were four votive platforms, each with five pillars, aligned with the four entrances. The surviving uprights, capping pieces, and slabs have been removed from the site and are displayed in various museums; the largest collection is at the Government Museum Chennai (Madras).

During the third century a number of changes were occurring in Buddhist religion and art. These are reflected in the structures at Nāgārjunakoṇḍa, the most important Buddhist settlement of the region, set in a valley delimited by the Kṛṣṇā river on the west. In the third and fourth centuries, when Nāgārjunakoṇḍa was the capital of the Ikṣvāku rulers, the successors of the Śatavāhanas, a large number of monasteries and stūpas were erected according to the cultic needs of various Buddhist schools, of which at least four were represented there. Here the great innovation is the wheel-shaped plan of the stūpas, demonstrating the transformation of a sacred Buddhist symbol into an architectural design. Each monastic unit consisted of a stūpa, a caitya hall, and a vihāra (monastic quarters). The residential unit would be generally separated from the stūpa by two caitya halls facing each other, one containing a stūpa and the other a buddha image, thus equating the stūpa with the buddha image. The stūpa and the image of the Buddha eventually coalesced in the fifth century in the AJAṆṬĀ caves. Although most of the excavated remains at Nāgārjunakoṇḍa were submerged under the waters of the Nāgārjuna Sagar, a few monuments were recreated on a hilltop, now an island in the middle of the lake. Limestone panels and friezes once decorating various monuments have been discovered, and together with the carvings found at Amarāvatī, they are the most important remains of the flourishing Buddhist art in the Deccan.

North and eastern India in the fifth to seventh centuries

The aesthetics of the Gandhāra and the Mathurā schools of Kushan art played a major role in the development of Gupta aesthetics. The Kushan power ebbed at the end of the third century C.E., and by the early fourth century the Gupta dynasty ruled over north and central India. Ancient sites connected with the Buddha, such as BODH GAYĀ (Bihar), were refurbished; Sārnāth, near Varaṇasī (the old Benares, in Uttar Pradesh), where the Buddha delivered his first sermon, became a major center of Buddhist learning and artistic development. The remains of two large stūpas, whose cores probably date from the Aśokan period, as well as of a number of monasteries, are still preserved there.

Another famous center of Buddhist learning was Nālandā, near Rājgir (Bihar). Despite its putative links to Gautama Buddha and to Aśoka, both of whom are said to have visited this site, no remains predate the fifth century C.E. The Stūpa/Temple 3 is the most prominent building at Nālandā. This monument underwent various phases of construction. At its core is a small stūpa set on a square base measuring 173 centimeters each side and 137 centimeters in height. It has been suggested that this could be an Aśokan stūpa, built on the caitya of ŚĀRIPUTRA, the Buddha's disciple renowned for his wisdom. It was further enlarged three more times. However, with the fifth enlargement, in the sixth century, the monument changed appearance and plan. It became a large-sized structure with four lavishly decorated towers at the corners. This monument was renovated twice more in the eleventh and twelfth centuries just before the decline of Buddhism in India.

The stūpa beyond India

The Buddhist doctrine was introduced in Sri Lanka in the third century B.C.E. During the subsequent centuries, a conspicuous number of *dagobas* or *dhātugopas* (relic-preservers) were built. Examples of this local version of the Indian stūpa are found at various sites, such as Anurādhapura, the ancient capital of Sri Lanka from around the second century B.C.E. to the ninth century C.E. Here are the oldest surviving *dagobas*, the largest of which is the Abhayagiri *dagoba.* Its diameter is about 110 meters and its height from the base to the spire about 82 meters. As is the case of the stūpa in India and Nepal, the *dagobas* of Sri Lanka have richly carved oblong projections at each cardinal point, which were probably thrones for the Dhyāni buddhas. More recent and smaller in size are the Buddhist remains at Polonnaruva, the capital of Sri Lanka from the ninth to the end of the thirteenth century C.E. The remains at this site are extremely important because these monuments were built at a time when Buddhists had greatly reduced, if not altogether ceased, their building activity in India. Furthermore, the architectural developments at Polonnaruva may constitute the link between the architecture on the Indian subcontinent and architecture overseas.

Buddhism arrived in Burma from important centers on the eastern coast of India, such as Amarāvatī and Nāgārjunakoṇḍa, in about the fifth century C.E. Both the MAINSTREAM BUDDHIST SCHOOLS and Mahāyāna were present at this early date as testified by archaeological evidence from the Pyu city of Śrī Kṣetra, near Prome. In time, further links with southern India and Sri Lanka, and subsequently with eastern India, were established, which had a seminal influence in the formation of Burmese architecture. The Burmese stūpa, an elegant, bell-shaped construction topped by a conical finial, is raised on a series of terraces or platforms; the most famous example is the great SHWEDAGON pagoda in Rangoon (ca. fifteenth century).

Mainstream Buddhism was prevalent in Indonesia until the end of the seventh century C.E. By the end of the century, however, the Mahāyāna school had risen in importance and soon became the only form of Buddhism followed there. One of the most significant Buddhist monuments of the world is BOROBUDUR in Java, dated to around 800. Every part of this magnificent building, from its maṇḍala-like layout to the tiniest detail of its decorative program, is imbued with a deep symbolic meaning. Here Buddhist doctrine, the structure of the universe, and the mystery of enlightenment are expressed through plan, architectural design, and sculpture.

See Monastic Architecture; Relics and Relics Cults

Bibliography

Dallapicccola, Anna Libera, and Zingel-Avé Lallemant, Stephanie, eds. *The Stūpa: Its Religious, Historical, and Architectural Significance.* Wiesbaden, Germany: Steiner, 1980.

Dehejia, Vidya. *Discourses in Early Buddhist Art: Visual Narratives of India.* New Delhi: Munshiram Manoharlal, 1997.

Dehejia, Vidya. *Indian Art.* London: Phaidon, 1997.

Hallade, Madeleine, *Gandharan Art of North India and the Graeco-Buddhist Tradition in India, Persia, and Central Asia.* New York: Harry N. Abrams, 1968.

Huntington, Susan, and Huntington, John C. *The Art of Ancient India.* New York and Tokyo: Weatherhill, 1985.

Isaacs, Ralph, and Blurton, T. Richard. *Visions from a Golden Land: Burma and the Art of Lacquer.* London: British Museum, 2000.

Knox, Robert. *Amaravati: Buddhist Sculpture from the Great Stūpa.* London: British Museum, 1992.

Marshall, John. *A Guide to Sāñcī,* 3rd edition. New Delhi: Manager of Publications, 1955.

Michell, George. *The Penguin Guide to the Monuments of India,* Vol. 1: *Buddhist, Jain, Hindu.* London: Viking, 1989.

Sarkar, H., and Misra, B. N. *Nāgārjunakoṇḍa,* 3rd edition. New Delhi: Director General, Archaeological Survey of India, 1980.

Volwahsen, Andreas. *Indien: Bauten der Hindus, Buddhisten, und Jains.* Munich: Hirmer Verlag, 1968.

Zwalf, Wladimir. *Buddhism: Art and Faith.* London: British Museum, 1985.

A. L. DALLAPICCOLA

SUFFERING. *See* **Duḥkha (Suffering)**

SUKHĀVATĪ. *See* **Pure Lands**

SUKHĀVATĪVYŪHA-SŪTRA

The title *Sukhāvatīvyūha-sūtra* (*Sūtra Displaying the Land of Bliss*) actually denotes two related but distinct texts, both of which narrate aspects of the mythic story of the buddha called AMITĀBHA or Amitāyus (Chinese, Amito; Japanese, Amida) and the paradise where he resides called Sukhāvatī. Following Chinese precedent, the two texts have commonly been distinguished as the *Larger Sūtra* (Chinese, *Wuliangshou jing, Dajing*; Japanese, *Muryōjukyō, Daikyō*; *Sūtra on the Buddha of Immeasurable Life*) and the *Smaller Sūtra* (*Amito jing, Amidakyō, Sūtra on Amitāyus Buddha*). These are early MAHĀYĀNA sūtras, probably composed in northwest India, and translations of the *Larger Sūtra* began in China in the second or third century. The pervasiveness of this belief is known by manuscripts of the *Larger Sūtra* also extant in Sanskrit, Tibetan, Khotanese, Uighur, and Xixia. Many core doctrines and practices of the Pure Land school in East Asia are based on the *Sukhāvatīvyūha* sūtras, but in fact there are 290 translated scriptures in the Chinese canon that discuss Amitābha Buddha and his realm.

The sūtras describe a cosmic order containing both a sacred realm inhabited by buddhas and bodhisattvas living in a paradise of fantastic proportions and an mundane realm inhabited by ordinary people, animals, ghosts, and so on, transmigrating but trapped. The sūtras also describe the promise by Amitābha Buddha to enable beings to transmigrate into his paradise. This is possible through his vows (Sanskrit, *praṇidhāna*) and the Mahāyāna doctrine of merit-transfer. Orthodox East Asian Pure Land thought views the Buddha's eighteenth vow in the Sanghavarman Chinese translation as the authoritative expression of the Buddha's commitment to help anyone, as it asks only that one sincerely hold in mind (or recite) the Buddha's name a minimum of ten moments in order to be reborn in his Pure Land.

See also: **Pure Land Schools**

Bibliography

Gómez, Luis, trans. and ed. *The Land of Bliss: The Paradise of the Buddha of Measureless Light, Sanskrit and Chinese Versions of the Sukhāvatīvyūha Sūtra.* Honolulu: University of Hawaii Press, 1996.

Inagaki, Hisao. *The Three Pure Land Sutras: A Study and Translation from Chinese.* Kyoto: Nagata Bunshodo, 1995.

MARK L. BLUM

SUKHOTHAI

Sukhothai, the first Thai kingdom, was founded around 1238 in the central part of present-day Thailand. In previous centuries, this area was under the sovereignty of Khmer kings who practiced Hinduism and MAHĀYĀNA Buddhism. The Thai, however, adopted THERAVĀDA Buddhism from Sri Lanka. Upon his return from Sri Lanka in the early 1330s, Si Satha, a high-ranking monk, introduced a new Sinhalese sect along with Buddha relics and artisans. The veneration of relics played a significant role in this sect, which dramatically transformed the architecture and plans of temple compounds. While earlier STŪPAS (Thai, *chedi*) in Sukhothai were in Khmer-tower form (*prang*; e.g., Wat Phraphai Luang), new innovative forms were built after 1340 as stūpas became the religious and ceremonial centers of monasteries.

The most important temple remains that reflect the development of Sukhothai architecture are at Wat Mahathat (Monastery of the Great Relic), located in the center of the city. Wat Mahathat was built during King Ramkhamhaeng's reign (ca. 1279–1298) and was renovated around 1340 during the reign of the pious King Loëthai (1298–1346/7). Many forms of stūpas can still be seen (Khmer-tower, lotus-bud, and bell-shaped types), as well as the ruins of the congregational hall (*ubosot* or *bot*) and an assembly hall (*wihan*). A unique Sukhothai-type of stūpa was built on a low pyramidal platform of three levels that supported a staggered shaft that housed the relic. Above it was a smoothly rounded ovoid bulb (lotus-bud stūpa), which would later be crowned with a spire. Eight subsidiary stūpas were linked to the center with connecting walls. The four axial towers built in Khmer style were decorated with stucco designs similar to those on the Lankatilaka Temple in Sri Lanka, dating to 1342. Themes from the historical Buddha's past lives, meant to inspire practitioners, decorated the Mahathat tympana.

Ubosot and *wihan* were commonly built of brick covered with plaster and decorated with stucco. Their roofs were made of wood covered with ceramic tiles; for the most part, only the columns stand today. *Ubosot* can be distinguished from *wihan* by the (typically eight) boundary stones (*sema*) that were generally placed around it.

See also: **Ayutthaya; Monastic Architecture; Southeast Asia, Buddhist Art in; Thailand**

Bibliography

Gosling, Betty. *Sukhothai: Its History, Culture, and Art.* Singapore and New York: Oxford University Press, 1991.

Griswold, Alexander B. *Towards a History of Sukhothai Art.* Bangkok: Fine Arts Department of Thailand, 1967.

Pattaratorn Chirapravati

SUMERU, MOUNT. *See* **Cosmology**

ŚŪNYATĀ (EMPTINESS)

Within the nature of reality in Mahāyāna ontology, emptiness (*śūnyatā*) must be realized en route to enlightenment. The term *śūnyatā* has been glossed as "openness," "inconceivability," or "unlimitedness," but is best translated as "emptiness" or "voidness." It refers to what dharmas (elements of reality) really are through what they are not: not as they appear, not conceptualizable, not distinguishable, and, above all, lacking permanent, independent, intrinsic existence.

Although emptiness is sometimes mentioned in non-Mahāyāna texts, where it describes, for example, the contents of an advanced meditative state, the nonexistence of a self, or the absence of defilements in Nirvāṇa, the Prajñāpāramitā literature of the Mahāyāna brought emptiness to prominence in Buddhist wisdom discourse. In paradoxical rhetoric, these sūtras describe emptiness as the true nature of all entities and concepts, from form through a buddha's awareness; thus, there really is no form, no buddha. This apparently nihilistic claim has been the subject of commentarial exegesis, philosophical disputation, meditative investigation, and ethical reflection throughout the Mahāyāna world. Still, emptiness is simply a radicalization and universalization of the earlier Buddhist idea of no-self (anātman), so that the view that there exists no unchanging subsisting person is extended to all possible objects and ideas, whether pure or impure, Buddhist or non-Buddhist—since grasping at true existence in any of them (including emptiness itself) will preclude the uprooting of defilements, hence the attainment of liberation and buddhahood.

In India, the most important philosophical reflection on emptiness emerged from the Madhyamaka school, beginning with Nāgārjuna (ca. second century C.E.), whose *Madhyamakakārikā* (*Verses on Madhyamaka*) uses reductive reasoning to demonstrate the untenability, hence emptiness, of various key concepts, including causation, time, and nirvāṇa. Nāgārjuna asserts, however, that emptiness is nihilistic only for those who ignore the distinction between two truths: the *ultimate,* in which everything truly lacks intrinsic existence; and the *conventional,* in which, precisely because they are empty (that is, interdependent), things exist and function, and concepts are valid. Subsequent Madhyamaka thinkers extended Nāgārjuna's analysis, reflecting on the implications of emptiness for such issues as the role of rationality on the path, the admissibility of syllogistic arguments "proving" emptiness, the "truth" value of conventional truths, the absoluteness of the negation involved in emptiness, the status of morality and compassion, the content of an awareness realizing emptiness, and the rapidity with which realization of emptiness effects enlightenment.

Other Mahāyānists analyzed emptiness, too. YOGĀCĀRA SCHOOL writers agreed on its ultimacy, but described it as the absence of concepts in perfected awareness, or as an external object's inseparability from the consciousness perceiving it. Texts on TATHĀGATAGARBHA (buddha-nature) sometimes implied that emptiness is different on different levels: Saṃsāric phenomena are empty of intrinsic existence, but buddha-awareness is empty of saṃsāric phenomena, itself being pure, permanent gnosis. In Tibet, these ideas were described as the *intrinsic emptiness* and *extrinsic emptiness* views, respectively. The HUAYAN JING (*Avataṃsaka-sūtra; Flower Garland Sūtra*) and East Asian schools based upon it, such as the Huayan school, portrayed emptiness as the perfect interpenetration of all phenomena. In tantric traditions, emptiness is the adamantine nature of reality, inseparable from a clear, blissful gnostic awareness; worlds and beings, MAṆḌALAS and deities, arise from and return to it, in reality as in meditative practice.

Discourse about emptiness was central to scholastic and meditative traditions in Tibet. It was also central to the philosophical treatises of the Sanlun, Huayan, and Tiantai schools of China, Korea, and Japan, and to the texts and praxis of East Asian Chan. Contemporary Buddhists, both Asian and Western, continue to explore the philosophical and practical implications of emptiness, reexamining traditional explanations of it, while aligning it with modern scientific and philosophical concepts, such as relativity, ecology, and deconstruction.

See also: **Anātman/Ātman (No-Self/Self); Chan School; Huayan School; Philosophy; Prajña (Wisdom); Tantra; Tiantai School**

Bibliography

Conze, Edward, trans. *The Perfection of Wisdom in Eight Thousand Lines and Its Verse Summary.* Bolinas, CA: Four Seasons Foundation, 1973.

Lopez, Donald S., Jr. *Elaborations on Emptiness: Uses of the Heart Sūtra.* Princeton, NJ: Princeton University Press, 1996.

Stearns, Cyrus. *The Buddha from Dolpo: A Study of the Life and Thought of the Tibetan Master Dolpopa Sherab Gyaltsen.* Albany: State University of New York Press, 1999.

Streng, Frederick. *Emptiness: A Study in Religious Meaning.* Nashville, TN: Abingdon, 1967.

ROGER R. JACKSON

SŪTRA

The Sanskrit word *sūtra* (Pāli, *sutta*), or "discourse," is the name generally given to any text said to contain the words or the teaching of the Buddha. Whether or not it actually does is another matter; many sūtras clearly postdate the Buddha's time. Typically, a sūtra begins with the phrase "Thus have I heard," which is presumed by tradition to be the words of the Buddha's attendant ĀNANDA repeating at the First Council what he heard the Buddha say at a given time and place. The *sūtra-piṭaka* (basket of discourses) represents one of three major divisions of the Buddhist CANON (Tripiṭaka), the others being the VINAYA and the ABHIDHARMA.

See also: **Āgama/Nikāya; Councils, Buddhist; Scripture**

JOHN S. STRONG

SŪTRA ILLUSTRATIONS

Sūtras were illustrated in many different formats and media, such as BIANXIANG (TRANSFORMATION TABLEAUX), but this entry is limited to manuscript illuminations and illustrations done primarily on palm leaf or paper.

Sūtra illustrations in South and Southeast Asia

In South and Southeast Asia the oral transmission of sūtras prevailed until the first century B.C.E. when written copies were first produced. By the tenth and eleventh centuries written sūtras were common and monastic complexes such as Nalanda produced illustrated texts. Sūtras were copied onto leaves of the tala or palmyra tree, the oldest extant example being one brought from China to Japan in 608. The palm leaves are approximately three to four inches wide by twelve to eighteen inches long. The text was written on both sides of the palm leaves, which were lacquered or prepared with pigments before the inscription of the texts. Strung together, the palm leaves were bound between covers of narrow boards upon which illustrations and decorative motifs were also drawn. Illustrated sūtras were also executed on paper that was cut, strung, and bound in the shape and style of palm-leaf sūtras.

The illustrations on these manuscripts were placed in single frames between lines of text or on the covers. Common subjects included individual deities and the

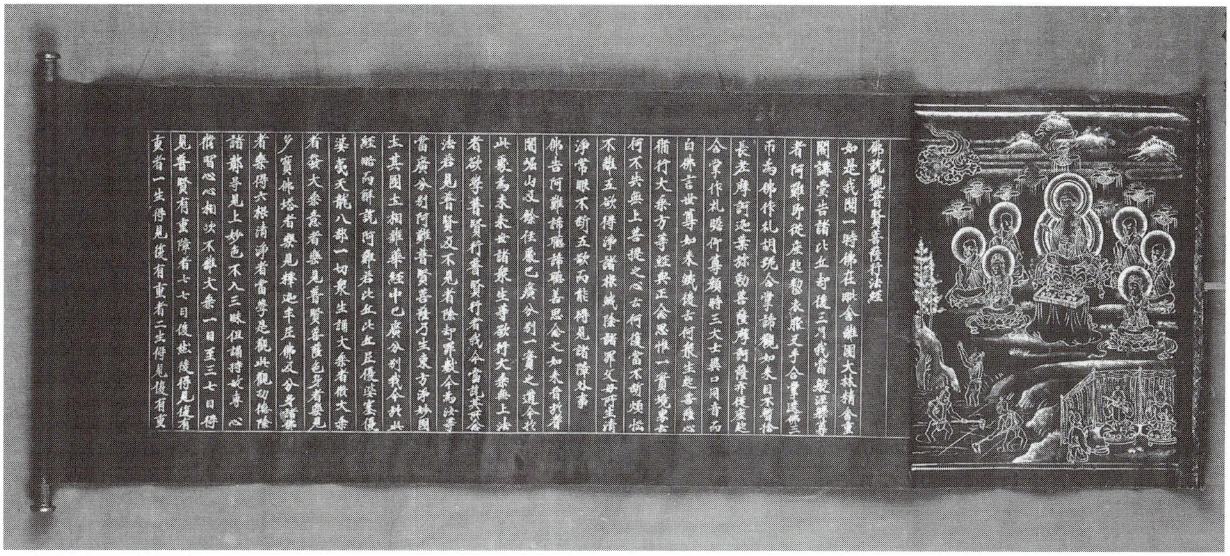

This twelfth-century Japanese work illustrates the Buddha preaching in the mountains, from the epilogue to the *Lotus Sūtra.* (Japanese, Heian period, 794–1185.) © Reunion des Musées Nationaux/Art Resource, NY. Reproduced by permission.

eight great events of Śākyamuni's life. In many instances, the figures depicted had no specific connection with the contents of the text and probably functioned as symbols of protection and reverence for the text. In other instances, particularly in later manuscripts, there were deities and narrative scenes based on the contents of the sūtra. The images were painted most often in ink and gouache, but also could have gold and silver accents. The miniaturization necessary to the format and the preeminence of the text hampered the development of continuous or complex narrative illustrations. Illuminated sūtras reached an artistic apogee in the eleventh and twelfth centuries, declined in number for several centuries, and experienced resurgence in number and quality in the sixteenth, seventeenth, and eighteenth centuries, especially in Nepal, Tibet, Thailand, and Burma.

Sūtra illustrations in East Asia

East Asian Buddhists copied sūtras from as early as the fourth century in China, where the development of and the Chinese reverence for the written word led to sūtra copying on a large scale. Sūtra copying reached its peak in the Tang period (618–907) in China, the Heian (794–1185) and Kamakura (1185–1333) periods in Japan, and the Koryŏ period (918–1392) in Korea. The sūtras were copied chiefly onto hand scrolls, but the folded book (Japanese, *orihon*), in which a scroll was folded in accordion fashion, and the bound book of separate sheets of paper were also used. Although the initial impetus was the need for copies of the text, the copied sūtras also were revered as evidence of the sponsor's piety and merit. The veneration of sūtras led to increasing adornment involving dyeing, marbling, decorative designs, and illustrations, as well as the use of gold and silver inks.

The most common form of sūtra illustration is the frontispiece painting found at the beginning of hand or folded book scrolls. These paintings were often executed in gold and silver inks and formed a style common to all East Asian cultures. The subject matter frequently centered upon the Buddha preaching to a group of BODHISATTVAS, deva, ARHATS, and practitioners. A printed version of the DIAMOND SŪTRA from DUNHUANG dated 868 is the earliest dated versions of such a frontispiece illustration. The scene of preaching did not always reflect the specific content of the text. However, some frontispiece paintings illustrated the main doctrines or stories of the text either as single illustrations or as additions to the preaching scene.

A second broad category of paintings evoked, rather than directly illustrated, the text's message. Japanese illustrations of the Heian and Kamakura periods sometimes referred to poetry or stories about the ideas and episodes in the sūtra. These illustrations appear to be unrelated to the text, but have hidden script and rebus that, when decoded, related to the specific sūtra. The Heike Nōkyō of 1164 is a good example of this evocative style of illustration.

Illustrations were also painted in the upper sections over text that was written in the lower sections, or the illustrations were interspersed between sections of the text. In both cases the text and picture were more closely interwoven than in frontispiece illustrations, and therefore these paintings were often more literal renditions of the text.

Finally, there were sūtra illustrations that had no relationship to the text. These illustrations were linked to the sponsor or copyist of the sūtra and thereby emphasized the person to whom merit accrued for copying the sūtra. It is believed that the fan-shaped booklets from the twelfth century at Shitennōji are examples of a sūtra written over paper painted with genre, courtier, and landscape scenes that once belonged to the sponsor of the copied sūtra.

Regardless of format or material, sūtra illustrations functioned in many ways: as illustrations and evocations of the sūtra's content, as protective talismans of the text, as emblems of the sponsor, and as pure adornment to an object of reverence.

See also: **Scripture**

Bibliography

Egami, Yasushi, ed. *Sôshkugyō* (*Nihon no Bijutsu* no. 278). Tokyo: Shibundō, 1989.

Ōyama, Ninkai, ed. *Shakyō* (*Nihon no Bijutsu* no. 156). Tokyo: Shibundō, 1979.

Pal, Pratapadtya, and Meech-Pekarik, Julia. *Buddhist Book Illuminations.* New York: Ravi Kumar, 1988.

Tanabe, Willa Jane. *Paintings of the Lotus Sutra.* New York: Weatherhill, 1988.

WILLA JANE TANABE

SUVARṆAPRABHĀSOTTAMA-SŪTRA

A MAHĀYĀNA sūtra likely compiled in northern Indic or Central Asian regions between the first and third centuries C.E., the *Suvarṇaprabhāsottama-sūtra* (*Sūtra of Golden Light*) is rich and varied in content. The nineteen chapters of the Sanskrit version preserved in the Nepalese tradition include a confession ritual, several chapters that prescribe rituals surrounding the preaching or hearing of the sūtra, two chapters dealing with medicine, and three tales of the Buddha's past lives (JĀTAKA), including a distinctive telling of the well-known "Tigress Story." Most of the sūtra's seemingly disparate parts share an emphasis upon the transformative power of the sūtra itself, represented as golden light that infuses its preachers and auditors. The role of the sūtra in protecting and sustaining the kingdom of the ruler who accords it appropriate respect is another dominant theme.

The transmission history of the text is particularly complex. The sūtra is partially or wholly extant in seven languages other than Sanskrit (Chinese, Tibetan, Khotanese, Sogdian, Tangut, Mongolian, and Old Uighur), in versions ranging from eighteen to thirty-one chapters in length. Both the Chinese and the Tibetan canons preserve several different versions of the sūtra. Many of the translations are based not on the Sanskrit sūtra but on YIJING's thirty-one chapter Chinese translation of the early eighth century. The Mongolian translations are based on the versions in the Tibetan canon. In both China and Japan the sūtra was a central text in imperial rituals and was the subject of several commentaries. In Tibet, the text was sometimes classified as a TANTRA rather than a sūtra.

See also: **Sanskrit, Buddhist Literature in**

Bibliography

Emmerick, R. E., trans. *The Sūtra of Golden Light, Being a Translation of the Suvarṇaprabhāsottama-sūtra,* 2nd edition. Oxford: Pāli Text Society, 1992.

NATALIE D. GUMMER

SUZUKI, D. T.

Daisetsu Teitarō Suzuki (1870–1966) was one of the most important individuals involved in the twentieth-century spread of Japanese Buddhism, particularly Zen, to the West. A lay popularizer of Japanese spirituality, Suzuki resided in the United States for two extended periods, in the early twentieth century and again in the 1950s. Through his distinctive lectures and voluminous, though idiosyncratic, writings in English, Suzuki sparked an interest in Zen and Japanese culture among many influential Western scholars, intellectuals, artists, and writers.

See also: **Chan School; Japan; Zen, Popular Conceptions of**

RICHARD M. JAFFE

SYNCRETIC SECTS: THREE TEACHINGS

While popular religious movements have left their marks in the Chinese historical record since the Eastern Han dynasty (25–220 C.E.), a new type of syncretic sectarianism emerged from the Yuan dynasty (1279–1368) onwards. Continuing trends begun under the preceding Song dynasty (960–1279), this age was characterized by expanding commerce, the spread of literacy, a flourishing printing and publishing industry, improved communication and transport systems throughout the empire, and increasing social and geographical mobility of the population. All of these factors facilitated the flow of religious ideas across regions, denominational boundaries, and classes, and thereby stimulated the emergence of new religious movements. The resulting syncretic proclivities of the age are part of a long history of negotiating the relationship of China's two major indigenous traditions (Confucianism and Daoism) with the foreign newcomer, Buddhism. Harmonizing tendencies constituted a strong intellectual undercurrent among the literati elite, while striking even deeper roots in popular religion, where a focus on family and the local community did not require exclusive affiliation with a particular teaching. Instead, each was seen to have its role to play in the life cycles of families and communities, and thus the concepts and religious specialists associated with each could be drawn upon as needed. This general outlook conditioned the efforts of popular religious virtuosi, creative individuals who possessed enough literacy to benefit from the burgeoning supply of printed texts, but lacked the formal education needed to gain access to literati circles. Many founders of popular sects from the Yuan dynasty onwards came from the ranks of these "folk intellectuals," who received inspiration from many sources and combined their ideas into new religious systems. These systems become visible to the historian of religion primarily in the texts composed by sectarian founders, texts that are treasure troves of information on the religious life of China throughout the Late Imperial period up into modern times.

This entry will focus on the contributions of Buddhism to the colorful world of Chinese popular sectarianism. The impact of Buddhist thought varied from sect to sect, with some movements being so strongly Buddhist in orientation that they have been regarded by outside observers as "lay" or "folk Buddhist" movements, while the teachings of others were more influenced by Daoism. Lin Zhao'en (1517–1598), for example, founded the Sanyi Jiao (Three-in-One sect), which sought to combine the Three Teachings, but in doing so emphasized Confucianism and the internal alchemy of Quanzhen (Complete Realization) Daoism over Buddhism. On the other hand, Luo Qing (1442–1527), founder of the Wuwei (Non-Action) sect, was a major figure in Buddhist-inspired sectarianism. Originally a soldier by profession, he set out on a quest for salvation, studied with various masters, and drew inspiration from a large number of texts, the majority of which were Buddhist in nature. Among these, the *Jin'gang keyi* (*Ritual Amplification of the Diamond Sūtra*) touched him particularly; he devoted three years of study to this text and frequently referred to it in his writings. His teachings show a strong influence of Chan Buddhism, with an emphasis on the individual's recovery of his or her innate buddha-nature, or TATHĀGATAGARBHA. For Luo Qing, the concept of ŚŪNYATĀ (EMPTINESS) collapsed all distinctions, including those between men and women, and clergy and laity, opening up release from SAṂSĀRA for all living beings. His writings were gathered in a collection called the *Wubu liuce* (*Five Books in Six Volumes*), which still enjoys the status of sacred scripture among present-day sects such as the Longhua Pai (Dragon Flower Sect) of southeastern China.

Alongside the "popular Chan" of Luo Qing, there developed a separate sectarian tradition of a millenarian nature. The first text to formulate this approach is, in fact, the earliest surviving sectarian scripture, dated to 1430: the *Foshuo huangji jieguo baojuan* (*Precious Volume Expounded by the Buddha on the [Karmic] Results of the [Teaching of the] Imperial Ultimate [Period]*). Here we find a Buddhist inspired view of the world as moving through three cycles: First there was the Ultimateless (*wuji*) period reigned over by the Lamplighter (Dīpaṃkara) Buddha (Randeng Fo); the present age is that of the Great Ultimate (*taiji*), governed by Śākyamuni Buddha; and now the world is about to enter the Imperial Ultimate (*huangji*) period of the Buddha MAITREYA. This three-stage COSMOLOGY with its eschatological expectation of a savior ushering in a new and better world became a powerful motif among later popular sects. It was modified somewhat by the introduction of a mother goddess, the Eternal Mother (Wusheng Laomu), who dispatched the various buddhas to the world so that her human children might return to their original home at their Mother's side. This return is becoming urgent as the world enters its final period and is on an inexorable course toward apocalyptic destruction. Sometimes, sectarian leaders themselves claimed to be Maitreya, sent by the Eternal Mother to gather in her children; occasionally, millenarian fervor initiated political action, as sects rebelled in an attempt to usher in the new age. The best-known modern representative of this millenarian tradition is the Yiguan Dao (Way of Unity), an influential religious movement in Taiwan and Hong Kong and among overseas Chinese, which was founded in the 1920s by a patriarch who claimed to be the Living Buddha Jigong, dispatched by the Eternal Mother to open up a path of salvation in this final age.

Thus, Buddhism historically served as an important source of inspiration for Chinese popular sects. Buddhist concepts and themes were integrated with Confucian and Daoist elements, as well as with elements of popular origin (such as mediumistic practices), to produce a variegated array of religious movements. The creativity of popular sectarianism has not ebbed in the modern age, as new sects keep emerging. Some of these draw on older sectarian traditions, while others make a fresh start by taking a new look at China's Three Teachings. A modern example of a sect that draws strongly on (in this case, tantric) Buddhist material is the Zhenfo Zong (True Buddha movement), founded by Lu Shengyan (1945–) in the 1980s. Headquartered in Seattle, Washington, it is particularly active among overseas Chinese. While usually eyed with some suspicion by the mainline SAṄGHA, the Buddhist borrowings of such syncretic sects are a testimony to the successful integration of Buddhism into Chinese popular culture and to its power to inspire religious innovation.

See also: **Confucianism and Buddhism; Daoism and Buddhism; Folk Religion, China; Millenarianism and Millenarian Movements**

Bibliography

Berling, Judith A. *The Syncretic Religion of Lin Chao-en.* New York: Columbia University Press, 1980.

Dean, Kenneth. *Lord of the Three in One: The Spread of a Cult in Southeast China.* Princeton, NJ: Princeton University Press, 1998.

Haar, Barend J. ter. *The White Lotus Teachings in Chinese Religious History.* Leiden, Netherlands: Brill, 1992.

Jordan, David K., and Overmyer, Daniel L. *The Flying Phoenix: Aspects of Chinese Sectarianism in Taiwan.* Princeton, NJ: Princeton University Press, 1986.

Ma Xisha, and Han Bingfang. *Zhongguo minjian zongjiaoshi.* Shanghai: Shanghai Renmin Chubanshe, 1992.

Overmyer, Daniel L. *Folk Buddhist Religion.* Cambridge, MA: Harvard University Press, 1976.

Overmyer, Daniel L. "Messenger, Savior, and Revolutionary: Maitreya in Chinese Popular Religious Literature of the Sixteenth and Seventeenth Centuries." In *Maitreya, the Future Buddha,* ed. Alan Sponberg and Helen Hardacre. Cambridge, UK: Cambridge University Press, 1988.

Overmyer, Daniel L. *Precious Volumes: An Introduction to Chinese Sectarian Scriptures from the Sixteenth and Seventeenth Centuries.* Cambridge, MA: Harvard University Asia Center, 1999.

Philip Clart

T

TACHIKAWARYŪ

Tachikawaryū is the name of a subschool of Shingon Buddhism, one of the two Japanese schools of tantric Buddhism. Probably founded by Ninkan, who was active in the early twelfth century, Tachikawaryū seems to have continued into the seventeenth century. The epithets often associated with it, "perverse teaching" or "perverse school," imply that this subschool taught a set of doctrines and rituals that were strongly sexualized. Tachikawaryū was denounced by Yūkai (1345–1416) and other representatives of the Buddhist orthodoxy during the Middle Ages, and most of the texts associated with the school are now lost. However, examination of the few extant texts that can be traced back to Tachikawaryū reveals that its teachings were not very different from those of the other Shingon subschools. In addition, a close reading of Shinjō's *Juhō-yōjin shū* (*Circumspect Acceptance of the Dharma*, 1268), the earliest text that is commonly believed to be a denunciatory account of Tachikawaryū practices, reveals that the sexual rituals described are not said to pertain to Tachikawaryū. Shinjō speaks simply of "these rituals," without naming them.

It is possible to distinguish at least two levels of sexual doctrines and rituals in medieval Japanese religion. First, in every lineage of what is usually called *kenmitsu* Buddhism, sexual elements were widely spread and practiced, at least in a metaphorical way. Tachikawaryū may well be counted as one of these lineages, although there were certainly more purist tendencies in each lineage. Second, the rituals described by Shinjō may have been taught and practiced only in a particular segment of this general movement. The rituals imply not only sexual intercourse, but also ritual use of a human skull.

See also: **Exoteric-Esoteric (Kenmitsu) Buddhism in Japan; Japan; Kamakura Buddhism, Japan; Shingon Buddhism, Japan; Shintō (Honji Suijaku) and Buddhism**

Bibliography

Kock, Stephen. "The Dissemination of the Tachikawa-ryū and the Problem of Orthodox and Heretic Teaching in Shingon Buddhism." *Studies in Indian Philosophy and Buddhism*, Tokyo University, 7 (2000): 69–83.

Sanford, James. "The Abominable Tachikawa Skull Ritual." *Monumenta Nipponica* 46, no. 1 (1991): 1–20.

NOBUMI IYANAGA

TAIWAN

Scholars can document the existence of Buddhism in Taiwan only from the migration of Chinese fleeing to the island after their failure to restore the fallen Ming dynasty in 1662. The "Southern Ming" court ruled Taiwan until the Qing dynasty captured the island in 1683. The subsequent history of Buddhism in Taiwan falls into three periods delimited by the three political regimes that followed: Qing rule (1683–1895); Japanese viceroyalty (1895–1945); and Han Chinese rule (1945–present).

The Southern Ming/Qing dynasty period

Chinese and Japanese scholars agree that knowledge and practice of Buddhism during this time was relatively unsophisticated. Taiwan was a land of pirates, typhoons, plagues, and headhunting natives, and did not attract China's social elite. Many of the "monks"

A row of golden Buddha statues at Fo Kuang Shan Monastery, Kaohsiung, Taiwan. © Michael S. Yamashita/Corbis. Reproduced by permission.

of this period were Ming loyalists who fled to the island in clerical disguise, and legitimate clerics were few in number and largely ignorant of Buddhist teachings. Those whose names appear in the records were noted for non-Buddhist accomplishments such as rainmaking, painting, poetry, and playing *go*. Most clerics functioned as temple caretakers and funeral specialists, and did not engage in teaching, meditation or other Buddhist practices.

The first known monk to migrate from the mainland is Canche (d.u.), who arrived in 1675. Chen Yonghua, a military commander, had built a monastery called the Dragon Lake Grotto (Longhu Yan), and invited Canche to serve as abbot. Canche later founded the Blue Cloud Monastery (Biyun-si) on Fire Mountain (Huoshan) near the present-day town of Chia-yi.

As the island became more settled, many more monasteries were founded, particularly around the capital city of Tainan. Notable among these early monasteries are the Zhuxi ("Bamboo Stream") Monastery (1664); the Haihui ("Ocean Assembly") Monastery (1680); the Fahua ("Dharma-Flower") Monastery (1683); the Mituo ("Amitābha") Monastery (d.u.); the Longshan ("Dragon Mountain") Monastery (1738); the Chaofeng ("Surpassing Peak") Monastery (registered 1763); and the Daxian ("Great Immortal") Monastery (d.u.). Despite this vigorous activity, most of the MONKS and NUNS in these monasteries had probably received only the novices' ordination; there was no ordaining monastery in Taiwan, and only scant records exist of those who journeyed to the mainland to receive the full PRECEPTS.

The Japanese colonial period

In 1895 the Chinese government ceded the island to Japan, and the Japanese troops brought Buddhist chaplains with them. These chaplains were eager to establish mission stations in order to propagate Japanese Buddhism to the native population, but funding from their head temples was insufficient, and only a very small percentage of the Chinese population ever enrolled in Japanese Buddhist lineages.

One of the most notable features of the Japanese period was, in fact, the effort on the part of the local

Buddhists to maintain their Chinese identity and traditions. This period saw the institution of the first facilities for transmitting the full monastic precepts in Taiwan. Four monasteries established "ordination platforms": The Lingquan ("Spirit Spring") Chan Monastery in Keelung, the Lingyun ("Soaring Cloud") Chan Monastery on Guanyin Mountain, the Fayun ("Dharma Cloud") Chan Monastery near Miaoli, and the Chaofeng ("Surpassing the Peak") Monastery in Kaohsiung County. The leaders of these monasteries all received ordination at the Yongquan ("Surging Spring") Monastery in Fuzhou, China, and they transmitted their tonsure-lineages to Taiwan. Monks and nuns ordained from these monasteries went forth and founded other monasteries, giving rise to the "four great ancestral lineages" that defined and organized Buddhism during this period.

At the same time, there were small groups of Chinese Buddhist monks who studied Marxism and advocated the relaxation of monastic discipline as a means to strengthen solidarity with ordinary people, while also resisting Japanese domination.

Even as Chinese Buddhism attempted to maintain its own distinctive identity, it still had to accommodate the government; thus clergy and laity joined together to form Buddhist organizations that functioned as governmental liaisons. The largest of these, founded in 1922 by Marui Keijirō, was called the South Seas Buddhist Association, which operated until 1945. These organizations were significant because they included members of *zhaijiao*, the "vegetarian religion"—a form of popular Buddhism that stood apart from the monastic establishment and rejected its oversight. Zhaijiao's participation in these Buddhist organizations marks the only time in history that they ever cooperated with monastic Buddhism. In 1945 they parted ways once again.

The Republican period (1945–present)

At the end of the Pacific War (known as World War II in the United States), Taiwan was returned to China, and the Japanese were evacuated. Four years later, in 1949, mainland China fell to the communists, and the nationalists fled to Taiwan. All of these events kept the political and economic situation in turmoil, and Buddhist clerics experienced difficulty keeping their monasteries viable. A few refugee Buddhist monks from the mainland, such as Cihang (1895–1954), were imprisoned on suspicion of spying. A few monks of national eminence also arrived, such as the Zhangjia Living Buddha (1891–1957), Baisheng (1904–1989), Wuming (1912–), and YINSHUN (1906–). They were the leaders of the newly revived Buddhist Association of the Republic of China (BAROC), and came to Taiwan for reasons that paralleled those of the nationalists: to use Taiwan as a base of operations until they could return home to rebuild Buddhism.

The BAROC mediated between Buddhism and the government in several ways: The government expected it to register all clergy and temples, organize and administer clerical ordinations, certify clergy for exit visas, and help in framing laws dealing with religion. The BAROC also confronted the government when it felt religious interests were threatened. Two notable controversies concerned the failure of the government to return confiscated Japanese-era monasteries to religious use, and the government's obstruction of efforts to establish a Buddhist university.

Because the laws on civic organizations allowed only one organization to fill any single niche in society, the BAROC enjoyed hegemony until the late 1980s. In 1989 the government stopped dealing with Buddhist monks and nuns separately, and registered them under their lay names as ordinary citizens. Thus, the BAROC was no longer needed to certify their status. That same year, a new law on civic organizations took effect, abolishing the "one niche, one organization" rule and opening the way for competition. In the ensuing period, other Buddhist organizations took root. Some grew out of preexisting groups, most notably Fo Kuang Shan and the Buddhist Compassionate Relief Tz'u-Chi Association. Others were newly founded, such as Dharma Drum Mountain.

Recent changes

Buddhism in Taiwan has undergone many changes during the last few decades as the island has shifted from an agrarian, village-based to an industrial, urban-based society. Four particularly prominent developments follow.

Historically, monks have predominated numerically over nuns in Chinese Buddhism. Since the 1950s the number of nuns in Taiwan has increased relative to the number of monks: Between 1953 and 1986 the BAROC ordained 2,030 men and 6,006 women. With more women than men seeking ordination, women are much more likely to be eliminated or given longer periods of testing. This has raised the overall quality and status of the nuns' order relative to the monks.

A ceremony at Fo Kuang Shan Monastery, Kaohsiung, Taiwan, 1987.

This first development must be seen against a backdrop of steadily decreasing ordinations overall. Between 1949 and 1989, when the population of Taiwan rose from 7.5 million to over 20 million, the number of new ordinations each year, especially male, did not keep pace. Many observers understand this phenomenon to be part of a trend in the Buddhist world at large, where laity has grown increasingly active and prominent.

Third, the ethical content of Buddhism in Taiwan has undergone change. Some organizations such as Fo Kuang Shan and the Buddhist Compassionate Relief Tz'u-Chi Association have propounded new precepts that followers formally undertake. The founder of Fo Kuang Shan, Xingyun (1927–), has published his vision of "Fo Kuang Buddhism" in several lectures and books, in which he seeks to turn followers' attention away from otherworldly concerns, such as rituals for the dead and rebirth in the Pure Land, and toward efforts to benefit living beings in this world. Likewise, the Buddhist Compassionate Relief Tz'u-chi Association under its founder Zhengyan (1937–) trains its followers to be of assistance within the present world. As an association composed almost entirely of laypeople, the focus is on social action rather than maintaining monastic roles. Individual monasteries such as the Nongchan Monastery in northern Taipei and the Faguang Monastery in downtown Taipei are two of many that no longer use disposable chopsticks and bowls due to a concern for the environment. In all these contexts, the slogan is "to build a Pure Land on Earth."

Finally, Buddhist monasteries in Taiwan have changed their fund-raising methods in response to developments in the economic sphere. In place of traditional methods of generating income, such as soliciting donations, providing funeral services, and renting land for agriculture, many monasteries seek to build bases of lay support in a more systematic, less overtly commercial way. They organize their core constituency into lay organizations, such as the Dharmapāla organization that supports Dharma Drum Mountain. They found collegiate Buddhist fellowships and lead students in meditation or Pure Land retreats. Some of the larger urban monasteries have publishing concerns.

However, the most universal means of raising money is still to hold "dharma meetings" (*fahui*), in which laypeople come to hear sūtras recited, see the ceremony of releasing living beings (*fangsheng*), or witness a ritual for the Release of the Burning Mouths (*yuqie yankou*), in which hungry ghosts are freed from their torments, fed, and receive teaching.

See also: **China; Colonialism and Buddhism; Pure Land Schools**

Bibliography

Jones, Charles B. *Buddhism in Taiwan: Religion and the State 1660–1990.* Honolulu: University of Hawaii Press, 1999.

Jones, Charles B. "Buddhism and Marxism in Taiwan: Lin Qiuwu's Religious Socialism and Its Legacy in Modern Times." *Journal of Global Buddhism* 1 (2000): 82–111.

Laliberté, André. "The Politics of Buddhist Organizations in Taiwan: 1989–1997." Ph.D. diss. University of British Columbia, 1999.

CHARLES B. JONES

TAIXU

Taixu (Lü Peilin, 1890–1947) was a Chinese Buddhist monk and reformer in the early Republican era (1912–1949). He was born on January 8, 1890, into a working-class family in Haining County of Zhejiang Province. In 1904 he joined the monastic order and received the Buddhist name *Taixu* (Supreme Emptiness). Several months later, Taixu formally took the Buddhist precepts at Tiantong Monastery in Ningbo, Zhejiang, where he studied Buddhism with a focus on MAHĀYĀNA texts and Chan meditation.

Taixu started his reform activity by founding *Jueshe* (Awakening Society) in Shanghai in 1918. Disregarding opposition from conservative Buddhists, Taixu campaigned for a socially engaged form of Buddhism and for a worldwide Buddhist mission. He aimed to organize the Buddhist clergy, revitalize Mahāyāna teachings, and propagate Buddhist studies. He also called for the government to preserve monastic resources. Under Taixu's leadership, the monthly periodical *Haichao yin* (*The Sound of the Sea Tide*) began publication in 1920, and the *Wuchang foxue yuan* (Wuchang Buddhist Institute) in Hubei, the first modern Chinese Buddhist seminary, was established in 1922. During the 1930s Taixu's leadership declined in the Chinese Buddhist Association, which had been established by the monk Yuanying (1878–1953) in Shanghai in 1929. But Taixu's involvement with political leaders such as Chiang Kai-shek (1887–1975) of the Nationalist government enabled him to continue his Buddhist reforms and trips abroad.

After the end of World War II in 1945, Taixu regained his influence and served on the *Zhongguo fojiao zhengli weiyuan hui* (Committee for the Reorganization of Chinese Buddhism). Hindered by the civil war (1946–1949) between the Communists and Nationalists, Taixu was unable to complete his reforms. He died on March 17, 1947, in Shanghai. His writings and lectures were posthumously published under the title *Taixu dashi quanshu* (*The Collected Works of Great Master Taixu*).

Taixu is regarded as the most important and controversial reformer in the history of modern Chinese Buddhism. His significance lies not in his reform movements, which in fact yielded limited results, but rather in his vision and ideas to modernize Chinese Buddhism through lay cooperation, intellectual promotion, social engagement, and international involvement.

See also: **China; Yinshun**

Bibliography

Pittman, Don A. *Toward a Modern Chinese Buddhism: Taixu's Reforms.* Honolulu: University of Hawaii Press, 2001.

Taixu dashi quanshu (*The Collected Works of Great Master Taixu*), 62 vols. Taibei: Haichao yin she, 1950–.

DING-HWA HSIEH

TAKUAN SŌHŌ

Takuan Sōhō (1573–1645) was a Japanese Zen (Chan) priest affiliated with the Daitokuji temple in Kyoto. In 1629 the Tokugawa government banished Takuan to northern Japan because of his open opposition to the new government regulations that had been imposed on the Zen monasteries of Kyoto. After his pardon in 1632, Takuan moved to Edo (modern Tokyo), where he eventually became adviser to the third Tokugawa shogun, Iemitsu (1604–1651). Today Takuan is best remembered for a letter he wrote to the fencing instructor Yagyū Munenori (1571–1646) in which he used swordsmanship as an example to explain the importance of imperturbability and mental freedom in the performance of one's duties. Reprinted under the title *Fudōchi shinmyōroku* (*Record of Marvelous Immovable Wisdom*), Takuan's treatise is frequently cited by people who advocate a connection between Buddhism, especially Zen, and Japanese martial arts.

See also: **Chan School; Martial Arts; Zen, Popular Conceptions of**

WILLIAM M. BODIFORD

TANTRA

Tantra in Western nomenclature has achieved forms of signification independent from its Sanskritic use and has become a somewhat promiscuous category applied to various RITUALS otherwise not easily classified. In general parlance, tantra indicates the pan-Indic religious system that became emulated in Buddhist, Hindu, and Jain circles, and tantra is often understood as having an erotic component. This entry will discuss the idea of tantra in India and in Central and East Asia.

India and Nepal

The word *tantra* in India was much more widely applied than might be understood from the modern explanation of its derivation from √*tan*—to weave. In medieval Sanskrit, the term signifies many forms of complex arrangement and may denote military deployment, a loom, certain forms of ritual, a political culture, a scriptural text emphasizing selected rituals, the pan-Indic religious aesthetic, and so on. In Buddhism, tantra is usually understood to include the use of MANTRAS authorized by a preceptor on a disciple during a complex initiation rite that confers the disciple with the authority to engage in many different kinds of ritual associated with a specific class of BUDDHAS, BODHISATTVAS, or Buddhist DIVINITIES. Included in the rituals are the construction or visualization of sacred circles (MAṆḌALA), the use of hand gestures (MUDRĀ), and the employment of fire sacrifice (*homa*), all of which may be for the purpose of specific soteriological or nonsoteriological goals. These latter are usually the four ritual actions of the pacification of obstacles, the increase of prosperity, the subjugation of difficulties, and the destruction of enemies; they may be performed for the practitioner's own ends or on behalf of a patron.

However, many of these elements had already enjoyed a lengthy precedent in Buddhist ritual long before the coalescence of mature esoteric Buddhism—to which tantra may properly be applied—in the late seventh and early eighth centuries. It is historically misleading to understand normative MAHĀYĀNA rituals as tantric in any significant sense, despite the fact that many of them make use of several of the elements eventually included in esoteric Buddhism. Moreover, many of the buddhas, bodhisattvas, and Buddhist divinities that originated in the Mahāyānist ritual environment eventually made the easy transition to the esoteric milieu. The primary difference between normative Mahāyāna and tantric Buddhism is that the latter appropriates an overarching political metaphor of overlordship in this very life, so that the INITIATION is performed in a manner derived from the coronation rituals of medieval Hinduism. Tantric Buddhism may be understood as a sacralization of the early medieval political and military fragmentation of North India, with its contentious rivalries between feudal clans. Consequently, it expresses an emphasis on secrecy, loyalty, allegiance, and unbreakable trust; on the visualization of self as a divine king (*devatārāja*) controlling complex spheres of dominion and power (maṇḍala); on new arrangements of vows; and on the use of any means necessary to achieve stated goals or secret ends. All of these items are generally absent from normative Mahāyānist rites.

Thus, replacing the self-sacrificial bodhisattva is the ideal of all-powerful siddha or MAHĀSIDDHA, the perfected being to whom no standards of behavior can apply. Siddhas also employed the methods of medieval sorcerers (VIDYĀDHARA)—such as the tantric feast (*gaṇacakra*) involving the sacramental employment of ritualized group sex and the ingestion of illicit substances like meat and liquor—in their search for magical powers. In imitation of the behavior of Śaiva and other ascetics, some siddhas wore ornaments of human bone, carried staffs of distinctive shapes, and frequented cremation grounds or forest areas. Their interest in tribal peoples is a theme in much of the later literature, and some siddhas were known to have spent time among the forest tribes of Central or Eastern India. From them, specific divinities appear to have been appropriated, possibly including Śaṃvara, Heruka, and Jāṅguli. Siddhas were also interested in herbs and drugs, and their use of intoxicants like datura is well attested. The tendency to group siddhas into various numbering systems (84 being most common, but 20, 40, 50, 80, and other numbers are also seen) occurred rather late and reflects Indian organizational strategies.

Siddhas may have been a minority, though, since Buddhist monks are quite frequently represented as Buddhist monastic *tāntrikas.* Monastic Buddhism apparently tried to displace overt siddha behavior with visualized or covert forms, and we occasionally read of monks becoming siddhas by being expelled from their cloisters for inappropriate behavior. Monks were responsible for domesticating the esoteric method by formulating it as on a continuum with monastic and Mahāyāna vows. This eighth-century hermeneutic was formalized in the triple discipline: The tantric master is expected to practice the vows of the monk (*prātimokṣasaṃvara*), the bodhisattva (*bodhisattvasaṃvara*), and the sorcerer (*vidyādharasaṃvara*). This reading emphasized that the esoteric system was a branch of the Mahāyāna—the mantra-method (*mantranaya*).

The maturation of tantric Buddhism happened surprisingly quickly. There is no concrete evidence for tantra prior to the late seventh century, and yet all the basic principles were in place a century later. It is also primarily a North and Central Indian phenomenon, with modest contributions from South India or Sri Lanka. The emphasis on PILGRIMAGE sites predominantly found in North and Central India, like the legendary Oḍiyāna (Swat Valley), reflect this reality. Because tantra arose in a culture of fragmentation, there is little textual unity, and the works classified by later authors as tantric may call themselves by other titles: discourse (sūtra), meditative aid (DHĀRAṆĪ), secret spell (MANTRA), incantation (*vidyā*), ritual (kalpa), as well as tantra. The textual sources gain added complexity through the tendency of later authors to read esoteric directions into earlier Buddhist scriptures and to incorporate these scriptures in their exegesis. Accordingly, the HEART SŪTRA is often taken as a tantric text, since it contains a mantra, even though this text predates any tantric Buddhism per se.

Classificatory systems thus had to wrestle with great differences in texts, and consequently there is no unanimity on tantric typology. Perhaps the most basic scheme is that employed by Buddhaguhya and others in the mid-eighth century: Tantras are those that emphasize external ritual activity (*kriyānaya-tantra*) or those that emphasize internal yogic practices (*yoganaya-tantra*). The fourfold classification favored by Tibetans has been often cited: Tantras are those that enjoin ritual action (*kriyā*), behavioral practice (*caryā*), meditation (yoga), or the highest yoga (*anuttarayoga-tantra*). Textual examples include the *Susiddhikara* (*kriyā*), the *Vairocanābhisambodhi* (*caryā*), the *Sarvatathāgatatattvasaṃgraha* (yoga), and the *Guhyasamāja* (*anuttara-yoga-tantra*). The latter category was often subdivided into two, with the *Guhyasamāja* being a *mahāyoga-tantra* and works like the *Cakrasaṃvara* classified as a *yoginī-tantra.* It must be emphasized, though, that there were many other typologies—some with seven or more categories. Neither was there unanimity on which texts actually belonged to which categories, irrespective of the number of categories. Some important texts, like the *Mañjuśrīnāmasaṃgīti* or the *Hevajra,* might be classified into two or three categories, depending on the interpretation.

Linguistically, the tantras reflect the regionalization of Indian society. They are written in regional or nonstandard Sanskrit—often influenced by colloquial expressions or grammar—and some of those composed in Eastern India use vernacular-based literary languages, such as Apabhraṃśa, in liturgical environments. Siddhas would also compose adamantine songs (*vajragīti*) to express their understanding or to critique others, and they often provided a signature line to identify the author. Consequently, tantric Buddhism returned to the autobiographical voice and the use of non-Sanskritic languages, as had been done in the early days of Buddhist literature but had been largely abandoned under the influence of the classical Mahāyāna.

Ritually, the fundamental meditative ritual became the sādhana, a rite wherein the meditator visualized the buddha or divinity as before him or identical to himself, prior to performing specific activities: recitation of mantras, yoga, fire sacrifice, initiation, tantric feast, and so on. The visualization sequence most often included imagining a royal palace inside a protective sphere, and visualizing a lotus on which is placed a seed syllable (*bījamantra*), which transforms first into a symbol of the divinity and then into the divinity itself. Thus, the syllable *om* might turn into a wheel and then into the Buddha Vairocana. If the practice contained a full maṇḍala of buddhas or divinities, the meditator would perform the same act (or an abbreviated version) for each figure. Because the maṇḍala is generated or born, this meditative form is sometimes called the birthing or developing process (*utpattikrama*).

Many of the later tantras also discuss an esoteric yogic physiology, sometimes called the *vajra*-body, in which the body contains psychic ganglia that may be represented in the form of wheels (cakra) or other arrangement. Generally, they contain the letters of the Sanskrit alphabet, the vowels (*āli*) and consonants (*kāli*), in one or another of many specified combinations.

Connecting the ganglia are channels (*nāḍi*) through which flows karmic winds (*karmavāyu*) that are closely involved with the physiological and psychological processes. The letters and winds may also be posited as being the internal representations of external phenomena, so that the meditator's perceptions are a result of the karmic relationship between the microcosm and macrocosm. The channels include a central channel and a left and right channel, eventually branching out into seventy-two thousand subsidiary channels that reach all areas of the body. In different visualizations, often called the perfecting process (*sampannakrama*), the meditator may imagine a flame below the navel or various lights in the wheels or employ a female sexual partner as a physical aid to harness the psychophysical process. By manipulating the winds that control his psychic processes, the meditator seeks eventually to drive these winds into some area of the central channel, an act that is said to transform the psychophysical winds into the gnostic wind (*jñānavāyu*). As the process is accomplished, a series of visions emerges, ending in an awareness of the illusory nature of interior and exterior phenomena, with all forms finally resolving into the clear light of ultimate reality.

Hayagrīva, a Buddhist wrathful deity, shown with his consort. (Tibetan sculpture, bronze, eighteenth century.) The Art Archive/Musée Guimet Paris/Dagli Orti. Reproduced by permission.

Central Asia and Tibet

Tantric Buddhism became quickly popular in the areas immediately contiguous to Northern India—Burma, Nepal, Tibet, Nanzhao—and spread into Central Asia and China. Tantric works were eventually translated into the Central Asian languages of Khotanese, Uighur, Tangut, and Mongolian, but TIBET became the most important area of tantric development. Three of the four major Tibetan orders—SA SKYA (SAKYA)-pa, BKA' BRGYUD (KAGYU)-pa, and Dga' ldan-pa (Gandenpa)—maintained a more or less conservative approach, following closely the later Indian tantras and other Indian scriptures translated in the astonishing efforts of the eighth through the fifteenth centuries.

The RNYING MA (NYINGMA)-pa order, however, continued the Indian culture of scriptural composition rather than the simply the conservation of received Indian works. As a result, the production of tantras in Buddhist Tibet equaled or exceeded the number and volume produced in Buddhist India, and these Tibetan works were collected together with a few important Indian tantras into the *Rnying ma rgyud 'bum* (*Old Tantric Canon*), beginning in the eleventh century. Most of these texts claim translation from a non-Tibetan source: from Oḍiyāna, Brusha, India, or the realm of the goddesses. Many are revealed in the process of the treasure (*gterma*) phenomenon in Tibet and are said to have been buried physically or spiritually on Tibetan soil by important saints of the eighth- to ninth-century royal dynastic period of Tibetan history.

While the content of many of the works is only beginning to be explored, our catalogues classify the *Old Tantric Canon* into the standard fourfold division accepted by most Tibetans (*kriyā*, etc.), with the difference that the Highest Yoga tantras are further divided into three: *mahāyoga*, *anuyoga*, and *atiyoga*. Generally, it is considered that the first two correspond in content to the division of Indian tantras into *mahāyoga* and *yoginī-tantras* (while the texts themselves are mostly different) but the *atiyoga* category is understood to be a Rnying ma category, even though the term was used in India to describe a stage of meditative ritual. In Rnying ma parlance, *atiyoga* is generally equated with the Great Perfection (*rdzogs chen*) and its literature is subdivided into three further varieties: the mental class (*sems sde*), the expanse class (*klong sde*), and the seminal drop class (*snying thig sde*). The first of these (mental class) appears to have evolved from the doctrines concerning the mind of awakening (*bodhicitta*), an important development in seventh- to eighth-century India based on an earlier Mahāyānist idea. The second and third classes, however, are Rnying ma contributions and represent in some sense the flowering of indigenous Tibetan spirituality, although they build on Indian ideas and practices. *Atiyoga* tantras are also qualitatively different from Indian works by their increased emphasis on doctrinal and philosophical expressions rather than performative ritual systems, so that they constitute some of the more interesting expressions of Buddhist ideology.

East Asia

The question of the existence and role of tantra in East Asia has provoked considerable disagreement. While the dissemination of South Asian texts, rituals, and ideas that may be designated as tantric was a major factor in the cultural milieus of China, Korea, and Japan from the eighth century onward, these developments were usually understood as new discursive and ritual extensions of the Mahāyāna. A survey of the Japanese *Bukkyō daijiten* (*Encyclopedia of Buddhism*) and the *Mikkyō daijiten* (*Encyclopedia of the Esoteric Teachings*) yields almost no references to tantra and the phrase "great teaching king" (*da jiao wang*) that sometimes served as a translation of *mahātantrarāja* is rare and occurs mostly in titles of a few Song dynasty (960–1279) translators. The scarcity of the designation is not merely an effect of an ideological rejection of later tantras, such as the *Hevajra*, by Japanese Shingon orthodoxy. Rather, the absence of a transliterated form of the term *tantra* in the context of assiduous transliteration of mantras and dhāraṇīs into Chinese underscores the irrelevance of the term throughout most of East Asia. While *tantra* is missing, mantra, dhāraṇī, *siddhi*, abhiṣeka, *homa*, *āveśa* (induced trance), and so on are well attested both in transliterated and translated forms.

Rather than either trying to apply a South Asian label that East Asians ignored or trying to measure Chinese and Korean religious history by the yardstick of Japanese sectarian developments, we do better asking a different set of questions, questions guided by the vocabulary that is present: Where do the ideas, discourses, pantheon, practices, and texts of South Asian tantra appear in East Asia? Who circulates them and what are the conditions of their reproduction, assimilation, and transformation?

A variety of tantras were quickly translated or summarized in Chinese. By the mid-eighth century the *Susiddhikara*, the *Vairocanābhisambodhi*, the *Sarvatathāgatatattvasaṃgraha*, and the *Subāhuparipṛcchā* had been translated, and we have evidence that the *Guhyasamāja* was known. So too, by the mid-eighth century, rituals to evoke or propitiate deities as diverse as Mārīcī, the lords of the Great Dipper, Buddhoṣṇīṣa, and the various *vidyārājas* had spread as far as Japan. By the end of the tenth century a version of the *Mañjuśrīmūlakalpa* and a complete version of the *Sarvatathāgatatattvasaṃgraha* had been translated into Chinese. By the twelfth century the full range of tantra, ritual manuals, and associated paraphernalia were available.

As in South Asia, in East Asia we find certain distinctive metaphors and practices connected with the circulation and assimilation of these texts. These include the pervasive use of the maṇḍala as an organizing principle and with it, its South Asian derived metaphors of sovereignty, unlimited power or *siddhi* (both for mundane and soteriological purposes), the notion of mantra, and rites of immolation (including those for pacification, increase of fortune, subjugation, and destruction), initiation, trance, and notions of secrecy. In the broadest sense, what we are dealing with is the afterlife of South Asian originated or inspired iconic discourses and ritual technologies for producing and manipulating the divine and the demonic in tangible form. In practice this adaptation of South Asian forms can range from the consecration of images to the induction of trance through possession, to the assumption of divine identity by the adept. The often trumpeted transgressiveness of tantra is a direct function of its core metaphors of kingship, its assertion of unlimited sovereignty, and the particular social locations of its practitioners. Thus, in East Asia the court was the natural locus of these systems. When located outside the court, "tantra" manifested in the pseudo KINGSHIP of siddhas and the occult.

China and Korea

The signature South Asian characteristic of tantra—its extensive application of the kingship metaphor deployed in maṇḍala and enacted in ritual—made it at once a possible threat to the Chinese imperial establishment and then a valued form of legitimation. Thus, the Indian missionary Śubhākarasiṃha (637–735) was initially treated with suspicion by emperor Xuanzong (r. 712–756). He was placed under house arrest, and his Sanskrit texts were impounded. But it soon became clear that the new teachings came along with considerable advances in mathematics and particularly calendrical astronomy, areas that were central to imperial ideology. The polymath monk Yixing (673–727) was assigned to spy on Śubhākarasiṃha, as much as to help him in his work of translation and dissemination of the *Vairocanābhisambodhi* and other mantra (Chinese, *zhenyan*) teachings, including the *Subāhuparipṛcchā*. A few years later in 720 C.E. the monk Vajrabodhi (671–741) arrived in the Chinese capital Chang'an (possibly from Śrīvijaya) and soon he and his chief disciple Amoghavajra (705–774) were, if not embraced by the court, at least given permission to translate texts and to take on disciples in exchange for performing ritual duties for the imperial house. Amoghavajra proved himself a valuable ally to the imperial house during the chaos of the An Lushan rebellion (755–763) and he gave emperor Suzong (r. 756–762) abhiṣeka as a cakravartin or world-ruling king. Under Suzong and then under his successor Daizong (r. 762–779), Amoghavajra and his disciples articulated an ideology of dual rulership with the cakravartin supported by his ācārya (religious preceptor) in a pattern remarkably similar to that found in South Asia. Amoghavajra not only produced translations of tantras and ritual manuals, but he also produced updated versions of some Mahāyāna texts, bringing their language into line with the latest esoteric or mantra discourses by adding dhāraṇī and ritual commentaries. The most prominent of these texts was the Chinese RENWANG JING (HUMANE KINGS SŪTRA), a scripture that melded traditional Chinese and Buddhist notions of rulership. Under Amoghavajra's tutelage the teachings associated with the *Sarvatathāgatatattvasaṃgraha* permeated much of the court, the military, and many imperial institutions. A ritual arena for *homa* and other practices was established in the imperial compound. Mañjuśrī replaced Piṇḍola in monastic refectories, large numbers of "tantric" ritual manuals were translated, and permanent altars for *homa* and abhiṣeka were constructed. Thematically speaking, Amoghavajra's Buddhism was, to borrow the Korean phrase, "State Protection Buddhism," and its most developed ritual dimensions concerned propping up the imperial house, ensuring the health of the emperor, giving succor to its ANCESTORS, helping to keep meterological and cosmic portents favorable, and generally esoterizing monastic establishments that were imperially funded. Although Daizong's successor Dezong (r. 779–805) initially severed lavish patronage to the mantra teachings, he later reversed his decision and supported the last of the great South Asian translators of the Tang, the monk Prajña (734–806?).

Imperial patronage henceforth was spotty. During the early Song dynasty the last group of great South Asian translators, Dharmapāla (963–1058), Dānapāla (fl. tenth century), and Fatian (d. 1001) produced more complete versions of the *Sarvatathāgatatattvasaṃgraha*, a version of the *Guhyasamāja*, and a translation of the *Śrīvajramaṇḍalāṃkāramahātantrarāja*. Patronage was, however, sporadic until the Mongols (Yuan dynasty, 1234–1368) and even later Ming (1368–1644) and Qing dynasty (1644–1911) patronage of Tibetan VAJRAYĀNA. Severed from the court and bereft of its natural metaphoric locale at the actual center of power, various elements of the system merged back into the stream of late Mahāyāna while others were simply rolled into Vajrayāna from Tibet. Indeed, the ritual technology associated with these teachings, especially that promising various forms of *siddhi* and connected with *homa* and *āveśa*, had an impact not only on the Mahāyāna in China, but also on Daoism and on local religious traditions. Perhaps more than all the divinities and complex ritual, Chinese traditions—Buddhist and non-Buddhist alike—found the ideology of hiddenness and the aura of the esoteric power of mantra most appealing. The idea of mantra had already been circulating from the second century onward and served as a model for the Brahmā-language of Daoist scripture. An exclusive focus on the short-lived presence of a sectarian tantric or esoteric "school" misses the point entirely. By the twelfth century there were esoteric CHAN SCHOOL transmissions, rites deriving directly from the tantras in use in PURE LAND SCHOOL circles and more generally for the salvation of the dead (the *shishi* or "distribution" of food to ghosts and the elaborate *shuilu* or Land and Water Masses). Popular accounts of the ācāryas celebrated their wielding of *siddhi* in a manner not unlike tales of siddhas found in South Asia and Tibet.

While a polity inspired by and enacted according to the *Sarvatathāgatatattvasaṃgraha* was made an actuality for some twenty-five years in China, we have no solid evidence that the teaching garnered full institutional support in Korea either under the Silla (668–935) or Koryŏ (918–1392) periods. Although the SAMGUK YUSA (MEMORABILIA OF THE THREE KINGDOMS) mentions two esoteric "sects" under the Koryŏ (Ch'ongji or Dhāraṇī school and the Sinin or Mudra school) the reliability of this source is questionable and there is no independent evidence of sectarian "schools." We know of a number of prominent Korean monks who studied with famous Chinese ācāryas—Pulgasaŭi (d.u.) with Śubhākarasiṃha, Hyech'o (fl. eighth century) with Amoghavajra, Hyeil (d.u.) and Ojin (d.u.) with Amoghavajra's disciple Huiguo (?–805)—and it appears that they brought full range of mantra teachings and ritual technology to the peninsula. The first edition of the Korean Tripiṭaka (produced 1029–1089 C.E.) contains the works of the Tang ācāryas as well as those of the Song ācāryas, and we have to assume that there was a ready market for these works among the Korean aristocracy. Apparently the mantra teachings were incorporated into Koryŏ Buddhism much as they had been into Tang and Song Buddhism, as new mantric ritual extensions of the Mahāyāna with new pantheons. While a full sectarian identity for the mantra teachings in the Silla and Koryŏ periods is suspect, we do have ample evidence of the spread of rituals in court circles. These included rites to Mārīcī, Mahāmāyūrī Vidyārājñī, Buddhoṣṇīṣa, Yamāntaka, and rites originating in the Tang and Song dynasties, including Land and Water Masses and rituals for protection of the state connected with the *Humane Kings Sūtra* and the SUVARṆAPRABHĀSOTTAMA-SŪTRA. As was the case in China, the rise of the Mongols and their influence over the Korean peninsula brought Tibetan LAMAS and the performance of Vajrayāna rituals to the court in the late thirteenth century. This presence, however, was fleeting.

Japan

Although we tend to equate the arrival of the tantras in Japan with KŪKAI (774–835) and Shingon, this is not wholly accurate. Indeed, Kūkai himself read the *Vairocanābhisambodhi* before he traveled to China and there is considerable evidence that teachings, texts, and ritual technology originating in South Asia had spread to Japan by the mid-eighth century and were known and in use in both monastic and *hijiri* (mountain ascetic) circles. The standard story of the foundation of the Shingon school by Kūkai on his return from the Tang court in 805 and the parallel esoterizing of the Tendai sect by SAICHŌ (767–822) that resulted in what later exegetes would dub Tōmitsu and Taimitsu, respectively, have recently come under scrutiny and have been shown to be, especially in the case of Kūkai and Shingon, a pious and anachronistic simplification. As was the case for Amoghavajra, Kūkai saw himself as introducing a distinctive inner teaching and a method of discourse and interpretation that extended and completed the Mahāyāna, and much of his work was aimed at and eventually embraced by the established Nara schools. It now appears that the synthesis of a system framed by two maṇḍalas drawn respectively from the *Vairocanābhisambodhi* and the *Sarvatathāgatatattvasaṃgraha* was in large part Kūkai's articulation of possibilities present but not expressed in the work of his Chinese teachers. Basing their system on these two texts Shingon apologists distinguish their Esoteric Buddhism (Mikkyō) from the corpus of texts described in the Vajrayāna as *anuttarayoga-tantra.* Accordingly they see their "pure" esoterism as untainted by influences originating in Śaivite Hinduism. One of Kūkai's most interesting innovations was his insistence that the esoteric teachings were preached directly by the Dharmakāya Buddha (the transcendent body of the Buddha).

But the sectarian history of Shingon and Tendai esoteric Buddhism does not fully capture the effect of the mantra teachings on Japanese culture. Scholars speak of the esoterizing of medieval Japanese culture and some of the most important effects of the tantras in Japan occurred in spite of Shingon's existence as a religious institution. For instance, Kakuban (1095–1143) explored the relationship between Shingon and Shintō, between Mahāvairocana, the great Sun Buddha, AMITĀBHA, and Amaterasu, the solar goddess progenitor of the imperial clan. Others explicated Pure Land and Zen in terms of the esoteric teachings. Mantras and dhāraṇīs spread through the culture and language, as did deities (Acala *vidyārāja*, for instance), and practices (*homa*). Antinomian tendencies surfaced in the so-called Tachikawa heresy with its promise of various *siddhi* and its employment of sexual techniques and skull rituals reminiscent of the Kāpālikas, and in the Pure Land/esoteric fusion of the "Secret Nenbutsu" (*himitsu nenbutsu*), which equated sexual action to the intake of breath and the chanting of the Buddha's name. The emergence of Ryōbu Shintō, a tradition that synthesized esoteric and indigenous traditions, is further evidence of the impact of the mantra teachings on medieval Japan. Perhaps the most important influence of the mantra teachings cannot be documented in a cause/effect fashion. It is nonetheless clear that the idea of mantra, of the *bīja* syllables (they adorn cemeteries and can be found on *homa* sticks in modern temples), were likely the inspiration for the *hiragana* syllabary.

See also: **Mijiao (Esoteric) School; Shingon Buddhism, Japan; Tiantai School**

Bibliography

Abé Ryūichi. *The Weaving of Mantra: Kūkai and the Construction of Esoteric Buddhist Discourse.* New York: Columbia University Press, 1999.

Achard, Jean-Luc. *L'essence perlée du secret: Recherches philologiques et historiques sur l'origine de la Grande Perfection dans la tradition rNying ma pa.* Turnhout, Belgium: Prepols Publishers, 1999.

Bailey, H. W. "Vajrayāna Texts from Gostana." In *Studies of Esoteric Buddhism and Tantrism.* Koyasan, Japan: Koyasan University, 1965.

Chou I-liang. "Tantrism in China." *Harvard Journal of Asiatic Studies* 8 (1945): 241–332.

Davidson, Ronald M. *Indian Esoteric Buddhism: A Social History of the Tantric Movement.* New York: Columbia University Press, 2002.

Davidson, Ronald M. "Reframing Sahaja: Genre, Representation, Ritual, and Lineage." *Journal of Indian Philosophy* 30 (2002): 45–83.

Faure, Bernard. "Japanese Tantra, the Tachikawa-ryū, and Ryōbu Shintō." In *Tantra in Practice,* ed. David G. White. Princeton, NJ: Princeton University Press, 2000.

Hakeda, Yoshito S., trans. and ed. *Kūkai: Major Works.* New York: Columbia University Press, 1972.

Jong, J. W. de. "A New History of Tantric Literature in India." *Acta Indologica* (Naratasan Shinshoji) 6 (1984): 91–113.

Kiyota, Minoru. *Shingon Buddhism.* Tokyo and Los Angeles: Buddhist Books International, 1978.

Lessing, Ferdinand D., and Wayman, Alex, trans. *Mkhas Grub Rje's Fundamentals of the Buddhist Trantras.* The Hague and Paris: Mouton, 1968.

Namai, Chishō Mamoru. "On Bodhicittabhāvanā in the Esoteric Buddhist Tradition." In *Tibetan Studies—Proceedings of the 7th Seminar of the International Association for Tibetan Studies, Graz 1995,* ed. Helmut Krasser et al. Vienna: Verlag der Österreichischen Akademie der Wissenschaften, 1997.

Nihom, Max. *Studies in Indian and Indo-Indonesian Tantrism: The Kuñjarakarṇadharmakathana and the Yogatantra.* Vienna: Institute of Indology, University of Vienna, 1994.

Orzech, Charles D. *Politics and Transcendent Wisdom: The Scripture for Humane Kings in the Creation of Chinese Buddhism.* University Park: Pennsylvania State University Press, 1998.

Przyluski, Jean. "Les Vidyārāja: Contribution à l'histoire de la magie dans les sects mahayanistes." *Bulletin d'École Francais d'Extrême-Orient* 23 (Hanoi, 1924): 301–318.

Regamey, Constantin. "Motifs vichnouites et śivaites dan le Kāraṇḍavyūha." In *Études tibétaines dédiées à la mémoire de Marcelle Lalou.* Paris: Librairie d'Amérique et d'Orient, 1971.

Sanford, James H. "The Abominable Tachikawa Skull Ritual." *Monumenta Nipponica* 46, no. 1 (1991): 1–15.

Smith, E. Gene. *Among Tibetan Texts: History and Literature of the Himalayan Plateau.* Boston: Wisdom, 2001.

Snellgrove, David L. "The Notion of Divine Kingship in Tantric Buddhism." *The Sacral Kingship: Contributions to the Central Theme of the Eighth International Congress for the History of Religions.* Leiden, Netherlands: Brill, 1959.

Snellgrove, David L. *Indo-Tibetan Buddhism: Indian Buddhists and Their Tibetan Successors,* 2 vols. Boston: Shambhala, 1987.

Sørensen, Henrik H. "Esoteric Buddhism in Korea." In *The Esoteric Buddhist Tradition,* ed. Henrik H. Sørensen. Copenhagen and Aarhus, Denmark: Seminar for Buddhist Studies, 1994.

Strickmann, Michel. *Mantras et mandarins: le bouddhisme tantrique en Chine.* Paris: Gallimard, 1996.

Van der Veere, Hendrik. *A Study into the Thought of Kōgyō Daishi Kakuban.* Leiden, Netherlands: Hotei, 2000.

Wallace, Vesna A. *The Inner Kālacakratantra: A Buddhist Tantric View of the Individual.* Oxford and New York: Oxford University Press, 2001.

Wayman, Alex. *Yoga of the Guhyasamājatantra: The Arcane Lore of Forty Verses.* Delhi: Motilal Banarsidass, 1977.

RONALD M. DAVIDSON
CHARLES D. ORZECH

TAOISM. *See* **Daoism and Buddhism**

TATHĀGATA

Tathāgata is the epithet used by the Buddha in referring to himself. In Sanskrit and Pāli, it can mean either "Thus-Gone-One" (*tathā-gata*) or "Thus-Come-One" (*tathā-āgata*). In translating the term, Tibetans generally opted for the former meaning, and East Asians for the latter. In either case, the implication is that the Buddha has come (or gone) in the same manner as his predecessors, the buddhas of the past.

See also: **Buddhahood and Buddha Bodies**

JOHN S. STRONG

TATHĀGATAGARBHA

The tathāgatagarbha ("matrix," "seed," or "treasure-store of the Tathāgata") is a MAHĀYĀNA Buddhist doctrine expressing the conviction that all beings have within themselves the virtues and wisdom of the TATHĀGATA (buddha), but that these are hidden by a covering of defilements (*kleśakośa*). The third-century scripture, the *Tathāgatagarbha-sūtra,* introduced the doctrine and illustrated it with nine similes based on the different meanings of the word *garbha,* such as womb, store, calyx, husk, and seed. The tathāgatagarbha is likened to a buddha hidden in the calyx of a flower; to a noble son hidden in the womb of a vile, ugly woman; to a seed hidden in a useless husk; and to a store of treasure hidden beneath a poor man's house. The compound therefore permits a wide range of legitimate translations including matrix, womb, embryo, germ, and treasure-store of the Tathāgata. Originally, the term *tathāgatagarbha* seems to have referred to beings themselves, who are *tathāgatagarbhas,* or "harborers of the Tathāgata."

The concept was developed further in later writings like the *Śrīmālādevī-sūtra* (*Discourse of Queen Śrīmālā*), where the term refers to an inner potential that enables beings to become buddhas. Were it not for the tathāgatagarbha, this sūtra states, beings would be unable to feel aversion for suffering or to seek NIRVĀṆA. The sūtra identifies the tathāgatagarbha as the dharmakāya of the buddha, which pervades all beings. The dharmakāya is said to have the four perfections (*guṇapāramitās*) of eternality, bliss, self, and purity, an assertion that has led some to question whether the tathāgatagarbha teaching might expound a form of Hindu monism, in which case it might contradict such fundamental Buddhist doctrines as ANITYA (IMPERMANENCE), ANĀTMAN/ĀTMAN (NO-SELF/SELF), and DUḤKHA (SUFFERING).

A closely related concept to the tathāgatagarbha is the *buddhadhātu,* usually translated as "buddha-nature," a term first used in the NIRVĀṆA SŪTRA with the famous phrase "all beings possess buddha-nature." Like the tathāgatagarbha, it expresses the Mahāyāna conviction that all beings have the potential for buddhahood.

The only Indian Buddhist treatise devoted to the tathāgatagarbha is the fifth-century *Ratnagotravibhāga* (Chinese, *Baoxing fenbie dacheng jiujing yaoyi lun*; *Analysis of the Source of the [Buddha] Jewel*). The *Ratnagotravibhāga* identified the tathāgatagarbha as "thusness mingled with pollution" (*samalā tathatā*), whereas the dharmakāya is identified as "thusness apart from pollution" (*nirmalā tathatā*). *Thusness* means supreme truth apprehended by nondiscriminating wisdom. The MADHYAMAKA SCHOOL understood *thusness* to mean the emptiness of all dharmas, but the *Ratnagotravibhāga* insisted that while the tathāgatagarbha is empty of *kleśas,* it is not empty of the virtues of the buddha, "which are more numerous than the sands of the Ganges." This assertion that something is ultimately "not empty" is also found in several YOGĀCĀRA SCHOOL texts. Additionally, the *Ratnagotravibhāga* uses traditional Yogācāra categories for analysis, which further suggests possible ties to the Yogācāra school.

A central teaching of the *Ratnagotravibhāga,* derived from the *Jñanālokālaṅkāra-sūtra* (*Discourse on the Ornamentation of Wisdom*), is that nirvāṇa, the noble truth of the cessation of suffering, ought to be understood as the nonorigination, rather than the extinguishing, of suffering and illusion. The mind is pure by nature, and suffering arises only when irrational thought (*ayoniśomanaskāra*) originates illusions, attachments, and cravings. One who has reached the truth does not give rise to illusions. The expression "cessation of suffering" refers to the dharmakāya of the Tathāgata, which is unborn and unproduced. Because all beings have the dharmakāya within them, they have the capacity not to originate suffering.

The tathāgatagarbha teaching was far more popular in East Asia than in India or Tibet. In India no school was organized around the tathāgatagarbha teaching, and in Tibet, only the Jo nang pa centered itself on the tathāgatagarbha teaching. But the *Ratnagotravibhāga* and the sūtras expounding the tathāgatagarbha were translated into Chinese shortly after their composition, and heavily influenced important Chinese treatises like the AWAKENING OF FAITH (DASHENG QIXIN LUN). An extensive debate over the buddha-nature of the ICCHANTIKA (the worst of beings), provoked further interest in the doctrine. The tathāgatagarbha teaching was accorded the highest place in the doctrinal classification schemes of such notable HUAYAN SCHOOL figures as FAZANG and ZONGMI (780–841), and became a focal point of both Tiantai and Chan school teachings.

See also: **Ālayavijñāna; Bodhicitta (Thought of Awakening); Chan School; Critical Buddhism (Hihan Bukkyō); Tiantai School**

Bibliography

Brown, Brian Edward. *The Buddha Nature: A Study of the Tathāgatagarbha and Ālayavijñāna.* Delhi: Motilal Banarsidass, 1991.

Gregory, Peter N. "Chinese Buddhist Hermeneutics: The Case of Hua-yen." *Journal of the American Academy of Religion* 51, no. 2 (1983): 231–249.

Grosnick, William H. "Nonorigination and Nirvāṇa in the Early Tathāgatagarbha Literature." *Journal of the International Association of Buddhist Studies* 4, no. 2 (1981): 33–43.

Ruegg, David Seyfort. *La théorie du tathāgatagarbha et du gotra: Études sur la sotériologie et la gnoséologie du bouddhisme.* Paris: École Française d'Extrème-Orient, 1969.

Takasaki, Jikido. *A Study on the Ratnagotravibhāga (Uttaratantra), Being a Treatise on the Tathāgatagarbha Theory of Mahāyāna Buddhism.* Rome: Istituto italiano per il Medio ed Estremo Oriente, 1966.

Wayman, Alex, and Wayman, Hideko, eds. *The Lion's Roar of Queen Śrīmālā: A Buddhist Scripture on the Tathāgatagarbha Theory,* tr. Alex Wayman and Hideko Wayman. New York: Columbia University Press, 1974.

WILLIAM H. GROSNICK

TEMPLE. *See* **Monastic Architecture; Monasticism**

TEMPLE SYSTEM IN JAPAN

The Japanese Buddhist temple system was established through legal decrees by the Tokugawa government (1603–1868) as a method to maintain secular control over Buddhist institutions. Overseen by the government's Office of Temples and Shrines, this administrative system involved a head-and-branch temple (*honmatsu*) organization. Each Buddhist sect designated a headquarters temple, which was approved by the government. With the headquarters temple at the top, all the sect's temples in Japan were linked through a hierarchical network. With links originally formed between teachers' (head temples) and disciples' temples (branch temples), a head temple often had a number of affiliated lineage branch temples. These linkages between generations of temples formed the basis for the concept that a particular temple was hierarchically superior to another.

Under the Tokugawa regime, informal lineage-based ties became formalized, and even temples that had no lineage ties were sometimes arbitrarily placed in head-and-branch relationships. This system consolidated sectarian hierarchies for all Buddhist temples by the early eighteenth century as the government perfected its control over Buddhist institutions. While the system developed out of a secular need for control, it also served each sect to establish organizational sectarian structures that persist into the modern period.

See also: **Japan**

Bibliography

Nosco, Peter. "Keeping the Faith: Bakuhan Policy towards Religions in Seventeenth-Century Japan." In *Religion in Japan: Arrows to Heaven and Earth,* ed. Peter Kornicki and Ian McMullen. Cambridge, UK: Cambridge University Press, 1996.

Williams, Duncan. "Representations of Zen: A Social and Institutional History of Sōtō Zen Buddhism in Edo Japan." Ph.D. diss. Harvard University, 2000.

DUNCAN WILLIAMS

TENDAI SCHOOL. *See* **Tiantai School**

THAI, BUDDHIST LITERATURE IN

Thai, the national language of Thailand, is closely related to Lao, the national language of neighboring LAOS, as well as the Shan language of northern Burma (MYANMAR) and several other languages and dialects in northern VIETNAM and southern CHINA. Together, they comprise the Tai language family. Approximately half of the more than sixty million residents of Thailand speak Thai as their mother tongue. Thai, and all Tai languages, are tonal languages in which a change of syllable tone results in a change of meaning.

The origin of the Thai script is credited to King Ramkhamhaeng the Great of Sukhothai and an inscription that dates from the latter part of the thirteenth century. While there is some debate about the authenticity of this inscription, it is generally held to be the first written evidence of the strong presence of Buddhism in Siam or Thailand. The Thai definition of literature is far reaching, and this inscription, which reads like a nation's constitution, is also viewed as a seminal piece of Buddhist literature. In it, the king states that he gives alms to the Mahāthera Saṅgharāja, a wise monk who has studied the Buddhist Pāli CANON (Tipiṭaka) from beginning to end (and who also likely came from Sri Lanka). The king also mentions that paying proper tribute to a divine spirit residing at a local mountain helps to ensure the prosperity of the kingdom. This blend of Buddhist practice and animistic elements continues to be characteristic of the Thai worldview.

The Thai imagination is most active in a work attributed to Phya Lithai, *Trai Phum Phra Ruang* (*The*

Three Worlds of King Ruang, 1345). Based on Buddhist canonical texts, local legends, and dreams, this detailed, full-blown COSMOLOGY serves as a road map to various HEAVENS and HELLS and the perils of lives lived at all levels of existence. In this work, gaps in Buddhist texts are filled in with speculation about the creation of life, while the spirit of other texts provides a springboard into rich pools of fantastic description that include falls from grace, detailed accounts of karmic consequences, and elaborated notions of a wheel-turning king whose right to rule is based on his righteousness.

One of the most enduring Thai literary works is the *Ramakian,* a uniquely Thai interpretation of the Indian epic, the *Rāmāyana.* While some people believe that the Thai version of the Rāma legend predated the establishment of the Kingdom of Sukhothai, the earliest archeological evidence for it was found in the ruins of the Kingdom of Ayudhaya, which was sacked by the Burmese in 1767. The destruction of Ayudhaya is considered one of the greatest losses of art and literature in Thai history. The longest version of the *Ramakian* was written by a group of poets in 1798 and was sponsored by the first king of the Chakri dynasty, Rāma I. Much has been written about the Indianization or Sanskritization of Southeast Asia, and the *Ramakian,* a blend of Thai legends, state rites, and Buddhist elements, stands as clear evidence of such influence.

The JĀTAKA tales, or birth stories of the Buddha, have held a prominent place in the imagination of the Thai people. Traditionally, the most popular tale describes the Buddha's penultimate life before attaining Buddhahood, that being the story of the generous Prince Vessantara (Sanskrit, VIŚVANTARA). This Job-like tale focuses on the sacrifices and merit made by Prince Vessantara. It includes demonstrations of the prince's nonattachment and giving—even the giving up of family members—in the process of demonstrating his commitment to generosity. The merit-making message of this tale is evidence of the importance of gift giving in Thai culture. Many monks continue the tradition of chanting, day and night, an elaborate version of this jātaka tale in an annual event called the Thet Mahachat (Sermon of the Great Life).

A further outgrowth of gift giving takes the form of an unusual genre of literature, the cremation volume. Souvenirs are often presented to attendees at the close of cremation rites. As early as the 1870s, with the advent of printing presses in Thailand, people began to distribute books at funerals. These volumes usually include a brief biography of the deceased; in addition, the publication of cremation volumes is a way of distributing and preserving literary, cultural, and religious information that families find meaningful. In a status-conscious society, these volumes also help to "place" people in the Thai social order. A collection of cremation volumes at Wat Bovoranives in Bangkok is cataloged according to an adaptation of the Dewey decimal system that reflects the status, ranks, and structure of Thai society.

Buddhist teachings and stories have been preserved through the strength of oral traditions and attention given to (palm leaf) manuscripts. The name of the Buddhist canon, the Tipiṭaka, presumably comes from an early filing system: putting the three parts of the canon—rules (VINAYA), teachings (*sutta*), and philosophical details (*abhidhamma*)—into separate baskets. While ideally monks should be well versed in all three of these dimensions, Buddhist tradition and subsequent curricula for monks focused on certain parts of the canon over others, making the observer often wonder which basket carries the most weight. For example, the meditative interests of forest monasteries tend to focus on texts (and biographies of local monks) dealing with such practices, while the leaders of some urban monasteries may favor other parts of the canon, including a fascination with the *abhidhamma.* The DHAMMAPADA has always been a popular text, and its inclusion in several levels of monks' Pāli exams has helped to maintain its popularity. Thai Buddhist laity are more likely to gain their knowledge of Buddhism from the influence of parents and teachers, and through listening to sermons and reading collections of proverbs, modern commentaries, or interpretations, rather than the canonical texts themselves.

Several modern figures have made major contributions to religious literature in Thailand. At the end of the nineteenth century, Prince-Patriarch Wachirayanwarorot (1860–1921, half-brother to King Chulalongkorn, Rama V) wrote a number of concise textbooks aimed at providing summaries of the important tenets of Buddhism. These texts were especially useful for people who ordained temporarily during the "rainy season retreat" (*vassa*) and they took an important place in the early curriculum for monks. BUDDHADĀSA Bhikkhu (1906–1993) fostered his own brave, innovative blend of Thai colloquial terms and interpretations of *dhamma* to spark more interest in Buddhist practice. His commentaries run many volumes, resembling a canon itself. In 1971 Prayudh

Payutto published the first edition of *Buddhadhamma,* a summary of major Buddhist principles, focusing especially on Buddhist notions of causality and interdependence. This major work has been expanded to over one thousand pages. And, not to be overlooked, modern Thai fiction itself is often a blend of romantic love, heroism, the life of the Buddha, and references to *jātaka* tales. While globalization refashions traditional belief, the Thai creative imagination continues to respond to modernity with its own distinctive synthesis of the past and present.

See also: **Southeast Asia, Buddhist Art in; Thailand**

Bibliography

Bofman, Theodora Helene. *The Poetics of the Ramakian.* DeKalb, IL: Northern Illinois University Center for Southeast Asian Studies, 1984.

Chamberlain, James F., ed. *The Ramkhamhaeng Controversy: Selected Papers.* Bangkok, Thailand: Siam Society, 1991.

Olson, Grant A. "Thai Cremation Volumes: A Brief History of a Unique Genre of Literature." *Asian Folklore Studies* 51 (1992): 279–294.

Payutto, Prayudh. *Buddhadhamma: Natural Laws and Values for Life,* tr. Grant A. Olson. Albany: State University of New York Press, 1995.

Reynolds, Frank E., and Reynolds, Mani B., trans. *Three Worlds According to King Ruang: A Thai Cosmology.* Berkeley, CA: Asian Humanities Press, 1982.

Rutin, Mattani Mojdara. *Modern Thai Literature: The Process of Modernization and the Transformation of Values.* Bangkok, Thailand: Thammasat University Press, 1988.

GRANT A. OLSON

THAILAND

The historical origins of Buddhism in the part of mainland Southeast Asia known today as Thailand are obscure. According to popular Thai tradition, Buddhism was propagated in the region south of present-day Bangkok by the monks Sona and Uttara, who were sent to Suvaṇṇabhūmi (the golden land) by the Mauryan king AŚOKA in the third century B.C.E. According to this view, from these beginnings Buddhism of a THERAVĀDA persuasion has dominated the country. Archaeological evidence confirms a flourishing Buddhist culture among the Mon at Dvāravatī in the region of Nakon Pathom thirty miles southwest of Bangkok as early as the fourth century C.E., but historical evidence fails to corroborate the legend of Aśoka's emissaries. Furthermore, while both archaeological and textual evidence suggest a strong Pāli Theravāda presence among the Mon states in Thailand and lower Burma (Myanmar), the Buddhist ubiety in the region was marked by diversity rather than uniformity. Indeed, prior to the establishment of the major Tai states of SUKHOTHAI and Chiang Mai in the thirteenth century, Buddhism in Thailand can only be characterized as eclectic. As part of the Indian cultural influence into "greater India," elements of MAHĀYĀNA, TANTRA, and MAINSTREAM BUDDHIST SCHOOLS entered different regions of Thailand through the Mon, the expansion of the Sumatran-based Śrivijāya kingdom into the southern peninsula, and the growing dominance of the Khmer empire in the west. These diverse Buddhist expressions, in turn, competed with Brahmanism, Hinduism, and autochthonous animisms. Rather than an organized sectarian lineage, the early religious amalgam in Thailand and other parts of Southeast Asia might be more accurately described as a syncretic collage of miraculous relics and charismatic monks, Hindu *dharmaśāstra,* Brahmanic deities, Mahāyāna buddhas, tantric practices, and Sanskrit Sarvāstivādin and Pāli Theravāda traditions.

Syncretism and tantric Theravāda

François Bizot describes the eclectic nature of Buddhism in premodern Thailand, Laos, and Cambodia as a congruence of Vedic Brahmanism, tantrism, and a pre-Aryan Austro-Asiatic cult of guardian spirits and protective divinities. Interacting with Mon Theravāda beliefs and practices, and possibly influenced by the Mūlasarvāstivādins, it resulted in what Bizot has characterized as "Tantric Theravāda," identified with a mystical tradition known as Yogāvacara (practitioner of the spiritual discipline). The features of this tantric Theravāda, at odds with the stereotypical view of classical Theravāda, include identifying one's body with the qualities of the Buddha; the use of esoteric syllables and words (DHĀRAṆĪ, MANTRA, yantra) to represent the identity of microcosm and macrocosm; the dharmic potency of sounds and letters; and esoteric initiation for the realization of both soteriological and mundane ends (Crosby).

By the twelfth and thirteenth centuries, Tai migrations from southwest China into Thailand resulted in the establishment of several petty kingdoms, most notably Chiang Mai under King Mangrai (r. 1292–1317) and Sukhothai under King Ramkhamhaeng (r. ca.

A restored statue of the Buddha at Sukhothai, the ancient capital of Thailand, which contains many temples and monasteries, some in ruins. © Lindsay Hebberd/Corbis. Reproduced by permission.

1279–1298). Somewhat earlier, the rise to power of the Sinhalese monarch Parakkama Bāhu I (r. 1153–1186) in Sri Lanka and the subsequent dominance of the Mahāvihāra monastic fraternity led to the missionary expansion of Sinhalese Theravāda into Burma and Thailand. A 1287 C.E. inscription at Sukhothai records that Ramkhamhaeng patronized monks of the Lanka order (*lankavaṃsa*), whom he invited from Nakon Sithammarāt, a Thai state located far to the south on the Gulf of Siam. Thai monks ordained in Burma and Sri Lanka brought lineages of Sinhala Theravāda to Thailand in the fourteenth and fifteenth centuries. Under Tilokarāt (r. 1441–1487) monks of the Mahāvihāra reformist tradition at the Red Forest Monastery (Wat Pā Daeng) in Chiang Mai gained a religious and political prominence that led to a council under royal sponsorship to regularize monastic teaching and practice. Nevertheless, although Buddhism in the Thai states from Nakon Sithammarāt in the south to AYUTTHAYA in central Thailand and Chiang Mai to the north came more under the sway of Sinhala Theravāda, it lacked the uniformity achieved with the formation of the modern nation-state around the turn of the twentieth century. Even today, Thai Buddhism is more complex and hybridized than the Pāli canon, the normative commentaries of BUDDHAGHOSA (fifth century C.E.), the Mahāvihāra *paritta* ritual handbook, and a national SAṄGHA organization created by the great Supreme Patriarch (*saṃgharāt*), Wachirayān (Vajirañāṇavarorasa, 1860–1921), would lead one to believe.

Syncretism continues to define many Thai religious practices. Temple festivals begin by invoking the guardian deities of the four quarters, zenith, and nadir. Monastic ordinations are often preceded by an elaborate spirit calling (*riak khwan*) ceremony. Yantric tattoos and magical amulets are worn by the devout to ward off danger. Offerings are made at the shrines of deities protecting mountain passes, and elaborate altars to the Hindu god Brahmā occupy a prominent place at the entrance to hotels. In Chiang Mai, northern Thais inaugurate the New Year by three sequential events: appealing to the spirit of a palladial buddha image; invoking the god, INDRA, resident in the city pillar; and sacrificing a buffalo to the spirits who guard the mountains overlooking the valley. The veneration of King Rāma V (Chulalongkorn, r. 1868–1910), which originated as a cult of his equestrian statue before the parliament building in Bangkok, has spread nationwide. And, as if to validate Bizot's theory of tantric Theravāda, Thailand's fastest-growing new Buddhist movement, Wat Thammakāi, espouses a Yogāvacara form of meditation claimed by the founder to be an ancient method rediscovered by the late abbot of Wat Paknām, a royal monastery located on Bangkok's Chao Phraya River.

Saṅgha and state

From the time of the Tai kingdoms in the thirteenth and fourteenth centuries, royal patronage of monks, monasteries, and monastic lineages has characterized the relationship between Buddhism and the state. Based on inscriptional and chronicle evidence, Ishii Yoneo observes in *Saṅgha, State, and Society* (1986) that state Buddhism in the Sukhothai and Ayutthaya kingdoms included the following elements: Kings conferred ecclesiastical ranks and controlled monastic appointments; kings appointed secular officials in charge of crown-saṅgha relationships; royal patronage included donating lands as well as building royal monasteries in the capital and provinces; kings ordained as monks for a limited time as an expression of piety; and kings helped settle saṅgha disputes. Accounts from the Thai Pāli chronicles, the *Jinakālamālīpakaraṇa* (*Sheaf of Garlands of the Epochs of the Conquerors*) and the *Cāmadevīvaṃsa* (*Legend of Queen Cāma*), link the spread of Buddhism and the legitimation of royal power with the veneration of magical BUDDHA IMAGES and relics, in particular the palladial Emerald Buddha now enshrined on the grounds of the grand palace in Bangkok.

In the *Trai Phūm Phra Ruang* (*Three Worlds According to King Ruang*), King Lithai of Sukhothai (1346/47–1368/74?) constructed a cosmological legitimation of Buddhist KINGSHIP and the state that in the Ayutthaya period (1569–1767) became a "galactic polity" through which the Ayutthayana monarchs dominated tributary states (Tambiah). It was certainly not a coincidence that when King Rāma I (r. 1782–1809) took over the reins of power at the new Thai capital in Thonburi/Bangkok after the Burmese sacked Ayutthaya in 1767, he sponsored a saṅgha council that included among its activities the production of a new edition of Lithai's *Trai Phūm Phra Ruang.*

In the early modern period, King Mongkut (r. 1851–1868) fully personified the close relationship between Buddhism and the state. Ordained a monk for twenty-seven years before he became king (Rāma IV), he founded a new monastic order, the Thammayut ("adhering strictly to the *dhamma*"), in 1829. In 1836 Mongkut was appointed abbot of Wat Bowoniwēt monastery in Bangkok, which was to become the headquarters of the Thammayut order and the home of its monastic university, Mahāmakut, founded in 1893. Mahāchulalongkorn was established as the university for the larger Mahānikāi (great congregation) order at its Bangkok headquarters, Wat Mahathāt. Both institutions figured prominently in the development of advanced monastic education during the twentieth century.

Buddhism as a civil religion was promoted by King Wachirawut (Rāma VI, r. 1910–1925) through the promulgation of the slogan, "nation, religion [Buddhism], king," symbolized by the country's tricolor national flag. During the regimes of the military strongmen Sarit Thanarat and Thanom Kittikachorn, who served as prime ministers from 1959 to 1973, new government programs, the Thammacarik (Dhamma Travelers) and Thammathūt (Dhamma Emissaries) were created to enlist saṅgha participation in the government's efforts to promote rural development, integrate the northern hill tribes into the Thai nation state, and encourage national loyalty in the face of perceived communist threats in sensitive border areas.

The symbiotic relationship between Buddhism and the state has not been without its tensions. Although royal patronage benefited the saṅgha, the power of the state restricted its freedom and authority; hence, on occasion, monks have challenged the state. In the 1930s the northern Thai monk, Khrūbā Sīwichai, was disciplined by the national saṅgha headquartered in Bangkok for following traditional northern Thai Buddhist practices that contravened the 1902 national saṅgha law. In the late nineteenth century, Āčhān Sao Kantasīlo and Āčhān Man Bhūridatto founded the modern forest WILDERNESS MONKS tradition. Although they remained Thammayut monks, the movement offered monks an avenue to pursue a spiritual practice freed from many of the constraints imposed by the national saṅgha. In the 1970s volatile political events saw an unprecedented left and right politicization of the saṅgha, and in what became the cause célèbre of the 1990s: Phra Bodhirak, who founded the Santi Asoka movement in the early 1970s, was defrocked because he ordained monks in defiance of government regulations.

Despite such tensions, state Buddhism has been an overriding feature of Thai history since the founding of Sukhothai and Chiang Mai. The prosperity of the saṅgha, the national system of monastic study and lay Buddhist education through both monastery and government schools, and the important place Buddhism holds in Thai culture and society has come about through the encouragement and patronage of the state. Thailand has a national saṅgha organization first enacted in 1902 during the reign of Rāma V. Its current form, set into law by the 1962 saṅgha ordinance, places a *saṅgharāja* (saṅgha king) and an appointed council at the head of a hierarchical structure organized into regions, provinces, districts, and subdistricts.

A standardized monastic curriculum was developed by Supreme Patriarch Wachirayān, an accomplished Pāli scholar in his own right and author of numerous books still in use throughout the nearly thirty thousand monasteries nationwide. The curriculum is divided into general Buddhist studies (*naktham*) and training in Pāli language. The three levels of Buddhist study include Buddhist doctrine, Buddhist history, the life of the Buddha and his most famous disciples, monastic discipline (VINAYA), and Buddhist rituals and ceremonies. The formal study of Pāli in Thailand began in the Ayutthaya period, although the system of nine grades or levels dates from the reign of Rāma II (1809–1824). Over the years its content has changed; today it includes study of Wachirayān's Pāli grammar, the DHAMMAPADA commentary, BUDDHAGHOSA's commentary on the vinaya and *Visuddhimagga* (*Path to Purification*), as well as study of the *abhidhamma* and the commentary on the *Maṅgalasutta* (*Maṅgalatthadīpanī*) written in 1525 C.E. by Sirimaṅgala, northern Thailand's greatest Pāli scholar.

Buddhism and Thai society

In times past it was said that to be Thai was to be Buddhist. Although the place of Buddhism as the linchpin of Thai identity has eroded due to the onslaught of globalization and rapid social change, the great majority of Thais still find Buddhism to be a locus of personal meaning and community identity. The Buddhist worldview continues to inform the lives of both urban and rural Thais: the transformative ideal of NIRVĀṆA; the natural law of cause and effect and its consequentialist ethic based on KARMA (ACTION) and REBIRTH; the values of generosity and hospitality; the ideals of equanimity, compassion, and nonviolence; the merit-making exchange that binds monk and laity together in a relationship of mutual reciprocity; and attitudes toward social hierarchy and gender.

These principles and values continue to be enacted in social relationships, including the ways in which children relate to parents, younger people to older people, and men to women. The rituals that define a life passage from birth to death and the festivals that mark a similar passage of the year, in the past tied more obviously to seasonal change and an agriculture calendar, have not disappeared even though they are attenuated in urban settings. Scores of young men still ordain annually as novice monks for a brief period, perhaps during a summer vacation rather than the traditional three-month rains-retreat from mid-July to mid-October. Temporary ordination has been the norm in Thailand for centuries, a very small percentage deciding to remain in the monkhood for a lifetime.

According to traditional lore, spending a few months as a monk "ripens" a young man and prepares him for responsible family and community life after he disrobes. Furthermore, ORDINATION not only functions as a male rite of passage into adulthood, it accrues special merit for one's parents, especially one's mother. Girls participate only as onlookers, unlike Burmese custom where both boys and girls are included in *shinbyu* ceremonies that end in temporary ordination for males and ear-boring for females. Anthropologists speculate that prostitution may have a perverse tie to the ideology of merit-making in Thailand. Since there is no women's saṅgha, females are denied the male opportunity to make merit for their parents; they can, however, help prevent their parents from falling into penury by supporting them from money earned as prostitutes (Muecke).

Other rites of passage continue to be observed in Thailand, often incorporating beliefs and practices more animistic than Buddhist. Life transitions of all kinds may be marked by spirit-calling rites (*pithī riak khwan*), and illness or other personal and community crises are occasions for life-extension (*sū'pčhatā*) rituals. Monks will be invited to conduct protective rituals (*suat mọn/tham yan*) for a new home, building, or business, and funerals at monasteries and in homes are such important ritual occasions that a unique chant style was developed for these occasions.

Annual festivals continue to serve as events where both men and women, young and old, experience a sense of belonging to a local community and a nation. For some, such as the Thai New Year celebrated at the end of April before the May monsoon rains, commercialism nearly overwhelms traditional practices. However, the old customs of paying respect to elders, building sand "mountains" (*čhēdī*) on the monastery grounds, and lustrating Buddha images and relics perdure. The annual preaching of the *Vessantara-jātaka* (*thēt mahāchāt*) in November has given way to movies, video, and rock concerts, but the Festival of the Floating Boats (*loi kratong*) held during the same month survives in altered form, with the traditional banana-leaf rafts floated on ponds, lakes, and rivers replaced by Styrofoam boats. Visākhā Pūjā, a celebration of the Buddha's birth, enlightenment, and death, and the beginning and end of the monastic rains-retreat endure not only as opportunities to make merit for the benefit of one's self and extended family both living and dead, but as an affirmation of one's identity as a Thai Buddhist.

Buddhism and the twenty-first century

To retain a continuing relevance to changing circumstances and conditions, religious traditions themselves must change. The Thailand of today differs vastly from the Tai kingdoms of the fourteenth century and also from the state Buddhism promoted by King Chulalongkorn and Supreme Patriarch Wachirayān in the early twentieth. Buddhism in Thailand today is marked

A Thai Buddhist lays an offering of flowers on the feet of a giant Buddha statue at Intaravehan Temple in Bangkok, Thailand, 1997. AP/Wide World Photos. Reproduced by permission.

by a cacophony of voices, a pluralism that includes a continuation of traditional forms and practices, a new sectarianism, an efflorescence of magical cults, a multifaceted reform movement, and an internationalism attuned to the emergent global community. Today, Thai Buddhist identity extends beyond the borders of a local community and the nation-state to an increasingly globalized world.

State Buddhism established at the beginning of the twentieth century and revised by the 1962 saṅgha law is still intact; however, calls for reforming the conservative, hierarchical saṅgha governance structure come from younger liberal monks as well as educated laity. There is increasing concern that mainstream civil Buddhism is out of tune with the times that in the affluent decades of the 1980s and 1990s became more complacent and materialistic. To be sure, in villages and towns throughout the country the monastery continues to serve important community functions, especially educating the rural poor, even though many of the roles once filled by monks are now the purview of civil servants. As a result there has been a general decline in the high regard and social status traditionally accorded monks. Several high-profile instances of immorality and rancorous division have also challenged the saṅgha's moral authority.

In the 1970s, partly in response to the changes brought about by globalization and challenges to the relevance of the saṅgha, two nationwide sectarian movements emerged, Santi Asok and Wat Thammakāi. Although Phra Bodhirak, Santi Asok's founder, was ordained into the Thammayut and then the Mahānikāi orders, in the mid-1970s Bodhirak and his fellow monks cut all ties with the national saṅgha. The movement continued to grow rapidly in the 1980s, and it gained special prominence through one of its members, General Chamlong Simuang, a former governor of Bangkok, member of parliament, and founder of the Phalang Dhamma political party. Santi Asok defined itself against the Thai mainstream, establishing centers where monks and laity observed a moderately ascetic regime, living in simple wooden huts, eating one vegetarian meal daily, and avoiding intoxicants, stimulants, and tobacco. In the view of mainstream Thai Buddhists, Santi Asok had overstepped acceptable limits both in terms of its independence and its

Thai Buddhists celebrate the new year by making merit. Here women give goods and flowers to Buddhist monks during a morning alms offering in Bangkok, Thailand, 2002. AP/Wide World Photos. Reproduced by permission.

outspoken criticisms of Thai society. In 1995 a court decision codified a 1988 recommendation by national saṅgha leaders to expel Bodhirak from the monkhood on the grounds that he had ordained monks and nuns without authorization and had contravened a vinaya prohibition forbidding claims to supernatural powers.

In several respects, Wat Thammakāi stands at the opposite end of the spectrum to Santi Asok. Also a product of the early 1970s, its imposing national headquarters at Prathum Thani near Bangkok represents a new version of state Buddhism with an aggressive, international perspective. Its founders, Phra Thammachayo and Phra Thattachīwo, were educated in marketing before becoming monks under the inspiration of the Venerable Monkhon Thēpmunī of Wat Paknām, who was noted for his unique visualization meditation method. The entrepreneurial skills they brought to the movement led to its considerable success but has also generated attacks on its commercialism and charges of financial irregularity.

A striking feature of the religious ethos in Thailand at the beginning of the twenty-first century is a burgeoning increase in cults. Although the veneration of relics and images of the Buddha has long played a central role in Buddhist devotional religion, its contemporary efflorescence is due in part to their commodification in the face of the cultural dominance of commercial values. The cult of images and relics, furthermore, is matched by the veneration of charismatic monks to whom are ascribed a wide range of apotropaic powers, including the generation of wealth. New cults, abetted by the financial crisis of 1997, include the veneration of images and other material representations of royalty, especially King Rāma V, and the popularity of the Bodhisattva Guanyin (Avalokiteśvara), which testifies to an increasing Chinese influence in the Thai economy.

One of the most encouraging developments in Thai Buddhism at the beginning of the twenty-first century is the movement toward change and reform generated by a loose agglomeration of monks and laity. This includes monks who have dedicated their lives to addressing a wide range of social, economic, and environmental problems faced by the people they serve in villages and towns throughout the country. One of the chief inspirations for Buddhist reformism has been

Phutathāt (Buddhadāsa Bhikkhu), whose innovative teaching and example continued to inspire the leading Buddhist reformist voices in the country, even after his death in 1993. Although regarded primarily as an outstanding Pāli scholar, Phra Thammapidok (Dhammapiṭaka), along with Phutathāt, have influenced numerous Buddhist social activists including Sulak Sivaraksa, a major figure in the international engaged Buddhist movement. Sulak's NGOs (nongovernmental organizations) include the International Network of Engaged Buddhists (INEB). The issues addressed by INEB range from assisting democracy activists persecuted by Myanmar's repressive military dictatorship to supporting the prominent Thai Buddhist academic, Chatsumarn Kabilsingh, who resigned her position in the philosophy department at Thammasat University to ordain in Sri Lanka as Samaneri Dhammānan with the hope of establishing an order of nuns in Thailand.

The international engaged Buddhist movement that includes reformers like Sulak advocates the integration of inner-personal and outer-social transformation. Progressive Thai Buddhists believe that the international problems of global poverty, economic exploitation, and violence require the practice of sustained awareness that lies at the heart of true compassion. Although awareness is an ancient Buddhist practice, its application to a Buddhist social ethic is an innovation that, while running the risk of diminishing its original intent, holds out the promise that the tradition will maintain its relevance to the dramatic dislocations of the postmodern world.

See also: **Amulets and Talismans; Engaged Buddhism; Merit and Merit-Making; Relics and Relics Cults; Thai, Buddhist Literature in**

Bibliography

Bizot, François. *Le Chemin de Lanka.* Paris: École Française d'Extreme-Orient, 1992.

Bizot, François. *Le Bouddhisme des Thais.* Bangkok, Thailand: Editions des Cahiers de France, 1993.

Buddhadasa Bhikkhu. *Me and Mine: Selected Essays of Bhikkhu Buddhadasa,* ed. Donald K. Swearer. Albany: State University of New York Press, 1989.

Crosby, Kate. "Tantric Theravāda: A Bibliographic Essay on the Writings of François Bizot and Others on the Yogāvacara Tradition." *Contemporary Buddhism: An Interdisciplinary Journal* 1, no. 2 (November 2000): 141–198.

Ishii Yoneo. *Saṅgha, State, and Society: Thai Buddhism in History,* tr. Peter Hawkes. Honolulu: University of Hawaii Press, 1986.

Jackson, Peter. *Buddhism, Legitimation, and Conflict: The Political Functions of Urban Thai Buddhism.* Singapore: Institute of Southeast Asian Studies, 1989.

Keyes, Charles. "Buddhist Politics and Their Revolutionary Origins in Thailand." *International Political Science Review* 10, no. 2 (1989): 121–142.

Muecke, Marjorie A. "Mother Sold Food, Daughter Sells Her Body: The Cultural Continuity of Prostitution." *Social Science Medicine* 35, no. 7 (1992): 891–901.

Ratanapañña Thera. *The Sheaf of Garlands of the Epochs of the Conqueror (Jinakalamalipakaranam),* tr. N. A. Jayawickrama. London: Luzac, 1968.

Reynolds, Frank E., and Reynolds, Mani B. *Three Worlds According to King Ruang: A Thai Buddhist Cosmology.* Berkeley, CA: Asian Humanities Press, 1982.

Swearer, Donald K. *The Buddhist World of Southeast Asia.* Albany: State University of New York Press, 1995.

Tambiah, Stanley J. *World Conqueror, World Renouncer: A Study of Buddhism and Polity in Thailand against a Historical Background.* Cambridge, UK: Cambridge University Press, 1976.

DONALD K. SWEARER

THERAVĀDA

Theravāda is the dominant form of Buddhism in Cambodia, Laos, Myanmar (Burma), Sri Lanka, and Thailand. It remains a central component of the Buddhism of Vietnam, even after its formal unification with MAHĀYĀNA forms in the 1960s. The tradition is followed by the Baruas, Chakma, and Magh ethnic groups in Bangladesh, and the Shans of southern China. Historically, the Theravāda school was also important in South India, and had a wider presence in South and Southeast Asia more generally, including Indonesia. In the modern period, Theravāda has spread worldwide through diaspora and mission. The school has been instrumental in the Buddhist revival in India and has begun to replace traditional Newari Buddhism in the Kathmandu valley of Nepal. Missionary monks worldwide serve both diasporic and convert Buddhists, often as separate congregations. In the two relatively recent phenomena of Western convert and ENGAGED BUDDHISM, Theravāda is likely to be universalized rather than culturally specific, and to be mixed or at least in dialogue with other forms of Buddhism and even other religions. There are an estimated 100 million Theravāda Buddhists worldwide.

Scriptural authority

Among the key features of traditional Theravāda Buddhism are the use of Pāli as a sacred language and the acceptance of the Pāli Buddhist CANON (*tipiṭaka*) as the highest scriptural authority. This remains true nominally even where the *tipiṭaka* is not directly relevant to belief or practice, and in spite of so-called APOCRYPHA and numerous other religious texts that teach noncanonical practices.

Theravāda's doctrinal tradition derives from the distinctive *Abhidhamma Piṭaka* of its aforementioned *tipiṭaka*. Because of the form of analytical doctrine (Pāli, *vibhajjavāda*) represented in this *abhidhamma* (Sanskrit, ABHIDHARMA) section of its canon, some scholars have suggested that Theravāda is better identified as the Vibhajjavāda school.

Theravāda is also characterized by an ORDINATION tradition based on its distinctive VINAYA *Piṭaka*. Although various branches of Theravāda may historically have used other vinayas, modern variations within the school relate principally to differing interpretations of the traditional 227 rules of conduct for monks outlined in the Pāli vinaya. Thus there are different *nikāyas* (ordination lineages) within Theravāda, and numerous sub-*nikāyas*.

Commentarial tradition and historiography

The scriptural authority of the Pāli *tipiṭaka* continues through strata of commentaries and compendia, dominated by works attributed to the fifth-century Indian scholar-monk BUDDHAGHOSA. Buddhaghosa is often considered to be the authoritative arbiter of Theravāda orthodoxy, although this status has been challenged, for example, by proponents of Burmese-style VIPASSANĀ (SANSKRIT, VIPAŚYANĀ) meditation in Sri Lanka in the twentieth century.

One explanation for Buddhaghosa's dominance over Theravāda scholasticism lies in the use made of him by another key figure in the commentarial tradition, the twelfth-century scholar-monk Sāriputta. Sāriputta emerged as the premier scholastic figure in Theravāda following King Parakramabahu I's unification of the central Sri Lankan saṅgha groups under the Mahāvihāra monastic tradition. Sāriputta based much of his interpretation of vinaya and doctrine on Buddhaghosa. Because of the political dominance of Sri Lanka at the time and the Mahāvihāra tradition's reputation as the representative of Theravāda orthodoxy and orthopraxy, many monks on mainland Southeast Asia sought ordination in the Mahāvihāra lineage. Mahāvihāra-derived lineages subsequently gained political support in mainland Southeast Asia, and Sāriputta's influence shaped literary developments within Theravāda over subsequent centuries.

The legacy of Mahāvihāra dominance has had an enormous impact on our understanding of the history of Theravāda more generally. Theravāda's own historiography is preserved mainly within the VAṂSA (chronicle) tradition of the Mahāvihāra and traditions derived from it. These chronicles emphasize the significance of the Mahāvihāra, Sri Lanka, and Pāli orthodoxy, and appear to have obscured local traditions.

According to the commentarial and *vaṃsa* tradition, Theravāda is original Buddhism. Like the *sutta* (Sanskrit, sūtra) and vinaya texts of its *tipiṭaka*, its *abhidhamma* texts too are attributed directly to the Buddha, who is said to have taught them to his mother in heaven, where they were witnessed for posterity by the Buddha's disciple Sāriputta (Sanskrit, ŚĀRIPUTRA). Theravāda even claims that its commentaries were compiled at the First Council following the Buddha's death. All the texts in its canon were rehearsed again at a second council one hundred years later. While the term *Theravāda*, meaning "doctrine of the elders," could be understood to indicate *Buddhism* in contrast to other religious traditions, the term becomes associated with a specific school in the Theravāda account of the schism between the MAHĀSĀṂGHIKA SCHOOL and more orthodox Sthaviras (the Sanskrit equivalent of the Pāli term *Thera*) that is said to have occasioned the Second Council. Theravāda sees itself as the continuation of this orthodox Sthavira branch of the early Buddhist tradition. The ambiguity of the term *theriya*, which can mean either "elder Buddhist monk" or "follower of the Thera school," complicates attempts to trace the school's early history. According to Theravāda tradition, its orthodoxy was again defended under Emperor AŚOKA in the third century B.C.E., this time against the corruption of heretics, which set a precedent for state intervention in the affairs of the saṅgha, which has shaped so much of the subsequent history of Theravāda.

After this purification, Aśoka had his son Mahinda and daughter Saṅghamitta ordained. They are credited with bringing Theravāda and its orthodox canon and commentaries to Sri Lanka, the same commentaries that Buddhaghosa later redacted back into the original Pāli from Singhalese. The *vaṃsas* also record that two monks, Soṇa and Uttara, took Theravāda to mainland Southeast Asia around this time. Trade links had certainly already been forged between the Indian mainland, Sri Lanka, and mainland Southeast Asia by the third century B.C.E., although archaeological evidence suggests that the introduction of Buddhism into these new regions occurred in piecemeal and diverse fashions.

Sometimes it is hard to relate inscriptions and other archaeological finds to a specific school and the association of Pāli exclusively with Theravāda may prove anachronistic. Theravāda seems to have flourished in parts of Burma and Thailand from the fourth century onward, becoming particularly strong in the lower Burmese kingdom of Pyu and the Dvāravatī polity of Thailand. While Theravāda on the whole seems to have coexisted in mainland Southeast Asia with other traditions of Buddhism, as it had to a lesser extent in Sri Lanka, it sometimes became almost a quasi-state religion. This happened, for example, under King Aniruddha of the Pagan kingdom of upper Burma in the eleventh century, under King Ramkhamhaeng of central Thailand in the thirteenth century, and under King Tilokarāt of northern Thailand in the fifteenth century.

Buddhology

The buddhology of Theravāda is dominated by the figure of Gotama (Sanskrit, Gautama) Buddha, the historical Buddha, who lived in the sixth century B.C.E. according to Theravāda chronology. Also important are the other four buddhas of the current world age, in particular the future buddha Metteyya (Sanskrit, MAITREYA). There is formally a tradition of twenty-four previous buddhas recorded in the *Buddhavaṃsa* (*Chronicle of the Buddhas*) text of the *Sutta Piṭaka,* but they rarely figure in iconography or narrative, except in relation to the career of Gotama Buddha in his former lives. Other important cultic figures include localized Indic and Buddhicized local deities, as well as heroic and mythic figures. Nāgas, mythical serpent beings that can take human form, are frequently represented as protectors of Buddhism. The process of localization, whereby DIVINITIES and spirits local to the host culture of Buddhism are adopted as protectors of Buddhism, has been important in Buddhism's adaptation to new cultures. As Theravāda ousted other forms of Buddhism in mainland Southeast Asia, it has incorporated figures such as UPAGUPTA, GAVĀṂPATI, and Piṇḍola Bhāradvāja, who are thought to have been more important originally in other Buddhist schools, such as the Sarvāstivāda. Consequently, the identity and significance of various deities and protective and other cultic figures varies greatly between different areas, and even between individual villages. They often serve some of the this-worldly functions of Theravāda religion.

Sacred landscape

The sacred landscape of Theravāda is dominated by monastic complexes. These complexes typically incorporate monastic dwellings, a building or area for sermons, a STŪPA in commemoration of the historical Buddha, a bodhi tree, a BUDDHA IMAGE, often in an enclosed temple, along with other traditional representations of the Buddha, such as his sacred footprint. In many villages the local temple is the dominant feature. Temples are often decorated with carvings outside and, inside, with paintings of episodes in Gotama Buddha's former lives (JĀTAKA) or final life, images of HELLS, and legends relating the coming of Buddhism to the region. Deities may also be featured in a subordinate position in the temple layout or contributory landscape. It is often believed that a guardian deity resides within the stūpa, tree, or image, in addition to the inherent Buddha power. Stūpas are often believed to contain relics of Gotama Buddha. Shrines, images, and stūpas are also found independent of the monastic complex. Other features of the sacred landscape are forest and mountain hermitage sites for meditation monks, and, since the 1950s, meditation and retreat centers for laypeople.

The three refuges in religious practice and the role of ordination

Much Theravāda practice revolves around the three REFUGES of the Buddha, *dhamma* (Sanskrit, dharma), and SAṄGHA. Appropriate treatment of all three is a key focus of MERIT AND MERIT-MAKING, a principal focus of religious practice in Theravāda.

WORSHIP of the Buddha varies from daily and incidental personal worship to annual festivals involving the entire community. The annual festival of Wesak, named after the lunar month in which it takes place (April/May), celebrates the Buddha's birth, enlightenment and death. Celebrations of other events, such as his former births, in particular the very popular *Vessantara-jātaka,* may also form a significant component of festivals that are not primarily Buddhist in focus, such as annual harvest festivals or ancestor rites. Occasional ceremonies include consecrations of images and inaugurations of both sacred and secular buildings. Worship involves offerings of flowers, rice, and lamps to the Buddha image and circumambulation of the stūpa. While the Buddha in human form may have died, his powers are thought to remain accessible through his relics and images. A legend known throughout the Theravāda world states that the Buddha himself commissioned his own first image, and imbued it with all his own qualities so that it might remain to protect the *dhamma*. Some relics and statues are associated with the security of the nation, as is the case with the tooth relic enshrined in Kandy, Sri Lanka, or the Emerald Buddha in Thailand. *Vaṃsas* record visits the Buddha made during his lifetime to the later strongholds of Theravāda Buddhism, in which he predicts the future glory of the religion and the monarchs who protect it in the region, and sometimes leaves behind relics. The predicted continuation of the *dhamma* in a particular region or in association with a particular royal lineage has been used to authorize the saṅgha-state interaction that dominates Theravāda history. Pilgrimages to sites associated with Gotama or previous buddhas—both in different Theravāda countries and the area of north India in which the historical Buddha lived—continue to be a popular form of merit-making.

The monk represents the ideal of enlightenment, even if this is nowadays thought by most to be unattainable, and in some traditions the ordinand ritually reenacts the life of the Buddha at ORDINATION. Ordination of men is mainstream. In Sri Lanka, lifelong ordination remains the dominant intention, although monks often secede from the order, sometimes after becoming established in a career, and there is an increasing tendency toward ordination as a form of retirement. In mainland Southeast Asian traditions that have not been undermined by communism, most Buddhist men will ordain at some point in their lives, even if only for a short period. In these societies, ordination fulfills the function of a coming-of-age ceremony and is also seen as a way of providing one's parents, in particular one's mother, with merit to ensure a heavenly REBIRTH, thus repaying her for the agony of childbirth. The earliest age for novice ordination (the lower of the two levels of ordination) varies from very young boys in Myanmar, to eight-year-olds and above in Sri Lanka, and teenagers and upward in Thailand. The availability of education through non-monastic state and private educational institutions has altered ordination patterns, as has the need to fit temporary ordination into the schedule of compulsory education. While temporary ordinations used to last for the three months of the annual rains-retreat, some are now designed to fit into the long university vacation. In communist countries, the loss of prestige and the lack of continuity in ordination traditions have reduced the dominance of ordination, especially in urban areas.

Full ordination for WOMEN died out in the medieval period and some Theravāda traditions have only recently attempted to revive it through reimportation of a Buddhist ordination lineage from East Asia (in 1996 in Sri Lanka, in 2002 in Thailand). For this reason, manifestations of female renunciation in the Theravāda school are quite diverse. Many women have pursued a life of celibate renunciation by undertaking either individually or in an institutionalized group most or all of the ten PRECEPTS traditionally undertaken by a novice monk. Sometimes nunneries are attached to monasteries, and NUNS may essentially serve the domestic needs of MONKS. Sometimes nuns have separate institutions and are independent of monks, a situation only fully possible in the absence of full ordination, since full ordination for women requires the participation of monks. The prestige and opportunities accorded Theravāda nuns have greatly increased over the past few decades. Nevertheless, it is the exception rather than the rule for nuns to form a significant focal point in the religious life of a Theravāda layperson.

By contrast, monks are the focus of lay religious practice at a whole range of ceremonies, from large annual celebrations to incidental homage paid when a layperson meets a monk. Perhaps the most significant of the annual ceremonies is the *kaṭhina* ceremony, at which robes (*kaṭhina*) and other gifts are offered to monks at the end of the rains-retreat.

In addition to representing and pursuing the ideal of nibbāna (Sanskrit, NIRVĀṆA), monks fulfill a number of other roles. They are the preservers and communicators of the *dhamma*. They are the formalized recipients of the generosity and esteem of laypeople and thereby serve as a source of merit for the laity. They act as spiritual teachers, particularly through providing sermons on holy days and on special occasions. They may act as advisers to rulers and governments. Some monks have even become members of parliament, trade union heads, and directors of charities. They have traditionally been educators, especially before the introduction of state education. Finally, monks fulfill the function of priests and ritual specialists, and sometimes even serve as astrologists. As ritual specialists monks have a role in administering the refuges and precepts to laypeople, and in performing funerals. They are often engaged to perform apotropaic rituals, which focus on the protective power of the Buddha and the *dhamma.*

Paritta

The most common manifestation of such protective rituals is the recitation of PARITTA AND RAKṢĀ TEXTS, which are considered to offer powerful protection in warding off dangers and appeasing malevolent spirits. *Paritta* recitation can last throughout the night or even for seven days and nights. During the ceremony further objects may be imbued with protective qualities, including string, sacred water, and AMULETS AND TALISMANS. In mainland Southeast Asia it is common for men to wear protective amulets in the form of small Buddha images, images of famous monks or kings, mythical figures, or even phallic shapes. Other forms of visual protection include *yantras,* which may be drawn on cloth or used as the pattern for a tattoo. They portray heroic figures and sacred writing of Buddhist formulae in Pāli, sometimes in the form of geometric designs and outlines of the Buddha.

Attempts to classify Theravāda

Much Theravāda religious activity includes ritualized interaction with the Buddha, *dhamma,* and saṅgha in combination in one or more of the forms described above. As such, Theravāda has much in common with other forms of Buddhism. In scholarship it is often strongly demarcated from other traditions, although the viability of such distinctions is currently under scrutiny.

One such distinction can be summarized on the basis of the relative value in Theravāda of self-transformation through MEDITATION and RITUAL. Paraphrasing the work of Melford Spiro, Theravāda religion may be said to fall into three categories. First, *nibbānic* Theravāda focuses on self-transformation, chiefly through meditations aimed at developing the emotional responses and level of insight of individuals so that they become enlightened and escape from SAṂSĀRA. Second, *kammatic* religion focuses on merit-making and ethical action, to improve one's future life and lives within saṃsāra. Third, apotropaic Buddhism uses magic in the form of amulets and rituals to deal with this-worldly concerns, either in distinction to or outside of the law of karmic cause and effect.

Tibetan Buddhism has been similarly categorized by Geoffrey Samuel. His three categories are: first, bodhi-oriented practices that focus on often ritualized altruism and higher levels of tantric ritual; second, karma-oriented merit-making to improve future life within saṃsāra; and third, pragmatic religion for this-worldly concerns, using tantric ritual.

If we align these two analyses we see that in terms of the two categories of seeking improved life within saṃsāra and this-worldly concerns, Theravāda and Tibetan Buddhism are directly parallel. It is at the soteriological end that Theravāda putatively eschews ritual and magic, whereas Tibetan Buddhism invokes it. However, there is a tradition of ritualized soteriology in Theravāda too that was found throughout the Theravāda world in the premodern period. This tradition involved ritual identification with the Buddha and the assimilation of the Buddha's qualities, much as are found in Tibetan tantra, yet using only Theravāda categories and nomenclature. Thus, Theravāda also employs ritual practices that might be designated magical at the *nibbānic*/bodhi end of the spectrum, a convergence that minimizes the distinction between Tibetan and Theravāda Buddhist practices. It further suggests that the apparent Theravāda focus on forms of meditation found in the *tipiṭaka* and Buddhaghosa may be the result of a narrowing of the tradition caused in part by the close state-saṅgha relationship that shaped dominant forms of Theravāda.

A more widespread generalization often made regarding Theravāda is that it is the sole surviving form of HĪNAYĀNA Buddhism. The supposed Mahāyāna-Hīnayāna dichotomy is so prevalent in Buddhist literature that it has yet fully to loosen its hold over scholarly representations of the religion. Hīnayāna (literally, "inferior way") is a polemical term, which self-described Mahāyāna (literally, "great way") Buddhist literature uses to denigrate its opponents. As such, Hīnayāna is a designation that has no clearly identifiable external referent. Some of the first attempts to categorize forms of Buddhism as either Hīnayāna or Mahāyāna are found in the accounts of early Chinese pilgrims to South Asia. But there are additional reasons for the modern association of Theravāda with Hīnayāna. The first is that one body of Mahāyāna texts, the PRAJÑĀPĀRAMITĀ LITERATURE, propounds the lack of self of all dharmas, a critique of the analytical categories of the abhidharma. This position is refuted in the *Kathāvatthu* (*Points of Controversy*), a text of the Theravāda *Abhidhamma Piṭaka,* which purports to discuss points of debate with other religious traditions raised at the Third Council. The second is that one supposed characteristic of the Mahāyāna involves the proliferation of multiple buddhas in parallel world systems. The possibility of more than one buddha living at a time is a view also rejected in the *Kathāvatthu.* The most common reason made to distinguish Mahāyāna and Theravāda is thoroughly flawed. This is the distinction made between Mahāyāna as the path of the BODHISATTVA and Theravāda as the path of the ARHAT or śravaka (disciple). Even Buddhaghosa recognized three levels of practice: that of the Buddha through the path of the *bodhisatta* (Sanskrit, bodhisattva); that of the *paccekabuddha* (Sanskrit, PRATYEKABUDDHA); and that of the arhat. Furthermore the bodhisattva ideal is present throughout Theravāda history, even if it never became ritualized and institutionalized to the same degree as it did in other Buddhist traditions. Although the bodhisattva ideal in Theravāda is more commonly associated with Gotama Buddha himself and with kings, it is also found expressed by those of humbler position. It is, for example, a common vow made by manuscript copyists in the colophons to Theravāda texts.

See also: **Cambodia; Commentarial Literature; Councils, Buddhist; Folk Religion, Southeast Asia; Laos; Mainstream Buddhist Schools; Myanmar; Pāli, Buddhist Literature in; Sri Lanka; Thailand; Theravāda Art and Architecture; Vietnam**

Bibliography

Assavavirulhakarn, Prapod. "The Ascendancy of Theravāda Buddhism in Southeast Asia." Ph.D. diss. University of California, Berkeley, 1990.

Crosby, Kate. "Tantric Theravāda: A Bibliographic Essay on the Writings of François Bizot and Other Literature on the Yogāvacara Tradition." *Journal of Contemporary Buddhism* 1, no. 2 (2000): 141–198.

Gombrich, R. F. *Theravāda Buddhism: A Social History from Ancient Benares to Modern Colombo.* London and New York: Routledge and Kegan Paul, 1988.

Gunawardana, R. A. L. H. *Robe and Plough: Monasticism and Economic Interest in Early Medieval Sri Lanka.* Tucson: University of Arizona Press, 1979.

Samuel, Geoffrey. *Civilized Shamans: Buddhism in Tibetan Societies.* Washington, DC, and London: Smithsonian Institution Press, 1993.

Samuels, Jeffrey. "The Bodhisattva Ideal in Theravāda Buddhist Theory and Practices: A Re-evaluation of the Bodhisattva-Śrāvaka Opposition." *Philosophy East and West* 47, no. 3 (1997): 399–415.

Smith, Bardwell L., ed. *Religion and Legitimation of Power in Sri Lanka.* Chambersburg, PA: ANIMA, 1978.

Spiro, Melford. *Buddhism and Society: A Great Tradition and Its Burmese Vicissitudes.* London: Allen and Unwin, 1971.

Swearer, Donald S. *The Buddhist World of Southeast Asia,* revised edition. Albany: State University of New York Press, 1995.

Terwiel, B. J. *Monks and Magic: An Analysis of Religious Ceremonies in Central Thailand* (1975), 3rd revised edition. Bangkok, Thailand: White Lotus Press, 1994.

KATE CROSBY

THERAVĀDA ART AND ARCHITECTURE

The focus of THERAVĀDA Buddhist art and architecture is Buddha Gautama, as revered teacher, exemplar of virtue and ethical conduct, role model for the SAṄGHA, and source of supernatural power. Thus the Theravāda monastery serves as a center for the dissemination of the Buddha's teachings, a gathering place for the practice and continuity of the religion, a dwelling place for monks, and a repository of sacred objects, including BUDDHA IMAGES and relics. Similarly, the majority of Theravāda art consists of sculptures and paintings depicting narratives about the historical Buddha's life and previous lives as lessons for the faithful.

In premodern times, Theravāda Buddhist monasteries were the focal point in the social and educational life of the community. Every village had at least one monastery and each town and city had several. While sociological, economic, and in some cases political changes—particularly in Cambodia and to a lesser degree in Laos—have disrupted many traditional patterns, the local monastery continues to occupy a significant place in the lives of individuals and communities.

A monastery compound typically includes an image hall for the monastery's principal Buddha image, an ordination hall, an assembly hall where laypeople gather to listen to sermons and recitations of sacred texts by the monks, a solid, dome-shaped reliquary, and residence buildings for the monks. Regional variations on this model exist, however; for example, in certain places the image hall and assembly hall are combined into one building. In other places the assembly hall and ordination hall are combined and the place reserved for ordinations is off-limits to women. Moreover, some monasteries have residences for nuns and lay meditators and some have a separate building for storing sacred scriptures. The latter, often referred to as a *Tripiṭaka hall* or library is usually raised on stilts to protect the books from water, insects, and rodents.

While the proportions and architectural features of monastery buildings vary from one region to another, certain features can be found throughout the Theravāda Buddhist world. Most obvious are the roofs, which are multitiered (especially for ordination halls and image halls) with an odd number of tiers, three being the most common. In addition, eaves brackets, gables, pillars, and doors are often decorated with carvings and paintings of mythical beings from Buddhist COSMOLOGY, such as ascetics, heavenly musicians, nāga serpents, lions, geese and other mythical birds, as well as plant motifs, particularly lotuses and vines. These motifs were among the repertoire of elements that both Buddhism and Hinduism inherited from the indigenous mythological landscape of India. Similarly, as Buddhism spread from India to Sri Lanka and Southeast Asia, it adapted to local preexisting spiritual beliefs by incorporating them into its narratives, rituals, and iconography. As examples, many Burmese monasteries contain statues of the thirty-seven *nats* (the indigenous deities representing natural phenomena and the spirits of ancestors who have met a violent death) and throughout the Theravāda world people place offerings at the foot of large banyan trees—both within monastery compounds and outside—to revere the spirits that dwell within.

Similarly, Hindu deities, such as Brahmā and INDRA, are frequently depicted as guardians of the Buddha to indicate the ascendancy of Buddhism over Hinduism, as are demonic figures that represent local spirits tamed by the Buddha's teachings. All of these elements contribute toward creating an elaborate, otherworldly atmosphere that calls to mind both local royal dwellings and higher realms of the Buddhist cosmos.

A generally more austere, but no less important, building in the monastery compound is the STŪPA or *cetiya,* a solid structure roughly resembling an inverted cone. The stūpa also varies greatly in shape, from broad bulbous bowl-shaped monuments in Sri Lanka to obelisk-shaped towers found at some sites in northeast Thailand (such as Phra Thāt Phanom), to elegant, attenuated lotus-bud *chedis* of the SUKHOTHAI kingdom in Thailand. While some stūpas contain relics of monks or monastery patrons, others are believed to hold bone fragments of the Buddha and are highly revered for their sacredness.

Laypeople's activities

Laypeople visit the monasteries for numerous reasons: to observe the lunar holy days (every full moon, waning moon, new moon, and waxing moon), to make merit for deceased relatives or for family member who are sick or in need, to consult with the monks about problems or about astrological considerations, to make merit for themselves in the hopes of fulfilling wishes, to seek advice or blessings, to be ordained, and to meditate.

Numerous monasteries are popular PILGRIMAGE sites because they are believed to contain sacred objects, such as an authentic bone fragment of the Buddha, a footprint left by the Buddha as delineated in a local chronicle, or historically significant images of the Buddha or of deceased monks famous for their supernatural powers. Devout Buddhists often make a special effort to pay reverence at these sites—sometimes in the hopes of obtaining a boon—with traditional offerings of flowers, incense, and candles. They usually return home with an amulet resembling the principal Buddha image commemorating the significance of the site.

At many monasteries pilgrims can purchase a small bird in a bamboo cage, circumambulate the monastery holding the birdcage, praying at various Buddha images along the way. Finally, they release the bird, appealing to the three JEWELS (Buddha, dharma, and saṅgha) to witness this act as sufficient merit.

Jātaka stories

Until modern times, the monastery's functions included the teachings of moral and religious teachings as well as basic literacy skills. With a largely illiterate population, monks relied on oral storytelling and the visual lessons of murals to teach Buddhist principles of ethics and morality through stories about the Buddha Gautama's life and previous lives. While key events from the Buddha's biography are frequently depicted in mural painting as well as in the miniature paintings of paper manuscripts, stories from his previous lives (JĀTAKAS, or birth stories, found in varied collections and totaling 500 to 547 stories) are equally, if not more, prevalent.

In Myanmar (Burma) terra-cotta plaques representing each of the *jātakas* can be found on the outside walls of some of the great monasteries of the ancient city of Pagan. In the mural painting of Thailand, Cambodia, and Laos, the last ten birth stories are found more frequently than the entire set. Each story represents one of the ten great virtues (renunciation, perseverance, loving kindness, resolution, wisdom, moral practice, forbearance, equanimity, truthfulness, and generosity) that the future Buddha perfected in order to attain enlightenment, and each has a predictable iconographic set of elements to identify it. For example, in the story demonstrating perseverance, the future Buddha, a prince who is separated from his kingdom at birth, survives a shipwreck to claim his throne. He is usually depicted swimming, surrounded by stylized waves and sea monsters, and rescued by a sea goddess.

The last of the ten, the Great Birth Story or *Vessantara Jātaka,* which exists in countless versions, or "tellings," is the most frequently depicted and recounted narrative of all, including the biography of the Buddha Gautama. Depending on the region, it is recited at the close of the Buddhist rains-retreat (around the time of the full moon in November) or during the months that follow. In parts of Thailand, Laos, Cambodia, and Burma, the recitation of this story is one of the most significant ceremonies of the year, lasting an entire day and a night. Painted banners depicting events in the story are hung around the inside of the monastery. Laypeople sponsor the reading of sections of the story and bring offerings of food and flowers. The motivation behind these activities is the widespread belief that a person who listens to the Great Birth Story recited in this context will be reborn during the time of the future Buddha MAITREYA. Those who hear Maitreya preach, according to this belief, will accomplish the very difficult goal of attaining NIRVĀṆA. While this doctrine may be technically outside the realm of what some would consider orthodox Theravāda teachings, it is an important aspect of practice and iconography in Theravāda regions.

Apart from these themes, other narratives depicted in murals, reliefs, and carvings are local histories describing the coming of Buddhism to the area, local folktales that are retold as birth stories of the Buddha, and the great *Rāmāyana* epic. While the latter is technically a Hindu story, it has long been popular in the Buddhist world and particularly in royally sponsored monasteries because of its association with kingship. Rāma, the story's hero, is a model of royal and familial righteousness. Monastery murals frequently depict his battles with the demonic forces to rescue his wife Sītā and restore order in his kingdom. They were commissioned by monarchs as a way of bringing to the earthly realm the power and symbolism of the heaven or macrocosm.

Murals and manuscripts depict the same themes and share similar stylistic features: abstract rather than realistic portrayal of figures, architecture, and landscape; and grouping of similar figures (such as warriors, attendants, dancers) in clusters that form one among several patterns within a space, with one figure echoing the others. Moreover, within these paintings one can also see a strong reflection of local dress, textile designs, indigenous physical characteristics, architecture, and customs.

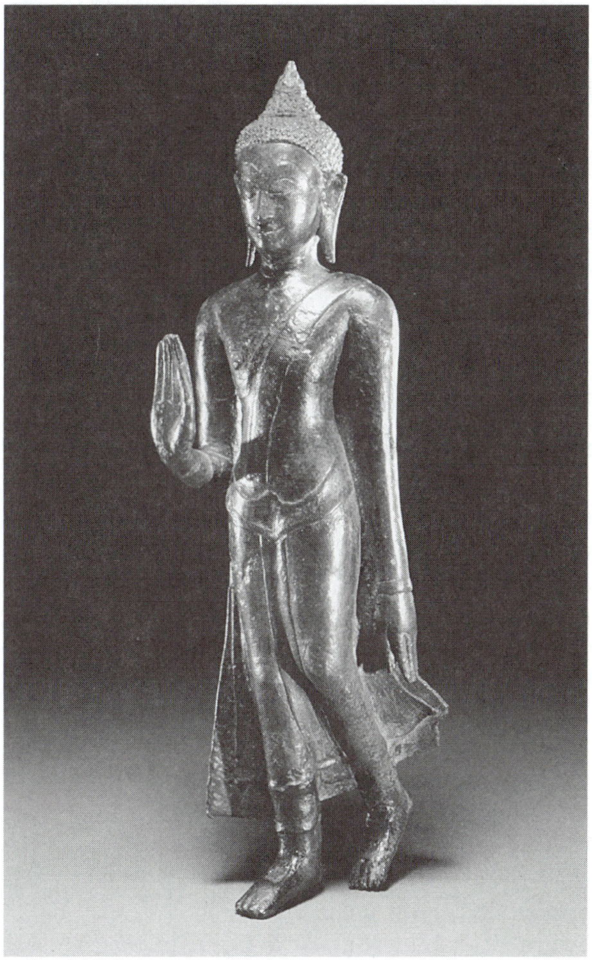

A bronze Buddha from the Thai "golden age." The Buddha is usually depicted standing, sitting, or lying down; the walking image is distinctively Thai. (Thai, Sukhothai period, fourteenth century.)

Sculpture

Sculptures representing the historical Buddha made of stone, bronze, terra-cotta, or wood can be found throughout the Theravāda world. They range in size from colossal images especially popular in Sri Lanka and Burma to miniature amulets encased in gold and worn on a necklace. The image serves as a reminder of the Buddha, his teachings, and his spiritual descendants—the monks, known collectively as the saṅgha. Images of the Buddha are always treated with utmost reverence and placed on a dais or altar above the heads of the people. It would be inappropriate to keep a Buddha image in a place other than a monastery, museum, or private home altar.

Images are believed to be repositories of potency and are often draped with orange robes resembling those worn by monks and worshiped with offerings of flowers, incense, and candles. Moreover, certain images are revered for miracles associated with them or legends surrounding their discovery. At many monasteries worshipers can purchase small squares of gold leaf to attach to images as acts of merit, and certain images, such as the Emerald Buddha in Bangkok, regularly receive offerings of special food thought to be their favorite from devotees requesting favors, such as a relative's good health.

Throughout Southeast Asia during the festivities revolving around the solar New Year in mid-April, images are carried in procession on elaborately decorated carts or trucks and bathed with fragrant water. Thus, even in a Theravāda context, Buddha images are treated in ways similar to those of statues of Hindu deities in India.

The most frequently seen postures and hand positions (MUDRĀ) in the Theravāda tradition are those depicting key events in the Buddha's life: meditating—seated cross-legged with hands folded in the lap; the enlightenment—a similar seated posture, but with the right hand at the right knee, fingers pointing downward toward the earth; teaching—standing with hands extended; and in nirvāṇa or death—lying on the right side, head supported by the right hand.

In Southeast Asia, the most popular posture by far is that of enlightenment, the posture known either as "touching the earth" or "victory over MĀRA" (the personification of darkness and delusion). In many monasteries, murals depicting this event cover the wall behind the main Buddha image. A central meditating figure of the Buddha is surrounded by Māra's army—a variety of demonic characters, some human, some animal, some hybrid—flinging arrows and other weapons. Below the Buddha is a standing female figure of the Earth Goddess, whom the Buddha has called to witness his enlightenment. She wrings out her long hair and from it flows the water that has collected from the acts of generosity that Gautama performed in his past lives, each time consecrating his donation by pouring water from an urn onto the ground. Theravāda Buddhists sometimes replicate this practice when they present offerings to the monks.

See also: **Amulets and Talismans; Buddha, Life of the, in Art; Merit and Merit-Making; Southeast Asia, Buddhist Art in; Sri Lanka, Buddhist Art in**

Bibliography

Boisselier, Jean. *The Heritage of Thai Sculpture.* New York: Weatherhill, 1975.

Döhring, Karl. *Buddhist Temples of Thailand: An Architectonic Introduction.* Bangkok, Thailand: White Lotus Press, 2000.

Gosling, Betty. *A Chronology of Religious Architecture at Sukhothai, Late Thirteeth to Early Fifteenth Century.* Ann Arbor, MI: Association for Asian Studies, 1996.

Gosling, Betty. *Old Luang Prabang.* New York and Kuala Lumpur, Malaysia: Oxford University Press, 1996.

Luce, Gordon H., *Old Burma—Early Pagan.* Locust Valley, NY: J. J. Augustin, 1969.

Matics, K. I. *Introduction to the Thai Temple.* Bangkok, Thailand: White Lotus Press, 1992.

Ringis, Rita. *Thai Temples and Temple Murals.* Singapore and New York: Oxford University Press, 1990.

Strachan, Paul. *Pagan: Art and Architecture of Old Burma.* Whiting Bay, Scotland: Kiscadale, 1989.

Vogel, Jean Philippe. *Buddhist Art in India, Ceylon, and Java.* New Delhi: Asian Educational Services, 1998.

Woodward, Hiram W. *The Sacred Sculpture of Thailand: The Alexander B. Griswold Collection, the Walters Art Gallery.* Baltimore, MD: The Walters Art Gallery; Seattle: University of Washington Press, 1997.

Woodward, Hiram W. *The Art and Architecture of Thailand: From Prehistoric Times through the Thirteenth Century.* Leiden, Netherlands, and Boston: Brill, 2003.

Wray, Elizabeth; Rosenfield, Clare; and Bailey, Dorothy. *Ten Lives of the Buddha: Siamese Paintings and Jataka Tales.* New York and Tokyo: Weatherhill, 1972.

BONNIE BRERETON

THICH NHAT HANH

Thich Nhat Hanh (Nguyen Xaun Bao, 1926–), a Vietnamese Buddhist monk and peace activist, coined the term ENGAGED BUDDHISM in the 1960s to describe the antiwar movement in his country. Nominated for the Nobel Peace Prize in 1967 by Martin Luther King, Jr., Nhat Hanh led the Buddhist delegation to the Paris peace talks and organized rescue missions to save the "boat people" fleeing Vietnam in the 1970s. Exiled from Vietnam since the 1960s, Nhat Hanh has taught MEDITATION and reconciliation to thousands of followers in the West. He founded the Tiep Hien Order (Order of Interbeing), has established retreat centers in Europe and North America, and has published more than one hundred books of poetry and prose. Stressing the oneness or "interbeing" of all existence, mindfulness in daily life, and service and nonviolent activism on behalf of those suffering tyranny and injustice, Thich Nhat Hanh is a leading preceptor of engaged Buddhism.

See also: **Europe; United States**

Bibliography

Nhat Hanh, Thich. *Being Peace.* Berkeley, CA: Parallax Press, 1987.

Nhat Hanh, Thich. *Love in Action: Writings on Nonviolent Social Change.* Berkeley, CA: Parallax Press, 1993.

CHRISTOPHER S. QUEEN

TIANTAI SCHOOL

Often described as the first genuinely Sinitic school of Buddhism, the Tiantai school traces its ancestry back to NĀGĀRJUNA (ca. second century C.E.) in India, not by any direct transmission but through the reading of translated texts by its proto-patriarchs, Huiwen (Beiqi *zunzhe,* mid-sixth century) and Huisi (Nanyue *chanshi,* 515–577). Very little is known of these two figures. Huiwen in particular is little more than a shadowy presence; traditional biographies report that he was active during China's Northern Qi dynasty (550–577), stressed strict meditation practice, and initiated the characteristic Tiantai emphasis on triplicity. In particular, Huiwen is reported to have emphasized the "simultaneity of the three contemplations," namely, the contemplation of each object as emptiness, provisional positing, and the "mean," as derived from a strong misreading of works attributed to Nāgārjuna. Huisi, on the other hand, authored several extant texts, and is credited with combining Huiwen's "three contemplations" with the teaching of the LOTUS SŪTRA (SADDHARMAPUṆḌARĪKA-SŪTRA), to which Huisi was especially devoted. This combination proved to be explosive.

Huisi interpreted the lotus from the title of this sūtra as a metaphor suggesting a special relationship between cause and effect, or practice and enlightenment. The lotus, he noted, is unusual in that it gives no flower without producing a fruit, that the fruit is concealed and copresent in the flower, and a single flower produces many fruits. This suggests that every practice leads to many different results, which are copresent in the practice, and yet unrevealed; every practice, even those that show no orientation toward buddhahood, lead to and are copresent with buddhahood. The translation of the *Lotus Sūtra* by KUMĀRAJĪVA (350–409/413 C.E.) characterizes "the ultimate reality" (literally, "real mark") "of all dharmas" in terms of "ten suchnesses" (literally, ten *like-this's*). They are:

1. like-this (suchlike) appearance
2. nature
3. substance
4. power
5. activity
6. cause
7. condition
8. effect
9. response
10. equality of ultimacy from beginning to end.

Huisi developed a special reading of this passage, facilitated by the peculiarity of the Chinese translation, where each phrase referred to every element of experience simultaneously as "empty," in addition to its literal reference to each as provisionally posited, referring to each specific differentiated aspect (i.e., appearance, nature, etc.). In Zhiyi's exfoliation of this interpretative move, each was also understood as the "mean." This bold hermeneutic approach and its threefold implication formed the basis for what would develop into the distinctive Tiantai conception of "the ultimate reality of/as all dharmas."

The de facto founder of the school, from whose part-time residence—Mount Tiantai in modern Zhejiang—the school gets its name, is ZHIYI (Tiantai Zhizhe *dashi,* 538–597). It was Zhiyi's numerous and voluminous works, most of which were transcribed by his disciple Guanding (Zhangan *dashi,* 561–632) from Zhiyi's lectures, that become authoritative for all later Tiantai tradition.

Provisional and ultimate truth: The *Lotus Sūtra* and the classification of teachings

Zhiyi constructed a vast syncretic system of MAHĀYĀNA thought and practice that aimed at giving a comprehensive overview of all of Buddhism and that found a place for all known modes of practice and doctrine.

Confronted with the massive influx of Mahāyāna texts translated into Chinese, many of which directly contradicted one another in matters of both doctrine and practice, Zhiyi was faced with the challenge of accommodating the claim that all these texts represented the authoritative teaching of the Buddha. The solution he arrived at can be described as an insight into the interconnection between two central Mahāyāna doctrines: the concept of UPĀYA (skillful means), particularly as presented in the *Lotus Sūtra,* and the concept of ŚŪNYATĀ (EMPTINESS), particularly as developed in the MADHYAMAKA SCHOOL. From the synthesis of these ideas, Zhiyi developed a distinctive understanding of the buddha-nature, rooted especially in the universalist exposition given in the NIRVĀṆA SŪTRA, and the identity between delusion and enlightenment as invoked in the *Vimalakīrtinirdeśa* and other sūtras, which entailed a reconfiguring of both *upāya* and śūnyatā as they had been understood in earlier Mahāyāna Buddhism.

The *Lotus Sūtra* asserts that the *śrāvakas* (HĪNAYĀNA disciples), who had hitherto been regarded as having no aspiration toward bodhisattvahood or buddhahood—indeed, as having explicitly repudiated these goals—are in fact BODHISATTVAS currently working toward buddhahood, although they are unaware of the real efficacy of their current practice. The text develops the idea that it is possible to be a bodhisattva without realizing it into a claim that in fact all Buddhist disciples are really bodhisattvas, and all who hear the *Lotus* teaching will finally attain buddhahood. Indeed, it is said in the text that no sentient being really knows what he or she is practicing, what the ultimate karmic efficacy of his or her deeds and cognitions is, nor what his or her own real identity is. Only buddhas know these things, and the real efficacy of all their deeds as thus known by the buddhas is that these deeds allow these beings eventually to become buddhas themselves. The non-bodhisattva practices and teachings are all skillful means provided by the Buddha, sometimes requiring an ignorance of the final goal in order to have efficacy toward reaching that goal. This is the teaching of the first half of the sūtra, which Zhiyi calls the "trace gate." Another wrinkle is given in the second half of the sūtra, which Zhiyi calls the "root gate." Here it is claimed that Śākyamuni Buddha did not attain buddhahood at BODH GAYĀ, but had actually been and would continue to be a buddha for countless eons, in spite of his apparent imminent decease. The implication is that while practicing the bodhisattva path, he was in fact already a buddha (leaving ambiguous his own degree of awareness of this fact at the time), and that being a buddha does not mean a transcendence of engagement in the intersubjective work of liberating SENTIENT BEINGS, but the mastering of all possible skillful means by which to accomplish this task, and a ceaseless indefatigable endeavor to do so.

Taken together then, the two halves of the sūtra suggest that all beings are bodhisattvas, and all bodhisattvas are buddhas. And yet this is only so if the division between them, the opacity and ignorance that keeps them from collapsing these identities, remains intact, just as the *upāyas* work only as long as they are not known as such. This means that the intersubjective liberative relationship between buddhas and sentient beings is primary and always operative, whichever role one may seem to be playing at any time. To be is to be intersubjective, and each being is always both liberating and being liberated by all others, even while also creating KARMA (ACTION) and DUḤKHA (SUFFERING). Ontology is here made soteriological: All existence is instructive and revelatory, and can be read as a salvational device put forth by a buddha to liberate sentient beings.

The relation between illusion and reality is thus reconfigured as the relation between provisional and ultimate truth in the Buddha's teaching. Zhiyi characterizes the *Lotus* teaching as the "opening of the provisional to reveal the real" (*kaiquan xianshi*), allowing one to see the provisional truths as both a means to and an expression of the ultimate truth. Provisional and ultimate truth are nondual, even while maintaining their strict opposition. Their relation is similar to that between the set-up and punch line of a joke; the punch line is funny only because the set-up was not, but once the punch line is understood, the set-up too is seen to have always been pervaded with the quality of humorousness, precisely by being contrastingly nonhumorous. On the basis of this doctrine, Zhiyi established a comprehensive system of "classification of teachings," which categorizes all Buddhist teachings as expressions of ultimate truth tailored to specific circumstances and listeners.

The Madhyamaka doctrine of "two truths" can be understood as asserting that ultimate truth is somehow more real than conventional truth, and indeed that while conventional truth covers both common language (i.e., the everyday use of terms like *I, you, cause, effect,* and the like) and verbal Buddhist teachings, the metaphysical claims of rival schools (i.e., attempts to make rigorous ultimate truths of causality, selfhood, a first cause, and so on) are not even conventional truth, but are simply falsehoods and errors. Zhiyi reinterprets the Madhyamaka position as implying the "three truths": emptiness, provisional positing, and the mean, which includes both and signifies their synonymy. The relation between these three is understood on the model of the *Lotus Sūtra*'s doctrine of "opening the provisional to reveal the real," which annuls any hierarchy between conventional and ultimate truth, and also expands conventional truth so as to include any provisionally posited assertion or cognition without exception. Zhiyi's claim is that these three aspects are not only on precisely equal footing and of equal ultimacy, but that each is in fact simply a way of stating the other two; the three are synonymous.

The three truths and the doctrine of inherent entailment

The reasoning behind the three truths doctrine follows the traditional Buddhist doctrine of PRATĪTYASAMUTPĀDA (DEPENDENT ORIGINATION), which holds that every element of experience necessarily appears "together with" other elements, which it depends upon for its existence and determinate character. These other, conditioning, elements, of course, also gain their determinate character only through their dependence on still other elements that simultaneously condition them. But it was this determinate character that was supposed to serve as a determining ground for the first element. If the determiner is not determinate, the determined also fails to be determined. Hence each element is coherent only locally, in relation to a limited set of these conditions; when all of its conditions—including contexts, components, and precedents—are considered, its coherence vanishes. There arises, then, no unambiguous particular element or entity with a univocally decidable nature. Precisely because all are determined in dependence on conditions, they are simultaneously without a fixed, determinate identity. This is the meaning of emptiness.

Elements of experience are normally taken to have definitive identities, to be determinate, to be finite, to have "simple location," and to have borders or boundaries between themselves and what is outside themselves. Tiantai MEDITATION, however, calls for an inquiry into the borders between being *X* and not being *X*, either in time, space, or conceptual space (i.e., the arising of a given state from its qualitatively different antecedents, conceptual contrasts, or efficient causes). To appear in experience at all, *X* must be "non-all," must be contrasted to some non-*X*, and must have an "outside." But to *necessarily* have an outside means the outside is not really outside; the relation between the internal and the external is itself internal. One can always ask: Is the border (spatial, temporal, or conceptual) part of the inside or the outside, both, or neither? There is no coherent way to answer these questions if to exist is assumed to mean "simply located." Hence, the interface always proves unintelligible, and the outside proves paradoxically both ineradicable and impossible, since it always proves to be equally internal, and hence not an outside at all. Therefore, the inside (*X*) is equally ineradicable and impossible (*bukede, bukeshe*). Like space, each determinate existent is simultaneously a merely nominal reality, is unobstructed and unobstructing, is beyond being and nonbeing, and is all-pervasive, present equally in the opposite of itself, in contrast to which it was originally defined. Precisely the same analysis applies to the difference between those defining borders that "determine as *X*" and those that "determine as *Y*," which is why Zhiyi goes on to assert that to be determined as *X* is always at the same time to be determined as *Y*, and all other possible quiddities.

In sum, what is only locally coherent is thereby globally incoherent. It is what it is only because the horizon of relevant contexts has been arbitrarily limited, but the fact that all being is necessarily contextualized (arises with qualitative othernesses) means that any such limit is ultimately arbitrary, and there are more relevant contexts that can be brought to bear in every case. The "mean" signifies that these two are merely alternate statements of the same fact, which necessarily appears in these two contrasted ways. Determinateness, thought through to the end, turns out to be ambiguity, and vice versa. Hence, ambiguity and determinateness are no longer "other" to one another, and each is itself, just as it is, "absolute" (i.e., free of dependence on a relationship to an outside). Therefore, *determinateness* is a synonym for *ambiguity*, and either is a synonym for *absoluteness* (the ultimate reality and value, "eternal, blissful, self, and pure"). Any of these always signifies all three aspects. Moreover, determinateness is never simply "determinateness as such or in general": It always means precisely *this* determinateness and precisely all other possible determinateness, which Zhiyi formulates for convenience as "the three thousand quiddities." Any possible experienced content is necessarily dependently co-arisen, which is to be provisionally posited as precisely this (like-this appearance, etc.), which is to be empty, which is to be readable equally as provisional positing and as emptiness, which is to be readable as precisely every other possible determinacy.

It is from the "mean" that the Zhiyi deduces the claim that all things are everywhere at once. For if to be definitively *X* and not definitively *X* are merely alternate ways of stating the same fact about *X*, the contrast between the absence and presence of *X* is annulled, and *X* is no more present here and now than it is present there and then. It is "simply located" at neither locus, but "virtually located" at both. It pervades all possible times and places to exactly the extent that it is present here at all. It can be read into any experience, and is here and now only because it has been so read into the here and now. *X*, in other words, is eternal and omnipresent, but only as "canceled," divested of the putative opacity of its simple location.

As an exfoliation of these claims, Zhiyi develops his theory of "the three thousand quiddities in each moment of experience," which implies the interinclusion of the ten realms of sentient experience: purgatories, hungry ghosts, asuras, animals, humans, devas, śrāvakas, PRATYEKABUDDHAS, bodhisattvas, and buddhas. Each realm is a process of causes and effects that inherently entails all the other realms. Each of these realms can at each moment be characterized by the ten "suchnesses" from the *Lotus Sūtra.* All of these may be understood either in terms of the sentient beings experiencing these realms, the environment conditioning these beings, or these beings considered in terms of their components. Ten realms, each including all the others, makes one hundred; multiplied by the ten suchnesses, one gets one thousand, and multiplied by the three aspects, three thousand. Zhiyi asserts that all of these qualities, which indicate not merely all things as considered from a single perspective, but all processes as simultaneously understood from the perspectives of all the cognitive misperceptions of all sentient beings, are inherently entailed in each moment of experience undergone by any sentient being at any time.

The three tracks and buddha-nature

The three truths are a name for the ultimate reality of all dharmas, or the ultimate reality as all dharmas, since to be is to be determinate as just these particular things, in their ambiguity and conditioning relationships. From various perspectives, the three truths can be renamed as a number of other triads, all of which maintain the same relation of interpervasive identity as difference. Zhiyi calls these parallel triads the "three tracks," which he characterizes as:

1. the track of contemplation and awareness (corresponding to emptiness)
2. the track of conditions for actualization or practice (provisional positing)
3. the track of the real nature or the absolute as such (the mean)

The triads belonging to these tracks include the three buddha-natures:

1. buddha-nature as manifesting cause (the awareness that allows the omnipresent buddha-nature to be made manifest)
2. buddha-nature as conditioning cause (practical and physical conditions that make this awareness possible)
3. buddha-nature as proper cause (the omnipresent absolute reality to be realized)

but also the three virtues of NIRVĀṆA:

1. prajñā (wisdom)
2. liberation
3. dharmakāya

and the three paths:

1. *kleśa* (delusion)
2. karma (activity as cause of suffering)
3. *duḥkha* (suffering)

Since all these triads are merely alternate names for the three truths and bear the same internally interinclusive relationship derived from the relation of *upāya* to ultimate truth, one arrives at the identity between delusion and wisdom, karma and liberation, dharmakāya and suffering. Each of these is eternal and omnipresent, always present in every possible quiddity. In addition, there is the identity between each of these as actualized realities and as potentials, between the virtues of nirvāṇa and the buddha-nature as potential, between buddha-nature and delusion-karma-suffering, and so on. These paradoxical identities between oppositely valued realities come to be the distinctive mark of the Tiantai school, culminating in its unique doctrine of "the evil inherent in the buddha-nature," the perfect interpervasion of delusion and enlightenment.

Zhanran and the buddha-nature of insentient beings

The Tiantai school fell into decline in the Tang dynasty (618–907), losing its imperial patronage and dominant influence to the newly arisen HUAYAN SCHOOL and CHAN SCHOOL. ZHANRAN (Jingxi *zunzhe,* 711–782) is credited with revitalizing the tradition, meeting the challenges of the new schools and consolidating and reorganizing Tiantai doctrine. The bulk of his writings concentrate on detailed commentaries to Zhiyi's works, but he is also responsible for adopting and adapting Huayan terminology into Tiantai doctrine while reasserting the distinctiveness of the Tiantai school, particularly noting the uniqueness of its doctrine of the evil inherent in the buddha-nature.

In his work *Jin'gangbei* (*Diamond Scalpel*), his only noncommentarial composition, Zhanran makes a frontal attack on the Huayan and early Chan doctrine that views the buddha-nature as an aspect of sentience, reasserting the Tiantai view that the buddha-nature is necessarily threefold from beginning to end, omnipresent in all three aspects, and impossible to restrict to sentient beings only. In fact, the threefold buddha-nature is another name for the three truths, which are the reality of any content of experience whatsoever, mind or matter, sentient or insentient. To be any one among them is to be all of them, so there can be no division of buddha-nature as the unconditioned essence of sentience and awareness as opposed to the passive inertness of insentient beings. Whenever one being attains buddhahood, all beings are buddha; whenever one entity is insentient, all beings are insentient. This is the interpervasion of all realms as understood in a Tiantai perspective; all possible predicates are always applicable to all possible beings.

The Song dynasty (960–1279) schism

Zhanran had imported certain formulations from Huayan thought into his teaching, most notably an interpretation of mind-only doctrine not found in Zhiyi, including the phrase "unchanging but following conditions, following conditions but unchanging," as a characterization of the mind and its nature, respectively, as derived from the Huayan patriarch FAZANG (643–712). In the Northern Song dynasty, some Tiantai writers later called the Shanwai (i.e., "off-mountain," or heterodox) began to adopt the privileging of "awareness" (*zhi*), or mind, that characterizes later Huayan and early Chan thought. Even in Fazang a similar tendency is arguably discernible. Here the mind in its present function is a transcendent category that produces all phenomena, and of which all phenomena are transformations; the mind is in this sense at least conceptually prior to these phenomena, and is their ontological base, although it is not a definite objective entity. Realizing this all-pervasive awareness as all things is equivalent to awakening, and so this mind is also called "ultimate reality." *Praxis* here means to see "the three thousand quiddities" as this present moment of mind, which is the transformation of mind, with nothing left out. Mind is the all-embracing "whole" that is uniquely capable of producing, determining, containing, and unifying all differentiated existences.

ZHILI (Siming Fazhi *fashi,* 960–1028) led an attack on this interpretation of Tiantai thought, developing a position that was later called the Shanjia (Mountain Masters, or orthodox) position. Zhili holds fast to the traditional Tiantai interpretation of the claim in the HUAYAN JING (Sanskrit, *Avataṃsaka-sūtra*) that "there is no difference between the mind, buddhas, and sentient beings," holding that this means that each of these three may be considered the creator of the other two, and vice versa. This interpretation rejects the assertion that mind is the real source that is able to create, or manifest itself, as either buddhas or sentient beings (as the Shanwai, Huayan, and Chan putatively claim), depending on whether it is enlightened or deluded. On the latter view, although buddhas and sentient beings could still be said to be "identical" to mind and hence to each other, this identity would be mediated by a one-way dependence relation. Zhili holds that this would not be real "identity," for mind has at least one quality that the other two lack: It is creator, as opposed to created. In Zhili's view, each is creator, each is created, and none is more ultimate than the others.

Zhili's teaching combats a one-sidedly "idealist" interpretation of Tiantai doctrine. He holds that while it is true to say that mind inherently entails all entities, it is equally true to say that form or matter inherently entails all entities, and not merely because matter is actually nothing but mind. Here Zhili is echoing Zhiyi's teaching that reality can be spoken of equally as mind-only, matter-only, taste-only, smell-only, touch-only, and so on. Zhili also insists that Tiantai meditation is a contemplation of the deluded mind, not directly of the pure or absolute mind that is the source and ground of all existence. The object of contemplation is the deluded process of differentiation itself, which is to be seen as creating the particular determinacies of the experienced world, then as inherently including all these determinacies, then as being identical to them all, and finally as itself determined, hence conditioned, hence empty, hence provisionally posited, hence the "mean." Once this is done, all other contents are equally seen as the three truths, but the process of transformation must begin with the deluded mind, the mind that mistakenly sees itself as "inside" as opposed to "outside," which makes arbitrary distinctions, and which is conditioned in a particular manner by particular causes. Only in this way, Zhili thinks, is practice both possible and necessary.

Zhili also reasserts the centrality of the doctrine of inherent evil, as is particularly evident in his teaching of "the six identities as applicable even to the dung beetle." The six identities were propounded by Zhiyi originally to maintain a balance to the claims of identity between sentient beings and buddhahood. All beings are identical to the Buddha (1) in principle; (2) in name, once they hear of this teaching and accept it intellectually; (3) in cultivation; (4) in partial attainment; (5) in approximation to final identity; and finally (6) when Buddhist practice is completed and one becomes explicitly a buddha. Zhili asserts that these six levels of difference and identity apply not only to the relations between sentient beings and buddhas, but also to the relations between any two sentient beings, any two determinations of any kind, indeed, even between any entity and itself. This means that prior to Buddhist practice one is identical to, say, a dung beetle in principle only, but as one's practice continues, one finally attains a more and more fully realized identity with the dung beetle, so that all the marks and names associated with dung beetle-hood become increasingly explicit and fully realized as practice continues. Evil, in other words, is not only what is cut off, but also what is more fully realized with practice; all things become more explicit together, and this full realization of their own determinate marks, by virtue of the three truths, is their liberation and transformation. This is the real goal of practice; indeed this is buddhahood itself.

Transmission to and development in Japan and Korea

Much of Zhili's concern in his polemic against the Shanwai and his defense of the doctrine of "inherent evil" was to maintain the seriousness of Tiantai ritual practice, an evil that he saw threatened by the "sudden" doctrines of Chan and the Shanwai. Zhili and his dharma-brother Zunshi (Ciyun *fashi,* 963–1032) were instrumental in combining Tiantai contemplation with the practice of the PURE LAND SCHOOLS, particularly the visualizations of AMITĀBHA, which were to be done in tandem with Tiantai doctrinal ruminations, "contemplating the image of the Buddha as an inherent aspect of the mind, utilizing the Buddha image to manifest the nature of mind." This was consistent with Zhili's general teaching that when any given content is made more explicit, it simultaneously makes all contents more explicit, as well as their interpervasion, the interpervasive three thousand being the realm of enlightenment.

In China, Tiantai and Pure Land practice came to be closely associated. A different development took place in Japan, where Tiantai, or Tendai in the Japanese pronunciation, became closely associated with esoteric Buddhism. Tiantai texts were first brought to Japan by the Chinese vinaya monk Jianzhen (687–763), but did not really take hold until the founding of the Japanese Tendai school by SAICHŌ (Dengyo *daishi,* 767–822). Saichō combined the Tiantai teachings he had studied in Tang China under Zhanran's disciple Daosui with elements of esoteric and Chan Buddhism. The tradition he founded later split into several rival schools, but Tendai remained for centuries the mainstream of Japanese Buddhism, providing the theoretical foundation of Buddhist practice to a much greater degree than was the case in China, where Huayan and Chan understandings of Buddhist doctrine arguably took a more preeminent position. Later Japanese Tendai contributed distinctive developments to the doctrines of ORIGINAL ENLIGHTENMENT (HONGAKU) and the buddhahood of inanimate objects, on which it laid special stress. All of the Buddhist reformers who created the new Japanese sects in the Kamakura period, including HŌNEN (1133–1212), SHINRAN (1173–1263), NICHIREN (1222–1282), and DŌGEN (1200–1253), were trained initially as Tendai monks.

Both Huisi and Zhiyi are said to have had direct disciples hailing from the Korean peninsula, and this tradition of exchange continued for many centuries. But it was not until 1097 that a separate Tiantai (Korean, Ch'ŏnt'ae) school was established there. Its founder, ŬICH'ŎN (1055–1101), hoped the new school would help reconcile the long-standing conflict in Korean Buddhism between scholastic studies and meditative practice. Ch'ŏnt'ae became one of the two main pillars of Korean Buddhism, together with Chan (Korean, Sŏn). The schools were unified under the auspices of a reconstituted Sŏn school in the early fifteenth century.

See also: **China; Japan; Korea; Vietnam**

Bibliography

Chan, Chi-wah. "Chih-li (960–1028) and the Crisis of T'ien-t'ai Buddhism in the Early Sung." In *Buddhism in the Sung,* ed. Peter N. Gregory and Daniel A. Getz, Jr. Honolulu: University of Hawaii Press, 1999.

Cleary, Thomas, trans. *Stopping and Seeing: A Comprehensive Guide to Buddhist Meditation* (a partial translation of Zhiyi's *Mohe zhiguan*). Boston: Shambhala, 1997.

Donner, Neal. "Chih-i's Meditation on Evil." In *Buddhist and Taoist Practice in Medieval Chinese Society,* ed. David W. Chappell. Honolulu: University Press of Hawaii, 1987.

Donner, Neal. "Sudden and Gradual Intimately Conjoined: Chih-i's T'ien-t'ai View." In *Sudden and Gradual: Approaches to Enlightenment in Chinese Buddhism,* ed. Peter N. Gregory. Honolulu: University of Hawaii Press, 1987.

Donner, Neal, and Stevenson, Daniel B. *The Great Calming and Contemplation: A Study and Annotated Translation of the First Chapter of Chih-i's Mo-ho chih-kuan.* Honolulu: University of Hawaii Press, 1993.

Gregory, Peter, and Getz, Daniel, eds. *Buddhism in the Sung.* Honolulu: University of Hawaii Press, 2001.

Hurvitz, Leon. *Chih-i (538–597): An Introduction to the Life and Ideas of a Chinese Buddhist Monk.* M'elange Chinois et Bouddhiques, vol. 12 (1960–1962). Brussels: Institut Belges Des Hautes Etudes Chinoises, 1980.

Ng Yu-kwan, *T'ien-t'ai Buddhism and Early Mādhyamika.* Honolulu: University of Hawaii Press, 1993.

Stevenson, Daniel. "The Four Kinds of Samādhi in Early T'ien-t'ai Buddhism." In *Traditions of Meditation in Chinese Buddhism,* ed. Peter N. Gregory. Honolulu: University of Hawaii Press, 1986.

Stone, Jacqueline. *Original Enlightenment and the Transformation of Medieval Japanese Buddhism.* Honolulu: University of Hawaii Press, 1999.

Swanson, Paul L. *Foundations of T'ien-t'ai Philosophy: The Flowering of the Two Truths Theory in Chinese Buddhism.* Berkeley, CA: Asian Humanities Press, 1989.

Ziporyn, Brook. "Anti-Chan Polemics in Post-Tang Tiantai." *Journal of the International Association of Buddhist Studies* 17, no. 1 (1994): 26–63.

Ziporyn, Brook. *Evil and/or/as the Good: Omnicentrism, Intersubjectivity, and Value Paradox in Tiantai Buddhist Thought.* Cambridge, MA: Harvard University Press, 2000.

BROOK ZIPORYN

TIBET

Tibet became one of the last major zones in Buddhist Asia to accept Buddhist ideology and rituals into its culture, which assumed a unique position as the perceived source for true dharma study during the twelfth to the twentieth centuries. Throughout their religious history, Tibetans have emphasized a balance of scholarship, contemplative MEDITATION, and the indivisibility of religious and secular authority; most of these values were formulated under the aegis of Buddhist tantrism. Tibetan Buddhism matured over the course of fourteen centuries and will be assessed in this entry in phases that, if somewhat contested in scholarly literature, still represent important stages in its development.

The Royal dynasty and the early translation period

Tibetan literature attributes the formal introduction of Buddhism to the reign of its first emperor, Srong btsan sgam po (Songtsen gampo, d. 649/650). Undoubtedly, though, proto-Tibetan peoples had been exposed to Buddhist merchants and missionaries earlier. There is a myth that the fifth king before Srong btsan sgam po, Lha tho tho ri gnyan btsan, was residing in the ancient castle of Yum bu bla mkhar when a casket fell from the sky. Inside were a gold RELIQUARY and Buddhist scriptures. While the myth is not early, it possibly reveals a Tibetan memory of prior missionary activity. We do know that official contact with Sui China was accomplished from Central Tibet in 608 or 609 and that, as Tibet grew more powerful, Buddhist contacts increased.

Nonetheless, two of Srong btsan sgam po's wives—Wencheng from China and Bhṛkuṭī from Nepal—were credited with constructing the temples of Magical Appearance (Sprul snang, or the JO KHANG) and Ra mo che. Other temples were built as well, and twelve were later considered limb-binding temples, where a demoness representing the autochthonous forces of Tibet was subdued by the sanctified buildings. Srong btsan sgam po is also credited with having one of his ministers, Thon mi Sambhota, create the Tibetan alphabet from an Indian script and write the first grammars.

Buddhist progress occurred with the successors to Srong btsan sgam po. Notable was the foundation of the first real monastery in Tibet, BSAM YAS (SAMYE, ca. 780) and the influx of Indian, Chinese, and Central Asian monks around that time. Particularly influential were Śāntarakṣita, an important Indian scholar, and his disciple Kamalaśīla. Śāntarakṣita and his entourage were responsible for the first group of six or seven aristocratic Tibetans to be ordained in Tibet. These authoritative monks did much to cement the relationship between Indian Buddhism and Tibetan identity. Another teacher, PADMASAMBHAVA, was a relatively obscure tantric guru whose inspiration became important later.

Translation bureaus in DUNHUANG and Central Tibet were opened by the Tibetan emperors, from Khri srong lde'u btsan (Trisong détsen, ca. 742–797) through Ral pa can (r. 815–838), but unofficial translations were recognized sources of concern. While the official bureaus emphasized the MAHĀYĀNA monastic texts, unofficial translations tended to feature more radical tantric works. During the reign of Sad na legs (r. 804–815) a council was convened to regularize Tibetan orthography and to establish both translation methods and a lexicon of equivalents for official translators. The result was the emergence of classical Tibetan, a literary language developed to render both sophisticated Buddhist terminology and foreign political documents into the rapidly evolving Tibetan medium.

Translations were initially made from several languages, but principally from Sanskrit and Chinese, so that a consistent tension between Indian and Chinese Buddhist practice and ideology marked this period. The Northern CHAN SCHOOL was present in Tibet, but from 792 to 794 a series of discussions between Indian and Chinese exegetes at the BSAM YAS DEBATE was ultimately decided in favor of the Indians. Eventually, Buddhist translations from Chinese were abandoned for exclusively Indic sources.

Fragmentation and the later spread of the dharma

The last of the emperors, Dar ma 'U dum btsan (r. 838–842) began a campaign of suppression of Buddhism contemporary to the Huichang suppression in China. Dar ma was assassinated by a Buddhist monk, and the vast Tibetan empire fragmented over imperial succession. The period from 850 to 950 was a chaotic time marked by popular revolts and warlordism. Surviving Buddhist monks fled, and monastic practice was eclipsed in Central Tibet for approximately a century. Aristocratic clans that had accepted Buddhism, however, continued to develop indigenous rituals and new literature based on the received tradition. This is the time that the classical persona of the nonmonastic religious teacher coalesced: the lay LAMA, sometimes a mystic inspired by visions of imperial preceptors. With the reestablishment of records in the late tenth century, we see active lay Buddhist behavior—PILGRIMAGE, lay rituals, autochthonous divinities as protectors, and so on—that was to endure to the present.

Yet the monastic religious form was closely allied to the memory of the empire, and Bsam yas stood empty. Eventually several Tibetans under the leadership of Klu mes from Central Tibet traveled to Dan tig Temple, in modern Xining, and received monastic ordination from Tibetan monks who had maintained it. Returning to Central Tibet around 980, Klu mes and others began to refurbish Bsam yas as well as construct networks of new temples. Their position, though, was often threatened by the lay lamas called Ban de, and the new monks were sometimes physically attacked.

One line of the imperial house established itself in Gu ge, in West Tibet, and some two dozen men, preeminently Rin chen bzang po (958–1055), were sent to study in Kashmir. Like the Tibetan emperors, the Gu ge kings supported Mahāyāna scholarship and were critical of extreme tantric behavior, whether Tibetan or Indian. While Rin chen bzang po principally translated esoteric works, many other translators, especially Ngog Blo ldan shes rab (1059–1109), specialized in Mahāyāna philosophical treatises, rendering many into Tibetan for the first time. Thus, the *Five Treatises of Maitreya* and much of the work of DHARMAKĪRTI and other scholastic authors were introduced to Tibetans through their activity. A great translator's convocation, where scholars discussed their texts and procedures, was called by the Gu ge king in 1076.

In Central Tibet, the later translation movement began with 'Brog mi (ca. 990–1060), who studied in Vikramaśīla and elsewhere in India. Following him, Dgos lo, Rwa lo, Mar pa, Kyung po rnal 'byor, and other scholars began the new translation or revision of Indian works. Many of these eleventh-century Central Tibetan translators were concerned with the newly evolving TANTRAS, which they presumed had not been revealed to earlier Tibetans. They also believed that the imperially sponsored systems had become mixed with indigenous Tibetan practices and derided them as "old style" (*rnying ma*).

For their part, certain RNYING MA (NYINGMA) teachers—especially Rong zom Chos kyi bzang po (late eleventh century)—were also translators and defended their own texts by decrying perceived inadequacies of the new translators and their Indian informants. Rong zom also composed the first synthetic Tibetan treatment of the Buddhist path in a detailed manual called the *Theg chen tshul 'jug* (*Entering the Method of the Mahāyāna*), which begins with monastic Buddhism and culminates in the Great Perfection (*rdzogs chen*) teaching. The Zur clan was also involved in Rnying ma defense, and Zur chen and Zur chung put together the earliest *Rnying ma rgyud 'bum* (*Old Tantric Canon*).

Another Rnying ma response became the development of the "treasure" literature (*gter ma*), grounded in indigenous scriptural composition during the tenth century, when Central Tibet was isolated. Scriptural composition was normative Buddhist behavior, liberating the intention of the Buddha from excessive literalness. In India, the practice was inhibited by various conservative strategies, but Tibetans began to stretch the form in creative ways. By the eleventh century, they realized that texts revealed in Tibet could not be justified on standard literary grounds. They therefore formulated the ideology that these works had been hidden, physically or spiritually, as treasures by saints of the Royal dynasty. Many of these early treasures were dedicated to the Great Perfection view and practices.

In 1042 the important Indian missionary, ATISHA Dīpaṃkara Śrījñāna (982–1054), arrived, invited by the Gu ge king. Atisha introduced the popular Bengali cult of the goddess Tārā and reframed tantric Buddhism as an advanced practice on a continuum with monastic and Mahāyāna Buddhism. This systematization, already known in India, became designated the triple discipline (*trisaṃvara*: the monastic, bodhisattva, and tantric vows) and Atisha embedded this ideal in his *Bodhipathapradīpa* (*Lamp for the Path to Awakening*). Atisha also promoted the basic Mahāyāna curriculum of his monastery Vikramaśīla, where works like ŚĀNTIDEVA'S BODHICARYĀVATĀRA (*Introduction to the Conduct That Leads to the Enlightenment*) were fundamental to monastic stability. Atisha's lay lama disciple 'Brom ston Rgyal ba'i byung gnas (1004–1064) founded the monastery of Rwa sgreng in Central Tibet (1057) and organized the Bka' gdams pa order.

The tantric orders evolved out of the activity of the early Central Tibetan translators. Preeminent were the various traditions of the Dwags po Bka' brgyud that derived from MAR PA (MARPA, 1002/1012–1097). While some of Mar pa's disciples were concerned with tantric scholarship, it was Mar pa's poet disciple MI LA RAS PA (MILAREPA, (1028/40–1111/23), and Milarepa's disciple Sgam po pa, who effectively grounded the tradition in both tantric and monastic practice. Likewise, 'Brog mi's center in Mu gu lung did not last, but his later follower 'Khon Dkon mchog rgyal po (1034–1102) founded SA SKYA (SAKYA) Monastery in 1073, and the Sa skya order became widely acknowledged through the influence and learning of 'Khon clan members. Beyond these, many smaller lineages were received from Indian masters but only partially succeeded in the institutionalization process of the twelfth century, eventually becoming subsets of one or another of the major orders.

Tanguts, Mongols, and Buddhist efflorescence in the twelfth to fourteenth centuries

By the twelfth century, small lineages began developing into specific orders that compiled the writings of exemplary figures. The initial cloisters were expanded, becoming "mother" monasteries for a series of satellite temples and monasteries. Orders established dominion in their areas, so that lay practice tended to come under the aegis of important teachers. Buddhist doctrinal and philosophical material became an important part of the curriculum. Translation activity continued, but with an emphasis on the revision of previous translations. A CANON of translated scripture and exegesis was compiled throughout this period, so that by the end of the fourteenth century its major outlines became relatively clear. Finally, the aura of the emerging orders attracted the interest of Central Asian potentates, beginning with the Tanguts and extending to the grandsons of Genghis Khan.

The Rnying ma order had coalesced around the received teachings derived from the Royal dynastic period, whether transmitted in a human succession (*bka' ma*) or as revealed treasure teachings (*gter ma*). Preeminently, Vimalamitra and Padmasambhava among the Indians, and Bai ro tsa na among the Tibetans, were the mythic sources for treasure scriptures. The important treasure finder Nyang ral Nyi ma 'od zer (1142–1192) and his school in southern Tibet promoted Padmasambhava over other figures. From Nyang ral's group came the *Maṇi Bka' 'bum,* the vehicle for the spread of the cult of Avalokiteśvara as the special protector of Tibet, purportedly embodied in Emperor Srong btsan sgam po. Treasure hagiographies of Padmasambhava by U rgyan gling pa (1323–?) have proven classics of the genre. Karma gling pa revealed the *Bar do thos grol,* widely known in the West as the TIBETAN BOOK OF THE DEAD. Although Rnying ma philosophical authors were relatively few, Klong chen rab 'byams pa (1308–1363) set the standard for tantric scholarship. Basing himself on treasures of the *Snying thig* (seminal drop) tradition of the Great Perfection, Klong chen pa authored important discussions of Rnying ma theory and practice.

A statue of Padmasambhava, who played a crucial role in the establishment of Buddhism in Tibet in the eighth century, at the Jo khang Temple, Lhasa, Tibet. © Craig Lovell/Corbis. Reproduced by permission.

The 'Khon clan continued to develop Sa skya Monastery, with the help of such individuals as Ba ri lo tsā ba (1040–1112), who assembled many relics at Sa skya. The great literary contributions, though, came from the five Sa skya masters: Sa chen Kun dga' snying po (1092–1158), Bsod nams rtse mo (1142–1182), Grags pa rgyal mtshan (1147–1216), SA SKYA PAṆḌITA (SAKYA PAṆḌITA, 1182–1251), and Chos rgyal 'Phags pa (1235–1280). Sa chen specialized in tantric scholarship, writing the first summary of the tantric path in Tibet and compiling eleven commentaries on the central text of the esoteric *Lam 'bras* (*Path and Fruit*), attributed to the Indian saint Virūpa. Sa chen's sons, Bsod nams rtse mo and Grags pa rgyal mtshan, contributed to the myth of the Buddha, established tantric exegesis, commented on Śāntideva's *Bodhicaryāvatāra*, and codified the Sa skya understanding of the tantric path. With Sa skya Paṇḍita, the Sa skya took to conservative philosophical scholarship, and the Sa skya order came to be known for its maintenance of the triple discipline and its defense of Dharmakīrti's epistemological system.

However, many original Tibetan contributions to Buddhism also came from this period. Among his innovations, Phya pa Chos kyi seng ge (1109–1169) developed philosophical definitions, doctrines of universals, and methods of argumentation; many challenged Indian assumptions, especially those of Dharmakīrti. In an entirely different direction, seminal BKA' BRGYUD (KAGYU) representatives, like Sgam po pa bsod nams rin chen (1079–1153), delineated the doctrines of the self-sufficient white remedy (*dkar po gcig thub*). These doctrines posited a soteriology of a single meditative method under the rubric of the Great Seal (*mahāmudrā*). Another Bka' brgyud pa, 'Bri gung 'Jig rten mgon po (1143–1217), additionally proposed that all the Buddha's statements were of definitive meaning (*nītārtha*), so that they all had the same intention (*dgongs gcig*). Also based on esoteric Buddhist ideals, Dol bu pa Shes rab rgyal mtshan (1292–1361) represented the newly formed Jo nang school, a tradition grounded in KĀLACAKRA exegesis. Dol bu pa's reading of ŚŪNYATĀ (EMPTINESS) emphasized an emptying of attributes from a ground of reality and became technically known as the "other emptiness" (*gzhan stong*). This position stood in opposition to the "self emptiness" (*rang stong*) of orthodox MADHYAMAKA SCHOOL philosophy. Like the ideology of the eighth-century Chinese Heshang Moheyan and the more radical Rnying ma doctrines, most of these Tibetan contributions became refuted by the orthodox, who adhered to a narrow definition of acceptable statements based on conformity to Indian texts by specific authors.

The Sa skya were granted control over Tibet during the Yuan dynasty, with the fifth of the great Sa skya teachers, 'Phags pa blo gros rgyal mtshan (1235–1280) proclaimed Kublai Khan's national preceptor in 1261. Sa skya leaders supported Mongol policies, such as the first census of Tibet, and some scholars became influenced by Mongol and Chinese literature, with Chinese imperial records translated into Tibetan. However, about 1350, during the Yuan decline, the Bka' brgyud pa monk Ta'i si tu Byang chub rgyal mtshan (1302–1364) challenged the Sa skya for control of Central Tibet. He was successful in some measure, and his Phag mo gru pa subtradition was the dominant political force for most of the next century.

One result was the formalization of the Tibetan canon under Ta'i si tu's patronage, by BU STON (BU TÖN) Rin chen grub (1290–1364). Bu ston catalogued the tantric canon (*rgyud 'bum*) section of the translated scriptures (*Bka' 'gyur*) and compiled the translated authoritative treatises (*Bstan 'gyur*). In the canonical compilation process, Bu ston wrote a history of the dharma, where scriptures and treatises were set out in a grand schematism of history, cosmology, and mythology. About the same time, the learned Sa skya hierarch, Bla ma dam pa Bsod nams rgyal mtshan (1312–1375), wrote the *Rgyal rabs gsal ba'i me long* (*Mirror Illuminating Royal Genealogy*), representing the popular mythology of the imperial period and origin of the Tibetan people.

Moreover, the peculiarly Tibetan office of the reincarnate lama became institutionalized. One of Sgam po pa's important disciples, the KARMA PA I Dus gsum mkhyen pa (1110–1193) was said to have prophesied his own rebirth as Karma pa II Karma Pakshi (1204–1283). While earlier teachers were said to be the reembodiment of specific saints or BODHISATTVAS, this was the first formalization of reincarnation, with the previous saint's disciples maintaining continuity and instructing his reembodiment. Following the lead of the Bka' brgyud pa, most traditions eventually appropriated the institution.

Great institutions and the Dga' ldan pa in the fifteenth and sixteenth centuries

If the previous three centuries represented an intense struggle with intellectual and canonical issues, the fifteenth and sixteenth centuries demonstrated the struggle for institutional authenticity. In part because of the political power wielded by the Sa skya and Bka' brgyud orders, many of the cloisters had become more social or political institutions, with religious involvement in the hands of the great clans or landed interests. Indeed, Tibetan monasteries were ripe for reformation, with great wealth and political authority eclipsing aspects of spirituality.

The most important event of this period was the rise and development of the reform order of TSONG KHA PA Blo bzang grags pa (1357–1419). Born in Amdo, Tsong kha pa originally studied in many traditions, but his most important intellectual influence was the Sa skya monk Red mda' ba (1349–1412), who had championed the radical Prāsaṅgika-Madhaymaka system of CANDRAKĪRTI (ca. 600–650). However, Tsong kha pa became dissatisfied with the contemporary understanding of monastic institutions and more general aspects of scholarship. With successive visions of Mañjuśrī, Tsong kha pa understood that he was to emphasize the system that Atisha had brought to Tibet. Eventually, after many years of wandering through Tibet bestowing instruction, he was persuaded to settle down and in 1409 founded the monastery of Dga' ldan, the Tibetan translation of Tuṣita, the name of MAITREYA's heaven. Tsong kha pa's order was called the Dga' ldan pa, although it was also known as the new Bka' gdams pa or the DGE LUGS (GELUK; Virtuous Order). He changed the color of their hats to yellow as well, giving them the name Yellow Hats in the West.

In a series of important treatises, he articulated a systematization of the exoteric Mahāyāna meditative path (*Lam rim chen mo*) and the esoteric practice according to the VAJRAYĀNA (*Sngags rim chen mo*). In the latter instance, he employed interpretive systems developed by exponents of the *Guhyasamāja tantra* to articulate a systematic HERMENEUTICS that could be applied to all tantras. Tsong kha pa, though, is best noted for his intellectual synthesis of the Madhyamaka and Yogācāra systems of Buddhism, using Indian treatises as a basis for his great commentaries and subcommentaries, and emphasizing the philosophical position of Candrakīrti.

Three of his disciples were most important in the continuation of his work. Rgyal tshab Dar ma rin chen (1364–1432) was Tsong kha pa's successor at Dga' ldan and was especially noted for his orthodox summaries and commentaries that became the basis for much of Dge lugs pa scholasticism. Mkhas grub Dge legs dpal bzang (1385–1438) succeeded him at Dga' ldan and was known for his acerbic tone toward his contemporaries as well as his epistemological treatises and his *Kālacakra tantra* exegesis. Dge 'dun grub pa (1391–1474, posthumously the first DALAI LAMA) founded the great monastery of Bkra shis lhun po in 1447 and was also noted for his scholarly work on epistemology. The rush to construct new Dga' ldan pa monasteries continued through the fifteenth century, with 'Bras spung (1416) and Se ra (1419) founded in the area of Lhasa, while others spread out east and west. Some of these monasteries eventually enrolled several thousand monks and were virtual religious cities. Part of this process led to the mission of Bsod nams rgya mtsho (1543–1588) to the Mongols, who had lapsed from Buddhist practice after their involvement with the Sa skya. Widely received, he was given the title Dalai Lama by Altan Khan, a title extended to his earlier incarnations beginning with Dge 'dun grub pa. Bsod nams rgya mtsho's reincarnation (Dalai Lama IV, Yon tan rgya mtsho, 1589–1616) was discovered as the great-grandson of Altan Khan, the only Dalai Lama not Tibetan by birth.

The intellectual and institutional vitality of the Dga' ldan pa did not go unopposed, and the Sa skya in particular found much to criticize. Interestingly, the Sa skya tradition also became involved in its own reform movement. Ngor chen Kun dga' bzang po (1382–1456) founded the monastery of Ngor E wam chos ldan in 1429 and established it as the most important tradition of esoteric Lam 'bras instruction, supplemented by the personality and work of Tshar chen Blo gsal rgya mtsho (1502–1566).

The sixteenth century was a high-water mark for scholarship in other traditions as well. Karma pa VIII, Mi bskyod rdo rje (1504–1557), questioned the basis for Dga' ldan pa confidence and provided a critique of the Rnying ma as well. The Bka' brgyud pa historians Dpa' bo Gtsug lag phreng ba (1504–1566) and 'Brug chen Pad ma dkar po (1527–1592) forcefully established their readings of Tibetan history and the tantric movement. Mnga' ris pan chen Pad ma dbang rgyal (1487–1542) formulated the classic Rnying ma statement of the triple discipline. Sog bzlog pa Blo gros rgyal mtshan (b. 1552) compiled the statements of Rnying ma opponents and established a defense of Rnying ma and treasure legitimacy.

The Dalai Lamas and Rnying ma revitalization in the seventeenth and eighteenth centuries

The Tibetan religious landscape changed dramatically again in the seventeenth century. Clans in the provinces of Dbus and Gtsang had been warring for several decades, and each had its associated religious affiliation. In Dbus, the fifth Dalai Lama—affectionately known to Tibetans as the Great Fifth (Za hor ban de Ngag dbang blo bzang rgya mtsho, 1617–1682)—had developed a base of power in 'Bras spung Monastery. The Great Fifth Dalai Lama was extraordinarily learned, with teachers from the Dga' ldan, Sa kya, Zha lu, and Rnying ma traditions. He was also highly ambitious and built on the previous Dalai Lamas' Mongolian connections, finally using the military might of Gushri Khan's Qoshot Mongols to solidify control over Tibet in 1642, inaugurating the reign of the Dalai Lamas.

Some traditions favored by the Great Fifth were greatly benefited. Because of his strong Rnying ma connections (he was one of the very few Dgan' ldan pa treasure finders) the Rnying ma tradition prospered. This was an important time for treasure traditions, with visionaries like Mi 'gyur rdo rje (1647–1667) and U rgyan gter bdag gling pa (1616–1714) revealing new textual cycles. Likewise, Rnying ma scholarship flourished, with scholars like Lo chen Dharma śrī (1654–1717). Virtually all the greatest Rnying ma monasteries were built during this period—Rdo rje brag (1632), Kaḥ tog (originally 1159 but resurrected in 1656), Dpal yul (1665), O rgyan smin grol gling (1670), Rdzogs chen (1685), and Zhe chen (1735). Despite a short-lived suppression from 1717 to 1720, the Rnying ma tradition in the eighteenth century was graced by exceptional figures as well, especially the historian Kaḥ tog rig 'dzin Tshe dbang nor bu (1698–1755) and the Omniscient 'Jigs med gling pa (1730–98). 'Jigs med gling pa was to dominate Rnying ma meditative traditions for the next two centuries with his Klong chen snying thig revelations.

Conversely, traditions not favored by the Great Fifth experienced significant problems. Most notoriously, he suppressed the Jo nang order, which had been undergoing a revival through the profound influence of Jo nang Tārānātha (1575–1634), an erudite scholar and historian. However, after 1642 the monastery was placed in Dga' ldan pa hands, the literature of the Jo nang pa was suppressed, and the order survived only in a few minor convents in far northeastern Tibet. The works of scholars critical of Tsong kha pa or his disciples were also suppressed, so that copies survived only in rare collections. The unfortunate sectarianism displayed by the Dga' ldan pa at this time was embodied in the literary form of the monastic syllabus (*yig cha*), the obligatory textbook of sectarian principles. Sectarianism was occasionally mitigated by open-minded Dga' ldan scholars like Lcang skya rol pa'i rdo rje (1717–1786).

This period was the great printing period for Tibetan Buddhism. Despite Tibetan forays into woodblock printing as early as the thirteenth century in Mongolia, the entire Tibetan canon (*Bka' 'gyur* and *Bstan 'gyur*) was not completely printed until the eighteenth century. The first *Bka' 'gyur* editions were printed under Chinese patronage, which continued through the eighteenth century (Yongle, 1410; Wanli, 1606; Kangxi, 1684–1692, 1700, 1717–1720; Qianlong, 1737). Editions produced in Tibet included the Li tang (1608–1621), Snar thang (1730–1732), Sde dge (1733), Co ni (1721–1731), and the Lha sa (1930s). The *Bstan 'gyur* editions include the Qianlong (1724), Sde dge (1737–1744), Snar thang (1741–1742), and Cho ni (1753–1773). In this same period, the collected works of the Sa skya masters were printed in Sde dge (ca. 1737), and 'Jigs med gling pa reorganized and expanded the *Old Tantric Canon*; it was eventually printed from 1794 to 1798.

Tibetan Buddhists prostrate themselves before the Jo khang Temple in Lhasa, Tibet. © Paula Bronstein/Getty Images. Reproduced by permission.

The modern nonsectarian movement and monastic intransigence in the nineteenth and twentieth centuries

The nineteenth century saw the rise of a nonsectarian movement in Eastern Tibet (Khams), where the Sa skya and the Rnying ma orders were especially supported. This movement tried to move Tibetans from a narrow view of lineage toward an ecumenical vision of Buddhist study and practice and specialized in the collection and publication of compendia of religious practice and ideas. 'Jam dbyang Mkhyen brtse'i dbang po (1820–1892) received training in both Sa skya and Rnying ma schools, and he promoted the study of their esoteric systems. Kong sprul Blo gros mtha' yas (1813–1899) developed a synthetic vision of treasure, one that integrated Rnying ma, Bon po, and Bka' brgyud systems all together in his great *Rin chen gter mdzod* (*Treasury of Gems*). In the Sa skya order, 'Jam dbyang Blo gter dbang po (1847–ca. 1914) brought together two great compendia of new translation practices, as well as editing and publishing the Sa skya esoteric system of the Lam 'bras in the face of criticism about the loss of secrecy. Two Rnying ma scholars established specifically Rnying ma scholastic syllabi: 'Ju Mi pham (1846–1912) and Mkhan po Gzhan dga' (1871–1927), the former studied by Rnying ma students, while Gzhan dga' was also favored by the Ngor pa subsect of the Sa skya.

By the turn of the twentieth century, Tibetans were becoming exposed to the wider world, especially through the Younghusband expedition (1904). With a British trade agent forcibly placed in Tibet, the Chinese responded, and the thirteenth Dalai Lama alternatively took refuge with the Chinese and the British, with Tibetans becoming aware that the world was unexpectedly changing. Sometimes this awareness had unforeseen consequences, and the scholar Dge 'dun chos 'phel (1901–1951) was especially provocative, as a monk with an interest in journalism, erotic literature, and intellectual criticism.

Communism and the Tibetan diaspora

The Communist Chinese military success of 1949 and subsequent invasion of Tibet in 1950 succeeded in subduing Tibet, where centuries of prior Chinese efforts had failed. For Buddhist traditions, the initial destruction of temples and monasteries in Eastern Tibet was still relatively modest, and many believed that Tibet could negotiate with Mao Zedong. The Great Proletarian Cultural Revolution of 1966 to 1976 changed everything, with the resultant massive destruction of virtually all monastic institutions and much of the religious art and literature. Some had read the signs, and Tibetans carried out or hid an astonishing amount of their portable art and books.

The fourteenth Dalai Lama had already fled Tibet in 1959, and over the next decade a steady stream of refugees began to populate the camps on Indian soil—perhaps 100,000 in all. Ever true to their traditions, Tibetans immediately set about to construct temples, monasteries, monastic schools, and print their sacred books. The latter project was assisted by the Public Law 480 Program of the United States, especially when directed by the brilliant Tibetologist E. Gene Smith, so that Tibetan (and other) books were purchased as part of Indian debt servicing to the United States. The Public Law 480 Program allowed foreign scholars access to Tibet's great literature for the first time, while publishers could provide monasteries with discounted copies of their literature.

Post-Maoist Tibet

Since the opening of Tibet after the Cultural Revolution, there has been a resurgence of Buddhist practice. The Chinese have resurrected religious buildings—the POTALA, Norbulinka, the Jo khang, and so on—as museums for tourism, and Tibet's cities have become Han Chinese enclaves, but Buddhism is thriving in the countryside. Ever suspicious of religion, the Chinese have sought to control monastic construction and the number of clergy. The participation of monks (and foreign sympathizers) in insurrections has exacerbated Beijing's mistrust. Even then, individual teachers have temporarily managed against great obstacles, although their building efforts are often dismantled. Certain lamas find allies in Han businessmen, who provide capital and political legitimacy to construction projects. China has also played politics with the process of reincarnation, installing its own PANCHEN LAMA and incarcerating the Dalai Lama's choice. More curiously, Tibetan publishing has taken off in the People's Republic of China since Mao's death, making many rare chronicles available for the first time.

The continued tug-of-war between the Dalai Lama's government in Dharamsala and Beijing over human rights and religious freedom is in part incomprehension by Beijing, in part stalling tactics until the Dalai Lama's death. Many young Tibetans in diaspora chafe at the Dalai Lama's pacifism, and there is unhappiness among some Tibetans in India or Nepal about either the Dalai Lama's policies or his ecumenical religious position. Some Dga' ldan pa sectarianism continues and promotes Rdo rje shugs ldan, a divinity representing the dominance of the Dga' ldan pa. American movie stars and the 1989 Nobel Prize for peace for the Dalai Lama have provided legitimacy to Tibetan aspirations, at the cost of some integrity. Yet, despite tensions inside Tibet and elsewhere, there can be little doubt that Buddhism and national identity are so intertwined in Tibetans' minds that the continuation of some sort of Buddhist practice by Tibetans is assured.

See also: **Apocrypha; Communism and Buddhism; Himalayas, Buddhist Art in**

Bibliography

Cabezón, José Ignacio, and Jackson, Roger R. *Tibetan Literature: Studies in Genre.* Ithaca, NY: Snow Lion, 1996.

Dreyfus, Georges B. J. *Recognizing Reality: Dharmakīrti's Philosophy and Its Tibetan Interpretations.* Albany: State University of New York Press, 1997.

Ekvall, Robert B. *Religious Observances in Tibet: Patterns and Function.* Chicago: University of Chicago Press, 1964.

Huber, Toni. *The Cult of the Pure Crystal Mountain: Popular Pilgrimage and Visionary Landscape in Southeast Tibet.* New York: Oxford University Press, 1999.

Jackson, David. *Enlightenment by a Single Means.* Vienna: Der Österreichischen Akademie der Wissenschaften, 1994.

Kapstein, Matthew T. *The Tibetan Assimilation of Buddhism: Conversion, Contestation, and Memory.* New York: Oxford University Press, 2000.

Nebesky-Workowitz, René de. *Oracles and Demons of Tibet: The Cult and Iconography of the Tibetan Protective Deities.* The Hague, Netherlands: Mouton, 1956.

Powers, John. *Introduction to Tibetan Buddhism.* Ithaca, NY: Snow Lion, 1995.

Ruegg, David Seyfort. *Buddha-nature, Mind, and the Problem of Gradualism in a Comparative Perspective.* London: School of Oriental and African Studies, 1989.

Shakabpa, Tsepon W. D. *Tibet: A Political History.* New Haven, CT: Yale University Press, 1967.

Smith, E. Gene. *Among Tibetan Texts: History and Literature of the Himalayan Plateau.* Somerville, MA: Wisdom, 2001.

Snellgrove, David. *Indo-Tibetan Buddhism: Indian Buddhists and Their Tibetan Successors.* Boston: Shambhala, 1987.

Stein, R. A. *Tibetan Civilization.* Stanford, CA: Stanford University Press, 1972.

Thondup, Tulku. *Hidden Teachings of Tibet: An Explanation of the Terma Tradition of the Nyingma School of Buddhism.* London: Wisdom, 1986.

Tucci, Giuseppe. *Tibetan Painted Scrolls.* Rome: La Libreria Dello Stato, 1949. Reprint, 3 vols., Bangkok, Thailand: SDI, 1999.

Tucci, Giuseppe. *The Religions of Tibet,* tr. Geoffrey Samuel. Berkeley: University of California Press, 1980.

RONALD M. DAVIDSON

TIBETAN BOOK OF THE DEAD

The *Tibetan Book of the Dead* is the title created by Walter Yeeling Evans-Wentz (1878–1965), its first Western-language editor, for a collection of Tibetan ritual and literary texts concerned with DEATH, INTERMEDIATE STATES (Sanskrit, *antarābhava*; Tibetan, *bar do*), and REBIRTH. In Tibetan the collection is actually titled *Bar do thos grol chen mo* (*Great Liberation upon Hearing in the Intermediate State*) and belongs to a much larger body of ritual and yogic literature called *Zhi khro dgongs pa rang grol* (*Self Liberated Wisdom of the Peaceful and Wrathful Deities*). Tradition attributes authorship of this cycle of funerary literature to the eighth-century Indian yogin PADMASAMBHAVA, who is believed to have concealed it as a religious "treasure" (Tibetan, *gter ma*) so that it could later be revealed at a more appropriate time. The basic texts of this hidden treasure were excavated by an obscure fourteenth-century "treasure-revealer" (Tibetan, *gter ston*) named Karma Gling pa. His "Tibetan Book of the Dead" tradition originated and was initially fostered in the southeastern Tibetan region of Dwags po and attracted followers from both the RNYING MA (NYINGMA) and BKA' BRGYUD (KAGYU) orders. Its rituals were refined and institutionalized sometime in the late fifteenth century in nearby Kong po, from where it was eventually transmitted throughout other parts of Tibet, Bhutan, Sikkim, Nepal, India, and later Europe and the United States.

The literature of the *Tibetan Book of the Dead* contains esoteric yoga teachings and liturgical directives focused on a MAṆḌALA of one hundred peaceful and wrathful deities (Tibetan, *zhi khro rigs brgya*) and includes detailed religious instructions to be employed at the moment of death and during the perilous intermediate state leading to a new existence. Its combination of ideas and practices are founded upon older conceptions originating in late Indian Buddhist tantra and in Tibetan Buddhist and non-Buddhist indigenous formulations that began to emerge in Tibet around the eleventh century. The literature's fundamental conceptual premises are derived essentially from the religious doctrines of the Great Perfection (Tibetan, *rdzogs chen*) tradition, an innovative Tibetan system standardized in the late fourteenth century and promoted especially by followers of the Rnying ma and non-Buddhist BON orders. According to this tradition, dying persons and those already deceased are presented during their last moments and in the interim period between lives with a series of diminishing opportunities for recognizing the true nature of reality. It is held that if the dying and deceased are capable of perceiving correctly the confusing and often terrifying death and postmortem visions as mental projections reflective of previous habitual thoughts and KARMA (ACTION), then enlightened liberation can be attained, leading directly to buddhahood. Failure to recognize the nature of these visions, however, leads eventually to rebirth and further suffering in the cycle of existence (SAṂSĀRA). Traditionally, to help the dying and the dead regain clarity of awareness at the moment of death and in the intermediate state, a LAMA (Tibetan, *bla ma*) or lay religious specialist will recite guiding instructions and inspirational prayers from the ritual cycle of the *Tibetan Book of the Dead.*

The Evans-Wentz edition of the *Tibetan Book of the Dead,* first published in 1927, was compiled from original Tibetan translations drawn up by the Sikkimese teacher Kazi Dawa Samdup (1868–1922). The book includes translations of only a small number of texts belonging to the literary tradition of the *Bar do thos grol chen mo.* The formal arrangement of this small group of texts as a unified and coherent "book" is misleading and obscures the fact that in Tibet there exists a variety of arrangements of this large ritual and literary cycle, each reflecting a different lineage of transmission and the localized interpretations of specific religious communities.

Popular enthusiasm for the *Tibetan Book of the Dead* has grown to such proportions that it now stands arguably as the most famous Tibetan book in the West. The Evans-Wentz edition has gone through numerous reprints in America and Europe, and it has inspired since 1927 several new translations from the original Tibetan texts.

See also: **Tibet**

Bibliography

Blezer, Henk. *Kar gliṅ Źi khro: A Tantric Buddhist Concept.* Leiden, Netherlands: Research School CNWS, 1997.

Cuevas, Bryan J. *The Hidden History of the Tibetan Book of the Dead.* New York: Oxford University Press, 2003.

Evans-Wentz, W. Y., and Kazi Dawa Samdup, ed. and trans. *The Tibetan Book of the Dead* (1927). Reprint, New York: Oxford University Press, 2000.

Fremantle, Francesca, and Chögyam Trungpa, trans. *The Tibetan Book of the Dead: The Great Liberation through Hearing in the Bardo.* Boston: Shambhala, 1975.

Lauf, Detlef Ingo. *Secret Doctrines of the Tibetan Books of the Dead,* tr. Graham Parkes. Boston: Shambhala, 1977.

Thurman, Robert, trans. *The Tibetan Book of the Dead: Liberation through Understanding in the Between.* New York: Bantam, 1994.

BRYAN J. CUEVAS

TIME. *See* **Cosmology; Decline of the Dharma; Millenarianism and Millenarian Movements**

TŌDAIJI. *See* **Hōryūji and Tōdaiji**

TOMINAGA NAKAMOTO

Tominaga Nakamoto (1715–1746) has often been included among a diverse group of rationalist or enlightenment (*keimō*) thinkers who emerged in eighteenth-century Japan. Counted among their numbers are medical doctors, scientists, economists, and others, all of whom shared a critical stance toward traditional religious authority and who believed that reliable knowledge could come only from the rigorous application of reason.

Born into the merchant class in Osaka, Tominaga was educated in a Confucian school, the Kaitokudō or Pavilion of Virtues, that his father and four other merchants had established. Tominaga was a brilliant student and by the age of fifteen he had completed his first study, *Setsuhei* (*Failings of the Classical Philosophers*), for which he was expelled from the school. The text is no longer extant, but passing references to it in later works suggest that it was a critical treatment of Confucianism. After his expulsion, he studied with other Confucian teachers, but he may also have read Buddhist texts at Manpukuji, a Zen monastery in Kyoto, where some believe he worked as a proofreader. The monastery was publishing a new edition of the Buddhist CANON at the time.

Tominaga died at the early age of thirty-one, but his breadth of knowledge of Confucianism, Buddhism, and Shintō enabled him to write two works that, after his death, had a revolutionary impact on Japanese religious history. In the short essay "Okina no fumi" ("The Writings of an Old Man," 1738) and in the much longer *Shutsujō gōgo* (*Talks after Emerging from Meditation,* 1745), he advanced the view that Japan's traditional religions were so historically and culturally conditioned that their claims to teach ultimate truth were untenable. In *Shutsujō gōgo* he focused his analysis on Buddhism in particular, contending that the texts of MAHĀYĀNA Buddhism, the dominant branch in Japan, were so different in language and content from the other sūtras that they could not be the direct teachings of the Buddha. Tominaga was the first person to systematically make this case in Japan. Viewed as a threat to the entire tradition, his position prompted numerous counterarguments from the Buddhist community. By the late nineteenth and early twentieth centuries, however, most Japanese Buddhist scholars accepted Tominaga's assertion about the later origins of Mahāyāna sūtras and embraced the critical historical approach to the study of texts that he had advanced.

See also: **Buddhist Studies; Confucianism and Buddhism; Japan**

Bibliography

Kato, Shuichi. "Okina no fumi: The Writings of an Old Man." *Monumenta Nipponica* 22, nos. 1–2 (1967): 194–210.

Kato, Shuichi. "Tominaga Nakamoto, 1715–1746: A Tokugawa Iconoclast." *Monumenta Nipponica* 22, nos. 1–2 (1967): 177–193.

Najita, Tetsuo. *Visions of Virtue in Tokugawa Japan: The Kaitokudō, Merchant Academy of Osaka.* Chicago: University of Chicago Press, 1987.

Pye, Michael. *Emerging from Meditation: Tominaga Nakamoto.* Honolulu: University of Hawaii Press, 1990.

PAUL B. WATT

TONSURE. *See* **Hair**

TRIPIṬAKA. *See* **Abhidharma; Canon; Commentarial Literature; Scripture; Vinaya**

TRIRATNA. *See* Refuges

TSONG KHA PA

Although Tsong kha pa (1357–1419) is considered by many as a seminal figure, the nature of his contribution is not always well understood. He is often presented as a reformer of Tibetan Buddhism or as being hostile to tantric practice. To correct these misapprehensions, he must be placed within his historical context before sketching some of his key ideas.

Tsong kha pa was born during a crucial period in the second development (*phyi dar*) of Tibetan Buddhism, which had started at the end of the tenth century. One of the important questions debated during this period was the relation between monasticism and tantric practice. A solution was initiated by the famous Indian teacher ATISHA (982–1054) and further developed by other Tibetan thinkers such as 'Brom ston (1055–1064) and SA SKYA PAṆḌITA (SAKYA PAṆḌITA) (1182–1251). According to this model, monasticism and tantric practices are included in the PATH of the BODHISATTVA, which provides the ethical framework for the entire range of Buddhist practices. In this perspective, higher tantric practices, ethically subordinated to the bodhisattva ideal, are the most effective way to realize this ideal, while monasticism is the best way of life to embody it.

Tsong kha pa devoted much of his work to the continuation of this moral tradition, as is made clear in his masterful *Lam rim chen mo* (*Extensive Stages of the Path to Enlightenment*). He regarded the promotion of monasticism as one of his central missions, as illustrated by his establishment in 1409 of the Great Prayer (*smon lam chen mo*) festival in Lhasa, which is said to have brought together eight thousand monks. Tsong kha pa's biographers consider this one of his most important deeds. It laid the ground for the foundation during the same year of the monastery Dga' ldan, one of the three main monasteries near Lhasa. The other two monasteries, 'Bras spung (pronounced Drepung) and Se ra, were founded shortly thereafter by two of Tsong kha pa's direct disciples, thus creating the famous three seats, the institutional basis for the future growth of his tradition.

Tsong kha pa's fame is also due to the quality of his works and the power of his ideas. He lived during the period in which Tibetans developed their own systematic presentation of the range of Buddhist materials they had received from India. Tsong kha pa's synthesis, which brings together the exoteric and esoteric aspects of the tradition, is not only masterful in the quality of its scholarship, it is also highly original and distinctive in its interpretations, particularly in the fields of the MADHYAMAKA SCHOOL and TANTRA, which Tsong kha pa considered his specialties.

Tsong kha pa's interpretation of Indian Madhyamaka is characterized by his strong preference for the Prāsaṅgika (consequentialist) approach of CANDRAKĪRTI (ca. 600–650 C.E.), which Tsong kha pa sees as the only fully correct view. In asserting the superiority of the Prāsaṅgika, Tsong kha pa adopts the views of earlier thinkers such as Spa tshab (b. 1055) and his followers, as well as Tsong kha pa's own main teacher Red mda ba (1349–1412). These teachers extolled Candrakīrti's Prāsaṅgika view of ŚŪNYATĀ (EMPTINESS) as being utterly beyond any description and hence beyond the reach of logical thinking. Tsong kha pa, however, insists on retaining a place for the traditional tools of Buddhist logic within this radical view, arguing that even in the context of the search for the ultimate one needs probative arguments.

This trust in Buddhist logic in a Prāsaṅgika context is unique to Tsong kha pa. Earlier thinkers such as Phya pa (1109–1169) had insisted on the importance of Buddhist LOGIC in Madhyamaka, but they followed the Svātantrika of BHĀVAVIVEKA (ca. 500–570 C.E.). Tsong kha pa adopted Phya pa's realist interpretation of Buddhist logic but integrated it into Candrakīrti's interpretation. This led to the creation of an audacious synthesis, which conciliates a radical undermining of essentialism and a realist confidence that thinking can apprehend reality, at least partly, and therefore can lead to insight into the ultimate nature of things.

For Tsong kha pa, this conviction is reflected in the development of the three types of critical acumen (*prajñā*; Tibetan, *shes rab or*) articulated by the Indian Buddhist tradition. First, one should study extensively both sūtras and tantras. Then one should start the process of internalization of the teachings by reflecting inwardly on them. This is the stage at which probative arguments are essential, because without proper inferences understanding remains superficial and fails to reach conviction in the Buddhist teaching in general and in the validity of the Prāsaṅgika view in particular. Finally, one should enter into prolonged meditative retreats to attain the experiential realization of the studied teachings, as Tsong kha pa did at

'Ol khar chos lung during the winter of 1392 to 1393. There he underwent several tantric retreats and received important visions, particularly that of Manjuśrī, his tutelary deity. This progression was particularly significant for Tsong kha pa, who saw his entire life accordingly.

As his practice makes clear, Tsong kha pa's work is not limited to the exoteric domains. In fact, the majority of his famous eighteen volumes of collected works are devoted to the study of tantras. For Tsong kha pa, the most important tantra is the *Guhyasamāja* cycle, which provides the key to the interpretation of the entire tantric corpus. Together with the *Yamāntaka* and *Cakrasaṃvara,* this tantra provides a map of the entire tantric practice, thus completing the vast synthesis of the tradition, from the most basic practices of monasticism to the highest yogic practices. For Tsong kha pa, tantric practice is central, but it is essential that it be undertaken gradually, as advocated by Atisha, after extensive preliminaries involving the study and assimilation of the entire exoteric path.

See also: **Dalai Lama; Dge Lugs (Geluk); Panchen Lama; Tantra; Tibet**

Bibliography

Dreyfus, Georges B. J. *Recognizing Reality: Dharmakīrti's Philosophy and Its Tibetan Interpreters.* Albany: State University of New York Press, 1997.

Hopkins, Jeffrey. *Meditation on Emptiness.* Boston: Wisdom, 1983.

Napper, Elizabeth. *Dependent-Arising and Emptiness: A Tibetan Buddhist Interpretation of Madhyamika Philosophy Emphasizing the Compatibility of Emptiness and Conventional Phenomena.* Boston: Wisdom, 1989.

Snellgrove, David, and Richardson, Hugh. *A Cultural History of Tibet.* Boston: Shambala, 1968.

Thurman, Robert, ed. *Life and Teachings of Tsong Khapa,* tr. Sherpa Tulku. Dharamsala, India: Library of Tibetan Works and Archives, 1982.

Tillemans, Tom J. F. *Scripture, Logic, Language: Essays on Dharmakīrti and His Tibetan Successors.* Boston: Wisdom, 1999.

Tsong kha pa. *The Great Treatise on the Stages of the Path to Enlightenment,* tr. the *Lamrim Chenmo* Translation Committee. Ithaca, NY: Snow Lion, 2000.

GEORGES B. J. DREYFUS

TULKU. *See* **Lama**

U

ŬICH'ŎN

Ŭich'ŏn (Taegak *kuksa*, 1055–1101) was the fourth son of King Munjong (r. 1047–1083) of the Korean Koryŏ dynasty. Ŭich'ŏn became the head of Buddhist saṅgha in Koryŏ at the age of thirteen. Well versed in Buddhist scriptures, particularly the teachings of the Hwaŏm (Huayan) school, he nevertheless decided to further his study in China after a long period of correspondence with the Song monk Jinshui Jingyuan (1011–1088). In 1085, after leaving a letter to his mother and his brother, the new King Sŏnjong (r. 1083–1094), Ŭich'ŏn surreptitiously boarded a merchant's ship and sailed to Song dynasty China to embark on his pilgrimage. During his fourteen-month sojourn in China, he met and consulted some fifty leading masters on the Chan, Huayan, and Tiantai schools of Buddhism, while studying with Jingyuan at Hiuyin Monastery in Hangzhou.

Ŭich'ŏn brought a number of important Huayan texts to China, which enabled Jingyuan to redefine the Huayan lineage. As Jingyuan's favorite disciple, Ŭich'ŏn was a prominent figure whose celebrity also helped boost the popularity of the master's monastery, which became known as the Koryŏ Monastery. After returning to Koryŏ and becoming the abbot of Hŭngwangsa, he managed to synthesize the Sŏn (Chinese, Chan; Japanese, Zen) school and the Kyo (scholastic) forms of Buddhism in Korea. He also founded a revitalized Ch'ŏnt'ae (Chinese, Tiantai) Buddhism in Koryŏ. In his monastery, Ŭich'ŏn built a library and a collection of important Buddhist texts, for which he compiled a catalogue called *Sin'pyŏn chejong kyojang ch'ongnok* (*New Catalogue of Buddhist Sectarian Writings*). The catalogue and his writings, the *Taegak kuksa munjip* and the *Taegak kuksa woejip*, remain important sources for the study of Korean Buddhism.

See also: **Huayan School; Tiantai School**

Bibliography

Huiyinsi zhi (*Record of Huiyin Monastery*). Taipei, Taiwan: Mingwen shuju, 1981.

Taegak kuksa munjip and Taegak kuksa woejip (*Collected Works of the National Preceptor Taegak*). Seoul: Kongguk University, 1974.

CHI-CHIANG HUANG

ŬISANG

Ŭisang (625–702) was the founder of the Hwaŏm school and an influential thinker in Korea and China. In 644 he was ordained a monk at Hwangboksa in Kyŏngju, the capital of Silla. Together with WŎNHYO (617–686), Ŭisang decided to study under Chinese masters. After a first unsuccessful attempt in 650, Ŭisang finally reached Tang China in 661, where he studied under Zhiyan (602–668), the second patriarch of the HUAYAN SCHOOL. Together with FAZANG (643–712), the future third patriarch of the Huayan school, Ŭisang became one of Zhiyan's chief disciples. In 668 Ŭisang wrote the *Hwaŏm ilsŭng pŏpkye to* (*Diagram of the Dharmadhātu According to the One Vehicle of Hwaŏm*), a poem epitomizing his understanding of Huayan philosophy. During the same year, Zhiyan died and Ŭisang took over teaching the disciples of his deceased master.

In 670 Ŭisang returned to Korea, warning King Munmu about an impending invasion of Silla by Tang army forces. In 676 Pusŏksa on Mount T'aebaek was built under royal decree and functioned as Ŭisang's main center for the propagation of the Hwaŏm school in Korea. Purportedly, Ŭisang gathered more than three thousand disciples and subsequently founded other monasteries throughout the country, further promoting Hwaŏm studies. Ŭisang's erudition was known both inside and outside of Korea. Fazang continued to correspond with Ŭisang, asking him to correct his manuscripts.

During the subsequent Koryŏ dynasty, CHINUL (1158–1210) copiously cited Ŭisang's works and King Sukjong conferred on him a posthumous title. Ŭisang's *Hwaŏm ilsŭng pŏpkye to* is often recited in modern Korean Buddhist liturgy.

Bibliography

Forte, Antonino. *A Jewel in Indra's Net: The Letter Sent by Fazang in China to Ŭisang in Korea.* Kyoto: Instituto Italiano di Cultura Scuola di Studi Sull'Asia Orientale, 2000.

Lee, Peter H., ed. *Sourcebook of Korean Civilization,* Vol. 1. New York: Columbia University Press, 1993.

Odin, Steve. *Process Metaphysics and Hua-yen Buddhism: A Critical Study of Cumulative Penetration vs. Interpretation.* Albany: State University of New York Press, 1982.

PATRICK R. UHLMANN

UNITED STATES

The American encounter with Buddhism dates from the start of systematic trade between China and the United States in 1784, when ships that docked along the eastern seaboard from Charleston, South Carolina, to Salem, Massachusetts, began to unload Asian artifacts. But during this period Americans, and Westerners more generally, had not yet identified Buddhism as a distinct religious tradition, perused translations of Buddhist sacred texts, or witnessed large-scale emigration of Buddhists from Asia. In that sense, the American contact with Buddhism did not begin in earnest until the 1840s and 1850s. In 1844 transcendentalist writer Elizabeth Palmer Peabody (1804–1894) translated an excerpt from a French edition of a Buddhist sacred text, the LOTUS SŪTRA (SADDHARMAPUṆḌARĪKASŪTRA), and that excerpt and commentary appeared in the magazine *The Dial* as "The Preaching of the Buddha." In the same year Edward Elbridge Salisbury (1814–1901), a professor of Sanskrit at Yale, read a paper on the history of Buddhism at the first annual meeting of the American Oriental Society, a group of scholars dedicated to the study of Asian cultures. These two events—Peabody's translation and Salisbury's paper—initiated systematic U.S. contact with Buddhism, and that encounter took on more significance in the next decade as Chinese immigrants landed on American shores. This initial period in the history of Buddhism in the United States would last until 1924, when Congress passed a restrictive immigration act. And the most recent era in America's encounter with Buddhism opened in 1965, when the immigration laws loosened to allow more Asians of Buddhist heritage to settle in the United States.

Encounters: 1844–1923

The public conversation, which began in the 1840s and peaked in the 1890s, included a wide range of voices—Christian travelers and missionaries, European and American scholars, as well as Buddhist sympathizers and converts. Much of the discussion—in magazines and books, in parlors and classrooms, in churches and lecture halls—focused on the sources of Buddhism's attraction (advocates claimed it was tolerant, egalitarian, and scientific) and the extent of its discontinuity with mainline Protestant beliefs and Victorian American values (critics found it pessimistic, atheistic, and passive). In books such as Samuel Henry Kellogg's *The Light of Asia and the Light of the World* (1885) Protestant critics of the Asian religion worried aloud about the increasing influence of Buddhism and countered with praise for Christianity. Henry M. King (1838–1919), a prominent Baptist clergyman who was troubled by the claims that it was "a most favorable time for the dissemination of Buddhistic views," even asked readers of one Christian periodical, "Shall We All Become Buddhists?" King offered a decisive *no,* and he and other Christian critics highlighted the ways that Buddhism seemed to diverge from widely shared beliefs and values—theism, individualism, activism, and optimism. But Buddhist sympathizers defended the tradition, as Paul Carus (1852–1919) did passionately in *Buddhism and Its Christian Critics* (1897).

Carus, one of the most influential participants in the public discussion, never affiliated formally or fully with Buddhism, but several thousand European Americans did during the first Buddhist vogue, from the 1880s to the 1910s. Attracted by Edwin Arnold's sympathetic life of the Buddha in verse, *The Light of Asia* (1879), and fascinated by the lectures and writings of two Asian Buddhists who spoke at Chicago's World Parliament of Religions in 1893, ANAGĀRIKA DHARMAPĀLA (1864–1933) and Sōen Shaku (1859–1919), some Americans turned East. Some in that first generation of American converts even traveled to Asia. Henry Steel Olcott (1832–1907), the first American convert in 1880, and Marie De Souza Canavarro (1849–1933), the first female convert in 1897, traveled to Ceylon (Sri Lanka). William Sturgis Bigelow (1850–1926) and Ernest Francisco Fenollosa (1851–1903) went to Japan, where they stayed for years and received the bodhisattva PRECEPTS of Tendai Buddhism at Homoyoin Monastery in 1885.

During this period, most Americans who would have claimed Buddhist identity never had the chance to encounter the tradition in Asia, and there were few Buddhist leaders, translations, and institutions to support their practice, which focused more on reading than meditation or chanting. Those who lived in San Francisco could take advantage of the Dharma Sangha of Buddha, a small Caucasian group founded in 1900 by Japanese Jōdo Shinshū (or True Pure Land Sect) missionaries, who also published a sophisticated English-language magazine, the *Light of Dharma* (1901–1907), which could boast of subscribers in twenty-five states. More than a decade earlier some readers encountered a distinctive blend of Swedenborgianism and Buddhism in another periodical, the *Buddhist Ray* (1888–1894), which was published in Santa Cruz, California, by a self-proclaimed convert, Herman C. Vetterling (1849–1931), who called himself Philangi Dasa. Yet most European Americans who sympathized with the tradition or thought of themselves as Buddhists had little support for their practice during this period.

Asian-American Buddhists, especially the Japanese, were a little less isolated. Immigrants from East Asia (China, Korea, and Japan) brought Buddhism to the United States during this period, starting with the Chinese in the 1850s. They settled along the West Coast to work as railroad laborers, miners, farmers, and domestics. In the 1850s and 1860s emigrants from China also landed in Hawaii to work on sugar plantations. And Buddhism was a part of the religious life of many of these Chinese migrants on the islands and on the mainland. It is difficult to say how many, since the Chinese did not keep clear records, establish vigorous organizations, or enjoy strong religious leadership. Further, as in their homeland, Buddhist beliefs and practices blended with Daoist, Confucian, and folk traditions in Chinese-American homes and temples. The Chinese established the first temple in the United States in 1853, in San Francisco's Chinatown. By the 1860s, tens of thousands of Chinese immigrants had some allegiance to Buddhism, and by the 1890s there were 107,488 Chinese in the United States. They could visit fifteen San Francisco temples, which enshrined Buddhist as well as Daoist images. Although no one could offer fully reliable figures, officials from the U.S. Bureau of the Census reported in 1906 that there were 62 Chinese temples and 141 shrines in 12 states, many of them in California.

The Japanese were the next Asian Buddhists to arrive. They began to travel to Hawaii in significant numbers during the 1860s, and by 1889 a Jōdo Shinshū priest, Soryu Kagahi, was ministering to Buddhist field workers there. In the next decade, the 1890s, thousands of Japanese migrants arrived in the American West, and almost from the start Japanese Buddhists were more organized than the Chinese. Religious leaders traveled from the homeland and formed religious institutions to support Buddhist practice. On September 2, 1899, the Honganji True Pure Land Buddhist organization in Kyoto sent two missionaries—Shuye Sonoda and Kakuryo Nishijima. By 1906 Japanese Pure Land Buddhists reported 12 organizations, 7 temples, and 14 priests in the United States. They also reported 3,165 members, although many more Japanese would have been loosely affiliated with the religion. Meanwhile, Buddhism continued to flourish among the Japanese in the Hawaiian Islands, which had become a U.S. possession in 1898. Chinese and Koreans on the islands also practiced Buddhism in this early period. For example, one scholar has estimated that at least half of the 7,200 Koreans who moved to Hawaii to labor on sugar plantations between 1903 and 1905 were Buddhists.

But, as they soon would discover, these pioneer Asian immigrants were not welcomed by all other Americans. They were, as some scholars have suggested, the ultimate aliens. Not only were they legally unable to become naturalized citizens, but they also were racially, linguistically, culturally, and religiously distinct from their neighbors. If Buddhism provided a source of identity and comfort, it also set them apart in a predominantly Christian nation. U.S. lawmakers targeted first the Chinese and later the Japanese. The Chinese Exclusion Act of 1882 set the tone, and by the time legislators passed the restrictive and racist 1924 immigration act, which included national quotas that in practical terms excluded Asians, the pattern was clear for the next period in U.S. Buddhist history.

Exclusions: 1924–1964

From the 1920s to the 1960s borders were closed to Asian immigrants, and interest contracted among European-American sympathizers and converts. Very few new Asian Buddhists arrived. The Chinese population fell, thriving Chinatowns declined, and some temples closed. Jōdo Shinshū, Sōtoshū, and Nichirenshū temples formed during the several decades after the Japanese arrival in the 1890s, but the immigrant population did not grow. The Japanese also suffered internment during World War II, when President Franklin Roosevelt's Executive Order 9066 incarcerated more than 120,000 Japanese Americans in assembly centers and internment camps in the Western states. Some Japanese stopped practicing Buddhism for fear of being labeled un-American, although most continued their religious practice and the Jōdo Shinshū mission, renamed the Buddhist Churches of America in 1944, survived the camps.

Japanese Buddhism even expanded between the 1920s and the 1960s. Sōto and Rinzai Zen leaders began to build on the foundations constructed earlier. Sōen, the first Zen teacher in America, had made a lecture tour in 1905 and 1906 and then published *Sermons of a Buddhist Abbot* (1906), the first book on Zen in the English language. Between 1925 and 1931 two of Sōen's students—Nyogen Senzaki (1876–1958) and Shigetsu Sasaki (later known as Sokei-an)—went on to establish Zen centers in Los Angeles, San Francisco, and New York. Other East Asian teachers, including Shunryu Suzuki, later founded Zen centers. Suzuki arrived in San Francisco in 1959 to serve the elderly Japanese-American congregation at Sokoji, the Sōto Zen temple that Hosen Isobe had built in 1934. Suzuki later established the San Francisco Zen Center and Tassajara Zen Mountain Center, the first Zen monastery in America. In 1960 SŌKA GAKKAI's president, Daisaku Ikeda, brought the practices of that Japanese religious movement to American shores.

If these and other teachers helped to build the institutions that nurtured Buddhist practice among converts and sympathizers after the 1960s, another Japanese Buddhist, D. T. SUZUKI (1870–1966), generated interest, especially in Zen, among intellectuals and artists. Suzuki, who had penned articles for the *Light of Dharma* and served as Sōen's translator at the Parliament and during his 1905 speaking tour, first stepped into the spotlight in 1927 when he published *Essays in Zen Buddhism.* Through his writings, translations, and lectures over the next four decades he influenced musicians, poets, choreographers, painters, theologians, and psychologists, including John Cage, Erich Fromm, and Thomas Merton—as well as Beat movement writers Allen Ginsberg, Gary Snyder, and Jack Kerouac, who looked to Buddhism as a spiritual alternative to their inherited traditions.

Another influence on the Beat generation was Dwight Goddard (1861–1939), a Baptist missionary who sailed for China to save the "heathen" and returned as a Buddhist convert committed to spreading the Asian tradition in the United States. It was Goddard's anthology of Buddhist scriptures, *The Buddhist Bible* (1932), that Kerouac's "dharma bums" carried with them on their spiritual journeys in Eisenhower's America. But neither Goddard, who had proposed an American Buddhist monastic community as early as 1933, nor Suzuki, who popularized Zen, could secure an enduring institutional foundation for Buddhist practice among converts. That would happen only after 1965.

Crossings: After 1965

Many things changed after 1965, even if cultural shifts in the preceding decades had helped prepare the way. Not only did the number of American converts swell, but more Buddhists arrived from Asia. All Buddhists also enjoyed increased support for their practice as more temples and centers dotted the American landscape. At the same time, Buddhism grew in visibility as it shaped elite and popular culture. There were multiple reasons for the changes. Cultural discontent during the tumultuous 1960s had opened Americans to new spiritual alternatives just as new translations of Buddhist texts made their way to bookstores and revised immigration laws opened the gates for Asian immigrants, including Buddhist teachers and followers. Starting in the 1970s, war-weary Buddhist refugees from Southeast Asia also began to settle in America after escaping political disruptions in their homelands.

So by the opening decade of the twenty-first century the United States was home to every form of Asian Buddhism—THERAVĀDA, MAHĀYĀNA, and VAJRAYĀNA. Cradle Buddhists, those born into the faith, and convert Buddhists, those who embraced it as adults, could practice in more than fifteen hundred temples or centers. No one knows for certain how many Americans think of themselves as Buddhists, since the U.S. census no longer gathers information about religious affiliation. Recent estimates range from 500,000 to over 5 million, with the average estimate about 2.3 million. Surveys in 2000—the General Social Survey (GSS), Monitoring the Future (MF), the

American Freshman (AF), and the American Religious Identification Survey (ARIS)—concluded that 1 million to 2.1 million adults (61% Asian American) and 1.4 million to 2.8 million in the total population affiliated with Buddhism. Scholars who defend the lower figure (1.4 million) argue that only the surveys of high school seniors and college freshmen (MF and AF) point toward the higher end. Those who concur with the larger estimate (2.8 million) note that the other studies (GSS and ARIS) were telephone surveys that excluded those who did not speak English and, therefore, undercounted Asian refugees and immigrants. Other evidence, or lack of evidence, also inclines some toward the high-end estimates: the religion survey (ARIS) failed to contact residents of Hawaii, which had the counties with the highest concentrations of Asian Americans according to the 2000 U.S. census, and the survey of high school seniors (MF) failed to include California, a state with a significant Buddhist presence.

To put these estimates in perspective, if we assume the lowest available figures, Buddhists still outnumbered more than seventeen U.S. Christian denominations, including the Disciples of Christ and the Quakers (ARIS). And even if the highest estimates—more than five million—seem exaggerated, they revealed two important features of the contemporary religious context, as demographer Tom Smith pointed out. First, observers might unwittingly inflate estimates of adherents because the building of Asian-American temples and the media's celebration of celebrity converts have made Buddhism more visible. Second, there are many sympathizers, or nightstand Buddhists, who read Buddhist popular books and practice meditation sporadically but do not affiliate formally or fully.

By almost any measure Buddhism had found its place in the American religious landscape by the start of the twenty-first century, and of those Americans who identified themselves as Buddhist adherents, approximately one-third were converts (ARIS). A small proportion were Asians who discovered or reaffirmed Buddhism in the United States, but most of the 341,000 (ARIS) to 800,000 (Baumann) converts were Americans of European or African descent. There was more diversity among converts who affiliated with Sōka Gakkai, the Japanese sect that venerates the teachings of NICHIREN (1222–1282). They were more ethnically diverse than both the U.S. population and other Buddhist converts: 15 percent African American, 15 percent "other," 23 percent Asian, and 6 percent Latino. However, most Buddhist converts tended to be white,

Thai-American Buddhists celebrate the Thai New Year festival at a temple in New York City, 2001. AP/Wide World Photos. Reproduced by permission.

as James William Coleman's study revealed. Converts also were middle and upper middle class, with a very high level of education: more than half (51%) held advanced degrees. Their range of religious backgrounds made them typical of the American population, except that convert Buddhists were disproportionately of Jewish heritage (16.5%, as compared with 3% in the U.S. population).

Although converts have embraced almost every form of Buddhism, since 1965 most have affiliated with one of several traditions. Through the efforts of American converts who had studied in Burma and Thailand during the 1960s, Theravāda Buddhism attracted interest, and efforts to transplant Southeast Asian Buddhism, especially VIPASSANĀ (or insight) meditation, took institutional form during the 1970s and 1980s. In 1975 Sharon Salzberg, Jack Kornfield, Joseph Goldstein, and others founded the Insight Meditation Society in Barre, Massachusetts. Soon after, teachers extended the movement to California: In 1977 Ruth Denison, who also had practiced in Asia, purchased property that would eventually become Dhamma Dena in Joshua Tree, and in 1988 Kornfield helped to establish another teaching, retreat, and training center at Spirit Rock, in Marin County.

Although W. Y. Evans-Wentz translated the TIBETAN BOOK OF THE DEAD in 1927 and Geshe Wangyal incorporated the first Tibetan Buddhist monastery in New Jersey in 1958, larger numbers of converts started turning to Vajrayāna traditions only in the late 1960s and early 1970s, when teachers such as Tarthang Tulku Rinpoche (1935–) in Berkeley, California, and Chogyam Trungpa Rinpoche (1939–1987) in Boulder, Colorado, established practice centers associated with the four main orders or schools of Tibetan Buddhism: BKA' BRGYUD (KAGYU), SA SKYA (SAKYA), RNYING MA (NYINGMA), and DGE LUGS (GELUK). And because the number of Tibetan exiles in the United States remains relatively small, Vajrayāna traditions are represented in America mostly by European-American converts and the Tibetan (or, increasingly, American) teachers who guide their practice.

Since the 1960s American converts also have practiced in centers associated with forms of Mahāyāna Buddhism. Sōka Gakkai International (SGI), a lay organization within Nichiren Shoshū until the bitter split in 1991, grew from its American origins in 1960 to attract approximately thirty-six thousand devotees, who chanted the title of the *Lotus Sūtra* in homes and centers across the United States by the turn of the century. Asian-born Zen teachers—Shunryu Suzuki (1904–1971) and Taizan Maezumi (1931–1995)—built on the foundations established earlier in the century, and their American-born "dharma heirs" went on to lead existing centers and found new ones. Philip Kapleau (1912–), Robert Aitken (1917–), Maurine Stuart (1922–1990), John Daido Loori (1931–), Richard Baker (1936–), and Bernard Glassman (1939–) all played important roles, and by 2000 their lineages had been extended, with later generations of American-born Sōto and Rinzai teachers, including many women, assuming positions of leadership.

Finally, Vietnamese Zen teacher THICH NHAT HANH (1926–) attracted sympathizers and converts, who are guided by the fourteen mindfulness trainings of his "ENGAGED BUDDHISM." He founded the Order of Interbeing (*Tiep Hien*) in the mid-1960s, when he was an internationally known peace activist, but the "core community" (the ordained) and the "extended community" (the unordained) began to grow in number and influence during the 1980s and 1990s through the writings and visits of the founder, who consecrated the Maple Forest Monastery in Hartland, Vermont, in 1997.

Nhat Hanh, the DALAI LAMA, and many other Asian- and American-born Buddhist teachers also shaped elite and popular culture. They filled bookstore shelves with accessible introductions to Buddhist practice that were read by tens of thousands of sympathizers who do not sign membership lists or formally take refuge in the Buddha but still find the tradition's teachings attractive. Buddhism also inspired American painters, architects, and sculptors. It shaped modern dance and contemporary music, from Philip Glass's new music to the Beastie Boys hip-hop. The pop star Tina Turner reported that chanting, a practice she learned from Nichiren Buddhism, granted her peace and prosperity. Buddhism influenced the sports world too: Phil Jackson, the professional basketball coach, credited Zen with his success in the game. How-to books promised improvement in everything from sex to business, if only readers would apply the principles of Zen or Tantric Buddhism. Inspired by Nhat Hanh's *Miracle of Mindfulness: A Manual on Meditation* (1975) and other texts and teachers, Duke University Medical Center and many other hospitals offered classes in "meditation-based stress reduction." Advertisers, fashion designers, scriptwriters, and filmmakers also used Buddhist images to move an audience or sell a brand. After celebrities confessed Buddhist affiliation and four films during the mid-1990s highlighted Buddhist themes (*Heaven and Earth, Little Buddha, Kundun,* and *Seven Years in Tibet*), a 1997 cover story in *Time* magazine celebrated "America's Fascination with Buddhism." A century after the peak of Victorian-American interest, a more intense and widespread Buddhist vogue seemed to have set in.

But cultural vogues come and go, and it is not yet clear whether the baby boomer converts will successfully pass on Buddhism to the next generation. So in many ways, the most culturally significant shift after 1965 has been the increased visibility and numbers of Buddhist immigrants and refugees from Asia. The 1965 revision of immigration laws swelled the foreign-born population. According to the 2000 U.S. census, 28.4 million Americans (10.4% of the population) were born outside the nation. Of those, 7.2 million emigrated from Asia, and approximately 665,000 foreign-born Asian Americans might be Buddhist, if we apply and extend the findings of the ARIS. In any case, if the same proportions hold as in that 2001 survey—61 percent of Buddhists were Asian American and 67 percent were born into the tradition—then about two-thirds of U.S. Buddhists are of Asian descent.

A small proportion of those Asian-American Buddhists trace their lineage to the Japanese, Koreans, and Chinese who arrived in the first wave of Asian migration, which brought forms of Mahāyāna Buddhism to the nation. Those third- and fourth-generation Japanese-American communities continue to practice their faith, as at the Seattle Buddhist Church (organized 1901), the fourth-oldest Jōdo Shinshū temple in the United States. But more recent immigrants and refugees have transplanted almost every form of Asian Buddhism. First-generation Americans from Sri Lanka, Thailand, Laos, and Cambodia have established Theravāda temples and retreat centers in more than thirty states, including Wat Carolina (dedicated 1988) in rural Bolivia, North Carolina, although temples predominate in cities in California, Texas, New York, and Illinois. In addition, Chinese, Koreans, and Vietnamese practice multiple forms of Mahāyāna Buddhism in hundreds of remodeled homes and new buildings, such as Oklahoma City's Chua Vien Giac, a Vietnamese temple dedicated in 1982, and Southern California's Hsi Lai Temple, a structure built by Chinese Americans in 1988 and still the largest Buddhist temple in America. More temples appear in the American landscape all the time. Asian-American Buddhists continue to organize groups, renovate homes, and build temples in urban, rural, and suburban communities across the nation. And many confront obstacles—from bomb threats to zoning laws.

Contemporary cradle and convert Buddhists also face many other issues. U.S. Buddhists must fashion identity and negotiate power in a culturally Christian nation, although Buddhism often has adapted to new cultures as it crossed cultural boundaries during its twenty-five-hundred-year history. Yet by the twenty-first century, American Buddhists had to confront not only divergent cultural values and the cultural clout of Christianity, but also an unprecedented array of others from the same tradition, for example at regular meetings of inter-Buddhist organizations across the country, including the Buddhist Sangha Council of Southern California (1980), the Buddhist Council of the Midwest (1987), and the Texas Buddhist Council (1992). Like other American immigrants before them, many post-1965 Asian-American Buddhists also face the challenges of intergenerational tensions and ponder how much to accommodate and how much to resist cultural practices in the United States—from meat eating to MTV. Some observers have trumpeted convert Buddhism's "democratic" impulses, which have opened participation and leadership to WOMEN and LAITY more than in most Asian cultures, but it remains to be seen how effectively they will extend that egalitarianism as they try to bridge racial divides among Asian, Caucasian, Latino/a, and African-American Buddhists. And it is not clear that the cultural dissenters who have been attracted to Buddhism will be able to build institutions that nurture children and youth and, thereby, assure the future vitality of the convert centers.

Finally, Buddhists encounter the U.S. legal and political systems. The federal courts have decided that even though they do not venerate a "supreme being," Buddhist conscientious objectors are protected under the Selective Service Training Act (*U.S. v. Seeger*) and that the First Amendment guarantees Buddhist prisoners "a reasonable opportunity" to practice the faith (*Cruz v. Beto*). There are even Buddhist chaplains serving soldiers in the U.S. military. But in a nation that still celebrates a theistic civil religion on its coins—"In God We Trust"—American Buddhists continue to struggle to make a place for those who take refuge in Buddha.

See also: **Buddhist Studies; Christianity and Buddhism; Europe; Zen, Popular Conceptions of**

Bibliography

Baumann, Martin. "The Dharma Has Come West: A Survey of Recent Studies and Sources." *Critical Review of Books in Religion* 10 (1997): 1–14.

Boucher, Sandy. *Turning the Wheel: American Women Creating the New Buddhism.* Boston: Beacon Press, 1993.

Coleman, James William. *The New Buddhism: The Western Transformation of an Ancient Tradition.* New York and Oxford: Oxford University Press, 2001.

Eck, Diana. *On Common Ground: World Religions in America,* 2nd ed. CD-ROM. New York: Columbia University Press, 2002.

Hammond, Phillip, and Machacek, David. *Soka Gakkai in America: Accommodation and Conversion.* New York and Oxford: Oxford University Press, 1999.

Kosmin, Barry A.; Mayer, Egon; and Keysar, Ariela. "The American Religious Identification Survey 2001." Graduate Center of the City University of New York, updated December 19, 2001.

Levinson, David, and Ember, Melvin, eds. *American Immigrant Cultures,* 2 vols. New York: Macmillan, 1997.

Morreale, Don, ed. *The Complete Guide to Buddhist America.* Boston and London: Shambhala, 1998.

Numrich, Paul David. *Old Wisdom in the New World: Americanization in Two Immigrant Theravada Buddhist Temples.* Knoxville: University of Tennessee Press, 1996.

Prebish, Charles S., and Tanaka, Kenneth K., eds. *The Faces of Buddhism in America.* Berkeley: University of California Press, 1998.

Seager, Richard Hughes. *Buddhism in America.* New York: Columbia University Press, 1999.

Smith, Tom W. "Religious Diversity in America: The Emergence of Muslims, Buddhists, Hindus, and Others." *Journal for the Scientific Study of Religion* 41 (2002): 577–585.

Tweed, Thomas A. "Night-stand Buddhists and Other Creatures: Sympathizers, Adherents, and the Study of Religion." In *American Buddhism: Methods and Findings in Recent Scholarship,* ed. Duncan Ryuken Williams and Christopher S. Queen. Surrey, UK: Curzon, 1999.

Tweed, Thomas A. *The American Encounter with Buddhism, 1844–1912: Victorian Culture and the Limits of Dissent.* Chapel Hill and London: University of North Carolina Press, 2000.

Tweed, Thomas A., and Prothero, Stephen, eds. *Asian Religions in America: A Documentary History.* New York and Oxford: Oxford University Press, 1999.

THOMAS A. TWEED

UPAGUPTA

Upagupta was a Buddhist saint and dharma master from Northwest India. He is unknown in the Pāli canon, but Sanskrit legends portray him as the fifth patriarch of the Buddhist tradition, in a line that stretches back through the disciples ĀNANDA and MAHĀKĀŚYAPA to the Buddha. He is associated with King AŚOKA (ca. 300–232 B.C.E.), whom he is said to have accompanied on a pilgrimage, but he is most famous for having tamed (some say converted) MĀRA. He is also said to have been cremated in Mathurā with the wooden tally-sticks (*śalākā*) of his many disciples.

In Myanmar (Burma), Upagupta is thought not to have died but to live on, in a meditative trance, in a pavilion in the midst of the southern ocean. From there, devotees invite him to come to their village to protect Buddhist festivals and rituals from disruptions caused by Māra, and to give people an opportunity to make merit. When his services are completed, devotees return Upagupta to his watery abode by floating his image downstream on a raft. His association with water and nāgas is also found in northern Thailand and Laos, where he is thought to reside in swamps or river bottoms.

Images of Upagupta commonly depict him as a seated monk looking up at the sun while eating from his alms bowl. He is said to have the power to stop the sun in its course, thus allowing him to eat after noon. In parts of Southeast Asia, it is thought that, on occasion, he may appear in person as a rough-looking monk. At such times, it is particularly beneficial to give him alms.

See also: **Arhat; Disciples of the Buddha**

Bibliography

Strong, John S. *The Legend and Cult of Upagupta.* Princeton, NJ: Princeton University Press, 1992.

JOHN S. STRONG

UPĀLI

Upāli, a disciple of Śākyamuni Buddha, attained the enlightened status of an ARHAT, or saint. Renowned for his knowledge of monastic discipline, he recited the VINAYA at the first Buddhist council in Rājagṛha.

Originally, Upāli had been a low-caste barber in the service of the Śākyan princes. When the princes leave in order to become monks, Upāli also decides to seek ORDINATION. Upāli attains a higher status in the monastic community than the princes because he is ordained before them. There are different accounts of Upāli's ordination in Buddhist literature. According to the Pāli vinaya, the high-caste Śākyan princes request that Upāli be ordained first so that they can learn to abandon their attachment to social status. In some Tibetan accounts, the arhat and disciple ŚĀRIPUTRA encourages Upāli to seek ordination when Upāli hesitates to do so because of his caste status.

Upāli's mother is credited in the Sanskrit MAHĀVASTU (*Great Story*) with arranging her son's first meeting with the Buddha. All accounts emphasize that caste has no bearing on a person's status in the monastic community. Upāli appears in the literature of different Buddhist schools as an expert on monastic and BODHISATTVA discipline. Like other arhats, he was the focus of worship already in ancient and medieval India. He figures in different Buddhist schools as the patron saint of specialists in vinaya. In Burma (Myanmar), Upāli is one of a set of eight arhats propitiated in protective rituals.

See also: **Councils, Buddhist; Disciples of the Buddha**

Bibliography

Malalasekera, G. P. "Upāli Thera." In *Dictionary of Pāli Proper Names* (1937–1938), 2 vols. New Delhi: Munshiram Manoharlal, 1995.

Strong, John S. *The Legend and Cult of Upagupta.* Princeton, NJ: Princeton University Press, 1992.

SUSANNE MROZIK

UPĀYA

Upāya is a central term in Buddhist HERMENEUTICS, SOTERIOLOGY, and ETHICS, especially in the MAHĀYĀNA tradition, where it refers to methods skillfully employed by BUDDHAS and BODHISATTVAS to assist SENTIENT BEINGS toward enlightenment.

In THERAVĀDA and Śrāvakayāna texts, *upāya* generally denotes a means or stratagem, and only occasionally refers to techniques employed by teachers on behalf of disciples. Still, the Buddha clearly was regarded as a masterful guide for sentient beings, adapting his message to the capacity of his audience, and encouraging promulgation of his doctrine in various languages.

Upāya gained prominence in early Mahāyāna sūtras, often as part of the compound *upāya-kauśalya,* which translates as skillful means, skill in means, or expedient. In many Prajñāpāramitā sūtras, *skillful means* refers to the multiple techniques used by buddhas or bodhisattvas to help worldly beings, and is explicitly linked with perfect wisdom as a requisite on the path. In the *Upāyakauśalya-sūtra,* immoralities attributed to bodhisattvas and weaknesses displayed by the Buddha are explained as the skillful means of beings whose compassion and insight preclude any immorality. In the *Vimalakīrtinirdeśa,* the layman VIMALAKĪRTI uses "inconceivable skillful means" to convert Vaiśālī's townsfolk. He enters such places as gambling halls and brothels to wean their denizens from vice, and he feigns illness so as to converse with śrāvakas and bodhisattvas, who fear his stinging rebukes, and puzzle at his insistence that passions be utilized rather than avoided. The LOTUS SŪTRA (SADDHARMAPUṆḌARĪKA-SŪTRA) uses both exposition and parables to describe the Buddha's skillful means for drawing beings to the One Vehicle (the Mahāyāna), including his promulgation of provisional truths that do not represent the "true" situation, but are appropriate to the capacities of certain disciples in certain contexts.

As Mahāyāna was systematized, *upāya* became increasingly central. In hermeneutics, the term explains apparent contradictions among the Buddha's teachings as rooted in his skillfully teaching his listeners what they needed to hear at a particular time, so that they would persevere on the path and eventually see things properly. Thus, Mahāyānists regarded HĪNAYĀNA teachings (and those of other traditions) as mere preludes to the definitive greater vehicle, and the Mahāyāna itself as containing more and less definitive doctrines. One source of this view was the SAṂDHINIRMOCANA-SŪTRA (*Sūtra Setting Free the [Buddha's] Intent*), which divides the Buddha's teachings into provisional and definitive. The scripture claims that, exercising skillful means, the Buddha turned the dharma-wheel thrice: provisionally in Hīnayāna scriptures (which incline to eternalism) and the Prajñāpāramitā sūtras (which incline to nihilism), and definitively in the *Saṃdhinirmocana* (which balances negation and affirmation). The three-wheel scheme became widespread in India and Tibet, though opinions varied as to the contents of the third turning (e.g., as YOGĀCĀRA, TATHĀGATAGARBHA, or TANTRA). In East Asia, the most influential hermeneutical scheme was that attributed to the Tiantai master ZHIYI (538–597), whose *panjiao* system identified five progressively higher stages of the Buddha's teaching, culminating in the *Lotus Sūtra.*

In mature Mahāyāna soteriology, *upāya* is, with wisdom, one of the two "sides" of the PATH perfected by bodhisattvas en route to buddhahood. Here, *upāya* refers to nearly any religious method not related directly to wisdom, and so includes the perfections of generosity, morality, patience, and effort; the practice of multifarious ritual and meditative techniques; and, above all, the development of the compassionately-motivated aspiration to achieve enlightenment for the sake of all beings (BODHICITTA). As perfecting wisdom or gnosis leads to attainment of a buddha's dharmakāya, the perfection of method results in the two "form bodies" that manifest for the sake of beings, the *saṃbhogakāya* and *nirmāṇakāya.* In some tantric traditions, where one "takes the result as path," wisdom and method were practiced simultaneously, for example as an cognition of emptiness appearing as a deity, or as a gnosis that sees emptiness while experiencing great bliss.

In Mahāyāna ethics, *skillful means* generally refers to compassionately motivated activity that benefits others, and corresponds well with traditional Buddhist morality. Certain texts suggest, however, that an advanced bodhisattva or buddha not only may, but must, break conventional precepts (including monastic vows) if doing so will be beneficial. Thus, sex, violence, lying, and stealing are sometimes claimed to be permissible. This "situational" ethic leaves moral decision making less rule-bound and more flexible, and defines virtue in terms of motive rather than conduct, thereby hinting at relativism and complicating judgments regarding one's own or others' behavior. Nevertheless, it was widely influential throughout the Mahāyāna world, where it was used to justify a range of actions, including trends toward laicization, particular political and military policies, erotic and terrifying elements in Tantra, and the behavior of spiritual masters. Especially in tantric and Chan traditions, training sometimes contravened standard morality and disciples were advanced using unorthodox techniques that sometimes included violence.

In contemporary Buddhism, *upāya* remains a crucial concept, helping to shape ongoing debates about how the dharma is to be expressed and transmitted, what range of practices is appropriate for Buddhists, how ethical decisions are to be made and judged, where WAR and politics fit into Buddhism, and what constitutes proper behavior by teachers toward their disciples.

See also: **Pāramitā (Perfection); Prajñā (Wisdom)**

Bibliography

Keown, Damien. *The Nature of Buddhist Ethics.* New York: Palgrave, 2001.

Lopez, Donald S., Jr., ed. *Buddhist Hermeneutics.* Honolulu: University of Hawaii Press, 1992.

Pye, Michael. *Skilful Means: A Concept in Mahāyāna Buddhism.* London: Duckworth, 1978.

Tatz, Mark, trans. *The Skill in Means (Upāyakauśalya) Sūtra.* Delhi: Motilal Banarsidass, 1994.

Thurman, Robert A. F., trans. *The Holy Teaching of Vimalakīrti: A Mahāyāna Scripture.* University Park: Pennsylvania State University Press, 1976.

Watson, Burton, trans. *The Lotus Sūtra.* New York: Columbia University Press, 1993.

ROGER R. JACKSON

USURY

Money lending is one of many business ventures practiced by Buddhist monks. Although commercial activities are not usually associated with Buddhism, from the inception of Buddhist communities as landowners to restaurants run by American Zen communities, monasteries have long been involved in a wide variety of economic enterprises. Because Buddhism identifies DESIRE, rather than the objects of desire, as a source of suffering, wealth per se is not condemned; on the contrary, the proper use and enjoyment of wealth is encouraged. Commercial operations within the monastery also reflect Buddhism's origins in the urban, mercantile centers of ancient India and in the systems of exchange, trade, and commerce, as well as the legal status of property and ownership, that developed there. The spread of Buddhism along trade routes meant that Buddhism and commerce traveled hand-in-hand. In China, for example, the innovation of lending banks was introduced by Buddhists traveling from India. The material needs of Buddhist devotional practice also encouraged the development of various crafts and guilds, as well as construction, agriculture, and other technologies.

Capital resources were provided by a model of the pure gift in which the laity contributed material goods to the monastic community (*dāna*) in return for religious merit (*puṇya*) that would enable better circumstances in future rebirths. As the wandering community of Buddhist renunciants quickly came to live the settled life of the vihāra (monastery), monastic regulations began to allow the accumulation of donations beyond the immediate needs of the community. Some communities permitted such surplus to be used to endow funds that would generate interest for the purchase of clothing, food, and other community needs, or even for reinvestment. Because the funds generated interest and the principal investment was not depleted, they were called "inexhaustible" or "permanent" goods (*akṣayanīvī*; Chinese, *wujinzai*). With the lands, serfs, livestock, grains, oil, cloth, gold, and silver thus acquired, renunciant communities were able to undertake a great variety of investment and commercial ventures. Later Chinese pilgrims reported that Indian monks supported themselves primarily by their land holdings and interest-bearing investments, rather than by daily rounds of alms seeking.

Lending at interest was one such practice. The assets lent from the inexhaustible goods could be commodities such as cloth, food, oils, seed, and other goods donated to the monastery. The lendable assets may also have included monies generated from land rents, commercial activities, and investments. The PRECEPTS of the various Indian schools give permission and rudimentary procedures for these lending practices. The Mūlasarvāstivāda-vinaya (*Monastic Code of the Mūlasarvāstivāda* [Group that Teaches that All Exists]), for example, gives specific instructions for lending the inexhaustible goods of the monastery, including details on the amount of collateral required (double the value of the loan), the form of the contract, the number of witnesses and guarantors needed, provisions for property seizure in the event of forfeiture, and other contractual details. The interest collected from monetary loans varied from as little as nothing to as high as 100 percent of the principal, but typically 50 percent of the principal was charged.

Although interest rates were frequently usurious, Buddhist monasteries were often the only source of large amounts of capital, so they performed an important and necessary social function that peasants, merchants, the gentry, and even monks took advantage of. At the same time, however, the vast wealth of the monasteries put them into competition for revenue with the state, so Buddhist economic enterprises were often attacked as corrupt and fraudulent. This was particularly true in China, where charges of financial impropriety were frequently raised during periods of imperial suppression of Buddhism.

The commercial activities of monasteries were not conducted solely for the purpose of economic gain—charitable lending and other social welfare institutions also developed. In China, for example, the Sanjie jiao (Three Stages school; late sixth–early eighth centuries), which operated several famous "Inexhaustible Storehouses," combined rules that provided for the endowment of inexhaustible funds with teachings from the *Huayan* (*Flower Garland*) and Vimalakīrti sūtras about the bodhisattva's inexhaustible storehouse of compassion for living beings. Their Inexhaustible Storehouse at the Huadu Monastery in Chang'an received donations from the faithful that were then lent out free of interest to the poor and needy of the empire. Because the goods of the storehouse were "inexhaustible," the donor acquired inexhaustible merit. This type of social welfare program was also seen in the development of pawnshops, another type of lending operation run by Buddhist monasteries.

Although in modern times many of the commercial ventures of Buddhist monasteries have been taken over by secular enterprise, the scope of Buddhist economic activities remains wide, and includes mutual-aid societies and cooperative banks, as well as modern forms of investment like credit cards and nonprofit corporations.

See also: **China; Economics; India; Monasticism**

Bibliography

Ch'en, Kenneth. *The Chinese Transformation of Buddhism.* Princeton, NJ: Princeton University Press, 1973.

Gernet, Jacques. *Buddhism in Chinese Society: An Economic History from the Fifth to the Tenth Centuries,* tr. Franciscus Verellen. New York: Columbia University Press, 1995.

Miller, Robert J. "Buddhist Monastic Economy: The Jisa Mechanism." *Comparative Studies in Society and History* 3, no. 4 (1961): 427–438.

Schopen, Gregory. "Doing Business for the Lord: Lending on Interest and Written Loan Contracts in the *Mūlasarvāstivāda-Vinaya.*" *Journal of the American Oriental Society* 114, no. 4 (1994): 527–554.

Schopen, Gregory. *Bones, Stones, and Buddhist Monks: Collected Papers on the Archaeology, Epigraphy, and Texts of Monastic Buddhism in India.* Honolulu: University of Hawaii Press, 1997.

Sizemore, Russell F., and Swearer, Donald K., eds. *Ethics, Wealth, and Salvation: A Study in Buddhist Social Ethics.* Columbia: University of South Carolina Press, 1990.

Jamie Hubbard

V

VAJRAYĀNA

Vajrayāna is an umbrella designation that denotes the final form of Buddhism to evolve in India; this term first comes into evidence in the eighth century. The Vajrayāna is often taken to be identical with Mantrayāna or Guhyamantrayāna, the vehicle of secret spells or incantations. In a very general sense, Vajrayāna means the vehicle (*yāna*) of the thunderbolt or of the adamantine scepter (*vajra*), although the designation of the male member as the *vajra* sometimes caused the Vajrayāna to be interpreted as the erotic vehicle, wherein sensuality may be employed for liberation. The modern attempt to proliferate terms with *-yāna* as a final element —(e.g., Kālacakrayāna, Sahajayāna, etc.) —is in error and none of these inauthentic neologisms appears in the literature. The Vajrayāna scriptures are the TANTRAS, and they with their commentaries present several different strategies to discuss the theoretical nature of this latest vehicle: Vajrayāna as a subset of the MAHĀYĀNA, Vajrayāna as the fruitional or advanced vehicle, and Vajrayāna as the third discipline of the sorcerer. Each of these will be considered in order.

Mahāyāna subset

According to this schematism, normative Indian Mahāyāna revealed two distinct ways (*naya*): the method of the perfections (*pāramitānaya*) and the method of MANTRAS (*mantranaya*). The former consists of the standard six or ten PĀRAMITĀ (PERFECTIONS) of the Mahāyāna and requires three incalculable eons to achieve the condition of buddhahood—the highest perfect awakening at the tenth or eleventh stage of the Mahāyānist path. The method of mantras, however, is said to confer this state in a single lifetime: buddhahood in this very body, as the literature affirms. This accelerated progress is possible because of the very powerful techniques associated with the use of mantras, so that the activity of the yogin's entire body, speech, and mind are employed in the process. Thus, the yogin visualizes BUDDHAS, BODHISATTVAS, or esoteric DIVINITIES either before him or identical to himself, recites mantras associated with such figures, and employs breathing techniques and other forms of physical yoga to accelerate the process of identification. Those following the esoteric path often maintain that the difference between the methods of perfection and the methods of mantras stems from their respective attitudes toward defilement. Whereas the method of perfections requires the elimination of defilement, in the method of mantras none of the physical or psychological functions are abandoned, but they are transformed into forms of the gnosis of awakening. In this light, the method of mantras was considered an easy path, without the difficulties inherent in the method of perfections. Similarly, the Vajrayāna was sometimes said to be preached as a response to the needs of those with inferior ability, who could not renounce the world but had to maintain a householder's position. However, as a subset of the Mahāyāna, a follower of the method of mantras is also expected to adhere to the vows of the bodhisattva, to practice the perfections as well and to operate on a continuum with the decorum expected of the bodhisattva.

Fruitional vehicle

The Vajrāyāna may also be called the fruitional vehicle (*phalayāna*), with the Mahāyāna classified as the causal vehicle (*hetuyāna*). In this schematism, the

Mahāyāna is a prelude to the Vajrayāna, for the latter is an advanced practice. Accordingly, one of the more important of the tantric scriptures, the *Guhyasamāja Tantra,* proclaims that the reason it had not been preached before was that there were no beings sufficiently advanced to hear it. It became revealed in the world once bodhisattvas with advanced practice arose to receive it. This means that the Vajrayāna is not just another, albeit faster, method but is inherently superior to normative Mahāyāna and not to be revealed to those of inferior faculties. In this way, the awakening conferred by the Vajrayāna was also different, for while the Mahāyāna led to the tenth or eleventh stage of the bodhisattva path, the citadel of the Eternal Buddha Vajradhara was said to be on the thirteenth stage, far advanced over the Mahāyānist idea of buddhahood.

The sorcerer's discipline

As the sorcerer's discipline (*vidyādharasaṃvara*), the Vajrayāna is laid out on a hierarchy of practice. The neophyte begins with the monastic discipline (*prātimokṣasaṃvara*), which may be formally that of the monk or of the devout layman (*upāsaka*) who has taken refuge and the five vows of the LAITY. Concomitantly, the views of the ABHIDHARMA and SAUTRĀNTIKA school may be studied. Once this practice is correctly established, then the practitioner may take the precepts of the bodhisattva (*bodhisattvasaṃvara*) and study the views of the YOGĀCĀRA SCHOOL and MADHYAMAKA SCHOOL. Finally, the precepts of the sorcerer may be taken through the rite of INITIATION, and they qualify the yogin to become the universal conqueror of the sorcerers (*vidyādharacakravartin*) so long as the PRECEPTS are scrupulously maintained. There are different lists of the precepts for the sorcerer's discipline, but the two most frequently encountered are vows to guard against the fourteen root transgressions:

1. Contempt for the teacher.
2. Transgressing the message of the Tathāgata.
3. Anger at members of the feast family.
4. Abandoning loving kindness.
5. Rejecting the thought of awakening.
6. Abusing the three vehicles.
7. Revealing secrets to unprepared people.
8. Disparaging the victor's body of instruction.
9. Doubt about the pure-natured dharma.
10. (Improper) love or dispassion toward evil people.
11. Imposition of other than nonduality upon reality.
12. Disparaging those with faith.
13. Not relying on the sacraments and vows.
14. Disparaging insight-filled women.

and the eight gross transgressions:

1. Seeking to take a consort who is without sacramental preparation.
2. Relying on unauthorized sacraments.
3. Arguing in the tantric feast.
4. Showing the secret dharma.
5. Teaching another dharma to those of faith, causing confusion.
6. Staying with śrāvakas for seven days.
7. Claiming the status of a *mantrin* without sufficient realization.
8. Teaching secrets to the unprepared.

The sorcerer's PRECEPTS were considered superior to those of the monk and bodhisattva, so that they took precedence in a hierarchy of value. If a yogin determined that observance of the sorcerer's precepts required the abandonment of one of the others, then some authorities considered this to be without fault, and many of the siddha hagiographies feature instances of exactly this behavior. Like other issues, though, this position was disputed, and much effort was expended by commentators to arrive at resolution of these problems. This question had a social component, for if the householder siddha was superior to the monk, then the latter should bow to him, despite the fact that prostrating before any layman is a clear violation of the monastic precepts.

The above analyses of the Vajrayāna reveal much inconsistency and a variety of opinions, which is not surprising for a complex and multifaceted system continuing to evolve over several centuries. As a result, among the many controversies that stirred discussion and polemical debate was whether the buddhahood of the Mahāyāna and the buddhahood of the Vajrayāna were in fact the same, or whether the latter was superior, with many subtle alternatives expressed. The relationship between practices and vehicles continued to be problematic so that as new practices arose, their precise placement and the shifting theoretical dynamic between the vehicles were extended topics of discussion. Particularly in Tibet, there tended to be a proliferation of vehicles, so that genres of literature came to represent new vehicles in the pages of some authors, although this was decidedly a minority opinion, found especially among the RNYING MA (NYINGMA).

See also: Tantra

Bibliography

Davidson, Ronald M. *Indian Esoteric Buddhism: A Social History of the Tantric Movement.* New York: Columbia University Press, 2002.

Lessing, Ferdinand D., and Wayman, Alex, trans. *Mkhas Grub Rje's Fundamentals of the Buddhist Trantras.* The Hague and Paris: Mouton, 1968.

Snellgrove, David L. *Indo-Tibetan Buddhism: Indian Buddhists and Their Tibetan Successors,* 2 vols. Boston: Shambhala, 1987.

Sobisch, Jan-Ulrich. *The Three-Vow Theories in Tibetan Buddhism: A Comparative Study of Major Traditions from the Twelfth through Nineteenth Centuries.* Wiesbaden, Germany: Reichert, 2002.

Strickmann, Michel. "The Consecration Sūtra: A Buddhist Book of Spells." In *Chinese Buddhist Apocrypha.*, ed. Robert E. Buswell, Jr. Honolulu: University of Hawaii Press, 1990.

Strickmann, Michel. *Mantras et mandarins: le bouddhisme tantrique en Chine.* Paris: Gallimard, 1996.

RONALD M. DAVIDSON

VAṂSA

The Pāli word *vaṃsa* literally refers to "lineage" or "bamboo," but it acquired the technical meaning of a "chronicle" early in the first millennium C.E. among THERAVĀDA Buddhists on the island of Sri Lanka. While many historical texts authored by Theravāda Buddhists in the ancient and medieval periods include the word *vaṃsa* in their titles, not all narrative accounts of the past are referred to in this way, nor do all *vaṃsas* share the same style and content. The *Mahāvaṃsa* (*Great Chronicle*) is arguably the best-known *vaṃsa* in modern times, yet its open-ended narrative, which has been periodically extended since the fifth century C.E., deviates from many other Theravāda *vaṃsas* whose narratives follow a discernible plot and reach a point of closure.

Modern scholars deduce that the *vaṃsa* genre of Buddhist literature grew out of ancient commentaries written on the Pāli CANON. The Theravāda tradition holds that these commentaries were brought to Sri Lanka by a monk named Mahinda in the third century B.C.E. Within a few centuries, excerpts dealing with the history of Buddhism in India and the events surrounding its establishment in Lanka were crafted into independent *vaṃsas* that recount events connected with the life of the Buddha and the historical instantiation of his teaching (*śāsana*; Pāli, *sāsana*). While Pāli *vaṃsas* appear well-suited to legitimate monastic lineages and inspire devotion in Buddhist communities, European scholars in the nineteenth and early twentieth centuries valued these texts for their detailed and fairly reliable accounts of South and Southeast Asian history. Still, many scholars point out that these texts mix historical facts with legendary embellishments.

Theravāda *vaṃsas* typically convey information about the life and death of the Buddha, the transmission of the dharma, and the establishment of the SAṄGHA (community of monks) and relics in other lands. Pious and sometimes heroic kings such as Duṭṭhagāmaṇī (161–137 B.C.E.) in Sri Lanka and Tilakapanattu (1495–1525 C.E.) in Thailand are regularly extolled, suggesting that the *vaṃsas* also provided images of virtuous and powerful Buddhist kings for later individuals to emulate. The oldest extant *vaṃsas*, the *Mahāvaṃsa* and its fourth-century predecessor the *Dīpavaṃsa* (*Chronicle of the Island*), recount the establishment of Buddhism in Sri Lanka. Other Sri Lankan *vaṃsas* written between the tenth and fourteenth centuries, such as the *Mahābodhivaṃsa* (*Chronicle of the Bodhi Tree*) and the *Thūpavaṃsa* (*Chronicle of the Relic Shrine*), often focus their narratives on particular relics of the Buddha that were purportedly brought from India and enshrined in Sri Lanka. The *Anāgatavaṃsa* (*Chronicle of the Future Buddha*) is distinguished by the fact that it narrates future events connected with the coming of the next Buddha MAITREYA (Pāli, Metteyya). Several of these *vaṃsas* were subsequently translated into a literary form of the vernacular Sinhala language, and their narratives were often substantially revised in the process.

The *vaṃsa* genre was passed along from Sri Lanka to the Buddhist lands of Southeast Asia, fulfilling many similar functions in legitimating Theravāda monastic lineages, deepening piety, and extolling kings. The sixteenth-century Pāli chronicle titled *Jinakālamālī* (*Sheaf of Garlands of the Epochs of the Conqueror*) details some of the historical events associated with the establishment of Theravāda Buddhism in Thailand. In Burma (Myanmar), the nineteenth-century *Sāsanavaṃsa* (*Chronicle of the Dispensation*) performs an analogous role, connecting Burmese Buddhist traditions with those found in India and Sri Lanka from an earlier age.

See also: **History; Sinhala, Buddhist Literature in**

Bibliography

Berkwitz, Stephen C. "Emotions and Ethics in Buddhist History: The *Sinhala Thūpavaṃsa* and the Work of Virtue." *Religion* 31, no. 2 (2001): 155–173.

Geiger, Wilhelm, trans. *The Mahāvaṃsa: Or the Great Chronicle of Ceylon* (1912), assisted by Mabel Haynes Bode. Reprint, London: Pali Text Society, 1980.

Jayawickrama, N. A., trans. *The Sheaf of Garlands of the Epochs of the Conqueror: Being a Translation of Jinakālamālīpakaraṇaṁ.* London: Pali Text Society, 1968.

Smith, Bardwell L., ed. *Religion and Legitimation of Power in Sri Lanka.* Chambersburg, PA: Anima Books, 1978.

Walters, Jonathan S. "Buddhist History: The Sri Lankan Pali Vaṃsas and Their Commentary." In *Querying the Medieval: Texts and the History of Practices in South Asia,* ed. Ronald Inden, Jonathan Walters, and Daud Ali. Oxford: Oxford University Press, 2000.

STEPHEN C. BERKWITZ

VASUBANDHU

While there is much disagreement concerning Vasubandhu's exact dates, most scholars agree that he lived sometime between the mid-fourth and mid-fifth centuries. Born in Puruṣapura (present-day Peshawar, Pakistan) to the same mother as his half-brother ASAṄGA, the putative founder of the YOGĀCĀRA SCHOOL, Vasubandhu left his Brahman upbringing to join the Vaibhāṣika Buddhists in their Kashmiri stronghold. While there he brilliantly and comprehensively summarized Vaibhāṣika doctrines in a roughly seven-hundred-stanza verse text entitled *Abhidharmakośa* (*Treasury of Abhidharma*). The prose autocommentary, ABHIDHARMAKOŚABHĀṢYA, that he wrote for these verses demonstrates his intellectual restlessness and growing dissatisfaction with Vaibhāṣika teachings as it critiques numerous Vaibhāṣika positions while siding with the positions of other Buddhist groups, most notably the SAUTRĀNTIKA. Vasubandhu eventually abandoned the teachings of the MAINSTREAM BUDDHIST SCHOOLS for MAHĀYĀNA, and he became a Yogācāra adept under Asaṅga's influence.

Vasubandhu's literary output was prodigious, and his works have had a deep impact on subsequent Buddhist developments. The *Abhidharmakośabhāṣya* continues to receive serious study by East Asian, Tibetan, and modern Western scholars, all of whom treat it as a major sourcebook for medieval Indian Buddhist doctrinal positions and terminology. Texts written during Vasubandhu's transitional period include *Karmasiddhiprakaraṇa* (*Investigation Establishing [the Correct Understanding] of Karma*), *Vādavidhi* (*Debate Methods*), and the *Pañcaskandhaprakaraṇa* (*Investigation of the Five Aggregates*). Vasubandhu's Yogācāra texts include the *Viṃśatikā* (*Twenty Verses*), the *Triṃśikā* (*Thirty Verses*), a crucial commentary on Maitreya-Asaṅga's *Madhyāntavibhāga* (*Madhyāntavibhāgabhāṣya*), and a commentary on Asaṅga's *Mahāyānasaṃgraha.* In addition, he is credited with commentaries on several Mahāyāna sūtras, including the DIAMOND SŪTRA, the NIRVĀṆA SŪTRA, the *Mañjuśrī Sūtra, Daśabhūmika-sūtra* (*Ten Stages Sūtra*), and the LOTUS SŪTRA (SADDHARMAPUṆḌARĪKA-SŪTRA). The latter two commentaries were especially influential in East Asian Buddhism.

Bibliography

Anacker, Stefan, trans. and ed. *Seven Works of Vasubandhu: The Buddhist Psychological Doctor.* Delhi: Motilal Banarsidass, 1984.

Kochumuttom, Thomas. *A Buddhist Doctrine of Experience: A New Translation and Interpretation of the Works of Vasubandhu the Yogacarin.* Delhi: Motilal Banarsidass, 1982. Reprint, 1999.

La Vallée Poussin, Louis de. *Abhidharmakośabhāṣyam,* 4 vols., tr. Leo M. Pruden. Berkeley, CA: Asian Humanities Press, 1988–1990.

DAN LUSTHAUS

VIDYĀDHARA

Vidyādhara (Pāli, *vijjādhara*; possessor of magical power) is a master of esoteric knowledge, a magician or sorcerer. In Indian Buddhist and Hindu sources the *vidyādhara* is depicted as a human or supernatural being who, by means of various occult sciences, develops the ability to perform marvelous feats like flying through the air, transmuting base metals into gold, becoming impervious to weapons, and so on. In the MAHĀYĀNA tantric tradition of Bengal, the term *vidyādhara* became a synonym for the MAHĀSIDDHA or "great accomplished one," a tantric master who attains liberation as an immortal wonder worker. Classically eighty-four in number, *mahāsiddhas* either ascend alive to the paradise of the ḌĀKINĪS or remain among humans until the advent of the Future Buddha MAITREYA (Pāli, Metteyya). From either abode, *mahāsiddhas* continuously protect the Buddha's religion and instruct worthy disciples in their liberating mysteries.

A similar tradition from Southeast Asia is the esoteric *weikza* cult of Burma (Myanmar). The Burmese *weikza* or *weikza-do* (from Pāli *vijjādhara*) is a kind of semi-immortal sorcerer committed to the protection of Buddhism and destined to remain alive until the coming of Metteyya. Possessed of an incorruptible body, the *weikza* teaches human disciples how to attain magical power and extraordinarily long life through such means as the recitation of spells, the casting of runes, and alchemy. It is a premise of the system that these techniques depend for the efficacy on a simultaneous mastery of meditative trance (*dhyāna*; Pali, *jhāna*). While almost certainly descended from the tantric tradition of Bengal, the *weikza* cult has long been domesticated to the dominant worldview of Burmese THERAVĀDA Buddhism and no longer retains any overt Mahāyāna elements.

Bibliography

Ferguson, John P., and Mendelson, E. Michael. "Masters of the Buddhist Occult: The Burmese *Weikzas*." *Contributions to Asian Studies* 16 (1981): 62–80.

Snellgrove, David. *Indo-Tibetan Buddhism: Indian Buddhists and Their Tibetan Successors.* Boston: Shambhala, 1987.

PATRICK A. PRANKE

VIETNAM

Although both THERAVĀDA and MAHĀYĀNA Buddhism exist in Vietnam, the kind of Buddhism that is most influential and most widely practiced by the majority of Vietnamese Buddhists is Sinitic Mahāyāna Buddhism. Indian and Chinese scholastic traditions have had little if any impact, while Chinese Chan and Pure Land are the only major schools that provide philosophical and religious foundations for the ideas and practices of Buddhism in Vietnam. Incorporation of popular religions and Vietnam's political involvement with China and France were also instrumental in shaping certain characteristics of Vietnamese Buddhism.

History

From the beginning to independence. Evidence indicates that Buddhism had come to Jiaozhou (as Vietnam, a Chinese protectorate, was then called) by the second century of the common era. Scattered hints in Chinese history inform us that Buddhism in Jiaozhou was consistent with the cultural and religious influences to which the religion was exposed in the first millennium C.E. The presence and activities of figures such as Mou Bo (second century C.E.) and Kang Senghui (third century C.E.) were indicative of the integration of Jiaozhou into the cosmopolitan Buddhist world of the time.

By the late sixth century C.E., Buddhism was already a part of the cultural and religious life of many people in Jiaozhou. Monks from various parts of Asia were regular visitors to Jiaozhou, and they contributed to Buddhist studies and activities there. They also inspired native monks to go on PILGRIMAGE to India or China to study the dharma. Little record of Buddhism in Vietnam during the Tang period (618–907) remains, but there are hints of a continuing pattern of links between Vietnam and other parts of the Buddhist world: visits to China by monks from Vietnam, or Chinese and Central Asian monks who stopped in Jiaozhou on their way to India. In addition, monks from Jiaozhou who made prolonged stays in China and India were well versed in Sanskrit and they assisted Indian and Central Asian monks in translation work.

Early Vietnamese dynasties (968–1010). By the time Vietnam gained independence from Chinese political hegemony in the tenth century, Buddhism had existed in Vietnam for nearly a millennium. The early Vietnamese dynasties found in the Buddhist clergy a cultural force that could assist them with their political agenda. The founder of the Đinh dynasty (968–980) instituted a system of hierarchical ranks for court officials, Buddhists monks, and Daoist priests. This indicates that Buddhist monks already held a recognized place in the social and cultural order of Vietnamese life, requiring the Đinh dynasty to integrate Buddhism into the structure of the state.

Lý dynasty (1010–1225). The Lý kings continued to draw support from Buddhism, and in return they patronized Buddhism on a large scale. Eminent monks served at court and exerted great influence in political

Monks dry rice at the Bat Temple at Soc Trang in the Mekong Delta, Vietnam, 1994. © Steve Raymer/Corbis. Reproduced by permission.

matters. The Lý kings also sent envoys to China to bring back Buddhist texts so that copies could be made and placed in the major monasteries. Some Chan classics, particularly those of the *chuandeng lu* (transmission of the lamp) and *yulu* (recorded sayings) genres, found their way to Vietnam and attracted the attention of learned monks. In brief, under the Lý, Chan became an integral part of the Vietnamese Buddhist worldview.

Trần dynasty (1225–1400). Under the Trần, Chan learning became more established with the arrival of Chinese Chan monks and literature. Starting from around the end of the Lý period, a number of Chinese Chan monks belonging to the Linji and Caodong schools came to Vietnam to spread Buddhism. Among their disciples were members of the Trần aristocracy, including the kings themselves. The Trúc Lâm *Thiền* (Chan) School, the first Vietnamese Chan Buddhist school, was founded by Trần Nhân Tông (1258–1309), the third king of the Trần dynasty. Unfortunately, only fragments of writings by the first three patriarchs of this school are extant. Through these writings we can see that Trúc Lâm Thiền modeled itself on Chinese patriarchal Chan. The most extensive Buddhist writing from the Trần is the *Khóa Hư Lục* (*Instructions on Emptiness*) composed by Trần Thái Tông (1218–1277), the founder of the Trần dynasty. The *Khóa Hu Lục* was the first collection of prose works on Buddhism in Vietnam. It includes essays written in different literary styles on a variety of subjects on Buddhist teachings and practices.

The most important accomplishment for Buddhism under the Trần was the composition of the *Thiền Uyển Tập Anh* (*Outstanding Figures of the Chan Community*) by an unknown author around the mid-fourteenth century. The author of the *Thiền Uyển* portrays Vietnamese Buddhism as the offshoot of Chinese Chan, an approach that left indelible traces on subsequent generations of historians of Vietnamese Buddhism.

The (later) Lý dynasty and the Northern-Southern dynasties (1428–1802). The advent of the Lý dynasty (1428–1527) marked a resurgence of Confucianism and the waning of Buddhist fortunes. Under the Lý and Trần, civil service examinations based on the Chinese classics were given to select men who were chosen to serve at court. This created a Confucian intelligentsia who became extremely influential and rivaled the influences of Buddhist monks. The Lý kings were ardent supporters of Confucianism and they passed restrictive measures on Buddhism, but they continued to support popular Buddhist activities. The period of the Northern/Southern division (1528–1802) was one of political turmoil, but Thiền Buddhism was not idle during this period, and there were efforts to revive Trúc Lâm Thiền. Chinese Linji and Caodong monks also came to Vietnam to teach, and several new Thiền schools were founded. The most influential were the two Linji sects: the Nguyên Thiền and the Liễu Quán in the south.

Nguyễn dynasty (1802–1945). The Nguyễn kings considered Confucianism to be a useful force in their efforts to centralize power, and there was an attempt to depoliticize Buddhism because it was considered detrimental to the Confucian hierarchy. Although the majority of court officials were Confucian and were averse to Buddhism, Buddhism was still appealing to aristocratic women and did not lose its grip on the masses. Buddhism also exerted great influence on some of the most eminent literati of the time, and the Nguyễn was a period of ardent Buddhist scholarly activity. However, the contributions of eminent monks of this period consisted mostly in compiling, editing, and publishing texts.

The French period. Vietnam was under French rule from 1883 to 1945, and French dominion presented new pressures for the Vietnamese Buddhists. Under foreign rule, Vietnamese Buddhists felt the need to create a more socially and politically engaged Buddhism. Many eminent monks were ardent patriots and leaders of insurgent movements; intellectual Vietnamese Buddhists were inspired by reformed movements in other East Asian countries in the 1920s and, in particular, by the Chinese monk TAIXU (1890–1947). Buddhist magazines and periodicals in colloquial Vietnamese (*quốc ngữ*) began to appear with a view to addressing political and social issues.

During the 1930s three new associations of Buddhist studies were established in the three parts of Vietnam. All were guided and supported by learned clergy and laypeople with exposure to Western culture. There were attempts at consolidating the three associations into a unified SAṄGHA, but the efforts were hindered by the repressive policy of the French and a lack of communication.

Postcolonial struggle. When Emperor Bảo Đại (1913–1997) assumed the role of head of state of South Vietnam he signed Decree No. 10, which followed the French policy of relegating all religions to the status of "public associations," with the exception of Catholic and Protestant missions. On assuming power in 1955, Ngô Đình Diệm (1901–1963) retained Decree No. 10. In 1957 Diệm also eliminated the Buddha's birthday (Vesak) from the list of official holidays.

Diệm's policy toward Buddhism led to many Buddhist resistance movements during the 1960s, which ultimately resulted in the overthrow of his government and inspired a Buddhist revival. The Vietnamese Unified Buddhist Church was founded in South Vietnam, Vạn Hạnh University, the first Buddhist university, was established in Saigon, and eminent monks such as Thích Trí Quang and Thích Tâm Châu became household names. A charismatic young monk with an American education, THICH NHAT HANH (1926–), the founder of School of Youth for Social Service at Vạn Hạnh University, became an overnight celebrity. However, due to inexperience on the part of the monks, division among the leadership, and a lack of a capable lay elite class, Vietnamese Buddhists failed to seize a rare opportunity to reform and explore the potential of Buddhist culture in their country.

From 1975 to the beginning of the twenty-first century. Vietnamese refugees began migrating to Europe and North America in 1975 in the aftermath of the fall of South Vietnam. In a relatively short time many temples were built as part of the emigrants' efforts to preserve their Vietnamese way of life. Buddhist practices at most such temples continued the patterns the patrons had followed in Vietnam. However, there has been a renewed interest in Thiền in the West, inspired by the popularity of Nhat Hanh. Some eminent Thiền teachers such as Thích Thanh Từ have been invited to the United States to give instructions on Chan meditation.

Practice

Little change or sectarian development has taken place in the practice of Vietnamese Buddhists since medieval times. This is probably due to the limited repertoire of Buddhist literature to which the tradition has been exposed. In brief, Vietnamese Buddhism is basically nonsectarian, and most Vietnamese Buddhists—cleric and

A monk sounds a bell at a Buddhist temple at My The in the Mekong Delta area of Vietnam. © Tim Page/Corbis. Reproduced by permission.

lay—regardless of their intellectual disparities, practice a composite form of Buddhism that runs the gamut of popular Buddhist practices in other East Asian countries. Although most clergy and educated lay Buddhists maintain that Vietnamese Buddhism is predominantly Chan with elements of Pure Land and TANTRA, Chan elements actually figure very little, if at all, in the practice of most Vietnamese Buddhists.

Vietnamese Buddhist practices can be conveniently outlined under two major headings: those that are limited to the clergy and those that involve lay participation. The first group of practices includes ritual ordinations, religious disciplines, monastic rituals, accession ceremonies, and summer retreats. The second group consists of religious observances and rituals that occur on a regular or occasional basis.

Occasional observances include celebrating the *vía* day of buddhas and bodhisattvas (i.e., their birthday or awakening day) and commemorative rituals relating to Śākyamuni Buddha (his birthday, his enlightenment, and his decease), taking the Bodhisattva precepts, taking the eight precepts (*bát quan trai*), participating in prayer services for peace (*cầu an*) and for rebirth in AMITĀBHA's Pure Land (*cầu siêu*), engaging in repentance, and freeing captured animals. Among these practices, praying for peace for the country and the world can be an individual or communal act. Repentance is a liturgy that takes place in the evening twice a month at the full moon and new moon. It consists of, among other things, the recitation of the names of 108 buddhas and bowing each time a buddha's name is recited. Freeing captured animals (*phóng sinh*) is one of the ways to accumulate merit (*phước*), an essential element of Vietnamese Buddhist practice. It is fair to say that most Vietnamese Buddhists are more concerned with accumulating merit than with cultivating wisdom. The most common forms of merit-making are contributing to the printing of Buddhist books, to the building and upkeep of temples, and to the support of monks and nuns.

Also included in this category of special practices are ceremonies and festivals that incorporate elements of folk beliefs, such as the New Year festival (Tết) and the Ullambana festival celebrating filial piety and commemorating past ancestors. These festivals and various death rituals involve the widest participation of the populace, including those who are only nominal Buddhists.

The most essential regular practice is daily chanting, which consists of three intervals of service performed at dawn, noon, and dusk. This practice includes chanting sūtras, reciting MANTRAS and DHĀRAṆĪs and buddhas' names, and circumambulation. A number of the principal Mahāyāna sūtras have been translated into Vietnamese, but not every sūtra is chanted. In most cases, only devotional sūtras or chapters from them are chanted. The three most chanted sūtras are the HEART SŪTRA, LOTUS SŪTRA (SADDHARMAPUṆḌARĪKA-SŪTRA), and *Amitābha Sūtra.*

Meditation is also an integral part of the Buddhist program of practice in Vietnam, and tends to include sitting quietly contemplating the magnificence of Amitābha Buddha's Pure Land or mentally reciting the names of buddhas and bodhisattvas. Most monks, nuns, and a number of laypeople sit in meditation occasionally, only a few regularly, but not every Vietnamese monastic is an adept in meditation.

See also: **Chan School; Festivals and Calendrical Rituals; Ghost Festival; Merit and Merit-Making; Pure**

Land Buddhism; Southeast Asia, Buddhist Art in; Vietnamese, Buddhist Influences on Literature in

Bibliography

Lê Mạnh Thát. *Lịch Sử Phật Giáo Việt Nam* (History of Vietnamese Buddhism), 3 vols. Hue, Vietnam: Thuận Hóa Publishing House, 1999–2000.

Mật Thể. *Việt Nam Phật Giáo Sử Lược* (A Brief History of Vietnamese Buddhism). Reprint, Saigon, Vietnam: Minh Đức, 1960.

Nguyen Cuong Tu. *Zen in Medieval Vietnam: A Study and Translation of the Thiền Uyển Tập Anh.* Honolulu: University of Hawaii Press, 1997.

Nguyễn Lang. *Việt Nam Phật Giáo Sử Luận* (Essays on History of Vietnamese Buddhism). Hanoi, Vietnam: Literature Publishing House, 2000.

Nguyễn Tài Thư. *Lịch Sử Phật Giáo Việt Nam* (History of Vietnamese Buddhism). Hanoi, Vietnam: Social Science Publishing House, 1988.

Thanh Từ Thích et al., eds. *Thiền Học Đời Trần* (Zen in the Tran Dynasty). Saigon, Vietnam: Saigon Institute of Vietnamese Buddhist Studies, 1992.

Thien-An Thich. *Buddhism and Zen in Vietnam.* Rutland, VT, and Tokyo: Charles E. Tuttle, 1975.

Trần Hồng Liên. *Đạo Phật trong Cộng Đồng Người Việt ở Nam Bộ – Việt Nam: Từ Thế Kỷ XVII đến 1975* (Buddhism in the Vietnamese Communities in South Vietnam: From 17th Century to 1975). Hanoi, Vietnam: Social Science Publishing House, 2000.

CUONG TU NGUYEN

VIETNAM, BUDDHIST ART IN.

See **Southeast Asia, Buddhist Art in**

VIETNAMESE, BUDDHIST INFLUENCES ON LITERATURE IN

Vietnam was ruled by the Chinese from 111 B.C.E. to the tenth century C.E. As a result, classical Chinese was the official language of Vietnam until around the middle of the nineteenth century. During the Trần dynasty (1225–1400) in medieval Vietnam there were sporadic efforts to create a system of demotic script (Nôm) to be used for transcribing vernacular Vietnamese. However, this script was based on Chinese radicals and phonetics and required fluency in classical Chinese, so it was never able to replace classical Chinese.

Vietnam came into contact with European countries, particularly France, in the seventeenth century. Within three centuries, and after various modifications, Vietnamese was written exclusively in the Roman alphabet, partly as a result of the work of Catholic missionaries. This romanized Vietnamese was referred to as *quốc ngữ* (national language) and it became the official language of the country in the middle of the nineteenth century.

From the thirteenth century C.E., when the first Buddhist writings were composed, to the early twentieth century, most Buddhist literature in Vietnam was in classical Chinese, although a number of texts contain chapters, glosses, or afterwords in Nôm. There were also some writings entirely in Nôm, but these works did not gain as wide a circulation as those written in Chinese.

Magazines and newspapers in *quốc ngữ* were first published in Vietnam as early as 1865, but most of these early *quốc ngữ* periodicals were published by the government and advanced particular political and propagandistic agendas. Buddhist literature in *quốc ngữ* did not appear until the 1920s; it was inspired by motivations to modernize Buddhism and to make it more appealing to the general populace. It was a time when classical Chinese studies was on the wane and educated Vietnamese Buddhists, both clerical and lay, believed that the use of *quốc ngữ* would help people through the transitional period.

Magazines and periodicals

The *Pháp Âm* (*Sounds of Dharma*) and *Phật Hóa Thanh Niên* (*Buddhist Teachings for the Youth*) were the first two Buddhist magazines published in *quốc ngữ* in the 1920s. In the 1930s, three more magazines, the *Từ Bi Âm* (*Sounds of Compassion*), the *Viên Âm* (*Sounds of Perfection*), and the *Đuốc Tuệ* (*Torch of Wisdom*), were launched by the three associations of BUDDHIST STUDIES in Saigon, Hue, and Hanoi, the major cities in the three parts of Vietnam. The articles in these magazines covered topics beyond the boundary of Buddhist doctrines and practices to address issues such as Buddhism and society, Buddhism and science, and Buddhism and modernization. This pattern continued in subsequent decades and reached a high point between 1954 and 1975. For example, *Tư Tưởng* (*Thought*), a journal published by Vạn Hạnh Buddhist University in Saigon in the late 1960s, was a pioneering effort in the comparative studies of Buddhism and continental philosophy.

Books

Vernacular Buddhist literature in the form of books can be divided into two categories: books on a variety of topics on Buddhism and translations, mostly from Chinese, of Buddhist texts. Around 1932 in Saigon, the lay Buddhist scholar Đoàn Trung Còn founded a publishing house named Phật Học Tùng Thư (*Buddhist Publications*), which published a number of books covering a wide range of Buddhist topics. In 1940 the Phật Học Tùng Thư began publishing books aimed at a young audience. Some of the most prolific authors in this period, such as the monk Thiện Chiếu, aimed at explaining Buddhism from a modern perspective to a new generation of intellectuals with a Western education. In sum, the majority of Vietnamese books on Buddhism were written with a view to making Buddhism accessible to the general populace. They range from Buddhist catechism to instructions on *niệm Phật* (contemplating the name of Amitābha Buddha, NENBUTSU).

Translations of Buddhist texts

Most Buddhist literature in *quốc ngữ* consists of translations of Buddhist texts from Chinese. *Quốc ngữ* translations of Buddhist texts began in the 1920s with the translation of the *Guiyuan zhizhi* (*Returning to the Sources*), a Chinese text on the practice of Pure Land Buddhism. During the 1930s the Phật Học Tùng Thư published translations of the major Mahāyāna sūtras and philosophical treatises such as the LOTUS SŪTRA (SADDHARMAPUṆḌARĪKA-SŪTRA), the *Amitābha Sūtra,* the LIUZU TAN JING (*Platform Sūtra),* the DIAMOND SŪTRA, and the AWAKENING OF FAITH (DASHENG QIXIN LUN). This effort continued in subsequent decades, and eventually other principal Mahāyāna sūtras, such as the *Perfection of Wisdom Sūtras,* the *Ratnakuṭa-sūtra,* and the *Śuraṅgama–sūtra,* were also translated into Vietnamese. In the 1970s the monk Thích Minh Châu, then rector of Vạn Hạnh Buddhist University, translated the Pāli *nikāyas* into *quốc ngữ*. Given the fact that Vietnamese Buddhism is predominantly Mahāyāna, Minh Châu's work was a remarkable contribution to the country's Buddhist literature. Since the fall of South Vietnam in 1975, there have been massive reprints of Buddhists texts, mostly *quốc ngữ* translations by Vietnamese Buddhists living overseas.

The most important vernacular Buddhist works in Vietnamese, however, are manuals for daily chanting and occasional rituals. These manuals vary from one temple to another, but they contain almost the same materials: complete or partial *quốc ngữ* translations or transliterations of the Buddhist texts that are used in daily and special rituals and observances.

In sum, Buddhist literature in *quốc ngữ* includes an array of writings on a variety of topics covering basic Buddhist teachings and practices, together with translations of the major Buddhist sūtras. Most were published for practical religious use and to address the immediate needs of Vietnamese Buddhists. Occasionally, books on aspects of Buddhist philosophy or translations of philosophical treatises are published. For instance, there are *quốc ngữ* translations of some principal treatises of the MADHYAMAKA and YOGĀCĀRA schools (the two major philosophical schools of Mahāyāna Buddhism), but these are intended more for personal intellectual gratification than as part of a larger systematic program of sectarian learning or practice.

See also: **Pure Land Buddhism; Ritual; Vietnam**

Bibliography

Nguyễn Khắc Kham. *Sơ-thảo mục-lục thư-tịch về Phật-Giáo Việt-Nam* (A Bibliography on Vietnamese Buddhism). Saigon, Vietnam: Ministry of National Education, 1963.

Nguyễn Lang. *Việt Nam Phật Giáo Sử Luận* (Essays on History of Vietnamese Buddhism). Hanoi, Vietnam: Literature Publishing House, 2000.

Phạm Thế Ngũ. *Việt Nam Văn Học Sử Giản Ước Tân Biên* (A New Concise History of Vietnamese Literature), Vol. 1. Saigon, Vietnam: Quốc Học Tùng Thư, 1961–1965.

Tran, Van Giap. *Contribution à l'Etude des Livres Annamites conservés à l'Ecole Francaise d'Extrême-Orient.* Tokyo: La Societe Internationale du Bouddhisme au Japon, 1943.

Trần Hồng Liên, *Phật Giáo Nam Bộ Từ Thế Kỷ 17 đến 1975* (Buddhism in the South: From 17th Century to 1975). Ho Chi Minh City, Vietnam: Phố Hồ Chí Minh City Publishing House, 1996.

CUONG TU NGUYEN

VIJÑĀNA. *See* **Consciousness, Theories of**

VIJÑĀNAVĀDA

The label Vijñānavāda (consciousness school) was applied to the epistemological and ontological positions of the YOGĀCĀRA SCHOOL and the Buddhist logic tradition in the polemical debate literature of their medieval

Indian opponents. These Buddhist and non-Buddhist disputants used the term *vijñānavāda* to emphasize the Yogācāra assertion that external objects do not exist, but consciousness does, thus inviting an idealist interpretation that these opponents (especially the realist schools, such as Nyāya, Mīmāṃsikā, and SAUTRĀNTIKA) refuted at great length. Aspects of Buddhist epistemology associated with the Vijñānavāda position include claims that parts, not wholes, are real; claims that particulars are real, not universals; the notion of momentariness; and the assertion that sense-objects (*viṣaya*), because they appear only within cognitive acts, are not external to the consciousness in which they appear.

The term *Vijñānavāda* was a misnomer because Yogācāra epistemology actually claimed that while cognitive objects (*viṣaya*) appearing in consciousness were real, the thing-itself (*vastu*)—which is singular, momentary, and causally produced—was not apprehended by ordinary perception. Yogācāra denies the realist claim that the perceptible object (*viṣaya*) has a corresponding *vastu* as its referent (*artha*), since a referent, whether perceptual or linguistic, is always a cognitive construction. However, once the consciousness stream is purified of emotional and cognitive obstructions (*kleśāvaraṇa* and *jñeyāvaraṇa*, respectively), a *vastu* can be cognized by direct, immediate cognition (jñāna), unmediated by cognitive, conceptual overlays (*prapañca, kalpanā, parikalpita*). This type of cognition is called *nirvikalpa* (devoid of conceptual construction).

Bibliography

Shastri, D. N. *The Philosophy of Nyāya-Vaiśeṣika and Its Conflict with the Buddhist Dignāga School (Critique of Indian Realism).* Reprint, New Delhi: Bharatiya Vidyā Prakashan, 1976.

Stcherbatsky, F. Theodore. *Buddhist Logic* (1930), 2 vols. Reprint, New York: Dover, 1962.

DAN LUSTHAUS

VIMALAKĪRTI

Vimalakīrti is a nonhistorical human BODHISATTVA known primarily as the main protagonist of an early MAHĀYĀNA sūtra called the *Vimalakīrtinirdeśa* (*The Teaching of Vimalakīrti*). Although a layman, Vimalakīrti is depicted as possessing the highest wisdom and attainment. Out of sympathy with the suffering of all beings and as a strategy for teaching (UPĀYA), he feigns a serious illness and, knowing this, the Buddha instructs each of his śrāvaka and bodhisattva disciples to ask after his health. All are reluctant to go, having been humiliated by Vimalakīrti's greater wisdom before, and only Mañjuśrī agrees. All the others follow to watch the encounter, the climax of which is a discussion in which Vimalakīrti asks each bodhisattva in turn how one enters nondualism. Mañjuśrī offers the ultimate insight that all dharmas are beyond discourse, but is trumped by Vimalakīrti, who remains silent when asked for his own answer. Vimalakīrti also displays a dry sense of humor, directed primarily against ŚĀRIPUTRA, as the main representative of the śrāvaka community.

As a spiritually accomplished layman Vimalakīrti offered an influential model for Buddhists in East Asia, where Indian Buddhist monasticism conflicted with Chinese social values. His popularity led to his depiction in painting and a number of lesser known texts in which he was the protagonist. The *Vimalakīrtinirdeśa* is also popular amongst Western Buddhists and has been translated into English several times.

See also: **Laity**

Bibliography

Lamotte, Étienne. *The Teaching of Vimalakīrti,* tr. Sara Boin. London: Pāli Text Society, 1976.

Watson, Burton. *The Vimalakīrti Sūtra.* New York: Columbia University Press, 1996.

ANDREW SKILTON

VINAYA

The word *vinaya* is derived from a Sanskrit verb that can mean to lead or take away, remove; to train, tame, or guide (e.g., a horse); or to educate, instruct, direct. All these meanings or shades of meaning intermingle in the Buddhist use of the term, where it refers both to the specific teachings attributed to the Buddha that bear on behavior, and to the literary sources in which those teachings are found. *Vinaya* is, in short, the body of teachings and texts that tell the ordained follower of the Buddha how he or she should or must behave. An ordained follower of the Buddha is one who has undergone a formal ritual of ORDINATION as a part of which he or she proclaims himself or herself able to follow the established rules. He or she does not—it is important to note—take a vow to do so. In fact, vows of the type that characterize Western monastic groups are unknown, at least in the Indian Buddhist world. Having undertaken the formal act of ordination, an individual becomes a bhikṣu (male) or *bhikṣuṇī* (female), and the vinaya, strictly speaking, applies only to bhikṣus and *bhikṣuṇīs*, although there are also rules for "novices."

Bhikṣu literally means a beggar or mendicant, but it is clear from their contents that by the time the vinaya texts that we have were compiled, many, perhaps most, bhikṣus did not beg for their food. This and the kind of commitment required by Buddhist ordination is nicely illustrated by the section in an ordination ceremony dealing with food. The officiant says to the individual seeking ordination: "Are you, named so-and-so, able to subsist, for as long as you live, with alms food?" The newly ordained must say: "I am able." Then the officiant immediately says: "Extra allowable acquisitions are boiled rice or porridge made from flour, water, melted butter, and pomegranate, etc., or made from milk, or soup made from cream, etc., or food provided on the fifth day festival, or the eighth or the fourteenth or the fifteenth day festival, or food regularly provided by donors . . . or again any other allowable alms food that might arise from the religious community itself or an individual—in regard to your acceptance of that, due measure must be practiced. Will you be fully and completely cognizant of such a condition?" The newly ordained must say: "I will be fully and completely cognizant."

Since all extant vinayas appear to have similar provisions, it must be obvious that Buddhist bhikṣus need not be—by virtue of their own rules—beggars. They had, or were allowed, rich foods, permanent provisions offered by the LAITY, and their religious community could also provide their food. In fact, both Buddhist vinaya texts and non-Buddhist literary sources indicate that Buddhist bhikṣus had a reputation for eating very well indeed. In the former there are stories of more than one Buddhist MONK dying as a result of overindulging in rich foods, and even accounts that suggest that the group's fine fare could motivate outsiders to seek admission. In the *Pravrajyāvastu* of the MŪLASARVĀSTIVĀDA-VINAYA, for example, a text begins, "A member of another religious group came to the Jetavana monastery. He saw that lovely seats had been arranged there and excellent food and drink had been prepared. He thought to himself: 'The enjoyment of worldly things by these Buddhist śrāmaṇas is lovely. . . . I am going to enter their order too.'" The text goes on to make a rule against admitting someone who also belonged to another religious group, but does not deny or criticize the characterization of Buddhist facilities as well appointed and possessed of "excellent food and drink." (The diet of most Western Christian monks also appears to have been far superior to that of ordinary people.)

But if a Buddhist bhikṣu was not—at least in the period of the vinaya texts—what he was called (e.g., a beggar), the question of what he was still remains. The term *bhikṣu* is usually, and conventionally, translated into English as "monk," and this rendering should help in understanding what a bhikṣu was, but it does so only with the addition of clear qualifications, in part, at least, because even in the West there has never been agreement on what a monk was—the entire history of Western monasticism can be viewed as a long, sometimes acrimonious, and unresolved debate about just this question. Moreover, most MONKS in the West were also not what they were called. The English word *monk* is derived from a Greek word that meant "(living) singly or alone," and yet almost all Western monks lived collectively in ordered, formally structured groups. In spite of that—and this is a particularly important obstacle to understanding the Buddhist bhikṣu—the figure of the monk in the modern West has been almost hopelessly romanticized as a simple, solitary figure given up to deep contemplation. The possibilities for misunderstanding here are very great.

Western monks—insofar as one can generalize—not only lived communally in usually well-endowed, permanent, and architecturally sophisticated complexes with an assured and usually abundant diet, they were also almost exclusively occupied with communally chanting or singing religious texts for the religious benefits or "merit" of their living and deceased donors and benefactors. If this is what a monk is understood to be, then a Buddhist bhikṣu might indeed be called a kind of monk. Certainly their vinayas are almost obsessed with avoiding any behavior that might alienate lay followers and donors, and they are saturated with rules designed, it seems, to make bhikṣus acceptable to donors as worthy objects of support and, consequently, as reliable means for donors to make merit. These "monks" too are in the service of the laity. Indeed, all Buddhist vinayas, it seems, contain detailed rules about a bhikṣu's obligations to the laity, one of which is to recite daily, both communally and individually, religious verses for the merit of their benefactors. Much to the chagrin of those modern scholars who want to maintain that MEDITATION was an important part of Buddhist monastic practice, moreover, the vinaya texts that we have say very little about meditation and allow very little room for its practice. They are equally chary of radical ASCETIC PRACTICES. This literature—and we have a very great deal of it—is concerned with maintaining and promoting a successful institution.

The extent of vinaya literature

The vinaya literature that has survived is enormous and still very little studied. It is commonly said that the vinayas of six Buddhist orders or schools have come down to us. Apart, however, from small fragments in Sanskrit from Central Asian manuscript finds, and the shortest section called the PRĀTIMOKṢA, the vinayas of four of these orders—the MAHĀSĀṂGHIKA, Sarvāstivāda, DHARMAGUPTAKA, and MAHĪŚĀSAKA—have survived exclusively in Chinese translations. The *Mūlasarvāstivāda-vinaya* has fared better: Large parts of it are available in a relatively early Sanskrit manuscript, large parts in a Chinese translation, and what may be the whole of it in a very literal Tibetan translation. The vinaya of the THERAVĀDA order, finally, is preserved entirely in Pāli, an Indian language, but scholars now agree that it too is a "translation" from some more original version.

At least two points, however, need to be noted in regard to all these vinayas. We do not know if any of these vinayas are complete because we do not actually know what a complete vinaya is. Until very recently the Theravāda or *Pāli Vinaya,* even though it was redacted in Sri Lanka, was taken as a model of what a complete vinaya in India would have looked like. Now, however, as the other vinayas are becoming better known, this has become problematic, and it is beginning to appear that the *Pāli Vinaya* is missing some potentially old sections that are found elsewhere under titles such as *Nidāna* (introductions) or *Mātṛkā* (matrices). This remains to be worked out, but the other important thing that needs to be noted is that none of the vinayas as we have them is early. The four vinayas preserved only in Chinese were all translated in the fifth century and consequently can represent only what these vinayas had become by that time—they do not necessarily tell us anything about what they looked like before then. The shape of the *Theravāda-vinaya* too cannot be taken back prior to the fifth century—its actual contents can only be dated from BUDDHAGHOSA's roughly fifth-century commentary on it, and even then both this commentary and the canonical text are known almost exclusively only on the basis of extremely late (eighteenth- and nineteenth-century) manuscripts. The *Mūlasarvāstivāda-vinaya* was not translated into Chinese until the eighth century, and into Tibetan only in the ninth, but it is the only vinaya for which we have significant amounts of actual manuscript material from, perhaps, the fifth, sixth, or seventh centuries. Regardless, then, of how one looks at it, the material we now have represents vinaya literature in a uniformly late stage of its development, and it can tell us very richly what it had become, and very poorly what it had earlier been.

The structure of vinaya literature

Perhaps not surprisingly almost all of these late vinayas look alike in broad outline. Almost all are, or were, structured in the same way and have basically the same component parts or sections. The shortest section, and the one that most scholars consider to be the oldest, is called the *Prātimokṣa,* a term that has been interpreted in a variety of ways. The *Prātimokṣa* is a list of graded offenses that begins with the most serious and continues with groups of offenses that are of lesser and lesser severity. The number of offenses for monks differs somewhat from order to order, the longest list (Sarvāstivāda) contains 263, the shortest (Mahāsāṃghika) has 218, but all use the same system of classification into named groups.

The most serious offenses, in the order given, are unchastity (in a startling variety of ways), theft, intentionally taking human life or instigating the taking of a life, and claiming to have religious attainments or supernatural powers that one does not have. The last of these is, of course, the only one that is unique to Buddhist vinaya, and is one that could have been a source of considerable friction and disruption for the communal life. It involved monks claiming a full understanding and perception of truths that they did not have; claims to stages of meditations and psychic powers that had not been achieved; and, interestingly, claims of regular and close relationships with DIVINITIES and a host of local spirits.

These four offenses are called *pārājikas,* a term commonly translated as "defeats," and it is still commonly asserted that the commission of any one of these by a bhikṣu or *bhikṣuṇī* resulted in his or her immediate and definitive expulsion from the order. This, however, was almost certainly not the case in India. Every vinaya except the *Pāli Vinaya* contains clear rules and ritual procedures that allowed a bhikṣu (and it seems a *bhikṣuṇī*) who had committed a *pārājika* to remain a member of the community, at a reduced status to be sure, but still with many of the rights and privileges of an ordained bhikṣu (or *bhikṣuṇī*). This is just one more way in which the *Pāli Vinaya* appears to be unrepresentative.

In addition to the *pārājikas*, the *Prātimokṣa* lists six further categories of offenses (a seventh outlines certain procedures), again in decreasing order of seriousness. These again involve issues of SEXUALITY and property, but overwhelmingly, perhaps, matters of proper decorum. Actual ethical concerns are surprisingly underdeveloped.

A second component part of the vinaya is called the *Vibhaṅga*, or explanation, and is closely related to the first. It is a kind of commentary on each of the rules listed in the *Prātimokṣa*, which typically describes the incident that gave rise to each of the rules, the conditions under which they must be applied, or in light of which an infraction of the rule does not actually constitute an offense. There are an impressive number of loopholes, and the dialectical ingenuity applied to the interpretation of the rules here is easily a match for that found in the higher reaches of Buddhist scholastic philosophy.

Although the bare *Prātimokṣa* was regularly recited at the fortnightly communal assembly of monks, it is unlikely that the rules themselves were ever actually applied without recourse to a *Vibhaṅga*, and this makes all the difference in the world. The Mūlasarvāstivāda *Prātimokṣa*, for example, has—like all the *Prātimokṣas*—a rule that would seem to forbid the engagement of bhikṣus in money transactions, but its *Vibhaṅga* unequivocally states that they must, for religious purposes, accept permanent money endowments and lend that money out to generate interest. This is but one of many possible examples.

A third component of Buddhist vinayas is what is called the *Vinayavastu* or *Khandhaka*, both *vastu* and *khandhaka* meaning here something like "division" or "chapter." There are generally between seventeen and twenty *vastus*, and they are named according to the main topic that they treat. There is, for example, a chapter on entering the religious life (Pravrajyāvastu), a chapter on the rainy season retreat (Varṣāvastu), a chapter on medicine (Bhaiṣajyavastu), a chapter on bedding and seats (Sayanāsanavastu), and so on. Like the *Vibhaṅga*, this part of a vinaya is large and very rich in both details and illustrative stories. The name of a *vastu* is, however, by no means an exhaustive indication of what it contains. The chapter on robes (Cīvaravastu), for example, does indeed deal with robes, but it also contains a good deal of material on Buddhist monastic inheritance law and the proper handling of a deceased monk's estate, which, in some cases at least, appears to have been very large. One of these *vastus*, the chapter on small matters (Kṣudrakavastu), is, ironically, so large that it sometimes is treated as a separate component.

What has so far been described refers strictly speaking to a vinaya for bhikṣus. But another component of a vinaya is both a separate *Prātimokṣa* and a separate *Vibhaṅga* for *bhikṣuṇīs*, a term that is usually translated as "nun." Although the number of rules for *bhikṣuṇīs*, or NUNS, in their *Prātimokṣas* is significantly larger than the rules for monks, the literature dealing with them is considerably smaller, and, for example, there appears not to have been a separate *Vinayavastu* for nuns, although the Pāli *Khandhaka* does contain a chapter on nuns, and a large part of one of the two volumes of the Mūlasarvāstivāda *Kṣudrakavastu* also is devoted to them.

Not so long ago a description of canonical vinaya literature would have ended here, with perhaps a nod toward the Pāli *Parivāra*, which is usually, but probably wrongly, described simply as an appendix. But very recent work has begun to look more carefully at the group of texts preserved in Chinese that are called *Nidānas* and *Mātṛkās*, and their counterparts preserved in the Tibetan translation of a large two-volume work called the *Uttaragrantha*. These texts seem to represent an independent ordering and treatment of vinaya rules, and there are some indications that this treatment may be older than that found in the better-known parts of the vinaya. This research, however, has only just begun, and the relative age of even the better-known parts of the vinaya is itself unresolved.

Theories on the date of vinaya literature

There are two general and opposed theories concerning the development of vinaya literature, both of which at least start from one of its most obvious characteristics: Although belonging to different orders or schools, the vinayas that have come down to us have, as already noted, a great deal in common, both in terms of their structure and their general contents. One theory would see these shared elements as early and argue that they predate the division of the Buddhist community into separate orders or schools. Another theory would see these same elements as late, as the result of mutual borrowing, conflation, and a process of leveling. There are, of course, arguments and evidence to support both theories.

Ancillary vinaya texts

In addition to canonical vinaya texts, there are, finally, large numbers of commentaries, subcommentaries, and handbooks. The last of these may have been particularly important since it seems likely that most monks did not actually read the enormous canonical vinayas, but relied instead on summaries, manuals, and such handbooks. But this too is a literature that has been very little explored and remains largely accessible only to specialists.

See also: **Festivals and Calendrical Rituals; Precepts; Robes and Clothing; Sarvāstivāda and Mūlasarvāstivāda**

Bibliography

Frauwallner, E. *The Earliest Vinaya and the Beginnings of Buddhist Literature.* Rome: Istituto Italiano per il Medio ed Estremo Oriente, 1956.

Hinüber, Oskar von. "Buddhist Law According to the Theravāda-Vinaya. A Survey of Theory and Practice." *Journal of the International Association of Buddhist Studies* 18, no. 1 (1995): 7–45.

Hinüber, Oskar von. *A Handbook of Pāli Literature.* Berlin and New York: Walter de Gruyter, 1996.

Hirakawa, Akira. *Monastic Discipline for the Buddhist Nuns.* Patna, India: Kashi Prasad Jayaswal Research Institute, 1982.

Horner, I. B., trans. *The Book of the Discipline.* London: Humphrey Milford, 1938–1966.

Lamotte, Étienne. *History of Indian Buddhism: From the Origins to the Saka Era,* tr. Sara Webb-Boin. Louvain, Belgium, and Paris: Peeters Press, 1988.

Pruitt, William, and Norman, K. R., eds. and trans. *The Pāṭimokkha.* Oxford: Pāli Text Society, 2001.

Schopen, Gregory. *Bones, Stones and Buddhist Monks: Collected Papers on the Archaeology, Epigraphy, and Texts of Monastic Buddhism in India.* Honolulu: University of Hawaii Press, 1997.

Schopen, Gregory. "Hierarchy and Housing in a Buddhist Monastic Code. A Translation of the Sanskrit Text of the Sayanāsanavastu of the Mūlasarvāstivādavinaya. Part One." *Buddhist Literature* 2 (2000): 92–196.

Schopen, Gregory. *Buddhist Monks and Business Matters: Still More Papers on Monastic Buddhism in India.* Honolulu: University of Hawaii Press, 2003.

GREGORY SCHOPEN

VIPASSANĀ (SANSKRIT, VIPAŚYANĀ)

Vipassanā (Sanskrit, *vipaśyanā*; insight) is direct intuition of the three marks that characterize all worldly phenomena: *anitya* (Pāli, *anicca*; impermanence), *duḥkha* (Pāli, *dukkha*; suffering), and anātman (Pāli, anatta; no-self). Buddhism classifies the cultivation of *vipassanā* as one of two modes of MEDITATION (*bhāvanā*), the other being tranquility (*śamatha*; Pāli, *samatha*). *Vipassanā* meditation entails perfecting the mental faculty of MINDFULNESS (*smṛti*; Pāli, *sati*) for the purpose of analyzing objects of meditation, such as mental states or the physical body, for manifestations of the three marks. When fully developed, *vipassanā* leads to the attainment of liberating prajñā (Pāli, *paññā*; wisdom) and the ultimate goal of NIRVĀṆA (Pāli, *nibbāna*) or the cessation of suffering and freedom from REBIRTH. *Samatha* meditation entails the cultivation of mental concentration (samādhi) for the purpose of strengthening and calming the mind. When fully developed it leads to the attainment of dhyāna (Pāli, *jhāna*), meditative absorption or trance, and the generation of various *abhijñā* (Pāli, *abhiññā*; higher knowledges).

The most common method of meditation described in the Pāli canon relies on *vipassanā* and *samatha* practiced together. In this method, *jhāna* is first induced through *samatha.* The meditator then exits from that state and reflects upon it with mindfulness to see that it is characterized by the three marks. In this way *jhāna* is made the object of *vipassanā* meditation. One who uses this method is called a tranquility worker (*samatha yānika*), and all buddhas and their chief disciples are described as having practiced in this way. A less common method found in the canon relies on *vipassanā* alone. Developing concentration to a lesser degree than *jhāna,* the meditator examines ordinary mental and physical phenomena for the three marks as described above. The meditator who uses this method is called a bare insight worker (*suddhavipassanāyānika*).

By the tenth century C.E., *vipassanā* meditation appears to have fallen out of practice in the THERAVĀDA school. By that time it was commonly believed that the religion of Gautama Buddha had so declined that liberation through insight could no longer be attained until the advent of the future Buddha Metteyya (Sanskrit, MAITREYA) many eons from now. In the early eighteenth century, however, renewed interest in the SATIPAṬṬHĀNA-SUTTA (*Discourse on the Foundations of Mindfulness*) led to a revival of *vipassanā* meditation in Burma (Myanmar). After encountering initial resistance, the practice of *vipassanā* was endorsed by the Burmese SAṄGHA and embraced by the royal court. By the late nineteenth century, a distinct praxis and organizational pattern had emerged that set the stage for the modern *vipassanā* movement of the twentieth century. Led chiefly by reform minded scholar-monks, a variety of simplified meditation techniques were devised based on readings of the *Satipaṭṭhāna-sutta,* the *Visuddhimagga* (*Path to Purification*), and related texts. These techniques typically follow the method of bare insight. The teaching of *vipassanā* also prompted the development of new Buddhist institutions called *wipathana yeiktha* or insight hermitages. Initially attached to monasteries, these evolved into independent lay oriented meditation centers. A related development was the rise of personality cults devoted to the veneration of prominent meditation teachers as living arhats. In terms of impact, the popularization of *vipassanā* represents the most significant development in Burmese Buddhism in the twentieth century. Thailand has also witnessed a revival of *vipassanā* practice in the modern period, and both Burmese and Thai meditation teachers have been instrumental in propagating *vipassanā* in Sri Lanka, India, and the West.

See also: **Abhijñā (Higher Knowledges); Anātman/Ātman (No-Self/Self); Anitya (Impermanence); Dhyāna (Trance State); Duḥkha (Suffering); Prajñā (Wisdom)**

Bibliography

Kornfield, Jack. *Living Buddhist Masters.* Santa Cruz, CA: Unity, 1977.

Mahasi Sayadaw. *The Progress of Insight through the Stages of Purification: A Modern Pāli Treatise on Buddhist Satipaṭṭhāna Meditation,* tr. Nyanaponika Thera. Kandy, Sri Lanka: Forest Hermitage, 1965.

Mendelson, E. Michael. *Sangha and State in Burma: A Study of Monastic Sectarianism and Leadership,* ed. John P. Ferguson. Ithaca, NY: Cornell University Press, 1975.

Swearer, Donald K. "The Way to Meditation." In *Buddhism in Practice,* ed. Donald S. Lopez, Jr. Princeton, NJ: Princeton University Press, 1995.

PATRICK A. PRANKE

VIPAŚYIN

The first of the so-called seven buddhas of the past, Vipaśyin is said to have lived in this world ninety-one eons (kalpas) ago. His career is discussed at length in the *Mahāpadāna-suttanta* (*Dīghanikāya,* no. 14) and more briefly in the *Buddhavaṃsa.* Despite his prominence in the list of seven, Vipaśyin does not appear to have become a major cultic figure.

See also: **Buddha(s)**

Bibliography

Horner, I. B., trans. *The Minor Anthologies of the Pāli Canon,* Part 3: *Buddhavaṃsa* and *Cariyapiṭaka.* London: Pāli Text Society, 1975.

Walshe, Maurice, trans. *Thus Have I Heard: The Long Discourses of the Buddha.* London: Wisdom Press, 1987.

JAN NATTIER

VIṢṆU

Viṣṇu is the Brahmanical god who preserves the universe, frequently as an *avatāra,* or descent. The Buddha is incorporated into Viṣṇu's mythology, most clearly in the *Gayā-mahātmya* (*Praises of the Greatness of Gayā*) section of the *Vāyu-purāṇa* (*Ancient Book of Vāyu*), in which Viṣṇu assumes the form of the Buddha and preaches false teachings to a group of asuras. Viṣṇu himself is not a particularly important textual presence, but in Sri Lanka he is frequently worshiped by Buddhists, often as one of the protectors of the religion and as a powerful, active force.

See also: **Divinities; Folk Religion, Southeast Asia; Hinduism and Buddhism**

Bibliography

Gonda, Jan. *Aspects of Early Viṣṇuism.* Delhi: Motilal Banarsidass, 1965.

The Vāyu Purāṇa, tr. G. V. Tagare. Delhi: Motilal Banarsidass, 1987.

JACOB N. KINNARD

VIŚVANTARA

The story of Prince Viśvantara (Pāli, Vessantara) is perhaps the most popular and well-known JĀTAKA (past-life story of the Buddha). It exists in many different versions and languages, and is a frequent subject of Buddhist art, ritual, and performance, particularly in THERAVĀDA countries of Southeast Asia.

In brief, the story involves a prince named Viśvantara who demonstrates the virtue of selfless generosity through a series of extraordinary gifts. First, he gives away his kingdom's most valuable elephant, an act that angers the citizenry and causes his father, King Saṃjaya, to reluctantly banish Viśvantara from the kingdom. After giving away all of his material possessions, Viśvantara embarks on a life of exile in the forest, accompanied by his wife and two children. When a cruel brahmin asks for the children as servants, Viśvantara willingly gives them away while his wife is off gathering food. Shortly thereafter, another brahmin supplicant asks for his wife, and Viśvantara again complies. This last supplicant reveals himself to be the god Śakra in disguise and immediately returns Viśvantara's wife to him. Meanwhile, full of remorse, King Saṃjaya ransoms Viśvantara's children from the cruel brahmin and then invites Viśvantara back from exile. In celebration, Śakra rains a shower of jewels from the sky.

Viśvantara never wavers from the harsh demands of universal generosity—giving children, wife, and material gifts to any and all who ask—yet everything is restored to him in the end. The story thus highlights the bodhisattva's "perfection of generosity," while also offering its listeners the promise of karmic rewards. Since Viśvantara loses his wife and children and becomes an ascetic in the forest (if only temporarily), the story also calls to mind the monk's renunciation of the world, as well as the life-story of the Buddha. Indeed, it has an especially close connection with the latter, for the birth as Viśvantara is understood to be the culmination of the Buddha's BODHISATTVA career and his last human rebirth before the final life as Siddhārtha Gautama. Moreover, when Siddhārtha battles against MĀRA underneath the Tree of Enlightenment, it is the merit acquired during his life as Prince Viśvantara that he invokes in order to secure Māra's defeat and thus attain buddhahood.

In line with its importance, the story of Viśvantara has been a popular subject of sermons, rituals, folk operas, dramas, and other forms of performance in many Buddhist cultures. In Thailand, for example, the Pāli *Vessantara-jātaka* is recited annually by monks during the Thet Mahachat festival, an act understood to produce abundant spiritual merit.

See also: **Buddha, Life of the; Entertainment and Performance; Folk Religion: An Overview; Folk Religion, Southeast Asia; Pāramitā (Perfection)**

Bibliography

Collins, Steven. "The *Vessantara Jātaka.*" In *Nirvāṇa and Other Buddhist Felicities: Utopias of the Pāli Imaginaire.* Cambridge, UK: Cambridge University Press, 1998.

Cone, Margaret, and Gombrich, Richard, trans. *The Perfect Generosity of Prince Vessantara: A Buddhist Epic.* Oxford: Clarendon Press, 1977.

REIKO OHNUMA

VOWS. *See* **Ordination; Precepts**

W

WAR

The list of the laureates of the Nobel Peace Prize in the twentieth century contains the names of two well-known Buddhist activists: Tenzin Gyatso (b. 1935), the fourteenth DALAI LAMA of Tibet, and Myanmar's Aung San Suu Kyi (b. 1945). Both have been deeply influenced by the rich traditions of Buddhist teachings and values. Their individual traditions may differ considerably, yet common to both figures is their rigorous stand against the employment of any kind of physical violence in pursuit of their aims for their people: religious freedom for the people of Tibet on the one hand and democratic structures and dignity for the people of Myanmar on the other. War as a legitimate means of acting in or reacting to a particular situation would not seem to harmonize with their understanding and practice of the Buddhist teaching. Nevertheless, history has known Buddhist kings and monks who engaged in warfare and, what is more telling, the transmitted literature of Buddhism is not devoid of stories and scattered textual passages that display a less vehement opposition to violence. Even warfare can, under certain circumstances, become a necessity.

The early times: Political neutrality

Hints about the political climate during the lifetime of the Buddha and a feel for his convictions may be found in the Pāli canon of the THERAVĀDA tradition of Buddhism. The first of the five major PRECEPTS taught by the Buddha, to refrain from injuring or killing any living being, would imply strict abstention from engaging in warfare, where the immediate practical aim usually involves the injury or annihilation of an enemy force. When asked by a military leader about the belief that a soldier who dies on the battlefield goes to heaven, the Buddha disappoints him with his response: Such a soldier will go to a specially prepared hell, owing to his evil state of mind, as manifested in his exerting himself to injure or kill his enemies (*Saṃyuttanikāya,* Woodward, vol. 4, pp. 216–219). This view must be judged as in sharp opposition to the dominant view of the time, according to which it was the particular duty of a kṣatriya, a member of the warrior caste, to fight and, if at all possible, to die on the battlefield. This would guarantee him the best karmic outcome.

This radical denial of the warrior ethic on an individual basis does not imply, however, that the Buddha necessarily tried to persuade rulers (in the main, kṣatriya kings) to refrain from all military activity, be it in defense of their realm or, as was the rule throughout India's history, in a war of aggression aimed at extending their territory. This may simply have been a pragmatic response to the realpolitik of those days. The rulers described in classical Indian literature, Machiavellian as they were, would hardly have welcomed a sermon on current power politics, much less advice on actual military operations, from a wandering ascetic. André Bareau describes this relationship between the spiritual power of the Buddha and the worldly concerns of contemporary sovereigns as an "equilibrium of forces" (p. 39). The Buddha would have realized the futility of interference in royal affairs. Moreover, wandering around the Ganges plain with his followers, he was mindful of the need to foster good relations with the rulers of the various realms in order to be granted entry and right of abode in their territories. Involvement in the political affairs of a neighboring kingdom could raise suspicion and might eventually put the whole community of his followers at risk.

One episode found in the Pāli recension of the MAHĀPARINIRVĀṆA-SŪTRA (*Great Discourse on the Extinction*; Collins, pp. 437–440) is typical of the kind of political neutrality the Buddha seems to have observed. In this passage, the wicked King Ajātasattu sends his chief minister to the Buddha in order to learn about his reaction to a planned attack on a neighboring people, the Vajjis. The chief minister informs the Buddha about the king's aggressive plan, but the text does not depict the Buddha as criticizing this cunning. Instead it has the Buddha listing seven kinds of behavior that, as long as the Vajjis stick to them, would keep them safe from the king's attack. The minister draws his own conclusion: The Vajjis cannot be overcome by warfare; other means have to be applied. And in fact, as the commentary explains, these means are undertaken by the minister, leading to the complete defeat of the Vajjis.

It is impossible to know whether this meeting between the chief minister and the Buddha ever took place. Nevertheless, the tradition has preserved this episode, which demonstrates that the Buddha's reported reaction was thought not to be unsuitable for him. There are, however, other transmitted passages in which the Buddha is confronted with conflicts of war; one of the best known, albeit from a considerably later source (*Kuṇālajātaka* [*Former Birth Story of the Buddha as Prince Kuṇāla*]), describes the conflict between the Sākyas and the Koliyas (Cowell, vol. 5, pp. 219–221). Here the Buddha is portrayed as a mediator between the two parties, who are on the verge of war over water rights. In this case, thanks to the Buddha's intervention, the conflict comes to an end.

From nonviolence to compassion

With the idea, which started to evolve in the first centuries of the common era, that the spiritual career of a BODHISATTVA is available to all, a clear shift in values becomes perceptible. If, until then, the principle of nonviolence (*ahiṃsā*) had governed the code of Buddhist ethics, KARUṆĀ (COMPASSION) now comes to the fore as the most essential element. The bodhisattva acts with compassion for the benefit of all living beings. The bodhisattva's own final awakening becomes secondary. It is against the background of this fundamental shift of values that violence became a more or less accredited means of action—unwholesome for its performer but benefiting the "victim." Take the case of a robber who tries to kill a group of spiritually highly developed persons. A bodhisattva aware of the situation and motivated by compassion will, if necessary, kill the potential wrongdoer in order to save him from the bad karmic consequences the murder would bring upon him. The bodhisattva, for his part, is willing to suffer the bad consequences caused by his violent act as part of this spiritual maturation (see the *Bodhisattvabhūmi* [*Bodhisattva Stages*], a text dating from the first centuries C.E.; in Tatz, pp. 70–71). As easily imaginable, this shift in values paved the way for justifying further means of violence, including war.

A Buddhist war ethic?

Throughout the more than two thousand years of compilation of literature among Buddhists, there is not a single text that could claim absolute authority in the matter of a "just war." As discussed above, Pāli texts portray the Buddha as reluctant to address the issue of war, thereby affirming the balance of powers. This lack of finality may have contributed to the very different stances on the issue of war that arose from early times on. Although there is no text dealing exclusively with the question of war and its ethical dimensions, relevant passages appear scattered throughout the literature. Their positions can vary between (1) an uncompromising rejection of any kind of participation in military activities; (2) a pragmatic approach shaped by the needs of a realistic royal policy, yet restricted by certain ethical considerations; and (3) a straightforward call for engagement in war in order to achieve a clearly defined goal.

Examples of the last position are extremely rare and not found in the earliest sources. One version of the Mahāyāna NIRVĀṆA SŪTRA, a text composed before the fifth century C.E., demands that lay followers protect the "true Buddhist teaching" with weapons. The killing of persons who oppose Mahāyāna is put on the same level as mowing grass or cutting corpses into pieces (Schmithausen, pp. 57–58). Similarly, the *Bodhisattvabhūmi* sanctions the overthrow of pitiless and otherwise oppressive kings and high officials, though it is quick to state that the bodhisattva is acting out of compassion so as to prevent these officials' accumulation of further demerit (Tatz, p. 71). Here, the shift from nonviolence to compassion is already fully operative.

A typical representative of the second position is a long chapter on royal ethics in the *Bodhisattvagocaropāyaviṇayavikurvaṇanirdeśa-sūtra* (*Sūtra That Expounds Supernatural Manifestations That Are Part of the Realm of Stratagems in the Bodhisattva's Field of Action*). This text, which probably originated in the fifth century C.E., propounds the bodhisattva ideal, although its actual influence on politics in India, Tibet, and China still remains to be investigated. The rele-

Buddha statues in the wreckage of Nagasaki, Japan, after the atomic bombing in 1945. © Getty Images. Reproduced by permission.

vant chapter is best read against the background of the traditional Machiavellian principles of rule in India to which it refers, and which it denounces as harmful and as a distortion of Buddhist morals. It is likely that the text aimed at supplying a practicable alternative and a more ethical set of rules for kings. It therefore had to come up with standards relating to war.

Surprisingly, the text includes no explicit prohibition against a war of aggression. The details, however, strongly suggest that what is being described are the rules for a defensive war. The king is advised to confront the hostile army with an attitude of kindness and to grant favors to the enemy. If this does not help, he should try to threaten his adversary by demonstrating (or pretending) military superiority. Such an approach, the text makes clear, is intended to prevent a war. If these actions prove futile, the king must remember his duty to protect his family and subjects, and so he may try to conquer the enemy by taking the hostile soldiers captive. As the next step, the king is described as addressing his army. The passage on war ends with the statement that even though a king may wound or slay his enemy, he will be without any blame. Immeasurable merit will fall to him who has done all this in a compassionate spirit and without resignation.

This passage allows for different interpretations. It likely expresses no more than the wish that a king fight and win a war by taking the enemy alive. But in the end, the text is ambiguous in that it absolves the king of blame in case he does kill somebody. Compassion is the essential element, and compassion automatically frees the king from the unwholesome consequences such acts would otherwise entail. Fighting a defensive war thus took on the guise of a morally correct endeavor, as long as the above rules were followed. Such an approach would enable a king to survive in hostile surroundings, while still basing his actions on Buddhist ethical foundations, which for pragmatic reasons had come to accommodate the needs of Indian realpolitik.

The first precept against killing mentioned above emphatically rejects the notion that somebody could become actively involved in a war without violating basic Buddhist tenets. This category tends to orthodoxy, and would not sanction compromises in the form of mechanisms undermining the precept of nonviolence for the sake of success in mundane affairs. Typically, compassion too is considered important, yet its incompatibility with violent actions is taken for granted. Buddhist royal politics that included guidelines for warfare could not evolve from this first position, as it could under the second pragmatic approach outlined above. In the final analysis, to be a Buddhist meant to refrain from any responsibilities or actions involving violence, let alone warfare.

CANDRAKĪRTI, a seventh-century Buddhist philosopher, consequently judges a king's presence on the battlefield as highly untoward, given that he "rushes around with rage and without affection, raising the weapon directed to the enemy's head in order to kill without any affection towards the other men" (Zimmermann, pp. 207–208). And a commentary on the ABHIDHARMAKOŚABHĀṢYA, an extremely influential Buddhist treatise of the fifth century C.E., states that even a soldier who has not killed anybody in a war is guilty, since he and his comrades have been inciting each other, and it would not matter who, in the last instance, has killed the enemy (Harvey, p. 254).

An even more orthodox approach is found in the FANWANG JING (BRAHMĀ'S NET SŪTRA), a sūtra most probably composed in Central or East Asia, which expounds the bodhisattva ideal. This text categorically forbids killing, ordering others to kill, and, with great forethought, the possession of weapons, contact with armies, and the instigation to war (Heinemann, pp. 114–123).

Compassionate killing

Given the plurality of positions described above, it is not surprising that Asia has experienced wars that have been fought on the basis of Buddhist arguments. It must be said, however, that these wars reached a degree of intensity and extent far lower than those witnessed by Christianity or Islam. Similarly, history knows of no ruler who engaged in war on the pretext of spreading Buddhism into non-Buddhist regions. However, one should not ignore the fact that Buddhist texts can be interpreted so as to serve as a reservoir of arguments for the justification of territorial expansion or economic and nation-building ambitions. Like most religious doctrines, Buddhist teachings can be turned into effective instruments in pursuit of highly mundane interests.

In *Zen at War* (1997), Brian Victoria demonstrates how the leaders and chief ideologists of Japan's Buddhist denominations hoped to gain the military government's sympathy before and during World War II by providing them with interpretations of scriptures that supported the country's war of expansion (pp. 79–94). The notion of a "war of compassion" appears frequently in their arguments. Such a "war which also benefits one's enemy" (pp. 86–91) was supposed to put an end to injustice and lawlessness and promote the advancement of society. One was not to go off and fight out of hatred or anger but—like a father punishing his child—out of compassion. To fight for a good reason would thus be in accord with the "great benevolence and compassion of Buddhism" (p. 87). The war's purpose would determine its rightfulness. In practice, however, this "just war" theory, based on Buddhist arguments, could easily be used to justify any armed conflict.

Other examples from the history of Buddhist countries that engaged in warfare might be added. Yet it must not be forgotten that besides the two Nobel laureates mentioned earlier, there is an incalculable number of individuals and organizations worldwide who, inspired by living Buddhist masters and the whole of the Buddhist tradition, take a clear stand in favor of a peace policy that advocates strict nonviolence as the only noble path.

See also: **Colonialism and Buddhism; Kingship; Modernity and Buddhism; Monastic Militias; Nationalism and Buddhism; Politics and Buddhism**

Bibliography

Bareau, André. "Le Bouddha et les rois." *Bulletin de l'École Française d'Extrême-Orient* 80, no. 1 (1993): 15–39.

Collins, Steven. *Nirvana and Other Buddhist Felicities: Utopias of the Pali Imaginaire.* Cambridge, UK: Cambridge University Press, 1998.

Cowell, Edward B., ed. *The Jātaka: Or, Stories of the Buddha's Former Births,* 6 vols., 1895–1907. Vol. 5 tr. Robert Chalmers. London: Pāli Text Society, 1906.

Demiéville, Paul. "Le Bouddhisme et la guerre." In *Choix d' Études Bouddhiques.* Leiden, Netherlands: Brill, 1973.

Harvey, Peter. *An Introduction to Buddhist Ethics: Foundations, Values and Issues.* Cambridge, UK: Cambridge University Press, 2000.

Heinemann, Robert K. *Der Weg des Übens im ostasiatischen Mahāyāna.* Wiesbaden, Germany: Harrassowitz, 1979.

Lang, Karen C. "Āryadeva and Candrakīrti on the Dharma of Kings." *Asiatische Studien* 46, no. 1 (1992): 232–243.

Schmidt-Leukel, Perry. "Das Problem von Gewalt und Krieg in der Buddhistischen Ethik." *Dialog der Religionen* 6, no. 2 (1996): 122–140.

Schmithausen, Lambert. "Aspects of the Buddhist Attitude towards War." In *Violence Denied: Violence, Non-Violence and the Rationalization of Violence in South Asian Cultural History,* ed. Jan E. M. Houben and Karel R. Van Kooij. Boston, Leiden, and Cologne: Brill, 1999.

Tatz, Mark, trans. *Asaṇga's Chapter on Ethics with the Commentary of Tsong-Kha-Pa, the Basic Path to Awakening, the Complete Bodhisattva.* Lewiston, NY: Mellen Press, 1986.

Victoria, Brian. *Zen at War.* New York and Tokyo: Weatherhill, 1997.

Woodward, Frank L., trans. *The Book of the Kindred Sayings or Grouped Suttas: Saṃyutta-Nikāya,* 5 vols. London: Pāli Text Society, 1917–1930.

Zimmermann, Michael. "A Mahāyānist Criticism of *Arthaśāstra*: The Chapter on Royal Ethics in the *Bodhisattvagocaropāya-viṇaya-vikurvaṇa-nirdeśa-sūtra.*" *Annual Report of the International Research Institute for Advanced Buddhology at Soka University for the Academic Year 1999* (2000): 177–211.

MICHAEL ZIMMERMANN

WILDERNESS MONKS

Wilderness plays three roles in early Buddhist texts: a place, a mode of livelihood, and an attitude toward practice. First, the wilderness is a place whose solitude, dangers, and rugged beauty provide an ideal environment for practice. The Buddha himself is said to have gained BODHI (AWAKENING) in the wilderness and to have encouraged his disciples to practice there as well. Monks could wander there during the dry season and settle there any time of the year. Nuns, though forbidden from settling or wandering alone in the wilderness, were required to go on a brief group wilderness tour annually after the Rains Retreat.

In addition to its role as a place, the wilderness functioned as a mode of livelihood. Monks and nuns, wherever they lived, were forbidden from engaging in the activities—farming, herding, and mercantile trade—that historically have set domestic civilization apart from the wilderness life of hunters and gatherers. Third and most important, monks and nuns were enjoined to cultivate wilderness as an attitude, an inner solitude and non-complacency transcending all external environments. Combined, this attitude and mode of livelihood provided the means by which Buddhist monastics were taught to straddle the line between civilization and the wilds.

Nevertheless, early texts show a division between monks who specialized in living either in the cities or in the wilderness. Although the portrayal of each type mixes criticism with praise, wilderness or forest monks on the whole enjoy the better press. MAHĀKĀŚYAPA, one of the Buddha's strictest and most respected disciples, is their model and ideal type, whereas city monks can claim no similar exemplar. Wherever the two types are directly compared—as in the accounts of the controversy at Kauśāmbī and of the Second Council—city monks are portrayed as intent on comfort and political power, contentious, unscrupulous, and undisciplined. The monks in Vaiśālī, whose behavior sparks the Second Council, are lax in their observance of the VINAYA (monastic rules). The Kauśāmbī monks, having split over a minor infraction, abuse the Vinaya to create an escalating war of accusations. Wilderness monks, in contrast, are portrayed as harmonious and unassuming, earnest meditators, strict and wise in their discipline.

The first praise for city monks appears in early MAHĀYĀNA texts. Whereas conservative versions of the bodhisattva path, derived from the early canons, take the wilderness monk living strictly by the Vinaya as their exemplar, more radical versions extol the city monk living in luxury as one who is not to be judged by outside appearances.

There are also reports, beginning with the early canons, of wilderness monks gone bad, using the psychic powers developed in their meditation for their individual fame and fortune to the detriment of the SAṄGHA (monastic community) as a whole. Although jealous city monks may have concocted these reports, they speak to a fear that has repeatedly been borne out in Buddhist history: that the respect shown for wilderness monks could create an opening for abuse. This possibility, combined with a general mistrust for the wilderness and the misfits who tended to settle there, led to an ambivalent attitude toward wilderness monks, which vacillated between reverence and wariness. During periods of relative stability, the uncertainty as to whether wilderness monks were charlatans, saints, or insane tended to discourage contact with them.

Their main role in shaping Buddhist history thus came in periods of crisis, when people in the centers of power lost faith in the domesticated Buddhism of the cities and, overcoming their fears, turned to wilderness monks to spearhead reforms. This pattern is especially marked in the THERAVĀDA tradition. In the thirteenth century, for instance, after a foreign invasion had threatened the revival of Theravāda in Sri Lanka, King Parakrāmabāhu II placed a contingent of forest/scholar monks, lead by a Sāriputta Bhikkhu, in charge of the saṅgha's unification. The system of governance and standards of scholarship thus formulated for the saṅgha proved influential in Theravāda countries well into the twentieth century. They also ensured that the traditions of the Mahāvihāra—the sect to which Sāriputta belonged—became the Theravāda norm.

Similarly, in the nineteenth century, when King Mindon of Burma (Myanmar), tried to revive classical Burmese culture in response to the British colonial threat, he invited wilderness monks to teach insight mediation (vipaśyanā; Pāli, VIPASSANĀ) to his court, in hopes that the resulting spiritual superiority of his government would dispel the barbarians at the gate. Despite its failure in this regard, his patronage of *vipassanā* established a precedent for high-ranking Burmese throughout the colonial period and for the Burmese government when it regained independence. This in turn fostered the development of distinct schools of *vipassanā* practice, such as the Mahasi Sayadaw and U Ba Khin methods, that have since spread around the world.

As the twenty-first century dawns, wilderness monk movements thrive in all the major Theravāda countries, examples being the forest/scholar brotherhoods founded in the twentieth century by Kaḍavädduvē Jinavaṁsa in Sri Lanka and Buddhadāsa Bhikkhu in Thailand. The most prominent wilderness movement, however, is the Kammaṭṭhāna (Meditation) tradition founded in Thailand in the late nineteenth century by Āčhān Sao Kantasīlo and Āčhān Man Bhūridatto. Building on the Dhammayut sect's reforms earlier in the century, this movement differed in two ways from the tantric wilderness movements extant in Thailand at its inception, both in its strict adherence to the Vinaya and in its championing of meditation techniques drawn from the Pāli canon. Before the close of the twentieth century, the movement spread beyond Thailand into other parts of Asia and the West.

Although some wilderness movements have left long-lasting marks on Buddhist history, they themselves have tended to be short-lived. Their very success in gaining support leads directly to their domestication and decline. In the past, the ubiquitous forest has served as the testing ground for new wilderness movements in Asia as older ones pass away. With the rapid deforestation of the continent, this source of regeneration and reform is in danger of disappearing. At the same time, with the spread of Buddhism beyond Asia, there is the question of whether wilderness in its three roles—as place, mode of livelihood, and attitude—will counterbalance the inevitable domestication of Buddhism as it settles into its new homes.

See also: **Ascetic Practices; Monasticism; Monks**

Bibliography

Carrithers, Michael. *The Forest Monks of Sri Lanka: An Anthropological and Historical Study.* Delhi: Oxford University Press, 1983.

Ray, Reginald A. *Buddhist Saints in India: A Study in Buddhist Values and Orientations.* Oxford: Oxford University Press, 1994.

Swearer, Donald K., ed. *Me and Mine: Selected Essays of Bhikkhu Buddhadāsa.* Albany: State University of New York Press, 1989.

Tambiah, Stanley Jeyaraja. *The Buddhist Saints of the Forest and the Cult of Amulets.* Cambridge, UK: Cambridge University Press, 1984.

Taylor, J. L. *Forest Monks and the Nation-state: An Anthropological and Historical Study in Northeastern Thailand.* Singapore: Institute for Southeast Asian Studies, 1993.

Teich, Anne, ed. *Blooming in the Desert: Favorite Teachings of the Wildflower Monk Taungpulu Sayadaw.* Berkeley, CA: North Atlantic Books, 1996.

Tiyavanich, Kamala. *Forest Recollections: Wandering Monks in Twentieth-Century Thailand.* Honolulu: University of Hawaii Press, 1997.

Thanissaro Bhikkhu. "The Customs of the Noble Ones" (1999). Available from *Access to Insight: Readings in Theravāda Buddhism* www.accesstoinsight.org.

THANISSARO BHIKKHU (GEOFFREY DEGRAFF)

WISDOM. *See* **Prajñā (Wisdom)**

WOMEN

A consideration of the role of women in Buddhism—as distinct from the symbolic role of the female—

proceeds in tension with several challenges. First, in much of Buddhist literature, female characters tend to function symbolically; their relationship to Buddhist women, by no means transparent, is contested within both academic and Buddhist communities. Secondly, the primacy of men in most historical Buddhist communities corresponds to a relative dearth of historical sources regarding the lives of women. Thirdly, women have been defined quite differently and have occupied quite distinct roles in different Buddhist cultures; the blanket term *women* can obscure this diversity. Finally, contemporary perspectives and controversies fundamentally shape our approach to this topic. With these caveats, however, a great deal can still be said.

Women and normative constructions of the female: Mothers, wives, objects of desire

Throughout the history of Buddhist communities, images of the feminine have played a central role in Buddhist thought and practice, and surely such images had a significant impact upon the lives of Buddhist women. It must be kept in mind, however, that these images were, for the most part, constructed by and for men. Still, conceptions of the female shaped and were shaped by the experiences of actual women in Buddhist communities, and thus represent an important, if problematic, resource for understanding the role of women in Buddhism.

Almost universally in premodern Buddhist communities, to be born a woman was considered a sign of unfavorable karmic propensities from past lives, and many texts portray REBIRTH as a man as a laudable soteriological goal, as, for instance, in the "Bhaiṣajyarāja" (Medicine King) chapter of the LOTUS SŪTRA (SADDHARMAPUṆḌARĪKA-SŪTRA). According to most normative texts, one of the eight conditions for receiving a prediction to buddhahood is a male body, and although women were often portrayed as capable of attaining BODHI (AWAKENING), many Buddhist sources suggest that final release requires rebirth in male form. Arguably, the female body's connection to birth (and thus to SAṂSĀRA itself) and its often noted capacity to arouse desire in men render it unfit for the highest soteriological attainments.

The death of the Buddha's own mother one week after his birth might be taken to signify not only the saṃsāric taint of giving birth, but also the great power of the bond between mother and child, one that had to be broken if the Buddha was to be able to renounce all worldly attachments. Pāli and MAHĀYĀNA sources often mention the infinite debt to one's mother and father; even if one were to carry one's parents on one's back for one hundred years, the *Kattaññu-sutta* of the *Aṅguttaranikāya* asserts, one could never repay the debt. Mothers, too, frequently figure in narrative literature as ultimate embodiments of attachment and the grief it brings (see, for instance, the chapter on "The Tigress" in the SUVARṆAPRABHĀSOTTAMA-SŪTRA). In such tales, the position of the mother remains ambiguous: The mother's experience of terrible grief because of her attachment to her children is presented very sympathetically, even as the goal of nonattachment is praised; sometimes the pain of motherhood itself becomes the basis for the realization of impermanence. Such sentiments are echoed in the colophons of manuscripts from DUNHUANG that were commissioned by mothers and wives to ensure the good rebirth of their deceased children and husbands.

The depth of a mother's love for her children is also the basis for the use of the figure of the mother as the paradigm of selfless compassion embodied in (usually male) BODHISATTVAS and BUDDHAS. In the bodhisattva vows of the MAHĀYĀNA, for instance, the bodhisattva is exhorted to be like a mother to all beings, and the Buddha himself is not infrequently described in motherly terms. The notion of the compassionate, loving mother is surely also at work in the characterization of certain prominent female bodhisattvas, such as Prajñāpāramitā (the "mother of all buddhas") and Tārā (embodiment of compassionate action) in Indo-Tibetan Buddhism, and female representations of Avalokiteśvara bodhisattva (Guanyin) in China. The latter bodhisattva appears in the form of "the giver of sons," and is propitiated to this day for assistance in obtaining (usually male) children.

Perhaps one of the most powerful normative images is that of the female as the primary object of male desire, and thus as the symbol of desire par excellence. Numerous passages in Buddhist canonical literature of all regions and schools warn monastic men against the dangers of sexual desire (almost always assumed to be heterosexual); a few virulently misogynistic passages attribute male desire to the degeneracy of women (Sponberg, pp. 18–23). Consideration of female sexual desire or its effect upon women, by contrast, is generally limited to the characterization of women as uncontrollable sexual beings that threaten male celibacy. Women are objects, not subjects, in many normative Buddhist constructions of desire; they are the lesser (and dangerous) "other" in relation to the male subject position, as discussed in further detail below.

But these normative constructions of the position of the female are not uncontested; tales of highly accomplished women—even stories of the bodhisattva in female form—are also found among Buddhist literary sources (for instance, the tale of "Rupāvatī" in the DIVYĀVADĀNA, and the "Padīpadāna-jātaka" in the *Paññāsa-jātaka* collection). Inscriptions and colophons in the broader Buddhist world attest both to the power of normative constructions and to alternative conceptions of women. Among the colophons of manuscripts at DUNHUANG, for instance, are found both women's prayers to leave behind a woman's "vile estate," and the dedications of wealthy and powerful female patrons whose words attest to their central role in lay life. Taking into account not only literary sources but also social-historical and anthropological materials enables a fuller and more complex appreciation of the position of women in Buddhist communities.

Women as patrons and rulers

Women have played central roles throughout Buddhist history as patrons of Buddhist institutions and practices. Indeed, this is the role of women most clearly attested in historical sources. Laywomen and NUNS (who clearly had access to economic resources in some Buddhist communities) figure prominently among the donors whose inscriptions and colophons survive across the Buddhist world, and they are depicted in murals such as those found at Dunhuang and AJAṆṬĀ. Female patronage was not only motivated by religious goals, but also by the relative freedom from social constraints that, in some Buddhist communities, association with Buddhism could offer. For instance, Jacques Gernet demonstrates how the support of Buddhist figures and institutions by aristocratic women during the Tang dynasty (618–907) in China could give such women access to considerable social and political power. Such instances make clear that, whatever the normative rhetoric about women may have been, individual women could appropriate Buddhist tropes and institutions for their own benefit.

Among the most famous female patrons of Buddhism is Empress Wu Zetian, whose occupation of the Tang dynasty throne in 690 C.E. (she had ruled unofficially since 665) heralded a time of great flourishing for Buddhism in China. For Empress Wu, Buddhism appears to have been both religiously fulfilling and politically expedient. Through the skillful reinterpretation of Buddhist texts that helped to identify her as both bodhisattva and cakravartin (wheel-turning monarch), her reign was legitimized and glorified. At the same time, her extremely generous patronage of Buddhist institutions, scholars, festivals, and arts greatly enhanced the wealth, power, and influence of Buddhists in the realm. While much maligned by premodern Chinese historians as a ruthless dictator, Empress Wu made extremely significant contributions not only to the development of Buddhist culture in China, but also to the betterment of the status of women at the time. Other powerful women, such as Queen Cāmadevī, the quasi-historical first ruler of the kingdom of Haripuñjāna in present-day northern Thailand, are also believed to have had a significant influence on the florescence of Buddhist culture in other times and places.

Women as renunciants

Due to the paucity of contemporaneous historical sources, the position of women in Buddhist renunciant communities prior to the first millennium of the common era must largely be surmised from literary sources, although inscriptional evidence should also be taken into account. Narratives in Pāli and Sanskrit canonical sources—perhaps most famously, the story of how the Buddha's stepmother, MAHĀPRAJĀPATĪ GAUTAMĪ, became the first nun—suggest that the position of women in the Buddhist community was viewed from multiple and often contradictory perspectives. Women were considered capable of attaining enlightenment, and were admitted, if somewhat grudgingly, into the community of renunciants. Canonical texts (see especially the *Therīgāthā*) tell of many prominent and accomplished female renunciants.

On the other hand, to be reborn a women was undeniably viewed as a lower birth, the fruit of negative KARMA (ACTION). According to the VINAYA, the most senior of female renunciants is inferior even to the youngest male novice, and must defer to him; in general, male monastic institutions have controlled monastic women. Moreover, the institution of female renunciation was undermined from the outset by the assertion that male renunciants represented a more fertile field of merit for the lay community than did female renunciants, as a result of which female renunciants appear frequently to have suffered from insufficient material and social support from the laity, as is confirmed by the eventual disappearance of the order of nuns in most of South and Southeast Asia. In Tibet, as well, the full ordination of women died out; only the novice (*śramaṇerikā*) level of ordination has been maintained to the present day. The full ordination of women has been preserved only in East Asia. Still, several contemporary movements seek to reestablish strong communities of female renunciants, with or without full ordination. Indeed, as Sid Brown indicates regarding Thai *maechi* (female renunciants), many women feel that renunciation without ordination is preferable, since they can thereby remain independent of male-dominated monastic institutions.

Women and the valorization of the female

Construed as the symbolic "other" of the male, feminine images have a potent function in Buddhist literature and practice. Since desire is conceived of as the fundamental cause of human suffering, the female, the paradigmatic object of male desire, frequently comes to represent the entrapment of saṃsāra itself. At the same time, the paradigmatic quality of the male/female hierarchical dichotomy lends itself to numerous other, quite different, manipulations. In the *Vimalakīrtinirdeśa,* for instance, a wise female deity transforms the hapless ŚĀRIPUTRA into a woman in order to demonstrate, through the apparent arbitrariness of GENDER, the principle of nonduality. While some scholars would see in this episode both a powerful female figure and the dismantling of gender categories (Schuster), it should also be noted that the female deity might be powerful in this context precisely because she is so unusual, so unconventional, and that gender breakdown might function as such a trenchant symbol of nonduality precisely because the gender hierarchy/dichotomy was so deeply entrenched in Buddhist communities. Herein lies the difficulty of interpreting female symbols in relation to women's lives: This story could be seen either as empowering women, or as revealing their social disempowerment—or both.

The role of women in tantric Buddhist contexts, where the symbol of the female is most highly valorized, is complex and controversial. While it is tempting to conflate the valorization of the female with the valorization of women, the texts of tantric Buddhism indicate that the glorification of the female most often presumes the perspective of the male practitioner and functions for his benefit. For instance, in the VAJRAYĀNA vows, the practitioner is exhorted not to disparage women; such an injunction indicates not only that women were likely disparaged, but also that the vows assume a male audience. Similarly, it is problematic to interpret the ubiquitous tales of highly realized (and usually very attractive) female figures, both human and divine, as corresponding to a historical reality, since these tales likely functioned primarily for male audiences. As is the case with Śāriputra's gender transformation, the valorization of the female may gain much of its potential symbolic power precisely from its transgression of historical realities. The construal of the female as the paradigmatic object of male desire likely underlies the manipulation of powerful female symbols by male practitioners: If the female is other, then the (male) self can be transformed through ritual identification or union with that symbolic other, an other that could be embodied in actual women who acted as sexual consorts.

On the other hand, the existence of such positive and powerful female symbols, whether or not they were intended to function primarily for men, obviously provided (and provides) productive resources for women wishing to subvert societal gender norms. While women within monastic institutions were generally subservient to men, legends of powerful female tantric practitioners open a space for virtuoso Buddhist women outside the monastic system—a space that many women surely occupied. Quasi-historical tales such as that of MA GCIG LAB SGRON (MACHIG LAPDÖN), the extraordinary female tantric practitioner who is said to have founded the practice of *gcod* (offering up one's body to undermine the notion of self) in Tibet, may attest to the relative freedom of some women. Virtuoso women, however rare, are still known to live itinerant (and highly esteemed) lives in contemporary Tibet; their existence points to a tradition that, for all the difficulty of locating its historical traces in Indo-Tibetan tantric literature, has a long lineage.

Contemporary appropriations and subversions

As notions of the equality of women in the contemporary world gain more widespread acceptance, female Buddhists not only in Europe and America but across the Buddhist world are grappling with the symbolic and institutional legacies of widely varied Buddhist conceptions of women. Buddhist women are beginning to ask how female symbols that were designed primarily for male practitioners relate to the lived religious experience of contemporary women. Can such images be appropriated to serve the religious goals of women, or are they inextricable from male-dominated thought and practice? Should women seek equality by attempting to gain recognition from institutions controlled by men, or should they establish their own communities and institutions that are not dependent on the still-pervasive authority of male figures? Can contemporary women simply dismiss as historical and cultural artifacts the ubiquitous references in Buddhism to the female body as an inherently lower form of birth? How do women, so often figured as the objects of male desire, create a subject position for themselves as Buddhist practitioners—or should this lack of a fully articulated "self" be viewed as an advantage on the Buddhist path? Such questions are hotly debated among practitioners and scholars alike; the fruits of these debates, whatever they may be, will surely herald significant shifts in the thought and practice of Buddhism for people of all genders.

Bibliography

Barnes, Nancy. "Buddhist Women and the Nuns' Order in Asia." In *Engaged Buddhism: Buddhist Liberation Movements in Asia,* ed. Christopher S. Queen and Sallie B. King. Albany: State University of New York Press, 1996.

Bartholomeusz, Tessa. *Women under the Bo Tree.* New York: Cambridge University Press, 1994.

Brown, Sid. *The Journey of One Buddhist Nun: Even against the Wind.* Albany: State University of New York Press, 2001.

Edou, Jérôme. *Machig Labdrön and the Foundations of Chöd.* Ithaca, NY: Snow Lion, 1996.

Falk, Nancy Auer. "The Case of the Vanishing Nuns." In *Unspoken Worlds: Women's Religious Lives in Non-Western Cultures,* ed. Nancy Falk and Rita Gross. San Francisco: Harper, 1980.

Findly, Ellison Banks, ed. *Women's Buddhism, Buddhism's Women: Tradition, Revision, Renewal.* Somerville, MA: Wisdom, 2000.

Gernet, Jacques. *Buddhism in Chinese Society: An Economic History from the Fifth to the Tenth Centuries,* tr. Franciscus Verellen. New York: Columbia University Press, 1995.

Klein, Anne Carolyn. *Meeting the Great Bliss Queen: Buddhists, Feminists, and the Art of the Self.* Boston: Beacon, 1995.

Lefferts, H. Leedom, Jr. "Textiles in the Service of Tai Buddhism." In *Textiles and the Tai Experience in Southeast Asia,* by Mattiebelle Gittinger and H. Leedom Lefferts, Jr. Washington, DC: Textile Museum, 1992.

Paul, Diana. "Empress Wu and the Historians." In *Unspoken Worlds: Women's Religious Lives in Non-Western Cultures,* ed. Nancy Falk and Rita Gross. San Francisco: Harper, 1980.

Paul, Diana. *Women in Buddhism: Images of the Feminine in the Mahayana Tradition,* 2nd edition. Berkeley: University of California Press, 1985.

Schopen, Gregory. *Bones, Stones, and Buddhist Monks: Collected Papers on the Archaeology, Epigraphy, and Texts of Monastic Buddhism in India.* Honolulu: University of Hawaii Press, 1997.

Schuster, Nancy. "Changing the Female Body: Wise Women and the Bodhisattva Career in Some Mahāratnakūṭasūtras." *Journal of the International Association of Buddhist Studies* 4, no. 1 (1981): 24–69.

Sponberg, Alan. "Attitudes toward Women and the Feminine in Early Buddhism." In *Buddhism, Sexuality, and Gender,* ed. José Ignacio Cabezón. Albany: State University of New York Press, 1992.

Strong, John S. *The Buddha: A Short Biography.* Oxford: Oneworld, 2001.

Swearer, Donald K. "Bimbā's Lament." In *Buddhism in Practice,* ed. Donald S. Lopez, Jr. Princeton, NJ: Princeton University Press, 1995.

Swearer, Donald K., and Premchit, Sommai. *The Legend of Queen Cāma: Bodhiraṃsi's Cāmadevīvaṃsi, a Translation and Commentary.* Albany: State University of New York Press, 1998.

Tsomo, Karma Lekshe, ed. *Buddhist Women across Cultures: Realizations.* Albany: State University of New York Press, 1999.

Van Esterik, Penny, ed. *Women of Southeast Asia.* DeKalb, IL: Southeast Asia Publications, 1996.

Willis, Janice D., ed. *Feminine Ground: Essays on Women and Tibet.* Ithaca, NY: Snow Lion, 1995.

NATALIE D. GUMMER

WŎN BUDDHISM. *See* **Wŏnbulgyo**

WŎNBULGYO

Wŏnbulgyo, a compound of the Korean *wŏn* (circle) and *pulgyo* (Buddhism), means literally "Circular Buddhism," or "Consummate Buddhism." It is the name of an indigenous religion founded in Korea in the twentieth century.

History

Pak Chung-bin (1891-1943; "Sot'aesan") attained great enlightenment in 1916 and had a precognition of the world entering an era of advancing material civilization, to which humans would be enslaved. The only way to save the world was by expanding spiritual power through faith in genuine religion and training in sound morality. With the dual aims to save sentient beings and cure the world of moral ills, Sot'aesan began his religious mission. He opened a new religious order with the *buddhadharma* as the central doctrine, establishing the Society for the Study of the Buddha-dharma at Iksan, North Cholla province, in 1924. He edified his followers with newly drafted doctrine until his death in 1943. The central doctrine was published in the *Pulgyo chŏngjŏn* (*The Correct Canon of Buddhism*) in 1943. In 1947 Song Kyu (1900–1962; "Chŏngsan"), the second patriarch, renamed the order *Wŏnbulgyo* (Wŏn Buddhism) and published the new canon, *Wŏnbulgyo kyojŏn* (*The Scriptures of Wŏn Buddhism*), in 1962.

Doctrine

The central doctrine lies in the tenets of *Irwŏnsang* (unitary circular form), Four Beneficences, and Threefold Practice. Just like a finger pointing at the moon, *Irwŏnsang*, enshrined as the symbol of the dharmakāya of the Buddha, refers to the Buddha-nature of the TATHĀGATHA and the fundamental source of the four beneficences (heaven and earth, parents, fellow beings, laws) to which one owes one's life. *Irwŏn* (unitary circle), the Wŏnbulgyo name for the Dharmakāya Buddha, is the noumenal nature of all beings of the universe, the original nature of all buddhas and patriarchs, and the Buddha-nature of all sentient beings. The worship of *Irwŏn* lies in requiting the four beneficences, as stated in the motto: "Requiting beneficence is making offerings to Buddha." The practice of *Irwŏn* lies in PRAJÑĀ (WISDOM), fostering (samādhi), and using (*śīla*), upon enlightenment to the Buddha-nature in mundane, daily life.

Practice

The requital of the four beneficences is carried out: (1) for heaven and earth, harboring no thought after rendering beneficence; (2) for parents, protecting the helpless; (3) for fellow beings, benefiting oneself by benefiting others; and (4) for laws, doing justice and forsaking injustice. The threefold practice is perfected by: samādhi, cultivation of spirit; prajñā, inquiry into facts and principles; and *śīla*, the heedful choice in karmic action. The threefold practice is carried out through timeless Zen, which holds as its central principle that when the six sense organs are at rest, one should nourish One Mind by clearing the mind of worldly thoughts; when they are at work, one should forsake injustice and cultivate justice.

Ceremonies

On Sundays, followers attend the dharma meeting at a Wŏn Buddhist temple, which includes seated meditation, prayers to the Dharmakāya Buddha, chanting, hymnals, and sermons. Two yearly memorial services (June 1 and December 1) for ancestors and four festival ceremonies (New Year's Day, the day of Sot'aesan's enlightenment and foundation of *Wŏnbulgyo*, Śākyamuni Buddha's birthday, and the day of Dharma authentication) are observed.

See also: **Chinul; Festivals and Calendrical Rituals; Hyujŏng; Korea; Wŏnhyo**

Bibliography

Chong, Key-ray. *Wŏn Buddhism: A History and Theology of Korea's New Religion.* Lewiston, NY: Mellen Press, 1997.

Chung, Bongkil. *The Scriptures of Wŏn Buddhism: A Translation of Wŏnbulgyo kyojŏn with an Introduction.* Honolulu: University of Hawaii Press, 2002.

Park, Kwang Soo. *The Wŏn Buddhism (Wŏnbulgyo) of Sot'aesan.* Bethesda, MD: International Scholars Publication, 1997.

BONGKIL CHUNG

WŎNCH'ŬK

Wŏnch'ŭk (Chinese, Yuance; Tibetan, Wen tshegs, 613–696) was a Korean expatriate scholar monk who lived in seventh-century China. Wŏnch'ŭk traveled to Tang China at the age of fifteen and studied YOGĀCĀRA SCHOOL texts based on PARAMĀRTHA's (499–569) translations under Fachang (567–645) and Sengbian (568–642). Later studying under XUANZANG (ca. 600–664), Wŏnch'ŭk joined the comprehensive project to translate Indian Buddhist texts into Chinese, marking the start of the so-called New Yogācāra. This movement was based specifically on these new translations and especially the compilation of the *Cheng weishi lun* (*Demonstration of Consciousness-Only*), in contrast to the so-called Old Yogācāra, which was based on Paramārtha's earlier translations. Wŏnch'ŭk's work appears to be an attempt to reconcile the doctrinal differences between those two distinctive trends of Chinese Yogācāra doctrine. His interpretation of Yogācāra diverges from the interpretations of KUIJI (631–682) and Xuanzang, while sometimes resonating with the work of Paramārtha. This led to severe criticism from the later disciples of Kuiji who started the FAXIANG SCHOOL, which took Kuiji as their first patriarch. Wŏnch'ŭk's extant works include the *Haesimmilgyŏng so,* a commentary on the SAṂDHINIRMOCANA-SŪTRA (the tenth and last fascicle is missing, but is available in Tibetan translation); the *Inwanggyŏng so,* a commentary on the RENWANG JING (HUMANE KINGS SŪTRA); and the *Pulsŏl panya paramilta simgyŏng ch'an,* a eulogy to the HEART SŪTRA. Unfortunately, Wŏnch'ŭk's *Sŏngyusingnon so,* a commentary on the *Cheng weishi lun,* which was probably his most representative work, is no longer extant and is known only through quotations.

With his vast scholarship on Yogācāra Buddhist doctrine and other philosophical trends within the Indian tradition, Wŏnch'ŭk significantly contributed to the development of Chinese Buddhism, influencing the doctrines of the Chinese HUAYAN SCHOOL and the especially the thought of FAZANG (643–712). However, Wŏnch'ŭk's influence was not limited to China. Even though he never returned to Korea, Wŏnch'ŭk's theories were inherited by the Korean monks Tojŭng (ca. 640–710) and T'aehyŏn (fl. 753), despite their lack of any direct contact with him. Wŏnch'ŭk also played an important role in the formation of the Japanese branch of Yogācāra, the Hossō (Chinese, Faxiang) school, and his works were admired by Gyōsin (ca. 750), Genjū (723–797), and Gomyō (750–834). The controversies and debates surrounding the issues that Wŏnch'ŭk and other Faxiang scholars explored in China challenged Japanese Yogācāra exegetes at the very moment that the school was founded during the Nara period. This admiration for Wŏnch'ŭk's scholarship changed around the end of Heian and into the Kamakura periods. At that time, the Hossō school instead took as authoritative the three patriarchs of Chinese Faxiang—namely Kuiji, Huizhao (650–714), and Zhizhou (668–723)—and Hossō monks designated some views as "orthodox" and others as "heretical." In addition, Wŏnch'ŭk's commentary on the *Saṃdhinirmocana-sūtra* was translated into Tibetan during the ninth century and was cited extensively by TSONG KHA PA (1357–1419) and his DGE LUGS (GELUK) successors. Wŏnch'ŭk's views were therefore influential in the subsequent development of Tibetan Buddhism.

Bibliography

Cho, Eunsu. "Wŏnch'ŭk's Place in the East Asian Buddhist Tradition." In *Currents and Countercurrents: Korean Influences on the East Asian Buddhist Traditions,* ed. Robert E. Buswell, Jr. Honolulu: University of Hawaii Press, 2004.

EUNSU CHO

WŎNHYO

Wŏnhyo (Break of Dawn, 617–686) is widely considered to be the most influential thinker, writer, and commentator in Korean Buddhist history. Arguably the first major contributor to the development of an indigenous approach to Korean Buddhist doctrine and practice, Wŏnhyo wrote over eighty treatises and commentaries on virtually every influential MAHĀYĀNA scripture then available in Korea, of which over twenty are extant. Reflecting the dynamic cultural exchanges and flourishing doctrinal scholarship and meditative practice occurring within East Asian Buddhism during his time, Wŏnhyo's scholarship embraced the full spectrum of East Asian Buddhism, from the Mahāyāna PRECEPTS to the emblematic teachings of Madhyamaka, Yogācāra, Tiantai, Pure Land, NIRVĀṆA, TATHĀGATAGARBHA, and Huayan. Wŏnhyo's writings were disseminated throughout East Asia and made important contributions to the development of Buddhist doctrinal exegesis.

Wŏnhyo's life has fascinated readers even in modern times and his biography has been the subject of novels, film, and television drama in Korea. Spending the early part of his career as a monk in Korea, Wŏnhyo made two attempts to travel to Tang China (618–907) with his lifelong friend ŬISANG (625–702) to study under XUANZANG (ca. 600–664), a Chinese scholar-pilgrim who was the most respected doctrinal teacher of his time. On the second attempt, Wŏnhyo's biographies state that he had an enlightenment experience that was intimately related to the *mind-only* theory of the YOGĀCĀRA SCHOOL. The accounts vary, but they all revolve around Wŏnhyo having a revelation after falling asleep one evening during his travels. In the most drastic version, recorded in a later Chan hagiographical collection, Wŏnhyo takes refuge from a storm in a sanctuary, but awakens thirsty in the middle of the night and looks in the dark for water. Finding a bowl of water, he drinks it and, satisfied, goes back to sleep. The next morning after he awakens, he finds to his disgust that the place where he had slept was in fact a crypt and what he had taken to be a bowl of water was actually offal in a human skull. Realizing that what he thought was thirst-quenching the night before was disgusting now, he reveled, "I heard that the Buddha said the three worlds are mind-only and everything is consciousness-only. Thus beauty and unwholesomeness depend on my mind, not on the water." The narrative power of this story helped shape East Asian images of enlightenment as a dramatic awakening experience. After this experience Wŏnhyo turned back from his journey, proclaiming that there was no need to search for truth outside one's mind. His friend Ŭisang, however, continued on to China, later returning home to found the Korean branch of the HUAYAN SCHOOL (Korean, Hwaŏm).

Wŏnhyo's later affair with a widowed princess produced a son, Sŏl Ch'ong (d.u.), one of the most famous literati in Korean history, and helped to seal his reputation as someone who transcended such conventional distinctions as secular and sacred. After an illustrious career as a writer and Buddhist thinker, Wŏnhyo lived primarily as a mendicant, wandering the cities and markets as a street proselytizer. As his biography in the SAMGUK YUSA (MEMORABILIA OF THE THREE KINGDOMS) states, "He used to . . . sing and dance his way through thousands of villages and myriad hamlets, touring while proselytizing in song. Thus, everyone in the country came to recognize the name 'Buddha' and recite 'Homage to Buddha.'" This same source relates that Wŏnhyo died in a hermitage in March 686, leaving no direct disciples. The *Samguk sagi* (*Historical Records of the Three Kingdoms*) also notes that he died as a householder (*kŏsa*), a male lay Buddhist.

Wŏnhyo's thought system is structured around the concept of "one mind," as illustrated in his commentaries to the AWAKENING OF FAITH (DASHENG QIXIN LUN). *One mind* is another term for the mind of SENTIENT BEINGS, which is intrinsically pure and unchanging, but appears externally to be impure and ephemeral. Even though every deluded thought arises from the mind, at the same time, it is that mind itself that provides the capacity to achieve enlightenment. Wŏnhyo outlines a threefold structure for experiencing enlightenment: ORIGINAL ENLIGHTENMENT (HONGAKU), nonenlightenment, and actualizing enlightenment, which are mutually contingent and mutually defining. Original enlightenment provides the theoretical basis for enlightenment; nonenlightenment is the misconception about the nature of original enlightenment; and actualizing enlightenment is the incitement to practice. Practice here is based on the conditional definition of nonenlightenment, that is, the insubstantiality of defilements. Practice, therefore, does not really involve removing something; it instead is correct knowledge that the defilements we experience in daily life are unreal. The distinction Wŏnhyo draws between original and nonenlightenments, and the attempts he makes to integrate the two, set the stage for notions of the universality of buddhahood in later East Asian Buddhism. The *Awakening of Faith* itself originally provided the conceptual frame for this notion, but it was Wŏnhyo's elaboration in his commentary to that treatise that provided a more coherent interpretation of this construct and proposed a solution to the tensions inherent in the definition of enlightenment in Buddhist history. This elaboration helped to establish a unique cognitive framework for East Asian Buddhism, and made Wŏnhyo's commentary one of the most influential texts in the East Asian Buddhist tradition.

See also: **Faxiang School; Korea; Madhyamaka School; Tiantai School**

Bibliography

Buswell, Robert E., Jr. *The Formation of Ch'an Ideology in China and Korea: The Vajrasamādhi-Sūtra, a Buddhist Apocryphon.* Princeton, NJ: Princeton University Press, 1989.

Buswell, Robert E., Jr. "Hagiographies of the Korean Monk Wŏnhyo." In *Buddhism in Practice,* ed. Donald S. Lopez, Jr. Princeton, NJ: Princeton University Press, 1995.

EUNSU CHO

WORSHIP

Worship in the Buddhist tradition takes many forms and is directed toward many different beings and objects, from images of the Buddha, to his physical remains (relics), to visualized BODHISATTVAS.

The question of the proper form and purpose of worship is addressed in several places in early Buddhist texts. Some texts stress that the Buddha should not be worshiped at all, but rather that the dharma (Pāli, *dhamma*) should be the focus of Buddhist practice. Thus, in the *Saṃyuttanikāya* (*Connected Discourses*), a monk named Vakkali expresses his desire to see and worship the Buddha, who sharply rebukes him: "What is the sight of this putrid body to you? He who sees the *dhamma,* Vakkali, he sees me; he who sees me, he sees the *dhamma*" (*SN* 3.120). Variations of this attitude toward worship of the Buddha can be found in a variety of early texts. In the *Dīghanikāya* (*Group of Long Discourses*), for instance, there is a scene in which the Buddha, having been showered by flowers from a blossoming tree, tells his chief disciple and faithful attendant, ĀNANDA, that such outward displays of worship are not appropriate; rather, the best form of worship of the Buddha is following the dharma (*DN* 2.138). Likewise, in the MAHĀPARINIRVĀṆA-SŪTRA (Pāli, *Mahāparinibbana-sutta*; *Great Discourse on the Nirvāṇa*), when Ānanda learns that the Buddha is about to die and is in anguish at the thought of the loss of his beloved teacher, the Buddha tells him that his physical presence is not necessary, for he has left the dharma, and that is the only guiding light that Ānanda and the other disciples will need. Scholars and Buddhists alike have frequently taken this famous episode as indicative of the Buddha's own attitude toward worship: Focus on learning and following the dharma, not on worshiping the physical form of the Buddha, which leads only to grasping.

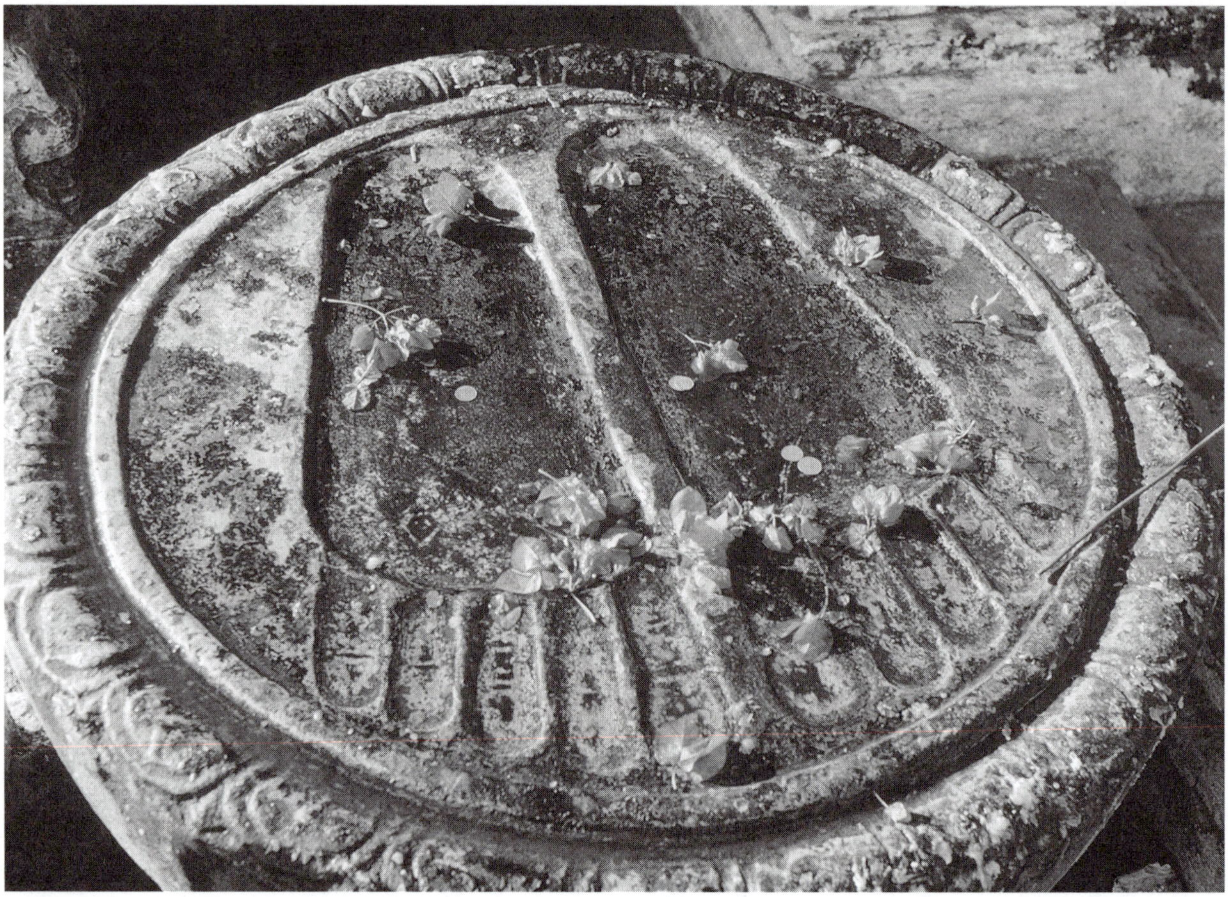

Lotus petals strewn on a sculptural representation of the Buddha's footprints at Bodh Gayā, site of the Buddha's enlightenment. © Hulton Archive by Getty Images. Reproduced by permission.

However, in another famous episode in the *Mahāparinirvāṇa-sūtra,* Ānanda asks the Buddha what should be done with his bones after his cremation, and he tells him that his remains should be gathered up and placed inside a STŪPA (Pāli, *thūpa*) built at the intersection of four great roads. There, the Buddha says, his followers can come to "offer a garland, or scent, or paint, or make a salutation, or feel serene joy in their heart, which will be to their benefit and well-being for a long time" (*DN* 2.142). This clearly sets a different precedent for worship, one that encourages worship of the physical objects related to the Buddha as an opportunity to honor the departed teacher and to establish an emotional connection to him. This practice, called *buddhānusmṛti* (Pāli, *buddhānusati*; recollection of the Buddha), involves the worshiper in creating through MEDITATION a mental image of the Buddha that can, then, be mentally worshiped. This form of worship is common in both the THERAVĀDA and MAHĀYĀNA school traditions.

The great Buddhist ruler AŚOKA (third century B.C.E.) is credited with having spread the relics and thus their worship by dividing the original eight portions into eighty-four thousand parts and enshrining them in stūpas throughout India. Such relics are often said to embody the Buddha, and thus are worshiped as extensions of his person. From at least the third century B.C.E. relic veneration has been one of the most important forms of worshiping the Buddha, and it continues to be at the core of worship in much of the Buddhist world. In contemporary Sri Lanka, for example, the Temple of the Tooth, which houses what is said to be one of the Buddha's canines, is visited by thousands of Buddhists daily and is perhaps the most important religious structure in the country.

In addition to the worship of the Buddha's physical remains, sculptural images are important objects of worship. Early Buddhism tended to represent the Buddha in iconic forms—via his footprints, an empty throne, the tree under which he attained enlightenment, the wheel of dharma—in order to emphasize his physical absence from the world and to prevent his followers from grasping on to the person of the Buddha. At both SĀÑCĪ and Bhārhut, two of the earliest Indian sites from which there are sculptural remains, there is evidence that such objects were worshiped in much the same way that the Buddha describes the proper worship of his relics: Offerings are made of flowers and the worshipers bow down in respect, forming the *añjali mudrā,* or gesture of reverence and respect.

Sculptural images of the Buddha himself began to appear sometime around the turn of the first millennium. These images focus on significant moments in the biography of the Buddha, such as his enlightenment or his defeat of MĀRA. In medieval India, a set of eight episodes from the Buddha's life—the *aṣṭamahāprātihārya*—became a common sculptural motif, and allowed the worshiper to honor and venerate the entire life of the Buddha in a single image.

Perhaps the most common form of worship in the Buddhist world is *buddha pūjā,* literally "honoring the Buddha," which can be performed both in the formal setting of a monastery or at a home shrine. It typically involves making some sort of offering to a Buddha image or relic or stūpa—a flower, a small lamp, food, or even money. When *buddha pūjā* is performed in a monastery, the worshiper first removes his or her shoes, washes the object to be offered to purify the offering, and then approaches the image or stūpa with hands clasped in the *añjali* gesture of respect. The object is then offered, and the worshiper bows down or prostrates before the image or stūpa. Such worship focuses the mind of the worshiper on the Buddha and his teachings and also generates merit. Although *buddha pūjā* can be performed at any time, it is particularly important to worship the Buddha in this manner on *poṣadha* (Pāli, *uposatha*) days and on special holidays, such as the Buddha's birthday, Vesak.

In the Mahāyāna tradition, in addition to worship that is directed toward the Buddha, bodhisattvas and other DIVINITIES (such as Tārā and Prajñāpāramitā) are objects of great devotion. In the PURE LAND SCHOOLS, AMITĀBHA in particular is worshiped; proper veneration of and faith in Amitābha, in some schools attained through the fervent recitation of his name, leads to rebirth in his Pure Land.

Finally, not only are buddhas and bodhisattvas the object of worship, but also MONKS, since one should honor and worship one's teacher as a living embodiment of the Buddha's teachings. In Thailand, the relics of famous monks are often objects of great devotion and worship. Likewise, in China and Japan, the mummified bodies of important monks are sometimes preserved as living presences, and in many Buddhist schools in Tibet, one worships one's LAMA in the same way that one would honor the Buddha himself.

See also: **Buddha Images; Buddhānusmṛti (Recollection of the Buddha); Dharma and Dharmas; Merit and Merit-Making; Relics and Relics Cults**

Bibliography

Eckel, Malcom David. *To See the Buddha: A Philosopher's Quest for the Meaning of Emptiness.* San Francisco: Harper, 1992.

Kinnard, Jacob N. *Imaging Wisdom: Seeing and Knowing in the Art of Indian Buddhism.* Richmond, UK: Curzon Press, 1999.

Trainor, Kevin. *Relics, Ritual, and Representation in Buddhism: Rematerializing the Sri Lankan Theravāda Tradition.* Cambridge, UK: Cambridge University Press, 1997.

JACOB N. KINNARD

X

XUANZANG

Xuanzang (Ci'en, ca. 600–664) was a renowned Chinese pilgrim to India and one of the most prolific Chinese translators. Due to his encompassing knowledge of Buddhist traditions, he was honored as *sanzang fashi* (Trepiṭaka Dharma Master).

Xuanzang became engrossed in Yogācāra thought at an early age, but came to realize that the scriptures of that school were only partially available in Chinese. It was particularly the absence of a full translation of the encyclopedic *Yogācārabhūmī-śāstra* (*Treatise on the Stages of the Yoga Masters*) that Xuanzang felt painfully. Therefore, he decided that in order to obtain an authentic interpretation of the teachings of the YOGĀCĀRA SCHOOL he had to travel to India. In 627 Xuanzang set out on his hazardous journey. On the way he relied on the support of many, lay and cleric, humble and noble, as well as on the saving power of the BODHISATTVAS, particularly of MAITREYA. Xuanzang spent fourteen years in India (629–643), venerating virtually all important sacred sites, collecting texts, and studying with teachers. The most important of his instructors was Śīlabhadra, a disciple of Dharmapāla, under whose guidance Xuanzang studied for five years at the monastic university of Nālandā. Besides Yogācāra, he studied Sarvāstivāda, Madhyamaka, and *hetuvidyā* (Buddhist LOGIC), as well as the Vedas and Sanskrit grammar. In Nālandā, Xuanzang figured among the most exalted scholars of his time, and he was enthusiastically entertained by the Indian kings Bhāskaravarman and Harṣa. After his return to Chang'an in 645, he was received by Emperor Tang Taizong, who funded Xuanzang's academy for the translation of sūtras and had him compile the *Da Tang xiyu ji* (*Record of Travels to the Western Regions*). This record, together with his biography, the *Ci'en zhuan* (*Biography of Xuanzang*) by Huili, remains the most important source for the Buddhism of his time.

During the nineteen years after his return, Xuanzang translated seventy-five of the 657 works he brought home. Among these his translations of ABHIDHARMA, Yogācāra, and *hetuvidyā* texts have secured him a foremost place in the annals of dharma transmission. Xuanzang did not work alone. The sources provide names of more than sixty major collaborators, some of them scholars famed for their exegetic work, including KUIJI, Jingmai, Shentai, WŎNCH'ŬK, Wenbei, Puguang, and Xuanying.

According to Xuanzang's biographers, among the questions he sought to answer were whether all beings possess an innate capacity to attain buddhahood, what awakening meant, and how the PATH is to be conceived. Whereas PARAMĀRTHA's translations supported the TATHĀGATAGARBHA (buddha-nature), the Yogācāra (Faxiang) teachings transmitted by Xuanzang included the notion of the Five Lineages (*pañcagotra*), one of which, the so-called ICCHANTIKA, was said not to possess the capacity for awakening. To many of Xuanzang's contemporaries, this sounded awkward. But, in fact, this teaching represented just one aspect of the highly sophisticated Yogācāra exegesis, which at the time constituted the sum of Buddhist learning because it incorporated the Abhidharma learning on a MAHĀYĀNA foundation. Xuanzang considered the faithful transmission and preservation of these teachings to be his duty. For him, it was pointless and an excessive simplification to assume that one should disregard the most refined teachings of the Indian sages. He summarized these teachings in the seminal *Cheng Weishi lun* (*Establishing the Exclusivity of Vijñāna*) a synoptic discussion of the Yogācāra doctrine following Dharmāpala's interpretation.

See also: **China; India; Pilgrimage; Silk Road**

Bibliography

Beal, Samuel, trans. *Si-yu-ki: Buddhist Records of the Western World.* London: Kegan Paul, 1906.

Grousset, René. *In the Footsteps of the Buddha.* London: Routledge, 1932.

La Vallée-Poussin, Louis de, trans. and ed. *Vijñaptimātratāsiddhi: La Siddhi de Hiuan-tsang.* Paris: Geuthner, 1928–1929.

Li, Rongxi, trans. *A Biography of the Tripitaka Master of the Great Ci'en Monastery of the Great Tang Dynasty.* Berkeley, CA: Numata Center for Buddhist Translation and Research, 1995.

Mayer, Alexander L., trans. *Xuanzang: Übersetzer und Heiliger.* Wiesbaden, Germany: Harrassowitz, 1992.

ALEXANDER L. MAYER

Y

YAKṢA

Yakṣa (Pāli, *yakkha*) are indigenous Indian tree spirits that are included in the list of the occupants of the lowest of the HELLS, where they torture beings, sometimes quite graphically. Either male or female, most yakṣas are wild, demonic, sexually prolific beings who live in solitary places and are hostile toward people, particularly monks and nuns, whose meditation they disturb by making loud noises. Yakṣas are associated variously with fertility, the earth, water, and trees, as well as with lust and delusion (māyā). Frequently, however, they are converted to Buddhism and "tamed," becoming active, positive forces in the world. Yakṣas appear in various JĀTAKA tales. In the *Devadhamma-jātaka,* for instance, the Buddha-to-be explains to a vicious *yakkha* that he has attained his lowly state due to his past KARMA (ACTION), and the *yakkha* converts to Buddhism and becomes a protector of the king. Vajrapāṇi, who becomes a particularly prominent divinity in the MAHĀYĀNA, is in early texts a yakṣa who protects Buddhism and serves as the Buddha's bodyguard. In other texts, though, yakṣas are considerably more fierce. In the *Valāhassana-jātaka,* for instance, there is a yakṣa city on an island (Sri Lanka) inhabited by female *yakṣinīs* who lure sailors with their apparent beauty, only to enslave, torture, and devour the sailors before they are rescued by the bodhisattva. In other early texts, such as the *Āḷavaka-sutta* of the *Sutta-nipāta,* the yakṣa frequently plays the role of the skeptic or reluctant convert, and thus serves as both a foil for the Buddha to preach the dharma and a metaphor for the power of the dharma to reform even the most wicked. Yakṣas are represented in Buddhist sculpture as early as the Mathurā period (fourth through second centuries B.C.E.), frequently as *caurī*-holding attendants and servants of the Buddha. They are especially prominent at SĀÑCĪ and Bhārhut.

See also: **Divinities; Ghosts and Spirits**

Bibliography

Coomaraswamy, Ananda K. *Yakṣas.* New Delhi: Munshiram Manoharlal, 1931.

Sutherland, Gail Hinich. *The Disguises of the Demon: The Development of the Yakṣa in Hinduism and Buddhism.* Albany: State University of New York Press, 1991.

JACOB N. KINNARD

YANSHOU

Yongming Yanshou (Zhijue, 904–975) was a major figure in the development of Chinese Buddhism after the Tang dynasty (618–907). Yanshou is particularly esteemed in the CHAN SCHOOL and PURE LAND SCHOOLS, where his memory is frequently invoked as an initiator of the Chan–Pure Land synthesis that dominated Chinese Buddhism after the Song dynasty (960–1279).

Yanshou lived during a period of upheaval between the Tang and Song, when China was divided into a number of de facto independent principalities, or kingdoms. In many respects, Yanshou represents a culmination of the scholastic style of Tang Buddhism. In other respects, Yanshou epitomized the syncretic style of Buddhism that became dominant during the Song. While Yanshou identified himself and was regarded as a Chan master, his scholastic style is more reminiscent of the major Tang Buddhist schools, Huayan and

Tiantai. His conception of Chan as the culmination of the Buddhist scriptural tradition, often rendered as "harmony between Chan and Buddhist teaching," stands in contrast to the independent claims of "a special transmission outside the teaching" identified particularly with the Linji lineage of Chan.

Within the Chan school, Yanshou is regarded as the third patriarch of the Fayan lineage. During the tenth century, Fayan monks played major roles at the courts of many southern kingdoms, especially Wuyue, where Tiantai Deshao (891–972) served as national preceptor or spiritual adviser to the Wuyue court. With the support of the Wuyue ruler, Deshao orchestrated the Buddhist revival in the region, most notably on Mount Tiantai, one of China's sacred mountains and Wuyue's spiritual center. Yanshou is regarded as Deshao's successor in the Fayan lineage; following Deshao's example, he served as a major prelate in Wuyue.

Little is known of Yanshou's life. Buddhist biographers suggest that Yanshou was a talented and pious youth who initially entered the civil service as a garrison commander (or an official in charge of military provisions, according to one source) at a sensitive border post in Wuyue. Moved by his Buddhist aspirations, Yanshou renounced his official duties to become a Chan monk. Later sources claim that Yanshou illicitly used government funds to buy captured fish and set them free as an expression of Buddhist altruism. Sentenced to death for his crime, Yanshou was eventually freed by the Wuyue ruler, who judged that Yanshou's motives were sincere when he faced death serenely. Yanshou's altruism became a major feature of his mythological image as a Buddhist savior, one who was able to escape death himself and to free others from the fate of purgatorial suffering. In this capacity, Yanshou became a devotional figure among Chinese Buddhists who enlisted Yanshou's assistance to gain birth in the Pure Land of AMITĀBHA Buddha. Yanshou's association with the Pure Land schools is largely the result of this.

After being granted official permission to leave government service and enter the Buddhist clergy, Yanshou studied and practiced for many years on Mount Tiantai. He commenced teaching on Mount Xuedou in 952. In 960 he was invited to serve as abbot of Lingyin Monastery, a major Buddhist institution in the Wuyue capital of Qiantang (present-day Hangzhou). The following year he was invited to assume abbot's duties at the recently constructed Yongming Monastery, also located in the capital and a major symbol of the Buddhist revival in Wuyue. In addition to his Chan scholasticism, Yanshou is particularly noted for his devotion to the LOTUS SŪTRA (SADDHARMAPUṆḌARĪKA-SŪTRA) and his promotion of Buddhist altruism through the performance of good deeds. He passed away on Mount Tiantai in 975 and was granted the posthumous name Zhijue by the Song emperor. Among his numerous works are the massive one-hundred-fascicle *Zongjing lu* (*Records of the Source-Mirror*), devoted to his vision of Chan as a pan-sectarian ideology espoused throughout Buddhism and not exclusive to the Chan lineage, and the *Wanshan tonggui ji* (*The Common End of Myriad Good Practices*), regarded in the later tradition as a testament to Chan–Pure Land syncretism, but actually espousing a broader syncretism encompassing the aims of the entire Buddhist tradition.

See also: **China**

Bibliography

Shih, Heng-ching, *The Syncretism of Chan and Pure Land Buddhism.* New York: Peter Lang, 1992.

Welter, Albert. "The Contextual Study of Chinese Buddhist Biographies: The Example of Yung-ming Yen-shou (904-975)." In *Monks and Magicians: Religious Biographies in Asia,* ed. Phyllis Granoff and Koichi Shinohara. Oakville, ON: Mosaic Press, 1988.

Welter, Albert. *The Meaning of Myriad Good Deeds: A Study of Yung-ming Yen-shou and the Wan-shan t'ung-kuei chi.* New York: Peter Lang, 1993.

ALBERT WELTER

YIJING

Yijing (635–713), together with FAXIAN and XUANZANG, is one of the most important Chinese pilgrims to travel to India. Yijing, who was honored during his lifetime with the title *sanzang fashi* (Master of the Tripiṭaka), was a prolific translator, particularly of the *Sarvāstivāda Vinaya.* In 671 he sailed to Śrīvijaya (Sumatra) and traveled from there to Tāmraliptī (eastern India), then to the monastic Buddhist university at Nālandā, where for nine years he studied *hetuvidyā* (logic), ABHIDHARMAKOŚABHĀṢYA, VINAYA, and MADHYAMAKA SCHOOL and YOGĀCĀRA SCHOOL philosophies. After further studies in Śrīvijaya, he returned to China in 695 and worked with ŚIKṢĀNANDA at his translation bureau in Luoyang. From 700 to 713 Yijing headed his own academy of translation. Altogether he translated approximately fifty-six works in 230 fascicles, including *Āgama*, AVADĀNA, and MAHĀYĀNA scriptures and treatises, tantras, and vinaya texts, particularly of the SARVĀSTIVĀDA, thus preserving one of the most important monastic traditions. His translations of Yogācāra texts and of Buddhist reasoning are equally important.

Yijing also wrote exegetic works and the earliest extant Sanskrit-Chinese dictionary (*Fanyu qianzi wen*). His two most important writings are *Nanhai jigui neifa zhuan* (*An Account of the Dharma Sent Back from the Southern Seas,* T 2125), which gives an account of Buddhist practices, showing the Chinese perceptions of the monastic regulations prevalent in India, and *Da Tang xiyu qiufa gaoseng zhuan* (*Record of Eminent Monks Who [Traveled to] India in Search of the Dharma during the Tang,* T 2066).

See also: **China; India; Pilgrimage; Silk Road**

Bibliography

Chavannes, Edouard, trans. *Mémoire composé à l'époque de la grande dynastie T'ang sur les religieux éminents qui allèrent chercher la loi dans les pays d'occident, par I-Tsing.* Paris: E. Leroux, 1894.

Takakusu Junjiro, trans. *A Record of the Buddhist Religion as Practised in India and the Malay Archipelago (A.D. 671–695) by I-Tsing.* Oxford: Clarendon, 1896.

ALEXANDER L. MAYER

YINSHUN

Widely considered to be the primary successor of the reform legacy of his teacher TAIXU (1890–1947), Yinshun Shengzheng (1906–) is an influential Buddhist scholar in modern Chinese Buddhist academe and a key architect of the Chinese Buddhist reform movement. He reformulated and added academic sophistication to the content of his late teacher's rallying rhetoric of "Buddhism for Human Life" (*Rensheng fojiao*) and coined the new slogan "Humanistic Buddhism" (*Renjian fojiao*) to promote his refined version of a modern "engaged" form of Buddhism.

In his writings, Yinshun proposed various periodization schemes outlining Buddhist doctrinal evolution, and polemically assessed the relevance of the different periods to modern Buddhist spirituality, as well as to what he considered to be the central, defining tenets of Buddhism. His positions challenged deeply cherished beliefs of Chinese Buddhists: his unsympathetic treatment of both the "transcendentalized" TATHĀGATAGARBHA or buddha-nature tradition, and the "vulgarized" popular Chinese schools like Pure Land and Chan.

No less impassioned and idealistic than his teacher Taixu in advancing his version of the bodhisattva path, Yinshun's copious works have left an indelible mark on the academic and religious discourse of modern Chinese Buddhist communities. Most of these works are collected in the massive *Miaoyun ji* (*Anthology of the Wondrous Clouds*) and the *Huayu ji* (*Anthology of the Flower Rains*). Other stand-alone volumes contain groundbreaking research on the Sarvāstivāda treatises and the Chinese *Samyuktāgama.*

See also: **China; Engaged Buddhism**

Bibliography

Pittman, Don A. *Toward a Modern Chinese Buddhism: Taixu's Reforms.* Honolulu: University of Hawaii Press, 2001.

Qiu Minjie. *Yinshun daoshi de foxue sixiang.* Taipei: Fajie, 1990.

WILLIAM CHU

YIXUAN

Yixuan (Linji Yixuan; Japanese, Rinzai Gigen; ?–866) was a famous Chinese master and an emblematic figure of the putative "golden age" of the CHAN SCHOOL of Buddhism. Early biographical sources agree on only a few details about his life. Linji's family name before becoming a monk was Jing; he was born in southwest Shandong province, studied under master Huangbo Xiyun (died ca. 850), visited various monasteries during his pilgrimage years, and finally taught at a monastery "near the ford" (*linji,* the origin of his name) in Hebei province, where he died. Most sources offer May 27, 866, as the date of his death.

In Chan circles, Linji's reputation as a forceful teacher fond of deafening shouts and unconventional teaching methods grew rapidly after his death. Notes of his sermons and conversations circulated, and such phrases as "Linji's True Man of No Rank" achieved wide renown. Nevertheless, almost three centuries passed before, in 1120, Yuanjue Zongyan (ca. late eleventh–twelfth century) compiled the *Linji lu* (*Record of Linji*), the most important extant source for

Linji's teaching. When this gem of a Chan text was published, Linji's reputation was already established as the founder of one of Chan's Five Houses, and his life story had become thoroughly embellished with colorful details.

Bibliography

Demiéville, Paul, trans. and ed. *Entretiens de Lin-tsi.* Paris: Fayard, 1972.

Miura, Isshū, and Sasaki, Ruth Fuller. *Zen Dust.* Kyoto: First Zen Institute of America in Japan, 1966.

Sasaki, Ruth Fuller, trans. *The Record of Lin-chi.* Kyoto: Institute for Zen Studies, 1975.

Watson, Burton, trans. *The Zen Teachings of Master Lin-chi.* Boston: Shambhala, 1993.

Yanagida, Seizan. "The Life of Lin-chi I-hsüan." *Eastern Buddhist* vol. V, no. 2 (1972): 70–94.

URS APP

YOGA. *See* Meditation

YOGĀCĀRA SCHOOL

The Yogācāra school, whose name is taken from one of its foundational texts, the *Yogācārabhūmi* (*Stages of Yoga Practice*), provided perhaps the most sophisticated examination and description in all of Buddhism of how the mind works—in psychological, epistemological, logical, emotional, cognitive, meditative, developmental, and soteriological modes. At once a rigorous, rational philosophy and an elaborate system of practice, it provided methods by which one could identify and correct the cognitive errors inherent in the way the mind works, since enlightenment meant direct, immediate, correct cognition.

The founding of Yogācāra, one of the two major Indian MAHĀYĀNA schools, is usually attributed to the half-brothers ASAṄGA and VASUBANDHU (fourth to fifth century C.E.), but most of its unique concepts had been introduced at least a century earlier in scriptures such as the SAṂDHINIRMOCANA-SŪTRA (*Sūtra Elucidating the Hidden Connections* or *Sūtra Setting Free the* [*Buddha's*] *Intent*). Yogācāra forged novel concepts and methods that synthesized prior Buddhist teachings into a coherent antidote (*pratipakṣa*) for eliminating the cognitive problems that prevented liberation from the karmic cycles of birth and death.

Historical overview

Key Yogācāra notions such as only-cognition (*vijñaptimātra*), three self-natures (*trisvabhāva*), the ĀLAYAVIJÑĀNA (warehouse consciousness), overturning the basis (*āśrayaparāvṛtti*), and the theory of eight consciousnesses were introduced in the *Saṃdhinirmocana-sūtra* and received more detailed, systematic treatment in the writings of Asaṅga and Vasubandhu. Born Brahmans in Puruṣapura (present-day Peshawar, Pakistan) to the same mother but different fathers, Asaṅga and his half-brother Vasubandhu became Buddhists, Asaṅga entering the MAHĪŚĀSAKA school, while Vasubandhu joined the Vaibhāṣikas in their stronghold in Kashmir. The literary core of Mahīśāsaka practice was the ĀGAMA/NIKĀYA corpus of the MAINSTREAM BUDDHIST SCHOOLS, while the Vaibhāṣikas excelled at ABHIDHARMA. The brothers' later writings reflect these backgrounds, since even Asaṅga's book on *abhidharma,* the *Abhidharmasamuccaya* (*Abhidharma Compilation*), cites only *āgamas,* not *abhidharma* texts.

According to tradition, after many years of fruitless practice and solitary meditation, in a moment of utter despair, Asaṅga began receiving instruction from the future Buddha, MAITREYA, who resides in the Tuṣita heaven. Maitreya dictated new texts for Asaṅga to disseminate. Asaṅga also composed works under his own name, though the Chinese and Tibetan traditions disagree about the attribution of these texts. For instance, both ascribe the *Mahāyānasaṃgraha* (*Mahāyāna Compendium*), *Abhidharmasamuccaya,* and *Mahāyānasūtrālaṃkāra* (*Ornament of Mahāyāna Sūtras*) to Asaṅga, and *Madhyāntavibhāga* (*Distinguishing the Middle and Extremes*) to Maitreya, but Chinese tradition attributes the *Yogācārabhūmi* to Maitreya, whereas Tibetans credit Asaṅga with this text. What gave the Maitreya-Asaṅga texts their lasting importance was not their mode of composition—receiving sacred scriptures from nonhuman sources is not uncommon in Asian traditions—but their content, that is, how they rethought Buddhism on a grand scale, as well as in its most minute details.

Vasubandhu grew dissatisfied with Vaibhāṣika doctrine and, after exploring other forms of Buddhism, became a Yogācāra through Asaṅga's influence. Asaṅga's magnum opus, the *Yogācārabhūmi,* is a comprehensive encyclopedia of Buddhist terms and models mapped according to a Yogācāra view of how one progresses along the stages of the path to enlightenment. Vasubandhu's pre-Yogācāra magnum opus, the ABHIDHARMAKOŚABHĀṢYA (*Treasury of Abhidharma*), also provides a comprehensive, detailed overview of the

Buddhist path with meticulous attention to nuances and differences of opinion on a broad range of exacting topics.

Vasubandhu's two main disciples (though they probably encountered his writings through intermediary generations of teachers) were DIGNĀGA (ca. 480–540 C.E.), who revolutionized Indian logic and epistemology, and Sthiramati (ca. 510–570), who wrote important commentaries on the works of Asaṅga and Vasubandhu, notably *Abhidharmasamuccayabhāṣya, Triṃśikāvijñaptiṭīkā,* and a subcommentary on Vasubandhu's commentary on the *Madhyāntavibhāga.* After Vasubandhu, Yogācāra developed into two distinct directions or branches: (1) a logico-epistemic tradition, exemplified by such thinkers as Dignāga, DHARMAKĪRTI, Śāntarakṣita, and Ratnakīrti; and (2) an *abhidharma*-style psychology, exemplified by such thinkers as Sthiramati, Dharmapāla, XUANZANG, and Vinītadeva. While the first branch focused on questions of epistemology and LOGIC, the other branch refined and elaborated the *abhidharma* analysis developed by Asaṅga and Vasubandhu. These branches were not entirely separate, and many Buddhists wrote works that contributed to both. Dignāga, for instance, besides his works on epistemology and logic, also wrote a commentary on Vasubandhu's *Abhidharmakośa.* What united both branches was a deep concern with the process of cognition, that is, analyses of how people perceive and think. The former branch approached that issue epistemologically, whereas the latter branch approached it psychologically and therapeutically. Both identified the root of all human problems as cognitive errors that needed correction.

The *abhidharma* branch faded in importance by the eighth century in India, while the logico-epistemic branch remained vital until the demise of Buddhism in India around the thirteenth century. Nonetheless, various Hindu and Jain schools have continued up to the present day to study and write about its arguments and contributions to Indian philosophy. Such literature usually labels the Yogācāra positions VIJÑĀNAVĀDA (consciousness school).

Yogācāra outside India

In the early sixth century in China, while translating Vasubandhu's commentary on the *Ten Stages Sūtra* (Sanskrit, *Daśabhūmikasūtropadeśa*; Chinese, *Dilun*), the two translators, Bodhiruci and Ratnamati, parted due to irreconcilable differences of interpretation. Bodhiruci favored a more orthodox Yogācāra approach, while Ratnamati was drawn to a Yogācāra-TATHĀGATAGARBHA hybrid ideology. The former emphasizes removing mental obstructions, whereas the latter stresses an ontological pure nature that shines forth once defilements are removed. Their feud had an immediate and lasting impact on Chinese Buddhism, with followers of Bodhiruci's interpretation developing into the so-called Northern Dilun school and Ratnamati's followers becoming Southern Dilun. That feud dominated contemporary Chinese Buddhism, and it intensified when in the mid-sixth century the Indian translator PARAMĀRTHA (499–569) introduced another version of Yogācāra, amenable to the tathāgatagarbha ideology, that reified a ninth consciousness (*amalavijñāna,* pure consciousness) that would emerge with enlightenment, even though no Indian text attests to this concept. Asaṅga's *Mahāyānasaṃgraha* (Chinese, *Shelun*) became the key text for Paramārtha's followers, so their school was dubbed Shelun.

In 629, seeking to resolve the disputes between these schools, Xuanzang (ca. 600–664) traveled to India, returning in 645 with over six hundred texts—seventy-four of which he translated—and a better understanding of Indian Yogācāra as taught at Nālandā (the prime seat of Buddhist learning at that time). His successor, KUIJI (632–682), founded the Weishi school (Sanskrit, Vijñaptimātra), also called FAXIANG (Dharma Characteristics). Students who had come from Korea and Japan to study with Xuanzang and Kuiji brought the teaching back to their countries, where it thrived for many centuries, and survives today in Japan as Hossō (the Japanese pronunciation of Faxiang). Although the Weishi school came under attack from the newly emerging sinitic Mahāyāna schools, such as the HUAYAN SCHOOL, for challenging ingrained orthodoxies, ironically those orthodoxies were themselves largely grounded in developments from the earlier Yogācāra-oriented Dilun and Shelun schools. The CHAN SCHOOL, which started to institutionalize around the time of Xuanzang and Kuiji, initially drew on the LAṄKĀVATĀRA-SŪTRA, a Yogācāra-tathāgatagarbha hybrid text, as one of its main scriptures. Thus, much of the later developments in East Asian Buddhism can be seen as arising out of inter-Yogācāra rivalries.

Yogācāra entered Tibet in the eighth century with Śāntarakṣita (ca. 725–790) and his disciple Kamalaśīla (ca. 740–795), who were among the earliest Buddhist missionaries there. While never established in Tibet as an independent school, Yogācāra teachings became part of the curriculum for other Tibetan schools, and exerted an influence on RNYING MA (NYINGMA) and Dzogs chen thought. TSONG KHA PA (1357–1419), founder of the DGE LUGS (GELUK) school, devoted considerable attention to Yogācāra, especially the works of Asaṅga and the *Saṃdhinirmocana-sūtra,* with particular attention to the Korean monk WŎNCH'ŬK's (613–696) commentary on the latter. Wŏnch'ŭk was a Korean disciple of Xuanzang; the final chapters of his *Saṃdhinirmocana* commentary are no longer extant in the original Chinese, the complete work surviving only in its Tibetan translation. The Tibetan understanding of Yogācāra, therefore, is drawn from East Asian as well as Indian sources. Many of the Tibetan debates on Yogācāra thought, which have continued until today, appear to be replays of the controversies that raged in China and East Asia centuries earlier, sometimes with new wrinkles.

Classic texts

The Maitreya-Asaṅga texts tend to be vast compendiums of models, technical terminology, and doctrinal lists that come alive only when one pays attention to their minutest details and contemplates their implications. The *Yogācārabhūmi,* which comprises one hundred fascicles in Xuanzang's Chinese translation (the complete Sanskrit is not available), describes seventeen stages (*bhūmis*) of practice, beginning with an exposition of what it means to have a body with the five sensory consciousnesses, and moving on to instructions on developing a vast array of mental and meditative capacities and on engaging the śrāvaka (HĪNAYĀNA), PRATYEKABUDDHA (one who achieves enlightenment independently without relying on Buddhism), and BODHISATTVA vehicles, culminating in NIRVĀṆA without remainder (*nirupādhikabhūmi*).

The first part of the *Abhidharmasamuccaya,* the *lakṣaṇasamuccaya* (compilation of definitions), offers detailed *abhidharma* lists and definitions of the five SKANDHAS (AGGREGATES), twelve sense-realms, and so on. The second part, *viniścayasamuccaya* (compilation of determinations), teaches how to activate the plethora of *abhidharma* lists and models, so that when applied to each other (rather than taken in isolation), they effect changes in the practitioner by deconstructing one's delusions, greed, and anger. The *Mahāyānasaṃgraha* details how hearing, thinking, and contemplating the Mahāyāna teachings destroys the *ālayavijñāna* from within, like a germ infecting a host, since the Buddha's word (*buddhavacana*) is ultimately irreducible to mental constructions; eliminating the *ālayavijñāna* therefore results in buddhahood. The *Madhyāntavibhāga,* implicitly deploying the theory of three natures (*trisvabhāva*) to define and explicate Buddhist practice, illustrates how ŚŪNYATĀ (EMPTINESS) and cultivating positive insight (*pariniṣpanna*) act as an antidote (*pratipakṣa*) to the pervasive false mental constructions (*parikalpita*) one projects as lived experience, resulting in reality being experienced just as it is (purified *paratantra*).

Vasubandhu's *Karmasiddhiprakaraṇa* (*Investigation Establishing* [*the Correct Understanding*] *of Karma*) discusses various Buddhist theories on how karma works, concluding that all is momentary but held together by causal chains, consequences of actions requiting their doer through mental causal chains embodied in the *ālayavijñāna.* The *Vādavidhi* (*Debate Methods*) is a proto-logic text on reasoning in arguments and debates, and a precursor of Dignāga's innovations in logic. *Pañcaskandhaprakaraṇa* (*Investigation of the Five Aggregates*) breaks down the aggregates into *abhidharma* categories and their constituents (dharmas), constructing a dharma system in transition between the seventy-five dharmas of his Vaibhāṣika *Abhidharmakośa* and his fully mature Yogācāra system of one hundred dharmas, later enumerated in his *Mahāyānaśatadharmāprakāśamukha-śāstra* (*One Hundred Dharma Treatise*). One can trace Vasubandhu's development from Vaibhāṣika to Yogācāra through these texts.

Vasubandhu's most important Yogācāra texts are his *Viṃśatikā* (*Twenty Verses*) with autocommentary and *Triṃśikā* (*Thirty Verses*), together sometimes called the Vijñaptimātra treatises. The *Triṃśikā* densely packs the entire Yogācāra system into thirty short verses. The *Viṃśatikā* refutes realist objections to Yogācāra. The realists contend that the objects in our perception exist outside of consciousness just as we perceive them, which is why they remain stable through (1) time and (2) space; why (3) people with different perceptions of a thing can reach a consensus about it; and why (4) the objective world operates by determinate causal principles, not through unreal, ineffective fantasies. Vasubandhu responds with numerous arguments to these four points, and he offers an analogy to DREAMS. Seemingly external objects appear in dreams, even though such objects are only mental fabrications with nothing external corresponding to them, proving that consciousness is a necessary and sufficient condition for objects to appear, but actual external objects are neither necessary nor sufficient. Ordinary perception is like a dream, a mental projection; that different beings perceive the supposed same thing differently proves this. To update Vasubandhu's example, that humans and flies perceive and react to excrement in radically different ways demonstrates that what each perceives is a projection based on its own conditioning, or its own mental "seeds" (*bījās*) acquired from past experiences (perhaps in past lives). KARMA (ACTION) is collective, in that we gravitate toward beings or types who perceive as we do, erroneously justifying the seeming universality of our group perspective. Thus the "varying perception" argument supports rather than undermines the Yogācāra position. Vasubandhu uses the example of a wet dream to demonstrate causal efficacy: Though the erotic cognitive object is a mental construction, without external or physical reality, it causes actual seminal emission, a physical effect produced outside the dream and recognized as such upon awakening. This means that even though dreams are only fantasies, they have real karmic consequences. The deluded mind produces real effects that can only be known after awakening, once delusion has ceased. Awakening means enlightenment—BODHI (AWAKENING) can also mean *enlightenment*—the cessation of the deluded mind. Even though we act in a collective deluded world of our own construction, our actions have real causal consequences.

To the objection that dream objects are usually not as stable as objects perceived while awake, Vasubandhu replies that objects and events seem less clear, less consistent in dreams than when awake because during sleep the mind is overcome by sleepiness and, thus, it is not "thinking clearly." Therefore, in a dream one does not know that the objects therein are only dream-objects until one awakens. Similarly, to the question of whether we can know other minds, Vasubandhu replies that even our own minds are opaque to us, since our mental capacities are dim and sleepy. An awakened one (the literal meaning of *buddha*), however, can know other minds more clearly than we know our own. So, not only can we know other minds (if we awaken), but we constantly influence each other for better and for worse (though we may not notice that within our individual dreams). Thus, karma is intersubjective. Moreover, since the more awake one is, the more causally effective one's mind becomes, sages and buddhas can exert powerful effects on the world, including devastating destruction, and even life and death.

Vijñaptimātra

Yogācāra encapsulates its doctrine in the term *vijñaptimātra* (often rendered "consciousness-only" or "representation-only"), which is not meant to suggest that only the mind is real. Consciousness (*vijñāna*) is not the ultimate reality or solution for Yogācāra, but rather the basic problem, as Vasubandhu's *Twenty Verses* illustrated. *Vijñapti* is grammatically a causative form, "what makes known," and thus indicates that what appears in cognition is constructed, projected by consciousness, rather than passively received from outside by consciousness. Since nothing appears to us except within our acts of consciousness, all is *vijñaptimātra*. The inability to distinguish between our interpretations of the world and the world itself is what Yogācāra calls *vijñaptimātra*. This problem pervades ordinary mental operations and can be eliminated only when those operations are brought to an end.

It is not that there is nothing real outside an individual mind. Yogācāra rejects solipsism and theories of a universal mind that subsumes individuals. According to Yogācāra, each individual is a distinct consciousness stream or mental continuum (*cittasantāna*), and individuals can communicate with each other, teach and learn from each other, and influence and affect each other. If this were not the case, learning about Buddhism would be impossible. Even *rūpa* (sensorial materiality) is accepted, if one realizes that physicality is only known as such through sensation and cognition. Everything we know, conceive, imagine, or are aware of, we know through cognition, including the notion that entities might exist independent of our cognition. Although the mind does not create the physical world, it generates the interpretative categories through which we know and classify the physical world, and it does this so seamlessly that we mistake our interpretations for the world itself. Those interpretations, which are projections of our desires and anxieties, become obstructions (*āvaraṇa*) preventing us from seeing what is actually the case. In simple terms, we are blinded by our own self-interests, our own prejudices, our desires. Unenlightened cognition is an appropriative act. Yogācāra does not speak about subjects and objects; instead, it analyzes perception in terms of graspers (*grāhaka*) and what is grasped (*grāhya*).

The Buddhist notion of karma is intimately connected to the notion of appropriation (*upādāna*). As the earliest Buddhist texts explained, suffering and ignorance are produced by karma. Karma, according to Buddhism, consists of any intentional activity of body, speech, or mind. Intention is the crucial factor, and intention is a cognitive condition, so whatever is devoid of cognition must be nonkarmic and nonintentional. Thus, by definition, whatever is noncognitive can have no karmic implications or consequences. Intention means desiring something. Physically, linguistically, or mentally, we try to "get it." Stated another way, only cognitive acts can have karmic repercussions. This would include meaningful bodily gestures that communicate intentions (such gestures are also called *vijñapti*). Since Buddhists seek to overcome ignorance and suffering by eliminating karmic conditioning, Buddhists need focus only on what occurs within the domain of cognitive conditions (*cittagocara*). Categories such as external object and materiality (*rūpa*) are cognitive constructions. *Materiality* is a word for the colors, textures, sounds, and so on that we cognize in acts of perception, and it is only to the extent that they are perceived and ideologically grasped, thereby becoming objects of attachment, that they have karmic significance. There is nothing intrinsically good or bad about gold, for example; rather our *ideas* about gold's value and uses, which we project and then act upon, lead to good or bad consequences. Materialism is not the problem. The incessant propensity (*anuśaya*) to appropriate (*upādāna*) what consciousness projects is the problem. These projections are not just things, but moral qualities, status, ideals, religious and national doctrines and identities, the *holding* of opinions, whatever we can make our own, or make ourselves to be.

A deceptive trick is built into the way consciousness operates at every moment. Consciousness constructs a cognitive object in such a way that it disowns its own creation, pretending the object is "out there," in order to render that object capable of being appropriated. Even while what we cognize is occurring within our act of cognition, we cognize it *as if* it were external to our consciousness. Realizing *vijñaptimātra* means exposing this trick at play in every act of consciousness, catching it in the act, as it were, and thereby eliminating it. Consciousness engages in this deceptive game of projection, dissociation, and appropriation because there is no "self." The deepest-seated erroneous view to which SENTIENT BEINGS cling, according to Buddhism, is *ātmadṛṣṭi*, the view that a permanent, eternal, immutable, independent self exists. No such self exists, and deep down we know that. This makes us anxious, since it entails that no self or identity endures forever. In order to alleviate that anxiety, we attempt to construct a self, to fill the anxious void, to do or acquire something enduring. The projection of cognitive objects for appropriation is consciousness's main tool for this construction. If I own things (ideas, theories, identities, material objects), then "I am." If there are eternal objects that I can possess, then I too must be eternal. To undermine this erroneous appropriative grasping, Yogācāra texts say: Negate the object, and the self is also negated (e.g., *Madhyāntavibhāga*, 1:4, 8).

Intentional acts also have moral motives and consequences. Since effects are shaped by their causes, an act with a wholesome intent would tend to yield wholesome fruits, while unwholesome intentions produce unwholesome effects.

Three natures (*trisvabhāva*)

Yogācāra devised a model of three self-natures (*trisvabhāva*) to explain *vijñaptimātra* more concisely. The pervasive mental constructions that obstruct our view of what truly is the case are called *parikalpita* (imaginative construction). The actual webs of causes and conditions at play are called *paratantra* (dependent on other [causes]). Other-dependence is so-called to emphasize that no thing exists as an independent, eternal self; everything arises dependent on causes and conditions other than itself, in the absence of which it ceases to be. Ordinarily *paratantra* is infested with *parikalpita*. *Pariniṣpanna* (consummation) is the removal of *parikalpita* from *paratantra*, leaving only purified *paratantra*.

Since the notion of "self-nature" is itself a parikalpic idea that presumes self-hood, it too must be eliminated. Thus the three self-natures are actually three non-self-natures (*tri-niḥsvabhāva*). *Parikalpita* is devoid of self-nature since it is unreal by definition. *Paratantra* lacks self-nature, since other-dependence precludes "self" nature. *Pariniṣpanna*—the Yogācāra counterpart to the Madhyamaka notion of śūnyatā (emptiness), which stands for the lack of self-nature in everything—is the antithesis of self-nature. Thus the three self-natures are ultimately understood as three non-self-natures.

Eight consciousnesses

Prior to Yogācāra, Buddhists discussed six types of consciousness: the five sensory consciousnesses (visual, auditory, gustatory, olfactory, and tactile) and mental consciousness (*manovijñāna*). The consciousnesses were said to be produced by contact between a sense organ (e.g., the eye) and its corresponding sense field or objects (e.g., colors, shapes). The mind (manas) operated like the other senses, mental consciousness arising from the contact between manas and mental objects (thoughts, ideas), though it could think about what the other senses perceived, while the five senses could not cognize each other's objects. Yogācāra found this theory sound but inadequate because it did not explain the origin of the sense of self-hood with its appropriative propensities, various problems with continuity of experience, or the projective activity of consciousness. If causality requires temporal contiguity, how can consciousness temporarily cease during sleep, unconscious states, certain forms of meditation, or between lives, and then suddenly recommence? Where did it reside in the interim? If karmic consequences occur long after the act they are requiting was committed, and there is no substantial self, what links the act to its eventual karmic effect, and in what does this linkage reside? Most importantly, how can consciousnesses that are derivative of contact between organs and objects become projective?

Yogācāra's eight consciousnesses theory answered these questions. *Manovijñāna* became the organ of the sixth consciousness, rather than its by-product; manas became the seventh consciousness, responsible for appropriating experience as "mine" and thus infesting experience with a sense of self-hood (and thus also called *ādānavijñāna,* "appropriative consciousness," and *kliṣṭamanas,* "defiled mind"). The eighth consciousness, the *ālayavijñāna* (warehouse consciousness), was Yogācāra's most important innovation.

Experiences produce seeds (*bījā*) and perfumings (*vāsanā*) that are deposited in the *ālayavijñāna.* These seeds, embodying wholesome or unwholesome implications, regenerate new seeds each moment. These causal seed chains remain latent until a new conscious experience causes the seed to sprout, infusing a new cognition. Hence the *ālayavijñāna* was also called *vipākavijñāna* (karmic requital consciousness). Like a warehouse, the *ālayavijñāna* serves as a repository for seeds that are stored there, across a lifetime or many lifetimes, until dispatched. So it was also called all-seeds consciousness (*sarvabījakavijñāna*). *Vāsanās* "perfume" the *ālayavijñāna,* like the smell of incense perfumes a cloth in its proximity. The smell may seem intrinsic to the cloth, but it is adventitious and can be removed, returning the cloth to its original state. Various Yogācāra texts debate whether seeds and perfuming describe the same phenomenon with different metaphors, or whether they are different types of mental events. In either case, the *ālayavijñāna* flows onward like a constant stream, changing each moment with each new experience, thus providing karmic continuity as the seeds reach fruition. The *ālayavijñāna* continues to function even while the other consciousnesses become temporarily inoperative, unconscious. Hence it is also called "foundational consciousness" (*mūlavijñāna*). Although it stores karmic seeds and engenders their projection, the *ālayavijñāna* is a karmically neutral mechanical process (*anivṛta, avyākṛta*). Manas appropriates the activities of the other consciousnesses, thinking they are "my" experience, and it appropriates the *ālayavijñāna* as a "self."

Karmic continuity ceases by overturning the basis (*āśrayaparāvṛtti*), in which the *ālayavijñāna* and the other consciousnesses cease to function. The consciousnesses (*vijñāna*) become direct cognitions (jñāna). *Ālayavijñāna* becomes the "great mirror cognition" (*mahādarśanajñāna*), no longer holding on to or engendering new seeds, but reflecting everything impartially in the present moment, like an unobstructed mirror. Manas loses its self-prejudicial nature and becomes the immediate cognition of equality (*samatājñāna*), equalizing self and other. *Manovijñāna,* which discriminates cognitive objects, becomes immediate cognitive mastery (*pratyavekṣaṇājñāna*), in which the general and particular characteristics of things are discerned just as they are. The five sense consciousnesses, now devoid of mental constructions, become immediate cognitions that accomplish what needs to be done (*kṛtyānuṣṭhānajñāna*), thereby engaging the world effectively. Yogācāra texts differ on which overturning occurs at which stage of practice, but they agree that full enlightenment entails accomplishing all of them.

Purification of the mental stream

Yogācāra practice consists of analyzing cognitive processes in order to purify the mental stream of pollutants (*āśrava*), removing all obstructions to unexcelled complete enlightenment (ANUTTARASAMYAKSAMBODHI). Bad seeds and perfumings need to be filtered out, while good seeds need to be watered and cultivated, so they will reach fruition. Mental disturbances (*kleśa*), such as greed, hatred, delusion, arrogance, wrong views, envy, shamelessness, and so on, are gradually eliminated, while karmically wholesome mental conditions, such as nonharming, serenity, carefulness, and equanimity, are strengthened. As the obstructions from emotional and mental obstructions (*kleśāvaraṇa*) are eliminated, purification continues until the deepest seated cognitive obstructions (*jñeyāvaraṇa*) are finally extinguished.

Yogācāra provides a vast and detailed literature on the various practices, meditations, and stages the Yogācāra adept undertakes. The details differ greatly across texts, with the *Yogācārabhūmi* enumerating seventeen stages, the *Daśabhūmikasūtropadeśa* ten stages, and other texts, such as the *Mahāyānasaṃgraha* and *Cheng weishi lun,* five stages. The five stages are:

1. The "provisioning" stage (*saṃbhārāvasthā*), during which one gathers and stocks up on "provisions" for the journey. These provisions primarily consist of orienting oneself toward the pursuit of the PATH and developing the proper character, attitude, and resolve to accomplish it. This stage commences at the moment the aspiration for enlightenment (BODHICITTA) arises. One relies on the four excellent powers (the causal force of one's seeds, good friends, focused attention, and provisions of merit and wisdom).
2. Next is the "experimental" stage (*prayogāvasthā*), where one begins to experiment with various Buddhist theories and practices, and doctrines are converted from theory to praxis. *Prayoga* also means "intensifying effort," or applying oneself with increasing vigilance. One trains in the four-stage samādhi (meditation): (1) meditation achieving initial illumination (into an issue), (2) meditation to increase that illumination, (3) meditation producing sudden insights, and (4) maintaining meditative awareness continuously and uninterruptedly. During this stage one begins to suppress the grasper-grasped relation and commences on a careful and detailed study of the relation between things, language, and cognition.
3. Continually honing one's discipline, eventually one enters the third stage, "deepening understanding" (*prativedhāvasthā*). Some texts refer to this as the path of corrective vision (*darśana-mārga*). Here one works on realizing the emptiness of self and dharmas while reducing the obstructions (*kleśāvaraṇa* and *jñeyāvaraṇa*). This stage ends once one has acquired some insight into nonconceptual cognition (*nirvikalpajñāna*), that is, cognition devoid of interpretive or imaginative overlay.
4. In this stage, the "path of cultivation" (*bhāvanā-mārga*), nonconceptual cognition deepens. The grasper-grasped relation is utterly eliminated, as are all cognitive obstructions. This path culminates in the full overturning of the basis, or enlightenment.
5. In the "final stage" (*niṣṭhāvasthā*), one abides in unexcelled, complete enlightenment and engages the world through the four immediate cognitions (mirror cognition, etc.). At this stage, all of one's activities and cognitions are "post-enlightenment" (*pṛṣṭhalabdha*), and other beings become one's sole concern because Mahāyāna adepts devote themselves not only to attaining enlightenment for themselves, but to helping all sentient beings to attain enlightenment as well. As Kuiji puts it in his *Heart Sūtra Commentary*: "This is the stage of liberation which comprises the three buddha bodies, the four kinds of perfect nirvāṇa, and the perfect fruition of buddhahood."

See also: **Consciousness, Theories of; Psychology**

Bibliography

Anacker, Stefan, trans. and ed. *Seven Works of Vasubandhu: The Buddhist Psychological Doctor.* Delhi: Motilal Banarsidass, 1984.

Buswell, Robert E., Jr. *The Formation of Ch'an Ideology in China and Korea: The Vajrasamādhi-Sūtra, a Buddhist Apocryphon.* Princeton, NJ: Princeton University Press, 1989.

Cook, Francis H., trans. *Three Texts on Consciousness Only.* Berkeley, CA: Numata Center, 1999.

Ganguly, Swati. *Treatise in Thirty Verses on Mere-Consciousness.* Delhi: Motilal Banarsidass, 1992.

Griffiths, Paul. *On Being Mindless: Buddhist Meditation and the Mind-Body Problem.* La Salle, IL: Open Court, 1986.

Griffiths, Paul; Hakamaya Noriaki; Keenan, John; and Swanson, Paul. *The Realm of Awakening: Chapter Ten of Asaṅga's Mahāyānasaṃgraha.* New York and Oxford: Oxford University Press, 1989.

Hayes, Richard P. *Dignāga on the Interpretation of Signs.* Dordrecht, Netherlands: Kluwer, 1988.

Hopkins, Jeffrey. *Reflections on Reality: The Three Natures and Non-Natures in the Mind-Only School.* Berkeley: University of California Press, 2002.

Kochumuttom, Thomas. *A Buddhist Doctrine of Experience: A New Translation and Interpretation of the Works of Vasubandhu the Yogacarin.* Delhi: Motilal Banarsidass, 1982. Reprint, 1999.

Lamotte, Étienne, trans. *Saṃdhinirmocana-sūtra.* Paris and Louvain, Belgium: Université de Louvain and Adrian Maisonneuve, 1935.

La Vallée Poussin, Louis de, trans. *Vijñaptimātratāsiddhi,* 2 vols. Paris: Geuthner, 1928.

Lusthaus, Dan. *Buddhist Phenomenology: A Philosophical Investigation of Yogācāra Buddhism and the Ch'eng wei-shih lun.* London: RoutledgeCurzon, 2002.

Nagao, Gadjin. *Mādhyamika and Yogācāra,* tr. Leslie Kawamura. Albany: State University of New York Press, 1991.

Powers, John. *The Yogācāra School of Buddhism: A Bibliography.* Metuchen, NJ: Scarecrow Press, 1991.

Powers, John. *Wisdom of the Buddha: The Saṃdhinirmocana Mahāyāna Sūtra.* Berkeley, CA: Dharma, 1995.

Rahula, Walpola, trans. *Le Compendium de la Super-Doctrine d'Asaṅga (Abhidharmasamuccaya).* Paris: Publications de l'École Française d'Extrême Orient, 1971. English translation, *Abhidharmasamuccaya: The Compendium of the Higher Teaching,* tr. Sara Webb-Boin. Fremont, CA: Asian Humanities Press, 2001.

Shih, Heng-ching, and Lusthaus, Dan, trans. *A Comprehensive Commentary on the Heart Sutra: Translated from the Chinese of K'uei-chi.* Berkeley, CA: Numata Center, 2001.

Sparham, Gareth, trans. *Ocean of Eloquence: Tsong kha pa's Commentary on the Yogācāra Doctrine of Mind.* Albany: State University of New York Press, 1993.

Tat, Wei, trans. *Ch'eng Wei-Shih Lun: The Doctrine of Mere Consciousness.* Hong Kong: Ch'eng Wei-Shih Lun Publication Committee, 1973.

Tatz, Mark. *Asaṅga's Chapter on Ethics with the Commentary of Tsong-kha-pa: The Basic Path to Awakening, the Complete Bodhisattva.* Lewiston, NY: Edwin Mellen Press, 1986.

DAN LUSTHAUS

YUJŎNG

The Korean Buddhist monk Yujŏng (1544–1610), better known as Samyŏng *taesa* (Great Master), lived during the middle of the Chosŏn dynasty (1392–1910), a period in which the country was invaded by the Japanese twice, in 1592 and 1597. Together with his teacher, HYUJŎNG (1520–1604), Yujŏng became a leader of the Buddhist MONASTIC MILITIA that defended the kingdom, and he remains an exemplar of patriotism.

Yujŏng was also known as Songun, and his secular name was Im Ŭnggyu; Yujŏng was his dharma name. Like many other Buddhist monks during the Chosŏn, when Confucianism was the orthodoxy, Yujŏng was educated in Confucian classics in his childhood. He was orphaned at age fifteen and became a Buddhist monk under Monk Shinmuk at Chikchisa. Early in his career as a monk Yujŏng studied both Buddhist and Confucian texts and he communicated with Confucian scholars. In 1557, no earlier than age thirty, he declined the king's appointment to become the abbot of Pongun Monastery, the head monastery of the Sŏn school, and he joined Hyujŏng at Mount Myohyang to practice meditation. Yujŏng is said to have attained enlightenment in 1586 at age forty-two.

In 1592 Yujŏng organized the monastic militia and helped lead a number of campaigns against the Japanese invasion. During and after the war he was appointed as a royal envoy and participated several times in peace negotiations with Japan. In 1604, after peace was established with Japan, Yujŏng returned to Korea with more than thirty-five hundred Korean war prisoners released by the Japanese. He petitioned the throne several times on what should be done for the defense of the country, including "building mountain fortresses" and "developing military weapons." Because of such patriotic activities, he appears in the Korean folk tradition as a heroic figure who uses supernatural powers to save the country. Even today, Yujŏng is related to various fascinating patriotic legends about the security of the country and the welfare of the people. One of the most compelling of these holds that whenever Korea is in danger, as it was during the Korean War or the time of the assassination of President Park Chung Hee in 1979, Yujŏng's posthumous stele in his hometown of Miryang (South Kyŏngsang province) sheds tears.

Yujŏng left only a few writings, which are published in his posthumous work, *Samyŏngdang taesajip* (*The Collected Works of Venerable Master Samyŏng*), in seven rolls.

Bibliography

An Kyehyŏn. "Chosŏn chŏn'gi ŭi sŭnggun" (The Monastic Militia in the Early Chosŏn Period). In *Han'guk Pulgyo sasangsa yŏn'gu* (*Studies on the History of Korean Buddhist Thought*). Seoul: Dongguk University Press, 1983.

U Chŏngsang. "Chosŏn pulgyo ŭi hoguk sasang e taehayo" (On State Protection Buddhism in the Chosŏn Period). In *Chosŏn chŏn'gi Pulgyo sasang yŏn'gu* (*Studies on Buddhist Thought in the Early Chosŏn Period*), ed. U Chŏngsang. Seoul: Dongguk University Press, 1985.

SUNGTAEK CHO

YUN'GANG

The Yun'gang CAVE SANCTUARIES are located sixteen kilometers west of Datong in Shanxi province in China. Begun around 460 C.E. as an attempt to atone the Buddhist PERSECUTION of 444, Yun'gang was associated with the imperial patronage of Buddhism of the Northern Wei dynasty, a nomadic empire that ruled China from 386 to 534. The colossal buddha images of caves 16 to 20 are said to commemorate the founder rulers of the Northern Wei, while members of the imperial family built many cave chapels until 494, when the capital was moved from Datong to Luoyang in central

China. Thereafter local Buddhists continued to dedicate small chapels until about 520. Carved into the sandstone cliffs are niches that contain statues of buddhas such as Śākyamuni and MAITREYA, as well as carvings of other Buddhist motifs. Passageways behind large statues or the construction of central pillars allow for ritual circumambulation. In sculptural style and iconography, strong Indian and Central Asian influences commingled with local elements to create a unique Yun'gang idiom, characterized by a robust figural form and an archaic smile. This idiom gradually gave way to a more elongated sinicized style that was associated with the sinification policies of the Northern Wei.

See also: **China, Buddhist Art in; Monastic Architecture**

Bibliography

Mizuno Seiichi, and Nagahiro Toshio. *Unkō sekkutsu* (*Yun'gang Cave-Temples*), 16 vols. Kyoto: Kyoto daigaku jimbun kagaku kenkyūsho, 1951–1956.

Su Bai. *Zhongguo shikusi yanjiu* (*A Study of the History of Chinese Cave-Temples*). Beijing: Wenwu Press, 1996.

Yungang Cave-Temples Cultural Relics Institute. *Yungang shiku* (*Yun'gang Cave-Temples*), 2 vols. Beijing: Wenwu Press, 1991.

DOROTHY WONG

Z

ZANNING

Zanning (Tonghui dashi, 919–1001) was a Buddhist scholar-official renowned for his knowledge of Buddhist history and institutions in China, although his knowledge extended beyond Buddhism to Confucian matters and details of Chinese history and culture. As an official and scholar, Zanning played a critical role in explaining and defining Buddhism for Song officials. Biographical records indicate that Zanning rose from humble beginnings and embarked on a monastic career at a young age, probably in 929 or 930. He received full ordination on Mount Tiantai while still in his teens and distinguished himself as a master of the VINAYA tradition. He became a leader of literary (*wen*) studies in his native Wuyue region (present-day Zhejiang province), and served in key government positions in Wuyue. Zanning also played a key role as the Wuyue representative in the return of the Wuyue region to Song control in 978.

Zanning reportedly made a great initial impression on the Song emperor Taizong (r. 976–997), who awarded him a high rank, an honorific robe, and a title. Buddhist sources report that Zanning was appointed to the prestigious Hanlin Academy of academicians, an extremely rare honor for a Buddhist, but this cannot be confirmed in non-Buddhist accounts. Zanning was also a member of the Society of Nine Elders, an elite group of literati-officials at the Song court responsible for managing imperially sponsored editorial projects. Among the surviving Buddhist works compiled by Zanning, two are of great interest to contemporary scholars: the *Song gaoseng zhuan* (*Song Biographies of Eminent Monks*) and the *Seng shilue* (*Historical Digest of the Buddhist Order*). As an official at the Song court, Zanning became the leading Buddhist cleric of the Song empire, first through appointment as chief lecturer on Buddhist sūtras and ultimately as Buddhist registrar of the right and left precincts of the capital, the leading position in the administration of Buddhist affairs.

See also: **Biographies of Eminent Monks (Gaoseng Zhuan); China**

Bibliography

Dahlia, Albert. "The 'Political' Career of the Buddhist Historian Tsan-ning." In *Buddhist and Taoist Practice in Medieval Chinese Society,* ed. David Chappell. Honolulu: University of Hawaii Press, 1987.

Welter, Albert. "Zanning and Chan: The Changing Nature of Buddhism in Early Song China." *Journal of Chinese Religions* 23 (1995): 105–140.

Welter, Albert. "A Buddhist Response to the Confucian Revival: Tsan-ning and the Debate Over Wen in the Early Sung." In *Buddhism in the Sung,* ed. Peter N. Gregory and Daniel A. Getz, Jr. Honolulu: University of Hawaii Press, 1999.

ALBERT WELTER

ZEN. *See* **Chan School**

ZEN, POPULAR CONCEPTIONS OF

Zen is the Japanese pronunciation of the Chinese character *chan,* itself a truncated transliteration of the Sanskrit term DHYĀNA (TRANCE STATE). In contemporary Japan, three monastic traditions, the Rinzai, Sōtō, and Ōbaku, now use the term to identify themselves as belonging to the common heritage of the CHAN SCHOOL, which they call *Zen* (*zenshū*). The word *Zen*, however, has also become part of the secular lexicon. Often appearing in the form of "the Zen of *x*" or "Zen and the art of *x*," the idea of Zen is pervasive in popular culture. In this context, Zen often denotes a sense of liberation, spontaneity, and oneness with the world that can be sought not only in highly technical forms of meditative practice but also in archery, gardening, tea ceremonies, and even the most mundane matters, such as motorcycle maintenance. No longer referring in a more technical sense to any specific Buddhist tradition in Asia, Zen is, as Alan Watts (1915–1973) puts it, "an ultimate standpoint from which 'anything goes.' "

This highly romanticized vision of Zen owes much to the writings of D. T. SUZUKI (1870–1966) and Beat generation authors, such as Watts, Gary Snyder (1930–), Jack Kerouac (1922–1969), and Allen Ginsberg (1926–1997). In his now classic novel, *The Dharma Bums,* Kerouac, for instance, sings of a "rucksack revolution" led by young American "Zen lunatics" armed with nothing but poetry and "visions of eternal freedom." Above all else, those who promoted this ideal of Zen as an alternative lifestyle vehemently opposed the rampant consumerism, materialism, and positivism of mid- to late-twentieth-century America and bemoaned the growing sense of alienation from nature and spirituality. Beatniks, hippies, and countercultural intellectuals celebrated a new "Zen" spirituality that ostensibly relied less on rational thought and more on the immediate, "mystical" experience of being.

Historians generally locate the origins of this particular understanding of Zen in a Buddhist reform movement that took place in Meiji (1868–1912) and post-Meiji Japan. Shortly after the emperor was restored to power in 1868, Buddhism came under heavy attack as a foreign, corrupt, and superstitious creed. As a result, numerous temples were abandoned and thousands of monks were returned to lay status under the slogan of *haibutsu kishaku,* "exterminate Buddhism and destroy Śākyamuni." In response to this threat, Zen apologists sought to defend their faith by advocating what they called a New Buddhism (*shin bukkyō*) that was thoroughly modern, nonsectarian, and socially engaged. In order to demonstrate their support of the colonial policies and military expansion of the newfound Japanese empire, adherents of New Buddhism went so far as to portray their new faith as consistent with *bushidō* (the way of the warrior), which they defined as the essence of Japanese culture.

A leading figure of this movement was the Rinzai priest Shaku Sōen (1859–1919) who, in 1893, visited Chicago as a representative of Zen at the World Parliament of Religions. In his *Sermons of a Buddhist Abbot,* the first book on Zen to appear in English, Sōen presented Buddhism as a rational and scientific religion well-suited to modern sensibilities. As in the case of all other so-called universal religions, Zen was no longer a strictly clerical concern but rather a spiritual insight accessible to all. Like his teacher Imagita Kōsen (1816–1892) before him, Sōen taught lay disciples at a *zazen* (seated meditation) society known as Ryōmōkyōkai in Tokyo and at the monastery Engakuji in Kamakura, where he served as abbot. Among those who found themselves studying meditation under Sōen at Engakuji was the young D. T. Suzuki.

With the help of Paul Carus (1852–1919), a strong proponent of "religion of science," Suzuki carried on Sōen's efforts to bring Zen into the modern world. Drawing upon the notion of "pure experience" (*junsui keiken*) from the writings of the American philosopher William James (1842–1910) and Nishida Kitaro (1870–1945), Suzuki moved beyond Carus's and Sōen's interest in the unity of rationality and faith and began to emphasize instead the importance of a mystical experience that underlies all religious truth. As the unmediated, direct experience of being, or what he called "isness" (*kono mama*), Zen experience, according to Suzuki, was beyond dualism and intellectualization, and hence was superior to all other forms of religious experience. Furthermore, by identifying Zen experience with the uniqueness of Japanese culture Suzuki was able to firmly establish a nationalistic discourse couched in seemingly benign and universalistic religious terms.

Hisamatsu Shin'ichi (1889–1980), a fellow Zen nationalist, similarly argued that the Japanese mind, unlike the discursive and logical mind of the West, was predisposed toward an "intuitive" mode of understanding and an innate love for nature and tranquility. Despite the lack of historical evidence to substantiate their claims, Suzuki and Hisamatsu described traditional Japanese art, most notably *haiku* poetry, stone gardens, and Noh drama, as quintessential expressions of Zen awakening (SATORI). For both Suzuki and Hisamatsu, Zen, and therefore Japanese culture, are unique in that they express the experience of awakening directly and immediately without having recourse to established conventions or discursive thought.

As cultural relativism and gnosticism displaced rationalism and Judeo-Christian values as the reigning ideology among twentieth-century intellectuals, many Americans and Europeans increasingly sought a viable alternative in Zen, oblivious of its nationalistic and racist overtones. The transcultural, unmediated status of Zen mysticism, for instance, offered dismayed Catholics like Kerouac an alternative to their own stifling tradition, yet paradoxically allowed them to remain loyal to their original faith. Similarly, large communities of lay practitioners who had little or no interest in monasticism flocked to Zen centers established by Yasutani Hakuun (1885–1973) and by his American disciples Philip Kapleau (1912–) and Robert Aitken (1917–), where the rapid attainment of *kenshō* (seeing one's true nature) and its certification known as *inka* were the only priority. This, however, stood in stark contrast to the disciplined lifestyle of a traditional Zen monk for whom such a certification bears more of an institutional than a personal significance. Zen, as we know it in the West, is thus significantly different from its more traditional counterpart; this difference, as we have seen, emerged from a cross-cultural dialogue that belongs exclusively neither to Japan nor to the West.

See also: **Critical Buddhism (Hihan Bukkyō); Engaged Buddhism; Meiji Buddhism Reform; Modernity and Buddhism; Nationalism and Buddhism**

Bibliography

Faure, Bernard. *Chan Insights and Oversights: An Epistemological Critique of the Chan Tradition.* Princeton, NJ: Princeton University Press, 1993.

Fields, Rick. *How the Swans Came to the Lake: A Narrative History of Buddhism in America,* 3rd edition. Boston: Shambhala, 1992.

Hisamatsu, Shin'ichi. *Zen and the Fine Arts,* tr. Gishin Tokiwa. Tokyo: Kodansha, 1971.

Kerouac, Jack. *The Dharma Bums.* New York: American Library, 1959.

Ketelaar, James Edward. *Of Heretics and Martyrs in Meiji Japan: Buddhism and Its Persecution.* Princeton, NJ: Princeton University Press, 1990.

Sharf, Robert H. "Sanbōkyōdan: Zen and the Way of the New Religions." *Japanese Journal of Religious Studies* 22, nos. 3–4 (1995): 417–458.

Sharf, Robert H. "The Zen of Japanese Nationalism." In *Curators of the Buddha: The Study of Buddhism under Colonialism,* ed. Donald S. Lopez, Jr. Chicago: University of Chicago Press, 1995.

Soyen, Shaku. *Sermons of a Buddhist Abbot.* Chicago: Open Court, 1906.

Suzuki, Daisetz T. *Zen and Japanese Culture.* Princeton, NJ: Princeton University Press, 1959.

JUHN AHN

ZHANRAN

Zhanran (Jingqi Zhanran and Miaole *dashi,* 711–782) is the ninth patriarch of the TIANTAI SCHOOL of Chinese Buddhism and the sixth patriarch following ZHIYI (538–597), the de facto architect of the tradition. Author of the first authoritative commentaries on the major works of Zhiyi, Zhanran revitalized and reformed Tiantai during the Tang dynasty (618–907).

Zhanran trained for twenty years on Mount Zuoji in Zhejiang under Xuanlang (673–754), who became the eighth patriarch, and he remained active in the southeast both in his native Jiangsu and in the environs of Mount Tiantai in Zhejiang. Avoiding the northern political centers, Zhanran declined several imperial invitations, but made pilgrimage to Mount Wutai in Shanxi and instructed the Huayan adept CHENGGUAN (738–838/840) in Suzhou, returning to Mount Tiantai in 775 for the last time. The veracity of his travels in the north has been challenged in the late-twentieth century. Included among Zhanran's disciples are the literati figures Li Hua (d.u.–ca. 774) and Liang Su (753–793), who wrote his memorial inscription.

Zhanran's most influential works are his *Zhiguan fuxing zhuanhong jue* (*Decisions on Supporting Practice and Broadly Disseminating* [*the Teachings of the Great*] *Calming and Contemplation*) and the *Jin'gangbei* (*Diamond Scalpel*). The first is a commentary on Zhiyi's MOHE ZHIGUAN (*Great Treatise on Calming and Contemplation*), which for the first time identifies that practice-oriented text with the LOTUS SŪTRA (SADDHARMAPUṆḌARĪKA-SŪTRA) and connects it to Zhiyi's two doctrinal commentaries on the *Lotus* to become the three quintessential texts of Tiantai. The *Jin'gangbei* is a polemical treatise on insentient TATHĀGATAGARBHA, an idea not articulated in early Tiantai. Since the last quarter of the twentieth century, scholars have also recognized that the famous Tiantai "five periods and eight teachings" (*wushi bajiao*) taxonomy attributed to Zhiyi, which elevates the *Lotus* as supreme among scriptures and emphasizes a transmission based on the received teaching, is not found in the writings of Zhiyi in the form relied upon by later Tiantai. Rather, it is a product of the times of Zhanran when issues of self-definition came to the fore. Zhanran's interpretations of Tiantai, which debate with the Buddhism of the mid-eighth century (in particular, the Huayan and Chan schools), further catalyzed much of the Tiantai on-mountain/off-mountain (*shanjia/shanwai*) debates of the Song dynasty (960–1279).

See also: **China**

Bibliography

Chen, Jinhua. *Making and Remaking History: A Study of Tiantai Sectarian Historiography.* Tokyo: International Institute for Buddhist Studies, 1999.

Penkower, Linda. "Making and Remaking Tradition: Chan-jan's Strategies toward a T'ang T'ien-t'ai Agenda." In *Tendai daishi kenkyū,* ed. *Tendai Daishi Kenkyū* Henshū I-inkai. Kyoto: Tendai Gakkai, 1997.

Ziporyn, Brook. *Evil and/or/as the Good: Omnicentrism, Intersubjectivity, and Value Paradox in Tiantai Buddhist Thought.* Cambridge, MA: Harvard University Asia Center, 2000.

LINDA PENKOWER

ZHAO LUN

Zhao lun (*The Treatises of [Seng]zhao*) is a collection of writings by Shi SENGZHAO (374–414), a primary disciple of KUMĀRAJĪVA (344–409/413). *Zhao lun* contains the following documents, considered to be chapters by some scholars and independent treatises by others: "Wu buqian lun" ("A Treatise on the Immutability of Things"); "Wu buzhen kong lun" ("A Treatise on the Emptiness of the Unreal"); "Bojo wuzhi lun" ("A Treatise on Prajñā as Distinguished from Ordinary Knowledge"); and "Niepan wuming lun" ("A Treatise on Nameless [Nature] of Nirvāṇa").

The first document dwells, for the most part, on the mysteries of time. It exposes NĀGĀRJUNA's (ca. second century C.E.) view that the dharmas are essentially beyond definition and without definite nature. Since all phenomena are dharmas, but dharmas themselves cannot be created or destroyed—they are without beingness or nonbeingness—the category of time is meaningless.

The second document illuminates Nāgārjuna's ideas about ŚŪNYATA (EMPTINESS) from a different perspective. In this treatise Sengzhao uses a renowned simile of a man created through magic. Since the person has been created through magic, he is not a real man, but within the frame of knowing that the man has been created through magic, such a man does exist. The simile explains how all phenomena are both existent and nonexistent at the same time.

The third treatise seeks to delineate *prajñāpāramitā* (perfection of wisdom) as a different state of mind than knowledge. Knowledge is obtained through the investigation of things that are believed to be real. It is marked by a struggle to reconcile beginnings and ends, past and future, and so on. The equality of all things can only be seen through *prajñāpāramitā,* where the oppositions of existence and nonexistence, future and past, and sorrow and joy are no longer relevant. Similar ideas are presented in the fourth piece in which NIRVĀṆA is approached through the use of core Madhyamaka terminology and epistemological devices. Adapting the principle of the four negations used by Buddha Śākyamuni, Nāgārjuna, and Kumārajīva (nirvāṇa is not a form of existence; nirvāṇa is not a form of nonexistence; nirvāṇa is not both existence and nonexistence; nirvāṇa is not neither existence nor nonexistence), Sengzhao speaks about nirvāṇa as being ultimately indefinable, that is, nameless. Along with this classical treatment of the subject, we find the beginnings of a new understanding of this important concept, in which nirvāṇa is equated with the TATHĀGATAGARBHA (*rulaizang*).

See also: **China; Prajñāpāramitā Literature**

Bibliography

Ch'en, Kenneth. *Buddhism in China: A Historical Survey.* Princeton, NJ: Princeton University Press, 1964.

Liebenthal, Walter, trans. and ed. *Chao lun: The Treatises of Seng-chao, a Translation with Introduction, Notes, and Appendices,* 2nd edition, vols. 1–2. Hong Kong: Hong Kong University Press, 1968.

TANYA STORCH

ZHILI

Zhili (Siming Fazhi *fashi,* 960–1028) reestablished the TIANTAI SCHOOL during China's Northern Song dynasty period by leading the Shanjia (orthodox) attack on the Shanwai (heterodox) interpretations of Tiantai doctrine and practice. Zhili stressed the uniqueness of Tiantai teaching as opposed to those of the HUAYAN SCHOOL and CHAN SCHOOL. He emphasized the doctrines of evil inherent in the buddha-nature, the contemplation of the deluded mind, the inherent entailment of all quiddities in each other, the existence of differentiated characteristics even in the absence of delusion, the simultaneous validity of both mind-only and matter-only doctrines, and "the ultimacy of the dung-beetle." The last-named doctrine was rooted in his claim that enlightenment was a state that made more explicit all determinate realities, good and evil, and disclosed each sentient being's identity not only with the Buddha, but with all other possible SENTIENT BEINGS in all their aspects, all of which were the ultimate reality.

Zhili was instrumental in combining Tiantai doctrine with Pure Land practice, and much of his doctrinal work can be understood as an attempt to provide an adequate framework for understanding the necessity and legitimacy of Buddhist ritual practice in the face of certain interpretations of "sudden enlightenment" that might threaten it. In 1017 he made a vow to commit SELF-IMMOLATION after three years of practicing the Lotus Repentance with a group of junior monks. He vowed to be reborn in AMITĀBHA's Pure Land. After defending his intention to commit this arguably sinful act in a series of letters, in which Zhili makes the notorious claim that "there is no Buddha but the Devil, and no Devil but the Buddha," he finally abandoned his plan, and was given a purple robe and the honorific name Fazhi (Dharma-wisdom) by the emperor.

See also: **Pure Land Buddhism**

Bibliography

Chan, Chi-wah. "Chih-li (960–1028) and the Crisis of T'ien-t'ai Buddhism in the Early Sung." In *Buddhism in the Sung,* ed. Peter N. Gregory and Daniel A. Getz, Jr. Honolulu: University of Hawaii Press, 1999.

Ziporyn, Brook. "Anti-Chan Polemics in Post-Tang Tiantai." *Journal of the International Association of Buddhist Studies* 17, no. 1 (1994): 26–63.

Ziporyn, Brook. *Evil and/or/as the Good: Omnicentrism, Intersubjectivity, and Value Paradox in Tiantai Buddhist Thought.* Cambridge, MA: Harvard University Press, 2000.

BROOK ZIPORYN

ZHIYI

Zhiyi (Tiantai Zhizhe *dashi*) (538–597) was the nominal third patriarch of the Chinese TIANTAI SCHOOL, but he was, in fact, its eponymous founder. Zhiyi was born in Jingzhou (present-day Hubei), and became a monk at the age of eighteen, taking the full precepts two years later. At the age of twenty-three, he went to study with Nanyue Huisi (d. 577), under whom he practiced the Lotus Samādhi, during which he had a breakthrough experience. At thirty, he went to Jinling, capital of the Chen kingdom, and began to lecture extensively.

Zhiyi taught for the rest of his life, his lectures transcribed by his disciples, most notably Guanding (561–632), who recorded the "three great works of Tiantai": *Fahua wenju* (*Commentary on the Lotus Sūtra*), *Fahua xuanyi* (*Profound Meaning of the Lotus Sūtra*), and MOHE ZHIGUAN (*Great Calming and Contemplation*), the first based on lectures given in 587 and the latter two based on lectures given in 593 and 594. Zhiyi also composed several works by his own hand, most notably a commentary on the *Vimalakīrtinirdeśa,* written at the request of the Jin ruling house.

Zhiyi's teaching stresses the simultaneous and equal development of both doctrinal understanding and meditative practice. He devised an elaborate system of classification of Buddhist teachings, making a coherent whole of the mass of Buddhist scriptures translated into Chinese, in accordance with his development of the true meaning of UPĀYA (skillful means) as expounded in the LOTUS SŪTRA and NIRVĀṆA SŪTRA. His teaching combined the *Lotus* notion of *upāya* and mutual entailment with Madhyamaka notions of ŚŪNYATĀ (EMPTINESS) and conventional truth and the buddha-nature concept from the *Nirvāṇa Sūtra,* by which Zhiyi devised the doctrine of the three truths—emptiness, provisional positing, and the mean—as a comprehensive template for understanding Buddhist teachings and practices. This doctrine holds that every element of experience is necessarily and simultaneously (1) determinate, (2) ambiguous, and (3) absolute, and that these three predicates are ultimately synonymous. This led to a distinctive understanding of the interpervasion of all dharmas as suggested in the HUAYAN JING, which in Zhiyi's understanding led to the doctrine of "the three thousand quiddities inherently entailed as each moment of experience," as well as the further doctrines of "the evil inherent in the Buddha-nature," the non-obstruction of enlightenment between delusion, and the equal ultimacy of all possible doctrinal positions, as mediated by the *Lotus* doctrine of *upāya.* Zhiyi also rewrote the Indian mind-only doctrine so that it could be equally restated as a claim that all reality is matter-only, or alternately scent-only, taste-only, touch-only, and so on. His ideas were influential in every aspect of later East Asian Buddhism; they were commented on and reinterpreted in every generation within the Tiantai school, and recast and responded to by the HUAYAN SCHOOL, which amended his classification scheme and reinterpreted the interpervasion of all dharmas in a new way. Zhiyi's hermeneutical technique, in particular his metaphorical "mind-contemplation gloss" for reading the scriptures, was instrumental in the early development of the CHAN SCHOOL.

Bibliography

Donner, Neal. "Chih-i's Meditation on Evil." In *Buddhist and Taoist Practice in Medieval Chinese Society,* ed. David W. Chappell. Honolulu: University Press of Hawaii, 1987.

Donner, Neal. "Sudden and Gradual Intimately Conjoined: Chih-i's T'ien-t'ai View." In *Sudden and Gradual: Approaches to Enlightenment in Chinese Buddhism,* ed. Peter N. Gregory. Honolulu: University of Hawaii Press, 1987.

Donner, Neal, and Stevenson, Daniel B. *The Great Calming and Contemplation: A Study and Annotated Translation of the First Chapter of Chih-i's Mo-ho chih-kuan.* Honolulu: University of Hawaii Press, 1993.

Hurvitz, Leon. *Chih-i (538–597): An Introduction to the Life and Ideas of a Chinese Buddhist Monk.* Brussels: Institut Belges Des Hautes Etudes Chinoises, 1980.

Ng Yu-kwan. *T'ien-t'ai Buddhism and Early Mādhyamika.* Honolulu: University of Hawaii, 1993.

Stevenson, Daniel. "The Four Kinds of Samādhi in Early T'ien-t'ai Buddhism." In *Traditions of Meditation in Chinese Buddhism,* ed. Peter N. Gregory. Honolulu: University of Hawaii Press, 1986.

BROOK ZIPORYN

ZHUHONG

Zhuhong Fohui (1532–1612) is known as one of the "Four Eminent Monks of the Ming Dynasty," who actively promoted the syncretistic fusion of Chan and Pure Land practices in China. Zhuhong's adolescence was steeped in Confucian learning and he only took refuge in Buddhism during his middle age.

Zhuhong's moral reputation and diligent practice of the "samādhi of Buddha-name recitation" (*nianfo sanmei*) was said to have transformed a dilapidated monastary in Mount Yunqi of Hangzhou, where he temporarily took up residence in 1571 as an itinerant novice, into a famous cultivation center to which people flocked to receive his tutelage.

Zhuhong associated widely with Confucian elites and, through his clout and eloquence, popularized what became prevailing modes of Buddhist pietistic activities in the late Ming. These included the institution of release grounds and protected reservoirs for animals and fish, observance of the Tantric ritual "relieving the sufferings of the hungry ghosts," and the use of a genre of "morality book" called "ledger of merit and demerit" (*gongguo ge*) for recording personal offenses and meritorious deeds by assigning prescribed numerical values of "merits" and "demerits" to each recorded action.

Zhuhong also started the practice of using Buddha statues as replacements for the living preceptors, whose presence was otherwise required by the VINAYA (monastic disciplinary codes) to transmit the full set of monastic precepts to novice monks. He did this to circumvent the political restrictions on the ordination of monks and nuns.

His writings spanned many subject matters including Chan, Pure Land, Huayan, Yogācāra, vinaya, and even non-Buddhist classics. They are preserved in the anthology *Yunqi fahui* (*Collected Dharma [Works by Venerable] Yunqi*).

See also: **Chan School; China; Pure Land Schools**

Bibliography

Greenblatt, Kristin. "Chu-hung and Lay Buddhism in the Late Ming." In *The Unfolding of Neo-Confucianism,* ed. William de Bary and the Conference on Seventeenth-Century Chinese Thought. New York and London: Columbia University Press, 1975.

Yü, Chun-fang. *Renewal of Buddhism in China: Chu-Hung and the Late Ming Synthesis.* New York: Columbia University Press, 1981.

WILLIAM CHU

ZONGGAO

Dahui Zonggao (Miaoxi; posthumous name Pujue; 1089–1163), a Chan master in the Yangqi branch of the Linji school in Song China (960–1279), played a pivotal role in the development of Chan *gong'an* (KŌAN) practice. Zonggao was born in Xuancheng in Anhui Province in southeast China. He left home in 1101 to join the monastic order, and in 1105 he received full ordination as a Buddhist monk. After seeking instructions from various Chan teachers, he became a disciple of the Linji master Yuanwu Keqin (1063–1135), the author of the famous *gong'an* anthology, the *Biyan lu* (*Blue Cliff Record*).

As one of the most influential Chan masters of his time, Zonggao had close associations with many powerful Confucian scholar-officials. His connection with the antipeace party led to his involvement in Song court factional strife, which resulted in his exile from 1143 to 1156 to the remote Hunan and Guangdong provinces. After the exile, however, Zonggao regained his prominence. He was summoned by the emperor to the court, where he was presented with a purple robe and given the cognomen Dahui (Great Wisdom). He spent his last years at Mount Jing in Zhejiang and died in 1163.

Dahui Zonggao is best known for his contribution to the evolution of Chan *gong'an* meditation. He advocated the use of *huatou,* the critical phrase of a *gong'an,* as a meditative object, and he emphasized the peculiar role of DOUBT in his teaching of *huatou* investigation. He believed that the practice of *huatou* was not only the most effective means to enlightenment but also a Chan practice that laypeople could easily adopt in the midst of their mundane activities. It was under Daihui Zonggao that *gong'an* Chan came to be known as *kanhua* Chan (Chan of investigating the [critical] phrase).

The chronology of Dahui Zonggao's life was recorded in detail by one of his disciples and attached to the *Dahui Pujue chanshi yulu* (*Discourse Record of the Chan Master Dahui Pujue*). Other works attributed to Dahui Zonggao include *Zongmen wuku* (*Arsenal of the Chan School*) and *Zhengfayan zang* (*Treasury of the True Dharma Eye*).

See also: **Chan School**

Bibliography

Buswell, Robert E., Jr. "The 'Short-cut' Approach of *K'an-hua* Meditation: The Evolution of a Practical Subitism in Chinese Ch'an Buddhism." In *Sudden and Gradual: Approaches to Enlightenment in Chinese Thought,* ed. Peter N. Gregory. Honolulu: University of Hawaii Press, 1987.

Cleary, Christopher, trans. *Swampland Flowers: Letters and Lectures of Zen Master Ta Hui.* New York: Grove Press, 1977.

Levering, Miriam L. "Ch'an Enlightenment for Laymen: Ta-hui and the New Religious Culture of the Sung." Ph.D. diss. Harvard University, 1978.

DING-HWA HSIEH

ZONGMI

Guifeng Zongmi (780–841) is a unique figure in the CHAN SCHOOL, who sought to bridge Chan and the canonical teachings (*jiao*) of Buddhism. His early education at home and at a Confucian academy gave him a background in the classical canon unknown to the typical Tang-dynasty Chan master. He trained under a master in the Shenhui lineage of Chan and practiced intense Chan sitting in remote settings for a decade, yet he also studied canonical exegesis for two years under the exceedingly erudite HUAYAN SCHOOL scholar CHENGGUAN (738–840).

Zongmi collected Chan texts into an enormous Chanzang (*Chan Piṭaka*), which has since been lost. His two most important extant works are his introduction to the *Chan Piṭaka,* titled *Chanyuan zhuquanji duxu* (*Prolegomenon to the Collection of Experience of the Chan Source*), and a short treatise titled *Pei Xiu shiyi wen* (*Imperial Redactor Pei Xiu's Inquiry [on Chan]*). Originality, creativity, and lack of bias are the hallmarks of these two works. The former propounds the identity of the canonical teachings and Chan, and champions all-at-once awakening and step-by-step practice; the latter provides a synopsis of the histories, teachings, and practices of the Chan houses of the day. The *Chan Prolegomenon* postulates three "theses" (*zong*) of Chan: Mind-Only Chan; Voidness Chan; and Dharma Nature Chan, which are expressions, geared to Chinese propensities and preferences, of the corresponding three types of Indian sūtras and treatises.

Zongmi's influence on later Chan was exceptionally strong in Korea, where the Chan tradition is known as Sŏn. Korean Sŏn's absorption of all the traditions of Buddhism coincides with Zongmi's orientation. CHINUL (1158–1210), one of the greatest figures of the Sŏn tradition, was a transmitter of Zongmi's stance; his magnum opus is based on *Pei's Inquiry.*

See also: **China**

Bibliography

Gregory, Peter N. *Tsung-mi and the Sinification of Buddhism.* Princeton, NJ: Princeton University Press, 1991.

Kamata Shigeo, ed. *Zengen shosenshū tojo,* tr. Kamata Shigeo. Zen no goroku 9. Tokyo: Chikuma shobō, 1971.

JEFFREY BROUGHTON

APPENDIX

TIMELINES OF BUDDHIST HISTORY

India

Southeast Asia

China

Japan and Korea

Tibet and the Himalayas

INDIA

ca. 566–486 or 488–368 B.C.E.	Possible dates of the Buddha's life. When the Buddha may have lived is a matter of scholarly debate; these time frames represent only two of many suggestions.
ca. 386 or 268 B.C.E.	Traditional dates—one hundred years after the Buddha's death—on which the first Buddhist Council is said to have been held at Vaiśālī, resulting in the first schism of the SAṄGHA or monastic community.
ca. 268–232 B.C.E.	Reign of King AŚOKA of India, who converted to Buddhism and became an important patron of the religion. Aśoka is said to have sent out missionaries to various lands after holding a Buddhist Council at Pāṭaliputra.
ca. 100 B.C.E.	Great stūpa at SĀÑCĪ built.
ca. 100 C.E.	LOTUS SŪTRA (SADDHARMAPUṆḌARĪKA-SŪTRA) and other influential Mahāyāna texts composed.
ca. 200	Philosopher and scholar NĀGĀRJUNA writes about ŚŪNYATĀ (EMPTINESS), establishing the MADHYAMAKA SCHOOL (the Middle Way).
ca. 320	Indian scholar and monk ASAṄGA (ca. 320–390) born. He becomes the founder of the YOGĀCĀRA SCHOOL of Buddhism.
ca. 320–550	Gupta Empire, during which Buddhism flourishes throughout the subcontinent.
ca. 500	Buddhist monastic university founded at Nālandā.
ca. 673	Chinese pilgrim YIJING (635–713) arrives in India.
1197	Destruction of the great monastic universities of Nālandā and Vikramaśīla, signaling the decline of Buddhism as a religious institution in India.

1891	ANAGĀRIKA DHARMAPĀLA (1864–1933) founds the Mahā Bodhi Society to restore the famous site of the Buddha's enlightenment.
1956	B. R. AMBEDKAR (1891–1956) renounces Hinduism and converts to Buddhism.

SOUTHEAST ASIA

247 B.C.E.	King AŚOKA of India (r. 268–232 B.C.E.) putatively sends his son, Mahinda, to SRI LANKA to introduce Buddhism to the island. King Devanāṃpiya Tissa of Sri Lanka converts to Buddhism.
240 B.C.E.	Mahinda establishes the Mahāvihāra (Great Monastery) in Anurādhapura in Sri Lanka. Mahinda's sister, Saṅghamittā, establishes the order of NUNS.
25 B.C.E.	Famine and schisms in Sri Lanka emphasize the need for the Buddhist CANON to be committed to writing. King Vaṭṭagāmiṇi oversees the recording of the Pāli canon on palm leaves.
ca. 100 C.E.	Monks from Sri Lanka first transmit THERAVĀDA Buddhism to Burma (MYANMAR) and THAILAND.
ca. 200	Chinese Buddhist missionaries travel to VIETNAM, establishing MAHĀYĀNA and non-Mahāyāna schools.
ca. 425	Buddhist scholar BUDDHAGHOSA collects Sinhalese COMMENTARIAL LITERATURE and oversees translation of this work into Pāli. With this translation, Sinhalese scholarship reaches the entire Theravāda world.
ca. 500	Indian Mahāyāna monks establish Buddhist communities throughout Indonesia on the islands of Java, Sumatra, and Borneo.
1057	King Anawartha of Pagan in Burma (Myanmar) conquers neighboring Thaton. Buddhist literature and arts flourish.
ca. 1153–1186	Reign of Sri Lankan king Parākramabāhu I. His rule reconstitutes the Buddhist SAṄGHA exclusively as a Theravāda order. Buddhist architecture and literature flourishes throughout the Polonnaruva era.
1181	King Jayavarman VII begins his reign in CAMBODIA. Under his orders the BAYON at Angkor is built.

1236	MONKS from Kañcipuram, INDIA, revive the Theravāda monastic line in Sri Lanka.
1279	Last extant inscriptions of any Theravāda nunnery in Burma (Myanmar).
1287	Pagan in Burma (Myanmar) looted by Mongol invaders; decline of Pagan monuments begins.
ca. 1300	A Sri Lankan tradition of WILDERNESS MONKS arrives in Burma (Myanmar) and Thailand. Theravāda Buddhism spreads to Laos. Thai Theravāda monasteries appear in Cambodia shortly before the Thais win their independence from the Khmers of Cambodia.
ca. 1500	In Cambodia, Viṣṇuite Temple at Angkor Wat (founded in the twelfth century as a site of Hindu worship) becomes a Buddhist center.
1753	King Kīrti Śrī Rājasiṃha reinstates Buddhism in Sri Lanka by inviting monks from the Thai court.
1777	King Rāma I founds the current dynasty in Thailand.
1803	Sri Lankans ordained in the Burmese city of Amarapura found the Amarapura Nikāya in Sri Lanka.
1829	Thailand's Prince Mongkut (later King Rāma IV) founds the Thammayut sect.
ca. 1862	Wilderness monks travel from Sri Lanka to Burma (Myanmar) for reordination, returning to establish the Ramañña Nikāya.
1871	Fifth Theravāda Council is held at Rangoon in Burma.
1873	Mohottivatte Gunananda defeats Christian missionaries in a public debate, sparking a nationwide revival of pride in Sri Lankan Buddhist traditions.
1879	Helena Blavatsky and Henry Steel Olcott, founders of the Theosophical Society, arrive in Sri Lanka from America and assist in a revival of Buddhism.
ca. 1900	Two wilderness monks, Āčhān Sao Kantasīlo and Āčhān Man Bhūridatto, revive the forest monk traditions in Thailand.
1956	The Sri Lanka Freedom Party wins a pivotal election in a landslide by promising that Sinhalese would become the national language and Buddhism the state religion.
1967	THICH NHAT HANH (1926–) is nominated for the Nobel Peace Prize, an acknowledgement of his antiwar work in Vietnam. Hanh coined the term ENGAGED BUDDHISM to describe practices that emphasize social service and nonviolent activism.
1970s	Refugees from war in Vietnam, Cambodia, and Laos settle in North America, Australia, and Europe, where they establish Buddhist communities.

China

67 C.E.	Two Indian Buddhist missionaries are reputed to arrive at the court of Emperor Ming (r. 58–75 C.E.) of the Han dynasty (206 B.C.E.–220 C.E.), where they translate the first Buddhist sūtras into Chinese.
148	The Parthian AN SHIGAO arrives in the Chinese capital of Luoyang; he translates forty-one scriptures of MAINSTREAM BUDDHIST SCHOOLS into Chinese.
366	Construction of Buddhist cave shrines at DUNHUANG begins.
399	Chinese scholar–pilgrim FAXIAN (ca. 337–ca. 418) departs for INDIA in search of Buddhist teachings.
401	KUMĀRAJĪVA (350–409/413), a Buddhist master from Kucha, arrives in the Chinese capital of Chang'an. He introduces numerous MAHĀYĀNA texts to CHINA.
402	HUIYUAN (334–416) assembles a group of monks and laymen before an image of the Buddha AMITĀBHA on Mount Lu and vows to be born in the Western Paradise of Sukhāvatī, starting the PURE LAND SCHOOLS of Buddhism.
460	The Northern Wei (386–534) begins to construct Buddhist cave sanctuaries at YUN'GANG and LONGMEN.
ca. 520	BODHIDHARMA, putative founder of the CHAN SCHOOL, is reputed to arrive in China from India.
ca. 585	ZHIYI (538–597) systematizes the TIANTAI SCHOOL of Chinese Buddhism, providing a distinctively Chinese conception of the Buddhist PATH in such texts as the MOHE ZHIGUAN (*Great Calmness and Contemplation*).
601	The Sui (581–618) court distributes the Buddha's relics throughout the country and begins a wave of pagoda construction.

645	XUANZANG (ca. 600–664) returns from his journey to India with twenty horse-loads of Buddhist texts, images, and relics and begins epic translation project.
699	FAZANG (643–712) lectures at the Wu Zetian court on the newly translated HUAYAN JING, signaling the prominence of the HUAYAN SCHOOL.
720	The arrival of Indian masters Vajrabodhi and Amoghavajra in the capital cities of China leads to a surge in popularity of the MIJIAO (ESOTERIC) SCHOOL.
745	Shenhui (684–758) arrives in the Eastern Capital and propagates the sudden-enlightenment teachings of HUINENG (638–713), the putative sixth patriarch of the CHAN SCHOOL.
845	Emperor Wuzong (r. 841–847) initiates the Huichang suppression of Buddhism, one of the worst PERSECUTIONS in Chinese Buddhist history.
972	The Song dynasty initiates a national project to prepare a woodblock printing of the entire Buddhist canon (completed 983).
ca. 1150	ZONGGAO (1089–1163) formalizes the KŌAN system of Chan MEDITATION.
1270	The Mongol Yuan dynasty (1234–1368) supports Tibetan Buddhist traditions in China.
ca. 1600	ZHUHONG (1532–1612) seeks to unify Chan and Pure Land strands of Chinese Buddhism.
1759	A compendium of Buddhist incantations in Chinese, Manchu, Mongolian, and Tibetan is compiled during the Qianlong reign (1736–1795) of the Manchu Qing dynasty (1644–1911).
1929	TAIXU (1890–1947) leads the Chinese Buddhist Association as part of his reform of Chinese Buddhist institutions.
1949	The communist victory in China forces many Buddhist MONKS, such as YINSHUN (1906–), to flee to TAIWAN.
1965	The Cultural Revolution is initiated by communist leader Mao Zedong (1893–1976), leading to widespread destruction of Buddhist sites in China.

JAPAN AND KOREA

372 C.E.	Buddhism is officially introduced to KOREA with the arrival of Chinese envoy and monk Sundo at the Koguryŏ court.
ca. 538 or 552	Buddhism is first introduced from the Korean peninsula to the rulers of JAPAN.
594	Prince SHŌTOKU (574–622), a major patron of Buddhism and national cultural hero, becomes regent in Japan.
ca. 670	WŎNHYO (617–686), a prolific and influential Korean commentator, seeks to reconcile doctrinal positions of different Buddhist texts.
668	The Silla kingdom (ca. 57 B.C.E.–936 C.E.), defeating Paekche (663) and Koguryŏ (668), unifies the Korean peninsula; Silla dynasty supports Buddhism as the state religion.
710	The Japanese capital of Nara is established with seven major Buddhist monasteries; the court later sponsors six official schools of NARA BUDDHISM.
822	SAICHŌ (767–822) establishes the Tendai school (the Japanese TIANTAI SCHOOL).
ca. 823	The Japanese monk KŪKAI (774–835) establishes SHINGON BUDDHISM.
828	The first mountain site in the NINE MOUNTAINS SCHOOL OF SŎN (the Korean CHAN SCHOOL) is founded; eight other sites are established over the next century.
918	Buddhism flourishes in Korea under the state patronage of the Koryŏ dynasty (918–1392).

1010	The Korean king Hyŏnjong (r. 1009–1031) orders the carving of woodblocks for a complete Buddhist CANON. This monumental undertaking is finished in 1087, but the woodblocks are destroyed by the Mongols in 1232.
1090	The Korean monk–prince ŬICH'ŎN (1055–1101) publishes a catalogue of 1,010 indigenous East Asian Buddhist works; woodblocks of these works are carved as a supplement to the first Koryŏ Buddhist canon, but these are burned by the Mongols in 1232.
1175	HŌNEN (1133–1212) founds Jōdōshū, an independent sect of Japanese PURE LAND BUDDHISM.
1200	CHINUL (1158–1210) revives Sŏn (Korean Chan school) and seeks to reconcile the doctrinal and meditative strands of Korean Buddhism.
1202	Eisai (1141–1215), with support of the Kamakura government, establishes the new Rinzai Zen sect (of the Japanese Chan school).
1233	DŌGEN (1200–1253) founds the Sōtō Zen sect.
1236	The Korean court orders the preparation of a second set of woodblocks for printing the Buddhist canon; this set of more than 80,000 woodblocks is completed in 1251 and is now stored at Haeinsa.
1253	NICHIREN (1222–1282), founder of NICHIREN SCHOOL of Japanese Buddhism, begins teaching.
1392	The Korean dynasty of Chosŏn (1392–1910) is founded; the new kingdom adopts neo-Confucianism as the state ideology, leading to some five centuries of persecution of Buddhism in Korea.
ca. 1570	Japanese general Oda Nobunaga (1534–1582) undertakes a military campaign to destroy Buddhism in Japan, eventually defeating Pure Land and Nichiren strongholds and burning Tendai head monasteries on Mount Hiei.
1592	Korea is invaded by Japanese general Hideyoshi Toyotomi (1536–1598), leading to widespread destruction of Buddhist sites; Korean monks HYUJŎNG (1520–1604) and YUJŎNG (1544–1610) establish a monk's militia, which played a major role in defeating the Japanese.
1868	The new Meiji government in Japan orders separation of Buddhism from Shintō, creating Shintō as an independent "ancient" state cult and suppressing Buddhism; the regime reduces the status of Buddhist clergy to that of ordinary "imperial subjects," and requires clergy to assume Japanese family names, attend compulsory education, eat meat, and marry.

1910	Japan colonizes Korea; the Japanese government-general eventually institutes Meiji-style reforms of the Buddhist order in Korea.
1955	After the Japanese defeat in World War II and the end of the Korean War, Korean monks launch a purification movement to remove all vestiges of Japanese colonial influence on Korean Buddhism and to restore celibacy and vegetarianism within the SAṄGHA.
1964	SŌKA GAKKAI sponsors foundation of the Kōmeitō (Clean Government) political party in Japan.

Tibet and the Himalayas

641 C.E.	King Srong btsan sgam po unifies TIBET and marries Chinese princess Wencheng, who putatively brings to Tibet an image of Śākyamuni Buddha, later enshrined at the JO KHANG.
775	King Khri srong lde btsan (r. 755–797) of Tibet invites yogin PADMASAMBHAVA to Tibet, and construction of BSAM YAS (SAMYE) Monastery begins.
ca. 797	Supporters of Indian Buddhism putatively prevail in debate with Chinese Buddhists (the BSAM YAS DEBATE), establishing an Indian Buddhist basis for Tibetan Buddhism.
840	King Dar ma 'U dum btsan (also known as Glang dar ma; r. 838–842) persecutes Tibetan Buddhists. A period of conflict and decline of Buddhist institutions begins.
1039	Tibetan translator MAR PA (MARPA) (1002/1012–1097), founder of the BKA' BRGYUD (KAGYU) school, travels to India and studies under NĀROPA (1016–1100).
1042	Indian scholar ATISHA (982–1054) arrives in Tibet.
1073	SA SKYA (SAKYA) Monastery established in Tibet.
ca. 1200	Buddhist MONKS flee INDIA in the wake of the destruction of such Buddhist centers as Nālandā, bringing their traditions to NEPAL and Tibet.
1247	SA SKYA PAṆḌITA (SAKYA PAṆḌITA) (1182–1251) submits to Gödan Khan, beginning the first priest/patron relationship between a Tibetan LAMA and a Mongol Khan.
1357	TSONG KHA PA (1357–1419) is born. He becomes an important Tibetan reformer and founder of DGE LUGS (GELUK; Yellow Hat) order.

1642	Gushri Khan enthrones the fifth DALAI LAMA as temporal ruler of Tibet.
1904	British troops enter Tibet and occupy Lhasa.
1912	Thub bstan rgya mtsho (Thubten Gyatso; 1876–1933), the thirteenth Dalai Lama, proclaims Tibet a "religious and independent nation."
1940	The five-year-old Bstan 'dzin rgya mtsho (Tenzin Gyatso) is enthroned as the fourteenth Dalai Lama.
1950	Chinese Communist troops invade Tibet.
1959	The Dalai Lama flees to India; thousands of Tibetans die in anti-Chinese revolt.
1989	The Dalai Lama receives the Nobel Peace Prize.
1995	The Dalai Lama recognizes six-year-old Dge 'dun chos kyi nyi ma (Gedhun Choekyi Nyima) as the eleventh PANCHEN LAMA. China denounces the choice, in favor of Rgyal mtshan nor bu (Gyaltsen Norbu).
2000	The seventeenth KARMA PA, O rgyan 'phrin las rdo rje (Orgyan Trinle Dorje), flees Tibet to join the Dalai Lama in exile at Dharamsala, India.

INDEX

Page numbers in **boldface** point to the main text entry for each subject; page numbers in *italics* refer to illustrations.

VOLUME 1, PP. 1–478: VOLUME 2, PP. 479–929

C

E

F

VOLUME 1, PP. 1–478: VOLUME 2, PP. 479–929

H

K

L

215, 226, 292, 332, 395, 412–413, **471–477,** 500, 532, 619, 693–694, 759, 772, 781, 871, 882. *See also* Nichiren school
and commentarial literature, 167
cult of, 594–598, 672
as protective text, 634
and sacred geography, 792
and Tiantai school, 845–847
Loulan, 125
Lōväda saṃgrahaya, 778
Luce, Gordon H., 302
Lumbinī, 83
lunar cycle, and time reckoning, 285
Lun Fogu biao (Han Yu), 759
Lung gi nye ma (Bu ston), 104
Lunyu, 172
Luohans, 151–152. *See also* arhat(s)
Luo Qing, 813
Luoyang, 146, 148, 535, 551
Luoyang qielan ji, 57, 516
Lushan, 348
Lu Shengyan, 814
Lüders, Heinrich, 97

M

Macy, Joanna, 248
Madhyamāgama, 11
Madhyamakahṛdayakārikā (Bhāvaviveka), 42, 481–482
Madhyamakakārikā (Nāgārjuna), 111, 581, 809
Madhyamakāloka (Kamalaśīla), 483
Madhyamaka school, 31–32, 42, 53, 77–78, 111, 144, 223–224, 470, **479–485,** 481–483, 581–582, 649, 680, 683, 749, 809, 827, 846–847, 855, 861–862
Madhyamakāvatāra (Candrakīrti), 111, 482, 604
Madhyāntavibhāga, 914, 916
Madhyāntika, 368, 750
maechi, 901
Maezumi, Taizan, 868
magazines and periodicals
Buddhist Ray (U.S.), 865
Light of Dharma (U.S.), 865
Vietnamese, 883
Ma gcig lab sgron (Machig Labdrön), **485–486,** 901
Mahābhārata, 331
Mahābodhi Temple, 50, 364, **486–487**
Mahābodhi Society, 16, 359, 448, 798
Mahābodhivaṃsa, 877
Mahāchulalongkorn, 832
Mahādeva, 504, 568
Mahādhamma Saṅkraṃ *Sāsanālaṅkāra cā tamʻʺ,* 102
Mahā Ghaṇṭā, 774
Mahā Ghosananda, 110
Mahākāla, 563
mahākalpa, 185
Mahākarma-vibhaṅga, 302
Mahākassapa (arhat). *See* Mahākāśyapa
Mahākāśyapa, 29, 84, 133, 188, 232, 354, **487,** 507, 542, 566, 576, 897
Mahāmakut, 832
Mahāmantrānudhāriṇī, 634
Mahāmaudgalyāyana, 232, 287, 290, 308–309, 317, 354, **487–488,** 542, 741, 750
Mahāmāyā, 238
Mahāmāyūrī, 634
mahāmudrā, **488–489,** 513
Mahānāman, 232
Mahānikāi order, 108
Mahāpadāna-suttanta, 72, 890
mahāpadeśa, 111
Mahāpadesa-sutta, 94
Mahāparinibbāna-sutta, 205–207, 626. *See also Mahāparinirvāṇa-sūtra*
Mahāparinirvāṇa-sūtra, 8, 84–85, 179, 300, **489,** 715, 894, 905–906
Mahāprajāpatī Gautamī, 83–84, 232, 238, 353, **489–490,** 607, 741
Mahāprajñāpāramitā-śāstra (Nāgārjuna), 214
Mahāprātisārā, 634
mahāpuruṣa, 80, 361
Mahārājakaniṣkalekha (Mātṛceṭa), 518
Mahārājavaṅʻ krīʺ (Ūʺ Kalā), 102
Mahāsaccaka-sutta, 83
Mahāsāṃghika school, 11, 77, 86, 113, 121, 188, 223–224, 354, 368, **490,** 491, 502–504, 538, 588, 674, 742
Mahāsāṃghika-vinaya, 887
mahāsammatta, 424–425
Mahāsāsrapramardiṇī, 634
Mahāsatipaṭṭhāna-sutta, 754
mahāsattva, 58, 61, 85
Mahāsena, 644
mahāsiddha, 488, **490–491,** 572, 583, 820–821, 878–879
Mahasi Sayadaw, 898
Mahāsthāmaprāpta, 15
mahāstūpa, 804
Mahathat Monastery, 39
Mahatisadda Ghaṇṭā, 774
Mahāvadāna-sūtra, 85–86
Mahāvagga, 231, 285
Mahāvagge Maṇḍapeyyakathā, 445
Mahāvairocana, 274, 373, 412, 473, 476, 764. *See also* Vairocana
Mahāvairocana-sūtra, 56, 254, 511, 534, 764
Mahāvaṃsa, 75, 95, 162, 333, 626, 644, 742, 777, 795–796, 877
Mahāvastu, 86, 230, **491,** 512, 538, 746
Mahāvessantara-jātaka, 422
Mahāvibhāṣā, 20, 166, 188, 377, 505
Mahāvihāra, 188, 644, 795, 837
Mahāvihāravāsins, 506
Mahāvīra, 383
Mahāvyutpatti, 87
Mahāyāna art, 372
Mahāyāna precepts in Japan, **499–501**
Mahāyānasaṃgraha (Asaṅga), 32, 59, 914–916
Mahāyāna school, 29, 33, 52, 211, 214, 239, 269, 309, 342, 419–420, 490, **492–499,** 525, 534, 616, 809–810, 871, 878
and apocrypha, 26–27
and *bodhicitta,* 54–56
and buddhahood, 77–78, 186–187, 219, 230, 378, 760
and Buddha images, 81, 88, 550
and buddhas, 13–14, 47, 71–74, 87, 234, 497, 743
in Cambodia, 106–107
in Central Asia, 120–121
in China, 143
"cult of the book," 474, 591, 717
and ethics, 262–263
and gender, 304–305
and initiation, 375–376
institutionalization of, 357–358
key texts, 113, 183, 227–228, 320, 456, 756
in Korea, 430–432, 904–905
and laity, 445, 447–448
and merit, 208, 532
in Nepal, 588, 593
and *nirvāṇa,* 603–604
and original enlightenment, 619–620
and path, 93, 636
and *prajñāpāramitā* literature, 665–667
precepts, 281–282, 675
and Pure Land Buddhism, 695–696, 698–699, 701, 707
rise of, 356–357, 369, 479, 507, 776
and spread of Buddhism in China, 140–141
and Tantra, 820, 852

VOLUME 1, PP. 1–478: VOLUME 2, PP. 479–929

O

Q

R

S

VOLUME 1, PP. 1–478: VOLUME 2, PP. 479–929

T

W

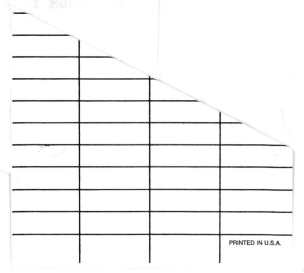